BUSINESS IN ETHICAL FOCUS

BUSINESS
IN
ETHICAL FOCUS

AN ANTHOLOGY

2 *nd edition*

EDITED BY

*Fritz Allhoff, Alexander Sager,
and Anand J. Vaidya*

broadview press

BROADVIEW PRESS — www.broadviewpress.com
Peterborough, Ontario, Canada

Founded in 1985, Broadview Press remains a wholly independent publishing house. Broadview's focus is on academic publishing; our titles are accessible to university and college students as well as scholars and general readers. With over 600 titles in print, Broadview has become a leading international publisher in the humanities, with world-wide distribution. Broadview is committed to environmentally responsible publishing and fair business practices.

The interior of this book is printed on 100% recycled paper.

Library and Archives Canada Cataloguing in Publication

Business in ethical focus : an anthology / edited by Fritz Allhoff,
    Alexander Sager and Anand J. Vaidya. — 2nd edition.

Includes bibliographical references.
ISBN 978-1-55481-251-6 (paperback)

    1. Business ethics. I. Allhoff, Fritz, editor II. Vaidya, Anand, editor
III. Sager, Alexander E. (Alexander Edward), editor

HF5387.B883 2016   174'.4   C2016-906981-8

Broadview Press handles its own distribution in North America
PO Box 1243, Peterborough, Ontario K9J 7H5, Canada
555 Riverwalk Parkway, Tonawanda, NY 14150, USA
Tel: (705) 743-8990; Fax: (705) 743-8353
email: customerservice@broadviewpress.com

Distribution is handled by Eurospan Group in the UK, Europe, Central Asia, Middle East, Africa, India, Southeast Asia, Central America, South America, and the Caribbean. Distribution is handled by Footprint Books in Australia and New Zealand.

Broadview Press acknowledges the financial support of the Government of Canada through the Canada Book Fund for our publishing activities.

Copy edited by Robert M. Martin
Book design by Michel Vrana

PRINTED IN CANADA

CONTENTS

ACKNOWLEDGMENTS

The editors would like to thank Stephen Latta for his support and for his valuable editorial guidance, Bob Martin for his careful and perspicuous copy-editing, and Tara Lowes for expertly shepherding the manuscript through production. We are also grateful to Sean McGuire and Richard Van Barriger for assistance with scanning and formatting texts and to Nate Ezra Lauffer for his work in editing the first edition case studies, proofreading introductory materials, and formatting the manuscript. We would like to extend our particular gratitude to Nicole Haley who provided integral editorial assistance throughout the entire process.

NOTE ON THE SECOND EDITION

Our goal in this anthology has been to give as comprehensive as possible a survey of the breadth and depth of business ethics. In selecting essays, we have aimed at providing theoretical work that is essential for understanding business ethics as an applied area of ethical inquiry. Each section includes articles that have achieved "classic" status in the discipline, combined with more recent works on urgent topics today. We have also sought to give readers articles that enable them to develop a good understanding of normative moral theory and other tools for doing ethics. This goal is to prepare the reader for the study of business ethics beyond this anthology.

For the second edition, we have sought to retain the strengths of the first edition and to add new articles to reflect developments in the field from the last eight years. We have strengthened the sections from the first edition with recent articles and created new sections such as Global Perspectives (with articles on Islamic, Confucian, and Buddhist business ethics) and Entrepreneurship, and the Not-for-Profit Sector. In addition, we have added 12 new detailed case studies with study questions that can be used to generate fruitful discussion.

PRELIMINARIES

INTRODUCTION: WHY STUDY BUSINESS ETHICS?

Anand J. Vaidya and Fritz Allhoff

THE WHAT AND WHY OF BUSINESS ETHICS

WHAT IS BUSINESS ETHICS, AND WHY STUDY IT? One good way to get an answer to this question is by taking note of what *business* is, what *ethics* is, and then tying the two together.

Business as will be understood here is the sum total of the relationships and activities that surround the trading of goods or services. In most cases, businesses seek to profit from their activities, though it is increasingly common for businesses such as social enterprises to operate as non-profits. As a category, business includes everything from the selling of handmade products between two neighboring villages in India to large-scale multinational corporations such as Nike and Microsoft engaged in global trade. Both the relationships between individuals involved in any aspect of business and the relationships between groups— corporations, divisions of them, unions, etc.—are important to understanding business as a whole.

Business ethics is important because it is involved centrally in most people's lives. Almost all people are consumers of commercial goods. Businesses also employ many people, giving them not only a wage, but in many cases an identity and an opportunity to express creativity.

Ethics, in its broadest sense, is an investigation into how humans *should* live. Ethics is distinct from law since laws themselves can be objects of ethical criticism. Within the confines of a moral investigation, one can inquire as to whether a legal statute is consistent with morality.[1] For example, slavery was once considered to be both morally permissible and legally permissible. Later many people disputed its morality even though it remained legally permissible.

Many ethicists divide their discipline into three branches: meta-ethics, normative ethics, and applied ethics. Meta-ethics explores conceptual and foundational questions in morality. Some of the questions are the following: Are there moral facts? Is morality objective? How do we come to know moral truths? Are moral claims the kinds of things that can be true or false, or are they simply expressions of emotion? What is the primary object of moral evaluation?

Normative ethics is the study of which principles determine the moral permissibility and impermissibility of an action, or, more simply, what constitutes right and wrong. One approach to this, deontology, holds that morality is constituted by rights and duties, and that those features take priority over the consequences of actions. An alternative approach, consequentialism, maintains that it is only the consequences of actions (often measured in terms of happiness and unhappiness) that determine the moral rightness of an action. Yet other theories, such as virtue theory, argue that actions are not the central objects of moral evaluation; rather, a person as a whole (and perhaps their character in particular) is the object of moral evaluation.

Applied ethics is the area which investigates specific problems and questions. Applied ethics includes such areas as biomedical ethics, computer ethics, environmental ethics, and, of course, business ethics. In applied ethics, for example, one may ask, "Is it just for companies to pursue profit within the confines of the law without considering if their actions further the public good?" or "Is it morally permissible to bribe government officials abroad when this practice is widespread?" In applied ethics, one is concerned with the specific ethical issues that arise from the area being investigated.

Philosophers dispute the precise relationship between meta-ethics, normative ethics, and applied ethics. Some philosophers hold that one's meta-ethical views and position in normative ethics have important implications for what one should claim when investigating specific ethical issues. Nonetheless, it is often possible to reach reasoned conclusions in applied ethics without settling contentious questions about the nature of morality or the content and justification of fundamental moral principles.

Putting together this understanding of business and ethics we arrive at the following conception of business ethics. *Business ethics* is the area of inquiry into issues that arise out of the relationships and activities surrounding the production, distribution, marketing, and sale of goods and services. We can further divide business ethics into micro, meso, and macro issues. Micro issues concern the behavior of individual workers and employers. Some of the questions revolve around the rights, responsibilities, and obligations that employees bear to each other and to their employers. Likewise there are questions about what rights, responsibilities, and obligations employers bear to employees. Does an employer have, for example, a right to information about the employee that is irrelevant to job performance? If not, how is the concept of job relevance to be defined? What set of rights, in general, do employees have when they sell their labor? Does this include a safe work environment? If so, is it the employer's obligation to provide it? What moral considerations help us understand why this is the case?

The meso level focuses on how businesses ought to be structured if they are to justly fulfill their role in society. The central debate has been over whether the sole responsibility of business is to maximize profit for shareholders or whether businesses also have significant moral responsibilities to stakeholders that go beyond profit maximization. This debate enquires into the immediate physical and social environment in which businesses are embedded, and to the future physical and social environment they will create. As a consequence, there are a host of ethical questions about the permissibility of polluting in the physical environment, and promoting socially important causes in the social environment.

A final set of questions for business ethics concerns macro level questions of political economy and distributive justice. Businesses operate in economic, legal, and social environments that both facilitate and constrain their actions and impact. Questions of corporate social responsibility and obligations to individual employees depend in part on our conclusions about a just society. What are the advantages and drawbacks of capitalism as an economic system? What constitutes a fair distribution of wealth? How do we understand democracy and to what extent should economic actors be subject to democratic control? In many cases, our conclusions about the macro, meso, and micro levels will inform each other, giving a more thorough ethical understanding of key issues faced by businesses, employees, and the public.

Finally we are left with the following question: Why study business ethics? The simple answer is that, if you are like most people, you will at some point enter some sector of the business world. And, if you are like most people, you will discover very quickly that there are significant questions about right and wrong that arise in this walk of life. The issues that this volume discusses can at least provide you with the following: an understanding of the issues one faces in the business world; some theoretical and practical tools one can use for analyzing ethical issues; and a framework for helping one construct an overall moral point of view. It is the hope of the editors of this book that everyone who takes to a serious study of this volume will come away with an appreciation for the role of morality within the world of business.

NOTE

1   We follow many philosophers in using "ethics" and "morality" synonymously in this introduction since within the discipline there is not an agreed upon distinction between the two terms.

—1—
ILL-FOUNDED CRITICISMS OF BUSINESS ETHICS

Anand J. Vaidya

IN THE WAKE OF CORPORATE SCANDALS SUCH AS Enron and WorldCom at the turn of the millennium, corporate executives and business schools were compelled to reflect on how to incorporate ethics into their organizations and curricula (Association to Advance Collegiate Schools of Business 2004). Nonetheless, one still finds a tendency amongst people to look at business ethics as not that relevant to doing good business. Insofar as the importance of business ethics is acknowledged, it is treated as a laundry list of codes that one must obey in order to avoid penalties, and that to a certain degree can be broken if one is careful. Cynical comments about business ethics as a contradiction in terms are common. Often people have in the back of their mind a conception of corporations ruthlessly seeking profit without regard to legal niceties or human cost.

The underlying assumption of this line of thought is that the concept of ethical conduct cannot be appropriately conjoined to the concept of business, that the concept of business transaction and negotiation is in tension with the concept of ethical conduct. At root the idea may be as simple as the claim that ethics is about a concern for the other at a possible cost to oneself, while business transactions are motivated by self-interest. Business, they say, involves wheeling and dealing, getting the better of your opponent; and, so they continue, business leaves ethics at the door. Ideas

like this are found in business literature starting as far back as the 1950s. Albert Z. Carr's "Is Business Bluffing Ethical?" (1958) argues that business is a lot like playing poker, and so one should adopt the ethics of poker, which is at odds with ethical codes prescribed by Christianity and other traditional religions.

Others point out that even when businesses adopt a "socially responsible" persona they do so out of the profit motive. Being socially responsible is *profitable*; if it weren't companies could not afford it. In order to survive in the marketplace one needs to make a profit; if being socially responsible requires sacrificing profits, then one could expect that their competitors will eventually force them out of the marketplace. The logic of competition puts socially responsible companies at a disadvantage. Competitors who decided not to be socially responsible would be able to displace socially responsible ones.

In order to clear the ground for the study of business ethics and to open the door to the fruits that may come from studying it, and from actually employing an ethical perspective in business, an end needs to be put to the idea that "business ethics" is an oxymoron, a somehow confused idea. In this essay I hope to exonerate business ethics of a couple of different criticisms that go together with the claim that it is an oxymoron. In section one, I will present the most common complaints about business ethics, and offer rebuttals. In section two, I will offer a diagnosis of the source of the view that business and ethics are incompatible, and show that it rests on a false understanding of what it takes for business to flourish.

1. COMMON COMPLAINTS ABOUT BUSINESS ETHICS

The four most common complaints about business ethics are that it is

- *Useless* because individuals upon reaching a certain age are incapable of changing the way in which they determine whether an action is morally permissible (i.e., good or bad).
- *Unfeasible* because the demands of market competition do not permit a sincere commitment to ethical considerations.
- *Indeterminate* because ethicists disagree over normative theories (e.g., consequentialism, deontology, virtue ethics) and principles (e.g., maximize happiness, distribute goods to the worst off, respect rights to private property, privacy, etc.) rendering decisive answers impossible, which consequently takes the *value* out of business ethics.
- *Beside the point* because ethical *inquiry* is not what is needed; rather individuals *behaving* ethically is what is needed.

Each of these complaints serves as a reason for avoiding business ethics discussions in the corporate world. And each of these can easily be shown to be unfounded.

The claim that business ethics is *useless* because by the time people enter the business world, roughly in their mid 20s to late 20s, their moral character has been, for the most part, formed for bad or good, rests on bad psychology, as well as bad reasoning.

First, consider the psychological assumption that a person's moral character is *static* rather than *revisable*. It may be true that it is harder for people to change how they morally evaluate a situation at

an older age than at a younger age, because certain moral habits or evaluative behaviors are more ingrained. And, it is probably true that most of us enter the work force at an age at which we have lots of opinions about what is morally right and wrong. However, it is false to say that it is impossible for one to change their moral viewpoint. More importantly, the attitude expressed by the "useless" argument is exactly the attitude that bars one from learning as a result of participation in community discussion about what is right and wrong. The fact is that we can change our moral point of view, and that listening and discussing things with others can have this result. Thus business ethics is important.

Second, critics of business ethics have argued that the nature of business, especially in a capitalist economy, makes ethical behavior impossible over the long run. On this account, business is committed to the logic of competition and profit maximization in the market place. In a capitalist economy, businesses that allow ethical considerations to impede focusing on the bottom line will not survive. Business leaders may *want* to act ethically, but those who allow corporate social responsibility or a commitment to sustainability as something more than a façade to attract consumers will find themselves replaced by boards looking after the interests of shareholders. One problem with this line of reasoning is that corporate social responsibility seems to have a neutral or slightly positive effect on the bottom line (Economist Intelligence Unit 2008). The claim that people in businesses must act unethically if they want to compete is probably false.

While some complain that business ethics is *useless or impossible*, a third complaint is that the real problem is that business ethics is *indeterminate*, and therefore *valueless*. The position they offer is not without initial plausibility. Anyone who has taken a freshman level course in ethics is aware that there are different schools of thought in ethics such as consequentialism, deontology, and virtue ethics. Each of these major schools of thought has its own criterion as to what constitutes right action or right living.

One brand of consequentialism, act-utilitarianism, says that the right action is that action from the set of available actions that maximizes aggregate happiness. One brand of deontology, Kantianism, says that the right action is that action whose maxim can be universalized without contradiction. Depending on which ethical school I subscribe to, I may give different answers as to the morality of any action I may have to take in the business world. So the critic of business ethics can argue: "What I wanted in the first place was to decide what to do based on what was morally permissible, but it is not possible for me to determine what is morally permissible until I know which school of moral thought is correct, and the ethicists have not settled that. Consequently, discussions of ethics in business will be indeterminate." And what is ultimately indeterminate, the critic of business ethics will argue, is without value. In order to understand this argument and locate the weakness in it, consider it in the following formal presentation.

1. Business ethicists disagree over first principles.
2. If theorists in a field disagree over first principles, then determinate answers cannot be reached.
3. If determinate answers cannot be reached in a field of inquiry, then that field of inquiry is without value.
4. Therefore, business ethics is without value.

Interestingly enough, we can formulate this argument with respect to any realm of inquiry where scholars of the discipline disagree over first principles and/or methodology. Consider the following argument about economics.

1. Economists disagree over first principles.
2. If theorists within a field of inquiry disagree over first principles, then determinate answers cannot be reached.
3. If determinate answers cannot be reached in a field of inquiry, then that field of inquiry is without value.
4. Therefore, economics is without value.

By looking at the mirror argument with respect to economics we can see the flaw in the critic's position. Before analyzing the premises we can note that while many in the business world feel comfortable offering the argument about business ethics, they would not feel as comfortable offering the corresponding argument for economics. Those that find themselves comfortable with the former argument, but not the latter put themselves in the following logical dilemma: accept the conclusion to both arguments, reject both arguments, or find the disanalogy between the two cases. In this case, we should reject both arguments as unsound because premises (2) and (3) are false.

First, regarding (2), it should be noted that the critic's use of "indeterminate" betrays an ambiguity. It does not follow from the claim that there are disputes over first principles within a discipline that all areas within the discipline are indeterminate. Economists, for example, may disagree in fundamental ways about human rationality, the tendency of markets to settle into equilibria, or government intervention, but nonetheless converge on specific issues. For example, almost all economists agree that international trade is beneficial on a whole, though specific segments of society may suffer when confronted with international competition. In some cases, there may not be major disputes about which tools from economics are useful for resolving an issue: for example, in public policy, few people deny that a cost-benefit-risk analysis is relevant for many decisions, even if they disagree about how this analysis is best conducted or about its weight compared to other considerations such as public support or civil rights.

This holds in the case of ethics as well. Though ethicists may disagree about ethical *theory*, their judgments may converge in many cases. For example, utilitarians, who base ethics on the promotion of happiness, will often call for the respect of rights and obligations. The reason is that societies in which most people's rights and obligations are honored tend to be happier. Indeed, a good deal of applied ethics occurs without explicit discussion of moral theory, since most ethical theorists agree that we should avoid harms and promote wellbeing, that we need to justify coercion, that under most circumstances discrimination and deception are wrong, and much else.

Regarding (3), it is hard to maintain that the indeterminacy within a discipline over first principles and methodology renders the discipline *valueless*. The main reason for this is the fact that *debates about principles and methodologies* are *themselves valuable* insofar as they can lead to clarification, resolution, and innovation.

Unlike the critic above who thinks that the indeterminacy of ethics renders it valueless, the frustrated critic of business ethics has recourse to a fourth complaint: business ethics is *beside the point* because we already know how people should act. The problem is getting them to act in that way. The members of Enron knew what they were doing was wrong when they committed fraudulent accounting practices to inflate their share price and engaged in insider trading, and they created a culture in which certain goals led to breaking the rules. What was needed was not more insight into what is wrong, but rather putting into play mechanisms that lead to people behaving morally.

While it is true that in general we would all benefit from everyone behaving morally, it is just false that we already, in general, know how to behave. Ethics is an on-going project; as technology advances and business takes on a new face, new ethical questions arise; and the answers to an ethical dilemma presented by new technology and business practice are not always answered by just looking at what we said in the past in the most relevantly similar cases.

But even if it were true that for the most part we know what the morally correct thing to do is in a given situation, it still would not be true that business ethics is beside the point. The underlying assumption required to make that inference is that *studying business ethics has no effect on our motivations.*

However, studying business ethics is not necessarily motivationally inefficacious. What is important is how we unpack the idea of "studying."

If studying business ethics just amounts to memorizing a bunch of codes and passing an exam, it is fair to say that studying it is likely to only provide one with knowledge of what codes and principles to obey. While this project might be worthy in itself, it does not come close to motivating one to be ethical. But there is another way of understanding the idea of "studying" business ethics. Being part of a business community where one can openly discuss how business should be conducted, and where one's contributions are taken seriously and reflected upon by others can often open one's mind to the possibility of change in light of the criticism of others.

Those who find that the pressure of the real world corporate environment pushes them away from the moral principles they believed in prior to entering the corporate world may discover that these principles are reactivated when they read case histories and debate what to do in particular and common situations. One of the best ways to learn about the consequences of cruelty is to read and discuss the great novels that portray it. Likewise, reading case histories representing common ethically relevant business situations, and discussing them, can reinforce values and bring clarity.

Secondly, ethics in general requires healthy debate and exchange of ideas. When a person offers an ethical position on a topic, and another disagrees, both parties have a prima facie obligation to offer reasons and justifications for their positions. Unlike disputes about what is the best flavor of ice cream, where opponents may disagree with one another with no other reason than that they like the particular flavor that they do, the nature of moral discussion requires that reasons be offered. Moral discussions are often about the possibility of harm to others, and most people in most cultures see the actions which have potential to harm others as requiring reasons and justifications. Consequently, and as a result of moral engagement, individuals can come to be motivated to act one way rather than another by acquiring new desires and beliefs through moral debate. It is often times noted that people feel most comfortable with an action they are about to take when they feel confident in the reasons they have for taking that action. Moral discussions can provide reasons, and confidence in those reasons.

Third, all of us at one time were new to the corporate environment and the pressures that arise in it, and most of us looked for guidance, not just from our colleagues and our bosses, but also from a source beyond them. One reason we searched for this was that we weren't always sure that our bosses and colleagues were doing the morally right thing, or, for that matter, that they were even concerned with the morally right thing to do. Clearly, business ethics can provide guidance here. The study of ethics can provide us with a firm grasp of principles that can be applied in new situations to help us determine for ourselves what the morally right action is. The ability to reason about ethics can provide us with that sense of independence in thought that allows us to judge for ourselves whether our actions are morally right, and to criticize others.

2. THE BAKER AND THE BUTCHER REVISITED

Let's go back to the beginning. Where does the idea that business and ethics do not fit together come from? One promising place to look would be at the role of *self-interest* in economics. There is a famous passage quoted from Adam Smith's 1778 *Wealth of Nations*:

> It is not from the benevolence of the butcher, the brewer, or the baker that we expect our dinner, but from their regard to their own interest. We address ourselves, not to their humanity but to their self-love ...

The standard story based on this passage is that the sellers want our money, we want their products, and the exchange benefits us all. As a result, there doesn't seem to be any need for ethics in the exchange matrix. Rational individuals pursuing their own self-interest are all it takes for day-to-day business dealings. Any imposition of ethical principles would be redundant.

While it is true that Smith paid tribute to self-interest in the passage above, it is a misreading of the passage, pointed out by Amartya Sen, to take it that it excludes ethics from the matrix of exchange. By locating the specific sense in which self-interest is being celebrated by Smith, Sen claims we can bring out the sense in which ethics is an essential component of a system of exchange. What Smith was saying is that our *motivation for exchange* is self-interest. We are motivated to come to the marketplace to exchange our goods, not out of love for the other, but out of the necessity of self-preservation. The butcher sells his meat, the brewer his beer, and the baker his bread out of the obvious desire to procure money in order to purchase the goods they desire. Smith is not saying that business can function without ethical principles to guide the exchange. By making a distinction between *the motivation for exchange* and *the features necessary for the flourishing of business* we can see the appropriate roles of self-interest and how business ethics makes sense.

Ethical principles and codes of conduct are what allow for a system of exchange to flourish over long periods of time. In order to see the necessity of ethical principles and codes of conduct in the marketplace it will be instructive to look at a point made by Socrates in Book 1 of *The Republic*.

In discussion with Thrasymachus, Socrates points out that if a group has a common goal and every member of the group acts unjustly, then the attainment of the common goal will be frustrated. His point is made in an attempt to praise justice against Thrasymachus' diatribe. Thrasymachus has praised the life of injustice and thievery because he understands justice to be a weakness, and injustice to be the power to take advantage of others with impunity. Socrates has pointed out that even though it is correct that thieves take advantage of others, and at times with impunity, it is not true that they live wholly unjust lives. In fact, Socrates points out, in their dealings with other thieves they obey rules, and have a code of conduct, that allows for their thievery in groups to prosper. Even in modern times Socrates' point is common knowledge. The mafia has their own code of conduct, and individuals within their circle obey a code of conduct out of fear of punishment. If you are convinced that "the ethics of the mafia" is not an oxymoron, then you should equally be convinced that "business ethics" is not an oxymoron.

Socrates' point connects well with the distinction between the motivation for exchange and those features of a system necessary for its flourishing. Codes of conduct, rules, and guidelines—ethical principles—are all required in order for business to flourish over time. Without ethical principles and rules the common goal of business—the exchange of goods for the benefit of all—would be frustrated, and less successful.

So, business and ethics do go together; and business ethics is not *useless, valueless* because *indeterminate*, or *beside the point*. Rather, ethics and business are connected in a way that is essential for the very flourishing of business.

BIBLIOGRAPHY

Association to Advance Collegiate Schools of Business, "Ethics Education in Business Schools: Report of the Ethics Education Task Force to AACSB International's Board of Directors." 2004. http://www.aacsb.edu/publications/researchreports/archives/ethics-education.pdf

Albert Z. Carr, "Is Business Bluffing Ethical?" *Harvard Business Review* (January/February 1968). See below, 526–34.

Economist Intelligence Unit, "Corporate Citizenship: Profiting from a Sustainable Business." (London: Economist Intelligence Unit, Ltd., 2008).

Plato, "Book 1," *Republic*, translated by G.M.A. Grube and revised by C.D.C. Reeve (Indianapolis, Indiana: Hackett Publishing Company, 1992).

Amartya Sen, "Does Business Ethics Make Economic Sense?" *Business Ethics Quarterly* 3.1 (January 1993). See below, 1–17.

Clarence C. Walton, "The State of Business Ethics," *Enriching Business Ethics* (New York: Plenum Press, 1990).

—2—

DOES BUSINESS ETHICS
MAKE ECONOMIC SENSE?

Amartya Sen

1. INTRODUCTION

I BEGIN NOT WITH THE NEED FOR BUSINESS ETHICS, but at the other end—the idea that many people have that there is no need for such ethics. That conviction is quite widespread among practitioners of economics, though it is more often taken for granted implicitly rather than asserted explicitly. We have to understand better what that conviction rests on, to be able to see its inadequacies. Here, as in many other areas of knowledge, the importance of a claim depends to a great extent on what it denies.

How did this idea of the redundancy of ethics get launched in economics? The early authors on economic matters, from Aristotle and Kautilya (in ancient Greece and ancient India respectively—the two were contemporaries, as it happens) to medieval practitioners (including Aquinas, Ockham, Maimonides, and others), to the economists of the early modern age (William Petty, Gregory King, François Quesnay, and others) were all much concerned, in varying degrees, with ethical analysis. In one way or another, they saw economics as a branch of "practical reason," in which concepts of the good, the right and the obligatory were quite central.

What happened then? As the "official" story goes, all this changed with Adam Smith, who can certainly be described—rightly—as the father of modern economics. He made, so it is said, economics scientific and hard-headed, and the new

economics that emerged, in the nineteenth and twentieth centuries, was all ready to do business, with no ethics to keep it tied to "morals and moralizing." That view of what happened—with Smith doing the decisive shooting of business and economic ethics—is not only reflected in volumes of professional economic writings, but has even reached the status of getting into the English literature via a limerick by Stephen Leacock, who was both a literary writer and an economist:

> Adam, Adam, Adam Smith
> Listen what I charge you with!
> Didn't you say
> In a class one day
> That selfishness was bound to pay?
> Of all doctrines that was the Pith.
>
> Wasn't it, wasn't it, wasn't it, Smith?[1]

The interest in going over this bit of history—or alleged history—does not lie, at least for this conference, in scholastic curiosity. I believe it is important to see how that ethics-less view of economics and business emerged in order to understand what it is that is being missed out. As it happens, that bit of potted history of "who killed business ethics" is altogether wrong, and it is particularly instructive to understand how that erroneous identification has come about.

2. EXCHANGE, PRODUCTION AND DISTRIBUTION

I get back, then, to Adam Smith. Indeed, he did try to make economics scientific, and to a great extent was successful in this task, within the limits of what was possible then. While that part of the alleged history is right (Smith certainly did much to enhance the scientific status of economics), what is altogether mistaken is the idea that Smith demonstrated—or believed that he had demonstrated—the redundancy of ethics in economic and business affairs. Indeed, quite the contrary. The Professor of Moral Philosophy at the University of Glasgow—for that is what Smith was—was as interested in the importance of ethics in behavior as anyone could have been. It is instructive to see how the odd reading of Smith—as a "no-nonsense" skeptic of economic and business ethics—has come about.

Perhaps the most widely quoted remark of Adam Smith is the one about the butcher, the brewer and the baker in *The Wealth of Nations*: "It is not from the benevolence of the butcher, the brewer, or the baker that we expect our dinner, but from their regard to their own interest. We address ourselves, not to their humanity but to their self-love...."[2] The butcher, the brewer and the baker want our money, and we want their products, and the exchange benefits us all. There would seem to be no need for any ethics—business or otherwise—in bringing about this betterment of all the parties involved. All that is needed is regard for our own respective interests, and the market is meant to do the rest in bringing about the mutually gainful exchanges.

In modern economics this Smithian tribute to self-interest is cited again and again—indeed with such exclusivity that one is inclined to wonder whether this is the only passage of Smith that is read these days. What did Smith really suggest? Smith did argue in this passage that the pursuit of self-interest would do fine to motivate the exchange of commodities. But that is a very limited claim, even though it is full of wonderful insights in explaining why it is that we seek exchange and how come exchange can be such a beneficial thing for all. But to understand the limits of what is being claimed here, we have to ask, first: Did Smith think that economic operations and business activities consist only of exchanges of this kind? Second, even in the context of exchange, we have to question: Did Smith think that the result would be just as good if the businesses involved, driven by self-interest, were to try to defraud the consumers, or the consumers in question were to attempt to swindle the sellers?

The answers to both these questions are clearly in the negative. The butcher-brewer-baker simplicity does not carry over to problems of production and distribution (and Smith never said that it did), nor to the problem as to how a system of exchange can flourish institutionally. This is exactly where we begin to see why Smith could have been right in his claim about *the motivation for exchange* without establishing or trying to establish *the redundancy of business or ethics* in general (or even in exchange). And this is central to the subject of this conference.

The importance of self-interest pursuit is a helpful part of understanding many practical problems, for example, the supply problems in the Soviet Union and East Europe. But it is quite unhelpful in explaining the success of, say, Japanese economic performance *vis-à-vis* West Europe or North America (since behavior modes in Japan are often deeply influenced by other conventions and pressures). Elsewhere in *The Wealth of Nations*, Adam Smith considers other problems which call for a more complex motivational structure. And in his *The Theory of Moral Sentiments*, Smith goes extensively into the need to go beyond profit maximization, arguing that "humanity, justice, generosity, and public spirit, are the qualities most useful to others."[3] Adam Smith was very far from trying to deny the importance of ethics in behavior in general and business behavior in particular.

Through overlooking everything else that Smith said in his wide-ranging writings and concentrating only on this one butcher-brewer-baker passage, the father of modern economics is too often made to look like an ideologue. He is transformed into a partisan exponent of an ethics-free view of life which would have horrified Smith. To adapt a Shakespearian aphorism, while some men are born small and some achieve smallness, the unfortunate Adam Smith has had much smallness thrust upon him.

It is important to see how Smith's wholeness tribute to self-interest as a motivation for exchange (best illustrated in the butcher-brewer-baker passage) can co-exist peacefully with Smith's advocacy of ethical behavior elsewhere. Smith's concern with ethics was, of course, extremely extensive and by no means confined to economic and business matters. But since this is not the occasion to review Smith's ethical beliefs, but only to get insights from his combination of economic and ethical expertise to understand better the exact role of business ethics, we have to point our inquiries in that particular direction.

The butcher-brewer-baker discussion is all about *motivation for exchange*, but Smith was—as any good economist should be—deeply concerned also with *production* as well as *distribution*. And to understand how exchange might itself actually work in practice, it is not adequate to concentrate only on the motivation that makes people *seek* exchange. It is necessary to look at the behavior patterns that could sustain a flourishing system of mutually profitable exchanges. The positive role of intelligent self-seeking in motivating exchange has to be supplemented by the motivational demands of production and distribution, and the systemic demands on the organization of the economy.

These issues are taken up now, linking the general discussion with practical problems faced in the contemporary world. In the next three sections I discuss in turn (1) the problem of organization (especially that of exchange), (2) the arrangement and performance of production, and (3) the challenge of distribution.

3. ORGANIZATION AND EXCHANGE: RULES AND TRUST

I come back to the butcher-brewer-baker example. The concern of the different parties with their own interests certainly can adequately *motivate* all of them to take part in the exchange from which each benefits. But whether the exchange would operate well would depend also on organizational conditions. This requires institutional development which can take quite some time to work—a lesson that is currently being learned rather painfully in East Europe and the former Soviet Union. That point is now being recognized, even though it was comprehensively ignored in the first flush of enthusiasm in seeking the magic of allegedly automatic market processes.

But what must also be considered now is the extent to which the economic institutions operate on the basis of common behavior patterns, shared trusts, and a mutual confidence in the ethics of the different parties. When Adam Smith pointed to the motivational importance of "regard to their own interest," he did not suggest that this motivation is all that is needed to have a flourishing system of exchange. If he cannot trust the householder, the baker may have difficulty in proceeding to produce bread to meet orders, or in delivering bread without prepayment. And the householder may not be certain whether he would be sensible in relying on the delivery of the ordered bread if the baker is not always altogether reliable. These problems of mutual confidence—discussed in a very simple form here—can be incomparably more complex and more critical in extended and multifarious business arrangements.

Mutual confidence in certain rules of behavior is typically implicit rather than explicit—indeed so implicit that its importance can be easily overlooked in situations in which such confidence is unproblematic. But in the context of economic development, across the Third World, and also of institutional reform, now sweeping across what used to be the Second World, these issues of behavioral norms and ethics can be altogether central.

In the Third World there is often also a deep-rooted skepticism of the reliability and moral quality of business behavior. This can be directed both at local businessmen and the commercial people from abroad. The latter may sometimes be particularly galling to well established business firms including well-known multinationals. But the record of some multinationals and their unequal power in dealing with the more vulnerable countries have left grounds for much suspicion, even though such suspicion may be quite misplaced in many cases. Establishing high standards of business ethics is certainly one way of tackling this problem.

There is also, in many Third World countries, a traditional lack of confidence in the moral behavior of particular groups of traders, for example merchants of food grains. This is a subject on which—in the context of the-then Europe—Adam Smith himself commented substantially in *The Wealth of Nations*, though he thought these suspicions were by and large unjustified. In fact, the empirical record on this is quite diverse, and particular experiences of grain trade in conditions of scarcity and famine have left many questions to be answered.

This is an issue of extreme seriousness, since it is now becoming increasingly clear that typically the best way of organizing famine prevention and relief is to create additional incomes for the destitute (possibly through employment schemes) and then to rely on normal trade to meet (through standard arrangements of transport and sales) the resulting food demand. The alternative of bureaucratic distribution of food in hastily organized relief camps is often much slower, more wasteful, seriously disruptive of family life and normal economic operations, and more conducive to the spread of epidemic diseases. However, giving a crucial role to the grain traders at times of famine threats (as a complement to state-organized employment schemes to generate income) raises difficult issues of trust and trustworthiness, in particular, that the traders will not manipulate the precarious situation in search of unusual profit. The issue of business ethics, thus, becomes an altogether vital part of the arrangement of famine prevention and relief.

The problem can be, to some extent, dealt with by skillful use of the threat of government intervention in the market. But the credibility of that threat depends greatly on the size of grain reserves the government itself has. It can work well in some cases (generally it has in India), but not always. Ultimately, much depends on the extent to which the relevant business people can establish exacting standards of behavior, rather than fly off in search of unusual profits to be rapidly extracted from manipulated situations.

I have been discussing problems of organization in exchange, and it would seem to be right to conclude this particular discussion by noting that the need for business ethics is quite strong even in the field of exchange (despite the near-universal presence of the butcher-brewer-baker motivation of "regard to their own interest"). If we now move on from exchange to production and distribution, the need for business ethics becomes even more forceful and perspicuous. The issue of trust is central to all economic operations. But we now have to consider other problems of interrelation in the process of production and distribution.

4. ORGANIZATION OF PRODUCTION: FIRMS AND PUBLIC GOODS

Capitalism has been successful enough in generating output and raising productivity. But the experiences of different countries are quite diverse. The recent experiences of East Asian economies—most notably Japan—raise deep questions about the modelling of capitalism in traditional economic theory. Japan is often seen—rightly in a particular sense—as a great example of successful capitalism, but it is clear that the motivation patterns that dominate Japanese business have much more content than would be provided by pure profit maximization.

Different commentators have emphasized distinct aspects of Japanese motivational features. Michio Morishima has outlined the special characteristics of "Japanese ethos" as emerging from its particular history of rule-based behavior pattern.[4] Ronald Dore has seen the influence of "Confucian ethics."[5] Recently, Eiko Ikegami has pointed to the importance of the traditional concern with "honor"—a kind of generalization of the Samurai code—as a crucial modifier of business and economic motivation.[6]

Indeed, there is some truth, oddly enough, even in the puzzlingly witty claim made by *The Wall Street Journal* that Japan is "the only communist nation that works" (30 January 1989, 1). It is, as one would expect, mainly a remark about the non-profit motivations underlying many economic and business activities in Japan. We have to understand and interpret the peculiar fact that the most successful capitalist nation in the world flourishes economically with a motivation structure that departs firmly—and often explicitly—from the pursuit of self-interest, which is meant to be the bedrock of capitalism.

In fact, Japan does not, by any means, provide the only example of a powerful role of business ethics in promoting capitalist success. The productive merits of selfless work and devotion to enterprise have been given much credit for economic achievements in many countries in the world. Indeed, the need of capitalism for a motivational structure more complex than pure profit maximization has been acknowledged in various forms, over a long time, by various social scientists (though typically not by many "mainstream" economists): I have in mind Marx, Weber, Tawney, and others.[7] The basic point about the observed success of non-profit motives is neither unusual nor new, even though that wealth of historical and conceptual insights is often thoroughly ignored in professional economics today.

It is useful to try to bring the discussion in line with Adam Smith's concerns, and also with the general analytical approaches successfully developed in modern microeconomic theory. In order to understand how motives other than self-seeking can have an important role, we have to see the limited reach of the butcher-brewer-baker argument, especially in dealing with what modern economists call "public good." This becomes particularly relevant because the overall success of a modern enterprise is, in a very real sense, a public good.

But what *is* a public good? That idea can be best understood by contrasting it with a "private good," such as a toothbrush or a shirt or an apple, which either you can use or I, but not both. Our respective uses would compete and be exclusive. This is not so with public goods, such as a livable environment or the absence of epidemics. All of us may benefit from breathing fresh air, living in an epidemic-free environment, and so on. When uses of commodities are non-competitive, as in the case of public goods, the rationale of the self-interest-based market mechanism comes under severe strain. The market system works by putting a price on a commodity and the allocation between consumers is done by the intensities of the respective willingness to buy it at the prevailing price. When "equilibrium prices" emerge, they balance demand with supply for each commodity. In contrast, in the case of public goods, the uses are—largely or entirely—non-competitive, and the system of giving a good to the highest bidder does not have much merit, since one person's consumption does not exclude that of another. Instead, optimum resource allocation would require that the *combined* benefits be compared with the costs of production, and here the market mechanism, based on profit maximization, functions badly.

A related problem concerns the allocation of private goods involving strong "externalities," with interpersonal interdependences working outside the markets. If the smoke from a factory makes a neighbor's home dirty and unpleasant, without the neighbor being able to charge the factory owner for the loss she suffers, then that is an "external" relation. The market does not help in this case, since it is not there to allocate the effects—good or bad—that work outside the market. Public goods and externalities are related phenomena, and they are both quite common in such fields as public health care, basic education, environmental protection, and so on.

There are two important issues to be addressed in this context, in analyzing the organization and performance of production. First, there would tend to be some failure in resource allocation when the commodities produced are public goods or involve strong externalities. This can be taken either (1) as an argument for having *publicly owned enterprises*, which would be governed by principles other than profit maximization, or (2) as a case for *public regulations* governing private enterprise, or (3) as establishing a need for the use of non-profit values—particularly of *social concern*—in private decisions (perhaps because of the goodwill that it might generate). Since public enterprises have not exactly covered themselves with glory in the recent years, and public regulations—while useful—are sometimes quite hard to implement, the third option has become more important in public discussions. It is difficult, in this context, to escape the argument for encouraging business ethics, going well beyond the traditional values of honesty and reliability, and taking on social responsibility as well (for example, in matters of environmental degradation and pollution).

The second issue is more complex and less recognized in the literature, but also more interesting. Even in the production of private commodities, there can be an important "public good" aspect in the production process itself. This is because production itself is typically a joint activity, supervisions are costly and often unfeasible, and each participant contributes to the over-all success of the firm in a way that cannot be fully reflected in the private rewards that he or she gets.

The over-all success of the firm, thus, is really a public good, from which all benefit, to which all contribute, and which is not parcelled out in little boxes of person-specific rewards strictly linked with each person's *respective contribution*. And this is precisely where the motives other than narrow self-seeking become productively important. Even though I do not have the opportunity to pursue the

point further here, I do believe that the successes of "Japanese ethos," "Confucian ethics," "Samurai codes of honor," etc., can be fruitfully linked to this aspect of the organization of production.

5. THE CHALLENGE OF DISTRIBUTION: VALUES AND INCENTIVES

I turn now to distribution. It is not hard to see that non-self-seeking motivations can be extremely important for *distributional* problems in general. In dividing a cake, one person's gain is another's loss. At a very obvious level, the contributions that can be made by ethics—business ethics and others—include the amelioration of misery through policies explicitly aimed at such a result. There is an extensive literature on donations, charity, and philanthropy in general, and also on the willingness to join in communal activities geared to social improvement. The connection with ethics is obvious enough in these cases.

What is perhaps more interesting to discuss is the fact that distributional and productional problems very often come mixed together, so that how the cake is divided influences the size of the cake itself. The so-called "incentive problem" is a part of this relationship. This too is a much discussed problem, but it is important to clarify in the present context that the extent of the conflict between size and distribution depends crucially on the motivational and behavioral assumptions. The incentive problem is not an immutable feature of production technology. For example, the more narrowly profit-oriented an enterprise is, the more it would, in general, tend to resist looking after the interests of others—workers, associates, consumers. This is an area in which ethics can make a big difference.

The relevance of all this to the question we have been asked to address ("Does business ethics make economic sense?") does, of course, depend on how "economic sense" is defined. If economic sense includes the achievement of a good society in which one lives, then the distributional improvements can be counted in as parts of sensible outcomes even for business. Visionary industrialists and businesspersons have tended to encourage this line of reasoning.

On the other hand, if "economic sense" is interpreted to mean nothing other than achievement of profits and business rewards, then the concerns for others and for distributional equity have to be judged entirely instrumentally—in terms of how they indirectly help to promote profits. That connection is not to be scoffed at, since firms that treat their workers well are often very richly rewarded for it. For one thing, the workers are then more reluctant to lose their jobs, since more would be sacrificed if dismissed from this (more lucrative) employment, compared with alternative opportunities. The contribution of goodwill to team spirit and thus to productivity can also be quite plentiful.

We have then an important contrast between two different ways in which good business behavior could make economic sense. One way is to see the improvement of the society in which one lives as a reward in itself; this works directly. The other is to use ultimately a business criterion for improvement, but to take note of the extent to which good business behavior could in its turn lead to favorable business performance; this enlightened self-interest involves an indirect reasoning.

It is often hard to disentangle the two features, but in understanding whether or how business ethics make economic sense, we have to take note of each feature. If, for example, a business firm pays inadequate attention to the safety of its workers, and this results accidentally in a disastrous tragedy, like the one that happened in Bhopal in India some years ago (though I am not commenting at present on the extent to which Union Carbide was in fact negligent there), that event would be harmful both for the firm's profits and for the general objectives of social well-being in which the firm may be expected to take an interest. The two effects are distinct and separable and should act cumulatively in an overall consequential analysis. Business ethics has to relate to both.

6. A CONCLUDING REMARK

I end with a brief recapitulation of some of the points discussed, even though I shall not attempt a real summary. First, the importance of business ethics is not contradicted in any way by Adam Smith's pointer to the fact that our "regards to our own interest" provide adequate motivation for exchange (section 2). Smith's butcher-brewer-baker argument is concerned (1) directly with *exchanges* only (not production or distribution), and (2) only with the *motivational aspect* of exchange (not its organizational and behavioral aspects).

Second, business ethics can be crucially important in economic organization in general and in exchange operations in particular. This relationship is extensive and fairly ubiquitous, but it is particularly important, at this time, for the development efforts of the Third World and the reorganizational attempts in what used to be the Second World (section 3).

Third, the importance of business ethics in the arrangement and performance of production can be illustrated by the contrasting experiences of different economies, e.g., Japan's unusual success. The advantages of going beyond the pure pursuit of profit can be understood in different ways. To some extent, this question relates to the failure of profit-based market allocation in dealing with "public goods." This is relevant in two different ways: (1) the presence of public goods (and of the related phenomenon of externalities) in the commodities produced (e.g., environmental connections), and (2) the fact that the success of the firm can itself be fruitfully seen as a public good (section 4).

Finally, distributional problems—broadly defined—are particularly related to behavioral ethics. The connections can be both direct and valuational, and also indirect and instrumental. The interrelations between the size of the cake and its distribution increase the reach and relevance of ethical behavior, e.g., through the incentive problem (section 5).

NOTES

1   Stephen Leacock, *Hellements of Hickonomics* (New York: Dodd, Mead & Co., 1936), p. 75.

2   Adam Smith, *An Inquiry into the Nature and Causes of the Wealth of Nations* (1776; republished, London: Dent, 1910), vol. I, p. 13.

3   Adam Smith, *The Theory of Moral Sentiments* (revised edition, 1790; reprinted, Oxford: Clarendon Press, 1976), p. 189.

4   Michio Morishima, *Why Has Japan "Succeeded"? Western Technology and Japanese Ethos* (Cambridge: Cambridge University Press, 1982).

5   Ronald Dore, "Goodwill and the Spirit of Market Capitalism," *British Journal of Sociology*, 34 (1983), and *Taking Japan Seriously: A Confucian Perspective on Leading Economic Issues* (Stanford: Stanford University Press, 1987).

6   Eiko Ikegami, "The Logic of Cultural Change: Honor, State-Making, and the Samurai," mimeographed, Department of Sociology, Yale University, 1991.

7   Karl Marx (with F. Engels), *The German Ideology* (1845–46, English translation, New York: International Publishers, 1947); Richard Henry Tawney, *Religion and the Rise of Capitalism* (London: Murray, 1926); Max Weber, *The Protestant Ethic and the Spirit of Capitalism* (London: Allen & Unwin, 1930).

—3—
MANAGING TO BE ETHICAL
Debunking Five Business Ethics Myths

Linda Klebe Treviño and Michael E. Brown

THE TWENTY-FIRST CENTURY HAS BROUGHT corporate ethics scandals that have harmed millions of employees and investors, and sent shock waves throughout the business world. The scandals have produced "perp walks" and regulatory backlash, and business ethics is once again a hot topic. Academics and managers are asking: What caused the recent rash of corporate wrongdoing, and what can we do, if anything, to prevent similar transgressions in the future? Perhaps because everyone has opinions about ethics and personal reactions to the scandals, a number of pat answers have circulated that perpetuate a mythology of business ethics management. In this article, we identify several of these myths and respond to them based upon knowledge grounded in research and practice.

MYTH 1: IT'S EASY TO BE ETHICAL

A 2002 newspaper article was entitled, "Corporate ethics is simple: If something stinks, don't do it." The article went on to suggest "the smell test" or "If you don't want to tell your mom what you're really doing ... or read about it in the press, don't do it." The obvious suggestion is that being ethical in business is easy if one wants to be ethical. A further implication is that if it's easy, it doesn't need to be managed. But that suggestion disregards the complexity surrounding ethical decision-making, especially in the context of business organizations.

Ethical Decisions Are Complex

First, ethical decisions aren't simple. They're complex by definition. As they have for centuries, philosophers argue about the best approaches to making the right ethical decision. Students of business ethics are taught to apply multiple normative frameworks to tough dilemmas where values conflict. These include consequentialist frameworks that consider the benefits and harms to society of a potential decision or action, deontological frameworks that emphasize the application of ethical principles such as justice and rights, and virtue ethics with its emphasis on the integrity of the moral actor, among other approaches. But, in the most challenging ethical dilemma situations, the solutions provided by these approaches conflict with each other, and the decision maker is left with little clear guidance. For example, multinational businesses with manufacturing facilities in developing countries struggle with employment practice issues. Most Americans believe that it is harmful and contrary to their rights to employ children. But children routinely contribute to family income in many cultures. If corporations simply refuse to hire them or fire those who are working, these children may resort to begging or even more dangerous employment such as prostitution. Or they and their families may risk starvation. What if respecting the rights of children in such situations produces the greater harm? Such business decisions are more complex than most media reports suggest, and deciding on the most ethical action is far from simple.

Moral Awareness Is Required

Second, the notion that "it's easy to be ethical" assumes that individuals automatically know that they are facing an ethical dilemma and that they should simply choose to do the right thing. But decision makers may not always recognize that they are facing a moral issue. Rarely do decisions come with waving red flags that say, "Hey, I'm an ethical issue. Think about me in moral terms!" Dennis Gioia was recall coordinator at Ford Motor Company in the early 1970s when the company decided not to recall the Pinto despite dangerous fires that were killing the occupants of vehicles involved in low-impact rear-end collisions. In his information-overloaded recall coordinator role, Gioia saw thousands of accident reports, and he followed a cognitive "script" that helped him decide which situations represented strong recall candidates and which did not. The incoming information about the Pinto fires did not penetrate a script designed to surface other issues, and it did not initially raise ethical concerns. He and his colleagues in the recall office didn't recognize the recall issue as an ethical issue. In other examples, students who download their favorite music from the Internet may not think about the ethical implications of "stealing" someone else's copyrighted work. Or, a worker asked to sign a document for her boss may not recognize this as a request to "forge" legal documents.

Researchers have begun to study this phenomenon, and they refer to it as moral awareness, ethical recognition, or ethical sensitivity. The idea is that moral judgment processes are not initiated unless the decision-maker recognizes the ethical nature of an issue. So, recognition of an issue as an "ethical" issue triggers the moral judgment process, and understanding this initial step is key to understanding ethical decision-making more generally.

T.M. Jones proposed that the moral intensity of an issue influences moral issue recognition, and this relationship has been supported in research. Two dimensions of moral intensity—magnitude of consequences and social consensus—have been found in multiple studies to influence moral awareness. An individual is more likely to identify an issue as an ethical issue to the extent that a particular decision or action is expected to produce harmful consequences and to the extent that relevant others in the social context view the issue as ethically problematic. Further, the use of moral language has been found to influence moral awareness. For example, in the above cases, if the words "stealing" music (rather than downloading) or "forging" documents (rather than signing) were used, the individual would be more likely to think about these issues in ethical terms.

Ethical Decision-Making Is a Complex, Multi-Stage Process

Moral awareness represents just the first stage in a complex, multiple-stage decision-making process that moves from moral awareness to moral judgment (deciding that a specific action is morally justifiable), to moral motivation (the commitment or intention to take the moral action), and finally to moral character (persistence or follow-through to take the action despite challenges).

The second stage, moral judgment, has been studied within and outside the management literature. Lawrence Kohlberg's well-known theory of cognitive moral development has guided most of the empirical research in this area for the past thirty years. Kohlberg found that people develop from childhood to adulthood through a sequential and hierarchical series of cognitive stages that characterize the way they think about ethical dilemmas. Moral reasoning processes become more complex and sophisticated with development. Higher stages rely upon cognitive operations that are not available to individuals at lower stages, and higher stages are thought to be "morally better" because they are consistent with philosophical theories of justice and rights.

At the lowest levels, termed "preconventional," individuals decide what is right based upon punishment avoidance (at stage 1) and getting a fair deal for oneself in exchange relationships (at stage 2). Next, the conventional level of cognitive moral development includes stages 3 and 4. At stage 3, the individual is concerned with conforming to the expectations of significant others, and at stage 4 the perspective broadens to include society's rules and laws as a key influence in deciding what's right. Finally, at the highest "principled" level, stage 5, individuals' ethical decisions are guided by principles of justice and rights.

Perhaps most important for our purposes is the fact that most adults in industrialized societies are at the "conventional" level of cognitive moral development, and less than twenty per cent of adults ever reach the "principled" level where thinking is more autonomous and principle-based. In practical terms, this means that most adults are looking outside themselves for guidance in ethical dilemma situations, either to significant others in the relevant environment (e.g., peers, leaders) or to society's rules and laws. It also means that most people need to be led when it comes to ethics.

The Organizational Context Creates Additional Pressures and Complexity

Moral judgment focuses on *deciding* what's right—not necessarily *doing* what is right. Even when people make the right decision, they may find it difficult to follow through and do what is right because of pressures from the work environment. Research has found that principled individuals are more likely to behave in a manner consistent with their moral judgments, and they are more likely to resist pressures to behave unethically. However, most people never reach the principled level. So, the notion that being ethical is simple also ignores the pressures of the organizational context that influence the relationship between moral judgment and action.

Consider the following ethical-dilemma situation. You find yourself in the parking lot, having just dented the car next to you. The ethical decision is relatively simple. It's about you and your behavior. No one else is really involved. You have harmed someone else's property, you're responsible, and you or your insurance company should pay for the repairs. It's pretty clear that you should leave a note identifying yourself and your insurance company. Certainly, there may be negative consequences if you leave that note. Your insurance rates may go up. But doing the right thing in this situation is fairly straightforward.

Contrast that to business-context situations. It is much harder to "just say no" to a boss who demands making the numbers at all costs. Or to go above the boss's head to someone in senior management with suspicions that "managing earnings" has somehow morphed into "cooking the books." Or to walk away from millions of dollars in business because of concerns about crossing an ethical line. Or to tell colleagues that the way they do business seems to have crossed that line. In these situations, the individual is operating within the context of the organization's authority structure and culture—and would likely be concerned about the consequences of disobeying a boss's order, walking away from millions of dollars in business, or blowing the whistle on a peer or superior. What would peers think? How would the leadership react? Would management retaliate? Is one's job at risk?

It may seem curious that people often worry about whether others will think of them as too ethical. But all of us recognize that "snitches" rarely fit in, on the playground or in life, and whistleblowers are frequently ostracized or worse. The reasons for their ostracism are not fully understood, but they may have to do with humans' social nature and the importance of social group maintenance. Research suggests that people who take principled stands, such as those who are willing to report a peer for unethical behavior, are seen as highly ethical while, at the same time, they are thought to be highly unlikable. Nearly a third of respondents to the 2003 National Business Ethics Survey said "their coworkers condone questionable ethics practices by showing respect for those who achieve success using them." Further, about forty per cent of respondents said that they would not report misconduct they observed because of fear of retaliation from management. Almost a third said they would not report misconduct because they feared retaliation from coworkers.

If you think this applies only to the playground or the factory floor, ask yourself why we haven't seen more CEOs proclaiming how appalled they are at the behavior of some of their peers after recent ethics scandals. Yes, we heard from a few retired CEOs. But very few active senior executives have spoken up. Why not? They're probably uncomfortable passing moral judgment on others or holding themselves up as somehow ethically better than their peers. So, social context is important because people, including senior executives, look to others for approval of their thinking and behavior.

In sum, being ethical is not simple. Ethical decisions are ambiguous, and the ethical decision-making process involves multiple stages that are fraught with complications and contextual pressures. Individuals may not have the cognitive sophistication to make the right decision. And most people will be influenced by peers' and leaders' words and actions, and by concerns about the consequences of their behavior in the work environment.

MYTH 2: UNETHICAL BEHAVIOR IN BUSINESS IS SIMPLY THE RESULT OF "BAD APPLES"

A recent headline was "How to Spot Bad Apples in the Corporate Bushel." The bad-apple theory is pervasive in the media and has been around a long time. In the 1980s, during a segment of the McNeil Lehrer Report on PBS television, the host was interviewing guests about insider trading scandals. The CEO of a major investment firm and a business school dean agreed that the problems with insider trading resulted from bad apples. They said that educational institutions and businesses could do little except to find and discard those bad apples after the fact. So, the first reaction to ethical problems in organizations is generally to look for a culprit who can be punished and removed. The idea is that if we rid the organization of one or more bad apples, all will be well because the organization will have been cleansed of the perpetrator.

Certainly there are bad actors who will hurt others or feather their own nests at others' expense—and they do need to be identified and removed. But, as suggested above, most people are the product of the context they find themselves in. They tend to "look up and look around," and they do what others around them do or expect them to do. They look outside themselves for guidance when thinking about what is right. What that means is that most unethical behavior in business is supported by the context in which it occurs—either through direct reinforcement of unethical behavior or through benign neglect.

An example of how much people are influenced by those around them was in the newspaper in November, 2002. Police in New Britain, Connecticut confiscated a 50-ft. long pile of stolen items, the result of a scavenger hunt held by the "Canettes," New Britain high school's all-girl drill team. According to the Hartford Courant, police, parents, and school personnel were astonished that 42 normally law-abiding girls could steal so many items in a single evening. But the girls had a hard time believing that they had done anything wrong. One girl said: "I just thought it was a custom ... kind of like a camaraderie thing, [and] if the seniors said it was OK and they were in charge, then it was OK!" In another incident in May 2003, suburban Chicago high school girls engaged in an aggressive and brutal "hazing ritual" that landed five girls in the hospital. We might say that these are teenagers, and that adults are different. But many of these teenagers are about to start jobs, and there are only a few years between these high school students and young people graduating from college. Most adults are more like these teens than most of us think or would prefer. The influence of peers is powerful in both cases.

When asked why they engaged in unethical conduct, employees will often say, "I had no choice," or "My boss told me to do it." Stanley Milgram's obedience-to-authority experiments, probably the most famous social psychology experiments ever conducted, support the notion that people obey authority figures even if that means harming another person. Milgram, a Yale psychologist, conducted his obedience-to-authority experiments in the Hartford community on normal adults. These experiments demonstrated that nearly two-thirds of normal adults will harm another human being (give them alleged electric shocks of increasing intensity) if asked to do so by an authority figure as part of what was billed as a learning experiment. Were these people bad apples? We don't think so. Most of them were not at all comfortable doing what they were being asked to do, and they expressed sincere concern for the victim's fate. But in the end most of them continued to harm the learner because the authority figure in a lab coat told them to do so.

How does this apply to work settings? Consider the junior member of an audit team who discovers something problematic when sampling a firm's financials and asks the senior person on the audit team for advice. When the leader suggests putting the problematic example back and picking another one, the young auditor is likely to do just that. The leader may add words such as the following: "You don't understand the big picture" or "Don't worry, this is my responsibility." In this auditing example, the harm being done is much less obvious than in the learning experiment and the junior auditor's responsibility even less clear, so the unethical conduct is probably easier to carry out and more likely to occur.

The bottom line here is that most people, including most adults, are followers when it comes to ethics. When asked or told to do something unethical, most will do so. This means that they must be led toward ethical behavior or be left to flounder. Bad behavior doesn't always result from flawed individuals. Instead, it may result from a system that encourages or supports flawed behavior.

A corollary of the bad-apples argument is that ethics can't be taught or even influenced

in adults because adults are autonomous moral agents whose ethics are fully formed by the time they join work organizations, and they can't be changed. This is simply not true. We know from many empirical studies that the large majority of adults are *not* fully formed when it comes to ethics, and they are not autonomous moral agents. They look outside themselves for guidance in ethical-dilemma situations, and they behave based to a large extent upon what those around them—leaders and peers—expect of them. So, we have to look at the very powerful signals that are being sent about what is expected. We also know that the development of moral reasoning continues into adulthood. Those who are challenged to wrestle with ethical dilemmas in their work will develop more sophisticated ways of thinking about such issues, and their behavior will change as a result.

MYTH 3: ETHICS CAN BE MANAGED THROUGH FORMAL ETHICS CODES AND PROGRAMS

If people in organizations need ethical guidance and structural support, how can organizations best provide it? Most large organizations now have formal ethics or legal compliance programs. In 1991 the US Sentencing Commission created sentencing guidelines for organizations convicted of federal crimes (see *www.ussc.gov* for information). The guidelines removed judicial discretion and required convicted organizations to pay restitution and substantial fines depending upon whether the organization turns itself in, cooperates with authorities, and whether it has established a legal compliance program that meets seven requirements for due diligence and effectiveness. These formal programs generally include the following key elements: written standards of conduct that are communicated and disseminated to all employees, ethics training, ethics advice lines and offices, and systems for anonymous reporting of misconduct. The Sarbanes-Oxley law, passed during the summer of 2002, requires corporations to set up an anonymous system for employees to report fraud and other unethical activities. Therefore, companies that did not previously have such reporting systems are busy establishing them.

Research suggests that formal ethics and legal compliance programs can have a positive impact.

For example, the Ethics Resource Center's National Business Ethics Survey revealed that in organizations with all four program elements (standards, training, advice lines, and reporting systems) there was a greater likelihood (78 per cent) that employees would report observed misconduct to management. The likelihood of reporting declined with fewer program elements. Only half as many people in organizations with no formal program said that they would report misconduct to management.

Yet, creating a formal program, by itself, does not guarantee effective ethics management. Recall that Enron had an ethics code, and the board voted to bypass its conflict-of-interest policy. Not surprisingly, research suggests that actions speak louder than words. Employees must perceive that formal policies go beyond mere window dressing to represent the real ethical culture of the organization. For example, the National Business Ethics Survey reports that when executives and supervisors emphasize ethics, keep promises, and model ethical conduct, misconduct is much lower than when employees perceive that the "ethics walk" is not consistent with the "ethics talk." In another study formal program characteristics were found to be relatively unimportant compared with more informal cultural characteristics such as messages from leadership at both the executive and supervisory levels. In addition, perceived ethics program follow-through was found to be essential. Organizations demonstrate follow-through by working hard to detect rule violators, by following up on ethical concerns raised by employees, and by demonstrating consistency between ethics and compliance policies and actual organizational practices. Further, the perception that ethics is actually talked about in day-to-day organizational activities and incorporated into decision-making was found to be important.

So, for formal systems to influence behavior, they must be part of a larger, coordinated cultural system that supports ethical conduct every day. Ethical culture provides informal systems, along with formal systems, to support ethical conduct. For example, the research cited above found that ethics-related outcomes (e.g., employee awareness of ethical issues, amount of observed misconduct, willingness to report misconduct) were much more positive to the extent that employees perceived that ethical conduct was rewarded and unethical conduct was punished in the organization. Further, a culture that demands unquestioning obedience to authority was found to be particularly harmful while a culture in which employees feel fairly treated was especially helpful.

The Fall of Arthur Andersen

Barbara Toffler's book *Final Accounting: Ambition, Greed, and the Fall of Arthur Andersen* (2003) can help us understand this notion of ethical (or unethical) organizational culture. Andersen transformed over a number of years from having a solid ethical culture to having a strong unethical culture. The company's complete demise is a rather dramatic example of the potential results of such a transformation.

In the mid-1990s, Arthur Andersen did not have a formal ethics office, but it did have formal ethical standards and ethics training. Ironically, it also established a consulting group whose practice was aimed at helping other businesses manage their ethics. Barbara Toffler was hired to run that practice in 1995 after spending time on the Harvard Business School faculty and in her own ethics consulting business. After joining Andersen, Toffler learned quickly that the firm's own ethical culture was slipping badly, and she chronicles that slippage in her book.

The book opens with the following statement "The day Arthur Andersen loses the public's trust is the day we are out of business." Steve Samek, country managing partner, made that statement on a CD-ROM concerning the firm's Independence and Ethical Standards in 1999. It was reminiscent of the old Arthur Andersen. Andersen's traditional management approach had been a top-down, "one firm" concept. Arthur Andersen had built a strong ethical culture over the years where all of the pieces fit together into a seamless whole that supported ethical conduct. No matter where they were in the world, if customers were dealing with Andersen employees, they knew that they could count on the same high-quality work and the same integrity. Employees were trained in the "Andersen Way," and that way included strong ethics. Training at their St. Charles, Illinois training facility was sacred. It created a cadre of professionals who spoke the same language and shared the same "Android" values.

Founders create culture and Arthur Andersen was no exception. Toffler says that in the firm's early days, the messages from the top about ethical conduct were strong and clear. Andersen himself said, "My own mother told me, 'Think straight—talk straight.' ... This challenge will never fail anyone in a time of trial and temptation." "Think straight, talk straight" became a mantra for decades at Arthur Andersen. Partners said with pride that integrity mattered more than fees. And stories about the founder's ethics became part of the firm's lore. At the young age of 28, Andersen faced down a railway executive who demanded that his books be approved—or else. Andersen said, "There's not enough money in the city of Chicago to induce me to change that report." Andersen lost the business, but later the railway company filed for bankruptcy, and Arthur Andersen became known as a firm one could trust. In the 1930s Andersen talked about the special responsibility of accountants to the public and the importance of their independence of judgment and action. Arthur Andersen died in 1947 but was followed by leaders with similar convictions who ran the firm in the 1950s and 1960s, and the ethical culture continued for many years. Pretty much through the 1980s, Andersen was considered a stable and prestigious place to work. People didn't expect to get rich—rather they wanted "a good career at a firm with a good reputation."

But, the ethical culture eventually began to unravel, and Toffler attributes much of this to the fact that the firm's profits increasingly came from management consulting rather than auditing. The leadership's earlier commitment to ethics came to be drowned out by the firm's increasing laser-like focus on revenues. Auditing and consulting are very different, and the cultural standards that worked so well in auditing didn't fit the needs of the consulting side of the business. But this mismatch was never addressed, and the resulting mixed signals helped precipitate a downward spiral into unethical practices. Serving the client began to be defined as keeping the client happy and getting return business. And tradition became translated into unquestioning obedience to the partner, no matter what one was asked to do. For example, managers and partners were expected to pad their prices. Reasonable estimates for consulting work were simply doubled or more as consultants were told to back into the numbers.

The training also began falling apart when it came to hiring experienced people from outside the firm—something that happened more and more as consulting took over. New employees had always been required to attend a three-day session designed to indoctrinate them into the culture of the firm, but new consultants were told not to forego lucrative client work to attend. So, Toffler never made it to the training, and many other consultants didn't either.

By the time Toffler arrived at Andersen, the firm still had a huge maroon ethics binder, but no one bothered to refer to it. Ethics was never talked about. And, she says, "when I brought up the subject of internal ethics, I was looked at as if I had teleported in from another world." The assumption, left over from the old days in auditing, was that "we're ethical people; we recruit people who are screened for good judgment and values. We don't need to worry about this stuff." But, as we all learned, their failure to worry about ethics led to the demise of the firm.

Could a formal ethics office have helped Arthur Andersen? Probably not, unless that office addressed the shift toward consulting, identified the unique ethical issues faced in the consulting side of the business, developed ethical guidelines for consulting, and so on. It is easy for formal ethics offices and their programs to be marginalized if they don't have the complete support of the organization's leadership and if they are inconsistent with the broader culture. In fact, Andersen still had ethics policies and they still talked about ethics in formal documents. But the business had changed along with the culture that guided employee actions every day, while the approach to ethics management had not kept pace.

MYTH 4: ETHICAL LEADERSHIP IS MOSTLY ABOUT LEADER INTEGRITY

In our discussion of Arthur Andersen, we suggested the importance of leadership. But what is executive ethical leadership? The mythology of ethical leadership focuses attention narrowly on individual character and qualities such as integrity, honesty, and fairness. The *Wall Street Journal* recently ran a story on its website entitled "Plain Talk: CEOs Need to Restore Character in Companies." It said, "The chief problem affecting corporate America right now is not the regulatory environment or snoozing board directors. It's character." But as Arthur Andersen demonstrated, leaders must be more than individuals of high character. They must "lead" others to behave ethically.

Recent research has found that certain individual characteristics are necessary but not sufficient for effective ethical leadership. Such leadership at the executive level is a reputational phenomenon. In most large organizations, employees have few face-to-face interactions with senior executives. So, most of what they know about a leader is gleaned from afar. In order to develop a reputation for ethical leadership, an executive must be perceived as both a "moral person" and a "moral manager."

Being perceived as a "moral person" is related to good character. It depends upon employee perceptions of the leader's traits, behaviors, and decision-making processes. Ethical leaders are

thought to be honest and trustworthy. They show concern for people and are open to employee input. Ethical leaders build relationships that are characterized by trust, respect and support for their employees. In terms of decision-making, ethical leaders are seen as fair. They take into account the ethical impact of their decisions, both short term and long term, on multiple stakeholders. They also make decisions based upon ethical values and decision rules, such as the golden rule.

But being perceived as a "moral person" is not enough. Being a "moral person" tells followers what the leader will do. It doesn't tell them what the leader expects *them* to do. Therefore, a reputation for ethical leadership also depends upon being perceived as a "moral manager," one who leads others on the ethical dimension, lets them know what is expected, and holds them accountable. Moral managers set ethical standards, communicate ethics messages, role model ethical conduct, and use rewards and punishments to guide ethical behavior in the organization.

Combining the "moral person" and "moral manager" dimensions creates a two-by-two matrix (see Figure 1). A leader who is strong on both dimensions is perceived to be an *ethical leader.* We can point to Arthur Andersen as an exemplar of ethical leadership. He was known as a strong ethical person who also clearly led his organization on ethics and values. People knew what they could expect of him, and they knew what he expected of them from an ethics perspective. Another example of ethical leadership is James Burke, CEO of Johnson & Johnson during the early 1980s Tylenol crisis (when Tylenol was laced with cyanide in the Chicago area). Burke handled that crisis masterfully, recalling all Tylenol at a huge financial cost to the firm. But his ethical leadership had begun much earlier when he first took the CEO helm. He focused the organization's attention on the company's long-standing credo and its values. He demanded that senior executives either subscribe to the credo or remove it from the wall. He didn't want to run a hypocritical organization. He also launched the credo survey, an annual survey that

Moral Person

	WEAK	STRONG
STRONG	*Hypothetical Leader* Jim Bakker Michael Sears	*Ethical Leader* Arthur Andersen James Burke Bill George
WEAK	*Unethical Leader* Al Dunlap Bernie Ebbers?	

(vertical axis label: Moral Manager)

◄——— *Ethically Silent Leader* ———► ?
Sandy Weill?

asks employees how the company is doing relative to each of the credo values. Bill George, recently retired CEO of Medtronic, is a more current example of an ethical leader. In his book *Authentic Leadership*, George calls for responsible ethical leadership in corporate America while recounting his own struggles to stay true to the company's mission and to himself.

A leader who is neither a moral person nor a moral manager is an *unethical leader*. In our research, Al Dunlap was frequently identified as an unethical leader. Subject of a book entitled *Chainsaw*, Dunlap was known as an expert turnaround manager. But while at Sunbeam, he also became known for "emotional abuse" of employees. As a result of his demands to make the numbers at all costs, employees felt pressure to use questionable accounting and sales techniques, and they did. Dunlap also lied to Wall Street, assuring them that the firm would reach its financial projections. In the end, Dunlap could no longer cover up the sorry state of affairs, and he left a crippled company when the board fired him in 1998. In 2002, he paid a $500,000 fine for financial fraud and agreed never to serve as an officer or director of a public corporation. Unfortunately, there are many candidates for a more current example of unethical leadership: Dennis Kozlowski from Tyco, Bernie

Ebbers from WorldCom, and Richard Scrushy from Health-South are just a few executive names attached to recent business scandals.

Leaders who communicate a strong ethics/values message (who are moral managers), but who are not perceived to be ethical themselves (they are not moral persons) can be thought of as *hypocritical leaders*. Nothing makes people more cynical than a leader who talks incessantly about integrity, but then engages in unethical conduct himself and encourages others to do so, either explicitly or implicitly. Hypocritical leadership is all about ethical pretense. The problem is that by spotlighting integrity, the leader raises expectations and awareness of ethical issues. At the same time, employees realize that they can't trust the leader.

Jim Bakker, the founder of PTL Ministries, is our favorite example of a hypocritical leader. At its peak, his television ministry had 2000 employees and reached more than ten million homes. Bakker preached about doing the Lord's work while raising funds for his Heritage USA Christian theme park. The problem was that he sold more memberships than could ever be honored. He tapped millions of dollars donated by his followers to support PTL operating expenses including huge salaries and bonuses for his family and high ranking PTL officials. PTL filed for bankruptcy in 1987, and Bakker spent eight years in prison.

Michael Sears, recently fired from Boeing for offering a job to an Air Force procurement specialist while she was overseeing negotiations with Boeing, represents a more recent example of a hypocritical leader. Sears had played a significant role at the Boeing Leadership Center which is known for its programs related to ethics. Also, shortly before his firing, Sears released advance copies of his book *Soaring Through Turbulence* which included a section on maintaining high ethical standards.

We call the final combination *ethically silent leadership*. It applies to executives who are neither strong ethical nor strong unethical leaders. They fall into what employees perceive to be an ethically neutral leadership zone. They may be ethical persons, but they don't provide leadership in the crucial area of ethics, and employees aren't sure where the leaders stand on ethics or if they care. The ethically silent leader is not perceived to be unethical but is seen as focusing intently on the bottom line without setting complementary ethical goals. There is little or no ethics message coming from the top. But silence represents an important message. In the context of all the other messages being sent in a highly competitive business environment, employees are likely to interpret silence to mean that the top executive really doesn't care how business goals are met, only that they are met, so employees act on that message. Business leaders don't like to think that their employees perceive them as ethically silent. But given the current climate of cynicism, unless leaders make an effort to stand out and lead on ethics, they are likely to be viewed that way.

Sandy Weill, CEO of Citigroup, may fit the ethically silent leader category. The company has been playing defense with the media, responding to ugly headlines about ethics scandals, especially at its Smith Barney unit where stock analysts were accused of essentially "selling" their stock recommendations for banking business. Weill's management style is to hire competent people to run

Citigroup's units and to let them do their jobs. That may work well for other aspects of the business, but ethics must be managed from the top and center of the organization. According to *Fortune* magazine, Weill has now "gotten religion," if a bit late. Weill has "told his board that he feels his most important job from now on is to be sure that Citigroup operates at the highest level of ethics and with the utmost integrity." New procedures and business standards are being developed at corporate headquarters, and a new CEO was appointed at Smith Barney. However, *Fortune* also cites cynicism about this recent turnabout, noting that Weill is often "tone deaf" on ethical issues.

So, developing a reputation for ethical leadership requires more than strong personal character. Employees must be "led" from the top on ethics just as they must be led on quality, competitiveness, and a host of other expected behaviors. In order to be effective ethical leaders, executives must demonstrate that they are ethical themselves, they must make their expectations of others' ethical conduct explicit, and they must hold all of their followers accountable for ethical conduct every day.

MYTH 5: PEOPLE ARE LESS ETHICAL THAN THEY USED TO BE

In the opening to this article, we said that business ethics has once again become a hot topic. The media have bombarded us with information about ethics scandals, feeding the perception that morals are declining in business and in society more generally.

According to a poll released by the PR Newswire in summer 2002, sixty-eight per cent of those surveyed believe that senior corporate executives are less honest and trustworthy today than they were a decade ago. But unethical conduct has been with us as long as human beings have been on the earth, and business ethics scandals are as old as business itself. The Talmud, a 1500-year-old text, includes about 2 million words and 613 direct commandments designed to guide Jewish conduct and culture. More than one hundred of these concern business and economics. Why? Because "transacting business, more than any other human activity, tests our moral mettle and reveals our character" and because "working, money, and commerce offer … the best opportunities to do good deeds such as … providing employment and building prosperity for our communities and the world."

So, unethical behavior is nothing new. It's difficult to find solid empirical evidence of changes over time. But studies of student cheating have found that the percentage of college students who admit to cheating has not changed much during the last thirty years. Some types of cheating have increased (e.g., test cheating, collaboration on individual assignments). Other types of cheating have declined (e.g., plagiarism, turning in another student's work). Certainly, given new technologies and learning approaches, students have discovered some clever new ways to cheat, and professors have their work cut out for them keeping up with the new methods. But the amount of overall cheating hasn't increased that much. Further, when employees were asked about their own work organizations, the 2003 National Business Ethics Survey found that employee perceptions of ethics are generally quite positive. Interestingly, key indicators have actually improved since the last survey conducted in 2000.

Alan Greenspan said it well on July 16, 2002: "It is not that humans have become any more greedy than in generations past. It is that the avenues to express greed [have] grown so enormously." So, unethical behavior is nothing new, and people are probably not less ethical than they used to be. But the environment has become quite complex and is rapidly changing, providing all sorts of ethical challenges and opportunities to express greed.

If ethical misconduct is an ongoing concern, then organizations must respond with lasting solutions that embed support for ethics into their cultures rather than short-term solutions that can easily be undone or dismissed as fads. The risk is that the current media focus on unethical conduct will result in "faddish" responses that offer overly simplistic solutions and that result inevitably in disillusionment and abandonment. Faddish solutions often result from external pressures to "do something" or at least look like you're doing something. The current focus on scandal certainly includes such pressures. But the recognition that unethical conduct is a continuing organizational problem may help to convince managers that solutions should be designed that will outlast the current intense media focus.

—4—
A BRIEF GUIDE TO THINKING ABOUT BUSINESS ETHICS

Alexander Sager

GRAVITY PAYMENTS, A CREDIT CARD PROCESSING company that serves small businesses, received national media coverage when founder and CEO Dan Price announced his plan to raise the salary of all employees to $70,000. Price claimed that his inspiration came from an article by Daniel Kahneman and Angus Deaton that reported emotional well-being does not increase over $75,000.[1] Price paid for the increase in wage for the company's 70 employees by cutting his own salary from $1.1 million to $70,000 and by diverting most of the company's anticipated profit to wages.[2] In an interview on the Today Show, Price said:

> I see everything I do as a responsibility and seeing growing inequality and how it's harder to just make ends meet and live the normal American dream. You know, things are getting more and more expensive, especially in a city like Seattle and the wages aren't keeping up. And so for me, we're here to serve our clients primarily and that's how we're going to be successful. It's not about making money. It's about making a difference.

Price's decision drew widespread praise, but also controversy. Some employees quit, outraged by colleagues in less skilled and demanding positions receiving large pay raises. Several customers ended their business with the firm, objecting to what they perceived as a political statement or fearing fee hikes despite reassurances that this would not occur.[3] As a result of legal fees and the use of profits and executive salary to fund the salary increase, Price had to rent out his house to make ends meet.[4]

Gravity Payment's story provides a helpful case for thinking about how to do business ethics. Business ethics courses ask students to analyze topics and cases from an ethical perspective. Many students wonder what this involves. Though ethical reasoning and decision-making plays a major role in our everyday lives, in many cases it is not explicit. Most of us make decisions about what to do, how to interact with others, and what values to endorse without considering ethics in detail. We take norms for granted, not devoting significant effort to asking if they are justified, how they fit with other norms, or how they should be applied. As a result, students taking an ethics class often wonder what it means to think philosophically about the ethical issues involved.

The first challenge that students face in business ethics is identifying *when* an ethical issue exists. Ethics is bound up with all aspects of social life. In our everyday interactions, ethics is embedded in our norms, customs, and habits. People are able to work together, to purchase what they need to live, or, for that matter, to walk down a busy street because they share ethical assumptions about promises, responsibility, fairness, rights, and much else. The challenge is that these are often not identified as *ethical* assumptions. In real life, ethical considerations are often implicit, bound up with other types of consideration such as efficiency, and embedded in largely unexamined rules, regulations, and habits. For example, in the infamous Ford Pinto case, Ford failed to recall cars that were prone to fires from low-level rear-end collisions. Though many people are outraged by what they perceive as Ford's pursuit of profit heedless of the cost of human lives, Linda Klebe Treviño and Michael E. Brown (Chapter 3) point out that it did not occur to the recall coordinator Dennis Gioia that an *ethical* issue was at stake. The danger posed by the Pinto did not register in the mental script that Gioia used to identify when a recall was warranted. Similarly, until recently, employers considered sexual harassment a personal issue, not a matter of ethics that needed to be addressed by workplace policies (see Chapters 66–69).[5] Some ethical wrongdoing occurs because the wrongdoers did not realize ethics was at stake.

How, then, do we identify when an ethical issue is present? Unfortunately, there is no straightforward answer or test. We come to identify ethical issues through exposure to them and through reflection. Thinking ethically involves what Aristotle called *phronesis* or practical wisdom (for more on this topic, see Chapter 7) which we acquire over time by experiencing and by working through ethical issues. It is hard to substitute for life experience, but we can prepare ourselves to confront ethical issues in the workplace by studying case studies that raise ethical issues. Moral cognition and imagination surrounding business can also be developed by reading novels, non-fiction (including biographies), and watching movies and television programs that explore moral issues involving work.[6]

Though there is no formula for identifying ethical issues, we can use clues to help determine if an ethical issue is at stake. Applied ethics often deals with the impact of individual conduct and institutions on well-being and freedom. Does business as a social institution contribute to well-being and human flourishing? Does it have an *obligation*

to do so? This is related to the topic of distribution: what role should business and the market have in determining the distribution of goods? For example, debates surrounding corporate social responsibility concern businesses' obligations—if any—to different stakeholders. Questions about freedom often address government regulations. When are governments morally justified in restricting what businesses can do? How much power ought democratic decision-making have over the private sector? Many other questions concern employees' rights. What rights do employees have and what do these imply for employers' obligations?

A reaction some people have to Gravity Payments' wage raise is that it is an *amoral* action, i.e., an action that is neither right nor wrong. On this view, Price's action is simply his choice and not one that can be criticized morally (though we might criticize its wisdom or view it as an action that we do not personally endorse). Though many of us would agree that Price had a right to raise his employees' salaries and that nobody should have had the power to stop him from doing so, the *ethics* of his decision is more complicated. That an agent has a right to do or not do something does not necessarily settle whether it is a moral (or the morally best) action, only that the agent should be allowed to perform it.

We can think about the Gravity Payments case on a number of levels. First, we can ask about the moral issues at stake in the workplace, especially those that concern managers and employees. Many issues in business ethics concern how corporations treat the people who work for them (and in some cases non-employees affected by their actions). Do businesses have a right to monitor their employees? Can they demand certain forms of behavior of their employees outside of working hours? What safety standards must they meet? How much do they have to compensate them? What control, if any, should employees have over company decisions?

In the case of Gravity Payments, many of the major ethical issues concern distributive justice—*who gets what for what reasons*? We can ask whether it was just for Price to have paid himself a $1.1 million salary in the first place. Though Price has suggested that his salary was set by the market rate, it appears that he received significantly more than other CEOs working at companies similar in size and profitability to Gravity Payments. Moreover, we can question if salaries should be set simply by what employees or CEOs can command on the market, as opposed to some other form of desert, need, equality, or other criteria. The view that Price received excessive compensation may also be at the heart of a lawsuit filed by his brother and major shareholder.[7]

Price's shift to radically egalitarian compensation where everyone makes $70,000 also raises issues of fairness and desert. Is it just for employees who contribute more with their education, skills, experience, and hours worked to receive the same compensation as employees who offer less? Even worker cooperatives such as Spain's Mondragon Corporation allow for some inequality in wages.[8] Morality may demand that workers be paid *differently*.

Beyond issues of compensation within the company, there are larger questions about the purpose of business and the nature of corporate social responsibility. Karen Weise from *Bloomberg Business* reports Price asking: "Is [the purpose of business] to maximize shareholder returns? Or is it to best serve the customers and provide for employees?"[9] Price represents himself as advocating a new vision of business where one set of stakeholders—in this case employees—benefits more than is typically the case. As the readings on corporate social responsibility in this anthology attest, this is a controversial view.

To see how this extends beyond Gravity Payment's shareholders (who may have a legitimate complaint at Price's decision to divert profits to employee wages), we can ask what would occur if all or even many businesses followed his lead. Ignoring the issue that part of the reason that Price *could* take this measure is that Gravity Payments is a small, privately owned company,[10] we can wonder how generalizing this policy would affect recruitment, motivation, investment, and much else. It may be that Price's ability to pay each worker significantly over the media wage is parasitical on a larger economic system where wages are largely set by supply and demand. If this is true, Gravity Payments cannot serve as a general model for corporate social responsibility.

How we view distributive justice within Gravity Payments will also be influenced by our macro-level views about how goods ought to be distributed. If we think that distributive justice mostly involves allowing the free market to allocate resources through supply and demand, then we will likely be attracted to a view of corporate social responsibility where businesses should focus on competing in the market. If our view of distributive justice instead emphasizes government redistribution to correct inequities caused by unbridled capitalism, then we may think corporations have broader obligations to diverse stakeholders.

MORAL THEORY AND BUSINESS ETHICS

So far I have tried to show that the case of Gravity Payments raises many fundamental issues in business ethics related to distribution and also to our vision of businesses' role in a just economy. Once we've identified ethical issues, the next step is analyzing them. How does one defend an ethical position?

Many people new to applied ethics imagine that applied ethics involves taking an ethical theory such as utilitarianism, Kantianism, virtue ethics, or care ethics (see Chapters 5–8) and applying it to the matter at hand. In fact, many early textbooks in applied ethics, including business ethics, took this approach. Though this approach is initially appealing and ethical theory is important, the role of ethical theory in the publications of most business ethicists is considerably more complex. *There is no formula for determining how to use moral theory in applied ethics.*

In order to see this, it is necessary to clarify what an ethical theory is. Ethical theories seek to provide a systematic account of ethical concepts and principles (or they explain why this isn't possible).[11] They advance some sort of test to guide actions such as asking if they maximize happiness or if proposed actions or principles would be assented to by an impartial observer. If successful, these tests would allow us to adjudicate between competing moral demands. A fully developed moral theory will provide guidance on how we should live and act.

Though applied ethicists sometimes work within an ethical theory when thinking through moral issues, this is rarely done through a straightforward top-down application of their preferred theory to an issue. Even if we accept that moral issues should ideally be addressed within an ethical theory, judgment is needed to determine what the ethical theory tells us. For example, a consequentialist may believe that ethical theory tells us we should strive to maximize happiness. Even if we can reach agreement on what happiness is (a topic of considerable disagreement among philosophers and psychologists), we still need to ask how to maximize happiness, when intervention is warranted, and who is responsible for acting. It is far from clear whether Dan Price's actions would be recommended by a consequentialist ethical theory.

A deeper concern with employing an ethical theory as the basis for ethical analysis in applied ethics is that philosophers have not reached an agreement about which ethical theory to endorse. Fundamental issues such as whether actions can be right or wrong independently of their consequences have not been resolved. This creates a problem: if we see applied ethics as the application of ethical theory, then it would seem that we need to resolve longstanding controversies about ethical theory first. This would be a bleak conclusion for anyone hoping that philosophical ethics can provide guidance for how we should live and act.

Fortunately, applied ethicists are able to proceed without relying on a developed ethical theory, drawing on widespread (though not universal) agreement about ethics. Often, moral issues can be analyzed based on factors that most people

and philosophers accept regardless of their ethical theory. Often moral theories are more controversial than many moral judgments. We do not need a moral theory to tell us that wanton cruelty is wrong or that causing harm is impermissible unless there are good reasons for it. In fact, if a moral theory implied that we should lie, cheat, steal, or murder, this would be evidence of the inadequacy of the theory, not of our moral judgments.

If it is possible to proceed in business ethics without explicit reference to an ethical theory, why learn about ethical theory? First, an awareness of ethical theory can sharpen our awareness of ethical issues and considerations. Asking ourselves what ethical theories say about a case can help alert us to morally salient information. Consequentialist theories based on maximizing happiness lead us to ask if policies and institutions promote the overall good. Theories that take their basis in the work of Immanuel Kant remind us of the importance of autonomy and of treating people as ends in themselves and not as mere means. Feminist theories alert us to the possibility of gender-based discrimination and oppression. The diversity of moral theories can help us recognize moral considerations that our preconceptions or prejudices may have led us to overlook.

For example, David Price claimed that his decision to raise wages was based on research suggesting about emotional well-being. Well-being is widely recognized as an important ethical value and consequentialist ethical theories tell us that in many cases we have a duty to promote well-being. Does Price's decision in fact improve the well-being of his employees and other stakeholders associated with Gravity Payments? Is it likely to do so in the long run? Consequentialist theories also address questions of distribution, possibly drawing on theories of distributive justice in political philosophy. What principles should be used to determine if a distribution is just? Few moral or political philosophers endorse Price's crude egalitarian principle that gives no weight to individual difference or merit. Knowledge of these theories helps us analyze and criticize Price's moral reasoning.

Knowledge of moral theory will also alert us to the possibility that well-being may not be all that matters. For instance, does Price's decision to pay all employees the same regardless of differences in their skills, educations, or position treat his employees with respect or as ends in themselves? Sometimes equitable treatment demands that we recognize differences. What employers owe to their stakeholders may not be simply to act in ways that maximize their well-being, but also to fulfil obligations. For example, even if Price does not have a legal obligation to shareholders such as his brother, there may be an implicit agreement that he do so. This may hold even if diverting profits to wages creates more overall wellbeing.

The study of ethical theory introduces us to many conceptual resources developed by philosophers to navigate moral controversies. Ethical theorists seek to systematize our intuitions about ethics and to defend their accounts against rival theories. As a result, they have developed distinctions to better fit their theories to our moral convictions. Distinctions between actions that are obligatory (we must perform them) and actions that are superogatory (performing them goes beyond what is morally required), between negative freedom (freedom from interference) and positive freedom (freedom to be able to do something) help us clarify what is at stake. An understanding of these distinctions gained by studying moral theory provides us with a toolkit for ethical analysis.

THE SOCIAL SCIENCES AND ETHICS

Knowledge of moral theory is important in business ethics, but it is also necessary to know a great deal about business, economics, law, psychology and other fields. People (including philosophers) who attempt to practice business ethics with little practical and theoretical knowledge of business often advance naïve and crude views. For example, the popular view that corporate leaders invariably seek to maximize profits or shareholder value regardless of the harm caused to stakeholders does not survive a cursory scrutiny of companies'

business practices. Some business leaders are ruthless and unscrupulous, but there are plenty of cases that indicate that businesses and their leaders can strive to meet moral ideals. Famous cases such as Aaron Feuerstein's commitment to rebuilding Malden Mills (Chapter 16), the Grameen Bank (Chapter 24), or Café Feminino (Chapter 88) rebut the claim that businesses practice corporate social responsibility only for public relations or because it is more profitable in the long run. Indeed, the practice of business ethics is largely premised on evidence that businesses sometimes meet ethical standards and that if they increasingly do so, it will increase their value to society.

Another reason why empirical knowledge is necessary in business ethics is that many ethical disputes turn on matters of fact rather than on values or moral principles. People often reach moral conclusions based on false, inaccurate, or one-side beliefs. For example, to effectively analyze Gravity Payments, it is important to understand that it is a private business. This is crucial for understanding Price's obligations to shareholders. If Gravity Payments were a publically traded company, Price would have faced legal constraints and quite possibly moral obligations to honor expectations and contracts.[12] Another fact to keep in mind is Gravity Payments is a small company, so a redistribution of executive compensation and profits made it possible to substantially raise wages. In firms that employ thousands or more workers, this would not substantially raise their salaries.[13] These facts alert us to the possibility that if our concern is equality, we might be better looking at other redistributive practices such as taxation, rather than salaries.

Ethical disputes may also depend on what empirical theories tell us about the world. Parties may generally agree on morally desirable outcomes, but dispute which institutions or social arrangements are most likely to produce these outcomes. Many of the most fundamental controversies in business ethics concern how markets function—or do not function—in different contexts. For example, advocates of shareholder conceptions of corporate social responsibility do not believe that shareholders are all that matter morally. Rather, their conviction is that when business is structured around benefiting shareholders, society benefits: competition between firms aiming to increase shareholder value increases efficiency, leading to lower prices for higher quality consumer goods.

To assess these debates, business ethicists need to understand markets, where they succeed and, perhaps even more importantly, under which circumstances they fail.[14] They need to understand firms and should acquire a working knowledge of areas such as institutional economics and theories such as agency theory (see Chapter 15). Business does not exist in a vacuum. Government regulation is also important. This brings in the study of law and policy and also of human psychology which is often relevant for business ethics. Learning these subjects can occupy a lifetime, but a basic knowledge of these subjects helps identify, understand, and assess authors' theoretical convictions. Perhaps even more importantly, learning a little bit about these topics should teach us modesty about the complexity of the world and the limits of our understanding. Applied ethics demands moral reflection with an invitation to learn more about the world: we need to make an effort to understand how things are to think about how they should be.

NOTES

1   Kahneman, D., and A. Deaton. 2010. "High Income Improves Evaluation of Life but Not Emotional Well-Being." *Proceedings of the National Academy of Sciences* 107 (38): 16489–93. doi:10.1073/pnas.1011492107.

2   Cohen, Patricia. 2015. "One Company's New Minimum Wage: $70,000 a Year." *New York Times*, April 13. http://www.nytimes.com/2015/04/14/business/owner-of-gravity-payments-a-credit-card-processor-is-setting-a-new-minimum-wage-70000-a-year.html.

3   Cohen, Patricia. 2015. "A Company Copes with Backlash Against the Raise That Roared." July 31. http://www.nytimes.com/2015/08/02/business/a-company-copes-with-backlash-against-the-raise-that-roared.html.

4   Howell, Kellan. 2015. "Dan Price, Seattle CEO Who Set Company Minimum Wage at $70K, Struggles to Make Ends Meet." *Washington Times*, August 1. http://www.washingtontimes.com/news/2015/aug/1/dan-price-seattle-ceo-who-set-company-minimum-wage/.

5   For an overview of the issue of sexual harassment in business ethics, see Dromm, Keith. 2012. *Sexual Harassment: An Introduction to the Conceptual and Ethical Issues*. Peterborough, Ontario: Broadview Press.

6   Kennedy, Ellen J., and Leigh Lawton. 1992. "Business Ethics in Fiction." *Journal of Business Ethics* 11 (3): 187–95.

7   Weise, Karen. 2015. "The CEO Paying Everyone $70,000 Salaries Has Something to Hide." *Bloomberg Business*, December 1. http://www.bloomberg.com/features/2015-gravity-ceo-dan-price/.

8   For an exploration of distributive justice, see the first two sections of Unit 6.

9   Weise 2015.

10   MacDonald, Chris. 2015. "Why Gravity Payments' $70,000 Minimum Salary, Sadly, Won't Catch On." *The Business Ethics Bowl*. April 16. http://businessethicsblog.com/2015/04/16/why-gravity-payments-70000-minimum-salary-sadly-wont-catch-on/.

11   Readers looking for a systematic overview of ethical theory may find useful Kagan, Shelly. 1998. *Normative Ethics*. Dimensions of Philosophy Series. Boulder, Colo: Westview Press.

12   Chris MacDonald raises this point.

13   Yglesias, Matthew. 2015. "What We Can Learn from the CEO Who Took a 93% Pay Cut to Give His Team a Raise." *Vox*, April 15. http://www.vox.com/2015/4/15/8420203/dan-price.

14   Two useful overviews of economics for the general reader are Wheelan, Charles J. 2010. *Naked Economics: Undressing the Dismal Science*. Fully rev. and updated. New York: W.W. Norton, and Chang, Ha-Joon. 2014. *Economics: The User's Guide*. New York: Bloomsbury Press.

—5—
UTILITARIANISM

David Meeler

IN EVERYDAY LIFE, WE MAKE A HOST OF VALUE judgments. Some of these have nothing to do with morality, such as which shoes are better for running or which restaurant has more tasty food. Other value judgments are obviously moral. For instance, many people think that murder is wrong or stealing violates basic human rights. Most of the ordinary claims we make can be tested for truth. If I say "The class average on the mid-term is 78," we can verify this. But how are we to test value claims? Suppose I say "Espresso is good." How can we determine if I am telling the truth? Maybe I just mean "I like espresso." Suppose instead that I say "Charity is good," or "Rape is wrong." Should the test be any different? Many people begin testing claims by checking for shared meaning of the terminology. If "espresso" is just my word for "mass murder" then we have a problem. Now, you and I probably won't have radical confusion between words like "espresso" and "mass murder," but terms like "good" and "bad" aren't always straightforward. So, one important way that many philosophers begin addressing issues in ethics is to investigate the *meaning* of our value terms. One of the factors differentiating utilitarians from other ethicists is their definition of value-terms, and this is where we'll start our look into utilitarianism.

To begin with, utilitarianism instructs us to do the greatest good we can for the greatest number of our ethical compatriots. Although some elements of utilitarian theory can be traced to Epicurus (341–270 BCE), its fullest form is that associated with Jeremy Bentham (1748–1832 CE) and John Stuart Mill (1806–73 CE). These two philosophers developed many of the principles and approaches still used by utilitarians today. Like many philosophical theories, it is easy to provide a quick statement of the key themes in utilitarianism, though it can be difficult to master the subtleties inherent in a richer understanding of the view. Let me start with a simplistic version.

In its most basic form, utilitarian thinking is associated with hedonism. Hedonism is the view that good and bad go along with pleasure and pain. Bentham's utilitarian foundations were hedonistic. In his investigation of how we use the word "good," Bentham noticed that it's usually when we are talking about things that bring us pleasure (or at least diminish our pain); and those things we call "bad" are those that cause us pain (or take away our pleasure). For instance, I get pleasure from chocolate-chip cookies, while you may find apples to be a source of endless joy. Similarly, studying for math tests always brought me distress, while some people are perpetually vexed by writing philosophy papers. In terms of a utilitarian theory then, the hedonist version says we should generate the most pleasure (or diminish as much pain) as we can for the relevant moral parties. This aspect of hedonism only describes how people use the terms, and as a result this is referred to as "descriptive" hedonism. From this simple beginning based on the psychological preferences of people, Bentham goes on to suggest that we *ought* to promote pleasure and diminish pain in our daily choices and activities. Thus, Bentham shifts from speaking descriptively about the world to offering the guidance of a standard for behavior, which is called a "norm." As a result, we say that this version is "normative" hedonism.

This view sounds simple enough, but almost immediately an interesting question emerges. Is it the cookie that is good? Or the pleasure the cookie causes? For hedonists, it is really the pleasure or pain, and not the cookie itself that is the root of our value terms. Cookies are good because they *generate* pleasure; of course, too many cookies are bad because that produces displeasure. But the pleasure or pain we feel is an *effect* of some other cause. The general approach that focuses on effects, or outcomes, is called consequentialism because the value of an action, or a thing, is found in the consequences that result. Consequentialism, in general, has a strong foothold in common sense. Most of us believe that we should endeavor to improve the world. At the least, most people try to make things better for themselves and their families. When we strive to make the world a better place, we are trying to achieve certain outcomes, or consequences that we think are good; and we judge the value of our choices in part by the quality of the results. For example, we often trade today's struggle for tomorrow's gain, such as studying hard and making good grades in order to get better jobs that make it easier to provide well for our families. And when we assess our actions (as well as the actions of others) we generally look to see what good came from our choices, or whether any harm was done. The old adages "All's well that ends well" and "No harm; no foul" nicely sum up this intuition. Hedonism is merely one kind of utilitarian theory. We can say that utilitarianism is the most famous consequentialist theory.

While the basic idea of hedonism has some intuitive appeal, several aspects remain unaddressed. For example, critics say when we rest our morality on mere pleasure we debase humanity. Common sense tells us that consequences are important, but it also seems that not all consequences are equal. The distinction that arises here is between the mere *amount* of pleasure (quantitative consequentialism) and the *kind* of pleasure we get (qualitative consequentialism). Jeremy

Bentham clearly seems to have advocated quantitative consequentialism, for he famously said that playing a simple board-game has as much value as reading fine poetry, so long as equal amounts of pleasure are created. After all, different people get pleasure from different activities. John Stuart Mill, on the other hand, favored qualitative consequentialism. Mill suggests that, like diamonds, pleasures can be divided into higher and lower grades. Higher pleasures include intellectual pleasures, such as working on mathematical proofs, while lower pleasures are more basic, like sensory experiences.

Having said that, Mill's choice of what kinds of activities we include in the higher and lower pleasures is not arbitrary. His strategy is quite interesting. Mill begins with the practical notion that we must ask people to judge whether pleasures of the intellect are qualitatively better than pleasures of the body. But there is a catch. We need only adhere to the opinions of *competent* judges. If someone can experience and appreciate both types of pleasure, then they are competent judges of the relative values. This also rests firmly on common sense. If you were going to ask someone whether reggae music is better than country music would you ask someone who only liked one and hated the other? Would you ask someone who hated both? No. Any time we make a comparative value judgment between things, Mill thinks it is important to first be capable of enjoying each. Only then will you be in a position to make the call. As it turns out, Mill says, all competent judges agree that intellectual pleasures are of a higher quality than physical pleasures. Mill's move from quantitative consequentialism to qualitative consequentialism is an important development in utilitarian ethical theories.

In addition to illustrating consequentialism, the example of pleasurable cookies highlights an important ethical distinction: that between intrinsic value and extrinsic value. Intrinsic value (which you can think of as "inside" value) is the value that a thing has in and of itself. Intrinsic value is also called "inherent" value. Extrinsic value (which you may think of as "outside" value) is when one thing is valuable because it leads to something else. Extrinsic value is also called "instrumental" value because one thing is valued as a tool, or an instrument, for getting something else. Money is often used as an example of something with only extrinsic value. When you think about it, money isn't really worth much in and of itself; the greatest value found in money is that other people are willing to trade things for it. So having at least average amounts of money usually brings pleasure to people because money is a general device that can be used to get the specific things that make us happy. As a result, money is valuable for what it can get you. But not all things are like this. If you are reading this book, it is highly probable that you are a university student. As such, you may have heard the saying "Education is its own reward." The meaning of this expression is built on the idea that education has intrinsic value. Of course, we all know education has extrinsic value as well. Studies indicate that college graduates have higher earning potential over the course of their lives. So your college education will likely lead to more money over the long term. Since education has both intrinsic and extrinsic value, ethicists say that education's value is "mixed." Many things in the world have mixed value because they are valued both intrinsically and extrinsically.

As well as making the switch from quantitative consequentialism to qualitative consequentialism, Mill made another important change to Bentham's basic utilitarian idea. Where Bentham focused his analysis of value terms on pleasure and pain, Mill's emphasis is on "happiness" more generally. Although Bentham speaks of happiness and Mill understood happiness (at least in part) as related to pleasure and pain, they each emphasized a different component. So Mill's idea represents a shift in utilitarian thinking. We can paraphrase Mill's understanding of utilitarianism as follows: produce the greatest balance of happiness over unhappiness for all members of our moral community. This focus on happiness rather than pleasure is one of the most fundamental changes Mill made to the utilitarian starting points elucidated by Bentham

in part because it *includes* the shift to qualitative consequentialism.

Moreover, Mill thinks that happiness holds a special place in the world: it is the only thing that we value *only* inherently. Mill's argument for this claim has two primary points. First, Mill suggests that happiness is a universal goal; the greatest proof of the desirability of happiness is the simple fact that everyone desires to be happy. Obviously, we don't all desire the same things because different things make each of us happy. But in the end, every person wants to be happy. So, one aspect of Mill's argument for the inherent value of happiness is that happiness is the end result of our various chains of extrinsically valued achievements. Perhaps you get good grades to get into a good law-school to get a high-paying job to make enough money to buy a Ferrari to make you happy. In short, we might say that all of our value-roads lead to happiness. The second important feature of Mill's argument is that happiness just doesn't work like money; we don't want happiness *because of* other things that happiness can bring. Granted, it is probably true that if you are happy then you will have more positive relationships, or make more lucrative sales, etc. Mill's point is that this is not the *reason why* we value happiness. We value happiness purely for its own sake, and not for the other things it gets us. As a general rule, we don't seek to *use* our happiness to get something else more desirable. Even asking what we expect happiness to get us reveals a fundamental misunderstanding of the inherent value we place on happiness.

Another aspect of utilitarianism—or consequentialism more generally—that we haven't addressed centers on the recipient of the outcome. Up to now I have spoken of generating good consequences for our "ethical compatriots," "members of our moral community," and for "all relevant parties," but I have left these groups undefined. So we don't know who belongs to these groups. As a result, one might readily ask some important questions of utilitarians: Should I generate good consequences for myself or my family? Should I generate good consequences for my community or for everyone?

In its weakest form, utilitarianism requires me to consider the impact of my actions on all those parties who are affected. But this apparently simple idea can quickly become complicated. First, it seems that many people can be affected by a single act. Imagine that I throw a glass bottle out of my car window, which breaks in the road. Another car drives over the glass and pops a tire. Changing the tire makes the driver late to get home, which irritates his wife so much that she kicks the family dog, which then runs out of the house down to the park and bites a child. Does the child's dog-bite *count* as part of the consequence of my littering? It is difficult to specify exactly how many extended consequences I should be held accountable for. In general, utilitarians suggest that the consequences I am responsible for are those relatively close to the action itself, so the dog-bite would not count. For most utilitarians, the driver's upset wife would not count either since there is no way I could reasonably foresee those events. However, the driver getting a flat tire does count because it is to be expected when you throw glass onto the road.

Secondly, I am probably much *more interested* in the consequences for me than I am in the consequences for others, especially those who aren't significant to me. Nevertheless, utilitarian ideals forbid me from giving more importance to my consequences over others who are affected by my actions. Traditional utilitarians like Bentham and Mill believed in strict equality among those affected by an action. In other words, when you assess the value of your actions, you must be impartial as to who gets the good or bad consequences. Benefits or burdens that fall on one person are just as important as those befalling another; even when the person is you. So I can't count my pain as more important than your pain. In fact, this facet of neutrality in classical utilitarianism requires me to treat the consequences for you as equally important as I treat the consequences for myself. From an impartial point of view, one person's happiness is as valuable as another's; and utilitarians think ethics should be done from an impartial point of view. This impersonal accounting is meant to prevent personal bias from entering our value judgments.

Third, even if we settle how many links in the consequence-chain are relevant, and I give no special weight to my own consequences, we might wonder whether the consequences for dogs, cows, chickens or fish should ever count. If the chain of consequences I am responsible for stops at the dog, then it couldn't possibly include the child's bite. According to utilitarianism, the pleasure or suffering of animals *is relevant*. For hedonists like Bentham the connection is straightforward since they focus on pleasure and pain, and many animals obviously feel both. When qualitative consequentialism like Mill's is preferred, we give intellectual happiness more weight than bodily pleasures. However, we are still required to count physical pleasures and pains as comparable to other physical effects. Intellectual pleasures might outweigh some physical suffering, but we must treat like pains alike; and since animals can feel physical pain, we must emphasize it as much as we do our own physical pain. Impartiality and universality are important features of all utilitarian thinking because utilitarians adhere to strict equality when counting the various consequences of our actions for all those affected. So the members of our moral community include all creatures capable of experiencing any *kind* of pleasure, pain, happiness or unhappiness we think is morally relevant for normal humans; and we must assess those consequences for all those closely affected by our actions.

In its most concise expression, utilitarianism instructs us to generate the greatest good for the greatest number. Perhaps many of our actions directly impact only a small number of people. However, if you are in a special role the scope of your actions might be enormous. Consider a state legislator. If you are one of the state-senators for your county, then you must consider the impact proposed laws will have on a vast number of people. Similarly, if you are a judge then your decisions will carry the weight of precedent for court cases that follow. Clearly, legislators must be concerned with the general welfare of the populace, and utilitarians say they should base their decisions on whether more overall happiness (or less overall unhappiness) will result for the largest number of people. Politicians are just as constrained by the limits of strict equality as the rest of us, which means they cannot work for special interests, for the benefit of themselves, for the benefit of their own class, or their own race, gender, etc. Strict egalitarianism requires government representatives to always work towards the maximum happiness for everyone equally.

Impartially generating happiness for as many sentient beings as you can might be all a utilitarian would need if we only assessed the value of actions *after* they occurred and the consequences could be readily determined. But when it comes to ethics, we often seek *guidance* on how we ought to act *before* we decide what to do. Thus another important distinction in utilitarian thinking is that between whether we are to focus our ethical evaluations on actual consequences or merely foreseeable consequences. On first appearance, this hardly seems like a significant distinction. Wouldn't we just use foreseeable consequences when deciding what to do ahead of time and use actual consequences when evaluating what has already been done? This is a good question, and the guidelines it suggests seem to work reasonably well much of the time. However, problem cases might emerge. Imagine that someone wants to generate substantial happiness, thinks carefully and foresees positive results; but when the plan is put in place, disastrous results follow. The foreseeable consequences were good but the actual consequences were bad. How should we assess the merits of this person and the action? Even though the results were bad, should we soften our judgment because the intentions were good? Classical utilitarians would not favor such an approach. Bentham and Mill both advocated expected utility (which is a form of foreseeable consequences) when we make plans and choose actions; they advocated judging actions based only on actual consequences. Over time, we can be expected to get better at making more accurate predictions of expected utility.

One final aspect that bears consideration is *how* consequences are to be weighted. For both Bentham and Mill, we should assess the value of our actions by determining the best balance of utility over disutility, but even that is not obviously straightforward. For instance, should we balance the *total* amount of happiness over unhappiness, or should we balance the *average* amounts of happiness and unhappiness? Traditionally, utilitarians like Bentham and Mill based their moral assessments on total happiness, rather than average happiness. Classical utilitarians said we should determine all the morally-relevant parties to the foreseeable consequences of an act, total the amount of happiness (remember, happiness is "good") that each party should get, and subtract off the total amount of unhappiness (or "bad"), and we'll have the net happiness for each person. Then we total all the net results (gains and losses) for each morally-relevant person to get a total net happiness for a proposed action. We do this for every option we are faced with, and then compare the expected total net results. We should choose to do whichever option yields the best total net outcome, regardless of who gets what allotment of happiness in each.

CRITICISM OF UTILITARIANISM

Traditionally, the philosophical criticism most often mounted against utilitarianism rests on the possibility that highly positive outcomes give good reasons for using horrendous measures to get them. The colloquial expression that captures this feature of utilitarian thinking is "the end justifies the means." Imagine the vast majority of the class decided that only one student will be responsible for doing all the assignments throughout the semester, for everyone; and they chose you. By heaping all the burdens on one person, everyone else benefits. Whenever those benefits outweigh the burdens, utilitarians say that nothing immoral has been done. On a larger scale, this means that some forms of slavery are permitted by utilitarian thinking. If enough happiness is generated for enough people to outweigh the unhappiness caused for the number of slaves, then the resulting happiness justifies the means of slavery. Critics point out that slavery is just plain wrong, regardless of how much happiness results. The mere fact that we *use* one person to generate happiness for another violates basic principles of justice, which require us to respect the value of persons. Such criticisms are often associated with ideas from Immanuel Kant because they are based on the inherent value of human life. Recall that utilitarians think happiness itself is the only thing that has purely inherent value, so a person's life is valuable only inasmuch as it is a source of happiness. It is this very rejection of inherent value of human life that makes utilitarianism seem so cold. *You* are not important to a utilitarian; only the happiness you experience is significant.

CASE EXAMPLE

A careful look at the mission statement from almost any large corporation operating in the twenty-first century will reveal a common idea. By and large, all corporations claim they seek to serve the long-term interests of their stakeholders. Stakeholders, generally, are understood as parties with a significant "stake" in the company's survival; so stakeholders tend to include such groups as investors (stockholders), employees (management and labor), customers, suppliers, and financiers (banks or other loan organizations). Naturally, the interests of the various stakeholder groups are frequently at odds with one another. For example, local communities want people employed, business taxes paid and their environment unpolluted, customers want lower priced goods while employees want higher wages, all of which compete with each other as well as cut into the higher profits desired by stockholders. So managing the overall strategy of the company means finding the best way to balance all these competing interests. In short, it means maximizing the overall long-term benefit for all.

Perhaps an example will help to illustrate both the positive and negative aspects of utilitarian principles in action. Consider the impact the last decade has had on the textile industry in the United States. Because textile plants historically relied on agricultural products, they are most often located in rural communities; and since these communities are generally small, the textile companies tend to be significant employers in these areas. Textile plants are also often primary employers of minorities and women in their communities, which has advanced social and economic justice in America. Textile workers tend to earn more in their communities, so the jobs are coveted by local workers. Around 1997, the dollar began rising in value as many currencies throughout Southeast Asia declined rapidly. As a result, it became more expensive to produce goods in America and less expensive to import goods from Asia. Since that time an increasing number of textile jobs have been lost in America while textile imports from Asia have increased dramatically. When major employers, like textile plants, close in small communities, the effects are far reaching. Local businesses cannot sell goods and services to people who no longer earn a living; burdens on local government support agencies increase; and contributions to charities and churches drop off precipitously.

Of course, we all exacerbate this situation on a daily basis because we usually look for low prices when we shop, and we rarely consider where goods are made. Stores even advertise, and position themselves, as "low price leaders." So consumers like you and me seem to prefer low prices and (perhaps inadvertently) choose to support the textile industries in other countries. Companies who supply goods to the retail market appreciate this, and therefore give us just what we demand: less expensive goods. So if manufacturers want to stay in business, they shift production to areas of the world where they can produce more goods at a lower cost. In short, our consumer demand for low-cost goods drives manufacturers to produce low-cost goods.

Naturally, corporate executives realize that individual people will lose their jobs during lay-offs or plant-closings; and they realize that in some cases entire communities will be very hard-hit. Of all the textile jobs lost in the US between 1997 and 2006, 88% were lost in North and South Carolina alone—where the bulk of the US textile manufacturing is located. But corporate executives are not trying to make decisions that destroy communities; rather they are trying to make decisions that ensure the long-term success of their companies as a whole, and this often means thinking about consequences on a global scale. Workers in the US may lose some jobs, while workers in another country gain jobs and a substantially improved lifestyle, and consumers in the US get cheaper goods, all while worldwide stockholder profits are maintained. Although one group's utility is decreased, many others are increased. Unsurprisingly, this probably does not comfort the worker who loses her job, but overall the benefits are substantial.

This style of utilitarian thinking is not confined to the overarching challenges of managing a global business. Most school children in the United States memorize the preamble to the Constitution which avows a deep concern to "promote the general welfare, and sustain the blessing of liberty" for all its citizens, now and in the future. Yet, this frequently means that government officials must balance a host of complex and competing interests in their pursuit of general welfare. For instance, after the Persian Gulf War in 1991, Turkey received a 50% increase in its textile importing quota from the US as a reward for its assistance during the war. Policy initiatives pursued by George W. Bush's administration in the years immediately following the terrorist attacks of September 11, 2001 were analogous. Subsequent to 9/11 the United States initiated a "free-trade" agreement with Jordan, the first ever for an Arab nation. Similarly, after Pakistan provided assistance in searching for Osama bin Laden and unseating the Taliban regime in Afghanistan, the Bush administration wanted to reward the Pakistani government. The most obvious way to do this was to soften the tariffs on Pakistani textiles. Textile manufacturing constitutes a significant portion of Pakistan's economy,

and disenchanted, unemployed Pakistanis are ripe recruits for extremist Islamic terrorist organizations who attack Americans as well as seek to destabilize pro-American governments like the one in Pakistan. So, if we can assist Pakistan's economy, then more Pakistanis will have a decent job, which in turn means there will be fewer possible recruits for terrorist organizations. Moreover, the Bush administration reasoned that Pakistani citizens would see the increase in jobs as a direct result of US measures on their behalf, and therefore they would feel affinity towards America. (The specific Bush plan to offer economic assistance to Pakistan's textile industry was not approved by the US Congress.)

Thus, pursuing a solution to one set of economic or geo-political problems may create new troubles; but these too can be addressed with some utilitarian thinking. As a result of the devastating effects the shift in worldwide textile production has had on communities in the American South, a large amount of US tax-dollars are spent on support services and career retraining for displaced textile workers. Expenditures through the Worker Adjustment and Retraining Notification Act (WARN) and the Trade Adjustment Act (TAA) are the most notable. Spreading the costs out in this way prevents those citizens in one area from bearing a disproportionate burden to support our consumer desire for cheap goods and our political desires to prevent terrorism.

So the US textile industry was hit hard at the turn of the twenty-first century in part due to utilitarian thinking at three different levels. First, consumers generally try to get the most good they can while incurring the lowest burden possible, which means they usually satisfy their preference for lower-priced goods. This first level of utilitarian thinking was augmented when the relative values of global currencies shifted in a way that made production in Asia more cost-effective. Consequently, corporate managers made the second round of utilitarian-style decisions when they responded by shifting production to more cost-effective locales, thus securing more long-term benefit for their companies. Finally, political initiatives that comprise part of America's foreign policy sometimes sacrifice an impact at home for a benefit abroad. We can say that utilitarian thinking contributed to, if not generated, difficulties for the American textile industry at the turn of the twenty-first century. But it is also utilitarian-style thinking that offers a solution to those difficulties, and hope to those displaced workers here in America. Our government policy-makers realize that international gains must be paid for, but justice and impartiality demand that no one group bears a disproportionate share of the burden. So when one segment of our economy is hard-hit, all Americans contribute tax dollars to the support, retraining, and revitalization of our workforce.

—6—
KANTIAN BUSINESS ETHICS

Heather Salazar

IMAGINE THAT YOU ARE THE OWNER OF A vitamin and supplement retail store. You must make many decisions about selling products that may be helpful, harmful, or ineffective. However, even ineffective and harmful supplements produce high profit-margins when they are in high-demand. For example, shark-cartilage has been touted as a cure for cancer based on the fact that sharks rarely contract cancer. Even though empirical studies on the impact of taking such supplements demonstrates no positive benefit apart from placebo effects, people who are in search for a cure for cancer often purchase large quantities of shark-cartilage, thus increasing the sales of vitamin and supplement retailers like you. The ethical question that you face is whether you should sell such products knowing that cancer patients are spending their money and hope for a lost cause as far as shark-cartilage goes.

An even more serious case involves selling products that are actually harmful to people who take them. For example, Ephedra is an herbal weight-loss supplement that was banned in the US in Feb. 2004 due to a large number of potentially fatal side-effects associated with its misuse, including over 155 reported deaths. But it was re-released in April 2006 because there was no proof of its harmfulness when taken according to the instructions. You know that if you stock your shelves with Ephedra it will produce incredible profits since it is in extremely high demand by the millions who are looking desperately for a solution to their obesity. Should you allow the consumer to determine for herself whether the risk of taking

these supplements is worth it? If you do, are you allowing consumers their autonomy or are you using desperate people in order to make a profit for yourself? This is obviously a difficult question as are so many of the ethical. Ethical theories help to guide people in their search for the correct decision in such complex cases.

The Kantian answer to whether you should sell ineffective and harmful supplements emphasizes, first, allowing and helping people to make rational decisions and, second, having a motivation that comes from what Kant calls the "good will," which means that your motivation is from duty and is not simply self-seeking. As the retailer, you can sell the supplements if you can do so while respecting people. One way you could respect people's autonomy and refrain from being paternalistic is by empowering people to make rational decisions about the supplements that they take. This would include making information available on the effectiveness and dangers of the supplements that you sell and helping people to use the resources that you provide. However, in order to be acting morally, in addition to providing such information, you must be motivated to do so because you know that this is the right thing to do, and not, for example, because you are afraid of creating a bad reputation for yourself. The Kantian principles will allow you to sell ineffective and harmful supplements if you are not deceiving or harming people, or otherwise using them for your own personal gain. When you help people to make the right decisions, by providing them with the best information that you have, you are respecting people and their ability to make good decisions.

The Kantian approach to business ethics, like Kantian ethics in general, emphasizes acting with respect toward all autonomous beings. It claims that we all have duties toward one another that depend on our relationships with one another, with the most basic and all-pervasive relationship between persons being that they are fellow members of humanity. As members of humanity, we each have value that stems from our rational and moral capacities, and we all ought to act in a way that shows appreciation for that value.

Kantian ethics differs from the other standard approaches, most notably rights-based theories and utilitarianism, in various significant ways. Unlike utilitarianism, it does not ask us to promote any particular value and it resists basing moral judgments on the quantification and/or aggregation of value. Like rights-based approaches, it proposes constraints on actions, giving us rules upon which to act. Duties are unlike rights, however, since although every right possessed by a person creates a respective duty for others to respect that right, some duties on a duty-based approach do not have correlate rights. That is: if I have a duty to do something for you, you don't necessarily have the right to demand it from me, or make me do it. For example, I have a duty to love my sister, but she does not have a right to my love. I have a duty to protect my country, perhaps, but my country does not have the right to use my labor and life in defense of itself.

Whether one has a duty to someone else depends not on the other's rights, as it does on a rights-based theory, but on the rational assessment of what is the right thing to do based on the various types of relationship that you have with the person. Morality for Kantians is constituted by how we ought to treat each other as fellow members of humanity, although other duties can arise for other types of relationships. In addition to this, it differs from rights-based approaches and utilitarianism by claiming that it is not only what you do that matters morally, but with what motivation you do it.

The crux of Kant's ethics resides in his startling claim that the only thing that is intrinsically good,

or good-in-itself, is the good will. He says that "There is no possibility for thinking of anything at all in the world, or even out of it, which can be regarded as good without qualification, except a *good will*" (MM 393). The will is the rational part of each person, and the good will is rationality which chooses to do what is right for the reason that it is good. This is why all members of humanity, or all rational beings, have value, and this is also the reason why these beings are the only thing of true value. The argument for the claim that the only thing that is good-in-itself is the good will relies on a further claim that it is the only thing that is truly under our control. Our external circumstances, like where, when and to whom we are born, are not under our control; so although it may be unfortunate that some, through no fault of their own, are living in absolute poverty with no hope of living happy or long lives, we cannot control these factors. Furthermore, although we can choose actions to better the situations of those who are less fortunate, the results of our actions are not fully under our control since they depend on external circumstances and other people. For example, I might donate money to UNICEF, but the money might never get to the destination to produce the help that is needed, if, for instance, there was a terrible hurricane that prevented the truck from delivering it or someone robbed it. The money might get to the needy families but it might not actually help them if they buy food with it and become ill due to contaminants in the food. These things are not under our control; the only thing that is truly under our control is our choices or our motivation with which we intend to act. Rationality enables me to reflect on the circumstances of others who are in need, and decide on a method of helping them. It allows me to intend to do what is good, but the results of my intentions and actions are not entirely up to me. So according to the Kantian, both the choice of what to do and the motivation are integral to the moral worth of the action. I have enumerated four simple steps for determining the moral worth of a choice below:

DETERMINING THE RIGHT ACTION AND MOTIVATION:

1. Formulate a Maxim-for-Action, that is, a principle for whether and when a type of action should be done.
2. Evaluate it as coming from the good will or not, that is, whether in willing actions according to that maxim you would have the right motivation.
3. If it is motivated by the good will, it is good, and you are good in doing it.
4. If it isn't motivated by the Good Will, but is *consistent* with it, then the action is good, but you are not doing it from the right motive and so you are not praiseworthy.

1. Maxims-for-Action

The first step in determining whether you should perform an action is to identify the action. Developing a maxim will allow you to determine whether the action is correct or not. Such maxims-for-action involve asserting what you will do and for what purpose you will do it. For example: I will take philosophy courses in order to learn how to reason well.

2.1. The Good Will: Right Actions

The second step asks you to evaluate the maxim-for-action as coming from the good will or not. The good will is the part of you that is motivated to do what is good for the right reasons so it involves evaluating (a) whether the action is the right action and (b) whether the action is rightly motivated.

For Kant, the right actions to take are those that are rational. This is because the will is the rational part of each of us, and so, if the maxim is rational, it is fit to be willed. Kant thinks that there are various tests that will allow us to see whether a maxim is rational or not, which we can call the Categorical Imperative Tests. The Categorical Imperative determines permissible, impermissible, and required actions.

Kant has three formulations of the Categorical Imperative, or what he takes to be the supreme law of pure rationality. These are often called "The Formula of Universal Law," "The Formula of Humanity," and "The Formula of Autonomy." According to Kant, all three of these formulations have the same results. In this explanation, I will focus on the first two formulations.

2.1.1. THE FORMULA OF UNIVERSAL LAW

In order to be rational, one must also be logical, and the most primary logical rule that should be observed is to be consistent; anything that is inconsistent is illogical and thus irrational and immoral for Kant. Kant's first formulation, the Formula of Universal Law, uses the rule of consistency to eliminate those maxims that are internally inconsistent, or impossible to will if everyone willed them. It states that you ought to "Act only according to that maxim whereby you can at the same time will that it should become a universal law" (Kant, MM 421).

After you have created a maxim, you must universalize it, which means that you must think of a law that everyone act according to the maxim that you have developed for yourself. A universalized maxim involves transforming my maxim "I will use my company's funds in order to woo prospective clients and gain business for the company," to a universalized maxim which states "Everyone will use their company's funds in order to woo prospective clients and gain business for the company."

Once it is universalized, you must check for inconsistencies. Ask yourself whether it is possible for everyone to will the maxim and to achieve their goals. For example, is everyone doing the action consistent with your achieving the purpose of your original maxim? If everyone used their company's funds to gain new clients, then companies would be investing in and obtaining new business by exerting their own resources. It would be possible for all companies to invest and gain new clients, including you. Therefore, the maxim is fit to be willed and it is a permissible action for you to perform.

Some maxims are inconsistent when universalized and thus irrational and impermissible to act on. For example, take the maxim, "I will embezzle my company's funds in order to obtain extra money rather than invest extra resources into the company." If universalized, everyone will be embezzling money from their companies and (1) the companies will not have enough money for people to embezzle and (2) the companies will know that everyone is embezzling money and they will stop people from embezzling money. If the companies do not have enough money for everyone to embezzle, then that defeats the purpose of your maxim, which is to gain money. It is therefore impermissible to act on that maxim. In addition, since the companies will know that you are trying to embezzle money, they will be able to stop you from doing so and punish you for it. This defeats the purpose of your maxim, as well, since they will stop you from embezzling the money. Since there is a contradiction in everyone willing this maxim, it is impermissible to act on it—i.e., it is required that you not act on it.

It is easy for people to misunderstand the Formula of Universal Law and think that the test requires that we see whether a good or a bad state of affairs *results* from the universalized version of the maxim. For example, someone might think that if the company knows that you are embezzling money you will be punished for it, and since you don't want to be punished, it is not a good maxim to act upon. Although it might be true that you should not act on maxims that will create bad outcomes, this is not what the Formula of Universal Law tests. It tests whether it is possible for everyone to will it and still achieve the purposes of the maxims.

By testing the universalizability of the maxim under scrutiny, the Formula of Universal Law prohibits people from making exceptions of themselves. It thus forbids, in general, all actions that rely on others not knowing what you are doing, which is a form of deceit. So stealing and lying are impermissible in any circumstance. And this has a tremendous impact on business as many of

business's ethical issues concern just these sorts of problems. For example, fraud, stock-market schemes, piggyback trading, deception in advertising and accounting, honesty in contracting and in lawsuits, and stealing company resources such as office supplies, taking extra time off, spending extravagantly, and pumping funds towards one's own investments.

2.1.2. THE FORMULA OF HUMANITY

The Formula of Humanity is a more intuitive version of the Categorical Imperative and it states to "Act in such a way that you treat humanity, whether in your own person or in the person of another, always at the same time as an end and never simply as a means" (Kant, MM 429). This statement, too, relies on the logical rule of consistency, but its focus is different. Humanity, which is the rational power within individuals, is valuable in itself, and is the only thing, according to Kant, that is valuable in itself. Because it is of value, and it is something that not only you possess, but all beings with rationality possess, everyone must respect each others' rationality. Respecting others' and your own rationality entails, according to this formulation, never treating it as mere means and always treating it as an end in itself. An end is something that is valuable in itself, and a means is something that is valuable only as a way to get what you want or to achieve an end. So we ought to always treat people's rationality as being valuable in itself. Therefore, we should allow people to use their rationality and we should use our own rationality, and we should never circumvent the use of rationality in order to get something that we desire, even something that we think of as rational and good.

This formulation, like the Formula of Universal Law, eliminates lying and deceit of any kind. Furthermore, it eliminates using ourselves without the consent of our rationality and it prohibits our use of other people without the consent of their rationality. This is not the same thing as getting someone's consent, since a person can give his or her consent without giving her *rational* consent.

Giving one's rational consent to something means reflecting on the action and its consequences, and examining whether it is a good thing for one to perform it. So someone might sign a contract for a credit card that charges an exorbitant amount of interest, but being charged this amount of interest is not what a rational person, under most circumstances, would choose. It is therefore impermissible and immoral for the person to sign the contract and it is impermissible and immoral for anyone to ask a person to sign such a contract.

In the Formula of Humanity it can also be seen quite clearly that people ought never to be unfair or treat people poorly. So issues in business that deal with inequities among the sexes, genders, races, and ages, and topics that concern the subjugation of individuals in unfair positions of bargaining power and sweatshop-like circumstances are also impermissible and immoral. All actions that are not impermissible, or do not involve the use of a person as a *mere* means, are permissible.

2.2. *The Good Will: Right Motivations*

After the maxim for action is evaluated as being permissible, impermissible, or required to act upon, and it passes the test, being either permissible or required to act upon, one must determine whether the motivation for acting on it is good. If the motivation is not good, then acting on it does not come from the Good Will. In order to distinguish the different kinds of motives that one may have in doing an action, let us first examine three different maxims and then the different motivations that accompany these maxims. Kant uses for this purpose an example that is relevant to businesses of a shopkeeper who treats his customers honestly for three distinct purposes.

Three Maxims in Kant's Shopkeeper:

1. I will be honest with my customers in order to gain their trust and get repeat-business.
2. I will be honest with my customers because I like them.

3. I will be honest with my customers because that's the right thing to do.

According to the Formula of Universal Law, it is permissible to treat one's customers honestly, no matter the purpose, because honesty never makes an exception of oneself. According to the Formula of Humanity, honesty is also good, because deceit involves using people by bypassing their rational consent. It may seem like the shopkeeper is using his customers in the first maxim that he devises since his purpose in being honest is to make money off of them, but this maxim is not eliminated by the Formula of Humanity as long as the shopkeeper respects the rationality of his customers while he intends to make a profit.

However, there is a moral difference in these three maxims even though each of them is permissible to act upon. These differences are revealed in the purposes within these maxims which correspond to three general types of motivation:

Three Types of Motivation:

A. Self-Interest (corresponding to (1))
B. Character or Sympathy (corresponding to (2))
C. The Moral Law or Duty (corresponding to (3))

Of these three kinds of motivation, Kant claims that the only good motivation is that which comes from the moral law or duty.

The reason why self-interest is eliminated as being a good motivation, where good is understood as "moral" or "praiseworthy" is fairly clear. Self-interested motivation does not consider others, so it cannot be a moral motivation, or one which aims to benefit humanity in general. In fact, actions that are performed for a person's self-interest and moral actions are frequently seen as opposed to one another since people can maximize their self-interest by harming other people.

The second type of motivation, which comes from character or sympathy, on the other hand, is not so obviously lacking goodness. Good people have good characters. They are kind, honest, and charitable. A good person will do good things, so the shopkeeper, if he is good, will be honest because that is the kind of person he is. Isn't the fact that he is a good person of credit to him? And, furthermore, ought not we all to try to become good people such that we do good just because that is the way we are? Kant's answer to this is that our characters at birth and throughout our lives are not wholly under our control and so we ought not to be credited for doing actions that naturally arise from our constitutions. Some people are born irritable and have difficulties in their families and environments that exacerbate these genetic tendencies. It is not these people's fault that they were born with such disadvantages. Likewise, motivations that come from sympathy have no moral worth for Kant because whether we like or dislike someone can change from moment to moment, and morality has a more solid foundation than this; unshakeable by our fleeting feelings and desires. If the objection arises that a person with a good character will have sympathetic reactions to others reliably, then his objection to motivations arising from character will emerge again. Motivations from character and sympathy can help us to act in accordance with the moral law, if they come from a good character, but they are not good in-themselves. Kant concludes that the only motivation that is under our control (and thus capable of being morally praiseworthy) and that will provide an unshakeable ground for morality is that motivation issuing directly from the will to obey the moral law. If we are motivated to do the right thing *because it is the right thing*, then we are performing actions that are not merely in accordance with morality, but are in fact moral.

3. CONCLUSION

Kantian ethics does not prohibit individuals from seeking their own happiness, which may include prosperity in business. However, it identifies constraints on what we may do in the pursuit of our happiness or profits: we must give equal respect to all rational individuals by exercising our own rationality and allowing others to do the same.

FOR FURTHER READING

Guyer, Paul. (1997). *Kant's Groundwork on the Metaphysics of Morals: Critical Essays.* Lanham, MD: Rowman & Littlefield Publishers, Inc.

Guyer, Paul. (2007). *Kant's Groundwork for the Metaphysics of Morals: A Reader's Guide.* London: Continuum International Publishing Group.

Kant, Immanuel. (2008). *Groundwork of the Metaphysics of Morals.* Trans. Thomas Kingsmill Abbott. Radford, VA: Wilder Publications.

Sedgwick, Sally. (2008). *Kant's Groundwork of the Metaphysics of Morals: An Introduction.* Cambridge: Cambridge University Press.

Sullivan, Roger J. (1994). *An Introduction to Kant's Ethics.* Cambridge: Cambridge University Press.

Wood, Allen W. (2007). *Kantian Ethics.* Cambridge: Cambridge University Press.

—7—

ARISTOTELEAN VIRTUE ETHICS AND THE RECOMMENDATIONS OF MORALITY

Richard M. Glatz

VIRTUE THEORIES OF ETHICS—NOTABLY, theories like those advanced by Aristotle and a number of other ancient philosophers—are markedly different from other, more "traditional" theories of ethics. In the (translated) words of Socrates, "ethics is no smaller matter than how one ought to live." In the more traditional kinds of ethical theories—consequentialist theories like John Stuart Mill's utilitarianism and deontological theories like that advanced by Immanuel Kant—the question of how one ought to live is answered on a case-by-case basis. Such traditional theories of ethics focus on individual actions and (in light of various factors including the circumstances under which the action is to be performed and the intentions or motives of the agent who is to perform the action) classify given actions as *right, wrong, obligatory, permissible, impermissible,* and the like. In this way, the non-virtue based theories of ethics offer a (often) formulaic and typically straightforwardly applicable procedure for determining which of the courses of action available to us at a given time is the course of action we ought to pursue.

Virtue theories of ethics are not like this, supplying neither a list of rules for conduct nor a procedure for picking the morally best course of action in a given situation. They issue neither universal moral principles such as "it is wrong to lie"

nor procedures for deriving circumscribed moral judgments such as "it would be wrong for John to lie to his wife about the fact that he lost their mortgage payment last night betting against the Bears." Virtue theories of ethics instead issue moral judgments such as "honesty is a virtue" and "John is vicious (viceful)."

The primary reason that virtue theories of ethics differ in this way from other approaches to ethics is that they take *agents* and their *characters* to be the primary objects of moral scrutiny. Whereas consequentialists and deontologists develop theories for morally evaluating particular *actions* (as performed in particular circumstances and for particular reasons), virtue theorists develop theories for morally evaluating the *character traits* that underlie agents' performances of those actions.

This aspect of the virtue theoretic approach to ethics is responsible not only for the fact that the judgments rendered by virtue theories differ so markedly from the judgments rendered by other kinds of theories of ethics; it is responsible also for a common objection to the virtue theoretic approach. It is thought by some that virtue ethics is unappealing because it does not provide action-guiding principles. Although it might be difficult to determine which action is the correct one on the basis of consequentialist or deontological principles, at least those principles provide some kind of basis for morally evaluating actions. Virtue theories of ethics, on the other hand, provide no basis for such an evaluation.

Even if this kind of objection does not show that virtue ethics is theoretically flawed, it does pose a particularly poignant problem for attempts (like those to be considered in this chapter) to employ a virtue theory of ethics to answer applied ethical questions. For this reason, the presentation of virtue ethics to follow is formulated with an eye on determining how virtue ethics can help us understand how to live our lives—our personal, as well as our professional, lives—and how that kind of understanding can help us make decisions when confronted by morally difficult situations.

1. ARISTOTLE'S VIRTUE ETHICS, IN SKETCH

It is fairly commonplace for us to think of ethics in terms of questions like "which actions are right and which are wrong?" and "which actions am I morally obligated to perform?" For Aristotle, however, the fundamental questions of ethics are instead questions like "what is a good *person*?" and "what is the best way *to live*?"

In pursuing answers to these questions Aristotle begins his principal ethical work—the *Nicomachean Ethics*—with a detailed discussion of "the good" for man. Through a variety of arguments that need not concern us here Aristotle reaches the conclusion that the highest good for man is *happiness*. Be warned, however, that the term Aristotle uses here, "*eudaimonea*," does not mean what we typically mean by "*happiness*." The English word "happiness" would be appropriate to describe the kind of *feeling* that I have when eating chocolate or the kind of *mood* into which most people are put by taking a walk on the beach with a lover. Aristotle's notion of *eudaimonea*, on the other hand, is meant to capture the kind of enduring *state* that one is in when, through *reasoned activity*, one has accomplished a life filled with all of the things that make a life wonderful and

"choiceworthy." It is often suggested that a more appropriate English translation of "*eudaimonea*" would be "(human) flourishing."

The foregoing characterization of *eudaimonea* is by no means a definition. The important thing to remember is that, unlike John Stuart Mill's notion of happiness as pleasure, *eudaimonea* is neither a *feeling* nor a *mood*. Rather, it is a *state of being* for which any reasonable person would strive. As such, Aristotle claims that *eudaimonea* is the chief good for man and the end to which all of our actions ultimately aim. It is also important to notice the role that is here played by the notion of *reasoned activity*. *Eudaimonea* is a state that is only attainable for rational beings that use their reason to achieve ends. It is a kind of *psychological* happiness that cannot be attained by creatures that lack the kinds of mental lives required to engage in projects or plan their lives.

In part to determine how a person can achieve *eudaimonea* and in part to show that *eudaimonea* really is the chief good for man, Aristotle takes up the question of what a *good person* is. It is instructive to look at this part of his investigation as a particular instance of a general question form, namely:

(Q1) What is a good *X*?

Aristotle takes it, perhaps mysteriously, that in order to answer an instance of (Q1) we must first find an answer to a subsidiary question of the following form:

(Q2) What is the *characteristic function* of an *X*?

As an example to see what Aristotle has in mind here, consider an axe. On Aristotle's view in order to find out what a good axe is we must first understand what the function of an axe is. Of course, axes may be put to various different uses— we might use an axe to split firewood, chop down a tree, drive a nail, slice a loaf of bread, kill an enemy, or even direct traffic. Some of these uses we regard as deviant (whether morally or merely socially) while others we regard as perfectly normal. The reason for this is that we understand that the characteristic function or purpose of an axe is to chop.

When it comes to *artifacts*—objects that have been created for a particular purpose—it is to be expected that the function of an artifact is the purpose for which it has been made. Aristotle's notion of a function extends beyond this, however. Indeed, the fact that artifacts have been constructed for a particular purpose only makes it easier to see what function they have. For Aristotle what the function of a thing is depends not upon how it is used or why it was made (if it was made) but on what activity that thing is best suited to do. Consider, for example, a person who has designed and uses a pair of tools—one for the slicing of bread and another for the chopping of firewood. Suppose that the tool created for the slicing of bread is exactly like what we call an "axe" and that the tool created for the chopping of firewood is exactly like what we call a "bread knife." When this artisan slices bread for his dinner he takes out his bread-slicing tool—a heavy, wedged blade attached to a meter long stick—and proceeds to hack at the loaf. The result is, of course, "slices" of bread that are mauled, flattened, and irregular. When the artisan chops wood for his fire, on the other hand, he takes out his wood-chopping tool—a lightweight, serrated blade attached to a hand-sized handle—and proceeds to saw, laboriously, at the logs. The process takes many hours and gives the artisan many splinters.

Holding aside judgment of the artisan regarding his rationality and intelligence, what is there to be said about his bread-slicer and wood-chopper? Although each has been made (and is used) for a particular purpose, it seems that the proper, characteristic *function* of the artisan's bread-slicer is to chop wood and that of the artisan's wood-chopper is to slice bread. If we approached the artisan as he swung his bread-slicer over his head, we would be correct to stop him, say "excuse me, but you are using that incorrectly," and hand him his wood-chopper. The reason for this is that the particular *qualities* of each tool make those tools especially suited for certain uses.

Let this serve, then, as a general approach for answering questions of the form (Q2) above. If a thing, *X*, has particular qualities that make it best suited for a certain activity, then that activity is (part of) the *function* of *X*. In light of this, what (if anything) might the function of a human be?[1]

Aristotle considers and rejects the suggestion that the function of a human is nourishment and growth. Given that these activities are common to plants, and given that Aristotle is looking for a function that is peculiar to humans, Aristotle concludes that nourishment and growth are not the function of humans. Aristotle also considers and rejects the suggestion that the function of a human is a life of perception or sensation as these are common to animals. Aristotle concludes that a life of *reasoned activity* is distinctively human and a kind of activity for which we are particularly well suited—indeed, it seems to be the activity that we are best at doing not only in the sense that we are best at doing *that activity* (from among activities that we do) but also in the sense that *we* (among beings who can engage in that activity) are the best at it. As a result, (if humans have a function, then) the function of a human is *to engage in reason-governed activity*—making plans, solving problems, communicating, interacting socially with other people, etc.

Let us assume that Aristotle is correct that humans have a function and that engaging in reason-governed activity is that function. We now have an answer to the question of form (Q2) above, but what of (Q1)?

Consider, again, an axe. What is a good axe? To answer this question we must first answer the subsidiary question "what is the *function* of an axe?" As discussed above, the function of an axe seems obviously to be *chopping*. What, then, is a good axe? An obvious and apparently trivial answer to this question is that a good axe is an axe that chops well. On Aristotle's view this is correct, but incomplete. In the direction of a complete answer, Aristotle would claim that a good axe is an axe that possesses the *excellences* of an axe, where the excellences of an axe are whatever *characteristics* an axe might have that contribute to the fulfillment or performance of the *function* of an axe. So the excellences of an axe are those characteristics that contribute to chopping—sharpness, weight (heavy but wieldable), balance (weighted near to head rather than the handle), sturdiness, etc. A good axe is one that possesses such characteristics.

A good person, similarly, is a person who possesses the excellences of a person, where the excellences of a person are whatever characteristics a person might possess that contribute to the fulfillment of the human function—engaging in reason-governed activity. These characteristics or excellences are the *virtues*.

Aristotle distinguishes between two kinds of virtues—intellectual virtues and moral virtues. Intellectual virtues are characteristics like practical wisdom (wisdom with respect to making plans and achieving one's goals), philosophical wisdom, intuitive reason, etc. About these I will say no more than to note that lacking the intellectual virtues, one would face great difficulties in successfully engaging in the kind of life planning and social interaction that Aristotle understands by *reason-governed activity*.

Aristotle defines the moral virtues to be *traits of character* that consist in a *disposition to choose the mean*. In many circumstances—facing fear, managing money, pursuing pleasures, etc.—there are two extremes, one of excess and the other of deficit. There are people who, in the face of frightful things, feel too much fear and are brought by their fear to flee from dangers that are minor or to "freeze up" and fail to accomplish important things. Such people are cowards and cowardice is their vice. On the other hand, there are people who, in the face of frightful things, feel too much confidence and are brought by their over-confidence to plunge into dangers that are beyond their abilities to handle. Such people are rash and rashness is their vice. A person is brave who, in the face of frightful things, feels the right amount of fear and the right amount of confidence and acts in accordance with these appropriate feelings.[2]

It is important to notice that Aristotle claims that it is virtuous to be disposed to choose the mean *relative to us*. What is excessive or deficient for one person might not be for another. A person trained in *khav magha* (the self-defence system used by the Israeli Defense Forces) might exhibit bravery by facing a mugger with a knife while a wimpy philosopher such as myself would almost certainly be exhibiting rashness by doing the same thing. As Aristotle says, "fear and confidence and appetite and anger and pity and in general pleasure and pain may be felt both too much and too little, and in both cases not well; but to feel them at the right times, with reference to the right objects, toward the right people, with the right motive, and in the right way, is what is both intermediate and best, and this is characteristic of virtue."[3] We must bear in mind, of course, that the right amount of an emotion to feel might depend upon the person who feels it.

According to Aristotle, then, possessing a virtue amounts to having the disposition to feel the right amount of a given emotion in the relevant circumstances and to act in accordance with that appropriately balanced emotion; possessing a vice amounts to having the disposition to feel either too much or too little of a given emotion in the relevant circumstances and to act in accordance with that inappropriately balanced emotion. Recall that Aristotle understands the virtues to be human excellences in the sense that they contribute to the well functioning of man—that is, to the successful engagement in reason-governed activity. When people engage in reason-governed activity they are bound to be confronted by situations that evoke some kind of emotional response—fear, anger, sympathy, and the like. When viceful people are confronted by such situations, their actions will be governed by inappropriate emotion responses—perhaps they will feel too much anger and behave wrathfully, or perhaps they will feel too little sympathy and behave callously. It is not Aristotle's position that their behavior then transgresses some kind of moral edict or law and is therefore wrong. Rather, their behavior fails to contribute to their success in whatever reason-governed activity in which they are engaged—be it business dealings, familial relations, or political decision-making. As the ultimate goal of all such activities is *eudaimonea*, the viceful person will not achieve true happiness. Only by possessing and acting from the *virtues* can we succeed in our reason-governed lives and thereby achieve *eudaimonea*.

It is important to note here that Aristotle places primary moral significance on the character of an agent but places a kind of derivative or secondary moral significance on the actions that the agent performs. Although it is, for Aristotle, something of a misnomer to characterize a particular action as a brave one, such characterizations are commonplace for us and even present in Aristotle's writing. Strictly speaking it is the *agent* who is brave when performing a particular action, not the action itself. We might be tempted to think of a brave action simply as whatever action a brave person would do, but it is very important for Aristotle that the action in question be performed *because* of the brave character of the agent. It is possible for an agent to exhibit cowardice when fleeing in the face of danger even if a brave agent would also flee in the same situation. If the agent in question flees as a result of overly pronounced fear, then the agent is not acting on the basis of feeling the right amount of fear given the situation. The fact that the situation calls for the agent to be afraid and flee does not change the fact that the agent in question actually did flee as a result of his cowardice.

There is another reason that actions themselves are morally significant on Aristotle's view. According to Aristotle, we develop and maintain the virtues through reflective training and habituation. Indeed, the root of the term "ethics" is "*ethos*," the Greek term for *habit*. People are neither virtuous nor vicious by nature. Rather, we become virtuous or vicious by repeatedly engaging in virtuous or vicious activity respectively. As a result, although virtue theories of ethics are not action-guiding in the same way that deontological and consequentialist theories are, virtue theories of ethics do call for us to routinely engage in the right kind of behavior. By engaging in viceful activity we damage our character and become vicious; only by engaging in virtuous activity do we develop and preserve a virtuous character and ensure that we will be neither overrun by our emotions nor emotionally detached in our dealings with others.[4]

2. TOWARD APPLIED VIRTUE ETHICS

The foregoing sketch of Aristotle's theory is meant to show how Aristotle approaches what he takes to be the fundamental questions of ethics—"what is a good person?" and "how ought one to live?" According to Aristotle, we ought to live in accordance with the virtues. As humans our function is to engage in reason-governed activity. The virtues are human excellences in the sense that they contribute to fulfilling this function; the vices are human defects in the sense that they detract from fulfilling this function. Good people develop and maintain the virtues through reflective habituation and thereby enable themselves to achieve *eudaimonea*—the highest good for man, true happiness.

For many of us, our professional lives are lives of reasoned-activity. Business interactions—buying, selling, producing, serving—are social interactions. Social interactions generally require communication, trust, agreements, etc., all of which require engaging one another in a reasoned way. No doubt, then, we are required to conduct ourselves in our professional lives in accordance with the virtues. In this way, virtue ethics applies to our professional lives just as it applies to our personal lives. A truly virtuous person would not simply exhibit the virtues while dealing with family and friends and then go to work and deal with co-workers, suppliers, customers, and bosses in non-virtuous ways. People who exhibit this kind of moral two-facedness between their private and professional lives really do not have the dispositions that embody the virtues—they are mere pretenders of virtue. Furthermore, those who leave virtue aside in their professional dealings would eventually habituate themselves contrary to the virtues and would become vicious.

There is another way in which to apply a virtue theory of ethics to the applied moral issues that face professionals. In what follows I will develop a certain Aristotelian view of what is often termed "role-differentiated morality." Discussions of role-differentiated morality are attempts to understand apparently different moral requirements that we face as a result of occupying certain roles. With respect to the welfare of a child, parents have different moral responsibilities than do teachers who have still different moral responsibilities than neighbors or strangers. By pursuing a career in law enforcement or medicine one chooses to place one's self in a *role* that carries different moral responsibilities than other lines of work. Following Aristotle we may arrive at a certain understanding of the moral significance of different roles as they apply to businesspeople.

To begin with an example to illustrate how this is to work, consider what makes a computer a good one. The Aristotelian analysis would begin by identifying the *function* of a computer and then identifying as *excellences* for a computer those characteristics that a computer might possess that would contribute to its performing its functioning well. There are, however, many different kinds of computers with various different functions. My computer does little beyond word processing and spreadsheet managing. My parents recently bought a computer especially designed for managing the many pictures of grandchildren that they now have. So-called "gamers" have computers especially designed for playing video games, often networked for multi-player gaming. The computers in many business offices have specialized software for whatever kind of computing is required for a business of that sort.

What all of these different kinds of computers have in common is that they all serve the function of running software, taking input from a user, and displaying output to that user. Excellences for computers *considered simply as computers* would

include characteristics that contribute to performing those functions well—fast, reliable processors, memory that can be written (and rewritten), user-friendly interfacing, etc. Such characteristics as these are analogous to the *human* virtues that Aristotle discusses—those being the excellences of a person *considered simply as a person*. Consider, however, a particular computer considered specifically as a *gaming* computer. The function of a gaming computer (beyond the basic function of a computer) is to allow the user to play games. To be a good gaming computer, then, a computer will need to have characteristics that contribute to that function—a high quality graphics card, suitable controller ports, hardware and software that enables fast, reliable networking, etc. While possessing such characteristics makes a gaming computer better, my glorified word-processor would not be improved by possessing those characteristics.

It is in this way that I suggest we handle the issue of role-differentiated morality from an Aristotelian perspective. Considering, for example, a corporate executive not simply as a person but *as a corporate executive* we might get some indication of how corporate executives ought to conduct themselves professionally. To do this, of course, we must first consider what the *function* of a corporate executive is.

This seems to be an easy question. The function of a corporate executive is to run a corporation or some aspect of its operation. Consider Melissa, the CEO of a pharmaceutical company. Melissa's function (considering her as the CEO of the pharmaceutical company) is to run that pharmaceutical company. To see how Melissa ought to conduct herself in the course of her job and to see what sorts of characteristics would contribute to Melissa's successful execution of her job we must first determine what successful running of the pharmaceutical company would amount to, and to determine this we must determine what the purpose of the pharmaceutical company is.

An overly cynical and simplistic answer that I would like to dismiss up front is that the purpose of the pharmaceutical company is to turn as large a profit as possible for the owners. Certainly part of the purpose or function of a corporation is to be profitable, but we must recognize that a pharmaceutical company is part of a wider social network that includes chemical companies (as suppliers), hospitals and private individuals (as customers), employees (as employees), and even other pharmaceutical companies (as competitors). I am not suggesting that it is the purpose of a company to operate for the advantage of each of these groups, but it must be understood how these groups socially interact with the company in question in determining how an executive ought to engage in the reason-governed activity that is her job.

This being said, I think that we should consider the purpose of a company like the pharmaceutical company imagined above in terms of the manufacture and distribution of pharmaceuticals. For a corporate executive like Melissa to fulfill her professional function well she must (at least) maintain trusting and mutually beneficial relationships among the parties involved in accomplishing these goals. In order to do this, Melissa should think of suppliers, employees, customers, and others not simply as entities that satisfy some need of the company, but as entities whose interests actually matter. I suspect that such an attitude will be engendered by the general human virtues as discussed by Aristotle—for according to those we must choose the mean even in pursuing such things as profit. Even so, there might be room here for some distinctively corporate

virtues. By following this kind of approach to role-differentiated morality we might be able to make some progress toward professional ethics in general and business ethics in particular.

NOTES

1 Aristotle offers no good argument for the conclusion that man has a function; he merely assumes it, and reasons on that basis.

2 Aristotle develops similar analyses regarding money, pleasure, honor, anger, social intercourse, etc.

3 Aristotle, *Nicomachean Ethics*, II: 6, 18–23 (W.D. Ross, transl.); from McKeon, Richard (ed.) *Introduction to Aristotle*, New York: Random House, 1947.

4 I have left out of this sketch of Aristotle's view the role that is played by external goods—wealth, health, good looks, pleasures, and other goods that Aristotle sees as necessary for *eudaimonea*. According to Aristotle, such external goods are achieved quite often by luck, seldom things that we have much control over. What we do have control over is the state of our character—whether we habituate ourselves to have the virtues or whether we habituate ourselves to have the vices. It would be nice if we could achieve eudaimonea simply by attending to our characters in this way, but Aristotle thinks that virtue is insufficient for eudaimonea. To achieve eudaimonea we must not only have a good character, we must also have the good fortune to have a life with sufficient external goods.

—8—
CARING AS AN ETHICAL PERSPECTIVE

Rita C. Manning

AN ETHIC OF CARE HAS EMERGED AS A NEW WAY to conceptualize some deeply held moral intuitions. It provides an important tool for analyzing, discussing, and ultimately shaping moral practice. In what follows, I will briefly describe an ethic of care. I shall then have something to say about how this perspective emerged and about how it differs from other moral orientations.

CARE FOR OTHERS AND FOSTERING RELATIONSHIPS

One characteristic of people with integrity is the ability to care for others and to foster good relationships. Caring for others is more than having sympathetic feelings for them; it requires that one take concrete action to look after the needs of others. Caring for others and fostering good relationships go together for two reasons. First, humans are essentially social creatures—we live and work in groups and most of us would be absolutely miserable if we didn't have meaningful relationships. So caring about persons means caring about their relationships. Second, we cannot accomplish many of the tasks we need to undertake unless we can foster good relationships. This includes the task of giving care to others.

Let's start with an example and see how caring works. Doug is concerned with trying to salvage an account and wants to send someone to visit the client. Ken is the most likely candidate since he has a good working relationship with the client, but he is scheduled to visit another client on a much bigger account. Susan has some experience with this client and has been known to save accounts in similar situations, so she is Doug's first choice. Carlos is a possibility, but he is not as familiar with the product as Susan. Doug recalls that Susan's father is in the last stages of his battle with congestive heart failure and he wonders whether it would be fair to ask her to go. He calls her into his office and Susan says that her father would probably want her to go. Satisfied, Doug sends Susan on the trip, but the account is lost anyway. Did Doug do the right thing? We can now answer this question by asking whether Doug was sufficiently caring.

CARE

Though not all defenders of an ethic of care see care as a virtue, I think this is the most plausible way to understand it. Like other virtues, care is a general disposition to behave in a particular way. Unlike other virtues, care is what I call a meta-virtue—that is it provides an organizing principle for all the other virtues. If my overall orientation is to be a caring person, then I will be courageous when what I value is at risk; I will be honest because honesty is usually the best way to care for others; I will want to be prudent because I recognize that I must balance the needs of others and my own needs. So the traditional virtues of courage, honesty and prudence are organized under the meta-virtue of care.

When Carol Gilligan first described the care orientation,[1] she described it as a typically female moral orientation. However, there is nothing gendered about caring; if it is more prevalent in women than in men, it is because women are socially conditioned to do much of society's caring work—they are more likely to be involved with caring for children and the sick, for example. Care is a basic human capacity and as such it is both possible and important for all of us to be caring persons. Developing one's capacity in giving care requires that we commit to this ideal and that we have practice exercising care. When we truly care about someone or something, we have certain emotions and motivations. If I see someone in dire need, for example, I will feel compassion and be motivated to do something to respond to the need. Finally, it is not enough to merely have the appropriate emotion and motivation; care involves an appropriate response.

Caring is a response to the variety of features of moral situations: need, harm, past promises, role relationships etc. In the case of need, our obligation to respond in an appropriately caring way arises when we are able to respond to need. We can roughly distinguish needs here from desires by describing needs as something that is basic to our survival and minimally decent life as opposed to something that we merely want. Humans need some things for their very survival: food, clothing, shelter, and health care are examples. There are also other things that we need for a minimally decent life: Aristotle cites friendship; Mill cites liberty and Rawls offers self-esteem as a need in this sense. Still, there is no universal, cross-cultural understanding of need. Rather, need is mediated by a number of factors including family, culture, economic class, gender and sexuality, disability and illness. Finally, as we respond to needs, we should recognize the vast differences in power that exist. Sometimes, people are unwilling to express their needs freely because they fear that their needs will not be met.

They may even be in such a state of dependence or despair that they are no longer able to identify their needs.

Need is not the only feature of moral situations. Harm, for example, is an important one to consider. Most people understand that being the cause of harming someone else creates an obligation to respond. But causation is a complex idea. We can be part of the causal story even when we don't think of ourselves as the primary cause. Suppose, for example, that you see the person sitting next to you in an exam cheating. Suppose further that this is an exam that is designed to demonstrate competence in a skill crucial for a health care practitioner. Suppose that you simply look the other way and later find out that a patient was seriously harmed because the practitioners really did not understand the procedure they should have followed, and that this procedure was the very one they were being tested on when you saw them cheating. Do you have a responsibility here? I would argue that you do, though it's not always clear what you can do after the fact. At the very least, you now know that you shouldn't look the other way when you see similar cheating in the future.

There are two other things that mark the moral dimension of a situation that are worth noting here—past promising and role responsibility. When we make a promise, we commit ourselves to a certain course of action. An ethic of care doesn't say that you are always committed to keeping a promise because sometimes doing so can be harmful to all concerned, but it does impose a moral obligation to respond. Similarly, being in a particular role, e.g., teacher, comes with a set of general obligations.

We've now looked at some of the features of situations that suggest that we have an obligation. In order to see what our obligations are in a particular situation, we need to look at the features of an ethic of care. There are four central ideas here: moral attention, sympathetic understanding, relationship awareness, and harmony and accommodation.

MORAL ATTENTION

Moral attention is the attention to the situation in all its complexity. When one is morally attentive, one wishes to become aware of all the details that will allow a sympathetic response to the situation. It is not enough to know that this is a case of a particular kind, say a case about lying or cruelty. In order to understand what our obligations are, we have to know all the details that might make a difference in our understanding and response to the particular situation at hand.

SYMPATHETIC UNDERSTANDING

When I sympathetically understand the situation, I am open to sympathizing and even identifying with the persons in the situation. I try to be aware of what the others in the situation would want me to do, what would most likely be in their best interests, and how they would like me to carry out their wishes and interests and meet their needs. I call this attention to the best interests of others maternalism. It is done in the context of a special sensitivity to the wishes of the other and with an understanding of the other's interest that is shaped by a deep sympathy and understanding. When it is hard to be sympathetic, one may try several strategies—perhaps imagining others as oneself in an earlier crisis. As one adopts this sympathetic attitude one often becomes aware of what others want and need. Finally, as we respond to others, we look to satisfy their needs in ways that will preserve their sense of competence and dignity while at the same time addressing their needs or even ameliorating their suffering.

RELATIONSHIP AWARENESS

There is a special kind of relationship awareness that characterizes caring. People recognize that others are in a relationship with them. First there is the most basic relationship, that of fellow creatures. Second there is the immediate relationship of need and ability to fill the need. Finally, one may be in some role relationship with the other that calls for a particular response, such as teacher-student. One is aware of all these relationships as one surveys a situation from the perspective of care. But there is another kind of relationship awareness that is involved as well. One can be aware of the network of relationships that connect humans, and care about preserving and nurturing these relationships. As caring persons think about what to do, they try not to undermine these relationships but rather to nurture and extend the relationships that are supportive of human flourishing.

ACCOMMODATION AND HARMONY

Related to the notion of relationship awareness is accommodation. When a problematic situation involves several people, how best to help is not obvious. The desire to nurture networks of care requires that one tries to accommodate the needs of all, including oneself. It is not always possible, or wise, to do what everyone thinks they need, but it is often important to do what you think is best while at the same time giving everyone concerned a sense of being involved and considered in the process. When we do this, we have a better chance of preserving harmony. If you do what you think is right without consulting anyone, you risk upsetting the harmony of the group. Of course not all harmony is worth preserving. The oppressive society may be stable and harmonious, but at the price of those at the bottom. An ethic of care would be opposed to this type of superficial harmony since it is dependent on treating some as though they do not deserve the same care as others. Ideally, we should aim for the harmonious society in which all are treated with care.

Let's return to Doug and see how he might have thought about the situation if he'd been more skillful at caring. Doug did not really think about Susan's situation very carefully. He should have realized that she was very upset about her father's illness. Since we are all distracted when something this serious is going on in our lives, she was probably also worried that her job performance might be affected. Doug should not have taken her words at face value because it's hard to believe that her father really wanted her to go. Perhaps he was just being a good father and trying to put Susan's needs above his own. Very likely, he was worried about how his illness was affecting her and might have told her to go to give her some time off or to protect her job. Doug also did not give much thought to how well Susan would be able to interact with the client while her father was dying miles away. The result of his action was a lost account and considerable discomfort for Susan. This lack of care on his part probably will affect his relationship with Susan and her effectiveness in future negotiations. Whenever she has to go visit a client, she will be reminded of that very precious time she lost with her father. Doug should have given more thought to finding other alternatives to sending Susan on the trip during this very trying time.

THE CARE VOICE AND THE JUSTICE VOICE

Now that we've seen how the care perspective works, let's turn to a brief history. Carol Gilligan's pioneering work, *In a Different Voice*, was the first systematic attempt to describe the voice of care and to distinguish it from what she called the voice of justice (Gilligan, 1982). Since then, psychologists and philosophers have been busy elucidating the central concepts and testing for various aspects of the two voices.

Gilligan began by responding to the views of Lawrence Kohlberg, who developed a theory about how people reason and develop morally.[2] His theory of moral reasoning posited that people reason morally by applying principles to cases, thus yielding judgments about what they ought to do. Moral development, in Kohlberg's account, is cognitive and proceeds to progressively more general principles, with ideal moral development culminating in principles that are universal and binding on all persons.

Gilligan noted that Kohlberg's subjects, though culturally diverse, were all male. She began to apply his tests to female subjects of various ages. Her conclusion was that some people, notably females, often used a different reasoning strategy than that described by Kohlberg and that they developed by moving through a different set of stages.

Gilligan theorized that some of her subjects appealed to an ethic of care. This involves a thorough understanding of the context, and a willingness to balance the needs of self and other in a way that preserves both. For Gilligan, moral development was both cognitive and emotional—the growth in the ability to see the situation from the perspective of self and other and to care about one's self as well as others.

She illustrated the differences in moral reasoning with two eleven year olds, Jake and Amy. Jake and Amy are both given Kohlberg's "Heinz dilemma" to solve. A druggist has invented a drug to combat cancer. Heinz's wife needs the drug but Heinz does not have the money to buy it and the druggist will not give it to him. The children are asked whether Heinz should steal the drug. Jake quickly answers affirmatively and defends his answer by appealing to the relative importance of life over property. Amy begins by saying that it depends. She points out all the things that could go wrong if Heinz steals the drug—perhaps he will get caught and go to jail and his wife will be worse off. She suggests instead that Heinz and the druggist should sit down and work it out to everyone's satisfaction.

Jake fits easily into Kohlberg's schemata: he imagines himself in Heinz's position and applies a principle that quickly yields an answer. He does not need any more information about Heinz, the druggist, Heinz's wife, etc. Amy, on the other hand, is virtually impossible to analyze on Kohlberg's scale because she never states or even implies a principle that will yield an answer. Instead, as she imagines herself in Heinz's shoes, she sees the complexity of the situation and realizes that its solution requires that Heinz and the druggist and Heinz's wife recognize their involvement in a relationship and that they honor this awareness by working out a solution that will enable them all to survive and, if possible, flourish.

For Jake the solution is cognitive: he merely reasons about the situation and can take action on the basis of that reasoning. Amy sees a real solution as necessarily involving growth in moral sensitivity and commitment.

On the basis of such differences in her subjects' responses, Gilligan posited a moral orientation, which she calls the voice of care, in addition to the justice orientation of Kohlberg. I propose an additional way of assessing the usefulness of the two: How does each voice answer two questions: What are moral agents like? What is the moral standing of persons and communities?

The justice voice models moral choice by imagining ideal moral agents as 1) isolated, abstract individuals who 2) follow general rules 3) in a cool and impartial manner. Thus real people fall considerably short of this ideal; but what this ideal observer would choose is supposed to tell us what we should aim at, because real justice is determined from this standpoint. The ideal moral agents are isolated in the sense that they are both independent of others and free to choose what relationship to have with others. The model of interaction is contractual—an individual as a moral agent chooses to whom s/he will be related and the conditions of the relationship. These ideal agents are abstract in the sense that their moral obligations are specified independently of any of the particular facts about them or about the situations they find themselves in. Their moral obligations are spelled out in abstract rules, rules that are general enough to bind similar cases. In following these general rules, these ideal agents must be cool and impartial. This requires unemotionally applying the rules in the same fashion regardless of the ties of affection and/or enmity that might call on them to be partial.

The voice of care, on the other hand, thinks of moral choices as made by agents who 1) are embedded in particular social contexts, relationships and personal narratives, 2) direct their moral attention to real others and 3) are open to sympathetic understanding and identification with those others.

In part because the justice voice conceives moral agency in the way it does, it gives the following answer to the question of the moral standing of persons and communities. 1) All persons are equally valuable—hence there are no special obligations to particular others. 2) Communities and relationships have no moral standing on their own account.

The care voice, on the other hand, believes that 1) though all persons are valuable, there are special obligations: those imposed by actual and potential relationships and those imposed by roles. Since it understands communities as more than mere aggregates of individuals and relationships as more than properties of individual persons, it is committed to saying that communities and relationships have moral standing and that they need to be included in our thought and action.

CARE, JUSTICE AND SELF-UNDERSTANDING

There is an additional way to sort out the differences between the care and justice voice and that is in terms of self-understanding. This was suggested by Nona Lyons, who argued that a particular self-understanding, a "distinct way of seeing and being in relation to others," explains the moral agent's preference for a particular moral voice.[3] Lyons identifies two different self-understandings: what she calls the separate/objective self and the connected self. Persons who fit the separate/objective self model describe themselves in terms of personal characteristics rather than connections to others. Connected selves, on the other hand, describe themselves in terms of connections to others: granddaughter of, friend of, etc. This suggests that the separate/objective self sees oneself as distinct from others in a more profound sense than does the connected self. The separate/objective self might, for example, see oneself as connected to others only through voluntary agreements. The separate/objective self might value autonomy more highly than good relationships with others.

Lyons describes further differences. Separate/objective selves recognize moral dilemmas as those that involve a conflict between their principles and someone else's desires, needs or demands. Connected selves, on the other hand, identify moral dilemmas as those that involve the breakdown of relationships with others.

Separate/objective selves fear connection and dependence, and hence value autonomy and independence. Connected selves fear separation and abandonment, and hence value connection and responsiveness.

We can see then how these self-understandings support different moral orientations. Separate selves understand themselves as distinct from others. They conceive moral dilemmas as arising from the conflict between their moral principles and the needs, demands, desires and principles of others. As such, they must mediate their interaction with others in the voice of justice—in terms of ground rules and procedures that can be accepted by all. This is the only foundation for interaction at all, since ties of affection are not seen as strong enough to provide a basis for interaction, especially in persons who fear connection and dependence. This fear of dependence and attachment also explains why they value the objectivity and impartiality that can stand between them and intimates. At the same time, separate/objective selves recognize that interaction with others plays a role in one's satisfaction, so they value community and relationship insofar as these play a role in individual satisfaction.

Connected selves see themselves in terms of others, so relationship is central to self-identity, rather than seen as voluntary and incidental. The problem of interaction is not then conceived of as how to get others to interact with oneself on terms that would be acceptable to all, but how to protect the ties of affection and connection that are central to one's very self-identity. Moral dilemmas arise over how to preserve these ties when they are threatened, and these dilemmas are mediated by the voice of care. Since the primary fear is of separation and abandonment, a strong value is placed on community and relationships.

CONCLUSION

An ethic of care is a moral orientation that is sorely needed in our increasingly fractured society. Whether we are managers or teachers or health care providers, an ethic of care provides guidance about how to live our lives. But it is not just a moral philosophy; it has a political dimension as well. If we are to meet our fellow creatures as caring individuals, we must rethink and, when necessary, restructure our institutions to make this possible.

NOTES

1   Gilligan, Carol. (1982). *In a Different Voice.* Cambridge, MA: Harvard University Press, 1982.
2   Kohlberg, Lawrence. (1981). *The Philosophy of Moral Development.* New York: Harper & Row.
3   Lyons, Nona. (1983). "Two Perspectives on Self, Relationship, and Morality," *Harvard Educational Review* 53 (1983): 125–45.

FOR FURTHER READING

Held, Virginia. (1993). *Feminist Morality.* Chicago: University of Chicago Press.

Holmes, Helen Bequaert, and Purdy, Laura (eds.). (1992). *Feminist Perspectives in Medical Ethics.* Bloomington and Indianapolis: Indiana University Press.

Kuhse, Helga. (1997). *Caring: Nurses, Women and Ethics.* Oxford: Blackwell Publishers Ltd.

Larrabee, Mary Jeanne (ed.). (1993). *An Ethic of Care.* New York and London: Routledge Press.

Manning, Rita. (1992). *Speaking from the Heart: A Feminist Perspective on Ethics.* Lanham, MD: Rowman and Littlefield.

Murdoch, Iris. (1971). *The Sovereignty of Good.* New York: Schocken Books.

Noddings, Nel. (1984). *Caring: A Feminine Approach to Ethics and Moral Education.* Berkeley: University of California Press.

CORPORATE SOCIAL RESPONSIBILITY

INTRODUCTION

Anand J. Vaidya

THE CENTRAL DEBATE IN BUSINESS ETHICS concerns the nature of corporations' social responsibilities. Are there any moral obligations that corporate executives/managers have other than to maximize profit for the stockholders? There are two standard responses to this question: stockholder theory and stakeholder theory.

Nobel Laureate economist Milton Friedman famously argued that the sole moral responsibility of a corporate executive is to do whatever is permissible within the confines of the law and local ethical customs in order to maximize profits for the stockholders. Friedman saw this as the moral obligation of corporations in general, in so far as one could speak of corporations having moral obligations. As an employee of a corporation, it would be morally *impermissible* for an executive to use funds allocated for profit maximizing ventures for "socially responsible" activities, such as funding charities, environmental clean up, or the building of local schools. According to Friedman, social responsibility is a governmental function. The government is responsible for correcting acknowledged social ills by allotting funds and setting up institutions to deal with them. In addition, people are responsible for voting for the political leaders whose agenda includes the social ills they wish to be corrected.

On the stockholder analysis of the moral obligations of corporations, executives are agents of the stockholders and thus are required to act on their behalf by striving to maximize share value. If executives were to take some of the stockholders' money and invest it in a specific public works project without the consent of the stockholders, they would be violating fiduciary obligations owed to the latter.

One critical response to Friedman's stockholder theory has been articulated by R. Edward Freeman and is known as stakeholder theory. Stakeholder theory maintains that stockholders are but one group *among others* that has a vested interest in a corporation's future. Freeman introduces the term "stakeholder" to refer to anyone who has a vested interest in the dealings of a corporation; that is anyone that has a stake in the future of the corporation. Under the narrow understanding of this term distributors, consumers, employees, manufacturers, and the local community in which the corporation is located are stakeholders because they have a vested interest in the corporation's survival and future well-being.

According to Freeman, stockholder theory is flawed because it does not accurately capture the fact that corporations are to be held accountable by interest groups that are not stockholders, such as environmental protection agencies and animal rights activist groups. An accurate theory of corporations would more accurately represent the real groups that an executive would have to take into consideration in making a decision for the future livelihood of the corporation. For example, employees depend on the corporations' continued success and future growth for their job security. Local communities depend on the corporation for jobs, producers and distributors depend on the corporation for contracts, and stockholders depend on the corporation for profits. A corporate executive must take into consideration these competing interests.

These two views present themselves as distinct accounts of what a corporation is and what its moral obligations are. According to stockholder theory, it appears as if it could never be the case that a corporate executive permissibly chooses a socially responsible action over pure profit maximization. For example, a corporate executive could not choose to spend some funds on building a school in the local community when that money could be used to fund research and development for a project that has a high probability of making profit for the stockholders. By contrast, it appears as if stakeholder theory allows for the possibility that a corporate executive may permissibly choose to fund the school project because his or her responsibility is not only to the stockholders, but also to the local community.

Although the two theories appear to be different, two things should be noted. First, the stockholder theory does not necessarily entail that a corporate executive cannot allocate funds for social projects. If the stockholders of a certain corporation *voted* to spend money on a public works project and not to pursue potential profits, then nothing in stockholder theory would block an executive from allocating funds and using them for that purpose. In recent years, the rise of B Corps and other companies that make corporate social responsibility part of their mission suggests that some investors not only tolerate, but demand that executives look beyond narrow profit maximization.

Second, on the plausible assumption that taking into consideration the interests of stakeholders is a good guide to maximizing profits for stockholders, stakeholder theory can be seen as a kind of special case of stockholder theory. In fact, a plausible assumption is that failing to pay attention to stakeholder interests often leads to poor long-term growth for a corporation. For example, closing down a car manufacturing facility in one town may, in the short term, increase profits by lowering costs; however it could lead to a loss in sales by boycotts prompted by the frustrated residents of the town. Overworking employees may lead to a strike. Failing to honor contracts with manufacturers and distributors because paying the cost of breaking the contract is less of a loss than living up to the contract may lead manufacturers and distributors to refrain from engaging in business with the corporation. Each of these considerations shows that recognizing and attempting to satisfy the interests of the various stakeholder groups may itself be a way of maximizing profit in the long term. Developing a more costly but environmentally sound product at a time where environmental soundness is in the eye of the consumer may actually lead consumers to buy the more expensive product over the less expensive and environmentally unsound product. The initial loss encumbered by research and development for the environmentally sound product is regained later by the future sustainability of the corporation as consumers' spending habits reflect concern for their environment.

A recent development influenced by debates on corporate social responsibility is that businesses have increasingly endorsed versions of corporate responsibility by stating that their mission is not simply to make profits, but also to do good. One concept that has had significant impact and requires conceptual and moral evaluation is "social entrepreneurship." Also, business ethicists have begun to turn their attention to the non-profit sector and the special moral dilemmas that arise in organizations that do not rely primarily on market mechanisms to dictate their success.

Finally, business ethics also benefits from dialogue with traditions that have developed sophisticated accounts of the moral obligations of business. As part of this dialogue, we have included articles on Islamic, Confucian, and Buddhist perspectives on corporate social responsibility.

—9—
CORPORATE SOCIAL RESPONSIBILITY THEORIES

Mapping the Territory

Elisabet Garriga and Domènec Melé

INTRODUCTION

SINCE THE SECOND HALF OF THE 20TH CENTURY A long debate on corporate social responsibility (CSR) has been taking place. In 1953, Bowen (1953) wrote the seminal book *Social Responsibilities of the Businessman*. Since then there has been a shift in terminology from the social responsibility of business to CSR. Additionally, this field has grown significantly and today contains a great proliferation of theories, approaches and terminologies. Society and business, social issues management, public policy and business, stakeholder management, corporate accountability are just some of the terms used to describe the phenomena related to corporate responsibility in society. Recently, renewed interest for corporate social responsibilities and new alternative concepts have been proposed, including corporate citizenship and corporate sustainability. Some scholars have compared these new concepts with the classic notion of CSR.

Furthermore, some theories combine different approaches and use the same terminology with different meanings. This problem is an old one. It was 30 years ago that Votaw wrote: "corporate social responsibility means something, but not always the same thing to everybody. To some it conveys the idea of legal responsibility or liability; to others, it means socially responsible behavior in the ethical sense; to still others, the meaning transmitted is that of 'responsible for' in a causal mode; many simply equate it with a charitable contribution; some take it to mean socially conscious; many of those who embrace it most fervently see it as a mere synonym for legitimacy in the context of belonging or being proper or valid; a few see a sort of fiduciary duty imposing higher standards of behavior on business men than on citizens at large" (Votaw, 1972, p. 25). Nowadays the panorama is not much better....

[O]ur aim here is to map the territory in which most relevant CSR theories and related approaches are situated. We will do so by considering each theory from the perspective of how the interaction phenomena between business and society are focused.

As the starting point for a proper classification, we assume as hypothesis that the most relevant CSR theories and related approaches are focused on one of the following aspects of social reality: economics, politics, social integration and ethics. The inspiration for this hypothesis is rooted in four aspects that, according to Parsons (1961), can be observed in any social system: adaptation to the environment (related to resources and economics), goal attainment (related to politics), social integration and pattern maintenance or latency (related to culture and values). This hypothesis permits us to classify these theories in four groups:

1. A first group in which it is assumed that the corporation is an instrument for wealth creation and that this is its sole social responsibility. Only the economic aspect of the interactions between business and society is considered. So any supposed social activity is accepted if, and only if, it is consistent with wealth creation. This group of theories could be called instrumental theories because they understand CSR as a mere means to the end of profits.
2. A second group in which the social power of corporation is emphasized, specifically in its relationship with society and its responsibility in the political arena associated with this power. This leads the corporation to accept social duties and rights or participate in certain social cooperation. We will call this group political theories.
3. A third group includes theories which consider that business ought to integrate social demands. They usually argue that business depends on society for its continuity and growth and even for the existence of business itself. We can term this group integrative theories.
4. A fourth group of theories understands that the relationship between business and society is embedded with ethical values. This leads to a vision of CSR from an ethical perspective and as a consequence, firms ought to accept social responsibilities as an ethical obligation above any other consideration. We can term this group ethical theories.

Throughout this paper we will present the most relevant theories on CSR and related matters, trying to prove that they are all focused on one of the forementioned aspects. We will not explain each theory in detail, only what is necessary to verify our hypothesis and, if necessary, some complementary information to clarify what each is about. At the same time, we will attempt to situate these theories and approaches within a general map describing the current panorama regarding the role of business in society.

INSTRUMENTAL THEORIES

In this group of theories CSR is seen only as a strategic tool to achieve economic objectives and, ultimately, wealth creation. Representative of this approach is the well-known Friedman view that "the only one responsibility of business towards society is the maximization of profits to the shareholders within the legal framework and the ethical custom of the country" (1970)....

Concern for profits does not exclude taking into account the interests of all who have a stake in the firm (stakeholders). It has been argued that in certain conditions the satisfaction of these interests can contribute to maximizing the shareholder value. An adequate level of investment in philanthropy and social activities is also acceptable for the sake of profits....

In practice, a number of studies have been carried out to determine the correlation between CSR and corporate financial performance. Of these, an increasing number show a positive correlation between the social responsibility and financial performance of corporations in most cases. However, these findings have to be read with caution since such correlation is difficult to measure.

Three main groups of instrumental theories can be identified, depending on the economic objective proposed. In the first group the objective is the maximization of shareholder value, measured by the share price. Frequently, this leads to a short-term profits orientation. The second group of theories focuses on the strategic goal of achieving competitive advantages, which would produce long-term profits. In both cases, CSR is only a question of enlightened self-interest since CSRs are a mere instrument for profits. The third is related to cause-related marketing and is very close to the second. Let us examine briefly the philosophy and some variants of these groups.

Maximizing the Shareholder Value

A well-known approach is that which takes the straightforward contribution to maximizing the shareholder value as the supreme criterion to evaluate specific corporate social activity. Any investment in social demands that would produce an increase of the shareholder value should be made, acting without deception and fraud. In contrast, if the social demands only impose a cost on the company they should be rejected. Friedman (1970) is clear, giving an example about investment in the local community: "It will be in the long run interest of a corporation that is a major employer in a small community to devote resources to providing amenities to that community or to improving its government. That makes it easier to attract desirable employees, it may reduce the wage bill or lessen losses from pilferage and sabotage or have other worthwhile effects." So, the socio-economic objectives are completely separate from the economic objectives.

Currently, this approach usually takes the shareholder value maximization as the supreme reference for corporate decision-making. The Agency Theory (Jensen and Meckling, 1976; Ross, 1973) is the most popular way to articulate this reference. However, today it is quite readily accepted that shareholder value maximization is not incompatible with satisfying certain interests of people with a stake in the firm (stakeholders). In this respect, Jensen (2000) has proposed what he calls 'enlightened value maximization.' This concept specifies long-term value maximization or value-seeking as the firm's objective. At the same time, this objective is employed as the criterion for making the requisite tradeoffs among its stakeholders.

STRATEGIES FOR ACHIEVING COMPETITIVE ADVANTAGES

A second group of theories are focused on how to allocate resources in order to achieve long-term social objectives and create a competitive advantage. In this group three approaches can be included: (a) social investments in competitive context, (b) natural resource-based view of the firm and its dynamic capabilities and (c) strategies for the bottom of the economic pyramid.

a) Social investments in a competitive context. Porter and Kramer (2002) have recently applied the well-known Porter model on competitive advantage (Porter, 1980) to consider investment in areas of what they call competitive context. The authors argue that investing in philanthropic activities may be the only way to improve the context of competitive advantage of a firm and usually creates greater social value than individual donors or government can. The reason presented—the opposite of Freidman's position—is that the firm has the knowledge and resources for a better understanding of how to solve some problems related to its mission....

b) Natural resource-based view of the firm and dynamic capabilities. The resource-based view of the firm maintains that the ability of a firm to perform better than its competitors depends on the unique interplay of human, organizational, and physical resources over time. Traditionally, resources that are most likely to lead to competitive advantage are those that meet four criteria: they should be valuable, rare, and inimitable, and the organization must be organized to deploy these resources effectively.

The "dynamic capabilities" approach presents the dynamic aspect of the resources; it is focused on the drivers behind the creation, evolution and recombination of the resources into new sources of competitive advantage. So dynamic capabilities are organizational and strategic routines, by which managers acquire resources, modify them, integrate them, and recombine them to generate new value-creating strategies. Based on this perspective, some authors have identified social and ethical resources and capabilities which can be a source of competitive advantage, such as the process of moral decision-making, the process of perception, deliberation and responsiveness or capacity of adaptation and the development of proper relationships with the primary stakeholders: employees, customers, suppliers, and communities....

c) Strategies for the bottom of the economic pyramid. Traditionally most business strategies are focused on targeting products at upper and middle-class people, but most of the world's population is poor or lower-middle class. At the bottom of the economic pyramid there may be some 4000 million people. On reflection, certain strategies can serve the poor and simultaneously make profits. Prahalad (2002), analyzing the India experience, has suggested some mind-set changes for converting the poor into active consumers. The first of these is seeing the poor as an opportunity to innovate rather than as a problem.

A specific means for attending to the bottom of the economic pyramid is disruptive innovation. Disruptive innovations (Christensen and Overdorf, 2000; Christensen et al., 2001) are products or services that do not have the same capabilities and conditions as those being used by customers in the mainstream markets; as a result they can be introduced only for new or less demanding applications among non-traditional customers, with a low-cost production and adapted to the necessities of the population. For example a telecommunications company inventing a small cellular telephone system with lower costs but also with less service adapted to the base of the economic pyramid.

Disruptive innovations can improve the social and economic conditions at the "base of the pyramid" and at the same time they create a competitive advantage for the firms in telecommunications, consumer electronics and energy production and many other industries, especially in developing countries.

Cause-Related Marketing

... [The goal of cause-based marketing] is to enhance company revenues and sales or customer relationship by building the brand through the acquisition of, and association with the ethical dimension or social responsibility dimension. In a way, it seeks product differentiation by creating socially responsible attributes that affect company reputation.... For example, a pesticide-free or non-animal-tested ingredient can be perceived by some buyers as preferable to other attributes of competitors' products.

Other activities, which typically exploit cause related marketing, are classical musical concerts, art exhibitions, golf tournaments or literacy campaigns. All of these are a form of enlightened self-interest and a win-win situation as both the company and the charitable cause receive benefits....

POLITICAL THEORIES

A group of CSR theories and approaches focus on interactions and connections between business and society and on the power and position of business and its inherent responsibility. They include both political considerations and political analysis in the CSR debate. Although there are a variety of approaches, two major theories can be distinguished: Corporate Constitutionalism and Corporate Citizenship.

Corporate Constitutionalism

Davis (1960) was one of the first to explore the role of power that business has in society and the social impact of this power. In doing so, he introduces business power as a new element in the debate of CSR. He held that business is a social institution and it must use power responsibly. Additionally, Davis noted that the causes that generate the social power of the firm are not solely internal of the firm but also external. Their locus is unstable and constantly shifting, from the economic to the social forum and from there to the political forum and vice versa.

Davis attacked the assumption of the classical economic theory of perfect competition that precludes the involvement of the firm in society besides the creation of wealth. The firm has power to influence the equilibrium of the market and therefore the price is not a Pareto optimum reflecting the free will of participants with perfect knowledge of the market.

Davis formulated two principles that express how social power has to be managed: "the social power equation" and "the iron law of responsibility." The social power equation principle states that "social responsibilities of businessmen arise from the amount of social power that they have" (Davis, 1967, p. 48). The iron law of responsibility refers to the negative consequences of the absence of use of power....

According to Davis, the equation of social power responsibility has to be understood through the functional role of business and managers. In this respect, Davis rejects the idea of total responsibility of business as he rejected the radical free-market ideology of no responsibility of business. The limits of functional power come from the pressures of different constituency groups.... The constituency groups do not destroy power. Rather they define conditions for its responsible use. They channel organizational power in a supportive way and to protect other interests against unreasonable organizational power.

Integrative Social Contract Theory

Donaldson (1982) considered the business and society relationship from the social contract tradition, mainly from the philosophical thought of Locke. He assumed that a sort of implicit social contract between business and society exists. This social contract implies some indirect obligations of business towards society. This approach would overcome some limitations of deontological and teleological theories applied to business.

Afterwards, Donaldson and Dunfee (1994, 1999) extended this approach and proposed an "Integrative Social Contract Theory" (ISCT) in order to take into account the socio-cultural context and also to integrate empirical and normative aspects of management. Social responsibilities come from consent. These scholars assumed two levels of consent. Firstly a theoretical macrosocial contract appealing to all rational contractors, and secondly, a real microsocial contract by members of numerous localized communities. According to these authors, this theory offers a process in which the contracts among industries, departments and economic systems can be legitimate. In this process the participants will agree upon the ground rules defining the foundation of economics that will be acceptable to them....

Corporate Citizenship

Although the idea of the firm as citizen is not new, a renewed interest in this concept among practitioners has appeared recently due to certain factors that have had an impact on the business and society relationship. Among these factors, especially worthy of note are the crisis of the Welfare State and the globalization phenomenon. These, together with the deregulation process and decreasing costs with technological improvements, have meant that some large multinational companies have greater economical and social power than some governments. The corporate citizenship framework looks to give an account of this new reality, as we will try to explain here.

In the 80s the term "corporate citizenship" was introduced into the business and society relationship mainly through practitioners. Since the late 1990s and early 21st century this term has become more and more popular in business and increasing academic work has been carried out.

Although the academic reflection on the concept of "corporate citizenship," and on a similar one called "the business citizen," is quite recent, this notion has always connoted a sense of belonging to a community. Perhaps for this reason it has been so popular among managers and business people, because it is increasingly clear that business needs to take into account the community where it is operating....

In spite of some noteworthy differences in corporate citizenship theories, most authors generally converge on some points, such as a strong sense of business responsibility towards the local community, partnerships, which are the specific ways of formalizing the willingness to improve the local community, and for consideration for the environment.

The concern for local community has extended progressively to a global concern in great part due to the very intense protests against globalization, mainly since the end of the 90s. This sense of global corporate citizenship led to the joint statement "Global Corporate Citizenship—the Leadership Challenge for CEOs and Boards," signed by 34 of the world's largest multinational corporations during the World Economic Forum in New York in January 2002....

INTEGRATIVE THEORIES

This group of theories looks at how business integrates social demands, arguing that business depends on society for its existence, continuity and growth. Social demands are generally considered to be the way in which society interacts with business and gives it a certain legitimacy and prestige. As a consequence, corporate management should take into account social demands, and integrate them in such a way that the business operates in accordance with social values.

So, the content of business responsibility is limited to the space and time of each situation depending on the values of society at that moment, and comes through the company's functional roles. In other words, there is no specific action that management is responsible for performing throughout time and in each industry. Basically, the theories of this group are focused on the detection and scanning of, and response to, the social demands that achieve social legitimacy, greater social acceptance and prestige.

Issues Management

Social responsiveness, or responsiveness in the face of social issues, and processes to manage them within the organization was an approach which arose in the 70s. In this approach it is crucial to consider the gap between what the organization's

relevant publics expect its performance to be and the organization's actual performance. These gaps are usually located in the zone that Ackerman (1973, p. 92) calls the "zone of discretion" (neither regulated nor illegal nor sanctioned) where the company receives some unclear signals from the environment. The firm should perceive the gap and choose a response in order to close it.

Ackerman (1973), among other scholars, analyzed the relevant factors regarding the internal structures of organizations and integration mechanisms to manage social issues within the organization. The way a social objective is spread and integrated across the organization, he termed "process of institutionalization." According to Jones (1980, p. 65), "corporate behavior should not in most cases be judged by the decisions actually reached but by the process by which they are reached." Consequently, he emphasized the idea of process rather than principles as the appropriate approach to CSR issues.

Jones draws an analogy with the political process assessing that the appropriate process of CSR should be a fair process where all interests have had the opportunity to be heard. So Jones has shifted the criterion to the inputs in the decision-making process rather than outcomes, and has focused more on the process of implementation of CSR activities than on the process of conceptualization....

Stakeholder Management

... "[S]takeholder management" is oriented towards "stakeholders" or people who affect or are affected by corporate policies and practices. Although the practice of stakeholder management is long-established, its academic development started only at the end of 70s. In a seminal paper, Emshoff and Freeman (1978) presented two basic principles, which underpin stakeholder management. The first is that the central goal is to achieve maximum overall cooperation between the entire system of stakeholder groups and the objectives of the corporation. The second states that the most efficient strategies for managing stakeholder relations involve efforts which simultaneously deal with issues affecting multiple stakeholders.

Stakeholder management tries to integrate groups with a stake in the firm into managerial decision making....

In recent times, corporations have been pressured by non-governmental organizations (NGOs), activists, communities, governments, media and other institutional forces. These groups demand what they consider to be responsible corporate practices. Now some corporations are seeking corporate responses to social demands by establishing dialogue with a wide spectrum of stakeholders.

ETHICAL THEORIES

There is a fourth group of theories or approaches that focus on the ethical requirements that cement the relationship between business and society. They are based on principles that express the right thing to do or the necessity to achieve a good society. As main approaches we can distinguish the following.

Universal Rights

Human rights have been taken as a basis for CSR, especially in the global market place. In recent years, some human-rights-based approaches for corporate responsibility have been proposed. One of them is the UN Global Compact, which includes nine principles in the areas of human rights, labor and the environment. It was first presented by the United Nations Secretary General Kofi Annan in an address to The World Economic Forum in 1999. In 2000 the Global Compact's operational phase was launched at UN Headquarters in New York. Many companies have since adopted it. Another, previously presented and updated in 1999, is The Global Sullivan Principles, which has the objective of supporting economic, social and political justice by companies where they do business. The certification SA8000 (www.cepaa.org) for accreditation of social responsibility is also based on human and labor rights. Despite using different approaches, all are based on the Universal Declaration of Human Rights adopted by the United Nations general assembly in 1948 and on other international declarations of human rights, labor rights and environmental protection....

Sustainable Development

Another values-based concept, which has become popular, is "sustainable development." Although this approach was developed at macro level rather than corporate level, it demands a relevant corporate contribution. The term came into widespread use in 1987, when the World Commission on Environment and Development (United Nations) published a report known as "Brundtland Report." This report stated that "sustainable development" seeks to meet "the needs of the present without compromising the ability of future generations to meet their own needs" (World Commission on Environment and Development, 1987, p. 8). Although this report originally only included the environmental factor, the concept of "sustainable development" has since expanded to include the consideration of the social dimension as being inseparable from development. In the words of the World Business Council for Sustainable Development (2000, p. 2), sustainable development "requires the integration of social, environmental, and economic considerations to make balanced judgments for the long term."

THE COMMON GOOD APPROACH

This third group of approaches, less consolidated than the stakeholder approach but with potential, holds the common good of society as the referential value for CSR.... This approach maintains that business, as with any other social group or individual in society, has to contribute to the common good, because it is a part of society. In this respect, it has been argued that business is a mediating institution. Business should be neither harmful to nor a parasite on society, but purely a positive contributor to the well-being of the society.

Business contributes to the common good in different ways, such as creating wealth, providing goods and services in an efficient and fair way, at the same time respecting the dignity and the inalienable and fundamental rights of the individual. Furthermore, it contributes to social well-being and a harmonic way of living together in just, peaceful and friendly conditions, both in the present and in the future.

To some extent, this approach has a lot in common with both the stakeholder approach and sustainable development, but the philosophical base is different. Although there are several ways of understanding the notion of common good, the interpretation based on the knowledge of human nature and its fulfillment seems to us particularly convincing. It permits the circumnavigation of cultural relativism, which is frequently embedded in some definitions of sustainable development.

The common good notion is also very close to the Japanese concept of Kyosei, understood as "living and working together for the common good," which, together with the principle of human dignity, is one of the founding principles of the popular "The Caux Roundtable Principles for Business" (www.cauxroundtable.org).

REFERENCES

Ackerman, R.W. 1973, 'How Companies Respond to Social Demands,' *Harvard University Review* 51(4), 88–98.

Christensen, C.M., T. Craig and S. Hart 2001, 'The Great Disruption,' *Foreign Affairs* 80(2), 80–96.

Christensen, C.M. and M. Overdorf 2000, 'Meeting the Challenge of Disruptive Change,' *Harvard Business Review* 78(2), 66–75.

Davis, K. 1960, 'Can Business Afford to Ignore Corporate Social Responsibilities?,' *California Management Review* 2, 70–76.

Davis, K. 1967, 'Understanding the Social Responsibility Puzzle,' *Business Horizons* 10(4), 45–51.

Donaldson, T. 1982, *Corporations and Morality* (Prentice Hall, Englewood Cliff, NJ).

Donaldson, T. and T.W. Dunfee 1994, 'Towards a Unified Conception of Business Ethics: Integrative Social Contracts Theory,' *Academy of Management Review* 19, 252–284.

Donaldson, T. and T.W. Dunfee 1999, *Ties That Bind: A Social Contracts Approach to Business Ethics* (Harvard Business School Press, Boston).

Emshoff, J.R. and R.E. Freeman 1978, 'Stakeholder Management,' Working Paper from the Wharton Applied Research Center (July). Quoted by Sturdivant (1979).

Friedman, M. 1970, 'The Social Responsibility of Business Is to Increase Its Profits,' *New York Times Magazine*, September 13th, 32–33, 122, 126.

Jensen, M.C. 2000, 'Value Maximization, Stakeholder Theory, and the Corporate Objective Function,' in M. Beer and N. Nohria (eds.), *Breaking the Code of Change* (Harvard Business School Press, Boston), pp. 37–58. Reprinted (2002) as 'Value Maximization, Stakeholder Theory, and the Corporate Objective Function,' *Business Ethics Quarterly* 12(2), 235–256.

Jensen, M.C. and W. Meckling 1976, 'Theory of the Firm: Managerial Behavior, Agency Cost, and Capital Structure,' *Journal of Financial Economics* 3(October), 305–360.

Jones, T.M. 1980, 'Corporate Social Responsibility Revisited, Redefined,' *California Management Review* 22(2), 59–67.

Parsons, T. 1961, 'An Outline of the Social System,' in T. Parsons, E.A. Shils, K.D. Naegie and J.R. Pitts (eds.), *Theories of Society* (Free Press, New York).

Porter, M.E. 1980, *Competitive Strategy: Techniques for Analyzing Industries and Competitors* (Free Press, New York).

Porter, M.E. and M.R. Kramer 2002, 'The Competitive Advantage of Corporate Philanthropy,' *Harvard Business Review* 80(12), 56–69.

Prahalad, C.K. 2002, 'Strategies for the Bottom of the Economic Pyramid: India as a Source of Innovation,' *Reflections: The SOL Journal* 3(4), 6–18.

Ross, S. 1973, 'The Economy Theory of the Agency: The Principal's Problem,' *American Economic Review* 63, 134–139.

Votaw, D.I. 1972, 'Genius Became Rare: A Comment on the Doctrine of Social Responsibility Pt 1', California Management Review 15(2), 25–31.

World Business Council for Sustainable Development 2000, Corporate Social Responsibility: Making Good Business Sense (World Business Council for Sustainable Development, Geneve).

World Commission on Environment and Development 1987, Our Common Future (Oxford University Press, Oxford).

—10—

THE SOCIAL RESPONSIBILITY OF BUSINESS IS TO INCREASE ITS PROFITS

Milton Friedman

WHEN I HEAR BUSINESSMEN SPEAK ELOQUENTLY about the "social responsibilities of business in a free-enterprise system," I am reminded of the wonderful line about the Frenchman who discovered at the age of 70 that he had been speaking prose all his life. The businessmen believe that they are defending free enterprise when they declaim that business is not concerned "merely" with profit but also with promoting desirable "social" ends; that business has a "social conscience" and takes seriously its responsibilities for providing employment, eliminating discrimination, avoiding pollution and whatever else may be the catchwords of the contemporary crop of reformers. In fact they are—or would be if they or anyone else took them seriously—preaching pure and unadulterated socialism. Businessmen who talk this way are unwitting puppets of the intellectual forces that have been undermining the basis of a free society these past decades.

The discussions of the "social responsibilities of business" are notable for their analytical loose-ness and lack of rigor. What does it mean to say that "business" has responsibilities? Only people can have responsibilities. A corporation is an arti-ficial person and in this sense may have artificial responsibilities, but "business" as a whole cannot be said to have responsibilities, even in this vague sense. The first step toward clarity in examining the doctrine of the social responsibility of business is to ask precisely what it implies for whom.

Presumably, the individuals who are to be responsible are businessmen, which means indi-vidual proprietors or corporate executives. Most of the discussion of social responsibility is directed at corporations, so in what follows I shall mostly neglect the individual proprietors and speak of corporate executives.

In a free-enterprise, private-property system, a corporate executive is an employee of the owners of the business. He has direct responsibility to his employers. That responsibility is to conduct the business in accordance with their desires, which generally will be to make as much money as possible while conforming to the basic rules of the society, both those embodied in law and those embodied in ethical custom. Of course, in some cases his employers may have a different objective. A group of persons might establish a corporation for an eleemosynary purpose—for example, a hos-pital or a school. The manager of such a corpora-tion will not have money profit as his objective but the rendering of certain services.

In either case, the key point is that, in his capacity as a corporate executive, the manager is the agent of the individuals who own the

corporation or establish the eleemosynary institution, and his primary responsibility is to them.

Needless to say, this does not mean that it
is easy to judge how well he is performing his
task. But at least the criterion of performance is
straightforward, and the persons among whom
a voluntary contractual arrangement exists are
clearly defined.

Of course, the corporate executive is also a
person in his own right. As a person, he may have
many other responsibilities that he recognizes or
assumes voluntarily—to his family, his conscience,
his feelings of charity, his church, his clubs, his city,
his country. He may feel impelled by these responsibilities to devote part of his income to causes he
regards as worthy, to refuse to work for particular
corporations, even to leave his job, for example, to
join his country's armed forces. If we wish, we may
refer to some of these responsibilities as "social
responsibilities." But in these respects he is acting
as a principal, not an agent; he is spending his own
money or time or energy, not the money of his
employers or the time or energy he has contracted
to devote to their purposes. If these are "social
responsibilities," they are the social responsibilities
of individuals, not of business.

What does it mean to say that the corporate executive has a "social responsibility" in
his capacity as businessman? If this statement
is not pure rhetoric, it must mean that he is to
act in some way that is not in the interest of his
employers. For example, that he is to refrain from
increasing the price of the product in order to
contribute to the social objective of preventing
inflation, even though a price increase would be
in the best interests of the corporation. Or that
he is to make expenditures on reducing pollution
beyond the amount that is in the best interests of
the corporation or that is required by law in order
to contribute to the social objective of improving
the environment. Or that, at the expense of corporate profits, he is to hire "hardcore" unemployed
instead of better qualified available workmen
to contribute to the social objective of reducing poverty.

In each of these cases, the corporate executive would be spending someone else's money
for a general social interest. Insofar as his actions
in accord with his "social responsibility" reduce
returns to stockholders, he is spending their
money. Insofar as his actions raise the price to
customers, he is spending the customers' money.
Insofar as his actions lower the wages of some
employees, he is spending their money.

The stockholders or the customers or the
employees could separately spend their own
money on the particular action if they wished to
do so. The executive is exercising a distinct "social
responsibility," rather than serving as an agent of
the stockholders or the customers or the employees, only if he spends the money in a different way
than they would have spent it.

But if he does this, he is in effect imposing
taxes, on the one hand, and deciding how the tax
proceeds shall be spent, on the other.

This process raises political questions on two
levels: principle and consequences. On the level
of political principle, the imposition of taxes and
the expenditure of tax proceeds are governmental
functions. We have established elaborate constitutional, parliamentary, and judicial provisions
to control these functions, to assure that taxes
are imposed so far as possible in accordance with
the preferences and desires of the public—after
all, "taxation without representation" was one of
the battle cries of the American Revolution. We
have a system of checks and balances to separate
the legislative function of imposing taxes and
enacting expenditures from the executive function
of collecting taxes and administering expenditure
programs and from the judicial function of mediating disputes and interpreting the law.

Here the businessman—self-selected or
appointed directly or indirectly by stockholders—
is to be simultaneously legislator, executive, and
jurist. He is to decide whom to tax by how much
and for what purpose, and he is to spend the proceeds—all this guided only by general exhortations
from on high to restrain inflation, improve the
environment, fight poverty and so on and on.

The whole justification for permitting the corporate executive to be selected by the stockholders is that the executive is an agent serving the interests of his principal. This justification disappears when the corporate executive imposes taxes and spends the proceeds for "social" purposes. He becomes in effect a public employee, a civil servant, even though he remains in name an employee of a private enterprise. On grounds of political principle, it is intolerable that such civil servants—insofar as their actions in the name of social responsibility are real and not just window-dressing—should be selected as they are now. If they are to be civil servants, then they must be elected through a political process. If they are to impose taxes and make expenditures to foster "social" objectives, then political machinery must be set up to make the assessment of taxes and to determine through a political process the objectives to be served.

This is the basic reason why the doctrine of "social responsibility" involves the acceptance of the socialist view that political mechanisms, not market mechanisms, are the appropriate way to determine the allocation of scarce resources to alternative uses.

On the grounds of consequences, can the corporate executive in fact discharge his alleged "social responsibilities?" On the other hand, suppose he could get away with spending the stockholders' or customers' or employees' money. How is he to know how to spend it? He is told that he must contribute to fighting inflation. How is he to know what action of his will contribute to that end? He is presumably an expert in running his company—in producing a product or selling it or financing it. But nothing about his selection makes him an expert on inflation. Will his holding down the price of his product reduce inflationary pressure? Or, by leaving more spending power in the hands of his customers, simply divert it elsewhere? Or, by forcing him to produce less because of the lower price, will it simply contribute to shortages? Even if he could answer these questions, how much cost is he justified in imposing on his stockholders,

customers, and employees for this social purpose? What is his appropriate share and what is the appropriate share of others?

And, whether he wants to or not, can he get away with spending his stockholders', customers' or employees' money? Will not the stockholders fire him? (Either the present ones or those who take over when his actions in the name of social responsibility have reduced the corporation's profits and the price of its stock.) His customers and his employees can desert him for other producers and employers less scrupulous in exercising their social responsibilities.

This facet of "social responsibility" doctrine is brought into sharp relief when the doctrine is used to justify wage restraint by trade unions. The conflict of interest is naked and clear when union officials are asked to subordinate the interest of their members to some more general purpose. If the union officials try to enforce wage restraint, the consequence is likely to be wildcat strikes, rank-and-file revolts, and the emergence of strong competitors for their jobs. We thus have the ironic phenomenon that union leaders—at least in the US—have objected to Government interference with the market far more consistently and courageously than have business leaders.

The difficulty of exercising "social responsibility" illustrates, of course, the great virtue of private competitive enterprise—it forces people to be responsible for their own actions and makes it difficult for them to "exploit" other people for either selfish or unselfish purposes. They can do good—but only at their own expense.

Many a reader who has followed the argument this far may be tempted to remonstrate that it is all well and good to speak of Government's having the responsibility to impose taxes and determine expenditures for such "social" purposes as controlling pollution or training the hard-core unemployed, but that the problems are too urgent to wait on the slow course of political processes, that the exercise of social responsibility by businessmen is a quicker and surer way to solve pressing current problems.

Aside from the question of fact—I share Adam Smith's skepticism about the benefits that can be expected from "those who affected to trade for the public good"—this argument must be rejected on grounds of principle. What it amounts to is an assertion that those who favor the taxes and expenditures in question have failed to persuade a majority of their fellow citizens to be of like mind and that they are seeking to attain by undemocratic procedures what they cannot attain by democratic procedures. In a free society, it is hard for "evil" people to do "evil," especially since one man's good is another's evil.

I have, for simplicity, concentrated on the special case of the corporate executive, except only for the brief digression on trade unions. But precisely the same argument applies to the newer phenomenon of calling upon stockholders to require corporations to exercise social responsibility (the recent GM crusade for example). In most of these cases, what is in effect involved is some stockholders trying to get other stockholders (or customers or employees) to contribute against their will to "social" causes favored by the activists. Insofar as they succeed, they are again imposing taxes and spending the proceeds.

The situation of the individual proprietor is somewhat different. If he acts to reduce the returns of his enterprise in order to exercise his "social responsibility," he is spending his own money, not someone else's. If he wishes to spend his money on such purposes, that is his right, and I cannot see that there is any objection to his doing so. In the process, he, too, may impose costs on employees and customers. However, because he is far less likely than a large corporation or union to have monopolistic power, any such side effects will tend to be minor.

Of course, in practice, the doctrine of social responsibility is frequently a cloak for actions that are justified on other grounds rather than a reason for those actions.

To illustrate, it may well be in the long-run interest of a corporation that is a major employer in a small community to devote resources to providing amenities to that community or to improving its government. That may make it easier to attract desirable employees, it may reduce the wage bill or lessen losses from pilferage and sabotage or have other worthwhile effects. Or it may be that, given the laws about the deductibility of corporate charitable contributions, the stockholders can contribute more to charities they favor by having the corporation make the gift than by doing it themselves, since they can in that way contribute an amount that would otherwise have been paid as corporate taxes.

In each of these—and many similar—cases, there is a strong temptation to rationalize these actions as an exercise of "social responsibility." In the present climate of opinion, with its widespread aversion to "capitalism," "profits," the "soulless corporation," and so on, this is one way for a corporation to generate goodwill as a by-product of expenditures that are entirely justified in its own self-interest.

It would be inconsistent of me to call on corporate executives to refrain from this hypocritical window-dressing because it harms the foundations of a free society. That would be to call on them to exercise a "social responsibility"! If our institutions, and the attitudes of the public make it in their self-interest to cloak their actions in this way, I cannot summon much indignation to denounce them. At the same time, I can express admiration for those individual proprietors or owners of closely held corporations or stockholders of more broadly held corporations who disdain such tactics as approaching fraud.

Whether blameworthy or not, the use of the cloak of social responsibility, and the nonsense spoken in its name by influential and prestigious businessmen, does clearly harm the foundations of a free society. I have been impressed time and again by the schizophrenic character of many businessmen. They are capable of being extremely far-sighted and clear-headed in matters that are internal to their businesses. They are incredibly short-sighted and muddle-headed in matters that are outside their businesses but affect the possible survival of business in general. This shortsightedness is strikingly exemplified in the calls from many businessmen for wage and price guidelines or controls or income policies. There is nothing that could do more in a brief period to destroy a market system and replace it by a centrally controlled system than effective governmental control of prices and wages.

The shortsightedness is also exemplified in speeches by businessmen on social responsibility. This may gain them kudos in the short run. But it helps to strengthen the already too prevalent view that the pursuit of profits is wicked and immoral and must be curbed and controlled by external forces. Once this view is adopted, the external forces that curb the market will not be the social consciences, however highly developed, of the pontificating executives; it will be the iron fist of Government bureaucrats. Here, as with price and wage controls, businessmen seem to me to reveal a suicidal impulse.

The political principle that underlies the market mechanism is unanimity. In an ideal free market resting on private property, no individual can coerce any other, all cooperation is voluntary, all parties to such cooperation benefit or they need not participate. There are no values, no "social" responsibilities in any sense other than the shared values and responsibilities of individuals. Society is a collection of individuals and of the various groups they voluntarily form.

The political principle that underlies the political mechanism is conformity. The individual must serve a more general social interest—whether that be determined by a church or a dictator or a majority. The individual may have a vote and say in what is to be done, but if he is overruled, he must conform. It is appropriate for some to require others to contribute to a general social purpose whether they wish to or not.

Unfortunately, unanimity is not always feasible. There are some respects in which conformity appears unavoidable, so I do not see how one can avoid the use of the political mechanism altogether.

But the doctrine of "social responsibility" taken seriously would extend the scope of the apolitical mechanism to every human activity. It does not differ in philosophy from the most explicitly collectivist doctrine. It differs only by professing to believe that collectivist ends can be attained without collectivist means. That is why, in my book *Capitalism and Freedom*, I have called it a "fundamentally subversive doctrine" in a free society, and have said that in such a society, "there is one and only one social responsibility of business—to use its resources and engage in activities designed to increase its profits so long as it stays within the rules of the game, which is to say, engages in open and free competition without deception or fraud."

—11—
THE SHAREHOLDER VALUE MYTH

Lynn A. Stout

SHAREHOLDER VALUE AND ITS DISAPPOINTMENTS

By the end of the 20th century, a broad consensus had emerged in the Anglo-American business world that corporations should be governed according to the philosophy often called shareholder primacy. Shareholder primacy theory taught that corporations were owned by their shareholders; that directors and executives should do what the company's owners/shareholders wanted them to do; and that what shareholders generally wanted managers to do was to maximize "shareholder value," measured by share price.

Today this consensus is crumbling. As just one example, in the past year no fewer than three prominent New York Times columnists have published articles questioning shareholder value thinking.[1] Shareholder primacy theory is suffering a crisis of confidence. This is happening in large part because it is becoming clear that shareholder value thinking doesn't seem to work, even for most shareholders.

Consider the example of the United States. The idea that corporations should be managed to maximize shareholder value has led over the past two decades to dramatic shifts in US corporate law and practice. Executive compensation rules, governance practices, and federal securities laws, have all been "reformed" to give shareholders more influence over boards and to make managers more attentive to share price. The results are disappointing at best. Shareholders are suffering their worst

investment returns since the Great Depression; the population of publicly-listed companies has declined by 40%; and the life expectancy of Fortune 500 firms has plunged from 75 years in the early 20th century to only 15 years today.

Correlation does not prove causation, of course. But in my book *The Shareholder Value Myth: How Putting Shareholders First Harms Investors, Corporations, and the Public*, I explore the logical connections between the rise of shareholder value thinking and subsequent declines in investor returns, numbers of public companies, and corporate life expectancy. I also show that shareholder primacy is an abstract economic theory that lacks support from history, law, or the empirical evidence. In fact, the idea of a single shareholder value is intellectually incoherent. No wonder the shift to shareholder value thinking doesn't seem to be turning out well—especially for shareholders.

DEBUNKING THE SHAREHOLDER VALUE MYTH: HISTORY

Although many contemporary business experts take shareholder primacy as a given, the rise of shareholder primacy as dominant business philosophy is a relatively recent phenomenon. For most of the twentieth century, large public companies followed a philosophy called managerial capitalism. Boards of directors in managerial companies operated largely as self-selecting and autonomous decision-making bodies, with dispersed shareholders playing a passive role. What's more, directors viewed themselves not as shareholders' servants, but as trustees for great institutions that should serve not only shareholders but other corporate stakeholders as well, including customers, creditors, employees, and the community. Equity investors were treated as an important corporate constituency, but not the only constituency that mattered. Nor was share price assumed to be the best proxy for corporate performance.

Go back further, to the very beginnings of business corporations, and we see even greater deviations from shareholder primacy. Many corporations formed in the late eighteenth and early nineteenth centuries were created specifically to develop large commercial ventures like roads, canals, railroads, and banks. Investors in these early corporations were usually also customers. They structured their companies to make sure the business would provide good service at a reasonable price—not to maximize investment returns.

So where did the idea that corporations exist only to maximize shareholder value come from? Originally, it seems, from free-market economists. In 1970, Nobel Prize winner Milton Friedman published a famous essay in the New York Times arguing that the only proper goal of business was to maximize profits for the company's owners, whom Friedman assumed (incorrectly, we shall see) to be the company's shareholders.[2] Even more influential was a 1976 article by Michael Jensen and William Meckling titled the "Theory of the Firm."[3] This article, still the most frequently cited in the business literature,[4] repeated Friedman's mistake by assuming that shareholders owned corporations and were corporation's residual claimants. From this assumption, Jensen and Meckling argued that a key problem in corporations was getting wayward directors and executives to focus on maximizing the wealth of the corporations' shareholders.

Jensen and Meckling's approach was eagerly embraced by a rising generation of scholars eager to bring the "science" of economics to the messy business of corporate law and practice. Shareholder primacy theory led many to

conclude that managerialism must be inefficient and outmoded, and that corporations needed to be "reformed" from the outside. (There is great irony here: free-market economist Friedrich Hayek would have warned against such academic attempts at economic central planning.) Shareholder primacy rhetoric also appealed to powerful interest groups. These included activist corporate raiders; institutional investors; and eventually, CEOs whose pay was tied to stock price performance. As a result, shareholder primacy rose from arcane academic theory in the 1970s to dominant business practice today.

DEBUNKING THE SHAREHOLDER VALUE MYTH: LAW

Yet it is important to note that shareholder primacy theory was first advanced by economists, not lawyers. This may explain why the idea that corporations should be managed to maximize shareholder value is based on factually mistaken claims about the law.

Consider first Friedman's erroneous belief that shareholders "own" corporations. Although laymen sometimes have difficulty understanding the point, corporations are legal entities that own themselves, just as human entities own themselves. What shareholders own are shares, a type of contract between the shareholder and the legal entity that gives shareholders limited legal rights. In this regard, shareholders stand on equal footing with the corporation's bondholders, suppliers, and employees, all of whom also enter contracts with the firm that give them limited legal rights.

A more sophisticated but equally mistaken claim is the residual claimants argument. According to this argument, shareholders are legally entitled to all corporate profits after the fixed contractual claims of creditors, employees, suppliers, etc., have been paid. If true, this would imply that maximizing the value of the shareholders' residual interest in the company is the same thing as maximizing the value of the company itself, which usually benefits society. But the residual claimants argument is also legally errone-ous. Shareholders are residual claimants only when failed companies are being liquidated in bank-ruptcy. The law applies different rules to healthy companies, where the legal entity is its own resid-ual claimant, meaning the entity is entitled to keep its profits and to use them as its board of directors sees fit. The board may choose to distribute some profits as dividends to shareholders. But it can also choose instead to raise employee salaries; invest in marketing or research and development; or make charitable contributions.

Which leads to the third legal error underlying shareholder primacy: the common but misleading claim that directors and executives are sharehold-ers' "agents." At law, a fundamental characteristic of any principal/agent relationship is the principal's right to control the agent's behavior. But sharehold-ers lack the legal authority to control directors or executives. Traditionally, shareholders' governance rights in public companies are limited and indirect, including primarily their right to vote on who sits on the board, and their right to bring lawsuits for breach of fiduciary duty. As a practical matter, nei-ther gives shareholders much leverage. Even today it remains very difficult for dispersed shareholders in a public corporation to remove an incumbent board. And shareholders are only likely to recover damages from directors in lawsuits involving breach of the duty of loyalty, meaning the directors were essen-tially stealing from the firm. Provided directors don't use their corporate powers to enrich them-selves, a key legal doctrine called the "business judg-ment rule" otherwise protects them from liability.

The business judgment rule ensures that, contrary to popular belief, the managers of public companies have no enforceable legal duty to maxi-mize shareholder value. Certainly they can choose to maximize profits; but they can also choose to pursue any other objective that is not unlawful, including taking care of employees and suppliers, pleasing customers, benefiting the community and the broader society, and preserving and protecting the corporate entity itself. Shareholder primacy is a managerial choice—not a legal requirement.

DEBUNKING THE SHAREHOLDER VALUE MYTH: EVIDENCE

Which leads to the question of the empirical evidence. As noted above, the law does not require corporate managers to maximize shareholder value. But this certainly is something managers can opt to do. And certain corporate governance strategies—putting more independent directors on boards, tying executive pay to share price, removing "staggered" board structures that make it harder to oust sitting directors—are widely recognized as effective means to make managers embrace raising share price as their primary objective. If share-holder primacy theory is correct, corporations that adopt such strategies should do better and produce higher investor returns than corporations that don't. Does the evidence confirm this?

Surprisingly, the answer to this question is "no." Researchers have spent decades and produced scores of studies seeking to prove that shareholder primacy generates superior business results. Yet there is a notable lack of replicated studies finding this. For example, one survey looked at more than a dozen studies of supposedly shareholder-hostile companies that used dual-class share structures to disenfranchise public investors. Some studies found dual-class structures had no effect on cor-porate performance; some found a mild negative effect; and some studies found a positive effect (in one case, a strongly positive effect), exactly the opposite of what shareholder primacy the-ory predicts.

But more important, studies that examine whether supposedly shareholder value-maximizing strategies improve the performance of an indi-vidual company for a year or two are looking in the wrong place and at the wrong time period. Individual shareholders may perhaps care only about their own investing returns in the near future. But policymakers and governance experts should care about public equity returns to inves-tors as a class, over longer periods. As already noted, if we look at returns to public equity inves-tors as a class, over time, the shift to shareholder primacy as a business philosophy has been accompanied by dismal results.

Why? The answer may lie in recognizing that shareholder value-increasing strategies that are profitable for one shareholder in one period of time can be bad news for shareholders collectively over a longer period of time. The dynamic is much the same as that presented by fishing with dynamite. In the short term, the fisherman who switches from using baited lines to using dynamite sees an increase in the size of his catch. But when many fishermen in the village begin using dynamite, after an initial increase, the collective catch may diminish steadily. Shareholders may experience the same regrettable result when they push managers to "maximize shareholder value."

THERE IS NO SINGLE SHAREHOLDER VALUE

To understand why shareholder primacy can be compared to fishing with dynamite, it is useful to start by recognizing an awkward reality: there is no single "shareholder value." Shareholder primacy looks at the world from the perspective of a Platonic shareholder who only cares about one company's share price, at one moment in time. Yet no such Platonic entity exists.

"Shareholders" actually are human beings who happen to own shares, and human beings have different interests and different values. Some shareholders plan to hold long-term, to save for retirement; others are speculators, eager to reap a quick profit and sell. Some shareholders want companies to make long-term commitments that earn the loyalty of customers, employees and suppliers; others may want to profit from opportunistically exploiting stakeholders' commitments. Some investors are undiversified (think of the hedge fund manager whose human and financial capital are both tied up in the fate of one or two securities). Most are diversified, and worry about the performance of multiple companies as well as their own health, employment prospects, and tax burdens. Finally, some shareholders may not care

if their companies earn profits by breaking the law, hurting employees and consumers, or damaging the environment. But others are "prosocial," willing to sacrifice at least some investment returns to ensure the companies they invest in contribute to, rather than harming, society.

It is these divisions between shareholders' interests that allow some shareholders to profit by pushing companies to adopt strategies that harm other shareholders. The divisions make it possible for shareholders to "invest with dynamite," as it were.

INVESTING WITH DYNAMITE

As an example, consider the conflict between short-term and long-term investors. It was once believed (at least by academic economists) that the market price of a company's stock perfectly captured the best estimate of its long-term value. Today this idea of a perfectly "efficient" stock market has been discredited, and it is widely recognized that some business strategies can raise share price temporarily while possibly harming the company's long-term prospects. Examples include cutting expenses for marketing or research and development; siphoning off cash that might otherwise be invested for the future through massive dividends or share repurchase plans; taking on risky leverage; and selling off all or part of the company. Hedge funds and other activist investors are famous for pushing boards to adopt such strategies. (Consider Carl Icahn's recent efforts to get Transocean to pay out dividends rather than reducing its debt.) This is profitable for the activists, who typically sell immediately after the share price rises. But over time, this kind of activism diminishes the size and health of the overall population of public companies, leaving investors as a class with fewer good investing options.

A similar dynamic exists when it comes to how companies treat stakeholders like employees and customers. Shareholders as a class want companies to be able to treat their stakeholders well, because this encourages employee and customer loyalty ("specific investment"). Yet individual shareholders can profit from pushing boards to exploit committed stakeholders—say, by threatening to outsource jobs unless employees agree to lower wages, or refusing to support products customers have come to rely on unless they buy expensive new products as well. In the long run, such corporate opportunism makes it difficult for companies to attract employee and customer loyalty in the first place. Some investors profit, but again, the size of the total investing "catch" declines.

Conflicts of interest between diversified and undiversified shareholders raise similar problems. For several years, BP paid large dividends and kept its share price high by cutting safety corners to keep expenses down. Undiversified investors who owned only BP common stock benefited, especially those lucky enough to sell before the Deepwater Horizon disaster. But when tragedy finally struck, the BP oil spill damaged not only the price of BP shares, but also BP bonds, other oil companies operating in the Gulf, and the Gulf tourism and fishing industries. Diversified investors with interests in these other ventures would have preferred that BP focused a bit less on maximizing shareholder value. Similarly, consider the irony of a pension fund portfolio manager whose job is to invest on behalf of employees pushing companies to raise share prices—by firing employees. This harms not only investors who are also employees, but all investors, as rising unemployment hurts consumer demand and eventually corporate profits.

Finally, consider the differing interests of asocial investors who do not care if companies earn profits from illegal or socially harmful behaviors, and prosocial investors who don't want the companies they invest in to harm others or violate the law. The first group wants managers to "unlock shareholder value" at any cost, without regard to any damage done to other people or to the environment. The second group does not. Asocial investing—one might even call it sociopathic investing—may not harm corporate profits in the long run. Thus it presents a different problem from other shareholder value strategies, discussed above, that reduce long-run investing returns. But it presents ethical, moral, and economic efficiency problems of its own.

WHICH SHAREHOLDERS AND WHOSE VALUES?

Closer inspection thus reveals the idea of a single "shareholder value" to be a fiction. Different shareholders have different values. Many, and probably most, have concerns far beyond what happens to the share price of a single company in the next year or two.

Some shareholder primacy advocates might nevertheless argue that we need to embrace share price as the sole corporate objective, because if we judge corporate performance more subjectively or use more than one criterion, managers become unaccountable. This argument has at least two flaws. First, we routinely judge the success of endeavors by multiple, often subjective, criteria. (Even eating lunch in a restaurant requires balancing cost against taste against calories against nutrition.) Second, the philosophy of "maximize shareholder value" asks managers to focus only on the share price of their own company, in the relatively near term. In other words, it resolves conflicts among shareholders by privileging the small subset of shareholders who are most short-sighted, opportunistic, undiversified, and indifferent to ethics or others' welfare—the lowest common human (perhaps subhuman) denominator. This seems a high price to pay for the convenience of having a single metric against which to measure managerial performance.

There may be a better alternative: replace corporate maximizing with corporate "satisficing."

THE SATISFICING ALTERNATIVE

Milton Friedman and other late twentieth-century academic economists were obsessed with optimizing: picking a single objective, then figuring out how to maximize it. This preference for analyzing problems from an optimizing perspective may reflect a taste for reductionism. It may also reflect a taste for mathematics. (Although math can help you figure out how to maximize a single variable, it is much less useful for telling you how to pick and choose among several.)

But optimization is rarely the best strategy for either organisms or institutions. For example, if biology favored optimizing a single objective, humans would not need to drag around the weight of an extra kidney. And if people made decisions by optimizing, we would not find ourselves debating between taste, calories, and nutrition in choosing what to eat for lunch. Similarly, Nobel Prize winning economist Herman Simon argued more than a half-century ago that corporations need not try to optimize a single objective. Rather, firms can pursue several objectives, and try to do decently well (or at least sufficiently well) at each rather than maximizing only one. Simon called this "satisficing," a word that combines "satisfy" with "suffice."[5]

Satisficing has many advantages as a corporate decision-making strategy. Most obviously, it does not try to resolve conflicts among different shareholders by maximizing only the interests of the small subset who are most short-term, opportunistic, undiversified, and asocial. It allows managers instead to try to decently (but not perfectly) serve the interests of many different shareholders—including long-term shareholders; shareholders who want the company to be able to keep commitments to customers and employees; diversified shareholders who want to avoid damaging their other interests as investors, employees, and consumers; and prosocial shareholders who want the company to earn profits in a socially and environmentally responsible fashion.

When managers are allowed to satisfice, they can retain earnings to invest in safety procedures, marketing, and research and development that contribute to future growth. They can eschew leverage that threatens the firm's stability. They can keep commitments that build customer and employee loyalty. They can protect their shareholders' interests as employees, taxpayers and consumers by declining to outsource jobs, lobby for tax loopholes, or produce dangerous products. Finally, they can respect the desires of their prosocial shareholders by trying to run the firm in a socially and environmentally responsible fashion.

Of course, if managers don't also earn profits, they won't be able to do these things for long. But the satisficing approach recognizes that while earning profits is necessary for the firm's long-term survival, it is not the only corporate objective. Once profitability is achieved, the firm can focus on satisfying other goals, including future growth, controlling risk, and taking care of its investors, employees, customers, even society. Our recent experience with the disappointing results of shareholder primacy suggest this approach may be better not only for shareholders, but for the rest of us as well.

NOTES

1   Jesse Eisinger, "Challenging the Long-Held Belief in 'Shareholder Values,'" *New York Times* (June 27, 2012); Joe Nocera, "Down with Shareholder Value," *New York Times* (August 10, 2012); Andrew Ross Sorkin, "Shareholder Democracy Can Mask Abuses," *New York Times* (February 25, 2013).

2   Milton Friedman, "The Social Responsibility of Business Is to Increase Its Profits," *New York Times Magazine* 32 (September 13, 1970).

3   Michael C. Jensen and William H. Meckling, "Theory of the Firm: Managerial Behavior, Agency Costs, and Ownership Structure," 3 *Journal of Financial Economics* 305 (1976).

4   Roger Martin, *Fixing the Game: Bubbles, Crashes, and What Capitalism Can Learn from the NFL* (2011).

5   Herbert A. Simon, *Administrative Behavior: A Study of Decision-Making in Administrative Organization* (1947).

—12—

PRIVATE CORPORATIONS AND PUBLIC WELFARE

George G. Brenkert

I

The doctrine of corporate social responsibility comes in many varieties. Its most developed version demands that corporations help alleviate "public welfare deficiencies," by which is understood problems of the inner city, drug problems, poverty, crime, illiteracy, lack of sufficient funding for educational institutions, inadequate health care delivery systems, chronic unemployment, etc.

In short, social responsibility, it is contended, requires that corporations assume part of the responsibility for the basic prerequisites of individual and social life within a community or society. Social responsibility demands this even though, it is claimed, corporations are not causally responsible for these conditions and doing so may not enhance their profits.

In response, corporations today provide job training for the hardcore unemployed, help renovate parks, sponsor clean-up programs, establish manufacturing plants in ghetto areas, offer seminars to high school students on how effectively to seek employment, support minority business adventures, provide educational films as well as additional instructors and tutors to public schools (i.e., "adopt" schools), etc.

Such projects have, seemingly, met with a great deal of approval. Indeed, during a time when the welfare of many is deficient, one wonders how anyone could object to such activities. It might seem that any objections to such corporate behavior would stem not from their participating in these activities, but from their not participating even more.

Nevertheless, a number of objections to corporations engaging in such activities have been raised and are well-known. Many of these criticisms are not very good and will not be reviewed here. There is, however, one objection that is much more interesting, even if it is rarely developed. The essence of this objection is that corporate social responsibility to produce directly the public welfare involves the illegitimate encroachment of private organizations into the public realm. There is much greater merit to it than might appear at first glance.

II

This objection takes various forms. Theodore Levitt, for example, claims that the essence of free enterprise is the production of high-level profits. Private business corporations tend to impose this narrowly materialistic view on whatever they touch. Accordingly, corporate responsibility for welfare threatens to reduce pluralism and to create a monolithic society. George C. Lodge similarly maintains that "the demand that business apply itself to problems which government is finding it increasingly difficult to comprehend or affect ... is ... absurd. Corporations, whatever else they may be, are not purveyors of social assistance."[1] Unelected businessmen, he claims, have "neither the right nor the competence" to define or establish the goals and the criteria by which society should repair or remake itself. Finally, Richard De George claims that

> there is great danger in expecting corporations to take upon themselves the production of public welfare, because they already have enormous power and are not answerable for its use to the general public. Politicians are elected by the public and are expected to have the common good as their end. We should not expect corporations to do what they are neither competent nor organized to do....[2]

These criticisms question the right as well as the competence of corporations to contribute directly to the public welfare. Further, they challenge the influence which corporations in so acting may gain over society. Both increased corporate power and a decrease of social pluralism are feared results.

Unfortunately, these criticisms are, more often than not, simply noted, rather than elaborated upon. In particular, the suggestion implicit within them that the provision of public welfare by private corporations runs afoul of an important distinction between what is public and what is private has not been discussed in recent literature. It is this point which requires greater attention.

The argument offered here is that corporate responsibility for public welfare threatens to reduce, transform, and in some cases eliminate important public dimensions of social life. For this reason we must be wary of it and reluctant to accept it in its present forms. Several characteristics of this argument should be noted at the outset. First, it does not pretend to show that all corporate measures that address public welfare deficiencies are (by themselves or individually) wrong, mischievous, or mistaken. Still, we must not be overly impressed by particular instances and thereby miss the systematic and general implications that are thereby promoted. It is not uncommon for individually rational actions to lead to collectively irrational or morally problematic results.

Second, this argument does not address corporate social responsibilities with regard to damages that corporations may themselves directly cause to the environment, employees, members of society, etc. For all these harms it is reasonable to believe that corporations do have responsibilities. The question this paper addresses concerns the implications of demanding that corporations go beyond correcting the damages they have brought about and assume responsibility for public welfare deficiencies for which they are not causally responsible.

Finally, if we could identify the harms that corporations directly *and* indirectly cause, then the arena of responsibilities that corporations have to society might significantly increase and the deficiencies in public welfare (assuming corporations fulfilled their responsibilities) might correspondingly decrease. This paper presupposes that, even in such a situation, there would remain public welfare deficiencies for which corporations are said to be socially responsible and for which they are neither directly nor indirectly causally responsible.

The present argument has four parts. To begin with, it is important to highlight the different relation that exists between an individual (or group) who is aided by a private corporation, and the relation between such an individual (or group) and public attempts to aid their welfare. The differences in these relations will, in practice, often be insignificant—especially when things go well. However, when problems arise theoretical and practical differences can be important. Surely cases could be identified in which corporations have successfully enhanced the public welfare. However, it is not to be expected that corporations will always act so successfully or so clearly in accord with public needs.

The point here is not that corporations may act in misguided ways so much as what happens in those instances where there are problems. Obviously appeals and complaints can be made to the corporation. However, the fact remains that appeals to the corporation tend to be appeals from external constituencies. Inasmuch as those aided by the corporation are not members of the corporation, they have no standing, as it were, within the corporation other than the one the corporation decides to give them. They have no "constitutional" rights against corporations as they do against public endeavors. They are not "citizens" of the corporation. Thus, they have, in principle, no internal access to the corporation's decision-making processes. They are part of that process only if the corporation allows it. Those who make the decisions to undertake various programs cannot be voted out of office—there is no political, and little legal control, over them. Accordingly, to advocate corporate provision of, and responsibility for, public welfare is to advocate that the basic requisites for human well-being are to be provided by institutions whose deliberations, at least at present, do not in principle include representation of those whose interests are affected. Those deficient in welfare lack formal control or power over those agencies from whom they obtain their welfare. Further, since those deficient in welfare tend to be those who are (in general) powerless, the advocacy of corporate responsibility for welfare tends to continue their powerlessness. Corporate social responsibility, in excluding any formal relation between those who are recipients of corporate aid and the corporation, maintains a division between the powerless and the powerful. A democratic society, one would suppose, would seek to moderate, rather than increase, the inequality presupposed in this division.

This situation contrasts with the state or other public bodies which provide, as part of their nature, various forms of administrative, legal and political redress. The state's activities on behalf of its citizenry are hemmed in (at least in principle) by safeguards and guarantees (voting, representation, public hearings, sunshine laws, etc.) which are not imposed on corporations. Indeed, such public forms of access and standing are generally said to be contrary to the corporation's private status. Accordingly, whenever people outside the private corporation are granted such access it is simply due to the benevolence of the corporation.

Now this different relation between individuals and the agencies (private or public) which provide support for them is particularly crucial when that support concerns their basic welfare, i.e., items to which one might reasonably claim a right: e.g., minimal health care, educational opportunities, physical security, shelter, and food. Surely various private institutions such as corporations, churches, etc. may appropriately give aid to those who are deficient in such welfare, when this occurs on an occasional or special basis. Accordingly, private institutions may aid the welfare of their members (those who have access and voice within the organization) as well as non-members (those who do not have such access and voice).

However, those who advocate that this become the normal situation are (implicitly at least) also advocating a condition that places the recipients in a tenuous position vis-à-vis the granting agencies. Though recipients may receive various goods and/or services they need from private corporations, not only are such individuals dependent on those agencies for the aid they receive, but they also lose any formal or "constitutional" voice in the agency which purports to aid them. In effect, any right they have to such welfare is degraded to an act of benevolence on the part of the contributing organization. They can no longer insist or demand that they be treated in various ways, but must play the role of supplicants.

It is in this kind of situation that the view attributed to Andrew Carnegie can arise unchecked by formal mechanisms to control it: "In the exercise of his trust he was responsible only to his own conscience and judgment of what was best for the community."[3] Recipients of such aid lack means of redress which, in matters of basic importance such as welfare, are terribly significant.

Furthermore, when the institutions (i.e., large business corporations) involved in providing welfare are not themselves dedicated to the welfare of others but primarily focused on their own self-interested economic ends, and when these organizations are extremely large and powerful, then we must reflect on the implications of the lack of membership, and hence the lack of redress and voice, within those organizations. Specifically, we need to consider whether these needs ought not to be met by organizations which will grant those receiving such aid the voice and access which has traditionally protected people who are dependent upon others.

In short, when corporations are asked to undertake public welfare on an ongoing basis, the welfare they give is privatized in a manner that eliminates an important relation for those receiving such welfare. To the extent that it formalizes a relation between the powerful and the powerless, it exposes the recipients of such aid to abuses of power. At the same time, the equality that democracy implies is also jeopardized.

Second, a variation on the preceding point concerns the standards by which decisions on the nature and means of implementing corporate welfare measures are made. Again, this might not appear to be a significant problem with regard to the construction or reconstruction of an inner-city park, a neighborhood clean-up campaign, or reading tutors in the schools. Surely corporations will, by and large, consult with the people involved to get their ideas and approval. On other occasions, the people involved will seek out a corporation to aid them. But this does not lay the issue to rest since the standards the corporation seeks to follow may be primarily private in nature, rather than public or general.

Suppose, for instance, that the welfare measures which the corporation seeks to provide (and to which their recipients agree) are of questionable constitutionality. They agree, perhaps, on educational films with a religious or a racist message for the public schools. Or, suppose they agree on an educational program but the corporation liberally sprinkles the presentation with its corporate logo, mascot, jingo, and the like. Suppose that in training of the hard-core unemployed they aim at white, rather than black or Hispanic, populations. The point at issue concerns the legitimacy of these decisions.

The standards according to which the public welfare is fulfilled must be a matter for the public (through its representatives) to determine, not the private corporation. Two reasons lie behind this claim. Such welfare concerns what is common among the citizens, what holds the members of a society together, and what is the nature of their basic prerequisites. It constitutes a statement about how we, as a community or society, believe that we should live. Fulfillment of welfare deficiencies for some that manifests prejudice against other groups, or works to their disadvantage, requires special justification and close public scrutiny, if it is allowed to stand.

In addition, to the extent that corporate contributions to public welfare are tax deductible, the foregone tax revenues constitute a public contribution to itself, through the agency of the corporation. Since public monies are committed through such contributions, the public has a right to assure itself that the standards according to which such monies are expended meet its (minimal) standards.

Accordingly, the legitimacy of the decisions the private corporation makes regarding public welfare cannot be judged simply according to its own private standards. Thus, if the corporation tries to impose its own view and standards, it is crossing an important line between the private and the public. It is naive, then, simply to argue that people's welfare is the responsibility of corporations, without providing for social determination and direction of the activities which corporations undertake.

In those instances in which corporate contributions are of a charitable (or prudential) nature *and* the objects of their actions are wholly private, it would seem that corporations might legitimately give to those individuals or organizations which promote their own values and ideas. In this way, their gifts may reflect their own idiosyncratic standards. Accordingly, some object to business giving to private universities whose faculty advocate ideas opposed to capitalism. However, in contrast, the direction and satisfaction of public welfare according to private standards is not appropriate, since the public welfare is not to be determined simply by this or that individual corporation's ideas and values, but by a political process and, ideally a community dialogue, on what those values should be.

Finally, if corporations are said to be responsible for remedying certain deficient levels of public welfare, but are not given control (both in terms of applicable standards and practical direction) over how such remedies are to be emplaced, then when these measures fail the corporation can hardly be held accountable. Nevertheless, since they will be associated with such efforts, they will often be faulted for their lack of success. Hence, if corporations are required to engage in social responsibility efforts, there will be an understandable tendency for them to seek control over the situations in which they participate. This means, however, supplanting (or reducing) public control and substituting their own judgments and standards for those of the public. Consequently, the demand for corporate social responsibility is a demand that encourages the substitution of private standards, authority and control for those of the public.

III

Third, the demand for corporate social responsibility arises, it has been assumed, due to deficient public welfare, which stems, at least in part, from inadequate public funding. Corporate opposition to higher taxes has played a contributing role to this situation, since taxes are viewed as coercive takings of corporate property. The lower the taxes the greater the return on investment corporations make and the greater the flexibility corporations have to use their resources as they choose. Part of the appeal of corporate social responsibility for public welfare is that the aid that is given is voluntary. Provision of such aid heads off higher taxes, government regulation and hence coercion. In short, behind the demand for corporate social responsibility is a view that holds that the public realm and the state constitute a sphere of coercion, while the private realm and the actions it takes are voluntary.

This is illustrated in Friedman's comment that "the political principle that underlies the political mechanism is conformity.... It is appropriate for some to require others to contribute to a general social purpose whether they wish to or not."[4] Corporate social responsibility, then, explicitly seeks to reduce the realm of the public, by reducing the area within which coercion and force might be used.

Now if the public were simply a realm of coercion, such a view would seem unexceptionable. On the contrary, however, such a view arguably distorts the realm of the public. Corporate social responsibility implies that the public is simply an area within which individual prudential interests are worked out and coercion imposed by the state. Both eliminate an important sense of the public.

The public is also the area within which general and common interests are articulated. It is what binds people together, in contrast to the private realm within which people are separated from each other and view each other as limitations upon their freedom. Accordingly, it is the realm of the "we," rather than the "you" or "I." It is what is done in all our names, and not just yours or mine. It is the area, some have even held, within which freedom is only possible. There is (or can be) a different sense of accomplishment when the community builds or creates something rather than simply this or that private organization. Conversely, there is a different sense of loss when a public figure, a President or Prime Minister dies, rather than the head of a private corporation.

Now charity is an extension of the private into this public realm. It is personal, self-given, and can't be demanded in particular cases. It need not be based on political discussion or compromise so much as on one's own willingness to aid others. Those who receive do not have grounds upon which they can demand or negotiate beyond which the charitable organization allows. Charity does not necessarily involve any political or public process by which recipient and contributor are bound together. Thus, Hannah Arendt comments, "The bond of charity between people ... is incapable of founding a public realm of its own...."[5] In short, charity cannot be the basis of a public or political dimension between people.

As such, corporate social responsibility drives out the political and the public. The appeal to corporate responsibility is a confession that the public or political realm has broken (or is breaking) down. It is an unwitting manifestation of liberal individualism extending the realm of the private to encompass the public.

Consequently, Friedman is quite wrong when he complains that the doctrine of social responsibility "taken serious would extend the scope of the political mechanism to every human activity."[6] This is plausible only in that case when the corporation and its executives both engage in social responsibility activities *and*, as a result, become subject to political election procedures since they are viewed as "civil servants."[7] On the other hand, if this does not happen (and there is little present evidence that it will), then the doctrine of social responsibility extends the nature of private activities to many activities in the public or political realm. In short, quite the opposite of what Friedman contends, it extends the scope of the private "to every human activity."

The problem with this approach is that it is implausible to treat society as simply an example of an ideal market situation. This is implied by the above comments on the nature of the public. Not all public (or private) values can be produced or sustained by market exchanges. Friedman slips from discussion of market activities to talk of society without argument. Thus, after he portrays the voluntary nature of the ideal free market, he immediately goes on (without argument) to equate such exchanges with society itself. However, it does not follow (and it is not plausible) to think of society as itself simply an ideal free market. Once again, then, corporate social responsibility involves views and demands which question legitimate distinctions between the private and the public.

IV

Finally, though the relation of the public and the private is a shifting relation, we must guard against collapsing one—either one—term of this relation into the other. The view that the public is simply the arena in which individual actions affect others without their voluntary approval impoverishes the notion of the public. As noted above, the public is more and different than this. The public is what binds a people together and relates them to each other. It is what is done in their common name; it is what makes them a people, rather than simply a random collection of individuals. It embodies the values, norms and ideals we strive towards even if we fail fully to achieve them. It is the responsibility of public agencies (the state or its government) to foster (at least) the minimal conditions under which the public may exist. To be a citizen is to owe allegiance to the government as it works to realize these principles and values.

Now suppose that the government does not fulfill its responsibilities to individuals for basic welfare. The demand that private corporations— other than the government—dispense public welfare is a step in the privatization of the public realm. The benefits that individuals receive from the government have long been thought to play an important role in their obligations to the state and, hence, their citizenship within the state. If these benefits come from private groups, rather than the state, then one would expect loyalties and obligations to be modified accordingly.

Consequently, if a corporation provides training for the hard-core unemployed, renovates the local park, or provides the house which shelters the sick, it is to the corporation that those aided will be grateful and indebted, not to the community or society of which they are members. It is the corporation to which one's loyalties will be turned, and not to the city or state of which one is a citizen. Indeed, the very notion of citizenship thereby becomes impoverished. The grounds upon which the state has been said to acquire the obligations of its citizenry have been narrowed. In its place develop isolated (groups of) individuals beholden to private institutions of which they are not members (or citizens) and over which they have no formal control.

Surely in these days of popular advertising, the corporation may seem more personal, less abstract, than the community or the state. Through logos, jingoes and mascots corporations seek to get people to identify with them and their products. And through corporate measures to aid their welfare, individuals would have concrete reason to be indebted to them, even if not members or citizens of them. But to accept or promote this situation, and the view of the individual's relations to private and public institutions which it involves, merely reveals the state of poverty to which our notions of the public and citizenship have come. Such corporations encourage us to seek a common identity, rather than to foster our common (public) interests. We are invited to replace the realm of the public which unavoidably involves impersonality with a personal and privatized realm. We transform a realm laden with political meanings into a private and psychologized realm.

However, the danger here does not simply stem from the implications of the altered identifications and loyalties that characterize citizens. The increasing privatization of the public realm that we see in shopping malls, corporate housing developments, the suburban environment, and corporate attempts to establish their own identity and role models within the schools carry other consequences to which we must be keenly sensitive. For example, in private shopping malls people may be prevented from political speech; in corporate housing developments, they may be prohibited from having children and remaining in their home; and cultural exhibits may be skewed to suit corporate purposes. Rights which all citizens share may be, wittingly or unwittingly, foregone through private efforts uninformed by public reflection and participation. In short, the public values and interests of a society can be threatened not simply by an authoritarian government but also by self-interested, though well-meaning, private groups and institutions which lack a sense of the significance of the public realm and the meaning of citizenship.

V

In conclusion, several comments are appropriate. First, it may be allowed that many objections which can be brought against corporate attempts to secure public welfare can also be brought against government or public attempts. Thus, both government and corporations may be inflexible, insensitive, impersonal, non-innovative, as well as hard to move or get through to. They may produce programs which are misconceived, uncoordinated, and/or precipitously stopped, leaving people in the lurch. The production of such programs may increase their power, size and influence; they may also deal paternalistically with those they seek to aid. One would be tempted to abandon all attempts to aid those deficient in welfare were it not for the fact that many people continue to suffer grievously from inadequate welfare. Thus, the question is a complex and messy one. There is no easy and neat answer.

Second, large corporations, however, will continue to be part of our social and political landscape. Their significant economic and political power are obvious. In this situation, the thrust of the public/private argument is two-sided. It can be taken to urge the separation of private corporations and public institutions. This is fraught with all the problems of bureaucratization, distant government, powerful but indifferent corporations, and failed efforts to satisfy public welfare needs. This is not to say that these problems could not be overcome within a fairly strict separation of the private and the public. Still, this would involve a recommitment (and rediscovery!) of the public realm that might be difficult in countries such as the US.

On the other hand, the above argument can also be taken to recommend that we require such large corporations be made more fully public, social organizations. Indeed, many argue that large corporations are no longer simply private organizations. George C. Lodge, for example, comments that "it is now obvious that our large public corporations are not private property at all ... The best we can say," he continues, "is that the corporation is a sort of collective, floating in philosophic limbo, dangerously vulnerable to the charge of illegitimacy and to the charge that it is not amenable to community control."[8] Thus, that corporations increasingly are called to participate in the production of public welfare is not so surprising given their present quasi-public nature. The further claim that has been made is that this quasi-public nature needs to be institutionalized so as to make it amenable to greater public control and direction. This direction, however, is one that others violently oppose.

Thus, we stand at a crossroads. This juncture is part and parcel of that "tension between self-reliant competitive enterprise and a sense of public solidarity espoused by civic republicans" that some have identified as "the most important unresolved problem in American history."[9] If one rejects the view that corporations must more fully take on the character of public institutions, then demands for corporate social responsibility for public welfare should be seriously curtailed.

The preceding arguments do not show conclusively that corporations ought never to aid public welfare. They are one set of considerations which might, in some circumstances, be overridden. However, they do indicate important reasons why we should be more reluctant to proceed down the path that many have been encouraging us to take. When we are repeatedly told that the sight of corporate social responsibility is so lovely, and that the prospects of corporate responsibility for public welfare are so rosy, one may rightfully come to suspect that we are being led down the garden path.

NOTES

1   George C. Lodge, *The New American Ideology* (New York: Alfred A. Knopf, 1975), p. 189.

2   De George, *Business Ethics*, 3rd ed. (New York: Macmillan Publishing Co., 1986), p. 171.

3   Robert H. Bremner, *American Philanthropy*, 2nd ed. (Chicago: The University of Chicago Press, 1988), p. 101.

4   Milton Friedman, "The Social Responsibility of Business Is to Increase Its Profits," in Milton Snoeyenbos, Robert Almeder, James Humber (eds.), *Business Ethics* (Buffalo, New York: Prometheus Books, 1983), p. 78.

5   Hannah Arendt, *The Human Condition* (Chicago: The University of Chicago Press, 1958), p. 53.

6   Milton Friedman, "The Social Responsibility of Business Is to Increase Its Profits," in Milton Snoeyenbos, Robert Almeder, James Humber (eds.), *Business Ethics* (Buffalo, New York: Prometheus Books, 1983), p. 79.

7   Friedman, "The Social Responsibility of Business Is to Increase Its Profits," p. 75.

8   Lodge, *The New American Ideology*, p. 18.

9   Bellah et al., *Habits of the Heart*, p. 256.

—13—

MANAGING FOR STAKEHOLDERS[1]

R. Edward Freeman

I. INTRODUCTION

The purpose of this essay is to outline an emerging view of business that we shall call "managing for stakeholders."[2] This view has emerged over the past thirty years from a group of scholars in a diverse set of disciplines, from finance to philosophy.[3] The basic idea is that businesses, and the executives who manage them, actually do and should create value for customers, suppliers, employees, communities, and financiers (or shareholders). And, that we need to pay careful attention to how these relationships are managed and how value gets created for these stakeholders. We contrast this idea with the dominant model of business activity; namely, that businesses are to be managed solely for the benefit of shareholders. Any other benefits (or harms) that are created are incidental.[4]

Simple ideas create complex questions, and we proceed as follows. In the next section we examine why the dominant story or model of business that is deeply embedded in our culture is no longer workable. It is resistant to change, not consistent with the law, and for the most part, simply ignores matters of ethics. Each of these flaws is fatal in the business world of the twenty-first century.

We then proceed to define the basic ideas of "managing for stakeholders" and why it solves some of the problems of the dominant model. In particular we pay attention to how using "stakeholder" as a basic unit of analysis makes it more difficult to ignore matters of ethics. We argue that the primary responsibility of the executive is to create as much value for stakeholders as possible, and

that no stakeholder interest is viable in isolation of the other stakeholders. We sketch three primary arguments from ethical theory for adopting "managing for stakeholders." We conclude by outlining a fourth "pragmatist argument" that suggests we see managing for stakeholders as a new narrative about business that lets us improve the way we currently create value for each other. Capitalism is on this view a system of social cooperation and collaboration, rather than primarily a system of competition.

II. THE DOMINANT STORY: MANAGERIAL CAPITALISM WITH SHAREHOLDERS AT THE CENTER

The modern business corporation has emerged during the twentieth century as one of the most important innovations in human history. Yet the changes that we are now experiencing call for its reinvention. Before we suggest what this revision, "managing for stakeholders" or "stakeholder capitalism," is, first we need to understand how the dominant story came to be told.

Somewhere in the past, organizations were quite simple and "doing business" consisted of buying raw materials from suppliers, converting it to products, and selling it to customers. For the most part owner-entrepreneurs founded such simple businesses and worked at the business along with members of their families. The development of new production processes, such as the assembly line, meant that jobs could be specialized and more work could be accomplished. New technologies and sources of power became readily available. These and other social and political forces combined to require larger amounts of capital, well beyond the scope of most individual owner-manager-employees. Additionally, "workers" or non-family members began to dominate the firm and were the rule rather than the exception.

Ownership of the business became more dispersed, as capital was raised from banks, stockholders, and other institutions. Indeed, the management of the firm became separated from the ownership of the firm. And, in order to be successful, the top managers of the business had to simultaneously satisfy the owners, the employees and their unions, suppliers and customers. This system of organization of businesses along the lines set forth here was known as managerial capitalism or laissez faire capitalism, or more recently, shareholder capitalism.[5]

As businesses grew, managers developed a means of control via the divisionalized firm. Led by Alfred Sloan at General Motors, the divisionalized firm with a central headquarters staff was widely adapted.[6] The dominant model for managerial authority was the military and civil service bureaucracy. By creating rational structures and processes, the orderly progress of business growth could be well-managed.

Thus, managerialism, hierarchy, stability, and predictability all evolved together, in the United States and Europe, to form the most powerful economic system in the history of humanity. The rise of bureaucracy and managerialism was so strong that the economist Joseph Schumpeter predicted that it would wipe out the creative force of capitalism, stifling innovation in its drive for predictability and stability.

During the last 50 years this "Managerial Model" has put "shareholders" at the center of the firm as the most important group for managers to worry about. This mindset has dealt with the increasing complexity of the business world by focusing more intensely on "shareholders" and "creating value for shareholders." It has become common wisdom to "increase shareholder value,"

and many companies have instituted complex incentive compensation plans aimed at aligning the interests of executives with the interests of shareholders. These incentive plans are often tied to the price of a company's stock, which is affected by many factors not the least of which is the expectations of Wall Street analysts about earnings per share each quarter. Meeting Wall Street targets and forming a stable and predictable base of quarter-over-quarter increases in earnings per share has become the standard for measuring company performance. Indeed, all of the recent scandals at Enron, Worldcom, Tyco, Arthur Anderson and others are in part due to executives trying to increase shareholder value, sometimes in opposition to accounting rules and law. Unfortunately, the world has changed so that the stability and predictability required by the shareholder approach can no longer be assured.

The Dominant Model Is Resistant to Change

The Managerial View of business with shareholders at the center is inherently resistant to change. It puts shareholders' interests over and above the interests of customers, suppliers, employees, and others, as if these interests must conflict with each other. It understands a business as an essentially hierarchical organization fastened together with authority to act in the shareholders' interests. Executives often speak in the language of hierarchy as "working for shareholders," "shareholders are the boss," and "you have to do what the shareholders want." On this interpretation, change should occur only when the shareholders are unhappy, and as long as executives can produce a series of incrementally better financial results there is no problem. According to this view the only change that counts is change oriented toward shareholder value. If customers are unhappy, if accounting rules have been compromised, if product quality is bad, if environmental disaster looms, even if competitive forces threaten, the only interesting questions are whether and how these forces for change affect shareholder value, measured by the price of the stock every day. Unfortunately, in today's world there is just too much uncertainty and complexity to rely on a single criterion. Business in the twenty-first century is global and multi-faceted, and shareholder value may not capture that dynamism. Or, if it does, as the theory suggests it must eventually, it will be too late for executives to do anything about it. The dominant story may work for how things turn out in the long run on Wall Street, but managers have to act with an eye to Main Street as well, to anticipate change to try and take advantage of the dynamism of business.[7]

The Dominant Model Is Not Consistent with the Law

In fact the clarity of putting shareholders' interests first, above that of customers, suppliers, employees, and communities, flies in the face of the reality of the law. The law has evolved to put constraints on the kinds of tradeoffs that can be made. In fact the law of corporations gives a less clear answer to the question of in whose interest and for whose benefit the corporation should be governed. The law has evolved over the years to give *de facto* standing to the claims of groups other than stockholders. It has in effect, required that the claims of customers, suppliers, local communities, and employees be taken into consideration.

For instance, the doctrine of "privity of contract," as articulated in *Winterbottom v. Wright* in 1842, has been eroded by recent developments in products liability law. *Greenman v. Yuba Power* gives the manufacturer strict liability for damage caused by its products, even though the seller has exercised all possible care in the preparation and sale of the product and the consumer has not bought the product from nor entered into any contractual arrangement with the manufacturer. *Caveat emptor* has been replaced in large part, with *caveat venditor*. The Consumer Product Safety Commission has the power to enact product recalls, essentially leading to an increase in the number of voluntary product recalls by companies

seeking to mitigate legal damage awards. Some industries are required to provide information to customers about a product's ingredients, whether or not the customers want and are willing to pay for this information. Thus, companies must take the interests of customers into account, by law.

A similar story can be told about the evolution of the law forcing management to take the interests of employees into account. The National Labor Relations Act gave employees the right to unionize and to bargain in good faith. It set up the National Labor Relations Board to enforce these rights with management. The Equal Pay Act of 1963 and Title VII of the Civil Rights Act of 1964 constrain management from discrimination in hiring practices; these have been followed with the Age Discrimination in Employment Act of 1967, and recent extensions affecting people with disabilities. The emergence of a body of administrative case law arising from labor-management disputes and the historic settling of discrimination claims with large employers have caused the emergence of a body of management practice that is consistent with the legal guarantee of the rights of employees.

The law has also evolved to try and protect the interests of local communities. The Clean Air Act and Clean Water Act, and various amendments to these classic pieces of legislation, have constrained management from "spoiling the commons." In an historic case, *Marsh v. Alabama*, the Supreme Court ruled that a company-owned town was subject to the provisions of the US Constitution, thereby guaranteeing the rights of local citizens and negating the "property rights" of the firm. Current issues center around protecting local businesses, forcing companies to pay the health care costs of their employees, increases in minimum wages, environmental standards, and the effects of business development on the lives of local community members. These issues fill the local political landscapes and executives and their companies must take account of them.

Some may argue that the constraints of the law, at least in the US, have become increasingly irrelevant in a world where business is global in nature. However, globalization simply makes this argument stronger. The laws that are relevant to business have evolved differently around the world, but they have evolved nonetheless to take into account the interests of groups other than just shareholders. Each state in India has a different set of regulations that affect how a company can do business. In China the law has evolved to give business some property rights but it is far from exclusive. And, in most of the European Union, laws around "civil society" and the role of "employees" are much more complex than even US law.

"Laissez faire capitalism" is simply a myth. The idea that business is about "maximizing value for stockholders regardless of the consequences to others" is one that has outlived its usefulness. The dominant model simply does not describe how business operates. Another way to see this is that if executives always have to qualify "maximize shareholder value" with exceptions of law, or even good practice, then the dominant story isn't very useful anymore. There are just too many exceptions. The dominant story could be saved by arguing that it describes a normative view about how business should operate, despite how actual businesses have evolved.[8] So, we need to look more closely at some of the conceptual and normative problems that the dominant model raises.

The Dominant Model Is Not Consistent with Basic Ethics

Previously we have argued that most theories of business rely on separating "business" decisions from "ethical" decisions.[9] This is seen most clearly in the popular joke about "business ethics as an oxymoron." More formally we might suggest that we define:

The Separation Fallacy

It is useful to believe that sentences like, "x is a business decision" have no ethical content or any implicit ethical point of view. And, it is useful to believe that sentences like "x is an ethical decision, the best thing to do all things considered" have no content or implicit view about value creation and trade (business).

This fallacy underlies much of the dominant story about business, as well as in other areas in society. There are two implications of rejecting the Separation Fallacy. The first is that almost any business decision has some ethical content. To see that this true one need only ask whether the following questions make sense for virtually any business decision:

The Open Question Argument

(1) If this decision is made for whom is value created and destroyed?

(2) Who is harmed and/or benefited by this decision?

(3) Whose rights are enabled and whose values are realized by this decision (and whose are not)?

(4) What kind of person will I (we) become if we make this decision?

Since these questions are always open for most business decisions, it is reasonable to give up the Separation Fallacy, which would have us believe that these questions aren't relevant for making business decisions, or that they could never be answered. We need a theory about business that builds in answers to the "Open Question Argument" above. One such answer would be "Only value to shareholders counts," but such an answer would have to be enmeshed in the language of ethics as well as business. Milton Friedman, unlike most of his expositors, may actually give such a morally rich answer. He claims that the responsibility of the executive is to make profits subject to law and ethical custom. Depending on how "law and ethical custom" is interpreted, the key difference with the stakeholder approach may well be that we disagree about how the world works. In order to create value we believe that it is better to focus on integrating business and ethics within a complex set of stakeholder relationships rather than treating ethics as a side constraint on making profits. In short we need a theory that has as its basis what we might call:

The Integration Thesis

Most business decisions, or sentences about business have some ethical content, or implicit ethical view. Most ethical decisions, or sentences about ethics have some business content or implicit view about business.[10]

One of the most pressing challenges facing business scholars is to tell compelling narratives that have the Integration Thesis at its heart. This is essentially the task that a group of scholars, "business ethicists" and "stakeholder theorists," have begun over the last 30 years. We need to go back to the very basics of ethics. Ethics is about the rules, principles, consequences, matters of character, etc., that we use to live together. These ideas give us a set of open questions that we are constantly searching for better ways to answer in reasonably complete ways.[11] One might define "ethics" as a conversation about how we can reason together and solve our differences, recognize where our interests are joined and need development, so that we can all flourish without resorting to coercion and violence. Some may disagree with such a definition, and we do not intend to privilege definitions, but such a pragmatist approach to ethics entails that we reason and talk together to try and create a better world for all of us.

If our critiques of the dominant model are correct then we need to start over by re-conceptualizing the very language that we use to understand how business operates. We want to suggest that something like the following principle is implicit in most reasonably comprehensive views about ethics.

The Responsibility Principle[12]

Most people, most of the time, want to, actually do, and should accept responsibility for the effects of their actions on others.

Clearly the Responsibility Principle is incompatible with the Separation Fallacy. If business is separated from ethics, there is no question of moral responsibility for business decisions; hence, the joke is that "business ethics" is an oxymoron. More clearly still, without something like the Responsibility Principle it is difficult to see how ethics gets off the ground. "Responsibility" may well be a difficult and multi-faceted idea. There are surely many different ways to understand it. But, if we are not willing to accept the responsibility for our own actions (as limited as that may be due to complicated issues of causality and the like), then ethics, understood as how we reason together so we can all flourish, is likely an exercise in bad faith.

If we want to give up the separation fallacy and adopt the integration thesis, if the open question argument makes sense, and if something like the responsibility thesis is necessary, then we need a new model for business. And, this new story must be able to explain how value creation at once deals with economics and ethics, and how it takes account of all of the effects of business action on others. Such a model exists, and has been developing over the last 30 years by management researchers and ethics scholars, and there are many businesses who have adopted this "stakeholder framework" for their businesses.

III. MANAGING FOR STAKEHOLDERS

The basic idea of "managing for stakeholders" is quite simple. Business can be understood as a set of relationships among groups which have a stake in the activities that make up the business. Business is about how customers, suppliers, employees, financiers (stockholders, bondholders, banks, etc.), communities and managers interact and create value. To understand a business is to know how these relationships work. And, the executive's or entrepreneur's job is to manage and shape these relationships; hence the title, "managing for stakeholders."

Figure 1 depicts the idea of "managing for stakeholders" in a variation of the classic "wheel and spoke" diagram.[13] However, it is important to note that the stakeholder idea is perfectly general. Corporations are not the center of the universe, and there are many possible pictures. One might put customers in the center to signal that a company puts customers as the key priority. Another might put employees in the center and link them to customers and shareholders. We prefer the generic diagram because it suggests, pictorially, that "managing for stakeholders" is a theory about management and business; hence, managers and companies in the center. But, there is no larger metaphysical claim here.

Figure 1

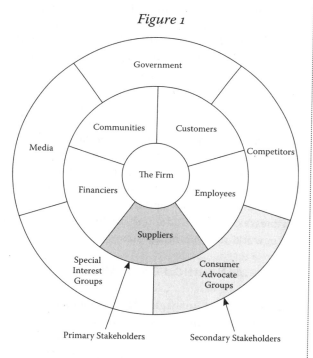

Primary Stakeholders   Secondary Stakeholders

Stakeholders and Stakes

Owners or financiers (a better term) clearly have a financial stake in the business in the form of stocks, bonds, and so on, and they expect some kind of financial return from them. Of course, the stakes of financiers will differ by type of owner, preferences for money, moral preferences, and so on, as well as by type of firm. The shareholders of Google may well want returns as well as be supportive of Google's articulated purpose of "Do No Evil." To the extent that it makes sense to talk about the financiers "owning the firm," they have a concomitant responsibility for the uses of their property.

Employees have their jobs and usually their livelihood at stake; they often have specialized skills for which there is usually no perfectly elastic market. In return for their labor, they expect security, wages, benefits and meaningful work. Often, employees are expected to participate in the decision making of the organization, and if the employees are management or senior executives we see them as shouldering a great deal of responsibility for the conduct of the organization as a whole. And, employees are sometimes financiers as well, since many companies have stock ownership plans, and loyal employees who believe in the future of their companies often voluntarily invest. One way to think about the employee relationship is in terms of contracts. Customers and suppliers exchange resources for the products and services of the firm and in return receive the benefits of the products and services. As with financiers and employees, the customer and supplier relationships are enmeshed in ethics. Companies make promises to customers via their advertising, and when products or services don't deliver on these promises then management has a responsibility to rectify the situation. It is also important to have suppliers who are committed to making a company better. If suppliers find a better, faster, and cheaper way of making critical parts or services, then both supplier and company can win. Of course, some suppliers simply compete on price, but even so, there is a moral element of fairness and transparency to the supplier relationship.

Finally, the local community grants the firm the right to build facilities, and in turn, it benefits from the tax base and economic and social contributions of the firm. Companies have a real impact on communities, and being located in a welcoming community helps a company create value for its other stakeholders. In return for the provision of local services, companies are expected to be good citizens, as is any individual person. It should not expose the community to unreasonable hazards in the form of pollution, toxic waste, etc. It should keep whatever commitments it makes to the community, and operate in a transparent manner as far as possible. Of course, companies don't have perfect knowledge, but when management discovers some danger or runs afoul of new competition, it is expected to inform and work with local communities to mitigate any negative effects, as far as possible.

While any business must consist of financiers, customers, suppliers, employees, and communities, it is possible to think about other stakeholders as well. We can define "stakeholder" in a number of ways. First of all we could define the term fairly narrowly to capture the idea that any business, large or small, is about creating value for "those groups without whose support, the business would cease to be viable." The inner circle of Figure 1 depicts this view. Almost every business is concerned at some level with relationships among financiers, customers, suppliers, employees, and communities. We might call these groups "primary" or "definitional." However, it should be noted that as a business starts up, sometimes one particular stakeholder is more important than another. In a new business start up, sometimes there are no suppliers, and paying lots of attention to one or two key customers, as well as to the venture capitalist (financier) is the right approach.

There is also a somewhat broader definition that captures the idea that if a group or individual can affect a business, then the executives must take that group into consideration in thinking about how to create value. Or, a stakeholder is any group or individual that can affect or be affected by the realization of an organization's purpose. At a minimum some groups affect primary stakeholders and we might see these as stakeholders in the outer ring of Figure 1 and call them "secondary" or "instrumental."

There are other definitions that have emerged during the last 30 years, some based on risks and rewards, some based on mutuality of interests. And, the debate over finding the one "true definition" of 'stakeholder' is not likely to end. We prefer a more pragmatist approach of being clear of the purpose of using any of the proposed definitions. Business is a fascinating field of study. There are very few principles and definitions that apply to all businesses all over the world. Furthermore, there are many different ways to run a successful business, or if you like, many different flavors of "managing for stakeholders." We see limited usefulness in trying to define one model of business, either based on the shareholder or stakeholder view, which works for all businesses everywhere. We see much value to be gained in examining how the stakes work in the value creation process, and the role of the executive.

IV. THE RESPONSIBILITY OF THE EXECUTIVE IN MANAGING FOR STAKEHOLDERS

Executives play a special role in the activity of the business enterprise. On the one hand, they have a stake like every other employee in terms of an actual or implied employment contract. And, that stake is linked to the stakes of financiers, customers, suppliers, communities, and other employees. In addition, executives are expected to look after the health of the overall enterprise, to keep the varied stakes moving in roughly the same direction, and to keep them in balance.[14]

No stakeholder stands alone in the process of value creation. The stakes of each stakeholder group are multi-faceted, and inherently connected to each other. How could a bondholder recognize any returns without management paying attention to the stakes of customers or employees? How could customers get the products and services they need without employees and suppliers? How could employees have a decent place to live without communities? Many thinkers see the dominant problem of "managing for stakeholders" as how to solve the priority problem, or "which stakeholders are more important," or "how do we make tradeoffs among stakeholders." We see this as a secondary issue.

First and foremost, we need to see stakeholder interests as joint, as inherently tied together. Seeing stakeholder interests as "joint" rather than opposed is difficult. It is not always easy to find a way to accommodate all stakeholder interests. It is easier to trade off one versus another. Why not delay spending on new products for customers in order to keep earnings a bit higher? Why not cut employee medical benefits in order to invest in a new inventory control system?

Managing for stakeholders suggests that executives try to reframe the questions. How can we invest in new products and create higher earnings? How can we be sure our employees are healthy and happy and are able to work creatively so that we can capture the benefits of new information technology such as inventory control systems? In a recent book reflecting on his experience as CEO of Medtronic, Bill George summarized the managing for stakeholders mindset:[15]

Serving all your stakeholders is the best way to produce long term results and create a growing, prosperous company.... Let me be very clear about this: there is no conflict between serving all your stakeholders and providing excellent returns for shareholders. In the long term it is impossible to have one without the other. However, serving all these stakeholder groups requires discipline, vision, and committed leadership.

The primary responsibility of the executive is to create as much value as possible for stakeholders.[16] Where stakeholder interests conflict, the executive must find a way to rethink the problems so that these interests can go together, so that even more value can be created for each. If tradeoffs have to be made, as often happens in the real world, then the executive must figure out how to make the tradeoffs, and immediately begin improving the tradeoffs for all sides. *Managing for stakeholders is about creating as much value as possible for stakeholders, without resorting to tradeoffs.*

We believe that this task is more easily accomplished when a business has a sense of purpose. Furthermore, there are few limits on the kinds of purpose that can drive a business. Wal-Mart may stand for "everyday low price." Merck can stand for "alleviating human suffering." The point is that if an entrepreneur or an executive can find a purpose that speaks to the hearts and minds of key stakeholders, it is more likely that there will be sustained success.

Purpose is complex and inspirational. The Grameen Bank wants to eliminate poverty. Fannie Mae wants to make housing affordable to every income level in society. Tastings (a local restaurant) wants to bring the taste of really good food and wine to lots of people in the community. And, all of these organizations have to generate profits, or else they cannot pursue their purposes. Capitalism works because we can pursue our purpose with others. When we coalesce around a big idea, or a joint purpose evolves from our day to day activities with each other, then great things can happen.

To create value for stakeholders, executives must understand that business is fully situated in the realm of humanity. Businesses are human institutions populated by real live complex human beings. Stakeholders have names and faces and children. They are not mere placeholders for social roles. As such, matters of ethics are routine when one takes a managing for stakeholders approach. Of course this should go without saying, but a part of the dominant story about business is that business people are only in it for their own narrowly defined self interest. One main assumption of the managerial view with shareholders at the center is that shareholders only care about returns, and therefore their agents, managers, should only care about returns. However, this does not fit either our experiences or our aspirations. In the words of one CEO, "The only assets I manage go up and down the elevators every day."

Most human beings are complicated. Most of us do what we do because we are self-interested and interested in others. Business works in part because of our urge to create things with others and for others. Working on a team, or creating a new product or delivery mechanism that makes customers lives better or happier or more pleasurable all can be contributing factors to why we go to work each day. And, this is not to deny the economic incentive of getting a pay check. The assumption of narrow self-interest is extremely limiting, and can be self-reinforcing—people can begin to act in a narrow self-interested way if they believe that is what is expected of them, as some of the scandals such as Enron, have shown. We need to be open to a more complex psychology—one any parent finds familiar as they have shepherded the growth and development of their children.

V. SOME ARGUMENTS FOR MANAGING FOR STAKEHOLDERS

Once you say stakeholders are persons then the ideas of ethics are automatically applicable. However you interpret the idea of "stakeholders," you must pay attention to the effects of your actions on others. And, something like the Responsibility Principle suggests that this is a cornerstone of any adequate ethical theory. There are at least three main arguments for adopting a managing for stakeholders approach. Philosophers will see these as connected to the three main approaches to ethical theory that have developed historically. We shall briefly set forth sketches of these arguments, and then suggest that there is a more powerful fourth argument.[17]

The Argument from Consequences

A number of theorists have argued that the main reason that the dominant model of managing for shareholders is a good idea is that it leads to the best consequences for all. Typically these arguments invoke Adam Smith's idea of the invisible hand, whereby each business actor pursues her own self interest and the greatest good of all actually emerges. The problem with this argument is that we now know with modern general equilibrium economics that the argument only works under very specialized conditions that seldom describe the real world. And further, we know that if the economic conditions get very close to those needed to produce the greatest good, there is no guarantee that the greatest good will actually result.

Managing for stakeholders may actually produce better consequences for all stakeholders because it recognizes that stakeholder interests are joint. If one stakeholder pursues its interests at the expense of all the others, then the others will either withdraw their support, or look to create another network of stakeholder value creation. This is not to say that there are not times when one stakeholder will benefit at the expense of others, but if this happens continuously over time, then in a relatively free society, stakeholders will either: (1) exit to form a new stakeholder network that satisfies their needs; (2) use the political process to constrain the offending stakeholder; or, (3) invent some other form of activity to satisfy their particular needs.[18]

Alternatively, if we think about stakeholders engaged in a series of bargains among themselves, then we would expect that as individual stakeholders recognized their joint interests, and made good decisions based on these interests, better consequences would result, than if they each narrowly pursued their individual self interests.[19]

Now it may be objected that such an approach ignores "social consequences" or "consequences to society," and hence, that we need a concept of "corporate social responsibility" to mitigate these effects. This objection is a vestigial limb of the dominant model. Since the only effects, on that view, were economic effects, then we need to think about "social consequences" or "corporate social responsibility." However, if stakeholder relationships are understood to be fully embedded in morality, then there is no need for an idea like corporate social responsibility. We can replace it with "corporate stakeholder responsibility" which is a dominant feature of managing for stakeholders.

The Argument from Rights

The dominant story gives property rights in the corporation exclusively to shareholders, and the natural question arises about the rights of other stakeholders who are affected. One way to understand managing for stakeholders is that it takes this question of rights, seriously. If you believe that rights make sense, and further that if one person has a right to X then all persons have a right to X, it is just much easier to think about these issues using a stakeholder approach. For instance, while shareholders may well have property rights, these rights are not absolute, and should not be seen as such. Shareholders may not use their property to abridge the rights of others. For instance, shareholders and their agents, managers, may not use corporate property to violate the right to life of others. One way to understand managing for stakeholders is that it assumes that stakeholders have some rights. Now it is notoriously difficult to parse the idea of "rights." But, if executives take managing for stakeholders seriously, they will automatically think about what is owed to customers, suppliers, employees, financiers and communities, in virtue of their stake, and in virtue of their basic humanity.

The Argument from Character

One of the strongest arguments for managing for stakeholders is that it asks executives and entrepreneurs to consider the question of what kind of company they want to create and build. The answer to this question will be in large part an issue of character. Aspiration matters. The business virtues of efficiency, fairness, respect, integrity, keeping commitments, and others are all critical in being successful at creating value for stakeholders. These virtues are simply absent when we think only about the dominant model and its sole reliance on a narrow economic logic.

If we frame the central question of management as "how do we create value for shareholders" then the only virtue that emerges is one of loyalty to the interests of shareholders. However if we frame the central question more broadly as "how do we create and sustain the creation of value for stakeholders" or "how do we get stakeholder interests all going in the same direction," then it is easy to see how many of the other virtues are relevant. Taking a stakeholder approach helps people decide how companies can contribute to their well-being and kinds of lives they want to lead. By making ethics explicit and building it into the basic way we think about business, we avoid a situation of bad faith and self-deception.

The Pragmatist's Argument

The previous three arguments point out important reasons for adopting a new story about business. Pragmatists want to know how we can live better, how we can create both ourselves and our communities in way where values such as freedom and solidarity are present in our everyday lives to the maximal extent. While it is sometimes useful to think about consequences, rights, and character in isolation, in reality our lives are richer if we can have a conversation about how to live together better. There is a long tradition of pragmatist ethics dating to philosophers such as William James and John Dewey. More recently philosopher Richard Rorty has expressed the pragmatist ideal.[20]

> ... pragmatists ... hope instead that human beings will come to enjoy more money, more free time, and greater social equality, and also that they will develop more empathy, more ability to put themselves in the shoes of others. We hope that human beings will behave more decently toward one another as their standard of living improves.

By building into the very conceptual framework we use to think about business a concern with freedom, equality, consequences, decency, shared purpose, and paying attention to all of the effects of how we create value for each other, we can make business a human institution, and perhaps remake it in a way that sustains us.

For the pragmatist, business (and capitalism) has evolved as a social practice; and important one that we use to create value and trade with each other. On this view, first and foremost, business is about collaboration. Of course, in a free society, stakeholders are free to form competing networks. But, the fuel for capitalism is our desire to create something of value, and to create it for ourselves and others. The spirit of capitalism is the spirit of individual achievement together with the spirit of accomplishing great tasks in collaboration with others. Managing for stakeholders makes this plain so that we can get about the business of creating better selves and better communities.

NOTES

1   The ideas in this paper have had a long development time. The ideas here have been reworked from R. Edward Freeman, *Strategic Management: A Stakeholder Approach* [Boston: Pitman, 1984]; R. Edward Freeman, "A Stakeholder Theory of the Modern Corporation, in T. Beauchamp and N. Bowie (eds.), *Ethical Theory and Business* [Englewood Cliffs: Prentice Hall, 7th edition, 2005], also in earlier editions coauthored with William Evan; Andrew Wicks, R. Edward Freeman, Patricia Werhane, Kirsten Martin, *Business Ethics: A Managerial Approach* [Englewood Cliffs: Prentice Hall, 2010]; and R. Edward Freeman, Jeffrey Harrison, and Andrew Wicks, *Managing for Stakeholders*, New Haven: Yale University Press, 2007. I am grateful to editors and coauthors for permission to rework these ideas here.

2   It has been called a variety of things from "stakeholder management," "stakeholder capitalism," "a stakeholder theory of the modern corporation," etc. Our reasons for choosing "managing for stakeholders" will become clearer as we proceed. Many others have worked on these ideas, and should not be held accountable for the rather idiosyncratic view outlined here.

3   For a stylized history of the idea see R. Edward Freeman, "The Development of Stakeholder Theory: An Idiosyncratic Approach" in K. Smith

and M. Hitt (eds.), *Great Minds in Management*, Oxford: Oxford University Press, 2005.

4   One doesn't manage "for" these benefits (and harms).

5   The difference between managerial and shareholder capitalism is large. However, the existence of agency theory lets us treat the two identically for our purposes here. Both agree on the view that the modern firm is characterized by the separation of decision making and residual risk bearing. The resulting agency problem is the subject of a vast literature.

6   Alfred Chandler's brilliant book, *Strategy and Structure*, Boston: MIT Press, 1970, chronicles the rise of the divisionalized corporation. For a not so flattering account of General Motors during the same time period see Peter Drucker's classic work, *The Concept of the Corporation*, New York: Transaction Publishers, Reprint Edition, 1993.

7   Executives can take little comfort in the adage that in the long run things work out and the most efficient companies survive. Some market theorists suggest that finance theory acts like "universal acid" cutting through every possible management decision, whether or not, actual managers are aware of it. Perhaps the real difference between the dominant model and the "managing for stakeholders" model proposed here is that they are simply "about" different things. The dominant model is about the strict and narrow economic logic of markets, and the "managing for stakeholders" model is about how human beings create value for each other.

8   Often the flavor of the response of finance theorists sounds like this. The world would be better off if, despite all of the imperfections, executives tried to maximize shareholder value. It is difficult to see how any rational being could accept such a view in the face of the recent scandals, where it could be argued that the worst offenders were the most ideologically pure, and the result was the actual destruction of shareholder value (see *Breaking the Short Term Cycle*, Charlottesville, VA: Business Roundtable Institute for Corporate Ethics/CFA Center for Financial Market Integrity, 2006). Perhaps we have a version of Aristotle's idea that happiness is not a result of trying to be happy, or Mill's idea that it does not maximize utility to

try and maximize utility. Collins and Porras have suggested that even if executives want to maximize shareholder value, they should focus on purpose instead, that trying to maximize shareholder value does not lead to maximum value (see J. Collins and J. Porras, *Built To Last*, New York: Harper Collins, 2002).

9   See R. Edward Freeman, "The Politics of Stakeholder Theory: Some Future Directions," *Business Ethics Quarterly* 4 (1994): 409–422.

10 The second part of the integration thesis is left for another occasion. Philosophers who read this essay may note the radical departure from standard accounts of political philosophy. Suppose we began the inquiry into political philosophy with the question of "how is value creation and trade sustainable over time" and suppose that the traditional beginning question, "how is the state justified" was a subsidiary one. We might discover or create some very different answers from the standard accounts of most political theory. See R. Edward Freeman and Robert Phillips, "Stakeholder Theory: A Libertarian Defense," *Business Ethics Quarterly*, Vol. 12, No. 3, 2002, pp. 331ff.

11 Here we roughly follow the logic of John Rawls in *Political Liberalism*, New York: Columbia University Press, 1995.

12 There are many statements of this principle. Our argument is that whatever the particular conception of responsibility there is some underlying concept that is captured like our willingness or our need to justify our lives to others. Note the answer that the dominant view of business must give to questions about responsibility. "Executives are responsible only for the effects of their actions on shareholders, or only insofar as their actions create or destroy shareholder value."

13 The spirit of this diagram is from R. Phillips, *Stakeholder Theory and Organizational Ethics* (San Francisco: Berret-Koehler Publishers, 2003).

14 In earlier versions of this essay in this volume we suggested that the notion of a fiduciary duty to stockholders be extended to "fiduciary duty to stakeholders." We believe that such a move cannot be defended without doing damage to the notion of "fiduciary." The idea of having a special duty to either one or a few stakeholders is not helpful.

15 Bill George, *Authentic Leadership*, San Francisco: Jossey Bass, Inc., 2004.

16 This is at least as clear as the directive given by the dominant model: Create as much value as possible for shareholders.

17 Some philosophers have argued that the stakeholder approach is in need of a "normative justification." To the extent that this phrase has any meaning, we take it as a call to connect the logic of managing for stakeholders with more traditional ethical theory. As pragmatists we eschew the "descriptive vs. normative vs. instrumental" distinction that so many business thinkers (and stakeholder theorists) have adopted. Managing for stakeholders is inherently a narrative or story that is at once: *descriptive* of how some businesses do act; *aspirational* and *normative* about how they could and should act; *instrumental* in terms of what means lead to what ends; and *managerial* in that it must be coherent on all of these dimensions and actually guide executive action.

18 See S. Venkataraman, "Stakeholder Value Equilibration and the Entrepreneurial Process," *Ethics and Entrepreneurship*, The Ruffin Series, 3 (2002): 45–57; S.R. Velamuri, "Entrepreneurship, Altruism, and the Good Society," *Ethics and Entrepreneurship*, The Ruffin Series, 3 (2002): 125–143; and, T. Harting, S. Harmeling, and S. Venkataraman, "Innovative Stakeholder Relations: When 'Ethics pays' (and When it Doesn't)," *Business Ethics Quarterly*, 16 (2006): 43–68.

19 Sometimes there are tradeoffs in situations that economists would call "prisoner's dilemmas" but these are not the paradigmatic cases, or if they are, we seem to solve them routinely, as Russell Hardin has suggested in *Morality within the Limits of Reason*, Chicago: University of Chicago Press, 1998.

20 E. Mendieta (ed.) *Take Care of Freedom and Truth Will Take Care of Itself: Interviews with Richard Rorty* (Stanford: Stanford University Press, 2006) p. 68.

—14—

BUSINESS ETHICS WITHOUT STAKEHOLDERS

Joseph Heath

OVER THE PAST TWO DECADES, THE "STAKE-holder paradigm" has served as the basis for one of the most powerful currents of thinking in the field of business ethics. Of course, stakeholder vocabulary is used even more widely, in areas where it is not necessarily intended to have any moral implications (e.g., in strategic management). In business ethics, however, the stakeholder approach is associated with a very characteristic style of normative analysis, viz. one that interprets ethical conduct in a business context in terms of a set of moral obligations toward stakeholder groups (or one that helps "to broaden management's vision of its roles and responsibilities to include interests and claims of non-stockholding groups"). Seen in this light, the primary moral dilemmas that arise in a business context involve reconciling these obligations in cases where stakeholder interests conflict. Thus ethicists who are impressed by the stakeholder paradigm have become highly adept at translating any moral problem that arises in the workplace into the language of conflicting stake-holder claims.

The question that I would like to pose in this paper is whether the stakeholder paradigm represents the most fruitful approach to the study of business ethics. The vocabulary of stakeholder obligations has become so ubiqui-tous that in many contexts it is simply taken for granted. Yet the stakeholder approach is one that comes freighted with very substantive—and

controversial—normative assumptions. Naturally, there are many who have criticized the stakeholder paradigm as part of a broader skeptical critique of business ethics in general, one which denies that firms have any "social responsibilities" beyond the maximization of profit. This is not my inten-tion here. I will argue that firms do have import-ant social responsibilities, ones that extend far beyond mere conformity to the law. The question is whether the stakeholder paradigm represents the best framework for articulating the logic and structure of these obligations.

In order to serve as a point of contrast, I would like to provide an outline of two other possible approaches to the study of business ethics: one, a more minimal conception, anchored in the notion of fiduciary obligations toward shareholders, and the other, a broader conception, focused on the regulatory environment in which firms operate. I will then attempt to show that the latter, which I refer to as a "market failures" approach, offers a more satisfactory framework for articulating the concerns that underlie traditional appeals for increased corporate social responsibility.

BUSINESS ETHICS AS PROFESSIONAL ETHICS

There is one point that all three of the approaches that I will be presenting here have in common. All three conceive of business ethics as a species of professional ethics. In the same way that medical ethics concerns, first and foremost, ethical questions that arise from the professional role of doctors, and legal ethics deals with questions that arise from the professional practice of lawyers, business ethics deals with questions that arise out of the professional role of managers. This is a narrower sense of the term "business ethics" than one sometimes encounters, but as we shall see, there are some advantages to be had from focusing on this somewhat constrained set of issues.

In each case, the assumption is that a professional role itself imposes its own set of obligations upon the person, which are not necessarily part of general morality (although they may be sanctioned by, or derived from, general morality). For example, both doctors and lawyers have a special obligation to protect client confidentiality, an obligation that arises out of their professional role. In other words, this obligation is one that is imposed upon each of them, not *qua* individual, but *qua* doctor, or *qua* lawyer. According to this conception, business ethics is concerned with the special obligations that arise out of the managerial role, and which are imposed upon the manager *qua* manager.

The reason that it is helpful to conceive of business ethics as a set of moral obligations arising out of the professional role of the manager is that it serves to head off the commonly expressed accusation that business ethics is just blue sky dreaming, or a wish list of things that ethicists would like corporations to do, many of which will turn out to be unrealistic in practice. According to the "professional ethics" view, business ethics represents an attempt to articulate a code of conduct that is *already implicit* both in the structure of corporate law and in the best practices of working managers. This helps to allay the suspicion that business ethics is some alien code, which ethicists seek to impose upon corporations from the outside.

Not everyone accepts the "professional ethics" view. There is an influential strain of thinking in business ethics that treats moral obligations as perfectly invariant across persons. (This tendency is perhaps summed up best in the title of John C.

Maxwell's recent book, *There Is No Such Thing as "Business" Ethics: There's Only One Rule for Making Decisions.*[1]) Thus some theorists begin by specifying an undifferentiated moral code (whether it be Kantian, utilitarian, Christian, Aristotelian, or what have you); they then treat business ethics as a subject concerned primarily with reconciling pressures that arise in a business context with the obligations that are imposed by this general morality (e.g., the Bible says "thou shalt not bear false witness," so what do you do when the boss asks you to lie to a client?). From this perspective, the managerial role shows up, not as a source of positive moral obligations, but primarily as a source of social pressures that may conflict with morality.

Absent from this perspective is any clear conception of the role that the professions play in a modern economic system (or of the way that a professional "ethos" can give rise to a system of distinctive moral constraints). The primary difference between having a job and practicing a profession involves the element of trust and fiduciary responsibility associated with the latter. In some situations, it is possible for parties in an employment relation to specify all the terms of the contract, to monitor performance completely, and to institute a system of incentives that guarantees perfect compliance. Stacking boxes in a warehouse is an example of an employment relation of this type. These are jobs, and in them, employees are not usually thought to have any special responsibilities beyond those specified in the contract, i.e., the terms of employment. Employees in these sorts of jobs are normally paid by the hour, and have a fixed workday, in recognition of the market-like structure of the transaction.

Things become more complicated, however, when it is impossible to specify the terms of an employment contract completely, imperfect observability of effort makes monitoring difficult, or information asymmetries make the design of a perfect system of performance incentives impossible. In such cases it is impossible to eliminate moral hazard, and so the purchaser of labor services must rely in large measure upon the voluntary cooperation of the seller in order to secure adequate work effort. Thus a certain amount of trust, or moral constraint, is required in these relationships. Contracts usually specify goals and obligations in very general terms, and the person supplying the services is expected to use his or her own judgment to decide how best these terms should be satisfied. The purchaser often lacks not only the information and skills to determine the best course on her own, but is often incapable of even verifying that the supplier has done so after the fact. This is the condition that Oliver Williamson refers to as "information impactedness," and it represents the primary force driving professionalization.[2]

In certain cases, reputation effects are enough to motivate good faith work effort for individuals in these roles. For example, most people have no ability to evaluate the claims and recommendations made by their auto mechanic, and the cost of getting a second opinion can be prohibitive (in both time and money). Thus they have no choice but to trust the mechanic. But as a result, reputation and "word-of-mouth" plays an important role in the market for automobile repairs. The market for contractors, plumbers, and hair stylists has a similar structure. These groups are not generally thought of as professionals, because the market still does a tolerable job of overcoming the important information asymmetries.

It is not an accident that these cases all involve purchases that consumers make frequently, where there is significant opportunity for repeat business. In markets where larger, more infrequent purchases are made, or where information asymmetries are even greater, it is much more difficult for purchasers of services to impose discipline upon suppliers through reputation mechanisms. As a result, suppliers who deploy highly specialized knowledge must work harder to secure the trust of potential clients, simply because the client may never have the opportunity to verify the quality or value of the services received. In some cases, the trust requirements are sufficiently high that these suppliers will form their own membership association, in order to impose an internal "code of conduct" more stringent than the requirements of general labor and contract law. The most well-known examples are the "bar" for lawyers, along with the various medical licensing boards for doctors. These sorts of associations are especially important in professions where the only people competent to evaluate a particular individual's performance are other members of that same profession.

Economists sometimes suggest that the function of these organizations is merely to cartelize a particular segment of the labor market. This is a good example of the "naïve cynicism" often exhibited in this field—where the automatic identification of pecuniary incentives as the dominant motive leads to sociologically naïve analyses of particular institutions. These associations also play an important socializing role, helping to instill genuine respect for a set of moral obligations that are often specific to the profession. For example, many engineers in Canada wear an iron ring on their little finger, which is conferred during a ceremony called "The Ritual of the Calling of an Engineer" (developed in 1925 by Rudyard Kipling). The ring is a symbol of the Pont de Québec Bridge, which collapsed in 1907 as it was nearing completion, killing seventy-six people. A subsequent Royal Commission declared that errors committed by the bridge's principal engineers were the primary cause of the tragedy. Initially, the rings were said to have been made with iron from the collapsed bridge. In the present day, the rings are intended simply to serve as a reminder to working engineers that the lives of many people depend upon their efforts. Engineers have more than just an obligation to put in a day's work for a day's pay, they must also consider the impact that their actions will have upon the eventual users of the structures or products they design. Many engineering students describe the ceremony as genuinely moving, and find that the ring serves as a constant reminder of their professional ethical obligations.

The existence of a professional association, a certification system, a common body of accepted knowledge, and a shared ethics code, are sometimes treated as the distinguishing marks of a genuine profession. This involves some confusion of cause and effect. What makes the complex body of knowledge important is that it generates an information asymmetry, which creates a moral hazard problem that threatens to undermine any market transaction involving such specialists. Thus specialists must work hard to cultivate trust among potential purchasers of their services. A certification system, along with a professional association that imposes a stringent code of conduct, is one way of achieving this objective. There may be cases, however, in which a certification system is difficult to devise, or a professional association difficult to organize. Such is the case, traditionally, with managers (especially during the era when most were promoted up from the shop floor). Nevertheless, the *economic role* that managers occupy is a professional one, precisely because of the information impactedness in the domain of services they provide. The nature of the managerial role is such that they *need* to be both trusted and trustworthy. This is reflected in the fact that most systems of corporate law treat senior managers as fiduciaries of the firm. Thus the mere fact that managers do not belong to professional associations does not mean that they are not professionals, or more importantly, that there is not a distinctive set of ethical obligations that arise out of their occupational role. The fact that they are in a position of trust is what matters.

Thinking of business ethics in terms of "professional ethics for managers" is an attractive perspective, insofar as it offers some relatively clear criteria for the evaluation of different "theories" or "paradigms" within the field. Managers who take social responsibility seriously already have some very firm intuitions about what constitutes ethical and unethical conduct. The question is whether the vocabulary and the principles that business ethicists develop offer a more or less perspicuous and coherent articulation of these intuitions—whether their theories help us to achieve greater clarity, or whether they sow confusion. This is the standard

that I shall be employing in this paper. Thus my criticism of the stakeholder approach to business ethics is not that it is false or incoherent. I shall merely try to show that the vocabulary, and the theory that underlies it, is *inherently misleading*, and thus does not promote useful ways of thinking about corporate social responsibility.

THE SHAREHOLDER MODEL

The managerial role arises as a consequence of the so-called separation of ownership and control in the modern corporation. In the early stages of development, most corporations are run by the founders, who are also generally the principal owners. At a later point, the owners may choose to employ managers to assist them in running the firm, or to take over that role entirely. In the same way that individuals employ lawyers in order to advance their interests in a legal context, owners hire managers in order to advance their interests in a business context. Of course, as the firm becomes more mature, this relationship becomes significantly more complex (leading many to argue that the shareholders in a publicly-traded corporation cannot be regarded as its "owners" in any coherent sense). Nevertheless, the fact that shareholders are residual claimants in a standard business corporation means that their interests are not protected by an explicit contract. As a result, there is a set of fiduciary principles governing the relationship between managers and shareholders. Because the fiduciary relationship imposes upon managers a very broad "duty of loyalty" and "duty of care" toward shareholders—concepts with explicit moral overtones—this particular relationship might be thought to serve as a natural point of departure for the development of a theory of business ethics (in the same way that duties toward the patient form the core of professional ethics for doctors, duties toward the client the core of professional ethics for lawyers, etc.).

Yet despite the fact that moral obligations toward shareholders are such a striking feature of the managerial role, in the business ethics literature they are the subject of considerable controversy, and are often downplayed or dismissed. (Marjorie Kelly, the editor of *Business Ethics* magazine, set the tone for one end of this discussion with the title of her article, "Why All the Fuss About Stockholders?")[3] There are several reasons for this relative neglect of the shareholder, some worse than others. In popular debates, there is a tendency when talking about "the corporation" simply to conflate to the two groups (managers and owners), or to assume that there is a greater identity of interests between them than is usually the case. The standard microeconomics curriculum encourages this, by starting out with the assumption that individuals maximize utility, but then aggregating consumers together into "households" and suppliers into "firms"—each of which is thought to maximize some joint utility function—without explaining the transition (this gets reserved for more advanced courses). Even though it is understood that "the firm" is something of a black box in this analysis, the result is still an unhelpful blurring of the distinction between the pursuit of self-interest on the part of individuals and the maximization of profit on the part of firms, and thus a tendency to overestimate the extent to which the latter flows naturally from the former. As a result, it is easy to underestimate the potential for moral hazard in the relationship between managers and shareholders.

The recent scandals at Enron, Parmalat, Tyco, WorldCom, Hollinger, and elsewhere, have shown that shareholders neglect these difficulties at their own peril. In each of the major scandals, managers were able to enrich themselves primarily at the expense of shareholders. (It may be helpful to recall that at its peak, Enron had 19,000 employees and a market capitalization of $77 billion. Thus for each employee who had to look for a new job as a result of the subsequent bankruptcy of the firm, shareholders lost at least $4 million.) The fact that most of these scandals involved illegal conduct should not distract us from the fact that each illegal act was surrounded by a very broad penumbral region of unethical conduct. For example,

it was never decided specifically whether the $2.1 million dollar party thrown by Tyco CEO Dennis Kozlowski for his wife's birthday, half paid out of company funds, constituted fraud or theft, but it most certainly represented a violation of his moral obligation to shareholders.

It is a mistake to believe that self-interest alone, combined with a few performance incentives, is able to achieve a harmony of interest between managers and shareholders. In this respect, a lot of the work done by economists (and game theorists) on the "theory of the firm" has been quite misleading. The overriding objective of many economists has been to extend the methodological tools—and in particular, the action theory—used in the analysis of markets to model the internal structure of organizations. Thus "principal-agent" theory has focused almost entirely upon the use of external incentives as a mechanism for overcoming collective action and control problems within the firm. In so doing, economists have dramatically underplayed the role that trust, values, social norms, and other aspects of "corporate culture" play in determining organizational behavior. Thus they have wasted considerable time and energy devising increasingly baroque performance pay schemes, while neglecting more obvious managerial strategies, such as encouraging employee loyalty to the firm, or cultivating a direct concern for customer satisfaction.

It is precisely because of the importance of these internal (i.e., moral) incentives, along with the enormous potential for abuse, that US corporate law essentially imposes a fiduciary relationship between senior managers and shareholders. It is helpful to recall, for example, the words of an influential US court judgment, concerning the obligations of managers:

> He who is in such a fiduciary position cannot serve himself and his cestius second. He cannot manipulate the affairs of his corporation to their detriment and in disregard of the standards of common decency and honesty. He cannot by the intervention of a corporate

entity violate the ancient precept against serving two masters. He cannot by the use of the corporate device avail himself of privileges normally permitted outsiders in a race of creditors. He cannot utilize his inside information and his strategic position for his own preferment. He cannot violate rules of fair play by doing indirectly through the corporation what he could not do directly. He cannot use his power for his personal advantage and to the detriment of the stockholders and creditors, no matter how absolute in terms that power may be and no matter how meticulous he is to satisfy technical requirements, for that power is at all times subject to the equitable limitation that it may not be exercised for the aggrandizement, preference, or advantage of the fiduciary to the exclusion or detriment of the cestuis. Where there is a violation of those principles, equity will undo the wrong or intervene to prevent its consummation.[4]

The obligations enumerated here are sufficiently broad that one could only imagine legal prosecution in cases of the most egregious violation. Thus a very robust theory of business ethics could be developed based simply on the injunction to respect the spirit of this judgment, along with the fiduciary obligations that it outlines toward shareholders. Yet despite this fact, far too little has been said on this subject. The dominant assumption has been that shareholders are able to take care of themselves. Many introductory business ethics textbooks cover topics like whistle-blowing, truth in advertising, pollution, discrimination, and health and safety issues, yet neglect to discuss more common ethical challenges that employees encounter in their day-to-day affairs, such as the temptation to abuse expense accounts. Strictly speaking, society should be no more willing to tolerate such abuses when carried out by business executives (wasting shareholders' money) than when carried out by politicians or civil servants (wasting taxpayers' money). The reality, needless to say, is quite different. Thus a simple duty of loyalty

toward shareholders precludes a lot of the everyday immorality that goes on in firms (but which attracts attention only when it reaches spectacular proportions, as with the recent spate of corporate scandals).

Thus the tendency to overestimate the degree of alignment of managerial and shareholder interests leads to more general failure to appreciate the extent to which shareholders are *vulnerable* in their relations with managers (just as patients are vulnerable in their relations with doctors, or clients are vulnerable in their dealings with lawyers). There is, however, also a more principled reason that obligations toward shareholders tend to get downplayed. There is a widespread perception that the fiduciary relationship between the manager and the shareholder cannot serve as a source of genuine moral obligation. Even though I am morally obliged to keep my promises, if I promise my friend that I will rob a bank that does not mean that I am then morally obliged to rob a bank. The same applies to fiduciary relations. Consider the following argument, due to Arthur Applbaum.[5] Imagine a Hobbesian state of nature, in which everyone treats everyone else abysmally. Such conduct is immoral. Now imagine that, in this state of nature, each person solemnly swears to stop pursuing his own interests, and to begin pursuing the interests of the person next to him. What changes? From the moral point of view, nothing much. It is still the war of all against all, except that now it is being carried out by proxy. Certainly the mere fact that each person is acting "altruistically"—advancing the interests of her neighbor, rather than her own—is not enough to transform this into a morally acceptable state of affairs. If it could, then the simple act of promising would permit unlimited "laundering" of immoral acts into moral ones.

Thus the discussion of the fiduciary responsibilities of managers quickly turns into a discussion of the moral legitimacy of the goals being pursued by shareholders. This in turn must lead to a discussion of the moral status of *profit* (since this is the interest of shareholders that managers are generally understood to be advancing). It is here that the "ethical" status of business ethics begins to seem problematic. Indeed, Milton Friedman's well-known article "The Social Responsibility of Business Is to Increase Its Profits," which presents the ethical obligation to maximize the returns of shareholders as the cornerstone of a conception of business ethics, usually shows up in business ethics textbooks, not as the point of departure for further development of the theory, but rather as an example of an instructively mistaken point of view. The problem is that "profit" is associated, in many people's minds, with "self-interest." "Ethics," on the other hand, is usually associated with behavior that is "altruistic," in some sense of the term. More precisely, morality can be understood as a "principled constraint on the pursuit of self-interest." If this is the case, then substituting "profit" for "self-interest" yields the conclusion that business ethics must represent some sort of principled constraint on the pursuit of profit—not an injunction to maximize it.

In the case of doctors, who must do everything in their power to promote the health of their patients, it is easy to see that health is a good thing, and so efforts to promote it in others must also be good. This is more difficult to see in the case of managers and wealth, especially in cases when increasing the wealth of shareholders can only be achieved at the expense of others. Yet managers who take their responsibilities toward shareholders seriously are often put in a situation where they must effect pure distributive transfers—often regressive ones between workers and shareholders. Here it becomes difficult to see what is so ethical about business ethics.

Thus in order to see managerial obligations toward shareholders as genuine moral obligations, one cannot merely point to their fiduciary status, one must also come up with some justification for the role that profit-taking plays in a capitalist economy. There are two general strategies for doing so. The first, which might be thought of as broadly Lockean, defends profits as the product of a legitimate exercise of the shareholder's property rights, under conditions of freedom of contract. According to this view, the shareholder is entitled to these profits for the same reason that the creditor is entitled to repayment with interest, or that the worker is entitled to her wages. This is not very compelling, however, because the Lockean theory is one that defines the individual's legal rights, but makes no pretense of accounting for her moral obligations. Thus, for example, the Lockean thinks that we have no legal obligation to give anything to charity, and our property rights protect us from any seizure of our assets for such purposes. But this does not mean that we have no moral obligation to give to charity. Ordinary morality tells us that wealth is not an overriding value, and so there would appear to be many cases where the profit motive is trumped by other considerations. This makes it unethical for shareholders to pursue profits in particular ways, and thus unethical for managers to assist them in carrying out such strategies.

The more promising defense of profit is the Paretian one, which points to the efficiency properties of the market economy as a way of justifying the profit orientation of firms. According to this view, the point of the market economy is not to respect individual property rights, but rather to ensure the smooth operation of the price system. The profit orientation is valued, not because individuals have a right to pursue certain interests, but rather because it generates the competition necessary to push prices toward the levels at which markets clear. When markets clear, it means that all resources will have been put to their best use, by flowing to the individuals who derive the most relative satisfaction from their consumption. The spirit of the Paretian approach is best expressed in the "invisible hand" theorem of welfare economics, which shows that the equilibrium of a perfectly competitive market will be Pareto-optimal (i.e., it will be impossible to improve anyone's conditions without worsening someone else's).

Yet this framework still seems to be, in many ways, not "ethical enough" to satisfy many people's intuitions. It offers a seal of approval, for instance, to a wide range of so-called sharp practices in market transactions (which, despite being legal, nevertheless offend our intuitive moral sensibilities). And while it has been pointed out many times that firms seldom profit in the long run from abusing employees, cheating customers, or taking advantage of suppliers, it nevertheless remains true that *in certain cases* it can be profitable to do so. In other words, it is simply not the case that the interests of shareholders always line up with those of workers, customers, suppliers, and other groups with an interest in the firm's decisions. There are genuine conflicts that arise, and it is not obvious that the ethical course of action for managers in every instance is to take the side of shareholders, respecting no constraints beyond those imposed by law. But if this is so, the question becomes how far one should go, as a manager, in advancing the interests of the principal, and when one should start showing more concern for others who are affected by one's actions. Yet even to pose the question in this way is to reveal the limitations of any theoretical approach to business ethics that takes obligations to shareholders as the sole criterion of ethical conduct in business.

THE STAKEHOLDER MODEL

The shareholder approach to business ethics suffers, first and foremost, from the taint of moral laxity. It does not seem to impose *enough* obligations upon managers to satisfy the moral intuitions of many people. In particular, it suggests that, as R. Edward Freeman puts it, "management can pursue market transactions with suppliers and customers in an unconstrained manner."[6] Thus the suggestion has been made that managers have moral obligations, not just to shareholders, but to other groups as well. Freeman introduced the term "stakeholders" as a "generalization of the notion of stockholders," in order to refer to "groups and individuals who benefit from or are harmed by, and whose rights are violated or respected by, corporate actions."[7] He went on to make the suggestion that managers have *fiduciary* obligations toward multiple stakeholder groups.

This overall approach has proven to be remarkably influential, and it is not difficult to see

why. After all, we understand quite clearly what it means for managers to have fiduciary obligations toward shareholders. By construing relations with "stakeholders" on analogy, Freeman provided an intuitively accessible framework for articulating the sorts of moral obligations that the shareholder model elides. (In the same way, the term "social capital" has become popular, precisely because people understand what capital is, and so construing social capital on analogy with real capital provides an intuitively accessible framework for thinking about collective action.)

Of course, the term "stakeholder" has been picked up and used quite widely, even by those who do not share Freeman's views on the structure of managerial obligations. For example, so-called strategic stakeholder theory argues that managers must exercise moral restraint in stakeholder relations *as a way of discharging their fiduciary obligations toward shareholders* (i.e., "ethics pays"). Freeman, on the other hand, claims that managers must exercise moral restraint in dealings with stakeholders *because managers have direct fiduciary obligations toward those stakeholders.* Shareholders, according to this view, are just one stakeholder group among many. Managers have fiduciary obligations toward shareholders only because shareholders are stakeholders, and managers have fiduciary obligations toward *all* stakeholders.

Thus Kenneth Goodpaster identifies the key characteristic of Freeman's theory when he refers to it as the "multi-fiduciary stakeholder" theory.[8] What matters is the idea that managers have fiduciary obligations toward multiple groups—regardless of whether these groups are called stakeholders or something else. Thus the two components of the theory are separable—one need not conceive of stakeholder relations as fiduciary relations. Nevertheless, stakeholder vocabulary is often used as a way of expressing tacit commitment to the multi-fiduciary view. As a result, some of the obvious weaknesses of the position tend to be overlooked. As Goodpaster observes, the fact that managers have moral obligations with respect to customers, employees, and other groups, does not mean that these obligations must take a fiduciary form. There is some danger of being seduced by the metaphor, leading one to think that the status of stakeholders is much closer to that of shareholders than it in fact is. For example, the manager might have an obligation to respect certain *rights* of customers, without also having a fiduciary duty to advance their *interests*.

If managers really are to be regarded as fiduciaries of stakeholder groups, it raises immediate difficulties with respect to questions of corporate governance. Freeman suggests that the manager must become like "King Solomon," adjudicating the rival claims of various stakeholder groups. Yet giving managers the legal freedom to balance these claims as they see fit would create extraordinary agency risks. On the one hand, managers would need to be protected from being fired by shareholders upset over the performance of their investments. But even more significantly, it would become almost impossible for members of any stakeholder group to evaluate the performance of management. It is difficult enough for shareholders to determine whether managers are actually maximizing profits, given available resources. But when profits can be traded off against myriad other objectives, such as maintaining employment, sustaining supplier relationships, and protecting the environment, while managers have the discretion to balance these objectives as they see fit, then there is really no alternative but to trust the word of managers when they say that they are doing the best they can. The history of state-owned enterprises shows that the "multiple objectives" problem can completely undermine managerial discipline, and lead to firms behaving in a *less* socially responsible manner than those that are explicitly committed to maximizing shareholder value.

Setting aside these practical difficulties, the plausibility of multi-fiduciary stakeholder theory also depends quite heavily upon how broadly the term "stakeholder" is understood. This so-called identification problem has attracted considerable attention. Freeman distinguishes between a "narrow definition" of the term, which refers to groups that are "vital to the success and survival of the firm," and a "wide definition," which refers to any group "who can affect or is affected by the achievement of the organization's objectives."[9] The former includes employees, customers, suppliers, but also, in most formulations of the theory, the local community. The wide definition, on the other hand, is so wide that it becomes equivalent to "all of society." (For example, every pricing decision made by the firm contributes to the national inflation rate, which in turn affects every member of society. So if a stakeholder is anyone affected by the corporation, then everyone is a stakeholder in everything.) Yet the idea that managers are fiduciaries for "all of society" simply collapses business ethics into general ethics (i.e., general utilitarianism, Kantianism, Christian ethics, or what have you). Thus theorists who believe that the managerial role imposes special obligations upon the individual have tended to stick to the narrower definition of the stakeholder.

From the moral point of view, however, there seems to be no reason for the firm to pay special attention to stakeholders in the narrow sense of the term. There are plenty of good *strategic* reasons for managers to worry most about those whose contribution is vital to the success of the firm, but it is difficult to see what moral ones there could be. The groups that are conventionally classified as stakeholders in the narrow sense are not necessarily those with the most at stake in a particular decision, in terms of their potential welfare losses. In fact, if one looks at the standard list of stakeholder groups (customers, suppliers, employees and the local community), it tends rather to be those who are the best organized, or who have the most immediate relationship to the firm, or who are best positioned to make their voices heard. Thus stakeholder theory often has a "squeaky wheel" bias. For example, when General Motors considers closing down a plant in Detroit and moving it to Mexico, a standard multi-fiduciary stakeholder theory would insist that managers take into account the impact of their decision, not just upon their workers in Detroit, but also upon other members of the community whose livelihood depends upon their wages. Thus the "local community" in Detroit where the plant is located would normally be counted as a "stakeholder." But what about the "local community" in Mexico, where the plant *would* be located? And what about the people there who *would* be getting jobs? Presumably they also have a lot at stake (possibly even more, in terms of welfare, given the relative poverty of the society in which they live). The fact that General Motors has built up a relationship over time with the people in Detroit may well count for something, but it cannot justify *ignoring* the interests of the people in Mexico. From the moral point of view, a potential relationship can be just as important as an actual one. The only real difference between the groups is that potential employees do not know who they are, and so are unable to organize themselves to articulate their interests or express grievances. But it is difficult to see why—from a moral, rather than a strategic point of view—this should give managers the freedom to leave potential employees, or potential "local communities," off the list of groups that the firm has an obligation to.

Because stakeholder theory focuses on the relationship between the manager and different "groups" within society, it tends to privilege the interests of those who are well-organized over those who are poorly organized, simply because it is the former who are able to present themselves as a coherent body with a common set of interests. To see this bias in action, one need only look at the difference in the way that different stakeholder theorists conceive of "social responsibility" and the way that *governments* have traditionally approached it. In this context, it is useful to recall that the widespread nationalization of industry that occurred in Western Europe after the Second World War was motivated, in large part, by the desire of democratic governments to make corporations behave in a more socially responsible manner. The thought was that corporations behaved irresponsibly because owners put their private interests ahead of the public good.

By transferring ownership to the state, the people as a whole would become the owners, and so the corporation would no longer have an incentive to pursue anything other than the public good.

Needless to say, this initiative did not have precisely the results that were anticipated. The interesting point, however, lies in the agenda that various governments initially laid out for these firms. First and foremost, state-owned enterprises were expected to play an important role in assisting the state to implement macroeconomic stabilization policies: attenuating the business cycle by making countercyclical investments; maintaining excess employment during recessionary periods; and following self-imposed wage and price controls when necessary, in order to control inflation. Similarly, state-owned enterprises were expected to serve the national interest in various ways, either by providing goods at discounted prices when supplying domestic industry, serving as a guaranteed market for domestically produced goods, or by assisting in the "incubation" of industries intended to bolster international competitiveness. They were of course also expected to act as model employers with respect to their workers, to refrain from polluting, to promote regional development, and so forth. While there is significant overlap between the latter set of objectives and the traditional concerns of many stakeholder theorists, there are also some striking differences. In particular, one can search the stakeholder literature long and hard without finding any mention of the way that firms can contribute to macroeconomic stability. The reason, I would suggest, is that there are no organized or clearly identifiable "stakeholder" groups in this case. After all, how does one identify those who are harmed by inflation? It is, by and large, an extremely diffuse group of individuals. As a result, business ethicists working within the stakeholder paradigm have had a tendency simply to ignore them. For example, I am not aware of anyone having suggested that managers should refrain from granting inflationary wage increases to workers (i.e., increases that are not funded by productivity gains). Governments, on the other hand, have traditionally been concerned with these questions, precisely because they do have a mandate to defend the welfare of all citizens, and to promote the public interest.

As a result, if one interprets the term "stakeholder" in the narrow sense, it introduces an unacceptable element of arbitrariness into business ethics. If one expands the definition, such that anyone affected by the firm's actions will be considered a stakeholder, multi-fiduciary stakeholder theory amounts to the claim that the manager should be motivated by general considerations of social justice. This risks rendering the stakeholder vocabulary nonsensical, since the concept of a "fiduciary" relation is inherently contrastive. Being a loyal fiduciary involves showing *partiality* toward the interests of one group, not an impartial concern for the interests of all. Furthermore, if the manager is obliged to show impartial concern, the question then becomes, is he or she the person best equipped, or best positioned, to be making these judgments? As Friedman pointed out long ago, normative issues at this level of generality seem to be a more appropriate topic for public policy and democratic deliberation. It is simply not obvious that the *manager's* obligations should be determined by these concerns.

Part of the unwillingness to accept this line of reasoning stems from a rejection of the idea that there might be an institutional "division of moral labor," such that not everyone is morally responsible for everything at all times. Many of the most subtle and difficult questions in professional ethics involves dealing with the way that obligations are divided up and parceled out to different individuals occupying different institutional roles. This is especially tricky in cases where the institution has an adversarial structure. For example, the role of a defense attorney in a criminal trial is to advance the interests of her client by mounting a vigorous defense. Naturally, the overall goal of the procedure is to see that "justice" is served. But that does not make the defense attorney *directly* accountable to what she thinks is "just" in any particular case. Her job is to defend her client (and

in fact, mounting a less-than-vigorous defense, because she happens to believe that her client is guilty, constitutes a serious violation of professional ethics). The victim of the crime is no doubt a "stakeholder" in these proceedings, but that does not mean that the defense attorney has a fiduciary obligation toward this individual. Both as a human being and as an officer of the court, she no doubt has ethical obligations toward victims of crime. But *qua* defense attorney, her obligation in many cases will be to disregard this everyday moral constraint. Justice arises through the interaction of her role-specific obligations with those of the crown prosecutor (or district attorney) and the judge. Of course, this is not to say that defense attorneys should do *anything* to secure the acquittal of their clients, or should not respect certain constraints in dealing with victims. There are clearly ethical and unethical ways to proceed. The point is that the vocabulary of fiduciary obligation does not provide a useful way of formulating these constraints. Furthermore, the idea that attorneys should seek to promote justice by balancing the interests of all affected parties is in tension with the role-differentiation that is a central component of the adversarial trial procedure.

Turning to business ethics, the first thing to note is that market transactions also have an adversarial structure (insofar as prices are competitively determined). One can see the problems that this creates for multi-fiduciary stakeholder theory by considering the attempts that have been made to classify "competitors" amongst the relevant stakeholder groups (or more often, the way that "competitors" are tacitly excluded without discussion). After all, competitors are clearly affected by many of the decisions taken by the firm. Furthermore, since competitors have the power to drive the firm into bankruptcy, their behavior is often vital to its success or failure. Yet it seems obvious that managers do not have any fiduciary obligations toward rival corporations. After all, the price mechanism functions only because of an unresolved collective action problem between firms. No company sets out with the intention of selling goods at a price that clears the market. Often no one even knows what that price is. It is only when firms compete with one another, undercutting each other's prices in order to increase their market share, that the selling price will be driven down to market-clearing levels. This is a classic form of non-cooperative behavior, since it is not normally profit-maximizing overall for firms to sell at this price level. They do it only because they are stuck in a collective action problem.

Thus there is a significant difference between market transactions and the administered transactions that occur within the organizational hierarchy of the firm. The former, because they are mediated through the price system, have an intrinsically adversarial element, since prices are supposed to be determined through competition (and considerable legal effort is invested in the task of keeping things that way). Since many of the socially desirable outcomes of the market economy are a consequence of the operation of the price mechanism, it is not clear that individual firms, much less managers, should be held directly accountable to them. Yet the possibility of such differentiated roles is tacitly denied by the wide version of stakeholder theory, which demands that the manager be ethically responsible for balancing the interests of everyone who is affected by the firm's actions, regardless of whether they are in a competitive or a cooperative relationship.

THE MARKET FAILURES MODEL

Despite these difficulties, the stakeholder paradigm still exercises an extraordinary grip over the imagination of many business ethicists. It is all too often assumed that the stakeholder theory and the shareholder theory exhaust the logical space of alternatives. As a result, theorists like Marjorie Kelly and Max Clarkson have sought to defend stakeholder theory by mounting increasingly spirited attacks on the idea that managers have any particular obligations to shareholders. The cornerstone of this "nothing special about shareholders" defense is the claim that shareholders are not really "owners" of the firm in any meaningful sense.[10] Thus Clarkson cites with approval the fact that "serious questions are being raised about the belief, widely held in North America, that the purpose of the corporation in society is to maximize profits and financial value for the primary benefit of its shareholders, who are also assumed, mistakenly, to be the corporation's owners."[11]

It is perhaps worth noting that this particular strategy for defending the stakeholder paradigm has the unhelpful effect of making business ethics extremely unintuitive for those who actually work in a standard corporate environment, where the understanding that shareholders own the firm is still widespread. In particular, the downgrading of shareholder claims creates an enormous tension with corporate law, which remains very much committed to the idea that shareholders have a special status within the firm, and that managers owe them fiduciary duties. Of course, it is always possible for the law to be unethical. Nevertheless, this problem is more serious than it would at first appear. If one could produce a sound argument for the conclusion that managers have fiduciary obligations toward various stakeholder groups, one would also have produced a strong *prima facie* argument for the legal enforcement of these obligations. Thus stakeholder theorists have invested some effort in attempting to show that corporate law has in fact been evolving in the direction of increased recognition of stakeholder claims. And it is here, I think, that one can see where the most instructive misunderstanding arises.

There can be no doubt that the development of the welfare state in the twentieth century has coincided with increased regulation of the market. Health and safety in the workplace, the minimum wage, unionization procedures, product warranties, "truth in advertising" and product labeling, toxic emission controls, environmental impact studies, even the size and location of commercial signage—have all become subject to increasingly strict controls. Furthermore, it is clear that all of these regulations respond, in one way or another, to the type of issues that have traditionally been of concern to business ethicists. Each regulation amounts to a legal prohibition of a form of corporate conduct that was at one time merely unethical. The question is how we should understand these developments. Freeman argues that the growth in regulation *constitutes an increased legal recognition of stakeholder claims.* This is, I will argue, a serious misunderstanding. The growth of regulation over the course of the twentieth century goes hand-in-hand with the increased positive economic role of the state in supplying public goods. Both represent strategies aimed at *correcting market failure.* As a result, I think that the concept of market failure provides a much more satisfactory framework for understanding the growth of regulation—and thus the increased legal entrenchment of the social responsibilities of business—than that of stakeholder claim recognition.

Setting aside Germany's "co-determination" arrangements, the closest one can find to an explicit recognition of stakeholder claims is the spread of statutes that allow boards of directors to consider the impact that a hostile takeover would have on non-shareholder groups in determining whether resistance to such takeovers would be "reasonable." These so-called other constituency statutes adopted in many US states (although not Delaware), typically permit (and occasionally require) "officers and directors to consider the impact of their decisions on constituencies besides shareholders."[12] Thomas Donaldson and Lee Preston describe this as a "trend toward stakeholder law."[13] It is significant, however, that these statutes do not impose fiduciary duties, and were largely motivated by a desire on the part of legislators to make hostile control transactions more difficult, based upon a perception that takeovers generate significant social costs. Thus "other constituency" statutes have a lot in common with enabling statutes for "poison pill" and "shark repellent" defenses. I would argue that they are therefore better understood as an attempt to curtail a (perceived) market failure in the stock market than as a legal recognition of stakeholder claims.

The politics of "other constituency" statutes is a complex issue, however, which I do not want to get into here. My primary concern is to illustrate the style of analysis suggested by the market failures perspective. A market failure represents a situation in which the competitive market fails to produce a Pareto-efficient outcome (or for our purposes, let us say, fails *egregiously* to produce an efficient outcome). There are two primary institutional responses to market failure. The first involves the creation of the corporation itself, which is based upon the substitution of an organizational hierarchy and a set of administered transactions for a competitive market. The central characteristic of the firm, as Ronald Coase observed in his classic work, is the internal elimination of market transactions and the "supersession of the price mechanism."[14] In more contemporary terms, we would say that the corporation substitutes a set of principal-agent relations for the non-cooperative relations of marketplace competition. However, because of the limitations of external incentive schemes, these agency relations can often be organized only through some combination of moral and prudential constraint. Thus the central focus of business ethics, in an *intrafirm* context, involves promoting cooperative behavior within these agency relationships (as Allen Buchanan has argued, in my view persuasively[15]). First and foremost among these obligations will be the fiduciary duty that managers have as the agents of shareholders. Thus when dealing with relationships or transactions "inside" the organizational hierarchy of the firm, the market failures approach to business ethics follows the shareholder-focused view quite closely. With respect to individuals who are "outside" the firm, on the other hand, it is quite different.

The second primary institutional response to market failure is less drastic than the first; it involves preservation of the market transaction, but subject to some more extensive set of legal, typically regulatory, constraints. To see the rationale for this strategy, it is helpful to recall that the point of permitting profit-maximizing behavior among firms in the first place is to promote price competition, along with all the beneficial "upstream" and "downstream" effects of such competition, such as technical innovation, quality improvement, etc. Under conditions of "perfect competition," lower price, improved quality and product innovation would be the *only* way that firms could compete with one another. We can refer to these as the set of *preferred* competitive strategies. Unfortunately, in the real world, the so-called Pareto conditions that specify the terms of perfect competition are never met. In order for competition to generate an efficient allocation of goods and services, there must be an absence of externalities (e.g., a complete set of property rights), symmetric information between buyers and sellers, a complete set of insurance markets, and rational, utility-maximizing agents with dynamically consistent preferences. Because of the practical impossibility of satisfying these constraints, firms are often able to make a profit using *non-preferred* competitive strategies, such as producing pollution, or selling products with hidden quality defects. This is what generates market failure. The basic rules for marketplace competition laid down by the state—including the system of property rights—are designed to limit these possibilities, in order to bring real-world competition closer to the ideal (or to bring *outcomes* closer to those that would be achieved under the ideal, in cases where a functional competition cannot be organized). This is the motivation that underlies not only direct state provision of public goods, such as roads, but also state regulation of negative externalities, such as pollution.

Unfortunately, the law is a somewhat blunt instrument. In many cases, the state simply lacks the information needed to implement the measures needed to improve upon a marketplace outcome (sometimes because the information does not exist, but often because the state has no way of extracting it truthfully from the relevant parties). Even when the information can be obtained, there are significant administrative costs associated with record-keeping and compliance monitoring, not

to mention the costs incurred by firms in an effort to evade compliance. Thus the deadweight losses imposed through use of the legal mechanism can easily outweigh whatever efficiency gains might have been achieved through the intervention. This often makes legal regulation unfeasible or unwise.

It is at this point that ethical constraints become germane. As we have seen, profit is not intrinsically good. The profit-seeking orientation of the private firm is valued only because of the role that it plays in sustaining the price system, and thus the contribution that it makes to the efficiency properties of the market economy as a whole. Ideally, the only way that a firm could make a profit would be by employing one of the preferred strategies. However, for strictly practical reasons, it is often impossible to create a system of laws that prohibits the non-preferred ones. Thus according to the market failures perspective, specifically ethical conduct in an *extrafirm* business context (i.e., when dealing with external parties) consists in refraining from using non-preferred strategies to maximize profit, even when doing so would be legally permissible. Put more simply, the ethical firm does not seek to profit from market failure. In many cases, doing so will be illegal—precisely because the state has tried, through increased regulation, to eliminate the use of non-preferred competitive strategies. Ethical constraint becomes relevant in the rather large penumbral region of strategies that are not illegal, and yet at the same time are not among the preferred.

Corporations, for instance, are often in a position where they can produce advertising that will be quite likely to mislead the consumer, but which stops short of outright falsity. In a perfect world, advertising would provide nothing more than truthful information about the qualities and prices of goods. However, the vagaries of interpretation make it impossible to prohibit anything but the most flagrant forms of misinformation. Thus misleading advertising stands to false advertising as deception does to fraud. It is something that would be illegal, were it not for practical limitations on the scope of the legal mechanism. Profiting from such actions is therefore morally objectionable, not because it violates some duty of loyalty to the customer (as stakeholder theory would have it), but because it undermines the social benefits that justify the profit orientation in the first place. (In a sense, the invisible hand no longer works to transform private vice into public virtue in this case, and so we are left merely with vice.)

In this respect, the market failures approach to business ethics is a version of what Bruce Langtry calls "tinged stockholder theory," which holds that "firms ought to be run to maximize the interests of stockholders, subject not only to legal constraints but also to moral or social obligations."[16] Indeed, it has been well understood for a long time that a shareholder-focused model with a set of deontic constraints (or "side constraints") on the set of permissible profit-maximizing strategies represents a plausible alternative to the stakeholder model. What distinguishes the market failures approach from other such proposals is the specific account of how these constraints should be derived. Rather than trying to derive them from general morality (as Langtry does by focusing on the "moral rights" of individuals affected by the firm, or as Goodpaster does even more explicitly through appeal to the "moral obligations owed by any member of society to others"), the market failures approach takes its guidance from the policy objectives that underlie the regulatory environment in which firms compete, and more generally, from the conditions that must be satisfied in order for the market economy as a whole to achieve efficiency in the production and allocation of goods and services. Furthermore, by focusing on the distinction between administered transactions and market transactions, it is able to offer a principled basis for the difference in structure between the intrafirm obligations owed to shareholders and the extrafirm obligations owed to other groups affected by the actions of the corporation.

When one adopts this market failures perspective, there is no reason to think that a conception of business ethics that continues to place primary emphasis upon the fiduciary responsibility toward shareholders cannot deal with the ethical obligations that have traditionally been described under the heading of "corporate social responsibility." What so often upsets people about corporate behavior—and what gives profit-seeking a bad name—is the exploitation of one or another form of market imperfection. People generally have no problem with companies that make money by providing good service, quality goods, low prices, and so forth. For example, if all companies fully internalized all costs, and charged consumers the full price that the production of their goods imposed upon society, I believe it would be impossible to make the case for any further "social responsibility" with respect to the environment. Thus the market failures approach to business ethics is able to retain the intuitively familiar idea that managers have fiduciary duties toward shareholders, and that the primary goal of corporations is to make a profit. Yet it is able to avoid the charge of moral laxity often leveled against the shareholder model of business ethics, because it imposes strict moral constraints on the range of permissible profit-maximization strategies.

There is a close analogy, from this perspective, between "corporate social responsibility" and the concept of "good sportsmanship" in competitive team sports. In the case of sports, the goal is clearly to win—but not by any means available. Every sport has an official set of rules, which constrain the set of admissible strategies. Yet it will generally be impossible to exclude strategies that respect the letter of the law, while nevertheless violating its spirit (e.g., taking performance-enhancing drugs that have other legitimate uses, and therefore have not been banned). "Good sportsmanship" consists in a willingness to refrain from exploiting these loopholes, while nevertheless retaining an adversarial orientation. In other words, the obligation is to be a team player and to compete fairly, but not necessarily to let the other side win. The fundamental problem with stakeholder theory is that it tries to eliminate the adversarialism of the managerial role, rather than merely imposing constraints upon it.

CONCLUSION

One of the charges that hostile critics frequently make against business ethicists is that they are implicitly, if not explicitly, anti-capitalist. Insofar as one equates business ethics with the stakeholder paradigm, there is more than a grain of truth in this accusation. Goodpaster was certainly not wrong to observe that the multi-fiduciary stakeholder theory "blurs traditional goals in terms of entrepreneurial risk-taking, pushes decision-making towards paralysis because of the dilemmas posed by divided loyalties and, in the final analysis, represents nothing less than the conversion of the modern private corporation into a public institution and probably calls for a corresponding restructuring of corporate governance (e.g., representatives of each stakeholder group on the board of directors)."[17] There is, of course, nothing wrong in principle with arguing for institutional reforms of this sort. But a theory that has this as its consequence is unlikely to provide much guidance when it comes to dealing with the ethical challenges that arise in the day-to-day operations of firms in an unreformed capitalist economy.

One of the central advantages of the market failures approach to business ethics is that, far from being antithetical to the spirit of capitalism, it can plausibly claim to be providing a more rigorous articulation of the central principles that structure the capitalist economy. If firms were to behave more ethically, according to this conception, the result would be an enhancement of the benefits that the market provides to society, and the elimination of many of its persistent weaknesses. It would help to perfect the private enterprise system, rather than destroy it.

Of course, none of this is intended to show that one *cannot* continue to talk about corporate social responsibility in terms of stakeholder interests. The question is simply whether this vocabulary encourages a more or less perspicuous articulation of the important moral issues. In this respect, it is important to remember that the term stakeholder was coined precisely in order to suggest an *analogy* between the relationship that managers have with shareholders and the relationship that they have with other interested parties. But as we have seen, the *moral* obligations that managers have toward these disparate groups are not analogous; in fact they are quite dissimilar. So while the term "stakeholder" may remain a useful piece of shop-talk in strategic management circles, as a piece of ethical vocabulary, for use in a theory that tries to articulate the central moral obligations of managers, it is inherently misleading. It creates considerable mischief in business ethics, while offering no real conceptual gain.

NOTES

1   John C. Maxwell, *There's No Such Thing as "Business" Ethics: There's Only One Rule for Making Decisions* (New York: First Warner, 2003).

2   Oliver Williamson, "Markets and Hierarchies: Some Elementary Considerations," *American Economic Review* Vol. 63 (1973): 316–25, at 318.

3   Marjorie Kelly, "Why All the Fuss about Stockholders?" reprinted in her *The Divine Right of Capital* (San Francisco: Berrett-Koehler, 2001).

4   *Pepper v. Litton* 308 US 295 (1939) at 311.

5   Arthur Isak Applbaum, *Ethics for Adversaries* (Princeton, NJ: Princeton University Press, 2000).

6   R. Edward Freeman, "A Stakeholder Theory of the Modern Corporation," in *The Corporation and Its Stakeholders*, ed. Max B.E. Clarkson (Toronto: University of Toronto Press, 1998), 126.

7   Freeman, "A Stakeholder Theory of the Modern Corporation," 129.

8   Kenneth Goodpaster, "Business Ethics and Stakeholder Analysis," *Business Ethics Quarterly* 1:1 (1991): 61–62.

9   The narrow definition is from Freeman, "A Stakeholder Theory of the Modern Corporation," 129; the wide is from Freeman, *Strategic Management*, 46.

10   Kelly, "Why All the Fuss About Stockholders?" Reprinted in her *The Divine Right of Capital* (San Francisco: Berrett-Koehler, 2001).

11   Clarkson, *The Corporation and Its Stakeholders*, 1.

12 John Boatright, "Fiduciary Duties and the Shareholder Managements Relation: or, What's So Special about Shareholders?" *Business Ethics Quarterly* Vol. 4 (1994): 393–407, at 402.

13 Donaldson and Preston, "The Stakeholder Theory of the Corporation," 76.

14 Ronald Coase, "The Nature of the Firm," *Economica* Vol. 4 (1937): 386–405, at 389. See also Williamson, "Markets and Hierarchies," 316.

15 Allen Buchanan, "Toward a Theory of the Ethics of Bureaucratic Organizations," *Business Ethics Quarterly* Vol. 6 (1996): 419–40.

16 Bruce Langtry, "Stakeholders and the Moral Responsibility of Business," *Business Ethics Quarterly* Vol. 4 (1994): 434–35.

17 Goodpaster, "Business Ethics and Stakeholder Analysis," 66.

—15—

BAD MANAGEMENT THEORIES ARE DESTROYING GOOD MANAGEMENT PRACTICES

Sumantra Ghoshal

THE CORPORATE SCANDALS IN THE UNITED States have stimulated a frenzy of activities in business schools around the world. Deans are extolling how much their curricula focus on business ethics. New courses are being developed on corporate social responsibility. Old, highly laudatory cases on Enron and Tyco are being hurriedly rewritten. "What more must we do?" the faculty are asking themselves in grave seminars and over lunch tables.

Business schools do not need to do a great deal more to help prevent future Enrons; they need only to stop doing a lot they currently do. They do not need to create new courses; they need to simply stop teaching some old ones. But, before doing any of this, we—as business school faculty—need to own up to our own role in creating Enrons. Our theories and ideas have done much to strengthen the management practices that we are all now so loudly condemning.

"The ideas of economists and political philosophers, both when they are right and when they are wrong, are more powerful than is commonly understood," wrote John Maynard Keynes (1953: 306). "Indeed the world is run by little else. Practical men, who believe themselves to be quite exempt from any intellectual influences are usually the slaves of some defunct economist.... It is ideas, not vested interests, which are dangerous for good or evil" Keynes (1953: 306).

This is precisely what has happened to management. Obsessed as they are with the "real world" and skeptical as most of them are of all theories, managers are no exception to the intellectual slavery of the "practical men" to which Keynes referred. Many of the worst excesses of recent management practices have their roots in a set of ideas that have emerged from business school academics over the last 30 years.

In courses on corporate governance grounded in agency theory (Jensen & Meckling, 1976) we have taught our students that managers cannot be trusted to do their jobs—which, of course, is to maximize shareholder value—and that to overcome "agency problems," managers' interests and incentives must be aligned with those of the shareholders by, for example, making stock options a significant part of their pay. In courses on organization design, grounded in transaction cost economics, we have preached the need for tight monitoring and control of people to prevent "opportunistic behavior" (Williamson, 1975). In strategy courses, we have presented the "five forces" framework (Porter, 1980) to suggest that companies must compete not only with their competitors but also with their suppliers, customers, employees, and regulators.

MBA students are not alone in having learned, for decades, these theories of management. Thousands—indeed, hundreds of thousands—of executives who attended business courses have learned the same lessons, although the actual theories were often not presented to them quite so directly. Even those who never attended a business school have learned to think in these ways because these theories have been in the air, legitimizing some actions and behaviors of managers, delegitimizing others, and generally shaping the intellectual and normative order within which all day-to-day decisions were made.

Why then do we feel surprised by the fact that executives in Enron, Global Crossing, Tyco, and scores of other companies granted themselves excessive stock options, treated their employees very badly, and took their customers for a ride when they could? Besides, the criminal misconduct of managers in a few companies is really not the critical issue. Of far greater concern is the general delegitimization of companies as institutions and of management as a profession caused, at least in part, by the adoption of these ideas as taken-for-granted elements of management practice....

I raise a very different concern: I argue that academic research related to the conduct of business and management has had some very significant and negative influences on the practice of management. These influences have been less at the level of adoption of a particular theory and more at the incorporation, within the worldview of managers, of a set of ideas and assumptions that have come to dominate much of management research. More specifically, I suggest that by propagating ideologically inspired amoral theories, business schools have actively freed their students from any sense of moral responsibility.

THE PRETENSE OF KNOWLEDGE

Our primary endeavor as business school academics over the last half century has been to make business studies a branch of the social sciences. Rejecting what we saw as the "romanticism" of analyzing corporate behaviors in terms of the choices, actions, and achievements of individuals, we have adopted the "scientific" approach of trying to discover patterns and laws, and have replaced all notions of human intentionality with a firm belief in causal determinism for explaining all aspects of corporate performance. In effect, we have professed that business is reducible to a kind of physics in which even if individual managers do play a role, it can safely be taken as determined by the economic, social, and psychological laws that inevitably shape peoples' actions. Legitimized by a set of influential reports and supported by significant investments by, among others, the Ford Foundation (about $250 million, in 2003 dollars), these beliefs have become dominant in business schools in the United States and around the world.

Adoption of scientific methods has undoubtedly yielded some significant benefits for both our research and our pedagogy, but the costs too have been high. Unfortunately, as philosophy of science makes clear, it is an error to pretend that the methods of the physical sciences can be indiscriminately applied to business studies because such a pretension ignores some fundamental differences that exist between the different academic disciplines.

... As Elster (1983) argued, from the perspective of philosophy of science, one must first distinguish between the natural sciences and the humanities. Within the natural sciences, there is a need to distinguish the study of inorganic nature, such as physics, and the study of organic nature, such as biology. Within the humanities, similarly, a distinction needs to be made between the social sciences, such as economics and psychology, and aesthetic disciplines, such as art. Eschewing for the moment the arguments of those who would classify management as a practicing art, let us accept the more common view and consider management-related theories as part of the social sciences.

His interests limited to the academic concerns of scholarship, Elster argued that the fundamental difference between these different fields lies neither in the method of inquiry nor in the interests they serve; it lies instead in the mode of explanation and theorizing that is appropriate for each. Categorizing such modes as causal, functional, and intentional, Elster demonstrated why for the sciences of inorganic matter, such as physics, the only acceptable mode of explanation is the causal mode. Functional explanations, based on notions such as benefits, evolution, or progress have no role in physics, nor is there any room for intentional or teleological explanations, such as those based on some notion of actor imagination or will.

Functional explanations, however, play an important role in the sciences of organic matter, such as biology. All one has to do to explain a particular feature of an organism, or some aspect of its behavior, is to demonstrate that the feature or behavior enhances its reproductive fitness. The reason such functional explanations are adequate, however, lies in the availability of an overarching causal theory: that of natural selection. There is no role of intentionality within biology because the process of evolution is driven by random error or mutation, over which the sources of variation or the units of selection have no influence.

The basic building block in the social sciences, the elementary unit of explanation, is individual action guided by some intention. In the presence of such intentionality, functional theories are suspect, except under some special and relatively rare circumstances, because there is no general law in the social sciences comparable to the law of natural selection in biology. As Elster explained, intentional adaptation differs from functional adaptation

in that the former can be directed to the distant future, whereas the latter is typically myopic and opportunistic. Intentional beings can employ such strategies as "one step backward, two steps forward," which are realized only by accident in biological evolution (1983: 36).

There is, of course, a role for causal theories in the social sciences, but it is a relatively limited one, suitable, for example, for the analysis of phenomena involving the interplay among a very large number of diverse actors (e.g., capital markets), where the intentions of individual actors can be ignored (similar to the analytical underpinnings of statistical quantum mechanics that does not intend to explain the outcomes for individual particles but makes statistical estimates of aggregate outcomes). However, for a vast range of issues relevant to the study of management, such conditions are not attained. For these issues, human intentions matter. And, intentions are mental states; so to say that a particular action of an individual was caused by a particular intention is not a causal explanation. To quote Elster, "using causal explanation, we can talk about all there is, including mental phenomena, but we shall not be able to single out mental phenomena from what else there is" (1983).

Management theories at present are overwhelmingly causal or functional in their modes of explanation. Ethics, or morality, however, are mental phenomena. As a result, they have had to be excluded from our theory, and from the practices that such theories have shaped. In other words, a precondition for making business studies a science as well as a consequence of the resulting belief in determinism has been the explicit denial of any role of moral or ethical considerations in the practice of management. No one has voiced this denial more strongly than Milton Friedman: "Few trends could so thoroughly undermine the very foundations of our free society as the acceptance by corporate officials of a social responsibility other than to make as much money for their stockholders as possible" (2002: 133).

To both the managers and the management academics who profess these beliefs, I refer the words of Isaiah Berlin: "One may argue about the degree of difference that the influence of this or that individual made in shaping events. But to try to reduce the behaviours of individuals to that of impersonal social forces not further analyzable into the conduct of men who ... make history ... is a form of false consciousness of bureaucrats and administrators who close their eyes to all that proves incapable of quantification, and thereby perpetrate absurdities in theory and dehumanisation in practice" (2002: 26)....

When managers, including CEOs, justify their actions by pleading powerlessness in the face of external forces, it is to the dehumanization of practice that they resort. When they claim that competition or capital markets are relentless in their demands, and that individual companies and managers have no scope for choices, it is on the strength of the false premise of determinism that they free themselves from any sense of moral or ethical responsibility for their actions.

It is not only morality, however, that has been a victim of this endeavor of business academics to make management a science; common sense, too, has suffered a toll. It is to this cost of losing the wisdom of common sense that Donald Campbell (1988) referred when he provided numerous examples of how the application of social theories had led to poor public policy decisions in the United States. As he wrote, referring to the application of scientific methods for the assessment of public programs, "if we present our resulting improved truth-claims as though they were definitive achievements comparable to those in the physical sciences, and thus deserving to override ordinary wisdom when they disagree, we can be socially destructive."

Friedrich von Hayek dedicated his entire Nobel Memorial Lecture to the danger posed by scientific pretensions in the analysis of social phenomena. Speaking as an economist and acknowledging that "as a profession we have made a mess of things," he placed the blame on "the pretense of knowledge," which is how he titled his talk (1989: 3–7). "It seems to me that this failure of economists to guide public policy more successfully is clearly connected with their propensity to imitate as closely as possible the procedures of the brilliantly successful physical sciences," said Hayek. Because of the very nature of social phenomena, which Hayek described as "phenomena of organized complexity," the application of scientific methods to such phenomena "are often the most unscientific, and, beyond this, in these fields there are definite limits to what we can expect science to achieve."

As an example of how this pretense of science affects management practice, consider the dictum of Milton Friedman that few managers today can publicly question, that their job is to maximize shareholder value. Where did the enormous certainty that this assertion seems to carry come from?

After all, we know that shareholders do not own the company—not in the sense that they own their homes or their cars. They merely own a right to the residual cash flows of the company, which is not at all the same thing as owning the company. They have no ownership rights on the actual assets or businesses of the company, which are owned by the company itself, as a "legal person." Indeed, it is this fundamental separation between ownership of stocks and ownership of the assets, resources, and the associated liabilities of a company that distinguishes public corporations from proprietorships or partnerships. The notion of actual ownership of the company is simply not compatible with the responsibility avoidance of "limited liability."

We also know that the value a company creates is produced through a combination of resources contributed by different constituencies: Employees, including managers, contribute their human capital, for example, while shareholders contribute financial capital. If the value creation is achieved by combining the resources of both employees and shareholders, why should the value distribution favor only the latter? Why must the mainstream of our theory be premised on maximizing the returns to just one of these various contributors?

The answer—the only answer that is really valid—is that this assumption helps in structuring and solving nice mathematical models. Casting shareholders in the role of "principals" who are equivalent to owners or proprietors, and managers as "agents" who are self-centered and are only interested in using company resources to their own advantage is justified simply because, with this assumption, the elegant mathematics of principal–agent models can be applied to the enormously complex economic, social, and moral issues related to the governance of giant public corporations that have such enormous influence on the lives of thousands—often millions—of people.

But then, to make the model yield a solution, some more assumptions have to be made. So, the theory assumes that labor markets are perfectly efficient—in other words, the wages of every employee fully represent the value of his or her contributions to the company and, if they didn't, the employee could immediately and costlessly move to another job. With this assumption, the shareholders can be assumed as carrying the greater risk, thus making their contribution of capital more important than the contribution of human capital provided by managers and other employees and, therefore, it is their returns that must be maximized (Jensen & Meckling, 1976).

The truth is, of course, exactly the opposite. Most shareholders can sell their stocks far more easily than most employees can find another job. In every substantive sense, employees of a company carry more risks than do the shareholders. Also, their contributions of knowledge, skills, and entrepreneurship are typically more important than the contributions of capital by shareholders, a pure commodity that is perhaps in excess supply. As Grossman and Hart (1986) showed, once we admit incomplete contracts, residual rights of control are optimally held by the party whose investments matter more in terms of creating value. If these truths are acknowledged, there can be no basis for asserting the principle of shareholder value maximization. There just aren't any supporting arguments.

Once again, Milton Friedman (1953) has provided a compelling counterargument: Don't worry if the assumptions of our theories do not reflect reality; what matters is that these theories can accurately predict the outcomes. The theories are valid because of their explanatory and predictive power, irrespective of how absurd the assumptions may look from the perspective of common sense.

What is interesting is that agency theory, which underlies the entire intellectual edifice in support of shareholder value maximization, has little explanatory or predictive power. Its solution to the agency model yields some relatively straightforward prescriptions: Expand the number and influence of independent directors on corporate boards so that they can effectively police management; split the roles of the chairman of the board and the chief executive officer so as to reduce the power of the latter; create markets for corporate control, that is, for hostile takeovers, so that raiders can get rid of wasteful managers; and pay managers in stock options to ensure that they relentlessly pursue the interests of the shareholders. The facts are that none of these factors have the predicted effects on corporate performance.

A review of 54 studies on the performance effects of board composition shows that the proportion of independent directors on the board has no significant effect on corporate performance. A similar review of 31 studies on the effects of separating leadership roles demonstrates that whether the same or different individuals occupy the positions of chairman and CEO does not affect corporate performance in any way. These studies cover companies based in different countries, and the conclusions are valid irrespective of whether performance is assessed in terms of market value of the company or accounting measures, such as return on capital employed (Dalton, Daily, Ellstrand, & Johnson, 1998)....

Unrealistic assumptions and invalid prescriptions—yet, the theory and the dictum it leads to remain absolute. As Margaret Blair (1995) has shown, it is this theory, amplified by the power of institutional investors and their political and academic supporters, that influenced both regulatory changes and court decisions in the United States, ultimately yielding to the argument a level of legitimacy and certainty that few managers or academics now dare question. At the same time, as Thomas Kochan has observed, the root cause of the recent corporate scandals in the United States lies in this "over-emphasis American corporations have been forced to give in recent years to maximizing shareholder value without regard for the effects of their actions on other stakeholders" (2002: 139).

What is most curious is that despite the lack of both face validity and empirical support, agency theory continues to dominate academic research on corporate governance. At the same time, despite the aberrations that have occurred in companies that fully conformed to the prescriptions of this theory—such as in Enron that had loaded its board with many (80%) high-profile independent directors who chaired most key committees, separated the chairman and chief executive roles, granted generous stock options to its senior managers, and operated in the economy with the most advanced market for corporate control—all regulatory reviews of corporate governance, such as by the SEC in the United States, by Derek Higgs in the United Kingdom, and by the Narayanamurthy Committee in India, are relying even more strongly on rigorous implementation of the same discredited prescriptions!

Why do we not fundamentally rethink the corporate governance issue? Why don't we actually acknowledge in our theories that companies survive and prosper when they simultaneously pay attention to the interests of customers, employees, shareholders, and perhaps even the communities in which they operate? Such a perspective is available, in stewardship theory for example (Davis, Schoorman, & Donaldson, 1997); why then do we so overwhelmingly adopt the agency model in our research on corporate governance, ignoring this much more sensible proposition?

The honest answer is because such a perspective cannot be elegantly modeled—the math does not exist. Such a theory would not readily yield sharp, testable propositions, nor would it provide simple, reductionist prescriptions. With such a premise, the pretense of knowledge could not be protected. Business could not be treated as a science, and we would have to fall back on the wisdom of common sense that combines information on "what is" with the imagination of "what ought to be" to develop both a practical understanding of and some pragmatic prescriptions for "phenomena of organized complexity" that the issue of corporate governance represents.

IDEOLOGY-BASED GLOOMY VISION

Currently influential theories of business and management span diverse academic disciplines including psychology, sociology, and, of course—preeminent of all—economics. Collectively, however, they have increasingly converged on a pessimistic view of human nature, on the role of companies in society, and of the processes of corporate adaptation and change. These negative assumptions are manifest in the strong form of determinism in both ecological and institutional analysis of organizations; in the denial of the possibility of purposeful and goal-directed adaptation in behavioral theories of the firm; in the focus on value appropriation rather than value creation in most theories of strategy; and in the assumptions about shirking, opportunism, and inertia in economic analysis of companies.

In his article "The Search for Paradigms as a Hindrance to Understanding," Albert Hirschman (1970) has traced the source of this pessimism to what he calls a "paradigm-based gloomy vision" that, as the title of his article suggests, he views as a critical barrier to developing effective understanding of complex social phenomena. Based essentially on an ideology, this gloomy vision is deeply embedded within the theories as starting assumptions—which, therefore, are exempt from the need for conforming either to common sense or to empirical evidence—and it is these pessimistic assumptions which have, through the self-fulfilling process we have described, curbed managers' ability to play out a more positive role in society.

Consider, for example, the assumptions regarding human nature. As Herbert Simon observed, "Nothing is more fundamental in setting our research agenda and informing our research methods than our view of the nature of human beings whose behaviours we are studying.... It makes a difference to research, but it also makes a difference for the proper design of ... institutions" (1985: 293).

Mainstream economics has, in the main, always worked on the assumption of *Homo Economicus*—a model of people as rational self-interest maximizers. Although recently, primarily in the field of behavioral economics, attention has been paid to systematic deviations from rationality in human behavior, such attention has largely been limited to "foolishness" and not to any aspect of other than-self-interested preferences of individuals.

Even practitioners of sociology and psychology, the starting points of which as academic fields were defined by the recognition that human behavior can be shaped by factors other than conscious, rational self-interest, have increasingly adopted the notion of behavior as being self-seeking as their foundational assumption. Friendship ties of people are now analyzed by sociologists as means for individuals to use social networks to enhance their personal influence, power, or pay. And social psychologists increasingly resort to the same assumption about human nature when studying how people interact with others.

Common sense has, of course, always recognized that human behavior can be influenced by other motives. Increasingly, empirical evidence provides overwhelming support to what common sense suggests. It is not only in behaviors such as mothers taking care of their children, people leaving a tip after a meal in restaurants they are unlikely to visit again, or Peace Corps volunteers toiling amid the depravations of impoverished countries that the limitations of the self-interest model become clear—they become manifest even in careful experiments devised by economists to test their theories under controlled conditions in which "aberrations," such as altruism or love are strictly excluded.

Consider, for example, the "ultimatum game" in which one player, designated as the proposer, is given the opportunity to propose a division of a certain sum—a gift—between herself and another player, designated as the responder. If the responder accepts the proposal, the sum is divided as proposed. If he rejects the proposal, neither player receives anything. In any variant of the self-interest-based model of human behavior, the proposer ought to offer only a token sum to the responder, keeping the bulk of the amount for herself, and the responder ought to accept the proposal, since even a token sum is more than nothing, which is the only alternative available to him.

Much to the dismay of all ardent supporters of the *Homo Economicus* model, including those who have proposed some relatively more sophisticated versions of the model, this outcome almost never materializes in experiments. Token offers are rarely made, and even more rarely accepted. Often proposers offer a 60:40 division, taking advantage of their position as first mover, but not exploiting that advantage fully because of their concerns for the responder. Most frequently, however, they propose a 50:50 split, out of a notion of fairness, which suggests that windfalls, that is, gains not merited through contributions but by chance, should be distributed equally among those involved in the event....

If both common sense and empirical evidence suggest the contrary, why does the pessimistic model of people as purely self-interested beings still so dominate management-related theories? The answer lies not in evidence but in ideology. Theories of social phenomena are, and have to be, ideologically motivated. Despite the pretense to be values-free, no social theory can be values-free. And, while no social science discipline makes a stronger claim to objectivity than economics, no domain of the social sciences is more values-laden in both its assumptions and its language than economics and all its derivatives, including much of modern finance and management theories. As Robert Nelson (2001) has observed, "[t]he closest predecessors for the current members of the economics profession are not scientists such as Albert Einstein or Issac Newton; rather, we economists are more truly the heirs of Thomas Acquinas and Martin Luther."

But what is the connection between ideology and pessimism? Why is the ideology pessimistic? Again, Milton Friedman (2002) has provided the most honest and direct answer. He labeled the ideology as "liberalism," cautioning at the same time, however, that his use of the term referred not to its corrupted association with concepts such as social welfare or equality, but to its earlier emphasis on "freedom as the ultimate goal and the individual as the ultimate entity in the society." He also recognized that the ideology was more commonly referred to as "conservatism," but he preferred "liberalism" because it sounded more "radical" (p. 6).

At the heart of this ideology lies two convictions. First, in Friedman's words, "a major aim of the liberal is to leave the ethical problem for the individual to wrestle with." In other words, it can and, indeed, must be excluded from social theory. The way to do so is to base all theories on the assumption of homogeneous human behavior based on self-interest. And, second, "the liberal conceives of men as imperfect beings ... and regards the problem of social organization to be as much a negative problem of preventing bad people from doing harm as of enabling good people to do good ..." (p. 12). And, given that much of social science until then had focused on the second part of the problem, the agenda of social scientists thereon, that is, for the last 40 years, has focused on the first part, that is, the "negative problem." Hence the pessimism, the ideology-based gloomy vision....

The roots of the ideology lie in the philosophy of radical individualism articulated, among others, by Hume, Bentham, and Locke (Berlin, 2002). While the philosophy has influenced the work of many scholars in many different institutions, its influence on management research has been largely mediated by the University of Chicago. It is in and through this institution that "liberalism," as Friedman called it, has penetrated economics, law, sociology, social psychology and most other core disciplines, yielding theories such as agency theory, transaction cost economics, game theory, social network analysis, theories of social dilemmas, and

so on, that we now routinely draw on both, radical individualism and Friedman's liberalism, to frame our research and to guide our teaching....

Combine ideology-based gloomy vision with the process of self-fulfilling prophecy and it is easy to see how theories can induce some of the management behaviors and their associated problems we have witnessed. Consider, for example, the case of transaction cost economics to which I referred at the beginning of this article. Oliver Williamson (1975), the most ardent champion of this theory, started from the Friedman position: Some people are opportunistic—not just self-interested, but worse. They make promises knowing full well that, should the benefits from breaking them exceed the costs, they would do so in an instant. They lie and cheat. While most people may not be like that, some are, and it is not possible to separate, ex-ante, those who are from those who are not. The "negative problem" this theory then focuses on is how organizations need to be managed so as to prevent these "bad" people from doing harm to others.

What follows from the theory is quite straightforward. The manager's task is to use hierarchical authority to prevent the opportunists from benefiting at the cost of others. To ensure effective coordination, managers must know what everyone ought to be doing, give them strict instructions to do those things, and use their ability to monitor and control and to reward and punish to ensure that everyone does what he or she is told to do. This is the exercise of "fiat."

What is the outcome of such a management approach? It is likely to be—and there is significant evidence that it indeed is—exactly the opposite of what Williamson's theory predicts: Instead of controlling and reducing opportunistic behavior of people, it is likely to actually create and enhance such behaviors (Ghoshal & Moran, 1996).

For managers, the net consequence of adopting Williamson's advice is what Strickland (1958) has described as "the dilemma of the supervisor": The situation when the use of surveillance, monitoring, and authority leads to management's distrust of employees and perception of an increased need for more surveillance and control. Because all behavior is seen by managers as motivated by the controls in place, they develop a jaundiced view of their people.

For the employees, the use of hierarchical controls signals that they are neither trusted nor trustworthy to behave appropriately without such controls. Surveillance that is perceived as controlling threatens peoples' personal sense of autonomy and decreases their intrinsic motivation. It damages their self-perception. One of the likely consequences of eroding attitudes is a shift from consummate and voluntary cooperation to perfunctory compliance.

The outcome of these negative feelings of both managers and employees is a pathological spiraling relationship, which has been described by psychologists Michael Enzle and Samuel Anderson (1993) as follows:

> Surveillants come to distrust their targets as a result of their own surveillance and targets in fact become unmotivated and untrustworthy. The target is now demonstrably untrustworthy and requires more intensive surveillance, and the increased surveillance further damages the target. Trust and trustworthiness both deteriorate.

Combine agency theory with transaction costs economics, add in standard versions of game theory and negotiation analysis, and the picture of the manager that emerges is one that is now very familiar in practice: the ruthlessly hard-driving, strictly top-down, command-and-control focused, shareholder-value-obsessed, win-at-any-cost business leader of which Scott Paper's "Chainsaw" Al Dunlap and Tyco's Dennis Kozlowski are only the most extreme examples. This is what Isaiah Berlin implied when he wrote about absurdities in theory leading to dehumanization of practice.

"As there is a degree of depravity in mankind which requires a certain degree of circumspection and distrust, so there are other qualities in human nature which justify a certain portion of esteem and confidence," wrote James Madison in the Federalist Papers (No. 55). What would happen if we acknowledged this complexity of human nature in our theories, this combination of good and evil, instead of focusing only on Friedman's "negative problem"? What would happen if we acknowledged the existence of other and process-regarding preferences, together with the self-regarding ones, in our assumptions about human nature? It would vastly change our theory.

The good news is that the endeavor appears to have already commenced. In the field of psychology, Martin Seligman—in his capacity as the president of the American Psychological Association in 1998—sponsored a new initiative that he referred to as positive psychology. Seligman argued that since World War II, research in psychology had been grounded in what he described as "a disease model of human nature." Human beings were seen as "flawed and fragile, casualties of cruel environments or bad genetics, and if not in denial then at best in recovery." Indeed, for psychologists, anything positive about people—hope, optimism, altruism, courage, joy, and fulfillment—had become suspect. While this focus on pathologies had produced important progress in understanding, treating, and preventing psychological discords, Seligman argued that the progress had come at some significant costs. It neglected human strengths and ignored what could go right with people (Peterson & Seligman, 2003).

Positive psychology, as framed by Seligman and his associates, proposes that it is time to correct this imbalance and to challenge the pervasive assumptions of the disease model. "Positive psychology calls for as much focus on strength as on weakness, as much interest in building the best things in life as in repairing the worst, and as much attention to fulfilling the lives of healthy people as to healing the wounds of the distressed."

In the field of economics, too, such an endeavor appears to be in progress as evidenced, for example, by the Conference on Economics, Values and Organization that took place at Yale University in April, 1996. The collected volume of conference papers, together with a foreword by Amartya Sen and an epilogue by Douglass North, explores "the two-way interaction between economic arrangements or institutions and preferences, including those regarding social status, the well-being of others, and ethical principles" (Ben-Ner & Putterman, 1998). As the volume editors argue, the time has arrived "when the questions of values and institutions can begin to be attacked using available and emerging analytical tools, without loss of rigour, but with much gain in relevance and generality." ...

But these are, as yet, the nascent efforts of a few. The mainstream of management theory is still dominated by the gloomy vision—indeed, if anything, the dominance is becoming stronger as the intellectual influence of the "Chicago agenda" is spreading to all the main areas of business school research. The positive perspective will not progress unless many scholars, including younger scholars, redirect their work, at considerable risk to their careers. For them to take such risks, much has to be done by many so as to reverse the overall trend of the last 50 years.

REVERSING THE TREND

Kurt Lewin argued that "nothing is as practical as a good theory" (1945: 129). The obverse is also true: Nothing is as dangerous as a bad theory. I have so far developed the proposition that bad management theories are, at present, destroying good management practices. I have traced the source of the "badness" to two trends that have powerfully influenced the nature of business school-based research over several decades. On the one hand, what Clegg and Ross-Smith (2003) have described as "the hubris of physics envy" has led us to increasingly adopt a narrow version of positivism together with relatively unsophisticated scientific methods to develop causal and testable theories. On the other hand, the growing dominance of a particular ideology has focused us on solving the "negative problem" of containing the costs of human imperfections. These two features of our

research, combined with the process of double hermeneutic, have led to our pessimism becoming a self-fulfilling prophecy.

I must emphasize, however, that by this analysis I do not at all intend to imply either that we should abandon the effort to develop systematic theory in the field of management or that we should not study some of the more distasteful aspects of individual and organizational behavior. My distinction between good and bad theory must not be taken to mean that the normative implications of a theory stand in isolation of its positive merits. A theory must illuminate and explain and, if it cannot do those things, it is not a theory—neither good nor bad. Wishes and hopes are not theory. Sermons and preaching are not theory either.

But the trouble with the social sciences is that the logic of falsification, which is so very essential for the epistemology of positivism, is very hard to apply with any degree of rigor and ruthlessness in the domain of social theories. Typically, no theory—which are all, by definition, partial—explains a "phenomenon of organized complexity" fully, and many different and mutually inconsistent theories explain the same phenomenon, often to very similar extents. As a result, nothing can be weeded out nor, given the very different framings, can anything be combined with anything else, except in a very synthetic and ad hoc manner.

The choice among theories, then, falls very much on a scholar's personal preferences rather than on either the discipline of empirical estimation or the rigor of formal, deductive logic. Combined with the possibility of self-fulfilling prophecy, it is this ambiguity that, in the social sciences, gives life to the distinction between good and bad theories.

Excessive truth-claims based on extreme assumptions and partial analysis of complex phenomena can be bad even when they are not altogether wrong. In essence, social scientists carry an even greater social and moral responsibility than those who work in the physical sciences because, if they hide ideology in the pretense of science, they can cause much more harm.

My contention here is that this is precisely what business school academics have done over the last 30 years.

Similarly, the criticism of negative assumptions does not in any way relate to what theorists choose to study or the conclusions they arrive at; I am not suggesting that business school academics should restrict themselves in any way from the spirit of free enquiry. My concern relates only to the practice of considering the premises as basic assumptions—often not even explicitly stated—instead of treating them as testable propositions. By treating them as assumptions, theorists exempt their own ideological biases from the need for either theoretical justification or empirical validation, and yet the same assumptions, through the self-fulfilling process of the double hermeneutic, influence the social and moral behaviors of people.

The ultimate goal must be to go from the pretense to the substance of knowledge. Physicists continue to seek a unifying grand theory that would combine both the particle and the wave nature of light. We too must seek the same with regard to the different and contradictory facets of human nature and organizational behavior. But, just as such a grand unification has eluded physics so far, so it is likely to elude us for a long time. In the meantime, just as physics has continued to make progress by independently investigating both the characters of light, so too must we make progress on both the negative and the positive problems described by Friedman. My contention is that the pretense of knowledge has led us to increasingly focus on only the negative problem as a result of which we have made little analytical progress in the last 30 years on the positive problem, at considerable cost to our students, to companies, and to society. I also suggest that to address the positive problem, we need to temper the pretense of knowledge and reengage with the scholarships of integration, application, and pedagogy to build management theories that are broader and richer than the reductionist and partial theories we have been developing over the last 30 years.

REFERENCES

Ben-Ner, A., & Putterman, L. (Eds.). 1998. *Economics, values, and organization: 7.*

Berlin, I. 2002. *Liberty: 26.* (Henry Hardy, Ed.). Oxford, England: Oxford University Press.

Blair, M. 1995. *Ownership and control.* Washington, DC: The Brookings Institution.

Boyer, E.L. 1990. *Scholarship reconsidered: Priorities of the professoriate.* Princeton, NJ: The Carnegie Foundation for the Advancement of Teaching.

Campbell, D.T. 1988. Can we be scientific in applied social science? In D.T. Campbell, *Methodology and epistemology for social science: Selected papers:* 315–333. [Originally published in *Evaluation Studies Review Annual* (1984): 26–48.] Chicago, IL: University of Chicago Press.

Clegg, S.R., & Ross-Smith, A. 2003. Revising the boundaries: Management education and learning in a postpositivist world. *Academy of Management Learning & Education,* 2(1): 85–98.

Dalton, D.R., Daily, C.M., Ellstrand, A.E., & Johnson, J.L. 1998. Meta-analytic reviews of board composition, leadership structure, and financial performance. *Strategic Management Journal,* 19: 269–290.

Davis, J.H., Schoorman, F.D., & Donaldson, L. 1997. Toward a stewardship theory of management. *Academy of Management Review,* 22: 20–47.

Elster, J. 1983. *Explaining technical change.* Cambridge, England: Cambridge University Press.

Enzle, M.E., & Anderson, S.C. 1993. Surveillant intentions and intrinsic motivation. *Journal of Personality and Social Psychology,* 64: 257–266.

Friedman, M. 1953. *Essays in positive economics.* Chicago: University of Chicago Press.

Friedman, M. 2002. *Capitalism and freedom* (40th Anniversary Edition). Chicago: The University of Chicago Press.

Ghoshal, S., & Moran, P. 1996. Bad for practice: A critique of the transaction cost theory. *Academy of Management Review,* 21(1): 13–47.

Grossman, S., & Hart, O. 1986. The costs of benefits of ownership: A theory of lateral and vertical integration. *Journal of Political Economy,* 94: 691–719.

Hayek, F.A. Von. 1989. The pretence of knowledge (Nobel Lecture). *American Economic Review*, December: 3–7.

Hirschman, A.O. 1970. The search for paradigms as a hindrance to understanding. *World Politics*, March.

Jensen, M., & Meckling, W. 1976. Theory of the firm: Managerial behaviour, agency costs and ownership structure. *Journal of Financial Economics*, 3: 305–360.

Keynes, J.M. 1953. *The general theory of employment, interest and money*. New York: Harcourt Brace Jovanovich.

Kochan, T.A. 2002. Addressing the crisis in confidence in corporations: Root causes, victims and strategies for reform. *Academy of Management Executive*, 16: 139–141.

Lewin, K. 1945. The research centre for group dynamics at Massachusetts Institute of Technology. *Sociometry*, 8: 126–135.

Nelson, R.H. 2001. *Economics as religion*. PA: The Pennsylvania State University.

Peterson, C.M., & Seligman, M.E.P. 2003. Positive Organizational Studies: Lessons from positive psychology. In K.S. Cameron, J.E. Dutton, & R.E. Quinn (Eds.). *Positive organizational scholarship*. San Francisco, CA: Berrett-Koehler.

Porter, M.E. 1980. *Competitive strategy: Techniques for analyzing industries and firms*. New York: Free Press.

Simon, H. 1985. Human nature in politics: The dialogue of psychology with political science. *American Political Science Review*, 79: 293–304.

Strickland, L.H. 1958. Surveillance and trust. *Journal of Personality*, 26: 200–215.

Williamson, O.E. 1975. *Markets and hierarchies: Analysis and antitrust implications*. New York: Free Press.

—16—

CASE STUDY

ACTIONS SPEAK LOUDER THAN WORDS

Rebuilding Malden Mills

David Meeler and Srivatsa Seshadri

BACKGROUND

FOUNDED IN 1906, MALDEN MILLS IS A PRIVATELY held textile mill located in Massachusetts. Like many other textile mills in the US, late in the twentieth century Malden Mills faced financial difficulty and eventually declared bankruptcy. If this were an average story of a bankrupt textile manufacturer in New England, Malden Mills would have folded long ago. But the owner, Aaron Feuerstein, spent millions of research dollars to develop entirely new fabrics, and re-opened the old mill right there in Massachusetts. By world-salary standards, this was an expensive move. The revolutionary new fabrics were Polartec® and Polarfleece®.

Polartec® and Polarfleece® are highly versatile and technical fabrics that hold little moisture, provide excellent insulation, offer low weight, etc. These fabrics are currently used by outdoor enthusiasts, extreme athletes, and various US Special Forces teams. Developing such a high-tech fabric might make you think that Malden Mills heavily emphasizes advanced research and development in their profit-making strategy. When speaking at MIT's Industrial Development lecture series in 1997, Feuerstein said,

You can have the best engineers, the best R&D guy, the best technical expert, figure out how to get better quality. But in the last analysis, it's the man on the floor who is going to get that quality for you. If he feels he's part of the enterprise and he feels he is treated the way he should be treated, he will go the extra mile to provide that quality.

In short, Aaron Feuerstein is committed to the idea that Malden's workers—white collar and blue collar alike—are the strongest asset the mill can have. A quick survey of any Fortune 500 company will reveal a publicly stated commitment to the value of their workers. For example, General Motors (whose devastating plant closing in Flint, MI was the subject of the film *Roger & Me*) states, "We are committed to developing and deploying employee skills, talent and potential effectively, improving the diversity of our workforce, influencing and shaping our performance to drive business outcomes and giving employees unmatched career opportunities. We see a clear link between our investment in human performance and our market performance and financial results." While many companies develop grandiose statements expressing a commitment to their employees, the fundamental difference between Malden Mills and other corporations, according to Feuerstein, "is that I consider our workers an asset, not an expense." Malden Mills demonstrates its appreciation of workers with actions, not mere words.

Developing new materials and re-opening the mill in an area requiring some of the highest wages in the world is not the only commitment Malden Mills made to its employees and communities. In 1995, a fire broke out at Malden Mills. The largest fire in Massachusetts for over 100 years destroyed three of Malden's 10 large buildings, ruining Polartec's® dyeing and finishing operations. A perfect opportunity, many would say, to relocate operations overseas and take advantage of lower wages and more liberal environmental regulations. Not so for Aaron Feuerstein. By the day after the fire, Feuerstein had announced that he would immediately rebuild the plant in Massachusetts, and keep employees on full salary for three months.

Employees at Malden Mills repaid this loyalty by going those extra miles. One building crucial to Polartec® was saved from the fire in part due to the efforts of 36 employees who helped fight the fire into the night. Afterwards, make-shift operations were put in place to compensate for the production capacity lost in the fire. Feuerstein was focused not only on his employees' welfare; he was also concerned with the communities where his facilities are located, and the environmental impact his company has on the world. The new Polartec® plant was the first textile mill built in Massachusetts in over a century. In rebuilding, Feuerstein constructed the plant as a high-tech and environmentally conscious facility complete with heat-recovery generators. These ultra-low-NOx systems decreased the facility's emissions by 40%—a savings equivalent to the annual emissions of 4,300 vehicles. During the rebuilding phase, Malden Mills set up an employee retraining center that included GED courses, English as a second language, and basic computer courses to prepare employees to work at the new state-of-the-art facility. When *60 Minutes* asked Feuerstein about his business choices after the fire, his reply was simple: "I think it was a wise business decision, but that isn't why I did it. I did it because it was the right thing to do."

ANALYSIS

One of the most important aspects we should note about the Malden Mills case is that at the time of the fire, it was privately owned. Without stockholders scrutinizing his business decisions, Feuerstein could do just about anything without fear of being sued. This is in sharp contrast to Henry Ford, whose stockholders sued him for continually reducing the sales-price of his Model T automobile. The Ford stockholders contended that the price could remain stable, and that by reducing the price Ford was giving away their profits. Feuerstein's decisions were obviously expensive. Construction costs, wages, and benefits are all higher in America, as is the expense of building environmentally friendly industrial facilities. But it was Feuerstein's money. He could do with it as he pleased.

In the months after the fire, Feuerstein was lauded as a model of executive heart. He was hailed for his courage and his honorable code of ethics. But the tale of Malden Mills is not a complete triumph. As a result of the fire, Malden Mills lost a great deal of international business supplying upholstery fabric, and eventually had to shut down its upholstery division. Try as he might, Feuerstein could not prevent a plant-shutdown or the layoffs of approximately 400 workers. Rebuilding after the fire also left the company with an enormous debt, and Malden Mills filed for Chapter 11 bankruptcy protection. Since large creditors then held a significant stake in Malden Mills, their voice would guide future business decisions. By the end of 2003, Malden Mills emerged from bankruptcy, and within six months Feuerstein was out and a new CEO took the reigns. Within one year Michael Spillane, President and CEO of Malden Mills, had put together a new senior management team and dedicated his tenure to increasing profitability, in part, through cost controls. By mid 2005, GE Commercial Finance, owner of Malden Mills, was looking for a buyer.

DISCUSSION QUESTIONS

1. Consider the actions of Feuerstein and his statement: "I think it was a wise business decision, but that isn't why I did it. I did it because it was the right thing to do." In hindsight, given that a small town lost a major employer when the upholstery division was shut down, employees lost jobs, the mill went into bankruptcy, the creditors got the raw end of the deal—in other words everyone suffered in the long-term—were the decisions of Feuerstein socially responsible? Why or why not?

2. Suppose that Malden Mills had been a publicly traded company in which you held stock. Upon hearing news of the fire and the CEO's decisions, how would you react? How would your reactions change if you were an employee? A customer? Was Feuerstein favoring the interests of some stakeholders over those of others?

3. If, through the good luck of substantial market demand, the mill had survived, would you view the ethics of the decisions differently?
   a. What if the good luck turned out to be an enormous contract to provide uniform clothing for military, police, or fire and rescue forces?
   b. What if the good luck turned out to be extremely high demand for the products from gang members? (Note: It is legal to be a gang member.)

FURTHER READINGS

Campbell, Kenneth. 1997. "Malden Mills Owner Applies Religious Ethics to Business." MIT News.

Rose, Charlie. 2003. "Kidnapped/Puzzle Master/Malden Mills." *60 Minutes*. Columbia Broadcasting System.

Seeger, Matthew W., and Robert R. Ulmer. 2001. "Virtuous Responses to Organizational Crisis: Aaron Feuerstein and Milt Colt." *Journal of Business Ethics* 31 (4): 369–76.

Ulmer, Robert R. 2001. "Effective Crisis Management through Established Stakeholder Relationships Malden Mills as a Case Study." *Management Communication Quarterly* 14 (4): 590–615.

—17—

CITIBANK AND COLLATERALIZED DEBT OBLIGATIONS

Tom McNamara and Irena Descubes

BACKGROUND

FOUNDED IN 1812, CITIBANK IS NOW PART OF Citigroup, one of the largest financial institutions in the world, with almost $2 trillion in assets. The bank has a storied past, with notable achievements including funding of the first trans-Atlantic telegraph cable in 1866, establishing one of the first foreign exchange offices for converting currencies in the late 1890s, and assisting in the financing of the construction of the Panama Canal in 1906. The company's operations even encompassed the exploration of space through Citigroup's involvement in a partnership that launched heavy-lift space vehicles.

But one of the company's more notorious activities, and one which would play a part in its almost going bankrupt, was its involvement in something known as collateralized debt obligations (CDOs). CDOs are complex financial contrivances originally designed to help commercial banks improve their financial positions by allowing them to remove loans from their balance sheets. CDOs are usually comprised of a mixture of commercial loans and other financial assets, all pooled into one tradable instrument. The different sorts of assets that go into a CDO usually have different levels of quality, meaning that they need to have different levels of reward for the investors who buy them. The solution is to cut the CDO into slices,

"tranches," with each having a different credit rating. The top slices are rated "AAA" and would therefore provide a lower rate of return, but with very low chance that investors would lose their investment. For those with greater fortitude and higher appetite for risk, a bottom slice can be bought which carries with it a greater chance of default, but which also provides a correspondingly higher rate of return. Ominously, these lower slices are often referred to as "toxic waste."

During the run-up to the Great Financial Panic of 2008, the toxic lower tranches were largely backed by questionable loans. In the early 2000s the United States, like many developed nations, experienced a housing bubble, with the price of an average home increasing by almost 100% between 2000 and 2006. Many housing mortgages were bundled into CDOs and sold to investors who saw this as a way to speculate and make money from the housing boom without necessarily having to buy a house. As the housing mania raged, lending standards slipped. So called "NINJA" loans ("No Income, No Job, No Assets") became more and more common. Experts assured us that none of this was cause for alarm. An authority no less than Alan Greenspan himself, former Chairman of the Federal Reserve ("The Fed"), had assured Americans that there was nothing to worry about. He was adamant that a speculative bubble in housing was impossible, due to the fact that a national housing market was really just a collection of smaller local markets. "Even if a bubble were to develop in a local market, it would not necessarily have implications for the nation as a whole," Greenspan assured the public.[1] Times were good and Citigroup, like the rest of Wall Street, was making money.

To understand how the crisis occurred, some knowledge of history and policy changes is needed. The entity that we now know as Citigroup came about in 1998 through a merger of what was then called Citicorp and the Travelers Group Inc., creating, at the time, the largest financial services company on the planet. Citicorp was primarily involved in banking activities, and the Travelers Group was an insurance company that also sold investors mutual funds. This was seen by many as a match made in heaven, since there was very little overlap between the two companies and a great potential for the cross selling of products, as well as "synergies." There was just one small problem with this arranged marriage—technically, it was illegal.

After the Great Crash of 1929, several laws were put in place to limit the types of speculative activities that banks could take part in. One of the most well known, and effective of these laws was the Glass-Steagall Act of 1933, which separated commercial from investment banking and made it illegal for a bank to own an insurance company and an insurance company to own a bank. Citigroup lobbied for Congress to overturn the Glass-Steagall Act, allowing the merger to go through. Most notably, Citigroup was supported by then Fed Chairman Alan Greenspan, by the Secretary of the Treasury at the time, Larry Summers, and by his immediate predecessor, former Secretary of the Treasury Robert Rubin. (Rubin would join Citigroup as a senior executive in 1999.)

In November of 1999 Congress passed the Financial Services Modernization Act (FSMA), cynically referred to by many as the "Citi-Travelers Act." Passage of the FSMA (effectively, the repeal of Glass-Steagall) is seen by many as the first step in the undoing of the legislation that had maintained relative financial stability in the US for 80

years, unleashing what would become known as "casino capitalism."

By the summer of 2007 cracks in the financial system were starting to show, in part because of the merger of commercial and investment banking. The strategy of giving mortgages to just about anyone who wanted one with no questions asked, and then bundling them into a CDO and selling them off to someone as soon as possible in order to get them off your books, was starting to show its problems. An early warning sign was the fact that during this period Citigroup was forced to buy back $25 billion of its own CDOs, due to poor investor demand. Citigroup responded by creating new CDOs to buy back the old CDOs, thus creating an even bigger, and more fragile, house of cards.

By the fall of 2008 all the steam had run out of the market and everything came to a crashing halt. The run up to the financial crisis of 2008 (followed by the subsequent Great Recession of 2008) saw the creation of the largest speculative bubble in history, greater even than the one experienced in Japan in the late 1980s or the Great Crash of 1929 in the US. The fallout for Citigroup was devastating. Caught short, illiquid and under billions of dollars of bad debt, the bank was virtually insolvent. In the immediate aftermath the US government invested $45 billion and took control of 36% of the company in an effort to stop the bleeding and restore confidence. Millions of people lost their jobs, their homes, and trillions in profits because of the collapse in house and stock prices. Between 2008 and 2009 the US economy shrank by almost 4%. The Federal Reserve has estimated that it will take at least until 2023 for the US economy to return to its pre-crisis rate of growth. This extended subpar performance is expected to result in between $6 trillion and $14 trillion of lost economic output.

Investor lawsuits and official investigations would soon follow. In July of 2014 Citigroup announced that it had reached a comprehensive settlement with the US Department of Justice and several other federal and state government agencies over various activities related to the company's issuance of CDOs between 2003 and 2008. Citigroup agreed to pay $4.5 billion in fines and charges, as well as provide $2.5 billion in "consumer relief," an act of penance in which the company provided financing for the construction of affordable housing, and reduced the principal on certain residential loans it had made. The company has until 2018 to make good on its promise to help consumers.

ANALYSIS

Business ethicists think about the ethics of the Citigroup case by analyzing the actions of the company and its senior managers, and the rules and regulations that enabled the financial crisis; and by assessing the distribution of harms and benefits in the aftermath of the crisis.

The most straightforward ethical objection to Citigroup's behavior is that it was criminal. Even Milton Friedman, who saw companies' responsibility to be to maximize profit for shareholders, insisted that actions follow the basic rules of society—law and ethical custom. A shareholder lawsuit filed in 2009 claimed that Citigroup knowingly engaged in deception and fraud, hiding tens of billions of dollars of toxic assets by repacking them as new CDOs. In 2011, Citigroup settled the lawsuit for $590 billion without admitting any wrongdoing.

Citigroup's actions also raise questions about the responsibilities of managers and regulators. Words like "crisis" and "panic" are often associated with the financial collapse of 2008, implying a certain randomness or unpredictability to events. But critics would counter that managers and regulators should have foreseen the impending threat to the economy from an unsustainable increase in asset prices, and from lax oversight and enforcement. For example, the former chairman of Citigroup, Robert Rubin (who in his role of Secretary of Treasury championed the 1998 merger that brought Citigroup into existence) testified that he wasn't aware of any problems with CDOs until the fall of 2007. Senior managers at best failed to meet their ethical responsibilities to properly oversee

Citigroup's investments and at worse abetted reckless and possibly criminal behavior. (Another concern exemplified by Rubin is the possibility of conflicts of interest due to the "revolving door" of people moving between senior positions in the public and private sectors.)

Another set of ethical questions concern the distributions of burdens resulting from the crisis. The people who had taken out sub-prime NINJA loans to buy houses were commonly blamed for causing the crisis. "These people should live up to their responsibilities and pay their bills" and "People should be held accountable for their poor life decisions" were often heard refrains. What was usually overlooked was the fact that on the other side of every irresponsible borrower was an irresponsible lender. Why was it that people with "no income, no job, and no assets" were being held to a higher standard than the bank presidents who lent them huge sums of money without due diligence?

Furthermore, rather than paying for their "poor life decisions," many on Wall Street were handsomely rewarded for them. About $140 billion in compensation was paid out by major US financial firms only one year after the worst financial crisis in living memory. This was estimated to be even larger than the amount earned by Wall Street in 2007, the year when the speculative bubble reached its peak. In 2009 the average salary in the financial industry was about $143,400. That same year, official unemployment hit a high of 10%, with a broader measurement of unemployment used by the Bureau of Labor Statistics reaching an astounding 17%.

Another criticism of the handling of the aftermath of the crisis was the immediacy with which banks such as Citigroup were in effect given blank checks, while the average Americans who lost their job or home were seen as getting very little in the way of help. "Wall Street got bailed out, Main Street got left out" was a popular cry.

By the end of 2008, while the ashes of the financial crash were still smoldering, the US government made available over $240 billion in aid to prop up faltering banks, mainly through the Treasury

Department's Troubled Asset Relief Program (TARP). According to Senator Elizabeth Warren, when one includes "secret" loans that the Fed made available to Wall Street banks, the cost of the bailout was much higher. In a Senate hearing, Senator Warren noted, "The biggest money for the biggest banks was never voted on by Congress. Instead, between 2007 and 2009, the Fed provided over $13 trillion in emergency lending to just a handful of large financial institutions. That's nearly 20 times the amount authorized in the TARP bailout."[2] In just one single lending scheme, the Fed handed out $9 trillion, with almost 70% going to just three banks: Citigroup, Morgan Stanley and Merrill Lynch. In another handout to Citigroup, the government stood ready to guarantee over $300 billion worth of toxic assets that the bank was holding.

In total, Citigroup would go on to receive an estimated $2 trillion in bailouts from the US taxpayer. And while the bank paid back all of the money it received in bailouts, many would argue that the bailouts themselves violated principles of justice. Disgruntlement resulted not only from the idea that harm caused by the crisis fell mainly on individuals losing their homes and jobs, while government assistance went mainly to Wall Street. It also came from the idea that the bailouts and the invocation of the "too big to fail" slogan violated principles of free competition central to a capitalist economy. As noted economist Joseph Schumpeter argued, at the heart of free market capitalism is the concept of "creative destruction," that is, that poorly run firms must be allowed to go extinct and die so that new dynamic ones can take their place. Nowhere in classical economics does one find the phrase "too big to fail." This also raises the argument that there are two types of capitalism in the US; one for well-connected and powerful banks who get saved no matter what the cost, another for the small business owner.

In an attempt to limit the chances of another financial meltdown, in 2010 the Dodd-Frank Act was passed. This law tries, once again, to restrict the speculative activities that banks can take part in. Disturbingly, a provision to the law was passed in December 2014 that lets banks use federally insured deposits to take part in speculation in the derivatives markets, the exact kind of behavior that led to the 2008 crisis. The main proponent for changing the Dodd-Frank Act? Citigroup.

DISCUSSION QUESTIONS

1. The crisis of 2008 was caused by poor government oversight, a poor understanding on the part of financial institutions of the products they were selling and a poor understanding on the part of investors of the products they were buying. Which party was most responsible for the crisis? Which party was least responsible? Why?

2. In the aftermath of the crisis, what do you believe the government did right? What do you believe the government did wrong? Explain.

3. Knowing what we know now about the crisis, how would you explain the dearth of criminal prosecution on the part of the Department of Justice justified in the immediate years following 2008?

4. Do you believe that there was a conflict of interest in former Secretary of the Treasury Robert Rubin taking a position at Citigroup so soon after he left public service?

NOTES

1 Testimony of Chairman Alan Greenspan, Monetary policy and the economic outlook, Before the Joint Economic Committee, US Congress, April 17, 2002. Accessed at: http://www.federalreserve.gov/boarddocs/testimony/2002/20020417/default.htm.

2 "Warren: Citigroup, Morgan Stanley, Merrill Lynch Received $6 Trillion Backdoor Bailout from Fed" by Pam Martens and Russ Martens, Wall Street on Parade, March 4, 2015. Accessed at: http://wallstreetonparade.com/2015/03/warren-citigroup-morgan-stanley-merrill-lynch-received-6-trillion-backdoor-bailout-from-fed/.

FURTHER READINGS

Bernstein, Jake, and Eisinger Jesse. 2010. "Banks' Self-Dealing Super-Charged Financial Crisis." *ProPublica*, August 26. http://www.propublica.org/article/banks-self-dealing-super-charged-financial-crisis.

Dash, Eric, and Julie Creswell. 2008. "Citigroup Saw No Red Flags Even as It Made Bolder Bets." *New York Times*, November 22.

The Economist. 2013. "The Origins of the Financial Crisis: Crash Course," September 7.

Krugman, Paul. 2009. "How Did Economists Get It So Wrong?" *New York Times*, September 2.

McLean, B., and Nocera, J. 2011. *All the Devils Are Here: The Hidden History of the Financial Crisis*. New York: Penguin.

Poole, W. 2010. "Causes and Consequences of the Financial Crisis of 2007–2009." *Harv. JL & Pub. Pol'y*, 33, 421.

Reich, Robert. 2015. "America's Biggest Banks Are Felons—Here's How to Make Them Pay." *Salon*, June 24. http://www.salon.com/2015/06/24/robert_reich_americas_biggest_banks_are_felons_heres_how_to_make_them_pay_partner/.

Weissman, Robert. 2009. "Reflections on Glass-Steagall and Maniacal Deregulation" *Common Dreams*, November 12. http://www.commondreams.org/views/2009/11/12/reflections-glass-steagall-and-maniacal-deregulation.

Wilmarth, A.E. 2014. "Citigroup: A Case Study in Managerial and Regulatory Failures." *Indiana Law Review*, 47, 69–137.

—18—

CORPORATE LOBBYING ON GMO LABELING LEGISLATION

Oregon Ballot Measure 92

Brad Berman

BACKGROUND

64 COUNTRIES CURRENTLY REQUIRE GENETICALLY engineered (GE) foods to be labeled as such. The United States is not among them. At both the state and federal level, labeling is strictly voluntary. If recently passed legislation in Vermont (Act 120) survives court challenges, this could change as early as July 2016.[1] But on the whole, legislative efforts to label GE foods have met with little success in the US.

In 2014, Oregon voters rejected one of the latest such efforts, a state ballot initiative (Measure 92) that would have required the labeling of broad classes of GE foods. Supporters grounded their core arguments for the measure in a presumed right of consumers to know how their food is produced. Mandatory labeling, they claimed, would enable consumers to make informed purchasing decisions, ones which reflect not only their values, ethical and otherwise, but also their own estimations of the relevant consequences of producing and consuming GE foods.

Grassroots support for Measure 92 was relatively strong. Thousands of individuals, mostly in-state, made small donations to PACs and campaigned on its behalf. Nonetheless, the measure's principal backers predominantly consisted of consumer advocacy groups, environmental organizations, and corporations—Dr. Bronner's Magic Soaps and Mercola.com Health Resources foremost among them—who collectively contributed millions in cash and in-kind support.

The results were the closest in state history with little more than one-twentieth of a percentage point separating the two sides. Initial polling, however, had shown overwhelming support for a mandatory labeling scheme. Just four months before the vote, for example, Oregon Public Broadcasting found 77% of residents to favor the labeling of GE foods.[2] Related ballot initiatives in the region, like California's Proposition 37 (2012) and Washington State's Initiative 522 (2013), were likewise voted down by narrow margins after early support eroded.

In each case, corporate lobbying played an outsized role in turning the tide of public opinion. In Oregon, in a campaign that shattered prior state spending records, the PAC opposing Measure 92 outspent its rivals by a nearly 2-to-1 margin. Well over 99% of its war chest was financed by national and multinational corporations.[3] Monsanto and DuPont Pioneer alone donated almost $11 million, effectively offsetting the entire fundraising effort in support of the measure. PepsiCo, Coca-Cola, and Dow AgroSciences also made seven-figure contributions to defeat the initiative, and another dozen companies, food and agrochemical conglomerates for the most part, donated sums in the hundreds of thousands.

A key stratagem that those donations financed focused on depicting Measure 92 as a poorly written piece of legislation. On the one hand, detractors argued that the measure went too far. They claimed, for example, that it would require some foods to bear a GE label despite neither containing nor being produced from GE ingredients.[4] On the other hand, and perhaps more surprisingly, detractors argued that the measure did not go far enough, citing exemptions for food prepared in restaurants, alcoholic beverages, and foods whose production indirectly involved genetic engineering, such as beef from cows fattened on GE feed.

That tactic might encourage the suggestion that Measure 92's corporate adversaries took issue more with the measure itself than with GE labeling generally. This construal of their target cannot be sustained. Those who donated to defeat Measure 92 in Oregon, with few exceptions, lobbied the US House of Representatives just a year later to pass H.R. 1599. In addition to prohibiting the FDA from requiring GE foods to be labeled as such, this federal bill, the so-called "Safe and Accurate Food Labeling Act of 2015," would preclude *any* further state-level GE labeling initiatives and invalidate those already passed.

ANALYSIS

The sheer volume of corporate donations and their disproportionate role in the campaigns for and against Measure 92 bred complaints that corporations had an undue influence on both the debate over the measure and its eventual fate. The extent to which corporate political activity can sway public opinion raises concerns about its appropriate place, if any, in a liberal democracy. Discussions of corporate lobbying thus often assume the burden of justifying such activity.

In the US, corporations have legal rights to various forms of political activity that, since the 1978 *First National Bank of Boston v. Bellotti* decision, have explicitly included a First Amendment right to contribute to ballot initiative campaigns. Insofar as corporations can direct their political activity to shaping public policy in ways that promote their competitive advantage, they often have strong financial incentives to exercise those legal rights. But whether it is ethically permissible for corporations to engage in political activity is another matter.

A principle of free expression commonly plays a crucial role in discussions to that end. The classic defense of free expression, Mill's *On Liberty*, hinges upon three points: that holding well-reasoned and true opinions is valuable, that we are fallible, and that the best, if not only, way to reliably improve our opinions is to subject them to unrestricted critical assessment. Free expression, on Mill's view, is both indispensable for personal autonomy, since it uniquely enables our development as reasonable persons, and conducive to the public good, since better decisions will be reached as more opinions— whatever their progeny or perceived merit—enter into in the public debate and challenge one another.

Still, one might wonder whether even a Millian advocate of free expression would sanction all the various forms of corporate speech engaged in over Measure 92.[5] The issuing of public statements expressing political opinions or reasons for them would seem to be most clearly protected, and all the more so if it is an extension of a corporation's public relations or branding platform since that would, in effect, associate those political views with the very identity of the corporation. Chipotle Mexican Grill's endorsement of Measure 92 is a good example on this front. As part of their "food with integrity" campaign, the company began disclosing which of their menu offerings contained GE ingredients in 2013 and, after developing suppliers, switched to solely serving non-GE foods in 2015.

Corporate campaign donations are a more complicated category of political activity to analyze. In the US, *Buckley v. Valeo* enshrined a line of legal interpretation taking political donations to constitute speech. In its decision, the Court argued that "because virtually every means of communicating ideas in today's mass society requires the expenditure of money," prohibiting or restricting the financing of political campaigns "necessarily reduces the quantity of expression by restricting the number of issues discussed, the depth of their exploration, and the size of the audience reached."[6]

On this point, it is perhaps useful to consider what the fight over Measure 92 might have looked like had corporate financing been removed from the process. The result would presumably have differed, but so, too, would the debate over GE labeling. Absent corporate funding, the No on 92 Coalition would have had roughly $1,000 to spend, leaving a non-negligible minority with few resources to publicly advance their case. A notable issue in their media campaign concerned the healthfulness of GE foods. Many supporting the measure appealed to "potential" but as-of-yet unknown health risks of consuming GE foods. Yet, for the most part, such fears are unfounded, or at least highly exaggerated in the public perception. The overwhelming scientific consensus is that consuming GE foods is no riskier than consuming their non-GE counterparts. Whether one concurs with that assessment or not, the debate over the measure was better for grappling with it.[7]

Nonetheless, the *Buckley v. Valeo* decision, which focuses on money as a *means* of effective political speech, remains controversial. One question that the fight over Measure 92 reiterates concerns the *content* of the speech that money might be said to constitute. Once money has been donated to a political action committee, the matter of how it is to be spent is often out of the donor's hands. It cannot be assumed, therefore, that Dupont Pioneer, for example, endorsed the views presented in ads commissioned and paid for by the No on 92 Coalition. At best, it supports the conclusion that Pioneer had an interest, self-appraised at no lower than $4.5 million, in seeing Measure 92 fail. If so, Pioneer's donations were plausibly a form of speech about a political issue, but not speech that, in itself, made a particularly valuable

contribution to the debate over that issue. Indeed, the speech in question might not even properly count as political speech, despite concerning a political topic, since the interest expressed could have had little to do with an estimation of the public good.

Should such corporate political speech be constrained then? If so, who should regulate it, in which circumstances, and in what way? Responses depend in large part upon the competing values one recognizes. In the present case, two are especially pressing. The first is a principle of equal political representation. As matters stand, those who have more money to spend have more power to impact the shape of the political debate. Corporate donations accounted for over 80% of the total spending on Measure 92, with 4 out of every 5 of corporate dollars going to defeat it. The overwhelming majority of corporate donors, to compound the issue, were headquartered out of state. Influence is of course harder to quantify than spending, but the conclusion that corporate donations cost citizens of Oregon control over at least some aspects of their election is hard to avoid.

A second challenge to free expression engages the nature of the measure, in contrast to the debate over it, more directly. Producers of GE foods contended that, in forcing them to label their products, Measure 92 would have compelled them to speak against their will. Supporters of the measure countered that mandatory labeling was needed to promote their personal autonomy. Without knowing how one's food is produced, supporters claimed, one's ability to make purchases in line with one's normative beliefs is undermined. The operative assumption here, typically unstated, is that one does not just buy a product, one buys into it, sharing in responsibility for the act of its production.

Hansen has argued that concerns for personal autonomy are not sufficient to justify the mandatory labeling of GE foods. She notes, first, that systematically enabling the choice between GE and non-GE foods would be achieved equally well by labeling the latter as by labeling the former. Second, she argues, the mandatory labeling of either category of food is excessive, at least for those who might wish to avoid GE foods, since those who want to do so already can. They need only assume that foods that are not reliably flagged as being GE-free—by, for example, bearing a USDA Organic label—may contain GE ingredients. As Rubel and Streiffer caution, though, most consumers, in point of fact, do not make that assumption.[8]

On the other hand, the distinction between GE and non-GE foods is perhaps not the appropriate place to focus with respect to labeling and autonomy, as few of the ethical issues raised by GE foods pertain to them as a class. But soybeans, Rainbow papayas, and Golden rice all routinely appear in discussions of the ethics of genetic engineering, but they typically do so to rather different ends. For this reason, the first state-wide labeling initiative in the US, 2002's failed Measure 27 in Oregon, proposed requiring far more specific information on GE food labels, including both the sources and purposes of genes transferred by genetic engineering techniques: for example, "this squash contains viral genetic information designed to make it resistant to viral infection."[9] While this information is often publicly available to consumers willing to do the research, the likelihood of its being required on US food labels any time soon is slim. For now, legal deference to free expression, corporate expression included, is simply too strong.

DISCUSSION QUESTIONS

1. Just whose speech is corporate speech? Whose opinions and interests should it represent and to what ends?
2. Political debates are notoriously suffused with rhetrickery. Is it fair to demand, then, that corporations meet higher standards when they enter those debates?
3. Does free expression live up to Mill's construal of its public good? In particular, does the debate over Measure 92 support his view, famously expressed by the Supreme Court, that truth will ultimately prevail in the marketplace of ideas?
4. To what extent, if any, are consumers ethically responsible for the actions that companies take to produce and market the goods they buy?
5. What kinds of information are companies ethically obliged to disclose to the public? What grounds those obligations?

NOTES

1 Maine and Connecticut have also passed mandatory labeling measures, though each made labeling conditional upon a critical mass of Northeastern states enacting coordinate legislation.

2 Devan Schwartz, "Most Northwest Residents Say They Want Labeling for Genetically Modified Food," *OPB*, July 7, 2014, http://www.opb.org/news/article/most-northwest-residents-say-they-want-labeling-fo/."URL":"http://www.opb.org/news/article/most-northwest-residents-say-they-want-labeling-fo/'," author":[{"family":"Schwartz","given":"Devan"}], "issued":{"date-parts":[["2014",7,7]]},"accessed":{"date-parts":[["2015",7,24]]}}}],"schema":"https://github.com/citation-style-language/schema/raw/master/csl-citation.json"}

3 The No on 92 Coalition received no more than a few dozen relatively small contributions from local industry associations and private individuals.

4 This claim is misleading, as nothing in the measure would have legally required such foods to bear a GE label. Yet, it is not unreasonable to think that, had the measure passed, GE labels would have been more liberally applied. Under the legislation's enforcement conditions, lack of a GE label would have potentially opened a food's producer to lawsuits, and so some producers, particularly small ones, might have opted to give their non-GE foods a GE label in an attempt to forestall costly, even if baseless, legal battles.

5 Other types of corporate political activity, while not properly speech, no doubt merit attention as well. For example, Ben & Jerry's served up free scoops of ice cream (an "in-kind" campaign contribution) at one of its Portland locations while the eponymous Jerry gave a talk promoting the

labeling of GE foods. The company regularly gives away its ice cream, but the context is here important since small gifts are a fairly effective means of influencing voter behavior. Such gifts are a far cry from the outright buying of votes, but they raise an analogous worry to the extent that they promote political decisions to be made independently of the actual issues in play.

6   *James L. Buckley, et al. v. Francis R. Valeo*, Secretary of the United States Senate, et al., 424 US 1 (1976).

7   On the other hand, many philosophically interesting arguments were given little attention even despite the massive media campaigns. A local chapter of the NAACP argued, for example, that increased food costs associated with labeling would disproportionately burden the poor since food purchases consume a larger share of their budget. The NAACP submitted the argument for inclusion in the voters' pamphlet, but it was not picked up for wider dissemination by the PAC challenging the measure and went largely unanswered.

8   On the prevalence of GE foods in the US and public misperception of it, see Maarten J. Chrispeels, "Yes Indeed, Most Americans Do Eat GMOs Every Day!," *Journal of Integrative Plant Biology* 56, no. 1 (2014): 4–6.

9   "Measure 27," in *Oregon Voters' Pamphlet: November 5th General Election* (Salem: Oregon Secretary of State, Elections Division, 2002), 116–37, http://library.state.or.us/repository/ 2010/201003011350161/ORVPGenMar i2002m.pdf.

FURTHER READINGS

Birnbaum, Jeffrey H. 1992. *The Lobbyists: How Influence Peddlers Get Their Way in Washington*. New York: Times Books.

Friesen, Mark. 2014. "2014 Oregon GMO Measure Fundraising." *OregonLive.com*. http://gov.oregonlive. com/election/2014/finance/measure-92/.

Hamilton, J. Brooke III, and David Hoch. 1997. "Ethical Standards for Business Lobbying." *Business Ethics Quarterly* 7 (3): 117–29.

Leong, Shane, James Hazelton, and Cynthia Townley. 2013. "Managing the Risks of Corporate Political Donations: A Utilitarian Perspective." *Journal of Business Ethics* 118 (2): 429–45.

"Measure 92." 2014. In *Oregon Voters' Pamphlet: November 4th General Election*, 137–53. Salem: Oregon Secretary of State, Elections Division. http://library.state.or.us/repository/2010/201003011350161/2014.pdf.

Singer, Alan E. 2013. "Corporate Political Activity, Social Responsibility, and Competitive Strategy: An Integrative Model." *Business Ethics: A European Review* 22 (3): 308–24.

Stark, Andrew. 2010. "Business in Politics : Lobbying and Corporate Campaign Contributions." In *The Oxford Handbook of Business Ethics*, edited by George G. Brenkert and Tom L. Beauchamp. Oxford: Oxford University Press.

Weirich, Paul, ed. 2007. *Labeling Genetically Modified Food: The Philosophical and Legal Debate*. Oxford; New York: Oxford University Press.

—19—
ISLAMIC ETHICS AND THE IMPLICATIONS FOR BUSINESS

Gillian Rice

INTRODUCTION

MY FOCUS IN THIS PAPER IS ON THE ETHICAL principles which relate to business and which are contained in the religion of Islam. Islam is generally misunderstood and it is often surprising to some that it contains an entire socio-economic system. In Islam, it is ethics that dominates economics and not the other way around (Naqvi, 1981). My purpose is twofold: (1) to share a perspective on business ethics, little known in the west, which may stimulate further thinking and debate on the relationships between ethics and business, and (2) to provide some knowledge of Islamic philosophy in order to help managers doing business in Muslim cultures deal with cultural differences....

THE ISLAMIC ETHICAL SYSTEM

Muslims derive their ethical system from the teachings of the Qur'an (which Muslims believe is a book revealed by God to Muhammad in seventh century Arabia), and from the *sunnah* (the recorded sayings and behavior of Muhammad). The goals of Islam are not primarily materialist. They are based on Islamic concepts of human wellbeing and good life which stress brotherhood/sisterhood and socioeconomic justice and require a balanced satisfaction of both the material and spiritual needs of all humans (Chapra, 1992).

A "MORAL FILTER"

There exists in most societies a relative scarcity of resources with unlimited claims upon them. A free-market capitalist economy uses market-determined prices as a filtering mechanism to distribute resources. The use of the price system alone, however, can frustrate the realization of socio-economic goals. Under a system of state control, the allocation of resources is in the hands of a bureaucracy, which is cumbersome and inefficient. According to Chapra (1992), the Islamic worldview implies that the market system should be maintained, but that the price mechanism be complemented with a device that minimizes unnecessary claims on resources. This device is the "moral filter." This means that people would pass their potential claims on resources through the "filter of Islamic values" so that many claims would be eliminated before being expressed in the marketplace. Resources would not be allowed to be diverted to the production of luxuries until the production of necessities was ensured in sufficient quantities (Siddiqi, 1981). The definition of luxurious or extravagant is related to the average standards of consumption in a society, the idea being that large departure from the standards would not be permissible.

Keynes' (1972) observations on this subject may be useful. He stated that even though "the needs of human beings may seem to be insatiable," ... "they fall into two classes—those needs which are absolute in the sense that we feel them whatever the situation of our fellow human beings may be, and those which are relative ones in the sense that their satisfaction lifts us above or makes us feel superior to others. Needs of the second class, which satisfy the desire for superiority, may indeed be insatiable; for the higher the general level, the higher still are they. But this is not so true of the absolute needs." Islamic jurists' categories of necessities (*daruri-yyat*), conveniences (*hayiyyat*) and refinements (*tahsiniyyat*) would fall into Keynes' first class of needs. These are any goods and services which fulfill a need or reduce a hardship and make a real difference in human well-being. Thus "comforts" are included here (Chapra, 1992). Luxuries (the second class of needs), however, are goods and services derived for their snob appeal and make no difference to a person's well-being. Galbraith (1958) refers to this second class of needs as "wants."

Consumer advocates in the US have long been critical of business practices that increase the desire for "wants" and subsequently have adverse cultural and social effects (Williams, 1993). For example, in pursuit of profit maximization, businesses often subject the consumer to advertising and sales promotion campaigns that appeal to the consumer's vanity, sex appetite and envy, either overtly or covertly. Consumers are encouraged to believe that their actualization and social esteem are dependent on the frequency and value of their purchases. This leads in turn to a tremendous amount of wasteful production, with adverse environmental as well as social implications. According to the United Nations Development Program (UNDP) Human Development Report (1994), the lifestyles of the rich nations must change; the north has a fifth of the world's population and four-fifths of its income and it consumes seventy percent of the world's energy, seventy-five percent of its metals and eighty-five percent of its wood. Even in these rich countries, some of the essential needs of the poor remain unfulfilled, and high pollution and rapid depletion of non-renewable resources occur.

The question, of course, is how to implement the "moral filter" without coercion or despotism. The filter mechanism of values must be socially-agreed upon and some way has to be devised to motivate consumers and businesspeople to abide by these values. From an Islamic point of view, social change must be gradual and cannot be achieved through force. The Qur'anic injunction "There is no compulsion in religion" (Qur'an 2:256) is relevant here. Change can occur by inviting people to alter their ways or by setting an example. Historically this is how Islam rapidly spread through a large part of the world in the seventh and eighth centuries (Eaton, 1994). For example, when Muslim merchants traveled to distant lands, the inhabitants of those lands were impressed by the traders' social and business conduct and so became curious about their beliefs. Many of these inhabitants subsequently became Muslims. · A parallel exists today with respect to the "green" movement which continues to spread around the globe. The adoption of environmentally conscious behavior is occurring through example, encouragement and education, as well as by legislation. Indeed, in the environmental context, legislation is insufficient. Only when the political will and support of the populace are strong enough, are environmental laws adequately enforced.

The Islamic ethical system contains specific guidelines for achieving the moral filter and for conducting business. These guidelines derive from the interrelated concepts of unity, justice and trusteeship which I explain below.

UNITY (*TAWHID*)

The key to the business philosophy of Islam lies in a person's relationship with God, His universe and His people. In common with other revealed religions is the moral appeal to humans to surrender themselves to the will of God. Islam goes beyond this exhortation and teaches that all life is essentially a unity because it also provides the practical way to pattern all facets of human life in accordance with God's will. There should be unity of ideas and actions in a person's existence and consciousness (Asad, 1993). Muslims believe that because people are accountable to God, and their success in the hereafter depends on their performance in this life on earth, this adds a new dimension to the valuation of things and deeds in this life (Siddiqi, 1981). Islam is simply a program of life in accord with the "laws of nature" decreed by God. A definite relationship between fellow humans is thus prescribed. This is the relationship of brotherhood or sisterhood and equality (Abu-Sulayman, 1976). In this sense, unity is a coin with two faces: one implies that God is the sole creator of the universe and the other implies that people are equal partners or that each person is a brother or sister to the other. As far as business is concerned, this means cooperation and equality of effort and opportunity.

JUSTICE (*ADALAH*)

Islam is absolutely unambiguous in its objective of eradicating from society all traces of inequity, injustice, exploitation and oppression. The Qur'an also condemns vicarious guilt or merit and teaches the greatest possible individualism "... no bearer of burdens can bear the burdens of another; ... man can have nothing but what he strives for ..." (Qur'an 53:38–9). This individualistic outlook on the spiritual destiny of humanity is counterbalanced by a rigorous conception of society and social collaboration. In their acquisition of wealth, however, people should not lie or cheat; they must uphold promises and fulfill contracts. Usurious dealings are prohibited. Islam teaches that all wealth should be productive and people may not stop the circulation of wealth after they have acquired it, nor reduce the momentum of circulation (Chapra, 1992).

The intense commitment of Islam to justice and brotherhood demands that Muslim society take care of the basic needs of the poor. Individuals are obliged to earn a living and only when this is impossible does the state intervene. The Islamic institution of *zakah*, that is, a wealth tax comprising compulsory charitable-giving for specially designated groups in society, facilitates the care of all members of society. The rich are not the real owners of their wealth; they are only trustees. They must spend it in accordance with the terms of the trust, one of the most important of which is fulfilling the needs of the poor. The word "*zakah*" means purification and as such, income redistribution is not only an economic necessity but also a means to spiritual salvation ("... of their wealth take alms so that you might purify and sanctify." Qur'an 9:103). Thus, economics is effectively integrated with ethics (Naqvi, 1981).

TRUSTEESHIP (*KHILAFAH*)

People are viewed as trustees of the earth on behalf of God. This does not mean a negation of private property but does have some important implications. No inhibitions attach to economic enterprise and people are encouraged to avail themselves of all opportunities available. There is no conflict between the moral and socio-economic requirements of life. There is a very wide margin in a person's personal and social existence. People may be ascetics or, after paying the wealth tax, may enjoy fully their remaining wealth. Yet, resources are for the benefit of all and not just a few and everyone must acquire resources rightfully. Although material prosperity is desirable, it is not a goal in itself. What is crucial is the motivation, the "ends" of economic activity. Given the right motivation, all economic activity assumes the character of worship (Siddiqi, 1982). Indulgence in luxurious living and the desire to show-off is condemned. Islam does not tolerate conspicuous consumption (Chapra, 1992).

Resources must also be disposed of in such a way as to protect everyone's well-being (Al-Faruqi, 1976). No one is authorized to destroy or waste God-given resources. This is very relevant to ethics concerning business and the environment: when Abu Bakr, the first ruler of the Islamic state after Muhammad, sent someone on a war assignment, he exhorted him not to kill indiscriminately or to destroy vegetation or animal life, even in war and on enemy territory. Thus there was no question of this being allowed in peacetime or on home territory. Trusteeship is akin to the concept of sustainable development. Models of sustainable development do not regard natural resources as a free good, to be plundered at the free will of any nation, any generation or any individual (UNDP, 1994). The notion of trusteeship is also common to the Jewish and Christian faiths; Green (1993) refers to Psalms 24:1, "The earth is the Lord's and the fullness thereof."

THE NEED FOR BALANCE

Muhammad advised Muslims to be moderate in all their affairs; he described Islam as the "middle way." A balance in human endeavors is necessary to ensure social well-being and continued development of human potential. Chapra (1992) notes that Islam recognizes what Marxism sought to deny: the contribution of individual self-interest through profit and private property to individual initiative, drive, efficiency and enterprise. At the same time, Islam condemns the evils of greed, unscrupulousness and disregard for the rights and needs of others, which the secularist, short-term, this-worldly perspective of capitalism sometimes encourages. The individual profit motive is not the chief propelling force in Islam (Siddiqi, 1981). Social good should guide entrepreneurs in their decisions, besides profit. A relevant saying of Muhammad is "work for your worldly life as if you were going to live forever, but work for the life to come as if you were going to die tomorrow."

Islam, like some other religions, places a greater emphasis on duties than on rights. The wisdom behind this is that if duties (relating to justice and trusteeship, for example) are fulfilled by everyone, then self-interest is automatically held within bounds and the rights of all are undoubtedly safeguarded. Society is the primary institution in Islam, not the state (Cantori and Lowrie, 1992). Chapra (1992) argues that in order to create an equilibrium between scarce resources

and the claims on them in a way that realizes both efficiency and equity, it is necessary to focus on human beings themselves, rather than on the market or the state. As emphasized by Cantori and Lowrie (1992), the Islamic jurists and the Islamic law or "shari'ah" (literally, "road") limit governmental power. The shari'ah is so all encompassing that there is less need for legislation regarding issues of ethics, social responsibility and human interaction. In particular, Muslims believe that the Qur'an contains a final and unambiguous statement of the truth, added to what had gone before (for example, the messages delivered to Moses and Jesus). The duty of the Muslim community is to preserve this message. Thus, Muslims have a profound horror of anything regarded as innovation in matters of religion, including what modern Christians interpret as necessary adaptations of religion to changing times (Eaton, 1994).

The emphasis is therefore on the human being rather than on state power. The real wealth of societies is with their people. An excessive obsession with the creation of material wealth can obscure the ultimate objective of enriching human lives. Humans are thus the ends as well as the means. Unless humans are motivated to pursue their self-interest within the constraints of economic well-being (the application of the "moral filter"), neither the "invisible hand" of the market nor the "visible hand" of central planning can succeed in achieving socioeconomic goals (Chapra, 1992).

SUMMARY

It should be emphasized that in Islam, business activity is considered to be a socially useful function; Muhammad was involved in trading for much of his life. Great importance is attached to views relating to consumption, ownership, goals of a business enterprise and the code of conduct of various business agents. Because Judaism, Christianity and Islam are closely related, many ethical principles such as honesty, trustworthiness and taking care of the less fortunate, are universal among the three religions, and indeed, among most moral codes. For example, as pointed out by Rossauw (1994), someone with a Christian understanding of the unconditional value of life cannot be careless in the workplace about product and quality standards that pose a threat to the lives of consumers or employees. However, Rossauw suggests that it is not the role of the church to approve or condemn economic systems. As economic systems are morally ambiguous, he encourages Christians to "keep a critical distance from the economic system in which they are working." In contrast, because Islam supplies a practical life-program, it is important to note that the Islamic socio-economic system includes detailed coverage of specific economic variables such as interest, taxation, circulation of wealth, fair trading, and consumption. Islamic law (shari'ah) derived from the Qur'an and sunnah also covers business relationships between buyers and sellers, employers and employees and lenders and borrowers (for full details, see for example, Keller, 1994). Note that there is no difference between Muslims and non-Muslims in legal rulings concerning commercial dealings. For example, it is unlawful to undercut another's price (whether that person be Muslim or non-Muslim) during a stipulated option to cancel period. A seller is not permitted to tell the buyer "cancel the deal and I'll sell you one cheaper." Also, whoever knows of a defect in an article he/she is selling is obliged to disclose it, to any buyer, Muslim or non-Muslim. Both Islamic and non-Islamic employees must be treated with the same just, equitable and honest approach.

Note that Islam is not an ascetic religion. Islam allows people to satisfy all their needs and to go beyond. The objective should not be to create a monotonous uniformity in Muslim society. Simplicity in consumption can be attained in lifestyles alongside creativity and diversity. Neither does Islam mean an absence of economic liberalization. There is a different kind of liberalization: one in which all private and public sector economic decisions are first passed through the filter of moral values before they are made subject to the discipline of the market. Undoubtedly, to implement the "moral filter" in practice requires the dedication of a large number of market participants. There is therefore frequently a wide gap between the philosophy and practice of Islamic ethics in countries with predominantly Muslim populations.

REFERENCES

Abu-Sulayman, A.A.: 1976, 'The Economics of Tawhid and Brotherhood', Contemporary Aspects of Economic Thinking in Islam (American Trust Publications, Indianapolis, IN).

Al-Faruqi, I.R.A.: 1976, 'Foreword', Contemporary Aspects of Economic Thinking in Islam (American Trust Publications, Indianapolis, IN).

Asad, M.: 1993, Islam at the Crossroads (Dar al-Andalus Ltd., Gibraltar).

Cantori, L.J. and A. Lowrie: 1992, 'Islam, Democracy, The State and The West', Middle East Policy 1, 49–61.

Chapra, M.U.: 1992, Islam and the Economic Challenge (International Institute of Islamic Thought, Herndon, VA).

Eaton, G.: 1994, Islam and the Destiny of Man (The Islamic Texts Society, Cambridge).

Galbraith, J.K.: 1958, The Affluent Society (Houghton Mifflin, Boston, MA).

Gould, S.J.: 1995, 'The Buddhist Perspective on Business Ethics: Experiential Exercises for Exploration and Practice', Journal of Business Ethics 14, 63–70.

Green, R.M.: 1993, 'Centesimus Annus: A Critical Jewish Perspective', Journal of Business Ethics 12, 945–954.

Keller, N.H.M., trans.: 1994, Reliance of the Traveller: A Classic Manual of Islamic Sacred Law by Ibn Naqib Al-Misri (Sunna Books, Evanston, IL).

Keynes, J.A.M.: 1972, The Collected Writings of John Maynard Keynes (Macmillan for the Royal Economic Society, London).

Naqvi, S.N.H.: 1981, Ethics and Economics: An Islamic Synthesis (The Islamic Foundation, Leicester).

Qur'an: undated, English translation of the meaning. Revised version of translation by Abdullah Yusuf Ali (The Presidency of Islamic Researches, King Fahd Holy Qur'an Printing Complex, Saudi Arabia).

Rossauw, G.J.: 1994, 'Business Ethics: Where Have All the Christians Gone?', *Journal of Business Ethics* 13, 557–570.

Sallam, H. and A.A. Hanafy: 1988, 'Employee and Employer: Islamic Perception,' *Proceedings of the Seminar on Islamic Principles of Organizational Behavior* (International Institute of Islamic Thought, Herndon, VA).

Siddiqi, M.N.: 1981, 'Muslim Economic Thinking: A Survey of Contemporary Literature,' in K. Ahmad (ed.), *Studies in Islamic Economics* (The Islamic Foundation, Leicester).

United Nations Development Program (UNDP): 1994, *Human Development Report*, 1994 (Oxford University Press, Oxford).

Williams, O.F.: 1993, 'Catholic Social Teaching: A Communitarian Democratic Capitalism for the New World Order,' *Journal of Business Ethics* 12, 919–932.

—20—

THE RELEVANCE AND VALUE OF CONFUCIANISM IN CONTEMPORARY BUSINESS ETHICS

Gary Kok Yew Chan

TO ADEQUATELY ASSESS THE CONTRIBUTION OF Confucian Ethics to the study of Business Ethics, one needs to first contend with more preliminary and broader questions as follows:

- Is Confucian Ethics relevant to the business arena?
- Is Confucianism compatible with Capitalism?

CONFUCIANISM AND PROFIT-MAKING

One major task pertaining to Confucian ethics in the business arena is to understand and explain the apparent negative attitude of Confucius against profit-making in business activities. In the Confucian classics, there are, admittedly, statements which indicate the association between "profit" and the "inferior man" (Analects, Book 4, Number 16) as well as the primacy of benevolence and righteousness over profit (Mencius, Book 1, Part 1, number 1; Chan, 1963, p. 60). In The Great Learning, it is stated that "[a] man of humanity develops his personality by means of his wealth, while the inhumane person develops wealth at the sacrifice of his personality" (Chan, 1963, p. 94).

In the context of governance and the state, The Great Learning also stated that "financial profit is not considered real profit whereas righteousness is considered the real profit" (Chan, 1963, p. 94).

Similarly, Mencius warned that excessive emphasis on "profits" will lead the country to ruin:

> If your Majesty [King Hui at Liang] asks what is profitable to your country, if the great officers ask what is profitable to their families, and if the inferior officers and the common people ask what is profitable to themselves, then both the superiors and the subordinates will try to snatch the profit from one another and the country will crumble (Chan, 1963, pp. 60–61).

It is important to note, however, that the above statements from the Confucian classics did not, taken as a whole, denigrate business activities per se. The main emphasis or lessons to be drawn from the statements are that one should strive to attain human virtues such as benevolence, righteousness, humanity and the development of one's personality. The Confucian statements collectively sought to remind the disciples of the significance of following the "Way" (Analects, Book 1, number 15).

In the course of advocating the virtues, the concept of profit-making was employed as a foil. Hence, in contrast to the aim of developing human virtues, the profit-making activity represents man's efforts to attain material wealth at the expense of virtuous living. It would be making a quantum leap, however, to argue from the above statements that Confucianism was necessarily against business and profit-making. In this regard, we note that Shibusawa Eiichi, the Japanese industrialist, had contended, consistent with the above statements in the Confucian classics, that Confucius did not condemn profit-making activities unless it was for selfish purposes and not for the good of the community (Ornatowski, 1999, 390). In addition, Jing Yuan-Shan (1841–1903), described as a "a Confucian merchant par excellence" from Shanghai, regarded moral attainment as more important than seeking material well-being (Tak and King, 2004, p. 248).

The question we need to address, therefore, is whether business is necessarily an activity or practice which seeks material wealth at the expense of human virtues in a manner incompatible with Confucian ethics....

CONFUCIAN APPROACHES TO BUSINESS AND CAPITALISM

The Confucian argument lies in moral self-cultivation and the development of human virtues, epitomised in the Confucian gentleman (*junzi*), instead of focusing on profits. I do not interpret Confucius in the classics as arguing for a cessation or impairment of business activities, but rather to emphasize the significance of human virtues as opposed to the mere fulfilment of selfish material desires. The Confucian approach suggests that one should adopt a proper focus towards the striving for human virtue and profits, respectively. Indeed, to reinforce this point, we can argue that the realm of economic or business activity is but one facet of man's life. Whilst man has been regarded as an economic being or having economic value within the capitalist framework, he is not solely defined by economic value....

There is no necessary incompatibility between Confucian ethics and capitalism. Nuyen (1999) has argued that Chinese philosophy including Confucianism is compatible with classical capitalism of perfect competition. In this regard, he refers to the writings of Francois Quesnay, the classical thinker. Quesnay stated that the economy is a self-regulating mechanism in accordance with the laws of nature and hence, a policy of laissez-faire should be adopted. This was adopted, as Nuyen described it, with a view to achieving "the goal of social harmony, and ultimately the harmony of the whole nature" (p. 75) which is consistent with the Confucian concept of *chung yung* (the Mean) and the way of the Tao (pp. 76–79).

However, whilst we attempt to integrate ethics and business holistically, the fact remains that we cannot completely eschew the reality that business objectives and life-objectives may conflict in at least some circumstances. The potential conflict between the personal morality of a company employee or agent and its "fiduciary duties" to the company is a case in point. This does not mean that business and the rest of one's life are or should be categorically treated as separate components. Indeed, we ought to, as Robert Solomon has argued, seek to integrate ethics and business in a more holistic fashion. But at the practical level, where there is a particular conflict between the attainment of business profits and the fundamental objectives of the whole life, it is logical and sensible that the latter should prevail. The objective of advancing human virtues should triumph over the narrower economic interests....

THE PRINCIPLE OF RECIPROCITY

When asked whether there is one word which would serve as a guiding principle for one's entire life, Confucius responded with the word "altruism" and the golden rule "Do not do to others what you do not want them to do to you" (Analects, Book XV, Number 23). The Chinese character for altruism (*shu*) encapsulates the concept of interpersonal care involving real and concrete individuals (Wang, 1999, p. 418).... In The Great Learning, the Confucian reciprocity principle is further reinforced, amongst others, in the context of the master–servant relationship:

What a man dislikes in his superiors, let him not display in the treatment of his inferiors: what he dislikes in inferiors, let him not display in the service of his superiors. (The Great Learning, X, ii)

According to the Analects (Book VI, Number 28), the person who abides by the principle of reciprocity is a man of humanity.

A man of humanity, wishing to establish his own character, also establishes the character of others, and wishing to be prominent himself, also helps others to be prominent. To be able to judge others by what is near to ourselves may be called the method of realizing humanity.

A man of humanity is one who practises the five virtues of "earnestness, liberality, truthfulness, diligence, and generosity" (Analects, Book 17, Number 6). In the book of Mencius, VII.A 4, the formula was specifically associated with the virtue of benevolence:

Try your best to treat others as you would wish to be treated yourself, and you will find that this is the shortest way to benevolence.

... The Confucian reciprocity principle appears to be qualified (and, indeed, complicated) by the apparent emphasis on familial relations. In the Analects, Confucius seemed to suggest that favoritism should be shown towards family members:

The Duke of She told Confucius, "In my country there is an upright man named Kung. When his father stole a sheep, he bore witness against him." Confucius said, "The upright men in my community are different from this. The father conceals the misconduct of the son and the son conceals the misconduct of the father. Uprightness is to be found in this (Book 13, Number 18).

In this regard, Mencius also favoured the Confucian emphasis on the five familial relations which are hierarchical in nature (Mencius, Book 3, Number 4). It should also be pointed out that Mencius had, in support of hierarchy at the familial level, opposed the principle of universal love without distinction advocated by the Moists (Mencius, Book 3, Number 5). The rationale appeared to be based on parents being the foundation of men. Mencius argued:

Mo advocated universal love which means a denial of the special relationship with the father. To deny the special relationship with the father ... is to become an animal ... If the principles of ... Mo are not stopped, and if the principles of Confucius are not brought to light, perverse doctrines will delude the people and obstruct the path of humanity and righteousness. When humanity and righteousness are obstructed, beasts will be led on to devour men, and men will devour one another (Chan, 1963, p. 72).

As Koehn and Leung (2004) have noted, the Confucian li (or rules of propriety) means that the concept of human dignity is not equal for everyone but is based on one's societal roles as well as family background and occupations (p. 269). Moreover, this notion of "role-based dignity" is, according to empirical studies, prevalent in the East Asian countries (Koehn and Leung, 2004, p. 273). In the employment context, a strictly hierarchical and authoritarian structure within the work organisation according to Confucian ethics would be contrary to the notion of participatory democracy in the workplace based on freedom and consent....

HUMAN VIRTUES AND THE MEAN

There are several commonalities between Confucian and Aristotelian ethics.... In particular, both philosophers believe in the significance of exemplary individuals for guidance and training in proper ethical behaviour (Sim, 2001). For Confucius, the person of exemplary virtue is junzi: for Aristotle, it is phronimos. Both junzi and phronimos exhibit desirable attributes of uprightness and other-regarding conduct. Second, Confucian and Aristotelian ethics are based on the need for the practice of such human virtues and the cultivation and development of one's character. For Aristotle, ethics is a "practical science", that is, it is concerned with action, rather than a set of theoretical knowledge about the right action. Aristotle said that "we become just by performing just acts, temperate by performing temperate ones, brave by performing brave ones" (The Nicomachean Ethics, p. 92). In the Analects, Confucius said that "[b]y nature men are alike. Through practice they have become far apart" (Book 17, Number 2). This emphasis on practice is also evident in Aristotle's statement in the Nicomachean Ethics that "[t]he moral virtues, then, are engendered in us neither by nor contrary to nature; we are constituted by nature to receive them, but their full development in us is due to habit" (p. 91).

... The Confucian individual is interpreted in connection with the community in which he or she is a part. The cultivation of the inner self is basically assessed by reference to ones external behaviour (Yao, 1996). The Confucian moral actor cleaves towards ethical standards to be found in a set of societal rituals and propriety though the self is not completely surrendered or submerged, as it were, in the sea of ritualised standards (Sim, 2003, 459)....

The other point of comparison between Confucian and Aristotelian ethics is the concept of the Mean in ethical conduct. For Aristotle, finding the ethical mean is intimately connected with the notion of human virtues. For each virtue, there is an appropriate mean. For example, we are exhorted to avoid the extremes of rashness and cowardice but to strive towards the mean, which is courage. Aristotle in the Nicomachean Ethics defines "virtue" as a "purposive disposition, lying in a mean that is relative to us and determined by a rational principle" (p. 101)....

The Confucian Doctrine of the Mean ... is based on the twin notions of centrality and balance (Chan, 1963, p. 16). This Confucian classic is concerned with human nature and being in harmony with the universe (Chan, 1963, pp. 95–96). The Mean is inextricably tied to human virtues: it is practised by the "superior man" whilst the "inferior man" acts contrary to the Mean (The Doctrine of the Mean, Stanza 2). Three virtues were highlighted in this Confucian classic: wisdom, humanity and courage (Stanza 20). Moreover, the value of sincerity to the superior man and humanity features prominently (Doctrine of the Mean, stanzas 24–26)....

CONCLUDING REMARKS

Confucian Ethics can and does play an important philosophical and practical role in impacting or influencing the direction of contemporary Business Ethics in the English-speaking world. With the growing stature of China's economy and businesses and the internationalisation of trade and commerce, it is likely that this influence will continue to be significant in the future....

REFERENCES

Chan, W.-T. 1963 *A Sourcebook of Chinese Philosophy.* Princeton University Press.

Nuyen, A.T.: 1999, "Chinese Philosophy and Western Capitalism," *Asian Philosophy* 9(1), 71–79.

Ornatowski, G.K. 1999 *Confucian Values, Japanese Economic Development, and the Creation of a Modern Japanese Ethics.* In Enderle, Georges (ed.), *International Business Ethics: Challenges and Approaches,* University of Notre Dame Press.

Wang, Q.J.: 1999, "The Golden Rule and Interpersonal Care—From a Confucian Perspective," *Philosophy East & West* 49(4), 415–438.

Yao, X.Z.: 1996, "Self-construction and Identity: The Confucian Self in Relation to Some Western Perceptions," *Asian Philosophy* 6(3), 1–17.

—21—

WESTERN ECONOMICS VERSUS BUDDHIST ECONOMICS

Laszlo Zsolnai

THE PROBLEM OF THE SELF

THOMAS SCHELLING RIGHTLY CHARACTERIZES modern Western economics as an egonomical framework. Modern Western economics is centered on self-interest understood as satisfaction of the wishes of one's body-mind ego. Buddhism challenges this view because it has a different conception of the self, which is *anatta*, the "no-self" (Elster 1985).

Anatta specifies the absence of a supposedly permanent and unchanging self in any one of the psychophysical constituents of empirical existence. What is normally thought of as the self is an agglomeration of constantly changing physical and mental constituents, which give rise to unhappiness if clung to as though this temporary assemblage represented permanence. The *anatta* doctrine attempts to encourage Buddhist practitioners to detach themselves from the misplaced clinging to what is mistakenly regarded as self, and from such detachment (aided by moral living and meditation) the way to *Nirvana* can be successfully traversed.

Modern neuroscience supports the Buddhist view of the self. What neuroscientists have discovered can be called the selfless (or virtual) self, a coherent global pattern, which seems to be centrally located, but is nowhere to be found, and yet is essential as a level of interaction for the behavior. The non-localisable, non-substantial self acts as if it were present, like a virtual interface (Varela 1999: 53, 61).

The Buddhist cosmology has the entire universe at its centre in contrast to the anthropocentric worldview of Western culture. For Buddhists human beings are humble in the totality and are essentially just grains of sand in the vast limitless ocean of space (Welford 2006).

The Four Noble Truths of the Buddha address the dynamics of human life:

(1) *Life is suffering.* This has to be comprehended. With the increasing secularism and dissociation from nature and the environment, and rising expectations inside and outside work, people are becoming less satisfied with life and lifestyles.

(2) *The cause of suffering is desire.* This has to be abandoned. Heightened dissatisfaction arguably has implications for consumerism. First, there is an erroneous perception that purchasing goods is going to make one happy; and second, we are increasingly dissatisfied and thus unhappy or stressed because we are unable to deal with what is needed to change.

(3) *The cessation of suffering is the cessation of desire.* This has to be realised. By becoming aware that there is a root to the general societal malaise and avoidance of environmental and social responsibilities, we can understand that there is a way of stopping such complacency and beginning a path to sustainability.

(4) *The path to the cessation of desire requires practice.* To cease doing what makes us dissatisfied, we have to realise the result of that dissatisfaction and keep trying to behave in a more sustainable manner. Buddhism shows us that this is difficult and requires ongoing commitment and practice.

Even if one gets what one desires, greater desires always emerge. The ego mindset cannot be fulfilled and its greed for more satisfaction and recognition becomes the source of its own destruction. This is a source of suffering because the human spirit becomes captured by the avaricious mind. The way through this life of constantly unsatisfied desires is the practice of non-attachment—in other words, developing a distance from all desires (Welford 2006).

PRINCIPLES OF BUDDHIST ECONOMICS

Minimising Suffering

While modern Western economics promotes doing business based on individual, self-interested, profit-maximising ways, Buddhism suggests an alternative strategy. The underlying principle of Buddhist economics is to *minimise suffering* of all sentient beings, including non-human beings.

From a Buddhist viewpoint a project is worthy to be undertaken if it can reduce the suffering of all those who are affected. Also, any change in economic-activity systems that reduces suffering should be welcomed.

The suffering-minimising principle can be formulated to reveal that the goal of economic activities is not to produce gains but to decrease losses....

Simplifying Desires

Modern Western economics cultivates desires. People are encouraged to develop new desires for things to acquire and for activities to do. The profit motive of companies requires creating more demand. But psychological research shows that materialistic value orientation undermines well-being. People who are highly focused on materialistic values have lower personal well-being and psychological health than those who believe that materialistic pursuits are relatively unimportant. These relationships have been documented in samples of people ranging from the wealthy to the poor, from teenagers to the elderly, and from Australians to South Koreans. These studies document that strong materialistic values are associated with a pervasive undermining of people's well-being, from low life satisfaction and happiness, to depression and anxiety, to physical problems such as headaches, and to personality disorders, narcissism, and antisocial behavior (Kasser 2002: 22).

Psychologists call the mechanism through which people seek to satisfy their desires auto-projection. It is a *loser strategy*, whether or not people achieve their desired goals. When they are not able to reach the goals they envision, they attribute their continuing dissatisfaction to their failure to reach the alleged corrective measures. When they succeed in attaining their goals, this usually does not bring what they hoped for and their feelings of discomfort are not relieved. So striving for satisfying desires never brings people the fulfilment they expect from it (Grof 1998: 207).

The Buddhist strategy is just the opposite of the Western one. It suggests not to multiply but to simplify our desires. Above the minimum material comfort, which includes enough food, clothing, shelter, and medicine, it is wise to try to reduce one's desires. Wanting less could bring substantial benefits for the person, for the community, and for nature.

Buddhism recommends moderate consumption and is directly aimed at changing one's preferences through meditation, reflection, analyses, autosuggestion and the like....

Desiring less is even fruitful in the case of money. Western economics presupposes that more money is better than less money. But, getting more money may have negative effects. Overpaid employees and managers do not always give high-level performance. Being underfinanced might be beneficial for a project. If people have smaller budgets, they may use the money more creatively and effectively.

Practicing Non-violence

In his monumental *Economics* textbook, Paul Samuelson selected the motto, Even a parrot can become an economist. All that he should learn is only two words: supply and demand. Modern Western economics aims to introduce markets wherever social problems need solving.

Karl Polanyi refers to the whole process of marketisation as "The Great Transformation", by which spheres of society became subordinated to the market mechanism (Polanyi 1946). In the age of globalisation we can experience this marketisation process on a much larger scale and in a speedier way than ever.

The market is a powerful institution. It can provide goods and services in a flexible and productive way; however, it has its own limitations. Limitations of the market come from *non-represented* stakeholders, *underrepresented* stakeholders, and *myopic* stakeholders.

Primordial stakeholders such as nature and future generations are simply not represented in the market because they do not have a vote in terms of purchasing power. They cannot represent their interests in the language of supply and demand. Other stakeholders such as the poor and marginalised people are underrepresented because they do not have enough purchasing power to signal their preferences in the market. Finally, stakeholders who are well represented in the market, because they have enough purchasing power, often behave in a myopic way; that is, they heavily discount values in space and time. Market prices usually reflect the values of the strongest stakeholders and favour preferences here and now. Because of these inherent limitations the market cannot give a complete, unbiased direction for guiding economic activities (Zsolnai and Gasparski 2002).

Non-violence (ahimsa) is the main guiding principle of Buddhism for solving social problems. It is required that an act does not cause harm to the doer or the receivers. Non-violence prevents doing actions that directly cause suffering for oneself or others and urges participative solutions.

The community-economy models are good examples. Communities of producers and consumers are formed to meet both their needs at the lowest cost and reduced risk by a long-term arrangement. Studying dozens of working models, Richard Douthwaite characterises community economy as follows (Douthwaite 1996):

> Community economy uses *local resources* to meet the needs of local people rather than the wants of markets far away. World prices do not determine what will be produced and the key production processes need to be run entirely without inputs from the world system.

Community economy is based on self-reliance that is closely linked to ecological sustainability. Practically speaking, *living within limits* and sustainability are one and the same thing. Every community should achieve ecological sustainability by exploiting the ecological niche available for itself. Achieving ecological sustainability and non-violence requires altering the underlying structure of dominating configurations of modern business. This means deemphasising profit maximisation and market systems and introducing small-scale, locally adaptable, culturally diverse ways of engaging in substantive economic activity.

BUDDHIST ECONOMICS AS A STRATEGY

Buddhist economics represents a *minimising framework* where suffering, desires, violence, instrumental use, and self-interest have to be minimised. This is why small is beautiful and less

Modern Western Economics versus Buddhist Economics

MODERN WESTERN ECONOMICS	BUDDHIST ECONOMICS
maximise profit	minimise suffering
maximise desires	minimise desires
maximise market	minimise violence
maximise instrumental use	minimise instrumental use
maximise self-interest	minimise self-interest
"bigger is better"	"small is beautiful"
"more is more"	"less is more"

is more nicely express the essence of the Buddhist approach to economic questions.

Modern Western economics represents a *maximising framework*. It wants to maximise profit, desires, market, instrumental use, and self-interest and tends to build a world where bigger is better and more is more (see the *table above*).

Buddhist economics does not aim to build an economic system of its own. Rather, it represents a strategy, which can be applied in any economic setting at any time. It helps to create livelihood solutions that reduce the suffering of all sentient beings through the practices of want negation, non-violence, caring and generosity.

In his paper Towards a Progressive Buddhist Economics, Simon Zadek asks the important question of whether Buddhist economics is able to penetrate the modern economy to prevent it from driving us along a materially unsustainable path, and to uproot its growing hold on our psychological conditions. And he concludes that we have no choice but to engage in modernisation in an attempt to redirect it or at least reduce its negative effects (Zadek 1997).

Today's dominating business models are based on and cultivates narrow self-centeredness. Buddhist economics points out that emphasising individuality and promoting the greatest fulfilment of the desires of the individual conjointly lead to destruction.

Happiness research convincingly shows that not material wealth but the richness of personal relationships determines happiness. Not things but people make people happy (Lane 1998). Western economics tries to provide people with happiness by supplying enormous quantities of things. But what people need are caring relationships and generous love. Buddhist economics makes these values accessible by direct provision.

Peace can be achieved in non-violent ways. Wanting less can substantially contribute to this endeavour and make it happen easier.

Permanence, or ecological sustainability, requires a drastic cutback in the present level of consumption and production globally. This reduction should not be an inconvenient exercise of self-sacrifice. In the noble ethos of reducing suffering it can be a positive development path for humanity.

REFERENCES

Bouckaert, L., Opdebeeck, H., Zsolnai, L. (eds) (2007): *Frugality: Rebalancing Material and Spiritual Values in Economic Life.* Oxford: Peter Lang Academic Publishers.

Douthwaite, R. (1996): *Short Circuit. Strengthening Local Economics for Security in an Unstable World.* The Lilliput Press.

Elster, J. (1985): Introduction. In: Elster, J. (ed.): *The Multiple Self*. Cambridge: Cambridge University Press, 1–34.

Grof, S. (1998): *The Cosmic Game. Explorations of the Frontiers of Human Consciousness*. Albany: State University of New York Press.

Kasser, T. (2002): *The High Price of Materialism*. Cambridge, MA: MIT Press.

Lane, R.E. (1998): The Joyless Market Economy. In: Ben-Ner, A., Putterman, L. (eds): *Economics, Values, and Organizations*. Cambridge: Cambridge University Press, 461–488.

Polanyi, K. (1946): *The Great Transformation. Origins of Our Time*. London: Victor Gollancz Ltd.

Schumacher, E.F. (1973): *Small Is Beautiful. Economics as if People Mattered*. Abacus.

Varela, F.J. (1999): *Ethical Know-How. Action, Wisdom, and Cognition*. Stanford: Stanford University Press.

Welford, R. (2006): Tackling Greed and Achieving Sustainable Development. In: Zsolnai, L. and Johannessen Ims, K. (eds): *Business within Limits: Deep Ecology and Buddhist Economics*. Oxford: Peter Lang Publisher, 25–52.

Zadek, S. (1997): Towards a Progressive Buddhist Economics. In: Watts, J., Senauke, A. and Bhikku, S. (eds): *Entering the Realm of Reality: Towards Dharmmic Societies*. Bangkok: INEB, 241–273.

Zsolnai, L. and Gasparski, W. (eds) (2002): *Ethics and the Future of Capitalism*. New Brunswick-London: Transaction Publishers.

—22—
THE MEANING OF "SOCIAL ENTREPRENEURSHIP"

J. Gregory Dees

THE IDEA OF "SOCIAL ENTREPRENEURSHIP" HAS struck a responsive chord. It is a phrase well suited to our times. It combines the passion of a social mission with an image of business-like discipline, innovation, and determination commonly associated with, for instance, the high-tech pioneers of Silicon Valley. The time is certainly ripe for entrepreneurial approaches to social problems. Many governmental and philanthropic efforts have fallen far short of our expectations. Major social sector institutions are often viewed as inefficient, ineffective, and unresponsive. Social entrepreneurs are needed to develop new models for a new century.

The language of social entrepreneurship may be new, but the phenomenon is not. We have always had social entrepreneurs, even if we did not call them that. They originally built many of the institutions we now take for granted. However, the new name is important in that it implies a blurring of sector boundaries. In addition to innovative not-for-profit ventures, social entrepreneurship can include social purpose business ventures, such as for-profit community development banks, and hybrid organizations mixing not-for-profit and for-profit elements, such as homeless shelters that start businesses to train and employ their residents. The new language helps to broaden the playing field. Social entrepreneurs look for the most effective methods of serving their social missions.

Though the concept of "social entrepreneurship" is gaining popularity, it means different things to different people. This can be confusing. Many associate social entrepreneurship exclusively with not-for-profit organizations starting for-profit or earned-income ventures. Others use it to describe anyone who starts a not-for-profit organization. Still others use it to refer to business owners who integrate social responsibility into their operations. What does "social entrepreneurship" really mean? What does it take to be a social entrepreneur? To answer these questions, we should start by looking into the roots of the term "entrepreneur."

ORIGINS OF THE WORD "ENTREPRENEUR"

In common parlance, being an entrepreneur is associated with starting a business, but this is a very loose application of a term that has a rich history and a much more significant meaning. The term "entrepreneur" originated in French economics as early as the 17th and 18th centuries. In French, it means someone who "undertakes," not an "undertaker" in the sense of a funeral director, but someone who undertakes a significant project or activity. More specifically, it came to be used to identify the venturesome individuals who stimulated economic progress by finding new and better ways of doing things. The French economist most commonly credited with giving the term this particular meaning is Jean Baptiste Say. Writing around the turn of the 19th century, Say put it this way, "The entrepreneur shifts economic resources out of an area of lower and into an area of higher productivity and greater yield." Entrepreneurs create value.

In the 20th century, the economist most closely associated with the term was Joseph Schumpeter. He described entrepreneurs as the innovators who drive the "creative-destructive" process of capitalism. In his words, "the function of entrepreneurs is to reform or revolutionize the pattern of production." They can do this in many ways: "by exploiting an invention or, more generally, an untried technological possibility for producing a new commodity or producing an old one in a new way, by opening up a new source of supply of materials or a new outlet for products, by reorganizing an industry and so on." Schumpeter's entrepreneurs are the change agents in the economy. By serving new markets or creating new ways of doing things, they move the economy forward.

It is true that many of the entrepreneurs that Say and Schumpeter have in mind serve their function by starting new, profit-seeking business ventures, but starting a business is not the essence of entrepreneurship. Though other economists may have used the term with various nuances, the Say-Schumpeter tradition that identifies entrepreneurs as the catalysts and innovators behind economic progress has served as the foundation for the contemporary use of this concept.

CURRENT THEORIES OF ENTREPRENEURSHIP

Contemporary writers in management and business have presented a wide range of theories of entrepreneurship. Many of the leading thinkers remain true to the Say-Schumpeter tradition while offering variations on the theme. For instance, in

his attempt to get at what is special about entrepreneurs, Peter Drucker starts with Say's definition, but amplifies it to focus on opportunity. Drucker does not require entrepreneurs to cause change, but sees them as exploiting the opportunities that change (in technology, consumer preferences, social norms, etc.) creates. He says, "this defines entrepreneur and entrepreneurship—*the entrepreneur always searches for change, responds to it, and exploits it as an opportunity.*" The notion of "opportunity" has come to be central to many current definitions of entrepreneurship. It is the way today's management theorists capture Say's notion of shifting resources to areas of higher yield. An opportunity, presumably, means an opportunity to create value in this way. Entrepreneurs have a mind-set that sees the possibilities rather than the problems created by change.

For Drucker, starting a business is neither necessary nor sufficient for entrepreneurship. He explicitly comments, "Not every new small business is entrepreneurial or represents entrepreneurship." He cites the example of a "husband and wife who open another delicatessen store or another Mexican restaurant in the American suburb" as a case in point. There is nothing especially innovative or change-oriented in this. The same would be true of new not-for-profit organizations. Not every new organization would be entrepreneurial. Drucker also makes it clear that entrepreneurship does not require a profit motive. Early in his book on Innovation and Entrepreneurship, Drucker asserts, "*No better text for a History of Entrepreneurship could be found than the creation of the modern university, and especially the modern American university.*" He then explains what a major innovation this was at the time. Later in the book, he devotes a chapter to entrepreneurship in public service institutions.

Howard Stevenson, a leading theorist of entrepreneurship at Harvard Business School, added an element of resourcefulness to the opportunity-oriented definition based on research he conducted to determine what distinguishes entrepreneurial management from more common forms of "administrative" management. After identifying several dimensions of difference, he suggests defining the heart of entrepreneurial management as "the pursuit of opportunity without regard to resources currently controlled." He found that entrepreneurs not only see and pursue opportunities that elude administrative managers; entrepreneurs do not allow their own initial resource endowments to limit their options. To borrow a metaphor from Elizabeth Barrett Browning, their reach exceeds their grasp. Entrepreneurs mobilize the resources of others to achieve their entrepreneurial objectives. Administrators allow their existing resources and their job descriptions to constrain their visions and actions. Once again, we have a definition of entrepreneurship that is not limited to business start-ups.

DIFFERENCES BETWEEN BUSINESS AND SOCIAL ENTREPRENEURS

The ideas of Say, Schumpeter, Drucker, and Stevenson are attractive because they can be as easily applied in the social sector as the business sector. They describe a mind-set and a kind of behavior that can be manifest anywhere. In a world in which sector boundaries are blurring, this is an advantage. We should build our understanding of social entrepreneurship on this strong tradition of entrepreneurship theory and research. Social entrepreneurs are one species in the genus entrepreneur. They are entrepreneurs with a social mission. However, because of this mission, they face some distinctive challenges and any definition ought to reflect this.

For social entrepreneurs, the social mission is explicit and central. This obviously affects how social entrepreneurs perceive and assess opportunities. Mission-related impact becomes the central criterion, not wealth creation. Wealth is just a means to an end for social entrepreneurs. With business entrepreneurs, wealth creation is a way of measuring value creation. This is because business entrepreneurs are subject to market discipline,

which determines in large part whether they are creating value. If they do not shift resources to more economically productive uses, they tend to be driven out of business.

Markets are not perfect, but over the long haul, they work reasonably well as a test of private value creation, specifically the creation of value for customers who are willing and able to pay. An entrepreneur's ability to attract resources (capital, labor, equipment, etc.) in a competitive marketplace is a reasonably good indication that the venture represents a more productive use of these resources than the alternatives it is competing against. The logic is simple. Entrepreneurs who can pay the most for resources are typically the ones who can put the resources to higher valued uses, as determined in the marketplace. Value is created in business when customers are willing to pay more than it costs to produce the good or service being sold. The profit (revenue minus costs) that a venture generates is a reasonably good indicator of the value it has created. If an entrepreneur cannot convince a sufficient number of customers to pay an adequate price to generate a profit, this is a strong indication that insufficient value is being created to justify this use of resources. A re-deployment of the resources happens naturally because firms that fail to create value cannot purchase sufficient resources or raise capital. They go out of business. Firms that create the most economic value have the cash to attract the resources needed to grow.

Markets do not work as well for social entrepreneurs. In particular, markets do not do a good job of valuing social improvements, public goods and harms, and benefits for people who cannot afford to pay. These elements are often essential to social entrepreneurship. That is what makes it social entrepreneurship. As a result, it is much harder to determine whether a social entrepreneur is creating sufficient social value to justify the resources used in creating that value. The survival or growth of a social enterprise is not proof of its efficiency or effectiveness in improving social conditions. It is only a weak indicator, at best.

Social entrepreneurs operate in markets, but these markets often do not provide the right discipline. Many social-purpose organizations charge fees for some of their services. They also compete for donations, volunteers, and other kinds of support. But the discipline of these "markets" is frequently not closely aligned with the social entrepreneur's mission. It depends on who is paying the fees or providing the resources, what their motivations are, and how well they can assess the social value created by the venture. It is inherently difficult to measure social value creation. How much social value is created by reducing pollution in a given stream, by saving the spotted owl, or by providing companionship to the elderly? The calculations are not only hard but also contentious. Even when improvements can be measured, it is often difficult to attribute them to a specific intervention. Are the lower crime rates in an area due to the Block Watch, new policing techniques, or just a better economy? Even when improvements can be measured and attributed to a given intervention, social entrepreneurs often cannot capture the value they have created in an economic form to pay for the resources they use. Whom do they charge for cleaning the stream or running the Block Watch? How do they get everyone who benefits to pay? To offset this value-capture problem, social entrepreneurs rely on subsidies, donations, and volunteers, but this further muddies the waters of market discipline. The ability to attract these philanthropic resources may provide some indication of value creation in the eyes of the resource providers, but it is not a very reliable indicator. The psychic income people get from giving or volunteering is likely to be only loosely connected with actual social impact, if it is connected at all.

DEFINING SOCIAL ENTREPRENEURSHIP

Any definition of social entrepreneurship should reflect the need for a substitute for the market discipline that works for business entrepreneurs.

We cannot assume that market discipline will automatically weed out social ventures that are not effectively and efficiently utilizing resources. The following definition combines an emphasis on discipline and accountability with the notions of value creation taken from Say, innovation and change agents from Schumpeter, pursuit of opportunity from Drucker, and resourcefulness from Stevenson. In brief, this definition can be stated as follows:

Social entrepreneurs play the role of change agents in the social sector, by:
- *Adopting a mission to create and sustain social value (not just private value),*
- *Recognizing and relentlessly pursuing new opportunities to serve that mission,*
- *Engaging in a process of continuous innovation, adaptation, and learning,*
- *Acting boldly without being limited by resources currently in hand, and*
- *Exhibiting heightened accountability to the constituencies served and for the outcomes created.*

This is clearly an "idealized" definition. Social sector leaders will exemplify these characteristics in different ways and to different degrees. The closer a person gets to satisfying all these conditions, the more that person fits the model of a social entrepreneur. Those who are more innovative in their work and who create more significant social improvements will naturally be seen as more entrepreneurial. Those who are truly Schumpeterian will reform or revolutionize their industries. Each element in this brief definition deserves some further elaboration. Let's consider each one in turn.

Change agents in the social sector: Social entrepreneurs are reformers and revolutionaries, as described by Schumpeter, but with a social mission. They make fundamental changes in the way things are done in the social sector. Their visions are bold. They attack the underlying causes of problems, rather than simply treating symptoms. They often reduce needs rather than just meeting them. They seek to create systemic changes and sustainable improvements. Though they may act locally, their actions have the potential to stimulate global improvements in their chosen arenas, whether that is education, health care, economic development, the environment, the arts, or any other social field.

Adopting a mission to create and sustain social value: This is the core of what distinguishes social entrepreneurs from business entrepreneurs even from socially responsible businesses. For a social entrepreneur, the social mission is fundamental. This is a mission of social improvement that cannot be reduced to creating private benefits (financial returns or consumption benefits) for individuals. Making a profit, creating wealth, or serving the desires of customers may be part of the model, but these are means to a social end, not the end in itself. Profit is not the gauge of value creation; nor is customer satisfaction; social impact is the gauge. Social entrepreneurs look for a long-term social return on investment. Social entrepreneurs want more than a quick hit; they want to create lasting improvements. They think about sustaining the impact.

Recognizing and relentlessly pursuing new opportunities: Where others see problems, social entrepreneurs see opportunity. They are not simply driven by the perception of a social need or by their compassion, rather they have a vision of how to achieve improvement and they are determined to make their vision work. They are persistent. The models they develop and the approaches they take can, and often do, change, as the entrepreneurs learn about what works and what does not work. The key element is persistence combined with a willingness to make adjustments as one goes. Rather than giving up when an obstacle is encountered, entrepreneurs ask, "How can we surmount this obstacle? How can we make this work?"

Engaging in a process of continuous innovation, adaptation, and learning: Entrepreneurs are innovative. They break new ground, develop new models, and pioneer new approaches. However, as Schumpeter notes, innovation can take many forms. It does not require inventing something wholly new; it can simply involve applying an existing idea in a new way or to a new situation. Entrepreneurs need not be inventors. They simply need to be creative in applying what others have invented. Their innovations may appear in how they structure their core programs or in how they assemble the resources and fund their work. On the funding side, social entrepreneurs look for innovative ways to assure that their ventures will have access to resources as long as they are creating social value. This willingness to innovate is part of the modus operandi of entrepreneurs. It is not just a one-time burst of creativity. It is a continuous process of exploring, learning, and improving. Of course, with innovation comes uncertainty and risk of failure. Entrepreneurs tend to have a high tolerance for ambiguity and learn how to manage risks for themselves and others. They treat failure of a project as a learning experience, not a personal tragedy.

Acting boldly without being limited by resources currently in hand: Social entrepreneurs do not let their own limited resources keep them from pursuing their visions. They are skilled at doing more with less and at attracting resources from others. They use scarce resources efficiently, and they leverage their limited resources by drawing in partners and collaborating with others. They explore all resource options, from pure philanthropy to the commercial methods of the business sector. They are not bound by sector norms or traditions. They develop resource strategies that are likely to support and reinforce their social missions. They take calculated risks and manage the downside, so as to reduce the harm that will result from failure. They understand the risk tolerances of their stakeholders and use this to spread the risk to those who are better prepared to accept it.

Exhibiting a heightened sense of accountability to the constituencies served and for the outcomes created: Because market discipline does not automatically weed out inefficient or ineffective social ventures, social entrepreneurs take steps to assure they are creating value. This means that they seek a sound understanding of the constituencies they are serving. They make sure they have correctly assessed the needs and values of the people they intend to serve and the communities in which they operate. In some cases, this requires close connections with those communities. They understand the expectations and values of their "investors," including anyone who invests money, time, and/or expertise to help them. They seek to provide real social improvements to their beneficiaries and their communities, as well as attractive (social and/or financial) return to their investors. Creating a fit between investor values and community needs is an important part of the challenge. When feasible, social entrepreneurs create market-like feedback mechanisms to reinforce this accountability. They assess their progress in terms of social, financial, and managerial outcomes, not simply in terms of their size, outputs, or processes. They use this information to make course corrections as needed.

SOCIAL ENTREPRENEURS: A RARE BREED

Social entrepreneurship describes a set of behaviors that are exceptional. These behaviors should be encouraged and rewarded in those who have the capabilities and temperament for this kind of work. We could use many more of them. Should everyone aspire to be a social entrepreneur? No. Not every social sector leader is well suited to being entrepreneurial. The same is true in business. Not every business leader is an entrepreneur in the sense that Say, Schumpeter, Drucker, and Stevenson had in mind. While we might wish for more entrepreneurial behavior in both sectors, society has a need for different leadership types and styles. Social entrepreneurs are one special breed of leader, and they should be recognized as such. This definition preserves their distinctive status and assures that social entrepreneurship is not treated lightly. We need social entrepreneurs to help us find new avenues toward social improvement as we enter the next century.

—23—

ETHICS AND NONPROFITS

Deborah L. Rhode and Amanda K. Packel

THOSE WHO WORK ON ISSUES OF ETHICS ARE among the few professionals not suffering from the current economic downturn. The last decade has brought an escalating supply of moral meltdowns in both the for-profit and the nonprofit sectors. Corporate misconduct has received the greatest attention, in part because the abuses are so egregious and the costs so enormous. Chief contenders for most ethically challenged include former Merrill Lynch & Co. CEO John Thain, who spent $1.22 million in 2008 to redecorate his office, including the purchase of a $1,400 trash can and a $35,000 antique commode, while the company was hemorrhaging losses of some $27 billion.[1]

Still, the corporate sector has no monopoly on greed. Consider EduCap Inc., a multibillion-dollar student loan charity. According to Internal Revenue Service records, the organization abused its tax-exempt status by charging excessive interest on loans and by providing millions in compensation and lavish perks to its CEO and her husband, including use of the organization's $31 million private jet for family and friends.[2]

Unsurprisingly, these and a host of other scandals have eroded public confidence in our nation's leadership. According to a CBS News poll, only a quarter of Americans think that top executives are honest. Even executives themselves acknowledge cause for concern. The American Management Association Corporate Values Survey found that about one-third of executives believed that their company's public statements on ethics sometimes conflicted with internal messages and realities. And more than one-third of the executives reported that although their company would follow the law, it would not always do what would be perceived as ethical.

Employee surveys similarly suggest that many American workplaces fail to foster a culture of integrity. Results vary but generally indicate that between about one-quarter and three-quarters of employees observe misconduct, only about half of which is reported.[3] In the 2007 National Nonprofit Ethics Survey, slightly more than half of employees had observed at least one act of misconduct in the previous year, roughly the same percentages as in the for-profit and government sectors. Nearly 40 percent of nonprofit employees who observed misconduct failed to report it, largely because they believed that reporting would not lead to corrective action or they feared retaliation from management or peers.[4]

Public confidence in nonprofit performance is similarly at risk. A 2008 Brookings Institution survey found that about one-third of Americans reported having "not too much" or no confidence in charitable organizations, and 70 percent felt that charitable organizations waste "a great deal" or a "fair amount" of money. Only 10 percent thought charitable organizations did a "very good job" spending money wisely; only 17 percent thought that charities did a "very good job" of being fair in decisions; and only one-quarter thought charities did a "very good job" of helping people.[5] Similarly, a 2006 Harris Poll found that only one in 10 Americans strongly believed that charities are honest and ethical in their use of donated funds. Nearly one in three believed that nonprofits have "pretty seriously gotten off in the wrong direction." These public perceptions are particularly troubling for nonprofit organizations that depend on continuing financial contributions.

Addressing these ethical concerns requires a deeper understanding of the forces that compromise ethical judgment and the most effective institutional responses. To that end, this article draws on the growing body of research on organizational culture in general, and in nonprofit institutions in particular. We begin by reviewing the principal forces that distort judgment in all types of organizations. Next, we analyze the ethical issues that arise specifically in the nonprofit sector. We conclude by suggesting ways that nonprofits can prevent and correct misconduct and can institutionalize ethical values in all aspects of the organization's culture.

CAUSES OF MISCONDUCT

Ethical challenges arise at all levels in all types of organizations—for-profit, nonprofit, and government—and involve a complex relationship between individual character and cultural influences. Some of these challenges can result in criminal violations or civil liability: fraud, misrepresentation, and misappropriation of assets fall into this category. More common ethical problems involve gray areas—activities that are on the fringes of fraud, or that involve conflicts of interest, misallocation of resources, or inadequate accountability and transparency.

Research identifies four crucial factors that influence ethical conduct:

1. Moral awareness: recognition that a situation raises ethical issues
2. Moral decision making: determining what course of action is ethically sound
3. Moral intent: identifying which values should take priority in the decision
4. Moral action: following through on ethical decisions.[6]

People vary in their capacity for moral judgment—in their ability to recognize and analyze moral issues, and in the priority that they place on moral values. They also differ in their capacity for moral behavior—in their ability to cope with frustration and make good on their commitments.

Cognitive biases can compromise these ethical capacities. Those in leadership positions often have a high degree of confidence in their own judgment. That can readily lead to arrogance, over-optimism, and an escalation of commitment to choices that turn out to be wrong either factually or morally.[7] As a result, people may ignore or suppress dissent, overestimate their ability to rectify adverse consequences, and cover up mistakes by denying, withholding, or even destroying information.[8]

A related bias involves cognitive dissonance: People tend to suppress or reconstrue information that casts doubt on a prior belief or action.[9] Such dynamics may lead people to discount or devalue evidence of the harms of their conduct or the extent of their own responsibility. In-group biases can also result in unconscious discrimination that leads to ostracism of unwelcome or inconvenient views. That, in turn, can generate perceptions of unfairness and encourage team loyalty at the expense of candid and socially responsible decision making.[10]

A person's ethical reasoning and conduct is also affected by organizational structures and norms. Skewed reward systems can lead to a preoccupation with short-term profits, growth, or donations at the expense of long-term values. Mismanaged bonus systems and compensation structures are part of the explanation for the morally irresponsible behavior reflected in Enron Corp. and in the recent financial crisis.[11] In charitable organizations, employees who feel excessive pressure to generate revenue or minimize administrative expenses may engage in misleading conduct.[12] Employees' perceptions of unfairness in reward systems, as well as leaders' apparent lack of commitment to ethical standards, increase the likelihood of unethical behavior.[13]

A variety of situational pressures can also undermine moral conduct. Psychologist Stanley Milgram's classic obedience to authority experiment at Yale University offers a chilling example of how readily the good go bad under situational pressures. When asked to administer electric shocks to another participant in the experiment, about two-thirds of subjects fully complied, up to levels marked "dangerous," despite the victim's screams of pain. Yet when the experiment was described to subjects, none believed that they would comply, and the estimate of how many others would do so was no more than one in 100. In real-world settings, when instructions come from supervisors and jobs are on the line, many moral compasses go missing.

Variations of Milgram's study also documented the influence of peers on individual decision making. Ninety percent of subjects paired with someone who refused to comply also refused to administer the shocks. By the same token, 90 percent of subjects paired with an uncomplaining and obedient subject were equally obedient. Research on organizational behavior similarly finds that people are more likely to engage in unethical conduct when acting with others. Under circumstances where bending the rules provides payoffs for the group, members may feel substantial pressure to put their moral convictions on hold. That is especially likely when organizations place heavy emphasis on loyalty and offer significant rewards to team players. For example, if it is common practice for charity employees to inflate expense reports or occasionally liberate office supplies and in-kind charitable donations, other employees may suspend judgment or follow suit. Once people yield to situational pressures when the moral cost seems small, they can gradually slide into more serious misconduct. Psychologists label this "the boiled frog" phenomenon. A frog thrown into boiling water will jump out of the pot. A frog placed in tepid water that gradually becomes hotter will calmly boil to death.

Moral blinders are especially likely in contexts where people lack accountability for collective decision making. That is often true of boards of directors—members' individual reputations rarely suffer, and insurance typically insulates them from personal liability. A well-known study by Scott Armstrong, a professor at the Wharton School of the University of Pennsylvania, illustrates the pathologies that too often play out in real life. The experiment asked 57 groups of executives and business students to assume the role of an imaginary pharmaceutical company's board of directors. Each group received a fact pattern indicating that one of their company's most profitable drugs was causing an estimated 14 to 22 "unnecessary" deaths a year. The drug would likely be banned by regulators because a competitor offered a safe medication with the same benefits at the same price. More than four-fifths of the boards decided to continue marketing the product and to take legal and political actions to prevent a ban. By contrast, when a different group of people with similar business backgrounds were asked for their personal views on the same hypothetical, 97 percent believed that continuing to market the drug was socially irresponsible.[14]

These dynamics are readily apparent in real-world settings. Enron's board twice suspended conflict of interest rules to allow CFO Andrew Fastow to line his pockets at the corporation's expense.[15] Some members of the United Way of the National Capital Area's board were aware of suspicious withdrawals by CEO Oral Suer over the course of 15 years, but failed to alert the full board or take corrective action.[16] Experts view the large size of some governing bodies, such as the formerly 50-member board of the American Red Cross, as a contributing factor in nonprofit scandals.[17]

Other characteristics of organizations can also contribute to unethical conduct. Large organizations facing complex issues may undermine ethical judgments by fragmenting information across multiple departments and people. In many scandals, a large number of professionals—lawyers, accountants, financial analysts, board members, and even officers—lacked important facts raising moral as well as legal concerns. Work may be allocated in ways that prevent decision makers from seeing the full picture, and channels for expressing concerns may be inadequate.

Another important influence is ethical climate—the moral meanings that employees give to workplace policies and practices. Organizations signal their priorities in multiple ways, including the content and enforcement of ethical standards; the criteria for hiring, promotion, and compensation; and the fairness and respect with which they treat their employees. People care deeply about "organizational justice" and perform better when they believe that their workplace is treating them with dignity and is rewarding ethical conduct. Workers also respond to moral cues from peers and leaders. Virtue begets virtue, and observing integrity in others promotes similar behavior.

ETHICAL ISSUES IN THE NONPROFIT SECTOR

These organizational dynamics play out in distinctive ways in the nonprofit sector. There are six areas in particular where ethical issues arise in the nonprofit sector: compensation; conflicts of interest; publications and solicitation; financial integrity; investment policies; and accountability and strategic management.

Compensation

Salaries that are modest by business standards can cause outrage in the nonprofit sector, particularly when the organization is struggling to address unmet societal needs. In a March 23, 2009, *Nation* column, Katha Pollitt announced that she "stopped donating to the New York Public Library when it gave its president and CEO Paul LeClerc a several hundred thousand-dollar raise so his salary would be $800,000 a year." That, she pointed out, was "twenty times the median household income." Asking him to give back half a million "would buy an awful lot of books—or help pay for raises for the severely underpaid librarians who actually keep the system going." If any readers thought LeClerc was

an isolated case, she suggested checking Charity Navigator for comparable examples.

The problem is not just salaries. It is also the perks that officers and unpaid board members may feel entitled to take because their services would be worth so much more in the private sector. A widely publicized example involves William Aramony, the former CEO of United Way of America, who served six years in prison after an investigation uncovered misuse of the charity's funds to finance a lavish lifestyle, including luxury condominiums, personal trips, and payments to his mistress.[18] Examples like Aramony ultimately prompted the IRS to demand greater transparency concerning nonprofit CEO compensation packages exceeding certain thresholds.[19]

Nonprofits also face issues concerning benefits for staff and volunteers. How should an organization handle low-income volunteers who select a few items for themselves while sorting through noncash contributions? Should employees ever accept gifts or meals from beneficiaries or clients? Even trivial expenditures can pose significant issues of principle or public perception.

Travel expenses also raise questions. Can employees keep frequent flyer miles from business travel? How does it look for cash-strapped federal courts to hold a judicial conference at a Ritz-Carlton hotel, even though the hotel offered a significantly discounted rate? The Panel on the Nonprofit Sector recommends in its *Principles for Good Governance and Ethical Practice* that organizations establish clear written policies about what can be reimbursed and require that travel expenses be cost-effective. But what counts as reasonable or cost-effective can be open to dispute, particularly if the nonprofit has wealthy board members or executives accustomed to creature comforts.

Conflicts of Interest

Conflicts of interest arise frequently in the nonprofit sector. The Nature Conservancy encountered one such problem in a "buyer conservation deal." The organization bought land for $2.1 million and added restrictions that prohibited development such as mining, drilling, or dams, but authorized construction of a single-family house of unrestricted size, including a pool, a tennis court, and a writer's cabin. Seven weeks later, the Nature Conservancy sold the land for $500,000 to the former chairman of its regional chapter and his wife, a Nature Conservancy trustee. The buyers then donated $1.6 million to the Nature Conservancy and took a federal tax write-off for the "charitable contribution."[20]

Related conflicts of interest arise when an organization offers preferential treatment to board members or their affiliated companies. In another Nature Conservancy transaction, the organization received $100,000 from SC Johnson Wax to allow the company to use the Conservancy's logo in national promotion of products, including toilet cleaner. The company's chairman sat on the charity's board, although he reportedly recused himself from participating in or voting on the transaction.[21]

These examples raise a number of ethical questions. Should board members obtain contracts or donations for their own organizations? Is the board member's disclosure and abstention from a vote enough? Should a major donor receive special privileges, such as a job or college admission for a child? In a recent survey, a fifth of nonprofits (and two-fifths of those with more than $10 million in annual expenses) reported buying or renting goods, services, or property from a board member or an affiliated company within the prior two years. In three-quarters of nonprofits that did not report any such transactions, board members were not required to disclose financial interests in entities doing business with the organization, so its leaders may not have been aware of such conflicts.[22]

Despite the ethical minefield that these transactions create, many nonprofits oppose restrictions because they rely on insiders to provide donations or goods and services at below-market rates. Yet such quid pro quo relationships can jeopardize an organization's reputation for fairness and integrity in its financial dealings. To maintain public trust and fiduciary obligations, nonprofits need detailed, unambiguous conflict of interest policies, including requirements that employees and board members disclose all financial interest in companies that may engage in transactions with the organization. At a minimum, these policies should also demand total transparency about the existence of potential conflicts and the process by which they are dealt with.

Publications and Solicitation

Similar concerns about public trust entail total candor and accuracy in nonprofit reports. The Red Cross learned that lesson the hard way after disclosures of how it used the record donations that came in the wake of the 9/11 terrorist attacks. Donors believed that their contributions would go to help victims and their families. The Red Cross, however, set aside more than half of the $564 million in funds raised for 9/11 for other operations and future reserves. Although this was a long-standing organizational practice, it was not well known. Donor outrage forced a public apology and redirection of funds, and the charity's image was tarnished.[23]

As the Red Cross example demonstrates, nonprofits need to pay particular attention to transparency. They should disclose in a clear and non-misleading way the percentage of funds spent on administrative costs—information that affects many watchdog rankings of nonprofit organizations. Transparency is also necessary in solicitation materials, grant proposals, and donor agreements. Organizations cannot afford to raise funds on the basis of misguided assumptions, or to violate public expectations in the use of resources.

Financial Integrity

Nonprofit organizations also face ethical dilemmas in deciding whether to accept donations that have any unpalatable associations or conditions. The Stanford Institute for Research on Women and Gender, for example, declined to consider a potential gift from the Playboy Foundation. By contrast, the ACLU's Women's Rights Project, in its early phase, accepted a Playboy Foundation gift, and for a brief period sent out project mailings with a Playboy bunny logo.[24] When Stanford University launched an ethics center, the president quipped about what level of contribution would be necessary to name the center and whether the amount should depend on the donor's reputation. If "the price was right," would the university want a Ken Lay or a Leona Helmsley center on ethics?

Recently, many corporations have been attempting to "green" their image through affiliations with environmental organizations, and some of these groups have been entrepreneurial in capitalizing on such interests. The Nature Conservancy offered corporations such as the Pacific Gas and Electric Co. and the Dow Chemical Co. seats on its International Leadership Council for $25,000 and up. Members of the council had opportunities to "meet individually with Nature Conservancy staff to discuss environmental issues of specific importance to the member company."[25]

There are no easy resolutions of these issues, but there are better and worse ways of addressing them. Appearances matter, and it sometimes makes sense to avoid affiliations where a donor is seeking to advance or pedigree ethically problematic conduct, or to impose excessive restrictions on the use of funds.

Investment Policies

Advocates of socially responsible investing argue that nonprofit organizations should ensure that their financial portfolio is consistent with their values. In its strongest form, this strategy calls for investing in ventures that further an organization's mission. In its weaker form, the strategy entails divestment from companies whose activities undermine that mission. The issue gained widespread attention after a Jan. 7, 2007, *Los Angeles Times* article criticized the Bill & Melinda Gates Foundation for investing in companies that contributed to the environmental and health problems that the foundation is attempting to reduce.

Many nonprofit leaders have resisted pressure to adopt socially responsible investing principles on the grounds that maximizing the financial return on investment is the best way to further their organization's mission, and that individual divestment decisions are unlikely to affect corporate policies. Our view, however, is that symbols matter, and that similar divestment decisions by large institutional investors can sometimes influence corporate conduct. Hypocrisy, as French writer François de La Rochefoucauld put it, may be the "homage vice pays to virtue," but it is not a sound managerial strategy. To have one set of principles for financial management and another for programmatic objectives sends a mixed moral message. Jeff Skoll acknowledged as much following his foundation's support of *Fast Food Nation*, a dramatic film highlighting the adverse social impacts of the fast-food industry. "How do I reconcile owning shares in [Coca-Cola and Burger King] with making the movie?" he asked.[26] As a growing number of foundations recognize, to compartmentalize ethics inevitably marginalizes their significance. About a fifth of institutional investing is now in socially screened funds, and it is by no means clear that these investors have suffered financial losses as a consequence.[27]

ACCOUNTABILITY AND STRATEGIC MANAGEMENT

By definition, nonprofit organizations are not subject to the checks of market forces or majoritarian control. This independence has come under increasing scrutiny in the wake of institutional growth. In 2006, after a $30 billion gift from Warren Buffet, the Gates Foundation endowment doubled, making it larger than the gross domestic product of more than 100 countries. In societies where nonprofits serve crucial public functions and enjoy substantial public subsidies (in the form of tax deductions and exemptions), this public role also entails significant public responsibilities. In effect, those responsibilities include fiduciary obligations to stakeholders—those who fund nonprofits and those who receive their services—to use resources in a principled way. As a growing body of work on philanthropy suggests, such accountability requires a well-informed plan for furthering organizational objectives and specific measures of progress. A surprising number of nonprofits lack such strategic focus. Many operate with a "spray and pray" approach, which spreads assistance across multiple programs in the hope that something good will come of it. Something usually does, but it is not necessarily the cost-effective use of resources that public accountability demands.

Money held in public trust should be well spent, not just well-intentioned. But in practice, ethical obligations bump up against significant obstacles. The most obvious involves evaluation. Many nonprofit initiatives have mixed or nonquantifiable outcomes. How do we price due process, wilderness preservation, or gay marriage?

Although in many contexts objective measures of progress are hard to come by, it is generally possible to identify some indicators or proxies. Examples include the number and satisfaction of people affected, the assessment of experts, and the impact on laws, policies, community empowerment, and social services. The effectiveness of evaluation is likely to increase if organizations become more willing to share information about what works and what doesn't. To be sure, those who invest significant time and money in social impact work want to feel good about their efforts, and they are understandably reluctant to spend additional resources in revealing or publicizing poor outcomes. What nonprofit wants to rain on its parade when that might jeopardize public support? But sometimes at least a light drizzle is essential to further progress. Only through pooling information and benchmarking performance can nonprofit organizations help each other to do better.

PROMOTING ETHICAL DECISION MAKING

Although no set of rules or organizational structures can guarantee ethical conduct, nonprofits can take three steps that will make it more likely.

Ensure Effective Codes of Conduct and Compliance Programs

One of the most critical steps that nonprofits can take to promote ethical conduct is to ensure that they have adequate ethical codes and effective compliance programs. Codified rules can clarify expectations, establish consistent standards, and project a responsible public image. If widely accepted and enforced, codes can also reinforce core values, deter misconduct, promote trust, and reduce the organization's risks of conflicting interests and legal liability.

Although the value of ethical codes and compliance structures should not be overlooked, neither should it be overstated. As empirical research makes clear, the existence of an ethical code does not of itself increase the likelihood of ethical conduct. Much depends on how standards are developed, perceived, and integrated into workplace functions. "Good optics" was how one manager described Enron's ethical code, and shortly after the collapse, copies of the document were selling on eBay, advertised as "never been read."[28]

A recent survey of nonprofit organizations found that only about one-third of employees believed that their workplace had a well implemented ethics and compliance program. This figure is higher than the corresponding figure for the business (25 percent) and government (17 percent) sectors, but still suggests ample room for improvement.[29] Part of the problem lies with codes that are too vague, inflexible, or narrow. Only about half of nonprofit organizations have conflict of interest policies, and fewer than one-third require disclosure of potentially conflicting financial interests.[30] A related difficulty is compliance programs that focus simply on punishing deviations from explicit rules, an approach found to be less effective in promoting ethical behavior than approaches that encourage self-governance and commitment to ethical aspirations.[31] To develop more effective codes and compliance structures, nonprofit organizations need systematic information about how they operate in practice. How often do employees perceive and report ethical concerns? How are their concerns addressed? Are they familiar with codified rules and confident that whistle-blowers will be protected from retaliation? Do they feel able to deliver bad news without reprisals?

Promote Effective Financial Management

Another step that nonprofits can take to foster ethical behavior and promote public trust is to use resources in a socially responsible way. In response to reports of bloated overhead, excessive compensation, and financial mismanagement, watchdog groups like Charity Navigator have begun rating nonprofits on the percentage of funds that go to administration rather than program expenditures. Although this rating structure responds to real concerns, it reinforces the wrong performance measure, distorts organizational priorities, and encourages disingenuous accounting practices. Groups with low administrative costs may not have the scale necessary for social impact. The crucial question that donors and funders should consider in directing their resources is the relative cost-effectiveness of the organization. Yet according to a 2001 study by Princeton Survey Research Associates, only 6 percent of Americans say that whether a program "makes a difference" is what they most want to know when making charitable decisions. Two-thirds expect the bulk of their donations to fund current programs and almost half expect all of their donations to do so. Such expectations encourage charities to provide short-term direct aid at the expense of building long-term institutional capacity.

Moreover, the line these donors draw between "overhead" and "cause" is fundamentally flawed. As Dan Pallotta notes in Uncharitable, "the distinction is a distortion." All donations are going to the cause, and "the fact that [a dollar] is not going to the needy now obscures the value it will produce down the road" by investing in infrastructure or fundraising capacity. Penalizing charities for such investments warps organizational priorities. It also encourages "aggressive program accounting,"

which allocates fundraising, management, and advertising expenses to program rather than administrative categories. Studies of more than 300,000 tax returns of charitable organizations find widespread violation of standard accounting practices and tax regulations, including classification of accounting fees and proposal writing expenses as program expenditures.[32]

To address these issues, nonprofit organizations need better institutional oversight, greater public education, and more transparent and inclusive performance measures. Ensuring common standards for accounting and developing better rating systems for organizational effectiveness should be a priority.

Institutionalize an Ethical Culture

In its National Nonprofit Ethics Survey, the Ethics Resource Center categorizes an organization as having a strong ethical culture when top management leads with integrity, supervisors reinforce ethical conduct, peers display a commitment to ethics, and the organization integrates its values in day-to-day decision making. In organizations with strong ethical cultures, employees report far less misconduct, feel less pressure to compromise ethical commitments, and are less likely to experience retaliation for whistle-blowing.[33] This survey is consistent with other research, which underscores the importance of factoring ethical concerns into all organizational activities, including resource allocation, strategic planning, personnel and compensation decisions, performance evaluations, auditing, communications, and public relations.

Often the most critical determinant of workplace culture is ethical leadership. Employees take cues about appropriate behavior from those at the top. Day-to-day decisions that mesh poorly with professed values send a powerful signal. No organizational mission statement or ceremonial platitudes can counter the impact of seeing leaders withhold crucial information, play favorites with promotion, stifle dissent, or pursue their own self-interest at the organization's expense.

Leaders face a host of issues where the moral course of action is by no means self-evident. Values may be in conflict, facts may be contested or incomplete, and realistic options may be limited. Yet although there may be no unarguably right answers, some will be more right than others—that is, more informed by available evidence, more consistent with widely accepted principles, and more responsive to all the interests at issue. Where there is no consensus about ethically appropriate conduct, leaders should strive for a decision making process that is transparent and responsive to competing stakeholder interests.

Nonprofit executives and board members also should be willing to ask uncomfortable questions: Not just "Is it legal?" but also "Is it fair?" "Is it honest?" "Does it advance societal interests or pose unreasonable risks?" and "How would it feel to defend the decision on the evening news?" Not only do leaders need to ask those questions of themselves, they also need to invite unwelcome answers from others. To counter self-serving biases and organizational pressures, people in positions of power should actively solicit diverse perspectives and dissenting views. Every leader's internal moral compass needs to be checked against external reference points.

Some three decades ago, in commenting on the performance of Nixon administration officials during the Watergate investigation, then-Supreme Court Chief Justice Warren Burger concluded that "apart from the morality, I don't see what they did wrong."[34] That comment has eerie echoes in the current financial crisis, as leaders of failed institutions repeatedly claim that none of their missteps were actually illegal. Our global economy is paying an enormous price for that moral myopia, and we cannot afford its replication in the nonprofit sphere.

NOTES

1   Jay Fitzgerald, "Treasury Gets Tough: Eyes Financial Bailout Abuse," Boston Herald, January 28, 2009: 25; Sheryl Gay Stolberg and Stephen Labaton, "Banker Bonuses Are 'Shameful,' Obama Declares," The New York Times, January 30, 2009: A1.

2   Sharyl Attkisson, "Student Loan Charity Under Fire: Is One Educational Charity Abusing Their Status with Lavish Travel and Huge Salaries?" CBS News, March 2, 2009; Sharyl Attkisson, "Loan Charity's High-Flying Guests Exposed: Educational Nonprofit Under Fire for Transporting Politicians with Money That Could Have Gone to Students," CBS News, March 3, 2009.

3   Deborah L. Rhode, "Where Is the Leadership in Moral Leadership?" D.L. Rhode, ed., Moral Leadership: The Theory and Practice of Power, Judgment, and Policy, San Francisco: Jossey-Bass, 2006: 13.

4   Ethics Resource Center, National Nonprofit Ethics Survey 2007, March 27, 2008: ix, 2–4, 19.

5   Paul C. Light, How Americans View Charities: A Report on Charitable Confidence, Washington, D.C.: Brookings Institution, April 2008.

6   James R. Rest, ed., Moral Development: Advances in Research and Theory, New York: Praeger Publishers, 1994: 26–39.

7   Rhode, "Where Is the Leadership in Moral Leadership?": 25.

8   Kimberly D. Krawiec, "Accounting for Greed: Unraveling the Rogue Trader Mystery," Oregon Law Review, 79(2), 2000: 309–10.

9   See Leon Festinger, Theory of Cognitive Dissonance, Stanford, Calif.: Stanford University Press, 1957: 128–34; Eddie Harmon-Jones and Judson Mills, eds., Cognitive Dissonance: Progress on a Pivotal Theory in Social Psychology, Washington, D.C.: American Psychological Association, 1999.

10 David M. Messick and Max H. Bazerman, "Ethical Leadership and the Psychology of Decision Making," MIT Sloan Management Review, 37(2), 1996: 76.

11 Ronald R. Sims and Johannes Brinkmann, "Enron Ethics (Or Culture Matters More Than Codes)," Journal of Business Ethics, 45(3), 2003: 243, 252.

12 See Panel on the Nonprofit Sector, Principles for Good Governance and Ethical Practice: A Guide for Charities and Foundations, October 2007: 27, which advises against compensating internal or external

fundraisers on the basis of a percentage of the funds raised.

13   Rhode, "Where Is the Leadership in Moral Leadership?": 17–18.

14   J. Scott Armstrong, "Social Irresponsibility in Management," Journal of Business Research, 5, September 1977: 185–213.

15   Barbara Kellerman, Bad Leadership: What It Is, How It Happens, Why It Matters, Boston: Harvard Business School Press, 2004: 146, 155.

16   Peter Whoriskey and Jacqueline L. Salmon, "Charity Concealed Pilfering: Auditors Had Flagged United Way Executive," Fort Wayne Journal Gazette, August 17, 2003: 7; Bill Birchard, "Nonprofits by the Numbers: In the Wake of Embarrassing Revelations, High-Profile Scandals, and Sarbanes-Oxley, Nonprofit CFOs Are Striving for Greater Transparency and Accountability," CFO Magazine, July 1, 2005.

17   Stephanie Strom, "Red Cross to Streamline Board's Management Role," The New York Times, October 31, 2006: A16.

18   Karen W. Arenson, "Ex-United Way Leader Gets 7 Years for Embezzlement," The New York Times, June 23, 1995: 14.

19   Internal Revenue Service, Form 990 Redesign for Tax Year 2008 Background Paper, December 20, 2007.

20   Joe Stephens and David B. Ottaway, "Conservancy Property Deals Benefit Friends," The Seattle Times, May 7, 2003: A12.

21   David B. Ottaway and Joe Stephens, "Conserving a Green Group's Public Image," Orlando Sentinel, May 18, 2003: G1; United States Senate Committee on Finance, Committee Report on The Nature Conservancy, Part III: 4.

22   Francie Ostrower, Nonprofit Governance in the United States, Washington, D.C.: The Urban Institute, 2007.

23   Birchard, "Nonprofits by the Numbers."

24   Fred Strebeigh, Equal: Women Reshape American Law, New York: W.W. Norton & Co., 2009: 46.

25   Ottaway and Stephens, "Conserving a Green Group's Public Image": G1.

26   Matthew Bishop and Michael Green, Philanthrocapitalism: How the Rich Can Save the World, New York: Bloomsbury Press, 2008: 167.

27   Paul Brest and Hal Harvey, Money Well Spent: A Strategic Plan for Smart Philanthropy, New York: Bloomberg Press, 2008: 127–30.

28   Peter S. Cohan, Value Leadership: The 7 Principles That Drive Corporate Value in Any Economy, San Francisco: Jossey-Bass, 2004: 2; Lynn Sharp Paine, Value Shift: Why Companies Must Merge Social and Financial Imperatives to Achieve Superior Performance, New York: McGraw-Hill, 2003: 36.

29   Ethics Resource Center, National Nonprofit Ethics Survey 2007: 2.

30   Ostrower, Nonprofit Governance in the United States: 9.

31   Melissa S. Baucus and Caryn L. Beck-Dudley, "Designing Ethical Organizations: Avoiding the Long-Term Negative Effects of Rewards and Punishments," Journal of Business Ethics, 56(4), 2005: 355.

32   Dan Pallotta, Uncharitable: How Restraints on Nonprofits Undermine Their Potential, Medford, Mass.: Tufts University Press, 2008: 41, 149–50, 162.

33   Ethics Resource Center, National Nonprofit Ethics Survey 2007: 1, 4–5, 10, 16.

34   Peter Goldman with Constance Wiley, "Inside the Burger Court," Newsweek, December 10, 1979: 76. See more at: http://ssir.org/articles/entry/ethics_and_nonprofits#sthash.iTsagFZG.dpuf

MICROLENDING AND THE GRAMEEN BANK

Ardhendu Shekhar Singh, Dilip Ambarkhane, and Bhama Venkataramani

BACKGROUND

THE GRAMEEN BANK HAS ITS ORIGINS IN AN experiment conducted by the economist Muhammad Yunus during the 1974 Bangladesh famine. In response to predatory lending that forced very poor people without collateral to pay exorbitant interest rates, Yunus lent $27 to a group of 42 people. To his surprise, the borrowers repaid these loans. This led him to expand and to test his ideas about microcredit with the Rural Economics Project at the University of Cittagong and ultimately to found the Grameen Bank in 1983. The bank's pioneering practice of microlending has been replicated in developing as well as developed nations, leading to Yunus and the Bank's joint reception of the Nobel Peace Prize.

ANALYSIS

The appeal of microcredit for many is that it serves (or is meant to serve) as a development tool by funding poor people's entrepreneurship rather than by providing charity. Microloans supply individuals with capital to carry out business projects that, if successful, will improve their lives. Unlike forms of aid in which donors fund agencies to carry out development projects, microloans go directly to the people who have obligations to repay their loans. This helps overcome information deficiencies of development agencies with a flawed understanding of local conditions and the preferences of the people they serve.

The Grameen Bank can be helpfully analyzed with the help of two concepts. First, its practices fit well with Prahalad and Hart's concept of the Bottom of the Pyramid (BoP).[1] This idea involves advocation of reducing/alleviating poverty through engaging the poor in income generating activities. Many organizations took the lead from the concept and have developed their strategies accordingly. A second concept of the "social enterprise" also characterizes the Grameen Bank. Social enterprises are businesses that compete against other businesses in the market with the objective of serving society. Profitability is still important, but the focus is on serving societal needs.

The value of these two concepts in understanding the Grameen Bank becomes clear when contrasting it with other microlenders such as Compartamos and SKS. These microlenders believe in commercialization of this sector and charge higher interest rates—sometimes more than 100 per cent—which can keep the poor indebted. Lenders justify their rates by citing the higher risk involved and the allegedly higher cost of serving these markets. From an ethical perspective, this neglects the information asymmetry between professionally run organizations and often illiterate customers with limited knowledge of the legal aspects and available alternatives.[2]

The Grameen Bank maintains much lower interest rates. In initial years, it solved the problem of how to include the poor with the help of subsidized capital, grants and volunteers. Over time the commercial principle of banking has assumed a more prominent role that at times may be at odds with its social mission. This raises questions about the ability of social enterprises to maintain their identity when their social functions conflict with profitability.

Though the Grameen Bank and its model have been widely praised, its practice of lending to groups, rather than individuals, has attracted controversy. The onus for repayment is on the group and the group is penalized if individuals fail to repay the loan. Consequently, groups tend not to include people from very poor families. Moreover, the practice of group lending creates a situation where borrowers who default compel successful members to pay for them. These successful members succumb to the pressure of defaulters because this system is their only source of credit (traditional financial players do not consider them creditworthy). It also relies on peer pressure and social embarrassment for defaulting members.

The Grameen Bank has responded to the exclusion of the poorest of the poor by creating a separate program that charges borrowers no interest. Though this program may seem uncontroversial, it is subsidized by other customers who are also poor, raising concerns about fairness.

DISCUSSION QUESTIONS

1. How should social enterprises navigate the potential tension between social mission and profitability?

2. Does the Grameen Bank's practice of cross-subsidizing the poor by charging higher interest rates to others raise ethical concerns?

3. Is it just for for-profit microlenders that do not see themselves as social enterprises to charge whatever interests rates that lenders will accept?

NOTES

1   Prahalad C.K. and Hart Stuart L. (2002), "The Fortune at the Bottom of the Pyramid," *Strategy+Business*, 26, 1–14.

2   Lewis, J.C. (2008). "Microloan Sharks." *Stanford Social Innovation Review*, 6(3), 54.

FURTHER READINGS

Ashta, A., & Bush, M. 2009. "Ethical Issues of NGO Principals in Sustainability, Outreach and Impact of Microfinance: Lessons in Governance from the Banco Compartamos' IPO." *Management Online Review*, 1–18.

Chakrabarty, S., & Bass, A.E. 2013. "Comparing Virtue, Consequentialist, and Deontological Ethics-based Corporate Social Responsibility: Mitigating Microfinance Risk in Institutional Voids." *Journal of Business Ethics*, 126(3), 487–512.

Hudon, M. 2011. "Ethics in Microfinance." In *The Handbook of Microfinance*, edited by B. Armendáriz and M. Labie. London: World Scientific.

"Signature of Change: The Grameen Bank in Bangladesh" (documentary by Mark Aardenburg).

Sinclair, H. 2012. *Confessions of a Microfinance Heretic: How Microlending Lost Its Way and Betrayed the Poor*. San Francisco: Berrett-Koehler Publishers.

Yunus, M. 1999. *Banker to the Poor*. New York: Public Affairs.

—25—

STUDENTS PROTEST UNIVERSITY INVESTMENTS

Vanderbilt's African Land-Grab

Joshua M. Hall

BACKGROUND

ON WEDNESDAY, JUNE 8, 2011, UK'S *THE GUARDIAN* reported that numerous US universities including Harvard and Vanderbilt were invested in companies that were buying large tracts of African farmland and kicking off the indigenous farmers in order for their employees (mostly non-Africans) to grow cash crops to sell to Europe.[1] Harms associated with this land-grabbing include, in addition to the evictions themselves, corruption among African governments and among absentee African land owners, increased food prices, and accelerated climate change.

The article mentions several specific examples of this land-grabbing practice. In Tanzania, Iowa University and a US corporation named AgriSol Energy planned to exile 162,000 people out of their refugee settlements, people who had been farming the land for 40 years. And in South Sudan, the Texas corporation Nile Trading and Development secured a 49-year long lease to all natural resources on 400,000 hectares of land (roughly half a million soccer fields in total size—a bit less than one-third the size of the land area of Connecticut), all for just $25,000. Altogether, the World Bank claims 60,000,000 hectares—the size of France—had been bought in this way in just the past three years alone.

The primary company in which Vanderbilt, Harvard and the other US schools were invested is EmVest (formerly Emergent Asset Management), based in London (and with offices in South Africa), and directed by investor Susan Payne and (former oil company geologist) David Murrin, former employees of JP Morgan and Goldman Sachs. The name of the fund is The African AgriLand Fund which controls 100,000 hectares of land, operates in Mozambique, South Africa, Swaziland, Zambia and Zimbabwe and openly utilizes tax havens all over Africa. It has a total investment estimated at $540,000,000, and projects an investment return of 25%. Also problematic is EmVest's strategy for capturing investors, which is to make doomsday projections about impending war between China and the West over limited food supplies.

According to the Oakland Institute, at least one of the villages affected by EmVest's African AgriLand Fund did not legally consent to the transfer of land, was not notified of the transfer in writing, and was experiencing greater difficulties getting enough food after the transfer. Additionally, there were few local jobs created (contrary to EmVest's promises to invest in local economic infrastructure); these jobs were mostly seasonal and low-paying, and some workers complained of not receiving their earned wages.

Vanderbilt's investments in EmVest and other morally questionable companies led to the formulation of an undergraduate organization, the Vanderbilt Responsible Endowment Campaign. In addition to the $26 million invested in EmVest (out of a total 2011 endowment of $3.3 billion), other problematic investments by Vanderbilt include an investment in a company that directly supported Apartheid in South Africa, and $145,000,000 in a hedge fund in the Cayman Islands (called Callao Partners Ltd Appleby Trust).[2]

The fight began when graduate students at Vanderbilt forwarded the Guardian article to Prof. Leslie Gill, Chair of the Anthropology Department, who then drafted a letter to Vice Chancellors Brett Sweet and Matthew Wright, requesting verification of the investment in EmVest. In support of this, a student also contacted Anuradha Mittal, director of the Oakland Institute, who encouraged them to begin the campaign. The group designed a proposal for an "Ethical Investing Policy" and eventually secured a meeting with Chancellor Wright (who had visited EmVest's site at Mozambique, but without meeting even a single local farmer). The group worked with Vanderbilt Students for Nonviolence to hold a teach-in in the administration building, submitted a letter to Chancellor Nicholas Zeppos, and constructed a tent city (from March to May of 2012) outside that building.

In response, an anonymous Trustee informed a student member of Vanderbilt Students for Nonviolence that the divestment had occurred (which remains the only official communication to that effect from the administration). The administration has still not, however, publicly acknowledged the divestment.

ANALYSIS

Some have argued that what are termed "land grabs" are actually of benefit to the people of the global South, in that they facilitate economic development of unused land, and provide jobs and infrastructure for the local communities. In its mission statement, EmVest asserts that it aims to provide food security to communities, regions, and countries in a social responsible, environmentally friendly, and sustainable manner.

As pointed out by the critics of land-grabbing, however, there is little to no empirical evidence of these alleged benefits, and significant evidence to the contrary. For example, one land grab in Malawi created only one permanent job and 200 seasonal jobs that paid only $0.70 per day.[3] Even if land grabs in general do in fact bring benefits to local populations, this case in particular raises several more fundamental issues regarding university ethics, including students' ethical obligations (including to themselves), and the ethical standards to which universities should be held.

Do undergraduate and/or graduate students have an ethical obligation to protest the investment decisions of their universities? Students not only share the same ethical obligations of all citizens, but are also members of the university and are likely better situated to learn about and take action against wrongdoings by their institutions. Since many ethicists hold that people have stronger obligations to perform duties that they are best qualified to do, students may actually have a greater responsibility than non-students to protest this sort of injustice.

On the other hand, might there be a competing ethical permission for students to protect themselves as vulnerable members of the institution? Students do have particular vulnerabilities not equally shared by non-students. For example, many undergraduates at Vanderbilt (and elsewhere) are from lower socioeconomic status backgrounds themselves, and depend on their scholarships in order to attend Vanderbilt. These protests could jeopardize their future academic and professional careers if they are pressured to leave, or unofficially blackballed by members of the administration. As anyone professionally involved in the academy is aware, even having a degree from a top-ranked US university is no guarantee of financial or professional success, unless there is also a functioning and supportive network in place.

And finally in regard to students, might it be "inappropriate" for students to intervene, as Vanderbilt's Vice Chancellor Matthew Wright, for one, initially claimed? In response, the Oakland Institute's Anuradha Mittal asks, "Since when can universities decide what students should be involved in, and not be involved in? And you hope that institutions of higher learning would really contribute to the buildup of democratic societies, where people can question, especially when the actions of the university are having a huge socioeconomic and environmental impact somewhere else."

Some might feel that this case and all of its publicity scapegoats Harvard and Vanderbilt. After all, the investment portfolios of most major US businesses are highly diversified and complex, and include ethically problematic aspects of which most shareholders are unaware. But a contrasting perspective is that universities' endowments should not be governed to maximize their value. Rather, the social function of universities to educate the next generation of leaders and citizens who will have major impacts on global justice gives rise to special obligations to make sure that their investments meet ethical standards. This perspective raises important questions about the nature of the university, its purposes (including its moral purposes) and the responsibilities of its administrators, faculty, and students.

More troubling than the potential scapegoating (of universities such as Vanderbilt) is the possibility that this story thereby distracts from more pervasive issues of global capitalism. After all, the total of universities' investments is minuscule compared to the total investments from the US government and companies. Should we not be focusing our critical energies on the companies which have the most power and influence in terms of the US's total investment portfolio? Perhaps we should be more concerned with the economic relationship between the global North and South as a whole, rather than fixating on the hypocrisy of the North's institutions of higher education.[4]

DISCUSSION QUESTIONS

1. Is the Oakland Institute correct that universities should be held to a distinct, more demanding ethical standard than other US American businesses?

2. Vice Chancellor Matthew Wright argued that it is "inappropriate" for undergraduates to involve themselves in their school's investments? Is he right? If not, why not?

3. What ethical obligations do American undergraduate and graduate students have (including obligations to themselves) when deciding whether to actively protest unethical investments at their colleges and universities?

4. Do reasonably well-functioning global markets fairly determine land usage and agricultural policies? If not, how should these be determined?

5. Compare and contrast the ethics of student self-protection, and their possible obligation to hold their institutions accountable for their investment decisions. How should these be balanced?

NOTES

1   See Vidal, John, and Claire Provost. "US Universities in Africa 'Land Grab,'" *The Guardian*, June 8, 2011, http://www.theguardian.com/world/2011/jun/08/us-universities-africa-land-grab.

2   Alexander Lavelle, "Aristotle, Justice, and Investment," unpublished manuscript.

3   Chinsinga, Blessings, Michael Chasukwa, and Sane Pashane Zuka. 2013. "The Political Economy of Land Grabs in Malawi: Investigating the Contribution of Limphasa Sugar Corporation to Rural Development." *Journal of Agricultural and Environmental Ethics* 26 (6): 1075.

4   This case study has benefited enormously from Alexander Lavelle's unpublished paper "Aristotle, Justice, and Investment" and from an interview conducted with Anuradha Mittal from the Oakland Institute.

FURTHER READINGS

Declaration on Land Issues and Challenges in Africa. 2009. Assembly of the African Union, Thirteenth Ordinary Session at Sirte, Libya, July 2009. http://www.uneca.org/sites/default/files/uploaded-documents/LPI/au_declaration_on_land_issues_eng.pdf.

Cotula, Lorenzo, Nat Dyer, and Sonja Vermeulen. 2008. *Fuelling Exclusion? The Biofuels Boom and Poor People's Access to Land.* London: International Institute for Environment and Development.

FAO. "Voluntary Guidelines on the Responsible Governance of Tenure of Land and Other Natural Resources, Zero Draft," April 18, 2011, Rome: *Food and Agriculture Organization of the United Nations,* http://www.fao.org/fileadmin/user_upload/nr/land_tenure/econsultation/english/Zero_Draft_VG_Final.pdf.

Hall, Ruth. 2011. "Land Grabbing in Southern Africa: The Many Faces of the Investor Rush," *Review of African Political Economy* 128: 193–214.

Stephens, Phoebe. 2011. "The Global Land Grabs: An Analysis of Land Governance Institutional," *International Affairs Review* 20 (1): 1–22.

Wolford, Wendy, Saturnino Borras, Jr., Ruth Hall, Ian Scoones, and Ben White. 2013. *Governing Global Land Deals: The Role of the State in the Rush for Land.* New York: Wiley-Blackwell.

GLOBALIZATION AND SUSTAINABILITY

INTRODUCTION

Alexander Sager and Anand J. Vaidya

BUSINESS TODAY TAKES PLACE IN A GLOBAL economy in which almost all goods are produced from materials and labor that compose complex, transnational supply chains. Even businesses that pride themselves on using local workers and suppliers own equipment and resources that have crossed multiple national borders. According to the World Bank, in 2014 merchandise exports totaled $19.13 trillion US and merchandise imports totaled $19.08 trillion US. International trade has created enormous wealth and is one of the effective mechanisms for development and for poverty reduction. Globalization also creates moral dilemmas for businesses.

Many complications arise from different labor standards and laws across jurisdictions. In recent decades, activists have vocally opposed overseas "sweatshops" thought to violate the rights of workers or to pay unacceptably low wages. How should businesses from countries such as the United States act when doing business in jurisdictions where wages or safety regulations are significantly lower than what would be acceptable at home?

On one hand, inequitable and arguably abusive treatment of workers seems morally unacceptable regardless of where they live. Many consumers in the industrialized West believe that purchasing goods manufactured under these conditions makes them complicit in the use of child labor, abusive working conditions, and exploitative wages. On the other hand, one of the most important advantages the developing world has over the industrialized West is cheap labor and fewer costly regulations.

If multinational corporations were to give workers the same labor rights and/or wages, they would lose the major incentive to expand beyond their borders.

It is sometimes assumed that there are universal standards for labor rights and fair wages, which can be applied across jurisdictions. One concern with this assumption is it does not address differences in cultural—and perhaps even moral—norms. Even if we reject moral relativism—the position that moral standards are relative to the norms or practices of particular groups—we cannot assume that the moral standards of the rich, developed world are the right ones.

Firms doing business in more than one country must decide how to navigate different norms. These issues arise when considering the issue of bribery, understood as the transfer of a gift, often money, in return for a favor that often involves breaking a law or policy, or which puts other competitors at an unfair disadvantage. When business is done globally, one has to take into consideration the perspective of other cultures and countries on the morality of gift giving and of the permissibility of bribery. In many places, offering a gift as part of a transaction is not considered bribery; it is simply understood as doing what it takes to get something done.

For example, suppose that getting a building permit in India takes four months and that applications are processed in the order in which they are received. But suppose that an American company building a hotel in India wants to have its permit filled in two months so that the project can get started. If members of the American firm were to pay government employees to process their paperwork sooner, then they would, under a classical Western analysis, be bribing government officials. However, from the context of what goes on in India, is this transaction of money for the processing of paperwork morally impermissible? In addition, in discussing bribery in the global context, norms vary about what kinds of gifts or payments are legitimate, and which ones are illegitimate.

The last section in this unit asks about the moral responsibilities of business to the environment in a globalized world. Local businesses have global effects, since waste and carbon emissions cross national lines. As a result, many of the most pressing environmental issues such as climate change, ocean pollution, and resource depletion cannot be solved locally.

Businesses wishing to be environmentally responsible also need to tackle difficult conceptual questions. Traditionally, businesses have treated the environment as an "externality," something to be consumed without affecting the cost of doing business. Water and air have been treated as infinite resources to be freely used without reflection on the costs. When calculating their net income, businesses have not usually taken into account the cost of environmental damage.

The reason for this neglect is not simply businesses' desire to reduce costs. There are controversial conceptual and philosophical questions concerning how to determine the worth of the environment. How should we quantify the value of things that are not priced on the market? What methods do we have to calculate benefits or harms to the environment? Can economic tools such as risk-cost-benefit analysis answer these questions or are their aspects of nature such as the survival of species that elude quantification? Ethically responsible businesses need to grapple with these types of questions.

—26—
INTERNATIONAL BUSINESS, MORALITY, AND THE COMMON GOOD

Manuel Velasquez

DURING THE LAST FEW YEARS AN INCREASING number of voices have urged that we pay more attention to ethics in international business, on the grounds that not only are all large corporations now internationally structured and thus engaging in international transactions, but that even the smallest domestic firm is increasingly buffeted by the pressures of international competition.[1] This call for increased attention to international business ethics has been answered by a slowly growing collection of ethicists who have begun to address issues in this field. The most comprehensive work on this subject to date is the recent book *The Ethics of International Business* by Thomas Donaldson.[2]

I want in this article to discuss certain realist objections to bringing ethics to bear on international transactions, an issue that, I believe, has not yet been either sufficiently acknowledged nor adequately addressed but that must be resolved if the topic of international business ethics is to proceed on solid foundations. Even so careful a writer as Thomas Donaldson fails to address this issue in its proper complexity. Oddly enough, in the first chapter where one would expect him to argue that, in spite of realist objections, *businesses* have international moral obligations, Donaldson argues only for the less pertinent claim that, in spite of realist objections, *states* have international moral obligations.[3] But international business organizations, I will argue, have special features that render realist objections quite compelling. The question I want to address, here, then, is a particular aspect of the question Donaldson and others have ignored: Can we say that businesses operating in a competitive international environment have any moral obligations to contribute to the international common good, particularly in light of realist objections? Unfortunately, my answer to this question will be in the negative.

My subject, then, is international business and the common good. What I will do is the following. I will begin by explaining what I mean by the common good, and what I mean by international business. Then I will turn directly to the question whether the views of the realist allow us to claim that international businesses have a moral obligation to contribute to the common good. I will first lay out the traditional realist treatment of this question and then revise the traditional realist view so that it can deal with certain shortcomings embedded in the traditional version of realism. I will then bring these revisions to bear on the question of whether international businesses have any obligations toward the common good, a question that I will answer in the negative. My hope is that I have identified some extremely problematic issues that are both critical and disturbing and that, I believe, need to be more widely discussed than they have been because they challenge our easy attribution of moral obligation to international business organizations.

I should note that what follows is quite tentative. I am attempting to work out the implications of certain arguments that have reappeared recently in the literature on morality in international affairs. I am not entirely convinced of the correctness of my conclusions, and offer them here as a way of trying to get clearer about their status. I should also note that although I have elsewhere argued that it is improper to attribute *moral responsibility* to corporate entities, I here set these arguments aside in order to show that even if we ignore the issue of moral responsibility, it is still questionable whether international businesses have obligations toward the common good.

I. THE COMMON GOOD

Let me begin by distinguishing a weak from a strong conception of the common good, so that I might clarify what I have in mind when I refer to the common good.

What I have in mind by a weak conception of the common good is essentially the utilitarian notion of the common good. It is a notion that is quite clearly stated by Jeremy Bentham:

The interest of the community then is—what? The sum of the interests of the several members who compose it.... It is vain to talk of the interest of the community, without understanding what is the interest of the individual. A thing is said to promote the interest or to be for the interest of an individual, when it tends to add to the sum total of his pleasure; or what comes to the same thing, to diminish the sum total of his pains.[4]

On the utilitarian notion of the common good, the common good is nothing more than the sum of the utilities of each individual. The reason why I call this the "weak" conception of the common good will become clear, I believe, once it is contrasted with another, quite different notion of the common good.

Let me describe, therefore, what I will call a strong conception of the common good, the conception on which I want to focus in this essay. It is a conception that has been elaborated in the Catholic tradition, and so I will refer to it as the Catholic conception of the common good. Here is how one writer, William A. Wallace, O.P., characterizes the conception:

A common good is clearly distinct from a *private* good, the latter being the good of one person only, to the exclusion of its being possessed by any other. A common good is distinct also from a *collective* good, which, though possessed by all of a group, is not really participated in by the members of the group; divided up, a collective good becomes respectively the private goods of the members. A true *common* good is universal, not singular or collective, and is distributive in character, being communicable to many without becoming anyone's private good. Moreover, each person participates in the whole common good, not merely in a part of it, nor can any one person possess it wholly.[5]

In the terms used by Wallace, the utilitarian conception of the common good is actually a "collective" good. That is, it is an aggregate of the private goods (the utilities) of the members of a society. The common good in the utilitarian conception is divisible in the sense that the aggregate consists of distinct parts and each part is enjoyable by only one individual. Moreover, the common good in the utilitarian conception is not universal in the sense that not all members of society can enjoy all of the aggregate; instead, each member enjoys only a portion of the aggregate.

By contrast, in the Catholic conception that Wallace is attempting to characterize, the common good consists of those goods that (1) benefit all the members of a society in the sense that all the members of the society have access to each of these goods, and (2) are not divisible in the sense that none of these goods can be divided up and allocated among individuals in such a way that others can be excluded from enjoying what another individual enjoys. The example that Wallace gives of one common good is the "good of peace and order."[6] Other examples are national security, a clean natural environment, public health and safety, a productive economic system to whose benefits all have access, a just legal and political system, and a system of natural and artificial associations in which persons can achieve their personal fulfillment.

It is this strong notion of the common good that the Catholic tradition has had in mind when it has defined the common good as "the sum total of those conditions of social living whereby men are enabled more fully and more readily to achieve their own perfection."[7] It is also the conception that John Rawls has in mind when he writes that "Government is assumed to aim at the common good, that is, at maintaining conditions and achieving objectives that are similarly to everyone's advantage," and "the common good I think of as certain general conditions that are in an appropriate sense equally to everyone's advantage."[8]

The Catholic conception of the common good is the conception that I have in mind in what follows. It is clear from the characterization of the common good laid out above that we can think of the common good on two different levels. We can think of the common good on a national and on an international level. On a national level, the common good is that set of conditions within a certain nation that are necessary for the citizens of that nation to achieve their individual fulfillment and so in which all of the citizens have an interest.

On an international level, we can speak of the global common good as that set of conditions that are necessary for the citizens of all or of most nations to achieve their individual fulfillment, and so those goods in which all the peoples of the world have an interest. In what follows, I will be speaking primarily about the global common good.

Now it is obvious that identifying the global common good is extremely difficult because cultures differ on their views of what conditions are necessary for humans to flourish. These differences are particularly acute between the cultures of the lesser developed third world nations who have demanded a "new economic order," and the cultures of the wealthier first world nations who have resisted this demand. Nevertheless, we can identify at least some elements of the global common good. Maintaining a congenial global climate, for example is certainly part of the global common good. Maintaining safe transportation routes for the international flow of goods is also part of the global common good. Maintaining clean oceans is another aspect of the global common good, as is the avoidance of a global nuclear war. In spite of the difficulties involved in trying to compile a list of the goods that qualify as part of the global common good, then, it is nevertheless possible to identify at least some of the items that belong on the list.

II. INTERNATIONAL BUSINESS

Now let me turn to the other term in my title: international business. When speaking of international business, I have in mind a particular kind of organization: the multinational corporation. Multinational corporations have a number of well known features, but let me briefly summarize a few of them. First, multinational corporations are businesses and as such they are organized primarily to increase their profits within a competitive environment. Virtually all of the activities of a multinational corporation can be explained as more or less rational attempts to achieve this dominant end. Secondly, multinational corporations are bureaucratic organizations. The implication of this is that the identity, the fundamental structure, and the dominant objectives of the corporation endure while the many individual human beings who fill the various offices and positions within the corporation come and go. As a consequence, the particular values and aspirations of individual members of the corporation have a relatively minimal and transitory impact on the organization as a whole. Thirdly, and most characteristically, multinational corporations operate in several nations. This has several implications. First, because the multinational is not confined to a single nation, it can easily escape the reach of the laws of any particular nation by simply moving its resources or operations out of one nation and transferring them to another nation. Second, because the multinational is not confined to a single nation, its interests are not aligned with the interests of any single nation. The ability of the multinational to achieve its profit objectives does not depend upon the ability of any particular nation to achieve its own domestic objectives.

In saying that I want to discuss international business and the common good, I am saying that I want to discuss the relationship between the global common good and multinational corporations, that is, organizations that have the features I have just identified.

The general question I want to discuss is straightforward: I want to ask whether it is possible for us to say that multinational corporations with the features I have just described have an obligation to contribute toward the global common good. But I want to discuss only one particular aspect of this general question. I want to discuss this question in light of the realist objection.

III. THE TRADITIONAL REALIST OBJECTION IN HOBBES

The realist objection, of course, is the standard objection to the view that agents—whether corporations, governments, or individuals—have moral obligations on the international level. Generally, the realist holds that it is a mistake to apply moral concepts to international activities: morality has no place in international affairs. The classical statement of this view, which I am calling the "traditional" version of realism, is generally attributed to Thomas Hobbes. I will assume that this customary attribution is correct; my aim is to identify some of the implications of this traditional version of realism even if it is not quite historically accurate to attribute it to Hobbes.

In its Hobbesian form, as traditionally interpreted, the realist objection holds that moral concepts have no meaning in the absence of an agency powerful enough to guarantee that other agents generally adhere to the tenets of morality. Hobbes held, first, that in the absence of a sovereign power capable of forcing men to behave civilly with each other, men are in "the state of nature," a state he characterizes as a "war ... of every man, against every man."[9] Secondly, Hobbes claimed, in such a state of war, moral concepts have no meaning:

> To this war of every man against every man, this also is consequent; that nothing can be unjust. The notions of right and wrong, justice and injustice have there no place. Where there is no common power, there is no law: where no law, no injustice.[10]

Moral concepts are meaningless, then, when applied to state of nature situations. And, Hobbes held, the international arena is a state of nature, since there is no international sovereign that can force agents to adhere to the tenets of morality.[11]

The Hobbesian objection to talking about morality in international affairs, then, is based on two premises: (1) an ethical premise about the applicability of moral terms and (2) an apparently empirical premise about how agents behave under certain conditions. The ethical premise, at least in its Hobbesian form, holds that there is a connection between the meaningfulness of moral terms and the extent to which agents adhere to the tenets of morality: If in a given situation agents do not adhere to the tenets of morality, then in that situation moral terms have no meaning. The apparently empirical premise holds that in the absence of a sovereign, agents will not adhere to the tenets of morality: they will be in a state of war. This appears to be an empirical generalization about the extent to which agents adhere to the tenets of morality in the absence of a third-party enforcer. Taken together, the two premises imply that in situations that lack a sovereign authority, such as one finds in many international exchanges, moral terms have no meaning and so moral obligations are nonexistent.

However, there are a number of reasons for thinking that the two Hobbesian premises are deficient as they stand. I want next, therefore, to examine each of these premises more closely and to determine the extent to which they need revision.

IV. REVISING THE REALIST OBJECTION: THE FIRST PREMISE

The ethical premise concerning the meaning of moral terms, is, in its original Hobbesian form, extremely difficult to defend. If one is in a situation in which others do not adhere to any moral restraints, it simply does not logically follow that in that situation one's actions are no longer subject to moral evaluation. At most what follows is that since such an extreme situation is different from the more normal situations in which we usually act, the moral requirements placed on us in such extreme situations are different from the moral requirements that obtain in more normal circumstances. For example, morality requires that in normal circumstances I am not to attack or kill my fellow citizens. But when one of those citizens is attacking me in a dark alley, morality allows me to defend myself by counterattacking or even killing that citizen. It is a truism that what moral principles require in one set of circumstances is different from what they require in other circumstances. And in extreme circumstances, the requirements of morality may become correspondingly extreme. But there is no reason to think that they vanish altogether.

Nevertheless, the realist can relinquish the Hobbesian premise about the meaning of moral terms, replace it with a weaker and more plausible premise, and still retain much of Hobbes' conclusion. The realist or neo-Hobbesian can claim that although moral concepts can be meaningfully applied to situations in which agents do not adhere to the tenets of morality, nevertheless it is not morally wrong for agents in such situations to also fail to adhere to those tenets of morality, particularly when doing so puts one at a significant competitive disadvantage.

The neo-Hobbesian or realist, then, might want to propose this premise: When one is in a situation in which others do not adhere to certain tenets of morality, and when adhering to those tenets of morality will put one at a significant competitive disadvantage, then it is not immoral for one to likewise fail to adhere to them. The realist might want to argue for this claim, first, by pointing out that in a world in which all are competing to secure significant benefits and avoid significant costs, and in which others do not adhere to the ordinary tenets of morality, one risks significant harm to one's interests if one continues to adhere to those tenets of morality. But no one can be morally required to take on major risks of harm to oneself. Consequently, in a competitive world in which others disregard moral constraints and take any means to advance their self-interests, no one can be morally required to take on major risks of injury by adopting the restraints of ordinary morality.

A second argument the realist might want to advance would go as follows. When one is in a situation in which others do not adhere to the ordinary tenets of morality, one is under heavy competitive pressures to do the same. And, when one is under such pressures, one cannot be blamed—i.e., one is excused—for also failing to adhere to the ordinary tenets of morality. One is excused because heavy pressures take away one's ability to control oneself, and thereby diminish one's moral culpability.

Yet a third argument advanced by the realist might go as follows. When one is in a situation in which others do not adhere to the ordinary tenets of morality it is not fair to require one to continue to adhere to those tenets, especially if doing so puts one at a significant competitive disadvantage. It is not fair because then one is laying a burden on one party that the other parties refuse to carry.

Thus, there are a number of arguments that can be given in defense of the revised Hobbesian ethical premise that when others do not adhere to the tenets of morality, it is not immoral for one to do likewise. The ethical premise of the Hobbesian or realist argument, then, can be restated as follows:

> In situations in which other agents do not adhere to certain tenets of morality, it is not immoral for one to do likewise when one would otherwise be putting oneself at a significant competitive disadvantage.

In what follows, I will refer to this restatement as the ethical premise of the argument. I am not altogether convinced that this premise is correct. But it appears to me to have a great deal of plausibility, and it is, I believe, a premise that underlies the feelings of many that in a competitive international environment where others do not embrace the restraints of morality, one is under no obligation to be moral.

V. REVISING THE REALIST OBJECTION: THE SECOND PREMISE

Let us turn, then, to the other premise in the Hobbesian argument, the assertion that in the absence of a sovereign, agents will be in a state of war. As I mentioned, this is an apparently empirical claim about the extent to which agents will adhere to the tenets of morality in the absence of a third-party enforcer.

Hobbes gives a little bit of empirical evidence for this claim. He cites several examples of situations in which there is no third party to enforce civility and where, as a result, individuals are in a "state of war."[12] Generalizing from these few examples, he reaches the conclusion that in the absence of a third-party enforcer, agents will always be in a "condition of war." But the meager evidence Hobbes provides is surely too thin to support his rather large empirical generalization. Numerous empirical counterexamples can be cited of people living in peace in the absence of a third-party enforcer, so it is difficult to accept Hobbes' claim as an empirical generalization.

Recently, the Hobbesian claim, however, has been defended on the basis of some of the theoretical claims of game theory, particularly of the prisoner's dilemma. Hobbes' state of nature, the defense goes, is an instance of a Prisoner's Dilemma, and *rational* agents in a Prisoner's Dilemma necessarily would choose not to adhere to a set of moral norms. Rationality is here construed in the sense that is standard in social theory: having a coherent set of preferences among the objects of choice, and selecting the one(s) that has the greatest probability of satisfying more of one's preferences rather than fewer.[13] Or, more simply, always choosing so as to maximize one's interests.

A Prisoner's Dilemma is a situation involving at least two individuals. Each individual is faced with two choices: he can cooperate with the other individual or he can choose not to cooperate. If he cooperates and the other individual also cooperates, then he gets a certain payoff. If, however, he chooses not to cooperate, while the other individual trustingly cooperates, the noncooperator gets a larger payoff while the cooperator suffers a loss. And if both choose not to cooperate, then both get nothing.

It is a commonplace now that in a Prisoner's Dilemma situation, the most rational strategy for a participant is to choose not to cooperate. For the other party will either cooperate or not cooperate. If the other party cooperates, then it is better for one not to cooperate and thereby get the larger payoff. On the other hand, if the other party does not cooperate, then it is also better for one not to cooperate and thereby avoid a loss. In either case, it is better for one to not cooperate.

Now Hobbes' state of nature, the neo-Hobbesian realist can argue, is in fact a Prisoner's Dilemma situation. In Hobbes' state of nature each individual must choose either to cooperate with others by adhering to the rules of morality (like the rule against theft), or to not cooperate by disregarding the rules of morality and attempting to take advantage of those who are adhering to the rules (e.g., by stealing from them). In such a situation it is more rational (in the sense defined above) to choose not to cooperate. For the other party will either cooperate or not cooperate. If the other party does not cooperate, then one puts oneself at a competitive disadvantage if one adheres to morality while the other party does not. On the other hand, if the other party chooses to cooperate, then one can take advantage of the other party by breaking the rules of morality at his expense. In either case, it is more rational to not cooperate.

Thus, the realist can argue that in a state of nature, where there is no one to enforce compliance with the rules of morality, it is more rational from the individual's point of view to choose not to comply with morality than to choose to comply. Assuming—and this is obviously a critical assumption—that agents behave rationally, then we can conclude that agents in a state of nature will choose not to comply with the tenets of ordinary morality. The second premise of the realist argument, then, can, tentatively, be put as follows:

> In the absence of an international sovereign, all rational agents will chose not to comply with the tenets of ordinary morality, when doing so will put one at a serious competitive disadvantage.

This is a striking, and ultimately revealing, defense of the Hobbesian claim that in the absence of a third-party enforcer, individuals will choose not to adhere to the tenets of morality in their relations with each other. It is striking because it correctly identifies, I think, the underlying reason for the Hobbesian claim. The Hobbesian claim is not an empirical claim about how most humans actually behave when they are put at a competitive disadvantage. It is a claim about whether agents that are *rational* (in the sense defined earlier) will adopt certain behaviors when doing otherwise would put them at a serious competitive disadvantage. For our purposes, this is significant since, as I claimed above, all, most, or at least a significant number of multinationals are rational agents in the required sense: all or most of their activities are rational means for achieving the dominant end of increasing profits. Multinationals, therefore, are precisely the kind of rational agents envisaged by the realist.

But this reading of the realist claim is also significant, I think, because it reveals certain limits inherent in the Hobbesian claim, and requires revising the claim so as to take these limits into account.

As more than one person has pointed out, moral interactions among agents are often quite unlike Prisoner's Dilemmas situations.[14] The most important difference is that a Prisoner's Dilemma is a single meeting between agents who do not meet again, whereas human persons in the real world tend to have repeated dealings with each other. If two people meet each other in a Prisoner's Dilemma situation, and never have anything to do with each other again, then it is rational (in the sense under discussion) from each individual's point of view to choose not to cooperate. However, if individuals meet each other in repeated Prisoner's Dilemma situations, then they are able to punish each other for failures to cooperate, and the cumulative costs of noncooperation can make cooperation the more rational strategy.[15] One can therefore expect that when rational agents know they will have repeated interactions with each other for an indefinite future, they will start to cooperate with each other even in the absence of a third party enforcer. The two cooperating parties in effect are the mutual enforcers of their own cooperative agreements.

The implication is that the realist is wrong in believing that in the absence of a third-party enforcer, rational individuals will always fail to adhere to the tenets of morality, presumably even when doing so would result in serious competitive disadvantage. On the contrary, we can expect that if agents know that they will interact with each other repeatedly in the indefinite future, it is rational for them to behave morally toward each other. In the international arena, then, we can expect that when persons know that they will have repeated interactions with each other, they will tend to adhere to ordinary tenets of morality with each other, assuming that they tend to behave rationally, even when doing so threatens to put them at a competitive disadvantage.

There is a second important way in which the Prisoner's Dilemma is defective as a characterization of real world interactions. Not only do agents repeatedly interact with each other, but, as Robert Frank has recently pointed out, human agents signal to each other the extent to which they can be relied on to behave morally in future interactions.[16] We humans can determine more often than not whether another person can be relied on to be moral by observing the natural visual cues of facial expression and the auditory cues of tone of voice that tend to give us away; by relying on our experience of past dealings with the person; and by relying on the reports of others who have had past dealings with the person. Moreover, based on these appraisals of each other's reliability, we then choose to interact with those who are reliable and choose not to interact with those who are not reliable. That is, we choose to enter Prisoner's Dilemmas situations with those who are reliable, and choose to avoid entering such situations with those who are not reliable. As Robert Frank has shown, given such conditions it is, under quite ordinary circumstances, rational to habitually be reliable since reliable persons tend to have mutually beneficial interactions with other reliable persons, while unreliable persons will tend to have mutually destructive interactions with other unreliable persons.

The implication again is that since signaling makes it rational to habitually cooperate in the rules of morality, even in the absence of a third-party enforcer, we can expect that rational humans, who can send and receive fairly reliable signals between each other, will tend to behave morally even, presumably, when doing so raises the prospect of competitive disadvantage.

These considerations should lead the realist to revise the tentative statement of the second premise of his argument that we laid out above. In its revised form, the second premise would have to read as follows:

In the absence of an international sovereign, all rational agents will chose not to comply with the tenets of ordinary morality, when doing so will put one at a serious competitive disadvantage, provided that interactions are not repeated and that agents are not able to signal their reliability to each other.

This, I believe, is a persuasive and defensible version of the second premise in the Hobbesian argument. It is the one I will exploit in what follows.

VI. REVISED REALISM, MULTINATIONALS, AND THE COMMON GOOD

Now how does this apply to multinationals and the common good? Can we claim that it is clear that multinationals have a moral obligation to pursue the global common good in spite of the objections of the realist?

I do not believe that this claim can be made. We can conclude from the discussion of the realist objection that the Hobbesian claim about the pervasiveness of amorality in the international sphere is false when (1) interactions among international agents are repetitive in such a way that agents can retaliate against those who fail to cooperate, and (2) agents can determine the trustworthiness of other international agents.

But unfortunately, multinational activities often take place in a highly competitive arena in which these two conditions do not obtain. Moreover, these conditions are noticeably absent in the arena of activities that concern the global common good.

First, as I have noted, the common good consists of goods that are indivisible and accessible to all. This means that such goods are susceptible to the free rider problem. Everyone has access to such goods whether or not they do their part in maintaining such goods, so everyone is tempted to free ride on the generosity of others. Now governments can force domestic companies to do their part to maintain the national common good. Indeed, it is one of the functions of government to solve the free rider problem by forcing all to contribute to the domestic common good to which all have access. Moreover, all companies have to interact repeatedly with their host governments, and this leads them to adopt a cooperative stance toward their host government's objective of achieving the domestic common good.

But it is not clear that governments can or will do anything effective to force multinationals to do their part to maintain the global common good. For the governments of individual nations can themselves be free riders, and can join forces with willing multinationals seeking competitive advantages over others. Let me suggest an example. It is clear that a livable global environment is part of the global common good, and it is clear that the manufacture and use of chloroflurocarbons is destroying that good. Some nations have responded by requiring their domestic companies to cease manufacturing or using chloroflurocarbons. But other nations have refused to do the same, since they will share in any benefits that accrue from the restraint others practice, and they can also reap the benefits of continuing to manufacture and use chlorofluorocarbons. Less developed nations, in particular, have advanced the position that since their development depends heavily on exploiting the industrial benefits of chlorofluorocarbons, they cannot afford to curtail their use of these substances. Given this situation, it is open to multinationals to shift their operations to those countries that continue to allow the manufacture and use of chlorofluorocarbons. For multinationals, too, will reason that they will share in any benefits that accrue from the restraint others practice, and that they can meanwhile reap the profits of continuing to manufacture and use chlorofluorocarbons in a world where other companies are forced to use more expensive technologies. Moreover, those nations that practice restraint cannot force all such multinationals to discontinue the manufacture or use of chlorofluorocarbons because many multinationals can escape the reach of their laws. An exactly parallel, but perhaps even more compelling, set of considerations can be advanced to show that at least some multinationals will join forces with some developing countries to circumvent any global efforts made to control the global warming trends (the so-called "greenhouse effect") caused by the heavy use of fossil fuels.

The realist will conclude, of course, that in such situations, at least some multinationals will seek to gain competitive advantages by failing to contribute to the global common good (such as the good of a hospitable global environment). For multinationals are rational agents, i.e., agents bureaucratically structured to take rational means toward achieving their dominant end of increasing their profits. And in a competitive environment, contributing to the common good while others do not, will fail to achieve this dominant end. Joining this conclusion to the ethical premise that when others do not adhere to the requirements of morality it is not immoral for one to do likewise, the realist can conclude that multinationals are not morally obligated to contribute to such global common goods (such as environmental goods).

Moreover, global common goods often create interactions that are not iterated. This is particularly the case where the global environment is concerned. As I have already noted, preservation of a favorable global climate is clearly part of the global common good. Now the failure of the global climate will be a one-time affair. The breakdown of the ozone layer, for example, will happen once, with catastrophic consequences for us all; and the heating up of the global climate as a result of the infusion of carbon dioxide will happen once, with catastrophic consequences for us all. Because these environmental disasters are a one-time affair, they represent a non-iterated Prisoner's Dilemma for multinationals. It is irrational from an individual point of view for a multinational to choose to refrain from polluting the environment in such cases. Either others will refrain, and then one can enjoy the benefits of their refraining; or others will not refrain, and then it will be better to have also not refrained since refraining would have made little difference and would have entailed heavy losses.

Finally, we must also note that although natural persons may signal their reliability to other natural persons, it is not at all obvious that multinationals can do the same. As noted above, multinationals are bureaucratic organizations whose members are continually changing and shifting. The natural persons who make up an organization can signal their reliability to others, but such persons are soon replaced by others, and they in turn are replaced by others. What endures is each organization's single-minded pursuit of increasing its profits in a competitive environment. And an enduring commitment to the pursuit of profit in a competitive environment is not a signal of an enduring commitment to morality.

VII. CONCLUSIONS

The upshot of these considerations is that it is not obvious that we can say that multinationals have an obligation to contribute to the global common good in a competitive environment in the absence of an international authority that can force all agents to contribute to the global common good. Where other rational agents can be expected to shirk the burden of contributing to the common good and where carrying such a burden will put one at a serious competitive disadvantage, the realist argument that it is not immoral for one to also fail to contribute is a powerful argument.

I have not argued, of course, nor do I find it persuasive to claim that competitive pressures automatically relieve agents of their moral obligations, although my arguments here may be wrongly misinterpreted as making that claim. All that I have tried to do is to lay out a justification for the very narrow claim that *certain very special kinds of agents, under certain very limited and very special conditions, seem to have no obligations with respect to certain very special kinds of goods.*

This is not an argument, however, for complete despair. What the argument points to is the need to establish an effective international authority capable of forcing all agents to contribute their part toward the global common good. Perhaps

several of the more powerful autonomous governments of the world, for example, will be prompted to establish such an international agency by relinquishing their autonomy and joining together into a coherently unified group that can exert consistent economic, political, or military pressures on any companies or smaller countries that do not contribute to the global common good. Such an international police group, of course, would transform the present world order, and would be much different from present world organizations such as the United Nations. Once such an international force exists, of course, then both Hobbes and the neo-realist would say that moral obligations can legitimately be attributed to all affected international organizations.

Of course, it is remotely possible but highly unlikely that multinationals themselves will be the source of such promptings for a transformed world order. For whereas governments are concerned with the well being of their citizens, multinationals are bureaucratically structured for the rational pursuit of profit in a competitive environment, not the pursuit of citizen well-being. Here and there we occasionally may see one or even several multinationals whose current cadre of leadership is enlightened enough to regularly steer the organization toward the global common good. But given time, that cadre will be replaced and profit objectives will reassert themselves as the enduring end built into the on-going structure of the multinational corporation.

NOTES

1   See, for example, the articles collected in W. Michael Hoffman, Ann E. Lange, and David A. Fedo, eds., *Ethics and the Multinational Enterprise* (New York: University Press of America, 1986).

2   Thomas Donaldson, *The Ethics of International Business* (New York: Oxford University Press, 1989).

3   Donaldson discusses the question whether *states* have moral obligations to each other in *op. cit.*, 10–29. The critical question, however, is whether *multinationals*, i.e., profit-driven types of

international organizations, have moral obligations. Although Donaldson is able to point out without a great deal of trouble that the realist arguments against morality among nations are mistaken (see 20–23, where Donaldson points out that if the realist were correct, then there would be no cooperation among nations; but since there is cooperation, the realist must be wrong), his points leave untouched the arguments I discuss below which acknowledge that while much cooperation among nations is possible, nevertheless certain crucial forms of cooperation will not obtain among multinationals with respect to the global common good.

4   J. Bentham, *Principles of Morals and Legislation*, 1.4–5.

5   William A. Wallace, O.P., *The Elements of Philosophy, A Compendium for Philosophers and Theologians* (New York: Alba House, 1977), 166–67.

6   *Ibid.*, 167.

7   "Common Good," *The New Catholic Encyclopedia*.

8   John Rawls, *A Theory of Justice* (Cambridge, MA: Harvard University Press, 1971), 233 and 246.

9   Thomas Hobbes, *Leviathan, Parts I and II* [1651] (New York: The Bobbs-Merrill, 1958), 108.

10   *Ibid.* As noted earlier, I am simply assuming what I take to be the popular interpretation of Hobbes' view on the state of nature. As Professor Philip Kain has pointed out to me, there is some controversy among Hobbes scholars about whether or not Hobbes actually held that moral obligation exists in the state of nature. Among those who hold that moral obligation does not exist in Hobbes' state of nature is M. Oakeshott in "The Moral Life in the Writings of Thomas Hobbes" in his *Hobbes on Civil Association* (Berkeley-Los Angeles: University of California Press, 1975), 95–113; among those who hold that moral obligation does exist in Hobbes' state of nature is A.E. Taylor in "The Ethical Doctrine of Hobbes" in *Hobbes Studies*, ed. K.C. Brown (Cambridge: Harvard, 1965), 41ff. Kain suggests that Hobbes simply contradicts himself—holding in some passages that moral obligation does exist in the state of nature and holding in others that it does not—because of his need to use the concept of the state of nature to achieve purposes that required incompatible conceptions of the state of nature; see his "Hobbes, Revolution and the Philosophy of History," in *Hobbes's 'Science of Natural Justice'*, ed. C. Walton and P.J. Johnson (Boston: Martinus Nijhoff, 1987), 203–18. In the present essay I am simply assuming without argument the traditional view that Hobbes made the claim that moral obligation does not exist in the state of nature; my aim is to pursue certain implications of this claim even if I am wrong in assuming that is Hobbes'.

11   See *ibid.*, where Hobbes writes that "yet in all times kings and persons of sovereign authority, because of their independency" are in this state of war.

12   *Ibid.*, 107–08.

13   See Amartya K. Sen, *Collective Choice and Social Welfare* (San Francisco: Holden-Day, 1970), 2–5.

14   See, for example, Gregory Kavka, "Hobbes' War of All Against All," *Ethics*, 93 (January, 1983), 291–310; a somewhat different approach is that of David Gauthier, *Morals By Agreement* (Oxford: Clarendon Press, 1986) and Russell Hardin, *Morality Within the Limits of Reason* (Chicago: University of Chicago Press, 1988).

15   See Robert Axelrod, *The Evolution of Cooperation* (New York: Basic Books, 1984), 27–69.

16   Robert Frank, *Passions Within Reason* (New York: W.W. Norton & Company, 1988).

—27—

VALUES IN TENSION

Ethics Away from Home

Thomas Donaldson

WHEN WE LEAVE HOME AND CROSS OUR NATION'S boundaries, moral clarity often blurs. Without a backdrop of shared attitudes, and without familiar laws and judicial procedures that define standards of ethical conduct, certainty is elusive. Should a company invest in a foreign country where civil and political rights are violated? Should a company go along with a host country's discriminatory employment practices? If companies in developed countries shift facilities to developing nations that lack strict environmental and health regulations, or if those companies choose to fill management and other top-level positions in a host nation with people from the home country, whose standards should prevail?

Even the best-informed, best-intentioned executives must rethink their assumptions about business practice in foreign settings. What works in a company's home country can fail in a country with different standards of ethical conduct. Such difficulties are unavoidable for businesspeople who live and work abroad.

But how can managers resolve the problems? What are the principles that can help them work through the maze of cultural differences and establish codes of conduct for globally ethical business practice? How can companies answer the toughest question in global business ethics: What happens when a host country's ethical standards seem lower than the home country's?

COMPETING ANSWERS

One answer is as old as philosophical discourse. According to cultural relativism, no culture's ethics are better than any other's; therefore there are no international rights and wrongs. If the people of Indonesia tolerate the bribery of their public officials, so what? Their attitude is no better or worse than that of people in Denmark or Singapore who refuse to offer or accept bribes. Likewise, if Belgians fail to find insider trading morally repugnant, who cares? Not enforcing insider-trading laws is no more or less ethical than enforcing such laws.

The cultural relativist's creed—When in Rome, do as the Romans do—is tempting, especially when failing to do as the locals do means forfeiting business opportunities. The inadequacy of cultural relativism, however, becomes apparent when the practices in question are more damaging than petty bribery or insider trading.

In the late 1980s, some European tanneries and pharmaceutical companies were looking for cheap waste-dumping sites. They approached virtually every country on Africa's west coast from Morocco to the Congo. Nigeria agreed to take highly toxic polychlorinated biphenyls. Unprotected local workers, wearing thongs and shorts, unloaded barrels of PCBs and placed them near a residential area. Neither the residents

198

nor the workers knew that the barrels contained toxic waste.

We may denounce governments that permit such abuses, but many countries are unable to police transnational corporations adequately even if they want to. And in many countries, the combination of ineffective enforcement and inadequate regulations leads to behavior by unscrupulous companies that is clearly wrong. A few years ago, for example, a group of investors became interested in restoring the SS *United States*, once a luxurious ocean liner. Before the actual restoration could begin, the ship had to be stripped of its asbestos lining. A bid from a US company, based on US standards for asbestos removal, priced the job at more than $100 million. A company in the Ukrainian city of Sevastopol offered to do the work for less than $2 million. In October 1993, the ship was towed to Sevastopol.

A cultural relativist would have no problem with that outcome, but I do. A country has the right to establish its own health and safety regulations, but in the case described above, the standards and the terms of the contract could not possibly have protected workers in Sevastopol from known health risks. Even if the contract met Ukrainian standards, ethical businesspeople must object. Cultural relativism is morally blind. There are fundamental values that cross cultures, and companies must uphold them.

At the other end of the spectrum from cultural relativism is ethical imperialism, which directs people to do everywhere exactly as they do at home. Again, an understandably appealing approach but one that is clearly inadequate. Consider the large US computer-products company that in 1993 introduced a course on sexual harassment in its Saudi Arabian facility. Under the banner of global consistency, instructors used the same approach to train Saudi Arabian managers that they had used with US managers: the participants were asked to discuss a case in which a manager makes sexually explicit remarks to a new

female employee over drinks in a bar. The instructors failed to consider how the exercise would work in a culture with strict conventions governing relationships between men and women. As a result, the training sessions were ludicrous. They baffled and offended the Saudi participants, and the message to avoid coercion and sexual discrimination was lost.

The theory behind ethical imperialism is absolutism, which is based on three problematic principles. Absolutists believe that there is a single list of truths, that they can be expressed only with one set of concepts, and that they call for exactly the same behavior around the world.

The first claim clashes with many people's belief that different cultural traditions must be respected. In some cultures, loyalty to a community—family, organization, or society—is the foundation of all ethical behavior. The Japanese, for example, define business ethics in terms of loyalty to their companies, their business networks, and their nation. Americans place a higher value on liberty than on loyalty; the US tradition of rights emphasizes equality, fairness, and individual freedom. It is hard to conclude that truth lies on one side or the other, but an absolutist would have us select just one.

The second problem with absolutism is the presumption that people must express moral truth using only one set of concepts. For instance, some absolutists insist that the language of basic rights provide the framework for any discussion of ethics. That means, though, that entire cultural traditions must be ignored. The notion of a right evolved with the rise of democracy in post-Renaissance Europe and the United States, but the term is not found in either Confucian or Buddhist traditions. We all learn ethics in the context of our particular cultures, and the power in the principles is deeply tied to the way in which they are expressed. Internationally accepted lists of moral principles, such as the United Nations' Universal Declaration of Human Rights, draw on many cultural and religious traditions. As philosopher Michael Walzer has noted, "There is no Esperanto of global ethics."

The third problem with absolutism is the belief in a global standard of ethical behavior. Context must shape ethical practice. Very low wages, for example, may be considered unethical in rich, advanced countries, but developing nations may be acting ethically if they encourage investment and improve living standards by accepting low wages. Likewise, when people are malnourished or starving, a government may be wise to use more fertilizer in order to improve crop yields, even though that means settling for relatively high levels of thermal water pollution.

When cultures have different standards of ethical behavior—and different ways of handling unethical behavior—a company that takes an absolutist approach may find itself making a disastrous mistake. When a manager at a large US specialty-products company in China caught an employee stealing, she followed the company's practice and turned the employee over to the provincial authorities, who executed him. Managers cannot operate in another culture without being aware of that culture's attitudes toward ethics.

If companies can neither adopt a host country's ethics nor extend the home country's standards, what is the answer? Even the traditional litmus test—What would people think of your actions if they were written up on the front page of the newspaper?—is an unreliable guide, for there is no international consensus on standards of business conduct.

BALANCING THE EXTREMES: THREE GUIDING PRINCIPLES

Companies must help managers distinguish between practices that are merely different and those that are wrong. For relativists, nothing is sacred and nothing is wrong. For absolutists, many things that are different are wrong. Neither extreme illuminates the real world of business decision making. The answer lies somewhere in between.

When it comes to shaping ethical behavior, companies must be guided by three principles.

1. Respect for core human values, which determine the absolute moral threshold for all business activities.
2. Respect for local traditions.
3. The belief that context matters when deciding what is right and what is wrong.

Consider those principles in action. In Japan, people doing business together often exchange gifts—sometimes expensive ones—in keeping with long-standing Japanese tradition. When US and European companies started doing a lot of business in Japan, many Western businesspeople thought that the practice of gift giving might be wrong rather than simply different. To them, accepting a gift felt like accepting a bribe. As Western companies have become more familiar with Japanese traditions, however, most have come to tolerate the practice and to set different limits on gift giving in Japan than they do elsewhere.

Respecting differences is a crucial ethical practice. Research shows that management ethics differ among cultures; respecting those differences means recognizing that some cultures have obvious weaknesses—as well as hidden strengths. Managers in Hong Kong, for example, have a higher tolerance for some forms of bribery than their Western counterparts, but they have a much lower tolerance for the failure to acknowledge a subordinate's work. In some parts of the Far East, stealing credit from a subordinate is nearly an unpardonable sin.

People often equate respect for local traditions with cultural relativism. That is incorrect. Some practices are clearly wrong. Union Carbide's tragic experience in Bhopal, India, provides one example. The company's executives seriously underestimated how much on-site management involvement was needed at the Bhopal plant to compensate for the country's poor infrastructure and regulatory capabilities. In the aftermath of the disastrous gas leak, the lesson is clear: companies using sophisticated technology in a developing country must evaluate that country's ability to oversee its safe use. Since the incident at Bhopal, Union Carbide has become a leader in advising companies on using hazardous technologies safely in developing countries.

Some activities are wrong no matter where they take place. But some practices that are unethical in one setting may be acceptable in another. For instance, the chemical EDB, a soil fungicide, is banned for use in the United States. In hot climates, however, it quickly becomes harmless through exposure to intense solar radiation and high soil temperatures. As long as the chemical is monitored, companies may be able to use EDB ethically in certain parts of the world.

DEFINING THE ETHICAL THRESHOLD: CORE VALUES

Few ethical questions are easy for managers to answer. But there are some hard truths that must guide managers' actions, a set of what I call *core human values*, which define minimum ethical standards for all companies. The right to good health and the right to economic advancement and an improved standard of living are two core human values. Another is what Westerners call the Golden Rule, which is recognizable in every major religious and ethical tradition around the world. In Book 15 of his *Analects*, for instance, Confucius counsels people to maintain reciprocity, or not to do to others what they do not want done to themselves.

Although no single list would satisfy every scholar, I believe it is possible to articulate three core values that incorporate the work of scores of theologians and philosophers around the world. To be broadly relevant, these values must include elements found in both Western and non-Western cultural and religious traditions. Consider the examples of values in the table.

WHAT DO THESE VALUES HAVE IN COMMON?

At first glance, the values expressed in the two lists seem quite different. Nonetheless, in the spirit of

what philosopher John Rawls calls *overlapping consensus*, one can see that the seemingly divergent values converge at key points. Despite important differences between Western and non-Western cultural and religious traditions, both express shared attitudes about what it means to be human. First, individuals must not treat others simply as tools; in other words, they must recognize a person's value as a human being. Next, individuals and communities must treat people in ways that respect people's basic rights. Finally, members of a community must work together to support and improve the institutions on which the community depends. I call those three values *respect for human dignity*, *respect for basic rights*, and *good citizenship*.

What Do These Values Have in Common?

NON-WESTERN	WESTERN
Kyosei (Japanese): Living and working together for the common good.	Individual liberty
Dharma (Hindu): The fullfillment of inherited duty.	Egalitarianism
Santutti (Buddhist): The importance of limited desires.	Political participation
Zakat (Muslim): The duty to give alms to the Muslim poor.	Human rights

Those values must be the starting point for all companies as they formulate and evaluate standards of ethical conduct at home and abroad. But they are only a starting point. Companies need much more specific guidelines, and the first step to developing those is to translate the core human values into core values for business. What does it mean, for example, for a company to respect human dignity? How can a company be a good citizen?

I believe that companies can respect human dignity by creating and sustaining a corporate culture in which employees, customers, and suppliers are treated not as means to an end but as people whose intrinsic value must be acknowledged, and by producing safe products and services in a safe workplace. Companies can respect basic rights by acting in ways that support and protect the individual rights of employees, customers, and surrounding communities, and by avoiding relationships that violate human beings' rights to health, education, safety, and an adequate standard of living. And companies can be good citizens by supporting essential social institutions, such as the economic system and the education system, and by working with host governments and other organizations to protect the environment.

The core values establish a moral compass for business practice. They can help companies identify practices that are acceptable and those that are intolerable—even if the practices are compatible with a host country's norms and laws. Dumping pollutants near people's homes and accepting inadequate standards for handling hazardous materials are two examples of actions that violate core values.

Similarly, if employing children prevents them from receiving a basic education, the practice is intolerable. Lying about product specifications in the act of selling may not affect human lives directly, but it too is intolerable because it violates the trust that is needed to sustain a corporate culture in which customers are respected.

Sometimes it is not a company's actions but those of a supplier or customer that pose problems. Take the case of the Tan family, a large supplier for Levi Strauss. The Tans were allegedly forcing 1,200 Chinese and Filipino women to work 74 hours per week in guarded compounds on the Mariana Islands. In 1992, after repeated warnings to the Tans, Levi Strauss broke off business relations with them.

Creating an Ethical Corporate Culture

The core values for business that I have enumerated can help companies begin to exercise ethical judgment and think about how to operate ethically in foreign cultures, but they are not specific enough to guide managers through actual ethical dilemmas. Levi Strauss relied on a written code of conduct when figuring out how to deal with the Tan family. The company's Global Sourcing and Operating Guidelines, formerly called the Business Partner Terms of Engagement, state that Levi Strauss will "seek to identify and utilize business partners who aspire as individuals and in the conduct of all their businesses to a set of ethical standards not incompatible with our own." Whenever intolerable business situations arise, managers should be guided by precise statements that spell out the behavior and operating practices that the company demands.

Ninety per cent of all *Fortune* 500 companies have codes of conduct, and 70 per cent have statements of vision and values. In Europe and the Far East, the percentages are lower but are increasing rapidly. Does that mean that most companies have what they need? Hardly. Even though most large US companies have both statements of values and codes of conduct, many might be better off if they didn't. Too many companies don't do anything with the documents; they simply paste them on the wall to impress employees, customers, suppliers, and the public. As a result, the senior managers who drafted the statements lose credibility by proclaiming values and not living up to them. Companies such as Johnson & Johnson, Levi Strauss, Motorola, Texas Instruments, and Lockheed Martin, however, do a great deal to make the words meaningful. Johnson & Johnson, for example, has become well known for its Credo Challenge sessions, in which managers discuss ethics in the context of their current business problems and are invited to criticize the company's credo and make suggestions for changes. The participants' ideas are passed on to the company's senior managers. Lockheed Martin has created an innovative site on the World Wide Web and on its local network that gives employees, customers, and suppliers access to the company's ethical code and the chance to voice complaints.

Many companies don't do anything with their codes of conduct; they simply paste them on the wall.

Codes of conduct must provide clear direction about ethical behavior when the temptation to behave unethically is strongest. The pronouncement in a code of conduct that bribery is unacceptable is useless unless accompanied by guidelines for gift giving, payments to get goods through customs, and "requests" from intermediaries who are hired to ask for bribes.

Motorola's values are stated very simply as "How we will always act: [with] constant respect for people [and] uncompromising integrity." The company's code of conduct, however, is explicit about actual business practice. With respect to bribery, for example, the code states that the "funds and assets of Motorola shall not be used, directly or indirectly, for illegal payments of any kind." It is unambiguous about what sort of payment is illegal: "the payment of a bribe to a public official or the kickback of funds to an employee of a customer...." The code goes on to prescribe specific procedures for handling commissions to intermediaries, issuing sales invoices, and disclosing confidential information in a sales transaction—all situations in which employees might have an opportunity to accept or offer bribes.

Codes of conduct must be explicit to be useful, but they must also leave room for a manager to use his or her judgment in situations requiring cultural sensitivity. Host-country employees shouldn't be forced to adopt all home-country values and renounce their own. Again, Motorola's code is exemplary. First, it gives clear direction: "Employees of Motorola will respect the laws, customs, and traditions of each country in which they operate, but will, at the same time, engage in no course of conduct which, even if legal, customary, and accepted in any such country, could be

deemed to be in violation of the accepted business ethics of Motorola or the laws of the United States relating to business ethics." After laying down such absolutes, Motorola's code then makes clear when individual judgment will be necessary. For example, employees may sometimes accept certain kinds of small gifts "in rare circumstances, where the refusal to accept a gift" would injure Motorola's "legitimate business interests." Under certain circumstances, such gifts "may be accepted so long as the gift inures to the benefit of Motorola" and not "to the benefit of the Motorola employee."

Striking the appropriate balance between providing clear direction and leaving room for individual judgment makes crafting corporate values statements and ethics codes one of the hardest tasks that executives confront. The words are only a start. A company's leaders need to refer often to their organization's credo and code and must themselves be credible, committed, and consistent. If senior managers act as though ethics don't matter, the rest of the company's employees won't think they do, either.

CONFLICTS OF DEVELOPMENT AND CONFLICTS OF TRADITION

Managers living and working abroad who are not prepared to grapple with moral ambiguity and tension should pack their bags and come home. The view that all business practices can be categorized as either ethical or unethical is too simple. As Einstein is reported to have said, "Things should be as simple as possible—but no simpler." Many business practices that are considered unethical in one setting may be ethical in another. Such activities are neither black nor white but exist in what Thomas Dunfee and I have called *moral free space*.[1] In this gray zone, there are no tight prescriptions for a company's behavior. Managers must chart their own courses—as long as they do not violate core human values.

Consider the following example. Some successful Indian companies offer employees the opportunity for one of their children to gain a job with the company once the child has completed a certain level in school. The companies honor this commitment even when other applicants are more qualified than an employee's child. The perk is extremely valuable in a country where jobs are hard to find, and it reflects the Indian culture's belief that the West has gone too far in allowing economic opportunities to break up families. Not surprisingly, the perk is among the most cherished by employees, but in most Western countries, it would be branded unacceptable nepotism. In the United States, for example, the ethical principle of equal opportunity holds that jobs should go to the applicants with the best qualifications. If a US company made such promises to its employees, it would violate regulations established by the Equal Employment Opportunity Commission. Given this difference in ethical attitudes, how should US managers react to Indian nepotism? Should they condemn the Indian companies, refusing to accept them as partners or suppliers until they agree to clean up their act?

Despite the obvious tension between nepotism and principles of equal opportunity, I cannot condemn the practice for Indians. In a country, such as India, that emphasizes clan and family relationships and has catastrophic levels of unemployment, the practice must be viewed in moral free space. The decision to allow a special perk for employees and their children is not necessarily wrong—at least for members of that country.

How can managers discover the limits of moral free space? That is, how can they learn to distinguish a value in tension with their own from one that is intolerable? Helping managers develop good ethical judgment requires companies to be clear about their core values and codes of conduct. But even the most explicit set of guidelines cannot always provide answers. That is especially true in the thorniest ethical dilemmas in which the host country's ethical standards not only are different but also seem lower than the home country's. Managers must recognize that when countries have different ethical standards, there are two types of conflict that commonly arise. Each type requires its own line of reasoning.

In the first type of conflict, which I call a *conflict of relative development*, ethical standards conflict because of the countries' different levels of economic development. As mentioned before, developing countries may accept wage rates that seem inhumane to more advanced countries in order to attract investment. As economic conditions in a developing country improve, the incidence of that sort of conflict usually decreases. The second type of conflict is a *conflict of cultural tradition*. For example, Saudi Arabia, unlike most other countries, does not allow women to serve as corporate managers. Instead, women may work in only a few professions, such as education and health care. The prohibition stems from strongly held religious and cultural beliefs; any increase in the country's level of economic development, which is already quite high, is not likely to change the rules.

To resolve a conflict of relative development, a manager must ask the following question: Would the practice be acceptable at home if my country were in a similar stage of economic development? Consider the difference between wage and safety standards in the United States and in Angola, where citizens accept lower standards on both counts. If a US oil company is hiring Angolans to work on an offshore Angolan oil rig, can the company pay them lower wages than it pays US workers in the Gulf of Mexico? Reasonable people have to answer yes if the alternative for Angola is the loss of both the foreign investment and the jobs.

Consider, too, differences in regulatory environments. In the 1980s, the government of India fought hard to be able to import Ciba-Geigy's Entero Vioform, a drug known to be enormously effective in fighting dysentery but one that had been banned in the United States because some users experienced side effects. Although dysentery was not a big problem in the United States, in India, poor public sanitation was contributing to epidemic levels of the disease. Was it unethical to make the drug available in India after it had been banned in the United States? On the contrary, rational people should consider it unethical not to do so. Apply our test: Would the United States, at an earlier stage of development, have used this drug despite its side effects? The answer is clearly yes.

But there are many instances when the answer to similar questions is no. Sometimes a host country's standards are inadequate at any level of economic development. If a country's pollution standards are so low that working on an oil rig would considerably increase a person's risk of developing cancer, foreign oil companies must refuse to do business there. Likewise, if the dangerous side effects of a drug treatment outweigh its benefits, managers should not accept health standards that ignore the risks.

When relative economic conditions do not drive tensions, there is a more objective test for resolving ethical problems. Managers should deem a practice permissible only if they can answer no to both of the following questions: Is it possible to conduct business successfully in the host country without undertaking the practice? and Is the practice a violation of a core human value? Japanese gift giving is a perfect example of a conflict of cultural tradition. Most experienced businesspeople, Japanese and non-Japanese alike, would agree that doing business in Japan would be virtually impossible without adopting the practice. Does gift giving violate a core human value? I cannot identify one that it violates. As a result, gift giving may be permissible for foreign companies in Japan even if it conflicts with ethical attitudes at home. In fact, that conclusion is widely accepted, even by companies such as Texas Instruments and IBM, which are outspoken against bribery.

Does it follow that all nonmonetary gifts are acceptable or that bribes are generally acceptable in countries where they are common? Not at all. What makes the routine practice of gift giving acceptable in Japan are the limits in its scope and intention. When gift giving moves outside those limits, it soon collides with core human values. For example, when Carl Kotchian, president of Lockheed in the 1970s, carried suitcases full of cash to Japanese politicians, he went beyond the norms established

by Japanese tradition. That incident galvanized opinion in the United States Congress and helped lead to passage of the Foreign Corrupt Practices Act. Likewise, Roh Tae Woo went beyond the norms established by Korean cultural tradition when he accepted $635.4 million in bribes as president of the Republic of Korea between 1988 and 1993.

GUIDELINES FOR ETHICAL LEADERSHIP

Learning to spot intolerable practices and to exercise good judgment when ethical conflicts arise requires practice. Creating a company culture that rewards ethical behavior is essential. The following guidelines for developing a global ethical perspective among managers can help.

Treat corporate values and formal standards of conduct as absolutes. Whatever ethical standards a company chooses, it cannot waver on its principles either at home or abroad. Consider what has become part of company lore at Motorola. Around 1950, a senior executive was negotiating with officials of a South American government on a $10 million sale that would have increased the company's annual net profits by nearly 25 per cent. As the negotiations neared completion, however, the executive walked away from the deal because the officials were asking for $1 million for "fees." CEO Robert Galvin not only supported the executive's decision but also made it clear that Motorola would neither accept the sale on any terms nor do business with those government officials again. Retold over the decades, this story demonstrating Galvin's resolve has helped cement a culture of ethics for thousands of employees at Motorola.

Design and implement conditions of engagement for suppliers and customers. Will your company do business with any customer or supplier? What if a customer or supplier uses child labor? What if it has strong links with organized crime? What if it pressures your company to break a host country's laws? Such issues are best not left for spur-of-the-moment decisions. Some companies have realized that. Sears, for instance, has developed a policy of not contracting production to companies that use prison labor or infringe on workers' rights to health and safety. And BankAmerica has specified as a condition for many of its loans to developing countries that environmental standards and human rights must be observed.

Allow foreign business units to help formulate ethical standards and interpret ethical issues. The French pharmaceutical company Rhône-Poulenc Rorer has allowed foreign subsidiaries to augment lists of corporate ethical principles with their own suggestions. Texas Instruments has paid special attention to issues of international business ethics by creating the Global Business Practices Council, which is made up of managers from countries in which the company operates. With the overarching intent to create a "global ethics strategy, locally deployed," the council's mandate is to provide ethics education and create local processes that will help managers in the company's foreign business units resolve ethical conflicts.

In host countries, support efforts to decrease institutional corruption. Individual managers will not be able to wipe out corruption in a host country, no matter how many bribes they turn down. When a host country's tax system, import and export procedures, and procurement practices favor unethical players, companies must take action.

Many companies have begun to participate in reforming host-country institutions. General Electric, for example, has taken a strong stand in India, using the media to make repeated condemnations of bribery in business and government. General Electric and others have found, however, that a single company usually cannot drive out entrenched corruption. Transparency International, an organization based in Germany, has been effective in helping coalitions of companies, government officials, and others work to reform bribery-ridden bureaucracies in Russia, Bangladesh, and elsewhere.

Exercise moral imagination. Using moral imagination means resolving tensions responsibly and creatively. Coca-Cola, for instance, has consistently turned down requests for bribes from Egyptian officials but has managed to gain political support and public trust by sponsoring a project to plant fruit trees. And take the example of Levi Strauss, which discovered in the early 1990s that two of its suppliers in Bangladesh were employing children under the age of 14—a practice that violated the company's principles but was tolerated in Bangladesh. Forcing the suppliers to fire the children would not have ensured that the children received an education, and it would have caused serious hardship for the families depending on the children's wages. In a creative arrangement, the suppliers agreed to pay the children's regular wages while they attended school and to offer each child a job at age 14. Levi Strauss, in turn, agreed to pay the children's tuition and provide books and uniforms. That arrangement allowed Levi Strauss to uphold its principles and provide long-term benefits to its host country.

Many people think of values as soft; to some they are usually unspoken. A South Seas island society uses the word *mokita*, which means, "the truth that everybody knows but nobody speaks." However difficult they are to articulate, values affect how we all behave. In a global business environment, values in tension are the rule rather than the exception. Without a company's commitment, statements of values and codes of ethics end up as empty platitudes that provide managers with no foundation for behaving ethically. Employees need and deserve more, and responsible members of the global business community can set examples for others to follow. The dark consequences of incidents such as Union Carbide's disaster in Bhopal remind us how high the stakes can be.

NOTE

1   Thomas Donaldson and Thomas W. Dunfee, "Toward a Unified Conception of Business Ethics: Integrative Social Contracts Theory," *Academy of Management Review*, April 1994; and "Integrative Social Contracts Theory: A Communitarian Conception of Economic Ethics," *Economics and Philosophy*, Spring 1995.

—28—

THE GREAT NON-DEBATE OVER INTERNATIONAL SWEATSHOPS

Ian Maitland

RECENT YEARS HAVE SEEN A DRAMATIC GROWTH in the contracting out of production by companies in the industrialized countries to suppliers in developing countries. This globalization of production has led to an emerging international division of labor in footwear and apparel in which companies like Nike and Reebok concentrate on product design and marketing but rely on a network of contractors in Asia and Central America, etc., to build shoes or sew shirts according to exact specifications and deliver a high quality good according to precise delivery schedules. These contracting arrangements have drawn intense fire from labor and human rights activists who charge that the companies are (by proxy) exploiting foreign workers. The companies stand accused of chasing cheap labor around the globe, failing to pay their workers living wages, using child labor, turning a blind eye to abuses of human rights, and being complicit with repressive regimes in denying workers the right to join unions and failing to enforce minimum labor standards in the workplace, and so on. Many companies have tried to address these concerns by developing codes of conduct for their overseas suppliers. This workshop will examine the desirability and pitfalls of such codes of conduct.

The campaign against international sweatshops has largely unfolded on television and, to a lesser extent, in the print media. What seems like no more than a handful of critics has mounted an aggressive, media-savvy campaign which has put the publicity-shy retail giants on the defensive. The critics have orchestrated a series of sensational "disclosures" on prime time television exposing the terrible pay and working conditions in factories making jeans for Levi's or sneakers for Nike or Pocahontas shirts for Disney. One of the principal scourges of the companies has been Charles Kernaghan who runs the National Labor Coalition (NLC), a labor human rights group involving 25 unions. It was Kernaghan who, in 1996, broke the news before a Congressional committee that Kathie Lee Gifford's clothing line was being made by 13- and 14-year olds working 20-hour days in factories in Honduras.

Kernaghan also arranged for teenage workers from sweatshops in Central America to testify before Congressional committees about abusive labor practices. At one of these hearings, one of the workers held up a Liz Claiborne cotton sweater identical to ones she had sewn since she was a 13-year old working 12 hour days. According to a news report, "[t]his image, accusations of oppressive conditions at the factory and the Claiborne logo played well on that evening's network news."[1] The result has been a circus-like atmosphere—as in Roman circus where Christians were thrown to lions.

Kernaghan has shrewdly targeted the companies' carefully cultivated public images. He has explained: "Their image is everything. They live and die by their image. That gives you a certain power over them." As a result, he says, "these companies are sitting ducks. They have no leg to stand on. That's why it's possible for a tiny group like us to take on a giant like Wal-Mart. You can't defend paying someone 31 cents an hour in Honduras...."[2] Apparently most of the companies agree with Kernaghan. Not a single company has tried to mount a serious defense of its contracting practices. They have judged that they cannot win a war of sound bites with the critics. Instead of making a fight of it, the companies have sued for peace in order to protect their principal asset—their image.

Major US retailers have responded by adopting codes of conduct on human and labor rights in their international operations. Levi-Strauss, Nike, Sears, JCPenney, Wal-Mart, Home Depot, Philips Van-Heusen now have such codes. As Lance Compa notes, such codes are the result of a blend of humanitarian and pragmatic impulses: "Often the altruistic motive coincides with 'bottom line' considerations related to brand name, company image, and other intangibles that make for core value to the firm."[3] Peter Jacobi, President of Global Sourcing for Levi-Strauss has advised: "If your company owns a popular brand, protect this priceless asset at all costs. Highly visible companies have any number of reasons to conduct their business not just responsibly but also in ways that cannot be portrayed as unfair, illegal, or unethical. This sets an extremely high standard since it must be applied to both company-owned businesses and contractors...."[4] And according to another Levi-Strauss spokesman, "In many respects, we're protecting our single largest asset: our brand image and corporate reputation."[5] Nike recently published the results of a generally favorable review of its international operations conducted by former American UN Ambassador Andrew Young.

Recently a truce of sorts between the critics and the companies was announced on the White House lawn with President Clinton and Kathie Lee Gifford in attendance. A presidential task force, including representatives of labor unions, human rights groups and apparel companies like L.L. Bean and Nike, has come up with a set of voluntary standards which, it hopes, will be embraced by the entire industry. Companies that comply with the code will be entitled to use a "No Sweat" label.

OBJECTIVE OF THIS PAPER

In this confrontation between the companies and their critics, neither side seems to have judged it to be in its interest to seriously engage the issue at the heart of this controversy, namely: What are appropriate wages and labor standards in international sweatshops? As we have seen, the companies have treated the charges about sweatshops as a public relations problem to be managed so as to minimize harm to their public images. The critics have apparently judged that the best way to keep public indignation at boiling point is to oversimplify the issue and treat it as a morality play featuring heartless exploiters and victimized third world workers. The result has been a great non-debate over international sweatshops. Paradoxically, if peace breaks out between the two sides, the chances that the debate will be seriously joined may recede still further. Indeed, there exists a real risk (I will argue) that any such truce may be a collusive one that will come at the expense of the very third world workers it is supposed to help.

This paper takes up the issue of what are appropriate wages and labor standards in international sweatshops. Critics charge that the present arrangements are exploitative. I proceed by examining the specific charges of exploitation from the standpoints of both (a) their factual and (b) their ethical sufficiency. However, in the absence of any well-established consensus among business ethicists (or other thoughtful observers), I simultaneously use the investigation of sweatshops as a setting for trying to adjudicate between competing views about what those standards should be. My examination will pay particular attention to (but will not be limited to) labor conditions at the plants of Nike's suppliers in Indonesia. I have not personally visited any international sweatshops, and so my conclusions are based entirely on secondary analysis of the voluminous published record on the topic.

What Are Ethically Appropriate Labor Standards in International Sweatshops?

What are ethically acceptable or appropriate levels of wages and labor standards in international sweatshops? The following four possibilities just about run the gamut of standards or principles that have been seriously proposed to regulate such policies.

(1) *Home-country standards*: It might be argued (and in rare cases has been) that international corporations have an ethical duty to pay the same wages and provide the same labor standards regardless of where they operate. However, the view that home-country standards should apply in host-countries is rejected by most business ethicists and (officially at least) by the critics of international sweatshops. Thus Thomas Donaldson argues that "[b]y arbitrarily establishing US wage levels as the bench mark for fairness one eliminates the role of the international market in establishing salary levels, and this in turn eliminates the incentive US corporations have to hire foreign workers."[6] Richard DeGeorge makes much the same argument: If there were a rule that said that "that American MNCs [multinational corporations] that wish to be ethical must pay the same wages abroad as they do at home, ... [then] MNCs would have little incentive to move their manufacturing abroad; and if they did move abroad they would disrupt the local labor market with artificially high wages that bore no relation to the local standard or cost of living."[7]

(2) *"Living wage" standard*: It has been proposed that an international corporation should, at a minimum, pay a "living wage." Thus DeGeorge says that corporations should pay a living wage "even when this is not paid by local firms."[8] However, it is hard to pin down what this means operationally. According to DeGeorge, a living wage should "allow the worker to live in dignity as a human being." In order to respect the human rights of its workers, he says, a corporation must pay "at least subsistence wages and as much above that as workers and their dependents need to live with reasonable dignity, given the general state of development of the society."[9] As we shall see, the living wage standard has become a rallying cry of the critics of international sweatshops. Apparently, DeGeorge believes that it is preferable for a corporation to provide no job at all than to offer one that pays less than a living wage.

(3) *Donaldson's test*: Thomas Donaldson believes that "it is irrelevant whether the standards of the host country comply or fail to comply with home country standards; what is relevant is whether they meet a universal, objective minimum."[10] He tries to specify "a moral minimum for the behavior of all international economic agents."[11] However, he concedes that this "leaves obscure not only the issue of less extreme threats but of harms other than physical injury. The language of rights and harm is sufficiently vague so as to leave shrouded in uncertainty a formidable list of issues crucial to multinationals."[12] He accepts that "many rights ... are dependent for their specification on the level of economic development of the country in question."[13] Accordingly, he proposes a test to determine when deviations from home-country standards are unethical. That test provides as follows: "The practice is permissible if and only if the members of the home country would, under conditions of economic development relevantly similar to those of the host country, regard the practice as permissible."[14] Donaldson's test is vulnerable to Bernard Shaw's objection to the Golden Rule, namely that we should not do unto others as we would they do unto us, because their tastes may be different. The test also complicates matters by introducing counterfactuals and hypotheticals (if I were in their place [which I'm not] what would I want?). This indeterminacy is a serious weakness in an ethical code: It is likely to confuse managers who want to act ethically and to provide loopholes for those don't.

(4) *Classical liberal standard*: Finally there is what I will call the classical liberal standard.

According to this standard a practice (wage or labor practice) is ethically acceptable if it is freely chosen by informed workers. For example, in a recent report the World Bank invoked this standard in connection with workplace safety. It said: "The appropriate level is therefore that at which the costs are commensurate with the value that informed workers place on improved working conditions and reduced risk."[15] Most business ethicists reject this standard on the grounds that there is some sort of market failure or the "background conditions" are lacking for markets to work effectively. Thus for Donaldson full (or near-full) employment is a prerequisite if workers are to make sound choices regarding workplace safety: "The average level of unemployment in the developing countries today exceeds 40 per cent, a figure that has frustrated the application of neoclassical economic principles to the international economy on a score of issues. With full employment, and all other things being equal, market forces will encourage workers to make trade-offs between job opportunities using safety as a variable. But with massive unemployment, market forces in developing countries drive the unemployed to the jobs they are lucky enough to land, regardless of the safety."[16] Apparently there are other forces, like Islamic fundamentalism and the global debt "bomb," that rule out reliance on market solutions, but Donaldson does not explain their relevance. DeGeorge, too, believes that the necessary conditions are lacking for market forces to operate benignly. Without what he calls "background institutions" to protect the workers and the resources of the developing country (e.g., enforceable minimum wages) and/ or greater equality of bargaining power exploitation is the most likely result. "If American MNCs pay workers very low wages ... they clearly have the opportunity to make significant profits."[17] DeGeorge goes on to make the interesting observation that "competition has developed among multinationals themselves, so that the profit margin has been driven down" and developing countries "can play one company against another."[18]

But apparently that is not enough to rehabilitate market forces in his eyes.

THE CASE AGAINST INTERNATIONAL SWEATSHOPS

To many of their critics, international sweatshops exemplify the way in which the greater openness of the world economy is hurting workers. According to one critic, "as it is now constituted, the world trading system discriminates against workers, especially those in the Third World."[19] Globalization means a transition from (more or less) regulated domestic economies to an unregulated world economy. The superior mobility of capital, and the essentially fixed, immobile nature of world labor, means a fundamental shift in bargaining power in favor of large international corporations. Their global reach permits them to shift production almost costlessly from one location to another. As a consequence, instead of being able to exercise some degree of control over companies operating within their borders, governments are now locked in a bidding war with one another to attract and retain the business of large multinational companies.

The critics allege that international companies are using the threat of withdrawal or withholding of investment to pressure governments and workers to grant concessions. "Today [multinational companies] choose between workers in developing countries that compete against each other to depress wages to attract foreign investment."[20] The result is a race for the bottom—a "destructive downward bidding spiral of the labor conditions and wages of workers throughout the world...."[21] Kernaghan claims that "It is a race to the bottom over who will accept the lowest wages and the most miserable working conditions."[22] Thus, critics charge that in Indonesia wages are deliberately held below the poverty level or subsistence in order to make the country a desirable location. The results of this competitive dismantling of worker protections, living standards and worker rights are predictable: deteriorating work conditions, declining real incomes for workers, and a widening gap between rich and poor in developing countries. I turn next to the specific charges made by the critics of international sweatshops.

Unconscionable wages: Critics charge that the companies, by their proxies, are paying "starvation wages"[23] and "slave wages."[24] They are far from clear about what wage level they consider to be appropriate. But they generally demand that companies pay a "living wage." Kernaghan has said that workers should be paid enough to support their families and they should get a "living wage" and "be treated like human beings."[25] Jay Mazur of the textile employees union (UNITE) says "On the question of wages, generally, of course workers should be paid enough to meet their basic needs—and then some."[26] According to Tim Smith, wage levels should be "fair, decent or a living wage for an employee and his or her family." He has said that wages in the maquiladoras of Mexico averaged $35 to $55 a week (in or near 1993) which he calls a "shockingly substandard wage," apparently on the grounds that it "clearly does not allow an employee to feed and care for a family adequately."[27] In 1992, Nike came in for harsh criticism when a magazine published the pay stub of a worker at one of its Indonesian suppliers. It showed that the worker was paid at the rate of $1.03 per day which was reportedly less than the Indonesian government's figure for "minimum physical need."[28]

Immiserization thesis: Former Labor Secretary Robert Reich has proposed as a test of the fairness of development policies that "Low-wage workers should become better off, not worse off, as trade and investment boost national income." He has written that "[i]f a country pursues policies that ... limit to a narrow elite the benefits of trade, the promise of open commerce is perverted and drained of its rationale."[29] A key claim of the activists is that companies actually impoverish or immiserize developing country workers. They experience an absolute decline in living standards. This thesis follows from the claim that the bidding war among developing countries is depressing wages. Critics deride the claim that sweatshops are benefiting the poor by means of a global version of "trickle down" economics. They reject as flawed "claims that US [free trade] policies are leading to the growth of huge middle classes—in such countries as China, India and Indonesia—that will drive the world economy in the twenty-first century."[30] This picture, they say, is belied by the fact that "Most of the 'global South'—some 45 per cent of humanity who reside mainly in the 140 poorest countries of the Third World—is locked in poverty and left behind as the richer strata grow...."[31]

Widening gap between rich and poor: A related charge is that international sweatshops are contributing to the increasing gap between rich and poor. Not only are the poor being absolutely impoverished, but trade is generating greater inequality within developing countries. Another test that Reich has proposed to establish the fairness of international trade is that "the gap between rich and poor should tend to narrow with development, not widen."[32] Critics charge that international sweatshops flunk that test. They say that the increasing GNPs of some developing countries simply mask a widening gap between rich and poor. "Across the world, both local and foreign elites are getting richer from the exploitation of the most vulnerable."[33] And, "The major adverse consequence of quickening global economic integration has been widening income disparity within almost all nations...."[34] There appears to be a tacit alliance between the elites of both first and third worlds to exploit the most vulnerable, to regiment and control and conscript them so that they can create the material conditions for the elites' extravagant lifestyles.

Collusion with repressive regimes: Critics charge that, in their zeal to make their countries safe for foreign investment, Third World regimes, notably China and Indonesia, have stepped up their repression. Not only have these countries failed to enforce even the minimal labor rules on the books, but they have also used their military and police to break strikes and repress independent unions. They have stifled political dissent, both to retain their hold on political power and to avoid any instability that might scare off foreign investors. Consequently, critics charge, companies like Nike are profiting from political repression. "As unions spread in [Korea and Taiwan], Nike shifted its suppliers primarily to Indonesia, China and Thailand, where they could depend on governments to suppress independent union-organizing efforts."[35]

EVALUATION OF THE CHARGES AGAINST INTERNATIONAL SWEATSHOPS

The critics' charges are undoubtedly accurate on a number of points: (1) There is no doubt that international companies are chasing cheap labor. (2) The wages paid by the international sweatshops are—by American standards—shockingly low. (3) Some developing country governments have tightly controlled or repressed organized labor in order to prevent it from disturbing the flow of foreign investment. Thus, in Indonesia, independent unions have been suppressed. (4) It is not unusual in developing countries for minimum wage levels to be lower than the official poverty level. (5) Developing country governments have winked at violations of minimum wage laws and labor rules. However, most jobs are in the informal sector and so largely outside the scope of government supervision. (6) Some suppliers have employed children or have subcontracted work to other producers who have done so. (7) Some developing country governments deny their people basic political rights. China is the obvious example; Indonesia's record is pretty horrible but had shown steady improvement until the last two years. But on many of the other counts, the critics' charges appear to be seriously inaccurate. And, even where the charges are accurate, it is not self-evident that the practices in question are improper or unethical, as we see next.

Wages and conditions: Even the critics of international sweatshops do not dispute that the wages they pay are generally higher than—or at least equal to—comparable wages in the labor markets where they operate. According to the International Labor Organization (ILO), multinational companies often apply standards relating to wages, benefits, conditions of work, and occupational safety and health, which both exceed statutory requirements and those practised by local firms. The ILO also says that wages and working conditions in so-called Export Processing Zones (EPZs) are often equal to or higher than jobs outside. The World Bank says that the poorest workers in developing countries work in the informal sector where they often earn less than half what a formal sector employee earns. Moreover, "informal and rural workers often must work under more hazardous and insecure conditions than their formal sector counterparts."[36]

The same appears to hold true for the international sweatshops. In 1996, young women working in the plant of a Nike supplier in Serang, Indonesia were earning the Indonesian legal minimum wage of 5,200 rupiahs or about $2.28 each day. As a report in the *Washington Post* pointed out, just earning the minimum wage put these workers among higher-paid Indonesians: "In Indonesia, less than half the working population earns the minimum wage, since about half of all adults here are in farming, and the typical farmer would make only about 2,000 rupiahs each day."[37] The workers in the Serang plant reported that they save about three-quarters of their pay. A 17 year-old woman said: "I came here one year ago from central Java. I'm making more money than my father makes." This woman also said that she sent about 75 per cent of her earnings back to her family on the farm. Also in 1996, a Nike spokeswoman estimated that an entry-level factory worker in the plant of a Nike supplier made five times what a farmer makes. Nike's chairman, Phil Knight, likes to teasingly remind critics that the average worker in one of Nike's Chinese factories is paid more than a professor at Beijing University. There is also plentiful anecdotal evidence from non-Nike sources. A worker at the Taiwanese-owned King Star Garment Assembly plant in Honduras told a reporter that he was earning seven times what he earned in the countryside. In Bangladesh, the country's fledgling garment industry was paying women who had never worked before between $40 and $55 a month in 1991. That compared with a national per capita income of about $200 and the approximately $1 a day earned by many of these women's husbands as day laborers or rickshaw drivers.

The same news reports also shed some light on the working conditions in sweatshops. According to the *Washington Post*, in 1994 the Indonesian office of the international accounting firm Ernst & Young surveyed Nike workers concerning worker pay, safety conditions and attitudes toward the job. The auditors pulled workers off the assembly line at random and asked them questions that the workers answered anonymously. The survey of 25 workers at Nike's Serang plant found that 23 thought the hours and overtime worked were fair, and two thought the overtime hours too high. None of the workers reported that they had been discriminated against. Thirteen said the working environment was the key reason they worked at the Serang plant while eight cited salary and benefits. The *Post* report also noted that the Serang plant closes for about ten days each year for Muslim holidays. It quoted Nike officials and the plant's Taiwanese owners as saying that 94 per cent of the workers had returned to the plant following the most recent break.

The *New York Times*'s Larry Rohter went to Honduras where he interviewed more than 75 apparel workers and union leaders and made visits to half a dozen plants, including the one that made clothes for the Gifford line. Workers and employers told Rohter that managers at some companies verbally abused their workers on a regular basis, but at other plants they treated their employees well. "What residents of a rich country see as exploitation," Rohter reported, "can seem a rare opportunity to residents of a poor country like Honduras, where the per capita income is $600 a year and unemployment is 40 per cent."[38]

There is also the mute testimony of the lines of job applicants outside the sweatshops in Guatemala and Honduras. According to Lucy Martinez-Mont, in Guatemala the sweatshops are conspicuous for the long lines of young people waiting to be interviewed for a job. Outside the gates of the industrial park in Honduras that Rohter visited "anxious onlookers are always waiting, hoping for a chance at least to fill out a job application [for employment at one of the apparel plants]."[39]

The critics of sweatshops acknowledge that workers have voluntarily taken their jobs, consider themselves lucky to have them, and want to keep them. Thus Barnet and Cavanagh quote a worker as saying, "I am happy working here. I can make money and I can make friends."[40] But they go on to discount the workers' views as the product of confusion or ignorance, and/or they just argue that the workers' views are beside the point. Thus, while "it is undoubtedly true" that Nike has given jobs to thousands of people who wouldn't be working otherwise, they say that "neatly skirts the fundamental human-rights issue raised by these production arrangements that are now spreading all across the world."[41] Similarly the NLC's Kernaghan says that "[w]hether workers think they are better off in the assembly plants than elsewhere is not the real issue."[42] Kernaghan, and Jeff Ballinger of the AFL-CIO, concede that the workers desperately need these jobs. But "[t]hey say they're not asking that US companies stop operating in these countries. They're asking that workers be paid a living wage and treated like human beings."[43] Apparently these workers are victims of what Marx called false consciousness, or else they would grasp that they are being exploited. According to Barnet and Cavanagh, "For many workers ... exploitation is not a concept easily comprehended because the alternative prospects for earning a living are so bleak."[44]

Immiserization and inequality: The critics' claim that the countries that host international sweatshops are marked by growing poverty and inequality is flatly contradicted by the record. In fact, many of those countries have experienced sharp increases in living standards—for all strata of society. In trying to attract investment in simple manufacturing, Malaysia and Indonesia and, now, Vietnam and China, are retracing the industrialization path already successfully taken by East Asian countries like Taiwan, Korea, Singapore and Hong Kong. These four countries got their start by producing labor-intensive manufactured goods (often electrical and electronic components, shoes, and garments) for export markets. Over time they graduated to the export of higher value-added items that are skill-intensive and require a relatively developed industrial base.

As is well known, these East Asian countries achieved growth rates exceeding eight per cent for a quarter century. As Gary Fields says, the workers in these economies were not impoverished by growth.[45] The benefits of growth were widely diffused: These economies achieved essentially full employment in the 1960s. Real wages rose by as much as a factor of four. Absolute poverty fell. And income inequality remained at low to moderate levels. It is true that in the initial stages the rapid growth generated only moderate increases in wages. But once essentially-full employment was reached, and what economists call the Fei-Ranis turning point was reached, the increased demand for labor resulted in the bidding up of wages as firms competed for a scarce labor supply.

Interestingly, given its historic mission as a watchdog for international labor standards, the ILO has embraced this development model. It recently noted that the most successful developing economies, in terms of output and employment growth, have been "those who best exploited emerging opportunities in the global economy."[46] An "export-oriented policy is vital in countries that are starting on the industrialization path and have large surpluses of cheap labour."[47] Countries which have succeeded in attracting foreign direct investment (FDI) have experienced rapid growth in manufacturing output and exports. The successful attraction of foreign investment in plant and equipment "can be a powerful spur to rapid industrialization and employment creation."[48] "At low levels of industrialization, FDI in garments and shoes and some types of consumer electronics can be very useful for creating employment and opening the economy to international markets; there may be some entrepreneurial skills created in simple activities like garments (as has happened in Bangladesh). Moreover, in some cases, such as Malaysia, the investors may strike deeper roots and invest in more capital-intensive technologies as wages rise."[49]

According to the World Bank, the rapidly growing Asian economies (including Indonesia) "have also been unusually successful at sharing the fruits of their growth."[50] In fact, while inequality in the West has been growing, it has been shrinking in the Asian economies. They are the only economies in the world to have experienced high growth *and* declining inequality, and they also show shrinking gender gaps in education.

This development strategy is working for Indonesia. According to a recent survey in the *Economist*, "Indonesia is now well and truly launched on the path of export-led growth already trodden by countries such as Malaysia, Thailand and South Korea."[51] "In 1967, when the president, Suharto, first took that job, Indonesia's GNP of $70 per person meant that it was twice as poor as India and Bangladesh. Since then Indonesia's economy has grown at a rate of almost 7 per cent a year in real terms.... By the early 1990s, average annual incomes had spurted to $650 a person—twice what they had been a decade earlier—as gross national product had expanded at an average clip of 6.8 per cent."[52] Indonesia has spent significant sums on health, education and the advancement of women and the provision of credit to low income families and small-scale entrepreneurs. It has also spread its wealth to the rural areas. Rural electrification and road construction have made rapid strides. By 1993, about half of the Indonesian countryside was expected to have electricity, up from 35 per cent the previous year. Largely because of improvements in rural medical facilities and sanitation, the infant mortality rate has fallen by nearly 60 per cent since the early 1970s. These facts are reviewed here because they are so starkly different from the much darker picture painted by the critics of international sweatshops.

Profiting from repression?: What about the charge that international sweatshops are profiting from repression? It is undeniable that there is repression in many of the countries where sweatshops are located. But economic development appears to be relaxing that repression rather than strengthening its grip. The companies are supposed to benefit from government policies (e.g., repression of unions) that hold down labor costs. However, as we have seen, the wages paid by the international sweatshops already match or exceed the prevailing local wages. Not only that, but incomes in the East Asian economies, and in Indonesia, have risen rapidly. Moreover, even the sweatshops' critics admit that the main factor restraining wages in countries like Indonesia is the state of the labor market. "Why is Indonesia the bargain basement of world labor?" ask Richard Barnet and John Cavanagh of the Institute for Policy Studies. Their principal explanation is that "[t]he reserve army of the unemployed is vast; 2.5 million people enter the job market every year."[53] The high rate of unemployment and underemployment acts as a brake on wages: Only about 55 per cent of the Indonesian labor force can find more than 35 hours of work each week, and about 2 million workers are unemployed.

The critics, however, are right in saying that the Indonesian government has opposed independent unions in the sweatshops out of fear they would lead to higher wages and labor unrest. But the government's fear clearly is that unions might drive wages in the modern industrial sector *above* market-clearing levels—or, more exactly, further above market. It is ironic that critics like Barnet and Cavanagh would use the Marxian term "reserve army of the unemployed." According to Marx, capitalists deliberately maintain high levels of unemployment in order to control the working class. But the Indonesian government's policies (e.g., suppression of unions, resistance to a higher minimum wage and lax enforcement of labor rules) have been directed at achieving exactly the opposite result. The government appears to have calculated that high unemployment is a greater threat to its hold on power. I think we can safely take at face value its claims that its policies are genuinely intended to help the economy create jobs to absorb the massive numbers of unemployed and underemployed.

LABOR STANDARDS IN INTERNATIONAL SWEATSHOPS: PAINFUL TRADE-OFFS

Who but the grinch could grudge paying a few additional pennies to some of the world's poorest workers? There is no doubt that the rhetorical force of the critics' case against international sweatshops rests on this apparently self-evident proposition. However, higher wages and improved labor standards are not free. After all, the critics themselves attack companies for chasing cheap labor. It follows that, if labor in developing countries is made more expensive (say, as the result of pressure by the critics), then those countries will receive less foreign investment, and fewer jobs will be created there. Imposing higher wages may deprive these countries of the one comparative advantage they enjoy, namely low-cost labor.

We have seen that workers in most "international sweatshops" are already relatively well paid. Workers in the urban, formal sectors of developing countries commonly earn more than twice what informal and rural workers get. Simply earning the minimum wage put the young women making Nike shoes in Serang in the top half of the income distribution in Indonesia. Accordingly, the critics are in effect calling for a *widening* of the economic disparity that already greatly favors sweatshop workers.

By itself that may or may not be ethically objectionable. But these higher wages come at the expense of the incomes and the job opportunities of much poorer workers. As economists explain, higher wages in the formal sector reduce employment there and (by increasing the supply of labor) depress incomes in the informal sector. The case against requiring above-market wages for international sweatshop workers is essentially the same as the case against other measures that artificially raise labor costs, like the minimum wage. In Jagdish Bhagwati's words: "Requiring a minimum wage in an overpopulated, developing country, as is done in a developed country, may actually be morally wicked. A minimum wage might help the unionized, industrial proletariat, while limiting the ability to save and invest rapidly which is necessary to draw more of the unemployed and nonunionized rural poor into gainful employment and income."[54] The World Bank makes the same point: "Minimum wages may help the most poverty-stricken workers in industrial countries, but they clearly do not in developing nations.... The workers whom minimum wage legislation tries to protect—urban formal workers—already earn much more than the less favored majority.... And inasmuch as minimum wage and other regulations discourage formal employment by increasing wage and nonwage costs, they hurt the poor who aspire to formal employment."[55]

The story is no different when it comes to labor standards other than wages. If standards are set too high they will hurt investment and employment. The World Bank report points out that "[r]educing hazards in the workplace is costly, and typically the greater the reduction the more it costs. Moreover, the costs of compliance often fall largely on employees through lower wages or reduced employment. As a result, setting standards too high can actually lower workers' welfare...."[56] Perversely, if the higher standards advocated by critics retard the growth of formal sector jobs, then that will trap more informal and rural workers in jobs which are far more hazardous and insecure than those of their formal sector counterparts.[57]

The critics consistently advocate policies that will benefit better-off workers at the expense of worse-off ones. If it were within their power, it appears that they would re-invent the labor markets of much of Latin America. Alejandro Portes' description seems to be on the mark: "In Mexico, Brazil, Peru, and other Third World countries, [unlike East Asia], there are powerful independent unions representing the protected sector of the working class. Although there rhetoric is populist and even radical, the fact is that they tend to represent the better-paid and more stable fraction of the working class. Alongside, there toils a vast, unprotected proletariat, employed by informal enterprises and linked, in ways hidden from public view, with modern sector firms."

Moreover the critics are embracing a development strategy—one that improves formal sector workers' wages and conditions by fiat—that has been tried and failed. It is in the process of being abandoned by Third World countries around the globe. Portes, who is no advocate of unfettered markets, has warned against the overregulation of labor markets in developing countries. He says: "For those who advocate a full set of advanced regulations to be implemented in all countries, I offer the example of those less developed nations which attempted to do so and failed. More often than not, their sophisticated legal codes did not so much reflect labor market realities as the influence and prestige of things foreign. The common end-result was an acute labor market dualism which protected a privileged segment of the labor force at the expense of the majority."[58] It is precisely to escape the web of overregulation of their own making that developing countries have established so-called "special production zones" (SPZs). The governments of "heavily regulated countries attempting to break into export markets have adopted the strategy of establishing [SPZs] in remote areas away from the centers of union strength. What is 'special' about these zones is precisely that provisions of the existing tax and labor codes do not apply to them and that they are generally 'union-free.'"[59]

Of course it might be objected that trading off workers' rights for more jobs is unethical. But, so far as I can determine, the critics have not made this argument. Although they sometimes implicitly accept the existence of the trade-off (we saw that they attack Nike for chasing cheap labor), their public statements are silent on the lost or forgone jobs from higher wages and better labor standards. At other times, they imply or claim that improvements in workers' wages and conditions are essentially free: According to Kernaghan, "Companies could easily double their employees' wages, and it would be nothing."[60]

In summary, the result of the ostensibly humanitarian changes urged by critics are likely to be (1) reduced employment in the formal or modern sector of the economy, (2) lower incomes in the informal sector, (3) less investment and so slower economic growth, (4) reduced exports, (5) greater inequality and poverty.[61] As Fields says, "The poor workers of the world cannot afford this."[62]

CONCLUSION: THE CASE FOR NOT EXCEEDING MARKET STANDARDS

It is part of the job description of business ethicists to exhort companies to treat their workers better (otherwise what purpose do they serve?). So it will have come as no surprise that both the business ethicists whose views I summarized at the beginning of this paper—Thomas Donaldson and Richard DeGeorge—objected to letting the market alone determine wages and labor standards in multinational companies. Both of them proposed criteria for setting wages that might occasionally "improve" on the outcomes of the market.

Their reasons for rejecting market determination of wages were similar. They both cited conditions that allegedly prevent international markets from generating ethically acceptable results. Donaldson argued that neoclassical economic principles are not applicable to international business because of high unemployment rates in developing countries. And DeGeorge argued that, in an unregulated international market, the gross inequality of bargaining power between workers and companies would lead to exploitation.

But this paper has shown that attempts to improve on market outcomes may have unforeseen tragic consequences. We saw how raising the wages of workers in international sweatshops might wind up penalizing the most vulnerable workers (those in the informal sectors of developing countries) by depressing their wages and reducing their job opportunities in the formal sector.

Donaldson and DeGeorge cited high unemployment and unequal bargaining power as conditions that made it necessary to bypass or override the market determination of wages. However, in both cases, bypassing the market in order to prevent exploitation may aggravate these conditions. As we have seen, above-market wages paid to sweatshop workers may discourage further investment and so perpetuate high unemployment. In turn, the higher unemployment may weaken the bargaining power of workers vis-à-vis employers. Thus such market imperfections seem to call for more reliance on market forces rather than less.

Likewise, the experience of the newly industrialized East Asian economies suggests that the best cure for the ills of sweatshops is more sweatshops. But most of the well-intentioned policies that improve on market outcomes are likely to have the opposite effect.

Where does this leave the international manager? If the preceding analysis is correct, then it follows that it is ethically acceptable to pay market wage rates in developing countries (and to provide employment conditions appropriate for the level of development). That holds true even if the wages pay less than so-called living wages or subsistence or even (conceivably) the local minimum wage. The appropriate test is not whether the wage reaches some predetermined standard but whether it is freely accepted by (reasonably) informed workers. The workers themselves are in the best position to judge whether the wages offered are superior to their next-best alternatives. (The same logic applies *mutatis mutandis* to workplace labor standards.)

Indeed, not only is it ethically acceptable for a company to pay market wages, but it may be ethically unacceptable for it to pay wages that exceed market levels. That will be the case if the company's above-market wages set precedents for other international companies which raise labor costs to the point of discouraging foreign investment. Furthermore, companies may have a social responsibility to transcend their own narrow preoccupation with protecting their brand image and to publicly defend a system which has greatly improved the lot of millions of workers in developing countries.

NOTES

1   Joanna Ramey and Joyce Barrett, "Apparel's Ethical Dilemma," *Women's Wear Daily*, March 18, 1996.

2   Steven Greenhouse, "A Crusader Makes Celebrities Tremble," *New York Times*, June 18, 1996, B4.

3   Lance A. Compa and Tashia Hinchliffe Darricarrere, "Enforcement Through Corporate Codes of Conduct," in Compa and Stephen F. Diamond, *Human Rights, Labor Rights, and International Trade* (Philadelphia: University of Pennsylvania Press, 1996) 193.

4   Peter Jacobi in Martha Nichols, "Third-World Families at Work: Child Labor or Child Care," *Harvard Business Review*, Jan.-Feb. 1993.

5   David Sampson in Robin G. Givhan, "A Stain on Fashion; The Garment Industry Profits from Cheap Labor," *Washington Post*, September 12, 1995, B1.

6   Donaldson, 98.

7   Richard DeGeorge, *Competing with Integrity in International Business* (New York: Oxford University Press, 1993) 79.

8   DeGeorge, *Competing with Integrity*, 356–57.

9   *Id.*, 78.

10   Thomas Donaldson, *The Ethics of International Business* (New York: Oxford University Press, 1989), 100.

11   Donaldson, *Ethics of International Business*, 145.

12   *Id.*, 100.

13   *Id.*, 101.

14   *Id.*, 103.

15   World Bank, *World Development Report 1995*, "Workers in an Integrating World Economy" (New York: Oxford University Press, 1995) 77.

16   Donaldson, *Ethics of International Business*, 115.

17   *Id.*, 358.

18   *Id.*

19   Kenneth P. Hutchinson, "Third World Growth," *Harvard Business Review*, Nov.-Dec. 1994. (In 1994, Hutchinson was executive director of the Asian-American Free Labor Institute in Washington, DC, an affiliate of the AFL-CIO.)

20   Terry Collingsworth, J. William Goold, Pharis J. Harvey, "Time for a Global New Deal," *Foreign Affairs*, Jan.-Feb. 1994, 8.

21   Collingsworth et al., 8.

22   David Holmstrom, "One Man's Fight Against Sweatshops," *Christian Science Monitor*, July 3, 1996.

23   *Nightline* (ABC), June 13, 1996.

24   Kernaghan cited in Larry Rohter, "To US Critics, a Sweatshop; for Hondurans, a Better Life," *New York Times*, July 18, 1996.

25   William B. Falk, "Dirty Little Secrets," *Newsday*, June 16, 1996.

26   Greenhouse, "Voluntary Rules."

27   Tim Smith, "The Power of Business for Human Rights," *Business & Society Review*, January 1994, 36.

28   Jeffrey Ballinger, "The New Free Trade Heel," *Harper's Magazine*, August 1992, 46–47. "As in many developing countries, Indonesia's minimum wage, ... is less than poverty level." Nina Baker, "The Hidden Hands of Nike," *Oregonian*, August 9, 1992.

29   Robert B. Reich, "Escape from the Global Sweatshop; Capitalism's Stake in Uniting the Workers of the World," *Washington Post*, May 22, 1994. Reich's test is intended to apply in developing countries "where democratic institutions are weak or absent."

30   Robin Broad and John Cavanaugh, "Don't Neglect the Impoverished South," *Foreign Affairs*, December 22, 1995, 18.

31   Broad and Cavanagh, "Don't Neglect the Impoverished South."

32   Reich, "Escape from the Global Sweatshop."

33   Hutchinson, "Third World Growth."

34   Broad and Cavanagh, "Don't Neglect the Impoverished South." See also Goozner, "Wages of Shame."

35   John Cavanagh and Robin Broad, "Global Reach; Workers Fight the Multinationals," *The Nation*, March 18, 1996, 21. See also Bob Herbert, "Nike's Bad Neighborhood," *New York Times*, June 14, 1996.

36   World Bank, *Workers in an Integrating World Economy*, 5.

37 Keith B. Richburg, Anne Swardson, "US Industry Overseas: Sweatshop or Job Source?: Indonesians Praise Work at Nike Factory," *Washington Post*, July 28, 1996.

38 .See also Henry Tricks, "Salvador Textile Workers Face Bad Times," Reuters, March 8, 1996; Freddy Cuevas, "Sweatshop, or a Boon?," *St. Paul Pioneer Press*, July 17, 1996; and Seth Mydans, "Tangerang Journal."

39 Rohter, "To US Critics, a Sweatshop."

40 Barnet and Cavanagh, *Global Dreams* (New York: Simon and Schuster, 1994) 327. Similarly, Nina Baker reported that "Tri Mugiyanti and her coworkers [at the Hasi plant in Indonesia] think they are lucky to get jobs at factories such as Hasi." Baker, "The Hidden Hands of Nike."

41 Barnet and Cavanagh, *Global Dreams*, 326.

42 Rohter, "To US Critics, a Sweatshop."

43 William B. Falk, "Dirty Little Secrets," *Newsday*, June 16, 1996.

44 Barnet and Cavanagh, "Just Undo It: Nike's Exploited Workers," *New York Times*, February 13, 1994.

45 Gary S. Fields, "Labor Standards, Economic Development, and International Trade," in Stephen Herzenberg and Jorge Perez-Lopez (eds.), *Labor Standards and the Development of the Global Economy* (Washington, DC: US Department of Labor, Bureau of International Affairs, 1990) 23.

46 ILO, 75.

47 *Id.*, 76.

48 *Id.*, 78.

49 *Id.*, 79.

50 World Bank, *The East Asian Miracle* (New York: Oxford University Press, 1993) 2.

51 Economist, "Wealth in Its Grasp."

52 Marcus W. Brauchli, "Indonesia Is Striving to Prosper in Freedom but Is Still Repressive," *Wall Street Journal*, October 11, 1994.

53 Barnet and Cavanagh, "Just Undo It: Nike's Exploited Workers."

54 Jagdish Bhagwati and Robert E. Hudec, eds. *Fair Trade and Harmonization* (Cambridge: MIT Press, 1996), vol. 1, 2.

55 World Bank, *Workers in an Integrating World Economy*, 75.

56 *Id.*, 77.

57 World Bank, *Workers in an Integrating World Economy*, 5.

58 Alejandro Portes, "When More Can Be Less; Labor Standards, Development, and the Informal Economy," in Herzenberg and Perez-Lopez, *Labor Standards and the Development of the Global Economy*, 234.

59 *Id.*, 228–29.

60 Rohter, "To US Critics, a Sweatshop."

61 Gary S. Fields, "Employment, Income Distribution and Economic Growth in Seven Small Open Economies," *The Economic Journal*, 94 (March 1984), 81.

62 Fields, "Labor Standards," 21.

—29—

ETHICS AND THE GENDER EQUALITY DILEMMA FOR US MULTINATIONALS

Don Mayer and Anita Cava

We hold these truths to be self-evident: that all men are created equal, and endowed by their creator with certain rights—life, liberty, and the pursuit of happiness.
—US DECLARATION OF INDEPENDENCE, 1776

All human beings are born free and equal in dignity and rights.
—UNITED NATIONS UNIVERSAL DECLARATION OF HUMAN RIGHTS, 1948

JUDGING FROM THE US DECLARATION OF Independence, gender equality was not self-evident in 1776. By 1948, however, the Universal Declaration of Human Rights took care not to exclude women from the ambit of declared rights. Since then, while gender equality has come a long way in the United States, many difficult and divisive issues remain unresolved. After completing a global inventory of attitudes on gender equality, Rhoodie (1989) concluded that many nations give only "lip service" to the goals of gender equality articulated in international conventions and declarations such as the UN Declaration of Human Rights (1948). Given the uneven progress of gender and racial equality in the world, it is inevitable that multinational enterprises (MNEs) encounter uneven ethical terrain.

Recently, the US Congress and the Supreme Court have differed markedly over how the principles of non-discrimination in Title VII of the Civil Rights Act of 1964 (Title VII) should be applied by US MNEs in their overseas activities. Both Congress and the Court recognized that US non-discrimination laws may create difficulties for US companies doing business in host countries where racial and/or gender discrimination is a way of life. But Congress, having the last word, decided in the Civil Rights Act of 1991 that Title VII protects US citizens from employment discrimination by US MNEs in their overseas operations.[1]

In so doing, Congress effectively reversed the Supreme Court, which only a few months earlier had decided that Title VII did not apply "extraterritorially" (*E.E.O.C. v. Aramco*, 1991).[2] According to the Court, to apply US laws abroad might cause "unintended clashes between our laws and those of other nations which could result in international discord." The majority of the Court wanted

Congress to be entirely clear about its intent before imposing the ethical values inherent in Title VII on the activities of a US company in a foreign country.

This reluctance is understandable. It seems logical to assume that companies would prefer not to have two personnel policies, one for US citizens and one for host country nationals and others. Human resource directors indicate a preference for following the laws and customs of the host country while doing business there, but a concern for furthering human rights values of the US.[3] Such a preference corresponds to other observed realities, since the recent history of law and business ethics shows that a number of US MNEs would engage in bribery in foreign countries, if that should be the custom, in order to remain "competitive." Similarly, many US MNEs were willing to acquiesce to *apartheid* in South Africa, despite the fact that such behavior would not be tolerated in the United States.

The multinational that adopts such a policy of moral neutrality follows what Bowie (1977) has identified as moral relativism. The approach of a moral relativism is characterized as—"When in Rome, do as the Romans do." This prescription has its arresting aspects. If Rome existed today as a commercial power, would US corporate executives entertain one another by watching slaves battle to the death, attending Bacchanalian orgies, or cheering while faithful but hapless Christians were being mauled by lions? While such practices do not have overt current counterparts, there are nonetheless substantial differences among cultures in matters of gender equality (Rhoodie, 1989).

How does the MNE deal ethically with such contrasts? Bowie suggests that while ethical relativism cannot support business ethics in the global economy, neither can we afford to be "ethnocentric" and assume that "our" way is the one "right way." Bowie uses the term "ethnocentric" to describe a view that "when in Rome, or anywhere else, do as you would at home" (Bowie, 1988; Wicks, 1990). Essentially, it was this concern that animated the Supreme Court's decision in *Aramco*, which explicitly worried about "unintended clashes" between US law and Saudi Arabian law. Further, it is this concern about "ethnocentrism" that fuels speculation that applying Title VII's equal opportunity provisions in countries like Japan is a recipe for corporate non-competitiveness and perhaps even a form of cultural imperialism.

This article explores some of the difficulties faced by US multinationals in complying with Title VII as applied abroad and examines the ethical arguments surrounding achieving the goal of gender equality. Part I discusses the current dilemma for international human resource managers and their employees, as well as for citizens of host countries. We focus on Japan as a model of a country in transition and consider the extreme situation of the Islamic countries as a counterpoint in the analysis. The emphasis is on practical and legal considerations. Part II returns to the issues of ethical relativism and cultural imperialism, and suggests that US multinationals should not opt for moral relativism by deferring entirely to cultural traditions in countries such as Japan, traditions that may be contrary to declared international standards for gender and racial equality and contrary to apparent global trends.

I. PERSPECTIVES ON THE CURRENT DILEMMA

Human resource managers, employees, and host country nationals will have varying perspectives on the application of US civil rights statutes for the promotion of gender equality in the foreign workplace. Each merits consideration in order to understand the framework within which an ethical analysis can be applied.

A. *The MNE Managerial Perspective*

For a MNE whose operations cover the US, Europe, Asia, and the Middle East, the differing cultural norms with respect to equal opportunity in the workplace are a bit unreal. Despite strong movements for gender equality in the Scandinavian countries and, to a lesser extent, in the US and Europe, the basic condition of women worldwide is largely "poor, pregnant, and powerless" (Rhoodie, 1989). The differences among various nations span a continuum from cultures with a strong commitment to gender equality in the workplace to those with strong commitments to keeping women out of the workplace entirely (Mayer, 1991).

For the MNE trying to "do the right thing," the situation suggests a kind of ethical surrealism, where reality retreats before an unreal mix of elements—social, cultural, legal, and philosophical. It seems natural that companies doing business abroad would want to follow host country laws and customs. Obviously, following US law only for US employees poses a dual dilemma. First, assuming that gender discrimination is culturally accepted and legally tolerated in many foreign countries, what should be the MNE personnel policy? The MNE has the option of designing a single non-discriminatory policy for all workers or creating a two-track system, protecting the legal rights of US nationals while accommodating the host country's norms for their nationals and others. Second, where the MNE has adopted a Code of Ethics for global application and the Code specifically refers to equal opportunity, can the MNE honor its commitment in a principled way?

Strict compliance with an ethical position would suggest a simple solution to this conundrum: Adopt an equal opportunity program, educate all employees, and enforce it consistent with Title VII's mandates across the board. Admittedly, however, following US law worldwide, for all employees, is surely "ethnocentric" and may also be unworkable. In some host countries, such as Saudi Arabia, the legal conflicts may be pronounced. In others, such as Japan, the cultural conflicts may undermine consistent enforcement of Title VII-oriented policies throughout the workforce.

Taking Japan as an example, the US MNE doing business in Tokyo is confronted with a patriarchal society in which women are expected to manage household work while men dominate the other forms of work (Lebra, 1984). Although men and women receive comparable educations

through the high school level, women are expected to marry by age 25. Employment after that age is generally discouraged (Prater, 1981). There is seldom, if ever, a managerial track for Japanese women: if employed by a major Japanese company, they are often given positions largely designed to make the office environment more comfortable (such as by serving tea and appearing "decorative"), and are not taken seriously as career office workers (Seymour, 1991).

For a US MNE to announce a policy of equal opportunity for Japanese operations, tie that policy to Title VII enforcement, and expect no negative results would require a supposition that the overwhelmingly male population of Japanese customers, suppliers, and government officials would treat US women and Japanese women equally. But, in fact, the sensitivity of Japanese males to sexual harassment issues is only dawning (Ford, 1992; Lan, 1991), and some other forms of overt discrimination are likely. Assuming, as seems warranted, that the MNE's female employees will be adversely affected to some degree by prevailing male attitudes in Japan, how would the company find that balanced approach that yields the least friction and the best results?

Such a question suggests that a utilitarian analysis, or some pragmatism, may be entirely appropriate here. It is well beyond the scope of this paper to suggest how absolute adherence to Title VII and equal opportunity principles should be tempered to achieve greater harmony with the host country culture, but a few observations are in order. First, Title VII's dictates may need to be culturally adjusted. An "appropriate" response to repeated incidents of Japanese males looking up female employees' skirts may be more educational than admonitory, at least for the first transgressions. Second, companies should be wary of any utilitarian or pragmatic approaches that predict a "non-competitive" result unless business hews to some perceived cultural norms. This point needs further elaboration.

In a country such as Saudi Arabia, the cultural norms and the sacred law, or *Shari'a*, are fairly congruent. The winds of change are not, seemingly, as strong as in other parts of the world. Japan, on the other hand, has demonstrated its willingness to adopt some "Western ways" in order to be part of the global economy, and there is considerable evidence that Japanese pragmatism has already created some new opportunities for women in the workplace (Prater, 1991). Moreover, legislation exists which purports to promote gender equality in the workplace, though some critics have questioned its efficacy (Edwards, 1988). In short, the "downside" of promoting equal opportunity in Japan because of cultural norms may easily be overstated; while Japanese males are not as sensitive to sexual harassment issues, for example, there are signs that they are becoming so (Lan, 1991).

For a host country culture that is less in flux, and whose culture and laws present a unified force against social change, the ethical issues change somewhat. This is because Title VII expressly allows discrimination in certain instances through the *bona fide* occupational qualification (BFOQ)[4] exception. The BFOQ exception provides that it will *not* be illegal to discriminate "on the basis of … religion, sex, or national origin in those certain instances where religion, sex, or national origin is a *bona fide* occupational qualification reasonably necessary to the normal operation of that particular business or enterprise."

In *Kern v. Dynalectron*,[5] for example, a company in the business of flying planes into the holy city of Mecca advised potential employees that Saudi Arabian law prohibited the entry of non-Muslims into the holy area under penalty of death. One pilot took instruction in the Muslim religion, but was Baptist at heart, and rescinded his "conversion." Returning to the US, he sued under Title VII for employment discrimination based on religion. The federal appeals court ultimately determined that Title VII applied but that being Muslim was, in this situation, a "*bona fide* occupational qualification" and not discriminatory.

It remains to be seen how gender qualifications may be raised and litigated for alleged discrimination overseas. But if those qualifications have the force of law, and are not the result of cultural preferences only, the most serious ethical dilemma is whether or not to do business in that country at all. To take an example based on racial classification, if South African law prohibited blacks from being hired by MNEs, the MNEs' only ethical choices would be to (1) do business in South Africa and comply with the law, (2) refuse to do business in South Africa, or (3) do business there and hire blacks anyway.

How are these three options analyzed from a perspective of ethics and the law? Option (3) may certainly be seen as an ethical policy, though probably of the "ethnocentric" variety, yet few ethicists and even fewer business executives would counsel such a course. Option (1) is well within the mainstream of ethical relativism, and, we would argue, is less ethical than choosing option (2). But again, *cultural* conflicts do not create such choices; legal mandates do. And countries whose cultural values are colliding with the values of "outsiders" may choose, at least temporarily, to preserve their culture through legal mandates. Saudi Arabia has laws which prohibit women from travelling alone, working with men, working with non-Muslim foreigners, and these laws apply to foreign women as well as host country women (Moghadam, 1988).

Even without such explicit laws of prohibition, MNEs and their human resource managers may hesitate to violate unwritten or cultural laws, and taking moral relativism's approach to the problem of gender equality in other countries may seem prudent. But such an approach seems to depend on a rather sketchy kind of utilitarian analysis: Engaging in overt equal opportunity policies will result in cultural condemnation, loss of customer and client contacts, and eventual unprofitability of the entire overseas enterprise. But in host countries whose culture is tied to the mainstream of world business, long-held attitudes will be difficult to maintain, and the negative impact of "doing things differently" should not be overestimated, nor should the definite benefits and opportunities of pursuing gender equality be overlooked (Lansing and Ready, 1988).

In this context, a comment about the employee's perspective seems appropriate. It might be difficult to generalize here because individual perspective often differs, depending upon personal ideology, situation, and career opportunities. However, from the viewpoint of a female manager in a US MNE, we will assume that the greatest good would be a business world safe for gender equality and supportive of same. Adler and others have noted the difficulty of persuading MNEs that women managers can succeed in many countries whose cultures actively promote gender inequality (Adler, 1984). Certainly, a US female manager's inability to obtain first-hand experience in dealing with Japanese businesses comes close to being a career handicap, and for Japanese women, the existence of opportunities outside the home may safely be regarded as benefits.

Ultimately, most American citizen employees of MNEs will test any policy by asking whether or not they are personally adversely affected. Companies that take care to structure career advancement opportunities such that experience in countries hostile to a protected class may find themselves with few employee complaints. However, MNEs not able to finesse the mandate of Title VII and the reality of certain foreign cultures will find themselves facing a similar set of choices described above with respect to apartheid. Now, however, a decision to accommodate host country norms must be accompanied by a fund out of which to pay judgments in Title VII litigation.

B. The Host Country's Perspective

From the overall Japanese societal perspective, the changes contemplated by a mandate of gender equality may indeed be troubling. The social structure that has built up over centuries, which has "worked" to achieve stability and a degree of consensus and comfort, could crumble if more and more women leave household work to obtain work in the "business world." Who will do the careful packing of lunches, the guidance for "cram courses" after school, tending to the children and dinner and bedtime while spouse is engaged in the obligatory socializing with office mates after hours? While Japanese men may now be undertaking more domestic duties, the differences are still staggering. One recent estimate suggested that Japanese women put in four to five hours of domestic work daily, while their husbands put in eight minutes (Watanabe, 1992).

Any change in the prescribed social order is bound to seem disruptive, and, therefore, negative. As one Islamic man declared to a National Public Radio correspondent during the Persian Gulf war, if women are allowed in the workplace, the forces of social decay would soon send the divorce and crime rates skyrocketing. This argument, a kind of utilitarian "parade of horribles,"[6] overtly trades on fear of change, is not empirically rigorous, and assumes that changes in the US over a fifty year period represent the ultimate result of mindless social tampering. For the Islamic, this particular proponent of gender inequality in the workplace has a back-up argument, the *Qur'an*.

By appeal to divine, or infinite wisdom, we find an argument more akin to natural law or universalism. The argument may even suppose that not only Islamic society, but all other societies, would be well advised to follow this divinely decreed social ordering. What is manifest to the Islamic mind is contrary, it would seem, to "Western" notions of gender equality. This conflict pits two "objective" or "universal" truths against one another: the "truth" of the *Qur'an* and the "truth" of the Universal Declaration of Human Rights. Is the moral relativist right, after all?

II. ETHICAL RELATIVISM AND ETHICAL ETHNOCENTRISM: A SYNTHESIS FOR OVERSEAS GENDER DISCRIMINATION ISSUES

In general terms, the theory of moral relativism holds that different moral standards are "equally valid or equally invalid," and there are no "objective standards of right and wrong or good and evil that transcend the opinions of different individuals or different societies."[7] At the opposite extreme of the continuum is the objective approach, which is premised on the notion that there are "transcultural" norms that are universally valid.

Bowie (1988) suggests that the proper view is a point closer to the latter position. Although he stops short of embracing universalism, Bowie believes there are minimum ethical principles that are universally evident such as "do not commit murder" and "do not torture." These principles, clearly, can be enforced without imposing ethnocentric (or imperialistic) views upon a host country. To these minimum universal principles, Bowie adds the "morals of the marketplace," which are required to support transactions in the business world. These include honesty and trust. The combination of these two strands of quasi-universalism is as far as Bowie will go in staking his claim on the continuum.

Consider again the dilemmas faced by a US MNE doing business in Japan, trying to integrate a tradition and practice of equal opportunity into a tradition and practice of unequal opportunity. One strategy for "blending in" with the Japanese market might be to adopt a thoroughly Japanese outlook and approach. That would include differing pay scales for men and women, actively discouraging women past the age of 25 from working with the company, and pointedly not inviting women employees to the after-five work/social functions that seem to play such an important part in an employee's successful corporate bonding.

Other than outright moral relativism, the social contract approach would appear to be the most likely proponent of such assimilation. Social contract theory examines the ethical foundations of societies by the relationships that exist within and between people, organizations, and groups. In an article on "extant social contracts," Dunfee (1991) explains and defends this communitarian approach to ethics, which appears grounded in relativism, but he also appears to offer an escape clause by way of a "filtering" device using utilitarian or deontological approaches. Dunfee would apparently recognize that racial discrimination is more widely condemned, and that gender discrimination is more widely tolerated, and conclude that perpetuating gender discrimination is less unethical than perpetuating racial discrimination. In a subsequent article, Dunfee and Donaldson (1991) retreat somewhat from the relativism approach and appear to suggest some dimensions of gender equality qualify as a "hypernorm," that is, a norm "recognized as core or foundational by most humans, regardless of culture." The example they give, however, is that of Saudi Arabia prohibiting women from driving, a rule that violates hypernorms of freedom of movement and rights of self-realization. Obviously, this issue does not approach the complexity posed by the international application of gender equality in the workplace.

In essence, what seems problematic for social contract theory is the substantial variance between the almost universally professed ideals of gender equality and the globally pervasive policies of gender inequality. If one looks to social practice for guidance as to what is ethical, gender inequality becomes relatively more ethical; yet if one looks to professed ideals and principles of equality, many existing forms of gender inequality (dowry deaths, female infanticide, widow-burning, and abortion based on male preference) (Howe, 1991) seem inexcusable. Ethical guidelines, apart from legal obligations, seem to require more explicit direction.

Bowie rejects relativism and argues for recognition of minimum universal principles and morals of the marketplace, an essentially deontological approach. He suggests that the latter may even control over the former where completely foreign agents meet to do business. Bowie draws upon democratic theory, torture and genocide, and examples based on bribery, apartheid, and political-economic values to make his point. He is, however, silent on gender discrimination. One wonders whether Bowie would view this issue as primarily social or as a political-economic priority on a plane with his other examples.

We take the position that neither relativism nor extant social contract theory are much help to

MNEs in a host country whose values run counter to the company's ethical code or the laws and traditions of its country of origin. Instead, the concepts of minimum universal principles and morals of the marketplace legitimately can be broadened to embrace gender equality. Support for this position is evident in the increasingly international consensus on this point.

For example, as Frederick (1991) has pointed out, the United Nations Universal Declaration of Human Rights, the OECD Guidelines for Multinational Enterprises, and the International Labor Office Tripartite Declaration all give support to "nondiscriminatory employment policies" and the concept of "equal pay for equal work." Note that neither of these policies is widespread in Japan. The United Nations Convention on the Elimination of All Forms of Discrimination Against Women (1979) was ratified by a large number of nations, both industrialized and developing. The European Community has passed a number of Council directives aimed at promoting gender equality in employment (Weiner, 1990).

We believe that by following policies which generally promote gender equality, without slavish adherence to all US judicial opinions on Title VII and with good faith adjustments where cultural conditions require, a US MNE in Japan can maintain its own code of ethics without the "inevitable" loss of "competitiveness." Moreover, it can do so without being "ethnocentric" or "imperialist," and by doing so it can avoid a kind of ethical balkanization that adherence to moral relativism would require. After all, a dozen different cultural traditions might require a dozen different HRM policies, each geared to the host country's dominant yet often changing traditions.

This does not mean that resort to more universal declarations of principle are based on a need for Wicks' "metaphysical comfort." We agree with Wicks that our grasp of certain principles in some sense depends on our own experience and what "works." Did the social movement toward greater gender and racial equality in the United States come about because of *a priori* arguments

on the ethical treatment of women and blacks, or because there was already equality in some areas and a perception that things "were not working"? There is no way to know with certainty, but there need be no need to identify either "ideal principles" or "real experience" as the mother lode for ethical discoveries.

Values, to be shared, must be mutually discovered. Universal standards, such as those proposed by the United Nations, come out of experience, and do not just emerge *a priori* (Frederick, 1991). Even without "metaphysical comfort," a MNE can be satisfied that there is an emerging consensus on gender equality. In going to a traditional culture where gender inequality is the norm, the MNE must be aware that there is another community emerging, one whose shape is as yet dimly perceived, but a community where goods, services, and information are traded with ever-increasing speed. Included in the information exchange is the communication of different values, and while these values are not being passed along in traditional ways, their transmission is inevitable. In this exchange of values and ideas, the ideals of equality are manifest in many ways. Any MNE, whatever the cultural norms it confronts in a particular country, would be wise to pay attention.

NOTES

1   Civil Rights Restoration Act of 1991, P.L. 102–166, Nov. 21, 1991, 105 Stat. 1071. For the purposes of this discussion, a US MNE is an enterprise with operations in one or more foreign countries.

2   *E.E.O.C. v. Aramco, Boureslan v. Aramco*, 111 S. Ct. 1227 (1991).

3   The authors mailed a survey entitled "Use of US Employment Discrimination Law Abroad" to human resource directors of 120 companies identified as multinational enterprises. In part, the questionnaire solicited information about whether or not the company felt it wise to apply Title VII abroad. The eight responses that were received provide anecdotal, as opposed to statistically significant, information. Six respondents indicated it would be

"unwise" to attempt to apply Title VII to US citizens working abroad. The reasons given appear predictable: it would be "difficult"; it is the "local manager's responsibility"; we "do not attempt" to impose our norms on others. Two respondents believed it would be wise to implement such a policy despite the obstacles discussed in this paper. Nonetheless, all respondents indicated that the policy is appropriately enforced in the US and two believed it would be wise to do so abroad as well.

4   42 U.S.C. §2000e-l (1988).

5   577 F. Supp. 1196, *affirmed* 746 F.2d 810 (1984).

6   George Christie, of Duke University Law School, coined this phrase in reference to attorneys, who learn to see the dark possibilities issuing from any proposed action and are prone to recite a "parade of horribles" to their clients.

7   Van Wyk, *Introduction to Ethics*, St. Martin's Press, New York (1990), 15.

REFERENCES

Adachi, K. 1989, "Problems and Prospects of Management Development of Female Employees in Japan," *Journal of Management Development* 8(4), 32–40.

Alder, N. 1984, "Women in International Management: Where Are They?," *California Management Review* 26, 78–89.

Bassiry, G.R. 1990, "Business Ethics and the United Nations: A Code of Conduct," *SAM Advanced Management Journal* (Autumn), 38–41.

Bellace, J. 1991, "The International Dimension of Title VII," *Cornell International Law Journal* 24, 1–24.

Bowie, N. 1988, "The Moral Obligations of Multinational Corporations," in Luper-Fay (ed.), *Problems of International Justice* (New York: Westview Press), 97–113.

Bowie, N. 1977, "A Taxonomy for Discussing the Conflicting Responsibilities of a Multinational Corporation," in *Responsibilities of Multinational Corporations to Society* (Arlington, VA: Council of Better Business Bureau), 21–43.

Carney, L. and O'Kelly. 1987, "Barriers and Constraints to the Recruitment and Mobility of Female Managers in the Japanese Labor Force," *Human Resource Management* 26(2), 193–216.

Daimon, S. 1991, "'Karoshi' Phenomenon Spreading to Female Workforce," *Japan Times Weekly* (Intl. Ed.), Sept. 30–Oct. 6, 7.

Donaldson, T. and T. Dunfee. 1991, "Social Contracts in Economic Life: A Theory," No. 91–156 (revised) Working Paper Series, Department of Legal Studies, The Wharton School, University of Pennsylvania, 27–32.

Dunfee, T. 1991, "Extant Social Contracts," *Business Ethics Quarterly* 1, 22–37.

Edwards, L. 1988, "Equal Employment Opportunity in Japan: A View from the West," *Industrial and Labor Relations Review* 41(2), 240–50.

Ford, J. 1992, "Sexual Harassment Taken for Granted," *Japan Times Weekly* (Intl. Ed.), Feb. 10–16, 4.

Frederick, W. 1991, "The Moral Authority of Transnational Corporate Codes," *Journal of Business Ethics* 10, 165–77.

Gundling, F. 1991, "Ethics and Working with the Japanese: The Entrepreneur and the Elite Coursel," *California Management Review* 33(3), 25–39.

Howe, M. 1991, "Sex Discrimination Persists, According to a UN Study," *New York Times* June 16, A4, col. 1.

Lan, S. 1991, "Japanese Businessman Produces Video to Prevent Lawsuits," *Japan Times Weekly* (Intl. Ed.), Nov. 11–17, 8.

Lansing, P. and K. Ready. 1988, "Hiring Women Managers in Japan: An Alternative for Foreign Employers," *California Management Review* 30(3), 112–21.

Lebra, D. 1984, *Japanese Women: Constraint and Fulfillment* (Honolulu: University of Hawaii Press).

Mayer, D. 1991, "Sex Discrimination Policies for US Companies Abroad," in Sanders, W. (ed.), *Proceedings of the Council on Employee Responsibilities and Rights*.

Moghadam, V. 1988, "Women, Work, and Ideology in the Islamic Republic," *International Journal of Middle East Studies* 20, 221–43.

Neff, R. 1991, "When in Japan, Recruit as the Japanese Do—Aggressively," *Business Week* June 24, 58.

Prater, C. 1991, "Women Try on New Roles; But Hopes Can Still Collide with Tradition," *Detroit Free Press*

November 27, 1 (5th in a series, later published in the *New York Times*).

Rhoodie, E. 1989, *Discrimination Against Women: A Global Survey of the Economic, Educational, Social and Political Status of Women* (London, UK: McFarland and Company).

Seymour, C. 1991, "The Ad-business: Talented Women Need Not Apply," *Japan Times Weekly* (Intl. Ed.), Dec. 9–15, 7.

Simon, H. and F. Brown, 1990/91, "International Enforcement of Title VII: A Small World After All?," *Employee Relations Law Journal* 16(3), 281–300.

United Nations. 1979, *Convention of the Elimination of All Forms of Discrimination Against Women*, UN Doc. A/34/36 (Dec. 18, 1979).

Watanabe, T. 1992, "In Japan, a 'Goat Man' or No Man; Women Are Gaining More Clout in Relationships," *Los Angeles Times* Jan. 6, A1, Col. 1.

Weiner, M. 1990, "Fundamental Misconceptions about Fundamental Rights: The Changing Nature of Women's Rights in the EEC and Their Application in the United Kingdom," *Harvard International Law Journal* 31(2), 565–74.

Wicks, A. 1990, "Norman Bowie and Richard Rorty on Multinationals: Does Business Ethics Need 'Metaphysical Comfort'?," *Journal of Business Ethics* 9, 191–200.

—30—

CASE STUDY

CHARITY BEGINS AT HOME

Nepotism

David Meeler and Srivatsa Seshadri

BACKGROUND

SULTAN HASEEM OPERATES THREE "MOM AND pop" retail stores in Karachi, Pakistan. His ten-employee operation consists of himself, and, being childless, his two nephews and seven others, mostly relatives. Tariq Mohammed, the older nephew, and Shaheed Hussain, the younger of the two nephews, were recruited in their teens and now, after 10 years, have been placed in charge of finance and purchasing respectively.

Wong Su Hong is the CEO of a not-for-profit organization in Kuala Lumpur, Malaysia. The 25-employee organization was created by leading business people to serve the under-privileged in the country. The organization, through a team of 100 volunteer-workers, collects left-over foods from restaurants and delivers them to the homeless the same day. Of the 25 employees, four are at management level, each responsible for fundraising, accounting, public relations, and liaison with the Malaysian government. All four managers were recruited by Hong himself and they are his brothers or brothers-in-law.

Camund Ltd. is a publicly traded, company based in Mumbai, India, with over 100,000 shareholders and yearly revenues of Rs. 2.5 billion (US: $50 million). The majority of the shares are owned by two families—the Bahais and the Sheths. The men at the helm of the company are from these families. These families control 11.3% of the equity

and all the directors and senior managers are family members. Recruitment is decentralized and each manager is free to recruit whoever they like. They tend to recruit friends, and kith and kin.

Ronald Whitefoot is the CEO of a large software company in San Jose, CA. The firm launched a successful IPO (initial public offering) two years ago increasing the firm's equity base to $50 million. Whitefoot still holds a 55% stake in the company and twelve of the fifteen Directors on the Board are his close relatives.

ANALYSIS

Nepotism is generally considered undesirable in the United States. It is defined by the Society for Human Resource Management as "Favoritism shown to relatives by individuals in a position of authority, such as managers or supervisors." Its most explicit nature is revealed in the recruiting of close friends or family members by managers. While it is not illegal in the United States it is generally frowned upon by US investors, since there is strong evidence that it leads to inefficiency and poor performance of the company.

In Asia however, nepotism is viewed quite differently. In Japan nepotism can almost be seen as the traditional model for business enterprises. For example, the keiretsu system establishes a mock "family" of companies intimately linked with one another. One's ethical obligations are thought

229

to be stronger to those who are closest to you. So members of a keiretsu family will do business primarily with one another. Family members are the closest, and those who are most different from you (i.e., foreigners) are the farthest away. This is why Western businesses often criticize the keiretsu system for being unfair. By its very nature, the kei-retsu system requires favoritism to other Japanese companies and reduced ethical obligations to foreign companies. For example, if a supplier in your keiretsu cannot provide the quality needed for your products, rather than switch suppliers, your company will work with your keiretsu-"sibling" to refine the production techniques until your quality standards have been met. Similar to this is the concept of Guanxi in China. Guanxi is loosely seen by Western businesses as "relationship circles" but it connotes more than that. Guanxi is also an obligation to return favors at some future time rather like blank IOUs. Thus this breeds nepotism. Asian countries see nepotism, not as an ethical issue, but good business sense. As one Asian busi-nessman once said, "Who better to trust than your own friends and family?" Asians tend to believe in "Better the devil you know than an unknown god." Additionally, a fatalistic attitude toward life in general allows them to attribute the negative consequences of nepotism to "acts of God" rather than questioning the tradition of nepotism.

DISCUSSION QUESTIONS

1. In which of the above four examples would you say the nepotism is a non-issue? In which of the examples is it ethically significant? Why or why not?

2. How would the financial performance (positive or negative) of a company where rampant nepotism exists affect your answers?

3. Suppose you are considering investing in a company, and as you read the annual report, you notice that several of the top executives are related. How does this affect your decision to invest? Would you invest in Whitefoot's software company?

4. What do you think is the role of culture in influencing the perception that nepotism is unethical behavior? Are there universal moral norms that should be followed by all multi-nationals, whether "in Rome" or not?

FURTHER READINGS

Abdallah, Hagen F., Ahmed S. Maghrabi, and Bel G. Raggad. 1998. "Assessing the Perceptions of Human Resource Managers toward Nepotism: A Cross-Cultural Study." *International Journal of Manpower* 19 (8): 554–70.

Chervenak, Frank A, and Laurence B. McCullough. 2007. "Is Ethically Justified Nepotism in Hiring and Admissions in Academic Health Centers an Oxymoron?" *The Physician Executive* 33 (5): 42–45.

Padgett, Margaret Y., and Kathryn A. Morris. 2005. "Keeping It 'All in the Family:' Does Nepotism in the Hiring Process Really Benefit the Beneficiary?" *Journal of Leadership & Organizational Studies* 11 (2): 34–45.

Vinton, Karn L. 1998. "Nepotism: An Interdisciplinary Model." *Family Business Review* 11 (4): 297–303.

—31—

CONFLICT MINERALS AND SUPPLY CHAIN MANAGEMENT

The Case of the DRC

Scott Wisor

BACKGROUND

THE DEMOCRATIC REPUBLIC OF CONGO IS HOME to arguably the deadliest conflict since World War II. Several million people have died in warfare and from war-related causes such as disease and malnutrition since 1998. The United Nations High Commissioner for Refugees reported in 2015 that 430,000 refugees remain in neighboring countries, and that 2.7 million internally displaced people within the country are unable to return to their homes. Though the civil war officially ended in 2003, multiple conflicts have continued to add to the causalities and to sexual violence against women, men, and children.

For many years the war in the DRC remained low on the agenda of international human rights organizations, despite the mounting death toll. But beginning in the late 2000s, advocacy organizations began to direct their attention to it. In particular, they focused on the role of the natural resource trade in fueling civil war. These organizations argued that armed militias were funded through the illicit trade in tungsten, tin, tantalum, gold, and other valuable minerals mined largely in the eastern provinces. Advocates claimed that these valuable minerals both financed armed militias and provided incentives for warring parties to continue fighting for territory in which these resources could be found.

To target the finances of armed groups in the DRC, advocacy organizations, led by the ENOUGH Project (an NGO working on atrocity prevention), launched a campaign focusing on the role of major electronics companies in sourcing minerals from the DRC. Drawing on campaigns targeting the 'blood diamonds' that fueled the wars in Liberia and Sierra Leone, they targeted major brands including Apple, Intel, and Motorola, arguing that the companies were using "conflict minerals."

In addition to exerting direct pressure on major electronics companies through savvy campaigns using well edited viral videos disseminated through social media, advocates also worked to change the laws regulating supply chain management. In the Dodd-Frank Wall Street Reform and Consumer Protection Act (2010), a small provision was added governing so-called conflict minerals. Section 1502 required companies listed on the SEC to report on whether they sourced minerals from provinces in conflict in the DRC, and if so, what steps they were taking to ensure that they were not complicit in funding armed groups.

A certification scheme was to be put in place to name mines that were "conflict free." These mines needed third party verification to be determined to be responsibly trading in conflict minerals. Similar legislation was considered in Europe and Canada as the movement to halt the civil war in the DRC focused on the natural resource sector spread internationally.

Feeling the pressure of both reputational risk and regulatory pressure, major brands revised their supply chain policies to avoid alleged complicity involved in trading in minerals sourced from the Democratic Republic of Congo. Many companies simply went Congo-free, ensuring that they did not source materials from the country, avoiding the risk that they would be inadvertently funding conflict in the region.

The passage of Dodd-Frank and the suspension of some commercial ties to the DRC were initially hailed as major achievements by some human rights organizations. But a growing chorus of critics argued that the campaign had been ill-conceived and was not only failing to end the conflict, but was actively harming workers in conflict-affected provinces and potentially exacerbating the deleterious role of mining in driving armed conflict in the DRC. A scathing open letter written by academic researchers and civil society representatives argued that four years after the passage of Dodd-Frank, external advocacy organizations had failed to listen to the relevant stakeholders among Congolese civil society and their employers, and to take account of ongoing efforts to reform the resource trade; and as a result they had caused great economic harm to communities dependent upon mining for their livelihoods.

Nearly four years after the passing of the Dodd-Frank Act, only a small fraction of the hundreds of mining sites in the eastern DRC have been reached by traceability or certification efforts. The rest remain beyond the pale, forced into either illegality or collapse as certain international buyers have responded to the legislation by going "Congo-free".

This in turn has driven many miners into the margins of legality (for instance, feeding into smuggling rackets), where armed actors return through the loopholes of transnational regulation. Others have simply lost their jobs, and in areas where mining has ceased, local economies have suffered.[1]

Congressional hearings received testimony noting the unintended and harmful consequences of 1502, and many media organizations began to cover "Obama's law," as it was known in the DRC, criticizing the alleged harmful impact it was having on local economies and artisanal miners.

Efforts to address the problem of mining in the DRC are an example of the more general trend toward institutional reform that attempts to mitigate the resource curse. The "resource curse" is a phenomenon that economists and political scientists argue affects national development. The idea here is that countries that have not yet developed high quality institutions (such as democratic, accountable government, the rule of law, a free and open media, etc.) and gain access to large reserves of oil or minerals, will be disproportionately likely to suffer from civil war, authoritarianism, gender inequality, and underperforming economic growth. In other words, if you don't have good institutions, and valuable natural resources come into production, your chances of institutional improvement decrease significantly.

There are several mechanisms that are thought to cause the resource curse. In conflict, valuable commodities may provide the capacity (by funding armed groups) and motivation (to gain control of valuable resources) for armed conflict where it would otherwise not exist, or not be as strong. Authoritarian governments get extra motivation in maintaining power when they are capturing the rents involved in mining; and this finances the armed forces that repress dissent, and purchase allegiance. Gender inequality is perpetuated due to the absence of stable democratic governments, under which effective women's rights movements might emerge, and due to the difficulty in establishing export-led economic growth, weakening economic opportunities for women outside the home. And when domestic currencies are buoyed by high resource prices, it is difficult to build a successful non-resource based exports sector, and poor economic performance results.

Efforts or proposals to address the resource curse include: transparency requirements specifying that extractives companies publish what initial and ongoing payments they make to governments to secure mineral rights; improvements in the process of bidding for and contracting the sale of mineral rights; targeted and general sanctions against resource-reliant regimes that abuse human rights; the establishment of trust funds to shield national budgets and domestic currencies from the boom-bust cycle of resource prices; and corporate social responsibility programs that include local communities in decision making about resource exploitation and in the benefits arising from resource extraction.

ANALYSIS

In the efforts to attempt to address the role of business in responding to the resource curse in the DRC and in other states, there are a number of ethical themes which emerge from the controversy over efforts to manage from afar the trade in natural resources.

The case of conflict minerals acutely raises the question of consumers', companies', and governments' moral responsibility for their consumption of products sourced from countries that are embroiled in violent conflict, plagued by human rights abuses, or governed by autocrats. Do such moral responsibilities exist, and if they do, how strong are they? How far down the supply chain do these responsibilities reach? When has a consumer or company done enough to address the problems facing innocent civilians and low wage miners in the DRC?

Responses to these questions track a more general issue that has animated contemporary moral and political philosophers. To what extent do moral and political obligations extend beyond one's own community? Are there duties of global ethics and justice, and if so, what do they require of individuals and corporations? On one line of

thinking, moral duties arise when certain structural relations hold between rights bearers and duty bearers. For example, consumers of products made in "sweatshops" or low wage conditions may have some duties to attempt to protect and promote the labor rights of workers in these industries. It is because enduring structural interactions are maintained between people vulnerable to low wages and exploitative work arrangements that such responsibilities are held by consumers and companies.

A closely related line of thought is that such duties arise when individuals are responsible for harming others, either directly or through the design of institutional arrangements. Institutional arrangements are thought to be harmful to others when they produce foreseeable human rights deficits and when feasible alternative institutional arrangements are available. For the theorists concerned with institutional harm, the argument is that consumers, companies, and governments have harmed innocent civilians in the DRC by permitting the natural resource trade to take place under rules and practices which incentivizes warfare, whereas alternative methods of engaging in this trade would not provide such incentives and therefore be less harmful.

An important question arises in light of the failure of 1502: how much evidence is needed to justify selecting feasible alternatives, especially under the conditions of complexity and uncertainty that are typical in these sorts of situations? The Congolese themselves do not appear to prefer the situation produced by that law to the previous anarchic trade.

A third line of thinking holds that ethical duties are established just in so far as some individuals are suffering and other individuals or institutions are in a position to provide assistance. These duties of beneficence are not specifically grounded in the relationships between companies and their supply chains. But it may be that companies sourcing materials from the DRC are better positioned to assist people who are suffering there, and so they have stronger humanitarian duties than other corporations who do not operate there.

Critics who reject such duties, especially with reference to the DRC, make several points. First, they argue that the alleged role of the resource trade in fueling warfare is overstated. There is a general war economy in the DRC, and all goods and services can be subject to the exploitative aims of armed groups; and it is far from clear that companies either have the knowledge or capacity to contribute to peace building in the region.

Second, it is not the primary task of corporations to secure basic human rights. This is the task of governance, and bad governance is the source of conflict in the DRC, not the minerals trade. Echoing classic opposition to corporate social responsibility from Milton Friedman, the business of business is to make profit, and the business of government is to secure rights.

Third, those corporations that have been targeted by advocacy campaigns have no direct presence in the DRC, and thus little standing to advocate for reform. They simply are the end users of natural resources that may passed through several different businesses before arriving in the finished product of a smartphone or laptop computer. To extend moral responsibility from these companies to their distant suppliers, many of whom may be unknown given their distance in the supply chain, is to exceed the plausible bounds of corporate responsibility. It is only the direct activities and relationships of a company that are properly subject to moral critique and legal regulation.

The Dodd-Frank legislation, which places obligations on companies to report on their supply chains, and which to some extent displaced or superseded other efforts to improve mining in the DRC, highlights the tension between legally binding regulatory efforts to improve corporate responsibility and voluntary initiatives that corporations choose to undertake to improve outcomes for relevant stakeholders. At the time that Dodd-Frank was passed, a number of other voluntary initiatives were under way to improve the conflict sensitivity of business practices affecting local communities in the DRC. These efforts often involved local civil society groups and companies who were at least somewhat interested in improving outcomes for relevant stakeholders.

Proponents of voluntary initiatives argue that they are likely to be better designed than formal regulation, to be more adaptable to changing circumstances, and to properly reflect the primary role of the business organization, which is responsibility for market activities, not for securing justice and human rights. Opponents of voluntary initiatives favor legally binding regulation. They argue that voluntary efforts often fall short of what is required to protect the rights of stakeholders, and that companies will undertake costly efforts to secure the rights of stakeholders only when legally compelled to do so.

A more general issue that arises from the attempts to regulate the resource trade in the DRC applies not only to the ethics of for-profit business enterprises but to the ethics of not-for-profit organizations. Innocent civilians harmed by either commercial activity or general conflict in the DRC are often neither able nor capable of being heard by major multinational corporations who may have links to the area of conflict. Non-governmental organizations often take it as their responsibility to speak on behalf of the victims of abuse, given that these victims might not have another outlet to exercise their voices. But with the power to speak for others comes the opportunity to misrepresent their views, to ignore internal disagreements among community members, to deny the agency of individuals and groups who were otherwise working to secure just outcomes, and to misdiagnose social and political problems.

Critics of the ENOUGH Project and their campaign to regulate the DRC's resource trade argue that their campaign was insensitive and unresponsive to the stated aims and goals of at least some members of civil society in the DRC, not to mention the commercial actors who were already undertaking efforts to improve supply chains in the DRC. While the problem of speaking for others is most apparent for non-governmental organizations that aim to speak on behalf of victims, it may also arise for business enterprises who may come to indirectly represent the interests of their customers or stakeholders' interests in various regulatory fora.

Operating in frontier markets plagued with authoritarian governance, human rights abuse, and civil conflict presents unique ethical challenges to companies and consumers. One option is of course simply not to operate there. But if companies halt operations in ethically risky areas, this may make populations in those areas worse off. Moral purity, in the form of non-participation, may be far worse than remaining in the country and attempting to negotiate the difficult ethical and policy terrain. There are two reasons for this. First, if a business departs and it is not replaced, this may mean fewer livelihood opportunities for people already facing significant material deprivation. Second, when a morally concerned business departs and is replaced by a less responsible corporate actor, there is less possibility for civilians to work with this new actor, or to establish good community relations, or to have in place a meaningful grievance procedure. The moral problem of worse actors suggests that in at least some cases, it is better for companies to continue operating with 'dirty hands' than to leave with 'clean hands'. This is not to deny that additional moral responsibilities are incurred by companies who do continue operations in conflict zones. These derivative duties to stakeholders will arise from the unique relations they have with them in highly non-ideal circumstances.

DISCUSSION QUESTIONS

1. If someone approaches you on the street, and offers to sell you stolen goods, is it wrong to purchase them? If a government plunders its natural resources to the detriment of its citizens, is it wrong for companies to buy these natural resources?
2. You likely own electronics that source materials from the DRC. Do you, as a consumer, bear responsibility for improving the situation in the country?
3. To what extent should companies make moral demands of the companies they do business

with, including companies that supply them raw materials?
4. To what extent should corporations be held responsible for the conduct of third party businesses from whom they purchase goods or materials?
5. If refraining from doing business in a particular country may harm workers in that country, do businesses have a responsibility to continue to work in countries that may present environmental and social risks?

NOTE

1   Vogel, Christoph. "An Open Letter." http://christophvogel.net/2014/09/09/conflict-minerals-an-open-letter/.

FURTHER READINGS

Haufler, Virginia. 2010. "Governing Corporation in Zones of Conflict: Issues, Actors, and Institutions," in *Who Governs the Globe?*, edited by Deborah Avant, Martha Finnemore, and Susan Sell. New York: Cambridge University Press.

Haufler, Virginia. 2009. "The Kimberley Process, Club Goods, and Public Enforcement of a Private Regime," in *Voluntary Programs: A Club Theory Approach*, edited by Aseem Prakash and Matthew Potoski. Cambridge, MA: MIT Press, 2009.

Rubenstein, Jennifer. 2014. "Why It Is Beside the Point That No One Elected Oxfam." *The Journal of Political Philosophy* 22: 204–230.

Ruggie, John. 2013. *Just Business: Human Rights and Multinational Corporations.* New York: W.W. Norton.

Seay, Laura. "What's Wrong with Dodd-Frank 1502? Conflict Minerals, Civilian Livelihoods, and the Unintended Consequences of Western Advocacy." Center for Global Development Working Paper 248.

Wenar, Leaf. 2008. "Property Rights and the Resource Curse." *Philosophy and Public Affairs* 36: 2–32.

Wisor, Scott. 2014. "The Moral Problem of Worse Actors." *Ethics and Global Politics* 7: 47–64.

—32—

CASE STUDY

GOOGLE IN CHINA

Censorship Requirements Challenge the Internet Company

Theresa Bauer

BACKGROUND

GOOGLE INC. SEES ITSELF AS A GOOD CORPORATE citizen. It follows the famous mission statement "Don't Be Evil," governs its business practices according to a code of conduct, and engages in philanthropy. Nevertheless, the company's compliance with censorship requirements in autocratic regimes such as China has attracted widespread criticism.

Since the Internet arrived in China in the 1990s, the response of the Chinese government has been twofold. Internet development has been supported as a chance to vitalize the economy. At the same time, the Chinese government has taken extensive measures to control online communication and suppress criticism, at least ostensibly to maintain political stability and social harmony. A number of laws have been developed to regulate the Internet, prohibiting the creation or dissemination of information that endangers national unification, damages the reputation of state organizations, instigates hatred or discrimination among nationalities, is sexually suggestive, or promotes gambling or violence. Chinese authorities police the Internet by screening websites, email and social media, stopping unwanted discussions, and arresting users who express negative opinions too freely.

In 2002, the "Golden Shield" project, also known as the "Great Firewall of China," was launched. This complex system automatically monitors the information flow within China and across borders through various techniques such as Internet address and domain name system tampering, IP address blocking, Web site blocking, and key-word filtering. Access to a number of websites (e.g., Human Rights Watch, Amnesty International) is completely blocked; in some cases users can access portions of websites while other parts (e.g., mentioning Tibet or Taiwan) are blocked.

Internet Service Providers are liable for all offensive content transmitted through their facilities. They are required to assist public security organizations in investigating breaches of the law and report illegal activities. Foreign companies wishing to obtain a Chinese operating license must sign the "Public Pledge on Self Discipline for the Chinese Internet Industry" (briefly "The Pledge"), which commits the companies to censor content on their websites and in search engine results, and to turn over the names of users who post objectionable content.

Even in light of these extensive regulations, Western Internet companies have a great interest in the Chinese market with its large and growing number of users. Google decided to launch its Chinese language search engine Google.cn in January 2006. Until then, Google.com could be accessed through Chinese local Internet providers, but the website was slow and unreliable inside China and results were automatically censored by the Great Firewall (though the wall only half-worked in Google's case, sometimes letting banned search results slip through). The new website Google.cn could operate more quickly and reliably. Yet, Google had to sign "The Pledge" committing itself to remove content banned under Chinese law. For example, when searching for "Tiananmen Square" Google.cn did not deliver any pictures of the crackdown on student protesters in 1989 (as a search on the conventional version does), but merely presented pictures of the square itself.[1] As a small measure of defiance, Google decided to display a pop-up warning to inform users when access had been restricted on certain search terms.

Google's decision to comply with Chinese Internet censorship laws stirred debate in the US and met with criticism from human rights organizations. In February 2006, company representatives, together with other US Internet companies operating in China, were called into Congressional hearings and had to defend their business practice in China.

Google changed its approach in 2010: In January, the company reported that hackers (allegedly on behalf of the Chinese government) had attempted to penetrate the Gmail accounts of human rights activists, and announced they would stop censoring results on Google.cn.[2] In March, Google began automatically redirecting Chinese users to unfiltered servers in Hong Kong, which is a special administrative region of China that is not subject to Chinese Internet censorship laws. After a warning by the Chinese government that the company's operating license would not be renewed if this practice continued, Google stopped the automatic rerouting in June 2010, but installed a landing page on Google.cn with a link to the Hong Kong website. However, observers noted Chinese authorities permitted only a tiny fraction of traffic to reach Google's servers in Hong Kong.[3]

In 2013, Google stopped notifying users when a search term was censored after Chinese authorities had found new ways to hamper the search engine. In 2014, Google began encrypting searches, thus making it difficult for Chinese authorities

to determine who was searching for illegal topics. Then all Google services were blocked in May 2014, including Google.hk and Google.com as well as products such as Gmail, Calendar and Translate.[4]

ANALYSIS

On what grounds could Google's decision to launch Google.cn and to follow Chinese censorship requirements be justified? Should Google have resisted Chinese requirements because of human rights concerns? Defenders of Google's presence in China have given economic, legal and moral justifications.

Google's decision to operate Google.cn could be justified on *economic* grounds. Most business ethicists see at least part of companies' obligations to be toward shareholders which include pursuing opportunities for profit when legal and in conformity with widely accepted ethical norms.[5] In 2006, Google faced growing competition in China as other Western companies such as Yahoo! Inc. were also present in the market and had chosen to follow censorship requirements. Most notably, Yahoo had surrendered emails and other information to the Chinese government in 2004, leading to the imprisonment of the pro-democracy journalist Shi Tao. Also, Chinese search engines had been developed and were gaining market share. Particularly the Beijing based Baidu arose as a strong competitor. In 2005, Google.com's new Chinese-character service had a search market share of 27 per cent, whereas Baidu was quickly gaining users and had amassed already nearly half of the Chinese search engine market.[6] Until the launch of Google.cn Google could offer only a slow version of its search engine in China and had to be prepared for complete blockades of its website Google.com with the consequence of further losing market share. Indeed, the search market share of Google.cn had fallen to a mere 1.7 per cent in October 2013. Though there were economic grounds for pursuing opportunities in China, they were not straightforward. One consideration was the economic effects of the blow to the company's reputation. Resisting Chinese censorship requirements might even make sense in the light of diminishing market share in the country, as such a practice can help avoid reputation loss in Western countries and hence be important for business success.

In addition to *economic* considerations, *legal* considerations about the regulatory framework need to be assessed. As Chinese law required Google to filter its content, Google.cn could not have been started without agreeing to assist in the censorship. This does not, however, settle matters. The fact that Google is an American company raises questions of jurisdiction: when operating abroad which laws and legal norms should it respect? How should a company act when confronted with a violation of the right to freedom of expression? Google also presented *moral* arguments to defend the start of Google.cn. In the congressional hearing in February 2006, Google's Vice President Elliot Schrage underlined the company's commitment to consider the moral implications of all business decisions. Schrage pointed out that the launch of Google.cn had been a difficult decision, but was justified, as Google.cn would "make a meaningful—though imperfect—contribution to the overall expansion of access to information in China."[7] Schrage also stressed the higher degree of transparency compared to competitors due to the notification when links had been removed from search results. In Schrage's point of view, this disclosure "allows users to hold their legal systems accountable."[8]

Google was attempting to justify its presence in China by arguing that this produced more overall benefits than the alternatives. One challenge to this type of argument is that it is difficult to assess whether benefits achieved by launching Google.cn actually outweighed the negative effects of censorship.[9] On one hand, Google contributed to increased access to information by delivering high quality search results. Even if politically sensitive websites had to be censored, Google "could still improve Chinese citizens' ability to learn about AIDS, environmental problems, avian flu, world

markets."[10] Besides, the censorship required by the Chinese government involved leeway for interpretation: Google—like the other signatories of "The Pledge"—had to follow the official guidelines on unwanted content, but these rules were often vague and Internet companies made different censoring choices. Hence, Google could attempt to censor less than its competitors. On the other hand, as US Representative Christopher Smith noted in 2006: "When Google sends you to a Chinese propaganda source on a sensitive subject, it's got the imprimatur of Google. And that influences the next generation—they think, maybe we can live with this dictatorship."[11]

Google's moral arguments face the criticism that they are incompatible with the universal concern for human rights, in particular the right to freedom of expression. Human rights are global, "inalienable rights of all members of the human family."[12] The right to freedom of expression includes the right to seek, receive and impart information and ideas; it is a negative right that protects the individual from abuses and interference (in the form of blocking access to information) by governments and private actors.

Human rights are moral rights, but have gained a legal basis through international covenants such as the Universal Declaration of Human Rights (UNUDHR) that was adopted by the United Nations General Assembly in 1948. The right to freedom of expression is guaranteed by Article 19 of the UNUDHR as well as by Article 19 of the International Covenant on Civil and Political Rights (ICCPR), a multilateral treaty adopted by the United Nations General Assembly in 1966.

The moral responsibility of companies to respect human rights has been increasingly recognized. The work by the United Nations (UN) Special Representative John Ruggie contributed to this development with the introduction of the UN "Protect, Respect and Remedy" Framework[13] and "Guiding Principles on Business and Human Rights."[14] According to Ruggie, companies must respect human rights and may not infringe on the rights of others as the baseline expectation. They should seek to prevent or mitigate adverse human rights impacts that are directly linked to their operations, products or services. Companies must also avoid becoming complicit in human rights violations, whereas complicity means any "indirect ways in which companies can have an adverse effect on rights through their relationships."[15]

The exact implications and limits of the concept of complicity are debated. Various categories of complicity have been identified: the idea of "direct complicity" is widely accepted, i.e. cases where the company knowingly "participates through assistance in the commission of human rights abuses"; "beneficial complicity" means a company benefits from human rights abuses without assisting or causing them; the most debated category is "silent complicity" that refers to failure to address human rights abuses with the appropriate authorities.[16]

Google's operations in China meant cooperating with the Chinese government in blocking websites. Google.cn restricted Chinese users in their access to websites to which they have a right of access. This kind of complicity has been called "obedient complicity" in which a company "follows laws or regulations of a government to act in ways that support its activities that intentionally and significantly violate people's human rights."[17]

Overall, does this mean Google should not have launched Google.cn due to human rights concerns? Although the right to freedom of expression has been violated, determining what Google should have done in 2006 (and what it should do today) is not straightforward. One may argue that this is a case where "moral compromise" is defensible, as the situation in 2006 was highly complex and exact consequences of the decision to launch Google.cn uncertain.[18] Besides, Google's management has not opted for the easy way out, but has been monitoring the situation in China constantly and has taken current assessments as the basis to decide what actions are required and acceptable with respect to censorship requirements. Correspondingly, it revised its decision to follow censorship requirements in 2010.

Censorship and filtering requirements continue to challenge Google and other Internet companies—not only in China, but in many countries around the world. This issue is complex, as it involves economic and legal issues, but also necessitates distinguishing just and unjust law and balancing freedom of expression and local cultural norms. One important step for Internet companies to clarify human rights obligations has been the start of the Global Network Initiative (GNI), co-founded by Google in 2008. The initiative commits participants to a set of principles, including respecting and protecting the freedom of expression of their users "by seeking to avoid or minimize the impact of government restrictions on freedom of expression" and by removing content or otherwise limiting access to information and ideas "in a manner inconsistent with internationally recognized laws and standards."[19]

DISCUSSION QUESTIONS

1. Google argued in 2006 that filtering Internet content is less harmful than not making its search engine available in the Chinese market. Do you agree? If this is true, does it justify Google doing business in China?
2. Is Google complicit in human rights abuses in China?
3. Some have dismissed the human rights approaches as a mere Western idea. Should the critics of the launch of Google.cn be castigated for their "ethical imperialism"?
4. Do governments of democratic countries have the responsibility to ensure proper conduct of internationally active companies abroad, i.e., should the US government prevent Google from working with autocratic regimes such as China?

NOTES

1   Brush, Silla, Knight, Danielle, and Fang, Bay. February 27, 2006. "Learning to Live with Big Brother." *US News & World Report* 140, no. 7: 29–d31.

2   David Drummond. January 12, 2010. "A New Approach to China." Official Google Blog, http://googleblog.blogspot.de/2010/01/new-approach-to-china.html.

3   Bradsher, Keith, and Mozursept, Paul. Sept. 21, 2014. "China Clamps Down on Web, Pinching Companies Like Google." *New York Times*, http://www.nytimes.com/2014/09/22/business/international/china-clamps-down-on-web-pinching-companies-like-google.html.

4   Levin, Dan. June 2, 2014. "China Escalating Attack on Google." *New York Times*, http://www.nytimes.com/2014/06/03/business/chinas-battle-against-google-heats-up.html?_r=0.

5   Economic responsibility can be conceptualized as one part of overall corporate responsibilities along with legal, ethical and philanthropic responsibilities. See Carroll, A.B. 1979. "A Three-Dimensional Conceptual Model of Corporate Social Performance." *Academy of Management Review* 4: 497–505.

6   Thompson, Clive. April 23, 2006. "Google's China Problem (and China's Google Problem)." *New York Times*, http://www.nytimes.com/2006/04/23/magazine/23google.html?pagewanted=all.

7   Schrage, Elliot. February 15, 2006. "Testimony of Google Inc. before the Subcommittee on Africa, Global Human Rights, and International Operations Committee on International Relations", United States House of Representatives, http://googleblog.blogspot.de/2006/02/testimony-Internet-in-china.html.

8   Ibid.

9   See Dann, Gary, and Neil Haddow. 2008. "Just Doing Business or Doing Just Business: Google, Microsoft, Yahoo! and the Business of Censoring China's Internet." *Journal of Business Ethics* 79, no. 3: 227.

10   Thompson, Clive. 2006. "Google's China Problem (and China's Google Problem)." *New York Times*, http://www.nytimes.com/2006/04/23/magazine/23google.html?pagewanted=all.

11   Thompson, Clive. 2006. "Google's China Problem (and China's Google Problem)." *New York*

Times, http://www.nytimes.com/2006/04/23/magazine/23google.html?pagewanted=all.

12   1948. UN General Assembly. "Universal Declaration of Human Rights." http://www.unhcr.org/refworld/docid/3ae6b3712c.html.

13   2008. United Nations. "Protect, Respect and Remedy: A Framework for Business and Human Rights Report of the Special Representative of the Secretary-General on the Issue of Human Rights and Transnational Corporations and Other Business Enterprises, John Ruggie. Human Rights Council, Eighth Session, a/Hrc/8/5." http://www.reports-and-materials.org/Ruggie-report-7-Apr-2008.pdf.

14   2011. United Nations. "Report of the Special Representative of the Secretary-General on the Issue of Human Rights and Transnational Corporations and Other Business Enterprises, Guiding Principles on Business and Human Rights: Implementing the United Nations "Protect, Respect and Remedy" Framework, Human Rights Council Seventeenth Session, a/Hrc/17/31." http://www.business-humanrights.org/media/documents/ruggie/ruggie-guiding-principles-21-mar-2011.pdf.

15   2008. United Nations. "Protect, Respect and Remedy: A Framework for Business and Human Rights. Report of the Special Representative of the Secretary-General on the Issue of Human Rights and Transnational Corporations and Other Business Enterprises, John Ruggie. Human Rights Council, Eighth Session, a/Hrc/8/5." http://www.reports-and-materials.org/Ruggie-report-7-Apr-2008.pdf: 3.

16   Clapham, Andrew, and Scott Jerbi. 2001. "Categories of Corporate Complicity in Human Rights Abuses." *Hastings International and Comparative Law Review* 24: 339–49.

17   Brenkert, George. 2009. "Google, Human Rights, and Moral Compromise." *Journal of Business Ethics* 85, no. 4: 459.

18   Ibid.

19   https://globalnetworkinitiative.org/principles/index.php.

FURTHER READINGS

Brenkert, George. 2009. "Google, Human Rights, and Moral Compromise." *Journal of Business Ethics* 85, no. 4: 453–78.

Dann, Gary, and Neil Haddow. 2008. "Just Doing Business or Doing Just Business: Google, Microsoft, Yahoo! and the Business of Censoring China's Internet." *Journal of Business Ethics* 79, no. 3: 219–34.

Eko, Lyombe, Anup Kumar, and Yao Qingjiang. 2011. "Google This: The Great Firewall of China, the It Wheel of India, Google Inc., and Internet Regulation." *Journal of Internet Law* 15, no. 3: 3–14.

Hamilton, J. Brooke, Stephen B. Knouse, and Vanessa Hill. 2009. "Google in China: A Manager-Friendly Heuristic Model for Resolving Cross-Cultural Ethical Conflicts." *Journal of Business Ethics* 86, no. 2: 143–57.

Thompson, Clive. April 23, 2006. "Google's China Problem (and China's Google Problem)." *New York Times*, http://www.nytimes.com/2006/04/23/magazine/23google.html?pagewanted=all.

—33—
GIFT GIVING, BRIBERY, AND CORRUPTION

Ethical Management of Business Relationships in China

P. Steidlmeier

GIFT GIVING IS A PREVALENT SOCIAL CUSTOM IN China in all areas of life: in family and in significant relationships (*guanxi*), as well as in dealing with political authorities, social institutions and business people. For all that, from an ethical perspective, it is very difficult to know when it is proper to give or receive a gift, what sort of gift is appropriate, or what social obligations gift giving imposes.

Anyone who has lived in a foreign culture knows how difficult it is to successfully adapt to the local way of doing things. One can spend many months learning how to behave, only to find it all too easy to still commit tremendous faux pas. For foreigners, the cultural logic and social practices of gift giving present one of the most difficult lessons in learning how to "do business right" in China. Not surprisingly, many Westerners unfamiliar with Chinese culture often make the easy identification of gifts with bribes and allege that the Chinese are promiscuously corrupt in their business practices. Such an easy identification is, however, incorrect. The Chinese themselves are well aware of the differences. There is hardly an issue that has so preoccupied the Chinese media and incited debate over the past years as bribery and corruption. Within Chinese culture itself, there are, indeed, moral parameters to distinguish morally proper gift giving from bribery and corruption.

In this paper I assess the cultural and moral differences between gift giving, bribery and corruption and set forth guidelines for managing business relations in China. I begin with a cultural framework of analysis and then proceed to analyze transactions based upon reciprocity in terms of 1) the action itself and 2) the moral intention of the agents. I conclude with moral guidelines for ethical management.

DEVELOPING A CULTURAL FRAMEWORK FOR RECIPROCITY

John Noonan (1984, p. 3) observes: "Reciprocity is in any society a rule of life, and in some societies at least it is the rule of life." China is one of those societies where reciprocity is a foundational pillar of social intercourse. To approach another and bring nothing is unusual, to say the least. To accept a gift and not reciprocate is perceived as morally wrong.

A social custom such as gift giving expresses deeper socially embraced behavioral ideals and norms of mutuality and "right relationships" between people. Practices of gift giving in China include visual behavioral patterns (organizational artifacts), which are enshrined in rites (*li*) of proper conduct. Such rites themselves are rooted in normative and prescriptive canons of righteousness

Table I: Cultural Databases

ARTIFACTS	Artifacts represent those things that can been seen or heard, e.g., what gifts are given to whom and under what circumstances; artifacts also include things as how offices are laid out, how people run meetings, how honorifics are used in situations of interaction and so forth. This level of the data base includes the "who-what-where-when" part of the story.
SOCIAL KNOWLEDGE	Social knowledge includes the social processes and values that people can offer as reasons when questioned, e.g., why and how people should act as they do. It provides the reason why it is proper to give a particular person a particular gift at a particular time, as well as the contrary. In this section of the database the "how" and "why" of gift giving is covered.
CULTURAL LOGIC	Cultural logic provides the worldview which rounds social behavior and knowledge. This part of the database provides the ideals, values and principles which serve as society's internal gyroscope. It provides a vision of the most fundamental relationships people have to others, to their environment, to truth and reality, to understanding human nature, to time.

(*yi*) and benevolence (*ren*), which express why such actions are culturally meaningful or logical. In general terms, cultural logic underscores the numerous socio-cultural values and beliefs that are embedded within organizations and function as a sort of internal gyroscope, which governs the social behavior of people. It is, nonetheless, difficult to discern when it is proper to give a gift, what its nature should be and to whom it should be given. Such discernment is ultimately a matter of social knowledge. Proper social knowledge represents the ability to align behavioral patterns with cultural logic.

In the area of business, a manager needs to gather and correlate such cultural information and its supporting ethical data in ways that make sense and render it usable. The three principal aspects of the cultural data base—artifacts, social knowledge and cultural logic—are summarized in Table I. In daily practice companies require a concrete understanding of acceptable business behavior patterns and an appreciation of why people do things in a certain way. To be successful business practices must be grounded in an accurate reading of these three levels of social meaning.

While cultural logic represents the transcendental values and worldview that underlie a culture, such as harmony, justice and right relations, artifacts represent the empirically observed behavior of people as they interact with one another, such as exchanging gifts, taking a certain place at table, or greeting a visitor at the airport. Social knowledge mediates between these two levels in determining what is appropriate. For example, if a visitor is coming from abroad, who is the proper person to meet him or her at the airport and what type of gift would be correct.

While the underlying traditional Chinese cultural logic provides the fundamental ethos of business practices, social knowledge provides a clearer map of "the rules of the game," through the mechanisms of routinely expected behavior patterns. The "rules of the game" reflect what people collectively, through social consensus and organizational will, find desirable. They provide specific ways of doing things within the overall structure of normative ethical parameters. Gift giving, for example, is expected behavior, which shows respect to another person and strengthens relationships. The practice is also bounded by rules of moral legitimacy, which may in the end lead to defining some gifts as illegitimate forms of corruption. Chinese sources themselves are well aware of this.

In China, gift giving forms part of a larger picture: belonging to a network of personal relationships (*guanxi*). That these relationships be "right" is a matter of utmost moral and practical concern. Gift giving is one of the ways of nurturing such relationships and strengthening the trust, caring, reciprocity and commitment between the parties. In practical terms, the quality of such relationships emerges as a universal primary reference point in judging what one ought to do. In day to day business, these realities lead to patterns of choice and the determination of priorities that are expressed in concrete deeds, such as favoring in commercial deals those people with whom one has close relationships or *guanxi*.

INTERACTING WITH OTHERS IN CHINA

Chinese culture exhibits a very nuanced social philosophy of relationships. These embody both the respect one person owes another in terms of face (*myan dz*) as well as obligations of mutual rights and duties (*quanli yu yiwu*), which bind people together. The predominant social structures of Chinese society are found in the web of significant relationships (*guanxi*), based upon family, geographic origin, school mates and so forth. A person's *guanxi* outlines who matters and how much they matter and provides the primary basis of moral claims for one person upon another.

Such relationships in China are not unidimensional. In fact, they embrace many different levels of intensity. Most generally, they are ranked in order of importance as follows: family, friends or fellows (school mates, colleagues, distant relatives, friends of friends), other Chinese, and the outside world. This ordering is also reflected within a business enterprise: the business itself is a quasi-family and evokes primary loyalties, followed by ties with the enterprise's principal alliances (with banks, suppliers, traders, customers), other Chinese

businesses and economic agents, and then the outside world. The principal challenge for a foreign corporation is to insert itself as closely as possible within the inner circles.

In dealing with the Chinese, it is very important to be aware of such things as practices of gift giving and receiving, the proper role for host organizations and guests, correct ways to handle introductions, etiquette in eating and drinking, proper decorum with superiors, peers and inferiors in the workplace, how to handle and express disagreements, proper dress and so forth.

Chinese social behavior has traditionally been quite prescriptive in terms of rites (*li*) and forms of courtesy, manners, politeness, and correct decorum (*li mao*). "*Li*" is highly ritualistic and expresses the proper public manner of relating to a superior, an equal or inferior in extending greetings, speaking, taking a seat, drinking or any expression of self towards another. As pointed out in the previous section, "*Li*" rests upon a broader normative ethic of "right relations," which, for instance, express the heart of ethical concerns in the Confucian tradition. In China, position within the group, rather than over the group or in distinction to it, is far more important than independence from the group. Likewise, respect for others ("face") is of paramount importance and is manifested through gift giving, deference, not publicly disagreeing, public honors within a group, and so forth. Both relationship networks (*guanxi*) and the social stature of face (*myan dz*) are enshrouded in public rituals (*li*), which express status, respect and bonding in formal terms.

Attention must first be paid to instrumental organizational dynamics of structure, control, incentives and time. Chinese organizations tend to emphasize high-status definition and follow the rules of *guanxi* and familial structures. US organizations are more low-status and more rule-based, closely following formal rules and regulations rather than "following relationships." Control mechanisms in the former tend to be more cooperative and based on personal trust, and incentives take forms that emphasize loyalty and security. In the West, control is often more conflictive and regulatory, with incentives based upon individual achievement and merit. In the West, time is a precious commodity as the slogan "time is money" suggests; in China time is put to the service of relationships.

Further, one must consider a central dynamic of personal organizational interaction that stands out: individualism versus group identity. In the West people often define themselves as standing out from the group, emphasizing individual creativity, achievement, reward and status. In China people are more at pains to define their place within a group. This becomes more evident when applying the cultural process to doing business in China.

According to William de Bary (1991, pp. 3–4):

> Reciprocity, then becomes the basis of self-cultivation. One defines ones "self" in relation to others and to the Way which unites them. Thus is constructed the web of reciprocal obligations or moral relations in which one finds oneself, defines oneself. Apart from these one can have no real identity. And yet these relations alone, it is equally important to recognize, do not define one totally.... [F]or Confucius the individual exists in a delicate balance with his social environment, reconciling his own self respect with respect for others, his inner freedom with the limiting circumstances of his own situation in life.

For Chinese, gift giving is a natural dynamic of any relationship: it shows a relationship is valued and is a means of expressing respect and honor for the other person. Gifts express good will and gratitude and, in many ways, can be considered a dynamic form of "social contracting." The difficult aspects of gift giving have more to do with assessing the proper proportionality between persons and the implied sense of obligation or reciprocity that is entailed in giving or receiving a particular gift. For example, in dealing with a Chinese delegation, the leader should receive a better gift than subordinates. One often must proceed by trial and error; however, exchanging equivalent gifts is not a bad rule of thumb: a meal for a meal, a pen for a pen. To avoid bribery, it is important to focus upon whether, through the gift, one is asking one party or other to engage in behavior that is not an integral or legitimate part of the set of transactions at hand, which form the backdrop for meeting in the first place. For example, depositing 1% of a multi-million dollar transaction's value in a Swiss bank account in order to get an official to sign off on a deal could not be construed as a gift....

MORAL ANALYSIS OF RECIPROCITY

How is reciprocity, as a general type of moral action, to be analyzed? To call what is empirically a transfer of resources between parties 1) giving a gratuity or 2) bribery, or 3) a commission involves interpreting the meaning of the empirically observed event. Such interpretation draws upon core human values, respect for local traditions, and an appreciation of context.

To label it "bribery" is already to make a moral judgment. For in ordinary English (or Chinese) the word bribery itself (*huilu*) connotes a wrongful transfer of resources between parties. Wrongful because the gift giver and receiver apparently strike a deal, which puts their own interests above other parties, who have legitimate prior claims in the transaction and on whose behalf the agents are acting. It not only breaks down trust between people and their agents but also undermines the legitimacy of social institutions. It is just this action which I wish to scrutinize before we characterize it with a label....

ANALYSIS OF RECIPROCITY AS A "TYPE OF MORAL ACTION"

In objective categories moral understanding of an existential kind of action demands clarification of values as well as concrete knowledge of ends, means and consequences. Moral judgment then seeks to decide:

1) whether as a type of action "x" is right or wrong 2) whether as a specific instance particular action "x" is good or bad, and 3) whether the parties (agents) involved are to be praised or blamed

The paying of a commission is ostensibly the least troublesome resource transfer. Morally, it is embedded in a freely undertaken and fair contract framework and represents remuneration in a transaction of mutually beneficial exchange. As a type of action the ends sought, means taken and consequences which ensue are usually justified in terms of instrumental values (efficiency, utility) and self-interest. Such an action is only morally correct if it is consistent with fundamental values of justice and basic moral virtues. Furthermore, the intentions of the parties must be honorable and neither their consciences nor freedom are impaired. However, all of this can be easily suborned. Values of self-interest can be transformed into raw selfishness and expediency replace justice. Some would argue that commissions have become the favorite form of bribery in the United States, because they offer the cloak of legality.

Giving a gratuity, such as a tip, is a bit more difficult to analyze. If it altruistically expresses gratitude—a bonus for a job well done and performance exceeding expectations—it is a sign of generosity and esteem for the other. But if the tippee somehow indirectly communicates that such remuneration is a precondition for good service, then it becomes coercive and a form of extortion. The problem is not with a 15% service charge announced as a matter of policy, but with coercive behavior. Such coercive behavior, in fact, is a partial breach of the contract which is implied when one buys a meal, takes a cab, or gets a haircut: the service promised for a certain price will not, in fact be delivered for that rate. In giving gratuities, people may respond immediately that there is both a commonly known socio-cultural expectation and approval of tipping in general. The "gratuity portion" of the tip is then reserved to the rate: whether 12% or 20%. In fact, tipping is usually considered part of the tippee's ordinary income. In that sense it represents a suitable means to a good end with beneficial consequences. It may be considered both a "right" type of action as well as a "good" action in the context of a particular tip.

The latter judgment could be altered, however, depending upon the subjective intentions of those involved and the degree of coercion. Tipping may, in fact, mask either bribery or extortion. In coercive tipping, the tipee extorts extra payments for a service. In bribery, the tipper may seek special consideration—the best table without having to either make reservations or wait. In the end, the overall analytical framework of values-end-means-consequences remains ambiguous. As with commissions, the phenomenon of giving gratuities can either be morally uplifting or an expression of corruption.

Bribery itself emerges as extremely complex. Defined as a type of action it is clearly wrong. However, as noted above, to say bribery is wrong is to utter a tautology. That is, bribery (*huilu*) defines a wrongful type of action. To use an example from Kant, we describe a type of action and its conditions (end, means, values, consequences), name it bribery, and then ask: would one want to make this action universal? The answer is "no." The previous discussion of epistemology and worldview are very important here. For if we asked the question in terms of Mill's utilitarianism (does it produce the greatest happiness for the greatest number?) the answer may well be quite different, whether considering bribery as an individual act or as a rule of behavior. To say that bribery is always wrong can only be established in the context of a specific worldview and a specific value set that one takes as universal and absolute. Subjectively, it is necessarily relative.

ANALYSIS OF RECIPROCITY IN TERMS OF MORAL AGENTS

It is important to move from the analysis of bribery as a type of action to a concrete situation. When one asks whether a particular instance of bribery may be good or bad or whether the parties involved may be praiseworthy or blameworthy, the analysis becomes considerably more nuanced because of the complexity of the concrete situation. In this context, the analyst must be particularly careful of ethnocentrism. To the point, to what degree does what appears to be bribery fulfill the conditions set forth in the abstract definition of bribery as a type of action?

This is further complicated when, in addition to grasping all the details of a situation, one tries to understand the moral agent him/herself: subjective factors of conscience, intention and degrees of freedom are factored in. In actions of reciprocity, where resources are exchanged between parties, the level of development of each party's conscience may enter in to mitigate circumstances. Bribery in the face of intractably corrupt officials and the certain closing of a plant due to a lost contract, differs from bribery to enrich oneself so as to build a third villa estate. Indeed, officials involved in the Lockheed case, argued the former case and that, in the end, they chose the lesser of two evils. In such cases one may arrive at different judgments of the agents being praiseworthy or blameworthy.

Attention must be paid to the social situation and context. I am not at this point arguing a situational ethics where a type of action is right or wrong according to the particular circumstances. Rather, the very concrete definition of the action taking place (i.e. of what is actually happening) derives from the socio-historical context in the first place. That is, the question is not whether "bribery" is all right in Shanghai but not in Kansas City. Rather, is this manner of reciprocity and resource transfer in Shanghai a bribe? This point is crucial to understanding the social purpose and consequences of the transaction and to judging whether this instance is good or bad and whether and to what degree the agents are morally blameworthy or praiseworthy. In many parts of the developing world what a Western observer would call a bribe is, in fact, closer to a tip or the socially expected form of the tippee's remuneration. That does not mean that "anything goes." The former Lockheed scandal and the recent "Recruit scandal"

in Japan as well as many instances of corruption cited in the Chinese press have clearly exceeded such bounds.

Even if the end or purpose of the transaction is good—the firm is engaged in selling a product very good for the people—the analyst must also ask whether the means adopted are suitable and whether the intentions of the parties are honorable. Phenomenologically, it is difficult to distinguish a bribe from a tip or a commission or consulting fee. In the end, moral judgment depends upon the social understanding of the meaning of the action as derived from analysis of ends and means, consequences and intentions.

Provided the end or purpose is good, the key difference seems to reside not in the phenomenology of the transaction itself in terms of means and consequences, but in the intention of those who are involved, conditioned by conscience and effective freedom. The essence of bribery is conflict of interest between self and one's publicly accepted fiduciary duties. Secondly, it affects the means a person employs to fulfill his or her fiduciary duty. The appropriateness of the resource transfer in a particular case and the praiseworthiness or blameworthiness of the parties depends upon the overall social consequences of the action and the intentions of the agents. What if the intentions of the briber are actually good with reference to the project and fulfilling his or her fiduciary duties but those of the briber are greed? Even then, the action may not be completely bad. Enter the principle of double effect: one may make the judgment that the success of the project is impossible without the bribe and the good consequences of the project clearly outweigh the evils of the bribe.

SOME GUIDELINES FOR "DOING BUSINESS RIGHT" IN CHINA

The guidelines I suggest below are based upon two sets of beliefs: 1) the moral ambiguity one experiences in differentiating bribes from gratuities and commissions and 2) the present situation in China with respect to political and business corruption.

From the above sections, it is clear that it is impossible to clearly distinguish gratuities, bribes and commissions on an empirical basis. Bribes can easily be dressed in the garb of "legitimate commissions" or gratuitous expressions of esteem. Furthermore, in analyzing whether a transaction is morally right or wrong and whether the agents are praiseworthy or blameworthy pivotal elements such as conscience, effective freedom, the determinative dynamics of the situation, and cumulative consequences are often beyond measurement. In the end, these facts attest to the reality that moral probity is ever a matter of discernment of what, in the Socratic tradition, is called wisdom: figuring out how to be excellent at being human.

From Chinese voices themselves, we know the following:

1. corruption is endemic, especially since the reforms of the last decades
2. corruption reaches the highest levels of the ruling elite
3. corruption flies in the face of Chinese (as well as Marxist) tenets and traditions of public morality and the moral dimensions of a public official's responsibility
4. the "corruption debate" among the Chinese also functions as cover for a power struggle or, perhaps more accurately, for multiple power struggles between factions in the post-Deng Xiaoping era
5. Chinese "rules of the game" lack transparency as well as universality across both a) regions and b) factions—leaving local officials with tremendous discretionary power

If the above observations regarding both ethical judgments, in general, and the Chinese social milieu, in particular, are substantially correct, what is a company doing business in China to do? ...

As a general rule of thumb, a US intelligence consultant, Kroll Associates (Asia) have suggested the following guidelines in choosing a local partner:

1. Investigate the backgrounds of local executives you place in charge of company matters. Did they do a good job for their previous company? Or did they leave after two years, taking the entire team with them? A common occurrence.
2. Ensure no one individual has total control over company matters.
3. Treat remarks such as "China is different" and "You shouldn't get involved" as a red light.
4. Establish regular and detailed auditing systems to ensure transparency.

To which I would add:

1. Be aware of the political standing of your counterparts and do not get caught in the cross fire of Chinese power struggles.
2. Explain your difficulties to the Chinese side (deriving from the US government, stockholders, competitors, ...) and offer alternatives that are legitimate—especially something that addresses key Chinese policy objectives (e.g. technology transfer), the attainment of which will give leverage.
3. As much as possible use Chinese sources themselves as the basis for your unwillingness to do corrupt deals.
4. Rather than becoming entangled in a specific minor bribe, place the whole matter in a broader context of negotiation. Rather than reactively saying "yes" or "no" to a specific bribe, proactively build up negotiating leverage and a viable set of alternatives at the outset.

This last point of building negotiating leverage is highly important. I conclude this article with a sketch of its basic elements. In the end, if one's objective is to attain "A", he/she should a) devise simultaneous and multiple means of doing so as well as b) build up negotiating leverage. This not only allows one's Chinese counterpart to save face by having a menu to consider, it secures effective freedom in negotiations....

There are no hard and fast rules for such negotiations. However, it is clear that companies that have a product, technology or service critical to China have far more leverage than those companies for whom China can find easy substitutes. Further, a company that has other viable partners and alternatives also gains negotiating leverage. Overall, it makes sense for a company to primarily attend to three things: First, to diversify its Chinese partners as well as Asia Pacific partners so that it does not become boxed in by a single deal. Regionally, China is very diverse and it is possible to have a number of partners. At the same time it is important to form partnerships from the outside. In this way a particular deal becomes part of a China strategy but not the only viable option.

Second, it is important to offer one's Chinese counterparts alternatives that are both legitimate and that address important needs in Chinese development. Rather than simply paying a bribe, one can offer a local official help in marketing local products or special training (as Japanese trading companies are prone to do) and other consulting services.

Third, a company can gain leverage by presenting their approach in China's own terms. It should become familiar with China's internal documentation and processes regarding corruption and economic development. Rather than preaching from a Western pulpit—which Chinese find easy to counter—they should arm themselves with the ideals and procedures embedded in China's own development policies. China ardently desires to be an integral part of world commerce. The case should be made that standard international fair business practices are in its own economic interests.

Negotiating is not to be a frontal attack, but rather a strategy of creative imagination. Diversification of both partners and alternative courses of action brings (moral) freedom and reduces risk. Such a diversified negotiating context will set the stage for more creative solutions that are both morally right and strategically sound. In many ways the most difficult part of ethics is not denouncing what is wrong but the creative imagination and courage to craft something new. Diversified negotiation helps create the effective freedom to do just that.

REFERENCES

de Bary, William Theodore: 1991, Learning for One's Self: Essay on the Individual in Confucian Thought (Columbia University Press, Lincolnwood, IL).

Noonan, John T., Jr.: 1984, Bribes (MacMillan and Co., New York, NY).

—34—

BUSINESS, GLOBALIZATION AND THE LOGIC AND ETHICS OF CORRUPTION

A.W. Cragg

THERE CAN BE FEW TOPICS AT THIS JUNCTURE OF the development of human civilization that are more in need of careful exploration than "Ethics and Capitalism." It is now the virtually unanimous view of leaders in both the industrialized and the developing world that capitalism, or, as some put it, a free market economy, is the only viable model for organizing efficient and productive economies. This view, emerging as it has from the dramatic, non-violent, worldwide collapse of communism,[1] is no longer remarkable. What is striking, however, is the way in which the emergence of this global consensus has been paralleled by the emergence of "a global market place."

The phenomenon of globalization is significant because of the way in which, increasingly, free and global markets appear to have undermined both the willingness and the capacity of governments to exercise their traditional responsibilities for coordinating economic with social development. The result is a global market whose operation appears often to be quite divorced from any recognition that development or increasing economic wealth is of value not for its own sake but only insofar as it leads to improvements in the quality of life of the people and the communities that make it possible.

This sense of political impotence on the part of individuals and governments is disturbing enough

in its own right. The accompanying unease is magnified, however, by the realization that many individuals and corporations doing business in the global market place have no clear sense of their responsibilities to the societies, cultures and individuals they encounter in the course of their international ventures. This is a cause for alarm since the activities of corporations operating multi nationally can have devastating as well as beneficial impacts on individuals, communities and even nation states.

My purpose in what follows is to examine a phenomenon that has accompanied globalization, namely corruption. It is clearly not the only challenge posed by globalization. It is, however, an important one. Further, although it is not often acknowledged, the long term viability of free markets is very much tied to the capacity of those in a position to provide leadership to respond to this and a number of other ethical challenges to which globalization has given rise.

PART ONE: IS CORRUPTION A SERIOUS PROBLEM?

Corruption is now widely thought to be thoroughly entrenched in the global market place. George Moody Stuart, the chairman of the British chapter of Transparency International, an international anti-corruption coalition headquartered in Berlin, Germany, suggests in a paper entitled "A Good Business Guide to Bribery"[2] that while there were pockets of corruption thirty years ago, the great majority of countries in the developing world at that time were "clean." By the mid-1970s, he contends, there was "a growing awareness of the rapid spread of grand corruption in Africa" aided and abetted by European contractors who were "all too willing to cooperate."[3] Nevertheless, he suggests, it was still possible for experienced business people to do business internationally without encountering corruption in a serious form.

Over the past ten years, however, there has been serious deterioration, with grand corruption now the general rule rather than the exception in major government connected contracts in the developing world. He concludes that in the nineties, "nobody in the business world pretends any more that it is not one of the most important and damaging factors in third world development."[4]

There is much to confirm these observations both here and abroad. Media descriptions of the machinations of Canadian gold mining companies in Indonesia, in response to the discovery of what was thought for a time to be one of the largest gold deposits in the world, reveal graphically both the problem that corruption can pose for multinational companies as well as the market and non-market solutions to which those companies turn to resolve it.[5]

Neither are the problems of corruption restricted to third world business transactions. Whatever else is to be learned from Canada's own airbus scandal, what emerges clearly from this unsettling incident in recent Canadian history is the wide spread belief in both government and corporate circles that bribery is widely used in the high technology sectors of the economies of the industrialized world to win contracts in the north and the south.[6]

There is a final clear signal that corruption is a serious problem. Informal discussion and class room debate shows unmistakably that the case against bribery and corruption as a business strategy is not at all obvious to many business and government leaders or to many students in business and management studies programs in Canada and abroad.

Some examples will serve to point to the magnitude of the problem. As recently as 1998, bribes were accepted as a legitimate, tax deductible, business expense throughout much of Europe. The result was that while it was illegal for a German company to bribe a German official, a bribe directed to a French or Canadian or any non German government official for the purpose of winning a contract, for example, was legal. Indeed, many European countries did not even require that payments identified as bribes be documented with receipts or invoices. What is more, until very recently most European and other western governments have resisted any suggestion for change in tax law or regulations in this regard.[7]

In Canada, companies have been blocked from treating bribes as a legitimate business expense only since 1993. Furthermore, until recently, the Canadian government has quietly resisted any effort to vigorously discourage bribery because of a fear of damaging the competitive position of Canadian companies. Neither, it would seem, has the Canadian government attempted to discourage crown corporations from using bribery where that appeared to be necessary for the procurement of foreign contracts. An example is the Canadian nuclear energy industry whose foreign sales are widely thought to have been procured in at least some cases with the assistance of substantial bribes to key decision makers of foreign countries in the market for nuclear generators.

Among the countries of the world, prior to 1998 only the United States had a foreign corrupt practices act aimed at curbing the corruption of foreign government officials in the pursuit of business contracts. Until recently all other OECD member governments have resisted following suit on the grounds that to do so would put their business community at a competitive disadvantage.[8]

PART TWO: THE PARADOX OF CORRUPTION

For many in the business community, the phenomenon of corruption has been treated in the past as no more than just another factor to be taken into account by those wishing to compete in the global market place. For those concerned about the defensibility of market economics, however, the willingness of the industrialized world to accept and adapt to corruption poses a genuine paradox. The reason should be readily apparent to any critical observer.

Corruption in the form of bribery, for example, is clearly a two way street. There must be a briber as well as a bribed. Hence, if corruption is wide spread, first world multi-national companies must be cooperating. This is paradoxical for many reasons. It is virtually universally accepted on the part of the corporate community in the industrialized world that accepting bribes is grounds for immediate dismissal for both private and public sector employees at all levels. Consistent with this ethic is the fact that preventing corruption is widely regarded as one of the central tasks of modern governments. Exposing corruption is thought by the media in democratic countries to be one of their central obligations. Indeed, one of the basic justifications of a free press is the need for an unfettered watch dog that can expose corruption without fear or favour.

It is worth noting, in this regard, that there are no pockets of popular or academic resistance to the legitimacy of these perspectives. No economists have suggested that the market economies of the developed world would work more efficiently were corruption to be encouraged. No corporate leaders have argued publicly for softening corporate or legal anti-corruption strictures.

Why, then, is it so widely thought throughout the western world that corporations are justified in using corrupt practices to secure contracts in foreign countries? This question, I suggest, deserves serious consideration. No doubt, a complete answer would include a review of the various vices to which human nature seems prone. I want to suggest, however, that at least part of the reason lies in the conjunction of two clusters of theories. One of those clusters takes management as its focus. The other emerges from moral theory. Let us look at the influence of each in turn.

The first is a cluster of theories whose purpose is to describe and explain role of management in the modern corporation. It draws on the language and explanatory models of economics. Its focus is individual self-interest and profit maximization. It is a cluster of theories in which the language of ethics is given little if any place. Neil Shankman describes it as lying at the root of many popular management theories or programs. He goes on to say that it is "perhaps the dominant metaphor underlying much of what is written in the popular financial press."[9] Two management theories illustrate the basic thrust of this cluster. The first, which I shall describe as the shareholder model of the firm, argues that a corporation's sole obligation is wealth maximization for the benefit of owners or shareholders. Popularized by Milton Friedman, an economist, this theory builds on the assumption that people who invest in corporations want "to make as much money as possible while conforming to the basic rules of society, both those embodied in law and those embodied in ethical custom."[10] In defending this view, Friedman argues that:

> Few trends could so thoroughly undermine the very foundations of our free society as the acceptance by corporate officials of a social responsibility other than to make as much money for their stockholders as possible.[11]

The second version of this view is captured by the agency theory of management. On this theory, managers are agents whose sole obligation is to pursue the goals of the owners of the corporation for which they work. It is a view that is grounded on the assumption that human economic behaviour is motivated exclusively by self-interest defined as the desire to maximize financial wealth. It gives pride of place to property and liberty rights, essentially the right of people to advance their interests through the free and unfettered exchange of goods and services. Where this is allowed to occur, it is argued, the social interests and needs of people and communities will be efficiently and effectively, though unintentionally satisfied and the moral aspirations of society effectively realized.

This cluster of theories is frequently characterized as the "traditional or historical model" of the corporation, a description, which though inaccurate, highlights its influence on management thought both in the academy and in the corporate board rooms of industrialized societies.

Neither of these theories taken either together or apart explicitly condones corrupt practices. To the contrary, because conventional western morality routinely condemns such things as bribery, both theories imply that it is not an acceptable way of winning business in the industrialized world. Nevertheless, this cluster of theories does have striking implications for management whose focus is the global market place. First, they strip management of moral agency and therefore of personal moral constraints. Managers on this view are instruments whose sole moral obligation is to maximize profits for the benefit of owners or shareholders. All other constraints are external and relate to the exigencies of law and conventional morality. Respect for the letter of the law, an awareness of local conventions, customs and laws and a willingness to work within their parameters are all that is required of corporations or their agents. Critical moral judgement or evaluation of the moral character of prevailing laws, conventions or customs is irrelevant to fulfilling managerial responsibilities.

What is important about this moral framework for our immediate purposes is that its focus is entirely local and its moral content entirely conventional. Two things follow from this. First, managers have no obligation to carry western moral strictures into the global market place. Secondly, what will count as corruption will be a function of the conventions and practices of the local cultures found in the geographical locations where business

is transacted. What we have then is an implicit theoretical justification for the popular maxim, "When in Rome do as the Romans do." The logic is clear and easy to follow. What is more important, the implications for the world of business are readily apparent.

The second cluster of theories of relevance for our purposes emanate from moral philosophy. They have been effectively articulated by liberal political and moral theorists for whom individual moral autonomy and political liberty are core values. Two important principles underlie the thinking of these theorists. First, there is no one correct moral vision of the good life. It follows that there may well not be solutions to fundamental disagreements about how people should live and the principles that should guide their lives as individuals and groups. Second, individuals should be allowed to build their lives either alone or collectively without impediment and to the fullest extent compatible with an equal freedom on the part of others to do likewise.

Liberal political and moral theory has and continues to influence patterns of political argument and social policy in the industrialized world in profound ways. It is reflected in policies that seek to resist efforts on the part of individuals and groups to impose their moral views on the public, a moral perspective that has been decisive in shaping public policy with regard to such controversial issues as abortion. The recently rekindled euthanasia debate revolves around the appropriate application of these same principles to arguments about the extent to which the law should control end of life decision making. Arguments calling for the separation of church and state rest on these same liberal foundations as do attacks on any attempt to limit reading material in libraries, publicly funded schools and courses in accordance with concepts of decency or appropriate moral behaviour however sincerely held.

In practice, what these kinds of theories appear to endorse is moral relativism, a view which now seems to be a deeply entrenched feature of popular culture.[12] ...

It would be a mistake to underestimate the power of these theories in the popular mind or their implications for understanding and responding to the phenomenon of corruption. For they too would appear to lend credibility to the slogan "When in Rome do as the Romans do," a view that often underlies the rationalization of behaviour that in a Canadian context, for example, would be rejected out of hand as morally unacceptable.

Closely related is the view that for countries like Canada to impose their definition of bribery and corruption on the global market place constitutes moral imperialism. We have no right to impose moral values that define corruption for us on cultures where what we call immoral is thought to be common place and widely accepted, or so some would argue.

What I am proposing, then, is that these two distinct clusters of theories have had the effect, in western management circles of rationalizing contradictory standards and patterns of behaviour, namely, the rejection as entirely unacceptable at home of behaviour that is nevertheless tolerated and condoned abroad.

PART THREE: THE ETHICS OF CORRUPTION

... What then is corruption and why is it so widely thought to be unethical?

Let me begin by defining as corrupt any attempt whether successful or not to persuade someone in a position of responsibility to make a decision or recommendation on grounds other than the intrinsic merits of the case with a view to the advantage or advancement of him or herself or another person or group to which he or she is linked through personal commitment, obligation, or employment or individual, professional or group loyalty. It should be clear that this definition is designed to be culturally neutral. It does not attempt to define what should constitute merit. It assumes only that people who are appointed to positions of responsibility have an obligation not to take advantage of their position to pursue

objectives that prevent them from fulfilling to the best of their ability the function for which they are paid. This, I suggest, is the rule that lies at the heart of efforts on the part of western societies to identify and condemn corruption in its various guises. It is a rule which is entirely consistent with values such as efficiency, effectiveness, productivity and competitiveness. Indeed, it would seem on the face of it to be essential to the realization of all of them.

What then are the ethical parameters of this quest? The ethical dimensions of practices can be evaluated against moral principles or values that are widely shared and consistent with critical morality. They can also be assessed in light of their consequences or impacts. Let us apply each of these tests to the issue of corruption taking bribery as the test case.

There are two moral principles that engage the issue. The first is the ethical obligation to be honest. The second is a principle of justice or fairness. Bribery fails on both counts. It is by its nature covert and deceitful. Payments intended as bribes are typically disguised. Double book keeping is often the strategy used to accomplish this objective. Secondly, whether it achieves its goal or not, bribery treats those who are deceived unfairly and unjustly, which is why deception is required. The reason is that the purpose of the bribe, as our definition makes clear, is to provide someone in a position of responsibility with an incentive the purpose of which is to ensure that a decision is made that favours the briber whether favoured treatment is justified on the merits of the case or not. Thus, it provides the briber with an unwarranted or unfair advantage.

The significance and relevance of this moral test is born out by examining the impact of bribery on those affected by it.

Let us examine first the impacts of bribery on corporations that accede to it in their efforts to compete successfully in global markets. For business, corruption increases uncertainty, reduces accountability, undermines control and introduces what can turn out to be significant risks, risks that are easily overlooked and hard to quantify. Michael Mackenzie, former supervisor of Canadian Financial Institutions and a former Treasurer of the Canadian chapter of Transparency International points out that:

> Generally speaking, the making of bribes and the taking of favours puts one into a system of organizations, politicians, government officials and others, and once into the system it is usually very difficult to get out. For example, it is common practice of those who take bribes to set aside a portion for the person making the payment sometimes without even letting him know at the time!

He goes on to say:

> Without extremely good records, it may not be possible always to be sure that the employees of the payer are not themselves "on the take."[13]

What this demonstrates is that bribery can have damaging implications for companies that offer bribes.

Additional less tangible implications also attach to activities of the sort under examination. Corruption typically generates contempt for those being corrupted since the acceptance of payments in exchange for favours implies a lack of moral integrity on their part. What is less obvious is the way in which contempt toward those receiving payment can turn into contempt and cynicism directed toward the company itself and its senior management. This potential impact on the way in which a company is perceived by its own employees is bound to be exacerbated if the company's public posture is one of denying any involvement in corrupt practices at home or abroad while at the same time engaging in them.

It is not uncommon for companies that engage in corrupt practices, particularly in developing countries, to assume that they can compartmentalize this kind of activity and the values associated with it and restrict its involvement to third world business transactions. What is too easily taken for granted, however, is that the people involved will be able to maintain the personal integrity required of them by the company in their dealings with the company itself and with the business world "back home" while condoning or engaging in behaviour in foreign settings that they know would never be tolerated within the company itself. That is to say, although a transnational company may choose to condone corrupt practices in its foreign operations, it will nevertheless be seen as essential for its own welfare that its employees and agents retain their loyalty to "first world values" when they come home and in all their internal dealings with the company.

The reasons are obvious. Internal corruption can not only impair, it can also cripple a corporation's capacity to compete effectively in a free market. For corruption by its nature undermines both the willingness and the ability of employees to advance the interests of the corporation as efficiently and effectively as their job and competition in the global market requires. This is because corruption distorts judgement; the right answer or the right decision is no longer what would best advance the interests of the corporation but rather what will best advance the interests of the decision maker.

Values, however, are not easily compartmentalized. It is a serious mistake for companies to assume that management can easily move from third world to first world "ways of doing things" where practices like bribery are involved. A little thought quickly indicates why this is the case. If the reason for engaging in corrupt activity in a third world setting is contracts and profits, it will be hard to reject similar reasoning should the need arise in first world settings. Further if advancing the interests of one's employer using unethical strategies is acceptable from a corporate or organizational perspective, why should the same strategies not be used where an employee's own interests are at stake. It is not surprising to learn, therefore, that reports of corrupt activities on the part of senior management in first world business settings are today quite common. In the global market place, Rome is as likely to be next door as half way around the world.

The implications of corruption for the public sector in both the industrialized and developing world is perhaps even more striking. Where political culture and institutions are concerned, the effect of corruption both in the short and medium term is to strengthen and consolidate the political status quo. There are many reasons for this. First, corruption generates significant financial and other rewards for office holders. Where corrupt practices are tolerated by the regime in power, the illicit financial benefits that accrue to office holders generate both dependence on and indebtedness to the system and the people to whom they owe their appointments. Inevitably, the criteria of appointment shift from competence as well as commitment to fulfilling responsibilities efficiently and effectively, to patronage and loyalty to the regime conferring the benefit. The effect is to entrench the political status quo.

Corruption also tends to generate financial wealth for the governing elite both collectively and individually just because those in power inevitably demand "a cut in the action." Resulting personal wealth enhances the status of the political leaders. And their access to "private" sources of financial wealth allows them to build a strong political apparatus which supports them in power. The end result is to strengthen both the appearance and the reality of political support for those in power.

Finally, corruption tends to strengthen the elite in power by undermining the rule of law. There are many reasons for this. Perhaps the most important is that no legal system anywhere formally condones practices like bribery. As a result, widespread corruption inevitably requires the connivance of law enforcement personnel as well as the courts. Respect for the law is an obvious casualty and with it public confidence in the law and legal institutions. This too serves to enhance the power of the governing elite since where the

law is not respected, those in power can use that power to protect and enhance their positions unrestrained by law.

Corruption also has significant economic repercussions particularly for countries caught in its grip. It distorts economic policy making. Projects are undertaken not for their potential public benefits but because of their potential to advance the financial interests of those responsible for choosing them. Suppliers and contractors are chosen not on grounds of merit but because of their willingness to divert funds for the private benefit of officials or advisors in positions of influence. The result is distorted economic priorities and the diversion of resources from public projects and activities to private bank accounts.

These observations are illustrated by a 1994 report emanating from Switzerland claiming that amounts in excess of $20 billion are currently held in Swiss banks for African leaders. In 1994, the Vice-President of Ecuador estimated that as much as a third of Third World debt may be a consequence of corruption and pointed out that even if only 10% to 15% of the debt of his own country were attributable to wasteful investment resulting from corruption together with the funds diverted from public use because of bribes, the sum would coincide with that part of its debt which at that time, Ecuador was unable to service.[14] ...

Finally, corruption distorts social relationships and exacerbates social tensions. Where corruption is wide spread, public status and privilege are not likely to be related to merit or contributions made to society or even to the capacity to contribute but rather to personal, tribal or ethnic connections. Those individuals and groups disadvantaged by prevailing social arrangements will almost certainly regard their treatment and that of their family, friends, tribe or ethnic group as unjust. Social tension or alternatively progressive alienation and disengagement is an obvious consequence. In the long term, the resulting social tensions provide the foundations for severe and violent social and political conflict.

PART IV: THE PARADOX OF CORRUPTION RECONSIDERED

The practice of bribery by multinational corporations, as we have already noted, is paradoxical. It is obviously incompatible with moral norms that are deeply embedded in the management of virtually all multinational corporations. These norms also have wide public endorsement. Many of these same people, however, regard corrupt practices to be an essential part of doing business in foreign business transactions. In response to this phenomenon, I have attempted to show first, that the rationalization of corruption in global markets is just that, a rationalization. The evidence for this view lies in the fact that corrupt practices like bribery are fundamentally immoral judged by ethical standards that are widely accepted. When we test the morality of corruption by evaluating the costs it imposes on its victims, once again the evidence points clearly to its unethical character. It is not surprising therefore that there is no legal system in the world that tolerates bribery.

How then are we to reconcile this finding with the dominant shareholder model of the corporation and agency theories of management? Further, can the view that corruption is immoral wherever it occurs be endorsed without falling prey to the evils of moral imperialism to which danger prevailing liberal moral and political theories have sensitized us?

Let us begin the discussion by recognizing that the shareholder model of the corporation is an abstraction that deviates in significant ways from the reality it purports to describe and explain. First, whatever the attractiveness of Milton Friedman's theory to some elements of the business and academic communities, even the most superficial review of business history will show that many corporations in the industrialized world have understood their social responsibilities to extend well beyond a single minded focus on maximizing profits. To describe shareholders as people exclusively interested in share value is equally distorting. Progressive companies have traditionally undertaken to connect to the communities in which they were located in mutually beneficial ways, whether that meant the sponsorship of local events or philanthropic contributions to local or national charitable organizations and projects. This is in part because shareholders are also citizens whose welfare is affected not simply by the value of their investments but the quality of the communities in which they live. While shareholders might be capable in the short term of ignoring the long term impacts of the corporations in which they invest on the communities in which they live, this stance is one that few can maintain for long in the face of such things as a deteriorating environment or disintegrating social systems. In short, it is widely accepted in the corporate community, though perhaps not always effectively communicated or argued, that corporations have social responsibilities that go well beyond maximizing shareholder financial wealth.

Agency theories of management, whatever their popularity in business schools, paint an equally distorted picture of management practice. Managers of corporations are not simply the agents of their owners. Indeed, any theory that implies that a manager's sole moral obligation is to facilitate the pursuit of the interests (narrowly defined as profit maximization) of the owners or shareholders is itself seriously deficient judged by the standards of liberal moral and political theory. For liberal moral theory projects moral agency on all individuals whatever their employment status. The agency theory of management, in contrast, has the opposite effect of stripping managers of their obligations as moral agents, picturing them not as morally autonomous individuals responsible for their actions to everyone impacted by them, but as the mere instruments of property owners who are themselves described by such theories as amoral profit maximizers.

In fact, few managers would deny that they have ethical obligations to a wide range of corporate stakeholders including employees, customers, suppliers and the public at large.

In short, management theories that appear to relieve managers of an obligation to evaluate corporate activities and policies from an ethical perspective are themselves open to serious moral criticism.

Neither is liberal moral and political theory a serious obstacle to confronting corruption in the global market. It is true that accusations of corruption can be culturally insensitive. Patterns of behaviour do vary from culture to culture. Gift giving at Christmas, for example, is widely practised by the business community in Canada. Gratuities for service are expected as a normal cost associated with restaurant dining throughout North America. Both practices would raise eyebrows in many countries in the world. But neither provide evidence of wide spread corruption as the term is normally used.

It is true that evaluating the behaviour of people of one culture by the standards of another culture does suggest a form of imperialism. However, requiring that people fulfil their responsibilities honestly and fairly in accordance with culturally appropriate criteria of evaluation is not an act of moral imperialism. To the contrary, it is a standard for doing business on which a market economy ultimately depends. In its absence, there can be no genuinely free market. Deception subverts the free and voluntary exchange of goods and services and undermines the conditions for competition on which the market relies. In this sense, double standards in cross cultural business dealings are as unpalatable from a moral perspective as double standards in culturally homogeneous settings.

NOTES

1   Excepting, of course, a few countries like Cuba that continue to struggle to organize their economic and political systems around socialist principles.
2   "A Good Business Guide to Bribery: Grand corruption in third world development," Berlin: Transparency International, 1994.
3   Ibid, p. 3.
4   Ibid, p. 3.
5   It is not irrelevant, here, that according to Transparency International's widely cited "Corruption Perceptions Index," Indonesia is widely perceived by those doing business around the world as one on the world's most corrupt countries.

6   The Canadian airbus scandal involved accusations that an Air Canada contract was won by the European manufacturers of the Airbus as a result of the payment of bribes to among others the Prime Minister of Canada. The accusations involved were never substantiated and the Canadian government eventually was required to apologize to the then Prime Minister, Brian Mulroney and to pay a very substantial out of court settlement for damages resulting from police investigations. Whatever the merits of the case, the fact that it was seriously entertained points to a wide spread belief that bribery plays a significant role in at least some areas of the economies of the industrialized world.

7   This in spite of the fact that the International Chamber of Commerce has been recommending that companies resist the use of bribes in international business transactions since the 1970's and the OECD has been urging that its member companies remove bribes as legitimate business expenses from tax regulations since 1994.

8   It is important to acknowledge that in the two years that have intervened since this article was first written there have been dramatic changes in this regard. In 1997, the twenty-nine OECD member countries plus five others signed a Convention committing their governments to introducing legislation criminalizing the bribery of foreign public officials and removing bribes as legitimate business expenses for tax purposes. The Convention came into force in 1999 with the enactment by Canada of Bill S-21, Canada's response to the OECD anti bribery convention. At the time of writing, more than fifteen of the signatory countries have introduced legislation designed to meet the requirements of the OECD convention. It is now anticipated that within a very short period of time, most of the remaining OECD countries will have followed suit. While these developments are remarkable in their own right, skeptics will remain unconvinced that they mark a significant change of direction until there is clear evidence that the new laws are going to be vigorously enforced.

9   "Reframing the Debate between Agency and Stakeholder Theories of the Firm," Journal of Business Ethics, Vol. 19, No. 4, May 1999.

10 See for example: "The Social Responsibility of Business Is to Increase Profits" in The New York Times Magazine (Sept. 13, 1970).

11 Quoted by Patricia Hogue Werhane in "Formal Organizations, Economic Freedom and Moral Agency," reprinted in Business Ethics in Canada (second edition), Scarborough Ontario: Prentice Hall Canada Inc. p. 91.

12 Whether they actually do or not will depend in part on the definition given to "moral relativism" and partly to the theorist and specific theory under discussion. (See, for example, my discussion of "Two Concepts of Community of Moral Theory and Canadian Culture" in Dialogue, Spring 1986, p. 31–52.

13 Quoted from the text of a speech made at the launch of the Canadian national section of Transparency International, November 17, 1996 in Toronto, Canada.

14 See "TI Country Program in Ecuador: A Practical Approach for Building Islands of Integrity" Transparency International, 1994.

CASE STUDY

BUYING INFLUENCE IN CHINA

The Case of Avon Products Incorporated

Peter Jonker

BACKGROUND

AVON PRODUCTS INCORPORATED IS A manufacturer of cosmetics and beauty related products. The company was founded in 1886 and is headquartered and listed in New York. With annual revenues of nearly USD 9 billion and over 30,000 employees,[1] Avon is one of the largest players in the market. Avon relies on a network of 6 million sales representatives to sell their products directly to customers.

In 2014, Avon and the US Department of Justice settled a corruption case related to Avon's operations in China with a Deferred Prosecution Arrangement (DPA).[2] The case involved violations of the US Foreign Corrupt Practices Act between 2004 and 2008 and resulted in a settlement for USD 135 million, an agreement to have an external monitor for 18 months and an obligation to report on the progress in its compliance efforts in the 18 months afterwards.

Until the law was changed in 2006, it was not possible for (foreign) companies to sell products in China via a direct selling approach. To ensure that it would be among the first companies to obtain a license to sell in China—a growing market of 1 billion consumers—Avon tried to influence Chinese government officials, offering them exclusive personal luxury items by Gucci or Louis Vuitton, dinners, entertainment, luxurious trips and even

cash between 2004 and 2008. According to the DPA with the US Department of Justice these payments amounted to around 8 million USD to buy influence, obtain licenses, avoid fines and avoid negative publicity.

Avon's revenues have been under pressure in recent years. Especially in China, sales targets were not achieved. Over the fiscal year 2014, the company reported a decline of its global sales of 18%. In China, sales dropped over 40%.[3]

ANALYSIS

There are several definitions of bribery in use and there is an ongoing debate on the scope of its definition. For example, the United States distinguishes between facilitation payments and bribes when it comes to enforcement of its Foreign Corrupt Practices Act. Facilitation payments are small payments to speed up administrative processes that one has a right to receive (e.g., paying a customs official a few dollars to process a shipment). Bribes are payments to induce officials to do things they would not otherwise necessarily do. Most international treaties and several countries do consider facilitation payments to be bribes.

We follow Transparency International, an internationally recognized NGO promoting the fight against corruption, in defining bribery as follows:

The offering, promising, giving, accepting or soliciting of an advantage as an inducement for an action which is illegal, unethical or a breach of trust. Inducements can take the form of gifts, loans, fees, rewards or other advantages (taxes, services, donations, favors etc.).

This is a broad definition, but the core is that the "advantage" offered leads to an action which is illegal, unethical or a breach of trust.

Many companies have defined gift policies these days, restricting routine external gifts to a maximum "nominal value." If the value of a gift surpasses a threshold of say USD 50, one should ask for internal approval or report it in a "gift register." Although this is an easy to understand rule, by focusing on the value of the gift, it diverts the attention from the real point; the intention behind the gift. If you are giving a gift to induce someone to do something illegal, it is a bribe.

Ethical questions surrounding bribery become especially complex in international business. In many countries, bringing gifts is a generally accepted business custom, which underscores the value of the relationship. In many Asian countries it is regarded disrespectful not to accept a gift. In the Middle East a gift is sometimes used to express how wealthy the giver is. People conducting business internationally need to navigate these customs while respecting legal and ethical obligations not to allow gifts to provide an unfair advantage.

According to the Statement of Facts in Avon's DPA with the US Department of Justice, Avon representatives offered Chinese officials gifts, entertainment and even cash "in order to obtain and retain direct selling licenses, avoid fines or negative media reports, obtain favorable judicial treatment and obtain government approval to sell nutritional supplements and healthcare apparel products, via direct selling, that did not meet or had yet to meet government standards."

The intention behind the gifts and entertainment was clearly to buy influence and make sure the government officials would rule in favor of Avon's petition for a license. A USD 8 million "investment" to secure potential revenues of hundreds of millions, could be viewed as making smart business sense. Executives and employees of Avon were very well aware of the sensitivity of their actions, as they deliberately changed the description of these expenses in their books and records, misleading or falsely describing them as "employee travel," "samples," or "public relations business entertainment." In addition, they also used a consulting company to send false invoices. Avon transferred money to this company, which then made payments into personal accounts of government officials. In 2005, the internal audit department of Avon made management aware of irregularities in China. But this did not lead to fundamental changes. After a whistleblower's report in 2008, Avon's Group management started a full-blown internal investigation and decided to voluntarily disclose its findings to the SEC.

Though Avon's wrongdoing in this case appears fairly straightforward, we need to inquire into the business environment that led them to bribe officials. Bribery is bad because it allows companies to receive contracts and licenses because of their ability to influence officials, not because of their ability to deliver goods and services more efficiently than their competition. The problem is that this does not explain why individual companies operating in an environment where corruption is widespread should refrain from bribery. Where governments are not committed to enforcing anti-corruption laws and bribery is widespread, companies that refuse to engage in corrupt practices may not be able to compete.

There are also complex questions remaining about the ethics of bribery and corruption from companies operating in multiple jurisdictions. As mentioned above, Avon was charged under the United States' Foreign Corrupt Practices Act which governs companies that have a "footprint" (e.g., a listing, subsidiary, or history of transactions in US dollars) in the US. Avon is a US company with a listing at the New York stock exchange so there is little confusion in this case. The legal and ethical ramifications are less clear for companies that have a more tangential connection to the United States. For example, the US's "extra-territorial" reach may be more problematic in cases where the US chooses to charge foreign companies that only have subsidiaries in the US. Questions of legitimate political authority are particularly pressing in international matters where parties affected do not have democratic representation. We can question the ethics of the US using its economic power to enforce regulations abroad, especially since these regulations do not command universal recognition: i.e., countries and cultures disagree about what constitutes bribery and when it is problematic.

In recent years, other countries have adopted laws governing corruption abroad. Until recently, the US was the only country that has vigorously enforced anti-corruption laws. Canada, the UK, and Brazil have all recently adopted laws with an extra-territorial reach. This raises practical and moral questions. In its anti-corruption law, Brazil, for instance, names penalties up to 20% of the company's annual revenue in corruption cases. Will they also go after Avon, for corruption in China, because Avon has a subsidiary in Brazil as well? And what is the role of China, the country where the corruption took place? Will they also take action against Avon? Who has a right to go after a company? In the case of Avon, would it be the US (as the company is listed at the NYSE), or China (as the crime happened there) or the UK (as Avon might have a "footprint" in the UK)? Could a company be fined more than once for the same scheme? Or, if the US collects a fine, should part of it be transferred to China, to support the Chinese government's efforts to tackle corruption?

A final question concerns the morality of punishment. Was the USD 135 million fine appropriate? When answering this question, it is important to reflect on all of the potential costs of the Deferred Prosecution Arrangement. One cost is the appointment of a Monitor, an independent external expert to monitor and report to the US authorities on the progress Avon makes in its anti-corruption and compliance efforts. Where

appropriate the Monitor decides to appoint additional external resources (for instance auditors) to verify the process. Avon must pay for the costs of those external consultants and invest internal management time to deal with compliance topics and improve processes and procedures, and also to report on progress and deal with authorities, legal experts and media.

Furthermore, the fine may impact the company's reputation and/or its share price and potentially lead to lower revenues. Other companies that have faced corruption issues have faced blacklisting with governments deciding not to buy products from them for a certain period of time. In China, Avon was also confronted with falling revenues and had to adjust its sales targets in recent years.

When assessing the fine imposed, we should ask about the function and proportionality of punishment. Is the purpose of the fine and accompanying actions to deter Avon and other companies from violating the Foreign Corrupt Practice Act? Is the punishment proportional? Is the fine comparable to what other companies have received for similar violations? Is a fine even the most appropriate punishment given that companies may come to see it as a cost of doing business, and merely take it into account in their overall plans. Are there any extenuating factors that deserve consideration? When considering this question, is it relevant that Avon had spent already USD 344 million on the investigation before the settlement?

DISCUSSION QUESTIONS

1. In his article A.W. Cragg cites the commonly expressed view that "we have no right to impose moral values that define corruption for us on cultures where what we call immoral is thought to be commonplace and widely accepted." In your view should all countries, like the US, UK, Brazil and Canada, start to implement and enforce laws against overseas bribery?

2. Avon settled with the US authorities for USD 135 million for improper payments of around 8 million. Do you think this is a fair and proportional penalty? Please explain your considerations.

3. There are different considerations to identify if a gift is "appropriate." What would be practical rules of thumb a company could use to define if a gift is "appropriate" or "lavish"?

NOTES

1   Avon, *Annual Report 2014*, http:// investor.avoncompany.com/GenPage. aspx?IID=3009091&GKP=210234.

2   *US Department of Justice v. Avon Products Inc.*, December 2014, http://www.justice.gov/criminal-fraud/case/ united-states-v-avon-products-inc-2014.

3   Avon, *Annual Report 2014*, page 40.

FURTHER READINGS

Baughn, Christopher, Nancy L. Bodie, Mark A. Buchanan, and Michael B. Bixby. 2010. "Bribery in International Business Transactions." *Journal of Business Ethics* 92 (1): 15–32.

Cleveland, Margot, Christopher M. Favo, Thomas J. Frecka, and Charles L. Owens. 2009. "Trends in the International Fight against Bribery and Corruption." *Journal of Business Ethics* 90 (S2): 199–244.

Transparency International, https://www.transparency. org/.

US Department of Justice, "*United States v. Avon Products Inc.*, Deferred Prosecution Agreement," http://www.justice.gov/file/188591/ download.

—36—
NATURAL CAPITALISM

Paul Hawken

SOMEWHERE ALONG THE WAY TO FREE-MARKET capitalism, the United States became the most wasteful society on the planet. Most of us know it. There is the waste we can see: traffic jams, irreparable VCRs, Styrofoam coffee cups, landfills; the waste we can't see: Superfund sites, greenhouse gases, radioactive waste, vagrant chemicals; and the social waste we don't want to think about: homelessness, crime, drug addiction, our forgotten infirm and elderly.

Nationally and globally, we perceive social and environmental decay as distinct and unconnected. In fact, a humbling design flaw deeply embedded in industrial logic links the two problems. Toto, pull back the curtain: The efficient dynamo of industrialism isn't there. Even by its own standards, industrialism is extraordinarily inefficient.

Modern industrialism came into being in a world very different from the one we live in today: fewer people, less material well-being, plentiful natural resources. As a result of the successes of industry and capitalism, these conditions have now reversed. Today, more people are chasing fewer natural resources.

But industry still operates by the same rules, using more resources to make fewer people more productive. The consequence: massive waste—of both resources and people.

Decades from now, we may look back at the end of the 20th century and ponder why business and society ignored these trends for so long—how one species thought it could flourish while nature ebbed. Historians will show, perhaps, how politics, the media, economics, and commerce created an industrial regime that wasted our social and natural environment and called it growth. As author Bill McKibben put it, "The laws of Congress and the laws of physics have grown increasingly divergent, and the laws of physics are not likely to yield."

The laws we're ignoring determine how life sustains itself. Commerce requires living systems for its welfare—it is emblematic of the times that this even needs to be said. Because of our industrial prowess, we emphasize what people can do but tend to ignore what nature does. Commercial institutions, proud of their achievements, do not see that healthy living systems—clean air and water, healthy soil, stable climates—are integral to a functioning economy. As our living systems deteriorate, traditional forecasting and business economics become the equivalent of house rules on a sinking cruise ship.

One is tempted to say that there is nothing wrong with capitalism except that it has never been tried. Our current industrial system is based on accounting principles that would bankrupt any company.

Conventional economic theories will not guide our future for a simple reason: They have never placed "natural capital" on the balance sheet. When it is included, not as a free amenity or as a putative infinite supply, but as an integral and valuable part of the production process, everything changes. Prices, costs, and what is and isn't economically sound change dramatically.

Industries destroy natural capital because they have historically benefited from doing so. As businesses successfully created more goods and jobs, consumer demand soared, compounding the destruction of natural capital. All that is about to change.

Everyone is familiar with the traditional definition of capital as accumulated wealth in the form of investments, factories, and equipment. "Natural capital," on the other hand, comprises the resources we use, both nonrenewable (oil, coal, metal ore) and renewable (forests, fisheries, grasslands). Although we usually think of renewable resources in terms of desired materials, such as wood, their most important value lies in the services they provide. These services are related to, but distinct from, the resources themselves. They are not pulpwood but forest cover, not food but topsoil. Living systems feed us, protect us, heal us, clean the nest, let us breathe. They are the "income" derived from a healthy environment: clean air and water, climate stabilization, rainfall, ocean productivity, fertile soil, watersheds, and the less-appreciated functions of the environment, such as processing waste—both natural and industrial. Nature's Services, a book due out this spring edited by Stanford University biologist Gretchen C. Daily, identifies trillions of dollars of critical ecosystem services received annually by commerce.

For anyone who doubts the innate value of ecosystem services, the $200 million Biosphere II experiment stands as a reality check. In 1991, eight people entered a sealed, glass-enclosed, 3-acre living system, where they expected to remain alive and healthy for two years. Instead, air quality plummeted, carbon dioxide levels rose, and oxygen had to be pumped in from the outside to keep the inhabitants healthy. Nitrous oxide levels inhibited brain function. Cockroaches flourished while insect pollinators died, vines choked out crops and trees, and nutrients polluted the water so much that the residents had to filter it by hand before they could drink it. Of the original 25 small animal species in Biosphere II, 19 became extinct.

At the end of 17 months, the humans showed signs of oxygen starvation from living at the equivalent of an altitude of 17,500 feet. Of course, design flaws are inherent in any prototype, but the fact remains that $200 million could not maintain a functioning ecosystem for eight people for 17 months. We add eight people to the planet every three seconds.

The lesson of Biosphere II is that there are no man-made substitutes for essential natural services. We have not come up with an economical way to manufacture watersheds, gene pools, topsoil, wetlands, river systems, pollinators, or fisheries. Technological fixes can't solve problems with soil fertility or guarantee clean air, biological diversity, pure water, and climatic stability; nor can they increase the capacity of the environment to absorb 25 billion tons of waste created annually in America alone.

Until the 1970s, the concept of natural capital was largely irrelevant to business planning, and it still is in most companies. Throughout the industrial era, economists considered manufactured capital—money, factories, etc.—the principal factor in industrial production, and perceived natural capital as a marginal contributor. The exclusion of natural capital from balance sheets was an understandable omission. There was so much of it, it didn't seem worth counting. Not any longer.

Historically, economic development has faced a number of limiting factors, including the availability of labor, energy resources, machinery, and financial capital. The absence or depletion of a limiting factor can prevent a system from growing. If marooned in a snowstorm, you need water, food, and warmth to survive. Having more of one factor cannot compensate for the absence of the other. Drinking more water will not make up for lack of clothing if you are freezing.

In the past, by increasing the limiting factor, industrial societies continued to develop economically. It wasn't always pretty: Slavery "satisfied" labor shortages, as did immigration and high birthrates. Mining companies exploited coal, oil, and gas to meet increased energy demands. The need for labor-saving devices provoked the invention of steam engines, spinning jennies, cotton gins, and telegraphs. Financial capital became universally accessible through central banks, credit, stock exchanges, and currency exchange mechanisms.

Because economies grow and change, new limiting factors occasionally emerge. When they do, massive restructuring occurs. Nothing works as before. Behavior that used to be economically sound becomes unsound, even destructive.

Economist Herman E. Daly cautions that we are facing a historic juncture in which, for the first time, the limits to increased prosperity are not the lack of man-made capital but the lack of natural capital. The limits to increased fish harvests are not boats, but productive fisheries; the limits to irrigation are not pumps or electricity, but viable aquifers; the limits to pulp and lumber production are not sawmills, but plentiful forests.

Like all previous limiting factors, the emergence of natural capital as an economic force will pose a problem for reactionary institutions. For those willing to embrace the challenges of a new era, however, it presents an enormous opportunity.

The value of natural capital is masked by a financial system that gives us improper information—a classic case of "garbage in, garbage out." Money and prices and markets don't give us exact information about how much our suburbs, freeways, and spandex cost. Instead, everything else is giving us accurate information: our beleaguered air and watersheds, our overworked soils, our decimated inner cities. All of these provide information our prices should be giving us but do not.

Let's begin with a startling possibility: The US economy may not be growing at all, and may have ceased growing nearly 25 years ago. Obviously, we are not talking about the gross domestic product (GDP), measured in dollars, which has grown at 2.5 percent per year since 1973. Despite this growth, there is little evidence of improved lives, better infrastructure, higher real wages, more leisure and family time, and greater economic security.

The logic here is simple, although unorthodox. We don't know if our economy is growing because the indices we rely upon, such as the GDP, don't measure growth. The GDP measures money transactions on the assumption that when a dollar changes hands, economic growth occurs. But there is a world of difference between financial exchanges and growth. Compare an addition to your home to a two-month stay in the hospital for injuries you suffered during a mugging. Say both cost the same. Which is growth? The GDP makes no distinction. Or suppose the president announces he will authorize $10 billion for new prisons to help combat crime. Is the $10 billion growth? Or what if a train overturns next to the Sacramento River and spills 10,000 gallons of atrazine, poisoning all the fish for 30 miles downstream? Money pours into cleanups, hatchery releases, announcements warning people about tainted fish, and lawsuits against the railroad and the chemical company. Growth? Or loss?

Currently, economists count most industrial, environmental, and social waste as GDP, right along with bananas, cars, and Barbie dolls. Growth includes all expenditures, regardless of whether society benefits or loses. This includes the cost of emergency room services, prisons, toxic cleanups, homeless shelters, lawsuits, cancer treatments, divorces, and every piece of litter along the side of every highway.

Instead of counting decay as economic growth, we need to subtract decline from revenue to see if we are getting ahead or falling behind. Unfortunately, where economic growth is concerned, the government uses a calculator with no minus sign.

Industry has always sought to increase the productivity of workers, not resources. And for good reason. Most resource prices have fallen for 200 years—due in no small part to the extraordinary increases in our ability to extract, harvest, ship, mine, and exploit resources. If the competitive advantage goes to the low-cost provider, and resources are cheap, then business will naturally use more and more resources in order to maximize worker productivity.

Such a strategy was eminently sensible when the population was smaller and resources were plentiful. But with respect to meeting the needs of the future, contemporary business economics is pre-Copernican. We cannot heal the country's social wounds or "save" the environment as long as we cling to the outdated industrial assumptions that the *summum bonum* of commercial enterprise is to use more stuff and fewer people. Our thinking is backward: We shouldn't use more of what we have less of (natural capital) to use less of what we have more of (people). While the need to maintain high labor productivity is critical to income and economic well-being, labor productivity that corrodes society is like burning the furniture to heat the house.

Our pursuit of increased labor productivity at all costs not only depletes the environment, it also depletes labor. Just as overproduction can exhaust topsoil, overproductivity can exhaust a workforce. The underlying assumption that greater productivity would lead to greater leisure and well-being, while true for many decades, has become a bad joke. In the United States, those who are employed, and presumably becoming more productive, find they are working 100 to 200 hours more per year than 20 years ago. Yet real wages haven't increased for more than 20 years.

In 1994, I asked a roomful of senior executives from Fortune 500 companies the following questions: Do you want to work harder in five years than you do today? Do you know anyone in your office who is a slacker? Do you know any parents in your company who are spending too much time with their kids? The only response was a few embarrassed laughs. Then it was quiet—perhaps numb is a better word.

Meanwhile, people whose jobs have been downsized, re-engineered, or restructured out of existence are being told—as are millions of youths around the world—that we have created an economic system so ingenious that it doesn't need them, except perhaps to do menial service jobs.

In parts of the industrialized world, unemployment and underemployment have risen faster than employment for more than 25 years. Nearly one-third of the world's workers sense that they have no value in the present economic scheme.

Clearly, when 1 billion willing workers can't find a decent job or any employment at all, we need to make fundamental changes. We can't—whether through monetary means, government programs, or charity—create a sense of value and dignity in people's lives when we're simultaneously developing a society that doesn't need them. If people don't feel valued, they will act out society's verdict in sometimes shocking ways. William Strickland, a pioneer in working with inner-city children, once said that "you can't teach algebra to someone who doesn't want to be here." He meant that urban kids don't want to be here at all, alive, anywhere on earth. They try to tell us, but we don't listen. So they engage in increasingly risky behavior—unprotected sex, drugs, violence—until we notice. By that time, their conduct has usually reached criminal proportions—and then we blame the victims, build more jails, and lump the costs into the GDP.

The theologian Matthew Fox has pointed out that we are the only species without full employment. Yet we doggedly pursue technologies that will make that ever more so. Today we fire people, perfectly capable people, to wring out one more wave of profits. Some of the restructuring is necessary and overdue. But, as physicists Amory Lovins and Ernst von Weizsäcker have repeatedly advised, what we should do is fire the unproductive kilowatts, barrels of oil, tons of material, and pulp from old-growth forests—and hire more people to do so.

In fact, reducing resource use creates jobs and lessens the impact we have on the environment. We can grow, use fewer resources, lower taxes, increase per capita spending on the needy, end federal deficits, reduce the size of government, and begin to restore damaged environments, both natural and social.

At this point, you may well be skeptical. The last summary is too hopeful and promises too much. If economic alternatives are this attractive, why aren't we doing them now? A good question. I will try to answer it. But, lest you think these proposals are Pollyannaish, know that my optimism arises from the magnitude of the problem, not from the ease of the solutions. Waste is too expensive; it's cheaper to do the right thing.

Economists argue that rational markets make this the most efficient of all possible economies. But that theory works only as long as you use financial efficiency as the sole metric and ignore physics, biology, and common sense. The physics of energy and mass conservation, along with the laws of entropy, are the arbiters of efficiency, not Forbes or the Dow Jones or the Federal Reserve. The economic issue is: How much work (value) does society get from its materials and energy? This is a very different question than asking how much return it can get out of its money.

If we already deployed materials or energy efficiently, it would support the contention that a radical increase in resource productivity is unrealistic. But the molecular trail leads to the opposite conclusion. For example, cars are barely 1 percent efficient in the sense that, for every 100 gallons of gasoline, only one gallon actually moves the passengers. Likewise, only 8 to 10 percent of the energy used in heating the filament of an incandescent lightbulb actually becomes visible light. (Some describe it as a space heater disguised as a lightbulb.) Modern carpeting remains on the floor for up to 12 years, after which it remains in landfills for as long as 20,000 years or more—less than .06 percent efficiency.

According to Robert Ayres, a leader in studying industrial metabolism, about 94 percent of the materials extracted for use in manufacturing durable products become waste before the product is even manufactured. More waste is generated in production, and most of that is lost unless the product is reused or recycled. Overall, America's material and energy efficiency is no more than 1 or 2 percent. In other words, American industry uses as much as 100 times more material and energy than theoretically required to deliver consumer services.

A watershed moment in the study of resource productivity occurred in 1976, when Amory Lovins published his now-famous essay "Energy Strategy:

The Road Not Taken?" Lovins' argument was simple: Instead of pursuing a "hard path" demanding a constantly increasing energy supply, he proposed that the real issue was how best to provide the energy's "end use" at the least cost. In other words, consumers are not interested in gigajoules, watts, or Btu, he argued. They want well-illuminated workspaces, hot showers, comfortable homes, effective transport. People want the service that energy provides. Lovins pointed out that an intelligent energy system would furnish the service at the lowest cost. As an example, he compared the cost of insulation with that of nuclear power. The policy of building nuclear power plants represented the "supply at any cost" doctrine that still lingers today. He said it made no sense to use expensive power plants to heat homes, and then let that heat escape because the homes lack insulation. Lovins contended that we could make more money by saving energy than by wasting it, and that we'd find more energy in the attics of American homes than in all the oil buried in Alaska. His predictions proved correct, although his proposals remained largely unheeded by the government. Today, the nuclear power industry has become moribund, not because of anti-nuclear protests but because it is uncompetitive.

In 1976, energy experts used to argue about whether the United States could achieve energy savings of 30 percent. Twenty-one years later, having already obtained savings of more than 30 percent over 1976 levels—savings worth $180 billion a year—experts now wonder whether we can achieve an additional 50 to 90 percent. Lovins thinks we might possibly save as much as 99 percent. That may sound ridiculous, but certainly no more so than the claim that textile workers could use gears and motors to increase their efficiency a hundred-fold would have sounded at the beginning of the Industrial Revolution. The resource productivity revolution is at a similar threshold. State-of-the-shelf technologies—fans, lights, pumps, superefficient windows, motors, and other products with proven track records—combined with intelligent mechanical and building design, could reduce energy consumption in American buildings by 90 percent. State-of-the-art technologies that are just being introduced could reduce consumption still further. In some cases—wind power, for example—the technologies not only operate more efficiently and pollute less, they also are more labor-intensive. Wind energy requires more labor than coal-generated electricity, but has become competitive with it on a real-cost basis.

The resource revolution is starting to show up in all areas of business. In the forest products industry, clearinghouses now identify hundreds of techniques that can reduce the use of timber and pulpwood by nearly 75 percent without diminishing the quality of housing, the "services" provided by books and paper, or the convenience of a tissue. In the housing industry, builders can use dozens of local or composite materials, including those made from rice and wheat straw, wastepaper, and earth, instead of studs, plywood, and concrete. The Herman Miller company currently designs furniture that can be reused and remanufactured a number of times; DesignTex, a subsidiary of Steelcase, a leading manufacturer of office furniture, sells fabrics that can be easily composted.

Although a new "hypercar" is now in development, "new urbanist" architects, such as Peter Calthorpe, Andres Duany, Elizabeth Plater-Zyberk, and others, are designing communities that could eliminate 40 to 60 percent of driving needs. (A recent San Francisco study showed that communities can decrease car use by 30 percent when they double population density.) Internet-based transactions may render many shopping malls obsolete. Down the road we'll have quantum semiconductors that store vast amounts of information on chips no bigger than a dot; diodes that emit light for 20 years without bulbs; ultrasound washing machines that use no water, heat, or soap; hyperlight materials stronger than steel; deprintable and reprintable paper; biological technologies that reduce or eliminate the need for insecticides and fertilizers; plastics that are both reusable and compostable; piezoelectric polymers that can generate electricity from the heel of your shoe or the force of a wave; and roofs and roads that do double duty as solar energy collectors. Some of these technologies, of course, may turn out to be impractical or have unwanted side effects. Nevertheless, these and thousands more are lining up like salmon to swim upstream toward greater resource productivity.

How can government help speed these entrepreneurial "salmon" along? The most fundamental policy implication is simple to envision, but difficult to execute: We have to revise the tax system to stop subsidizing behaviors we don't want (resource depletion and pollution) and to stop taxing behaviors we do want (income and work). We need to transform, incrementally but firmly, the sticks and carrots that guide business.

Taxes and subsidies are information. Everybody, whether rich or poor, acts on that information every day. Taxes make something more expensive to buy; subsidies artificially lower prices. In the United States, we generally like to subsidize environmental exploitation, cars, big corporations, and technological boondoggles. (We don't like to subsidize clean technologies that will lead to more jobs and innovation because that is supposed to be left to the "market.") Specifically, we subsidize carbon-based energy production, particularly oil and coal; we massively subsidize a transportation system that has led to suburban sprawl and urban decay; we subsidize risky technologies like nuclear fission and pie-in-the-sky weapons systems like Star Wars. (Between 1946 and 1961 the Atomic Energy Commission spent $1 billion to develop a nuclear-powered airplane. But it was such a lemon that the plane could not get off the ground. History's dustbin also includes a nuclear-powered ship, the Savannah, that was retired after the Maritime Administration found she cost $2 million more per year than other ships.)

We subsidize the disposal of waste in all its myriad forms—from landfills, to Superfund cleanups, to deep-well injection, to storage of nuclear waste. In the process, we encourage an economy where 80 percent of what we consume gets thrown away after one use.

As for farming, the US government covers all the bases: We subsidize agricultural production, agricultural non production, agricultural destruction, and agricultural restoration. We provide price supports to sugarcane growers, and we subsidize the restoration of the Everglades (which sugarcane growers are destroying). We subsidize cattle grazing on public lands, and we pay for soil conservation. We subsidize energy costs so that farmers can deplete aquifers to grow alfalfa to feed cows that make milk that we store in warehouses as surplus cheese that does not get to the hungry.

Then there is the money we donate to dying industries: federal insurance provided to floodplain developers, cheap land leases to ski resorts, deposit insurance given to people who looted US savings and loans, payments to build roads into wilderness areas so that privately held forest product companies can buy wood at a fraction of replacement cost, and monies to defense suppliers who have provided the Pentagon with billions of dollars in unnecessary inventory and parts.

Those are some of the activities we encourage. What we hinder, apparently, is work and social welfare, since we mainly tax labor and income, thereby discouraging both. In 1994, the federal government raised $1.27 trillion in taxes. Seventy-one percent of that revenue came from taxes on labor—income taxes and Social Security taxes. Another 10 percent came from corporate income tax. By taxing labor heavily, we encourage businesses not to employ people.

To create a policy that supports resource productivity will require a shift away from taxing the social "good" of labor, toward taxing the social "bads" of resource exploitation, pollution, fossil fuels, and waste. This tax shift should be "revenue neutral"—meaning that for every dollar of taxation added to resources or waste, one dollar would be removed from labor taxes. As the cost of waste and resources increases, business would save money by hiring less-expensive labor to save more-expensive resources. The eventual goal would be to achieve zero taxation on labor and income.

The purpose of this tax shift would be to change what is taxed, not who is taxed. But no tax shift is uniform, and without adjustments for lower incomes, a shift toward taxing resources would likely be regressive. Therefore, efforts should be made to keep the tax burden on various income groups more or less where it is now. (There are numerous means to accomplish this.) The important element to change is the purpose of the tax system because, other than generating revenue, the current tax system has no clear goal. The only incentive provided by the Internal Revenue Code, with its 9,000 sections, is to cheat or to hire tax lawyers.

A shift toward taxing resources would require steady implementation, in order to give business a clear horizon in which to make strategic investments. A time span of 15 to 20 years, for example, should be long enough to permit businesses to continue depreciating current capital investments over their useful lives.

Of course, a tax shift alone will not change the way business operates; a broad array of policy changes on issues of global trade, education, economic development, econometrics (including measures of growth and well-being), and scientific research must accompany it. For the tax shift to succeed, we must also reverse the wrenching breakdown of our democracy, which means addressing campaign finance reform and media concentration.

It is easier, as the saying goes, to ride a horse in the direction it is going. Because the costs of natural capital will inevitably increase, we should start changing the tax system now and get ahead of the curve. Shifting taxes to resources won't—as some in industry will doubtless claim—mean diminishing standards of living. It will mean an explosion of innovation that will create products, techniques, and processes that are far more effective than what they replace.

Some economists will naturally counter that we should let the markets dictate costs and that using taxation to promote particular outcomes is interventionist. But all tax systems are interventionist; the question is not whether to intervene but how to intervene.

A tax system should integrate cost with price. Currently, we dissociate the two. We know the price of everything but the cost of nothing. Price is what the buyer pays. Cost is what society pays. For example, Americans pay about $1.50 per gallon at the gas pump, but gasoline actually costs up to $7 a gallon when you factor in all the costs. Middle Eastern oil, for instance, costs nearly $100 a barrel: $25 to buy and $75 a barrel for the Pentagon to keep shipping lanes open to tanker traffic. Similarly, a pesticide may be priced at $35 per gallon, but what does it cost society as the pesticide makes its way into wells, rivers, and bloodstreams.

In 1750, few could imagine the outcome of industrialization. Today, the prospect of a resource productivity revolution in the next century is equally hard to fathom. But this is what it promises: an economy that uses progressively less material and energy each year and where the quality of consumer services continues to improve; an economy where environmental deterioration stops and gets reversed as we invest in increasing our natural capital; and, finally, a society where we have more useful and worthy work available than people to do it.

A utopian vision? No. The human condition will remain. We will still be improvident and wise, foolish and just. No economic system is a panacea, nor can any create a better person. But as the 20th century has painfully taught us, a bad system can certainly destroy good people.

Natural capitalism is not about making sudden changes, uprooting institutions, or fomenting upheaval for a new social order. (In fact, these consequences are more likely if we don't address fundamental problems.) Natural capitalism is about making small, critical choices that can tip economic and social factors in positive ways.

Natural capitalism may not guarantee particular outcomes, but it will ensure that economic systems more closely mimic biological systems, which have successfully adapted to dynamic changes over millennia. After all, this analogy is at the heart of capitalism, the idea that markets have a power that mimics life and evolution. We should expand this logic, not retract it.

For business, the opportunities are clear and enormous. With the population doubling sometime in the next century, and resource availability per capita dropping by one-half to three-fourths over that same period, which factor in production do you think will go up in value—and which do you think will go down? This basic shift in capital availability is inexorable.

Ironically, organizations like Earth First!, Rainforest Action Network, and Greenpeace have now become the real capitalists. By addressing such issues as greenhouse gases, chemical contamination, and the loss of fisheries, wildlife corridors, and primary forests, they are doing more to preserve a viable business future than are all the chambers of commerce put together. While business leaders hotly contest the idea of resource shortages, there are few credible scientists or corporations who argue that we are not losing the living systems that provide us with trillions of dollars of natural capital: our soil, forest cover, aquifers, oceans, grasslands, and rivers. Moreover, these systems are diminishing at a time when the world's population and the demand for services are growing exponentially.

Looking ahead, if living standards and population double over the next 50 years as some predict, and if we assume the developing world shared the same living standard we do, we would have to increase our resource use (and attendant waste) by a factor of 16 in five decades. Publicly, governments, the United Nations, and industries all work toward this end. Privately, no one believes that we can increase industrial throughput by a factor anywhere near 16, considering the earth's limited and now fraying life-support systems.

It is difficult for economists, whose important theories originated during a time of resource abundance, to understand how the decline in ecosystem services is laying the groundwork for the next stage in economic evolution. This next stage, whatever it may be called, is being brought about by powerful and much-delayed feedback from living systems. As we surrender our living systems, social stability, fiscal soundness, and personal health to outmoded economic assumptions, we are hoping that conventional economic growth will save us. But if economic "growth" does save us, it will be anything but conventional.

So why be hopeful? Because the solution is profitable, creative, and eminently possible. Societies may act stupidly for a period of time, but eventually they move to the path of least economic resistance. The loss of natural capital services, lamentable as it is in environmental terms, also affects costs. So far, we have created convoluted economic theories and accounting systems to work around the problem.

You can win a Nobel Prize in economics and travel to the royal palace in Stockholm in a gilded, horse-drawn brougham believing that ancient forests are more valuable in liquidation—as fruit crates and Yellow Pages—than as a going and growing concern. But soon (I would estimate within a few decades), we will realize collectively what each of us already knows individually: It's cheaper to take care of something—a roof, a car, a planet—than to let it decay and try to fix it later.

While there may be no "right" way to value a forest or a river, there is a wrong way, which is to give it no value at all. How do we decide the value of a 700-year-old tree? We need only ask how much it would cost to make a new one. Or a new river, or even a new atmosphere.

Despite the shrill divisiveness of media and politics, Americans remain remarkably consistent in what kind of country they envision for their children and grandchildren. The benefits of resource productivity align almost perfectly with what American voters say they want: better schools, a better environment, safer communities, more economic security, stronger families and family support, freer markets, less regulation, fewer taxes, smaller government, and more local control.

The future belongs to those who understand that doing more with less is compassionate, prosperous, and enduring, and thus more intelligent, even competitive.

-37-

A DEFENSE OF RISK-COST-BENEFIT ANALYSIS

Kristin Shrader-Frechette

ENVIRONMENTALISTS OFTEN CRITICIZE SCIENCE. They frequently argue for a more romantic, sensitive, holistic, or profound view of the world than science provides. William Bees, for example, criticizes economics on the grounds that it falls victim to scientific materialism; he says we need a new paradigm, other than economics, for achieving sustainable development. Similarly, Mark Sagoff, also writing in this text, criticizes the economic model of benefit-cost analysis and argues that it is not always the proper method for making environmental decisions. In particular, he criticizes benefit-cost analysis as utilitarian.

This essay argues that environmentalists' criticisms of science often are misguided. The criticisms err mainly because they ignore the fact that good science can help environmental causes as well as hinder them. Economic methods, for example, can show that nuclear power is not cost effective, that it makes little economic sense to bury long-lived hazardous wastes, and that biological conservation is extraordinarily cost effective. One reason some environmentalists are antiscience or antieconomics—and ignore the way science can help environmentalism—is that they misunderstand science. They attribute flaws to science when the errors are the result of how people use, interpret, or apply science, not the result of science itself. Rees, for example, criticizes economics as guilty of scientific materialism, yet this essay will show that economics

(benefit-cost analysis) can be interpreted in terms of many frameworks, not just scientific materialism. Similarly, Sagoff criticizes benefit-cost analysis as utilitarian, yet this essay will show that the technique is neither *purely* utilitarian, nor utilitarian in a flawed way, because those who use benefit-cost analysis can interpret it in terms of Kantian values, not just utilitarian ones. If this essay is right, then the ethical problems with economics are not with the science itself but with us, humans who interpret and use it in biased ways. In other words, the real problems of economics are the political and ethical biases of its users, not the science itself. To paraphrase Shakespeare: The fault, dear readers, is not with the science but with ourselves, that we are underlings who use it badly.

Consider the case of risk-cost-benefit analysis and attacks on it. Risk-cost benefit analysis (RCBA), the target of many philosophers' and environmentalists' criticisms, is very likely the single, most used economic method, at least in the United States, for evaluating the desirability of a variety of technological actions—from building a liquefied natural gas facility to adding yellow dye number 2 to margarine. The 1969 National Environmental Policy Act requires that some form of RCBA be used to evaluate all federal environment-related projects. Also, all US regulatory agencies—with the exception perhaps of only the Occupational Health and Safety Administration

(OSHA)—routinely use RCBA to help determine their policies.

Basically, RCBA consists of three main steps. These are (1) identifying all the risks, costs, and benefits associated with a particular policy action; (2) converting those risk, cost, and benefit values into dollar figures; and (3) then adding them to determine whether benefits outweigh the risks and costs. Consider the proposed policy action of coating fresh vegetables with a waxy carcinogenic chemical to allow them to be stored for longer periods of time. Associated with such a policy would be items such as the risk of worker carcinogenesis or the cost of labor and materials for coating the vegetables. The relevant benefits would include factors such as increased market value of the vegetables since the preservative coating would reduce spoilage and losses in storage.

Those who favor RCBA argue that this technique—for identifying, quantifying, comparing, and adding all factors relevant to an economic decision—ought to be one of the major considerations that any rational person takes into account in developing social policy. To my knowledge, no economist or policymaker ever has argued that RCBA ought to be the sole basis on which any social or environmental choice is made. Despite the fact that RCBA, an application of welfare economics, dominates US decision making regarding environmental and technological issues, it continues to draw much criticism. Economists, industrial representatives, and governmental spokespersons tend to support use of RCBA, but philosophers, environmentalists, and consumer activists tend to criticize its employment.

This essay (1) summarizes the three main lines of criticism of RCBA, (2) outlines arguments for objections to RCBA, (3) shows that the allegedly most devastating criticisms of RCBA are at best misguided and at worst incorrect, and (4) reveals the real source of the alleged deficiencies of RCBA. Let us begin with the three main criticisms of RCBA. These are objections to RCBA (1) as a formal method, (2) as an economic method, and (3) as an ethical method.

OBJECTION 1: RCBA AS A FORMAL METHOD

The most strident criticisms of RCBA (as a *formal* method for making social decisions) come from phenomenologically oriented scholars, such as Hubert and Stuart Dreyfus at Berkeley. They argue that, because it is a rigid, formal method, RCBA cannot model all instances of "human situational understanding."[1] For example, say Stuart Dreyfus, Lawrence Tribe, and Robert Socolow, whenever someone makes a decision, whether about playing chess or driving an automobile, he or she uses intuition and not some analytic, economic "point count."[2] They claim that formal models like RCBA fail to capture the essence of human decision making. The models are too narrow and oversimplified in focusing on allegedly transparent rationality and scientific know-how. Rather, say Dreyfus and others, human decision making is mysterious, unformalizable, and intuitive, something close to wisdom. This is because the performance of human decision making requires expertise and human skill acquisition that cannot be taught by means of any algorithm or formal method like RCBA.

Moreover, say Robert Coburn, Amory Lovins, Alasdair MacIntyre, and Peter Self, humans not only do not go through any formal routine like RCBA, but they could not, even if they wanted to. Why not? Humans, they say, often can't distinguish costs from benefits. For example, generating increased amounts of electricity represents a cost for most environmentalists, but a benefit for most economists. Lovins and his colleagues also claim that people don't know either the probability of certain events, such as energy-related accidents, or the consequences likely to follow from them; they don't know because humans are not like calculating machines; they cannot put a number on what they value.[3]

Although these criticisms of RCBA are thought provoking, they need not be evaluated in full here, in part because they are analyzed elsewhere.[4] Instead, it might be good merely to sketch the sorts of arguments that, when developed, are capable of answering these objections to the use of RCBA. There are at least six such arguments.

The first is that, since Dreyfus and others merely point to deficiencies in RCBA without arguing that there is some less deficient decision method superior to RCBA, they provide only necessary but not sufficient grounds for rejecting RCBA. A judgment about sufficient grounds for rejecting RCBA ought to be based on a relative evaluation of all methodologic alternatives because reasonable people only reject a method if they have a better alternative to it. Showing deficiencies in RCBA does not establish that a better method is available.

A second argument is that Dreyfus, Tribe, Socolow, and others have "proved too much." If human decision making is unavoidably intuitive and its benefits are indistinguishable from costs, as they say, then no rational, debatable, nonarbitrary form of technologic policymaking is possible. This is because rational policymaking presupposes at least that persons can distinguish what is undesirable from what is desirable, costs from benefits. If they cannot, then this problem does not count against only RCBA but against any method. Moreover, Dreyfus and others ignore the fact that no policymaking methods, including RCBA, are perfect. And if not, then no theory should be merely criticized separately, since such criticisms say nothing about which theory is the least desirable of all.

Another argument, especially relevant to Dreyfus's claims that RCBA is not useful for individual tasks, such as the decision making involved in driving a car, is that many of the objections to RCBA focus on a point not at issue. That RCBA is not amenable to individual decision making is not at issue. The real issue is how to take into account millions of individual opinions, to make societal decisions. This is because societal decision making presupposes some unifying perspective or method of aggregating preferences of many people, a problem not faced by the individual making choices. Of course, accomplishing RCBA is not like individual decision making, and that is precisely why

social choices require some formal analytic tool like RCBA.

Criticisms of RCBA as a formal method are also questionable because Dreyfus and others provide an incomplete analysis of societal decision making in making appeals to wisdom and intuition. They fail to specify, in a political and practical context, whose wisdom and intuitions ought to be followed and what criteria ought to be used when the wisdom and intuitions of different persons conflict in an environmental controversy. RCBA answers these questions in a methodical way.

A final argument against criticisms of RCBA, as a formal method, is that Dreyfus and others are incomplete in using policy arguments that ignore the real-world importance of making decisions among finite alternatives and with finite resources. Wisdom may tell us that human life has an infinite value, but the scientific and economic reality is that attaining a zero-risk society is impossible and that there are not enough resources for saving all lives. In dismissing RCBA, Dreyfus and others fail to give their answers to the tough question of what criterion to use in distributing environmental health and safety. If we do not use RCBA, what informal method is a bigger help? That realistic question they do not answer. If not, RCBA may be the best method among many bad methods.

OBJECTION 2: RCBA AS AN ECONOMIC METHOD

Although these six argument-sketches are too brief to be conclusive in answering objections to RCBA as a formal method, let us move on to the second type of criticism so that we can get to the main focus of this essay. Philosophers of science and those who are critical of mainstream economics, like Kenneth Boulding, most often criticize RCBA as a deficient economic method. Perhaps the most powerful methodologic attack on RCBA deficiencies focuses on its central methodologic assumption: Societal welfare can be measured as the algebraic sum of compensating variations (CVs). By analytically unpacking the concept of compensating variation, one can bring many RCBA deficiencies to light.

According to RCBA theory, each individual has a CV that measures the change in his or her welfare as a consequence of a proposed policy action. For example, suppose a university was considering raising the price of student parking permits from $200 per year to $400 per year and using the additional money to build a parking garage on campus. Suppose also that the university would decide whether this act or policy was desirable on the basis of the way it affected all the students. Raising the parking fees and building a garage would affect the welfare of each student differently, depending on her (or his) circumstances. According to economic theory, the CV of each student would measure her particular change in welfare. To find exactly how each student would measure her CV, her change in welfare because of the changed parking fees, we would ask her to estimate it. For example, suppose Susan drives to campus each day and has a part-time job off campus, so she cannot carpool or ride a bus because she needs her car to move efficiently between campus and work. Susan wants to have the parking garage, however, because she has to look nice in her part-time job. If the university builds the parking garage, she will not get wet and muddy walking to her car and will not have to spend 20 minutes searching for a parking place. If someone asked Susan to put a monetary value on paying $200 more per year for parking in a garage, she might say this change was worth an additional $100, and that, even if the fees increased by $300, would rather have the parking garage. That is, Susan would say her CV was +$100 because she would gain from the new plan. However, suppose Sally also drives to campus each day and suppose her welfare is affected negatively by the increase in parking fees and the proposed parking garage. Because Sally lives at an inconvenient location two hours away, she must drive to campus and park her car every day. But because she lives so far away, has no part-time job, and is going to school with savings, Sally wants to pay as little as possible for parking and prefers the existing muddy, uncovered parking lots. If someone asks Sally to put a monetary value on paying $200 more per year for parking in a garage, she might say this change harmed her by $200. That is, Sally would say her CV was -$200. Economists who use RCBA believe that, in order to determine the desirability of building the parking garage and charging $200 more per year, they should add all the CVs of gainers (like Susan) and losers (like Sally) and see whether the gains of the action outweigh the losses.

Or consider the case of using CVs to measure the effects of building a dam. The CVs of some persons will be positive, and those of others will be negative. Those in the tourism industry might be affected positively, whereas those interested in wilderness experiences might be affected negatively. The theory is that the proposed dam is cost-beneficial if the sum of the CVs of the gainers can outweigh the sum of the CVs of the losers. In more technical language, according to economist Ezra Mishan, a CV is the sum of money that, if received or paid after the economic (or technologic) change in question, would make the individual no better or worse off than before the change. If, for example, the price of a bread loaf falls by 10 cents, the CV is the maximum sum a man would pay to be allowed to buy bread at this lower price. Per contra, if the loaf rises by 10 cents, the CV is the minimum sum the man must receive if he is to continue to feel as well off as he was before the rise in price.[5] Implied in the notion of a CV are three basic presuppositions, all noted in standard texts on welfare economics and cost-benefit analysis: (1) the compensating variation is a measure of how gains can be so distributed to make everyone in the community better off; (2) the criterion for whether one is better off is how well off feels subjectively; and (3) one's feelings of being well off or better off are measured by a sum of money judged by the individual and calculated at the given set of prices on the market.

According to the critics of RCBA, each of the three presuppositions buys into the concept of a CV that contains controversial assumptions. The first presupposition, that CVs provide a measure of how to make everyone better off, is built on at least two questionable assumptions: Gains and losses, costs and benefits, for every individual in every situation can be computed numerically. A second questionable assumption built into this presupposition is that employing an economic change to improve the community welfare is acceptable, even though distributional effects of this change are ignored. Many people have argued that the effect of this assumption is merely to make economic changes that let the rich get richer and the poor get poorer, thus reflecting the dominant ideologies of the power groups dominating society.

The second presupposition built into the notion of CV, that the criterion for whether one is better off is how one feels subjectively, as measured in quantitative terms, also embodies a number of doubtful assumptions. Some of these are that, as Kenneth Arrow admits, individual welfare is defined in terms of egoistic hedonism;[6] that the individual is the best judge of his welfare, that is, that preferences reveal welfare, despite the fact that utility is often different from morality; that summed preferences of *individual* members of a group reveal *group* welfare; and that wealthy and poor persons are equally able to judge their well-being. This last assumption has been widely criticized since willingness to pay is a function of the marginal utility of one's income. That is, rich people are more easily able to pay for improvements to their welfare than poor people are. As a consequence, poor persons obviously cannot afford to pay as much as rich persons in order to avoid the risks and other disamenities of technology-related environmental pollution. That is why poor people are often forced to live in areas of high pollution, while wealthy people can afford to live in cleaner environments.

Continuing the analysis of CV, critics of RCBA point out that the third presupposition built into the notion of CV also involves a number of questionable assumptions. The presupposition that one's feelings of being better off are measured by money, and calculated in terms of market prices, includes at least one highly criticized assumption—that prices measure values. This assumption is controversial on a number of grounds. For one thing, it begs the difference between wants and morally good wants. It also ignores economic effects that distort prices. Some of these distorting effects include monopolies, externalities, speculative instabilities, and "free goods," such as clean air.

Because methodologic criticisms such as these have been a major focus of much contemporary writing in philosophy of economics and in sociopolitical philosophy, discussion of them is extremely important. However, economists generally *admit* most of the preceding points but claim that they have no better alternative method to use than RCBA. If their claim is at least partially correct, as I suspect it is (see the previous section of this essay), then many of the preceding criticisms of RCBA are beside the point. Also, both economists and philosophers have devised ways of avoiding most of the troublesome presuppositions and consequences of the assumptions built into the notion of compensating variation. Chief among these ways of improving RCBA are use of alternative weighting schemes and employment of various ways to make the controversial aspects of RCBA explicit and open to evaluation. Use of a weighting scheme for RCBA would enable one, for example, to "cost" inequitably distributed risks more than equitably distributed ones. Also, if one desired, it would be possible to employ Rawlsian weighting schemes for promoting the welfare of the least-well-off persons. One of the chief reforms, important for addressing the economic deficiencies of RCBA, would be to employ a form of adversary assessment in which alternative RCBA studies would be performed by groups sharing different ethical and methodologic presuppositions. Such adversary assessment has already been accomplished, with success, in Ann Arbor, Michigan, and in Cambridge, Massachusetts. Hence, at least in theory, there are ways to avoid the major economic deficiencies inherent in RCBA.

OBJECTION 3: RCBA AS AN ETHICAL METHOD

The most potentially condemning criticisms of RCBA come from the ranks of moral philosophers. Most of those who criticize RCBA on ethical grounds, as one might suspect, are deontologists who employ standard complaints against utilitarians. Philosophers, such as Alasdair MacIntyre and Douglas MacLean, claim that some things are priceless and not amenable to risk-benefit costing. Alan Gewirth argues that certain commitments— for example, the right not to be caused to contract cancer—cannot be traded off (via RCBA) for some utilitarian benefit.[7] In sum, the claim of these ethicist critics of RCBA is that moral commitments, rights, and basic goods are inviolable and incommensurable and hence cannot be "bargained away" in a utilitarian scheme like RCBA, which is unable to take adequate account of them and of values like distributive justice.

Of course, the linchpin assumption of the arguments of Gewirth, MacLean, and others is that RCBA is indeed utilitarian. If this assumption can be proved wrong, then (whatever else is wrong with RCBA) it cannot be attacked on the grounds that it is utilitarian.

Misguided Ethical Criticism of RCBA

RCBA is not essentially utilitarian in some damaging sense for a number of reasons. First of all, let's admit that RCBA is indeed utilitarian in one crucial respect: The optimal choice is always determined by some function of the utilities attached to the consequences of all the options considered. Hence reasoning in RCBA is unavoidably consequentialist.

Because it is unavoidably consequentialist, however, means neither that RCBA is consequentialist in some *disparaging* sense, nor that it is only consequentialist, both points that are generally begged by deontological critics of RCBA. Of course, RCBA is necessarily consequentialist, but so what? Anyone who follows some deontological theory and ignores consequences altogether is just as simplistic as anyone who focuses merely on consequences and ignores deontological elements. This is exactly the point recognized by Amartya Sen when he notes that Jeremy Bentham and John Rawls capture two different but equally important aspects of interpersonal welfare considerations.[8] Both provide necessary conditions for ethical judgments, but neither is sufficient.

Although RCBA is necessarily consequentialist, there are at least four reasons that it is not only consequentialist in some extremist or disparaging sense. *First*, any application of RCBA principles presupposes that we make some value judgments that cannot be justified by utilitarian standards alone. For example, suppose we are considering which of a variety of possible actions (e.g., building a nuclear plant, a coal plant, or a solar facility) ought to be evaluated in terms of RCBA. A utilitarian value judgment would not suffice for reducing the set of options. It would not suffice for deciding which of many available chemicals to use in preserving foods in a given situation, for example, because we would not have performed the utility weighting yet. Usually we use deontological grounds for rejecting some option. For instance, we might reject chemical X as a food preservative because it is a powerful carcinogen and use of it would threaten consumers' rights to life.

Second, RCBA also presupposes another type of nonutilitarian value judgment by virtue of the fact that it would be impossible to know the utilities attached to an infinity of options because they are infinite. To reduce these options, one would have to make some nonutilitarian value judgments about which options not to consider. For example, suppose chemical Z (considered for preserving food) were known to cause death to persons with certain allergy sensitivities or to persons with diabetes. On grounds of preventing a violation of a legal right to equal protection, analysts using RCBA could simply exclude chemical Z from consideration, much as they exclude technically or economically infeasible options for consideration.

Also, in the course of carrying out RCBA calculations one is required to make a number of nonutilitarian value judgments. Some of these are: (1) There is a cardinal or ordinal scale in terms of which the consequences may be assigned some number, (2) a particular discount rate ought to be used, (3) or certain values ought to be assigned to certain consequences. For example, if policy-makers subscribed to the deontological, evaluative judgment that future generations have rights equal to our own, then they could employ a zero discount rate. Nothing in the theory underlying RCBA would prevent them from doing so and from recognizing this deontological value.

Third, one could weight the RCBA parameters to reflect whatever value system society wishes. As Ralph Keeney has noted, one could always assign the value of negative infinity to consequences alleged to be the result of an action that violated some deontological principle.[9] Thus, if one wanted to avoid any technology likely to result in violation of people's rights not to be caused to contract cancer, one could easily do so.

Fourth, RCBA is not necessarily utilitarian, as Patrick Suppes points out, because the theory could, in principle, be adopted (without change) to represent a "calculus of obligation and a theory of expected obligation"; in other words, RCBA is materially indifferent, a purely formal calculus with an incomplete theory of rationality.[10] This being so, one need not interpret only market parameters as costs. Indeed, economists have already shown that one can interpret RCBA to accommodate egalitarianism and intuitionism as well as utilitarianism. More generally, Kenneth Boulding has eloquently demonstrated that economic supply-demand curves can be easily interpreted to fit even a benevolent or an altruistic ethical framework, not merely a utilitarian ethical framework.

THE REAL SOURCE OF RCBA PROBLEMS

If these four arguments, from experts such as Suppes and Keeney, are correct, then much of the criticism of RCBA, at least for its alleged ethical deficiencies, has been misguided. It has been directed at the formal, economic, and ethical *theory* underlying RCBA, when apparently something else is the culprit. This final section will argue that there are at least two sources of the problems that have made RCBA so notorious. One is the dominant political ideology in terms of which RCBA has been interpreted, applied, and used. The second source of the difficulties associated with RCBA has been the tendency of both theorists and practitioners—economists and philosophers alike—to claim more objectivity for the conclusions of RCBA than the evidence warrants. Let's investigate both of these problem areas.

Perhaps the major reason that people often think, erroneously, that RCBA is utilitarian is that capitalist utilitarians first used the techniques. Yet, to believe that the logical and ethical presuppositions built into economic methods can be identified with the logical and ethical beliefs of those who originate or use the methods is to commit the genetic fallacy. *Origins* do not necessarily determine *content*. And, if not, then RCBA has no built-in ties to utilitarianism. What has happened is that, in practice, one *interpretation* of RCBA has been dominant. This interpretation, in terms of capitalist utilitarianism, is what is incompatible with nonutilitarian values. But this means that the problem associated with the dominant political ideology, in terms of which RCBA is interpreted, has been confused with RCBA problems. Were the methods interpreted according to a different ideology, it would be just as wrong to equate RCBA with that ideology.

Confusion about the real source of the problems with RCBA has arisen because of the difficulty of determining causality. The cause of the apparent utilitarian biases in RCBA is the dominant *ideology* in terms of which people interpret it. The cause is not the method itself. This is like the familiar point, which often needs reiteration, that humans, not computers, cause computer errors. Given this explanation, it is easy to see why C.B. MacPherson argues that there is no necessary incompatibility between maximizing utilities and maximizing some nonutilitarian value. The alleged incompatibility arises only after one interprets the nonutilitarian value. In this case, the alleged incompatibility arises only when one interprets utilities in terms of unlimited individual appropriations and market incentives.

If the preceding view of RCBA is correct and if people have erroneously identified one—of many possible—interpretations of RCBA with the method, then obviously they have forgotten that RCBA is a formal calculus to be used with a variety of interpretations. But if they have forgotten that RCBA is open to many different interpretations, then they have identified one dominant political interpretation with RCBA itself, then they have forgotten that because of this dominant interpretation, RCBA is politically loaded. And if they have forgotten that they are employing a utilitarian *interpretation* that is politically loaded, then they probably have assumed that RCBA is objective by virtue of its being part of science.

Utilitarian philosophers and welfare economists have been particularly prone to the errors of believing that utilitarian interpretations of decision making are objective and value-free. Utilitarian R.M. Hare argues in his book, for example, that moral philosophy can be done without ontology;[11] he also argues that moral philosophy can be done objectively and with certainty, that there are no irresolvable moral conflicts;[12] and that objective moral philosophy is utilitarian in character.[13] Hare even goes so far as to argue that a hypothetical-deductive method can be used to obtain moral evaluations and to test them.[14] Hare, one of the best moral philosophers of the century, equates utilitarian tenets with value-free, certain conclusions obtained by the scientific method of hypothesis-deduction. His error here means that we ought not to be surprised that lesser minds also have failed to recognize the evaluative and interpretational component in utilitarianism and in the utilitarian interpretations of RCBA. Numerous well-known practitioners of RCBA have argued that the technique is objective, and

they have failed to recognize its value component. Milton Friedman calls economics "objective,"[15] and Chauncey Starr, Chris Whipple, David Okrent, and other practitioners of RCBA use the same terminology; they even claim that those who do not accept their value-laden interpretations of RCBA are following merely "subjective" interpretations.

Given that both moral philosophers and practitioners of RCBA claim that their utilitarian analyses are objective, they create an intellectual climate in which RCBA is presumed to be more objective, value-free, and final than it really is. Hence, one of the major problems with RCBA is not that it is inherently utilitarian but that its users erroneously assume it has a finality that it does not possess. It is one of many possible techniques, and it has many interpretations. Were this recognized, then people would not oppose it so vehemently.

SUMMARY AND CONCLUSIONS

RCBA has many problems. As a formal method, it suggests that life is more exact and precise than it really is. As an economic method, it suggests that people make decisions on the basis of hedonism and egoism. As an ethical method, people have interpreted it in utilitarian ways, in ways that serve the majority of people, but not always the minority.

Despite all these criticisms, RCBA is often better than most environmentalists believe. It is better because criticisms of RCBA often miss the point in two important ways. First, the criticisms miss the point that society needs some methodical way to tally costs and benefits associated with its activities. While it is true that RCBA has problems because of its being a formal, economic method, this criticism of it misses the point. The point is that we humans need some clear, analytic way to help us with environmental decision making. Most people would not write a blank check in some area of personal life, and no one ought to write a blank check for solving societal problems. Not using some technique like RCBA means that we would be writing a blank check, making decisions and commitments without being aware of their costs, benefits, and consequences. All that RCBA asks of us is that we add up all the risks, benefits, and costs of our actions. It asks that we not make decisions without considering all the risks, costs, and benefits. The point is that RCBA does not need to be perfect to be useful in societal and environmental decision making; it needs only to be useful, helpful, and better than other available methods for making societal decisions.

Second, criticisms of RCBA miss the point because they blame RCBA for a variety of ethical problems, mainly problems associated with utilitarianism. RCBA, however, is merely a formal calculus for problem solving. The users of RCBA are responsible for the capitalistic, utilitarian interpretation of it. If so, then what needs to be done is neither to abandon RCBA, nor to condemn it as utilitarian, but to give some philosophical lessons in the value ladenness of its interpretations. We need more ethical and epistemological sensitivity among those who interpret RCBA, and we need to recognize practical, political problems for what they are. The problem is with us, with our values, with our politics. The problem is not with RCBA methods that merely reflect our values and politics.

NOTES

1   Stuart E. Dreyfus, "Formal Models vs. Human Situational Understanding: Inherent Limitations on the Modeling of Business Expertise," *Technology and People* Vol. 1 (1982): 133–65.

2   S. Dreyfus, "Formal Models," op. cit., note 6, 161.

3   Peter Self, *Econocrats and the Polity Process: The Politics and Philosophy of Cost-Benefit Analysis* (London: Macmillan, 1975), 70; Alasdair MacIntyre, "Utilitarians and Cost-Benefit Analysis," in D. Scherer and T. Attig, eds., *Ethics and the Environment*, op. cit., note 7, 143–45; and Amory Lovins, "Cost-Risk-Benefit Assessment in Energy Policy," *George Washington Law Review* Vol. 45, no. 5 (August 1977): 913–16, 925–26. See also Robert Coburn, "Technology Assessment, Human Good, and Freedom," in K.E. Goodpaster and K.M. Sayer,

eds., *Ethics and Problems of the 21st Century* (Notre Dame: University of Notre Dame Press, 1979), 108; E.J. Mishan, *Cost-Benefit Analysis* (New York: Praeger, 1976), 160–61; Gunnar Myrdal, *The Political Element in the Development of Economic Theory*, Paul Steeten, trans. (Cambridge: Harvard University Press, 1955), 89; and A. Radomysler, "Welfare Economics and Economic Policy," in K. Arrow and T. Scitovsky, eds., *Readings in Welfare Economics* (Homewood, IL: Irwin, 1969), 89.

4   See K.S. Shrader-Frechette, *Science, Policy, Ethics, and Economic Methodology* (Boston: Reidel, 1985), 38–54. See also K.S. Shrader-Frechette, *Risk and Rationality* (Berkeley: University of California Press, 1991), 169–96.

5   Mishan, *Cost-Benefit Analysis*, op. cit., note 10, 391.

6   Cited in V.C. Walsh, "Axiomatic Choice Theory and Values," in Sidney Hook, ed., *Human Values and Economic Policy* (New York: New York University Press, 1967), 197.

7   Lovins, "Cost-Risk-Benefit Assessment," op. cit., note 10, 929–30; Douglas MacLean, "Qualified Risk Assessment and the Quality of Life," in D. Zinberg, ed., *Uncertain Power* (New York: Pergamon, 1983), Part V; and Alan Gewirth, "Human Rights and the Prevention of Cancer," in D. Scherer and T. Attig, eds., *Ethics and the Environment*, op. cit., note 7, 177.

8   Amartya K. Sen, "Rawls versus Bentham," in N. Daniels, ed., *Reading Rawls* (New York: Basic Books, 1981), 283–92.

9   Ralph G. Keeney mentioned this to me in a private conversation at Berkeley in January 1983.

10 Patrick Suppes, "Decision Theory," in P. Edwards, ed., *Encyclopedia of Philosophy*, Vol. 1 and 2 (New York: Collier-Macmillan, 1967), 311.

11 R.M. Hare, *Moral Thinking* (Oxford: Clarendon Press, 1981), 6 (see also 210–11).

12 Ibid., 26.

13 Ibid., 4.

14 Ibid., 12–14.

15 Milton Friedman, "Value Judgments in Economics," in S. Hook, ed., *Human Values and Economic Policy*, op. cit., note 19, 85–88.

—38—

RECONCILING THE IRRECONCILABLE

The Global Economy and the Environment

Deborah C. Poff

FOR THE PAST DECADE, WE HAVE BEEN LISTENING to a number of inconsistent and irreconcilable recommendations for solving the serious economic and environmental problems in both domestic and international economies. Our current language with respect to the significant sea changes we have witnessed in the global economy over the past decade is filled with, to use that most appropriate euphemism of the 1980s, disinformation.

This discussion will focus on how the relationship among structural adjustment policies and practices, the business activities of transnational corporations and what Robert Reich has called "the coming irrelevance of corporate nationality" makes environmental sustainability impossible. To begin, a brief discussion of the global economy and its relation to the diminishing significance of national boundaries will set the context.

THE GLOBAL ECONOMY AND THE EROSION OF STATEHOOD

In their 1989 book, *For the Common Good*, Daly and Cobb argued that if Adam Smith were alive today, he would probably not be preaching free trade. Their argument is based on what they believe to have been a necessary commitment of the 18th century capitalist to a sense of community and to an identification with his own nationhood. On this point, Smith is perhaps most universally known. He states, "By preferring the support of domestic to that of foreign industry, he (i.e., the

capitalist) intends only his own security; and by directing that industry in such a manner as its produce may be of the greatest value, he intends only his own gain, and he is in this, as in many other cases, led by an invisible hand to promote an end which was no part of his intention" (Smith, 1776, 423). Daly and Cobb argue that the cornerstone of the free trade argument, capital immobility, that factored so strongly into Smith's belief that the capitalist was committed to investing in his or her own domestic economy has been eroded by

> A world of cosmopolitan money managers and transnational corporations which, in addition to having limited liability and immortality conferred on them by national governments, have now transcended those very governments and no longer see the national community as their residence. They may speak grandly of the "world community" as their residence, but in fact, since no world community exists, they have escaped from community into the gap between communities where individualism has a free reign. (Daly and Cobb, 215)

These capitalists, as Daly and Cobb rightly note, have no disinclination to move their capital abroad for the slightest favourable preferential rate of return. The concern which Daly and Cobb articulate here is frequently posed as a question or series of questions. For example, "with the globalization of the economy are we living in a world system in which national economies are merely vestigial remnants of modernity or the earlier industrial period?," or, "are nations as political and social regulatory systems necessary agents for global economic negotiation and cooperation?" And what we've had as answers to these questions is essentially political positioning in two oppositional camps. As MacEwan and Tabb (1989) summarize this debate,

> The extreme globalist position often carries the implication that no change is possible except on the international level, and since there is no political mechanism for such change—aside from that of formal relations among governments—oppositional political activity is easily seen as useless. On the other extreme, those who view the national economic system as a viable unit are led to formulate programs that ignore the importance of economic forces which transcend national boundaries. Such an outlook can lead to both unrealistic programs which fail because of capital's international flexibility and implicit alliances with reactionary nationalist groups to advocate, for example, increased "competitiveness." (24)

Now while I will later argue that both of these alternatives are inadequate. I'd like first to spend some time discussing how we've gotten into our current economic crisis and that means a brief sojourn into the world of structural adjustment, the world we have essentially been living in for much of the past decade.

STRUCTURAL ADJUSTMENT

I am going to address structural adjustment only as a consequence of the debt crisis and the stagnation and economic insecurity of the 1980s. Those familiar with the literature on the current economic crisis know that a complete picture starts with the Bretton Woods conference of 1944 which set guidelines for what was to become the International Monetary Fund and the International Bank for Reconstruction and Development (the

World Bank as it is now known). Bretton Woods also guaranteed the dominance of the United States in the world economy. As Jamie Swift notes, "the US dollar, linked to gold, would be the world's most important reserve currency and the United States effectively became banker to the Western world, with the right to print and spend the principal currency" (82). What ensued in the next forty plus years is too complex to examine here. It is sufficient to note that during that time, Japan and Germany rebuilt, the United States faced with a growing trade deficit and budget deficits abandoned the gold standard, and an unprecedented exchange of world currency as commodities ensued. This was followed by extensive loans to third world countries. And with those loans went conditionality, that conditionality being structural adjustment.

Structural adjustment as the salvation from national and international economic insecurity was a natural by-product of the Reagan-Thatcher-Mulroney era posited as it is on an idealized nineteenth-century laissez-faire. It comes from, as Foster (1989) notes, a "renewed faith in the rationalizing effect of market forces in the face of economic stagnation" (281).

Structural adjustment involves, in fact, a number of complementary actions, all mutually targeted to producing on a global scale, a so-called level playing field. These actions include privatization, deregulation and liberalization of national economies. Much of this is familiar to Canadians for this is precisely what the Canadian government has been pursuing in concert with the Canadian-American Free Trade agreement and with the North American Free Trade Agreement. The impact of structural adjustment it is assumed will remove the supposed artificial obstacles and allow for the rational correction of the current crisis by removing the obstructions to natural market forces. Part of adjusting to create a level playing field, however, means, to quote Rosenberg (1986) "a weakened, restructured labour force with lowered expectations" (as quoted in Foster, 281). Thus, part of the restructuring for global competitiveness has meant deregulating or decertifying unions in the United Kingdom, New Zealand and elsewhere in the developed world. In the developing world, it has meant devalued domestic currencies, high unemployment, increased poverty and starvation, inflation of the cost of living and, as a strategy for global competitiveness, the establishment of free trade zones within a number of these countries.

Furthermore, within the developing nations all of these factors have led to disproportionately increased poverty among women. This appears somewhat paradoxical given that much of this increase in poverty happened during the second half of the United Nations Decade for Women. However, since women are the poorest and most politically and economically vulnerable members of the global community (the UN 1980 data argued that women do two-thirds of the world's labour, earn one-tenth of the world's income and own one-one hundredth of the world's property), they also represent the largest so called surplus labour force. Hence we have the incongruity that while both nationally and internationally, more equity legislation was introduced into charters and constitutions and international agreements than ever before in recorded history, at the same time, the transnational corporations of advanced economies were utilizing the world's poor women as an avenue out of the stagnation of their own domestic economies by moving some of their operations to free trade zones. As Beneria (1989) states,

> The existence of a large pool of female labour at a world scale is being used to deal with the pressures of international competition, profitability crises, and economic restructuring that characterize the current reorganization of production. The availability of cheap female labour has also been an instrumental factor in the export-led policies of their world countries shifting from previous import-substitution strategies. (250)

The United Nations World Survey on Women (1989) concludes that "[t]he bottom line shows that, ... economic progress for women has virtually stopped, social progress has slowed, social well-being in many cases has deteriorated and, because of the importance of women's social and economic role, the aspirations for them in current development strategies will not be met" (xiv).

ENVIRONMENTAL SUSTAINABILITY

Having briefly outlined the parameters of structural adjustment, we can now ask: "What does it mean for environmental sustainability?" Well, if it is not already evident, any attempt to repay debts and remain competitive in such a global market under such conditions is almost impossible for a third world country and increasingly difficult for developed nations like Canada. To look first at the seemingly more favourable conditions in Canada, consider that environmental protection in developed nations like our own is only a relatively recent phenomenon. Snider (1993) argues that even within the boundaries of a nation state where a conflict arises between business interests and environmental protection, business wins. Thus, she states that both in Canada and the United States "environmental protection varies from poor to nonexistent, basically ... because of the power of business" (194). When we add to this the power of transnational corporations which take on supernumerary roles, traversing the globe and engaging in negotiations that change the quality of life and laws in various domestic economies, we begin to realize the resistance which any attempt to protect the environment meets. To again quote Snider with respect to the situation in Canada,

> As with occupational health and protection laws, provinces and countries fear they will be at a competitive disadvantage if they strengthen environmental regulations unilaterally. Industries have always tried to minimize the costs of operation by moving to the cheapest locations they can find. Free trade between Canada and the United States has often resulted in industries from Canada

and northern US states relocating to the less regulated south.... With an extension of the free trade agreement to Mexico, many can be expected to join the already extensive migration, ... taking advantage of cheap labour and lax environmental regulations there. (194)

In developing countries, the situation is exacerbated by the very nature of their so-called competitive edge as outlined by Snider (i.e., cheap labour, lax environmental regulations). The result of a heavy debt load, structural adjustment, and a radical change in the basis of domestic economies in third world nations guarantees that such nations cannot put the environment before economic survival. As Swift (1991) summarizes the problem,

> It is simply not possible to push the idea of sustainable development while insisting also on debt repayment, favourable access to minerals and agricultural resources for transnational corporations, and cuts in the public sector and lower levels of social spending by Third World governments. Such an economic model is bound to focus not on environmental safeguards but on achieving a better trade and payments balance—the kind of policy package known as "structural adjustment." The notion that the same ideologies of industrial growth that created the environmental crisis can bring about "sustainable growth" is, in the end, not only puzzling but also dangerous. (215–16)

The perversity of food-aid distribution over the past decade to countries where predictably famine follows deforestation and desertification and developed nation dogooders attempt to teach starving people in the third world modern farming methods to previously agrarian peoples who destroyed their environment cash-cropping for markets in the developed world, is sufficiently mind-boggling as to make us search for alternative, more coherent explanations to the problem. Essentially, we have here three cycles of activity. The first is the externally imposed requirement within a third

world country to move from traditionally agrarian subsistence farming to large-scale cash crop farming. This results in a cycle of famine. And this, in turn, results in foreign food-aid and the attempt by non-profit organizations from industrialized countries to bring modern agricultural farming methods to the famine-stricken area along with the food-aid as a means of eliminating starvation. The latter cycle is initially done in relative ignorance by well-intentioned individuals who are unaware that the cycle of famine was predictably engineered by previous development strategies. Rather, it assumed that there is an inability among poor nations to deal with what are believed to be natural disasters like famine in Ethiopia or flooding in Bangladesh. However, as Berlan (1989) notes these disasters are not caused by whims of nature. Nor are they caused by the ignorance of peoples who merely need instruction in ecological conservation. Rather, "Third World countries are caught up in a desperate and vicious process of destroying their natural resources simply to service debt and allow short-term survival" (222). And they are doing so because they have lost control of their domestic economy and of national self-governance. The environmental damage seems reminiscent and evocative. It brings to mind images of the pollution and environmental degradation which was endemic to the Industrial Revolution. The difference here is that the negotiations and damages incurred by development have been transnational in nature and have seemingly gone beyond the capacity of nation-states to effectively control. This is not just a difference in scale but a difference in kind. As Berlan summarizes the problem,

> Transnational companies are involved in all manner of hazardous ventures in Third World countries. They are building nuclear power plants, constructing massive dam projects, undertaking large mining and mineral-processing ventures, and investing in manufacturing that uses dangerous chemicals and produces hazardous wastes. In most Third World countries health and safety regulations

inside plants are either non-existent or weak. Environmental standards to govern industry are just starting to be taken seriously. Most Third World governments are so desperate to attract investment that companies are in a good position to reduce their costs by saving on expensive pollution controls and health and safety equipment for workers. (221–22)

Such radical shifts in power from national economies to transnational corporations and supranational monetary funds has led some intellectuals to embrace a new political cynicism and existential ennui captured by the general heading, postmodernism. David Harvey summarizes this state as a loss of faith in progress, science and technology and a total agnosticism with respect to any political or collective solutions. At least psychologically, if not epistemologically, this is similar to the political inertia noted at the beginning of this paper, the position of the extreme globalist which "carries the implication that no change is possible except on the international level, and since there is no political mechanism for such change—aside from that of formal relations among governments—oppositional political activity is easily seen as useless" (x).

THE REMNANT STATE?

This brings us to the final questions; "Do we have both conceptually and factually or descriptively an erosion of nationhood or statehood?" And, if so, "What does this mean for such global problems as environmental sustainability?"

Robert Reich (1991) argues that it is no longer meaningful to speak of nations in terms of national economies because the emerging global economy has rendered those economies irrelevant. He states,

As almost every factor of production—money, technology, factories, and equipment—moves effortlessly across borders, the very idea of an American economy is becoming meaningless, as are the notions of an American corporation, American capital, American products, and American technology. A similar transformation is affecting every other nation, some faster and more profoundly than others. (8)

This perspective is echoed in the discussion of national governance in the UN World Investment Report (1991). The report notes,

One of the trends highlighted in the present volume is the growing regionalization of the world economy. National economies are becoming increasingly linked in regional groupings, whether through initiatives at the political level, as in the case of the integration of the European Community, or through activities at the private-sector level…. As described in this report, regionalization is one of the important factors behind the recent growth of foreign direct investment and its growing role in the world economies. (40)

For those concerned with Canada's involvement in free trade agreements and the protection of Canada's natural resources in those agreements, the question of Canadian sovereignty is central. As Bienefeld (1991) notes with respect to financial deregulation, "the political content of financial regulation is usually entirely neglected when the multilateral agencies stress the importance of international regulation while advocating national deregulation even though this means giving up a large degree of autonomy in domestic ... policy" (50). To this, Easter (1992) adds "In Canada, our true sovereignty as a nation is being lost as we replace political debate and decision-making for community goals, with the absolute rule of the market…. Almost all ... [good policies] ... are now being lost or rendered useless under the 'competitiveness' and 'open borders'" (93).

But there is something to remain cognizant of when we look at the literature on the loss of national economic autonomy and sovereignty and that is that it is nations that are the key agents in negotiating deregulation, privatization and free trade deals. In the worst literature on the globalization of the economy it is as if Adam Smith's invisible hand had been replaced by the invisible man for all we hear about are global economic forces that require structural adjustments.

Nation states which, in liberal democracies, we view as protectors of basic rights, both positive and negative, and basic civil liberties are, in fact, involved in global negotiations which may erode the very principles on which they are based. And this not only affects rights meant to ensure the quality of life, including the right to live in a clean and sustainable environment, within given nations but also diminishes the possibility for the growth of democracy and democratic rights on a global scale. As Foster points out, "as each state makes its economy leaner and meaner to enlarge its own internally generated profits and export the crisis to others, the stress on the world economy intensifies, and international cooperation—always a dim possibility—becomes more remote" (294). Interestingly, as regional deprivation within developed economies more and more mirrors the economies in developing nations, we witness what we previously only saw in countries, like India, where prior to Bhopal, the prime minister of the country was willing to put jobs at any cost before anything else; safety, environment, quality of work life, etc. As we add the nations of the former Soviet Union to this mix, we observe with seeming fatalism the bottom-rung position which both environmental protection and quality of life issues take in the turmoil of establishing political and economic security.

Not only, however, do forward-looking principles of rights and benefits get undermined as nation after nation positions for a competitive advantage that results in levelling to the lowest common denominator, but global negotiation coupled with financial deregulation and the development of information technology has resulted in unbridled corruption and crime. As chief financial officer of the Bank of Montreal noted,

I can hide money in the twinkling of an eye from all of the bloodhounds that could be put on the case, and I would be so far ahead of them that there would never be a hope of unravelling the trail.... Technology today means that that sort of thing can be done through electronic means. (quoted in Naylor, 1987, 12)

In a related argument, Thomas (1989) claims that "the contradictory development of bureaucracy in the face of ideological assaults on the state ... includes a burgeoning growth of corruption, which has reached such staggering proportions that some social scientists see it as an 'independent productive factor'" (337).

With respect to the environment, this level of corruption coupled with desperation has been evidenced in the third world as nations vie for position to accept toxic waste from developed countries in contravention to international law.

So, does all of this mean that indeed the notion of statehood has shifted, diminished or been eroded? I would say unequivocally not. What has been eroded here is not statehood but democracy and the ability for citizens within democratic states to exercise democratic rights. Democracy has been undermined or subverted and people have been disempowered, but states have not. And this is not only true with respect to developed countries which have some type of democratic governance but it also bodes ominously for the establishment of new fledgling democracies. Not only is Canada less democratic to the extent that deregulation, privatization and economic liberalization has been accomplished, but to the extent that nations are willing to use such factors as economic bargaining chips, so is the possibility for democracy in other nations. With deregulation, privatization and economic liberalization, environmental sustainability becomes one more barrier to competitiveness, as do social programs and other quality of life indicators.

Assuming as I do that democracy is a good thing, what should be done about this? At the beginning of this paper, I pointed out what I thought were false alternatives, on the one hand extreme globalism that accepts the world defeat of nationhood and, on the other, naive nationalism which we encounter frequently in Canada these days as Canadians try to claw back Canada's social democracy from its recent demise. So, what's my solution? Well, it is not a new idea. Essentially all nations need to negotiate internationally from a position where they can set their own national priorities with respect to the social, political and economic needs of their citizens. This is something that increasingly has been given up even in nations like Canada where there is still the possibility of exercising collective political will. All nations have to negotiate from a position of national self-sufficiency. Transnational corporations have a political and undemocratic message that citizens in all nations have to be more competitive and that that is to be accomplished by dismantling national institutions, social programs and environmental protections. The fact that competitiveness without the protection of our natural resources, our infrastructure and social programs amounts to mass suicide is rarely considered. And what I am going to conclude with here may sound reminiscent of the cultural imperialism of a former era but it behooves those of us with the privilege to still resist global degradation and the erosion of basic rights and freedoms to do so and not allow our nations to bargain away the world. As Keynes noted in 1933,

The divorce between ownership and the real responsibility of management is serious within a country when, as a result of joint-stock enterprise, ownership is broken up between innumerable individuals who buy their interest today and sell it tomorrow and lack altogether both knowledge and responsibility towards what they monetarily own. But when this same principle is applied internationally, it is, in times of stress, intolerable—I am irresponsible towards what I own and those who operate what I own are irresponsible towards me. (193)

And the solution to the problem of divorce here is reconciliation rather than resignation and resistance to the false and alarming rhetoric of global greed that has benumbed our better sensibilities.

REFERENCES

Berlan, J.P. 1989, "Capital Accumulation, Transformation of Agriculture, and the Agricultural Crisis: A Long-Term Perspective," in *Instability and Change in the World Economy*.

Bienefeld, M. 1992, "Financial Deregulation: Disarming the Nation State," *Studies in Political Economy* 37, 31–58.

Daly, H. and J. Cobb. 1989, *For the Common Good: Redirecting the Economy toward Community, the Environment and a Sustainable Future* (Boston: Beacon Press).

Easeer, W. 1992, "How Much Lower Is Low Enough?" in J. Sinclair (ed.), *Crossing the Line* (Vancouver: New Star Books).

Foster, J.B. 1989, "The Age of Restructuring," in *Instability and Change in the World Economy*.

Keynes, J.M. 1933, "National Self-Sufficiency," in D. Moggeridge (ed.), *The Collected Writings of John Maynard Keynes*, Vol. 21 (London: Cambridge University Press).

MacEwan, A. and W. Tabb (eds.). 1989, *Instability and Change in the World Economy* (New York: Monthly Review Press).

Naylor, R. 1987, *Hot Money and the Politics of Debt* (Toronto: McClelland and Stewart).

Reich, R. 1991, *The Work of Nations: Preparing Ourselves for 21st Century Capitalism* (New York: Alfred Knopf).

Snider, L. 1993, *Bad Business: Corporate Crime in Canada* (Toronto: Nelson).

Swift, J. and the Ecumenical Coalition for Economic Justice. 1991, "The Debt Crisis: A Case of Global Usury," in J. Swift and B. Tomlinson (eds.), *Conflicts of Interest: Canada and the Third World* (Toronto: Between the Lines).

Swift, L. 1991, "The Environmental Challenge: Towards a Survival Economy," in *Conflicts of Interest: Canada and the Third World*.

Thomas, C. 1989, "Restructuring of the World Economy and Its Political Implications for the Third World," in A. MacEwan and W. Tabb (eds.), *Instability and Change in the World Economy* (New York: Monthly Review Press).

United Nations. 1989, *1989 World Survey on the Role of Women in Development* (New York: United Nations).

United Nations. 1991, *World Investment Report: The Triad in Foreign Direct Investment* (New York: United Nations).

Wood, R. 1989, "The International Monetary Fund and the World Bank in a Changing World Economy," in *Instability and Change in the World Economy*.

—39—

BUSINESS, ETHICS, AND GLOBAL CLIMATE CHANGE

Denis G. Arnold and Keith Bustos

IN YEARS PAST, THERE WAS SUBSTANTIAL DEBATE over the existence of global warming. Today, the debate is largely over. A consensus has emerged in the global scientific community that global climate change (GCC) is occurring and that it will have a dramatic and adverse impact on ecosystems, non-human species populations, and human populations.[1] In a recent review essay in *Ethics*, Stephen Gardiner notes that despite the fact that GCC is widely regarded by scientists, policy analysts, and politicians as an ethical issue, the philosophical literature on the ethics of GCC is surprisingly underdeveloped.[2] The primary subjects of ethical analysis identified by Gardiner are states, and the primary ethical issues he identifies are the fair distributions of burdens among states in reducing emissions.[3] However, what ethical obligations, if any, the business organizations that produce these emissions—either directly or indirectly—have regarding GCC is not addressed. This is not surprising, for the possibility that business organizations can have ethical obligations concerning GCC is almost entirely absent from the existing literature on the ethics of GCC.[4]

The organization of this essay is as follows. First, an overview and brief history of the discovery of GCC is provided. Second, the influential position that holds that free markets and responsive democracies relieve business organizations of any special obligations to protect the environment is explained. Next, five objections to this "free market

solution" to environmental problems, concerning GCC, are presented with special attention given to the transportation and electricity generation sectors' contribution to GCC. Finally, the ethical obligations of business in the transportation and energy sectors are identified with regard to their contribution to GCC, and preliminary policy recommendations are offered.

GLOBAL CLIMATE CHANGE

There is a vast amount of conflicting information concerning GCC available to anyone surfing the web, browsing headline articles in national newspapers, or scanning library collections. When trying to determine the scientific facts concerning GCC, it can be difficult to know which sources to trust. However, the most widely cited, peer-reviewed sources are the assessment reports produced by the Intergovernmental Panel on Climate Change (IPCC). In 1988, the IPCC was jointly established by the World Meteorological Organization (WMO) and the United Nations Environment Programme (UNEP) with the purpose of assessing the available scientific and socioeconomic information on climate change in order to provide expert advice to the Conference of the Parties to the United Nations Framework Convention on Climate Change. Since 1990, the IPCC has relied upon hundreds of expert scientists to produce a series of reports and papers that have become standard works of reference used by policy makers, scientists, and other agencies such as the Energy Information Administration (EIA), a division of the United States Department of Energy.[5]

Before getting to the IPCC's position on GCC, we should be clear about what factors contribute to this phenomenon. As solar radiation enters the Earth's atmosphere, atmospheric greenhouse gases (GHGs) (such as water vapor, carbon dioxide, methane, and others) trap some of this radiation as it travels back out of the atmosphere, retaining heat much like glass in a greenhouse. Even though water vapor is by far the most abundant greenhouse gas in the Earth's atmosphere, human activities have a negligible effect on the atmospheric concentrations of water vapor, and for this reason, it is not figured into national greenhouse gas emission inventories. Many of the GHGs (carbon dioxide, methane, nitrous oxide) are produced by both natural and anthropogenic processes, and there are natural mechanisms that remove significant amounts of GHGs from the atmosphere. However, anthropogenic emissions have increased the total concentration of GHGs beyond the Earth's natural capacity to remove these gases from the atmosphere. Of these GHGs, CO_2 (carbon dioxide) is the most abundant in the Earth's atmosphere due to burning fossil fuels. CO_2 is the most recalcitrant of the GHGs, since it does not decompose easily in the atmosphere (taking anywhere from 50–200 years to decompose). This means that a significant decrease in atmospheric CO_2 levels will not be realized for many years after anthropogenic CO_2 emissions drop. Incidentally, the US has ranked first in the world for CO_2 emissions for decades and has been responsible for about twenty-four percent of the total world CO_2 emissions for the past decade and is projected to hover between twenty-three percent and twenty-four percent until 2025.

According to the IPCC, approximately seventy-five percent of the atmospheric CO_2 stemming from human activity (world-wide) over the past twenty years is due to burning fossil fuel, and the other twenty-five percent is largely due to changes in land-use, mainly deforestation. Due to an increase in atmospheric concentrations of CO_2, "the globally averaged surface temperatures have increased by $0.6 \pm 0.2°C$ over the 20th century." Furthermore, the IPCC projects that "the globally averaged surface air temperature is projected ... to warm 1.4 to 5.8°C by 2100 relative to 1990." This warming trend is projected to continue at a rate of about 0.1 to 0.2 degrees Celsius per decade for the next few decades. The IPCC has also found evidence indicating that regional changes in temperature have already affected a variety of physical and biological systems world wide, such as shrinking glaciers, lengthening of mid to high-latitude growing seasons, poleward migration of plant and animal ranges, and declines of some plant and animal populations.

Generally speaking, an increase in average global temperatures is likely (sixty to ninety percent chance) to lead to altered weather patterns resulting in a greater risk of droughts (due to extreme drying) and floods (due to intense rainfall events) in many different regions, and the global mean sea level is projected to rise between 0.09 to 0.88 meters by 2100. Also, natural systems (such as coral reefs, mangroves, boreal and tropical forests, and prairie wetlands to name a few) are vulnerable to climate changes due to their inability to adapt to rapid environmental changes. Some of the more vulnerable species risk extinction, and the extent of damage or loss of biodiversity is sure to increase with the magnitude and rate of climate change.

The human systems that are highly susceptible to climate change are water resources, agriculture, forestry, fisheries, energy production, industry, insurance and other financial services, and human health (particularly a net increase in the geographic range of malaria and dengue). A nation's ability to cope with and adapt to climate change depends on such factors as wealth, available technology, education, access to information, skills, infrastructure, access to resources, and management capabilities. The most important thing to note is that the impacts of future climate changes will most likely be disproportionately borne by the world's poor.

As for the impact on the global financial sector, the extreme weather events anticipated to accompany climate change would increase actuarial uncertainty in risk assessment, which would result in increased insurance premiums or could possibly lead to the withdrawal of coverage in certain situations altogether. In either case, the need for government-funded compensation following natural disasters is sure to increase (particularly here in the US)....

THE MARKET "SOLUTION"

In his classic and widely reprinted essay "Money, Morality and Motor Cars" Norman Bowie takes on environmentalists who believe that businesses have special obligations to protect the environment.[6] Bowie is skeptical that an adequate defense of the environmentalist position has been mounted, and so he assumes the role of "devil's advocate" in arguing that businesses have no special obligation to protect the environment above and beyond what is required by law. Bowie begins by endorsing the commonly accepted principle that "no one has a right to render harm on another unless there is a compelling, overriding moral reason to do so."[7] He points out that this *prima facie* duty is commonly understood to apply to individual persons, not ecosystems, species, or even individual animals. Bowie next points out that when it comes to the manufacture and marketing of consumer goods, businesses must factor the cost of avoiding harm into the price of the product. He illustrates this claim with the example of automobiles. In 2003 there were 33,471 passenger fatalities in the US. Death is an obvious harm. When it comes to passenger safety, all cars are not created equal. Inexpensive cars typically have fewer safety features than more expensive cars. Customers who cannot afford to pay for safer, more expensive cars, buy inexpensive ones with comparatively few safety features. Other customers may prefer to pay more for a car that has particular engine performance or style qualities, despite the fact that it has a poor safety record. While still other consumers will emphasize safety as an overriding preference and purchase their vehicles from companies that emphasize safety such as the

Volvo division of Ford. If many automobile manufacturers emphasized safety in all their models, then on Bowie's analysis, consumers would not buy as many cars from those manufacturers and those automobile companies would lose money. Given the varied preferences of consumers, Bowie concludes that "an automobile company does not violate its obligation to avoid harm and hence is not in violation of the moral minimum if the trade-off between potential harm and the utility of the products rests on social consensus and competitive realities."[8]

Bowie then extends this analysis to the question of harm to the environment. He points out that consumers often rebuff businesses that embrace environmentally friendly practices. For example,

> The restaurant chain Wendy's tried to replace foam plates and cups with paper, but customers in the test markets balked. Proctor and Gamble offered Downey fabric softener in a concentrated form that requires less packaging than ready-to-use products; however the concentrate version is less convenient because it has to be mixed with water. Sales have been poor. Proctor and Gamble manufactures Vizar and Lenor brands of detergents in concentrate form, which the customer mixes at home in reusable bottles. Europeans will take the trouble; Americans will not. Kodak tried to eliminate its yellow film boxes but met customer resistance....[9]

Given this type of consumer behavior, Bowie concludes that legal harm to the environment caused by businesses is regarded as morally permissible by society. As such, he believes that "current legal activities by business organizations that harm the environment do not violate the avoid-harm criterion."[10]

In cases of market failure, where citizens recognize that their individual preference satisfaction is harming the environment in undesirable ways, Bowie points out that citizens in democracies have the ability to impose regulations to correct market failures. For example, when consumers purchase

SUVs and conventional automobiles, their use of those vehicles contributes to GCC. Citizens who choose to purchase such vehicles may nonetheless grant tax relief for purchasers of hybrid electric vehicles, thereby encouraging others to purchase low emission vehicles that contribute much less to GCC. Given the importance of this ability to correct for market failures, together with the fact that businesses justify their environmental practices by appealing to consumer preferences, Bowie concludes that businesses have an obligation to refrain from opposing the preferences of consumers regarding environmental protection.

Bowie does not explicitly take up the issue of GCC. However, it is not difficult to extrapolate the obligations of business with regard to GCC, at least in democracies, according to his analysis. These are, first, to obey the law. Second, to refrain from opposing the collective will of citizens as expressed through the legislative process and the law regarding GCC. Third, to respond to consumer demand regarding GCC. Businesses that do these things will have no ethical obligations regarding GHG emissions and GCC beyond those stipulated by law.

MARKET FAILURES AND ETHICAL OBLIGATIONS

Bowie's arguments have received surprisingly little criticism in the literature. However, there are serious difficulties with his defense of the market solution to environmental problems. In what follows we raise five of the most substantial objections, focusing in particular on the roles of business organizations in the transportation and electricity generation sectors regarding GCC.

Objection One: The Absence of Democracy

This objection has two parts. First, many of the nations in which MNCs conduct business lack important democratic institutions such as equal voting rights, multiple political parties, democratic elections, politically neutral militaries, and an independent judiciary. Thirty-eight percent of

the world's sovereign states and colonial units—home to forty-two percent of the world's population—have nondemocratic forms of government. Bowie's defense of the ethical obligations of business concerning the environment are conceptually incoherent when applied to MNCs that operate in nondemocratic nations. It is conceptually incoherent because in order to provide normative guidance it must assume the existence of democratic institutions where they do not exist. Second, the elevated GHG emissions that are permitted in the US will harm not merely US citizens, but the entire population of the planet. Yet the preferences regarding the potential harm to non-US citizens remain unaccounted for on Bowie's analysis. The fact that voters accept a particular level of harm does not make such harm morally legitimate. This might be the case if the harm is restricted to those who accept it, but GCC will not only affect US citizens, but the entire population of the planet and future generations of persons who cannot yet register their preferences in the market or in the political process. Yet the preferences regarding the potential harm to non-US citizens and future generations remain unaccounted for on Bowie's analysis.

Objection Two: The Roles of Consumers

It is unreasonable to believe that most consumers have an accurate understanding of the causes of global climate change, or an accurate understanding of the role of their own consumer choices regarding global climate change. With regard to complex environmental problems such as GCC, it is reasonable to conclude that most consumers lack an understanding of the causes of climate change, or its likely harm to their welfare and the welfare of future generations. However, the large businesses that dominate the transportation and electricity sectors of the global economy typically have a sophisticated understanding both of GCC, and the extent to which their own production, products, and services contribute to GCC. This sophisticated knowledge allows them to make changes regarding their practices, and to develop environmentally friendly products and services, which consumer preference satisfaction by itself could never achieve. Bowie cites examples of failed environmentally friendly initiatives on the part of businesses. However, as with any new product offering, marketing the initiative to consumers must be regarded as an important priority. And just as the marketing of a new toothpaste or soda flavor can be a failure, so too can the marketing of an environmentally friendly product. Not all environmentally friendly products will be successful. However, we should not become too cynical as a result of failed product launches. There are many examples of businesses that have brought environmentally friendly products to market successfully. And it is worth noting that despite modest initial resistance from consumers, Wendy's and nearly all fast-food restaurants have successfully switched from foam plates and cups to paper.

Objection Three: Consumer Choice

Bowie's analysis presumes that if businesses are to protect the environment above and beyond the law, it must be as a result of consumer preferences. However, there are two difficulties with this claim. First, consumer preferences are not always satisfied by businesses. For example, consumers who are concerned about GCC and wish to purchase hybrid electric vehicles (HEV) currently have few options. There are waiting lists for many HEV vehicles. But as automobile manufacturers are well aware, consumers purchase vehicles based on the ability of the vehicle to meet a variety of needs. Fuel efficiency and emissions may be important to a consumer, but so are things like passenger capacity, acceleration, and luxury qualities. At present there are no HEV minivans or HEV luxury sedans, so consumers who would prefer more environmentally friendly minivans or luxury sedans are left without options.

Second, consumers often have little or no influence with regard to the environmental practices of businesses. For example, a consumer who recognizes that coal-fired power plants emit harmful levels of GHGs into the atmosphere, may strongly prefer to purchase electricity from an energy provider that relies more on wind, solar, or hydroelectric energy sources. However, energy providers typically have a monopoly over consumers, so the consumer cannot take her business elsewhere. Furthermore, the consumer *qua* citizen typically has no direct way to regulate energy providers.

Objection Four: Harm to Others

As noted above, the impact of GCC will affect every person on Earth, and not merely the consumers of specific products or services. The atmosphere is a common resource, one that US consumers share with the global community. As Will Kymlicka and Henry Shue have argued, preferences typically entail a claim on resources.[11] The preference satisfaction of US consumers, for example, makes use of a per-capita disproportionate level of atmospheric resources. At the same time, the harm caused to present generations of non-US consumers will be disproportionate to their use of atmospheric resources. So too, presumably, will be the harm to future generations. These future persons will have preferences that require due consideration.[12] The mere preference satisfaction of present-day US consumers cannot by itself justify this harm to others.

Objection Five: Responsibility for the Past

A basic principle of justice holds that it is unfair to require others to pay for the costs of benefits one has secured for oneself without their uncoerced consent. Those who enjoy the benefits resulting from burning fossil fuels, and thereby contribute to GCC, ought to pay more for such benefits than those who do not enjoy such benefits. In the US the transportation sector and the electricity generation sector are the two most carbon intensive sectors, and thus the two sectors that contribute the most to the total US CO_2 emissions. The reason for these two sectors being so carbon intensive is due to their heavy dependence upon fossil fuel combustion. The transportation sector is more carbon intensive than the electricity generation sector because the former is almost completely dependent upon petro-fuels....

Given the transportation and electricity generation sectors' large contribution to GCC, it is reasonable to hold them accountable for the proportional harm to the atmosphere that they have caused historically. In particular, there are good reasons for holding them accountable for the impact of at least some of their GHG emissions on GCC to date.

THE WAY FORWARD

As we have seen, there is clear scientific evidence documenting the contribution of anthropogenic GHGs to climate change. Changes in the global climate are expected to produce chaotic and extreme weather events throughout the world. While we have a moral obligation to mitigate avoidable large-scale harm, it is important to note that there is no need to be immediately alarmed by the potential negative effects of GCC, for catastrophic effects will not begin to manifest for several decades and possibly not for a hundred years or so. However, we ought to still be concerned about GCC, as GHG emissions have been proven to exacerbate the onset of GCC. To draw an analogy for the sort of concern that we ought to have, consider the example of steering an ocean liner. If the captain spots an iceberg in the path of the liner a fair distance off, he would want to begin altering the course of his ship to avoid the obstacle. He would not order the ship to be turned sharply; instead he would order a gradual change in the course. Similarly, we need not radically alter our current business practices so as to immediately stop emitting GHGs (specifically CO_2); instead we need to begin altering business practices so as to gradually, and deliberately, reduce GHG emissions. Such a course of action calls for individual firms to start taking proactive measures to abate their CO_2 emissions....

POLICY IMPLICATIONS

How should we determine the appropriate level of GHG abatement? What would an appropriate abatement plan look like? What time frame should it have? The two extremes that set our boundaries are (1) do too little, and cause substantial harm to future generations; or (2) take drastic action too soon thus incurring unnecessary costs. It seems reasonable to suggest that we adopt a moderate approach, which means that if we are to avoid the predicted catastrophes related to GCC, then we need to reduce CO_2 emissions below 1990 levels within a few decades, and then continue to decrease CO_2 steadily thereafter. The long-term goal is to reduce CO_2 emissions to a small fraction of what they are today. The need to engage in aggressive, but not frantic, CO_2 abatement is due to the fact that this GHG has an atmospheric lifetime of 50–200 years. This means that even an aggressive plan of action will not reverse GCC, it will only stabilize it since the CO_2 we produce today can continue to contribute to GCC for up to 200 years into the future. So, we contend that business organizations that are responsible for substantial CO_2 emissions have a moral obligation to be engaged in aggressive proactive measures to abate their CO_2 emissions is deserving of disapprobation.

Before discussing what sort of punishments and incentives might be invoked to help business organizations comply with such a moral duty, it must be noted that we do not believe that merely complying with the current US regulations satisfies the duties of business organizations regarding GHG abatement and GCC mitigation. In order to avoid censure, a business organization must go beyond mere compliance, for current US legislation does not bode well for mitigating GCC.

The problem with determining the actual degree and type of proactive measures that a business organization must engage in, so as to meet this moral demand, is that there are numerous ways to go beyond compliance and still miss the mark. That is, just because a firm engages in beyond-compliance practices does not necessarily mean that it is doing all that it is morally obligated to do regarding GCC. Conversely, just because a business organization is guilty of a few environmental transgressions does not mean that it is failing to take appropriate action regarding GCC. Just as there are" shades of green" within the corporate world, there are also shades of brown....

The position that we have argued for is that individual business organizations are morally responsible for their contribution to GCC and the resulting harm. And, in order for firms to reduce their contribution to the harm that will inevitably befall persons in the future due to the extreme and chaotic weather events caused by GCC, they must take aggressive proactive measures to abate their respective CO_2 emissions. Ideally, this is a moral obligation that should be voluntarily embraced by individual firms. However, we realize that placing such a moral responsibility on firms may be too much to ask of them on their own, so we also call for the help of the government in abating industrial CO_2 emissions. Such governmental assistance would come in the form of imposing a tax on carbon emissions, and this expense can then be internalized by individual firms and incorporated in the price of their goods, thereby requiring consumers to bear a fair price for the pollution produced when manufacturing the goods that they consume. Also, the revenue generated from the carbon tax can be used to fund or subsidize further abatement measures so as to help the US reduce its contribution to GCC.

NOTES

1   Within popular discourse, global warming and global climate change are used interchangeably. However, these two terms refer to different but related issues. Specifically, as the average global temperatures rise due to an increase in greenhouse gas emissions, the elevated temperatures contribute to distinctive changes in the global climate patterns. The latter has been the focus of this paper. Refer to: Intergovernmental Panel on Climate Change, Climate Change 2001: Impacts, Adaptation, and Vulnerability (New York: Cambridge University Press, 2001), 3–17.

2   Stephen M. Gardiner, "Ethics and Global Climate Change," *Ethics*, 114 (April 2004), 555–600. This overview of the literature is highly recommended.

3   Henry Shue, "Environmental Change and the Varieties of Justice," in *Earthly Goods: Environmental Change and Social Justice*, eds. Fen Osler Hampson and Judith Reppy (Ithaca, NY: Cornell University Press, 1996), 9–29; Matthew Paterson, "Principles of Justice in the Context of Global Climate Change," in *International Relations and Global Climate Change*, eds. Urs Luterbacher and Detlef Sprinz (Cambridge, MA: Cambridge University Press, 2001); and Peter Singer, "One Atmosphere," in *One World: The Ethics of Globalization* (New Haven, CT: Yale University Press, 2002).

4   For example, while a special issue of *Business Ethics Quarterly* was devoted to "Environmental Challenges to Business," none of the eighteen essays published therein focuses on global climate change. See *Business Ethics Quarterly*, The Ruffin Series No. 2: "Environmental Challenges to Business," 2000. The most important exception to this rule is R. Edward Freeman, Jessica Pierce, and Richard H. Dodd, *Environmentalism and the New Logic of Business: How Firms Can Be Profitable and Leave Our Children a Living Planet* (Oxford: Oxford University Press, 2000).

5   Ibid.

6   Norman E. Bowie, "Money, Morality and Motor Cars," in W.M. Hoffman, R. Frederic, and E. Petry (eds.) *Business, Ethics, and the Global Environment* (New York: Quorum Books, 1990), 89–97.

7   Bowie, "Money, Morality and Motor Cars," 90.

8   Bowie, "Money, Morality and Motor Cars," 92.

9   Ibid., 93.

10 Ibid., 93.

11 Will Kymlicka, *Liberalism, Community, and Culture* (New York: Oxford University Press, 1989), 37–38; Henry Shue, *Environmental Change and the Varieties of Justice*, 9–29.

12 The importance of the preferences of future generations is sometimes said to require "discounting." We discuss this objection below.

—40—

THE DEEPWATER HORIZON OIL SPILL

Cyrlene Claasen and Tom McNamara

BACKGROUND

THE PETROLEUM INDUSTRY, ONE OF THE MOST profitable on the planet, is also one that is fraught with risk and danger. This became apparent on April 20, 2010, when the Deepwater Horizon, an oil rig operated by a company called Transocean under contract for British Petroleum (BP), exploded, caught fire and sank in the Gulf of Mexico. Eleven workers lost their lives and millions of barrels of oil spilled into the Gulf of Mexico over the course of 87 days, devastating marine life and damaging hundreds of miles of sensitive nearby coastline. It would turn out to be the biggest oil spill in US history.

BP realized immediately that they were the ones who would be ultimately held responsible in any legal judgements. The company set aside about $42 billion to cover the cost of cleanup, fines and compensation to victims, with $36 billion of this money already being paid out or assigned by February of 2013. In the immediate aftermath of the explosion, the US government forbade BP from bidding on any federal contracts and sought $21 billion in compensation for the environmental damage (according to the Clean Water Act, for each barrel of oil spilled a polluter can be fined the basic penalty of $1,100, or up to $4,300, depending on the degree of negligence).

Deep-sea drilling for oil, a highly technical and demanding task, has been going on for decades. The companies that engage in this type of activity have millions of hours of experience. So what exactly went wrong one mile below the surface of the ocean? The cause of the accident appears to have been an accumulation of errors and mistakes.

One of the major dangers associated with deep-sea drilling is "kicks," powerful disruptions experienced when a drill comes into contact with a pocket of natural gas. Ominously, Deepwater Horizon was experiencing an unusually large number of these kicks, but BP played down their risk. In order to diminish the threat from explosion, cement is applied to the outside of the bore piping used in the drilling. This is supposed to create a type of seal which prevents flammable gas from working its way back up the drill pipes. A second line of defense is something known as a blowout preventer, basically a giant pair of scissors that sits at the bottom of the ocean and is designed to cut the drilling pipe in the event of an explosion. In the case of Deepwater Horizon, both of these devices apparently failed. It is believed that the explosion was a result of the initial failure of the contracted company Halliburton to properly mix the cement supplied for the seal on the Gulf's floor. This was then compounded by a lack of care and diligence on the part of the rig operators, with the result of the explosion and catastrophic environmental disaster.

BP's actions afterwards also deserve scrutiny. The company claimed that about 1,000 barrels of oil per day were flowing into the Gulf of Mexico. Later a government scientist estimated the flow at nearly 5,000 barrels, but said he could not vouch for the accuracy of that figure. Complicating matters further, BP's response included using a highly toxic chemical, Corexit, in the cleanup of the Gulf. Corexit contains five chemicals associated with cancer, 10 chemicals that may be harmful to the kidneys, as well as other potentially dangerous chemicals; it is said to be 50 times more toxic than oil itself. Sweden and the United Kingdom (where BP is based) have banned Corexit. 771,000 gallons (2,900,000 L) of this chemical dispersant were injected into the flow of oil near the seafloor to break up oil droplets and cause them to disperse or sink to the seafloor. So, rather than waiting for the oil to rise to the surface and removing it with specialized equipment, BP flooded the Gulf with chemicals which, scientists say, poison coral reefs and other marine life. Not surprisingly, cleanup crews began complaining about health problems during their shifts, ranging from nausea and vomiting to dizziness and chest pains. The Government Accountability Project collected stories from BP cleanup crews, and blood tests confirmed that the majority of these whistleblowers had highly elevated levels of toxins in their blood. It is believed that there is a link between these illnesses, Corexit and petroleum exposure.

In response to these troubles, workers filed a class-action lawsuit against BP for damages associated with Corexit. Over 12,000 claims were included and to date, over 700 people have been compensated. In May 2010, the US Environmental Protection Agency (EPA) directed BP to switch to less-toxic dispersants but the company said that it could not find any suitable alternatives. The EPA has proposed rules that would strengthen standards for dispersants used in oil spill cleanups. This would allow the agency to "delist" certain dispersants that are highly toxic and require companies to find alternatives. The EPA has already received hundreds of comments on the rules, including industry opposition to any restrictions.

Five years after the disaster, wildlife is still struggling to rebound. A new report, released by the NWF, suggests that at least 20 species are still being affected by the spill. "This report, more so than any, shows that science is certain that this is a long-term problem," said Ryan Fikes, a scientist with NWF. "But it's going to take even more time to understand the true magnitude of this." In another scientific study, as part of an unusual mortality event investigation, a team of scientists has discovered that dead bottlenose dolphins stranded in the northern Gulf of Mexico since the start of the *Deepwater Horizon* oil spill have lung and adrenal lesions consistent with petroleum product exposure. While some phenomena in the Gulf—people getting sick, fishing nets coming back empty—are hard to pin conclusively on BP, experts say the signs of ecological and economic loss that followed the spill are deeply concerning for the future of the Gulf.

In January of 2013 BP pleaded guilty to manslaughter charges over the deaths of the 11 rig workers. It also agreed to a deal in which it would pay $4 billion in fines and penalties (at the time, a record) to the US Justice Department. None of these actions absolved the company of the civil claims it was facing from the federal government.

In September of 2014 a judge arrived at a ruling on the disaster. It was determined that BP would be assigned 67% of the blame, with the rig's owner Transocean getting 30% and Halliburton getting stuck with 3%. In the 153-page court decision, the presiding judge said that BP had shown negligence and was primarily concerned with making "profit-driven decisions" during the exploration activities that immediately preceded the deadly explosion. The ruling meant that BP was now liable for penalties under the Clean Water Act, which theoretically could add up to over $17 billion. In response, BP said that it would appeal the ruling.

In June of 2015 the US Supreme Court rejected BP's bid to have the 2014 ruling against it thrown out. Part of the company's argument was that it should not be held responsible for oil spilled due to equipment failure on a drilling rig that it did not own. For its part, in 2014, Transocean (the rig's owner) agreed to pay the US government $1 billion in fines and penalties for its role in the spill.

Finally, in July of 2015, BP announced that it had reached a settlement. The company said that it had agreed to pay a record $18.7 billion in damages to the US government and the five states directly affected by the spill (Alabama, Florida, Louisiana, Mississippi and Texas). The terms of the agreement give the company 18 years to pay out any monies related to civil claims and environmental restoration. BP's chief executive Mr. Bob Dudley said, "This is a realistic outcome which provides clarity and certainty for all parties" and that "this agreement will deliver a significant income stream over many years for further restoration of natural resources and for losses related to the spill."[1]

In the aftermath of the Deepwater Horizon oil spill, BP has tried to address its badly dented corporate image by ramping up its effort to convince consumers that life is returning to normal on the Gulf coast. The company has released public relation materials that highlight the Gulf's resilience, as well as a report compiling scientific studies that suggest the area is making a rapid recovery. However, affected communities are not in agreement with the company and its reassurances have done little to quell people's fear. Activists and residents of the area surrounding the Gulf of Mexico say that oil is still being found on beaches, on private land and in the water. They complain that in addition to having to deal with economic hardships and environmental damage, BP's insistence that everything is getting better and its numerous doubtful explanations merely act as salt on a not-yet-healed wound. For example, on Pointe à la Hache, about 45 minutes south of New Orleans, oystermen say their catches dropped after the spill, and have been decreasing ever since. BP shot back by saying that depleted oyster beds could be due to a variety of factors other than the spill—including the divergence of fresh water from the Mississippi into coastal marshes.

ANALYSIS

The BP oil spill raises many questions about environmental ethics and companies' responsibilities toward employees, nature and the communities and other stakeholders dependent on the natural environment for economic survival. Environmental ethics is the study of human interaction with nature. In a business situation, environmental ethics is concerned with a company's responsibility to protect the environment in which it operates.

Businesses have traditionally shown indifference towards the environment and environmental protection was seldom seen as a priority. People saw the natural world as a free and unlimited good which could be exploited without any morally significant harm done. Pollution could damage the environment, but the damage done was considered to be unimportant because the world was seen as such a large place. In recent decades, business leaders and policy makers have come to realize that resources aren't unlimited and to address the harms to people, animals, and ecosystems.

The petroleum industry repeatedly causes harm to the environment. Oil exploration and production involve risky processes but the industry thrives because it offers significant economic rewards. The industry is prone to what some describe as "incidents," especially in the drilling procedure. On the one hand there are accidents due to unanticipated malfunctions, failures, or side-effects of technological systems. On the other hand, there are those episodes which are a direct result of deliberate unethical and irresponsible behaviors that benefit the company at the expense of the environment, and the safety, health and even lives of employees.

BP has been found guilty of the latter—deliberate disregard of warnings that imminent danger was looming. According to various sources, immediately after the explosion, BP, the rig operator Transocean and the Obama administration were of the opinion that the disaster was an unpredictable event. However, interviews with workers, information gathered by researchers and testimony given to Congressional and Coast Guard hearings prove that there was in fact abundant evidence that an explosion could take place.

BP and its partners Transocean and Halliburton ignored the forewarnings without fearing much reprisal as the Mineral Management Service (MMS) of the Department of the Interior had long ago ceded all immediate and important regulatory control to the industry itself. The US Department of Labor's Occupational Safety and Health Administration (OSHA) and the Department of Environmental Protection (DEP) also regulate specific aspects of the industry but are said to be more reactionary than proactive in enforcing safety and environmental protection laws. The extent of self-regulation became obvious when Captain Nguyen, the co-chairman of the Coast Guard Inquiry questioned the rig safety measures, specifically regarding the blow-out preventers: "So my understanding is that it is designed to industry standard, manufactured to industry standard, installed by industry, with no government oversight of the construction or the installation. Is that correct?" Interior Department regulator Michael Saucier replied, "That would be correct."

Further, instead of taking responsibility for the 11 deaths and the inestimable damage caused to the environment, BP blamed Transocean (now the world's largest offshore drilling contractor). At the same time, numerous industry experts and fellow oil executives accused BP of cutting corners in order to save time and money. One of the concerns was that BP was not sufficiently reactive when its crew experienced continuous and repeated problems related to powerful "kicks" of surging gas, which, according to employees, resulted in the jobs falling behind schedule and costing BP millions of dollars in rental fees. During all of this the workers contended with stuck drilling pipes and broken tools. Moreover, the company used a well design that presented few barriers to high-pressure gas rising up, skipped a crucial $128,000 test of the quality of the cementing, and failed to install capping devices at the top of the well that could

also have prevented gas from lifting a critical seal. Chairman of the House Energy and Commerce Committee, Henry A. Waxman said that "BP has cut corner after corner to save $1 million here, a few hours or days there, and now the whole Gulf Coast is paying the price."

BP's negligence of failing to implement industry-wide safety standards against the loss of human life and extraordinary environmental damage is well-established. This case is also relevant to more controversial questions in business and environmental ethics. One question considers how societies should regulate potentially risky activities: in what circumstances should regulation be left to the industry and in what circumstances is government oversight required? As we saw above, industry determined and implemented rig safety measures with no government oversight. When pondering this question, we should keep in mind that government regulation can be costly and inefficient, especially in areas where considerable technological competence is required and that industry may be more likely to endorse voluntary standards.

Second, there are questions of corporate social responsibility and sustainability: what are the responsibilities of companies to the community and to the environment when there are risks of substantial damage? On the shareholder account of corporate social responsibility, a company has an obligation to follow the law and widely accepted industry standards, but no further obligations to take actions that might harm the bottom line. On stakeholder and sustainability accounts, BP's obligations to the community and environment might go considerably further. For example, the use of Corexit was approved by the United States Environmental Protection agency at the time BP chose to use it. Did BP have an obligation nonetheless to look for less toxic alternatives to the cleanup? Does BP have moral obligations beyond its legal settlements to remediate the environmental damage?

Critics of BP and other drilling and mining companies say that businesses need to invest more in safety, training and environmental remediation, rather than just trying to greenwash their operations by finding excuses for the harm caused. It is also argued that efforts should be made to make extraction operations less intrusive and more sustainable. Pressure to do so is mounting as human needs expand, the costs engendered by deteriorating ecosystems rise, and the environmental awareness of consumers increases. Companies, including BP already address environmental challenges by adopting techniques such as environmental auditing and corporate environmental reporting. BP says that since the 1970s, no major BP oil or gas project has moved forward until independent experts have assessed the environmental impact. According to the company, these reviews are thorough and look at potential problems and at the best ways to address them.

DISCUSSION QUESTIONS

1. BP was found responsible for the Deep Horizon oil spill. However, in the immediate aftermath of the disaster, the company blamed Transocean (the rig's owner) for the catastrophe. What were BP's arguments for this? What are some of the consequences of this denial of responsibility?

2. The petroleum industry is strongly involved in self-regulation. What are the reasons for this? Might this arrangement suit certain parties? Which are these? What are the consequences?

3. Do you think that it is BP's responsibility to reinvest in the environment since it already pays heavy taxes? Is this not the responsibility of the government?

4. Who pays for the loss of income of communities in areas affected by human-made disasters such as the Deep Horizon oil spill? Can this loss be measured? What are the implications for future generations?

5. Who are the actors involved in the Deep Horizon oil spill? Who has the power to assert their positions and stakes? Who has less or more power? Why?

NOTE

1 "BP Settles 2010 Gulf Oil Spill Claims with US States for Record $18.7bn" by Julia Bradshaw, *The Telegraph*, July 2, 2015. Accessed on July 2, 2015 at: http://www.telegraph.co.uk/finance/newsbysector/energy/oilandgas/11713507/BP-to-settle-2010-Gulf-oil-spill-claims-with-US-states.html.

FURTHER READINGS

Deepwater Horizon Study Group. (2011). "Final Report on the Investigation of the Macondo Well Blowout." Center for Catastrophic Risk Management, University of California at Berkeley. Accessed on July 1, 2015 at: http://ccrm.berkeley.edu/pdfs_papers/bea_pdfs/dhsgfinalreport-march2011-tag.pdf.

Kujawinski, E.B., Kido Soule, M.C., Valentine, D.L., Boysen, A.K., Longnecker, K., & Redmond, M.C. (2011). "Fate of Dispersants Associated with the Deepwater Horizon Oil Spill." *Environmental Science & Technology*, 45 (4), 1298–1306.

Smith, L.C., Smith, M., & Ashcroft, P. (2011). "Analysis of Environmental and Economic Damages from British Petroleum's Deepwater Horizon Oil Spill." *Albany Law Review*, 74 (1), 563–585.

Water, D. (2011). "The Gulf Oil Disaster and the Future of Offshore Drilling. Report to the President." https://www.gpo.gov/fdsys/pkg/GPO-OILCOMMISSION/content-detail.html.

RIGHTS AND OBLIGATIONS OF EMPLOYEES AND EMPLOYERS

INTRODUCTION

Anand J. Vaidya

ONE OF THE MOST BASIC RELATIONS IN THE BUSI-ness world is the relationship between an employer and an employee. Regarding this basic relationship, a pair of related ethical questions arises. What are the rights and obligations of employers with respect to their employees? Correspondingly, what are the rights and obligations of employees with respect to their employer? In this unit we focus on employment at will, whistleblowing, drug testing, and safety in the workplace.

Employment at will is the doctrine that employment is voluntary and of indefinite duration for both employers and employees. With regard to the employer, it means that the employer may release or fire an employee at any time for no reason whatsoever. What employment at will means is that an employer voluntarily offers work to an employee and consequently the employer may take it away at any time without having to offer a reason. Given that employment is a social good, the employment at will doctrine is ethically controversial. Job insecurity means there is a potential for exploitation. In a situation in which there are many people seeking work, the fact that an employer can simply discharge an employee for no reason may allow the employer to pay employees unjustly low wages or impose onerous work conditions.

Employment at will also means that the employee may leave work at any time. Although it is less common to talk of potentials for abuse by the employee, this is clearly possible. Consider a company that is working on a project which is due in two weeks. Suppose that one employee of the company has specialized skills which cannot be readily replaced from elsewhere. Further suppose that, without this employee, the project cannot continue. If this employee decides to suddenly leave the corporation during this crucial period, then the company would suffer a serious loss.

Another central topic is whistleblowing, the practice of outing a corporation for illegal or suspect practices of which the general public should have knowledge. One could, for example, blow the whistle on a car company for not meeting the safety standards required for motor vehicles, or on a company for filing false reports on their earnings, as occurred in the Enron scandal. The main ethical issues that surround whistleblowing have to do with what kinds of things one should blow the whistle on, and what steps should be taken *prior* to going public with information that could potentially discredit the company.

In general, most ethicists agree that if one suspects or has evidence that a company is acting irresponsibly or illegally, then one should first attempt to solve the problem through some internal channel, since this is both less destructive and, potentially, more efficacious. An employee not only has an obligation to the public to inform them of any irresponsible or intentional wrong doing on the part of the company, but also an obligation to not cause undue harm to the welfare of the company and its employees. In addition, employees have an obligation not to blow the whistle on a company unless the evidence they have reasonably shows that specific members are violating explicit policies of the corporation, are in violation of specific external ethical codes that regulate the corporation, or else are working against the welfare of the community at large. Because there is a potential for unfounded (or, even worse, malicious) whistleblowing, a person considering blowing the whistle must first take certain steps.

Personnel drug testing is an issue that arises in business, but also in the military, education, and athletics. The ethical question here is: What information about an employee or potential employee is an employer entitled access to? In choosing to hire an employee, is an employer entitled to know a candidate's political beliefs, sexual practices, personal habits, or religious beliefs? In choosing to promote, retain, and evaluate an employee, is an employer allowed to do so on the basis of information about the client's voting practices, eating habits, and extracurricular activities? The central issue is what kind of information is job-relevant. Many ethicists agree over the following principle. If a piece of information is not job-relevant, then an employer may not use it in choosing to hire, retain, promote, or evaluate an employee. The substantive question is whether a specific piece of information, such as drug use, is job-relevant.

One could argue that, for certain kinds of jobs, whether an employee uses drugs is simply job-irrelevant. For example, on the one hand commercial airplane pilots must undergo drug testing, since drugs affect pilot performance, and could put passengers at risk. On the other hand, mail clerks need not undergo drug testing, since drug use does not create risk. Alternatively, one might think that an employer has a *right* to know whatever they would like to know, regardless of the grounds. In addition, one might worry that the use of "job relevance" as a criterion in the argument may be too vague, insofar as it might allow for the possible justification of acquiring information about too many aspects of employees' lives, for example, their sleeping and eating habits.

Historically, one issue that has been of central importance for workers has been safety in the workplace. This issue becomes even more salient in a situation where there is a surplus of labor, and because of this, an employer could simply choose not to provide high enough safety standards in order to attract and retain employees. So, there is both a question of what are the minimal safety standards to which an employee is entitled, and a question about the grounds of this entitlement. It is sometimes claimed, for example, that workers could simply choose not to work at a sweatshop if they believe that the hours are too long and the safety standards and pay are too low. However, this claim fails to take into consideration the circumstances that bring about the possibility of sweatshop labor in the first place.

—41—
EMPLOYMENT AT WILL AND DUE PROCESS

Patricia H. Werhane and Tara J. Radin

THE PRINCIPLE OF EMPLOYMENT AT WILL (EAW) is a common-law doctrine that states that, in the absence of law or contract, employers have the right to hire, promote, demote, and fire whomever and whenever they please. In 1887, the principle was stated explicitly in a document by H.G. Wood entitled *Master and Servant.* According to Wood, "A general or indefinite hiring is prima facie a hiring at will."[1] Although the term "master-servant," a medieval expression, was once used to characterize employment relationships, it has been dropped from most of the recent literature on employment.

In the United States, EAW has been interpreted as the rule that, when employees are not specifically covered by union agreement, legal statute, public policy, or contract, employers "may dismiss their employees at will ... for good cause, for no cause, *or even for causes morally wrong,* without being thereby guilty of legal wrong."[2] At the same time "at will" employees enjoy rights parallel to employer prerogatives, because employees may quit their jobs for any reason whatsoever (or no reason) without having to give any notice to their employers. "At will" employees range from part-time contract workers to CEOs, including all those workers and managers in the private sector of the economy not covered by agreements, statutes, or contracts. Today at least 60% of all employees in the private sector in the United States are "at will" employees. These employees have no rights

to due process or to appeal employment decisions, and the employer does not have any obligation to give reasons for demotions, transfers, or dismissals. Interestingly, while employees in the *private* sector of the economy tend to be regarded as "at will" employees, *public* sector employees have guaranteed rights, including due process, and are protected from demotion, transfer, or firing without cause.

Due process is a means by which a person can appeal a decision in order to get an explanation of that action and an opportunity to argue against it. Procedural due process is the right to a hearing, trial, grievance procedure, or appeal when a decision is made concerning oneself. Due process is also substantive. It is the demand for rationality and fairness: for good reasons for decisions. EAW has been widely interpreted as allowing employees to be demoted, transferred or dismissed without due process, that is, without having a hearing and without requirement of good reasons or "cause" for the employment decision. This is not to say that employers do not have reasons, usually good reasons, for their decisions. But there is no moral or legal obligation to state or defend them. EAW thus sidesteps the requirement of procedural and substantive due process in the workplace, but it does not preclude the institution of such procedures or the existence of good reasons for employment decisions.

EAW is still upheld in the state and federal courts of this country, although exceptions are made when violations of public policy and law are at issue. According to the *Wall Street Journal*, the court has decided in favor of the employees in 67% of the wrongful discharge suits that have taken place during the past three years. These suits were won not on the basis of a rejection of the principle of EAW but, rather, on the basis of breach of contract, lack of just cause for dismissal when company policy was in place, or violations of public policy. The court has carved out the "public policy" exception so as not to encourage fraudulent or wrongful behavior on the part of employers, such as in cases where employees are asked to break a law or to violate state public policies, and in cases where employees are not allowed to exercise their fundamental rights, such as the rights to vote, to serve on a jury, and to collect worker compensation. For example, in one case, the court reinstated an employee who was fired for reporting theft at his plant on the grounds that criminal conduct requires such.[3] In another case, the court reinstated a physician who was fired from the Ortho Pharmaceutical Corporation for refusing to seek approval to test a certain drug on human subjects. The court held that safety clearly lies in the interest of public welfare, and employees are not to be fired for refusing to jeopardize public safety.[4]

During the last ten years, a number of positive trends have become apparent in employment practices and in state and federal court adjudications of employment disputes. Shortages of skilled managers, fear of legal repercussions, and a more genuine interest in employee rights claims and reciprocal obligations have resulted in a more careful spelling out of employment contracts, the development of elaborate grievance procedures, and in general less arbitrariness in employee treatment. While there has not been a universal revolution in thinking about employee rights, an increasing number of companies have qualified their EAW prerogatives with restrictions in firing without cause. Many companies have developed grievance procedures and other means for employee complaint and redress.

Interestingly, substantive due process, the notion that employers should give good reasons for their employment actions, previously dismissed as legal and philosophical nonsense, has also recently developed positive advocates. Some courts have found that it is a breach of contract to fire a long-term employee when there is not sufficient cause—under normal economic conditions even when the implied contract is only a verbal one. In California, for example, 50% of the implied contract cases (and there have been over 200) during the last five years have been decided in favor of the employee, again, without challenging EAW. In light of this recognition of implicit contractual obligations between employees and employers, in some unprecedented court cases *employees* have been held liable for good faith breaches of contract, particularly in cases of quitting without notice in the middle of a project and/or taking technology or other ideas to another job.

These are all positive developments. At the same time, there has been neither an across-the-board institution of due process procedures in all corporations nor any direct challenges to the *principle* (although there have been challenges to the practice) of EAW as a justifiable and legitimate approach to employment practices. Moreover, as a result of mergers, downsizing, and restructuring, hundreds of thousands of employees have been laid off summarily without being able to appeal those decisions.

"At will" employees, then, have no rights to demand an appeal to such employment decisions except through the court system. In addition, no form of due process is a requirement preceding any of these actions. Moreover, unless public policy is violated, the law has traditionally protected employers from employee retaliation in such actions. It is true that the scope of what is defined as "public policy" has been enlarged so that "at will" dismissals without good reason are greatly reduced. It is also true that many companies have grievance procedures in place for "at will" employees. But such procedures are voluntary, procedural due process is not *required*, and companies need not give any reasons for their employment decisions.

In what follows we shall present a series of arguments defending the claim that the right to procedural and substantive due process should be extended to all employees in the private sector of the economy.

EAW is often justified for one or more of the following reasons:

1. The proprietary rights of employers guarantee that they may employ or dismiss whomever and whenever they wish.
2. EAW defends employee and employer rights equally, in particular the right to freedom of contract, because an employee voluntarily contracts to be hired and can quit at any time.
3. In choosing to take a job, an employee voluntarily commits herself to certain responsibilities and company loyalty, including the knowledge that she is an "at will" employee.
4. Extending due process rights in the workplace often interferes with the efficiency and productivity of the business organization.
5. Legislation and/or regulation of employment relationships further undermine an already overregulated economy.

Let us examine each of these arguments in more detail. The principle of EAW is sometimes maintained purely on the basis of proprietary rights of employers and corporations. In dismissing or demoting employees, the employer is not denying rights to *persons*. Rather, the employer is simply excluding that person's *labor* from the organization.

This is not a bad argument. Nevertheless, accepting it necessitates consideration of the proprietary rights of employees as well. To understand what is meant by "proprietary rights of employees" it is useful to consider first what is meant by the term "labor." "Labor" is sometimes used collectively to refer to the workforce as a whole. It also refers to the activity of working. Other times it refers to the productivity or "fruits" of that activity. Productivity, labor in the third sense, might be thought of as a form of property or at least as something convertible into property, because

the productivity of working is what is graded for remuneration in employee-employer work agreements. For example, suppose an advertising agency hires an expert known for her creativity in developing new commercials. This person trades her ideas, the product of her work (thinking), for pay. The ideas are not literally property, but they are tradable items because, when presented on paper or on television, they are sellable by their creator and generate income. But the activity of working (thinking in this case) cannot be sold or transferred.

Caution is necessary, though, in relating productivity to tangible property, because there is an obvious difference between productivity and material property. Productivity requires the past or present activity of working, and thus the presence of the person performing this activity. Person, property, labor, and productivity are all different in this important sense. A person can be distinguished from his possessions, a distinction that allows for the creation of legally fictional persons such as corporations or trusts that can "own" property. Persons cannot, however, be distinguished from their working, and this activity is necessary for creating productivity, a tradable product of one's working.

In dismissing an employee, a well-intentioned employer aims to rid the corporation of the costs of generating that employee's work products. In ordinary employment situations, however, terminating that cost entails terminating that employee. In those cases the justification for the "at will" firing is presumably proprietary. But treating an employee "at will" is analogous to considering her a piece of property at the disposal of the employer or corporation. Arbitrary firings treat people as things. When I "fire" a robot, I do not have to give reasons, because a robot is not a rational being. It has no use for reasons. On the other hand, if I fire a person arbitrarily, I am making the assumption that she does not need reasons either. If I have hired people, then, in firing them, I should treat them as such, with respect, throughout the termination process. This does not preclude firing. It merely asks employers to give reasons for their actions, because reasons are appropriate when people are dealing with other people.

This reasoning leads to a second defense and critique of EAW. It is contended that EAW defends employee and employer rights equally. An employer's right to hire and fire "at will" is balanced by a worker's right to accept or reject employment. The institution of any employee right that restricts "at will" hiring and firing would be unfair unless this restriction were balanced by a similar restriction controlling employee job choice in the workplace. Either program would do irreparable damage by preventing both employees and employers from continuing in voluntary employment arrangements. These arrangements are guaranteed by "freedom of contract," the right of persons or organizations to enter into any voluntary agreement with which all parties of the agreement are in accord. Limiting EAW practices or requiring due process would negatively affect freedom of contract. Both are thus clearly coercive, because in either case persons and organizations are forced to accept behavioral restraints that place unnecessary constraints on voluntary employment agreements.

This second line of reasoning defending EAW, like the first, presents some solid arguments. A basic presupposition upon which EAW is grounded is that of protecting equal freedoms of both employees and employers. The purpose of EAW is to provide a guaranteed balance of these freedoms. But arbitrary treatment of employees extends prerogatives to managers that are not equally available to employees, and such treatment may unduly interfere with a fired employee's prospects for future employment if that employee has no avenue for defense or appeal. This is also sometimes true when an employee quits without notice or good reason. Arbitrary treatment of employees or employers therefore violates the spirit of EAW—that of protecting the freedoms of both the employees and employers.

The third justification of EAW defends the voluntariness of employment contracts. If these are agreements between moral agents, however, such agreements imply reciprocal obligations between the parties in question for which both are accountable. It is obvious that, in an employment contract, people are rewarded for their performance. What is seldom noticed is that, if part of the employment contract is an expectation of loyalty, trust, and respect on the part of an employee, the employer must, in return, treat the employee with respect as well. The obligations required by employment agreements, if these are free and noncoercive agreements, must be equally obligatory and mutually restrictive on both parties. Otherwise one party cannot expect—morally expect—loyalty, trust, or respect from the other.

EAW is most often defended on practical grounds. From a utilitarian perspective, hiring and firing "at will" is deemed necessary in productive organizations to ensure maximum efficiency and productivity, the goals of such organizations. In the absence of EAW unproductive employees, workers who are no longer needed, and even troublemakers, would be able to keep their jobs. Even if a business could rid itself of undesirable employees, the lengthy procedure of due process required by an extension of employee rights would be costly and time-consuming, and would likely prove distracting to other employees. This would likely slow production and, more likely than not, prove harmful to the morale of other employees.

This argument is defended by Ian Maitland, who contends,

> [I]f employers were generally to heed business ethicists and institute workplace due process in cases of dismissals and take the increased costs or reduced efficiency out of workers' paychecks—then they would expose themselves to the pirating of their workers by other employers who would give workers what they wanted instead of respecting their rights in the workplace.... In short, there is good reason for concluding that the prevalence of EAW does accurately reflect workers' preferences for wages over contractually guaranteed protections against unfair dismissal.[5]

Such an argument assumes (a) that due process increases costs and reduces efficiency, a contention that is not documented by the many corporations that have grievance procedures, and (b) that workers will generally give up some basic rights for other benefits, such as money. The latter is certainly sometimes true, but not always so, particularly when there are questions of unfair dismissals or job security. Maitland also assumes that an employee is on the same level and possesses the same power as her manager, so that an employee can choose her benefit package in which grievance procedures, whistleblowing protections, or other rights are included. Maitland implies that employers might include in that package of benefits their rights to practice the policy of unfair dismissals in return for increased pay. He also at least implicitly suggests that due process precludes dismissals and layoffs. But this is not true. Procedural due process demands a means of appeal, and substantive due process demands good reasons, both of which are requirements for other managerial decisions and judgments. Neither demands benevolence, lifetime employment, or prevents dismissals. In fact, having good reasons gives an employer a justification for getting rid of poor employees.

In summary, arbitrariness, although not prohibited by EAW, violates the managerial ideal of rationality and consistency. These are independent grounds for not abusing EAW. Even if EAW itself is justifiable, the practice of EAW, when interpreted as condoning arbitrary employment decisions, is not justifiable. Both procedural and substantive due process are consistent with, and a moral requirement of, EAW. The former is part of recognizing obligations implied by freedom of contract, and the latter, substantive due process, conforms with the ideal of managerial rationality that is implied by a consistent application of this common law principle.

NOTES

1   H.G. Wood, *A Treatise on the Law of Master and Servant* (Albany, NY: John D. Parsons, Jr., 1877), 134.

2   Lawrence E. Blades, "Employment at Will versus Individual Freedom: On Limiting the Abusive Exercise of Employer Power," *Colombia Law Review* 67 (1967), 1405, quoted from *Payne v. Western*, 81 Tenn. 507 (1384), and *Hutton v. Watters*, 132 Tenn. 527, S.W. 134 (1915).

3   *Palmateer v. International Harvester Corporation*, 85 Ill. App. 2d 124 (1981).

4   *Pierce v. Ortho Pharmaceutical Corporation*, 845 N.J. 58, 417 A.2d 505 (1980). See also Brian Hershizer, "The New Common Law of Employment: Changes in the Concept of Employment at Will," *Labor Law Journal*, 36 (1985), 95–107.

5   Ian Maitland, "Rights in the Workplace: A Nozickian Argument," in Lisa Newton and Maureen Ford, eds., *Taking Sides* (Guilford, CT: Dushkin Publishing Group), 1990, 34–35.

—42—

IN DEFENSE
OF THE CONTRACT AT WILL

Richard A. Epstein

THE PERSISTENT TENSION BETWEEN PRIVATE ordering and government regulation exists in virtually every area known to the law, and in none has that tension been more pronounced than in the law of employer and employee relations. During the last fifty years, the balance of power has shifted heavily in favor of direct public regulation, which has been thought strictly necessary to redress the perceived imbalance between the individual and the firm. In particular the employment relationship has been the subject of at least two major statutory revolutions. The first, which culminated in the passage of the National Labor Relations Act in 1935, set the basic structure for collective bargaining that persists to the current time. The second, which is embodied in Title VII of the Civil Rights Act of 1964, offers extensive protection to all individuals against discrimination on the basis of race, sex, religion, or national origin. The effect of these two statutes is so pervasive that it is easy to forget that, even after their passage, large portions of the employment relation remain subject to the traditional common law rules, which when all was said and done set their face in support of freedom of contract and the system of voluntary exchange. One manifestation of that position was the prominent place that the common law, especially as it developed in the nineteenth century, gave to the contract at will.

The basic position was set out in an oft-quoted passage from *Payne v. Western & Atlantic Railroad*:

> [M]en must be left, without interference to buy and sell where they please, and to discharge or retain employees at will for good cause or for no cause, or even for bad cause without thereby being guilty of an unlawful act per se. It is a right which an employee may exercise in the same way, to the same extent, for the same cause or want of cause as the employer.[1]

* * *

In the remainder of this paper, I examine the arguments that can be made for and against the contract at will. I hope to show that it is adopted not because it allows the employer to exploit the employee, but rather because over a very broad range of circumstances it works to the mutual benefit of both parties, where the benefits are measured, as ever, at the time of the contracts formation and not at the time of dispute. To justify this result, I examine the contract in light of the three dominant standards that have emerged as the test of the soundness of any legal doctrine: intrinsic fairness, effects upon utility or wealth, and distributional consequences. I conclude that the first two tests point strongly to the maintenance of the at-will rule, while the third, if it offers any guidance at all, points in the same direction.

I. THE FAIRNESS OF THE CONTRACT AT WILL

The first way to argue for the contract at will is to insist upon the importance of freedom of contract as an end in itself. Freedom of contract is an aspect of individual liberty, every bit as much as freedom of speech, or freedom in the selection of marriage partners or in the adoption of religious beliefs or affiliations. Just as it is regarded as prima facie unjust to abridge these liberties, so too is it presumptively unjust to abridge the economic liberties of individuals. The desire to make one's own choices about employment may be as strong as it is with respect to marriage or participation in religious activities, and it is doubtless more pervasive than the desire to participate in political activity. Indeed for most people, their own health and comfort, and that of their families, depend critically upon their ability to earn a living by entering the employment market. If government regulation is inappropriate for personal, religious, or political activities, then what makes it intrinsically desirable for employment relations?

It is one thing to set aside the occasional transaction that reflects only the momentary aberrations of particular parties who are overwhelmed by major personal and social dislocations. It is quite another to announce that a rule to which vast numbers of individuals adhere is so fundamentally corrupt that it does not deserve the minimum respect of the law. With employment contracts we are not dealing with the widow who has sold her inheritance for a song to a man with a thin mustache. Instead we are dealing with the routine stuff of ordinary life; people who are competent enough to marry, vote, and pray are not unable to protect themselves in their day-to-day business transactions.

Courts and legislatures have intervened so often in private contractual relations that it may seem almost quixotic to insist that they bear a heavy burden of justification every time they wish to substitute their own judgment for that of the immediate parties to the transactions. Yet it is hardly likely that remote public bodies have better information about individual preferences than the parties who hold them. This basic principle of autonomy, moreover, is not limited to some areas of individual conduct and wholly inapplicable to others. It covers all these activities as a piece and admits no ad hoc exceptions.

This general proposition applies to the particular contract term in question. Any attack on the contract at will in the name of individual freedom is fundamentally misguided. As the Tennessee Supreme Court rightly stressed in *Payne*, the contract at will is sought by both persons.[2] Any limitation upon the freedom to enter into such contracts limits the power of workers as well as employers and must therefore be justified before it can be accepted. In this context the appeal is often to an image of employer coercion. To be sure, freedom of contract is not an absolute in the employment context, any more than it is elsewhere. Thus the principle must be understood against a backdrop that prohibits the use of private contracts to trench upon third-party rights, including uses that interfere with some clear mandate of public policy, as in cases of contracts to commit murder or perjury.

In addition, the principle of freedom of contract also rules out the use of force or fraud in obtaining advantages during contractual negotiations, and it limits taking advantage of the young, the feeble-minded, and the insane. But the recent wrongful discharge cases do not purport to deal with the delicate situations where contracts have been formed by improper means or where individual defects of capacity or will are involved. Fraud is not a frequent occurrence in employment contracts, especially where workers and employers engage in repeat transactions. Nor is there any reason to believe that such contracts are marred by misapprehensions, since employers and employees know the footing on which they have contracted: the phrase "at will" is two words long and has the convenient virtue of meaning just what it says, no more and no less.

An employee who knows that he can quit at will understands what it means to be fired at will, even though he may not like it after the fact. So long as it is accepted that the employer is the full owner of his capital and the employee is the full owner of his labor, the two are free to exchange on whatever terms and conditions they see fit, within the limited constraints just noted. If the arrangement turns out to be disastrous to one side, that is his problem, and once cautioned, he probably will not make the same mistake a second time. More to the point, employers and employees are unlikely to make the same mistake once. It is hardly plausible that contracts at will could be so pervasive in all businesses and at all levels if they did not serve the interests of employees as well as employers. The argument from fairness then is very simple, but not for that reason unpersuasive.

II. THE UTILITY OF THE CONTRACT AT WILL

The strong fairness argument in favor of freedom of contract makes short work of the various for-cause and good-faith restrictions upon private contracts. Yet the argument is incomplete in several respects. In particular, it does not explain why the presumption in the case of silence should be in favor of the contract at will. Nor does it give a descriptive account of *why* the contract at will is so commonly found in all trades and professions. Nor does the argument meet on their own terms the concerns voiced most frequently by the critics of the contract at will. Thus, the commonplace belief today (at least outside the actual world of business) is that the contract at will is so unfair and one-sided that it cannot be the outcome of a rational set of bargaining processes any more than, to take the extreme case, a contract for total slavery. While we may not, the criticism continues, be able to observe them, defects in capacity contract formation nonetheless must be present: the ban upon the contract at will is an effective way to reach abuses that are pervasive but difficult to detect, so that modest government interference only strengthens the operation of market forces.

In order to rebut this charge, it is necessary to do more than insist that individuals as a general matter know how to govern their own lives. It is also necessary to display the structural strengths of the contract at will that explain why rational people would enter into such a contract, if not all the time, then at least most of it. The implicit assumption in this argument is that contracts are typically for the mutual benefit of both parties. Yet it is hard to see what other assumption makes any sense in analyzing institutional arrangements (arguably in contradistinction to idiosyncratic, non-repetitive transactions). To be sure, there are occasional cases of regret after the fact, especially after an infrequent but costly, contingency comes to pass. There will be cases in which parties are naive, befuddled, or worse. Yet in framing either a rule of policy or a rule of construction, the focus cannot be on that biased set of cases in which the contract aborts and litigation ensues. Instead, attention must be directed to standard repetitive transactions, where the centralizing tendency powerfully promotes expected mutual gain. It is simply incredible to postulate that either employers or employees, motivated as they are by self-interest, would enter routinely into a transaction that leaves them worse off than they were before, or even worse off than their next best alternative.

From this perspective, then, the task is to explain how and why the at-will contracting arrangement (in sharp contrast to slavery) typically works to the mutual advantage of the parties. Here, as is common in economic matters, it does not matter that the parties themselves often cannot articulate the reasons that render their judgment sound and breathe life into legal arrangements that are fragile in form but durable in practice. The inquiry into mutual benefit in turn requires an examination of the full range of costs and benefits that arise from collaborative ventures. It is just at this point that the nineteenth-century view is superior to the emerging modern conception. The modern view tends to lay heavy emphasis on the need to control employer abuse. Yet, as the passage from *Payne* indicates, the rights under the contract at will are fully bilateral, so that the employee can use the contract as a means to control the firm, just as the firm uses it to control the worker.

The issue for the parties, properly framed, is not how to minimize employer abuse, but rather how to maximize the gain from the relationship, which in part depends upon minimizing the sum of employer and employee abuse. Viewed in this way the private contracting problem is far more complicated. How does each party create incentives for the proper behavior of the other? How does each side insure against certain risks? How do both sides minimize the administrative costs of their contracting practices? ...

1. *Monitoring Behavior.* The shift in the internal structure of the firm from a partnership to an employment relation eliminates neither bilateral opportunism nor the conflicts of interest between employer and employee. Begin for the moment with the fears of the firm, for it is the firm's right to maintain at-will power that is now being called into question. In all too many cases, the firm must contend with the recurrent problem of employee theft and with the related problems of unauthorized use of firm equipment and employee kickback arrangements.... [The] proper concerns of the firm are not limited to obvious forms of criminal misconduct. The employee on a fixed wage can, at the margin, capture only a portion of the gain from his labor, and therefore has a tendency to reduce output. The employee who receives a commission equal to half the firm's profit attributable to his labor may work hard, but probably not quite as hard as he would if he received the entire profit from the completed sale, an arrangement that would solve the agency-cost problem only by undoing the firm....

The problem of management then is to identify the forms of social control that are best able to minimize these agency costs.... One obvious form of control is the force of law. The state can be brought in to punish cases of embezzlement or fraud. But this mode of control requires extensive cooperation with public officials and may well be frustrated by the need to prove the

criminal offense (including mens rea) beyond a reasonable doubt, so that vast amounts of abuse will go unchecked. Private litigation instituted by the firm may well be used in cases of major grievances, either to recover the property that has been misappropriated or to prevent the individual employee from further diverting firm business to his own account. But private litigation, like public prosecution, is too blunt an instrument to counter employee shirking or the minor but persistent use of firm assets for private business....

Internal auditors may help control some forms of abuse, and simple observation by coworkers may well monitor employee activities. (There are some very subtle tradeoffs to be considered when the firm decides whether to use partitions or separate offices for its employees.) Promotions, bonuses, and wages are also critical in shaping the level of employee performance. But the carrot cannot be used to the exclusion of the stick. In order to maintain internal discipline, the firm may have to resort to sanctions against individual employees. It is far easier to use those powers that can be unilaterally exercised: to fire, to demote, to withhold wages, or to reprimand. These devices can visit very powerful losses upon individual employees without the need to resort to legal action, and they permit the firm to monitor employee performance continually in order to identify both strong and weak workers and to compensate them accordingly. The principles here are constant, whether we speak of senior officials or lowly subordinates, and it is for just this reason that the contract at will is found at all levels in private markets....

In addition, within the employment context firing does not require a disruption of firm operations, much less an expensive division of its assets. It is instead a clean break with consequences that are immediately clear to both sides. The lower cost of both firing and quitting, therefore, helps account for the very widespread popularity of employment-at-will contracts. There is no need to resort to any theory of economic domination or inequality of bargaining power to explain at-will contracting, which appears with the same tenacity in relations between economic equals and subordinates and is found in many complex commercial arrangements, including franchise agreements, except where limited by statutes.

Thus far, the analysis generally has focused on the position of the employer. Yet for the contract at will to be adopted ex ante, it must work for the benefit of workers as well. And indeed it does, for the contract at will also contains powerful limitations on employers' abuses of power. To see the importance of the contract at will to the employee, it is useful to distinguish between two cases. In the first, the employer pays a fixed sum of money to the worker and is then free to demand of the employee whatever services he wants for some fixed period of time. In the second case, there is no fixed period of employment. The employer is free to demand whatever he wants of the employee, who in turn is free to withdraw for good reason, bad reason, or no reason at all.

The first arrangement invites abuse by the employer, who can now make enormous demands upon the worker without having to take into account either the worker's disutility during the period of service or the value of the worker's labor at contract termination. A fixed-period contract that leaves the worker's obligations unspecified thereby creates a sharp tension between the parties, since the employer receives all the marginal benefits and the employee bears all the marginal costs.

Matters are very different where the employer makes increased demands under a contract at will. Now the worker can quit whenever the net value of the employment contract turns negative. As with the employer's power to fire or demote, the threat to quit (or at a lower level to come late or leave early) is one that can be exercised without resort to litigation. Furthermore, that threat turns out to be most effective when the employer's opportunistic behavior is the greatest because the situation is one in which the worker has least to lose. To be sure, the worker will not necessarily make a threat whenever the employer insists that the worker accept a less favorable set of contractual terms, for sometimes the changes may be accepted as an

uneventful adjustment in the total compensation level attributable to a change in the market price of labor. This point counts, however, only as an additional strength of the contract at will, which allows for small adjustments in both directions in ongoing contractual arrangements with a minimum of bother and confusion....

2. *Reputational Losses.* Another reason why employees are often willing to enter into at will employment contracts stems from the asymmetry of reputational losses. Any party who cheats may well obtain a bad reputation that will induce others to avoid dealing with him. The size of these losses tends to differ systematically between employers and employees—to the advantage of the employee. Thus in the usual situation there are many workers and a single employer. The disparity in number is apt to be greatest in large industrial concerns; where the at-will contract is commonly, if mistakenly, thought to be most unsatisfactory because of the supposed inequality of bargaining power. The employer who decides to act for bad reason or no reason at all may not face any legal liability under the classical common law rule. But he faces very powerful adverse economic consequences. If coworkers perceive the dismissal as arbitrary, they will take fresh stock of their own prospects, for they can no longer be certain that their faithful performance will ensure their security and advancement. The uncertain prospects created by arbitrary employer behavior is functionally indistinguishable from a reduction in wages unilaterally imposed by the employer. At the margin some workers will look elsewhere, and typically the best workers will have the greatest opportunities. By the same token the large employer has more to gain if he dismisses undesirable employees, for this ordinarily acts as an implicit increase in wages to the other employees, who are no longer burdened with uncooperative or obtuse coworkers.

The existence of both positive and negative reputational effects is thus brought back to bear on the employer. The law may tolerate arbitrary behavior, but private pressures effectively limit its scope. Inferior employers will be at a perpetual competitive disadvantage with enlightened ones and will continue to lose in market share and hence in relative social importance. The lack of legal protection to the employees is therefore in part explained by the increased informal protections that they obtain by working in large concerns.

3. *Risk Diversification and Imperfect Information.* The contract at will also helps workers deal with the problem of risk diversification.... Ordinarily, employees cannot work more than one, or perhaps two, jobs at the same time. Thereafter the level of performance falls dramatically, so that diversification brings in its wake a low return on labor. The contract at will is designed in part to offset the concentration of individual investment in a single job by allowing diversification among employers *over time*. The employee is not locked into an unfortunate contract if he finds better opportunities elsewhere or if he detects some weakness in the internal structure of the firm. A similar analysis applies on the employer's side where he is a sole proprietor, though ordinary diversification is possible when ownership of the firm is widely held in publicly traded shares.

The contract at will is also a sensible private adaptation to the problem of imperfect information over time. In sharp contrast to the purchase of standard goods, an inspection of the job before acceptance is far less likely to guarantee its quality thereafter. The future is not clearly known. More important, employees, like employers, *know what they do not know*. They are not faced with a bolt from the blue, with an "unknown unknown." Rather they face a known unknown for which they can plan. The at-will contract is an essential part of that planning because it allows both sides to take a wait-and-see attitude to their relationship so that new and more accurate choices can be made on the strength of improved information. ("You can start Tuesday and we'll see how the job works out" is a highly intelligent response to uncertainty.) To be sure, employment relationships are more personal and hence often stormier than those that exist in financial markets, but that is no warrant for replacing the contract at will with a for-cause contract provision. The proper question is: will the shift in methods of control work a change for the benefit of both parties, or will it only make a difficult situation worse?

4. *Administrative Costs.* There is one last way in which the contract at will has an enormous advantage over its rivals. It is very cheap to administer. Any effort to use a for-cause rule will in principle allow all, or at least a substantial fraction of, dismissals to generate litigation. Because motive will be a critical element in these cases, the chances of either side obtaining summary judgment will be negligible. Similarly, the broad modern rules of discovery will allow exploration into every aspect of the employment relation. Indeed, a little imagination will allow the plaintiff's lawyer to delve into the general employment policies of the firm, the treatment of similar cases, and a review of the individual file. The employer for his part will be able to examine every aspect of the employee's performance and personal life in order to bolster the case for dismissal....

III. DISTRIBUTIONAL CONCERNS

Enough has been said to show that there is no principled reason of fairness or utility to disturb the common law's longstanding presumption in favor of the contract at will. It remains to be asked whether there are some hitherto unmentioned distributional consequences sufficient to throw that conclusion into doubt....

The proposed reforms in the at-will doctrine cannot hope to transfer wealth systematically from rich to poor on the model of comprehensive systems of taxation or welfare benefits. Indeed it is very difficult to identify in advance any deserving group of recipients that stands to gain unambiguously from the universal abrogation of the at-will contract. The proposed rules cover the whole range from senior executives to manual labor. At every wage level, there is presumably some differential in workers' output. Those who tend to slack off seem on balance to be most vulnerable to dismissal under the at-will rule; yet it is very hard to imagine why some special concession should be made in their favor at the expense of their more diligent fellow workers.

The distributional issues, moreover, become further clouded once it is recognized that any individual employee will have interests on both sides of the employment relation. Individual workers participate heavily in pension plans, where the value of the holdings depends in part upon the efficiency of the legal rules that govern the companies in which they own shares. If the regulation of the contract at will diminishes the overall level of wealth, the losses are apt to be spread far and wide, which makes it doubtful that there are any gains to the worst off in society that justify somewhat greater losses to those who are better off. The usual concern with maldistribution gives us situations in which one person has one hundred while each of one hundred has one and asks us to compare that distribution with an even distribution of, say, two per person. But the stark form of the numerical example does not explain how the skewed distribution is tied to the concrete choice between different rules governing employment relations. Set in this concrete context, the choices about the proposed new regulation of the employment contract do not set the one against the many but set the many against each other, all in the context of a shrinking overall pie. The possible gains from redistribution, even on the most favorable of assumptions about the diminishing marginal utility of money, are simply not present.

If this is the case, one puzzle still remains: who should be in favor of the proposed legislation? One possibility is that support for the change in common law rules rests largely on ideological and political grounds, so that the legislation has the public support of persons who may well be hurt by it in their private capacities. Another possible explanation could identify the hand of interest group politics in some subtle form. For example, the lawyers and government officials called upon to administer the new legislation may expect to obtain increased income and power, although this explanation seems insufficient to account for the current pressure. A more uncertain line of inquiry could ask whether labor unions stand to benefit from the creation of a cause of action for wrongful discharge. Unions, after all, have some skill in working with for-cause contracts under the labor statutes that prohibit firing for union activities, and they might be able to promote their own growth by selling their services to the presently nonunionized sector. In addition, the for-cause rule might give employers one less reason to resist unionization, since they would be unable to retain the absolute power to hire and fire in any event. Yet, by the same token, it is possible that workers would be less inclined to pay the costs of union membership if they received some purported benefit by the force of law without unionization. The ultimate weight of these considerations is an empirical question to which no easy answers appear. What is clear, however, is that even if one could show that the shift in the rule either benefits or hurts unions and their members, the answer would not justify the rule, for it would not explain why the legal system should try to skew the balance one way or the other. The bottom line therefore remains unchanged. The case for a legal requirement that renders employment contracts terminable only for cause is as weak after distributional considerations are taken into account as before....

CONCLUSION

The recent trend toward expanding the legal remedies for wrongful discharge has been greeted with wide approval in judicial, academic, and popular circles. In this paper, I have argued that the modern trend rests in large measure upon a misunderstanding of the contractual processes and the ends served by the contract at will. No system of regulation can hope to match the benefits that the contract at will affords in employment relations. The flexibility afforded by the contract at will permits the ceaseless marginal adjustments that are necessary in any ongoing productive activity conducted, as all activities are, in conditions of technological and business change. The strength of the contract at will should not be judged by the occasional cases in which it is said to produce unfortunate results, but rather by the vast run of cases where it provides a sensible private response to the many and varied problems in labor contracting. All too often the case for a wrongful discharge doctrine rests upon the identification of possible employer abuses, as if they were all that mattered. But the proper goal is to find the set of comprehensive arrangements that will minimize the frequency and severity of abuses by employers and employees alike. Any effort to drive employer abuses to zero can only increase the difficulties inherent in the employment relation. Here, a full analysis of the relevant costs and benefits shows why the constant minor imperfections of the market, far from being a reason to oust private agreements, offer the most powerful reason for respecting them. The doctrine of wrongful discharge is the problem and not the solution. This is one of the many situations in which courts and legislatures should leave well enough alone.

NOTES

1   *Payne v. Western Atl. RR*, 81 Tenn. 507, 518–19 (1884), overruled on other grounds, *Hutton v. Watters*, 132 Tenn. 527, 544, 179 S.W. 134, 138 (1915)....

2   Ibid.

—43—

EMPLOYEE VOICE IN CORPORATE GOVERNANCE

A Defense of Strong Participation Rights

John J. McCall

1. INTRODUCTION

Participative Management. "Employee Involvement." "Flattened Hierarchies." "Employee Voice." As these current buzzwords of management literature indicate, the topic of employee participation decision making has arrived in the US. Once a mantra of left-wingers that was inaudible in mainstream discussions of corporate governance, concern with employee participation promises to spread in the current economic and political climate. It is urged by former Clinton administration players (Labor Secretary Robert Reich and chief economist Laura D'Andrae Tyson), promoted as an essential element of the future American workplace by the blue ribbon "Dunlop Commission on the Future of Labor–Management Relations" and embraced by some labor readers. However, aside from a continuing few in academic circles (e.g., Marxist social scientists, philosophers and some devotees of the Critical Legal Studies movement), praise of employee participation is purely instrumental. Its entry into the mainstream is as a device for increasing labor productivity and/or for improving the competitiveness of US industry. In contrast to such views, this article argues that strong forms of employee participation should be recognized as a matter of right, as they have been for decades in Western Europe.

A few distinctions concerning rights will be helpful in understanding the thesis I wish to urge. First, a right, as understood here, involves a valid claim that some interest of an individual deserves protection. Such claims can be moral or legal. A legal right is one that is, explicitly or implicitly, contained in a given system of positive laws and the principles reflected by those laws. A moral right, on the other hand, is a protection for an individual's interest that is dictated by the principles and values of a moral system. Secondly, rights can be basic or derivative. They are basic when they are essential for treating individuals with dignity and respect. They are derivative when their validity rests on values that are more fundamental, values that the right is instrumental in achieving. For instance, some argue that a right to free speech is basic in that prohibiting freedom of speech cuts at the very heart of what it means to be an autonomous, reasoning person. A right to property, on the other hand, is usually understood as derivative, gaining its importance because it is instrumental in protecting other more fundamental goods such as autonomy or democracy. Thirdly, rights can either be already recognized within a society or they can be, to borrow Joel Feinberg's phrase, manifesto rights. It should be uncontroversial to note that a manifesto right could be a valid right, on that a particular society, even on its own professed values, ought to, but does not yet, acknowledge (e.g., universal suffrage in America at the turn of the century).

I want to argue that a strong form of employee participation is at least a derivative moral right. It is also obviously a manifesto right in the United States since that society does not as yet recognize workers as having a valid claim to a substantial share in workplace governance and decision-making authority.

In order to understand what I intend to argue, it will also be helpful to catalog some of the forms of employee participation that are possible. Participation can vary in scope and cover issues from the most mundane, shop-floor questions (e.g., coffee break scheduling) through mid-level decisions (hiring and firing) to the most far reaching upper-level issues (plant closures or relocations). It can be implemented through purely advisory mechanisms such as quality circles or through stronger mechanisms that confer actual control over decision making. Among the latter are works councils with powers to make and implement policy, Employee Stock Ownership Plans (ESOPS) where employees obtain voice as voting shareholders, and worker representation on corporate boards. Finally, participation in decision making by employees can be either direct, where the employees themselves make decisions about, for example, the distribution of work assignments within their own group, or it can be representative, for example, where the employees elect one or more of their number to serve on a works council.

I will argue that workers have a right to co-determine policy at all levels of the corporation. Hence, the argument will support at least employee-employer workplace committees and equal employee representation on corporate boards. In essence, I will be arguing for the adoption in the US of a model of employee participation in corporate governance along the lines of that found in some European nations.

2. DEFENSES

Employee participation rights can be defended on a number of grounds. Since the primary thrust of this paper is to respond to certain objections to these rights, I will merely sketch some of the defenses here.

A. Dignity

First, most approaches to morality that emphasize rights do so because their adherents believe that persons somehow have inherent value and should be treated with dignity. A long tradition explains that inherent value as deriving from the ability to deliberate rationally and choose freely how to live, that is, from autonomy. Traditional hierarchical patterns of work organization, of course, treat employees as anonymous and replaceable "human resources" that are to be "managed" for the goal of corporate profit. An authentic social commitment to the dignity and autonomy of individuals would challenge that tradition. Since we spend one-third to one-half of our adult lives at work, since our work experience influences the character of even our non-working hours and since work in our culture plays such a dominant role in defining us as individuals and in establishing our social worth, a commitment to dignity and autonomy should urge that workers have some ability to exercise control over their work lives. That control can only be more than token when it is possessed in amounts equal to that of management.

B. Fairness

Second, participation rights can be derived from modern Western moral norms that profess a commitment to the equal dignity of each person. While no social system could guarantee that all the interests of it members are accommodated, the commitment to equality requires that decisions affecting those interests, and especially decisions affecting important or basic interests, be made fairly. Clearly, many policy decisions made in corporations are capable of great impact on the most basic interests of workers. What more effective guarantee of fairness and accountability could there be than allowing workers to represent their own interests in the decision-making process? In order for that guarantee to be effective, however, the mechanism of participation must provide real authority. And, since a balanced and fair consideration of all interests is more likely when opposing parties have roughly equal institutional power, employees deserve an amount of authority that enables them to resist policies that unfairly damage their interests. That, of course, means a right to co-determine policy at all levels.

C. Self-Respect

Third, it is now a psychological commonplace that a person's sense of self-worth is largely conditioned by the institutional relationships she has and by the responses from others she receives in those relationships. Of course, in contemporary America, the development of both the division of labor and hierarchical authority structures leaves little room for most workers to exercise their autonomy or to feel that their opinions are influential. The frequent consequence of such work structures is worker burnout and alienation. Workers dissociate themselves from a major portion of their lives, often with the consequence of a sense of impotence and unimportance. However, these results are less likely when workers are given opportunities for autonomous action and for the exercise of judgment. Since participation in decision making can reaffirm the employees' sense of influence and self worth, there is a presumptive reason for implementing it in the workplace.

It should be noted that this defense of participation rights does not require that those rights be rights to co-determine policy. The concerns expressed by this defense could potentially be satisfied by forms of participation that were merely advisory, if those advisory mechanisms in fact increased employees' subjective sense of influence and self-worth. It is also worth noting, however,

that purely advisory mechanisms of participation carry the danger that workers, after an initial decrease in feelings of alienation, might become cynical about the real impact of the participatory structures. Cases of this abound in corporations that implemented quality circles without a strong commitment to altering traditional hierarchical and autocratic structures. The history of the General Foods Topeka plant's experiment with participation programs is a classic example (Zwerdling, 1980). These same points apply as well to the defenses of participation that follow immediately below.

D. Health

Fourth, if as was just suggested, contemporary work organization is an important cause of alienation, work may provide the stressors that lead to both physical and mental health problems. Some evidence indicates, however, that stress is inversely related to perceived control over one's work environment (Fletcher, 1991; Karasek and Theorell, 1990). Thus, if employees were granted some measure of control over workplace decisions, stress and attendant health difficulties might be reduced. In fact, data exist which show increased levels of work satisfaction when workers believe they are able to influence corporate policies. Additionally, there is evidence that employee voice in the workplace through participatory committees makes more effective regulatory initiatives aimed at health and safety (Rogers, 1995). Since health is a basic interest, there are presumptive reasons for programs, such as employee participation, that might reduce threats to it.

E. Democracy

Finally, some have argued that only by increasing citizens' sense of power over more local and immediate aspects of their lives will we be able to reverse trends toward voter apathy and disengagement from active participation in the political process, trends that so threaten the vitality of our democracy. Of course, the workplace is a prime example of the kind of environment where persons can learn lessons either of impotence or efficacy. Hence, participation mechanisms can be instrumental in protecting the health of democratic politics by encouraging people toward greater civic involvement.

This brief summary reveals strong presumptive grounds for extending a right to participate in corporate decision making. In terms of the categories identified above, such a right would be a derivative one grounded in moral values of fairness, autonomy democracy and utility (this last since, presumably, an increase in sense of self-worth and a decrease in alienation for large numbers of employees would mean an increase in collective welfare).

3. PROPERTY RIGHTS OBJECTIONS

While the foregoing arguments provide some support for a right to participate in corporate decision making, that support is only presumptive. That is, whether we ought to finally recognize such a right will depend on the strength of competing considerations.

Some objections to strong forms of worker participation arise from efficiency concerns. The most serious objections from a moral perspective, however, derive from property rights claims and it is on those that the remainder of this paper focuses.

The property objection presents a serious obstacle (at least rhetorically) to the acceptance of a manifesto right to strong employee participation. That objection asserts that extending to workers partial control over enterprise decisions is a violation of the corporate owners' property rights. Clearly, if property rights mean anything, they mean that the title holder has more or less exclusive rights to control the use of property. Of course shareholders might allow their agents, management, to introduce participatory schemes if that were a beneficial strategy. That, however, is a far cry from claiming that employees are entitled to participation as a matter of right. Since rights to private property are so central to the ideology of our culture, this objection has a rhetorical seriousness that threatens to undermine the presumptive grounds for participation.

Some reject this corporate property rights argument on the basis of a fact that was forcefully identified by Berle and Means over 50 years ago—in contemporary corporations, ownership is separated from control. Some might suggest that since owners have already ceded control to management, there is no conflict between shareholders' property rights and an employee share of decision making control.

We might do well to resist this conclusion as too hasty. While it is true that contemporary corporate forms separate owners from substantial control of their property, there are still a number of reasons why corporate property rights might be seen as in conflict with strong employee participation rights.

First, even if owners have ceded control, they arguably have done so under the assumption that management will act as their fiduciary and will promote the interests of shareholders alone. Some ongoing debates about corporate control and the agency problems of corporate structures indicate that there is a serious concern that management might not focus sufficiently on shareholder benefit and might instead opportunistically use their powers to promote their own financial gain. Thus, the mere separation of ownership and control does not necessarily make it any easier to defend mechanisms of participation, especially if those mechanisms might force corporate decisions to give more consideration to the interests of employees.

Second, one could imagine, as the law sometimes seems to, that the property is the corporation's and that management has a quasi-ownership right to control the corporate assets. Under this interpretation, the right to control decisions is still vested in another constituency whose interests are in potential conflict with the interests of employees. A defense of strong employee participation rights must still, then, confront a property rights objection.

However, before we accede to such an objection and allow private property rights to "trump" rights to co-determination, we need to ask about the status of private property rights themselves. While they are undoubtedly a permanent part of our moral landscape, we need to question whether they are basic or derivative and, if derivative, from what values do they acquire their importance?

Interestingly enough, private property has traditionally been justified by appeals to autonomy, democracy, fairness and utility. Private possession of property has been defended as providing the greatest incentive for people to work and invest, thus raising the total amount of economic activity and goods produced and, in turn, increasing the aggregate standard of living (utility). It has been described as the only approach that rewards labor properly because it allows one who "mixes his labor with nature" to enjoy the fruits of that labor (fair return). It has been urged as an external check on government abuse that protects democracy by providing a countervailing locus of power. And it has been presented as maintaining autonomy by allowing property owners to have a stable and secure material base that frees them from over-reliance on the largesse of others.

Whatever one thinks of these traditional defenses of private property, the important thing for our purposes is that they reveal property rights to be derivative rights that have the same moral foundations as do the manifesto right of employee participation. As a consequence, it will not be possible for opponents of participation rights to brush them aside by an appeal to owner's rights to control property. Before that conclusion can be drawn, further argument is necessary.

4. ADJUDICATING THE RIGHTS CONFLICT

What form must such further argument take? When two claimed rights rest on the same moral grounds, a theoretical defense for the priority of one over the other must show that the justifying values are more centrally at stake in the one taking priority. We must ask whether the values promoted by the property rights would be compromised seriously by allowing encroachment in order to sustain another person's competing right claim. Can it be shown that property will take priority over participation rights, that autonomy, fairness and utility are more jeopardized by granting participation rights than by denying them?

A. Autonomy

Certainly, there seems little threat to owners' autonomy from the marginal decrease in the owners' control over their property that would be required to recognize a workers' right to co-determine corporate policy. For even if workers were given a right to co-determination, owners still would have a large bundle of rights associated with share ownership. In addition to a significant right to control through voting privileges, and a representation of their interests by management, owners retain the ability to sell their shares. Further, the evidence indicates that a well-designed program of participation does no necessary damage to productivity or profitability. There is increasing empirical and theoretical evidence that employee participation either improves productivity and/or profitability or is at least neutral with regard to those. And, so, corporate property owners would still have the financial "cushion" of their investment. Since the autonomy promoting aspect of corporate share ownership is the greater economic independence and greater control over life-choices that such ownership provides, employee participation rights seem to pose no substantial threat to owners' autonomy.

However, even if, hypothetically, participation would cause decreases in share value, opposition to it based on owners' autonomy would have to argue that the lost autonomy due to decreases in share value exceeds the autonomy gained by giving workers a say in their workplace. Available evidence suggests that any negative impact is likely to be small and unlikely, therefore, to outweigh the substantial increase in employees' control over crucial parts of their lives. The change in property rights created by recognizing an employee right to co-determination, then, is an improbable source for an autonomy-based objection.

Note, however, that these last points admit the relevance of questions concerning the economic impact of participation in deciding on its status as a derivative right. If the economic consequences of participation were to be disastrous, the impact would befall owners and workers alike. Both depend on the viability of business enterprises for economic security and the control over one's life that such security provides. If firms were not productive and profitable, neither owners nor workers would gain in autonomy. In such a case, no autonomy argument for derivative participation rights would be convincing. The same analysis, of course, holds for any other derivative right defended on autonomy grounds, including the right to privately own productive enterprises. Happily, the evidence seems to indicate that neither the right to private property, properly constrained, nor a right to employee participation, properly designed, has these negative economic results. Nonetheless, close attention must be paid to how both rights are implemented in practice.

In spite of the preceding analysis, some would argue that even this marginal change in owners' property rights is not necessary for protecting employees. They would claim that neither autonomy nor fairness would be denied employees if we failed to grant a right to participate in corporate decision-making. According to some proponents of this perspective, corporations exist as a "nexus of contracts" where the parties to the contracts can freely negotiate whatever terms they are willing and able to pay for. Workers could, on this view, bargain for participation rights in the same way that they bargain for health benefits or paid vacation days. Thus, according to the argument, the competitive marketplace itself guarantees fair treatment and autonomy for workers. The fact hat workers do not possess participation rights shows not that their autonomy is jeopardized but only that they are not sufficiently interested

in co-determination to be willing to pay for the privilege.

A response to this argument requires that we investigate both the meaning of autonomy and the degree to which the actual labor market possesses the characteristics of the economists' ideal market, especially full knowledge of alternatives, mobility between alternatives and, of course, the existence of such alternatives.

It should be clear that the actual market either does or does not possess these ideal characteristics. If it does, we would expect to see a wage premium for workers who choose not to pay for co-determination rights. There seems no reason to suppose that such a wage premium exists, however. This is true whether one compares American workers without participation rights to either their European counterparts or their American counterparts with participation rights. Part of the problem, of course, will be the impossibility of isolating the effect of the innumerable variables that influence wages. One could argue, however, that there is reason to suspect that employees with participation rights have even better compensation packages than those without. Evidence shows that strong participation programs are often found among high wage workers (Buechtemann, 1993).

Some might suggest that the absence of a discoverable wage premium merely shows how little workers value participation. That flies in the face of numerous survey data (Adams, 1990; Freeman and Rogers, 1994; Witte, 1980) that show very significant interest in institutional representation for workers within the corporation (82 percent even of those workers who are opposed to unions in the Freeman and Rogers survey).

If, on the other hand, as the previous passage suggests, the labor market does not possess the characteristics of the economists' ideal market, the argument that competitive markets assure autonomy and fairness is seriously undermined. Under this assumption, the fact that the market does not force management to share control may suggest not that workers do not want participation but rather that employers possess more power at the bargaining table. There are reasons to believe that this inequality of bargaining does obtain. Usually, corporations can forego the employment of an individual worker more easily than that individual can forego his/her particular job. That should be a surprise to no one except those captured by the ideology of free markets.

This real imbalance of bargaining power in the labor market weakens the claim that strong participation rights are not needed to protect autonomy and fairness. However, even if the demand for labor exceeded the supply and even if the transaction costs for workers moving between jobs was low, the labor market would still not satisfy the criteria for an ideal market unless those other jobs presented real alternatives to the non-participatory job options. The current labor market in the United States, of course, does not provide many alternatives where employees have the right to co-determine policy.... The issue is not whether employees have the freedom to change jobs but the degree of control they have over their lives on the job.

This last point forces us to consider more carefully what we mean by autonomy and why we attach moral value to it. Autonomy is the ability to make reasoned choices about how to live one's life. It has as a necessary component some measure of control over important aspects of one's life (Dworkin, 1988). Real autonomy must involve more than merely the ability to accept or reject whatever offers are made by the marketplace or government or other persons. If autonomy meant only that, if it placed no constraints on the kinds of choices that a person might be forced to choose between, it would be difficult to account for its moral significance. For consider that if autonomy meant merely having choices, we would be forced to admit that an oppressive totalitarian regime respected autonomy if it permitted free emigration. Or for that matter, we would be forced to admit the same of the gunman who offers me the choice of "your money or your life." If autonomy is only the formal ability to make reasoned choices, then autonomy is a morally empty ideal.

Rather, for autonomy to be worthy of its moral import, it must require that the offers we can choose from do not place important human interests in jeopardy. It must, therefore, allow individuals some core level of control over their lives without having to pay for that control by sacrificing the conditions that constitute a decent human existence. In practice, then, an adequate analysis of autonomy cannot be separated from ideas about the elements that are constitutive of human good. This picture of autonomy presumptively suggests that, given the centrality of work in our lives, employees deserve to be able to jointly control those corporate policies that crucially affect them.

The alternative market picture of autonomy seems too weak by comparison. It believes that autonomy is sufficiently respected when formal freedom of contract is present in the marketplace. However, freedom of contract is valuable merely as one mechanism for helping to assure autonomy in its more full-bodied sense—the ability to exercise control over important aspects of life. To presume that freedom of contract takes precedence over a right to participate, also a mechanism aimed at assuring autonomy is to beg the question of this debate.

We can locate the circularity in the freedom of contract argument more precisely if we recognize that what is at issue here is not freedom of contract itself but the presupposed background conditions of the bargaining. The free contract argument implicitly accepts property rights as granting owners a sole right to direct corporate property. It then suggests that workers who wish some control in the corporation must purchase participation rights from employers, if the employers are willing to sell them. But, of course, this presupposed understanding of property is just what is in dispute between those who defend and those who reject employee participation rights. The debate is precisely over whether an analysis of autonomy will allow property rights to trump rights to participation.

Once this presupposition of the free contract argument is understood, we have to see that the argument provides no independent reasons for claiming that autonomy is sufficiently respected in the market. While it is true that such market freedom allows workers to purchase a right to participate, that is not the question. The question, rather, is whether the right to participate is one that should be guaranteed or merely one available for purchase in the marketplace. The real question, then, is what background entitlements we ought to establish as setting the context for freely negotiated contracts....

The argument that individual autonomy is adequately respected by the actual labor market is unconvincing. Rather, I would argue that autonomy is better promoted by extending participation rights to workers and marginally reducing current conceptions of corporate property owners' rights to control. With such an extension of participation rights, employees gain the ability to exert strong influence over decisions that can potentially have major impacts on their lives. Individual owners lose some theoretical amounts of control but do not have the value of their investment placed at seriously greater risk than would exist without participation (especially given the data on participation and productivity).Thus the individual owners may still retain the autonomy provided by the secure possession of a base of material wealth.

B. Fairness

A similar analysis may hold for the relative impact of participation and property rights on the shared foundational value of fairness. One could imagine an argument that with strong participation rights workers gain greater guarantees that their interests will be considered fairly, and individual owners retain rights over their corporate assets substantial enough to provide for a fair return on investment. At the very most, owners might suffer some loss of profits returned as dividends if workers were better able to protect their interests (e.g., by gaining more safety equipment). But in assessing the fairness of this, one could argue that workers with co-determination rights assure a fairer distribution of surplus revenue than would be the case under traditional arrangements where management alone determines the distribution.

The typical replies to this suggestion are that investors deserve the return either because they took the risk or because their investment created the enterprise. This, however, ignores the facts that employees face substantial risks at work and are also essential contributors to the enterprise. Neither risk exposure nor contribution, as we will see presently, will provide grounds sufficient for the claim that investors deserve sole rights to control.

Clearly, shareholders and employees are both necessary contributors to the enterprise; the absence of either would mean the corporation would cease to exist. Some might suggest, though, that, since they initiated the process that created the organization, shareholders deserve control over the enterprise. For most contemporary corporations, however, stockholders are not temporally prior participants in the organization. I would hazard that most stock now owned was obtained after the firm was actively involved in production. In any case, it is not clear that being temporally first in involvement with the organization would carry sufficient moral weight to justify exclusion of other contributors from a say in the operation of the firm. What seems more relevant is that the contributions of both constituencies are logically necessary for any production to occur.

As for risk, it is often suggested that shareholders, as the residual risk bearers, deserve greater control. Employees, it is claimed, have already been compensated for their risks by the wage they negotiated. This position, however, fails on a number of grounds. Employees face risks to life and health at work. These risks are differentially distributed across and within occupational categories. No evidence suggests, though, that there is a risk premium given to all whose work is more risky, as this position would imply.

Employees also face risks that the firm will lose money and that they will then be out of a job. While shareholders can diversify against such risk by owning a broad portfolio of stock, employees generally cannot have simultaneous careers in multiple corporations. Hence, there is reason for finding that employees, too, face significant economic risk in choosing to work for a given corporation.

More importantly, it is problematic to claim that employees have been compensated for their risk and efforts by their past wages. This claim ignores the importance of internal labor markets for understanding the economics of employment. Typically, workers, after some job-hopping while young, develop long-term relationships with firms. As workers stay in a firm's employment for longer periods, they gradually and increasingly make "investments" in the firm. Clearly, workers develop social attachments in their workplaces that are not easily replaced. They acquire firm specific skills that are not easily transferable nor as valuable in the external labor market as they are within the firm. They also typically gain seniority benefits (increased wages, first preference for new positions, greater opportunities for promotion, less exposure to layoffs when there are cyclic downturns in demand) and pension vesting. Given these firm-specific investments, it is not surprising that evidence indicates that the costs of being laid-off rise with the length of a worker's job tenure. Workers with all these investments are likely to have a difficult time matching their old income and benefits in a new job, especially since new jobs will often begin at the lowest seniority levels.

Recent economic and industrial relations analyses explain the presence of some of these internal job characteristics by pointing out the benefits firms achieve by structuring their internal labor market in these ways. Many of these practices serve to bond the worker to the firm by making quitting more expensive. Firms thus reduce the possible loss of hiring and training costs when a worker leaves voluntarily. Firms that increase wages or that increase the value of pension benefits over a worker's job tenure also solve problems associated with monitoring a worker's performance. If future earnings are likely to rise, firms create an incentive mechanism that decreases a worker's probability of slacking on the job while simultaneously decreasing the need for constant and costly performance monitoring. Since workers have more to lose if they are fired for insufficient performance, the frequency of monitoring may be reduced. Essentially, firms promise delayed, future compensation as a vehicle for achieving high productivity at reduced management costs. Thus, the longer workers remain with a firm, the more they have invested in their jobs.

These employee investments, however, are subject to predatory and opportunistic abuse by employers. The implicit bargain of higher future wages and/or benefits for current effort and loyalty to the firm is not an enforceable one. For instance, in recent cases, moneys invested in corporate pension funds on the basis of actuarial projections of future earnings of workers (so as to assure that pension benefits were based on wage levels just before retirement) were raided during hostile take-overs because of a technicality in pension law. After the takeover, employees lost substantial value in the expected pension. Similarly, in plant closings and layoffs, discharged workers are denied the implicitly promised future benefits. If we recognize, as economists and industrial relations specialists increasingly do, that the promise of higher wages and benefits in the future is part of an economic bargain that employers strike for their own benefit, it is very clear that employees have quite a bit at risk in the corporation. It is also clear that past wages and benefits cannot be seen as sufficient compensation for employees' effort and risk. The claim that they are sufficient treats labor markets as ordinary commodity markets. The above characteristics of internal labor markets, however, cannot be explained if the markets are viewed as simple commodity markets.

Thus, it does not seem that the value of fairness, whether it is understood as grounded in contribution or in risk, can provide easy theoretical grounds for a claim that property rights "trump" the manifesto right of employees to co-determination. Rather, it seems that since risk and contribution are shared between owners and employees, then both ought to be able to exercise control over corporate decisions. That, of course, is tantamount to recognition of co-determination rights for employees.

Some, of course, will attempt to take a tack similar to that taken above with respect to autonomy. They argue that the interests of workers can be protected from unfair treatment by other mechanisms such as union negotiation or government regulation. If that is true, a concern for fairness does not demand that we recognize an employee right to co-determine corporate policy.

The proposed protective mechanisms, however, provide insufficient guarantees of fair treatment. Union power to bargain effectively has been seriously jeopardized by the increasing willingness of employers to follow President Reagan's example and hire permanent replacements. Thus the most effective weapon in the union arsenal has been rendered largely impotent. Employers are also increasingly resisting union organizing attempts with aggressive (and sometimes illegal) tactics. Further, the ability of unions to protect employees would apply only to a small fraction of the US workforce. Union membership is now in the low to mid-teens as a percentage of the total workforce.

Government regulatory protections appear somewhat more promising as a mechanism for guaranteeing worker interests are treated fairly. But even this is insufficient. Consider two government regulatory actions, OSHA rules and the Worker Adjustment and Retraining Notification Act (WARN).

According to one analysis, only "20 percent of all workplace accidents are covered by OSHA standards, which means ... that even full compliance by employers ... would produce only a modest reduction in employee injuries" (Weiler, 1990). Another recent report found that 75 percent of workplaces experiencing serious accidents in 1994 and the first four months of 1995 had not been inspected in the prior five years (Port and Solomon, 1995).

The much debated WARN Act tried to provide protection for employees from the costs of plant closings by requiring advance notice of closings and layoffs. A study by the General Accounting Office in 1993, however, found that businesses were exploiting significant loopholes in the law or merely ignoring its provisions. It also found that government enforcement was lacking in the extreme. According to the study, fully two-thirds of the employers covered by the Act failed to comply.

Similar stories can be told about much protective government regulation. Its enforcement is contingent on the direction of the political winds. The legislation writing and rule making process is ripe for influence by lobbyists seeking loopholes. Even the substantial fines that are sometimes possible are nearly always reducible on appeal. Government regulation is at best an insecure mechanism for protecting workers. It might supplement but cannot replace the greater self-protection powers provided when workers have co-determination rights. In fact, some suggest directly that participation rights are highly effective in improving the quality of regulatory programs (Rogers, 1995).

These difficulties with the usually proposed external protective mechanisms point to an ironic dilemma for those opposed to strong employee participation. If the corporation is understood along the lines of the traditional shareholder model as requiring management to maximize owners' wealth, then the need for mechanisms to protect employee interests becomes all that more important. Since the external mechanisms of union representation and government regulation are often ineffective, there is greater urgency to the moral arguments for strong participation. However, if the corporation is understood along the lines of a stakeholder model (where the corporation must be run in a way that respects the interests of all constituencies), then there is less reason for exclusive representation of owners in corporate governance, less basis for moral resistance to strong forms of employee participation....

5. CONCLUSION

The argument of this paper has been that an employee right to co-determine corporate policy has presumptive force. Its force is based on the very same values that have traditionally been used to support a right to private property. While the former right is not currently recognized, the moral commitments of the culture dictate that it ought to be. Such a recognition sets up a potential conflict between participation and property as it is now understood. I have argued that conflict should be resolved by asking which has the greater impact on the underlying values: rejecting the right to co-determination or marginally changing current understandings of corporate property rights. I have also argued both that the marginal change to property rights does least violence to those underlying values and that those who claim that participatory rights are unnecessary for achieving the underlying values are mistaken.

REFERENCES

Adams, George W. 1990. Worker Participation in Corporate Decision-Making: Canada's Future. Queen's Papers in Industrial Relations. Kingston, Ont.: Industrial Relations Centre.

Buechtemann, Christopher F. 1993. "Employment Security and Labor Markets." In *Employment Security and Labor Market Behavior*, ed. C. Buechtemann. Ithaca, N.Y.: ILR Press.

Fletcher, Ben C. 1991. *Work, Stress, Disease and Life Expectancy*. New York: John Wiley and Sons.

Freeman, Richard and Rogers, Joel. 1994. *Worker Representation and Participation Survey: A Report on the Findings*. Princeton N.J.: Princeton Survey Research Associates.

Karasek, Robert and Tores Theorell. 1990. *Healthy Work: Stress, Productivity, and the Reconstruction of Working Life*. New York: Basic Books.

Post, Bob and John Solomon. 1995. "More Than a Third of Union Complaints to OSHA Result in No Violations." *Associated Press*, September 6.

Rogers, Joel. 1995. "United States: Lessons from Abroad and Home." In *Works Councils*, ed. Joel Rogers and Wolfgang Streeck. Chicago: University of Chicago Press.

Weiler, Paul. 1990. *Governing the Workplace*. Cambridge, Mass.: Harvard University Press.

Zwerdling, Daniel. 1980. *Workplace Democracy*. New York: Harper and Row.

LIFESTYLES AND YOUR LIVELIHOOD

Getting Fired in America

David Meeler and Srivatsa Seshadri

BACKGROUND

DEBORAH HOBBS, WHO LIVED WITH HER boyfriend, was given three options by her boss: Get married, move out, or be fired. Lynne Gobbell put a John Kerry campaign sticker on her car and was given two options: Remove it or be fired. Boeing CEO Harry Stonecipher was fired for having consensual sex with another company executive. Employees at Weyco, Inc. lost their jobs when they refused to quit smoking after work. Michael Hanscom was fired from Microsoft and Ellen Simonetti was fired from Delta Airlines for pictures they posted on their personal websites. US Senate staffer Jessica Cutler lost her job for chronicling her off-hour sexcapades. In today's digital and confessional age, the message is clear: companies feel free to dictate and scrutinize appropriate personal behavior for their employees.

Before we get too outraged, we should note that many of these firings were probably legitimate. After several earlier scandals, Boeing's new CEO, Harry Stonecipher, hyped the company's new company policies as evidence of the kinds of progress Boeing had made to clean up its operations. Those same policies explicitly forbade intimate relationships between workers and superiors. Since Stonecipher's affair was with a woman over whom he had no direct supervision, the board concluded that he had not violated the letter of the code. However, given recent scandals, they felt many of the details and circumstances surrounding Stonecipher's affair indicated poor judgment, which impaired his ability to retain confidence and lead the company forward. Michael Hanson worked for Xerox under a contract with Microsoft, and was bound by nondisclosure agreements when he posted a photograph of Apple computers being offloaded at his Microsoft jobsite. Although he found it humorous, the photographs clearly violated the explicit policies governing his employment. Ellen Simonetti was happy to be a flight attendant, and in her personal blog-gallery she posted some photographs of herself in uniform and on a plane, in pin-up style poses. Although Ellen was fully clothed and Delta was never able to specify exactly which company policy she violated, the pictures can be seen to reflect poorly on Delta. Ellen represented Delta airline when she wore company attire in a public forum.

Like many other companies in America, Weyco was ostensibly concerned about its growing healthcare costs. But things are not always as they appear. As a former football coach, Howard Weyers, president of Weyco, brings his in-control, non-nonsense judgment to his management decisions. He was quoted in a New York Times article saying, "I spent all my life working with young men, honing them mentally and physically to a high performance. And I think that's what we need to do in the workplace.... You work for me, this is what I expect. You don't like it? Go someplace else."

It seems that whatever activities Howard doesn't approve of, his employees had better not engage in—even in the privacy of their own homes. At least Weyco can claim that firing employees who fail their random nicotine tests helps the company reduce healthcare costs.

Still, other of these cases are harder to justify. Lynne Gobbell's boss exercised his right to political speech by having pro-Bush flyers inserted into each employee's paycheck; but Lynne has no legal recourse after losing her job. Deborah Hobbs was faced with the consequences of a law initially passed in 1805 and that was ruled unconstitutional in 2006 after the ACLU sued to have it overturned. While Washington insiders expended great effort to deduce the identities of Jessica's lovers from clues in her blog, Ms. Cutler has kept the names of her lovers secret to this day. Little could be more personal than intimate sexual encounters, and being fired for chronicling your exploits seems intuitively unfair.

Perhaps it is most important to note that corporate intrusion into our off-the-clock lives is not a new phenomenon. By all accounts, Henry Ford was an innovative industrialist who brought prosperity and opportunity to hundreds of thousands of people. He is well known for implementing modern machine techniques in automobile production, but less well known for his social ideals. Henry Ford had no qualms about hiring immigrants and offered English classes to immigrant workers, and even started a nationwide phenomenon when he began hiring ex-convicts. Henry Ford was committed to bringing the benefits of an industrial society to everyone. The price of his cars actually went down year in and year out. Between 1910 and 1915, the price of Ford's *Model T* was reduced by more than half. At the same time, Ford paid his workers $5 a day—twice the average wage for an auto-worker. But Ford's benefits came with a price. The "Five Dollar Day" was split between wages and profit-sharing; and employees would get profits only after they were approved by Ford's "sociology department." One of the first requirements for the five dollar wage was fluency in English, combined with abandoning the customs of your native country and mandatory attendance at "community values" classes. Investigators from the sociology department checked on how clean the worker's home was, how personal finances were spent, whether alcohol or tobacco were being used (both of which were forbidden), church attendance, and even sexual habits. Ford didn't want anything to diminish his worker's capacity to be as efficient as possible.

ANALYSIS

The United Nations Declaration of Human Rights includes a right to privacy. While governments might not intrude into our private lives, employers are using their economic power to control our personal lives. How is it that companies can demand so much from their employees in the 9–5 world, and then dictate their personal behavior outside of work? The answer is quite simple: the vast majority of employees in the US are "at will." In brief, being employed "at will" means that you can quit your job at any time, for any reason. But it also means that you can be fired at any time, for almost any reason, including good reasons, bad reasons, or no reason at all. Unless you have an individual work contract or are governed by a collective bargaining agreement, you are an at-will employee. At-will employees can be hired, fired, demoted, promoted, transferred, etc., at any time so long as it is consistent with statutory law. Federally, there are a few grounds on which you cannot be fired. If you are fired on the basis of sex, religion, age, race, etc., then you have some legal recourse. But if you are fired because your cologne offends the boss, there is little you can do. Some states add other protections. For instance, five states have laws that forbid firing someone based on her political view or affiliations.

This trend is identified more broadly as "Lifestyle Discrimination." Most aspects of lifestyle discrimination are putatively tied to economics. Like Weyco, many companies look down on risky activities that are linked with increased costs.

As early as 1988 an Administrative Management Society survey revealed that approximately 6,000 companies in the US were discriminating against off-duty smokers. The ACLU suggests that discrimination against overweight employees is comparable.

DISCUSSION QUESTIONS

1. In your opinion, are any of the above firings ethical? Why or why not? Of those firings you think are unethical, what is unethical about them?
2. What recourse can an employee who was a victim of unethical (not illegal) conduct of the employer take against the ex-employer?
3. Suppose these employees had been asked by their employers to stop those behaviors, and given an opportunity to change. How do the arguments you put forth for Question 1 above change? In a case like Weyco's, would it make a difference if the employers offered financial assistance with a smoking-abatement program?

FURTHER READINGS

Barry, Bruce. 2007. "The Cringing and the Craven: Freedom of Expression in, around, and beyond the Workplace." *Business Ethics Quarterly* 17 (2): 263–96.

Byers, Shelbie J. 2007. "Untangling the World Wide Weblog: A Proposal for Blogging, Employment-at-Will, and Lifestyle Discrimination Statutes." *Val. UL Rev* 42.

Kirkland, Aaron. 2006. "You Got Fired on Your Day Off: Challenging Termination of Employees for Personal Blogging Practices." *UMKC L. Rev* 75.

—45—
WHISTLEBLOWING

Richard T. De George

WE SHALL RESTRICT OUR DISCUSSION TO A specific sort of whistleblowing, namely, *non-governmental, impersonal, external whistleblowing.* We shall be concerned with (1) employees of profit-making firms, who, for moral reasons, in the hope and expectation that a product will be made safe, or a practice changed, (2) make public information about a product or practice of the firm that due to faulty design, the use of inferior materials, or the failure to follow safety or other regular procedures or state of the art standards (3) threatens to produce serious harm to the public in general or to individual users of a product. We shall restrict our analysis to this type of whistleblowing because, in the first place, the conditions that justify whistleblowing vary according to the type of case at issue. Second, financial harm can be considerably different from bodily harm. An immoral practice that increases the cost of a product by a slight margin may do serious harm to no individual, even if the total amount when summed adds up to a large amount, or profit. (Such cases can be handled differently from cases that threaten bodily harm.) Third, both internal and personal whistleblowing cause problems for a firm, which are for the most part restricted to those within the firm. External, impersonal whistleblowing is of concern to the general public, because it is the general public rather than the firm that is threatened with harm.

As a paradigm, we shall take a set of fairly clear-cut cases, namely, those in which serious bodily harm—including possible death—threatens either the users of a product or innocent bystanders because of a firm's practice, the design of its product, or the action of some person or persons within the firm. (Many of the famous whistleblowing cases are instances of such situations.) We shall assume clear cases where serious, preventable harm will result unless a company makes changes in its product or practice.

Cases that are less clear are probably more numerous, and pose problems that are difficult to solve, for example, how serious is *serious* and how does one tell whether a given situation is serious? We choose not to resolve such issues, but rather to construct a model embodying a number of distinctions that will enable us to clarify the moral status of whistleblowing, which may, in turn, provide a basis for working out guidelines for more complex cases.

Finally, the only motivation for whistleblowing we shall consider here is moral motivation. Those who blow the whistle for revenge, and so on, are not our concern in this discussion.

Corporations are complex entities. Sometimes those at the top do not want to know in detail the difficulties encountered by those below them. They wish lower-management to handle these difficulties as best they can. On the other hand, those in lower management frequently present only good news to those above them, even if those at the top do want to be told about difficulties. Sometimes, lower-management hopes that things will be straightened out without letting their superiors know that anything has gone wrong. For instance, sometimes a production schedule is drawn up, which many employees along the line know cannot be achieved. Each level has cut off a few days of the production time actually needed, to make his projection look good to those above. Because this happens at each level, the final projection is weeks, if not months, off the mark. When difficulties develop in actual production, each level is further squeezed and is tempted to cut corners in order not to fall too far behind the overall schedule. The cuts may be that of not correcting defects in a design, or of allowing a defective part to go through, even though a department head and the workers in that department know that this will cause trouble for the consumer. Sometimes a defective part will be annoying; sometimes it will be dangerous. If dangerous, external whistleblowing may be morally mandatory.

The whistleblower usually fares very poorly at the hands of his company. Most are fired. In some instances, they have been blackballed in the whole industry. If they are not fired, they are frequently shunted aside at promotion time, and treated as pariahs. Those who consider making a firm's wrongdoings public must therefore be aware that they may be fired, ostracized, and condemned by others. They may ruin their chances of future promotion and security; and they also may make themselves a target for revenge. Only rarely have companies praised and promoted such people. This is not surprising, because the whistleblower forces the company to do what it did not want to do, even if, morally, it was the right action. This is scandalous. And it is ironic that those guilty of endangering the lives of others—even of indirectly killing them—frequently get promoted by their companies for increasing profits.

Because the consequences for the whistleblower are often so disastrous, such action is not to be undertaken lightly. Moreover, whistleblowing may, in some cases, be morally justifiable without being morally mandatory. The position we shall develop is a moderate one, and falls between two extreme positions: that defended by those who claim that whistleblowing is always morally justifiable, and that defended by those who say it is never morally justifiable.

WHISTLEBLOWING AS MORALLY PERMITTED

The kind of whistleblowing we are considering involves an employee somehow going public, revealing information or concerns about his or her firm in the hope that the firm will change its product, action, or policy, or whatever it is that the whistleblower feels will harm, or has harmed others, and needs to be rectified. We can assume that when one blows the whistle, it is not with the consent of the firm, but against its wishes. It is thus a form of disloyalty and of disobedience to the corporation. Whistleblowing of this type, we can further assume, does injury to a firm. It results in either adverse publicity or in an investigation of some sort, or both. If we adopt the principle that one ought not to do harm without sufficient reason, then, if the act of whistleblowing is to be morally permissible, some good must be achieved that outweighs the harm that will be done.

There are five conditions, which, if satisfied, change the moral status of whistleblowing. If the first three are satisfied, the act of whistleblowing will be morally justifiable and permissible. If the additional two are satisfied, the act of whistleblowing will be morally obligatory.

Whistleblowing is morally permissible if—

1. The firm, through its product or policy, will do serious and considerable harm to the public, whether in the person of the user of its product, an innocent bystander, or the general public.

Because whistleblowing causes harm to the firm, this harm must be offset by at least an equal amount of good, if the act is to be permissible. We have specified that the potential or actual harm to others must be serious and considerable. That requirement may be considered by some to be both too strong and too vague. Why specify "serious and considerable" instead of saying, "involve more harm than the harm that the whistleblowing will produce for the firm?" Moreover, how serious is "serious?" And how considerable is "considerable?"

There are several reasons for stating that the potential harm must be serious and considerable. First, if the harm is not serious and considerable, if it will do only slight harm to the public, or to the user of a product, the justification for whistleblowing will be at least problematic. We will not have a clear case. To assess the harm done to the firm is difficult; but though the harm may be rather vague, it is also rather sure. If the harm threatened by a product is slight or not certain, it might not be greater than the harm done to the firm. After all, a great many products involve some risk. Even with a well-constructed hammer, one can smash one's finger. There is some risk in operating any automobile, because no automobile is completely safe. There is always a trade-off between safety and cost. It is not immoral not to make the safest automobile possible, for instance, and a great many factors enter into deciding just how safe a car should be. An employee might see that a car can be made slightly safer by modifying a part, and might suggest that modification; but not making the modification is not usually grounds for blowing the whistle. If serious harm is not threatened, then the slight harm that is done say by the use of a product, can be corrected after the product is marketed (e.g., as a result of customer complaint). Our society has a great many ways of handling minor defects, and these are at least arguably better than resorting to whistleblowing.

To this consideration should be added a second. Whistleblowing is frequently, and appropriately, considered an unusual occurrence, a heroic act. If the practice of blowing the whistle for relatively minor harm were to become a common occurrence, its effectiveness would be diminished. When serious harm is threatened, whistleblowers are listened to by the news media, for instance, because it is news. But relatively minor harm to the public is not news. If many minor charges or concerns were voiced to the media, the public would soon not react as it is now expected to react

to such disclosures. This would also be the case if complaints about all sorts of perceived or anticipated minor harm were reported to government agencies, although most people would expect that government agencies would act first on the serious cases, and only later on claims of relatively minor harm.

There is a third consideration. Every time an employee has a concern about possible harm to the public from a product or practice we cannot assume that he or she makes a correct assessment. Nor can we assume that every claim of harm is morally motivated. To sift out the claims and concerns of the disaffected worker from the genuine claims and concerns of the morally motivated employee is a practical problem. It may be claimed that this problem has nothing to do with the moral permissibility of the act of whistleblowing; but whistleblowing is a practical matter. If viewed as a technique for changing policy or actions, it will be justified only if effective. It can be trivialized. If it is, then one might plausibly claim that little harm is done to the firm, and hence the act is permitted. But if trivialized, it loses its point. If whistleblowing is to be considered a serious act with serious consequences, it should be reserved for disclosing potentially serious harm, and will be morally justifiable in those cases.

Serious is admittedly a vague term. Is an increase in probable automobile deaths, from 2 in 100,000 to 15 in 100,000 over a one-year period, serious? Although there may be legitimate debate on this issue, it is clear that matters that threaten death are prima facie serious. If the threatened harm is that a product may cost a few pennies more than otherwise, or if the threatened harm is that a part or product may cause minor inconvenience, the harm—even if multiplied by thousands or millions of instances—does not match the seriousness of death to the user or the innocent bystander.

The harm threatened by unsafe tires, which are sold as premium quality but that blow out at 60 or 70 mph, is serious, for such tires can easily lead to death. The dumping of metal drums of toxic waste into a river, where the drums will rust, leak, and cause cancer or other serious ills to those who drink the river water or otherwise use it, threatens serious harm. The use of substandard concrete in a building, such that it is likely to collapse and kill people, poses a serious threat to people. Failure to x-ray pipe fittings, as required in building a nuclear plant, is a failure that might lead to nuclear leaks; this involves potential serious harm, for it endangers the health and lives of many.

The notion of serious harm might be expanded to include serious financial harm, and kinds of harm other than death and serious threats to health and body. But as we noted earlier, we shall restrict ourselves here to products and practices that produce or threaten serious harm or danger to life and health. The difference between producing harm and threatening serious danger is not significant for the kinds of cases we are considering.

2. Once an employee identifies a serious threat to the user of a product or to the general public, he or she should report it to his or her immediate superior and make his or her moral concern known. Unless he or she does so, the act of whistleblowing is not clearly justifiable.

Why not? Why is not the weighing of harm sufficient? The answer has already been given in part. Whistleblowing is a practice that, to be effective, cannot be routinely used. There are other reasons as well. First, reporting one's concerns is the most direct, and usually the quickest, way of producing the change the whistleblower desires. The normal assumption is that most firms do not want to cause death or injury, and do not willingly and knowingly set out to harm the users of their products in this way. If there are life-threatening defects, the normal assumption is, and should be, that the firm will be interested in correcting them—if not for moral reasons, at least for prudential reasons, viz., to avoid suits, bad publicity, and adverse consumer reaction. The argument from loyalty also supports the requirement that the firm be given the chance to rectify its action or procedure or policy before

it is charged in public. Additionally, because whistleblowing does harm to the firm, harm in general is minimized if the firm is informed of the problem and allowed to correct it. Less harm is done to the firm in this way, and if the harm to the public or the users is also averted, this procedure produces the least harm, on the whole.

The condition that one report one's concern to one's immediate superior presupposes a hierarchical structure. Although firms are usually so structured, they need not be. In a company of equals, one would report one's concerns internally, as appropriate.

Several objections may be raised to this condition. Suppose one knows that one's immediate superior already knows the defect and the danger. In this case reporting it to him or her would be redundant, and condition two would be satisfied. But one should not presume without good reason that one's superior does know. What may be clear to one individual may not be clear to another. Moreover, the assessment of risk is often a complicated matter. To a person on one level what appears as unacceptable risk may be defensible as legitimate to a person on a higher level, who may see a larger picture, and knows of offsetting compensations, and the like.

However, would not reporting one's concern effectively preclude the possibility of anonymous whistleblowing, and so put one in jeopardy? This might of course be the case; and this is one of the considerations one should weigh before blowing the whistle. We will discuss this matter later on. If the reporting is done tactfully, moreover, the voicing of one's concerns might, if the problem is apparent to others, indicate a desire to operate within the firm, and so make one less likely to be the one assumed to have blown the whistle anonymously.

By reporting one's concern to one's immediate superior or other appropriate person, one preserves and observes the regular practices of firms, which on the whole promote their order and efficiency; this fulfills one's obligation of minimizing harm, and it precludes precipitous whistleblowing.

3. If one's immediate superior does nothing effective about the concern or complaint, the employee should exhaust the internal procedures and possibilities within the firm. This usually will involve taking the matter up the managerial ladder, and, if necessary—and possible—to the board of directors.

To exhaust the internal procedures and possibilities is the key requirement here. In a hierarchically structured firm, this means going up the chain of command. But one may do so either with or without the permission of those at each level of the hierarchy. What constitutes exhausting the internal procedures? This is often a matter of judgment. But because going public with one's concern is more serious for both oneself and for the firm, going up the chain of command is the preferable route to take in most circumstances. This third condition is satisfied of course if, for some reason, it is truly impossible to go beyond any particular level.

Several objections may once again be raised. There may not be time enough to follow the bureaucratic procedures of a given firm; the threatened harm may have been done before the procedures are exhausted. If, moreover, one goes up the chain to the top and nothing is done by anyone, then a great deal of time will have been wasted. Once again, prudence and judgment should be used. The internal possibilities may sometimes be exhausted quickly, by a few phone calls or visits. But one should not simply assume that no one at any level within the firm will do anything. If there are truly no possibilities of internal remedy, then the third condition is satisfied.

As we mentioned, the point of the three conditions is essentially that whistleblowing is morally permissible if the harm threatened is serious, and if internal remedies have been attempted in good faith but without a satisfactory result. In these circumstances, one is morally justified in attempting to avert what one sees as serious harm, by means that may be effective, including blowing the whistle.

We can pass over as not immediately germane the questions of whether in nonserious matters one has an obligation to report one's moral concerns to one's superiors, and whether one fulfills one's obligation once one has reported them to the appropriate party.

WHISTLEBLOWING AS MORALLY REQUIRED

To say that whistleblowing is morally permitted does not impose any obligation on an employee. Unless two other conditions are met, the employee does not have a moral obligation to blow the whistle. To blow the whistle when one is not morally required to do so, and if done from moral motives (i.e., concern for one's fellow man) and at risk to oneself, is to commit a supererogatory act. It is an act that deserves moral praise. But failure to so act deserves no moral blame. In such a case, the whistleblower might be considered a moral hero. Sometimes he or she is so considered, sometimes not. If one's claim or concern turns out to be ill-founded, one's subjective moral state may be as praiseworthy as if the claim were well-founded, but one will rarely receive much praise for one's action.

For there to be an obligation to blow the whistle, two conditions must be met, in addition to the foregoing three.

4. The whistleblower must have, or have accessible, documented evidence that would convince a reasonable, impartial observer that one's view of the situation is correct, and that the company's product or practice poses a serious and likely danger to the public or to the use of the product.

One does not have an obligation to put oneself at serious risk without some compensating advantage to be gained. Unless one has documented evidence that would convince a reasonable, impartial observer, one's charges or claims, if made public, would be based essentially on one's word. Such grounds may be sufficient for a subjective feeling of certitude about one's charges, but they are not usually sufficient for others to act on one's claims. For instance, a newspaper is unlikely to print a story based simply on someone's undocumented assertion.

Several difficulties emerge. Should it not be the responsibility of the media or the appropriate regulatory agency or government bureau to carry out an investigation based on someone's complaint? It is reasonable for them to do so, providing they have some evidence in support of the complaint or claim. The damage has not yet been done, and the harm will not, in all likelihood, be done to the complaining party. If the action is criminal, then an investigation by a law-enforcing agency is appropriate. But the charges made by whistleblowers are often not criminal charges. And we do not expect newspapers or government agencies to carry out investigations whenever anyone claims that possible harm will be done by a product or practice. Unless harm is imminent, and very serious (e.g., a bomb threat), it is appropriate to act on evidence that substantiates a claim. The usual procedure, once an investigation is started or a complaint followed up, is to contact the party charged.

One does not have a moral obligation to blow the whistle simply because of one's hunch, guess, or personal assessment of possible danger, if supporting evidence and documentation are not available. One may, of course, have the obligation to attempt to get evidence if the harm is serious. But if it is unavailable—or unavailable without using illegal or immoral means—then one does not have the obligation to blow the whistle.

5. The employee must have good reason to believe that by going public the necessary changes will be brought about. The chance of being successful must be worth the risk one takes and the danger to which one is exposed.

Even with some documentation and evidence, a potential whistleblower may not be taken seriously, or may not be able to get the media or government agency to take any action. How far should one go, and how much must one try? The more serious the situation, the greater the effort required. But unless one has a reasonable expectation of success, one is not obliged to put oneself at great risk. Before going public, the potential whistleblower should know who (e.g., government agency, newspaper, columnist, TV reporter) will make use of his or her evidence, and how it will be handled. He or she should have good reason to expect that the action taken will result in the kind of change or result that he or she believes is morally appropriate.

The foregoing fourth and fifth conditions may seem too permissive to some and too stringent to others. They are too permissive for those who wish everyone to be ready and willing to blow the whistle whenever there is a chance that the public will be harmed. After all, harm to the public is more serious than harm to the whistleblower, and, in the long run, if everyone saw whistleblowing as obligatory, without satisfying the last two conditions, we would all be better off. If the fourth and fifth conditions must be satisfied, then people will only rarely have the moral obligation to blow the whistle.

If, however, whistleblowing were mandatory whenever the first three conditions were satisfied, and if one had the moral obligation to blow the whistle whenever one had a moral doubt or fear about safety, or whenever one disagreed with one's superiors or colleagues, one would be obliged to go public whenever one did not get one's way on such issues within a firm. But these conditions are much too weak, for the reasons already given. Other, stronger conditions, but weaker than those proposed, might be suggested. But any condition that makes whistleblowing mandatory in large numbers of cases, may possibly reduce the effectiveness of whistleblowing. If this were the result, and the practice were to become widespread, then it is doubtful that we would all be better off.

Finally, the claim that many people very often have the obligation to blow the whistle goes against the common view of the whistleblower as a moral hero, and against the commonly held feeling that whistleblowing is only rarely morally mandatory. This feeling may be misplaced. But a very strong argument is necessary to show that although the general public is morally mistaken in its view, the moral theoretician is correct in his or her assertion.

A consequence of accepting the fourth and fifth conditions stated is that the stringency of the moral obligation of whistleblowing corresponds with the common feeling of most people on this issue. Those in higher positions and those in professional positions in a firm are more likely to have the obligation to change a firm's policy or product—even by whistleblowing, if necessary—than are lower-placed employees. Engineers, for instance, are more likely to have access to data and designs than are assembly-line workers. Managers generally have a broader picture, and more access to evidence, than do nonmanagerial employees. Management has the moral responsibility both to see that the expressed moral concerns of those below them have been adequately considered and that the firm does not knowingly inflict harm on others.

The fourth and fifth conditions will appear too stringent to those who believe that whistleblowing is always a supererogatory act, that is always moral heroism, and that it is never morally obligatory. They might argue that, although we are not permitted to do what is immoral, we have no general moral obligation to prevent all others from acting immorally. This is what the whistleblower attempts to do. The counter to that, however, is to point out that whistleblowing is an act in which one attempts to prevent harm to a third party. It is not implausible to claim both that we are morally obliged to prevent harm to others at relatively little expense to ourselves, and that we are morally obliged to prevent great harm to a great many others, even at considerable expense to ourselves.

The five conditions outlined can be used by an individual to help decide whether he or she is morally permitted or required to blow the whistle. Third parties can also use these conditions when attempting to evaluate acts of whistleblowing by others, even though third parties may have difficulty determining whether the whistleblowing is morally motivated. It might be possible successfully to blow the whistle anonymously.

But anonymous tips or stories seldom get much attention. One can confide in a government agent, or in a reporter, on condition that one's name not be disclosed. But this approach, too, is frequently ineffective in achieving the results required. To be effective, one must usually be willing to be identified, to testify publicly, to produce verifiable evidence, and to put oneself at risk. As with civil disobedience, what captures the conscience of others is the willingness of the whistleblower to suffer harm for the benefit of others, and for what he or she thinks is right.

PRECLUDING THE NEED FOR WHISTLEBLOWING

The need for moral heroes shows a defective society and defective corporations. It is more important to change the legal and corporate structures that make whistleblowing necessary than to convince people to be moral heroes.

Because it is easier to change the law than to change the practices of all corporations, it should be illegal for any employer to fire an employee, or to take any punitive measures, at the time or later, against an employee who satisfies the first three aforementioned conditions and blows the whistle on the company. Because satisfying those conditions makes the action morally justifiable, the law should protect the employee in acting in accordance with what his or her conscience demands. If the whistle is falsely blown, the company will have suffered no great harm. If it is appropriately blown, the company should suffer the consequences of its actions being made public. But to protect a whistleblower by passing such a law is no easy matter. Employers can make life difficult for whistleblowers without firing them. There are many ways of passing over an employee. One can be relegated to the back room of the firm, or be given unpleasant jobs. Employers can find reasons not to promote one or to give one raises. Not all of this can be prevented by law, but some of the more blatant practices can be prohibited.

Second, the law can mandate that the individuals responsible for the decision to proceed with a faulty product or to engage in a harmful practice be penalized. The law has been reluctant to interfere with the operations of companies. As a result, those in the firm who have been guilty of immoral and illegal practices have gone untouched even though the corporation was fined for its activity.

A third possibility is that every company of a certain size be required, by law, to have an inspector general or an internal operational auditor, whose job it is to uncover immoral and illegal practices. This person's job would be to listen to the moral concerns of employees, at every level, about the firm's practices. He or she should be independent of management, and report to the audit committee of the board, which, ideally, should be a committee made up entirely of outside board members. The inspector or auditor should be charged with making public those complaints that should be made public if not changed from within. Failure on the inspector's part to take proper action with respect to a worker's complaint, such that the worker is forced to go public, should be prima facie evidence of an attempt to cover up a dangerous practice or product, and the inspector should be subject to criminal charges.

In addition, a company that wishes to be moral, that does not wish to engage in harmful practices or to produce harmful products, can take other steps to preclude the necessity of whistleblowing. The company can establish channels whereby those employees who have moral concerns can get a fair hearing without danger to their position or standing in the company. Expressing such concerns, moreover, should be considered a demonstration of company loyalty and should be rewarded appropriately. The company might establish the position of ombudsman, to hear such complaints or moral concerns. Or an independent committee of the board might be established to hear such complaints and concerns. Someone might even be paid by the company to present the position of the would-be whistleblower, who would argue for what the company should do, from a moral point of view, rather than what those interested in meeting a schedule or making a profit would like to do. Such a person's success within the company could depend on his success in precluding whistleblowing, as well as the conditions that lead to it.

—46—

DOES IT MAKE SENSE TO BE A LOYAL EMPLOYEE?

Juan M. Elegido

INTRODUCTION

IT HAS BECOME COMMONPLACE THAT THE OLD implied employment contract under which employers offered employment for life in return for the employees' undivided attention and devotion is dead. Supposedly, modern economic conditions put a premium on employer flexibility and employee mobility and have rendered that implied contract unviable. However, serious questions have been raised on how prevalent that supposed implied employment contract ever was, at least in the Western world, on the extent to which the old contract is gone, and on the economic advantages of the free-agent model. However that may be, my own experience and that of other academics who teach in programmes addressed to management practitioners is that many young managers do not think of their relationship to their current or future employers in terms of loyalty. Much of the motivation for my writing this article stems from my belief that these young managers are missing something potentially important for their lives when they so casually dismiss the possibility of a loyal relationship with their employers.

Irrespective of the prevailing values in the world of practice, the issue of loyalty is very much alive in business ethics journals and books. The appropriateness or otherwise of giving or expecting loyalty in modern corporations keeps being discussed, as the many references provided in this article attest. However, no clear conclusion seems to emerge from the recent work on loyalty....

Perhaps that lack of clear conclusions derives from the fact that the contemporary academic discussion of loyalty addresses many different issues. Among others: How should loyalty be defined? Do employers have a moral duty to be loyal to their employees? Does the manager's loyalty to her subordinates clash with her fiduciary duties? Do employees have a moral duty to be loyal to their employers? If this duty exists, does it clash with other duties (i.e., that of blowing the whistle in appropriate occasions)? In which ways and within what limits should loyalty towards employers be manifested?

To increase the chances of making progress in the investigation of loyalty in work settings, I will focus as sharply as possible the discussion and will confine myself to studying whether, and under what conditions, from the point of view of the employee's fulfilment, it is advisable that he offer loyalty to his employer. I will not even pause to ask whether employees have a moral duty to show loyalty to their employers.

The employee fulfilment to which I refer in this article should not be understood as being better off in purely financial or hedonic terms. Throughout the article I have in mind an inclusive conception of human flourishing according to which a person has lived a fulfilling life if at the end it is possible to make an overall judgement that that life was a good life, even if many particular aims of that person were frustrated or had to be sacrificed, either because of unfavourable circumstances or in order to attain more important goals. Of course, there are many conceptions of what is a good life, but in the context of this article I wish to leave this question as open as possible as the thesis I defend here is compatible with many of them. Broadly speaking, it should be possible to accommodate the theses I uphold in this article within many types of preference-satisfaction and objective-list conceptions of a good life.

The point of departure of many academic discussions of this topic is the ordinary meaning of the term loyalty. This has hampered the emergence of shared views as the term loyalty can be defined in many different, though related, ways and none of these is specially geared to making it easier to arrive at definite conclusions in a process of moral reasoning. To avoid these problems I will try to be very clear about the concept of loyalty I use and, though I will endeavour not to stray too far from common usage in stipulating my use of the term, the main consideration I will have in mind in fashioning my definition is to arrive at a definition of loyalty that is suitable for the purpose of moral argument and takes into account the lessons of past discussions of professional loyalty.

So, my plan is to start by putting forward a clear definition of loyalty. Then I will investigate whether, and under what circumstances, it makes sense for an employee to offer loyalty (in the sense defined) to her employer by exploring in detail the arguments that can be offered in favour of, and against, the thesis that professional loyalty is conducive to an employee's fulfilment.

A DEFINITION OF EMPLOYEE'S LOYALTY

For my purposes in this article, I wish to stipulate that when I use the term loyalty I will be referring to:

A deliberate commitment to further the best interests of one's employer, even when doing so may demand sacrificing some aspects of one's self-interest beyond what would be required by one's legal and other moral duties.

I do not put forward this definition because I think it corresponds better than other alternative definitions which could be offered to the way the term "loyalty" is commonly used. While this definition is not purely idiosyncratic, the main reason I offer it is that, at least under some circumstances, acting in that way towards their employers is likely to make employees better off. I have crafted this definition with an eye to staking out a defensible moral position in the tradition of virtue ethics represented by philosophers like Aristotle, Aquinas and MacIntyre.

This definition describes loyalty as a deliberate commitment. By choosing this characterization I am dissociating myself from an understanding of loyalty that sees it as a sentiment, feeling, emotion or passion....

I want to make it clear, however, that by defining loyalty as a deliberate commitment I am not trying to suggest that loyalty is, or should be, detached from emotion. As a matter of fact, the deliberate commitment will often be motivated by feelings of attachment. In other cases what started as a deliberate choice will eventually produce those feelings of attachment. Most commonly, the deliberate commitment and the feelings of attachment will have grown in parallel and, as I will discuss below, this fact provides a reason why the deliberate commitment is worth making.

My definition also makes reference to the fact that loyalty may demand sacrificing some aspects of one's self-interest.... For loyalty as I define it to exist, the loyal subject does not have to be willing to sacrifice everything for the employer to which he is loyal; the readiness to sacrifice some aspects of one's self-interest will suffice.... Loyalty is better understood as a continuum than as a binary phenomenon; accordingly, in my definition loyalty to an employer is not necessarily a matter of all or nothing but admits of degrees, of more and less, and the fact that it is not wholehearted does not imply that it does not exist at all. Thus understood, it should also be noted that loyalty does not have to be exclusive as could be the case if I had defined it in a more totalizing way. It is possible for a person to have several loyalties simultaneously.... Again, it should also be noted that, because of the relative modesty of the definition of loyalty I offer, no presumption arises that, as defined by me, loyalty has to be uncritical.

The definition refers to furthering the best interests of one's employer. The employer does not necessarily have to be a business organization.... The employer could be a university, an NGO, a research institute, a government department or agency, a health organization, or a church. It has great interest for my discussion that many young people nowadays are opting to work for such employers rather than for business organizations, often at a significant financial cost to themselves. It is also important to notice that while, as we will see below, the great majority of arguments against employee loyalty are based on developments in the business world, in practice they have induced a general mistrust against the idea of loyalty to employers of all types. By bringing other types of employers explicitly into my discussion of this issue I hope to be able to assess openly all relevant considerations.

The definition refers to the employer's interests. These interests can be furthered in many ways, and it is important to stress that being loyal to one's employer is not just a question of persisting in that employment relationship for a very long time. One can express one's loyalty in other ways such as avoiding gossip, mentoring younger employees, going the extra mile with a customer, taking pains with one's work, and being ready to work overtime even when that is not personally convenient, among many others. We can even talk of post-exit loyalty when a former employee maintains a readiness to foster the interest of a former employer after the employment connection has been terminated. Also, the mere fact of persisting in one's employment for a long time will not necessarily express loyalty in terms of my definition as it

may not result from a willingness to further one's employer's interests, but may instead be the result of purely self-regarding considerations.

It is well known that in most countries the economy nowadays is much more dynamic than it was some decades ago: companies are born and die more frequently and leading companies lose their leadership positions faster. It is a necessary consequence of this that employees will have to change employment more frequently and therefore to promise a life-long employment relationship may well be a very rash action. But this in no way shows that other aspects of employee loyalty make no sense any longer. In this article I assume that an employee's commitment to the interests of the employer will often most naturally be expressed in a readiness to persist in the employment relationship for the long term. But how long this relationship will last, and even whether this way of expressing loyalty is appropriate, will much depend on many circumstantial factors and very especially on the other commitments of the employee (for very good reasons, loyalty to their employers will not be the only loyalty, nor the most important one for most employees) and the characteristics of the employer. At any rate, even if a long-term relationship is not appropriate in a given case, it by no means follows that other ways of expressing the employee's commitment will also be inappropriate.

The definition I have put forward refers to a commitment to further the employer's best interests, not her every want.

My definition also refers to sacrificing one's interests beyond what would be required by one's legal and other moral duties. I take it for granted in this article that there are very good reasons for employees to comply not only with all the legal duties which attach to their position as employees (among which is the legal duty of loyalty, that is to say, the legal duty to act solely for the benefit of the employer when engaging in any conduct that relates to the employment), but also with any general moral duties such as those which may result from previous (though perhaps not legally enforceable) promises or from the fact of the employee being given significant decision powers in the understanding that they will be exercised to foster the interests of the employer. It would be a false dichotomy to assume that the only alternative to an employee being loyal (in the sense of my definition) is for her to be disloyal. It is possible not to be loyal without being disloyal or in any other way unethical. As Pfeiffer (1992: 536) has observed: "One may be described or viewed as a valued employee at the same time one is not properly a loyal one (sic). One can do one's job well, be respected and valued by one's employer, yet plainly lack any particular allegiance to the employer. One might explain that one is looking for a better job, is happy to have this one for now, and will work honestly and well until the better one arrives. An employer may accept this explanation, not branding the employee as the least bit disloyal." What I am trying to investigate in this article is whether there are good reasons for employees to go voluntarily beyond the demands of this legal and moral baseline.

Finally, it will be useful to point out that my definition does not require that loyalty be reciprocal. Even though I have explicitly introduced my own definition as a stipulative one and therefore, strictly speaking, it needs no defence but only consistency in my use of it, as so many, and so competent, writers have taken a line different from mine, it may be useful if I try to account for my own approach. In the first place, I have tried to avoid being idiosyncratic. Cases like the mother who persists in being loyally committed to her disloyal son, show that common usage does not insist on reciprocity as a requirement of loyalty.... Finally, it may be useful to note that several of the philosophers who include reciprocity in their treatment of loyalty are well-known Aristotelians who probably have in mind the paradigmatic case of loyalty between friends. Aristotle famously taught that mutuality is a requirement of friendship. For my own purpose of studying the attitudes appropriate to an employee who is seeking fulfilment in his work, importing into my discussion the stronger requirements of friendship in its focal instances makes little sense.

ARGUMENTS FOR LOYALTY TO ONE'S EMPLOYER

A committed and loyal relationship between employee and employer has been seen as a desirable arrangement by many people. Even if, as it has been widely reported, many employers and employees no longer see it as practicable, or even desirable, in current circumstances, it will be useful to try and start by understanding its potential benefits. I will pay no attention here to the likely advantages to the employer from that type of relationship (except insofar as they may result in benefits for the employee), as doing so would lead me beyond the scope of this article. I will concentrate instead on examining the arguments which can be offered in defence of the position that for an employee to offer loyalty—as defined above—to her employer might indeed be conducive to making for herself the best life she possibly can.

At this stage it may be useful to repeat that it is not my purpose to argue that employees generally have a duty of loyalty to their employers. My aim in this article is just to show that it may well be in the interests of the employees themselves to be loyal, in the sense that adopting this attitude towards their employers may help them to live a more fulfilling life.

Loyalty and Human Flourishing

As the main point of this article is that being loyal as an employee can be conducive to human flourishing it may be useful to clarify the relationship between loyalty and human flourishing.

Loyalty, along the lines I defined it above is a form of commitment, and for my purposes here can be best understood as an aspect of friendship. A useful approach to this matter can be found in the interpretation that the Oxford philosopher John Finnis offers of the work of Aristotle on friendship. As Finnis understands this, the core of a relationship of friendship is that two parties "are in such a relationship to each other that each wants the other to be better off, and find some satisfaction or even joy in the other's ... success." (Finnis, 2011: 99). Like Aristotle, Finnis considers that the central case of friendship is that in which each friend is identified with the other on account of the other being a lovable person.

For Aristotle friendship is an important aspect of human flourishing and he says things such as: "a good friend is by nature desirable for a good man," "[friendship] is necessary for living," "the happy man needs friends," "[n]obody would choose to live without friends even if he had all the other good things" and "friends are considered to be the greatest of external goods" (Nicomachean Ethics VIII, I and IX, ix)....

Very few people would like to have to deny the value of friendship; and even though it is possible for somebody to deny it verbally, that person will be unable to avoid inconsistency for he or she will act in many ways which are only explicable on the basis of an implicit acceptance of that value of friendship which he or she denies.

A possible difficulty in approaching loyalty to one's employer as a form of friendship is that Aristotle himself, near the beginning of his treatment of friendship (Nichomachean Ethics VIII, iii), distinguishes three varieties or species of friendship: friendship of goodness, friendship of pleasure and friendship of utility and he explicitly states that only the first class is "true friendship" (VIII, vi), perfect of its kind, while the last two are "secondary forms of friendship" (VIII, vi), "are grounded on an inessential factor" (VIII, iii), are "of a less genuine kind" (VIII, iv) and can easily be dissolved (VIII, iii). Should we conclude from this that a relationship with one's employer can at best become one of these inferior types of friendship and that, though perhaps it may be useful for some purposes, it cannot possibly be an aspect of true human flourishing? This conclusion would most likely not be justified even in respect of Aristotle. In his discussion of friendship he makes reference to many other types of friendship that, while they are not instances of the focal case of friendship between two mature good men, are not either instances of any of the two secondary forms of friendship

(pleasure and utility) which he specifically identifies. Examples are the "mutual friendliness between members ... of the human species" (VIII, i); friendship among the members of a community (VIII, i and ix) or the citizens of a state (IX, vi), between parents and their children (VIII, i), brothers (VIII, ix), and husband and wife (VIII, vii), among those serving on the same ship or in the same force (VIII, ix) or among members of the same social club (VIII, xi). All these cases of friendship can be best thought of as derivative instances of the concept (because—in Aristotle's view—they do not instantiate to the full all the traits of the central case) but are still good and valuable as they exhibit some of these traits.

I hope these summary comments go some way towards clarifying both how the relationship among the members of a large body can display this type of valuable harmony, and that that harmony is indeed a form of friendship whose intrinsic value, as illuminated by the consideration of more focal cases of friendship, derives from the members of that body sharing in common goals and being committed to the well-being of the other members, though perhaps without the intensity and even exclusivity that is typical of the central cases of friendship....

Loyal Employees Improve the Performance of the Organizations for Which They Work and in This Way Benefit Themselves

The ways in which a work organization benefits from having loyal employees have been well studied. Organizations with loyal employees save on significant replacement costs. An organization can more confidently delegate authority to a loyal employee without fearing that the authority will be misused in self-serving ways and in the complex and fast-changing environments which are characteristic nowadays, the ability to delegate authority to employees who are closer to the action is advantageous; conversely, a work organization that is not able to delegate decision making authority to employees lower in the hierarchy is hampered in its ability to react fast and appropriately to changes in its environment. There are other ways—highly beneficial to itself—in which an organization can act with regards to loyal employees, which are not available, at least to the same extent, in relation to employees which are not loyal. Examples include making significant investments in the training of employees and disclosing to them confidential information. Loyal employees who remain long-term with an organization are also essential for the preservation of the organization's institutional memory. Hirschman (1970, 1974) has argued that organizational deficiencies can be corrected either by "voice" (expressing dissatisfaction and making efforts to improve things) or by "exit" (leaving the organization when its performance declines) and that loyalty delays exit and encourages voice, which is more effective in improving organizations. Finally, organizations are more effective when loyal employees exhibit organizational citizenship behaviour, that is to say, when they act in sponta-neous and innovative ways which go beyond role requirements, especially in the fast-expanding ser-vice sector in which it is more difficult to directly supervise employees.

Having a single loyal employee is valuable, but the organization which has a critical mass of such employees enjoys a definite strategic advantage: such organization will be able to act in ways which other organizations working in the same field will find it difficult to imitate.

In itself all that the argument set out in the two preceding paragraphs shows is that having loyal employees is very advantageous for the orga-nizations which employ them, not immediately for the employees themselves. However, in so far as working for a more successful employer makes the employee better off, this is already an employee benefit and, more significantly, in so far as employ-ees are loyal towards their employers and identify with them, the distinction between the interests of the employer and those of the employee blurs: if I identify with the objectives of my employer and her goals (or at least some of them) are my own

goals, the fact that my employer is more successful in reaching its goals makes me ipso facto more successful in reaching my own goals.

Loyal Employees Make a Special Contribution to the Wider Society

By being loyal employees also contribute to the general good of the society, not only to the pros-perity of their own employers. Loyal employees make it easier for new organizations to grow and existing ones to survive in ways that are favourable to the creation and preservation of social capital (Hirschman, 1970, 1974). In other words, when employees are loyal, at least to a certain extent, to their own employers, they protect valuable social institutions that contribute to the satisfaction of human needs. As the previous one, this argument is not directly an argument that the employee is better off for being loyal. But so far as the employ-ees care not only for their own immediate interests, but also for those of the wider society, they are better off by the society being better off.

Loyalty at Work Makes It Easier to Have Committed Relationships in Other Areas of the Employee's Life

Fears have been expressed that a strong commit-ment by employees to their jobs or their employers will make it difficult for them to accommodate strong commitments in other aspects of their lives. However, research on employee commitment has found a positive relationship between the work and non-work attitudes of employees. This is not surprising. A basic insight of virtue ethics, which many who are not paid-up members of this school of thought accept, is that our choices, especially important choices made repeatedly, shape our character. An employee who often chooses not to act loyally in occasions when acting loyally could be appropriate is shaping himself—*pro tanto*—as a person for whom loyalty is not a valued trait of character. Therefore, acting without loyalty in a significant area of our lives such as work will tend to make it more difficult to be consistently loyal in other spheres such as marriage, family or friendships. Of course, less loyal marriages, families or friendships just mean less strong marriages, families or friendships, as loyalty in those relationships is constitutive of the relationships themselves....

Loyal Employees Help Make the Organization a True Community

If a critical mass of the employees of a work organization become loyal, in the sense I have defined, then in the words of Gilbert, "strangers grow into neighbours and collaborators" (2001: 5) and the organization can become a true community in which the members have a sense of belonging, in which there is a certain identification of interests among them, and in which they can find social and emotional support and practical assistance when they face difficulties at work or in their personal lives outside work. Also, in so far as an organization is a community the quality of social interaction and personal relationships in it is enhanced.

A work organization whose members are totally lacking in loyalty and commitment towards it does not necessarily have to be a terrible place. Even in the absence of any loyalty or commitment, and even if ultimately each participant is exclusively interested in advancing his own interests, it is still possible, at least in principle, to have an arms-length relationship in which all parties are strictly dutiful and law-abiding and punctiliously do all they undertook to do. But even in this best of all possible alternatives to loyal relationships something of great importance for human flourishing would be missing. The dynamics of such workplace would force each employee to restrict his concern to the defence of his own individual interests and to try to get as much as possible for himself at the least possible cost. To work for an organization in which that is everybody's attitude would entail that the aspect of a person's life to which she devotes the greatest number of hours and one of those that she perceives as more significant, would have to be organized along the lines of a strict individualism,

which excludes radically any bonds of solidarity. Any ethical doctrine that considers that attitudes like identification with others, love of neighbour, or solidarity, are fundamental requirements of personal fulfilment will necessarily perceive fundamental defects in such a workplace....

Loyal Relationships Have an Inherent Value

Up to this point I might have given the impression that the value of loyalty to one's employer is purely instrumental. But that is not the case. It is true that being a loyal employee is instrumental for many other benefits that stand outside loyalty itself, but this is not incompatible with loyalty towards one's employer having also an intrinsic value, even in cases where that loyalty may not be corresponded or, more generally, in cases in which for one reason or another, the benefits to which I have made reference in the preceding paragraphs may fail to materialize....

In which way does loyalty to one's employer have inherent value? Assuming that one's employer is contributing in an ethical way to the satisfaction of some personal or social needs, the mere fact that a loyal employee has been engaged creatively and with effort, for an extended period of time, in trying to sustain and increase the ability of her employer to operate more effectively has value in itself, independently of the eventual results of her efforts. Of course, it is better to try and succeed than to try and fail, but it in no way follows that an attempt that fails is valueless. Both history and literature afford us many examples of people who tried to achieve valuable objectives, often against great odds... but did not succeed. The lives of such people are not "wasted" but rather good and meaningful along a variety of dimensions. In many ways they may well have been richer and better than those of other, outwardly more successful, individuals.

I focused in the preceding paragraph on the extreme case of the employee who, alone among her fellow employees, is committed to her employer. In many cases, however, there will be in a given organization more than one committed employee. In many such cases the common commitment that such employees have issues in mutual relationships of mutual help and loyalty. Again, such relationships are intrinsically valuable independently of whether or not the efforts of these people are successful.

ARGUMENTS AGAINST LOYALTY TO ONE'S EMPLOYER

A variety of arguments have been offered which purport to show that being loyal towards one's employer is misguided and I will now proceed to consider them. I will only consider here arguments which have prima facie force against the definition of loyalty I have offered.

It Is Possible to Participate in the Value of Loyalty in Other Ways

Even if it is granted that engaging in loyal relationships can be an important aspect of a person's flourishing, would it not be possible, as a reviewer has asked, to capture the inherent, flourishing-inducing value of loyalty by being loyal to one's profession or community, without necessarily being a loyal employee? Indeed it is possible, and because of this the large number of people who for one reason or the other are precluded from engaging in a loyal relationship with their employers are not thereby condemned to lead unfulfilled lives. Many other forms of loyalty and of friendship are open to them, and so are many other aspects of human flourishing such as, to name only a few, knowledge, play, work, and religion. But the issue is not whether there are alternative ways to flourish, but whether it is reasonable not to take advantage of this one when the opportunity of doing so presents itself. And in making this decision, three factors to which I already referred above in slightly different contexts are especially relevant: very often there is no reason why one form of loyalty should be exclusive and preclude others; work is the activity to which most

of us devote most of our waking hours and therefore excluding loyal relationships from this area of our lives can have great significance; and many people nowadays have too few realistic alternative poles of significant loyal relationships to casually discard the possibility of finding one in their working life.

Loyalty Makes the Employee Vulnerable

My definition emphasises that loyalty requires sacrificing one's own interests and that in itself is a prima facie argument against loyalty, one which, as far as I can judge from the arguments my own students often put forward in discussing this topic, has a good deal of practical importance. Why should I sacrifice my interests, for instance by failing to take advantage of an alternative higher-paying, or in other ways more attractive, employment offer; or by engaging in behaviours which demand an investment of effort but are not demanded by my contract of employment and nobody is likely to notice or reward?

Of course, no sane person would recommend self-sacrifice for its own sake but it may be useful to point out that perhaps this argument tries to prove too much. After all, the element of self-sacrifice is not something exclusive to professional loyalty. Every commitment (including those of love and friendship) demands self-sacrifice, makes us vulnerable and may easily become a source of suffering. But in the same way that most sane people would be slow to conclude from this that one should avoid entanglements and try to live as unattached a life as possible, one should also be slow in drawing such conclusions in the area of professional loyalties.

Even after considering this point, someone might still see a contradiction in my argument in this paper. According to the definition I have offered, loyalty "may demand sacrificing some aspects of one's self-interest beyond what would be required by one's legal and other moral duties." However, in the preceding section I have argued that loyalty may make employees better off. As what makes me better off is precisely what is in my self-interest, I would seem to be contradicting myself: loyalty would be and would not be in the employee's self-interest.

The contradiction is only apparent, however. Loyalty may demand, and in practice it often does demand, "sacrificing some aspects of one's self-interest", but as I have argued in the preceding section it also advances our interests in very important ways. One cannot decide whether it is worthwhile paying a certain price until one has considered the value of what one acquires. All of us daily sacrifice some interests ... in order to advance other interests that seem more important to us and there is nothing surprising in these trade-offs.

In order to assess some of these trade-offs, it is important to remember my remarks above on the issue of commitment leading to identification. I have mentioned that by being loyal I help my employing organization to be more productive and more of a community. At first sight it might appear that these are not part of my own interests. However, in so far as I identify myself with my employer, it is progressively less a question of balancing my own interests with those of my employer, because I now increasingly see my employer's interests as my own.... The question now becomes, even in relation to these interests that might seem to lie outside myself, whether it makes sense to sacrifice some of my interests in order to advance other interests *of mine*.

Other interests that an employee can advance by being loyal are more obviously his own. As we saw before, such interests include increasing one's work motivation, developing one's character in ways that make it easier for one to have committed relationships in other areas of one's life, adding meaning to one's life, and achieving greater unity in one's life. I have also pointed out that, beyond the interests of the employee that loyalty to her employer may advance, which ultimately may be frustrated by circumstances beyond the employee's control, a loyal relationship is in itself something inherently valuable and worth participating in, whatever other results may ultimately flow from it.

I do not want to conclude from this that the benefits of loyalty to one's employer are such that they justify any sacrifices that such loyalty may entail, as I am not trying to argue that loyalty is always, or even most often, justified (or not justified for that matter). My point in this section is more limited: the fact that employee loyalty may demand the sacrifice of some of the employee's interests does not automatically entail that such loyalty is excluded.

There is an especially prominent personal sacrifice that loyalty would seem to demand in some cases which should be given special attention here. I refer to the danger of the employee becoming an "organization man," so fully devoted to the interests of his organization that it becomes the sole source of his identity; such an employee can become fully dependent on his employer and stop being an autonomous individual with interests and projects of his own and a capacity to think critically and make his own decisions.

A well-known way of avoiding such a danger is to avoid loyalty to one's employer being the exclusive loyalty in one's life, or even the paramount one. But, more generally, it was precisely with this danger in view that I defined the loyalty I was interested in as a commitment which will sacrifice *some* aspects of one's self-interest and explicitly rejected definitions which speak of *thoroughgoing or wholehearted devotion*....

The Profit-making Nature of Business Enterprises

Duska (1997: 338), in an article first published in 1985, has put forward the following argument:

> To think we owe a company or corporation loyalty requires us to think of that company as a person or as a group with a goal of human fulfillment. If we think of it in this way we can be loyal. But this is the wrong way to think. A company is not a person. A company is an instrument, and an instrument with a specific purpose, the making of profit. To treat an instrument as an end in itself ... does

give the instrument a moral status it does not deserve.

For good measure, he adds:

> There is nothing as pathetic as the story of the loyal employee who, having given above and beyond the call of duty, is let go in the restructuring of the corporation. He feels betrayed because he mistakenly viewed the company as an object of his loyalty.

To begin with, it should be noted that while the focus of my interest in this article is all types of work relationships, Duska's argument is restricted to business organizations. Therefore it does not even pretend to touch the very large number of employers who are not organized on a for-profit basis. Still, I do not believe the argument is valid, or at least generally valid, even in regard to for-profit organizations.

Duska's statement that "[a] company is an instrument ... with a specific purpose, the making of money" has to be considered carefully. Many work organizations are organized on a for-profit basis but may in fact pursue at the same time several different objectives. Think, for instance, of a newspaper whose primary objective is to advance a certain political or cultural agenda; or of a wealthy businesswoman who keeps a factory operating in her town, even though this location is not optimal from an economic point of view, in order to preserve as many jobs as possible in the area. None of these examples is purely imaginary and many similar ones could be offered, all tending to show the rich variety and complexity of actual motivations which we find in the business world.

I would agree that if profit maximization were the single factor driving decisions in a business organization, to the exclusion of everything else except (by hypothesis) the organization's legal obligations, that is to say to the exclusion of gratitude, consideration, aesthetics, respect for people and the environment, and ethical concerns generally, then, in most cases, that organization would not be a fit object for loyalty. In the first place, an organization which is exclusively profit-driven will, by definition, at all times do what maximizes its profits and therefore cannot be relied upon to reciprocate any past loyalty. Still, this is not a knock-out argument as I did not include reciprocity in my definition of loyalty and gave reasons for that choice. Secondly, and more importantly, there are many other candidates for my commitment that are more appealing than money, especially in the many societies which nowadays live well above the limits of subsistence and are not forced to subordinate everything else to securing the essentials of survival. But purely profit-driven employers will not be fit objects of loyalty in most cases, rather than invariably. A profit-driven fund manager in charge of the savings of many retirees could be an appropriate focus of loyalty for its employees; in a society living on the brink of survival, profit-focused organizations could deserve loyalty....

Loyalty Stifles Rational Criticism

Dogs provide many outstanding examples of unswerving loyalty to their masters, to the point of death in some cases. But the very fact that many dogs exhibit this attitude may lead us to suspect that loyalty may not, after all, be appropriate for human beings.

It is often argued that being loyal is incompatible with thinking critically of those one is loyal to or with scrutinising untrustingly their instructions. There have even been well-known cases in which it was incontestable that the behaviour required from a subordinate was unethical but in which it was argued that the sacrifice of the subordinate's own principles and personal convictions would only prove that his loyalty was great enough, up to the demands of this very special sacrifice. Totalitarian leaders have been notable for demanding the unswerving and unquestioning loyalty of their subjects with well-known consequences. The frequency with which a claim of loyalty has been used to demand unethical behavior from subordinates lends resonance to the saying that "when an organization wants you to do right, it asks for your integrity; when it wants you to do wrong, it demands your loyalty" (Kleinig, 2008: 4).

This unsavoury side of loyalty can infect work relationships as much as any others. The chronicles of many business scandals feature episodes in which some employees had discovered that their employers were doing seriously harmful things, but were induced by an appeal to their loyalty to co-operate in their employers' wrongs, or at least to refrain from reporting them to the appropriate authorities. Some people conclude that if loyalty is capable of making people suspend in this way their capacity for moral judgment it would seem something to be avoided rather than recommended.

At this point also, it may be useful to point out that similar arguments could be put forward against any other type of loyalty and commitment. If we do not believe that the argument is strong enough to justify the decision to pursue a life totally free from attachments, we may be less impressed by it in the specific area of work relationships.

Business ethicists have treated this issue most frequently in the context of whistleblowing. They have generally concluded that, provided that other avenues for stopping the harm the employer is doing seem not practicable and that there is proportionality between that harm and the harms that the employer and its stakeholders will suffer by the employee's denunciation of the employer's inappropriate behaviour to the authorities or to the general public, a sane loyalty would not be incompatible with blowing the whistle, far less would it require active co-operation with the employer's unethical behaviour. Different writers frame this general conclusion in different ways, depending on their respective conceptions of loyalty and their general ethical positions. On my own part, it should be enough to point out that nothing in the definition of loyalty I offered above would commit anybody who concludes that offering such loyalty to her employer is a desirable thing to feel obliged to suspend her moral judgment or to override her conclusions on what is the right thing to do.

CONCLUSIONS

I have examined several ways in which a loyal commitment towards one's employer can make one's life significantly richer. I believe that an attentive consideration of the arguments I have reviewed provides strong reasons not to be hasty in embracing the popular dismissal of professional loyalty as irrelevant to modern conditions. However, it is important to realize that, if they are examined carefully, all the arguments in favour of loyalty to one's employer that I have discussed tend to show that a certain (and variable) degree of loyalty is likely to be appropriate provided that the objectives and values of an organization are appealing. As far as I can see, none of them provides conclusive reasons to act loyally "without restrictions or qualifications" and "no matter the circumstances." In other words, all of the reasons in favour of being a loyal employee that I have discussed above are conditional in nature: they only show that in so far as some conditions obtain, being loyal in some ways towards one's employer can be one way of leading a more fulfilling life.

Something similar can be said of all the objections to the idea of being a loyal employee that I have examined. None of them provides an absolute argument, valid at all times and in all contexts, against being loyal to one's employer. However, they succeed in making it clear that in certain situations loyalty will be misguided and also that loyalty should have limits. While generally speaking, a loyal relationship with his employer may be conducive to an employee's fulfilment, this will not be necessarily so in relation to all employers and even less so in relation to all the different ways in which loyalty can be expressed. A consideration of the objections against loyalty which I have discussed will help the reader to better appreciate my decision to stay clear of a totalizing conception of loyalty in my definition and to opt instead for defining it in a way that admits of more and less; some of the arguments I examined show that in many circumstances a hundred-per-cent commitment to an employer would not make sense: Many employers may deserve some commitment, but not a total commitment; there may well be some doubt that some employers will keep deserving in future the same degree of commitment they deserve now; there is always an element of risk that the employer may fail to reciprocate the commitment it is given and it may be appropriate to take precautions to minimize one's losses if that were to be the case. Even accepting the arguments in favour of loyalty and agreeing that there are many ways in which a loyal relationship with one's employer may be a very fine thing, all of these factors will often tend to recommend to express one's loyalty in some ways but not in others, and to accept a certain degree of self-denial in acting loyally, but not a greater one.

REFERENCES

Duska, R. 1997. Whistle-blowing and employee loyalty. In T.L. Beauchamp and N.E. Bowie (Eds.), *Ethical theory and business*. Upper Saddle River, NJ: Prentice Hall.

Finnis, J. 2011. "Bernard Williams on truth's values", in John Finnis, *Reason in Action: Collected Essays: Volume I*. Oxford: Oxford University Press, pp. 92–103.

Gilbert, D.R. 2001. *An extraordinary concept in the ordinary service of management*. Business Ethics Quarterly, 11 (1): 1–9.

Hirschman, A.O. 1970. *Exit, voice, and loyalty: Response to decline in firms, organizations and states*. Cambridge, MA: Harvard University Press.

——. 1974. *Exit, Voice, and Loyalty: Further Reflections and a Survey of Recent Contributions*. Social Science Information, 13 (1): 7–26.

Kleinig, J. 2008. Loyalty. The Stanford encyclopedia of philosophy (Fall 2008 Edition), <http://plato.stanford.edu/archives/fall2008/entries/loyalty/>.

Pfeiffer, R.S. 1992. Owing loyalty to one's employer. *Journal of Business Ethics*, 11: 535–43.

—47—

WHISTLE-BLOWING, MORAL INTEGRITY, AND ORGANIZATIONAL ETHICS

George G. Brenkert

WHISTLE-BLOWING HAS ATTRACTED CONSIDER-able interest, both popular and academic, during the past one hundred years. Although one can find examples of whistle-blowing prior to the twentieth century, whistle-blowing is largely a contemporary phenomenon that has increased in frequency and extent. Changes in job structures, attitudes toward authority, and the size and complexity of organizations are among the reasons cited for this increase.

Whistle-blowers evoke widely different responses. On the one hand, some are perceived as brave and even heroic. Jeffrey Wigand, who exposed the actions of Brown & Williamson, a tobacco company that allegedly manipulated the effects of nicotine in cigarettes, has generally been portrayed in the media as a courageous person. Three whistle-blowers, Sherron Watkins, Cynthia Rowland, and Coleen Rowley, were celebrated as "Persons of the Year" in 2002 by Time magazine. On the other hand, whistle-blowers are also viewed as snitches, traitors, and spies. The former president of General Motors, James Roche, is frequently quoted as calling whistle-blowers the "enemies of business" and accusing them of "spreading disunity and creating conflict."[1]

Business ethicists have examined this important phenomenon by considering, in general, two major issues. First, how may we best analyze the concept of whistle-blowing? Since the term is recent, answers to this question are not simply reports of how the term is standardly defined, but are attempts to identify the phenomenon to be analyzed. How may we best capture the characteristics to which people refer when they speak of whistle-blowing? Second, ethical discussions of whistle-blowing have tended to focus on the question of how, if at all, whistle-blowing may be justified in individual cases. This is an ethical problem of enormous significance for those directly involved. It deserves the ethical consideration it has received.

Nevertheless, there are other important issues to which answers regarding the justification of this or that act of whistle-blowing may only be a partial, and frequently ineffective, response. Accordingly, a third issue business ethicists need to consider concerns whistle-blowing in its organizational and social context. What problem does whistle-blowing answer and how effectively does it do so? If the difficulties that give rise to whistle-blowing can be reduced or eliminated, we may be able to avoid the moral dilemmas and predicaments that whistle-blowing raises. This broader set of questions looks to the nature of the ethical organization and its implications for whistle-blowing, rather than simply at the harms or injuries to which particular acts of whistle-blowing may seek to respond.

WHAT IS WHISTLE-BLOWING?

Many definitions of whistle-blowing have been offered over the past half century. Some are relatively informal and careless in their formulation, others more meticulous. Many include the following conditions: (1) An individual has some privileged status with regard to an organization (usually he or she is a member or former member) that permits knowledge of inside, confidential, or private information regarding activities undertaken by individuals within the organization; (2) This individual reports some activity that he or she considers to be illegal, immoral, or opposed to the basic values or purposes of the organization; (3) The reporting may be done internally or externally to person(s), not in the direct line of reporting, who is (are) believed to be capable and willing to stop or prevent such wrongdoing either directly or indirectly; (4) The wrongdoing is of a substantive or serious nature; (5) This wrongdoing affects the public interest, though not necessarily immediately or directly. Hence, cases of sexual harassment or racial discrimination that applied only to members of an organization might prompt whistle-blowing, because they are matters of significant public interest.

Accordingly, John Boatright suggests that whistle-blowing is the voluntary release of nonpublic information, as a moral protest, by a member or former member of an organization outside the normal channels of communication to an appropriate audience about illegal and/or immoral conduct in the organization or conduct in the organization that is opposed in some significant way to the public interest.[2] Norman Bowie holds that

> a whistle blower is an employee or officer of any institution, profit or nonprofit, private or public, who believes either that he/she has been ordered to perform some act or he/she has obtained knowledge that the institution is engaged in activities which (a) are believed to cause unnecessary harm to third parties, (b) are in violation of human rights or (c) run counter to the defined purpose of

the institution and who inform the public of this fact.[3]

Much more simply, Sissela Bok says that "whistle-blowers sound an alarm from within the very organization in which they work, aiming to spotlight neglect or abuses that threaten the public interest."[4] Finally, Janet Near and Marcia Miceli contend that whistle-blowing is "the disclosure by organization members (former or current) of illegal, immoral, or illegitimate practices under the control of their employers, to persons or organizations that may be able to effect action."[5] This last definition has been widely used in social scientific discussions of whistle-blowing.

These definitions differ in various ways among themselves and from the characteristics I noted above. The following paragraphs offer a resolution of these differences in the pursuit of a coherent account concept of whistle-blowing.

First, whistle-blowers do not have to be current members of the organization. They can be former members, applicants, suppliers, or auditors. The Sarbanes-Oxley Act of 2002, a federal law enacted in response to corporate and accounting scandals, recognizes both present and former employees, as well as applicants, as whistle blowers. More generally, it seems that the whistle-blower is a person "with privileged access to an organization's data or information" that he has gained due to his official relationship with the organization. Because of one's relationship with the organization, one is assumed to have obligations of confidentiality and loyalty to the organization. Thus a potential whistle-blower must be bound by norms of confidentiality, privacy, and loyalty that govern the operations of that organization.

Second, whistle-blowing may occur inside or outside an organization. Some reject this view and argue that whistle-blowing within an organization involves processes and procedures that are part of the organization. Thus, one who reports internally is not whistle-blowing but only following standard procedures. This view is mistaken. There are many examples in which people have blown the whistle within their organizations—Cynthia Cooper blew the whistle internally on accounting practices at WorldCom. The mistake made by those who oppose the notion of internal whistle-blowing is the failure to see that one can report "bad" information internally in ways that do not follow the normal chain of command and which are not, therefore, simply standard procedures. When I inform my supervisor that something wrong or harmful is going on, that is fulfilling my role responsibility. When I have to circumvent my supervisor because he will not do something to correct a harm or wrong, but tries to block the information from getting to appropriate individuals, then a situation of internal whistle-blowing arises. Accordingly, Sarbanes-Oxley speaks of whistle-blowing in an internal context. Near and Miceli capture the underlying point when they note that whistle-blowing is "a challenge to the organization's authority and therefore threatens its basic mode of operation."[6] And, "It is this characteristic that, in part, makes the specter of whistle-blowing anathema to organizations."[7]

Third, whistle-blowing is a deliberate act. One does not blow the whistle by accident. Instead, one must decide and initiate a course of action to release confidential information in order to correct a wrong the whistle-blower believes someone in the organization is committing. If an employee accidentally left a document detailing wrongdoing within an organization on the desk of a journalist or a top executive in the organization who might redress that wrongdoing, it would not be a case of whistle-blowing.

Even though whistle-blowing must be a deliberate act, any particular whistle-blower might not want his or her name associated with the act of whistle-blowing. He or she may seek to blow the whistle anonymously. Sarbanes-Oxley explicitly mandates the possibility of anonymous whistle-blowing. The implications of anonymity for the justification of any particular case of whistle-blowing are strongly disputed. Particularly in Europe, anonymous whistle-blowing has been viewed as unjustified. Whichever route one takes to blow the whistle may have practical consequences for the whistle-blower and the charges brought against him or her, but it does not alter the fact that he or she has engaged in an act of whistle-blowing.

Fourth, the wrongdoing that is the object of whistle-blowing must be substantial. Very minor transgressions in a firm or organization might be the occasion for someone to report their occurrence to someone outside the chain of command or even to people outside the organization. For example, suppose someone goes to a person higher in the hierarchy or to the press with a report that someone has taken a few pencils home from work, charging that this act is theft and ought to be stopped. The person revealing this action does what a whistle-blower would do, but the object of the action lacks the significance whistle-blowing requires. To begin with, the wrong is a common one, and though organizations oppose employees taking company property home for their personal use, this is not the appropriate occasion for complaining to higher officials or the press. It is too minor. Further, whistle-blowing occurs within a context in which the act and/or information regarding the act is not public or open. Indeed it is viewed as confidential or secret to the organization. The potential whistle-blower is viewed as having an obligation not to make the information known to the public. In trivial matters such confidentiality and obligations are themselves trivial or nonexistent. The situation does not rise to the level of whistle-blowing. However, this does not mean that there are any sharp lines here. There are not. Those who say that "an opportunity for whistle-blowing occurs with every questionable activity ... [and that] therefore, the potential for whistle-blowing is widespread"[8] are exaggerating. Instead, as Bowie and Duska correctly note, "whistle-blowing is reserved conceptually only for ... serious moral faults."[9] And although other faults might be involved, for example, legal ones, they are correct on the required serious or substantial nature of the situation that may occasion whistle-blowing.

Fifth, in blowing the whistle, an individual must direct his or her report at some person or organization (e.g., a newspaper) that the whistle-blower believes can do something to correct the purported wrongdoing. Since what one divulges may relate to past, present, or future wrongdoings, the whistle-blower's report seeks to stop, prevent, or rectify some wrongdoing. In any case, the report must be to someone the whistle-blower believes can set in process changes that will accomplish these aims. Hence, whistle-blowing need not be to someone in authority, though frequently it will be. It would not be whistle-blowing if one simply told one's spouse or a friend.

An ironical result of this analysis is that whistle-blowing, so understood, is a complex phenomenon that has evolved away from its simpler origins in sporting activities, where the referee or umpire "blows the whistle" to stop some infraction. In sports, it is the role of the officials to blow the whistle; they are (in general) respected parts of the game; they are not members of a team, but outsiders, hired by the league; what they "reveal" is not something hidden or confidential, but something that has occurred in public that they have witnessed and any careful spectator might also have seen. Though whistle-blowers do still try to stop infractions, the preceding characteristics of officials in sports are not replicated in whistle-blowing as we know it today....

AN INTEGRITY THEORY
OF WHISTLE-BLOWING

In formulating an integrity theory, I will begin by focusing on the notion of wrongdoing and the responsibilities one has to report wrongdoing associated with the organization of which one is a member. Through one's association or membership with an organization, one takes on certain responsibilities one would not otherwise have. In considering this role or position, I concentrate on wrongdoing rather than harm that occurs through one's organization, since some harm might be justifiably imposed on others. For an example, a supervisor might desire to learn certain intimate details about an employee's private life, but though this desire is harmed when it is blocked, still it is

justified to block that desire. The supervisor has not been wronged. Such incidents are not an occasion for whistle-blowing. Instead, it is unjustified harms, or wrongs that raise the issue of whistle-blowing. The action or policy that is the object of whistle-blowing must violate some important rule, law, or value according to which the business, or those within the business, should operate.

In such a context, I will argue that in accordance with a Principle of Positional Responsibility (PPR) a person has a responsibility to blow the whistle. The scope and stringency of this responsibility is dependent, in part, upon one's other responsibilities to the organization, the possibility of effectively reporting the wrongdoing, and the risks to oneself, one's other responsibilities and projects. However, only some whistle-blowing is obligatory. Other acts of whistle-blowing are supererogatory. Whether one is justified in blowing the whistle, all things considered, depends on how one's responsibility under the Principle of Positional Responsibility coheres with other responsibilities and ideal forms of behavior to which the person is also committed. Which are most important? Which should take precedence? In acting in accord with the Principle of Positional Responsibility or other responsibilities and values one holds, how may one best maintain one's integrity? In each situation potentially involving whistle-blowing, one must not simply consider whether there are good moral reasons to blow the whistle but also whether one should, all things considered, blow the whistle given the balance of responsibilities and ideal forms of behavior to which he or she is committed. This is a question of one's integrity.

Thus, this account is a two-part, mixed account of justified whistle-blowing: a Principle of Positional Responsibility and the integrity considerations of one's commitment to PPR and other normative demands and values that define one....

THE PRINCIPLE OF
POSITIONAL RESPONSIBILITY

Underlying our responsibility to report wrongdoing is a Principle of Positional Responsibility. This principle morally obliges people to report wrong-doings to those who might prevent or rectify them, when the wrongdoings are of a significant nature (either individually or collectively), when one has special knowledge due to one's circumstances that others lack, when one has a privileged relationship with the organization through which the wrong-doing is occurring (or has occurred), and when others are not attempting to correct the wrongdoing.[10]

This is not a general principle of doing good or even preventing harm. It is a limited principle of reporting wrongdoing, under specific circumstances and conditions, with the intention of preventing or stopping it. We do not have a general duty to correct the wrongs of the world. If we did, we would be constantly involved in the affairs of others in order to fulfill our moral obligations. And, since we have limited time, abilities, and means, we would also need some means to distinguish among the various wrongs that deserved our attention. However, the Principle of Positional Responsibility tells us that due to a special organizational or situational position we occupy involving knowledge of wrongdoing, as well as our ability to have an effect on correcting a wrong of some importance through making it known, a person acquires a responsibility to speak out. That is, through these special circumstances we have a specific duty or responsibility to take steps that will lead to the correction of wrongs.

This principle concerns wrongdoings that are of a serious nature. Though this notion lacks specificity and precision, so too does much of life in business.[11] Still, we can differentiate between those wrongs that might regard small or inconsequential matters and those involving matters of great importance and/or harm to large numbers of people. The elevator inspector who shut down poorly operating elevators that were improperly licensed was addressing a serious wrongdoing.[12] An employee who reports on improper city road contracts is also concerned about serious matters, as was the FAA flight controller who worried about colliding planes.[13] Sometimes the wrongdoing is much more abstract as when it involves accounting procedures.

For example, at WorldCom various expenditures were treated as capital expenditures rather than ordinary expenses. This different accounting approach allowed WorldCom to record significant profits when, according to ordinary accounting rules, it was losing money. Part of the reason that the wrongdoing must be serious is that if a person sought to report a trivial matter, for example, a few missing pencils, to someone in upper management or to the media, he would be viewed as an annoyance, rather than a whistle-blower. If the wrongdoing were very minor, it would not rise to the level of whistle-blowing, whether or not it was justified in the particular case.

The Principle of Positional Responsibility requires, it should be noted, that one is connected with the organization (or situation) through which one or more people are engaged in wrongdoing. It does not tell us, absent this connection, that one has any particular responsibilities. In short, it is this connection that gives a person the position or "standing" to reveal and attempt to correct the wrongs of others. This "standing" arises because as a member of the organization (or one who has privileged access) one supports the organization through one's actions (or even sometimes one's inactions), one is more likely to have verifiable knowledge unavailable to others through such an association, and by having access to officials in the organization there may be an initial presumption one may more easily and effectively bring about change. It is true that through the media and the Internet one might become aware of a host of wrongdoings around the world. But that knowledge is not part of the special circumstances in which one is a member of an organization through which wrongdoing is taking place.

Finally, this principle requires that we can have some effect to stop the wrongdoing or to correct it, though we need not be able to do this directly or individually. It is sufficient that the whistle-blower provide the impetus or the occasion that may lead, through others, to the correction of this wrongdoing. The whistle-blower need not be able to change the situation all by herself. However, by shining the light of day upon the wrongdoing, her reporting may play a crucial role in the correction process.

It is worth noting that the Principle of Positional Responsibility is compatible with widely held views regarding an individual's responsibility to report and, if possible, prevent wrongdoings associated with one's position, knowledge, and abilities. Some of this is captured in the law. For example, as earlier noted, one might be accused of a "misprision of a felony" if one fails to report felonious behavior of which one is aware.

Nonlegal, moral examples would include our responsibility to alert our neighbors and the police if we know that someone is breaking into our neighbor's house. Under these circumstances we have a responsibility to report crimes in our neighborhoods in the city. Crime Awareness campaigns and Neighborhood Crime Reports build on this notion of responsibility to report wrongs of which one becomes aware. These are responsibilities we have both as moral agents and as members of society....

THE SCOPE OF THE PRINCIPLE OF POSITIONAL RESPONSIBILITY

Previously, I have identified an employee-based responsibility to inform or report to one's supervisor, as well as duties of loyalty, obedience, and confidentiality. How do these norms relate to the Principle of Positional Responsibility when one's supervisor has told one that one's concerns regarding some putative wrongdoing are not serious or relevant and that one should get back to work? What does this principle direct one to do? How far should one proceed in reporting? This is one way to approach questions of the scope or extent of this principle.

We may begin by assuming that some serious wrong is being done to someone or some group and that all the conditions for PPR are relevantly fulfilled. Prima facie, one ought to report the wrongdoing. Similarly, one's other duties of loyalty, obedience, as well as respect for those one works for are also prima facie. They can be overridden in serious cases. Consequently, PPR might, given appropriate circumstances, override them.

One's obligation to report should be directed internally (at least initially and subject to overriding conditions) because the source of the wrongdoing comes through the organization. One's loyalty is not simply to one's supervisor but also to the organization.[14] The wrongdoing may also have significant implications for the organization (loss of reputation, legal fees, fines). Under these circumstances, to permit those closest to the wrongdoing (and responsible to correct it) the opportunity to do so is to respect their authority and self-determination. To report externally, as long as there were other reasonable internal venues, would be to undercut their responsibilities and not give them a chance to do what they should do. In addition, the internal route might also be the most efficient way to address the situation. The organization could then deal with the fact that a serious legal or moral wrong has been done. In the case of a serious legal wrongdoing, the corporation would have to self-report the problem to legal authorities. This inside approach would give the leadership of the organization a chance to know about the problem before the media or court system does, to announce the problem to the responsible legal officials, and to begin to address the organizational dimensions of the problem even before a full legal accounting took place. In general, this would be desirable both practically and ethically for an organization. However, should the internal route pose significant danger to the potential whistle-blower or the strong likelihood of a pointless result, then one's obligation to report would be to external agents.

An employee does not have a responsibility to challenge insurmountable barriers. He or she does not have a responsibility to reform the organization so that reports of wrongdoing make it to the top levels. If each person the whistle-blower goes to in the hierarchy does not act on the information but resists and punishes the whistle-blower, then there is something wrong with the organization, its processes, and procedures. Though many organizations have rules and policies requiring employees to report wrongdoing, still, the de facto corporate culture may oppose such reporting as a form of snitching or betrayal. The more a business undercuts the conditions required for the fulfillment of one's responsibility to report internally, the weaker is this responsibility to the organization. It is not surprising that one of the reasons empirical accounts report why people do not blow the whistle is that they believe nothing will be done. This is a direct reflection on the failure of the organization's internal mechanisms and culture.

If under these circumstances, an employee continues to try to report up the corporate chain of command, then they go above and beyond the call of duty. Doing so may even be foolish. It may also be that one's actions are of a supererogatory nature, presenting us with an ideal, if not heroic, form of loyalty. However, morality does not require that one take such steps or that one uselessly sacrifice oneself in this manner, even if the aim is noble. Instead, one's reporting responsibility is to make genuine efforts to report the wrongdoing to responsible officials. When it becomes clear that the organizational response is not going to change, it would be unreasonable to require one to go through each level of the organization. Instead, the Principle of Positional Responsibility and loyalty require that one give the organization a fair and meaningful chance to address the charges and to correct the problem....

THE STRINGENCY OF THE PRINCIPLE OF POSITIONAL RESPONSIBILITY

The question of the weight or stringency that one should attribute to the principle of positional responsibility arises also with regard to risks to oneself. There are different studies on this topic, but there is certainly the possibility that one will suffer—perhaps even dramatically—if one reports wrongdoing, but particularly if one does so externally. Some businesses have responded with a viciousness that is appalling. The treatment of Dan Gellert by Eastern Airlines is a good example. As a pilot at Eastern Airlines, Gellert became aware of a defect in the autopilot control system on Lockheed 1011 aircraft. At times it would disengage

in a manner that could lead to a crash. In fact, one plane did crash. Others had near crashes. For his efforts to bring this situation to the attention of management and get it corrected, he was given flight schedules that tested his physical well-being, mental exams that challenged his psychological fitness, told to appear in courtrooms in other cities in a time frame that was impossible, and so on. All this was part of an effort to discredit him. In short, what a whistle-blower should know is that her life will change—and may change significantly—as a result of her report.

This risk to oneself directly affects one's moral responsibility to blow the whistle since it may negatively affect many of one's other responsibilities, important interests, and projects. One has multiple responsibilities and interests that have defined one's life prior to this unexpected event. One has built up relationships at work and outside of work that depend upon one fulfilling the responsibilities that constitute these other relationships. Will one act consistently on these principles, or will one compromise some of them? Which principles and values are most important? How courageous is one prepared to be? How courageous is one capable of being? How would other moral agents who are courageous act, and what risks would they undertake, in this situation? What about one's duty of confidentiality and obedience that are part of one's job? What about one's responsibilities to one's peers and one's family? The Principle of Positional Responsibility, by itself, cannot answer these questions.

The extent of one's responsibilities under this principle will be difficult to determine in any particular case and certainly cannot be ascertained precisely in many cases. A soldier's responsibilities may include placing himself in harm's way such that he might possibly be killed. A physician has a responsibility to his patients that may involve contracting life-threatening sicknesses. However, employees do not, ordinarily, have a responsibility—unless they so choose—to sacrifice their health, lives, or futures for a business by helping to prevent the damage that the wrongdoing of others may do to them. Rather, their whistle-blowing responsibilities are tied, most closely, to those who are wronged (or may be wronged) by the employees of the business for which they work.

Assuming that some serious wrongdoing has taken (or will take) place, that the person has reasonable evidence of this wrongdoing, that the agents normally responsible are not fulfilling their duties, and that one has a reasonable prospect of effectively changing the situation, one has a responsibility to proceed with bringing the wrongdoing to the attention of others who can do something about it. And, particularly, if whistle-blowing would have very minimal, short-term effects on one's life, but correct a serious wrong, then an employee has a responsibility to try to make the information public.

However, if the chance of success is limited and the implications for the whistle-blower are themselves so significant that his or her life will be dramatically injured as a result, it is much less obvious that the person is responsible to blow the whistle. After all, the wrongdoing is not itself a failure of the potential whistle-blower, but of others in the organization. Further, it is plausible that a person does not have an obligation to report the wrongdoings of others when doing so will destroy himself or turn him simply into a means whereby the organization's wrongs are corrected....

INTEGRITY CONSIDERATIONS

In making these decisions regarding whistle-blowing, one must place the Principle of Positional Responsibility within the context of other values and norms one justifiably stands for. We are concerned in whistle-blowing situations with one's faithfulness or commitment not only to this principle but also to other important values, norms, and ideals that define one. Is one prepared to act and live by them even when confronted with situations that impose threats and costs—sometimes even of a considerable nature—on one? These are considerations of integrity, inasmuch as a person of integrity will defend her values and norms even

when doing so is inconvenient or difficult. As Lynn Sharp Paine says, "persons of integrity have a set of anchoring beliefs or principles that define who they are and what they believe in. They stand for something and remain steadfast when confronted with adversity or temptation."[15]

Beyond this, assuming that our values, responsibilities, and ideals may conflict at times, a person of integrity will integrate these normative facets of her life into some reasonably coherent whole. Those responsibilities and values of greatest importance will receive the greatest priority. Integrity, we are told, "involves recognition that some desires are more important and more desirable than others; that some commitments make a greater claim upon us than others; that some values are deeper than others; and that some principles take priority over others."[16] Which of these principles, ideals, and values are the most important ones to support and at what cost to oneself as well as others? To which values and norms is one prepared to remain faithful? Is one prepared to sacrifice other important values (e.g., family, career) to correct the wrongdoing one has discovered?

When an instance of whistle-blowing arises, the justified course of action will be filtered through these different normative dimensions of one's justified values and norms. Does this area central to who a person is shrink, at such times, to a small island focused simply on protecting oneself? Does it encompass others and the full range of one's values, norms, and ideals? The decision one makes on implementing the Principle of Positional Responsibility will be a decision regarding one's integrity as one decides what one justifiably stands for. One might say that this situation is the flip side of complicity. It is not because one is involved in wrongdoing that one must decide whether or not one will blow the whistle, but because one must choose between the different principles of obligation and duty that pertain to one, the ideals by which one lives, and the kind of person one wishes to be. Even with internal whistle-blowing, one must decide to step outside the security, protections, and relative anonymity of the normal hierarchy to make a moral stand for what ought to be done. It is inherently a situation that requires courage and commitment to one's values and principles.

Consider then an employee, Debra, who knows of wrongdoing in the business for which she works; others who work there are afraid to say anything. Her supervisor and peers say that she ought to forget it about it: "That's just the way things are done around here." Debra is certain that wrongdoing is going on and has evidence to back up her view. This wrongdoing bothers her greatly; she understands the implications of PPR. Thus, Debra takes her information to top management or goes to an outside source to change things, even knowing that there are considerable risks. However, in doing so she does not blow the whistle simply because this is the implication of PPR, but because it fits with her ongoing concerns for honesty, for not wronging others, and for accountability. These values and norms have defined Debra's life and her relations with others. Not to blow the whistle would be to retreat and compromise these, as well as PPR. It is a question of integrity—of knowing what was going on, of having certain values and views, and of living them. Contrariwise, if she had these values, norms, and character traits and did not act on them, she would be a hypocrite and her integrity tarnished.

Contrast this with Jim, who comes to know of serious wrongdoing that is going on regarding accounting measures at his firm. No one is being physically harmed, but the company is misreporting its financial status and various activities. When this fraud becomes known, this will affect investors and possibly employees and suppliers. Jim reports his knowledge of the wrongdoing to his supervisor, who says that he will take care of it and that Jim should stick to his own job. There are suggestions that if he does not do this he will be in trouble. Jim is convinced that the supervisor will do nothing, and if he (Jim) does not do anything else, this wrongdoing will continue (at least for the present). Though there are other people (with authority) in the organization who know the wrong doing is going on, there is a conspiracy of silence amongst a small group of people. Jim is aware of the implications of PPR, but Jim has other important responsibilities as well that have shaped his life. He is the sole provider for his family. He is also the chairperson of a regional group that focuses on providing disadvantaged children with educational support. His role has been critical in moving this group from one that is largely ineffective to one that makes an important impact on children in the area. Since this area is conservative, Jim believes that if he became involved in revealing the corporate wrongdoing his position in this regional organization would be jeopardized and the aid they are providing disrupted. He is also not certain that if he blew the whistle anyone would listen. He knows about the retaliation against other whistle-blowers, and he has his family to think about. He decides that there are other, more important things he should be doing than correcting this particular wrong in his company by whistle-blowing. He also has other, more direct responsibilities that would be crippled if he blew the whistle. Ideally, of course, he would do both. But this is not an ideal world. He can maintain his integrity by resigning, even if it means taking a lower-paying job, while fulfilling the other important responsibilities he has undertaken and which are crucial to him and those to whom he is responsible.

In each of these cases, the integrity of those involved has played a role in how the Principle of Positional Responsibility is applied. If one's responsibility to blow the whistle does not significantly disrupt one's other responsibilities and projects, one has a responsibility to blow the whistle. One would be wrong not to do so, whether internally or, if necessary, externally. However, all too frequently, in deciding to blow the whistle, one may be making a life-altering decision that will affect oneself as well as others. It is not like calling the police to report a neighborhood crime, which may take a few minutes or few hours, after which it will be over. Due to the responses of fellow workers, the recrimination to which one may render oneself vulnerable, the amount of time and money one must expend to defend one's claims, the pressures it will place on one's personal life and family relationships, whistle-blowing may simply change the course of one's life. It is too easy to say, abstractly considered, one has a moral obligation to blow the whistle without placing this obligation within the broader context of the other responsibilities, values, and practical implications for the whistle-blower. One cannot appropriately respond to PPR by simply considering this principle itself, separated from the rest of one's life. Instead, one's response must arise out of how this principle, in a particular set of circumstances, coheres with the rest of who we are, namely, our other values, principles, and ideals as we have integrated them into our lives. The question is not simply and abstractly, "Would it be justified for some person or other to blow the whistle in this situation?" But rather the question is, "Would it be justified for this person in this situation to blow the whistle?" Here the risks a person must take play a legitimate role in her decision as well as how this action coheres with other values and norms she supports. In answering these questions, one defines what kind of person one is and reaffirms (or undercuts) one's integrity.

Hence, the present account of justified whistle-blowing is a mixed one. The Principle of Positional Responsibility and integrity play joint roles. But because PPR plays its role within the broader context of our integrity, I have called it the Integrity Theory.

WHISTLE-BLOWING AND THE DESIGN OF ORGANIZATIONS

The preceding accounts of whistle-blowing ask what justifies an individual engaging in whistle-blowing. The Integrity Theory, I believe, is the best response to that question. However, focusing on this question distracts us from the underlying problem of the misconduct occurring in (or through) organizations that organizations themselves fail to identify and correct. Whistle-blowers have played a vital role in bringing to light many of these wrong-doings. They have provided an admirable service to the public. For this they deserve protection.

However, depending on the measures adopted, this way of correcting wrongdoing may not be very successful. In any case, such an approach treats the symptoms and not the underlying problems. It is a Band-Aid approach.

Accordingly, we should also be asking about the situation that gives rise to the need for individual whistle-blowing. What, in short, is the problem to which whistle-blowing is the supposed answer? What is the design problem (as McDonough would say) to which blowing the whistle is the answer?[17] The unsurprising, but important, answer is whistle-blowing is necessary when there has been a failure within the organization. It is one way by which we discover and seek to correct important wrongs or abuses by organizations when some of their members do not wish to recognize or correct them. In short, the wrong doing whistle-blowers target is both an individual and an organizational failure.

There are two striking features of this answer. First, this answer tends to imperil, and sometimes destroy, the people who report the wrongdoing. There are numerous reports of the terrible retaliation whistle-blowers have experienced.[18] And though the empirical evidence does not demonstrate that all whistle-blowers suffer significant retaliation, far too many do.[19] Second, whistle-blowing is, often, not terribly effective. The evidence regarding how often claims of whistle-blowing successfully result in the wrongs or harms reported being corrected is extremely difficult to come by, given the nature of these actions.[20] One measure is to consider those who have filed under the Whistle-blower Protection Act. On this score, whistle-blowers have had "a minuscule success rate. Only 1 percent of such cases since 2001 was referred to agency heads for investigation. Of the last 95 such cases that reached the federal circuit court of appeals, only one whistle-blower won."[21] Accordingly, whistle-blowing as a response to wrongdoing by organizations and the people in them has considerable weaknesses. The whistle-blowing answer to our design problem is not an obviously good answer—even if an individual is justified in blowing the whistle. Those who blow the whistle are themselves often wronged or abused. And the result of their efforts is quite frequently that needed changes do not take place. Yet these changes were the point of the whistle-blowing. As such, the current focus on individual whistle-blowing is often the justification of sacrificial victims on behalf of ineffective efforts.

This suggests that we need more discussion of organizational conditions that would forestall the necessity of whistle-blowing. If organizations were designed to obviate the necessity of whistle-blowing, then the gut-wrenching stories of the fate of whistle-blowers might be considerably reduced and the occasions of individual whistle-blowing become much more infrequent. In short, the discussion of organizational designs that would reduce or eliminate the need for whistle-blowing should be primary, and any justification of individual whistle-blowing should be secondary.

The real ethical problem whistle-blowing raises is how do we create self-correcting organizations that catch violations by themselves and do not rely on individuals (who experience retaliation) to identify and demand their correction? How can we avoid the results of bureaucracies and organizations that devote "inordinate amounts of energy to the construction of barriers to review and account"?[22] For such self-correcting organizations, individual whistle-blowing would be, at best, a second—or third choice—as a way to address these problems.

Needless to say, the solution to this problem is something that I can only briefly touch upon here. However, for present purposes I do not need to provide a complete account. Instead, what I must do is to indicate the general features of self-correcting organizations that would work to obviate the necessity of whistle-blowing.

The relevant design question regarding organizations is not simply a matter of trying to protect whistle-blowers but of creating organizations in which external whistle-blowing is not necessary (or at the least minimized), and in which internal whistle-blowing (should it be necessary) is received with a positive response. Such organizations must be able to detect and acknowledge mistakes or wrongful acts, receive bad news, and take steps to correct those problems. Unless organizations are serious about this, we cannot be serious about whistle-blowing. If they were serious, they would be self-regulating and self-enforcing organizations. Such organizations would, thereby, be faithful to their own values, purposes, and legitimating bases. They would be organizations of integrity.

Self-Correcting Organizations

What features would characterize a self-correcting organization?

First, they would seek information regarding problems and violations from all those who are members of (or who have a privileged relation with) the organization. They cannot rely simply on monitors, auditors, or the like. If an organization's self-correcting method is dependent simply on monitors or auditors to detect its problems, then it will always be inadequate since such an approach can never have a monitor in each office and for every action.

Second, the members of organizations must also have an acknowledged responsibility to come forward when they see misconduct. Organizations can seek to capture this responsibility in codes of ethics, through ethics and compliance programs, and those in charge of overseeing ethical and legal complaints. Nevertheless, these methods will not be adequate unless this responsibility is acknowledged through a corporate culture that values, rather than denigrates, the reporting of bad news and misconduct. The most direct way for this to occur is for those involved to self-report problems, errors, wrongful acts, and so on. As in experimental sciences, these failures may be the occasion of important learning and redirection of the individuals, departments, and businesses involved.

Third, there must be means to receive the reports and to initiate examination of them and, as appropriate, institute needed changes. The point, after all, of bringing such charges forward is, when warranted, to make changes. At the same time, there are stories about employees being told they have a responsibility to report misconduct and then not being protected when they do.[23] Both these situations suggest the importance of structural and cultural changes. These do not, however, take place spontaneously. They require the good will of management and executives, the "buy-in" of employees, but also the need of the law, social pressures, and stakeholder pressures on behalf of such behavior. The law must play an important role here, giving not only some measure of protection to whistle-blowers but also incentives to organizations to be self-correcting.

Fourth, self-correcting organizations would have to institute measures to foster an attitude among employees willing to push back against directions to engage in illegal or unethical behaviors. They would have to encourage them to fulfill their responsibilities to identify substantive wrong-doings and to resist efforts to remain quiet. This would require important cultural changes for many organizations and individuals. In particular, cultural changes are necessary to address the situation that has often been reported of insiders who see wrong things being done but tend not to report them.[24]

The other side of this equation would require that organizations be structured, and their members trained, to accept bad news, to confront wrong-doing, and seek ways to change it. To encourage these attitudes it is necessary to address negative attitudes employees and supervisors may have regarding resistance to their views and the reporting of misconduct. This involves, but is not limited to, integrating ethics into performance evaluations and feedback surveys, linking the value of loyalty to the legitimating bases of the organization, and protecting and commending those who identify problems and misconduct. This involves programs and initiatives far beyond whistle-blowing situations. These initiatives speak to a general condition for how those who have power and authority over others should treat those subordinate to them when the latter inform their leaders of illegal, immoral, or illegitimate activities going on in the organization. The organizational dimension of this question is the fundamental ethical issue that whistle-blowing raises.

Finally, since an organization is not a wholly self-contained system but exists only within the political, economic, social, and legal context of its time, there is a role for the broader social and political system in the preceding, for example, for the government to provide penalties for harming or harassing whistle-blowers and incentives for whistle-blowers to come forward with valuable information. Since we are dealing with "the crooked timber" of humanity, there must always be means, internally and externally, for people in an organization to circumvent wrongdoers when these are the people to whom one would ordinarily report the wrongdoing. More generally, however, we should work to create organizations and a social and political system that renders whistle-blowing and such sacrifices unnecessary. We need to transform organizations that shape and form our lives so that the wrong, the harms, and the abuses that occur through them can be identified and corrected. We may not be able to ensure that this is always the case, but we can do a better job than we have.

The preceding points are not designed simply to protect whistle-blowers. Rather, they are about how organizations ought to be designed so that the need for whistle-blowing is minimized and not the only answer to the correction of wrongdoing within or through organizations. Since there are different kinds of organizations, the answers here will vary. They may seek to accomplish their ends in a variety of ways. But the general points made above remains the same.

This is the project on which those truly concerned about whistle-blowing should be focused. It is this project of revising corporate activities that will address the real problem that lies behind whistle-blowing.

NOTES

1   James M. Roche, "The Competitive System to Work, to Preserve, and to Protect," *Vital Speeches of the Day* (May 1971): 455.

2   John R. Boatright *Ethics and the Conduct of Business*, 3rd ed. rev. (Upper Saddle River, N.J.: Prentice-Hall, 2000), 109.

3   Norman Bowie *Business Ethics* (Englewood Cliffs, N.J.: Prentice-Hall, Inc., 1982), 142.

4   Sissela Bok "Whistleblowing and Professional Responsibility," *New York University Education Quarterly* 11 (1980): 2.

5   Janet Near and Marcia Miceli "Organizational Dissidence: The Case of Whistle-Blowing," *Journal of Business Ethics* 4 (1985): 4.

6   Ibid.

7   Ibid.

8   Marcia P. Miceli and Janet P. Near *Blowing the Whistle* (New York: Lexington, 1992), 3, 19–20.

9   Norman E. Bowie and Ronald F. Duska *Business Ethics*, 2nd ed. rev. (Englewood Cliffs, N.J.: Prentice-Hall, 1990), 74.

10 These conditions draw upon the Kew Gardens principle that Simon, Power, and Gunneman have set out. See John G. Simon Charles W. Powers and Jon P. Gunneman *The Ethical Investor: Universities and Corporate Responsibility* (New Haven, Conn.: Yale University Press, 1972), 22–25.

11 Both De George and Bowie link whistle-blowing with serious harms or wrongdoings. See De George, *Business Ethics*, 308–9; Bowie, *Business Ethics*, 142, 144.

12 Yolanda Woodlee, "Former D.C. Workers Say Law Doesn't Prevent Retaliation," *The Washington Post*, April 28, 2008, B1.

13 Del Quentin Wilber, "More Step Up to Complain about FAA," *The Washington Post*, May 31, 2008, D1.

14 See Vandekerckhove and Commer, "Whistle Blowing and Rational Loyalty." Also *Restatement of Agency*.

15 Lynn Sharp Paine "Integrity," in *The Blackwell Encyclopedic Dictionary of Business Ethics*, ed. Patricia H. Werhane and R. Edward Freeman (Malden, Mass.: Blackwell, 1997), 335.

16 Damian Cox Marguerite La Caze and Michael P. Levine *Integrity and the Fragile Self* (Aldershot, U.K.: Ashgate, 2003), 8.

17 See William A. McDonough, "A Boat for Thoreau," in *Business Ethics Quarterly*: Ruffin Series, vol. 2, "Environmental Challenges to Business" (2000), 115– 133.

18 Marlene Winfield "Whistleblowers as Corporate Safety Net," in *Whistleblowing: Subversion or Corporate Citizenship?* ed. Gerald Vinten (New York: St. Martin's, 1994), 22.

19 Near and Miceli report that "fewer than half of the responding whistle-blowers [in a study they made] reported that they experienced any retaliation." See Janet P. Near and Marcia P. Miceli "Whistle-blowers in Organizations: Dissidents or Reformers?" in *Research in Organizational Behavior*, ed. B.M. Staw and L.L. Cummings (Greenwich, Conn.: JAI Press, 1987), 356. The data for this finding were gathered from the public sector where there are (were) greater protections for whistle-blowers.

20 See Marica P. Miceli and Janet P. Near "Understanding Whistle-Blowing Effectiveness: How Can One Person Make a Difference?" in *The Accountable Corporation: Business-Government Relations*, vol. 4, ed. Marc J. Epstein and Kirk O. Hanson (Westport, Conn.: Praeger, 2006).

21 Mark Clayton, "Hard Job of Blowing the Whistle Gets Harder," *The Christian Science Monitor* (January 20, 2005), http://www.csmonitor.com/2005/0120/p13s02-sten.html (accessed March 14, 2016). We should also consider the many employees who simply do not speak out but remain silent witnesses to wrongdoing; see Marcia P. Miceli and Janet P. Near *Blowing the Whistle* (New York: Lexington, 1992).

22 Martin Landau, "On the Concept of a Self-Correcting Organization," *Public Administration Review* (Nov.–Dec. 1973): 534.

23 See Marlene Winfield, "Whistleblowers as Corporate Safety Net," 27.

24 Miceli and Near, "Understanding Whistle-Blowing Effectiveness: How Can One Person Make a Difference?" 201.

OBLIGATIONS, RESPONSIBILITY, AND WHISTLEBLOWING

A Case Study of Jeffrey Wigand

Brian J. Collins

BACKGROUND

JEFFREY WIGAND IS ONE OF THE MOST FAMOUS "whistleblowers" in American history due to the portrayal of his story in the 1999 film *The Insider*. The film, starring Russell Crowe as Wigand and Al Pacino as CBS *60 Minutes* producer Lowell Bergman, details Wigand's struggle as he decides whether or not he will break his confidentiality agreement with former employer Brown & Williamson and expose the tobacco company's disturbing secrets.

The term "whistleblower" originates from a nineteenth-century British expression referring to the practice of unarmed police and merchants blowing an actual whistle to alert bystanders of crimes such as pickpocketing and shoplifting. When the expression "blowing the whistle" emerged in the American vernacular in the early twentieth century it had transformed slightly, now conjuring an image of a referee putting an end to a match or stopping play to call a penalty. Though the expression simply meant to put a stop to something, it now carried with it a strong negative connotation that was used to brand individuals as "snitches" who "squealed" to authorities. However, beginning in the 1960s a young attorney and consumer advocate, Ralph Nader, helped to rehabilitate the word "whistleblower" back to the morally praiseworthy association tied to the origin of the expression. Advocating for consumers and workers, Nader called for civic minded "whistleblowers" in the government and private sectors to do their part by reporting fraud and generally poor policy and oversight. Nader's work, and the whistleblowers who stepped forward, helped lead to many consumer-protection laws such as the National Traffic and Motor Vehicle Safety Act (1966) which set new safety standards for vehicles and roadways and the Wholesome Meat Act (1967) which set new regulations for the inspection of slaughterhouses and meat packing facilities.[1]

In 1970 the Occupational Safety and Health Act (OSH) was passed into law by Congress to act as whistleblower protection. It prohibits "employers from discriminating against their employees for exercising their rights under the OSH Act. These rights include filing an OSHA [Occupational Safety and Health Administration] complaint, participating in an inspection or talking to any inspector, seeking access to employer exposure and injury records, reporting an injury, and raising a safety or health complaint with the employer."[2] Legally, a whistleblower is anyone who reports illegal or unsafe activities or conditions within a business or organization.

This brings us back to the case of Jeffrey Wigand and Brown & Williamson. After completing his B.A., M.A., and Ph.D. in biochemistry, Wigand began a career in the healthcare industry. For seventeen years he worked in various roles for several healthcare companies such as Pfizer, Johnson & Johnson, and Biosonics. Then in 1989, somewhat surprisingly, Wigand accepted a lucrative offer from the tobacco company Brown & Williamson (B&W) (owned by British American Tobacco–BAT Industries). He was named the head of Research & Development to lead the department with an annual budget of $30 million and a staff of 243. Almost immediately there was tension between Wigand and his colleagues as he felt that the level of testing and research was not up to par. Additionally, Wigand quickly began to feel that his scientific concerns over certain additives being used in the manufacturing process of tobacco products and his ethical concerns about marketing tobacco products to teenagers were not being taken seriously by company executives. Finally, after four years of increasing tension and disagreement, Wigand was fired on March 24, 1993.

In order to keep his severance package, including medical benefits for his family, Wigand reluctantly signed a comprehensive lifelong confidentiality agreement with B&W that would keep him from discussing *anything* about the company. However, in February of 1994 Wigand was sought out by Lowell Bergman, a producer at CBS's *60 Minutes*, to analyze some documents Bergman had obtained concerning Philip Morris (a competitor of B&W). This would be the beginning of a relationship that would eventually lead to Wigand breaking his confidentiality agreement and coming forward publically as a whistleblower against B&W and the tobacco industry. Before coming forward publically, Wigand worked privately (with his identity protected) with the Food and Drug Administration advising them on cigarette chemistry and some of the dangerous chemical additives. While Wigand remained hesitant to share everything he knew for fear of being sued by B&W and losing his family's medical benefits (on which one

of his daughters depended on to cover her medical expenses associated with spina bifida), he began to work with Bergman and *60 Minutes*. Then on November 29, 1995, Wigand gave a deposition in a case the state of Mississippi brought against the tobacco companies. Portions of this testimony were eventually published in *The Wall Street Journal* and on February 4, 1996, CBS finally aired the story and interview with Wigand. In these acts of whistleblowing Wigand contended that B&W manipulated the nicotine and chemical additives in cigarettes, lied about their knowledge concerning the addictiveness of cigarettes, and failed to work towards developing "safer" cigarettes.

Wigand's decision to blow the whistle on B&W and the tobacco industry did not come without personal cost. In dealing with the pressure and stress, Wigand struggled personally with drinking, legal problems, and divorce. B&W engaged in a brutal smear campaign against Wigand and he received several death threats and faced other forms of intimidation severe enough to require a full-time bodyguard to help ensure his safety. Ultimately though, his actions helped lead to the Master Settlement Agreement (1998) between the four largest tobacco companies and forty-six states. In this settlement the tobacco companies agreed to change marketing practices and pay over $200 billion dollars to help compensate for state-funded medical costs associated with smoking-related diseases.

ANALYSIS

We now know that cigarettes are addictive and dangerous to health. Jeffrey Wigand helped bring these facts, and the tobacco companies' suppression of this information, into the open. This high profile case is valuable because it provides a sort of arena where we can test and examine our concepts. We can use this case to frame questions about whistleblowing, such as: When is it morally *permissible* for someone to blow the whistle? When is it morally *required*? What is one supposed to do when other moral obligations are in conflict with whistleblowing (e.g., one's contractual obligations)?

One useful way of beginning to address these questions is to use Richard T. De George's well-known analysis of the morality of whistleblowing. De George offers five conditions that help determine when and under what conditions employees should blow the whistle. The first three of De George's conditions attempt to specify when the act of whistleblowing is morally justifiable and *permissible*.

Following Michael W. Hoffman and Mark Schwartz, we will call the first condition the "Harm Principle."[3] It states that the company, through its product or policy, must be doing or risking serious and considerable harm to employees or to the public. How does Wigand's case fare in relation to this first criterion? Brown & Williamson was aware of the harmful effects of smoking and knew that the nicotine in its cigarettes was addictive; they were manipulating the nicotine levels and other chemical additives in the tobacco for exactly these reasons. These circumstances appear to meet De George's "Harm Principle" perfectly. B&W product *and* policies were doing serious harm to people and, by covering up the information they had about addictiveness and the negative health effects of smoking, threatening even a greater number of people. So Wigand's case meets the first of De George's criteria for his act of whistleblowing to be morally justified and permissible.

De George's second and third conditions are closely related to one another; we'll call them the "Internal Reporting Principles." They state that once the serious harm or threat has been identified it must first be reported to an immediate superior. If the immediate superior does not effectively address the concern, then one can take the concern up the managerial ladder. De George contends that if these first three conditions are met the act of whistleblowing is morally justified and permissible. In the case of Wigand and B&W, Wigand did report his findings to his superiors and attempted to move up the corporate chain when he was not satisfied with the responses he was receiving. Consequently, Wigand meets the first three of De George's criteria thereby classifying his act of whistleblowing as morally justified and permissible. However, these criteria do not seem to take into account the fact that Wigand signed a contract that forfeited his right to talk publically about information he had concerning B&W.

De George stresses that simply because an action is *morally permissible* does not mean that we must perform it. After all, whistleblowers face significant costs that need to be considered. De George offers two additional criteria that strengthen the moral status of whistleblowing from being merely permissible to being morally *obligatory*. We will call his fourth condition the "Evidentiary Principle." It states that the whistleblower must have documented evidence of the serious harm or threat that would convince a reasonable and impartial observer. This condition is offered with the idea that one need not come forward publicly without substantial evidence because without such support the individual would be taking a significant personal risk without a reasonable expectation that any advantage will be gained (i.e., that the harm or threat will be remedied). In Wigand's case he had documented scientific evidence that the nicotine in cigarettes was addictive and that the chemical additives being incorporated into the tobacco products had potential long-term health effects. In addition, Wigand had some evidence that the executives of B&W knew these things and were ignoring or even suppressing this information. However, given the money and power possessed by the tobacco company and the circumstances of Wigand's daughter's medical condition, it is not immediately clear that the personal risk was outweighed by the chance of success. B&W did not have an explicit anti-retaliation policy and Wigand correctly feared that he would be met with hostility and backlash from his employer. Additionally, B&W was willing and able to threaten massive lawsuits against any media outlet who even showed signs that they were considering investigating the story.

These questions concerning cost/benefit analysis relate to De George's fifth condition, which we will call the "Make a Difference Principle." This final criterion states that the individual must have good reason to think the chances that the whistleblowing will succeed in stopping the serious harm or threat outweigh the risk one takes in going public. Given the monetary resources and power of B&W it does not seem immediately clear that Wigand's personal risk was outweighed by a reasonable expectation that any advantage would be gained. If Wigand's case meets De George's first three criteria but does not meet the fourth and/or fifth, then De George's analysis would be that whistleblowing would be morally justified and permissible but *not* something that Wigand was morally obligated to do.

DISCUSSION QUESTIONS

1. If Wigand had not come forward, would he be morally responsible for future individuals becoming addicted to and getting sick and dying from cigarette use?
2. How strong are contractual obligations? What are some examples when it would be morally permissible to break one's contract? What are some examples of when it would be morally impermissible to break one's contract?
3. Many people intuitively believe that employees ought to be loyal to their employers. Why do you think an obligation of loyalty might exist for an employee?
4. How much moral responsibility do the media have for making sure that morally justified acts of whistleblowing succeed in stopping the harm or threat?

5. Should the moral permissibility of whistleblowing depend on the motivations of the individual blowing the whistle? Do one's motivations affect the moral praiseworthiness of whistleblowing? What, if any, difference is there between moral permissibility, praiseworthiness, and obligation?

NOTES

1   Zimmer, Ben. 2013. "The Epithet Nader Made Respectable." *The Wall Street Journal*, http://www.wsj. com/articles/SB10001424127887323 368704578596083294221030.
2   United States Department of Labor. 2015. "The Whistleblower Protections Programs." http://www.whistleblowers.gov/.
3   Hoffman, W. Michael and Schwartz, Mark S. 2014. "The Morality of Whistleblowing: A Commentary on Richard T. De George," *Journal of Business Ethics*, 771–781.

FURTHER READINGS

Brenner, Marie. May 1996. "The Man Who Knew Too Much," *Vanity Fair*.

Hoffman, W. Michael and Schwartz, Mark S. 2014. "The Morality of Whistleblowing: A Commentary on Richard T. De George," *Journal of Business Ethics*, 771–781.

—49—
DRUG TESTING IN EMPLOYMENT

Joseph DesJardins and Ronald Duska

ACCORDING TO ONE SURVEY, NEARLY ONE-HALF of all Fortune 500 companies were planning to administer drug tests to employees and prospective employees by the end of 1987.[1] Counter to what seems to be the current trend in favor of drug testing, we will argue that it is rarely legitimate to override an employee's or applicant's right to privacy by using such tests or procedures.[2]

OPENING STIPULATIONS

We take privacy to be an "employee right" by which we mean a presumptive moral entitlement to receive certain goods or be protected from certain harms in the workplace. Such a right creates a *prima facie* obligation on the part of the employer to provide the relevant goods or, as in this case, refrain from the relevant harmful treatment. These rights prevent employees from being placed in the fundamentally coercive position where they must choose between their job and other basic human goods.

Further, we view the employer-employee relationship as essentially contractual. The employer-employee relationship is an economic one and, unlike relationships such as those between a government and its citizens or a parent and a child, exists primarily as a means for satisfying the economic interests of the contracting parties. The obligations that each party incurs are only those that it voluntarily takes on. Given such a contractual relationship, certain areas of the employee's life remain their own private concern and no employer has a right to invade them. On these presumptions we maintain that certain information about an employee is rightfully private, i.e., the employee has a right to privacy.

THE RIGHT TO PRIVACY

According to George Brenkert, a right to privacy involves a three-place relation between a person A, some information X, and another person B. The right to privacy is violated only when B deliberately comes to possess information X about A, and no relationship between A and B exists which could justify B's coming to know X about A.[3] Thus, for example, the relationship one has with a mortgage company would justify that company's coming to know about one's salary, but the relationship one has with a neighbor does not justify the neighbor's coming to know that information. Hence, an employee's right to privacy is violated whenever personal information is requested, collected and/or used by an employer in a way or for any purpose that is *irrelevant to* or in *violation of* the contractual relationship that exists between employer and employee.

Since drug testing is a means for obtaining information, the information sought must be relevant to the contract in order for the drug testing not to violate privacy. Hence, we must first decide if knowledge of drug use obtained by drug testing is job-relevant. In cases where the knowledge of drug use is not relevant, there appears to be no justification for subjecting employees to drug tests. In cases where information of drug use is job-relevant, we need to consider if, when, and under what conditions using a means such as drug testing to obtain that knowledge is justified.

IS KNOWLEDGE OF DRUG USE JOB-RELEVANT INFORMATION?

There seem to be two arguments used to establish that knowledge of drug use is job-relevant information. The first argument claims that drug use adversely affects job performance thereby leading to lower productivity, higher costs, and consequently lower profits. Drug testing is seen as a way of avoiding these adverse effects. According to some estimates twenty-five billion dollars ($25,000,000,000) are lost each year in the United States because of drug use.[4] This occurs because of loss in productivity, increase in costs due to theft, increased rates in health and liability insurance, and such. Since employers are contracting with an employee for the performance of specific tasks, employers seem to have a legitimate claim upon whatever personal information is relevant to an employee's ability to do the job.

The second argument claims that drug use has been and can be responsible for considerable harm to the employee him/herself, fellow employees, the employer, and/or third parties, including consumers. In this case drug testing is defended because it is seen as a way of preventing possible harm. Further, since employers can be held liable for harms done both to third parties, e.g., customers, and to the employee or his/her fellow employees, knowledge of employee drug use will allow employers to gain information that can protect themselves from risks such as liability. But how good are these arguments? We turn to examine the arguments more closely.

THE FIRST ARGUMENT: JOB PERFORMANCE AND KNOWLEDGE OF DRUG USE

The first argument holds that drug use leads to lower productivity and consequently implies that knowledge of drug use obtained through drug testing will allow an employer to increase productivity. It is generally assumed that people using certain drugs have their performances affected by such use. Since enhancing productivity is something any employer desires, any use of drugs that reduces productivity affects the employer in an undesirable way, and that use is, then, job-relevant. If such production losses can be eliminated by knowledge of the drug use, then knowledge of that drug use is job-relevant information. On the surface this argument seems reasonable. Obviously some drug use in lowering the level of performance can decrease productivity. Since the employer is entitled to a certain level of performance and drug use adversely affects performance, knowledge of that use seems job-relevant.

But this formulation of the argument leaves an important question unanswered. To what level of performance are employers entitled? Optimal performance, or some lower level? If some lower level, what? Employers have a valid claim upon some *certain level* of performance, such that a failure to get form up to this level would give the employer a justification for disciplining, firing or at least finding fault with the employee. But that does not necessarily mean that the employer has a right to a maximum or optimal level of performance, a level above and beyond a certain level of acceptability. It might be nice if the employee gives an employer a maximum effort or optimal performance, but that is above and beyond the call of the employee's duty and the employer can hardly claim a right at all times to the highest level of performance of which an employee is capable.

That there are limits on required levels of performance and productivity becomes clear if we recognize that job performance is person-related. It is person-related because one person's best efforts at a particular task might produce results well below the norm, while another person's minimal efforts might produce results abnormally high when compared to the norm. For example a professional baseball player's performance on a ball field will be much higher than the average person's since the average person is unskilled in baseball. We have all encountered people who work hard with little or no results, as well as people who work little with phenomenal results. Drug use in very talented people might diminish their performance or productivity, but that performance would still be better than the performance of the average person or someone totally lacking in the skills required. That being said, the important question now is whether the employer is entitled to an employee's maximum effort and best results, or merely to an effort sufficient to perform the task expected.

If the relevant consideration is whether the employee is producing as expected (according to the normal demands of the position and contract), not whether he/she is producing as much as possible, then knowledge of drug use is irrelevant or unnecessary. Let's see why.

If the person is producing what is expected, knowledge of drug use on the grounds of production is irrelevant since, *ex hypothesi* the production is satisfactory. If, on the other hand, the performance suffers, then, to the extent that it slips below the level justifiably expected, the employer has *prima facie* grounds for warning, disciplining or releasing the employee. But the justification for this is the person's unsatisfactory performance, not the person's use of drugs. Accordingly, drug use information is either unnecessary or irrelevant and consequently there are not sufficient grounds to override the right of privacy. Thus, unless we can argue that an employer is entitled to optimal performance, the argument fails.

This counter-argument should make it clear that the information which is sub-relevant, and consequently which is not rightfully private, is information about an employee's level of performance and not information about the underlying causes of that level. The fallacy of the argument which promotes drug testing in the name of increased productivity is the assumption that each employee is obliged to perform at an optimal, or at least quite high, level. But this is required under

few, if any, contracts. What is required contractually is meeting the normally expected levels of production or performing the tasks in the job-description adequately (not optimally). If one can do that under the influence of drugs, then on the grounds of job-performance at least, drug use is rightfully private. If one cannot perform the task adequately, then the employee is not fulfilling the contract, and knowledge of the cause of the failure to perform is irrelevant on the contractual model.

Of course, if the employer suspects drug use or abuse as the cause of the unsatisfactory performance, then she might choose to help the person with counseling or rehabilitation. However, this does not seem to be something morally required of the employer. Rather, in the case of unsatisfactory performance, the employer has a *prima facie* justification for dismissing or disciplining the employee.

Before turning to the second argument which attempts to justify drug testing, we should mention a factor about drug use that is usually ignored in talk of productivity. The entire productivity argument is irrelevant for those cases in which employees use performance enhancing drugs. Amphetamines and steroids, for example, can actually enhance some performances. This points to the need for care when tying drug testing to job-performance. In the case of some drugs used by athletes, for example, drug testing is done because the drug-influenced performance is too good and therefore unfair, not because it leads to inadequate job-performance. In such a case, where the testing is done to ensure fair competition, the testing may be justified. But drug testing in sports is an entirely different matter than drug-testing in business.

To summarize our argument so far: Drug use may affect performance, but as long as the performance is at an acceptable level, the knowledge of drug use is irrelevant. If the performance is unacceptable, then that is sufficient cause for action to be taken. In this case an employee's failure to fulfill his/her end of a contract makes knowledge of the drug use unnecessary.

The Second Argument: Harm and the Knowledge of Drug Use to Prevent Harm

Even though the performance argument is inadequate, there is an argument that seems somewhat stronger. This is an argument based on the potential for drug use to cause harm. Using a type of Millian argument, one could argue that drug testing might be justified if such testing led to knowledge that would enable an employer to prevent harm. Drug use certainly can lead to harming others. Consequently, if knowledge of such drug use can prevent harm, then, knowing whether or not one's employee uses drugs might be a legitimate concern of an employer in certain circumstances. This second argument claims that knowledge of the employee's drug use is job-relevant because employees who are under the influence of drugs can pose a threat to the health and safety of themselves and others, and an employer who knows of that drug use and the harm it can cause has a responsibility to prevent it. Employers have both a general duty to prevent harm and the specific responsibility for harms done by their employees. Such responsibilities are sufficient reason for an employer to claim that information about an employee's drug use is relevant if that knowledge can prevent harm by giving the employer grounds for dismissing the employee or not allowing him/her to perform potentially harmful tasks. Employers might even claim a right to reduce unreasonable risks, in this case the risks involving legal and economic liability for harms caused by employees under the influence of drugs, as further justification for knowing about employee drug use.

This second argument differs from the first in which only a lowered job performance was relevant information. In this case, even to allow the performance is problematic, for the performance itself, more than being inadequate, can hurt people. We cannot be as sanguine about the prevention of harm as we can about inadequate production. Where drug use can cause serious harms, knowledge of that use becomes relevant if the knowledge of such use can lead to the prevention of harm and drug testing becomes justified as a means for obtaining that knowledge.

As we noted, we will begin initially by accepting this argument on roughly Millian grounds where restrictions on liberty are allowed in order to prevent harm to others. (The fact that one is harming oneself, if that does not harm others is not sufficient grounds for interference in another's behavior according to Mill.) In such a case an employer's obligation to prevent harm may override the obligation to respect an employee's privacy.

But let us examine this more closely. Upon examination, certain problems arise, so that even if there is a possibility of justifying drug testing to prevent harm, some caveats have to be observed and some limits set out.

JOBS WITH POTENTIAL TO CAUSE HARM

To say that employers can use drug testing where that can prevent harm is not to say that every employer has the right to know about the drug use of every employee. Not every job poses a serious enough threat to justify an employer coming to know this information.

In deciding which jobs pose serious enough threats certain guidelines should be followed. First the potential for harm should be *clear* and *present*. Perhaps all jobs in some extended way pose potential threats to human well-being. We suppose an accountant's error could pose a threat of harm to someone somewhere. But some jobs like those of airline pilots, school bus drivers, public transit drivers and surgeons, are jobs in which unsatisfactory performance poses a clear and present danger to others. It would be much harder to make an argument that job performances by auditors, secretaries, executive vice-presidents for public relations, college teachers, professional athletes, and the like, could cause harm if those performances were carried on under the influence of drugs. They would cause harm only in exceptional cases.

NOT EVERY PERSON
IS TO BE TESTED

But, even if we can make a case that a particular job involves a clear and present danger for causing harm if performed under the influence of drugs, it is not appropriate to treat everyone holding such a job the same. Not every job-holder is equally threatening. There is less reason to investigate an airline pilot for drug use if that pilot has a twenty-year record of exceptional service than there is to investigate a pilot whose behavior has become erratic and unreliable recently, or than one who reports to work smelling of alcohol and slurring his words. Presuming that every airline pilot is equally threatening is to deny individuals the respect that they deserve as autonomous, rational agents. It is to ignore previous history and significant differences. It is also probably inefficient and leads to the lowering of morale. It is the likelihood of causing harm, and not the fact of being an airline pilot *per se*, that is relevant in deciding which employees in critical jobs to test.

So, even if knowledge of drug use is justifiable to prevent harm, we must be careful to limit this justification to a range of jobs and people where the potential for harm is clear and present. The jobs must be jobs that clearly can cause harm, and the specific employee should not be someone who is reliable with a history of such reliability. Finally, the drugs being tested should be those drugs, the use of which in those jobs is really potentially harmful.

LIMITATIONS ON DRUG
TESTING POLICIES

Even when we identify those jobs and individuals where knowledge of drug use would be job-relevant information, we still need to examine whether some procedural limitations should not be placed upon the employer's testing for drugs. We have said that in cases where a real threat of harm exists and where evidence exists suggesting that a particular employee poses such a threat, an employer could be justified in knowing about drug use in order to prevent the potential harm. But we need to recognize that as long as the employer has the discretion for deciding when the potential for harm is clear and present, and for deciding which employees pose the threat of harm, the possibility of abuse is great. Thus, some policy limiting the employer's power is called for.

Just as criminal law places numerous restrictions protecting individual dignity and liberty on the state's pursuit of its goals, so we should expect that some restrictions be placed on an employer in order to protect innocent employees from harm (including loss of job and damage to one's personal and professional reputation). Thus, some system of checks upon an employer's discretion in these matters seems advisable. Workers covered by collective bargaining agreements or individual contracts might be protected by clauses on those agreements that specify which jobs pose a real threat of harm (e.g., pilots but not cabin attendants) and what constitutes a just cause for investigating drug use. Local, state, and federal legislatures might do the same for workers not covered by employment contracts. What needs to be set up is a just employment relationship—one in which an employee's expectations and responsibilities are specified in advance and in which an employer's discretionary authority to discipline or dismiss an employee is limited.

Beyond that, any policy should accord with the nature of the employment relationship. Since that relationship is a contractual one, it should meet the condition of a morally valid contract, which is informed consent. Thus, in general, we would argue that only methods that have received the informed consent of employees can be used in acquiring information about drug use.

A drug testing policy that requires all employees to submit to a drug test or to jeopardize their job would seem coercive and therefore unacceptable. Being placed in such a fundamentally coercive position of having to choose between one's job and one's privacy does not provide the conditions for truly free consent. Policies that are unilaterally established by employers would likewise be unacceptable. Working with employees to develop company policy seems the only way to ensure that the policy will be fair to both parties. Prior notice of testing would also be required in order to give employees the option of freely refraining from drug use. It is morally preferable to prevent drug use than to punish users after the fact, since this approach treats employees as capable of making rational and informed decisions.

Further procedural limitations seem advisable as well. Employees should be notified of the results of the test, they should be entitled to appeal the results (perhaps through further tests by an independent laboratory) and the information obtained through tests ought to be kept confidential. In summary, limitations upon employer discretion for administering drug tests can be derived from the nature of the employment contract and from the recognition that drug testing is justified by the desire to prevent harm, not the desire to punish wrongdoing.

EFFECTIVENESS OF DRUG TESTING

Having declared that the employer might have a right to test for drug use in order to prevent harm, we still need to examine the second argument a little more closely. One must keep in mind that the justification of drug testing is the justification of a means to an end, the end of preventing harm, and that the means are a means which intrude into one's privacy. In this case, before one allows drug testing as a means, one should be clear that there are not more effective means available.

If the employer has a legitimate right, perhaps duty, to ascertain knowledge of drug use to prevent harm, it is important to examine exactly how effectively, and in what situations, the *knowledge* of the drug use will prevent the harm. So far we have just assumed that they will prevent the harm. But how?

Let us take an example to pinpoint the difficulty. Suppose a transit driver, shortly before work, took some cocaine which, in giving him a feeling of invulnerability, leads him to take undue risks in his driving. How exactly is drug testing going to contribute to the knowledge which will prevent the potential accident?

It is important to keep in mind that: (1) if the knowledge doesn't help prevent the harm, the testing is not justified on prevention grounds; (2) if the testing doesn't provide the relevant knowledge, it is not justified either; and finally, (3) even if it was justified, it would be undesirable if a more effective means for preventing harm were discovered.

Upon examination, the links between drug testing, knowledge of drug use, and prevention of harm are not as clear as they are presumed to be. As we investigate, it begins to seem that the knowledge of the drug use even though relevant in some instances, is not the most effective means to prevent harm.

Let us turn to this last consideration first. Is drug testing the most effective means for preventing harm caused by drug use?

Consider. If someone exhibits obviously drugged or drunken behavior, then this behavior itself is grounds for preventing the person from continuing on the job. Administering urine and blood tests, sending the specimens out for testing and waiting for a response, will not prevent harm in this instance. Much drug testing, because of the time lapse involved, is equally superfluous in those cases where an employee is in fact under the influence of drugs, but exhibits no or only subtly impaired behavior.

Thus, even if one grants that drug testing somehow prevents harm an argument can be made that there might be much more effective methods of preventing potential harm such as administering dexterity tests of the type employed by police in possible drunk-driving cases, or requiring suspect pilots to pass flight simulator tests. Eye-hand coordination, balance, reflexes, and reasoning ability can all be tested with less intrusive, more easily administered, reliable technologies which give instant results. Certainly if an employer has just cause for believing that a specific employee presently poses a real threat of causing harm, such methods are just more effective in all ways than are urinalysis and blood testing.

Even were it possible to refine drug tests so that accurate results were immediately available, that knowledge would only be job-relevant if the drug use was clearly the cause of impaired job performance that could harm people. Hence, testing behavior still seems more direct and effective in preventing harm than testing for the presence of drugs *per se.*

In some cases, drug use might be connected with potential harms not by being causally connected to motor-function impairment, but by causing personality disorders (e.g., paranoia, delusions, etc.) that affect judgmental ability. Even though in such cases a *prima facie* justification for urinalysis or blood testing might exist, the same problems of effectiveness persist. How is the knowledge of the drug use attained by urinalysis and/or blood testing supposed to prevent the harm? Only if there is a causal link between the use and the potentially harmful behavior, would such knowledge be relevant. Even if we get the results of the test immediately, there is the necessity to have an established causal link between specific drug use and anticipated harmful personality disorders in specific people.

But it cannot be the task of an employer to determine that a specific drug is causally related to harm-causing personality disorders. Not every controlled substance is equally likely to cause personality changes in every person in every case. The establishment of the causal link between the use of certain drugs and harm-causing personality disorders is not the province of the employer, but the province of experts studying the effects of drugs. The burden of proof is on the employer to establish that the substance being investigated has been independently connected with the relevant psychological impairment and then, predict on that basis that the specific employee's psychological judgment has been or will soon be impaired in such a way as to cause harm.

But even when this link is established, it would seem that less intrusive means could be used to detect the potential problems, rather than relying upon the assumption of a causal link.

Psychological tests of judgment, perception and memory, for example, would be a less intrusive and more direct means for acquiring the relevant information which is, after all, the likelihood of causing harm and not the presence of drugs *per se.* In short, drug testing even in these cases doesn't seem to be very effective in preventing harm on the spot.

Still, this does not mean it is not effective at all. Where it is most effective in preventing harm is in its getting people to stop using drugs or in identifying serious drug addiction. Or to put it another way, urinalysis and blood tests for drug use are most effective in preventing potential harm when they serve as a deterrent to drug use *before* it occurs, since it is very difficult to prevent harm by diagnosing drug use *after* it has occurred but before the potentially harmful behavior takes place.

Drug testing can be an effective deterrent when there is regular or random testing of all employees. This will prevent harm by inhibiting (because of the fear of detection) drug use by those who are occasional users and those who do not wish to be detected.

It will probably not inhibit or stop the use by the chronic addicted user, but it will allow an employer to discover the chronic user or addict, assuming that the tests are accurately administered and reliably evaluated. If the chronic user's addiction would probably lead to harmful behavior of others, the harm is prevented by taking that user off the job. Thus regular or random testing will prevent harms done by deterring the occasional user and by detecting the chronic user.

There are six possibilities for such testing:

1. regularly scheduled testing of all employees;
2. regularly scheduled testing of randomly selected employees;
3. randomly scheduled testing of all employees;
4. randomly scheduled testing of randomly selected employees;
5. regularly scheduled testing of employees selected for probable cause; or finally,
6. randomly scheduled testing of employees selected for probable cause.

Only the last two seem morally acceptable as well as effective.

Obviously randomly scheduled testing will be more effective than regularly scheduled testing in detecting the occasional user, because the occasional users can control their use to pass the tests, unless of course tests were given so often (a practice economically unfeasible) that they needed to stop altogether. Regular scheduling probably will detect the habitual or addicted user. Randomly selecting people to test is probably cheaper, as is random scheduling, but it is not nearly as effective as testing all. Besides, the random might miss some of the addicted altogether, and will not deter the risk takers as much as the risk aversive persons. It is, ironically, the former who are probably potentially more harmful.

But these are merely considerations of efficiency. We have said that testing without probable cause is unacceptable. Any type of regular testing of all employees is unacceptable. We have argued that testing employees without first establishing probable cause is an unjustifiable violation of employee privacy. Given this, and given the expense of general and regular testing of all employees (especially if this is done by responsible laboratories), it is more likely that random testing will be employed as the means of deterrence. But surely testing of randomly selected innocent employees is as intrusive to those tested as is regular testing. The argument that there will be fewer tests is correct on quantitative grounds, but qualitatively the intrusion and unacceptability are the same. The claim that employers should be allowed to sacrifice the well-being of (some few) innocent employees to deter (some equally few) potentially harmful employees seems, on the face of it, unfair. Just as we do not allow the state randomly to tap the telephones of just any citizen in order to prevent crime, so we ought not allow employers to drug test all employees randomly to prevent harm. To do so is again to treat innocent employees solely as a means to the end of preventing potential harm.

This leaves only the use of regular or random drug testing as a deterrent in those cases where probable cause exists for believing that a particular employee poses a threat of harm. It would seem that in this case, the drug testing is acceptable. In such cases only the question of effectiveness remains: Are the standard techniques of urinalysis and blood testing more effective means for preventing harms than alternatives such as dexterity tests? It seems they are effective in different ways. The dexterity tests show immediately if someone is incapable of performing a task, or will perform one in such a way as to cause harm to others. The urinalysis and blood testing will prevent harm indirectly by getting the occasional user to curtail their use, and by detecting the habitual or addictive user, which will allow the employer to either give treatment to the addictive personality or remove them from the job. Thus we can conclude that drug testing is effective in a limited way, but aside from inhibiting occasional users because of fear of detection and discovering habitual users, it seems problematic that it does much to prevent harm that couldn't be achieved by other means.

Consider one final issue in the case of the occasional user. They are the drug users who do weigh the risks and benefits and who are physically and psychologically free to decide. The question in their case is not simply "will the likelihood of getting caught by urinalysis or blood testing deter this individual from using drugs?" Given the benefits of psychological tests and dexterity tests described above, the question is "will the rational user be more deterred by urinalysis or blood testing than by random psychological or dexterity tests?" And, if this is so, is this increase in the effectiveness of a deterrent sufficient to offset the increased expense and time required by drug tests? We see no reason to believe that behavioral or judgment tests are not, or cannot be made to be, as effective in determining what an employer needs to know (i.e., that a particular employee may presently be a potential cause of harm). If the behavioral, dexterity and judgment tests can be as effective in determining a potential for harm, we see no reason to believe that they cannot be as effective a deterrent as drug tests. Finally, even if a case can be made for an increase in deterrent effect of drug testing, we are skeptical that this increased effectiveness will outweigh the increased inefficiencies.

In summary, we have seen that deterrence is effective at times and under certain conditions allows the sacrificing of the privacy rights of innocent employees to the future and speculative good of preventing harms to others. However, there are many ways to deter drug use when that deterrence is legitimate and desirable to prevent harm. But random testing, which seems the only practicable means which has an impact in preventing harm, is the one which most offends workers' rights to privacy and which is most intrusive of the rights of the innocent. Even when effective, drug testing as a deterrent must be checked by the rights of employees.

ILLEGALITY CONTENTION

At this point critics might note that the behavior which testing would try to deter is, after all, illegal. Surely this excuses any responsible employer from being overly protective of an employee's rights. The fact that an employee is doing something illegal should give the employer a right to that information about his private life. Thus, it is not simply that drug use might pose a threat of harm to others, but that it is an illegal activity that threatens others. But again, we would argue that illegal activity itself is irrelevant to job performance. At best conviction records might be relevant, but, of course, since drug tests are administered by private employers we are not only exploring the question of conviction, we are also ignoring the fact that the employee has not even been arrested for the alleged illegal activity.

Further, even if the due process protections and the establishment of guilt is acknowledged, it still does not follow that employers have a claim to know about all illegal activity on the part of their employees.

Consider the following example: Suppose you were hiring an auditor whose job required certifying the integrity of your firm's tax and financial records. Certainly, the personal integrity of this employee is vital to the adequate job performance. Would we allow the employer to conduct, with or without the employee's consent, an audit of the employee's own personal tax return? Certainly if we discover that this person has cheated on his/her own tax return we will have evidence of illegal activity that is relevant to this person's ability to do the job. Given one's own legal liability for filing falsified statements, the employee's illegal activity also poses a threat to others. But surely, allowing private individuals to audit an employee's tax returns is too intrusive a means for discovering information about that employee's integrity. The government certainly would never allow this violation of an employee's privacy. It ought not to allow drug testing on the same grounds. Why tax returns should be protected in ways that urine, for example, is not, raises interesting questions of fairness. Unfortunately, this question would take us beyond the scope of this paper.

VOLUNTARINESS

A final problem that we also leave undeveloped concerns the voluntariness of employee consent. For most employees, being given the choice between submitting to a drug test and risking one's job by refusing an employer's request is not much of a decision at all. We believe that such decisions are less than voluntary and thereby would hold that employers cannot escape our criticisms simply by including within the employment contract a drug testing clause. Furthermore, there is reason to believe that those most in need of job security will be those most likely to be subjected to drug testing. Highly skilled, professional employees with high job mobility and security will be in a stronger position to resist such intrusions than will less skilled, easily replaced workers. This is why we should not anticipate surgeons and airline pilots being tested, and should not be surprised when public transit and factory workers are. A serious question of fairness arises here as well.

Drug use and drug testing seem to be our most recent social "crises." Politicians, the media, and employers expend a great deal of time and effort addressing this crisis. Yet, unquestionably, more lives, health, and money are lost each year to alcohol abuse than to marijuana, cocaine and other controlled substances. We are well-advised to be careful in considering issues that arise due to such selective social concern. We will let other social commentators speculate on the reasons why drug use has received scrutiny while other white-collar crimes and alcohol abuse are ignored. Our only concern at this point is that such selective prosecution suggests an arbitrariness that should alert us to questions of fairness and justice.

In summary, then, we have seen that drug use is not always job-relevant, and if drug use is not job-relevant, information about it is certainly not job-relevant. In the case of performance it may be a cause of some decreased performance, but it is the performance itself that is relevant to an employee's position, not what prohibits or enables him to do the job. In the case of potential harm being done by an employee under the influence of drugs, the drug use seems job-relevant, and in this case drug testing to prevent harm might be legitimate. But how this is practicable is another question. It would seem that standard motor dexterity or mental dexterity tests, immediately prior to job performance, are more efficacious ways of preventing harm, unless one concludes that drug use invariably and necessarily leads to harm. One must trust the individuals in any system in order for that system to work. One cannot police everything. It might work to randomly test people, to find drug users, and to weed out the few to forestall possible future harm, but are the harms prevented sufficient to override the rights of privacy of the people who are innocent and to overcome the possible abuses we have mentioned? It seems not.

Clearly, a better method is to develop safety checks immediately prior to the performance of a job. Have a surgeon or a pilot or a bus driver pass a few reasoning and motor-skill tests before work.

The cause of the lack of a skill, which lack might lead to harm, is really a secondary issue.

DRUG TESTING FOR PROSPECTIVE EMPLOYEES

Let's turn finally to drug testing during a pre-employment interview. Assuming the job description and responsibilities have been made clear, we can say that an employer is entitled to expect from a prospective employee whatever performance is agreed to in the employment contract. Of course, this will always involve risks, since the employer must make a judgment about future performances. To lower this risk, employers have a legitimate claim to some information about the employee. Previous work experience, training, education, and the like are obvious candidates since they indicate the person's ability to do the job. Except in rare circumstances drug use itself is irrelevant for determining an employee's ability to perform. (Besides, most people who are interviewing know enough to get their systems clean if the prospective employer is going to test them.)

We suggest that an employer can claim to have an interest in knowing (a) whether or not the prospective employee *can* do the job and (b) whether there is reason to believe that once hired the employee *will* do the job. The first can be determined in fairly straightforward ways: past work experience, training, education, etc. Presumably past drug use is thought more relevant to the second question. But there are straightforward and less intrusive means than drug testing for resolving this issue. Asking the employee "Is there anything that might prevent you from doing this job?" comes first to mind. Hiring the employee on a probationary period is another way. But to inquire about drug use here is to claim a right to know too much. It is to claim a right to know not only information about what an employee can do, but also a right to inquire into whatever background information *might* be (but not necessarily is) causally related to what an employee *will* do. But the range of factors that could be relevant here, from medical history to psychological dispositions to family plans, is surely too open-ended for an employer to claim as a *right* to know.

It might be responded that what an employee is entitled to expect is not a certain level of output, but a certain level of effort. The claim here would be that while drug use is only contingently related to what an employee can do, it is directly related to an employee's motivation to do the job. Drug use then is *de facto* relevant to the personal information that an employer is entitled to know.

But this involves an assumption mentioned above. The discussion so far has assumed that drugs will adversely affect job performance. However, some drugs are performance enhancing whether they are concerned with actual output or effort. The widespread use of steroids, painkillers, and dexadrine among professional athletes are perhaps only the most publicized instances of performance enhancing drugs. (A teacher's use of caffeine before an early-morning class is perhaps a more common example.) More to the point, knowledge of drug use tells little about motivation. There are too many other variables to be considered. Some users are motivated and some are not. Thus the motivational argument is faulty.

We can conclude, then, that whether the relevant consideration for prospective employees is output or effort, knowledge of drug use will be largely irrelevant for predicting. Employers ought to be positivistic in their approach. They should restrict their information gathering to measurable behavior and valid predictions (What has the prospect done? What can the prospect do? What has the prospect promised to do?), and not speculate about the underlying causes of this behavior. With a probationary work period always an option, there are sufficient non-intrusive means for limiting risks available to employers without having to rely on investigations into drug use.

In summary, we believe that drug use is information that is rightfully private and that only in exceptional cases can an employer claim a right to know about such use. Typically, these are cases in which knowledge of drug use could be used to prevent harm. However, even in those cases we believe that there are less intrusive and more effective means available than drug testing for gaining the information that would be necessary to prevent the harm. Thus, we conclude that drug testing of employees is rarely justified, and mostly inefficacious.

NOTES

1   *The New Republic*, March 31, 1986.

2   This trend primarily involves screening employees for such drugs as marijuana, cocaine, amphetamines, barbiturates, and opiates (e.g., heroin, methadone and morphine). While alcohol is also a drug that can be abused in the workplace, it seldom is among the drugs mentioned in conjunction with employee testing. We believe that testing which proves justified for controlled substances will, *a fortiori*, be justified for alcohol as well.

3   "Privacy, Polygraphs, and Work," George Brenkert, *Business and Professional Ethics Journal*, Vol. 1, no. 1 (Fall 1981). For a more general discussion of privacy in the workplace see "Privacy in Employment" by Joseph DesJardins, in *Moral Rights in the Workplace*, edited by Gertrude Ezorsky (SUNY Press, 1987). A good resource for philosophical work on privacy can be found in "Recent Work on the Concept of Privacy" by W.A. Parent, in *American Philosophical Quarterly* (Vol. 20, Oct. 1983) 341–56.

4   *US News and World Report*, Aug. 1983; *Newsweek*, May 1983.

—50—

DRUG TESTING AND THE RIGHT TO PRIVACY

Arguing the Ethics of Workplace Drug Testing

Michael Cranford

DRUG TESTING IS BECOMING AN INCREASINGLY accepted method for controlling the effects of substance abuse in the workplace. Since drug abuse has been correlated with a decline in corporate profitability and an increase in the occurrence of work-related accidents, employers are justifying drug testing on both legal and ethical grounds. Recent estimates indicate that the costs to employers of employee drug abuse can run as high as $60 billion per year.[1] Motorola, before implementing its drug testing program in 1991, determined that the cost of drug abuse to the company—in lost time, impaired productivity, and health care and workers compensation claims—amounted to $190 million in 1988, or approximately 40% of the company's net profit for that year.[2] As these effects on the workplace are viewed in light of a much larger social problem—one which impacts health care and the criminal justice system, and incites drug-related acts of violence—advocates of drug testing argue that the workplace is an effective arena for engaging these broader concerns. The drug-free workplace is viewed as causally antecedent and even sufficient to the development of drug-free communities.

The possibility of using workplace drug interventions to effect social change may obscure the more fundamental question of whether or not drug testing is an ethical means of determining employee drug abuse. While admitting that drug testing could mitigate potential harms, some CEOs have elected not to follow the trend set by Motorola and an estimated 67% of large companies,[3] and instead argue that drug testing surpasses the employer's legitimate sphere of control by dictating the behavior of employees on their own time and in the privacy of their own homes.[4] Recent arguments in favor of a more psychologically-sensitive definition of employee privacy place employer intrusions into this intimate sphere of self-disclosure on even less certain ethical grounds.[5] The ethical status of workplace drug testing can be expressed as a question of competing interests, between the employer's right to use testing to reduce drug-related harms and maximize profits, over against the employee's right to privacy, particularly with regard to drug use which occurs outside the workplace.

In this paper I will attempt to bring clarity to this debate and set the practice of workplace drug testing on more certain ethical grounds by advancing an argument which justifies workplace drug testing. I will begin by showing that an employee's right to privacy is violated when personal information is collected or used by the employer in a way which is irrelevant to the contractual relationship which exists between employer and employee. I will then demonstrate that drug testing is justified within the terms of the employment contract, and therefore does not amount to a violation of an employee's right to privacy. After responding to a battery of arguments to the contrary, I will propose that while drug testing can be ethically justified under the terms of an employment contract, it still amounts to treating employees as a means to an economic end, and is therefore fundamentally inconsistent with a substantive valuation of human worth and dignity.

PRIVACY AND PERFORMANCE OF CONTRACT

Legal definitions of privacy inevitably rely on the 1890 *Harvard Law Review* article "The Right to Privacy" by Samuel Warren and Louis Brandeis. This article offered an understanding of privacy for which a constitutional basis was not recognized until the 1965 case *Griswold v. Connecticut* (381 US 479). In both instances, privacy was understood as an individual's right "to be let alone," with the Griswold decision according citizens a "zone of privacy" around their persons which cannot be violated by governmental intrusion. This definition, utilized by the Court in numerous decisions since the 1965 ruling, will not be adequate for describing the employee's claim to privacy in an essentially social and cooperative setting like the workplace. In such a condition an absolute right "to be let alone" cannot be sustained, and it may well prove impossible for an employee to maintain a "zone of privacy" when the terms of employment entail certain physical demands. This is not to argue that a right to privacy does not exist in this setting; rather, we must conclude that the aforementioned conditions are not necessary components in such a right.

A more useful definition begins with the idea of a person's right to control information about herself and the situations over which such a right may be legitimately extended. For example, information to the effect that an individual possesses a rare and debilitating disease is generally considered private, but a physician's coming to know that a patient has such a disease is not an invasion of privacy. One might also note that while eavesdropping on a conversation would normally constitute an invasion of privacy, coming to know the same information because the individual inadvertently let it slip in a casual conversation would not. These and other examples demonstrate that the right to privacy is not violated by the mere act of coming to know something private, but is instead contingent on the relationship between the knower and the person about whom the information is known.

George Brenkert formulates this understanding as follows: Privacy involves a relationship between a person A, some information X, and another individual Z. A's right of privacy is violated only when Z comes to possess information X and no relationship exists between A and Z that would justify Z's coming to know X.[6] Brenkert notes that what would justify Z coming to know X is a condition in which knowing X and having a certain access to A will enable Z to execute its role in the particular relationship with A. In such a case, Z is entitled to information X, and A's privacy is in no way violated by the fact that Z knows. Thus, a physician is justified in coming to know of a patient's disease (say, by running certain diagnostic tests), since knowing of the disease will enable her to give the patient medical treatment. One cannot be a physician to another unless one is entitled to certain information and access to that person. Conversely, one can yield one's right to privacy by disclosing information to another that the relationship would not normally mandate. To maintain a right to privacy in a situation where another would normally be entitled to the information to enable them to fulfill the terms of the relationship is, quite simply, to violate the terms of the relationship and make fulfillment of such terms impossible. In the case of our earlier example, to refuse a physician access to the relevant points of one's health status is to make a physician-patient relationship impossible. Similarly, to refuse an employer access to information regarding one's capability of fulfilling the terms of an employment contract is to violate an employer-employee relationship.

The argument advanced at this point is that drug testing involves access to and information about an employee that are justified under the terms of the implicit contractual agreement between employer and employee. An employer is therefore entitled to test employees for drug use. This statement relies on at least two important assumptions. First, a contractual model of employer-employee relations is assumed over against a common law, agent-principal model. It is not the case that employees relinquish all privacy rights in return for employment, as the common law relationship may imply, but rather that the terms of the contract, if it is valid, set reasonable boundaries for employee privacy rights consistent with the terms and expectations of employment. The argument offered here is that drug testing does not violate those boundaries. I am also assuming that drug abuse has a measurable and significant impact on an employee's ability to honor the terms of the employment contract. Employers are entitled to know about employee drug abuse on the grounds that such knowledge is relevant to assessing an employee's capability to perform according to the terms of the agreement. Without arguing for the connection between drug abuse and employee performance at length, the reader's attention is directed to studies which, if not absolutely incontestable in their methodology, are nonetheless reasonably set forth.

In support of this argument, I would first direct attention to other types of information about an employee that an employer is entitled to know, and in coming to know such information does not violate the employee's privacy. Employers are entitled to information about a current or prospective employee's work experience, education, and job skills—in short, information relevant for determining whether or not the employee is capable of fulfilling her part of the contract. More critically, the employer is not only entitled to such information, but is entitled to obtain such information through an investigatory process, both to confirm information the employee has voluntarily yielded about her qualifications, as well as to obtain such relevant information as may be lacking (i.e., inadvertently omitted or, perhaps, intentionally withheld).

Brenkert further adds that an employer is entitled to information which relates to elements of one's social and moral character:

> A person must be able not simply to perform a certain activity, or provide a service, but he must also be able to do it in an acceptable manner—i.e., in a manner which is approximately as efficient as others, in an honest manner, and in a manner compatible with others who seek to provide the services for which they were hired.[7]

Again, the employer is entitled to know, in the case of potential employees, if they are capable of fulfilling their part of the contract, and, in the case of existing employees, if they are adhering to the terms and expectations implicit in the contract. While this latter case can often be confirmed by direct observation of the employee's actions at the work site, on occasion the employer is entitled to information regarding behavior which can be observed at the workplace but originates from outside of it (such as arriving at work late, or consuming large quantities of alcohol prior to arriving). As all of these actions may be in violation of the term of employment, the employer is entitled to know of them, and in coming to know of them does not violate the employee's privacy.

My point in offering these examples is to suggest that drug testing is a method of coming to know about an employee's ability to fulfill the terms of contract which is analogous to those listed. An exploratory process, in seeking to verify an employee's ability to do a certain job in connection with reasonable expectations for what that job entails, may also validly discover characteristics or tendencies that would keep the employee from performing to reasonable expectations. Drug testing is precisely this sort of process. As a part of the process of reviewing employee performance to determine whether or not they are fulfilling the terms and expectations of employment satisfactorily, drug testing may be validly included among other types of investigatory methods, including interviews with coworkers, skills and proficiency testing, and (in some professions) medical examinations. The fact that an employee may not want to submit to a drug test is entirely beside the point; the employee may just as likely prefer not to include a complete list of personal references, or prefer that the employer not review her relations with other employees. In all these cases, the employer is entitled to know the relevant information, and in coming to know these things does not violate the employee's privacy. The employee may withhold this information from the employer, but this action is tantamount to ending the employer-employee relationship. Such a relationship, under the terms of employment, includes not only each party's commitment to benefit the other in the specific way indicated, but also entitles each to determine if the other is capable of performance according to the terms of contract. In this way, each retains the free ability to terminate the relationship on the grounds of the other's nonperformance.

Of course, not just any purpose of obtaining information relevant to evaluating performance under the terms of contract can automatically be considered reasonable. For instance, an employer cannot spy on a prospective employee in her own home to determine if she will be a capable employee. I offer the following criteria as setting reasonable and ethical limits on obtaining relevant information (though note that the requirement of relevancy is in each case already assumed).

1. *The process whereby an employer comes to know something about an employee (existing or prospective) must not be unnecessarily harmful or intrusive*

The information may not result from investigatory processes which are themselves degrading or humiliating by virtue of their intrusiveness (e.g., strip searches, spying on an employee while they use the bathroom, interviewing a divorced spouse, or searching an employee's locker) or which may prove unhealthy (e.g., excessive use of x-rays, or torture). (Note: Degrading processes of securing information must be distinguished from processes of securing information which is itself degrading. The latter is not necessarily in violation of this or successive criteria.)

2. *The process whereby an employer comes to know something about an employee must be efficient and specific*

The information must result from an efficient and specific process—i.e., a process which is the most direct of competing methods (though without compromising point 1 above), and should result in information which corresponds to questions of performance under the terms of the employment contract, and should not result in information that does not so correspond. For example, detailed credit checks may help a bank decide whether a prospective employee is a capable manager of finances, but not directly (only inferentially), and it would also provide a great deal of information that the employer is not entitled to see. Consulting the employee's previous employer, on the other hand, may provide the relevant information directly and specifically.

3. *The process whereby an employer comes to know something about an employee must be accurate, or if not itself precise, then capable of confirmation through further investigation*

The information must result from a dependable source; if a source is not dependable and is incapable of being verified for accuracy, the employer is not justified in pursuing this avenue of discovery. Thus, the polygraph must be excluded, since it is occasionally inaccurate and may in such cases result in information that cannot be verified. In addition, disreputable sources of information, or sources that may have an interest in misrepresenting the information being sought, should not be used.

Having outlined these, I offer my argument in full: Drug testing is not only a method of coming to know about an employee's ability to fulfill the terms of contract which is analogous to those listed earlier, but which also is reasonable under the criteria listed above.

1. Drug Testing Is Not Harmful or Intrusive

In the Supreme Court case *Samuel K. Skinner v. Railway Labor Executives' Association* (489 US 602), the Court determined that both blood and urine tests were minimally intrusive.[8] While the Court acknowledged that the act of passing urine was itself intensely personal (Ibid., 617), obtaining a urine sample in a medical environment and without the use of direct observation amounted to no more than a minimal intrusion (Ibid., 626). The Court justified not only testing of urine but also testing of blood by focusing on the procedure of testing (i.e., "experience ... teaches that the quantity of blood extracted is minimal," Ibid., 625) and pointing out that since such tests are "commonplace and routine in everyday life," the tests posed "virtually no risk, trauma, or pain" (Ibid., 625). The Court's findings on this case are compelling, and are consistent with my contention that drug testing is not unnecessarily harmful or intrusive. While such testing does amount to an imposition upon an employee (i.e., by requiring her to report to a physician and provide a urine sample) in a way that may not be commonplace for many employees, the Court ruled that since this takes place within an employment context (where limitations of movement are assumed), this interference is justifiable and does not unnecessarily infringe on privacy interests (Ibid., 624–25).

2. Drug Testing Is Both Efficient and Specific

In fact, drug testing is the most efficient means of discovering employee drug abuse. In addition to providing direct access to the information in question, the results of drug testing do not include information that is irrelevant. The test targets a specific set of illegal substances. It can be argued (and has been) that drug testing is not efficient because it does not test for impairment—only for drug use. But this point ignores the fact that the test is justified on a correlation between drug abuse and employee productivity more generally; impairment is itself difficult or impossible to measure, since the effects of a given quantity of substance vary from individual to individual and from one incidence of use to another. The fact that impairment is an elusive quantity cannot diminish the validity of testing for drug abuse. This criticism also ignores the fact that the test is an effective means of deterring impairment, providing habitual users a certain expectation that their drug use will be discovered if it is not controlled.

3. Drug Testing Can Be Conducted in a Way Which Guarantees a High Degree of Precision

It is well known that the standard (and relatively inexpensive) EMIT test has a measurable chance of falsely indicating drug use, and is also susceptible to cross-reactivity with other legal substances. But confirmatory testing, such as that performed using gas chromatography/mass spectrometry, can provide results at a high level of accuracy. This confirmatory testing, as well as a host of other stringent safeguards, is required of all laboratories certified by the National Institute on Drug Abuse.[9]

In summary, my contention is that an employer is entitled to drug test on the grounds that the information derived is relevant to confirm the employee's capacity to perform according to the terms of employment, and that such testing is a reasonable means of coming to know such information. Other points in favor of drug testing, which are not essential to my preceding argument but congruent with it, include the following two items.

First, drug testing is an opportunity for employer beneficence. Testing permits the employer to diagnose poor employee performance and require such individuals to participate in employer-sponsored counseling and rehabilitative measures. Employers are permitted to recognize that drug abuse is a disease with a broad social impact that is not addressed if employees who perform poorly as a result of drug abuse are merely terminated. Second, a specific diagnosis of drug abuse in the case of poor employee performance might protect the employer from wrongful termination litigation, in the event that an employee refuses to seek help regarding their abuse. The results of drug testing might confirm to the court that the termination was effected on substantive and not arbitrary grounds.

DRUG TESTING AND QUESTIONS OF JUSTIFICATION

A number of arguments have been offered which suggest that drug testing is not justified under terms of contract, or is not a reasonable method by which an employer may come to know of employee drug abuse, and therefore amounts to a violation of employee privacy. These arguments include a rejection of productivity as a justification for testing, charges that testing is coercive, and that it amounts to an abuse of employee privacy by controlling behavior conducted outside the workplace. I will respond to each of these in turn.

First, some have charged that arguing from an employer's right to maximize productivity to a justification for drug testing is problematic. DesJardins and Duska point out that employers have a valid claim on some level of employee performance, such that a failure to perform to this level would give the employer a justification for firing or finding fault with the employee. But it is not clear that an employer has a valid claim on an optimal level of employee performance, and that is what drug testing is directed at achieving. As long as drug abuse does not reduce an employee's performance beyond a reasonable level, an employer cannot claim a right to the highest level of performance of which an employee is capable.[10]

DesJardins and Duska further point out the elusiveness of an optimal level of performance. Some employees perform below the norm in an unimpaired state, and other employees might conceivably perform above the norm in an impaired state. "If the relevant consideration is whether the employee is producing as expected (according to the normal demands of the position and contract) not whether he/she is producing as much as possible, then knowledge of drug use is irrelevant or unnecessary."[11] This is because the issue in question is not drug use *per se*, but employee productivity. Since drug use need not correlate to expectations for a given employee's productivity, testing for drug use is irrelevant. And since it is irrelevant to fulfillment of the employment contract, testing for drugs is unjustified and therefore stands in violation of an employee's privacy.

While I agree that it is problematic to state that an employer has a right to expect an optimal level of performance from an employee, I would argue that the employer does have a right to a workplace free from the deleterious effects of employee drug abuse. Drug testing, properly understood, is not directed at effecting optimal performance, but rather performance which is free from the effects of drug abuse. Since the assessment which justifies drug testing is not based on the impact of drug abuse on a given employee's performance, but is correlated on the effects of drug abuse on workplace productivity more generally, drug testing does measure a relevant quantity.

It is also overly simplistic to state that employers need not test for drugs when they can terminate employees on the mere basis of a failure to perform. Employers are willing to tolerate temporary factors which may detract from employee performance; e.g., a death in the family, sickness, or occasional loss of sleep. But employers have a right to distinguish these self-correcting factors from factors which may be habitual, ongoing, and increasingly detrimental to productivity, such as drug abuse. Such insight might dramatically impact their course of action with regard to how they address the employee's failure to perform. It is therefore not the case, as DesJardins and Duska suggest, that "knowledge of the cause of the failure to perform is irrelevant."[12]

A more critical series of arguments against basing drug testing on an employer's right to maximize productivity has been leveled by Nicholas Caste. First, Caste attacks what he identifies as "the productivity argument":

> The productivity argument essentially states that since the employer has purchased the employee's time, the employer has a proprietary right to ensure that the time purchased is used as efficiently as possible.... The employer must be concerned with "contract enforcement" and must attempt somehow to motivate the employee to attain maximal production capacity. In the case of drug testing, the abuse of drugs by employees is seen as diminishing their productive capacity and is thus subject to the control of the employer.[13]

From this argument, Caste states, one can infer that any manipulation is acceptable as long as it is maximizing productivity, and he defines manipulation as an attempt to produce a response without regard for that individual's good, as he or she perceives it.[14] Caste goes on to give two examples of hypothetical drugs which, assuming the productivity argument, an employer would be justified in requiring employees to take. The first drug increases employee productivity while also increasing pleasure and job satisfaction. The second drug increases productivity while inflicting painful side-effects on the employee. The fact that the productivity argument appears to sanction the use of both drugs, and in fact cannot morally distinguish between them, seems to argue for its invalidity. Since the productivity argument cannot distinguish between causing an employee pleasure or pain, by adopting its logic one would be forced to the morally unacceptable conclusion that an employee's best interests are irrelevant.

Caste points out that what is wrong with the second drug is not that it causes pain "but that it is manipulatively intrusive. It establishes areas of control to which the employer has no right."[15] He concludes that what is wrong with the productivity argument is that it is manipulative. And what is wrong with manipulation is not the effects it produces (which may, coincidentally, be in the subject's best interests) but rather that it undermines the subject's autonomy by not allowing their desires to be factored into the decision making process. Since drug testing is justified by appeal to productivity arguments, it also is fundamentally manipulative and results in a morally unacceptable degree of employee control. Drug testing is therefore unethical, and should be rejected.

One could point out that our system of modern law regulates behavior in a way that would also have to be considered manipulative, according to Caste's definition, but he avoids this counterexample by stating that in a democratic system, citizens have a chance to participate in the legislative process. Since their desires participate through the election of representatives who make the laws, Caste argues that our legal system does not destroy autonomy the way mandatory drug testing does, by dictating behavior without any room for autonomy.[16] Before I address the critical oversight here, I should point out that one might rescue drug testing from the charge of being manipulative by using the same argument that Caste did to rescue our legal system. One can exercise the same degree of autonomy with respect to drug testing legislation as one currently does with legislation generally by participating in our electoral system. Since employees have an ability to elect representatives who can limit the use of drug testing, one could argue that drug testing also "does not destroy the individual's autonomy in that he or she retains the capability of input into the governing process."[17] In point of fact, individual autonomy is limited in both cases, as it must necessarily be in any contractual obligation, making any expressed distinction here trivial.

The failure of Caste's argument becomes clear when we realize that, if he is correct, virtually every action required of an employee at a work site would qualify as manipulative—whether the action in question was in her best interests or not, and whether or not she desired to comply, since Caste defines manipulation as a function of restricting autonomy. Dress codes, starting times, and basic performance expectations all may be similarly justified by appeal to the productivity argument—but most of us are not prepared to count these things as manipulative or unjustified. Requirements of this sort are not instances of manipulation, but are justified expectations which honor a contractual agreement. Similarly, an employee who demands a paycheck of her employer is engaging in manipulation, according to Caste's definition—but this cannot be correct. In the contract, each party is apprised that the other has a right to benefit from the arrangement, and each has a commensurate responsibility to uphold their part. Accountability to the terms of the contract does not amount to manipulation when the accountability in question is reasonable. In agreement with Caste's original criticism, it is not true that an employer has a right to ensure maximal productivity. But an employer does have the right to hold an employee accountable to the terms of the contract, which express reasonable expectations of productivity. From this it cannot be inferred, however, that just any activity to maximize (or even minimally ensure) productivity is justifiable, since the contractual model expressly allows that the employee has certain morally justified claims that cannot be bargained away in return for employment. Since the productivity argument, as Caste depicts it, is in fact not a justification for drug testing under a contractual model, it is not the case that drug testing must be rejected.

In a similar vein, some argue that any testing which involves coercion is inherently an invasion of employee privacy. Placing employees in a position where they must choose between maintaining their privacy or losing their jobs is fundamentally coercive. "For most employees, being given the choice between submitting to a drug test and risking one's job by refusing an employer's request is not much of a decision at all."[18] While Brenkert's arguments against the use of the polygraph are directed at that device's inability to distinguish the reason behind a positive reading (which may not,

in many instances, indicate an intentional lie), his argument that the polygraph is coercive is pertinent to the question of drug testing as well.

Brenkert notes that if an employee

> ... did not take the test and cooperate during the test, his application for employment would either not be considered at all or would be considered to have a significant negative aspect to it. This is surely a more subtle form of coercion. And if this be the case, then one cannot say that the person has willingly allowed his reactions to the questions to be monitored. He has consented to do so, but he has consented under coercion. Had he a truly free choice, he would not have done so.[19]

Brenkert's point is surprising, in that his own understanding is that A's privacy is limited by what Z is entitled to know in order to execute its role with respect to A. If Z (here, the corporation) is entitled to know X (whether or not the employee abuses drugs) in order to determine if A (the employee) is capable of performing according to the terms of employment, then the employee has no right to privacy with respect to the information in question. While this does not authorize the corporation to obtain the information in just any manner, the mere fact that the employee would *prefer* that the employer not know cannot be sufficient to constitute a right to privacy in the face of the employer's legitimate entitlement. The employee can freely choose to withhold the information, but this is not so much invoking a right to privacy as it is rejecting the terms of contract.

If Brenkert's criticism of employer testing were valid, then potentially all demands made by the employer on the employee—from providing background information to arriving at work on time—would count as coercive, since in every case where the employee consents to the demand there is a strong possibility that she would not have consented if she was offered a truly free choice. But these demands are reasonable, and the employer is entitled to demand them under the terms of employment, just as the employee is entitled to profit by acceding to such demands.

The final argument considered here is the charge that drug testing is an attempt to "control the employee's actions in a time that has not actually been purchased."[20] Even if we assume that an employer has the right to maximize profitability by controlling the employee's behavior during normal work hours, the employer has no right to control what an employee does in her free time. To attempt to do so is a violation of employee rights. This argument also falls flat, however, when we realize that the demands of a standard employment contract inherently place limitations on an employee's free time. In a sense, the employment contract demands priority, requiring the employee to organize her free time around her employment schedule in a way that permits her to honor the contractual obligation. For instance, time traveling to and from work occurs during an employee's "free time," and is dependent on the employee's own personal resources, but is rightfully assumed within the terms of the contract. Time and money spent shopping for work attire also falls outside the normal time of employment, but is essential for honoring a mandatory dress code. These are not normally considered violations of an employee's private life, or unethical "controls" placed on an employee by an employer, but are justified, again, under the terms of contract. Drug testing is justified similarly.

RESERVATIONS AND POLICY RECOMMENDATIONS

At least one troubling aspect of drug testing remains to be considered prior to recommendations on policy, and that is the ethics of profit maximization as a justification for including employee testing under the terms of an employment agreement. As Caste correctly observed, the fact that drug testing may be in the best interests of employees is ancillary to the employer's productivity goals.[21] While drug testing may turn out to further the interests of employees by forcing them

to confront self-destructive behavior, this correlation between employee's interests and the financial goals of the corporation is merely fortuitous. If drug testing were not perceived as being in the best interests of the company from a financial point of view, then drug testing would not be the issue it is today.

In counterpoint, one could argue that the financial status of the company is inherently intertwined with the good of employees; as the corporation becomes increasingly profitable, employees are increasingly benefited. One might even argue that, in light of such a framework, profit maximization is central to society and therefore inherently consistent with its values. This model is overly simplified, however; we can easily envision a situation where a corporation, attempting to maximize its profits, does so in a way that is inconsistent with a substantive social ethic but is not otherwise limited by market values. Appealing to profit maximization as a social ethic does not alleviate these tensions.

It is the position adopted in this article that a corporation is entitled to drug test its employees to determine employee capacity to perform according to the terms of the employment contract. That drug testing is not, however, in the large majority of cases, directed at maximizing the employee's best interests, suggests that employers should avail themselves of their right to drug test within reasonable limits. In light of this conclusion, the following policy recommendations are directed at employers, with the goal of balancing the employer's right to drug test with a more substantive regard for the dignity and privacy of employees.

4. *Testing should focus on a specifically targeted group of employees*

In the case of employers who are testing without regard for questions of safety, I would strongly urge that testing only be done when probable cause exists to suspect that an employee is using controlled substances. Probable cause might include uncharacteristic behavior, obvious symptoms of impairment, or a significantly diminished capacity to perform their duties. Utilizing probable cause minimizes the intrusive aspect of testing by yielding a higher percentage of test-positives (i.e., requiring probable cause before testing will inherently screen out the large majority of negatives). Even with this stipulation, a drug program may provide a reasonable deterrence factor at the workplace.

It should be noted that this qualification does not apply in cases of job applicants. Employers who insist on testing potential employees will typically do so under a general suspicion of drug use, and may in that case assume a condition of probable cause.

5. *When testing is indicated, it should not be announced ahead of time*

Regularly scheduled testing runs the risk of losing its effectiveness by providing an employee sufficient time to contrive a method of falsifying the sample. Drug testing, if it is to be used at all, should be used in a way which maximizes its effectiveness and accuracy.

6. *Employees who test positive for drug abuse should be permitted the opportunity to resolve their abusive tendencies and return to work without penalty or stigma*

Employees should only be terminated for an inability to resolve their abuse, once early detection and substantial warning have been made. Employers can mitigate the dehumanizing aspect of this technology by using it as an opportunity to assist abusive employees with their problems, and permitting them to return to their old positions if they can remedy their habitual tendencies. Toxicological testing should therefore be accompanied by a full range of employee assistance interventions.

NOTES

1 According to SAMHSA (Substance Abuse and Mental Health Services Administration), cited in Ira A. Lipman, "Drug Testing Is Vital in the Workplace," *USA Today Magazine* 123 (January 1995), 81.

2 Dawn Gunsch, "Training Prepares Workers for Drug Testing," *Personnel Journal* 72 (May 1993), 52.

3 According to the US Bureau of Labor Statistics, cited in Rob Brookler, "Industry Standards in Workplace Drug Testing," *Personnel Journal* 71 (April 1992), 128.

4 See Lewis L. Maltby, "Why Drug Testing Is a Bad Idea," *Inc.* (June 1987), 152.

5 On this point see Michele Simms, "Defining Privacy in Employee Health Screening Cases: Ethical Ramifications Concerning the Employee/Employer Relationship," *Journal of Business Ethics* 13 (1994), 315–25.

6 George G. Brenkert, "Privacy, Polygraphs, and Work," *Business and Professional Ethics Journal* 1 (1981), 23. In agreement see DesJardins, "An Employee's Right to Privacy," 222; Joseph DesJardins and Ronald Duska, "Drug Testing in Employment," *Business and Professional Ethics Journal* 6 (1987), 3–4.

7 Brenkert, "Privacy, Polygraphs, and Work," 25.

8 While the legal opinion itself only summarizes and does not in and of itself justify a moral argument, it does in this case demonstrate a broad consensus and both rational and intuitive appeals to the matter at hand.

9 See Brookler, "Industry Standards in Workplace Drug Testing," 129.

10 DesJardins and Duska, "Drug Testing in Employment," 5.

11 Ibid., 6.

12 Ibid.

13 Nicholas J. Caste, "Drug Testing and Productivity," *Journal of Business Ethics* 11 (1992), 301.

14 Ibid., 302.

15 Ibid., 303.

16 Ibid., 302.

17 Ibid.

18   DesJardins and Duska, "Drug Testing in
      Employment," 16–17. This is also implied in
      DesJardins, "An Employee's Right to Privacy," 226,
      but in neither case is the argument fully developed.
19   Brenkert, "Privacy, Polygraphs, and Work," 28–29.
20   Caste, "Drug Testing and Productivity," 303. See also
      Maltby, "Why Drug Testing Is a Bad Idea," 152.

21   Caste, "Drug Testing and Productivity," 302. Caste
      goes too far when he attributes to corporations
      following the productivity argument an "absence
      of concern for the individual employee" (303), but
      I am in agreement that employer beneficence is, in
      the case of drug testing, at best an afterthought.

—51—
GENETIC TESTING IN THE WORKPLACE

The Employer's Coin Toss

Samantha French

A TOSS OF THE COIN BY THE MODERN-DAY employer reveals two options regarding genetic testing in the workplace. The employer may choose to take advantage of increasingly precise, available, and affordable genetic testing in order to ascertain the genetic characteristics—and deficiencies—of its employees. This outcome exposes the employer to a vast array of potential litigation and liability relating to the Americans with Disabilities Act, the Fourth Amendment, Title VII of the Civil Rights Act, and state legislation designed to protect genetic privacy. Alternatively, the employer may neglect to indulge in this trend of genetic testing and may face liability for employer negligence, violations of federal legislation such as OSHA regulations, and increased costs associated with insuring the health of genetically endangered employees. In the rapidly developing universe of genetic intelligence, the employer is faced with a staggering dilemma.

THE MOST RECENT DEVELOPMENT: AN OVERVIEW

Equal Employment Opportunity Commission v. Burlington Northern Santa Fe Railway

On May 6, 2002, the Equal Employment Opportunity Commission ("EEOC") settled its case against Burlington Northern Santa Fe Railway ("Burlington"). Thirty-six Burlington employees walked away with $2.2 million. What did Burlington do wrong?

"Burlington admitted no wrongdoing and there has been no determination that what it did was illegal. What it did according to Burlington was fairly benign," said Hunter Hughes, mediator of the settlement proceedings.

Then why did the case settle before trial? In the EEOC's first case challenging genetic testing of employees, the defendant railway company admitted to conducting undisclosed genetic testing on its employees after the workers complained of carpal tunnel syndrome ("CTS") stemming from work-related activities. It hoped to use a pilot DNA test to confirm the existence of the condition in conjunction with a comprehensive medical exam. Undoubtedly, Burlington felt compelled to react to its employees' complaints or risk accusations of employer negligence and failure to comply with federal safety regulations, to name a few potentially-devastating outcomes. How far was it required to proceed in its investigation of the employees' grievances?

If a new genetic test was available to test for the presence of CTS, should the railway have employed such an innovative device? What would have been the outcome if it had not?

The Significance of the Burlington Case

The Burlington case was decided at a crucial moment in time. In the summer of 2002, Senator Tom Daschle and several other Democratic Senators plan to co-sponsor a bill about genetic testing and discrimination. The bill, entitled the Genetic Nondiscrimination in Health Insurance and Employment Act, would prevent insurance companies from using genetic information to deny medical coverage or boost premiums and would bar employers from using such information in hiring, promotion, or salary decisions. Additionally, the bill would allow victims of genetic discrimination to sue for unlimited, uncapped damage amounts from their employers or insurers. Opposition from Republican leaders, as well as employer organizations and coalitions such as the Health Insurance Association of America, threatens the passage of such legislation.

A careful balance of competing interests is necessary before such a bill is adopted into law. The politically popular stance is one that readily protects privacy interests and is openly suspicious of the potential evils of genetic testing. Former President Clinton issued an executive order in February 2000 banning the use of predictive genetic information against federal employees; current President Bush has similarly signaled his support for genetic privacy legislation, and, as the former governor of Texas, signed a genetic privacy bill. Americans want to be assured that their genetic compositions are being protected by lawmakers, but what of the employers who face increasing pressure to make use of readily-available genetic tests? Indeed, employers are caught between a rock and a hard place, with no clear-cut federal legislation or case precedent to guide their actions. The choice to use or refrain from using genetic testing in the workplace is riddled with risky consequences.

A BREAKDOWN OF CURRENT LAWS SURROUNDING GENETIC TESTING

There are several avenues of recourse available to an employee who believes his or her rights have been violated by the use of genetic testing in the workplace:

· The Americans with Disabilities Act ("ADA")
· The Fourth Amendment's constitutional prohibition on illegal searches and seizures
· Title VII of the Civil Rights Act of 1964
· Individual state legislation prohibiting discrimination in the workplace based on the results of genetic tests

The Americans with Disabilities Act of 1990, which expanded the Civil Rights Act of 1964, protects individuals with disabilities from discrimination. The ADA is considered the most significant piece of federal legislation pertaining to employer-based genetic discrimination; however, it does not explicitly or completely address genetic testing. A person is protected by the ADA only if he is disabled. The ADA defines "disability" as "(A) a physical or mental impairment that substantially limits one or more of the major life activities ... (B) a record of such an impairment; or (C) being regarded as having such an impairment." Since 1995, the EEOC has been involved in an elaborate effort to classify genetically predisposed individuals as possessing an "impairment" under section C and thereby qualifying for protection under the auspices of the ADA. Its efforts have met with moderate success; though it has added a clarification of its position to its compliance manual, the ADA has not been formally amended to include such a provision. Thus, the ADA does not prevent employers from requiring pre-placement medical exams, which may include physical exams and genetic tests, and employers are still not prevented from requiring workers to consent to general medical record release or family history including genetic information at various points in the application or employment phases.

In the first case it has initiated involving genetic testing, the EEOC attempted to include the Burlington workers under its definition of those suffering from an "impairment" under section C. Is this feasible? The ADA explicitly protects only those employees with a proven, qualifying "disability." "Persons with mere predispositions to genetic disorders do not fall within the ADA's definition of disability because they display no present symptoms that substantially limit a major life activity."[1] The inclusion of the Burlington workers found to possess a CTS genetic disorder would seem to constitute a substantial expansion of the currently-accepted definition of disability; however, "the ADA was created to protect only those persons that are presently disabled, and interpreting it to include all persons with a potential to become disabled in the future, including those persons genetically predisposed to becoming disabled, would violate the original intent of the ADA."[2] Additionally, a genetic predisposition for a disease is only an indicator that a person may become afflicted; genetic testing is by no means a dispositive predictor of an individual's future health. "When scientists genetically test an individual for a disease such as breast, ovarian, or prostate cancer, a positive test result only indicates a susceptibility to, and not an absolute certainty of, developing the disease."[3] How should this ultimate uncertainty affect the labeling of a genetic predisposition as a "disability" or "impairment"? As the EEOC concedes, no action was taken to discriminate against the Burlington workers based on the results of the genetic test performed; none of the workers tested were found to possess the chromosome characteristic at issue. Thus there appears to be no question of a genetic "disability" or "impairment" and hence no valid ADA claim.

Additionally, the ADA gives added protection for things required to maintain a viable business environment. Specifically, the ADA permits employers to conduct medical examinations of current employees if they are "job-related and consistent with business necessity." In Burlington, there is no opposition to the railway's claim that it used genetic testing only as a diagnostic tool for a particular genetic trait, one which was the subject of inquiries and complaints by its employees. Thus the railway can argue that it reacted out of business necessity, employing its right to use all information necessary to make an important work-related safety evaluation. "Particularly where this use is motivated by non-discriminatory purposes, it should be protected, despite the limitations of the ADA, as a necessary element of conducting business."[4]

The constitutionally protected right to privacy has developed and expanded from its initially narrow and constrictive "penumbra" as defined in *Griswold v. Connecticut* to encompass medical information and its confidentiality. In *Whalen v. Roe*, the United States Supreme Court recognized a right to privacy in medical information. In *Doe v. Attorney General of the United States*, the Ninth Circuit confirmed the privacy interest inherent in medical confidentiality by stating that "there are few matters that are quite so personal as the status of one's health, and few matters the dissemination of which one would prefer to maintain greater control over." In *Norman-Bloodsaw v. Lawrence Berkeley Laboratory*, the Ninth Circuit further concluded that one who consents to a general medical examination does not waive a basic privacy right not to be tested for intimate, personal matters involving his or her health. Specifically, while the taking of a bodily fluid sample implicates one's privacy interests, "the ensuing chemical analysis of the samples to obtain physiological data is a further intrusion of the tested employee's privacy interests."

However, the court in Norman-Bloodsaw dealt only with undisclosed testing for conditions unrelated to the workplace environment or job performance, stating that "there was little, if any, 'overlap' between what plaintiffs consented to and the testing at issue here." In contrast, in Burlington the employer tested for a specific condition that both affects and is affected by the workers' daily employment tasks. Based on the Norman-Bloodsaw language, one could tentatively conclude that the employees' expectations of privacy were lowered because the condition subject to testing had a connection to their work. Further, the employees basically solicited the testing performed in Burlington. After experiencing problems with their arms, they complained to their union and to their employer, and ultimately sought attention. There is an argument that the employees' actions constituted consent to an invasive procedure, one targeted at exploring and diagnosing conditions related to CTS (the source of their initial complaint). Whether consent to generalized medical testing also extends to genetic testing remains to be considered by a court of law.

Under Title VII of the Civil Rights Act of 1964, the unauthorized retention of sensitive medical information on the basis of race or sex constitutes an "adverse effect" or injury. In Norman-Bloodsaw, genetic tests were performed on female employees for the purpose of testing for pregnancy and on black employees for the purpose of testing for sickle cell trait, a condition present almost exclusively in the African-American population. Genetic testing becomes a straightforward violation of Title VII when employees or applicants are singled out based on race or sex. Burlington did not violate Title VII because the railway chose only those employees at risk for CTS based on work environment and without regard to race or sex. In fact, Title VII could be construed as a preventative measure that could be used to support the existence of genetic testing in the workplace. If companies select subjects for testing according to neutral, non-biased qualifying characteristics, as Burlington did, the provision may well serve its intended purpose of preventing racial and gender discrimination in the workplace.

Federal law does not explicitly restrict the use of genetic testing in employment. Because of a growing need for more stringent regulation, virtually every state has adopted legislation aimed at more careful management of this novel capability. There are three types of legislation that various states have elected to pass into law. First, in the 1970s, in response to discrimination against carriers of sickle cell trait, almost every state passed laws prohibiting discrimination in employment based on genetic characteristics. A second type of legislation passed by a significant number of states prohibits employers from requiring applicants or employees to undergo genetic testing. The third

type of legislation bans discrimination based on genetic test results or the refusal to take a genetic test, while at the same time banning discrimination based on mere genetic information, such as that which might be provided by an employee on a simple medical questionnaire. As an example of the second type of law, in 1996 New York passed a law restricting genetic testing by disallowing the use of such testing as a condition of employment, membership or licensure. Further, employers, employment agencies, labor organizations, and licensing agencies are prohibited from purchasing or otherwise acquiring such test results. The law has a very broad impact, as it decreases the minimum number of employees required in order to classify one as an employer to four, thereby narrowing the requirements set forth by the ADA and Title VII (each require at least fifteen employees for coverage).

Public policy underlying such statutes is relatively clear and straightforward, with little variation among the various states. Legislators are worried about the uncertainty inherent in genetic tests, which remain relatively new and imprecise in many respects. Additionally, concern over the creation of a "genetic underclass" defined by genetic defects has prompted lawmakers to use caution when considering genetic testing in work environments. Lastly, legislators are apprehensive regarding the use of genetic tests to test for conditions unrelated to job performance. Where an employee may be at risk or places co-workers at risk, the necessity for genetic diagnostic testing may be increased and its use justified.

Because of the traditional exception that is made for situations in which genetic testing is required in the name of workplace safety, Burlington may have been able to make a case that its employees required such testing to remain safe on the job. Even Minnesota's law, one of the most liberal and far-reaching in terms of protecting employees' right of privacy from genetic testing invasion, allows for immunity for those tests required to measure an individual's ability to perform job-related functions. The Minnesota Human Rights Act ("MHRA") is the only state or federal law to require that all medical exams be strictly limited to those related to workplace performance ability. Ironically, however, its progressive legislation is in direct support of the kind of test that was performed by Burlington's medical staff. There is no evidence that the railway tested its employees for anything other than CTS, and it is admitted by both sides that there was no attempt to use this limited information for screening purposes. Some say that "the MHRA represents the most promising legislative approach for protecting the confidentiality of individual medical records and preventing employers from obtaining access to or basing employment decisions on such records."[5] In sum, since Burlington did not violate the most progressive and protective state legislation, and existing state legislation is admittedly much more constrictive than the federal law, was the railway truly at fault?

On the other side of the coin, there are several reasons why an employer should worry about not utilizing genetic testing to its utmost potential:

· Possible tort liability under theories of employer negligence, specifically with respect to third parties
· Fear that workers' compensation programs do not address genetic predispositions and thus leave the employer liable to its employees
· Mandatory federal regulatory legislation (like OSHA) requiring workplace safety
· Cost containment

Employers have a duty of good faith and due care toward their employees, most notably in the prevention of unnecessary work-related injuries. An employer in the modern age of technology and genetic savvy may be found liable for manifestations of genetic conditions of which it should have been aware. Under the tort theories of negligent hiring, retention, and entrustment, employers are held directly liable for injuries caused by the acts of their employees, whether within or outside the scope of their employment.

According to the theory of negligent hiring, an employer may be found liable to third parties for the torts of its employee beyond the scope of employment "where it knew or had reason to know of the [employee's] particular unfitness, incompetence or dangerous attributes ... and could reasonably have foreseen that such qualities created a risk of harm to other persons."[6] This tort claim may go directly to the quality and thoroughness of an employer's pre-employment investigation into the health and competence of job applicants. Because an employer bears the responsibility of assessing the degree of risk that its employees pose to third parties, it has a significant, vested interest in ascertaining whether or not an employee possesses characteristics that will instill dangerous propensities in the workplace. The increasingly available and affordable nature of genetic testing is a method through which employers can more accurately and thoroughly predict the extent of liability they will incur by hiring a certain employee. For example, as genetic tests become more and more prevalent in society, an employer who refuses to utilize them will be held liable to third parties for the damages sustained by an employee whose genetic condition causes lapses of consciousness or incapacity. The costs that Burlington incurred as a result of its settlement pale in comparison to the costs it may have suffered as a result of a lawsuit brought by victims of a train wreck if that accident was caused by improper laying of track due to an employee's genetically-predictable CTS condition. Employers may well have too much to lose through tort claims based on negligent hiring to justify refusing to make use of valuable genetic testing.

Negligent retention tort claims are based on the theory that an employer has a continuing duty to retain only those employees who are fit and competent. An employer may be held liable for negligent retention if it (1) had "reason to know of the particular unfitness, incompetence or dangerous attributes of the employee" and (2) "could reasonably have foreseen that such qualities created a risk of harm to other persons." If an employer conducts routine genetic monitoring of employees in the workplace, it will be particularly susceptible to this tort claim once it is made aware of the employee's condition or propensity. In Burlington, negligent retention is relevant in that the railway had been put on notice of its employees' questionable CTS affliction at the time the employees filed complaints. A failure to fully investigate such claims would have rendered the company vulnerable to claims of negligent retention. Tort damages may well have exceeded the amount of settlement for the railway company.

A third type of employer negligence, that of negligent entrustment, occurs "where the employer supplies an employee with a chattel knowing the employee to be likely … to use it in a manner involving unreasonable risk of physical harm to himself and others." Individual states vary as to the level of care that must be demonstrated by the employer. A Georgia appeals court ruled that "the employer must look into all available information in order to satisfy its burden of ordinary care." In Burlington, the available information included the genetic test for CTS, which had been developed and promulgated by a licensed physician. Without clear federal, state, or administrative regulations banning the use of genetic testing, the employer could be induced to make use of the genetic testing available in order to protect itself from a negligent entrustment claim. Additionally, without a full disclosure of the complainant's CTS condition, Burlington may have been liable to the employees themselves for injuries caused by job-related work. If an employer has access to genetic tests revealing a condition that might impact an employee's work related abilities and overall well-being, it might be found negligent for failing to exercise its ordinary duty of care by not performing and acting upon the test results.

In these types of employer negligence cases, third parties are the intended beneficiaries, as employees are normally precluded from filing tort claims due to the principles embodied in state workers' compensation programs. Currently, workers compensation guidelines contain no provisions that deal explicitly with genetic testing. Whether or not genetic tests will be incorporated into these guidelines has yet to be determined. Permitting the disqualification from workers' compensation of individuals at genetically increased risk of occupational disease would violate important public policies; for example, it would eliminate employers' incentives to clean up the workplace and replace harmful production materials and processes with safer and healthier ones, and it would treat genetically at-risk employees less favorably than other employees with occupational disease in direct violation of the aims of many states to reduce or eliminate genetic discrimination. However, genetically predisposed individuals are neither included nor disqualified under current state workers' compensation programs; whether they are free to sue their employer for its failure to implement genetic testing under any of the theories of employer negligence remains to be seen.

By virtue of its fiduciary position, an employer is charged with responsibility for the safety of its employees. The Occupational Safety and Health Act of 1970 (OSHA) was passed into law with the intent to reduce risk of injury in the workplace. OSHA invokes a long history of employer-conducted medical examinations, specifically requiring biological monitoring of employees through "periodic analysis of body fluids, tissues and excreta in order to measure the impact of the body's exposure to chemical agents and to evaluate the health risks these chemicals pose." Genetic testing may be used to warn people with particular genetic dispositions to avoid certain jobs that may trigger an adverse condition; because of such precautionary abilities, it is likely that, for the purpose of protection of employees, OSHA will require the most precise testing available in order to further ensure the safety of workers. In particular, OSHA is concerned with regulating employee well-being with respect to cancer-causing agents. In fact, one section of OSHA provides that "before an employee is assigned to enter a regulated area, a pre-assignment physical examination by a physician shall be provided. The examination shall include the personal history of the employee, family and occupational background, including genetic and environmental factors." Further, because the ADA does not protect workers from post-employment requirements or requests to provide genetic information, the employer can follow these OSHA requirements without violating the ADA. In effect, the regulations promulgated by OSHA "seem to allow for the implementation of a company-wide genetic monitoring or screening program to improve employee health or safety."[7] Therefore, existing federal safety regulations and developing case law place upon the employer the burden of responsibility for the well-being of his employees as well as the public. When genetic testing offers a more certain method of assuring such safeguarding and is accompanied by federal statutory encouragement such as OSHA, the employer may be compelled to make full use of it.

Employers have an interest in hiring and retaining healthy, productive employees. Unhealthy workers can cost employers money through absenteeism, insurance costs, and the retraining required to replace those who ultimately leave the workplace. Most notably among these incentives to implement genetic testing in the workplace is the cost of health insurance, which continues to rise by twenty percent each year. As costs associated with retention of a sick employee (or one that is genetically predisposed to become sick) rise and the cost of genetic tests falls, employers will be further compelled to use such devices to eliminate high insurance premiums associated with those who possess genetic predispositions to prolonged, costly afflictions. Additionally, due to the increasing costs of health insurance coverage as well as to the Employee Retirement Income Security Act of 1974 ("ERISA"), employers are increasingly electing to self-insure. Those who do self-insure are excluded from high premiums as well as from all types of state insurance regulations, including state legislation that prohibits genetic discrimination.

A recent amendment to ERISA, the Health Insurance Portability and Accountability Act of 1996 ("HIPAA"), was intended to prevent even self-insured employers from establishing different rules for employee health insurance eligibility based on genetic information. However, this amendment contains numerous exceptions "that tend to deemphasize the extent of these expressed rights" and can best be summarized only as "a promising start to future legislation."[8] Therefore, the increasing numbers of employers who self-insure retain the privilege of choosing who they will and will not cover for their employees. Such incentive will create a much more volatile situation, one in which discrimination in health care insurance will predominate.

Cost containment for the employer must be a consideration in the development of clear-cut legislation to address the issue of genetic testing in the workplace. As has been demonstrated, it was likely the main consideration in Burlington's decision to make use of genetic tests for CTS and its decision to settle the lawsuit, as any other decision may have resulted in a far greater expense to the railway.

CONCLUSION

Burlington Northern Santa Fe Railway Co. purposefully and readily agreed to an unfavorable settlement prior to trial. Why? There exists a clear lack of federal prohibition with regard to the use of genetic testing in the workplace. Furthermore, there was an admitted non-presence of any evidence on the part of the EEOC to suggest that Burlington had used the genetic information to discriminate against its employees based on the test results or to screen for conditions unrelated to the workplace; consequently, the railway did not violate the ADA. Burlington settled to avoid the expense and publicity associated with a full-blown trial. "The fact that the case was high profile that got significant attention from the EEOC and was a very emotional matter for many of the individuals involved certainly affected the settlement process."[9] Burlington, while offering no admission of liability, realized that reacting to the concerns of its employees using genetic testing had resulted in criticism and stigmatism. Heads, Burlington lost. But what was the alternative? Claims of negligence and OSHA violations, branding as a company who does not react to its employees' conditions and concerns to the fullest extent possible. Tails, Burlington would have lost.

NOTES

1   Steinforth, Kimberly A. "Bringing Your DNA to Work: Employers' Use of Genetic Testing Under the Americans with Disabilities Act," 43 Ariz. L. Rev. 965, 968–69 (2001).

2   Id. at 969.

3   Smith, Nathalie. "The Right to Genetic Privacy? Are We Unlocking the Secrets of the Human Genome Only to Risk Insurance and Employment Discrimination?" 2000 Utah L. Rev. 705, at 726.

4   Steinforth, supra note 1, at 969.

5   Rothstein, Mark A. "Protecting Genetic Privacy by Permitting Employer Access Only to Job-Related Employee Medical Information: Analysis of a Unique Minnesota Law," 24 Am. J.L. and Med. 399, 1998, at 416.

6   *Di Cosala v. Kay*, 450 A.2d 508, 516 (N.J. 1982).

7   Weaver, Kirke D. "Genetic Screening and the Right Not to Know," 13 Issues L. & Med. 243, 268–68 (1997).

8   Smith, supra note 3, at 742.

9   Interview with Hunter Hughes, mediator of the settlement proceedings.

—52—

ELECTRONIC MONITORING AND PRIVACY ISSUES IN BUSINESS-MARKETING

The Ethics of the DoubleClick Experience

Darren Charters

"If we would've known we wouldn't have done it. We moved into a grey area where there's a tremendous amount of confusion and that's not good. We're a very innovative company and sometimes you get ahead. We made a mistake."
(Mr. Kevin O'Connor, CEO DoubleClick Inc.)

INTRODUCTION

BUSINESSES HAVE LONG BEEN AWARE OF THE value of targeted advertising. DoubleClick Inc. (DoubleClick) is an advertising company that operates in the Internet banner and pop-up advertising business space. The ability to continually tailor Internet advertising to the interests of a user is an advance on previous advertising mediums and represents an opportunity to develop a competitive advantage in the industry. Once trends are detected in a user's Internet activity advertising can be customized to the user's revealed interests.

A company such as DoubleClick sits between the advertiser and the end user and acts as a facilitator between companies who want to advertise to specific types of users and users who may be interested in receiving such advertising. End users arguably benefit as they obtain the advantages of customized advertising content while the receipt of unwanted advertising is minimized. Until November 1999, DoubleClick had always tracked user activity by attaching user histories to anonymous user identifications. Accordingly, while user activity could be tracked, the actual identity of the user was unknown. However, the ability to further refine data profiles was made possible through a series of acquisitions of other companies and their proprietary databases.

In November 1999 DoubleClick announced an amendment to its existing practice. DoubleClick intended to match anonymous existing data with specific user names, personal information, and e-mail addresses. There was no initial public response to the proposed activity. However, in February 2000 the Electronic Privacy Information Center, a privacy advocate, publicly stated that the linkage of such information might have negative implications for users. The negative public response after the statement was immediate and forceful. DoubleClick was forced to back away from the proposed activity. DoubleClick's CEO offered the comment preceding the introduction in response to DoubleClick's failed proposal.

Mr. O'Connor's statement suggests that DoubleClick did nothing wrong from an ethical perspective. Rather, if DoubleClick was guilty of anything, it was just of being too far ahead in anticipating customer tolerance for such activity. Reflecting on the aborted initiative, Mr. O'Connor indicated that DoubleClick would not combine personally identifiable information with anonymous user activity profiles until such time as industry-wide privacy standards exist. Once again, however, there was no suggestion that DoubleClick will not engage in such activity, only that it would wait until some standards are developed before doing so.

This paper will discuss electronic monitoring from an ethical perspective. The discussion will deal generally with ethical issues involved in electronic monitoring for business-marketing purposes, and the DoubleClick experience specifically. The analysis will begin with a brief overview of the basic technology that has permitted the development of such monitoring and move into a discussion of three general concepts of privacy relevant to electronic monitoring. The paper will continue with an examination of the two primary ethical foundations, Utilitarianism and Kantianism, which underpin the various privacy concepts. Once completed, the various privacy principles and ethical foundations will be discussed in the specific context of electronic monitoring. The paper will conclude with an ethical evaluation of Doubleclick's response to the situation in which it found itself and a suggested alternative approach for ethically justifying electronic monitoring....

COOKIES AND ELECTRONIC MONITORING

i. Cookie Technology

Cookies are small data structures used by websites or servers to store and retrieve information on the user's side of the Internet connection. They are sent by a host website or server and reside in the user's computer. A cookie allows websites and servers to "remember" information about specific users. Cookies are a relatively recent phenomenon and were created with very early editions of Internet browsers. In the brief period following the introduction of cookies but prior to the development of the Internet as a medium for commerce the primary use for cookies was as a tool of convenience. For example, cookies could be used to store password codes so that a user would not have to re-type a password when re-entering a site. The intent behind cookies was not to create a tool for gathering knowledge about users but to benefit users through increased convenience. More recently this user convenience has also manifested itself in the ability to create customized content through personalized news service subscriptions and other services.

As business has developed on the Internet cookies have been adapted for business purposes including "shopping carts" for carrying electronic purchases and tracking website activity. By downloading a cookie, servers hosting a website have the power to track and record information such as the previous website from which the user arrived, all web pages the user visits while on the given site, and finally the website address to which the user departs. This information is multiplied in power if the user can be successfully prompted to provide personal information and data while at the site. The knowledge can then be tied to a specific individual. This power has been taken one step further by Internet marketers, who developed the ability to monitor and profile user activity across thousands of sites. In addition the ability to tie such history to a specific individual has been achieved, not just through the voluntary action of users, but also through industry wide database consolidation.

ii. Browser Capabilities

Practically speaking, most Internet users would have no knowledge as to when their Internet activity is being electronically monitored. The normal practice is to download cookies onto a user's hard drive without notice to the user. In this respect there is no choice given to the user, and the downloading and subsequent monitoring is involuntary from the user's perspective.

However, it must be acknowledged that software already exists that can give users complete power with respect to what cookies, if any, are allowed to be stored on a computer. More recent Internet browser versions have given users the ability to control cookies. Users can elect to prohibit all cookie downloads or, alternatively, be notified of, and have the right to accept or reject, any attempted cookie downloads by a server. Based on this it might be asserted that users cannot take the position that there is an ethical issue created by, or an invasion of privacy resulting from, electronic monitoring when it is within their power to completely prohibit or selectively control the activity.

On a theoretical level this argument may have some merit, but it fails for three practical reasons. First, Internet users may still be utilizing browser software that does not contain such cookie control options. Second, even if all users had such browser software, it is a distinct possibility that many users would still be unaware of the capability such software contained. Many computer and Internet users regularly utilize, and only have limited knowledge of, a minimal amount of a software program's capabilities. Third, and most important, the technology that enables electronic monitoring is constantly evolving.

Soon after technology was developed that gave control of cookies to users, marketers seized on new technologies, such as web "bugs," that can evade user detection thus allowing continued surveillance. The ongoing tension between user and marketer control in the development of surveillance technology ensures that the ethics of electronic monitoring will be a relevant issue for the foreseeable future. Further, while the technological means to monitor electronically may differ the same ethical issues are poised to play themselves out, or are already emerging in other spheres of business activity. For example the same issues are already developing in the field of telecommunications. In addition, the same issues will likely surface in the context of location based wireless Internet advertising, thus providing additional incentive to develop a greater understanding of the ethical principles involved in the current Internet advertising debate.

PRIVACY

As a concept, the notion of privacy is grounded in individual rights. Most theorists agree that privacy is a bona fide concept that is fundamentally important to human experience but there is no unanimous agreement on what that concept means or exactly what it encompasses. This is important because it essentially means that privacy has developed as a weaker right. Strong rights tend to have clear definitions and often remain inviolable notwithstanding any other ethical appeals to limit them. The protection of the right to free speech by American courts is one such example. Since the right to privacy is a weak right it has not provided the quality of individual protection that other rights might provide. As a result, it is possible to justify an invasion of the right to privacy on another ethical basis. In effect, what results is an ethical invasion of privacy.

With respect to defining a right of privacy some theories focus on the existence and delineation of a private sphere. Other privacy theories concentrate on actions or conduct that, if carried out, will result in a violation of privacy. No one concept of privacy has been delineated that suitably applies to every situation. The concept has been expanded and extrapolated over time with the result that a number of acceptable concepts of privacy now exist. The privacy issues raised by electronic monitoring are not groundbreaking in that existing concepts of privacy adequately capture the current concerns surrounding electronic monitoring....

ii. Privacy as the Right to Control Access to One's Personal Information

There are a number of various privacy theories that can, in their essence, be reduced to the right to control access to information about the self. These more recent theories of the right to privacy better address the distinction between privacy and liberty (Boatright, 2000). The basic theory represents a refinement of the Warren and Brandeis definition in that it eliminates potential confusion with the right to liberty. It does this by focusing on privacy of personal information. Privacy is conceived of as a right of an individual to determine to what extent, if at all, information about him or herself will be revealed to others (McCloskey, 1980). In this respect privacy is almost akin to a property right. It is to be dealt with as the owner wishes and no other individual has a right to exploit or appropriate it (McCloskey, 1980). An individual is free to be extremely conservative or cavalier with respect to publicizing or allowing access to their personal information.

A variation of this concept of privacy is the right to control access to the realm of the individual. It is a variant on the above in that it recognizes the private sphere does not solely include factual information. It includes elements of individuality (i.e., private motivations) that may not be recordable or quantifiable but are capable of observation. Such information is also considered private and individuals should be able to control access to it (McCloskey, 1980).

Upon initial examination, the idea of personal control may seem an enviable concept as it places control of information with the individual. It is a cohesive fit with western liberal-democratic ideals of individualism and choice and finds favour from that perspective. It is not, however, without criticism. As noted by McCloskey, people may consent to significant invasions or losses of privacy if they place low personal value on the right, or have simply become apathetic due to the continual assault on the sanctity of their personal affairs (McCloskey, 1980). It has also been noted that this approach effectively equates privacy with control when such a linkage is not appropriate. There could well be a loss of privacy in the free disclosure of very personal information without any individual loss in control (Boatright, 2000).

iii. Privacy as the Right to Withhold Certain Facts from Public Knowledge

The final notion of privacy to be discussed here is the concept of privacy that is premised on the notion that there is a definable private sphere and that a person is in a state of privacy when information within this sphere is unknown to others (Boatright, 2000). Parent defines this private realm as, "the condition of not having undocumented personal knowledge about one possessed by others" (Parent 1983, p. 269). Undocumented personal knowledge is conceived of as personal information that is not part of the public record and that most individuals in a society at a given time would not want widely known (Boatright, 2000). This approach implies that this private sphere should generally remain so notwithstanding an individual's casual willingness to surrender it. Also implicit in this approach to privacy is the recognition that there is, at any given point in time, some general community consensus as to personal information individuals would prefer not be available for public consumption. The foregoing definition attempts to refine the preceding concept of privacy by focusing on what information is, or should be, included in the private sphere. If a sphere of private information based on a general community consensus could be ascertained then most, if not all, actions that intrude on this sphere would be a violation of the right to privacy. This concept also has application to the electronic monitoring debate in the sense that if Internet activity were determined to be in the private realm, there would be few situations in which electronic monitoring could be ethically justified.

However, as with the other theories of privacy, there are difficulties with this definition. First, even within a single cultural community people have very different understandings of what is or is not private which makes the likelihood of ascertaining a general consensus elusive. Second, external factors continually impact the ability to invade privacy and as a result the concept is necessarily fluid. For example, it is foreseeable that many activities that were formerly public in nature (i.e., shopping purchases etc.) will become increasingly private as technology gives individuals the ability to carry out such activities in relative privacy. The countervailing trend is that even this activity is increasingly capable of being monitored. If it is acknowledged that the sphere of what is private is fluid, and can be expanded or contracted, than delineating a private sphere is a venture fraught with significant difficulty.

ETHICAL PRINCIPLES UNDERLYING THE RIGHT TO PRIVACY

As with most, if not all, moral and legal rights there is an ethical basis underpinning the right. The right to privacy is no exception. It is built on both Utilitarian and Kantian foundations:

i. Utilitarian Foundation

The Utilitarian basis for acknowledging a right to privacy is two-fold (Boatright, 2000). First, there is the concern that the invasion of privacy can result in significant actual harm to individuals. To evaluate whether a practice is ethical in Utilitarian terms, the harm realized is measured against the benefit flowing from the activity. The ethical evaluation is based on the collective benefits and collective harm resulting to society, although each is experienced at the individual level. If the overall harm exceeds the overall benefit then the practice is deemed to be unethical.

In the context of electronic marketing the potential harm results from the fact that the organization developing user profiles can accumulate potentially sensitive information about a user, based on his or her Internet activities. For example, a gay individual may have elected not to publicly disclose his or her sexual orientation. However, the same individual may, with presumed anonymity, visit websites with gay content or participate as part of a gay Internet community. A company that is able to electronically monitor the individual's computer use could potentially gain intimate knowledge of the individual's situation as a result of the Internet sites the individual visited. The organization developing the profile may intend to use such information solely for the purpose of advertising, however it is not difficult to see the potential harm to the individual's practical interests if such information came into the hands of another party. Another example is potentially sensitive medical condition that might be accessed by employers doing pre-hiring checks or insurers contemplating the issuance of a policy. Profile information generated by electronic monitoring has the potential to be used against the individuals in a manner that harms their personal practical interests.

Opponents of electronic marketing frequently dwell on potential harm but little mention is made of an actual weighing of harms against benefits. The balancing in the electronic monitoring context involves weighing potential serious harm to a limited number of people against the marginal benefit, such as increased convenience and knowledge of consumer products, which might flow to many people from such activity. If the total harm exceeds the total benefit the invasion of privacy through electronic monitoring cannot be considered ethical.

However, if it can be claimed that benefits exceed harm the foundation exists for an ethical invasion of privacy.

The second utilitarian basis for acknowledging a right to privacy is based on a wider concept of harm. As stated succinctly by Boatright, "a certain amount of privacy is necessary for the enjoyment of some activities, so that invasions of privacy change the character of our experiences and deprive us of the opportunity for gaining pleasure from them" (Boatright, 2000, p. 169). The "harm" resulting from the loss of the ability to gain maximum pleasure is presumed to exceed any benefit, such as increased convenience in the electronic monitoring context, such activity might have. A similar argument is that invasions of privacy harm the development and maintenance of personal identity, and that such harm exceeds all benefits (Boatright, 2000).

There has been little reference to either of the above arguments made by privacy advocates in the electronic monitoring debate.

ii. Kantian Foundation

The right to privacy can also be supported on the basis of Kant's second categorical imperative. It provides that individuals should act in a manner that treats other individuals as an end and never as a means only (Boatright, 2000). This imperative captures the themes that people should be respected and treated as autonomous individuals capable of rational choice. To quote Stanley Benn:

> Covert observation—spying—is objectionable because it deliberately deceives a person about his world, thwarting ... his attempts to make a rational choice. One cannot be said to respect a man ... if one knowingly and deliberately alters his conditions of action, concealing the fact from him (cited in Boatright, 2000, p. 170).

Arguments against electronic monitoring that are premised on Kantianism base their position on the argument that electronic monitoring violates the principle of respect for individuals and prohibits them from acting as autonomous beings capable of rational choice.

To date, there has been little public opposition expressed against electronic monitoring on the foregoing basis. However, this is not surprising. In terms of generating public support against electronic monitoring, concerns over potential harm will have a greater mobilizing influence than a more esoteric, albeit relevant, ethical theory such as Kantianism. The fact that Kantian theories supporting a right to privacy have not been part of popular debate makes them no less a valid basis on which to base an objection to, or alternatively support for, electronic monitoring.

PRIVACY AND ETHICAL THEORIES APPLIED

i. Electronic Monitoring and Privacy

Reduced to its simplest form, electronic monitoring as it is currently practiced amounts to unauthorized observance. Many individuals using the Internet have no knowledge of when their online activity is being monitored for the purpose of developing an advertising profile. When discussing concepts of privacy theorists have sometimes resorted to the analogy of one individual watching another individual in a shower without the showering individual's knowledge or consent (McCloskey, 1980). Such action is almost always considered an unethical invasion of privacy. The foregoing analogy generally applies to the context of electronic monitoring. The fundamental similarity is that Internet users can be observed without knowledge or express consent. That said, personal reaction to such observance by users has ranged from significant concern to complete disinterest. Although many people consider their bodies to be a very private aspect of themselves, they may feel less so about Internet activities that are capable of being observed electronically. Accordingly, this may account for the relative indifference of some users.

When the previously discussed concepts of privacy are considered, one would conclude that electronic monitoring without consent constitutes an invasion of privacy. Electronic monitoring violates the right to privacy if it is conceived of as the right to be left alone, or the right to control access to one's personal information. There is a possible argument that there is no violation of the right to withhold certain facts from public knowledge. It might be argued that if current user apathy about electronic monitoring is substantial, most users have little concern over whether their activity is widely known. As such, electronic monitoring does not meet the threshold test that most members of society consider it to be information that should not be widely known. However this argument can just as easily be made the opposite way. As such, even considering the various understandings attached to the concept of privacy it is difficult to argue that electronic monitoring does not violate the privacy right.

ii. Electronic Monitoring and Ethical Foundations

The interesting fact is that electronic monitoring still occurs notwithstanding that it amounts to an invasion of privacy. The justification for, and tolerance of, electronic monitoring rests in the minor differences that exist with the shower analogy. With electronic monitoring the observed information may be electronically collected, organized, and distilled before another individual views it. It is even possible that another individual will never view such information and that any advertising that is tailored to an Internet user will be done completely by electronic intelligent agents. The possibility of harm is minimized still further once Internet advertising companies such as DoubleClick make additional efforts to ensure user profiles remain anonymous.

From a Kantian perspective the minimization of harm is relatively meaningless in terms of ethically justifying the activity. If electronic monitoring is carried out in such a way that it fundamentally respected the autonomy of individuals then it is ethically permissible on a Kantian basis even with isolated incidents of harm. It is still ethically permissible in instances of significant harm provided the principle of individual autonomy is respected. Using Benn's quote above as the analytical tool, it is evident that the guarantee that profiles will not be matched against other identifying information is meaningless in terms of making the practice of electronic monitoring ethical from a Kantian perspective. Most users still had no knowledge of the situation and DoubleClick and other companies could not, from an ethical perspective, be judged to be treating users as individuals capable of rational choice.

However, the minimization of harm is fundamental to justifying electronic monitoring on a Utilitarian basis. As noted above the right to privacy is a relatively weak right. Accordingly, it is open to being subverted based on an appeal to Utilitarianism. Utilitarian based arguments would allow electronic monitoring regardless of its design provided the harms do not exceed its benefits to society as a whole. On this basis, the argument is that any serious albeit intermittent harm that comes to individuals (i.e., the example of the user and the medical condition) is more than offset by the benefits that accrue to the public. Advertising promotes economic efficiency, and advertising that can be tailored directly to individuals, only serves to further promote economic efficiency and thus, generally benefits the public. Further, by initiating the blind profile Internet advertisers could claim that the potential for harm was significantly minimized. Proponents of electronic monitoring could then claim the invasion of privacy was ethically justified. In reality, it was only justifiable based on one ethical perspective, Utilitarianism.

Further, in Doubleclick's situation, had it proceeded with its intention to link user profiles with identified individuals it would have undermined the very ethical foundation that justified its electronic monitoring practice.

DOUBLECLICK'S RESPONSE TO OPPOSITION

It is apparent from the foregoing discussion that linking user data to personally identifiable information could result in a formerly ethical invasion of privacy becoming unethical. DoubleClick responded to the privacy concerns in a variety of ways after aborting its plan. DoubleClick also initiated a significant media campaign to explain how users could opt-out of DoubleClick's service. DoubleClick had an operable opt-out service for over three years preceding the most recent controversy but had not promoted it extensively. The opt-out mechanism requires a user to visit a site and download a cookie. This cookie serves as notice to DoubleClick that they are not to download any cookies on the user's computer. DoubleClick would be free to download a cookie onto a hardrive as long as the "opt-out cookie" is not present.

In theory, it could be argued that this gives autonomous individuals a choice with respect to electronic monitoring and thus provides a Kantian justification for the activity. However, this option is little known and is likely to remain so notwithstanding advertising efforts. Accordingly it is difficult to claim that this truly gives control to users and respects their individual autonomy.

A Chief Privacy Officer (CPO) was also hired along with a Privacy Advisory Board Chair to act as a consumer ombudsman. Overall the response was indicative of a company that developed a greater sensitivity to privacy issues (perhaps for commercial reasons) but that had not developed a deeper understanding of the ethical issues at stake. That is, the actions do not suggest that they have analyzed and understood the ethical issues and tried to develop a principled response. To give DoubleClick some benefit of the doubt, it may be that the new CPO and privacy advisory board chair will infuse the organization with a deeper understanding of the ethical issues at stake and develop ethically based approaches to dealing with such issues. Doubleclick's share price largely recovered after the implementation of the foregoing measures suggesting that even if the response was ethically unsatisfactory in the short term, at least the market was satisfied with Doubleclick's immediate response.

As noted above DoubleClick indicated it would not engage in such activity until such time as industry wide privacy standards were developed. This was relevant in that DoubleClick could still justify its electronic monitoring on a Utilitarian basis. That said, they probably lost some degree of public trust on the issue. DoubleClick has been directly involved in the development of the Interactive Advertising Bureau's (IAB) recently developed Privacy Guidelines. The Privacy Guidelines are intended to form the foundation of a self-regulatory regime with respect to personally identifiable information gathered by electronic means on the Internet. Unfortunately, regarding the use of cookies in electronic monitoring, the guidelines state only that IAB member organizations should notify users, through privacy policies, of such technologies in use and provide users the ability to disable such cookies or other information gathering system. This represents no change from the current situation and for the reasons outlined above, does not provide a proper foundation for the ethical use of cookies in electronic monitoring.

The Privacy Guidelines have also proposed measures that allow individuals to place limits on the use of personally identifiable information that an organization may possess. Once again, it is premised on an opt-out format. That is, organizations are generally free to collect and use personally identifiable information in the first instance subject to an individual informing an organization of limits to be placed on use of such information. It is an ingenious approach that appears to place control of personally identifiable information in the hands in individuals that, realistically, requires minimal change in the current practices of organizations that use electronic monitoring to gather such information.

Further, the Privacy Guidelines have a fundamental problem in that their only real value is as a tool of moral suasion. Although the Privacy Guidelines encourage Internet businesses to adopt the practices established therein, there is no mechanism whatsoever for disciplining businesses who elect to ignore them. For all the effort put into the exercise, the Privacy Guidelines amount to nothing more than best practice suggestions for Internet marketers with respect to privacy issues.

If DoubleClick respects the initial basis on which it proceeded with electronic monitoring, it can claim to have an ethical basis for such conduct. However, considering Doubleclick's willingness to discontinue the previously protective practice one has to wonder how vigilant DoubleClick, or other companies, will be about supporting the privacy of Internet users in a highly competitive market. Since DoubleClick maintains profiles for their own business benefit, it is not possible to claim that they stand in a position of trust with respect to managing such information. However, their position is ethically more sensitive than they appeared to originally comprehend. Based on this, there is cause to argue that it is no longer sufficient to continue to permit electronic monitoring in its current state. This is buttressed by the inherent weakness of relying on a self-regulatory regime that effectively has no sanctioning authority or disciplinary power.

The alternative, and it is not a mutually exclusive option, would be move to a permission based form of electronic monitoring....

AN ALTERNATIVE ETHICAL JUSTIFICATION

If one accepts that privacy is the right to control access to information about one's self then the solution to electronic monitoring is apparent. The choice about whether or not to be monitored in the first instance should be made by the individual user. In fact, in the wake of the DoubleClick experience many commentators and privacy advocates have taken the position that express consent by a user should be a regulatory precondition to downloading cookies that enable electronic monitoring. Placing the power to control electronic monitoring with users is ethically justifiable on a Kantian basis.

First, giving users a choice to be monitored gives individuals autonomy and appears to respect their capabilities of rational choice. However, it could be argued in a wider sense that Internet advertisers are still utilizing individuals as a means to profit and that this violates Kant's second categorical imperative. However, if an individual knowingly and rationally elects to permit such monitoring this must undermine, at least to a minimum degree, such an argument. Accordingly, any electronic monitoring that occurs with express rational permission can be claimed to be ethical on a Kantian basis. This is a significant step, because it provides an alternative basis for ethically justifying electronic monitoring.

A corollary to the foregoing discussion is that while electronic monitoring is most frequently opposed on the basis of potential harm, which is a Utilitarian concern, the permission-based approach in no way guarantees an outcome that will make the practice ethically justifiable on a Utilitarian basis. In other words, the solution being proposed by many commentators is at ethical odds to the frequency stated concern of potential significant harm. If everyone freely elects to permit electronic monitoring the potential for harm is no different than it was prior to such a practice. For example, it is not difficult to imagine that information based on website usage, if in the hands of certain groups, could be used to make decisions about individuals that cause harm. The only difference is that now users have voluntarily accepted the risk. It should also be recognized however, that providing choice to users necessarily undermines the concept that there is a private sphere that should generally be respected irrespective of individual opinion. As such, it is a fundamental rejection of one concept of the right to privacy.

Even if the foregoing is accepted it has little application to the profiles that have been generated to date. In fact there will likely be continual pressure to exploit the marketing advantages that such databases provide. Further, there appears to be limited willingness for companies to zealously regulate themselves at an individual or even an industry-wide level. In this respect there is a regulatory role for governments to play. There is a possibility that individual harm will result from such database consolidation. In addition, regulations should be developed which aim to provide at least minimal individual privacy protection with respect to such database management and/or consolidation. It is apparent that this represents as much a threat to individual privacy as electronic monitoring in the first instance.

REFERENCES

Boatright, M. 2000, 'Privacy', *Ethics and the Conduct of Business*, 3rd ed. (Prentice-Hall, Saddle River New Jersey), pp. 159–183.

McCloskey, H. 1980, 'Privacy and the Right to Privacy', *Philosophy* 55(211), 17–38.

Parent, W.A. 1982, "Privacy, Morality, and the Law." *Philosophy and Public Affairs* 12(4), 269–288.

—53—

E-MAIL AND PRIVACY

A Novel Approach

Mike Bowern

BACKGROUND[1]

SOFTWARE IMPROVEMENTS PTY. LTD. IS A SMALL company located in Canberra, Australia. The company has a number of lines of business, which include selling software tools for modeling and development support; developing their own project support products; consulting; and developing and supporting an advanced electronic voting and vote counting system (eVACS®). The total number of people in the company varies between six and ten, including the managing director, depending on the work in hand.

Each member of the company has a specific area of responsibility, and while there is very little overlap of these areas, it is usual for another person to have a working knowledge of an associated field of the business. The company has adopted some of the ideas of Ricardo Semler,[2] including corporate planning, selection of new people, and setting salaries.

As with any organization, communication within the company is very important. A small office makes face-to-face meetings easy, and there are regular, formal company meetings over lunch. E-mail is the primary medium for communication with outside organizations, including customers, prospects, business partners and contacts, and people working away from the office.

Since the mid-1990s the company has had an open e-mail policy, whereby everyone receives all incoming e-mail messages, regardless of the addressee. Sent messages are regularly copied to others in the company, for example on matters on which the managing director needs to be kept informed. All messages are also copied to the office manager, who archives these together with all incoming e-mail. There has never been any objection from the people in the company to this practice.

Software Improvements believes they gain great benefit from this approach. It provides to each person a daily snapshot of what is happening in the company and its business areas. Regularly, a person not specifically part of an exchange of e-mails has been able to offer some advice or a useful comment on the particular matter being discussed. This is a good example of practical knowledge management.

If an urgent message arrives for a person who may not be available at the time, the office manager forwards the message to the addressee; and replies to the sender saying the person is currently unavailable but knows of the message, and will respond in due course. This is a good example of practical customer service.

Outgoing messages are not monitored or available to all people in the company. A person may send a private message, in the knowledge that any reply may be seen by all. In practice this tends to limit the types of message sent. For example, one would not usually send e-mails about personal finance or health matters. However one may send messages about activities with a professional society, in the knowledge that the replies could be read and could advertise the professional activities.

The people in the company decided to implement this practice in a democratic way at one of the regular staff meetings. There were no arguments against the proposal. If a person does not want messages from particular people to be read by others, he or she asks these people to send their messages to a private e-mail address. People joining the company are told of this policy, and usually accept this method of working. To date, no one has objected to this practice, but if they did object, the e-mail system could be configured to filter their messages to the one recipient.

While some customers and others outside the company are aware of this e-mail practice, there is no conscious effort made to inform all customers and others that their e-mails may be read by all people in the company.

ANALYSIS

This is a simple case about the matter of privacy of e-mail messages. Some people have argued that e-mail messages should be regarded as postal mail and treated with the same level of privacy. Postal mail is treated as private between the sender and recipient, and generally it is against the law for mail in the postal system to be tampered with in any way.

Company e-mails are, or should be, written for business purposes, in the company's time, using equipment and software provided by the company. So managers could argue that the company has the right to monitor and access e-mail messages sent and received on its facilities. However, if a company has this right it also has an obligation to inform its employees that it monitors and accesses the e-mail messages they send and receive. The employees can then accept this situation, perhaps negotiate different arrangements, or leave the company; but these choices may not be as simple as this, and the result may be a matter of coerced consent rather than fully informed consent. For

example, leaving the company may not really be an option in times when, or places where, there are few employment opportunities. Also negotiating different arrangements may not be easy if only one or a few employees are involved.

Wherever there is a policy of e-mail monitoring in the workplace, there should also be a policy of informed consent, whereby employees may give their consent to e-mail monitoring after they have been provided with the policy and all other relevant information about the monitoring process. James H. Moor[3] has proposed a number of principles to guide the setting of policies for privacy and the use of cyber-technology. These are:

1. *The Publicity Principle*—where the rules and conditions (i.e., policies) governing privacy aspects should be clearly defined and known to those people affected by them, thus enabling informed consent.
2. *The Justification of Exceptions Principle*—which allows for the privacy policy to be breached under certain circumstances, when the harm done by the breach of privacy is less than that if the policy were followed.
3. *The Adjustment Principle*—which allows for changes to the policy to be made and publicized.

The e-mail monitoring policy in Software Improvements has generally followed these principles. The policy, as such, is not written down, but the decisions relating to e-mail access are documented in the notes of the regular staff meetings. The Publicity Principle was well and truly followed, since all of the staff were parties to making the decision.

Since this is an open policy, an exception would be for someone *not* to be able to see all incoming e-mail messages. If a person decided they did not want to see all messages, for example a part-time contractor who did not need this facility, then the e-mail system can be configured to enable this. Therefore the requirements of the Justification of Exceptions Principle can be met.

A point for debate in this case could be the matter of e-mail senders not knowing that their messages can be read by all of the people in the company. Often, when you make a telephone call to the Help Desk of a service provider, you hear a message to the effect that "your call may be monitored for training and quality purposes," and you have the option for this not to happen. This is a simple example of informed consent. If Software Improvements decides to inform their business contacts and others about their open e-mail policy then the Adjustment Principle could be followed to make and publicize the changes to their policy.

DISCUSSION QUESTIONS

1. Do you accept the reasons that Software Improvements gives for adopting this practice of e-mail management? Could you work in such an environment? What objections might you have to this approach? Does the overall company benefit override the privacy of the individual?
2. Software Improvements is a small company, with about 10 people. The obvious response is that any more people would make this approach unworkable; but would it? Could other technology help to make this work in an organization of any size? For example could it be arranged for each project team to work in this way?
3. Do managers have a valid argument that the company has the right to monitor and access e-mail messages sent and received on its hardware and software facilities? Would the

same argument apply to monitoring telephone usage for private calls, or private use of a car or a cell phone provided by the company?
4. Do you think that anybody sending a message to Software Improvements should be aware that it may be read by everyone in the company? How could they be made aware of this practice?

NOTES

1   This case has been published with the permission of Software Improvements Pty. Ltd.
2   Semler, Ricardo. 1993. *Maverick*. New York: Warner Books.
3   Moor, James H. "Towards a Theory of Privacy in the Information Age." 1997. *Computers and Society* 27 (September): 27–32.

FURTHER READINGS

Mishra, Jitendra M., and Suzanne M. Crampton. 1998. "Employee Monitoring: Privacy in the Workplace?" *SAM Advanced Management Journal* 63: 4–14.

Moor, James H. 1997. "Towards a Theory of Privacy in the Information Age." *Computers and Society* 27 (3): 27–32.

Nord, G. Daryl, Tipton F. McCubbins, and Jeretta Horn Nord. 2006. "E-Monitoring in the Workplace: Privacy, Legislation, and Surveillance Software." *Communications of the ACM* 49 (8): 72–77.

Weisband, Suzanne P., and Bruce A. Reinig. 1995. "Managing User Perceptions of Email Privacy." *Communications of the ACM* 38 (12): 40–47.

—54—
THE EMPLOYER-EMPLOYEE RELATIONSHIP AND THE RIGHT TO KNOW

Anita M. Superson

I

DANGERS LURK IN THE WORKPLACE. IT HAS BEEN reported that more than 2,200,000 workers are disabled, and more than 14,000 are killed annually as a result of accidents on the job.[1] The causes include safety hazards such as fires, explosions, electrocution, dangerous machinery, as well as health hazards such as loud noise, harmful dusts, asbestos particles, toxic gases, carcinogens, and radiation.[2] The fact that these and other dangers exist is problem enough; but even more problematic is that an employee's awareness of such dangers, prior to being exposed to them, is often minimal, at best. If an employee is to have any say in what happens to his person, what needs to be established—at least more firmly than it is currently—is an employee's[3] right to know about the presence of health and safety hazards in the workplace.

In what follows, I shall first examine the current status of an employee's right to know. I shall argue that it is the very nature of the employer-employee relationship that gives rise to an employee's limited awareness of on-the-job hazards. Next, I shall offer what I think are the philosophical justifications for an employee's right

to know. Finally, in light of these justifications, I shall argue that establishing an employee's right to know will, in fact, benefit both the employee and the employer, and be one step toward achieving a fiduciary relationship.

Throughout this essay, I compare the employer-employee relationship to that of the physician and patient. Although there are some disparities between the two, the comparison is helpful in that it points out that the moral basis for establishing a right to know for a patient is the same as for an employee, yet the two are not accorded the same recognition by the law. To show that the right to know for patients is not recognized as being the same for employees, yet that it is based on the same philosophical foundation for the same reasons, only strengthens the argument for establishing a right to know in the workplace.

II

In the medical setting a person's right to know about risks involved in different kinds of treatment has been recognized under the guise of informed consent. Recently, there have been many attempts in the law and in various health codes to ensure that patients have given informed consent

411

to medical treatments or experimentation. In *Canterbury v. Spence*, 1972, Circuit Court Judge Spotswood W. Robinson III rules that since "every human being of adult years and sound mind has a right to determine what shall be done with his own body," a physician has a "duty of reasonable disclosure of the choices with respect to proposed therapy and the dangers inherently and potentially involved."[4] Similarly, the American Hospital Association's *Patient's Bill of Rights* (1973) states that "The patient has the right to receive from his physician information necessary to give informed consent prior to the start of any procedure and/or treatment."[5] Again, the Nuremberg Code, which focuses on guidelines used in human experimentation carried out in Nazi Germany, specifies that the human subject "should have sufficient knowledge and comprehension of the elements of the subject matter involved as to enable him to make an understanding and enlightened decision."[6] These and other such examples show that through informed consent, a patient's or research subject's right to know about the risks and hazards involved in medical procedures is firmly entrenched. We shall see later that this right is protected by the law. Though the amount of information given to patients may vary among physicians, consent forms must be signed by the patient or by his next of kin. This is true for all patients undergoing most invasive forms of treatment (e.g., surgery).

But the headway that has been made in the medical setting is, unfortunately, unparalleled in the workplace. It was not until 1980 that the Occupational Safety and Health Administration (OSHA) of the United States Department of Labor established the legal right of an employee to "access to employer maintained exposure and medical records relevant to employees exposed to toxic substances and harmful physical agents."[7] In 1983, OSHA issued a final rule requiring

> chemical manufacturers and importers to assess the hazards of chemicals which they produce and import, and all employers having workplaces in the manufacturing division ...

to provide information to their employees concerning hazardous chemicals by means of hazard communication programs including labels, material safety data sheets, training, and access to written records. In addition, distributors of hazardous chemicals are required to ensure that containers they distribute are properly labeled, and that a material safety data sheet is provided to their customers....[8]

On the same note, the National Institute for Occupational Safety and Health (NIOSH) reported that workers had the right to know whether or not they were exposed to hazardous chemical and physical agents regulated by the Federal Government.[9] Finally, the National Labor Relations Act (NLRA) recognizes a labor union's right to information that is relevant to a collective bargaining issue, including safety rules and practices.[10] Although these regulations are a step in the direction of securing a worker's right to know, they are insufficient.

First, though the OSHA rulings recently have been expanded from simply permitting access to an employer's exposure and medical records to requiring assessment of the hazards of chemicals and providing information about such chemicals to an employee by means of labels and material safety data sheets, they fail to extend protection through information to many workers. The 1983 regulation applies only to employees in the manufacturing division, yet does not apply to employees in other divisions such as mining, construction, trade, etc. The reasoning underlying OSHA's restriction to manufacturing is that it has determined that the employees in this division "are at the greatest risk of experiencing health effects from exposure to hazardous chemicals."[11] The agency thus hoped to regulate that sector in which it could be most effective for the greatest number of employees. So, although warning labels and safety data sheets, as well as the assessment of hazards which they necessitate, certainly are positive steps toward securing a worker's right to know, they apply to about only fifty per cent of all workers.[12]

Second, the OSHA rulings apply only to employees which the agency defines as "a current employee, a former employee, or an employee being assigned or transferred to work where there will be exposure to toxic substances or harmful physical agents."[13] The rulings exclude provision of information regarding hazards to the *prospective* employee. This is problematic because the prospective employee is faced with a similar choice, that is, the choice of whether or not to take on a job which entails working in hazardous conditions. Yet providing this information to prospective employees may raise problems in itself. Employers may find this too time-consuming a task to perform for *each* person contending for a position; or, they may feel an obligation to provide this information only to employees since it is this group of persons which has pledged some degree of loyalty to the company. These problems, though, should be worked around for the sake of the prospective employee who will avoid the trouble of committing himself to a job if he knows in advance that the hazardous working conditions outweigh the benefits of taking on the job.

Third, the OSHA rulings do not apply to all safety and health hazards. The 1980 ruling regulates "toxic substances and harmful physical agents," and the 1983 ruling regulates "hazardous chemicals." Clearly, these rulings do not account for a whole spectrum of on-the-job hazards, some of which were mentioned at the outset of this essay. A worker's right to know of these hazards has yet to be firmly established.

This is not to imply that an employer has no responsibility to keep his workplace safe. In fact, in 1970, the Occupational Safety and Health Act (OSHAct) was passed, establishing safety and health standards for all workers other than those employed by federal, state, and local governments. The Act requires an employer to ensure that his workplace is "free from recognized hazards that are causing or likely to cause death or serious physical harm."[14] But this Act, too, is insufficient. It has been reported[15] that the Act protects against only "recognized hazards," defined as those which "can

be detected by the common human senses, unaided by testing devices, and which are generally known in the industry to be hazards." Indeed, this leaves many hazards unaccounted for. It is those hazards not prohibited by law about which the employee may not be informed.

The NIOSH report is inadequate in similar ways. The Institute recognizes a worker's right to know only whether or not they were exposed to hazardous chemical and physical agents regulated by the Federal Government. Its inadequacies are that it does not recognize a right to know of hazards prior to exposure to them, and that like the OSHA rulings, it applies only to chemical and physical agents, rather than all on-the-job hazards.

Finally, the National Labor Relations Act accords some protection to employees who belong to labor unions but is also limited. It established that labor unions had a right to "information that is in the hands of the employer and is relevant to bargainable issues."[16] An employee's right to know about hazardous working conditions is usually recognized as being "relevant to bargainable issues." But what sometimes occurs is a conflict between the employee's right to know and the company's right to keep trade secrets. A trade secret has been defined under the *Restatement of Torts* as "any formula, device, or information, used in a business which gives its holder a competitive advantage over those without the secret."[17] Now if a labor union requests information about job hazards, but this information will expose an employer's trade secrets, thereby jeopardizing his competitive advantage, the employer need not necessarily release this information. And in different cases, the law has favored both sides.

In *Borden Chemical*, an administrative law judge of the National Labor Relations Board determined that Borden had refused to bargain in good faith when it failed to release information to the labor union. It was then ordered to supply the information to the union. The reason behind the ruling was that Borden failed to show that disclosure of the information would damage its competitive position.[18] Essentially, Borden failed to show how its trade secrets would reach its competitors.[19] In

Colgate-Palmolive, however, an administrative law judge ruled that the employer was obliged to reveal a list of chemicals in the workplace *except* those constituting trade secrets.[20] Colgate-Palmolive apparently showed how it would be disadvantaged were its trade secrets to be revealed. We can surmise from these two cases and from the OSHA and NIOSH rulings that an employee's right to know is not accorded full protection by the law, and, in fact, may be denied by the law.

III

Why is the right to know in the workplace not firmly grounded? It is the argument of this section that protection of such a right is limited because of the very nature of the employer-employee relationship.

This relationship can be best defined as a nonfiduciary one, meaning that there is little or no trust on behalf of each party in the actions of the other party. This lack of trust stems from the expectations each party has for forming a personal relationship. In most cases, the expectations dictate a non-personal interaction. The employee often feels the same; he views himself as a person for hire, whose function is to perform a certain job for the company or institution in exchange for wages and perhaps a few fringe benefits. If the employee does not like his job for whatever reason, he is free to leave. The employer is also free (for the most part) to fire any employee who is not performing his job in what the employer judges to be a favorable way. As a result, many employees remain with a certain company for only a short period of time, thus making it difficult to come to know their employer personally, if this be at all possible.

Both the employer and employee normally do not enter into their relation thinking that they can trust each other to look out for the other's best interests. Probably the only form of trust existent between the two parties is that the employer will pay the employee a wage that at least matches the work he puts out, and that the employee will perform the job he is asked to do in a way that is normally expected. These are the roles both the employer and employee expect each other to take on. It would be difficult to establish a fiduciary relationship under such expectations. What adds to the difficulty is that often the employer and employee do not even know each other at any kind of personal level. I ask rhetorically: How can a fiduciary relationship be established if no relationship has been established?

Another feature of the employer-employee relationship which adds to its nonfiduciary nature is the reasons both the employee and the employer have for entering into their relationship. The employee enters a relationship with his employer primarily for monetary reasons; he seeks employment in order to earn wages with which he can secure the goods he needs to live. The employer, on the other hand, enters a relationship primarily for the sake of profit-making. His position in respect to that of the employee is one of power. It derives its power from the fact that the employer offers the employee a benefit—wages—if he accepts and performs a job. The employer stands to benefit directly from his employee. He needs a certain job to be done; the company's profits depend upon whether the task is accomplished. And the financial success of the company is directly related to the employer.

Both the expectations of the employee and employer, as well as the reasons for each entering into the relationship, make it likely that an employer would use his employee merely as a means to his own end, to borrow a notion from Kant. That is, the employer, seeking to augment his profits (the end), may use the employee merely as a means to achieve that end. One way in which he could do this is to fail to inform an employee about hazardous work conditions. Failure to inform an employee about these hazards is to deny him information that may affect his decision to stay on the job. And by remaining on the job, the employee works in part for the employer's benefit, that is, to increase the company's profits. In this way, the employee is used as a means to the employer's end.

More specifically, if the expectations of both the employer and employee of each other are as I have described, it is easy for the former to use the latter as a means to an end because being so far removed on a personal level from the employee, he does not feel a sense of obligation towards the employee's welfare. All he has invested in the relationship is that the job gets done. And since the employee does not view the relationship as a fiduciary one, he has no basis for trusting the employer to ensure that the workplace is free from hazards, or at least to inform him of the hazards that do exist. Indeed it would be nice for the employer to do either; yet the employee probably does not expect it, and certainly cannot trust his employer to do so.

And, if the reasons the employer and employee have for entering their relationship are as I have described, this is another reason why an employer may use his employee merely as a means to his own end. If the employer is aware of the power he holds over his employee, that is, that he to a large extent controls the employee's means of livelihood, he may feel no obligation to inform the employee about on-the-job hazards. In fact, somewhat ironically, the employer may even go so far as to view the employee as using *him*, the *employer*, as a means to an end. This belief is based upon the fact that the employee may take on a job solely for the purpose of obtaining money, perhaps with minimum effort put forth, and that the employee is free to leave when he so desires. If the employer has this attitude toward his employee, it becomes easier for him not to inform the employee of hazards in the workplace.

The nature of the employer-employee relationship differs from that of the physician-patient in these two respects. Specifically, the expectations of the physician and patient are of a much more trusting nature. Oftentimes, the physician and patient have established a personal relationship; they, for example, know somewhat about each other's lifestyles, values, etc. Patients generally expect and trust their physician to act in their best interests. They expect that physicians will inform them of the hazards and risks involved in various medical treatments, and that together they will arrive at a decision about what is the best course of action to

take. And if the physician fails to inform his patient about these hazards and risks, the patient usually assumes that the information was withheld for his, the patient's, own benefit.

Furthermore, the reasons for the patient and physician entering a relationship are different from that of the employer and employee. Patients seek the advice of a physician because, simply put, they want to be treated for an illness. They expect that the physician will do this, and will give the patient information on forms of treatment. This is what the patient pays for, and thus expects to receive. The physician, in turn, should feel that he has an obligation to provide this information to the patient, unless he can justify withholding it.

The physician's reasons for entering the relationship are different from the employer's. Rather than being solely, or at least primarily, profit-motivated, physicians often view their role as one of benefitting the sick. Certainly there are many physicians who enter the profession for monetary reasons: I do not wish to deny this. Yet, as any physician would admit, there are easier ways to make money. Still, the physician, like the employer, is in a power position. But the source of the physician's power is different. He does not stand to benefit from performing a certain therapy on any *particular* patient (unless, of course, the patient is indeed unique), for it is likely that another patient will choose to undergo that treatment. And, more importantly, physicians will always have patients seeking their services because persons will always get sick. Unless a physician is so inadequate, he can rest assured that he will be in business for a long time. This gives him less reason to deny patients information they need concerning the hazards of treatment. Thus, a physician's power position is not as threatened by loss of profit as is an employer's. He therefore has less reason than an employer to use a person merely as a means to his own end.

Moreover, an employer's reasons for withholding information are often different from those of the physician. While the physician may feel he is acting in the patient's best interests (whether or not he is certainly is open to debate) when he withholds information concerning the risks of treatment, this is not often the case with the employer. The employer withholds information about on-the-job hazards not because he wishes to protect the employee, or to act in the employee's best interests, but because he wants to protect his own interests. He wants the company to profit, and this may be possible only if certain hazardous assignments are made. The employer may feel that he is justified in withholding information about risks from the employee. After all, the employee does not have to stay on *this* job; he is free to leave. The employer's reasons for withholding information are thus, unlike those of most physicians, self-interested. It is these features of the employer-employee relationship, namely, the expectations of both parties, their reasons for entering into the relationship, and the employer's reasons for withholding information, which all contribute to the nonfiduciary nature of this relationship. These features may, of course, all be a result of the capitalist system. If this be so, some persons may argue that the very nature of the employer-employee relationship can be changed only by changing the socio-economic system. I believe this is false, and in Section V I will argue that establishing an employee's right to know will, in fact, make headway in changing the relationship into one that is fiduciary in nature.

IV

We have seen that the nature of the employer-employee relationship is such that it is difficult to establish an employee's right to know. Employers, on the one hand, find little or no reason to give their employees information about hazards in the workplace. In turn, employees find little or no reason to expect to receive this information. The differences in the nature of the relationship are, in all probability, responsible for the dissimilarities in the establishment of the right to know. But should this difference exist? Is there a difference in the choices faced by a person as patient versus a person as employee that will justify the difference in the recognition of the right to know?

I suggest that there is not. Although many disparities exist between the relationships, an important similarity grounds the right to know. It is this: in both cases, the person wants to know the dangers involved for the *same* reasons. He wants to know the risks that may be incurred to his body so that he can decide whether or not to expose himself to those risks. The information is needed for him to make a reasonable choice.

In both situations, the moral basis of the right to know lies in the principle of autonomy. Much talk has been generated about this principle since Mill and Kant recognized its importance. Although the literature offers a variety of definitions, this principle is usually defined in such a way as to include the notion of making one's own decisions affecting one's own life without coercion from others. In order for one to make a responsible decision, he must be informed about the choices with which he is faced. Just as a patient must be informed about the risks involved in a certain treatment in order for him to decide if he wants that treatment, an employee, too, must be informed about the hazards involved in working under certain conditions if he is to make a responsible, autonomous choice about whether or not to subject his person to such risks. In either case, if such information is not disclosed, the person's autonomy has been placed in jeopardy.

The choice faced by both the patient and the employee is one of whether or not to subject one's person to risk of harm. It may be objected that the harms which may be incurred in the workplace are less serious than those which may be incurred in the medical setting. But this is simply not true. The harms incurred in the workplace may be just as serious, and may not be as immediate as those incurred in the medical setting. For example, side-effects from an operation or from taking certain drugs are often known by the patient and/or his physician soon after they are incurred. Harms resulting from on-the-job hazards, however, often take considerable time to manifest themselves, and often require long-term exposure to take effect. For example, chronic berylliosis, constituted by coughing, dyspnea, and anorexia, may appear years after exposure to beryllium.[21] And cancer may take years to manifest itself after exposure to coal tar, paraffin, asbestos, vinyl chloride, and benzene. Other toxic materials do not produce side-effects in the exposed person, but instead in his or her children. These are either mutagenic in nature, in which case they change the genetic makeup of the offspring, or teratogenic, in which case they are capable of causing birth defects in the offspring.[22] This is not to imply that all harms incurred in the medical setting are immediate, and those incurred on the job are made manifest years after exposure; instead the point is that many do follow this pattern.

Because the harms incurred in the workplace often are made manifest years later, it is more difficult for an employer to face liability charges. In the medical realm, patients can be awarded damages either in battery or in negligence. Traditionally, patients can sue physicians for damages in battery if they are touched, treated, or researched upon without consent.[23] In a British Columbia case, it was reported[24] that a patient who suffered loss of smell and partial loss of taste after surgery was awarded damages in battery because she was unaware of these risks at the time of her consent. In America, failure to disclose risks to patients "is considered a breach of the physician's general duty to care to give reasonable information and advice to his patient."[25] To be awarded damages in battery, the patient need only establish that "what was done differed substantially from that to which he assented."[26]

Patients can sue also for damages in negligence. In Canada, it is reported that the physician should inform the patient of the nature and seriousness of treatment lest he be held negligent. The duty in negligence "is based on the nature of the physician-patient relationship as a trust," thus imposing a "basic requirement of honesty upon the physician."[27] In order for a physician to be found negligent, the patient must show that there was a breach of the duty of disclosure and that he, the patient, would not have consented had

the required disclosure been given, and that he suffered a loss as a result.[28]

Although a patient can sue for damages in either battery or negligence, an employee has no such privilege. Establishment of workmen's compensation has prevented the right to sue in tort.[29] Prior to the establishment of workmen's compensation, employees could settle under tort law and receive payments for both loss of income as well as for "pain and suffering." Workmen's compensation statutes, however, include payment for loss of income, but only limited payment for "pain and suffering."[30] One source reports that no payment for pain and suffering is included.[31] Thus, employers do not have to pay for the full consequences of their negligence. Employees themselves must shoulder most of the burden of costs for employer negligence. This seems especially unjust when we are reminded of the fact that an employee's right to know is not firmly established.

One basis, then, for establishing a right to know in the workplace is that it ensures that an employee is given information necessary for him to be able to make a choice which may significantly affect his life. Informing an employee of workplace hazards puts him in the position of deciding whether or not he wants to be exposed to hazards, and thereby is one step in the direction of promoting his autonomy. Establishment of a right to know is especially important for the worker since he does not have much recourse against his employer if damages ensue.

Another basis for establishing this right lies in the notion of fairness of contract. When a person is hired for a job, there is an implicit contract made between the employer and employee, the terms of which spell out that person X will do job A and will be paid by person Y. This contract requires, like any fair contract, that both parties know what they are contracting to. It is insufficient that an employee know he is consenting to do a certain job in a certain way at a certain pace, and so on. If hazards which may produce harm to his person are involved, he should be made aware of them before he enters the contract. If he is not made aware of the hazards, and enters the contract with the employer, he is not giving fully informed consent to the relevant terms of the contract. The contract is thus unfair.

A third basis for establishing an employee's right to know is partly economic, partly moral. It lies in Milton Friedman's notion of business' social responsibility, namely "to use its resources and engage in activities designed to increase its profits so long as it stays within the rules of the game, which is to say, engages in open and free competition, without deception or fraud."[32] The moral justification for the right to know, using Friedman's terms of business' social responsibility, lies in his normative judgment that business should not engage in deceptive practices. Though Friedman does not spell out what this entails, surely withholding information from the prospective employee—information which is likely to influence his decision—is a deceptive practice, prohibited even on Friedman's libertarian analysis of business in the free market system.

An economic justification for the right to know also can be found in Friedman and other free market advocates. It is this: in order to ensure that the free market really is free, persons should be able to enter the occupation of their choosing (at least insofar as they meet the qualifications). This choice must be informed. If information about job hazards is withheld, the choice will not be fully informed. And if the choice is not fully informed, it is not truly free. Thus, ignoring the right to know, besides violating moral principles such as autonomy and fairness of contract, violates one of the fundamental economic bases of the free market system.

V

If an employee's right to know becomes firmly established, certain implications are likely to follow. On the negative side, the employer will be faced with the difficult task of determining how much and what kind of information ought to be given to the employee. The employer will have to devote time and effort to find out just what hazards exist, and to convey the results of his findings to the employee. And if the risks involved in taking on a certain job are very high, or very serious, the employer may have difficulty in hiring someone for the job. Also, the company's trade secrets undoubtedly will sometimes be revealed.

While I do not wish to diminish the inconvenience these implications bring to the employer, none is too important to override the employee's right to know. Indeed, there certainly are ways to lessen the inconvenience while still bringing about the desired effects.

More importantly though, it is reasonable to assume that both parties are likely to benefit by establishing an employee's right to know.

It benefits the employee in several ways. First, since the employer will have to ascertain what are hazards in the workplace, he may eliminate at least some of them for the sake of attracting employees. Thus, the environment may be safer for the employee. Second, if the employee is presented with the relevant information about on-the-job hazards, it places into the hands of the employee the informed decision of whether or not to accept a position. The employee can then make his own choice of whether or not to expose himself to those hazards. Moreover, informing the employee of hazards in the workplace ensures him that the contract made with his employer is fair and not based upon deception. In these ways, it establishes trust in the employer.

The employer, too, benefits. Once he has given such information to his employee, if the employee willingly accepts the job knowing that to which he has consented, and is in some way harmed, the employer would decrease his liability in many cases. After all, it was the employee's decision to expose himself to the hazards. He knew what to expect, and is responsible for his decision. The employer, in many cases, will avoid paying compensation.

Most important is that the right to know may go so far as to establish a fiduciary relationship between employer and employee, much the same as that existent between many patients and their physicians. Part of what is involved in such a relationship is that both parties trust each other to look after each other's best interests. The employer can accomplish this by improving his work environment, by informing his employee of existent hazards, and the like.

The employee, also, can look out for his employer's best interests by unifying his goals with the goals of his employer. If the employee is made aware of risks involved in taking on a certain job, and yet he consents to taking on that job (assuming, of course, that he understands the risks and is not coerced into the job perhaps by another person or because he is unable to find an alternative), he has invested a part of himself into that relationship. He admits his willingness to work for an employer to achieve his employer's goals. The goals of the employer are then shared with the employee. And since the employee knows he is not being deceived about the conditions under which he works, he may have more incentive to do his job well. This, too, is likely to benefit the employer.

It is interesting to note, in conclusion, that the very nature of the employer-employee relationship which makes it difficult to secure an employee's right to know can, in fact, be changed into one of a fiduciary nature through the establishment of a right to know. We have seen that though the philosophical basis for securing a right to know in the workplace is the same as in the medical setting and that the harms which may possibly be incurred are similar, this right is more firmly grounded in the medical setting than in the workplace. What needs to be firmly established for the benefit of both the employer and employee in order to make headway in achieving a fiduciary relationship is an employee's right to know.

NOTES

1   Manuel G. Velasquez, *Business Ethics: Concepts and Cases* (Englewood Cliffs, NJ: Prentice-Hall, Inc., 1982), 311.

2   See Nicholas A. Ashford, *Crisis in the Workplace: Occupational Disease and Injury* (Cambridge, MA: The MIT Press, 1976), 68–83, for a thorough and interesting description of these hazards.

3   Although I shall use the term "employee" throughout this essay, my arguments shall apply also to the prospective employee since he is faced with a similar choice, that is, whether or not to accept a job in a hazardous work environment.

4   *Canterbury v. Spence*, US Court of Appeals, District of Columbia Circuit, May 19, 1972, 464 Federal Reporter, 2nd Series, 772.

5   "A Patient's Bill of Rights," American Hospital Association, reprinted in Mappes and Zembaty (eds.), *Biomedical Ethics* (New York: McGraw-Hill, Inc., 1981), 87–89.

6   "Declaration of Helsinki," World Medical Association, reprinted in Mappes and Zembaty, *op. cit.*, 145–47.

7   *Federal Register*, Vol. 45 no. 102, Friday, May 23, 1980, Rules and Regulations, Dept. of Labor, Occupational Safety and Health Administration, 23CFR Part 1910, 35212.

8   *Federal Register*, Vol. 48 no. 228, Friday, November 25, 1983, Rules and Regulations, Dept. of Labor, Occupational Safety and Health Administration, 29CFR Part 1910, 53280.

9   Ruth R. Faden and Tom L. Beauchamp, "The Right to Risk Information and the Right to Refuse Health Hazards in the Workplace," in *Ethical Theory of Business* (2nd ed.), Tom L. Beauchamp and Norman E. Bowie, eds. (Englewood Cliffs, NJ: Prentice-Hall, Inc., 1983), 196–206.

10   Tim D. Wermager, "Union's Right to Information vs. Confidentiality of Employer Trade Secrets: Accommodating the Interests through Procedural Burdens and Restricted Disclosure," 66 *Iowa Law Review*, 1333–51, July, 1981.

11   *Federal Register*, Vol. 48 no. 228, Friday, November 25, 1983, Rules and Regulations, Dept. of Labor, Occupational Safety and Health Administration, 29CFR Part 1910 53284.

12   Ibid., Table 1, 53285.

13   Ibid., Vol. 45, 35215.

14 The Occupational Safety and Health Act of 1970
    (Public Law 91-596), Section 5(a)(1), reprinted in
    Ashford, 545–75.

15 Robert Stewart Smith, *The Occupational Safety
    and Health Act: Its Goals and Its Achievements*
    (Washington, DC: American Enterprise Institute for
    Public Policy Research, 1976), 9.

16 Wermager, *op. cit.*, 1333.

17 David Carey Fraser, "Trade Secrets and the NLRA:
    Employee's Right to Health and Safety Information,"
    14 *University of San Francisco Law Review*, 495–524,
    Spring, 1980.

18 Wermager, *op. cit.*, 1335–36.

19 Wermager, *op. cit.*, 1343.

20 Wermager, *op. cit.*, 1345.

21 Ashford, *op. cit.*, 76.

22 Ashford, *op. cit.*, 78.

23 Karen Lebacqz and Robert J. Levine, "Informed
    Consent in Human Research: Ethical and Legal
    Aspects," in *Encyclopedia of Bioethics*, Vol. 2,
    Warren T. Reich, editor-in-chief (New York: The
    Free Press, 1978), 755–62.

24 Gilbert Sharpe, LLM, "Recent Canadian Court
    Decisions on Consent," *Bioethics Quarterly*, Vol. 2
    No. 1 (Spring, 1980), 56–63.

25 Sharpe, ibid., 58.

26 Sharpe, ibid., 61.

27 Janice R. Dillon, "Informed Consent and the
    Disclosure of Risks of Treatment: The Supreme
    Court of Canada Decides," *Bioethics Quarterly*, Vol.
    3 No. 3 and 4 (Fall/Winter, 1981), 156–62.

28 Dillon, ibid., 160.

29 Ashford, *op. cit.*, 350.

30 Ashford, *op. cit.*, 392.

31 "Occupational Health Risks and the Worker's Right
    to Know," 90 *Yale Law Journal*, 1792–1810, July, 1981.

32 Milton Friedman, *Capitalism and Freedom*
    (Chicago: The University of Chicago Press, 1962), 13.

—55—

HUMAN RIGHTS, WORKERS' RIGHTS, AND THE "RIGHT" TO OCCUPATIONAL SAFETY

Tibor R. Machan

INTRODUCTION

I TAKE THE POSITION OF THE NONBELIEVER.[1] I DO not believe in special workers' rights. I do believe that workers possess rights as human beings, as do publishers, philosophers, disc jockeys, students, and priests. Once fully interpreted, these rights may impose special standards at the workplace, as they may in hospitals, on athletics fields, or in the marketplace.

Human Rights

Our general rights, those we are morally justified to secure by organized force (e.g., government), are those initially identified by John Locke: life, liberty, and property. That is, we need ask no one's permission to live, to take actions, and to acquire, hold, or use peacefully the productive or creative results of our actions. We may, morally, resist (without undue force) efforts to violate or infringe upon our rights. Our rights are (1) absolute, (2) unalienable, and (3) universal: (1) in social relations no excuse legitimatizes their violation; (2) no one can lose these rights, though their exercise may be restricted (e.g., to jail) by what one chooses to do; and (3) everyone has these rights, whether acknowledged or respected by others or governments or under different descriptions (within less developed conceptual schemes).[2]

I defend this general rights theory elsewhere.[3] Essentially, since adults are rational beings with the moral responsibility to excel as such, a good or suitable community requires these rights as standards. Since this commits one to a virtuously self-governed life, others should respect this as equal members of the community. Willful invasion of these rights—the destruction of (negative) liberty—must be prohibited in human community life.

So-called positive freedom—that is, the enablement to do well in life—presupposes the prior importance of negative freedom. As, what we might call, self-starters, human beings will generally be best off if they are left uninterfered with to take the initiative in their lives.

WORKERS' RIGHTS

What about special workers' rights? There are none. As individuals who intend to hire out their skills for what they will fetch in the marketplace, however, workers have the right to offer these in return for what others (e.g., employers) will offer in acceptable compensation. This implies free trade in the labor market.

Any interference with such trade workers (alone or in voluntary cooperation) might want to engage in, with consent by fellow traders, would violate both the workers' and their traders' human rights. Freedom of association would thereby be abridged. (This includes freedom to organize into trade associations, unions, cartels, and so forth.)

Workers' rights advocates view this differently. They hold that the employee-employer relationship involves special duties owed by employers to employees, creating (corollary) positive rights to be treated with care and considerations that governments, given their purpose, should also protect.

This, however, is a bad idea. Not to be treated with care and consideration can be open to moral criticism. And lack of safety and health provisions may mean the neglect of crucial values to employees. In many circumstances employers should, morally, provide them.

This is categorically different from the idea of enforceable positive rights. (Later I will touch on unfulfilled reasonable expectations of safety and health provisions on the job!) Adults aren't due such service from free agents whose conduct should be guided by their own judgments and not some alien authority. This kind of moral servitude (abolished after slavery and serfdom) of some by others has been discredited.

Respect for human rights is necessary in a moral society—one needn't thank a person for not murdering, assaulting, or robbing one—whereas being provided with benefits, however crucial to one's well being, is more an act of generosity than a right.

Of course moral responsibilities toward others, even strangers, can arise. When those with plenty know of those with little, help would ordinarily be morally commendable. This can also extend to the employment relationship. Interestingly, however, government "regulation may impede risk-reducing change, freezing us into a hazardous present when a safer future beckons."[4]

My view credits all but the severely incapacitated with the fortitude to be productive and wise when ordering their affairs, workers included. The form of liberation that is then viral to workers is precisely the bourgeois kind: being set free from subjugation to others, including governments. Antibourgeois "liberation" is insultingly paternalistic.[5]

ALLEGING SPECIAL WORKERS' RIGHTS

Is this all gross distortion? Professor Braybrooke tells us, "Most people in our society ... must look for employment and most (raking them one by one) have no alternative to accepting the working conditions offered by a small set of employers—perhaps one employer in the vicinity."[6] Workers need jobs and cannot afford to quibble. Employers can wait for the most accommodating job prospects.

This in part gives rise to special workers' rights doctrines, to be implemented by government occupational safety, health and labor-relations regulators, which then "makes it easier for competing firms to heed an important moral obligation and to be, if they wish, humane."[7]

Suppose a disadvantaged worker, seeking a job in a coal mine, asks about safety provision in the mine. Her doing so presupposes that (1) she has other alternatives, and (2) it's morally and legally optional to care about safety at the mine, not due to workers by right. Prior to government's energetic prolabor interventions, safety, health, and related provisions for workers had been lacking. Only legally mandated workers' rights freed workers from their oppressive lot. Thus, workers must by law be provided with safety, health care, job security, retirement, and other viral benefits.

Workers' rights advocates deny that employers have the basic (natural or human) private property rights to give them full authority to set terms of employment. They are seen as nonexclusive stewards of the workplace property, property obtained by way of historical accident, morally indifferent historical necessity, default, or theft. There is no genuine free labor market. There are no jobs to offer since they are not anyone's to give. The picture we should have of the situation is that society should be regarded as a kind of large team or family; the rights of its respective parts (individuals) flow not from their free and independent moral nature, but from the relationship of the needs and usefulness of individuals as regards the purposes of the collective.

By this account, everyone lacks the full authority to enter into exclusive or unilaterally determined and mutual agreements on his or her terms. Such terms—of production, employment, promotion, termination, and so on—would be established, in line with moral propriety, only by the agency (society, God, the party, the democratic assembly) that possesses the full moral authority to set them.

Let us see why the view just stated is ultimately unconvincing. To begin with, the language of rights does not belong within the above framework. That language acknowledges the reality of morally free and independent human beings and includes among them workers, as well as all other adults. Individual human rights assume that within the limits of nature, human beings are all efficacious to varying degrees, frequently depending upon their own choices. Once this individualist viewpoint is rejected, the very foundation for rights language disappears (notwithstanding some contrary contentions).[8]

Some admit that employers are full owners of their property, yet hold that workers, because they are disadvantaged, are owed special duties of care and considerateness, duties which in turn create rights the government should protect. But even if this were right, it is not possible from this position to establish enforceable *public* policy. From the mere existence of *moral* duties employers may have to employees, no enforceable public policy can follow; moral responsibilities require freely chosen fulfillment, not enforced compliance.

Many workers' rights advocates claim that a free labor market will lead to such atrocities as child labor, hazardous and health-impairing working conditions, and so forth. Of course, even if this were true, there is reason to think that OSHA-type regulatory remedies are illusionary. As Peter Huber argues, "regulation of health and safety is not only a major obstacle to technological transformation and innovation but also often aggravates the hazards it is supposed to avoid."[9]

However, it is not certain that a free labor market would lead to child labor and rampant neglect of safety and health at the workplace. Children are, after all, dependents and therefore have rights owed them by their parents. To subject children to hazardous, exploitative work, to deprive them of normal education and health care, could be construed as a violation of their individual rights as young, dependent human beings. Similarly, knowingly or negligently subjecting workers to hazards at the workplace (of which they were not made aware and could not anticipate from reasonable familiarity with the job) constitutes a form of actionable fraud. It comes under the prohibition of the violation of the right to liberty, at times even the right to life. Such conduct is actionable in a court of law and workers, individually or organized into unions, would be morally justified, indeed advised, to challenge it.

A consistent and strict interpretation of the moral (not economic) individualist framework of rights yields results that some advocates of workers' rights are aiming for. The moral force of most attacks on the free labor market framework tends to arise from the fact that some so-called free labor market instances are probably violations of the detailed implications of that approach itself. Why would one be morally concerned with working conditions that are fully agreed to by workers? Such a concern reflects either the belief that there hadn't been any free agreement in the first place, and thus workers are being defrauded, or it reflects a paternalism that, when construed as paternalism proper instead of compassion, no longer carries moral force.

Whatever its motives, paternalism is also insulting and demeaning in its effect. Once it is clear that workers can generate their own (individual and/or collective) response to employers' bargaining power—via labor organizations, insurance, craft associations, and so on—the favorable air of the paternalistic stance diminishes considerably. Instead, workers are seen to be regarded as helpless, inefficacious, inept persons.

THE "RIGHT" TO OCCUPATIONAL SAFETY

Consider an employer who owns and operates a coal mine. (We could have chosen any firm, privately or "publicly" owned, managed by hired executives with the full consent of the owners, including interested stockholders who have entrusted, by their purchase of stocks, others with the goal of obtaining economic benefits for them.) The firm posts a call for jobs. The mine is in competition with some of the major coal mines in the country and the world. But it is much less prosperous than its competitors. The employer is at present not equipped to run a highly-polished, well-outfitted (e.g., very safe) operation. That may lie in the future, provided the cost of production will not be so high as to make this impossible.

Some of the risks will be higher for workers in this mine than in others. Some of the mineshafts will have badly illuminated stairways, some of the noise will be higher than the levels deemed acceptable by experts, and some of the ventilation equipment will be primitive. The wages, too, will be relatively low in hopes of making the mine eventually more prosperous.

When prospective employees appear and are made aware of the type of job being offered, and its hazards they are at liberty to (a) accept or reject, (b) organize into a group and insist on various terms not in the offing, (c) bargain alone or together with others and set terms that include improvements, or (d) pool workers' resources, borrow, and purchase the firm.

To deny that workers could achieve such things is not yet to deny that they are (negatively) free to do so. But to hold that this would be extraordinary for workers (and thus irrelevant in this sort of case) is to (1) assume a historical situation not in force and certainly not necessary, (2) deny workers the capacity for finding a solution to their problems, or (3) deny that workers are capable of initiative.

Now suppose that employers are compelled by law to spend the firm's funds to meet safety requirements deemed desirable by the government regulators. This increased cost of production reduces available funds for additional wages for present and future employees, not to mention available funds for future prospect sites. This is what has happened: The employee-employer relationship has been unjustly intruded upon, to the detriment not only of the mine owners, but also of those who might be employed and of future consumers of energy. The myth of workers' rights is mostly to blame.

CONCLUSION

I have argued that the doctrine of special workers' rights is unsupported and workers, accordingly, possess those rights that all other humans possess, the right to life, liberty, and property. Workers are not a special species of persons to be treated in a paternalistic fashion and, given just treatment in the community, they can achieve their goals as efficiently as any other group of human beings.[10]

NOTES

1   I also wish to thank Bill Puka and Gertrude Ezorsky for their very valuable criticism of an earlier draft of this essay, despite their very likely disapproval of my views.

2   This observation rests, in part, on epistemological insights available, for example, in Hanna F. Pitkin, *Wittgenstein and Justice* (Berkeley, CA: University of California Press, 1972).

3   Tibor R. Machan, "A Reconsideration of Natural Rights Theory," *American Philosophical Quarterly* 19 (January 1980): 61–72.

4   Peter Huber, "Exorcists vs. Gatekeepers in Risk Regulation," *Regulation* (November/December 1983), 23.

5   But see Steven Kelman, "Regulation and
     Paternalism," *Rights and Regulation*, ed. T.R.
     Machan and M.B. Johnson (Cambridge, MA:
     Ballinger Publ. Co., 1983), 217–48.
6   David Braybrooke, *Ethics in the World of Business*
     (Totowa, NJ: Rowman and Allanheld, 1983), 223.
7   Ibid., 224.
8   For an attempt to forge a collectivist theory of rights,
     see Tom Campbell, *The Left and Rights* (London
     and Boston: Routledge and Kegan Paul, 1983).
9   Huber, "Exorcists vs. Gatekeepers," 23.
10   Ibid. Huber observes that "Every insurance
     company knows that life is growing safer, but the
     public is firmly convinced that living is becoming
     ever more hazardous" (23). In general, capitalism's
     benefits to workers have simply been acknowledged,
     especially by moral and political philosophers!
     It is impossible to avoid the simple fact what the
     workers of the world believe differs judging by what
     system they prefer to emigrate to whenever possible.

—56—
OCCUPATIONAL SAFETY AND PATERNALISM

Machan Revisited

Earl W. Spurgin

MACHAN'S ARGUMENT

IN 1987, MACHAN PROVIDED A LIBERTARIAN CASE against the right to occupational safety.[1] Since before Machan's essay appeared, many business ethicists and legal scholars have given considerable attention, both pro and con, to the overall position Machan endorses: the acceptance of employment at will and the rejection of employee rights.[2] No one yet has given adequate attention, however, to the fact that Machan's argument against the right to occupational safety actually stands or falls independently of his overall position on employee rights. I will attempt to do so in this paper. My analysis of Machan's argument reveals that it ultimately rests on two values: the promotion of employee interests and anti-paternalism. These values, however, often are shared by supporters of the right to occupational safety. Supporters of the right who share these values must find a strategy for opposing Machan's argument that preserves the values. The goal of this paper is to find that strategy....

The first step toward giving Machan's argument against the right to occupational safety the attention it deserves is to recognize that it can be interpreted as two distinct arguments. I will call the first the "general argument" since it draws an entailment from Machan's general position on employee rights. I will call the second the "specific argument" since one could accept it even if one rejects Machan's general position on employee rights. The general argument Machan argues is that persons possess only the basic human rights to life, liberty, and property. No other special moral right accrues to any person by virtue of being a member of a specific group.[3] Employees, then, have no special rights as employees. They, like the members of any group, have the rights to life, liberty, and property, but no other moral rights.[4] This position on rights in general leads to an obvious conclusion regarding the right to occupational safety: It does not exist. The argument is as follows:

1. There are no special moral rights beyond the basic rights to life, liberty, and property that all persons possess.
2. The right to occupational safety would be a special moral right.
3. Therefore, there is no right to occupational safety.

The argument hinges on the success of the first premise. Machan defends the premise by arguing that the enforcement of employee rights impeded free trade in the labor market. He writes,

> As individuals who intend to hire out their skills for what they will fetch in the

marketplace, ... workers have the right to offer these in return for what others ... will offer in acceptable compensation. This implies free trade in the labor market. Any interference with such trade ... would violate both the workers' and their traders' human rights.[5]

An employee right can be enforced only by preventing either employees or employers from making the agreements that they wish to make in free exchanges of labor for compensation.

Essentially, Machan is applying Nozick's theory of distributive justice to the labor market. Nozick argues that any attempt by government to produce a specific social outcome necessarily will violate the rights of some person or set of persons. He writes,

> ... no ... distributional patterned principle of justice can be continuously realized without continuous interference with people's lives.... To maintain a pattern one must either continually interfere to stop people from transferring resources as they wish to, or continually (or periodically) interfere to take from some persons resources that others for some reason chose to transfer to them.[6]

For Machan, employee rights come at the same cost that Nozick attributes to any social outcomes that government might try to bring about: the erosion of someone's freedom. Employers and employees, like all persons, should have equal freedoms. Absent employee rights, Machan argues, they do. The parties are equally free to bargain in an unimpeded labor market in which wages are exchanged for labor. In the course of that bargaining, the parties are free to accept or reject the terms offered. Assuming there is no employment contract to which both parties have agreed, after bargaining has ended and employment has begun, employees are free to quit at any time and employers are free to fire at any time. Enforcing employee rights, on the other hand, destroys this equality of freedoms.

When government enforces an employee right, it does so by preventing either employees or employers from making the agreements that they wish both during the pre-employment bargaining period and after employment has begun. For this reason, Machan concludes, employees, like all persons, have only the rights to life, liberty, and property.

Many, however, reject the idea that employees have only the three basic rights that Machan endorses. Although the objections come in various forms, one developed initially by Werhane and later by Werhane and Radin, is especially useful here.[7] Werhane and Radin agree with Machan that equal freedoms for employers and employees is desirable, but, because of the power differences, employee rights are necessary to produce the desired equal freedoms. Without some rights, the more vulnerable positions of employees make them less free than employers. They argue that Nozickian free trade in the labor market ignores the reality of the relationships between employees and employers. Under normal circumstances, the relative power differences are too great to conclude that an unimpeded labor market produces equal freedoms for the bargaining parties. They write, "Except under conditions of very low unemployment, employers ordinarily stand in a position of power relative to prospective employees, and most employees, at any level, are replaceable with others."[8] Given this power differential, the claim that employees and employers are equally free when they bargain in a free labor market unimpeded by employee rights is mistaken. Employees simply lack the power that is necessary to be as free as employers unless they are granted certain rights that lead to more equal grounds on which the parties can bargain....

JUSTIFICATION FOR EXAMINATION OF THE SPECIFIC ARGUMENT

Suppose that Werhane's and Radin's objection or some other objection to the first premise of the general argument is decisive. Such an objection proves that employees possess some set of moral rights beyond the basic human rights to life, liberty, and property. Such an objection does not prove, however, that employees possess any specific right X. To prove that right X is a member of the set of employee rights, one must provide a sound argument for that right.

Typically, to make the case for a set of employee rights, proponents argue for some specific right to demonstrate why they believe employment at will is misguided. For example, Werhane and Radin argue for the right to due process while McCall argues for the right not to be dismissed without just cause.[9] No one, however, has made the case against employment at will by arguing for the right to occupational safety. Consequently, no one has addressed Machan's specific argument against the right.

This does not meant that no business ethicists support the right to occupational safety. Many do, but they argue for the employee rights to be informed of hazardous working conditions and to refuse hazardous work.[10] Arguments for the former right, however, do not address Machan's position at all while arguments for the latter right must respond to the specific argument in order to succeed. With respect to the right to be informed of hazardous working conditions, there is very little difference between Machan's position and that of those who argue for the right. Machan denies that employees have a right to occupational safety. He does not deny that employees have the right to know that working conditions are unsafe. He writes of instances where employers do not inform employees of dangerous working conditions,

> ... knowingly or negligently subjecting workers to hazards at the workplace (of which they were not made aware and could not anticipate from reasonable familiarity with the job) constitutes a form of actionable fraud. It comes under the prohibition of the violation of the right to liberty, at times even the right to life. Such conduct is actionable in a court of law

and workers ... would be morally justified ... to challenge it.[11]

In the case of a particular hazard, there may be disagreement between Machan and others over whether it is reasonable to expect employees to anticipate that hazard in the workplace, and such disagreement may result in differing judgments about whether the employer is obligated to inform employees of the hazard. Nevertheless, there is no disagreement over the central point that employees have a right to know that the hazard exists.

The matter is more complicated with respect to the right to refuse hazardous work. Machan describes employees' options in this way:

> When prospective employees ... are made aware of the type of job being offered, and its hazards they are at liberty to (a) accept or reject, (b) organize into a group and insist on various terms not in the offing, (c) bargain alone or together with others and set terms that include improvements, or (d) pool workers' resources, borrow, and purchase the firm.[12]

In a trivial sense, Machan's position does not differ from that of his opponents. Clearly, employees can refuse hazardous work. To deny that claim would be to accept a form of slavery. In a more substantive way, however, Machan's position differs dramatically. For Machan, an employer is not obligated to retain the services of a fully informed employee who refuses hazardous work. For his opponents, the fact that dismissal is a possible consequence of refusing hazardous work is tantamount to denying employees the right to refuse the work. To defeat Machan's position, one must provide a convincing case for the right to occupational safety. Only with that right in force can employees refuse hazardous work without opening themselves up to possible dismissal by their employers.[13] To accomplish that, however, one must defeat Machan's specific argument against the right to occupational safety.

THE SPECIFIC ARGUMENT

The specific argument is based on Machan's antipaternalism: the view that governments and societies should not control adults for the purposes of promoting the adults' own good. Machan believes that employees are competent adults who are capable of negotiating for themselves the terms of employment. He writes, "My view credits all but the severely incapacitated with the fortitude to be productive and wise when ordering their affairs, workers included."[14] The right to occupational safety, Machan argues, is paternalistic because it prevents employees from ordering their affairs as they wish for the purposes of promoting their own good.

This anti-paternalist position on which the specific argument is based applies only to adults.[15] Machan recognizes the potential problem raised by children in the workforce. He argues, however, that they have parents or guardians who are morally bound to protect them from dangers such as unsafe working conditions. He writes, "Children ... have rights owed them by their parents. To subject children to hazardous, exploitative work ... could be construed as a violation of their individual rights as young, dependent human beings."[16] For Machan, children have the rights to life, liberty, and property that all persons have. Since they do not yet have the capacities to make their own decisions regarding how to secure and act on those rights, however, it falls to parents and guardians to make such decisions for them. Parents and guardians must protect children from dangerous work so that they can develop their capacities to make their own decisions in the future. One can glean the specific argument from Machan's example of a coal mining company that lacks the financial resources to operate as safely as its competitors.[17] Machan writes,

> ... suppose that employers are compelled by law to spend the firm's funds to meet safety requirements.... This increased cost of production reduces available funds for additional wages for present and future employees.... This is what has happened: The employee–employer relationship has been unjustly intruded upon, to the detriment not only of mine owners, but also of those who might be employed.... The myth of workers' rights is mostly to blame.[18]

The most striking feature of this passage is that Machan appeals to the interests of the employees themselves. This does not mean that the interest of employers do not figure in his reasoning. Undoubtedly they do since he supports the basic rights to life, liberty, and property for all persons. His appeal to the interests of employees is striking, however, because he claims that the right to occupational safety actually makes employees worse off than they would be without the right. We rarely think of rights as harmful to us; rather, we think of them as helpful in our attempts to satisfy our needs and wants.

For Machan, the right to occupational safety prevents employees from ordering their working lives as they wish by removing certain options that some employees might choose. The specific argument is as follows:

1. Paternalism, restricting persons' freedom for their own good, is unjustified.
2. The right to occupational safety restricts employees' freedom for their own good.
3. Therefore, the right to occupational safety is unjustified.

PREMISE 1, MILL, AND ANTI-PATERNALISM

Essentially, Machan supports premise 1 by adopting Mill's classic opposition to paternalism. For Mill, one is in the best position to determine what is in one's own interests. Mill writes,

> ... neither one person, nor any number of persons, is warranted in saying to another

human creature of ripe years that he shall not do with his life for his own benefit what he chooses to do with it. He is the person most interested in his own well-being: the interest which any other person, except in cases of strong personal attachment, can have in it is trifling compared with that which he himself has; the interest which society has in him individually (except as to his conduct to others) is fractional and altogether indirect, while with respect to his own feelings and circumstances the most ordinary man or woman has means of knowledge immeasurably surpassing those that can be possessed by anyone else.[19]

Early in this passage, Mill seems to suggest that, close acquaintances aside, one is always the person most concerned with one's own interests. That view, however, is implausible. As Bishop Butler points out, often individuals do not look out for their own interests.[20] He writes about individuals, "... they are often set on work by the particular passions themselves, and a considerable part of life is spent in the actual pursuit of them, that is, is employed, not by self-love, but by the passions."[21] He adds, "Men daily, hourly sacrifice the greatest known interest to fancy, inquisitiveness, love, or hatred, any vagrant inclination. The thing to be lamented is not that men have so great a regard to their own good or interest in the present world, for they have not enough...."[22] Those who abuse dangerous drugs, pursue extreme thrills without taking appropriate care, and otherwise abuse their bodies provide ample evidence for Butler's claim. Given this, Mill seems to base his opposition to paternalism on an implausible premise.

Mill, however, need not, and likely does not, actually hold such an implausible premise. Instead, he need only hold the view that one is more likely to be correct about what is in one's own interests than are others. The remainder of the quoted passage from Mill points in this direction. He claims that while others have only indirect access, one has direct access to one's own needs, wants, and desires. Others who try to dictate one's good

generally do so from positions of ignorance. Thus, their judgments about one's good are more likely to be erroneous than are one's own judgments. Mill supports this view further when he writes,

The interference of society to overrule his judgment and purposes in what only regards himself must be grounded on general presumptions which may be altogether wrong and, even if right, are as likely as not to be misapplied to individual cases, by persons no better acquainted with the circumstances of such cases than those are who look at them from without.[23]

Not only are others more likely to dictate one's good from positions of ignorance, they are more likely to be motivated by concerns other than one's interest. In fact, the remainder of the last sentence quoted from Butler explains why. The entire sentence is as follows: "The thing to be lamented is not that men have so great a regard to their own good or interest in the present world, for they have not enough; but that they have so little to the good of others."[24] Even though, in a particular case, one may well not be motivated by one's own interest, another person who controls one is even more likely not to be motivated by one's interest....

Mill believes that competent adults are more likely to get it right about their own interests than are other parties. For that reason, Mill believes we should avoid paternalism.

PREMISE 2 AND MACHAN'S COAL MINING COMPANY EXAMPLE

Although one can glean Machan's support for premise 2 from his coal mining company example, the example does not highlight the crucial issue of employee options. A modified version of Machan's example better highlights that issue and, consequently, better illustrates how Machan would defend premise 2.

Suppose the company operates several mines that are all equipped with safety features that meet or exceed government regulations. In addition to the operational mines, the company owns another mine that has not been in operation for decades. Operations in it were suspended at that time because the state of mining technology would not allow the company to extract additional coal even though the company scientists estimated that the reserves were not yet depleted. Suppose, further, that a recent breakthrough in mining technology would allow the company to reopen the mine and extract the remaining reserves. Even with the costs of the new mining equipment, there are enough reserves for the company to turn a profit. Unfortunately, the mine is so far behind the current safety regulations that the company cannot afford to purchase the new mining equipment and update the safety features. Suppose, however, that the company executives determined that the company could afford to purchase the new equipment if it could avoid the costs of updating the safety features by giving employees hazardous-duty pay of twice their normal income to move from the safe mines in which they currently work to the unsafe mine. The right to occupational safety, however, prevents the company from making the offer to employees. If it is to reopen the mine, the company must update the mine so that it meets current safety regulations. This requirement removes the option to work for hazardous-duty pay from employees in order to protect them from unsafe working conditions. Many employees might be willing to take the risk for the additional income, but they will never have that opportunity.

MACHAN, MORAL RIGHTS, AND LEGAL RIGHTS

Before turning to possible objections to the specific argument, some clarification concerning the distinction between moral and legal rights is necessary. When discussing the right to occupational safety, Machan conflates the moral right and the legal right. He moves easily between the two and treats them almost as though they are one and the same. The moral and legal rights, however, are conceptually distinct. I have a moral right not to have my confidence violated by a friend, but I have no such legal right. Suppose I tell a friend about my infatuation with a mutual acquaintance after securing from the friend a promise not to tell the acquaintance. If the friend breaks that promise, then the friend violates my moral right but violates no legal right. Likewise, one might argue that some rights, such as the right of states to execute criminals, are legal rights with no corresponding moral rights. Finally, one might argue that some rights, such as the right to free speech, are both moral and legal rights.

Although Machan begins with the concept of moral rights, both the general argument and the specific argument depend on government enforcement of the right to occupational safety. As I will address shortly, one might argue that he should keep his focus on the moral right and avoid conflating it with the legal right. In one sense that claim is correct and accords with my interest in defending a moral right to occupational safety that employers should acknowledge and respect.

There are good reasons, however, not to quibble with Machan's conflation of moral and legal rights in this context. First, as Machan rightly points out, the right to occupational safety is one that is currently enforced by law and that enforcement has important implications for employers and employees. Second, Machan conceives of the right to occupational safety as a positive right. He writes of advocates of employee rights, "They hold that the employee–employer relationship involves special duties owed by employers to employees, creating (corollary) rights that governments ... should protect. Aside from negative rights, workers are owed respect of their positive rights to be treated with care and consideration."[25] As a positive right, the right to occupational safety runs counter to one of the basic tenets of libertarianism that Machan follows. On the Nozickian grounds described earlier, libertarians reject positive rights because they necessarily infringe on the liberty of some person or set of persons.[26] As Machan envisions it, the positive right to occupational safety entitles employees to safe working conditions and requires that employers provide those conditions. In this way, the right to occupational safety is quite different from the negative rights to life, liberty, and property that Machan endorses. As negative rights, they entitle one to freedom from others taking one's life, liberty, or property, but they do not require others to take steps to secure one's life, liberty, or property.

The second point is the more important reason for ignoring Machan's conflation of the moral and legal rights to occupational safety. He is correct in that the vast majority of those who support the moral right also support government enforcement when employers do not acknowledge and respect it. This does not mean that government should seek to enforce all moral rights. Some moral rights, such as that in the earlier example of the friend who breaks a promise, are not significant enough to justify government enforcement. Such exhaustive government enforcement of moral rights is undesirable for two reasons. First, governments simply do not have the resources to enforce all moral rights. Second, and moral importantly, doing so would constitute too great an invasion of citizens' lives. On the other hand, some moral rights, such as the right to freedom from slavery, are so significant that government enforcement is justified. Although the right to occupational safety is not on a par with the right to freedom from slavery, most supporters see it as significant enough to justify government enforcement....

THE MORAL RIGHT OBJECTION

One might object that Machan sees the right to occupational safety as paternalistic because he conflates the moral right to occupational safety with its legal recognition. It is the legal recognition of the right that is paternalistic, not the moral right itself. If we focus on the moral right itself rather than the legal enforcement of it, we can see that Machan has overstated what the moral right to occupational safety actually requires of employers. Even as a positive right, the moral right requires only that employers do not subject employees to dangerous working conditions without their consent. When fully informed employees agree to accept hazardous duty pay, they grant their consent to the dangerous working conditions. Seen in this way, the moral right to occupational safety does not remove options from employees at all. If government intrudes and enforces the right in such a way that it removes options from employees, then government is being paternalistic in its legal recognition of the right. If government enforced the right by requiring employers to provide safe working conditions or obtain legitimate consent from employees to work in unsafe conditions, then the enforcement would not be paternalistic. If, on the other hand, government enforced the right by requiring employers to provide all employees with safe conditions, then the enforcement would be paternalistic. The moral right to occupational safety, so the objection would run, requires the former, not the latter. The right itself, as a moral right, is not paternalistic and, consequently, premise 2 is false.

Although the objection is based on a vision of the right to occupational safety that would produce circumstances with which Machan would be sympathetic, he likely would respond by claiming that the legal ramifications of the right cannot be ignored. It is hard to imagine legal recognition of the right that allows employers to make offers of hazardous duty pay. Given that, Machan likely would argue that we must look at the legal ramifications of the right to determine its standing with respect to paternalism.

Another concern about this objection, albeit one with which Machan would be unsympathetic, is perhaps more important. We cannot overlook the problem of whether employees are in positions to grant legitimate consent if their employers propose options to work for hazardous-duty pay. In fact, it is quite likely that this problem gives rise to the legal recognition of the right to occupational safety that is the target of the objection. Although I cannot work out a full account of legitimate consent here, one salient feature of legitimate consent illustrates the problem. To consider that feature, set aside the positions of employees and consider the concept of consent in the abstract. In order to give legitimate consent in any matter, one must have a live option to do otherwise. Imagine one consents to X because another person is holding a gun to one's head. In a trivial sense, one could choose to accept the bullet rather than consent to X. That option, however, is not a live option for the vast majority of people. As William James writes, to be a live option it must make "... some kind of appeal, however small, to your belief."[27] For an option to be live, one's belief system must be such that it allows one to consider the option a real possibility. Most of us do not have belief systems that allow us to consider choosing death in the described circumstances a real possibility. For this reason, one's consent to X is not legitimate....

Often, employees feel that refusing to consent to their employers' wishes is not a live option. An unskilled employee may feel that rejecting an employer's offer is tantamount to asking to be fired. In most cases, as Werhane and Radin argue, employers are in stronger positions than are employees. This is especially true during tough economic periods with high unemployment. Even in good economic times, however, particular employees may feel pressured to agree to work for hazardous-duty pay because educational backgrounds, lack of experience, spotty work histories, or criminal records limit their employment opportunities. Although it does not involve hazardous duty pay, a real scenario that my mother faced helps to illustrate this point. She married quite young, never completed high school, and did not work until she reached her thirties. During a recent holiday visit when the subject of business ethics arose, she recounted a time several years earlier when her employer asked her to do some personal errands for him that fell outside her job description. Despite feeling angered and believing that the employer's request was morally wrong, she did the errands. When I asked why she did them, she replied, "I didn't have a choice. I had to keep the job. Without a high school education I couldn't find another job. This town's not very big you know." She had no live option to refuse because she knew that she had no other opportunities for work and her employer could easily find a replacement for her....

Globalization worsens this problem for many employees. With greater opportunities in other countries, the pool of prospective employees has been greatly enlarged for employers in many industries. Generally, these are industries that do not depend on a well-educated, high-tech labor force. As many people who have called a computer manufacturer's helpline can attest, however, even some high-tech positions are moving to other countries. The upshot is that in such industries, globalization has made it even easier for employers to reject employees' demands. They have more places to which they can turn for employees who are not in positions to make those demands.

Moreover, one important fact about capitalism strengthens employers' positions in most cases. Policymakers in capitalist societies often strive for full employment, but, as Porket writes, "... unemployment is a phenomenon which no modern economy can escape (as long as labour and the labour market are free) and without which no modern economy can thrive...."[28] Essentially, the capitalist market system results in some level of unemployment....

The concern over whether employees are in a position to grant legitimate consent should not be pushed too far. To do so would be to fall into the very paternalism that I wish to join Mill and Machan in opposing. Nevertheless, it casts serious doubt, albeit not for reasons Machan would endorse, on the moral rights objection to premise 2. Because of that doubt, we should look elsewhere for a successful objection.

THE OPTIONS OBJECTION

Machan describes the view of employee right advocates that he rejects as follows:

Prior to government's energetic prolabor interventions safety, health, and related provisions for workers had been lacking. Only legally mandated workers' rights freed workers from their oppressive lot. Thus, workers must by law be provided with safety, health care, job security, retirement, and other vital benefits.[29]

Although Machan did not intend it, his words point to a successful objection to premise 2.

The difficulty for Machan lies in his view that the right to occupational safety restricts the freedom of employees. When considered from the perspective of the modified version of Machan's coal mining company example, it appears that the right does just that. Due to legal recognition of the right, employers cannot offer hazardous-duty pay to employees who are willing to work in unsafe conditions. This example, however, takes the right out of its historical context. When viewed in that historical context, the right actually has broadened rather than restricted the freedom of employees. The right and legal recognition of it played an important role in the emergence of the many opportunities employees have to work in safe conditions. Historical evidence shows that, without the right to occupational safety supported by legislation, the playing field was tilted in favor of employers in such a way that many employees lacked the necessary conditions to bring about positive changes in their working conditions in the way that Machan himself suggests that they should. Without a right to occupational safety supported by legislation, too many employees would be destined to work in unsafe conditions without the options to work in safe conditions.

One need only consider the coal miners that Machan uses in his example to find evidence for this. Historically, when miners tried to organize so that they could cause changes in their working conditions such as improved safety, mine owners used violence and intimidation to block their efforts. Owners often hired armed agents to threaten and intimidate miners. Corbin writes of an actual event in West Virginia in 1920, "One hundred miners met at Roderfield, McDowell County, to form a local.... [T]he county sheriff and a squad of Baldwin–Felts guards (who were also deputy sheriffs) arrived to break up the meeting and the local, a gun battle ensued, leaving four dead and four wounded."[30] He also writes of coal mining companies' attitudes toward unions and their efforts to stop union activities:

> The Mingo County operators were not about to surrender to the institution that they hated and that they claimed would cause the downfall of the United States. They brought in trainloads of strikebreakers from the South and New York and Chicago to run the mines and imported more and more guards to protect their plants and strikebreakers.[31]

Brit Hume makes clear the characteristics of the agents owners hired to confront the miners. He writes, "During a strike in 1920, the operators had imported a brigade of hired thugs from the infamous Baldwin–Felts Detective agency to evict miners from their company-owned houses. After they had done their dirty work...."[32] H.B. Lee, Attorney General of West Virginia (1925–1933), writes of the agency,

> This Agency ... was a ruthless, strikebreaking organization headed by William G. Baldwin and Thomas L. Felts—the two most feared and hated men in the mountains. For more than thirty years, its employees, called "Baldwin Thugs" and mine guards by the workers, had ruled the coal fields, fought strikes and strikers, and otherwise tyrannized over the miners.[33]

Lee points to the owners' use of the so-called "Yellow-Dog Contract" as an especially intimidating tactic employed to prevent miners from organizing. He writes, "It acquired this scurrilous title because miners were compelled to sign it in order to secure or hold employment in the mines."[34] He presents the following as a typical form of the contract:

CONTRACT OF EMPLOYMENT

I am employed by and work for the _____ Company, of _____, West Virginia, with the express understanding that I am not a member of the United Mine Workers of America, and will not become so while an employee of said _____ Company; that said company agrees to run an "Open Shop" while I am employed by said _____ Company. If at any time I want to join or become connected with the United Mine Workers of America, or any affiliated organization, I agree to withdraw from the employment of said Company, and I further agree that while I am in the employ of said Company that I will not make any efforts amongst its employees to bring about the unionization of said employees against the Company's wishes. I have either read the above or it has been read to me. Dated this _____ day of _____, 19____.

(Signed)[35]

Lee adds, "This little contract proved to be the most powerful weapon ever devised for excluding the miners' union from West Virginia's coal fields...."[36]

One might object, on behalf of Machan, that Lee exaggerates the effect of the yellow-dog contract. After all, one might argue, the miners were not compelled to sign. They could have refused employment in mines that required acceptance of the yellow-dog contract.

Such an argument, however, does not give adequate attention to the hardships that the miners faced, nor does it recognize how limited was the availability of alternative work for the miners. Lee describes the situation dramatically when he writes,

As a bitter aftermath of those strikes, Yellow-Dog Contracts, and injunctions, in the years between 1920 and 1925, no fewer than 50,000 men, women, and children were evicted from their homes in southern West Virginia. They found shelter under cliffs, in tents, and in improvised shacks built by the union. Year after weary year they lived and starved in those unwholesome surroundings. Malnutrition and unsanitary conditions increased the death rate to appalling figures, especially among the children. But there was no relenting by the coal barons. To many of them their hungry, protesting workers were pariahs or outcasts, who had to be starved until hunger forced them to return to the service of their masters.

In the end, hunger won, and the workers slunk back to the mines with hearts filled with hate and minds embittered by the memory of the wrongs they had suffered.[37]

The evictions to which both Hume and Lee refer point to another important aspect of the intimidation miners faced. Because many mine owners actually owned the entire towns in which they operated, they were able to use various forms of economic intimidation....

Circumstances such as those faced by the coal miners who sought to organize and struggle for improvements in their working conditions demonstrate that too often employees lack the necessary conditions to bring about such changes. The coal miners needed government intervention so that they could have live options to do something about their working conditions. Without it, they faced force, intimidation, coercion, and duress that prevented them from taking steps to bring about the positive changes they so desperately needed. In this way, government intervention actually enhanced employees' options rather than, as Machan believes, reduced them. The government intervention was freedom-enhancing rather than, as Machan believes, paternalistic.

This does not mean, however, that employees always need the help of government intervention in order to achieve their desired goals. In many cases, such as when employees possess unique talents that are hard to find in other potential employees, they can succeed quite well on their own. Also, it does not mean that all positive changes in workplace safety are the results of the right to occupational safety and its supporting legislation. Clearly, many improvements in workplace safety are the result of technological innovations. One need only think of the development of now commonplace items such as safety glasses, safety belts, and hardhats to find technological innovations that make workplaces safer. Nevertheless, the historical evidence demonstrates how many employees need the right to occupational safety and its supporting legislation so that they are in positions where they can take the steps that are necessary to bring about positive changes in their working conditions....

This point about owners' efforts to stop miners from organizing bears directly on Machan's position regarding the options of workers who are unhappy with their working conditions. Recall that Machan claims that one option for such workers is to "... organize into a group and insist on various terms not in the offing...."[38] He, too, assumes that the miners had the ability to organize even though the owners impeded it with violence and intimidation.

Given the impact that owners' efforts had on the options of employees, Machan's view that the right to occupational safety reduces the freedom of employees is mistaken and premise 2 of the specific argument is false. It is true that the right removes one option from employees. In that sense, the right is restrictive. Employees cannot opt to work for hazardous-duty pay. This restriction and lost option, however, does not reduce employees' freedom. In fact, we cannot evaluate their freedom by looking merely at this one lost option. We must consider the host of options to work in safe conditions that the right has helped to provide employees. The additional options are valuable options and the right helps to maximize them. In this way, the right enhances employees' freedom. Thus, the right is far from paternalistic. It has enhanced the freedom of employees by maximizing their valuable options.

NOTES

1   See Machan (1987).

2   Some of those who have argued either for or against employment at will are: DesJardins (1985), DesJardins and McCall (1985), Epstein (1984), Freed and Polsby (1989), Hiley (1985), Larson (1986–87), Maitland (1989), McCall (2003), Phillips (1992), Posner (1989), Power (1983), Radin and Werhane (2003), Sass (1985), Werhane (1983 and 1988), and Werhane and Radin (1996).

3   Accordingly, Machan believes that governments should enforce only the rights to life, liberty, and property. To enforce other types of moral rights, such as employee rights, would be to enforce non-existent rights.

4   Machan (1987, pp. 45–46).

5   Machan (1987, p. 46).

6   Nozick (1974, p. 163).

7   See Radin and Werhane (2003), Werhane (1983 and 1988), and Werhane and Radin (1996).

8   Radin and Werhane (2003, p. 115).

9   See Werhane and Radin (1996) and McCall (2003).

10 See Faden and Beauchamp (1988), Sass (1986), and Superson (1983).

11 Machan (1987, p. 48).

12 Machan (1987, p. 49).

13 Neither Machan nor his opponents believe that an employee who has agreed to do a dangerous job such as a police officer or firefighter can refuse to do the job any time it becomes unsafe. Such jobs are inherently dangerous. Machan's opponents do believe, however, that employees should be able to refuse hazardous work without fear of dismissal when employers provide conditions that make the work more dangerous than is necessary. Machan does not hold that view.

14 Machan (1987, p. 47).

15 For this reason, the paternalism at issue in the remainder of this paper will be paternalism directed toward adults.

16 Machan (1987, p. 48).

17 Machan (1987, pp. 49–50).

18 Machan (1987, p. 50).

19   Mill (1859; 1978, p. 74).

20   I am indebted to an anonymous reviewer who cited Butler.

21   Butler (1726; 1983, p. 20).

22   Butler (1726; 1983, p. 21).

23   Mill (1859; 1978, p. 74).

24   Butler (1726; 1983, p. 21).

25   Machan (1987, p. 46).

26   I will not try to defend Machan's rejection of positive rights since it is one of the tenets of libertarianism I reject.

27   James (1896; 1984, p. 309).

28   Porket (1995, p. 19).

29   Machan (1987, p. 47).

30   Corbin (1981, p. 196).

31   Corbin (1981, p. 202).

32   Hume (1971, p. 113).

33   Lee (1969, p. 53).

34   Lee (1969, p. 78).

35   Lee (1969, p. 78).

36   Lee (1969, p. 78).

37   Lee (1969, p. 83).

38   Machan (1987, p. 49).

—57—

THE RANA PLAZA COLLAPSE

Alexander Sager

BACKGROUND

ON APRIL 24, 2013, THE EIGHT STORY RANA PLAZA in Bangladesh collapsed killing 1,129 people, many employed in garment factories serving international brands that included Benetton, the Children's Place, Joe Fresh, Mango, and Walmart. The collapse was one of a recent series of highly publicized tragedies in Bangladesh's garment industry, which directly or indirectly employs four million people and composes 80% of Bangladesh's $21 billion export market, making up 18% of the country's GDP in 2013.

The collapse was in many ways predictable. The owners had added additional stories to a building without receiving a permit to do so. The building was not designed for industrial use, but much of the space had been leased to garment factories with heavy machinery. Despite police warnings to evacuate and employee protests at the new cracks that had appeared in the building, managers ordered garment workers to come to work.

The Rana Plaza Collapse exemplifies the political corruption and economic pressures that contribute to widespread labor abuses in Bangladesh's and many other developing countries' export sectors. It was preceded by the April 11, 2005, collapse of the Spectrum-Sweater factor in Savar that killed sixty four people. The November 24, 2012, Dhaka fire killed 117 people and injured many more, because of the lack of emergency exits. Many more incidents go unreported in the international news. The avoidable deaths of workers is only the most extreme example of widespread, questionable labor practices in the developing world that include slavery and indentured labor, child labor, physical and sexual abuse, exposure to hazardous chemicals, and low wages.

There have been a number of responses that address safety and working conditions in Bangladesh, including a National Action Plan to review fire safety and structural integrity for buildings with ready-made garment factories and a compact between the government of Bangladesh, the European Union, the United States, and the International Labor Organization to improve working conditions. The International Labor Organization has established a fund to compensate victims of the Rana Plaza collapse. As of June 2014, the fund had received less than half of the $40 million target and half of the companies associated with manufacturing in the Rana Plaza failed to contribute.

On May 23, 2013, international retailers and Bangladeshi trade unions released the *Accord on Fire and Building Safety in Bangladesh* calling for increased inspections, remediation, and training, as well as contributions from signatory companies. The *Accord* is a legally binding document, which requires companies to fix buildings that fail safety standards and to continue to employ and compensate workers while repairs are taking place. Though many major international brands have signed the accord, Walmart, Gap Inc., and H&M refused. Walmart and Gap Inc. later joined a coalition of major North American apparel companies, retailers, and brands to form the Alliance for Bangladesh Worker Safety and created the Bangladesh Worker Safety Initiative.

It is too early to know the long term effects of these initiatives, but there are some grounds for concern about their scope, efficacy, and broader effects. Though the Institute for Global Labour and Human Rights reports successes from a collaboration between Bangladeshi workers, the Institute, Gap and H&M in improving conditions and wages and benefits for factories in the Ha-Meem and Windy Groups of factories, these groups compose only a fraction of Bangladesh's garment factories. Even leaving aside widely recognized problems with corruption, the Bangladeshi government does not currently have enough staff to rigorously inspect all of its factories.

Inspections can also harm workers that they are designed to help. The *New York Times* reports that inspections organized through the Bangladesh Accord Foundation have led to the closing of some factories, leaving thousands of workers unemployed and uncompensated as repairs are made.[1] Factory owners and labor unions have asked international brands to pay wages, but so far have had limited success.

ANALYSIS

The Rana Plaza collapse clearly involved negligence on the part of the building owner, the garment factories leasing space, and the public officials expected to oversee safety compliance. Workers should not be subjected to easily preventable, immanent, life-threatening danger, a conviction expressed by the arrest and conviction of building owner Mohammed Sohel Rana and factory owner Bazlus Samad Adnan who employed 1,700 people at the Rana Plaza. But the reason that this case is interesting for business ethics is that issues surrounding the collapse raises broader issues about safety, working condition, and wages.

Working conditions in the developing world often appear unacceptable from the perspective of people in affluent, Western countries. Nonetheless, workers routinely accept risks and choose to labor for what seem like low wages because jobs in the export sector are better than other alternatives open to them. In fact, companies serving international brands often pay higher wages than local companies. Moreover, the only reason that developing world countries are able to attract business for their export sectors is because they offer plentiful cheap labor. Though many developed world consumers take pride in paying more for clothing made by unionized workers in their country, refusing to buy cheap foreign goods may very well slow economic development and harm the global poor. The imposition of safer worker conditions by international firms under pressure from consumers abroad may be welcome, but it can also be an imposition for workers who lose wages or their jobs when the companies they work for do not meet standards.

In 2014, Bangladesh raised the minimum wage 79 per cent to $68 per month without overtime (adjusted for purchasing power parity), cutting into profit margins and contributing to a slowdown in the garment industry. One consequence of the international focus on Bangladesh is that factory owners reported that export orders fell to rivals.[2] The disproportionate focus on Bangaldesh after the Rana Plaza collapse is questionable since there are similar labor practices in many countries, including major rivals such as China, Vietnam, Indonesia, and Cambodia.

How do we decide what just labor standards are? Should this question be largely determined by supply and demand on the market in which workers and firms negotiate wages and working conditions? Are there universal minimal standards that all ethical employers must respect? Should citizens decide labor practices through democratic processes? Are multinational corporations bound by the labor standards of the countries in which they operate or of the countries in which they are based? Or do they need to find some sort of compromise? Should countries comply with standards set by the International Labor Organization or another international body? What role should consumers play? These are complicated questions.

One concern that many people have about overseas labor is that it is exploitative. Though theorists have understood exploitation in various ways, a core idea is that exploitation occurs when one party is able to take unfair advantage of the other, usually because the exploiting party enjoys more power or possesses information that the exploited party lacks. Notably, exploitation is often mutually beneficial. For example, low-wage labor under unpleasant conditions is often better than the alternative of unemployment. Nonetheless, critics retort that it is exploitative because workers are not in a position to bargain for something better.

The challenge for any account of exploitation is to explain when an agreement is unfair. Broad accounts of exploitation hold that most agreements reached between parties with unequal bargaining power are unfair. One concern, though, is that this may entail that most employees are exploited, including relatively well paid employees in developed countries. Narrower accounts of exploitation locate unfairness against a baseline of what would be determined under conditions of perfect competition: if workers are being paid less than they would in a free market, they are exploited. These accounts raise the opposite concern: if markets are reasonably efficient, then almost nobody can claim to be exploited.

Some business ethicists have preferred to distinguish questions of safety and working conditions from questions of wages. After all, even advocates of low-wage overseas labor condemn businesses that enslave workers, use physical violence to compel workers to meet quotas, or force children to work long hours. Regarding questions of safety, business ethicists sometimes invoke rights such as the right to life or notions of human dignity. For example, Denis Arnold and Norman Bowie have argued from a Kantian perspective that respect for persons requires that employers guarantee minimal health and safety conditions and that they inform workers of any workplace hazards so that they can make rational decisions about accepting work.

Critics from libertarian market-based perspectives have responded that it is illegitimate to distinguish between wages and improvements to worker safety and health. The cost of a salary increase and the cost of a sprinkler system have the same effect on a company's bottom line. In contrast, they place the emphasis on worker choice and view the market as providing sufficient information to allow employees to choose rationally whether they wish to assume the risks.

This debate raises two issues. First, are market mechanisms the right tools for determining just labor conditions and wages? Libertarians contend that if workers have freely decided to sell their labor in a competitive market, then competition will lead employers to offer wages and working conditions that satisfy workers' preferences. Workers are usually the best judges of their needs and their tolerance for risk, and this should be respected. In response, critics contend that labor conditions should not be set solely by supply and demand; they prefer instead to invoke independent standards such as basic human rights, or to have these questions be determined by democratic processes.

A second, related issue concerns the extent to which imperfect and asymmetrical information, barriers to entry, monopoly power, and background political and social conditions impair the market from functioning efficiently. Libertarians who oppose regulation gain traction from the assumption that markets are fairly efficient in practice. Where this turns out not to be the case, the market should not be relied on to set just labor conditions, even if this would be best in an ideal world of perfect competition.

Leaving aside questions of safety and fair wages, who is responsible for labor abuses and workplace dangers? Often critics of oversea labor conditions place the primary responsibility and blame on multinational companies. For example, Kalpona Akter, executive director of the Bangladesh Center for Worker Solidarity, commented on the Rana Plaza collapse: "After the Tazreen fire, it was a cemetery, human bodies all over the floor. And now we have another one ... American companies, they know this is happening. We've told them: Remember these human faces. You killed these girls."[3]

Is Akter right that American companies are to blame for these tragedies? The answer to this question turns on whether or not American (and other) companies failed to meet moral obligations they had to workers in the supply chain. In order to determine companies' obligations, it may also be necessary to determine other agents' moral obligations. Another complex question concerns how moral responsibility should be reassigned if some parties fail to fulfill their obligations. For example, presumably local suppliers and governments have obligations toward the safety of workers. In fact, H&M's reason for rejecting the *Accord on Fire and Building Safety in Bangladesh* was that it thought responsibility for safety standards rested in the factories and in the local government. A further concern is that foreign corporations or consumers are imposing their labor standards on the developing world with limited knowledge of local conditions, and that this is condescending and paternalistic.

The Bangladeshi government has labor standards in place, but they are often not enforced due to corruption or lack of capacity. If local companies fail to meet their obligations, do these obligations automatically fall on companies further up in the supply chain? To answer this, we need to determine what role that multinational companies play and can play in working conditions. Did the fact that Bangladesh factories manufacture clothes for export to international brands play a significant role in the working conditions, or are workers poorly paid or mistreated because of vulnerabilities caused primarily by local conditions? How we answer this question will affect where we should direct our attention in identifying potential for reform. Should we think of overseas working conditions in terms of corporate social responsibility or as question of government regulation and reform (keeping in mind that it might be both)?

Another question concerns the moral obligations of parties in a commodity chain. The fair trade movement places moral obligations on consumers with the conviction that they can pressure companies into improving conditions. One reason why many people focus on large, multinational companies is the conviction that they have the power and responsibility to change practices and conditions in companies that supply them. If we believe companies have some obligations, there are further questions. How much knowledge do companies need to acquire about their contractors, keeping in mind the many challenges of effectively monitoring practices abroad? What if contractors subcontract some work to other companies? When answering these questions, it is important to keep in mind that monitoring and compliance have costs that may impact vulnerable workers.

Another question concerns the type of measures that ought to be adopted and who should determine their content. Should labor standards be determined primarily by regulation or by voluntary compliance? The Accord on Fire and Building Safety in Bangladesh gives trade unions a major role in setting policies and also serves as a binding agreement. The International Labor Organization serves as an independent chair. One drawback to this sort of agreement is that companies may be reluctant to join. For example, Gap refused to be part of the Accord because it feared that it might result in lawsuits and that it would require them to fund safety upgrades. In contrast, the Bangladesh Worker Safety Initiative was founded by retailers and takes more of a corporate social responsibility approach. Though companies may have less reluctance to become involved in this sort of initiative, one concern is that it gives workers and unions limited power to help set the agenda and that it lacks independent monitoring.

Finally, we can ask about the role of the global capitalist economy in putting pressure on production and arguably contributing to a race to the bottom. In recent years, textile companies' product life cycles have become shorter, with new collections appearing monthly and even weekly (as opposed to bi-yearly cycles in the past). Shorter lead times and last minute changes lead factories to subcontract to second and third tier suppliers over which there is limited control. Furthermore, buyers place enormous pressure on price, leading suppliers to frequently switch to new factories or new countries to meet demands. The result is that factories have no guarantee of work in the future; this removes the incentive to invest in safety and better equipment and motivates them to cut corners to meet demands. Addressing these concerns involves suppliers and buyers, but also requires structural changes in the industry and in consumer attitudes and demands.[4]

DISCUSSION QUESTIONS

1. Is Kalpona Akter correct that American companies are morally culpable for the deaths of the people who died in the Tazreen fire?
2. The economist Paul Krugman echoes the conviction of many of his colleagues that we should in fact praise cheap labor. Why do you think he believes this? Is he right? If not, why not?
3. What moral obligations (if any) do consumers in the developed world have when deciding to buy clothing made abroad?
4. Do reasonably well-functioning markets fairly set wages and working conditions? If not, how should these be determined?
5. Compare and contrast the Accord on Fire and Building Safety in Bangladesh and the Bangladesh Worker Safety Initiative. What are the advantages and shortcomings of each?

NOTES

1 Greenhouse, Steven. "Bangladesh Inspections Find Gaps in Safety." *New York Times*, March 11, 2014, http://www.nytimes.com/2014/03/12/business/safety-flaws-found-in-new-inspections-of-factories-in-bangladesh.html?_r=0.

2 Quardir, Serajul. "Rising Wages Squeeze Bangladesh Garment Makers as Factories Await Upgrades." *Reuters*, April 13, 2014, http://www.reuters.com/article/2014/04/13/us-bangladesh-garments-idUSBREA3CoN520140413.

3 Stillman, Sarah. "Death Traps: The Bangladesh Garment Factory Disaster." *The New Yorker*, May 1, 2013.

4 I'm grateful to Peter Jonker for his comments on this case study and his insights on the textile industry.

FURTHER READINGS

Arnold, Denis G., and Norman E. Bowie. 2003. "Sweatshops and Respect for Persons." *Business Ethics Quarterly* 13 (2): 221–42.

Accord on Fire and Building Safety in Bangladesh, http://bangladeshaccord.org/.

Bangladesh Worker Safety Initiative, http://www.bangladeshworkersafety.org/.

Bhagwati, Jagdish. 2004. *In Defense of Globalization.* New York: Oxford University Press.

Institute for Global Labour and Human Rights. October 2014. Unprecedented Changes: Garment Workers in Bangladesh Fight Back and Win, http://www.globallabourrights.org/reports/document/1410-IG-LHR-Bangladesh-UnprecedentedChanges.pdf.

Klein, Naomi. 2000. *No Logo: Taking Aim at the Brand Bullies.* New York: Picador.

Krugman, Paul. "In Praise of Cheap Labor." *Slate*, March 21, 1997, http://www.slate.com/articles/business/the_dismal_science/1997/03/in_praise_of_cheap_labor.html.

Locke, Richard M. "Opening the Debate: Can Global Brands Create Just Supply Chains? A Forum on Corporate Responsibility for Factory Workers." *Boston Review*, May 21, 2013, http://www.bostonreview.net/BR38.3/ndf_richard_locke_global_brands_labor_justice.php.

Poulton, Lindsay, Francesca Panetta, Jason Burke, David Levene, and the Guardian Interactive Team. "The Shirt on Your Back: the Human Cost of the Bangladeshi Garment Industry," *The Guardian*, April 16, 2014, http://www.theguardian.com/world/ng-interactive/2014/apr/bangladesh-shirt-on-your-back.

JUSTICE AND FAIR PRACTICE

INTRODUCTION

Anand J. Vaidya

IN THIS UNIT, OUR ATTENTION WILL FOCUS ON issues of diversity and affirmative action, sexual harassment, bluffing, and advertising.

In recent decades, businesses and other institutions have sought to better understand and address the challenges arising from a more diverse workplace. Groups such as women and racial and ethnic minorities that were historically excluded from many sectors have made progress in many fields, but still face discrimination in hiring and in the workplace.

Affirmative action is the practice of hiring or promoting a person in part on the basis of belonging to a group that faces discrimination, often due to race, ethnicity, or gender. The practice has been, and still is, controversial. On the one hand, some people think that it either remedies past injustices or promotes important social goals, such as workplace diversity. On the other hand, critics see affirmative action as a sort of reverse discrimination that runs contrary to important meritocratic principles and sets up unqualified job candidates for failure and stigma.

Sexual harassment is constituted by unwelcome sexual advances or conduct. It often takes one of these two forms: (1) *quid pro quo* (something for something) employment decisions such as hiring or promotion are made contingent on accepting sexual advances or conduct; (2) hostile workplace sexual harassment, interfering with the victim's ability to perform her or his job. Defining harassment and sexual harassment in particular raises difficult conceptual and normative issues. The definition must not be too narrow so as to

exclude activity that is problematic. For example, sexual harassment cannot be limited to physical contact, since verbal actions can be equally harmful. The definition must also not be so broad as to preclude friendly contact between workers. There is additional concern about the rights of the accuser and of the accused.

Bluffing is yet another practice in business that deserves ethical analysis. On the face of it, bluffing appears to be an immoral practice, given that it seems to be a form of lying: when two negotiators bluff, they each make false claims about something (e.g., their "reserve prices," or the price at which they would consent to a transaction). However, several philosophers have argued that bluffing is actually morally permissible in the business context, sometimes attempting to identify features of business negotiation that distinguish importantly between bluffing and lying. For example, Albert Carr argues, based on an analogy with poker, that bluffing is permissible in a business negotiation. Just as poker players understand that other players may be bluffing about the cards they hold in their hand, people in business understand the "rule of the game" allows for deception that in other contexts would be morally problematic. The appropriateness of this analogy has been discussed by Thomas Carson and Fritz Allhoff, who present alternative arguments for the moral legitimacy of bluffing. John Carson deepens the discussion of deception by extending the analysis to sales.

Advertising raises a number of central questions for business ethicists. First, one might legitimately ask how much information about a product is a corporation morally required to provide. Are they required to give all of the information or only some, and if only some, which information is morally required?

Second, given that corporations have to provide some information, what are the requirements on how that information is presented? In other words, are there certain ways of presenting the information that are impermissible? Consider information about the possible harmfulness of a product. What if this information is presented in a way unlikely to be understood by a normal consumer: has the corporation satisfied its requirement to provide the information?

Third, are corporations required to tell the truth about their products? What are consumers' rights regarding truth-telling and accurate representation in advertisements? Quite often we see advertisements that use statistical claims (e.g., ninety per cent of doctors endorse some product). However, it is well-known that statistical information can be represented in ways to make a claim look stronger than the evidence warrants. When is this an ethical violation? And consider the practice of claiming that a group of "experts" supports a product, what constitutes an "expert"?

Besides these questions about the representation of information, there are also deep philosophical questions about advertising. One of them has to do with the creation of desire. Some philosophers and economists have argued that various forms of advertising are immoral because they override an agent's autonomy—independence in thought and action. Often advertising functions by feeding off basic human desires or by selectively presenting information in a way that predictably leads to false or incomplete beliefs. If I buy a product that I know pollutes the environment, then it would seem that I am responsible for that outcome. However, if the advertising process overrides my autonomy, so that I am not really acting as myself, but am being manipulated, then I am not responsible for the harm caused.

Another important question concerning consumers is whether *targeting* a certain group of people for advertising is permissible. Targeting is the practice of intentionally aiming at a certain group of consumers. Suppose commercials for a specific kind of medicine are always run at a certain time of night when older people who are more likely to have the associated condition are watching television. We might conclude in this case that targeting these individuals by running a commercial at a time when they are more likely to watch it is morally permissible, perhaps because we deem the product to be healthy. But what about commercials that promote unhealthy snack foods during children's programming? In this case, corporations are targeting children and creating in them the desire for certain unhealthy snacks. Many people hold that targeting children is impermissible not only because the product may be harmful, but also because of doubts that children are capable of accurately assessing the reliability of advertising or fully understanding their own needs.

A final issue concerns how advertising interacts with gender inequality, for example by perpetrating stereotypes or representing women in ways that contribute to their objectification or subordination. Do businesses have a responsibility to advertise in ways that support—or at least do not undermine—goals such as gender equality? Do governments have a right to regulate advertising to support such goals?

—58—
WHAT IS WRONG WITH REVERSE DISCRIMINATION?

Edwin C. Hettinger

MANY PEOPLE THINK IT OBVIOUS THAT REVERSE discrimination is unjust. Calling affirmative action reverse discrimination itself suggests this. This discussion evaluates numerous reasons given for this alleged injustice. Most of these accounts of what is wrong with reverse discrimination are found to be deficient. The explanations for why reverse discrimination is morally troubling show only that it is unjust in a relatively weak sense. This result has an important consequence for the wider issue of the moral justifiability of affirmative action. If social policies which involve minor injustice are permissible (and perhaps required) when they are required in order to overcome much greater injustice, then the mild injustice of reverse discrimination is easily overridden by its contribution to the important social goal of dismantling our sexual and racial caste system.

By "reverse discrimination" or "affirmative action" I shall mean hiring or admitting a slightly less well qualified woman or black, rather than a slightly more qualified white male, for the purpose of helping to eradicate sexual and/or racial inequality, or for the purpose of compensating women and blacks for the burdens and injustices they have suffered due to past and ongoing sexism and racism. There are weaker forms of affirmative action, such as giving preference to minority candidates only when qualifications are equal, or providing special educational opportunities for youths in disadvantaged groups. This paper seeks to defend the more controversial sort of reverse discrimination defined above. I begin by considering several spurious objections to reverse discrimination. In the second part, I identify the ways in which this policy is morally troubling and then assess the significance of these negative features.

SPURIOUS OBJECTIONS

1. Reverse Discrimination as Equivalent to Racism and Sexism

In a discussion on national television, George Will, the conservative news analyst and political philosopher, articulated the most common objection to reverse discrimination. It is unjust, he said, because it is discrimination on the basis of race or sex. Reverse discrimination against white males is the same evil as traditional discrimination against women and blacks. The only difference is that in this case it is the white male who is being discriminated against. Thus if traditional racism and sexism are wrong and unjust, so is reverse discrimination, and for the very same reasons.

But reverse discrimination is not at all like traditional sexism and racism. The motives and intentions behind it are completely different, as are its consequences. Consider some of the motives underlying traditional racial discrimination. Blacks were not hired or allowed into schools because it was felt that contact with them was degrading, and sullied whites. These policies were based on contempt and loathing for blacks, on a feeling that blacks were suitable only for subservient positions and that they should never have positions of authority over whites. Slightly better qualified white males are not being turned down under affirmative action for any of these reasons. No defenders or practitioners of affirmative action (and no significant segment of the general public) think that contact with white males is degrading or sullying, that white males are contemptible and loathsome, or that white males—by their nature—should be subservient to blacks or women.

The consequences of these two policies differ radically as well. Affirmative action does not stigmatize white males; it does not perpetuate unfortunate stereotypes about white males; it is not part of a pattern of discrimination that makes being a white male incredibly burdensome. Nor does it add to a particular group's "already overabundant supply" of power, authority, wealth, and opportunity, as does traditional racial and sexual discrimination. On the contrary, it results in a more egalitarian distribution of these social and economic benefits. If the motives and consequences of reverse discrimination and of traditional racism and sexism are completely different, in what sense could they be morally equivalent acts? If acts are to be individuated (for moral purposes) by including the motives, intentions, and consequences in their description, then clearly these two acts are not identical.

It might be argued that although the motives and consequences are different, the act itself is the same: reverse discrimination is discrimination on the basis of race and sex, and this is wrong in itself independently of its motives or consequences. But discriminating (i.e., making distinctions in how one treats people) on the basis of race or sex is not always wrong, nor is it necessarily unjust. It is not wrong, for example, to discriminate against one's own sex when choosing a spouse. Nor is racial or

sexual discrimination in hiring necessarily wrong. This is shown by Peter Singer's example in which a director of a play about ghetto conditions in New York City refuses to consider any white applicants for the actors because she wants the play to be authentic.[1] If I am looking for a representative of the black community, or doing a study about blacks and disease, it is perfectly legitimate to discriminate against all whites. Their whiteness makes them unsuitable for my (legitimate) purposes. Similarly, if I am hiring a wet nurse, or a person to patrol the women's change rooms in my department store, discriminating against males is perfectly legitimate.

These examples show that racial and sexual discrimination are not wrong in themselves. This is not to say that they are never wrong; most often they clearly are. Whether or not they are wrong, however, depends on the purposes, consequences, and context of such discrimination.

2. Race and Sex as Morally Arbitrary and Irrelevant Characteristics

A typical reason given for the alleged injustice of all racial and sexual discrimination (including affirmative action) is that it is morally arbitrary to consider race or sex when hiring, since these characteristics are not relevant to the decision. But the above examples show that not all uses of race or sex as a criterion in hiring decisions are morally arbitrary or irrelevant. Similarly, when an affirmative action officer takes into account race and sex, use of these characteristics is not morally irrelevant or arbitrary. Since affirmative action aims to help end racial and sexual inequality by providing black and female role models for minorities (and non-minorities), the race and sex of the job candidates are clearly relevant to the decision. There is nothing arbitrary about the affirmative action officer focusing on race and sex. Hence, if reverse discrimination is wrong, it is not wrong for the reason that it uses morally irrelevant and arbitrary characteristics to distinguish between applicants.

3. Reverse Discrimination as Unjustified Stereotyping

It might be argued that reverse discrimination involves judging people by alleged average characteristics of a class to which they belong instead of judging them on the basis of their individual characteristics, and that such judging on the basis of stereotypes is unjust. But the defense of affirmative action suggested in this paper does not rely on stereotyping. When an employer hires a slightly less well qualified woman or black over a slightly more qualified white male for the purpose of helping to overcome sexual and racial inequality, she judges the applicants on the basis of their individual characteristics. She uses this person's sex or skin color as a mechanism to help achieve the goals of affirmative action. Individual characteristics of the white male (his skin color and sex) prevent him from serving one of the legitimate goals of employment policies, and he is turned down on this basis.

Notice that the objection does have some force against those who defend reverse discrimination on the grounds of compensatory justice. An affirmative action policy whose purpose is to compensate women and blacks for past and current injustices judges that women and blacks on the average are owed greater compensation than are white males. Although this is true, opponents of affirmative action argue that some white males have been more severely and unfairly disadvantaged than some women and blacks. A poor white male from Appalachia may have suffered greater undeserved disadvantages than the upper-middle class women or blacks with whom he competes. Although there is a high correlation between being female (or being black) and being especially owed compensation for unfair disadvantages suffered, the correlation is not universal.

Thus defending affirmative action on the grounds of compensatory justice may lead to unjust treatment of white males in individual cases. Despite the fact that certain white males are owed greater compensation than are some women or blacks, it is the latter that receive compensation.

This is the result of judging candidates for jobs on the basis of the average characteristics of their class, rather than on the basis of their individual characteristics. Thus compensatory justice defenses of reverse discrimination may involve potentially problematic stereotyping. But this is not the defense of affirmative action considered here.

4. Failing to Hire the Most Qualified Person Is Unjust

One of the major reasons people think that reverse discrimination is unjust is because they think the most qualified person should get the job. But why should the most qualified person be hired?

a. *Efficiency.* One obvious answer to this question is that one should hire the most qualified person because doing so promotes efficiency. If job qualifications are positively correlated with job performance, then the more qualified person will tend to do a better job. Although it is not always true that there is such a correlation, in general there is, and hence this point is well taken. There are short term efficiency costs of reverse discrimination as defined here.

Note that a weaker version of affirmative action has no such efficiency costs. If one hires a black or woman over a white male only in cases where qualifications are roughly equal, job performance will not be affected. Furthermore, efficiency costs will be a function of the qualifications gap between the black or woman hired, and the white male rejected: the larger the gap, the greater the efficiency costs. The existence of efficiency costs is also a function of the type of work performed. Many of the jobs in our society are ones which any normal person can do (e.g., assembly line worker, janitor, truck driver, etc.). Affirmative action hiring for these positions is unlikely to have significant efficiency costs (assuming whoever is hired is willing to work hard). In general, professional positions are the ones in which people's performance levels will vary significantly, and hence these are the jobs in which reverse discrimination could have significant efficiency costs.

While concern for efficiency gives us a reason for hiring the most qualified person, it in no way explains the alleged injustice suffered by the white male who is passed over due to reverse discrimination. If the affirmative action employer is treating the white male unjustly, it is not because the hiring policy is inefficient. Failing to maximize efficiency does not generally involve acting unjustly. For instance, a person who carries one bag of groceries at a time, rather than two, is acting inefficiently, though not unjustly.

It is arguable that the manager of a business who fails to hire the most qualified person (and thereby sacrifices some efficiency) treats the owners of the company unjustly, for their profits may suffer, and this violates one conception of the manager's fiduciary responsibility to the shareholders. Perhaps the administrator of a hospital who hires a slightly less well qualified black doctor (for the purposes of affirmative action) treats the future patients at that hospital unjustly, for doing so may reduce the level of health care they receive (and it is arguable that they have a legitimate expectation to receive the best health care possible for the money they spend). But neither of these examples of inefficiency leading to injustice concern the white "male victim" of affirmative action, and it is precisely this person who the opponents of reverse discrimination claim is being unfairly treated.

To many people, that a policy is inefficient is a sufficient reason for condemning it. This is especially true in the competitive and profit oriented world of business. However, profit maximization is not the only legitimate goal of business hiring policies (or other business decisions). Businesses have responsibilities to help heal society's ills, especially those (like racism and sexism) which they in large part helped to create and perpetuate. Unless one takes the implausible position that business' only legitimate goal is profit maximization, the efficiency costs of affirmative action are not an automatic reason for rejecting it. And as we have noted,

affirmative action's efficiency costs are of no help in substantiating and explaining its alleged injustice to white males.

b. *The Most Qualified Person Has a Right to the Job.* One could argue that the most qualified person for the job has a right to be hired in virtue of superior qualifications. On this view, reverse discrimination violates the better qualified white male's right to be hired for the job. But the most qualified applicant holds no such right. If you are the best painter in town, and a person hires her brother to paint her house, instead of you, your rights have not been violated. People do not have rights to be hired for particular jobs (though I think a plausible case can be made for the claim that there is a fundamental human right to employment). If anyone has a right in this matter, it is the employer. This is not to say, of course, that the employer cannot do wrong in her hiring decision; she obviously can. If she hires a white because she loathes blacks, she does wrong. The point is that her wrong does not consist in violating the right some candidate has to her job (though this would violate other rights of the candidate).

c. *The Most Qualified Person Deserves the Job.* It could be argued that the most qualified person should get the job because she deserves it in virtue of her superior qualifications. But the assumption that the person most qualified for a job is the one who most deserves it is problematic. Very often people do not deserve their qualifications, and hence they do not deserve anything on the basis of those qualifications. A person's qualifications are a function of at least the following factors:

A. innate abilities,
B. home environment,
C. socioeconomic class of parents,
D. quality of the schools attended,
E. luck, and
F. effort or perseverance.

A person is only responsible for the last factor on this list, and hence one only deserves one's qualifications to the extent that they are a function of effort.

It is undoubtedly often the case that a person who is less well qualified for a job is more deserving of the job (because she worked harder to achieve those lower qualifications) than is someone with superior qualifications. This is frequently true of women and blacks in the job market: they worked harder to overcome disadvantages most (or all) white males never faced. Hence, affirmative action policies which permit the hiring of slightly less well qualified candidates may often be more in line with considerations of desert than are the standard meritocratic procedures.

The point is not that affirmative action is defensible because it helps ensure that more deserving candidates get jobs. Nor is it that desert should be the only or even the most important consideration in hiring decisions. The claim is simply that hiring the most qualified person for a job need not (and quite often does not) involve hiring the most deserving candidate. Hence the intuition that morality requires one to hire the most qualified people cannot be justified on the grounds that these people deserve to be hired.

d. *The Most Qualified Person Is Entitled to the Job.* One might think that although the most qualified person neither deserves the job nor has a right to the job, still this person is entitled to the job. By "entitlement" in this context, I mean a natural and legitimate expectation based on a type of social promise. Society has implicitly encouraged the belief that the most qualified candidate will get the job. Society has set up a competition and the prize is a job which is awarded to those applying with the best qualifications. Society thus reneges on an implicit promise it has made to its members when it allows reverse discrimination to occur. It is dashing legitimate expectations it has encouraged. It is violating the very rules of a game it created.

Furthermore, the argument goes, by allowing reverse discrimination, society is breaking an explicit promise (contained in the Civil Rights Act of 1964) that it will not allow race or sex to be used against one of its citizens. Title VII of that Act prohibits discrimination in employment on the basis of race or sex (as well as color, religion, or national origin).

In response to this argument, it should first be noted that the above interpretation of the Civil Rights Act is misleading. In fact, the Supreme Court has interpreted the Act as allowing race and sex to be considered in hiring or admission decisions. More importantly, since affirmative action has been an explicit national policy for the last twenty years (and has been supported in numerous court cases), it is implausible to argue that society has promised its members that it will not allow race or sex to outweigh superior qualifications in hiring decisions. In addition, the objection takes a naive and utopian view of actual hiring decisions. It presents a picture of our society as a pure meritocracy in which hiring decisions are based solely on qualifications. The only exception it sees to these meritocratic procedures is the unfortunate policy of affirmative action. But this picture is dramatically distorted. Elected government officials, political appointees, business managers, and many others clearly do not have their positions solely or even mostly because of their qualifications. Given the widespread acceptance in our society of procedures which are far from meritocratic, claiming that the most qualified person has a socially endorsed entitlement to the job is not believable.

5. Undermining Equal Opportunity for White Males

It has been claimed that the right of white males to an equal chance of employment is violated by affirmative action. Reverse discrimination, it is said, undermines equality of opportunity for white males.

If equality of opportunity requires a social environment in which everyone at birth has roughly the same chance of succeeding through the use of his or her natural talents, then it could well be argued that given the social, cultural, and educational disadvantages placed on women and blacks, preferential treatment of these groups brings us closer to equality of opportunity. White males are full members of the community in a way in which women and blacks are not, and this advantage is diminished by affirmative action. Affirmative action takes away the greater than equal opportunity white males generally have, and thus it brings us closer to a situation in which all members of society have an equal chance of succeeding through the use of their talents.

It should be noted that the goal of affirmative action is to bring about a society in which there is equality of opportunity for women and blacks without preferential treatment of these groups. It is not the purpose of the sort of affirmative action defended here to disadvantage white males in order to take away the advantage a sexist and racist society gives to them. But noticing that this occurs is sufficient to dispel the illusion that affirmative action undermines the equality of opportunity for white males.

LEGITIMATE OBJECTIONS

The following two considerations explain what is morally troubling about reverse discrimination.

1. Judging on the Basis of Involuntary Characteristics

In cases of reverse discrimination, white males are passed over on the basis of membership in a group they were born into. When an affirmative action employer hires a slightly less well qualified black (or woman), rather than a more highly qualified white male, skin color (or sex) is being used as one criterion for determining who gets a very important benefit. Making distinctions in how one treats people on the basis of characteristics they cannot help having (such as skin color or sex) is morally problematic because it reduces individual autonomy. Discriminating between people on the basis of features they can do something about is preferable, since it gives them some control over how others act towards them. They can develop the characteristics others use to give them favorable treatment and avoid those

characteristics others use as grounds for unfavorable treatment.

For example, if employers refuse to hire you because you are a member of the American Nazi party, and if you do not like the fact that you are having a hard time finding a job, you can choose to leave the party. However, if a white male is having trouble finding employment because slightly less well qualified women and blacks are being given jobs to meet affirmative action requirements, there is nothing he can do about this disadvantage, and his autonomy is curtailed.

Discriminating between people on the basis of their involuntary characteristics is morally undesirable, and thus reverse discrimination is also morally undesirable. Of course, that something is morally undesirable does not show that it is unjust, nor that it is morally unjustifiable.

How morally troubling is it to judge people on the basis of involuntary characteristics? Notice that our society frequently uses these sorts of features to distinguish between people. Height and good looks are characteristics one cannot do much about, and yet basketball players and models are ordinarily chosen and rejected on the basis of precisely these features. To a large extent our intelligence is also a feature beyond our control, and yet intelligence is clearly one of the major characteristics our society uses to determine what happens to people.

Of course there are good reasons why we distinguish between people on the basis of these sorts of involuntary characteristics. Given the goals of basketball teams, model agencies, and employers in general, hiring the taller, better looking, or more intelligent person (respectively) makes good sense. It promotes efficiency, since all these people are likely to do a better job. Hiring policies based on these involuntary characteristics serve the legitimate purposes of these businesses (e.g., profit and serving the public), and hence they may be morally justified despite their tendency to reduce the control people have over their own lives.

This argument applies to reverse discrimination as well. The purpose of affirmative action is to help eradicate racial and sexual injustice. If affirmative action policies help bring about this goal, then they can be morally justified despite their tendency to reduce the control white males have over their lives.

In one respect this sort of consequentialist argument is more forceful in the case of affirmative action. Rather than merely promoting the goal of efficiency (which is the justification for businesses hiring naturally brighter, taller, or more attractive individuals), affirmative action promotes the non-utilitarian goal of an egalitarian society. In general, promoting a consideration of justice (such as equality) is more important than is promoting efficiency or utility. Thus in terms of the importance of the objective, this consequentialist argument is stronger in the case of affirmative action. If one can justify reducing individual autonomy on the grounds that it promotes efficiency, one can certainly do so on the grounds that it reduces the injustice of racial and sexual inequality.

2. Burdening White Males without Compensation

Perhaps the strongest moral intuition concerning the wrongness of reverse discrimination is that it is unfair to job-seeking white males. It is unfair because they have been given an undeserved disadvantage in the competition for employment; they have been handicapped because of something that is not their fault. Why should white males be made to pay for the sins of others?

It would be a mistake to argue for reverse discrimination on the grounds that white males deserve to be burdened and that therefore we should hire women and blacks even when white males are better qualified. Young white males who are now entering the job market are not more responsible for the evils of racial and sexual inequality than are other members of society. Thus reverse discrimination is not properly viewed as punishment administered to white males.

The justification for affirmative action supported here claims that bringing about sexual and racial equality necessitates sacrifice on the part of white males who seek employment. An important step in bringing about the desired egalitarian society involves speeding up the process by which women and blacks get into positions of power and authority. This requires that white males find it harder to achieve these same positions. But this is not punishment for deeds done.

Thomas Nagel's helpful analogy is state condemnation of property under the right of eminent domain for the purpose of building a highway.[2] Forcing some in the community to move in order that the community as a whole may benefit is unfair. Why should these individuals suffer rather than others? The answer is: Because they happen to live in a place where it is important to build a road. A similar response should be given to the white male who objects to reverse discrimination with the same "Why me?" question. The answer is: Because job-seeking white males happen to be in the way of an important road leading to the desired egalitarian society. Job-seeking white males are being made to bear the brunt of the burden of affirmative action because of accidental considerations, just as are homeowners whose property is condemned in order to build a highway.

This analogy is extremely illuminating and helpful in explaining the nature of reverse discrimination. There is, however, an important dissimilarity that Nagel does not mention. In cases of property condemnation, compensation is paid to the owner. Affirmative action policies, however, do not compensate white males for shouldering this burden of moving toward the desired egalitarian society. So affirmative action is unfair to job-seeking white males because they are forced to bear an unduly large share of the burden of achieving racial and sexual equality without being compensated for this sacrifice. Since we have singled out job-seeking white males from the larger pool of white males who should also help achieve this goal, it seems that some compensation from the latter to the former is appropriate.

This is a serious objection to affirmative action policies only if the uncompensated burden is substantial. Usually it is not. Most white male "victims" of affirmative action easily find employment. It is highly unlikely that the same white male will repeatedly fail to get hired because of affirmative action. The burdens of affirmative action should be spread as evenly as possible among all the job-seeking white males. Furthermore, the burden job-seeking white males face—of finding it somewhat more difficult to get employment—is inconsequential when compared to the burdens ongoing discrimination places on women and blacks. Forcing job-seeking white males to bear an extra burden is acceptable because this is a necessary step toward achieving a much greater reduction in the unfair burdens our society places on women and blacks. If affirmative action is a necessary mechanism for a timely dismantlement of our racial and sexual caste system, the extra burdens it places on job-seeking white males are justified.

Still the question remains: Why isn't compensation paid? When members of society who do not deserve extra burdens are singled out to sacrifice for an important community goal, society owes them compensation. This objection loses some of its force when one realizes that society continually places undeserved burdens on its members without compensating them. For instance, the burden of seeking efficiency is placed on the shoulders of the least naturally talented and intelligent. That one is born less intelligent (or otherwise less talented) does not mean that one deserves to have reduced employment opportunities, and yet our society's meritocratic hiring procedures make it much harder for less naturally talented members to find meaningful employment. These people are not compensated for their sacrifices either.

Of course, pointing out that there are other examples of an allegedly problematic social policy does not justify that policy. Nonetheless, if this analogy is sound, failing to compensate job-seeking white males for the sacrifices placed on them by reverse discrimination is not without precedent. Furthermore, it is no more morally troublesome than is failing to compensate less talented members of society for their undeserved sacrifice of employment opportunities for the sake of efficiency.

CONCLUSION

This article has shown the difficulties in pinpointing what is morally troubling about reverse discrimination. The most commonly heard objections to reverse discrimination fail to make their case. Reverse discrimination is not morally equivalent to traditional racism and sexism since its goals and consequences are entirely different, and the act of treating people differently on the basis of race or sex is not necessarily morally wrong. The race and sex of the candidates are not morally irrelevant in all hiring decisions, and affirmative action hiring is an example where discriminating on the basis of race or sex is not morally arbitrary. Furthermore, affirmative action can be defended on grounds that do not involve stereotyping. Though affirmative action hiring of less well qualified applicants can lead to short run inefficiency, failing to hire the most qualified applicant does not violate this person's rights, entitlements, or deserts. Additionally, affirmative action hiring does not generally undermine equal opportunity for white males.

Reverse discrimination is morally troublesome in that it judges people on the basis of involuntary characteristics and thus reduces the control they have over their lives. It also places a larger than fair share of the burden of achieving an egalitarian society on the shoulders of job-seeking white males without compensating them for this sacrifice. But these problems are relatively minor when compared to the grave injustice of racial and sexual inequality, and they are easily outweighed if affirmative action helps alleviate this far greater injustice.

NOTES

1   Peter Singer, "Is Racial Discrimination Arbitrary?" *Philosophia*, Vol. 8 (November 1978), 185–203.
2   Nagel, "A Defense of Affirmative Action." Testimony before the Sub-committee on the Constitution of the Senate Judiciary Committees (June 18, 1981).

—59—
THE MORAL STATUS OF AFFIRMATIVE ACTION

Louis P. Pojman

"A ruler who appoints any man to an office, when there is in his dominion another man better qualified for it, sins against God and against the State." (The Koran)

"[Affirmative Action] is the meagerest recompense for centuries of unrelieved oppression." (quoted by Shelby Steele as the justification for Affirmative Action)

I. DEFINITIONS

FIRST LET ME DEFINE MY TERMS:

Discrimination is simply judging one thing to differ from another on the basis of some criterion. "Discrimination" is a good quality, having reference to our ability to make distinctions. As rational and moral agents we need to make proper distinctions. To be rational is to discriminate between good and bad arguments, and to think morally is to discriminate between reasons based on valid principles and those based on invalid ones. What needs to be distinguished is the difference between rational and moral discrimination, on the one hand, and irrational and immoral discrimination, on the other hand.

Prejudice is a discrimination based on irrelevant grounds. It may simply be an attitude which never surfaces in action, or it may cause prejudicial actions. A prejudicial discrimination in action is immoral if it denies someone a fair deal. So discrimination on the basis of race or sex where these are not relevant for job performance is unfair. Likewise, one may act prejudicially in applying a relevant criterion on insufficient grounds, as in the case where I apply the criterion of being a hard worker but then assume, on insufficient evidence, that the black man who applies for the job is not a hard worker.

There is a difference between prejudice and bias. *Bias* signifies a tendency toward one thing rather than another where the evidence is incomplete or is based on non-moral factors. For example, you may have a bias toward blondes and I toward redheads. But prejudice is an attitude (or action) where unfairness is present—where one *should* know or do better—as in the case where I give people jobs simply because they are redheads. Bias implies ignorance or incomplete knowledge, whereas prejudice is deeper, involving a moral failure—usually a failure to pay attention to the evidence. But note that calling people racist or sexist without good evidence is also an act of prejudice.

Equal opportunity exists when everyone has a fair chance at the best positions that society has at its disposal. Only native aptitude and effort should be decisive in the outcome, not factors of race, sex, or special favors.

Affirmative Action is the effort to rectify the injustice of the past as well as to produce a situation closer to the ideal of equal opportunity by special policies. Put this way, it is Janus-faced or ambiguous, having both a backward-looking and a forward-looking feature. The backward-looking feature is its attempt to correct and compensate for past injustice. This aspect of Affirmative Action is strictly deontological. The forward-looking feature is its implicit ideal of a society free from prejudice, where one's race or gender is irrelevant to basic opportunities. This is both deontological and utilitarian: deontological in that it aims at treating people according to their merits or needs, utilitarian in that a society perceived as fair will be a happier society.

When we look at a social problem from a backward-looking perspective, we need to determine who has committed or benefited from a wrongful or prejudicial act and to determine who deserves compensation for that act.

When we look at a social problem from a forward-looking perspective, we need to determine what a just society (one free from prejudice) would look like and how to obtain that kind of society. The forward-looking aspect of Affirmative Action is paradoxically race-conscious, because it uses race to bring about a society that is not race-conscious—that is color blind (in the morally relevant sense of this term).

It is also useful to distinguish two versions of Affirmative Action. *Weak Affirmative Action* involves such measures as the elimination of segregation (namely the idea of "separate but equal"), widespread advertisement of job opportunities to groups not previously represented in certain privileged positions, special scholarships for the disadvantaged classes (such as the poor), using under-representation or a history of past discrimination as a tie breaker when candidates are relatively equal, and the like.

Strong Affirmative Action involves more positive steps to eliminate past injustice, such as reverse discrimination, hiring candidates on the basis of race and gender in order to reach equal or nearly equal results, and proportionate representation in each area of society....

III. ARGUMENTS FOR AFFIRMATIVE ACTION

Let us now survey the main arguments typically cited in the debate over Affirmative Action. I will briefly discuss seven arguments on each side of the issue.

1. Need for Role Models

This argument is straightforward. We all have need of role models, and it helps to know that others like us can be successful. We learn and are encouraged to strive for excellence by emulating our heroes and role models.

However, it is doubtful whether role models of one's own racial or sexual type are necessary for success. One of my heroes was Gandhi, an Indian Hindu, another was my grade school science teacher, one Miss DeVoe, and another was Martin Luther King. More important than having role models of one's own type is having genuinely good people, of whatever race or gender, to emulate. Furthermore, even if it is of some help to people with low self-esteem to gain encouragement from seeing others of their particular kind in leadership roles, it is doubtful whether this need is a sufficient condition to justify preferential hiring or reverse discrimination. What good is a role model who is inferior to other professors or business personnel? Excellence will rise to the top in a system of fair opportunity. Natural development of role models will come more slowly and more surely. Proponents of preferential policies simply lack the patience to let history take its own course.

2. The Need of Breaking the Stereotypes

Society may simply need to know that there are talented blacks and women, so that it does not automatically assign them lesser respect or status. We need to have unjustified stereotype beliefs replaced with more accurate ones about the talents of blacks and women. So we need to engage in preferential hiring of qualified minorities even when they are not the most qualified.

Again, the response is that hiring the less qualified is neither fair to those better qualified who are passed over nor an effective way of removing inaccurate stereotypes. If competence is accepted as the criterion for hiring, then it is unjust to override it for purposes of social engineering. Furthermore, if blacks or women are known to hold high positions simply because of reverse discrimination, then they will still lack the respect due to those of their rank. In New York City there is a saying among doctors, "Never go to a black physician under 40," referring to the fact that AA has affected the medical system during the past fifteen years. The police use "Quota Cops" and "Welfare Sergeants" to refer to those hired without passing the standardized tests. (In 1985, 180 black and hispanic policemen, who had failed a promotion test, were promoted anyway to the rank of sergeant.) The destruction of false stereotypes will come naturally as qualified blacks rise naturally in fair competition (or if it does not—then the stereotypes may be justified). Reverse discrimination sends the message home that the stereotypes are deserved—otherwise, why do these minorities need so much extra help?

3. Equal Results Argument

Some philosophers and social scientists hold that human nature is roughly identical, so that on a fair playing field the same proportion from every race and gender and ethnic group would attain to the highest positions in every area of endeavor. It would follow that any inequality of results itself is evidence for inequality of opportunity. John Arthur, in discussing an intelligence test, Test 21, puts the case this way.

> History is important when considering governmental rules like Test 21 because low scores by blacks can be traced in large measure to the legacy of slavery and racism: segregation, poor schooling, exclusion from trade unions, malnutrition, and poverty have all played their roles. Unless one assumes that blacks are

naturally less able to pass the test, the conclusion must be that the results are themselves socially and legally constructed, not a mere given for which law and society can claim no responsibility.

> The conclusion seems to be that genuine equality eventually requires equal results. Obviously blacks have been treated unequally throughout US history, and just as obviously the economic and psychological effects of that inequality linger to this day, showing up in lower income and poorer performance in school and on tests than whites achieve. Since we have no reason to believe that difference in performance can be explained by factors other than history, equal results are a good benchmark by which to measure progress made toward genuine equality.[1]

The result of a just society should be equal numbers in proportion to each group in the work force.

However, Arthur fails even to consider studies that suggest that there are innate differences between races, sexes, and groups. If there are genetic differences in intelligence and temperament within families, why should we not expect such differences between racial groups and the two genders? Why should the evidence for this be completely discounted?

Perhaps some race or one gender is more intelligent in one way than another. At present we have only limited knowledge about genetic differences, but what we do have suggests some difference besides the obvious physiological traits.[2] The proper use of this evidence is not to promote discriminatory policies but to be *open* to the possibility that innate differences may have led to an over-representation of certain groups in certain areas of endeavor. It seems that on average blacks have genetic endowments favoring them in the development of skills necessary for excellence in basketball.

Furthermore, on Arthur's logic, we should take aggressive AA against Asians and Jews since they are over-represented in science, technology, and medicine. So that each group receives its fair share, we should ensure that 12% of the philosophers in the United States are black, reduce the percentage of Jews from an estimated 15% to 2%—firing about 1,300 Jewish philosophers. The fact that Asians are producing 50% of PhDs in science and math and blacks less than 1% clearly shows, on this reasoning, that we are providing special secret advantages to Asians.

But why does society have to enter into this results game in the first place? Why do we have to decide whether all difference is environmental or genetic? Perhaps we should simply admit that we lack sufficient evidence to pronounce on these issues with any certainty—but if so, should we not be more modest in insisting on equal results? Here is a thought experiment. Take two families of different racial groups, Green and Blue. The Greens decide to have only two children, to spend all their resources on them, to give them the best education. The two Green kids respond well and end up with achievement test scores in the 99th percentile. The Blues fail to practice family planning. They have 15 children. They can only afford two children, but lack of ability or whatever prevents them from keeping their family down. Now they need help for their large family. Why does society have to step in and help them? Society did not force them to have 15 children. Suppose that the achievement test scores of the 15 children fall below the twenty-fifth percentile. They cannot compete with the Greens. But now enters AA. It says that it is society's fault that the Blue children are not as able as the Greens and that the Greens must pay extra taxes to enable the Blues to compete. No restraints are put on the Blues regarding family size. This seems unfair to the Greens. Should the Green children be made to bear responsibility for the consequences of the Blues' voluntary behavior?

My point is simply that Arthur needs to cast his net wider and recognize that demographics and childbearing and -rearing practices are crucial factors in achievement. People have to take some responsibility for their actions. The equal results argument (or axiom) misses a greater part of the picture.

4. The Compensation Argument

The argument goes like this: blacks have been wronged and severely harmed by whites. Therefore white society should compensate blacks for the injury caused them. Reverse discrimination in terms of preferential hiring, contracts, and scholarships is a fitting way to compensate for the past wrongs.

This argument actually involves a distorted notion of compensation. Normally, we think of compensation as owed by a specific person A to another person B whom A has wronged in a specific way C. For example, if I have stolen your car and used it for a period of time to make business profits that would have gone to you, it is not enough that I return your car. I must pay you an amount reflecting your loss and my ability to pay. If I have only made $5,000 and only have $10,000 in assets, it would not be possible for you to collect $20,000 in damages—even though that is the amount of loss you have incurred.

Sometimes compensation is extended to groups of people who have been unjustly harmed by the greater society. For example, the United States government has compensated the Japanese-Americans who were interred during the Second World War, and the West German government has paid reparations to the survivors of Nazi concentration camps. But here a specific people have been identified who were wronged in an identifiable way by the government of the nation in question.

On the face of it the demand by blacks for compensation does not fit the usual pattern. Perhaps Southern States with Jim Crow laws could be accused of unjustly harming blacks, but it is hard to see that the United States government was involved in doing so. Furthermore, it is not clear that all blacks were harmed in the same way or whether some were *unjustly* harmed or harmed more than poor whites and others (e.g., short people). Finally, even if identifiable blacks were harmed by identifiable social practices, it is not clear that most forms of Affirmative Action are appropriate to restore the situation. The usual practice of a financial payment seems more appropriate than giving a high level job to someone unqualified or only minimally qualified, who, speculatively, might have been better qualified had he not been subject to racial discrimination. If John is the star tailback of our college team with a promising professional future, and I accidentally (but culpably) drive my pick-up truck over his legs, and so cripple him, John may be due compensation, but he is not due the tailback spot on the football team.

Still, there may be something intuitively compelling about compensating members of an oppressed group who are minimally qualified. Suppose that the Hatfields and the McCoys are enemy clans and some youths from the Hatfields go over and steal diamonds and gold from the McCoys, distributing it within the Hatfield economy. Even though we do not know which Hatfield youths did the stealing, we would want to restore the wealth, as far as possible, to the McCoys. One way might be to tax the Hatfields, but another might be to give preferential treatment in terms of scholarships and training programs and hiring to the McCoys.[3]

This is perhaps the strongest argument for Affirmative Action, and it may well justify some weak versions of AA, but it is doubtful whether it is sufficient to justify strong versions with quotas and goals and time tables in skilled positions. There are at least two reasons for this. First, we have no way of knowing how many people of group G would have been at competence level L had the world been different. Secondly, the normal criterion of competence is a strong prima facie consideration when the most important positions are at stake. There are two reasons for this: (1) society has given people expectations that if they attain certain levels of excellence they will be awarded appropriately and (2) filling the most important positions with the best qualified is the best way to insure efficiency in job-related areas and in society in general. These reasons are not absolutes. They

can be overridden. But there is a strong presumption in their favor so that a burden of proof rests with those who would override them.

At this point we get into the problem of whether innocent non-blacks should have to pay a penalty in terms of preferential hiring of blacks. We turn to that argument.

5. Compensation from Those Who Innocently Benefited from Past Injustice

White males as innocent beneficiaries of unjust discrimination of blacks and women have no grounds for complaint when society seeks to rectify the tilted field. White males may be innocent of oppressing blacks and minorities (and women), but they have unjustly benefited from that oppression or discrimination. So it is perfectly proper that less qualified women and blacks be hired before them.

The operative principle is: He who knowingly and willingly benefits from a wrong must help pay for the wrong. Judith Jarvis Thomson puts it this way. "Many [white males] have been direct beneficiaries of policies which have down-graded blacks and women ... and even those who did not directly benefit ... had, at any rate, the advantage in the competition which comes of the confidence in one's full membership [in the community], and of one's right being recognized as a matter of course."[4] That is, white males obtain advantages in self respect and self-confidence deriving from a racist system which denies these to blacks and women.

Objection. As I noted in the previous section, compensation is normally individual and specific. If A harms B regarding x, B has a right to compensation from A in regards to x. If A steals B's car and wrecks it, A has an obligation to compensate B for the stolen car, but A's son has no obligation to compensate B. Furthermore, if A dies or disappears, B has no moral right to claim that society compensate him for the stolen car—though if he has insurance, he can make such a claim to the insurance company. Sometimes a wrong cannot be compensated, and we just have to make the best of an imperfect world.

Suppose my parents, divining that I would grow up to have an unsurpassable desire to be a basketball player, bought an expensive growth hormone for me. Unfortunately, a neighbor stole it and gave it to little Lew Alcindor, who gained the extra 18 inches—my 18 inches—and shot up to an enviable 7 feet 2 inches. Alias Kareem Abdul Jabbar, he excelled in basketball, as I would have done had I had my proper dose.

Do I have a right to the millions of dollars that Jabbar made as a professional basketball player—the unjustly innocent beneficiary of my growth hormone? I have a right to something from the neighbor who stole the hormone, and it might be kind of Jabbar to give me free tickets to the Laker basketball games, and perhaps I should be remembered in his will. As far as I can see, however, he does not *owe* me anything, either legally or morally.

Suppose further that Lew Alcindor and I are in high school together and we are both qualified to play basketball, only he is far better than I. Do I deserve to start in his position because I would have been as good as he is had someone not cheated me as a child? Again, I think not. But if being the lucky beneficiary of wrong-doing does not entail that Alcindor (or the coach) owes me anything in regards to basketball, why should it be a reason to engage in preferential hiring in academic positions or highly coveted jobs? If minimal qualifications are not adequate to override excellence in basketball, even when the minimality is a consequence of wrongdoing, why should they be adequate in other areas?

6. The Diversity Argument

It is important that we learn to live in a pluralistic world, learning to get along with those of other races and cultures, so we should have fully integrated schools and employment situations. Diversity is an important symbol and educative device. Thus preferential treatment is warranted to perform this role in society.

But, again, while we can admit the value of diversity, it hardly seems adequate to override considerations of merit and efficiency. Diversity for diversity's sake is moral promiscuity, since it obfuscates rational distinctions, and unless those hired are highly qualified the diversity factor threatens to become a fetish. At least at the higher levels of business and the professions, competence far outweighs considerations of diversity. I do not care whether the group of surgeons operating on me reflect racial or gender balance, but I do care that they are highly qualified. And likewise with airplane pilots, military leaders, business executives, and, may I say it, teachers and professors. Moreover, there are other ways of learning about other cultures besides engaging in reverse discrimination.

7. Anti-Meritocratic (Desert) Argument to Justify Reverse Discrimination: "No One Deserves His Talents"

According to this argument, the competent do not deserve their intelligence, their superior character, their industriousness, or their discipline; therefore they have no right to the best positions in society; therefore society is not unjust in giving these positions to less (but still minimally) qualified blacks and women. In one form this argument holds that since no one deserves anything, society may use any criteria it pleases to distribute goods. The criterion most often designated is social utility. Versions of this argument are found in the writings of John Arthur, John Rawls, Bernard Boxill, Michael Kinsley, Ronald Dworkin, and Richard Wasserstrom. Rawls writes, "No one deserves his place in the distribution of native endowments, any more than one deserves one's initial starting place in society. The assertion that a man deserves the superior character that enables him to make the effort to cultivate his abilities is equally problematic; for his character depends in large part upon fortunate family and social circumstances for which he can claim no credit. The notion of desert seems not to apply to these cases."[5] Michael Kinsley is even more adamant:

Opponents of affirmative action are hung up on a distinction that seems more profoundly irrelevant: treating individuals versus treating groups. What is the moral difference between dispensing favors to people on their "merits" as individuals and passing out society's benefits on the basis of group identification?

Group identifications like race and sex are, of course, immutable. They have nothing to do with a person's moral worth. But the same is true of most of what comes under the label "merit." The tools you need for getting ahead in a meritocratic society—not all of them but most: talent, education, instilled cultural values such as ambition—are distributed just as arbitrarily as skin color. They are fate. The notion that people somehow "deserve" the advantages of those characteristics in a way they don't "deserve" the advantage of their race is powerful, but illogical.[6]

It will help to put the argument in outline form.

1. Society may award jobs and positions as it sees fit as long as individuals have no claim to these positions.
2. To have a claim to something means that one has earned it or deserves it.
3. But no one has earned or deserves his intelligence, talent, education or cultural values which produce superior qualifications.
4. If a person does not deserve what produces something, he does not deserve its products.
5. Therefore better qualified people do not deserve their qualifications.
6. Therefore, society may override their qualifications in awarding jobs and positions as it sees fit (for social utility or to compensate for previous wrongs).
7. So it is permissible if a minimally qualified black or woman is admitted to law or medical school ahead of a white male with excellent credentials or if a less qualified person from an "underutilized" group gets a professorship ahead of a far better qualified white male.

Sufficiency and underutilization together outweigh excellence.

Objection. Premise 4 is false. To see this, reflect that just because I do not deserve the money that I have been given as a gift (for instance) does not mean that I am not entitled to what I get with that money. If you and I both get a gift of $100 and I bury mine in the sand for 5 years while you invest yours wisely and double its value at the end of five years, I cannot complain that you should split the increase 50/50 since neither of us deserved the original gift. If we accept the notion of responsibility at all, we must hold that persons deserve the fruits of their labor and conscious choices. Of course, we might want to distinguish moral from legal desert and argue that, morally speaking, effort is more important than outcome, whereas, legally speaking, outcome may be more important. Nevertheless, there are good reasons in terms of efficiency, motivation, and rough justice for holding a strong prima facie principle of giving scarce high positions to those most competent.

The attack on moral desert is perhaps the most radical move that egalitarians like Rawls and company have made against meritocracy, but the ramifications of their attack are far reaching. The following are some of its implications. Since I do not deserve my two good eyes or two good kidneys, the social engineers may take one of each from me to give to those needing an eye or a kidney—even if they have damaged their organs by their own voluntary actions. Since no one deserves anything, we do not deserve pay for our labors or praise for a job well done or first prize in the race we win. The notion of moral responsibility vanishes in a system of levelling.

But there is no good reason to accept the argument against desert. We do act freely and, as such, we are responsible for our actions. We deserve the fruits of our labor, reward for our noble feats and punishment for our misbehavior.

We have considered seven arguments for Affirmative Action and have found no compelling case for Strong AA and only one plausible argument (a version of the compensation argument) for

Weak AA. We must now turn to the arguments against Affirmative Action to see whether they fare any better.[7]

IV. ARGUMENTS AGAINST AFFIRMATIVE ACTION

1. Affirmative Action Requires Discrimination against a Different Group

Weak Affirmative Action weakly discriminates against new minorities, mostly innocent young white males, and Strong Affirmative Action strongly discriminates against these new minorities. As I argued in III.5, this discrimination is unwarranted, since, even if some compensation to blacks were indicated, it would be unfair to make innocent white males bear the whole brunt of the payments. In fact, it is poor white youth who become the new pariahs on the job market. The children of the wealthy have no trouble getting into the best private grammar schools and, on the basis of superior early education, into the best universities, graduate schools, managerial and professional positions. Affirmative Action simply shifts injustice, setting blacks and women against young white males, especially ethnic and poor white males. It does little to rectify the goal of providing equal opportunity to all. If the goal is a society where everyone has a fair chance, then it would be better to concentrate on support for families and early education and decide the matter of university admissions and job hiring on the basis of traditional standards of competence.

2. Affirmative Action Perpetuates the Victimization Syndrome

Shelby Steele admits that Affirmative Action may seem "the meagerest recompense for centuries of unrelieved oppression" and that it helps promote diversity. At the same time, though, notes Steele, Affirmative Action reinforces the spirit of victimization by telling blacks that they can gain more by emphasizing their suffering, degradation and helplessness than by discipline and work. This message holds the danger of blacks becoming permanently handicapped by a need for special treatment. It also sends to society at large the message that blacks cannot make it on their own.

Leon Wieseltier sums up the problem this way.

> The memory of oppression is a pillar and a strut of the identity of every people oppressed. It is no ordinary marker of difference. It is unusually stiffening. It instructs the individual and the group about what to expect of the world, imparts an isolating sense of aptness.... Don't be fooled, it teaches, there is only repetition. For that reason, the collective memory of an oppressed people is not only a treasure but a trap.
>
> In the memory of oppression, oppression outlives itself. The scar does the work of the wound. That is the real tragedy: that injustice retains the power to distort long after it has ceased to be real. It is a posthumous victory for the oppressors, when pain becomes a tradition. And yet the atrocities of the past must never be forgotten. This is the unfairly difficult dilemma of the newly emancipated and the newly enfranchised: an honorable life is not possible if they remember too little and a normal life is not possible if they remember too much.[8]

With the eye of recollection, which does not "remember too much," Steele recommends a policy which offers "educational and economic development of disadvantaged people regardless of race and the eradication from our society—through close monitoring and severe sanctions—of racial and gender discrimination."[9]

3. Affirmative Action Encourages Mediocrity and Incompetence

Last spring Jesse Jackson joined protesters at Harvard Law School in demanding that the law

School faculty hire black women. Jackson dismissed Dean of the Law School, Robert C. Clark's standard of choosing the best qualified person for the job as "Cultural anemia." "We cannot just define who is qualified in the most narrow vertical academic terms," he said. "Most people in the world are yellow, brown, black, poor, non-Christian and don't speak English, and they can't wait for some White males with archaic rules to appraise them."[10] It might be noted that if Jackson is correct about the depth of cultural decadence at Harvard, blacks might be well advised to form and support their own more vital law schools and leave places like Harvard to their archaism.

At several universities, the administration has forced departments to hire members of minorities even when far superior candidates were available. Shortly after obtaining my PhD in the late 1970s I was mistakenly identified as a black philosopher (I had a civil rights record and was once a black studies major) and was flown to a major university, only to be rejected for a more qualified candidate when it discovered that I was white.

Stories of the bad effects of Affirmative Action abound. The philosopher Sidney Hook writes that "At one Ivy League university, representatives of the Regional HEW demanded an explanation of why there were no women or minority students in the Graduate Department of Religious Studies. They were told that a reading knowledge of Hebrew and Greek was presupposed. Whereupon the representatives of HEW advised orally: 'Then end those old fashioned programs that require irrelevant languages. And start up programs on relevant things which minority group students can study without learning languages.'"[11]

Nicholas Capaldi notes that the staff of HEW itself was one-half women, three-fifths members of minorities, and one-half black—a clear case of racial over-representation.

In 1972 officials at Stanford University discovered a proposal for the government to monitor curriculum in higher education: the "Summary Statement ... Sex Discrimination Proposed HEW Regulation to Effectuate Title IX of the Education Amendment of 1972" to "establish and use internal procedure for reviewing curricula, designed both to ensure that they do not reflect discrimination on the basis of sex and to resolve complaints concerning allegations of such discrimination, pursuant to procedural standards to be prescribed by the Director of the office of Civil Rights." Fortunately, Secretary of HEW Caspar Weinberger when alerted to the intrusion, assured Stanford University that he would never approve of it.[12]

Government programs of enforced preferential treatment tend to appeal to the lowest possible common denominator. Witness the 1974 HEW Revised Order No. 14 on Affirmative Action expectations for preferential hiring: "Neither minorities nor female employees should be required to possess higher qualifications than those of the lowest qualified incumbents."

Furthermore, no tests may be given to candidates unless it is *proved* to be relevant to the job.

No standard or criteria which have, by intent or effect, worked to exclude women or minorities as a class can be utilized, unless the institution can demonstrate the necessity of such standard to the performance of the job in question.

Whenever a validity study is called for ... the user should include ... an investigation of suitable alternative selection procedures and suitable alternative methods of using the selection procedure which have as little adverse impact as possible.... Whenever the user is shown an alternative selection procedure with evidence of less adverse impact and substantial evidence of validity for the same job in similar circumstances, the user should investigate it to determine the appropriateness of using or validating it in accord with these guidelines.[13]

At the same time Americans are wondering why standards in our country are falling and the Japanese are getting ahead. Affirmative Action with its twin idols, Sufficiency and Diversity, is the enemy of excellence. I will develop this thought below (IV.6).

4. Affirmative Action Policies Unjustly Shift the Burden of Proof

Affirmative Action legislation tends to place the burden of proof on the employer who does not have an "adequate" representation of "underutilized" groups in his work force. He is guilty until proven innocent. I have already recounted how in the mid-eighties the Supreme Court shifted the burden of proof back onto the plaintiff, while Congress is now attempting to shift the burden back to the employer. Those in favor of deeming disproportional representation "guilty until proven innocent" argue that it is easy for employers to discriminate against minorities by various subterfuges, and I agree that steps should be taken to monitor against prejudicial treatment. But being prejudiced against employers is not the way to attain a just solution to discrimination. The principle: innocent until proven guilty, applies to employers as well as criminals. Indeed, it is clearly special pleading to reject this basic principle of Anglo-American law in this case of discrimination while adhering to it everywhere else.

5. An Argument from Merit

Traditionally, we have believed that the highest positions in society should be awarded to those who are best qualified—as the Koran states in the quotation at the beginning of this paper. Rewarding excellence both seems just to the individuals in the competition and makes for efficiency. Note that one of the most successful acts of integration, the recruitment of Jackie Robinson in the late 1940s, was done in just this way, according to merit. If Robinson had been brought into the major league as a mediocre player or had batted .200 he would have been scorned and sent back to the minors where he belonged.

Merit is not an absolute value. There are times when it may be overridden for social goals, but there is a strong prima facie reason for awarding positions on its basis, and it should enjoy a weighty presumption in our social practices.

In a celebrated article Ronald Dworkin says that "Bakke had no case" because society did not owe Bakke anything. That may be, but then why does it owe anyone anything? Dworkin puts the matter in Utility terms, but if that is the case, society may owe Bakke a place at the University of California/Davis, for it seems a reasonable rule-utilitarian principle that achievement should be rewarded in society. We generally want the best to have the best positions, the best qualified candidate to win the political office, the most brilliant and competent scientist to be chosen for the most challenging research project, the best qualified pilots to become commercial pilots, only the best soldiers to become generals. Only when little is at stake do we weaken the standards and content ourselves with sufficiency (rather than excellence)—there are plenty of jobs where "sufficiency" rather than excellence is required. Perhaps we now feel that medicine or law or university professorships are so routine that they can be performed by minimally qualified people—in which case AA has a place.

But note, no one is calling for quotas or proportional representation of *underutilized* groups in the National Basketball Association where blacks make up 80% of the players. But if merit and merit alone reigns in sports, should it not be valued at least as much in education and industry?

6. The Slippery Slope

Even if Strong AA or Reverse Discrimination could meet the other objections, it would face a tough question: once you embark on this project, how do you limit it? Who should be excluded from reverse discrimination? Asians and Jews are over-represented, so if we give blacks positive quotas, should we place negative quotas to these other groups? Since white males, "WMs," are a minority which is suffering from reverse discrimination, will we need a New Affirmative Action policy in the twenty-first century to compensate for the discrimination against WMs in the late twentieth century?

Furthermore, Affirmative Action has stigmatized the *young* white male. Assuming that we accept reverse discrimination, the fair way to make sacrifices would be to retire *older* white males who are more likely to have benefited from a favored status. Probably the least guilty of any harm to minority groups is the young white male—usually a liberal who has been required to bear the brunt of ages of past injustice. Justice Brennan's announcement that the Civil Rights Act did not apply to discrimination against whites shows how the clearest language can be bent to serve the ideology of the moment.[14]

7. The Mounting Evidence against the Success of Affirmative Action

Thomas Sowell of the Hoover Institute has shown in his book *Preferential Policies: An International Perspective* that preferential hiring almost never solves social problems. It generally builds in mediocrity or incompetence and causes deep resentment. It is a short term solution which lacks serious grounding in social realities.

For instance, Sowell cites some disturbing statistics on education. Although twice as many blacks as Asians students took the nationwide Scholastic Aptitude Test in 1983, approximately fifteen times as many Asian students scored above 700 (out of a possible 800) on the mathematics half of the SAT. The percentage of Asians who scored above 700 in math was also more than six times higher than the percentage of American Indians and more than ten times higher than that of Mexican Americans—as well as more than double the percentage of whites. As Sowell points out, in all countries studied, "intergroup performance disparities are huge" (108).

There are dozens of American colleges and universities where the median combined verbal SAT score and mathematics SAT score total 1200 or above. As of 1983 there were less than 600 black students in the entire US with combined SAT scores of 1200. This meant that, despite widespread attempts to get a black student "representation" comparable to the black percentage of the population (about 11%), there were not enough black students in the entire country for the Ivy League alone to have such a "representation" without going beyond this pool—even if the entire pool went to the eight Ivy League Colleges.[15]

Often it is claimed that a cultural bias is the cause of the poor performance of blacks on SAT (or IQ tests), but Sowell shows that these test scores are actually a better predictor of college performance for blacks than for Asians and whites. He also shows the harmfulness of the effect on blacks of preferential acceptance. At the University of California, Berkeley, where the freshman class closely reflects the actual ethnic distribution of California high school students, more than 70% of blacks fail to graduate. All 312 black students entering Berkeley in 1987 were admitted under "Affirmative Action" criteria rather than by meeting standard academic criteria. So were 480 out of 507 Hispanic students. In 1986 the median SAT score for blacks at Berkeley was 952, for Mexican Americans 1014, for American Indians 1082 and for Asian Americans 1254. (The average SAT for all students was 1181.)

The result of this mismatching is that blacks who might do well if they went to a second tier or third tier school where their test scores would indicate they belong, actually are harmed by preferential treatment. They cannot compete in the institutions where high abilities are necessary.

Sowell also points out that Affirmative Action policies have mainly assisted the middle class black, those who have suffered least from discrimination. "Black couples in which both husband and wife are college-educated overtook white couples of the same description back in the early 1970s and continued to at least hold their own in the 1980s" (115).

Sowell's conclusion is that similar patterns of results obtained from India to the USA wherever preferential policies exist. "In education, preferential admissions policies have led to high attrition rates and substandard performances for those preferred students ... who survived to graduate." In all countries the preferred tended to concentrate in less difficult subjects which lead to less remunerative careers. "In the employment market, both blacks and untouchables at the higher levels have advanced substantially while those at the lower levels show no such advancement and even some signs of retrogression. These patterns are also broadly consistent with patterns found in countries in which majorities have created preferences for themselves ..." (116).

The tendency has been to focus at the high level end of education and employment rather than on the lower level of family structure and early education. But if we really want to help the worst off improve, we need to concentrate on the family and early education. It is foolish to expect equal results when we begin with grossly unequal starting points—and discriminating against young white males is no more just than discriminating against women, blacks or anyone else.

CONCLUSION

Let me sum up. The goal of the Civil Rights movement and of moral people everywhere has been equal opportunity. The question is: how best to get there. Civil Rights legislation removed the legal barriers to equal opportunity, but did not tackle the deeper causes that produced differential results. Weak Affirmative Action aims at encouraging minorities in striving for the highest positions without unduly jeopardizing the rights of majorities, but the problem of Weak Affirmative Action is that it easily slides into Strong Affirmative Action where quotas, "goals," and equal results are forced into groups, thus promoting mediocrity, inefficiency, and resentment. Furthermore, Affirmative Action aims at the higher levels of society—universities and skilled jobs—yet if we want to improve our society, the best way to do it is to concentrate on families, children, early education, and the like. Affirmative Action is, on the one hand, too much, too soon and on the other hand, too little, too late.

Martin Luther said that humanity is like a man mounting a horse who always tends to fall off on the other side of the horse. This seems to be the case with Affirmative Action. Attempting to redress the discriminatory iniquities of our history, our well-intentioned social engineers engage in new forms of discriminatory iniquity and thereby think that they have successfully mounted the horse of racial harmony. They have only fallen off on the other side of the issue.[16]

NOTES

1   John Arthur, *The Unfinished Constitution* (Belmont, CA, 1990), 238.

2   See Phillip E. Vernon's excellent summary of the literature in *Intelligence: Heredity and Environment* (New York, 1979) and Yves Christen "Sex Differences in the Human Brain," in Nicholas Davidson (ed.), *Gender Sanity* (Lanham, 1989) and T. Bouchard, *et al.*, "Sources of Human Psychological Differences: The Minnesota Study of Twins Reared Apart," *Science*, Vol. 250 (1990).

3   See Michael Levin, "Is Racial Discrimination Special?" *Policy Review*, Fall issue (1982).

4   Judith Jarvis Thomson, "Preferential Hiring," in Marshall Cohen, Thomas Nagel and Thomas Scanlon (eds.), *Equality and Preferential Treatment* (Princeton, 1977).

5   John Rawls, *A Theory of Justice* (Cambridge, 1971), 104; See Richard Wasserstrom, "A Defense of Programs of Preferential Treatment," *National Forum* (Phi Kappa Phi Journal), Vol. 58 (1978). See also Bernard Boxill, "The Morality of Preferential Hiring," *Philosophy and Public Affairs*, Vol. 7 (1978).

6   Michael Kinsley, "Equal Lack of Opportunity," *Harper's*, June issue (1983).

7   There is one other argument which I have omitted. It is one from precedence and has been stated by Judith Jarvis Thomson in the article cited earlier:

Suppose two candidates for a civil service job have equally good test scores, but there is only one job available. We could decide between them by coin-tossing. But in fact we do allow for declaring for *A* straightaway, where *A* is a veteran, and *B* is not. It may be that *B* is a non-veteran through no fault of his own.... Yet the fact is that *B* is not a veteran and *A* is. On the assumption that the veteran has served his country, the country owes him something. And it is plain that giving him preference is not an unjust way in which part of that debt of gratitude can be paid. (379f)

The two forms of preferential hiring are analogous. Veteran's preference is justified as a way of paying a debt of gratitude; preferential hiring is a way of paying a debt of compensation. In both cases innocent parties bear the burden of the community's debt, but it is justified.

My response to this argument is that veterans should not be hired in place of better qualified candidates, but that benefits like the GI scholarships are part of the contract with veterans who serve their country in the armed services. The notion of compensation only applies to individuals who have been injured by identifiable entities. So the analogy between veterans and minority groups seems weak.

8 Quoted in Jim Sleeper, *The Closest of Strangers* (New York, 1990), 209.

9 Shelby Steele, "A Negative Vote on Affirmative Action," *New York Times*, May 13, 1990 issue.

10 *New York Times*, May 10, 1990 issue.

11 Nicholas Capaldi, op. cit., 85.

12 Cited in Capaldi, op. cit., 95.

13 *Ibid.*

14 The extreme form of this New Speak is incarnate in the Politically Correct Movement ("PC" ideology) where a new orthodoxy has emerged, condemning white, European culture and seeing African culture as the new savior of us all. Perhaps the clearest example of this is Paula Rothenberg's book *Racism and Sexism* (New York, 1987) which asserts that there is no such thing as black racism; only whites are capable of racism (6). Ms. Rothenberg's book has been scheduled as required reading for all freshmen at the University of Texas. See Joseph Salemi, "Lone Star Academic Politics," No. 87 (1990).

15 Thomas Sowell, op. cit., 108.

16 I am indebted to Jim Landesman, Michael Levin, and Abigail Rosenthal for comments on a previous draft of this paper. I am also indebted to Nicholas Capaldi's *Out of Order* for first making me aware of the extent of the problem of Affirmative Action.

—60—

GENDER MATTERS,
SO DO RACE AND CLASS

Experiences of Gendered Racism on the Wal-Mart Shop Floor

Sandra E. Wessinger

IN THIS CASE STUDY, INEQUITABLE ACCESS TO power found within one particular institution, Wal-Mart stores, is examined. As the largest corporation in the world—with revenues larger than those accumulated by Switzerland and outselling Target, Home Depot, Sears, Kmart, Safeway, and Kroger combined—the company is quite powerful both in the United States and abroad. In the US, 1.3 million are employed within the four thousand stores across the nation. Because the lives of so many converge there, Wal-Mart has the potential to mirror many of the oppressive practices observed in social relationships outside of the stores. For this reason, the statements given by Wal-Mart employees are telling of the robust and adaptive nature of discriminatory practices, regardless of geographic location. Within Wal-Mart, the multidimensional nature of inequality can be illuminated as gender, race, and class intersect and shape the experiences of the women that work at these stores.

CASE BACKGROUND

In 2004, 1.6 million plaintiffs were granted class action status, making theirs the largest sex discrimination case seen in US courts. The suit, *Dukes v. Wal-Mart Stores Inc.*, began when current and former female Wal-Mart employees from across the United States claimed that the retailer discriminated against them in terms of access to promotions, wages similar to their male colleagues, and their job tasks. Individual employees examined their personal issues and developed a sociological imagination (Mills 2000 [1959])—the ability to see that the treatment they were subject to was shared, at least in part, by those with similar biographical characteristics. For example, when her supervisor referred to her as a "Mexican princess" in front of her peers, Gina Espinoza-Price (a plaintiff) was humiliated. She also realized that others were being treated in a similar unprofessional fashion.

Wal-Mart's defense lawyers posed several challenges to the plaintiffs; the most important was whether their case qualified as a class action suit. If the case had not qualified, plaintiffs would have had to file individual suits against the corporation. At best, this could produce rulings that benefited an individual plaintiff but failed to bring about large-scale changes to Wal-Mart's employment and promotions procedures that would benefit all employees. This suit is the impetus behind changes in Wal-Mart's human resources departments nationwide. All employees can now view and apply for all positions. They are also given the opportunity to officially declare their career goals in their computerized personnel file.

The plaintiff for whom the case is named, Betty Dukes, is still employed at Wal-Mart. Dukes has stated that her motivation to continue speaking about employment practices at Wal-Mart comes from her religious background as a Christian minister. According to Dukes, "I am participating in this case in order to insure that young women such as my nieces and other women are treated fairly at every Wal-Mart store. The time has surely come for equality for women" (Rosen 2004). Dukes's statement is unique in that she sees her actions today as connected to the lives of others who will come after her. Although the other plaintiffs did not specifically list similar motivations, all of the plaintiffs made claims concerning inequality. These claims have been bolstered by the statistical findings of Drogin (2003), who found that across geographic locations, women working for Wal-Mart earn less than male employees who occupy the same positions. In addition, Drogin found that women were promoted into management positions at lower and slower rates than male employees.

The Dukes suit rightly identifies the effects of sex-based discrimination that are generalizable across women's experiences within Wal-Mart stores. To provide another vantage point from which to understand the effects of the discrimination experienced by these employees (and perhaps those at corporations that seek to model their businesses after Wal-Mart), I contend that discrimination due to biological sex differences alone does not explain the range of the plaintiffs' experiences or properly gauge individual and social damages caused when one must navigate treacherous environments on a daily basis. Rather, I argue, those individuals who are targeted for mistreatment experience such treatment as equally raced, classed, and gendered people whose lives exist within a web of intersecting and relational inequalities. Therefore, a reexamination of what plaintiffs of the class action suit said about their employment experiences (when guided by a gender primacy framework) is necessary so that the multiple and differing daily work experiences of the plaintiffs can be illuminated, adding to sociological knowledge concerning the work lives of women across standpoints. Reexamination is needed not simply to see difference in lives, but to reveal the persistence of inequality and the multiple ways discriminatory work atmospheres are maintained....

METHODOLOGY

Theoretically, I adhere to the argument that biography matters in terms of understanding the experiences articulated by participants. Marshall (2003) speaks about how people develop frames to understand the world, in part due to their biography. Mills (2000 [1959]) argues that biography matters in shaping the development of individuals' sociological imaginations. To that end, I implement an intersectional methodological framework when analyzing data. By doing so I seek to first highlight difference in terms of biography, locating multiple characteristics of speakers. In this work I identify six biographical characteristics most plaintiffs mentioned in their declarations: gender, race, class, family makeup, geographic location, and age. To be clear, I do not argue that one area of oppression or facet of one's biography is more important than another. My argument is not one that posits that there is a monolithic or authentic experience either. Certainly, lived experiences can be similar and should be juxtaposed against one another for analysis. Rather, I argue that each employee had rich and unique work experiences resulting from the intersecting characteristics that make up their biographies. I focus on how the intersections of race, class, and gender shape each plaintiff's experience mainly because these characteristics were available in 13 of the plaintiffs' statements. After noting differences in biography, I examined the statements for similarities and relationships across class and race, concluding that different work experiences can be attributed to the intersection of biography, location, and time period. Past studies have failed to examine women's work experiences outside of the gender lens. Questioning how the multiple features of each plaintiff's biography influence and shape the stories they tell about work life at Wal-Mart is at the heart of this work.

One hundred ten declarations have been made available by the plaintiffs' team of lawyers. Although gender is highlighted in every statement and class is noted in the majority of declarations, most plaintiffs do not make mention of their race. This serves as a research limitation. Because most plaintiffs failed to mention race, the sample size was reduced from 110 to 13. Of the 13 who mentioned race, 11 were people of color. Even when the plaintiffs wanted to see themselves as equal coworkers whose race, gender, and class were inconsequential, those they had contact with at the stores would not let them forget that they were raced, classed, and gendered individuals, as observed in their retelling of work events. That is, much of the harassment these women were subject to occurred because of their obvious differences when compared to their assailants.

In the 110 statements, only two people identified as white. This shows how race (including whiteness), gender, and class shaped their everyday lives on the Wal-Mart shop floor through the retelling of "insider" or "backstage" comments by white male supervisors (Picca and Feagin 2007). As noted earlier, the majority of declarations did not mention the race of the plaintiff unless the individual was a person of color. This omission highlights how certain racial groups are forced to identify, or show themselves as different when compared against those seen as the norm. This is a function of race based, in this case white, privilege. Eight of those who identified as women of color clearly stated their race at the beginning of their declarations. When describing the Wal-Mart culture and their experiences while on the job, three noted specific instances when coworkers and superiors, often by way of a joke or as an explanation for their slow promotion, acknowledged their race.

Plaintiffs whose declarations were examined for this essay mentioned race and gender in their statements. This subsample was chosen so experiences could be compared across race, class, and gender. The vast majority of the declarations described in detail the job duties of the plaintiffs; therefore, I use job position as a proxy for class and

am able to compare statements across these three areas of difference.

FINDINGS

Insider Outsider Statuses

Very few white plaintiffs mentioned their race but when they did, it was in relation to the race of others. These statements were made when the plaintiff reflected on "backstage" (Picca and Feagin 2007), private conversations they engaged in with white male supervisors. The failure of white women plaintiffs to mention race, except when noting the difference between themselves and people of color, illustrates that "whiteness is unmarked because of the pervasive nature of white domination" (Blee 2002:56). To illuminate this argument, the following excerpts show how two white women who held positions of authority at Wal-Mart stores addressed race.

The first quote is from Ms. Lorie Williams, the youngest declarant in this sample (twenty-six years old) and a single mother who supports her child as a "Front End Manager," the lowest ranking management position in the occupational hierarchy at the stores.

In 1996, I became the front-end manager. With no training, I was single-handedly responsible for hiring door greeters, cart pushers, over sixty new cashiers, and preparing the entire front end in order to transition the Collierville Wal-Mart into a Supercenter. Almost immediately, Co-Manager Doug Ayerst and new Store Manager Robert Hayes (he replaced Wes Grab in 1996) began criticizing the way in which I was managing the front end. They repeatedly complained to me about problems in the front end but did not give me any practical management advice and often gave inconsistent instructions. Store Manager Hayes once told me that the problem was that there were "too many damn women in the front end." On another occasion, Store Manager Hayes and

Co-Manager Jim Belcoff pulled me aside to tell me that I needed to "whiten up [the staff of] the front end." Both of these statements seemed to indicate that they wanted me to stop hiring women and African-American cashiers. When I asked why, they indicated that the staff was "intimidating" to the clientele. I tried to explain that I did not believe this was true and that I was hiring the individuals whom I believed were the most qualified applicants. They were unresponsive.

Here, plaintiff Lorie Williams comments on the lack of support and job training she received. She argues that this occurred because of her gender. In reflecting about her experiences with two white male supervisors, she notes how their comments were not helpful as "practical management advice." In addition to the lack of support she received, her statement highlights shared backstage information she had access to because of her job position (class), race (white), and gender (female). The white male supervisors felt comfortable chastising Lorie Williams' hiring decisions, telling her that the problems she experienced were not due to poor training, but because she was a poor manager and worker, like the white women she hired. She was also chastised for hiring people of color because these workers "intimidated" clients. In these statements, these men played on stereotypes held by society concerning aspects of Lorie Williams' biography as well as stereotypes concerning the "intimidating" nature of people of color. They questioned her competence due to her gender and spoke to her, backstage, about the "others" she hired as help. In addition, they failed to include her in important networking and training activities that would have helped her manage her department better.

In the second example, the words of Melissa Howard, a 35 year-old white woman who had risen to the rank of Store Manager while raising her biracial child in the Midwest, are examined.

In July 1997, I was promoted to the position of Store Manager in Marysville, Kansas. I drove with my daughter's father, who is African-American, to find a place to live there. When we arrived in town, we were treated hostilely by a clerk in the local Wal-Mart store, the town realtor, and by a number of prospective landlords because we were a mixed-race family. At the last rental we visited, the landlord told us that my daughter was not safe and that we needed to be out of town by dark. I knew then that I could not move my family to this place. I called the Regional Personnel Manager Gary Coward, explained what had happened and asked to be placed as a store manager anywhere else. He refused and told me that I would have to go to Marysville as planned or accept a demotion and return as an assistant manager to the 86th Store in Indianapolis, one of the worst stores in the area. I took the demotion.... This was particularly humiliating because my employees in Plainfield had just thrown me a big going-away party to celebrate my promotion.

Melissa Howard was chastised by a male supervisor not just because of her gender, but because she broke a racialized stereotype of white women's chasteness. By breaking this stereotype, her colleagues and supervisors saw her as a lower class white. As a result of this construction, the unequal ways individuals have access to power are produced and upheld. As a white woman in an interracial relationship, Melissa Howard was punished and seen as an outsider by the white people with whom she interacted. It was as though she created the problems she and her family experienced in Kansas.

In both examples, these white women were treated as incompetent and at fault for the problems they experienced. In turn, this affected their work. In these examples it is clear that while these women faced oppression due to their gender, rules and relationships to power are established for individuals based on the multiple, and differently valued, statuses they hold. Melissa Howard seemingly rose above the occupational glass ceiling noted by many plaintiffs. However, her failure to adhere to dating rules held by those with power, including landlords, realtor, and the Wal-Mart Regional Manager, created experiences of discrimination. As an insider due to her race, but a subordinate due to gender and class, Lorie Williams was able to attain a lower-level management position, but was chastised and belittled because she hired men of color and women.

These stories illustrate the lived experiences of white women who work at Wal-Mart. To succeed, they were socialized to accept and replicate discrimination against people of color. Similarly, workers are trained to follow rules of "respectability" concerning their actions. Insiders like Lorie Williams who hold beliefs that make them outsiders, need support so they will continue to believe that the long-term benefits of their actions will outweigh the short-term punishments they endure for failing to replicate discriminatory practices.

The Continuing Significance of Race

Although all women of color mentioned race in their declarations, some only did so when describing a work event that reminded them of the significance of race to how others viewed them. For example, Theresa Collier, received a master's degree in public administration and was honorably discharged from the United States Navy after running a successful pediatric trauma unit. She began to work as an Assistant Manager for Wal-Mart to be close to an ailing family member. The following excerpt describes one of many incidents that motivated her to seek employment elsewhere.

> Prior to beginning at the Geneva store, I had been scheduled to attend a leadership training school. Once in Geneva, Mr. Lawrence did not think I should attend, but District Manager Hart intervened and advocated on my behalf. After that, I was touring the store with Mr. Lawrence, and—in a tone of disgust—he told me that as a "black" and as

a "woman," I would go far with Wal-Mart. I knew from his tone of voice that he would never give me a fair chance to succeed.

Theresa Collier understood that her opportunities for additional training would be limited under the supervision of her direct supervisor due to his belief that she should not engage in leadership training. Her fears were confirmed in later discussions when he described how he viewed her. She would go far not because she was motivated or talented or because she was highly educated or disciplined, but only because of the features of her biography observable to others: race, gender, and though unspoken, class. Regardless of what Theresa Collier could offer the company, a man with authority used his energy to deter and deflect her potential rather than nurture it.

In the following statement, it is clear subordinates also draw on racial and gendered privileges to gain power, even in instances in which they occupy lower class positions. In her statement, Ms. Jennifer Johnson, a Black woman with a community college degree, describes her interpersonal relationships with store staff.

> In 1991, Mr. Pshek was promoted to District Manager in a different district. He told me that if I was willing to relocate to a store in his district, that he would promote me to Assistant Manager, a position that I had sought for some time. I agreed, although I knew that Scott Schwalback, Mark Melatesta, and a male named Rick had been promoted to Assistant Manager without having to switch districts. I was transferred to the Eustis, Florida store as an hourly employee. I worked in that store as a Department Manager for approximately five months without receiving the promotion to Assistant Manager that Mr. Pshek had promised. Finally, I spoke with Bob Hart, Regional Vice President, about the situation, and he told me I had to wait another three to fourth months to be promoted to Assistant Manager. I was

finally promoted in February 1992. Both Scott Schwalback and Rick (a Department Manager in Furniture) became Department Managers after I had, since I had worked for Wal-Mart for longer, but they were both promoted to Assistant Manager positions before I was. Thus, I worked much longer as a Department Manager before being promoted to Assistant Manager than similarly qualified men had. Shortly after I was promoted to Co-Manager, one of the male Assistant Managers who reported to me was disrespectful and avoided doing work I assigned him. I spoke to my Store Manager Kevin Robinson about it. He told me that the man was upset that I had been promoted instead of him, and said "you have two strikes against you: 1) you're a woman; 2) you're black."

Jennifer Johnson described the years of obstacles she navigated to gain promotions. Even with her experience and dedication, others reduced her accomplishments and used them to treat her with disdain. For her and other women of color, working in these stores means that they must not only do their jobs well, but they must also navigate a workplace where others use them as scapegoats for their own frustrations, block them from training opportunities, or sabotage them by not doing work these women of color assign them. In addition, those with the power to chastise offenders and influence workplace discussions of inequality did nothing. Therefore, women of color had to find their own ways to overcome inequality.

The above examples illustrate blatant, hostile racism. But racism is not always aggressively expressed. Feagin (1991) argues after a lifetime of experiencing discrimination, people of color develop a special lens through which to recognize even subtle discrimination. For example, joking can be a subtle medium through which people of color experience belittlement and struggles for dominance. Ms. Gina Espinoza-Price, an energetic, innovative woman, worked her way up to become the District Manager of Mexico. She provided an example of how a white man used joking to force others to acknowledge the labels he created for them and to show dominance. Because he knew he would not face a penalty for his actions, he was able to set a behavioral example for other men under his supervision.

Male Photo Division Management behaved in ways that demeaned and belittled women and minorities. In fall 1996, there was a Photo District Manager meeting in Valencia, California. Wal-Mart had just hired a second female Photo District Manager for the western region, Linda Palmer. During dinner, Jeff Gwartney introduced all of the District Managers to Ms. Palmer using nicknames for the minorities and women. I was introduced as Gina, "the little Mexican princess." I was very offended by Mr. Gwartney's comment and left the dinner early. Throughout the meeting, men made sexual statements and jokes that I thought were very offensive. For example, a flyer with an offensive joke about women being stupid was left on my belongings. In February 1997, during an evaluation, I complained to One-hour Photo Divisional Manager Joe Lisuzzo about harassment based on gender at the previous Photo District Manager meeting. He replied that he would take care of it. I knew from trainings on Wal-Mart's sex harassment policy given by Wal-Mart Legal Department employee Canetta Ivy that company policy mandates that when someone complains of sexual harassment, an investigation must begin within twenty-four hours. Therefore, I expected to be interviewed as a part of an investigation. I was never called. A couple of weeks later, in March 1997, I saw Mr. Lisuzzo at a meeting. I asked him if he had been conducting an investigation of my sexual harassment complaint. He replied that it was being taken care of. I was never aware of any action taken in response to my complaint. Six weeks after complaining about sexual harassment, I was terminated.

Gina Espinoza-Price's statement highlights blatant examples of racism and sexism as well as subtle, institutional examples of discrimination as carried out by individuals who occupied similar class positions, but different status levels. Mr. Lisuzzo's handling of the sexual harassment claim filed by the plaintiff is an example of how the concerns of people are ignored, requiring victims of harassment and discrimination to waste emotional energy rationalizing their own reactions and creating coping tactics to help them interact with hostile colleagues. In addition, it shows how racist joking is often coupled with class and gender. In this case, Mr. Gwartney created an environment of fear for the subordinates at the dinner table. These individuals did not correct him for fear of creating an even more uncomfortable atmosphere. His actions clearly indicate how white male dominance is rewarded by Wal-Mart, as Mr. Gwartney held a high occupational position in which racism, sexism, classism, and elitism could be reproduced. This excerpt further shows that people of color and white women who have risen to high ranks within Wal-Mart and earn middle class salaries are guaranteed neither fair treatment nor respect based on their work records. Rather, discrimination is found at all levels within the job hierarchy at these stores.

Class Matters

In this section I highlight the sex discrimination experienced by women based on their class level. Just as some women enjoy privilege and opportunities based on their race, class also shapes their experiences and actions. The following excerpts demonstrate the difficulties and frustrations of women of color who are single mothers trying to support their families with Wal-Mart wages.

The first story is from Ms. Mary Crawford, a mother living in South Carolina.

In approximately 1995, a female cashier at the York store told me that Store Manager John Locklear was sexually harassing her. As an Assistant Manager, I understood that I was required to take action on her complaint. I informed District Manager Michael Gillespie of the Cashier's complaint. I did this with some hesitation, as I had observed that District Manager Gillespie was a personal friend of Mr. Locklear. After another female employee also lodged a sexual harassment complaint against Mr. Locklear, Mr. Locklear was demoted and transferred out of the York store. After Mr. Locklear was demoted, Mr. Gillespie began to harass and intimidate me on the job. It felt as though he was blaming me for Mr. Locklear's demotion. Although I had always received good evaluations and had no coaching as an Assistant Manager, Mr. Gillespie began to criticize my performance and blame me for errors in departments that were not my responsibility as Assistant Manager. I used the Open Door to discuss this with Mr. Gillespie, and let him know that his treatment of me was unfair and unjustified. Mr. Gillespie responded, "What are you going to do about it?" I took his comment to mean that he was going to continue harassing me in retaliation for reporting Mr. Locklear's behavior, and I felt that there was, in fact, not much I could do about Mr. Gillespie's treatment of me. I had already seen how male managers supported one another. In the face of Mr. Gillespie's direct threat to retaliate against me if I used the Open Door regarding Mr. Gillespie's behavior, I decided that I would probably lose my job if I used the Open Door again. Shortly after this conversation, I reluctantly requested and received a demotion to Department Manager. At the time I was separated from my husband and raising my children on one paycheck. I could not afford to lose my job.

Although Mary Crawford was only trying to do her job, her supervisor bullied her. She felt that taking a demotion was the best survival tactic in a hostile work environment if she was to continue to support her children. The white male manager responsible for this intimidation leveraged his power to reinstate a job ceiling over Mary Crawford, blocking her ability to gain greater access to the upper echelons of career options with the retailer—jobs filled at the time by mostly white men (a claim supported by Drogin 2003).

Ms. Uma Jean Minor, a single mother living in Alabama, also described the need to remain gainfully employed.

> As a single mother, I could not support my family on this wage [paid by Wal-Mart] and was forced to take a second, full-time day job at Food Fair. At the time, I planned to work this second job only until I was able to move to a higher paying position at Wal-Mart. I had no idea that it would take me another seven years to obtain a management position at Wal-Mart and that I would be working two full-time jobs for this entire period.

In this example, Uma Jean Minor notes that her Wal-Mart wages were not sufficient to lift her out of poverty, an argument echoed by living wage supporters throughout the United States (see McCarthy and Ciokajlo 2006; Talbott and Dolby 2003; Warren 2005). Though she shows a tremendous amount of will power, motivation, and agency, her actions would not be sustainable for most women in her position as a single mother of five. Missing from her declaration are the stories of fear, if not hardship, she lived through raising five children and working two full time jobs. In addition, we do not know if she had a network of kin or fictive kin on which she could rely. Therefore, we can only guess at the psychological and material effects discrimination had on her and her children.

Clearly, the effects of sex-based discrimination at Wal-Mart shape the lives of women and their families in different and important ways. For Uma Jean Minor, sex-based discrimination meant she could not reach her highest potential and she needed another full time job that kept her from her family for seven years. Uma Jean Minor's children, who were in their formative years at the time, had less interaction and possibly fewer chances to learn tactics or ways to move in the world from their mother. Thus these children were placed at greater risk of experiencing a range of society's harsh realities early in their lives.

For female heads of household whose families depend on their earnings, the wages, difficult decisions about how to navigate work, and workplace stress factor into whether it is worthwhile to work for poverty wages. Studies like that of Edin and Lein (1997) have demonstrated that the benefits lost by taking a low wage job are detrimental to these women's children, who lose state funded health care, housing assistance, and food support. For women like the defendants, work provides another burden; because they need these jobs, they must sometimes sacrifice their dignity and morals in the face of oppressive supervisors (like Mary Crawford) and glass ceilings (like Uma Jean Minor) for the sake of their children.

DISCUSSION AND CONCLUSION

The findings demonstrate how biographical characteristics provided certain women with insider knowledge and many more with penalties for attempting to challenge widely accepted patterns of behavior and caste-like occupational opportunities within Wal-Mart stores. In every example, instances of multidimensional discrimination are observable. Melissa Howard was treated as a woman who could pass for white. I use the word "pass" to highlight how other whites in her statement reclassified her once they realized she was partnered with a person of color. She might have served as an extraordinary store manager who mentored young, innovative potential store leaders through her example. This did not come to pass because whites who worked with her actively reinforced a barrier, thereby redirecting her career path. In this case we see Melissa Howard's wasted energy as she defended herself and her family; on the part of the people in Marysville as they plotted to harm the Howard family; and on the part of the regional manager who disempowered Melissa Howard instead of helping her navigate the discrimination she faced. Melissa Howard's potential was stunted, as was the potential of the employees at the Maryville store that might have benefited from the unique frame and experiences Melissa Howard had.

Women, regardless of race, who chose to live their lives in ways that differed from what powerful socialization agents felt was acceptable were subject to marginalization. The store manager and co-manager invested a significant amount of time communicating with each other and Lorie Williams about their vision to further disempower "women and African-Americans" who sought cashier positions at the Collierville Wal-Mart. In addition to their discriminatory actions, the supervisors wasted opportunities to train Lorie Williams, giving her "inconsistent instructions." If they treated Lorie Williams this way, it is fair to assume that they treated those without management status in similar if not worse ways. In effect, they maintained the gap between the elite and marginal lower status people by looking for ways to "whiten up the front end." The social frames from which people with power view the world shapes what opportunities are available and how individuals are tracked into positions based on biography and stereotypes rather than on their talent and potential.

The Geneva store manager did his best to exclude Theresa Collier from additional job training. He took the time to argue with his supervisor about curtailing Theresa Collier's opportunities and, therefore, to limit her potential. Upon failing, he let the plaintiff know that he would continue to monitor her work, making Theresa Collier exert emotional energy wondering how she would navigate work life when her boss had made it clear that he would not give her a fair chance to succeed. Like Theresa Collier, Gina Espinoza-Price was forced to spend time negotiating her place as the subordinate to a racist supervisor. She spent energy filing a claim with the legal department of the company, time she could have spent creating new manuals or innovative ways to operate the Photo Department—activities for which she had received multiple accolades during her tenure at

Wal-Mart (see the declaration for Gina Espinoza-Price at www.walmartclass.com). These examples illustrate the intersectional nature of how women experience discrimination. Marginalization occurs regardless of one's educational attainment and class position and because of these statuses.

These plaintiffs did not experience the waste of their talent, energy, and potential in the same way. Rather, it can be observed that the Dukes case is a collection of varying vignettes through which social scientists can observe how some women have more access to power and resources, leaving others to struggle because of their marginalized positions in the power hierarchy. To be clear, although some of the women at Wal-Mart have suffered because of sexism, gender abuse takes multiple forms allowing certain women privilege (even in their oppression) because power is not distributed equally.

If the experiences of the thirteen women in this study are representative of the other 1.6 million Wal-Mart workers, it is important for scholars to investigate the following questions: What is the difference between declarants and other women who work for Wal-Mart who are not involved in the lawsuit? How do men working for the retailer experience work life across race and class? How are workers' collectives that challenge the employment practices of Wal-Mart addressing the multiple ways employees experience oppression?

Overall, I discovered that the women's experiences and tactics for navigating discrimination were quite different. The effort each put forward came at a cost to the women, their families, and the work communities of which they are a part. Even when given positions of authority, plaintiffs were often stymied by those who, in the short term, felt they could gain more power from the marginalization of these plaintiffs.

REFERENCES

Blee, Kathleen M. 2002. *Inside Organized Racism: Women in the Hate Movement.* Berkeley: University of California Press.

Drogin, Richard. 2003. *Statistical Analysis of Gender Patterns in Wal-Mart Workforce*. Retrieved from www.walmartclass.com on 22 Sept 2008.

Edin, Kathryn and Lein, Laura. 1997. *Making Ends Meet: How Single Mothers Survive Welfare and Low-Wage Work*. New York: Russell Sage Foundation.

Feagin, Joe R. 1991. "The Continuing Significance of Race: Antiblack Discrimination in Public Places." *American Sociological Review* 56 (1): 101–116.

Marshall, Anna-Maria. 2003. "Injustice Frames, Legality, and the Everyday Construction of Sexual Harassment." *Law & Social Inquiry* 28 (3): 659–689.

Mills, C. Wright. 2000 [1959]. *The Sociological Imagination*. Oxford: Oxford University Press.

Picca, Leslie Houts and Feagin, Joe R. 2007. *Two-Faced Racism: Whites in the Backstage and Frontstage*. New York: Routledge.

Rosen, Ruth. 2004. *Big-Box Battle: A Review of Selling Women Short: The Landmark Battle for Workers' Rights at Wal-Mart*, by Liza Featherstone. Retrieved from http://www.longviewinstitute.org/research/rosen/walmart/sellingwomenshort on 14 October 2008.

—61—
A FEMINIST DEFINITION OF SEXUAL HARASSMENT

Anita M. Superson

1. INTRODUCTION

BY FAR THE MOST PERVASIVE FORM OF DISCRIMI-nation against women is sexual harassment (SH). Women in every walk of life are subject to it, and I would venture to say, on a daily basis.[1] Even though the law is changing to the benefit of victims of SH, the fact that SH is still so pervasive shows that there is too much tolerance of it, and that victims do not have sufficient legal recourse to be protected.

The main source for this problem is that the way SH is defined by various Titles and other sources does not adequately reflect the social nature of SH, or the harm it causes all women. As a result, SH comes to be defined in subjective ways. One upshot is that when subjective definitions infuse the case law on SH, the more subtle but equally harmful forms of SH do not get counted as SH and thus not afforded legal protection.

My primary aim in this paper is to offer an objective definition of SH that accounts for the group harm all forms of SH have in common. Though my aim is to offer a moral definition of SH, I offer it in hopes that it will effect changes in the law. It is only by defining SH in a way that covers all of its forms and gets at the heart of the problem that legal protection can be given to all victims in all circumstances.

I take this paper to be programmatic. Obviously problems may exist in applying the definition to cases that arise for litigation. In a larger project a lot more could be said to meet those objections. My goal in this paper is merely to defend my definition against the definitions currently appealed to by the courts in order to show how it is more promising for victims of SH. I define SH in the following way:

> Any behavior (verbal or physical) caused by a person, A, in the dominant class directed at another, B, in the subjugated class, that expresses and perpetuates the attitude that B or members of B's sex is/are inferior because of their sex, thereby causing harm to either B and/or members of B's sex.

II. CURRENT LAW ON SEXUAL HARASSMENT

Currently, victims of SH have legal recourse under Title VII of the Civil Rights Act of 1964, Title IX of the 1972 Education Amendments, and tort law.

The Civil Rights Act of 1964 states:

a) It shall be an unlawful employment practice for an employer—

(1) to fail or refuse to hire or to discharge any individual; or otherwise to discriminate against any individual with respect to his

compensation, terms, conditions, or privileges of employment because of such individual's race, color, religion, sex, or national origin....[2]

Over time the courts came to view SH as a form of sex discrimination. The main advocate for this was Catharine MacKinnon, whose book, *Sexual Harassment of Working Women*,[3] greatly influenced court decisions on the issue. Before it was federally legislated, some courts appealed to the Equal Employment Opportunity Commission (EEOC) *Guidelines on Discrimination Because of Sex* to establish that SH was a form of sex discrimination. The *Guidelines* (amended in 1980 to include SH) state that

> Harassment on the basis of sex is a violation of Sec. 703 of Title VII. Unwelcome sexual advances, requests for sexual favors, and other verbal or physical conduct of a sexual nature constitute sexual harassment when (1) submission to such conduct is made either explicitly or implicitly a term or condition of an individual's employment, (2) submission to or rejection of such conduct by an individual is used as the basis for employment decisions affecting such individual, or (3) such conduct has the purpose or effect of unreasonably interfering with an individual's work performance or creating an intimidating, hostile, or offensive working environment.[4]

In a landmark case,[5] *Meritor Savings Bank, FSB v. Vinson* (1986),[6] the Supreme Court, relying on the EEOC *Guidelines*, established that SH was a form of sex discrimination prohibited under Title VII. The case involved Mechelle Vinson, a teller-trainee, who was propositioned by Sidney Taylor, vice president and branch manager of the bank. After initially refusing, she agreed out of fear of losing her job. She allegedly had sexual relations with Taylor 40 or 50 times over a period of four years, and he even forcibly raped her several times, exposed himself to her in a restroom, and fondled her in public.[7]

Sexual harassment extends beyond the workplace. To protect students who are not employees of their learning institution, Congress enacted Title IX of the Education Amendments of 1972, which states:

> No person in the United States shall, on the basis of sex, be excluded from participation in, be denied the benefits of, or be subjected to discrimination under any educational program or activity receiving federal financial assistance.[8]

Cases of litigation under Title IX have been influenced by Meritor so that SH in educational institutions is construed as a form of sex discrimination.

The principles that came about under Title VII apply equally to Title IX. Under either Title, a person can file two different kinds of harassment charges: *quid pro quo*, or hostile environment. *Quid pro quo* means "something for something."[9] *Quid pro quo* harassment occurs when "an employer or his agent explicitly ties the terms, conditions, and privileges of the victim's employment to factors which are arbitrary and unrelated to job performance."[10] Plaintiffs must show they "suffered a tangible economic detriment as a result of the harassment."[11] In contrast, hostile environment harassment occurs when the behavior of supervisors or co-workers has the effect of "unreasonably interfering with an individual's work performance or creates an intimidating, hostile, or offensive environment."[12] Hostile environment harassment established that Title VII (and presumably Title IX) were not limited to economic discrimination, but applied to emotional harm, as well. The EEOC *Guidelines* initiated the principle of hostile environment harassment which was used by the courts in many cases, including *Meritor*.

For each kind of SH (*quid pro quo* or hostile environment), courts can use one of two approaches: disparate treatment, or disparate impact. *Black's Law Dictionary* defines disparate treatment as "[d]ifferential treatment of employees or applicants on the basis of their race, color, religion, sex, national origin, handicap, or veteran's status."[13] The key is to establish that the person was harassed because of her sex, and not because of other features (e.g., hair color). Disparate impact, in contrast, "involves facially neutral practices that are not intended to be discriminatory, but are discriminatory in effect."[14] Disparate *impact* came about because the facts did not always show that an employer blatantly discriminated on the basis of sex,[15] but the employer's practices still worked to the disadvantage of certain groups. Allegedly, "[f]or both *quid pro quo* and hostile environment sexual harassment, courts use disparate treatment theory."[16]

For women who are harassed other than in an employment or an educational setting, tort law [A *tort* is a private or civil, as opposed to public, wrong. We thus speak of civil as opposed to criminal offenses in the law.] can offer legal remedy. Also, torts can accompany a claim invoking Title VII (and presumably, Title IX). Criminal suits apply only if the victim of harassment "is a victim of rape, indecent assault, common assault, assault causing bodily harm, threats, intimidation, or solicitation,"[17] and in these cases the suit will usually be for one of these charges, not harassment. To be taken seriously, the action requires police charges, a difficulty in SH cases.

Civil torts are a more promising way to go for victims of SH, though with limitations. The battery tort prohibits battery which is defined as "an intentional and unpermitted contact, other than that permitted by social usage."[18] The intent refers to intent to contact, not intent to cause the harm that may result from the contact. The assault tort prohibits assault, which is defined as "an intentional act, short of contact, which produces *apprehension* of battery."[19] The defendant must have intended to arouse psychic apprehension in his victim.[20] Victims can also appeal to the tort of intentional infliction of emotional distress. According to Section 46 of the *Restatement of Torts*,

Liability has been found only where the conduct has been so outrageous in character, and so extreme in degree, as to go beyond all possible bounds of decency, and to be regarded as atrocious, and utterly intolerable in a civilized community. Generally, the case is one in which the recitation of the facts to an average member of the community would arouse his resentment against the actor, and lead him to exclaim, "Outrageous."[21]

"[M]ere insults, indignities, threats, annoyances, petty oppression, or other trivialities" will not result in tort action because a person must be "hardened to a certain amount of rough language."[22] *The Restatement of Torts* invokes the reasonable man standard, claiming that the emotional distress must be "so severe that no reasonable man could be expected to endure it."[23] Moreover, the conduct must be done intentionally or recklessly.

Despite major advances made in the last few decades in the law on SH, I believe the law is still inadequate. The main problem in my view is that the law, reflecting the view held by the general public, fails to see SH for what it is: an attack on the group of *all* women, not just the immediate victim. Because of this, there is a failure to recognize the group harm that all instances of SH, not just the more blatant ones, cause all women. As a result, the law construes SH as a subjective issue, that is, one that is determined by what the victim feels and (sometimes) what the perpetrator intends. As a result, the burden of proof is wrongly shifted to the victim and off the perpetrator with the result that many victims are not legally protected.

For instance, victims filing complaints under Title VII (and presumably Title IX) are not protected unless they have a fairly serious case. They have to show under hostile environment harassment that the behavior unreasonably interfered with their work performance, and that there was a pattern of behavior on the defendant's behalf.

Regarding the latter point, the EEOC *Guidelines* say that:

> In determining whether alleged conduct constitutes sexual harassment, the Commission will look at the record as a whole and at the totality of the circumstances, such as the nature of the sexual advances and the context in which the alleged incidents occurred.[24]

It seems unlikely that the victim of isolated incidents of SH could have her complaint taken seriously under this assessment. Under *quid pro quo* harassment, the victim must show she suffered a tangible economic detriment. Disparate treatment cases might be difficult to show because not *all* members of the victim's class (e.g., the group of all females) are likely to be harassed by the defendant. This makes it unlikely that the victim will be able to show she was harassed because of her sex, and not because of some personal feature she has that others lack. Victims who are harassed outside of the workplace and educational institutions have to rely on tort law to make their case, but under it, defendants have a way out by claiming innocence of intention. Under the tort of intentional infliction of emotional distress, victims must have an extreme case in order to get protection.

Victims not protected include the worker who is harassed by a number of different people, the worker who suffers harassment but in small doses, the person who is subjected to a slew of catcalls on her two mile walk to work, the female professor who is subjected to leering from one of her male students, and the woman who does not complain out of fear. The number of cases is huge, and many of them are quite common....

III. THE SOCIAL NATURE OF SEXUAL HARASSMENT

Sexual harassment, a form of sexism is about domination, in particular, the domination of the group of men over the group of women.[25] Domination involves control or power which can be seen in the economic, political, and social spheres of society. Sexual harassment is not simply an assertion of power, for power can be used in beneficial ways. The power men have over women has been wielded in ways that oppress women. The power expressed in SH is oppression, power used wrongly.

Sexual harassment is integrally related to sex roles. It reveals the belief that a person is to be relegated to certain roles on the basis of her sex including not only women's being sex objects, but also their being caretakers, motherers, nurturers, sympathizers, etc. In general, the sex roles women are relegated to are associated with the body (v. mind) and emotions (v. reason).

When A sexually harasses B, the comment or behavior is really directed at the group of all women, not just a particular woman, a point often missed by the courts. After all, many derogatory behaviors are issued at women the harasser does not even know (e.g., scanning a stranger's body). Even when the harasser knows his victim, the behavior is directed at the particular woman because she happens to be "available" at the time, though its message is for all women. For instance, a catcall says not (merely) that the perpetrator likes a woman's body but that he thinks women are at least primarily sex objects and he—because of the power he holds by being in the dominant group—gets to rate them according to how much pleasure they give him. The professor who refers to his female students as "chicks" makes a statement that women are intellectually inferior to men as they can be likened to non-rational animals, perhaps even soft, cuddly ones that are to serve as the objects of (men's) pleasure. Physicians' using Playboy centerfolds in medical schools to "spice up their lectures" sends the message that women lack the competence to make it in a "man's world" and should perform the "softer tasks" associated with bearing and raising children.[26]

These and other examples make it clear that SH is not about dislike for a certain person; instead, it expresses a person's beliefs about women as a group on the basis of their sex, namely, that they are primarily emotional and bodily beings. Some theorists—Catharine MacKinnon, John Hughes and Larry May—have recognized the social nature of SH. Hughes and May claim that women are a disadvantaged group because

1. they are a social group having a distinct identity and existence apart from their individual identities,
2. they occupy a subordinate position in American society, and
3. their political power is severely circumscribed.[27]

They continue:

> Once it is established that women qualify for special disadvantaged group status, all practices tending to stigmatize women as a group, or which contribute to the maintenance of their subordinate social status, would become legally suspect.[28]

This last point, I believe, should be central to the definition of SH.

Because SH has as its target the group of all women, this *group* suffers harm as a result of the behavior. Indeed, when any one woman is in any way sexually harassed, all women are harmed. The group harm SH causes is different from the harm suffered by particular women as individuals: it is often more vague in nature as it is not easily causally tied to any particular incident of harassment. The group harm has to do primarily with the fact that the behavior reflects and reinforces sexist attitudes that women are inferior to men and that they do and ought to occupy certain sex roles. For example, comments and behavior that relegate women to the role of sex objects reinforce the belief that women *are* sex objects and that they *ought to* occupy this sex role. Similarly, when a female professor's cogent comments at department colloquia are met with frowns and rolled eyes from her colleagues, this behavior reflects and reinforces

the view that women are not fit to occupy positions men arrogate to themselves.

The harm women suffer as a group from any single instance of SH is significant. It takes many forms. A Kantian analysis would show what is wrong with being solely a sex object. Though there is nothing wrong with being a caretaker or nurturer, etc., *per se*, it is sexist—and so wrong—to assign such roles to women. In addition, it is wrong to assign a person to a role she may not want to occupy. Basically women are not allowed to decide for themselves which roles they are to occupy, but this gets decided for them, no matter what they do. Even if some women occupy important positions in society that men traditionally occupy, they are still viewed as being sex objects, caretakers, etc., since all women are thought to be more "bodily" and emotional than men. This is a denial of women's autonomy, and degrading to them. It also contributes to women's oppression. The belief that women must occupy certain sex roles is both a cause and an effect of their oppression. It is a cause because women are believed to be more suited for certain roles given their association with body and emotions. It is an effect because once they occupy these roles and are victims of oppression, the belief that they must occupy these sex roles is reinforced.

Women are harmed by SH in yet another way. The belief that they are sex objects, caretakers, etc., gets reflected in social and political practices in ways that are unfair to women. It has undoubtedly meant many lost opportunities that are readily available to men. Women are not likely to be hired for jobs that require them to act in ways other than the ways the sex roles dictate, and if they are, what is expected of them is different from what is expected of men. Mothers are not paid for their work, and caretakers are not paid well in comparison to jobs traditionally held by men. Lack of economic reward is paralleled by lack of respect and appreciation for those occupying such roles. Certain rights granted men are likely not to be granted women (e.g., the right to bodily self-determination, and marriage rights).

Another harm SH causes all women is that the particular form sex stereotyping takes promotes two myths: (1) that male behavior is normally and naturally predatory, and (2) that females naturally (because they are taken to be primarily bodily and emotional) and even willingly acquiesce despite the appearance of protest.[29] Because the behavior perpetuated by these myths is taken to be normal, it is not seen as sexist, and in turn is not counted as SH.

The first myth is that men have stronger sexual desires than women, and harassment is just a natural venting of these desires which men are unable to control. The truth is, first, that women are socialized *not* to vent their sexual desires in the way men do, but this does not mean these desires are weaker or less prevalent. Masters and Johnson have "decisively established that women's sexual requirements are no less potent or urgent than those of men."[30] But second, SH has nothing to do with men's sexual desires, nor is it about seduction; instead, it is about oppression of women. Indeed, harassment generally does not lead to sexual satisfaction, but it often gives the harasser a sense of power.

The second myth is that women either welcome, ask for, or deserve the harassing treatment. Case law reveals this mistaken belief. In *Lipsett v. Rive-Mora*[31] (1987), the plaintiff was discharged from a medical residency program because she "did not react favorably to her professor's requests to go out for drinks, his compliments about her hair and legs, or to questions about her personal and romantic life."[32] The court exonerated the defendant because the plaintiff initially reacted favorably by smiling when shown lewd drawings of herself and when called sexual nicknames as she thought she had to appease the physician. The court said that "given the plaintiff's admittedly favorable responses to these flattering comments, there was no way anyone could consider them as 'unwelcome.'"[33] The court in *Swentek v. US Air*[34] (1987) reacted similarly when a flight attendant who was harassed with obscene remarks and gestures was denied legal recourse because previously she used vulgar language and openly discussed her sexual encounters. The court concluded that "she was the kind of person who could not be offended by such comments and therefore welcomed them generally."[35]

The idea that women welcome "advances" from men is seen in men's view of the way women dress. If a woman dresses "provocatively" by men's standards, she is said to welcome or even deserve the treatment she gets. One explanation harassing professors give for their behavior is that they are bombarded daily with the temptation of physically desirable young women who dress in what they take to be revealing ways. When the case becomes public, numerous questions arise about the attractiveness of the victim, as if she were to blame for being attractive and the consequences thereof. Catcallers often try to justify their behavior by claiming that the victim should expect such behavior, given her tight-fitting dress or shorts, low-cut top, high heels, etc. This way of thinking infests discussions of rape in attempts to establish that women want to be raped, and it is mistaken in that context, too. The myth that women welcome or encourage harassment is designed "to keep women in their place" as men see it. The truth of the matter is that the perpetrator alone is at fault.

Both myths harm all women as they sanction SH by shifting the burden on the victim and all members of her sex: women must either go out of their way to avoid "natural" male behavior, or establish conclusively that they did not in any way want the behavior. Instead of the behavior being seen as sexist, it is seen as women's problem to rectify.

Last, but certainly not least, women suffer group harm from SH because they come to be stereotyped as victims. Many men see SH as something they can do to women, and in many cases, get away with. Women come to see themselves as victims, and come to believe that the roles they can occupy are only the sex roles men have designated for them. Obviously these harms are quite serious for women, so the elimination of all forms of SH is warranted.

I have spoken so far as if it is only men who can sexually harass women, and I am now in a position to defend this controversial view. When a woman engages in the very same behavior harassing men engage in, the underlying message implicit in male-to-female harassment is missing. For example, when a woman scans a man's body, she might be considering him to be a sex object, but all the views about domination and being relegated to certain sex roles are absent. She cannot remind the man that he is inferior because of his sex, since given the way things are in society, he is not. In general, women cannot harm or degrade or dominate men as a group, for it is impossible to send the message that one dominates (and so cause group harm) if one does not dominate. Of course, if the sexist roles predominant in our society were reversed, women could sexually harass men. The way things are, any bothersome behavior a woman engages in, even though it may be of a sexual nature, does not constitute SH because it lacks the social impact present in male-to-female harassment. Tort law would be sufficient to protect against this behavior, since it is unproblematic in these cases that tort law fails to recognize group harm.

IV. SUBJECTIVE V. OBJECTIVE DEFINITIONS OF SEXUAL HARASSMENT

Most definitions of "sexual harassment" make reference to the behavior's being "unwelcome" or "annoying" to the victim. *Black's Law Dictionary* defines "harassment" as a term used "to describe words, gestures and actions which tend to annoy, alarm and abuse (verbally) another person."[36] The *American Heritage Dictionary* defines "harass" as "to disturb or irritate persistently," and states further that "[h]arass implies systematic persecution by besetting with annoyances, threats, or demands."[37] The EEOC *Guidelines* state that behavior constituting SH is identified as "unwelcome sexual advances, requests for sexual favors, and other verbal or physical conduct of a sexual

nature."[38] In their philosophical account of SH, Hughes and May define "harassment" as "a class of annoying or unwelcome acts undertaken by one person (or group of persons) against another person (or group of persons)."[39] And Rosemarie Tong takes the feminists' definition of noncoercive SH to be that which "denotes sexual misconduct that merely annoys or offends the person to whom it is directed."[40]

The criterion of "unwelcomeness" or "annoyance" is reflected in the way the courts have handled cases of SH, as in *Lipsett*, *Swentek*, and *Meritor*, though in the latter case the court said that the voluntariness of the victim's submission to the defendant's sexual conduct did not mean that she welcomed the conduct. The criterion of unwelcomeness or annoyance present in these subjective accounts of harassment puts the burden on the victim to establish that she was sexually harassed. There is no doubt that many women *are* bothered by this behavior, often with serious side-effects including anything from anger, fear, and guilt, to lowered self-esteem and decreased feelings of competence and confidence, to anxiety disorders, alcohol and drug abuse, coronary disturbances, and gastro-intestinal disorders.

Though it is true that many women are bothered by the behavior at issue, I think it is seriously mistaken to say that whether the victim is bothered determines whether the behavior constitutes SH. This is so for several reasons.

First, we would have to establish that the victim was bothered by it, either by the victim's complaints, or by examining the victim's response to the behavior. The fact of the matter is that many women are quite hesitant to report being harassed, for a number of reasons. Primary among them is that they fear negative consequences from reporting the conduct. As is often the case, harassment comes from a person in a position of institutional power, whether he be a supervisor, a company-president, a member of a dissertation committee, the chair of the department, and so on. Unfortunately for many women, as a review of the case law reveals, their fears are warranted. Women have been fired, their jobs have been made miserable forcing them to quit, professors have handed out unfair low grades, and so on. Worries about such consequences means that complaints are not filed, or are filed years after the incident, as in the *Anita Hill v. Thomas Clarence* case. But this should not be taken to imply that the victim was not harassed.

Moreover, women are hesitant to report harassment because they do not want anything to happen to the perpetrator, but just want the behavior to stop. Women do not complain because they do not want to deal with the perpetrator's reaction when faced with the charge. He might claim that he was "only trying to be friendly." Women are fully aware that perpetrators can often clear themselves quite easily, especially in tort law cases where the perpetrator's intentions are directly relevant to whether he is guilty. And most incidents of SH occur without any witnesses—many perpetrators plan it this way. It then becomes the harasser's word against the victim's. To complicate matters, many women are insecure and doubt themselves. Women's insecurity is capitalized upon by harassers whose behavior is in the least bit ambiguous. Clever harassers who fear they might get caught or be reported often attempt to get on the good side of their victim in order to confuse her about the behavior, as well as to have a defense ready in case a charge is made. Harassers might offer special teaching assignments to their graduate students, special help with exams and publications, promotions, generous raises, and the like. Of course, this is all irrelevant to whether he harasses, but the point is that it makes the victim less likely to complain. On top of all this, women's credibility is very often questioned (unfairly) when they bring forth a charge. They are taken to be "hypersensitive." There is an attitude among judges and others that women must "develop a thick skin."[41] Thus, the blame is shifted off the perpetrator and onto the victim. Given this, if a woman thinks she will get no positive response—or, indeed, will get a negative one—from complaining, she is unlikely to do so.

Further, some women do not recognize harassment for what it is, and so will not complain. Sometimes this is because they are not aware of their own oppression, or actually seem to endorse sexist stereotypes. I recall a young woman who received many catcalls on the streets of Daytona Beach, Florida during spring break, and who was quite proud that her body could draw such attention. Given that women are socialized into believing their bodies are the most important feature of themselves, it is no surprise that a fair number of them are complacent about harassing behavior directed at them. Sandra Bartky provides an interesting analysis of why every woman is not a feminist, and I think it holds even for women who understand the issue.[42] Since for many women having a body felt to be "feminine" is crucial to their identity and to their sense of self "as a sexually desiring and desirable subject," feminism "may well be apprehended by a woman as something that threatens her with desexualization, if not outright annihilation."[43] The many women who resist becoming feminists are not likely to perceive harassing behavior as bothersome. It would be incorrect to conclude that the behavior is not harassment on the grounds that such victims are not bothered. What we have is a no win situation for victims: if the behavior bothers a woman she often has good reason not to complain; and if it does not bother her, she will not complain. Either way, the perpetrator wins. So we cannot judge whether women are bothered by the behavior on the basis of whether they say they are bothered.

Moreover, women's *behavior* is not an accurate indicator of whether they are bothered. More often than not, women try to ignore the perpetrator's behavior in an attempt not to give the impression they are encouraging it. They often cover up their true feelings so that the perpetrator does not have the satisfaction that his harassing worked. Since women are taught to smile and put up with this behavior, they might actually appear to enjoy it to some extent. Often they have no choice but to continue interacting with the perpetrator, making it very difficult to assert themselves. Women often make up excuses for not "giving in" instead of telling the perpetrator to stop. The fact that their behavior does not indicate they are bothered should not be used to show they were not bothered. In reality, women are fearful of defending themselves in the face of men's power and physical strength. Given the fact that the courts have decided that a lot of this behavior should just be tolerated, it is no wonder that women try to make the best of their situation.

It would be wrong to take a woman's behavior to be a sign that she is bothered also because doing so implies the behavior is permissible if she does not seem to care. This allows the *perpetrator* to be the judge of whether a woman is harassed, which is unjustifiable given the confusion among men about whether their behavior is bothersome or flattering. Sexual harassment should be treated no differently than crimes where harm to the victim is assessed in some objective way, independent of the perpetrator's beliefs. To give men this power in the case of harassment is to perpetuate sexism from all angles.

An *objective* view of SH avoids the problems inherent in a subjective view. According to the objective view defended here, what is decisive in determining whether behavior constitutes SH is not whether the victim is bothered, but whether the behavior is an instance of a practice that expresses and perpetuates the attitude that the victim and members of her sex are inferior because of their sex. Thus the Daytona Beach case counts as a case of SH because the behavior is an instance of a practice that reflects men's domination of women in that it relegates women to the role of sex objects.

The courts have to some extent tried to incorporate an objective notion of SH by invoking the "reasonable person" standard. The EEOC *Guidelines*, as shown earlier, define SH partly as behavior that "has the purpose or effect of unreasonably interfering with an individual's work performance...." The *Restatement of Torts*, referring to the tort of intentional infliction of emotional distress, states that the emotional distress must be "so severe that no *reasonable* man could be expected to endure it."[44]

In various cases the courts have invoked a reasonable man (or person) standard, but *not* to show that women who are not bothered still suffer harassment. Instead, they used the standard to show that even though a particular woman *was* bothered, she would have to tolerate such behavior because it was behavior a reasonable person would not have been affected by. In *Rabidue v. Osceola Refining Co.*[45] (1986), a woman complained that a coworker made obscene comments about women in general and her in particular. The court ruled that "a reasonable person would not have been significantly affected be the same or similar circumstances,"[46] and that "women must expect a certain amount of demeaning conduct in certain work environments."[47]

But the reasonable man standard will not work, since men and women perceive situations involving SH quite differently. The reasonable person standard fares no better as it becomes the reasonable man standard when it is applied by male judges seeing things through male eyes. Studies have shown that sexual overtures that men find flattering are found by women to be insulting. And even when men recognize behavior as harassment, they think women will be flattered by it. The differences in perception only strengthen my point about the group harm that SH causes all women: unlike women, men can take sexual overtures directed at them to be complimentary because the overtures do not signify the stereotyping that underlies SH of women. A reasonable man standard would not succeed as a basis upon which to determine SH, as its objectivity is outweighed by the disparity found in the way the sexes assess what is "reasonable."

Related to this last topic is the issue of the harasser's intentions. In subjective definitions this is the counterpart to the victim's being bothered. Tort law makes reference to the injurer's intentions: in battery tort, the harasser's intent to contact, in assault tort, the harasser's intent to arouse psychic apprehension in the victim, and in the tort of intentional emotional distress, the harasser's intent or recklessness, must be established in order for the victim to win her case.

But like the victim's feelings, the harasser's intentions are irrelevant to whether his behavior is harassment. As I just pointed out, many men do not take their behavior to be bothersome, and sometimes even mistakenly believe that women enjoy crude compliments about their bodies, ogling, pinching, etc. From perusing cases brought before the courts, I have come to believe that many men have psychological feelings of power over women, feelings of being in control of their world, and the like, when they harass. These feelings might be subconscious, but this should not be admitted as a defense of the harasser. Also, as I have said, many men believe women encourage SH either by their dress or language, or simply by the fact that they tolerate the abuse without protest (usually out of fear of repercussion). In light of these facts, it would be wrongheaded to allow the harasser's intentions to count in assessing harassment, though they might become relevant in determining punishment. I am arguing for an objective definition of SH: it is the attitudes embedded and reflected *in the practice* the behavior is an instance of, not the attitudes or intentions of *the perpetrator*, that makes the behavior SH.

Yet the idea that the behavior must be directed at a certain person in order for it to count as harassment, seems to suggest that intentions do count in assessing harassment. This feature is evident both in my definition, as well as in that found in *Black's Law Dictionary* which takes harassment to be conduct directed against a specific person causing substantial emotional distress. If conduct is directed at a particular individual, it seems that the person expressing himself must be intentionally singling out that individual, wanting to cause her harm.

I think this is mistaken. Since the harasser can subconsciously enjoy the feeling of power harassing gives him, or might even consider his behavior to be flattering, his behavior can be directed at a specific person (or group of persons)

without implying any ill intention on his part. By "directed at a particular individual," I mean that the behavior is in some way observed by a particular person (or persons). This includes, for example, sexist comments a student hears her professor say, pornographic pictures a worker sees, etc. I interpret it loosely enough to include a person's overhearing sexist comments even though the speaker has no idea the person is within earshot (sometimes referred to as "nondirected behavior"). But I interpret it to exclude the bare knowledge that sexist behavior is going on (e.g., female employees knowing that there are pornographic pictures hidden in their boss's office). If it did not exclude such behavior it would have to include knowledge of *any* sexist behavior, even if no person who can be harmed by it ever observes it (e.g., pornographic magazines strewn on a desert island). Though such behavior is sexist, it fails to constitute SH.

V. IMPLICATIONS OF THE OBJECTIVE DEFINITION

... [An] implication of my definition is that it gives the courts a way of distinguishing SH from sexual attraction. It can be difficult to make this distinction, since "traditional courtship activities" are often quite sexist and frequently involve behavior that is harassment. The key is to examine the practice the behavior is an instance of. If the behavior reflects the attitude that the victim is inferior because of her sex, then it is SH. Sexual harassment is not about a man's attempting to date a woman who is not interested, as the courts have tended to believe; it is about domination, which might be reflected, of course, in the way a man goes about trying to get a date. My definition allows us to separate cases of SH from genuine sexual attraction by forcing the courts to focus on the social nature of SH.

Moreover, defining SH in the objective way I do shifts the burden and the blame off the victim. On the subjective view, the burden is on the victim to prove that she is bothered significantly enough to win a tort case, or under Title VII, to show that the behavior unreasonably interfered with her work. In tort law, where the perpetrator's intentions are allowed to figure in, the blame could easily shift to the victim by showing that she in some way welcomed or even encouraged the behavior thereby relinquishing the perpetrator from responsibility. By focusing on the practice the behavior is an instance of, my definition has nothing to do with proving that the victim responds a certain way to the behavior, nor does it in any way blame the victim for the behavior.

Finally, defining SH in a subjective way means that the victim herself must come forward and complain, as it is her response that must be assessed. But given that most judges, law enforcement officers, and even superiors are men, it is difficult for women to do so. They are embarrassed, afraid to confront someone of the same sex as the harasser who is likely not to see the problem. They do not feel their voices will be heard. Working with my definition will I hope assuage this. Recognizing SH as a group harm will allow women to come to each other's aid as co-complainers, thereby alleviating the problem of reticence. Even if the person the behavior is directed at does not feel bothered, other women can complain, as they suffer the group harm associated with SH.

NOTES

1   Rosemarie Tong, "Sexual Harassment," in *Women and Values*, Marilyn Pearsall, ed. (Belmont, CA: Wadsworth Publishing Company, 1986), 148–66. Tong cites a *Redbook* study that reported 88 per cent of 9,000 readers sampled experienced some sort of sexual harassment (149).

2   Civil Rights Act of 1964, 42 USC Sec. 2000e-2(a) (1982).

3   Catharine A. MacKinnon, *Sexual Harassment of Working Women: A Case of Sex Discrimination* (New Haven: Yale University Press, 1979).

4   EEOC *Guidelines on Discrimination Because of Sex*, 29 C.F.R Sec. 1604.11(a) (1980).

5   The case was a landmark case because it established (1) federal legislation that SH is a form of sex discrimination, (2) that just because the victim "voluntarily" submitted to advances from her employer, it did not mean she welcomed the conduct, (3) that victims could appeal on grounds of emotional harm, not merely economic harm. For an excellent discussion of the history of the case as it went through the courts, see Joel T. Andreesen, "Employment Discrimination—The Expansion in Scope of Title VII to Include Sexual Harassment as a Form of Sex Discrimination," *Meritor Savings Bank, FSB v. Vinson, The Journal of Corporation Law*, Vol. 12, No. 3 (Spring, 1987), 619–38.

6   *Meritor Savings Bank, FSB v. Vinson*, 477 US 57 (1986).

7   Joyce L. Richard, "Sexual Harassment and Employer Liability," *Southern University Law Review*, Vol. 12 (1986), 251–79. See 272–75 for an excellent discussion of the case.

8   Title IX of the Education Amendments of 1972, 20 USC. Sec. 1681 (1982).

9   *Black's Law Dictionary*, 6th ed. (St. Paul, MN: West Publishing Co., 1990), 1248.

10   Michael D. Vhay, "The Harms of Asking: Towards a Comprehensive Treatment of Sexual Harassment," *The University of Chicago Law Review*, Vol. 55 (Winter, 1988), 334. In the case of students, *quid pro quo* harassment can take the form of a professor threatening the student with a lower grade if she does not comply with his demands.

11   Ellen Frankel Paul, "Sexual Harassment as Sex Discrimination: A Defective Paradigm," *Yale Law & Policy Review*, Vol. 8, No. 2 (1990), 341.

12   EEOC *Guidelines, op. cit.*, at Sec. 1604.11(a).

13   *Black's Law Dictionary, op. cit.*, 470. It cites *Rich v. Martin Manetta Corp.*, D.C.Colo., 467 F.Supp. 587, 608.

14   *Topical Law Reports* (New York: Commerce Clearing House, Inc., 1988), 3030.

15   John C. Hughes and Larry May, "Sexual Harassment," *Social Theory and Practice*, Vol. 6, No. 3 (Fall, 1980), 260.

16   Frankel Paul, *op. cit.*, 337.

17   Rosemarie Tong, *Women, Sex, and the Law* (Savage, MD: Rowman and Littlefield Publishers, Inc., 1984), 71.

18 Frank J. Till, *Sexual Harassment: A Report on the Sexual Harassment of Students* (Washington, DC: National Advisory Council on Women's Educational Programs, 1980), pt. II, 13.

19 Ibid., 14.

20 Tong, *Women, Sex, and the Law, op. cit.*, 73.

21 *Restatement (Second) of Torts* Sec.46 (1965) comment a.

22 Ibid.

23 Ibid., comment j.

24 EEOC *Guidelines*, 29 C.F.R, Sec. 1604.11(b) (1985).

25 This suggests that only men can sexually harass women. I will defend this view later in the paper.

26 Frances Conley, a 50-year-old distinguished neurophysician at Stanford University, recently came forward with this story. Conley resigned after years of putting up with sexual harassment from her colleagues. Not only did they use Playboy spreads during their lectures, but they routinely called her "hon," invited her to bed, and fondled her legs under the operating table. *Chicago Tribune*, Sunday, June 9, 1991. Section 1, 22.

27 Hughes and May, *op. cit.*, 264–65.

28 Ibid., 265.

29 These same myths surround the issue of rape. This is discussed fruitfully by Lois Pineau in "Date Rape: A Feminist Analysis," *Law and Philosophy*, Vol. 8 (1989), 217–43.

30 MacKinnon, *op. cit.*, 152, is where she cites the study.

31 *Lipsett v. Rive-Mora*, 669 F.Supp. 1188 (D. Puerto Rico 1987).

32 Dawn D. Bennett-Alexander, "Hostile Environment Sexual Harassment: A Clearer View," *Labor Law Journal*, Vol. 42, No. 3 (March, 1991), 135.

33 Lipsett, op. cit., Sec. 15.

34 *Swentek v. US Air*, 830 F.2d 552 (4th Cir. 1987).

35 *Swentek v. US Air*, Ibid., 44 Epd at 552.

36 *Black's Law Dictionary, op. cit.*, 717.

37 *American Heritage Dictionary of the English Language* (New York: American Heritage Publishing Co., Inc., 1973), 600.

38 EEOC *Guidelines, op. cit.*, Sec. 1604.11(a).

39 Hughes and May, *op. cit.*, 250.

40 Tong, *Women, Sex, and the Law, op. cit.*, 67.

41 See Frankel Paul, *op. cit.*, 333–65. Frankel Paul wants to get away from the "helpless victim syndrome," making women responsible for reporting harassment, and placing the burden on them to develop a tough skin so as to avoid being seen as helpless victims (362–63). On the contrary, what Frankel Paul fails to understand is that placing these additional burdens on women detracts from the truth that they are victims, and implies that they deserve the treatment if they do not develop a "tough attitude."

42 Sandra Bartky, "Foucault, Femininity and the Modernization of Patriarchal Power," in Sandra Bartky, *Femininity and Domination: Studies in the Phenomenology of Oppression* (New York: Routledge, Chapman, and Hall, Inc., 1990), 63–82. See especially 77–78.

43 Ibid., 77.

44 *Restatement (Second) of Torts*, Sec. 146, (1965), comment j, my emphasis.

45 *Rabidue v. Osceola Refining Co.*, 805 F2d (1986), Sixth Circuit Court.

46 Ibid., at 622.

47 Ibid., at 620–22.

—62—

SEXUAL HARASSMENT AND THE RIGHTS OF THE ACCUSED

Stephen Griffith

MUCH OF AMERICA SAT TRANSFIXED BEFORE their television sets during the Supreme Court confirmation hearings for Judge Clarence Thomas while Anita Hill accused him of sexual harassment. The main topic of debate for most people following the hearings was whether it was Anita Hill or Clarence Thomas that was telling the truth, since their testimony was directly contradictory and there was essentially no independent evidence on either side. From a philosophical point of view, however, the most important issue illustrated by this whole affair concerns the nature of sexual harassment in itself. What is sexual harassment anyway, and why is it wrong, if it is? Even if Clarence Thomas did everything Anita Hill says he did, was his behavior seriously immoral, so much so as to justify denying him a seat on the Supreme Court? Opinions on this subject seem to range from saying that behavior of the sort alleged is the moral equivalent of rape to saying that it is simply a bit rude and inappropriate in the context within which it supposedly occurred. More recently, the President of the United States himself has been accused of sexual harassment. Although many people have reacted differently to this case than to that involving Justice Thomas, the wide variety of reactions to both of these cases and the vehemence of many of those reactions suggest that there is considerable confusion concerning the broad issue of sexual harassment which a careful philosophical analysis might help to alleviate.

Sexual misconduct of various sorts has become an increasingly serious problem in our society and must be dealt with both carefully and effectively whenever and wherever it occurs. All too frequently, individuals are sexually abused or assaulted by spouses, lovers, or total strangers, coerced into unwanted sexual activity by superiors, or subjected to unwanted sexual attention or embarrassment.[1] In response to these problems, a just society must have just and effective legislation: public and private institutions and corporations must have effective and fair policies and procedures; both this legislation and these policies and procedures must be consistent with the basic principles of justice, morality and fairness. The case for developing and implementing such legislation and policies has been made often and well, much progress along these lines has been made, and much more still needs to be done. Unfortunately, however, as is often the case in situations involving deeply felt causes, the understandable zeal for dealing with these problems has produced definitions of sexual harassment and attendant legislation and policies which contain the potential for serious abuse of human rights, especially the rights of the accused, and judging from various reports appearing in the media, the implementation of such policies and procedures has actually resulted in such abuse in some cases, especially in the groves of academe. The problem has been well expressed by a character in *Disclosure*, Michael Crichton's novel about sexual harassment:

"the problem is that there's that third category, somewhere in the middle, between the two extremes," Fernandez said. "Where the behavior is gray. It's not clear who did what to whom. That's the largest category of complaints we see. So far, society's tended to focus on the problems of the victim, not the problems of the accused. But the accused has problems, too. A harassment claim is a weapon, Bob, and there are no good defenses against it. Anybody can use the weapon—and lots of people have."[2]

With regard to the problems of the accused, Maatman says the following:

Many times the accused harasser must prove a negative: that harassment never took place. Putting aside legal liability, the mere charge of unwelcome sexual conduct itself can oftentimes destroy a career or stamp the accused as being of suspect morals and deficient judgment. Not surprisingly, sexual harassment complaints have the potential for malicious use, whereby an employee falsely asserts the charge as a weapon of retaliation, extortion, or to prevent or insulate a critical review of their own job performance.[3]

Although abuses of this sort may happen and continue to happen in only a small percentage of cases, the fact that any one instance of such abuse can deprive an innocent person of a livelihood, a career, or a good name suggests that we should be mindful of such possible abuses and take steps to minimize this possibility. My purpose in this paper is to suggest the adoption of a more precise definition of sexual harassment than those usually given and to illustrate how some of the abuses which are possible in the implementation of typical existing policies and procedures might thereby be avoided without significantly weakening the legitimate protections afforded by such policies.

The definition of sexual harassment given by the Equal Employment Opportunity Commission illustrates many of the problems referred to above. According to the EEOC,

Unwelcome sexual advances, requests for sexual favors, and other verbal or physical conduct of a sexual nature constitute sexual harassment when

(1) submission to such conduct is made either explicitly or implicitly a term or condition of an individual's employment;
(2) submission to, or rejection of, such conduct by an individual is used as the basis for employment decisions affecting such, individual; or
(3) such conduct has the purpose or effect of substantially interfering with an individual's work performance or creating an intimidating, hostile, or offensive working environment.[4]

The forms of conduct referred to in (1) and (2) fall under the rubric of what will be referred to in this paper as sexual coercion, a serious sexual offense which must be dealt with firmly and effectively whenever and wherever it occurs. Clause (3), on the other hand, taken at face value, could in principle be interpreted so as to apply to a wide variety of behaviors, some of which might not even be offensive to most normal people. This definition thus illustrates a regrettable tendency on the part of those most concerned with the issue of "sexual harassment" to define it much too broadly, so that all sorts of behavior, ranging from such serious sexual misconduct as rape to such relatively inconsequential behavior as the use of "inappropriate innuendo," are placed on a continuum and regarded as different forms of sexual harassment.[5] Thus, for example, gender harassment, seductive behavior, sexual bribery, sexual coercion, and sexual assault are all regarded by some writers as forms of sexual harassment.[6] Defining sexual harassment this broadly not only confuses the issue, but also has the unfortunate consequence that persons who have been accused of relatively minor offenses, often involving behavior which is not even morally blameworthy, are painted with the same accusatory brush as those accused of relatively serious crimes.[7] This has the doubly unfortunate effect of not only making relatively trivial offenses seem more serious than they are but also of trivializing more serious offenses.

There are several other problems with the EEOC definition of sexual harassment. In the first place, the crucial term "sexual" is left undefined, which leaves the entire scope of this definition unacceptably vague, as does the use of the term "substantially" in clause (3). In addition, its use of such subjective terms as "intimidating," "hostile," and "offensive" allows the accuser to define the offense, and the use of the expression "or effect" encourages us to ignore the intentions of the accused. Neither of these tendencies seems consistent with sound jurisprudence.

All of the above-mentioned defects in the EEOC definition of sexual harassment can be (and to a certain extent have been) substantially mitigated in courts of law. Some of the vagueness has been removed by precedent, and much potential abuse of the EEOC guidelines has doubtless been avoided by fair and experienced judges, impartial juries, rules of evidence, and all the other protections afforded the accused in our legal system. Unfortunately, however, the EEOC definition has also been used as a guideline for many corporate and institutional policies which are implemented in the absence of any of these protections, and it is here that most abuses have occurred.

I. NARROWING THE SCOPE

The use which the term "sexual harassment" has come to have in both legal contexts and in scholarly work on this topic has probably become too entrenched to permit any hope that a narrower meaning can be given to the term at this time, but we can at least hope to distinguish more clearly among the wide variety of behaviors which are currently listed together under this heading. In particular, we can distinguish between those forms of behavior which ought reasonably to have been regarded as sexual harassment *per se* and other forms of sexual misconduct which have inappropriately come to be regarded as such.

A. Discrimination Based on Gender

As a first step, we can distinguish sexual misconduct in general from those offenses which involve unjustifiable discrimination on the basis of gender. Although most discrimination based on gender cannot be justified and should be eliminated whenever and wherever possible, a person's gender and sexual orientation must obviously play a differentiating role in that person's social interaction with other persons. Even if we find it prudent or necessary to limit the types of interaction which are permitted or encouraged in academic or workplace settings, it is not reasonable to stigmatize someone by accusing that person of sexual harassment simply in virtue of the fact that that person treats men and women differently in some respects in situations where this could reasonably be expected. Chivalry, for example, may be dead, and it is certainly "sexist," but its vestigial remnants are not offensive to reasonable people and can hardly be regarded as immoral.

What is more important, however, is that even unjustifiable discrimination on the basis of gender should not be regarded as an instance of "sexual" misconduct. It is simply an accident of the English language that the word "sex" and its cognates can refer either to sexual activity or to gender. It is perniciously discriminatory, for example, to prohibit women from pursuing certain careers on morally irrelevant grounds, but a person who does this is not thereby guilty of immoral sexual activity, and might in fact lead a morally exemplary life in that respect, despite having "sexist" views. It could be argued, of course, that there are in many cases important sociological and psychological links between discrimination on the basis of gender and what is here being referred to as sexual misconduct, and this is surely why they are so often regarded as different forms of the same thing (i.e., sexual harassment), but a similar point could be made concerning alcohol abuse. There are strong links of an even more obvious sort between alcohol abuse and sexual abuse, but that is no reason to regard alcohol abuse as a form of sexual misconduct or harassment. For most people, the term "sexual misconduct" and the term "discrimination" both have negative connotations, and appropriately so, but the former has a sort of "sleaziness" to it that the latter lacks. They imply completely different sorts of character flaws on the part of those to whom they can truthfully be applied, and this alone is reason enough to regard them as significantly different sorts of offenses. "Sexual" misconduct, including sexual harassment, ought to be defined as involving, either directly or indirectly, sexual activity of some sort, and discrimination on the basis of gender is not necessarily sexual in this sense.

B. Other Forms of Sexual Misconduct

Having distinguished discrimination based on gender from sexual misconduct, we must now distinguish various forms of sexual misconduct from each other. It will be useful to comment briefly upon those forms of sexual misconduct which have inappropriately become regarded as forms of sexual harassment before attempting to define sexual harassment *per se* more precisely.

1. SEXUAL ASSAULT

The most serious and most obviously immoral type of sexual offense is sexual assault. This would apply not only to forcible rape as traditionally understood, but also to any form of clearly sexual behavior involving the use of physical force against a person without that person's consent. This is sometimes called "sexual imposition," especially in connection with less physically invasive forms of assault. Forcible rape, the most serious type of sexual assault, has long been regarded as a serious crime, and rightly so. It is clear that we must continue to develop and improve laws and institutional policies which deal effectively not only with forcible rape but also with other forms of sexual

assault Although the EEOC definition does not regard sexual assault as a form of sexual harassment, there is a tendency among writers on this topic to list it as such, which may be motivated by an understandable desire on the part of those enraged by sexual harassment to taint it with the opprobrium commonly occasioned by instances of rape. Unfortunately, this runs the risk of having the Opposite effect of making sexual assault seem less serious than it is, especially since the vast majority of behaviors commonly regarded as sexually harassing are clearly less serious than sexual assault.

2. SEXUAL COERCION

The most serious type of sexual misconduct encompassed (inappropriately, according to our present argument) by the EEOC definition of sexual harassment is sexual coercion. It would be beyond the scope of this paper to attempt to define coercion *per se* in any detail. It will be sufficient for our present purposes simply to say that we are being coerced to do something if and only if (1) we are doing something which we would prefer not to do, and (2) we are doing that thing primarily or entirely because someone else has unjustifiably threatened to harm us in some way if we do not. One is then guilty of sexual coercion if and only if one has coerced someone into engaging in sexual activity. In other words, sexual coercion is coercive for the same reasons that other forms of coercion are coercive, and its coercive nature is sufficient in itself to make it wrong, whether or not there are additional reasons for so regarding it.

To the extent that coercion in general involves the threat of harm, the threatened harm may be either physical or nonphysical in nature. Sexual coercion involving the threat of physical harm thus differs from sexual assault as defined above in that the victim of sexual coercion has a "choice," in an admittedly perverse sense, whether to accede to the offender's demands or run the risk of suffering the threatened harm, whereas a victim of sexual assault has no choice in any sense of the term.

It is important to note that successful sexual coercion involving the threat of physical harm can often be more harmful to the victim than the corresponding form of sexual assault, since the victim must suffer not only the indignity of compliance with the offender's demands but also the psychological trauma of feeling partially responsible for the outcome, which trauma often occurs despite assurances to the victim that resistance should not have been expected given the nature of the threats involved and the unlikelihood that the resistance would have been successful. This may help to explain why coercing persons to engage in sexual intercourse by threatening them with physical harm has traditionally been regarded as a form of rape, even if no overpowering force is used and no physical harm of the sort threatened ensues.

Whether the threatened harm is physical or nonphysical, it is important to note that coercion takes place only when it is both reasonable for the purported victim to believe that a threat has been made and unreasonable for the purported offender to deny that a threat has been made. The mere fact that a potential offender is in a position to inflict harm upon a potential victim clearly does not imply that the potential victim has been threatened with this harm. Moreover, the mere fact that a potential victim *feels* threatened, and thus fears that harm will occur unless sexual favors are granted, does not imply that a threat has occurred, even if the potential victim subsequently engages in unwanted sexual activity solely as a result of this fear.

It is important to point out that this can be true even in some cases where the fear in question is perfectly reasonable. If Smith knows or reasonably believes that persons answering some particular description often inflict harm upon persons like him in certain sorts of circumstances, and if he encounters Jones, a person of this description, in these circumstances, it is perfectly reasonable for Smith to fear Jones. Unless, however, Jones or these circumstances are described in such a way as to be inherently threatening (e.g., "a man

brandishing a knife" or "during an armed robbery"), Jones cannot be accused of coercing Smith simply because Jones makes a request of Smith that Smith grants only or primarily because of this reasonable fear. In other words, Jones cannot be held responsible for the fact that persons like Jones sometimes or even often harm others in similar circumstances. This is a perfectly general point that applies to any situation involving encounters between persons of different general descriptions who have been stereotyped in some way.[8]

The point here is not that threats must be explicitly stated in order to be coercive. Brandishing a weapon is clearly a threat of physical harm, and threats can often be subtle and covert but nonetheless conveyed and received. The point here, once again, is that a person is not guilty of sexual coercion unless that person's behavior is truly threatening, which implies not only that the purported victim can reasonably regard the purported offender's behavior as threatening, but also that the purported offender realizes (or is at least in such a position that he or she can reasonably be faulted for not realizing) that this behavior is likely to be regarded as threatening. Thus, engaging in sexual activity with someone who is in a position to inflict some sort of harm, even if one does so solely because one is fearful that this harm will otherwise ensue, does not by itself entail that one is a victim of sexual coercion. One is coerced only when one is actually threatened with harm.

Unlike sexual assault, which has always been regarded as a serious offense, sexual coercion has traditionally been recognized as such only when the victim has been threatened with bodily harm. One positive development in recent years has been that legal and institutional protection, largely under the rubric of the first two clauses in the EEOC definition of sexual harassment, has been extended to potential victims of sexual coercion involving threats of other types of harm, such as harm to their educational or professional careers. Sexual coercion of this sort is the most serious offense typically regarded as a form of sexual harassment. As is true, albeit to a lesser extent, in the case of sexual assault, there are both concep- tual and practical difficulties involved in trying to decide how to handle sexual coercion. Suppose, for example, that a spouse or lover threatens to break off a relationship unless sexual favors are granted, as often happens. Breaking off a relation- ship could often be regarded as Potentially harmful to the threatened person, and threatening to do so for this reason might be morally opprobrious but it is nevertheless difficult to see how we could justify making such behavior illegal. Laws and policies concerning sexual coercion are most easily justified in cases where there is an institutional or corporate "power differential" between potential offenders and victims, and there would now be at least a rough consensus that this form of behav- ior is morally unacceptable and should be dealt with effectively when it occurs within this sort of context. It would also appear that there would be no insuperable difficulties involved in reaching a consensus as to how these offenses should be defined.[9] The seriousness of this offense, and the relative ease with which a consensus could be reached concerning not only how to define it but also that it is morally unacceptable, provide ample justification for regarding sexual coercion as a spe- cific type of sexual offense, differing both from the equally serious offense of sexual assault and from less serious forms of sexual misconduct, including sexual harassment *per se.*

3. SEXUAL OFFERS

Another sort of behavior sometimes regarded as a form of sexual harassment might be called a "sexual offer." Sexual offers are of two sorts. The first sort of sexual offer is one in which a person offers to confer an otherwise undeserved benefit in exchange for sexual favors. The second sort of sex- ual offer is one in which a person offers to confer sexual favors in exchange for an otherwise unde- served benefit. Since the refusal to confer sexual favors or undeserved benefits cannot be regarded as "harmful" in the relevant sense, sexual offers do not constitute coercive threats and cannot be

regarded as a special case of sexual coercion. There is a clear moral difference between using or threat- ening to use one's power to harm someone, which is *prima facie* immoral, and using or offering to use one's power to benefit someone, which is not. Moreover, the so-called power differential which looms so large in most cases of sexual coercion is not so clearly relevant here. Any situation in which a person who has the "power" to confer an unde- served benefit in exchange for sexual favors is likely to make such an offer is also a situation in which the person to whom such an offer is made has the "power" to offer sexual favors in exchange for these benefits. It cannot be assumed that the lure of undeserved benefits to someone in a position to confer sexual favors is any more "powerful" than the lure of sexual favors to someone in a position to confer undeserved benefits, so the "power" in such cases is reciprocal. Finally, if *making* a sexual offer is to be regarded as an offense, it is presum- ably because the relationship that would ensue if the offer were accepted would be in some way illicit or inappropriate. It therefore follows that if making such an offer is to be regarded as an offense, accepting one should also be so regarded, and for the same reason. Thus, other things being equal, making or accepting either sort of sexual offer must be equally offensive, and any policy which mandates sanctions for making one sort of offer must mandate similar sanctions for making the other and for accepting either sort of offer as well.

Sexual offers as here defined are commonly referred to in sexual harassment literature as "sexual bribery." Referring to them in this way is problematic for several reasons, some of which are inherent in the concept of bribery itself. In general, bribery is regarded as an offense primarily in a political context. It occurs when a public official who is in a position to confer benefits as a result of holding the position that she holds confers unmerited benefits on someone in exchange for personal gain. It is regarded as an offense partly because it is unjust to those who actually deserve but do not receive the benefits thus conferred and also because it contradicts the purpose for which the official has been given the authority to bestow the benefits in question. Suppose, however, that an elected public official exercises her legitimate authority in such a way that it happens to benefit certain constituents more than others, and suppose that those particular constituents contribute heavily, but in accordance with (admittedly nonexistent) campaign financing laws generally regarded as fair, to the reelection campaign of that official. This would not constitute bribery unless there was an explicit or tacit understanding between the official and her constituents that the benefits in question were to be conferred in exchange for the contributions. The mere fact that benefits have been conferred and contributions made does not imply that bribery occurred or was even attempted. Finally, it could be argued that any law which flatly prohibits public officials from benefiting their constituents or flatly prohibits those constituents from contributing to the campaigns of the elected officials of their choice is at least an infringement, if not a violation, of their rights.[10]

Similar considerations apply in the case of so-called sexual bribery. Offering sexual favors, even to someone in a position to confer undeserved benefits, may be immoral for some reason, but does not necessarily constitute attempted bribery. Neither does requesting such favors from persons one is in a position to benefit constitute soliciting a bribe, even if it is immoral for some other reason. It is only when granting the benefit or favor is made conditional on granting the other that something resembling bribery has occurred or been attempted. Unless this condition is stated explicitly, which is not often the case, any allegation of bribery would have to be based on the contention that the condition was somehow implicit in the context in which the behavior took place. In cases of this sort, the motives and intentions of the parties involved are of paramount importance, and these are often not entirely clear, even to the persons themselves. A person may convince himself that he is acquiescing to a request for sexual favors from his superior because he is in love with her when he really just wants a promotion, and a person may convince herself that an underling who has acquiesced to her request for sexual favors really deserves a promotion, when she is really just in love with him. Great care must therefore be taken in attempting to adjudicate a situation in which someone is accused of sexual bribery. Sexual offers of either sort may be immoral for a variety of reasons, and it may be prudent for institutions to develop policies which attempt to regulate and monitor such behavior, but it could be argued that any policy which flatly prohibits competent adults from making or accepting unconditional sexual offers or requests is an infringement if not a violation of their rights, even if making or accepting such offers or requests is often morally opprobrious in many cases.

4. SEXUAL BOORISHNESS

Sexual boorishness is nonthreatening, expressive behavior of a sexual nature which is patently offensive to a morally decent and psychologically normal adult of either gender. Obscene gestures, the public display of obscene or pornographic photographs or drawings, the use of obscene language, and otherwise rude sexual comments can all be examples of sexual boorishness in a wide variety of circumstances. Sexual boorishness is most appropriately regarded as sexual misconduct under two circumstances. The first is when it is directed against a particular person and constitutes an instance of sexual harassment *per se*, as will be explained later. The second is when it creates what is sometimes misleadingly referred to as a "hostile environment."[11] This typically refers to a situation in which a person cannot participate in some particular educational experience or engage in some particular mode of employment without being subjected to what has been defined above as sexually boorish behavior. The point of referring to an "environment" here is to emphasize the fact that the behavior in question need not be directed at any one individual in particular. If it seems to be directed toward or primarily offensive to persons of some particular sexual orientation or gender, it can be regarded as a form of discrimination and treated as such. The term "hostile," however, is misleading in this context, because it can refer either to the motives of those responsible for the environment or to those aspects of the environment which render it harmful independently of their source. It is appropriate to hold someone morally responsible for a hostile environment only if they themselves have hostile motives or are indifferent to various consequences of their behavior which they know to be harmful to others. Human beings often express hostility toward one another in a wide variety of ways and for a wide variety of reasons, having to do with race, religion, politics, and moral beliefs, as well as sex and gender, and those who do so can be held morally responsible for the consequences of their actions, but we are understandably reluctant to impose sanctions on persons who engage in such behavior except in highly specific circumstances. For one thing, various persons might unknowingly contribute to a "hostile" environment by unintentionally bringing about certain physically or psychologically harmful aspects of that environment. There is no evidence, other than pseudo-Freudian generalizations of various sorts, that persons who indulge in sexual innuendo or humor, for example, are necessarily expressing hostility toward members of the opposite sex, or realize that their behavior is offensive or harmful in any way, even if, as a matter of fact, it is. The remedy in this case is communication, not punishment, and not "counseling" of a sort which implies that the accused person is somehow mentally ill. Some people are brought up using ethnic slurs without even realizing that they are doing so.[12] The same is true of at least some sexual boorishness. In both cases, the persons in question are often unaware that their behavior is even offensive.

Although sexual boorishness can be morally opprobrious even when it does not constitute a sanctionable offense, any attempt to legislate it, either legally or through corporate or institutional policy, must take both cultural differences and the right to freedom of expression into account. Respect for cultural and personal differences is especially important in connection with comments concerning a person's sexual attractiveness, since comments of this sort which are enthusiastically welcomed by some persons may be offensive to others. It is a plain and simple fact, for example, that some persons are pleased and flattered when someone describes them as "sexy," whereas others are embarrassed or even deeply offended. This does not imply that we must tolerate behavior of the extreme sort common in the most sexist societies, but it does imply that we must avoid adopting sexually repressive codes of behavior favored only by those at the opposite end of the spectrum, who have no more right to impose their values on others than anyone else does.

II. SEXUAL HARASSMENT PER SE

Sexual coercion and sexual assault are clearly unacceptable and ought to be dealt with effectively and fairly whenever and wherever they occur. Sexual boorishness and sexual offers are more problematic. It would be beyond the scope of this paper to attempt the difficult task of deciding exactly when such forms of behavior are justifiably sanctionable and when they are not, but with appropriate and important qualifications, we might be able to justify laws and policies which regulate or prohibit these sorts of behavior in certain circumstances. With regard to sexual harassment *per se*, the challenge is to define it in such a way as not only to distinguish it from unjustifiable discrimination based on gender and the various sorts of sexual misconduct discussed above, but also in such a way as to enable us to determine, at least in principle, whether someone is or is not guilty of this offense. Unless we are able to do this, it is difficult to justify either legal or institutional sanctions concerning sexual harassment.

It would seem that the proper place to begin in an attempt to define sexual harassment would be to say that it must be both clearly sexual in nature and clearly a form of harassment.[13] It would thus be useful at this point to discuss both what it means to say that a form of behavior is sexual in nature and what it means to say that it is a form of harassment.

A. Sexual Behavior

With regard to the term "sexual," there is both a broad and a narrow use of the term. In the broad sense of the term, psychologists and others constantly remind us that almost any form of behavior can be regarded as sexual in some context or other. Since in cases of alleged sexual harassment, the question as to whether a particular bit or pattern of behavior constitutes an offense so often hinges on whether that behavior is or is not "sexual" in nature, it is especially important for the purpose of crafting a policy statement concerning sexual harassment to adopt, at least at the outset, a more narrow definition. Otherwise, we run the risk of being forced to regard far too many different sorts of behavior as instances of sexual harassment, especially if we give the term "harassment" an equally broad or vague definition. Any law or policy which is sufficiently vague so as to enable us to regard almost anything as an offense is obviously both unwise and unjustifiable. (Cf. the charges brought against Socrates in Athens.)

It will thus be useful at this point to distinguish among (1) behavior which is *prima facie* sexual in nature, (2) behavior which is *prima facie* nonsexual, and (3) behavior which is neither. To say that a bit of behavior is *prima facie* sexual is simply to say that, due to some. inherent features of the behavior in itself, it is sexual *unless* there are contextual circumstances which render it nonsexual. Thus, for example, behavior involving physical contact with genitalia is ordinarily sexual in nature, but would not ordinarily be considered sexual in those cases in which it occurred in connection with some justifiable medical procedure. Similarly, behavior is *prima facie* nonsexual if there is nothing inherent in that behavior which renders it sexual. It can therefore be presumed to be nonsexual in nature *unless* there is something extraordinary about the circumstances in which it occurs which

renders it sexual. Such things as playing chess or reading a novel, for example, could be regarded as sexual activities only in highly extraordinary circumstances. Finally, and most importantly within the present context, there are bits of behavior which cannot be *presumed* to be either sexual or nonsexual independently of the context in which they occur. On being told, for example, that X kissed Y, we are not justified in presuming either that X's behavior was sexual or that it was nonsexual unless we know something about the context. Kissing is often a sexual activity, but parents kissing their children on the forehead are seldom if ever engaged in sexual activity, unless we define the term "sexual" much too broadly to be useful in the present context. The foregoing distinctions are applicable to all forms of sexual misconduct, but will be seen to be especially important in the context of sexual harassment.

B. Harassment

With regard to harassment, *Black's Law Dictionary* defines it as a "petty misdemeanor" which involves the use of "words, gestures, and actions which tend to annoy, alarm, and abuse (verbally) another person."[14] It does not ordinarily refer to any form of coercion or assault. If I attempt to coerce someone or strike them in such a way as to physically harm them, I am guilty of something significantly more serious than harassment. Moreover, offering to reward someone for doing something they would not otherwise do, or to do something of this sort in exchange for a reward, even in cases where it is morally unacceptable to do so, would not ordinarily be considered a form of harassment. In general terms, harassment refers only to behavior which is annoying or offensive, not to behavior which is seriously harmful, threatening, or tempting in a morally pernicious manner. It also seems clear that typically A is harassing B only if A is engaged in behavior toward B which is unwanted by B, is known by A to be unwanted by B, and which is nevertheless repeated by A. Thus, for example, if I tap someone on the shoulder and ask a reasonable question, this would not ordinarily be regarded as harassment. If, however, I continue to do so even after the person in question has made it clear that he would prefer that I not do so, this might constitute harassment, even though my behavior in this instance is not inherently immoral. We might add that a bit of behavior would not ordinarily be regarded as a form of harassment unless it is of a sort which a reasonable person might find objectionable or annoying. If I regularly say "good morning" to my neighbor as I drive off to work in the morning and he is offended by this, I can hardly be accused of harassment, especially if he does not indicate that he is offended by it. Moreover, if I regularly wear a blue shirt and he is offended by this, I cannot be accused of harassing him even if he *does* tell me it offends him. In fact, any attempt on his part to discourage or prevent me from wearing blue shirts might constitute harassment on *his* part, or even worse.

C. Sexual Harassment

It would seem that similar considerations should apply to sexual harassment. Roughly speaking, sexual harassment is simply harassment in which the offending behavior is sexual in nature. In other words, to parallel what was said above about harassment in general, the term "sexual harassment" should not be applied to sexual coercion or sexual assault, nor should it be applied to situations in which persons are tempted to voluntarily engage in sexual behavior for morally inappropriate reasons. It should be applied only to sexual behavior which is merely annoying or offensive, not to behavior which is seriously harmful, threatening, or tempting in a morally pernicious manner. A person (A) should be said to be sexually harassing another person (B) only if A is engaged in sexual behavior toward B which is unwanted by B, is known by A to be unwanted by B, and which is nevertheless repeated by A. Finally, a bit of behavior would not ordinarily be regarded as

a form of sexual harassment unless it is of a sort which a reasonable person might find objectionable or annoying.

Since the more intimate forms of sexual activity are those in which consent is clearly called for, it would be inappropriate to refer to any such behavior as sexual harassment. If consent is not given, a person who initiates such activity is guilty of sexual assault. If consent *is* given, initiating such behavior might be immoral for a variety of reasons, but it cannot be a clearly sanctionable offense unless it involves a morally unjustifiable sexual offer or is coercive. Since none of these three types of offenses are properly regarded as types of sexual harassment, it follows that sexual harassment cannot involve intimate sexual activity, but must involve sexual activity of a less intimate sort. It must, in other words, involve behavior which is clearly sexual in nature, but not especially intimate.

We are now in a position to see why sexual harassment is so difficult to define, much less adjudicate. Most behavior which is *prima facie* sexual in nature is fairly intimate. Although, as mentioned above, intimate sexual behavior might sometimes involve morally unjustifiable sexual offers or constitute a form of sexual coercion or assault, it seldom if ever constitutes sexual harassment. Typical cases of sexual harassment involve behavior which is *not prima facie* sexual in nature, but is sexual due to its context, if at all. Most often, behavior which is not *prima facie* sexual in nature is clearly sexual only when it constitutes a sexual advance, but behavior of this sort which constitutes a sexual advance in one set of circumstances might not do so in another. Moreover, in many cases of purported sexual harassment, both parties will agree that certain behavior has occurred, but will strongly disagree as to how that behavior should be interpreted or described. For example, a purported victim of sexual harassment (A) may claim that a purported offender (B) has persisted in making "unwanted sexual advances" toward A by engaging in behavior toward A which A, but not B, regards as sexual in nature. If the behavior of B is *prima facie* sexual as defined above, the burden of proof will be on B to show that it was not sexual, and if this behavior is *prima facie* nonsexual, the burden of proof will be on A to show that it is sexual. But what if, as is often if not usually the case, it is neither? Since many types of sexual advance involve behavior which is not *prima facie* sexual in nature, there is often considerable disagreement between purported victims and purported offenders in such cases concerning whether the behavior of the purported offender was in fact a sexual advance. It thus becomes problematic whether any such bit of behavior satisfies one of the necessary conditions which such a bit must satisfy in order to be an instance of sexual harassment.

There are several logically possible ways of resolving this difficulty. One way would be to allow the precise nature of the purported offender's behavior to be subjectively determined by the purported victim. In other words, we might simply say that if the purported victim regards the purported offender's behavior as a sexual advance, then that settles the matter. The problem with this procedure, of course, is that there does not seem to be any *a priori* reason to prefer the subjective opinions of the purported victim to those of the purported offender. For one thing, the latter is surely in a better position to know the inherent nature of his or her motives or intentions.[15] In addition, since the guilt or innocence of the purported offender might well hinge on our determination of whether his or her behavior is sexual in nature, the principle that an accused person is innocent until proven guilty clearly implies that we should give the benefit of the doubt to the accused. But to accept the subjectively determined opinions of accused persons concerning their own behavior as definitive in such cases is to leave potential victims essentially unprotected, since accused persons will almost always describe their own motivations in such a way as to support a claim of innocence.

What is clearly called for here is some objective basis for determining whether a person's behavior is sexual in the relevant sense. Since we are now discussing behavior which is not *prima facie* sexual in nature, any determination must be based on contextual considerations. Among things to be considered will be the intentions and other psychological states of the accused and various social conventions pertaining to interpersonal relationships. In an increasingly multi-cultural world, however, there must be a wide variety of interpretations of what is to constitute a sexual advance, and a correspondingly wide variety of socially acceptable behaviors. Judas, for example, was not making or even pretending to make a homosexual advance when he betrayed Jesus with a kiss, and even today, Arab men often kiss and hold hands with no implication of homosexuality. Similarly, in most cultures and subcultures, including those of the United States, there are many social contexts in which heterosexual embracing, kissing, and other forms of physical affection are not ordinarily considered to be sexual advances, even though there are some persons who seem to regard almost any sort of physical contact whatsoever as a sexual advance. As mentioned previously, we need not tolerate the sorts of behavior which would be regarded as acceptable in the most extremely sexist societies, but we also need not adopt a code of behavior so sexually repressive that we are required to regard all forms of unconsented-to physical contact or affection as sexual advances. No one narrow segment of society should be permitted to impose its interpretation of what constitutes a sexual advance or its views concerning what is socially acceptable on the rest of society. For all these reasons, great care must be taken in formulating legislation or institutional policies according to which a sexual advance can sometimes be a sanctionable offense. In particular, the term "sexual advance" cannot be defined in such a way as to automatically apply to bits of behavior which are often nonsexual in nature. Moreover, persons chosen to exercise judgment concerning whether a given bit of behavior constitutes a sexual advance in some particular context must be sufficiently broad-minded so as to instill confidence in all parties that such judgments will reflect an understanding of all the considerations referred to above.

D. Defining the Term

We are now in a position to attempt a more precise definition of sexual harassment. As a first approximation, consider the following:

(1) Person A is guilty of sexually harassing person B iff:

> (a) A's behavior toward B is clearly sexual in nature, but does not involve a morally unjustifiable sexual offer or constitute either sexual coercion or sexual assault.
> (b) A's behavior toward B is clearly unwanted by B.

The difficulty with this definition is that, depending on what we mean by "clearly" in (b), a person might be guilty of sexual harassment without having any way of being aware of that fact. It might be clear to any number of people that A's behavior is unwanted by B, but unless it is (or at least should be) clear to A, it is difficult to see how A's behavior can be morally sanctionable, unless, of course, it is inherently so for some reason.

Consider now the following substitute for (1), which is derived by substituting (b*) for (b) in (1):

(1*) Person A is guilty of sexually harassing person B iff:

> (a) A's behavior toward B is clearly sexual in nature, but does not involve a morally unjustifiable sexual offer or constitute either sexual coercion or sexual assault.
> (b*) A's behavior toward B is known by A to be unwanted by B.

A good case can be made for the view that if A's behavior satisfies both of these conditions, A's behavior is morally objectionable. It is perfectly reasonable to claim that there is something morally objectionable about engaging in sexual behavior toward a person when we know that that person does not want us to do so. The difficulty with this definition is that

it excludes too much. Suppose, for example, A does not *know* that the behavior in question is unwanted by B, but has good reason to *believe* that it is. A's lack of *knowledge* of B's feelings would certainly not excuse A's behavior in this instance.

Perhaps, then, we can revise our definition again, by substituting (b**) for (b*):

(1**) Person A is guilty of sexually harassing person B iff:

> (a) A's behavior toward B is clearly sexual in nature, but does not involve a morally unjustifiable sexual offer or constitute either sexual coercion or sexual assault.
> (b**) A has good reason to believe that A's behavior toward B is unwanted by B.

Condition (b**), however, is still too strong. Suppose that A and B are total strangers, that they meet in circumstances in which it would ordinarily be thought inappropriate to make sexual advances (e.g., in a supermarket) and that A makes a sexual advance toward B which is *prima facie* sexual in nature. Unless it is argued (implausibly) that no one ever wants to be propositioned by a total stranger, A might truthfully claim that although she has no good reason to believe that her behavior is wanted by B, she also has no good reason to believe that her behavior toward B is unwanted. We might nevertheless argue that A's behavior in this case might constitute at least a mild form of sexual misconduct. One way of doing so is to point out that such behavior is offensive to most people, whether or not it is offensive to everyone, and that it is morally unacceptable to behave in a way which is offensive to most people in this respect, even if there may be some people who do not find this behavior offensive.

This suggests a further modification in our proposed definition, as follows:

(1***) Person A is guilty of sexually harassing person B iff:

(a) A's behavior toward B is clearly sexual in nature, but does not involve a morally unjustifiable sexual offer or constitute either sexual coercion or sexual assault.

(b***) A has no reason to believe that A's behavior toward B might be wanted by B.

This definition clearly applies to behavior of the sort described above, but instead of excluding too much, it suffers from the opposite defect. Social conventions being what they are, there are many situations in which behavior satisfying both of these conditions would be perfectly acceptable. In the first place, if A and B know each other well enough, a sexual advance which is *prima facie* sexual in nature might be perfectly appropriate. In the second place, if A and B do not know each other well, sometimes the most appropriate way to determine whether a sexual advance is or is not wanted is simply to make one, especially if it is one which is *not prima facie* sexual in nature. There is clearly something amiss in our attempt to define sexual harassment so far.

Sexual relationships cannot exist unless they are initiated by someone. If doing something to initiate a sexual relationship is regarded as "making a sexual advance," it follows that sexual relationships cannot exist unless someone makes a sexual advance. Moreover, the first person to make such an advance in a sexual relationship must do so without knowing whether such an advance is wanted by the other person. The reason for this is that anything the other person did which would suffice to indicate that a sexual advance *was* wanted (or was even not unwanted) could be regarded as a sexual advance on the part of the other person, in which case, contrary to hypothesis, the person in question could not be the first person to make such an advance. Moreover, given this understanding of what constitutes a sexual advance, asking permission to make one is also tantamount to making one. Thus, sexual relationships cannot exist unless someone makes a sexual advance without knowing whether it is wanted.

What follows from this is that making sexual advances, even when it is not known whether they are or are not wanted, cannot be *prima facie* morally unacceptable, so that sexual harassment, if it is to be regarded as morally unacceptable, cannot be defined simply in terms of unwanted sexual advances. Many sexual advances which seem to be morally unacceptable, such as the example given above involving total strangers in the supermarket, are best regarded as instances of mere sexual boorishness, and not as forms of sexual harassment. In order to define sexual harassment correctly we must once again attend to the meaning of the term "harassment."

As we have seen, to harass someone is to *repeatedly* engage in behavior toward that person despite our knowledge or belief that the behavior is unwanted. The fact that the behavior is repeated is especially important in the case of sexual harassment. In the first place, since the only reasonable way to ascertain that a sexual advance is unwanted is often to make it, there are many cases in which one cannot be blamed for making one unless one has already made one and been rebuffed. In the second place, sexual harassment occurs most often among people who know each other but are not involved in a serious romantic or sexual relationship. Since it is considered excessively crude to attempt to initiate such a relationship by making sexual advances which are *prima facie* sexual in nature, people typically do so by making sexual advances which are *not prima facie* sexual in nature. This enables those who wish to reject such an advance to do so by simply responding to it as if it were not such an advance, and it enables those whose advances have been rebuffed to save face by pretending that they were not really making such an advance. The intent in these cases is not to deceive, but simply to minimize hurt feelings and embarrassment. Since, however, sexual advances of this kind are by hypothesis patterns of behavior that need not be regarded as sexual advances at all, it follows that people must often engage in the same patterns of behavior without intending to make any sexual advances. For this reason, it often happens that one person will interpret another person's behavior as a sexual advance when no such advance was intended. This alone is sufficient reason for not defining sexual harassment in terms of such ambiguous behavior.

It also explains, however, why it is so important that the behavior be repeated. Suppose that person A engages in behavior toward person B which A does not regard as sexual in nature but B does. As previously implied, the burden of proof will be on A if the behavior in question is *prima facie* sexual and on B if it is *prima facie* nonsexual. Moreover, even when it is neither, and regardless of what A or B claim to believe about the behavior in question, the context can sometimes make it clear whether this behavior is or is not sexual in nature. The problem is that, even when the context is completely specified, there are many cases in which there may be no clear consensus as to whether the behavior should be regarded as sexual or not. In a single instance of this sort, the benefit of the doubt must be given to the accused. Since, however, by hypothesis, the behavior in question is not *prima facie* nonsexual it could under some conceivable circumstances be regarded as sexual. Thus, if A knows that B regards it as sexual, whether or not A also so regards it, A cannot continue to engage in this behavior toward B without presupposing that B will interpret A's behavior as sexual. Thus, unless A has sufficient reason to believe that B desires or at least has no objection to A's engaging in sexual behavior toward B, A's continuing to engage in the behavior in question shows disrespect toward B of a very serious sort.

We are now in a position to try once again to define sexual harassment. Consider the following:

(2) Person A is guilty of sexually harassing person B iff:

(a) A has engaged in behavior toward B which is either *prima facie* sexual in nature or is such that B could reasonably regard it as such, but which does not constitute either sexual coercion, sexual assault, or a morally unjustifiable sexual offer.

(b) A knows or has adequate reason to believe that B reasonably regards A's behavior as sexual in nature.
(c) A knows or has adequate reason to believe that B does not want A to continue behaving in this manner toward B.
(d) A continues to behave in the same manner toward B.

There are several noteworthy aspects of this definition. The first is that condition (a) is necessary but not sufficient. A single, isolated instance of sexual coercion, sexual assault, or a morally unjustifiable sexual offer constitutes a sexual offense, but no isolated bit of behavior can constitute an instance of sexual harassment. Sexual harassment does not involve behavior which is inherently immoral. It occurs only when persons engage in sexual behavior or behavior which could reasonably be interpreted as such toward persons whom they know or have reason to believe may not want them to engage in such behavior. No one can reasonably be expected to continually provide each person they encounter in their daily lives with a detailed description of all those forms of behavior which they regard as sexual, nor can they provide each person with a list of those forms of behavior which they would prefer the person in question not exhibit toward them. For this reason, it often happens that persons engage in such behavior without realizing that it is offensive to others. If those others never indicate in any way that they are offended, or if the behavior in question is such that no reasonable person would be offended by it, the person engaging in it cannot be regarded as having committed an offense.

NOTES

1   Although it seems obvious that the vast majority of victims of these offenses are women, the moral dimensions of the problem are gender-neutral and will be treated as such wherever possible in this paper.

2   Michael Crichton, *Disclosure* (Knopf, 1994), 397. For a realistic fictional account of the abuse of sexual harassment policies in academe, see *Oleanna*, a play by David Mamet (New York: Pantheon, 1992).

3   Gerald R. Maatman, Jr., "Primer on the Law of Sexual Harassment," *Federation of Insurance & Corporate Counsel Quarterly* 42, No. 3 (1992), 320.

4   Michele A. Paludi and Richard B. Barickman, *Academic and Workplace Sexual Harassment: A Resource Manual* (Albany: SUNY Press, 1991), 3.

5   Cf. F.M. Christensen, "'Sexual Harassment' Must Be Eliminated," *Public Affairs Quarterly* 8, No. 1 (1994).

6   Cf., e.g., Fitzgerald et al., *Journal of Vocational Behavior* 32, 152–75.

7   Behavior which is not morally blameworthy may sometimes be justifiably prohibited and thus regarded as an "offense" in appropriate institutional or corporate settings. In particular, it may be prohibited when it seriously detracts from institutional or corporate goals and when this prohibition is not itself a violation of the rights of those engaging in the behavior in question. The point here is thus not that only morally blameworthy behavior may be prohibited, but rather that those who engage in behavior which is not morally blameworthy, even when it is contrary to some morally justifiable policy, ought to be treated differently than those whose behavior is clearly and seriously immoral or illegal.

8   I have a gainfully employed, law-abiding, African-American male friend who once walked into a convenience market on a very cold day wearing a ski mask. The female clerk, who was alone in the store at the time, saw him and immediately started to hand him the contents of the cash register. Given her own past experience and her knowledge of crime statistics in that neighborhood, it could be argued that her fear of my friend was quite reasonable, and she certainly acted as she did because of this reasonable fear. My friend, however, could certainly not have been accused of coercion. He would not, of course, have been justified in keeping the contents of the cash register in these circumstances, and would probably have been prosecuted for doing so, since it was obvious that the clerk acted out of fear in this case. Suppose, however, that he had simply approached a stranger on the street and asked for a simple favor. If the stranger, without showing any fear, nevertheless granted the favor for

this reason, could my friend have been accused of coercion?

9   The interpretation of the first two clauses of the EEOC statement is continually being refined in the courts, and even though there is no comparable refining process in academe, reasonable people could probably reach a consensus as to how such cases could be resolved there as well.

10 The problem here has been expressed fairly well in a form letter written by US Representative Barney Frank to his contributors, which I will quote at length. "Writing a thank-you note to campaign contributors in today's climate forces me to emulate Rube Goldberg without pictures. That is, I have to write something that reflects (1) my deep genuine gratitude on a personal level for your sending me a contribution to help me stay in Congress, counterbalanced by (2) my concern that someone reading this might infer something disparaging about your motives in engaging in the sinister process of 'campaign finance,' itself counterbalanced by (3) my interest in keeping you sufficiently happy with me—or insufficiently unhappy—so that you will continue to contribute, in turn counterbalanced by (4) my fear that the media will denounce me for accepting campaign contributions and thereby subjecting myself to improper influence, albeit from proper people." Reprinted in *Harper's*, August 1994, 17.

11 Cf. clause (3) of the EEOC statement.

12 My first landlord, an immigrant from Greece, informed me that the term "Greek" is an ethnic slur (the proper term is "Grecian"), but that it did not offend him, since the people that use this term are all "barbarians" anyway.

13 One virtue of the EEOC definition is that it does at least make it clear that only behavior which is sexual in nature can be regarded as a form of sexual harassment, although it unfortunately leaves the term "sexual" undefined.

14 *Black's Law Dictionary*, 5th edition, West, St. Paul, 645.

15 Many chronic sex offenders, of course, are subject to various types of self-deception concerning their own motives and behavior, but to the extent that this is true, it would seem to render them less responsible for their behavior and to make it more difficult to justify using sanctions against them.

—63—

DISCRIMINATION, HARASSMENT, AND THE GLASS CEILING

Women Executives as Change Agents

Myrtle P. Bell, Mary E. McLaughlin, and Jennifer M. Sequeira

ALTHOUGH SEX DISCRIMINATION IS PROHIBITED by law in the United States and various other regions, it continues to be a widespread problem for working women.[1] Title VII of the Civil Rights Act of 1964, amended in 1991 to include punitive damages, prohibits sex discrimination in the US in all employment-related matters. Women in the US have made considerable progress in organizations in the nearly 40 years since Title VII was passed and affirmative action for women was implemented. Nonetheless, women in the US earn only about 76 cents to the dollar that men earn, are more concentrated in lower earning industries and organizations than are men, and are under-represented in managerial and executive positions—positions of power, decision-making, and influence. Though comprising almost 50% of the US workforce, women occupy only about 30% of all salaried manager positions, 20% of middle manager positions, and about 5% of executive level positions. These disparities in earnings, status, and position cannot be completely or largely explained by differences in the education, job tenure, or experience of working women, leaving much to be attributed to employment discrimination.

As in the US, discrimination against women is a continuing problem around the world. Various countries provide prohibitions against discrimination. The Sex Discrimination Act of 1975 in the United Kingdom, the Canadian Human Rights Act, the Sex Discrimination Acts of 1984 and 1992 in Australia and the Hong Kong Sex Discrimination Ordinance of 1996 all prohibit discrimination on the basis of sex. These prohibitions provide criminal and/or individual penalties for such behavior. Nonetheless, despite bans against sex discrimination, in most countries, as in the US, women's lower earnings, status, and occupation of managerial positions when compared with men's provide evidence of its continued existence.

In this article, we discuss the relationships between discrimination, harassment, and the glass ceiling, arguing that many of the factors that preclude women from occupying executive and managerial positions also foster sexual harassment. We suggest that measures designed to increase representation of women in higher level positions will also reduce sexual harassment. We first define and discuss discrimination, harassment, and the glass ceiling, relationships between each, and relevant legislation. We next discuss the relationships between gender and sexual harassment, emphasizing the influence of gender inequality on sexual harassment. We then present recommendations for organizations seeking to reduce sexual harassment, emphasizing the role that women executives may play in such efforts and, importantly, the recursive effects of such efforts on increasing the numbers of women in higher level positions in organizations. Though much of the discussion focuses on US women, because discrimination and harassment are issues for working women worldwide, we include available references to such issues in various regions outside of the US. In addition, our suggestions for addressing discrimination and harassment should be useful for organizations worldwide, particularly given the increasing recognition of the problems of discrimination and harassment for working women around the world.

DISCRIMINATION, HARASSMENT, AND THE GLASS CEILING

We propose three forms of sex discrimination that affect women in organizations: overt discrimination,[2] sexual harassment, and the glass ceiling. Though by no means exhaustive of discriminatory acts, each has negative effects on women's status and therefore on women's ability to effect change regarding such discrimination. We discuss each form of discrimination, their shared antecedents, and a possible solution below.

Overt Discrimination

Overt discrimination is defined as the use of gender as a criterion for employment-related decisions. This type of discrimination was targeted by Title VII of the Civil Rights Act of 1964, which prohibited making decisions based on sex (as well as on race/ethnicity, national origin, and religion) in employment-related matters such as hiring, firing, and promotions. Overt discrimination includes, but is not limited to, such behaviors as refusing to hire women, paying them inequitably, or steering them to "women's jobs." Overt discrimination has long been a factor in women's employment experiences, yet its inclusion in Title VII is said to have been an "after-thought" perceived as certain to ensure its failure to pass.

Along with societal norms and perceptions of gender-appropriate occupations, overt discrimination led to occupational sex segregation. Occupational sex-segregation, in which at least 75% of workers in an occupation are male or female, has declined somewhat in the past three decades, however, most jobs remain fairly well sex-segregated. In the US, women constitute the majority of nurses, flight attendants, and secretaries, in positions supportive of men, who comprise the majority of physicians, pilots, and executives, respectively. Indeed, 7 of the 10 most common jobs for women are sex segregated (secretaries, cashiers, registered nurses, nursing aides/orderlies/assistants, elementary school teachers, and servers). These jobs are characterized by low pay, low status, and short career ladders.

Women's occupational sex segregation, and the concomitant low status, short career ladders, and low pay, are common in other regions around the world. In the US and other countries, women who are low in organizational status, have low organizational power, and who earn significantly less than men are more frequent targets of sexual harassment. Further, in these lower status positions, and many others that women occupy, women are considerably more likely to be supervised or managed by men than by women, which increases the risk that they will be harassed by their male superiors.

Sexual Harassment

Sexual harassment, a form of sex discrimination, is but one manifestation of the larger problem of employment-related discrimination against women. It now appears obvious that sexual harassment is a form of sex discrimination. However, its inclusion under Title VII was not the original intent of the act. Early legal cases under Title VII questioned whether sexual harassment constituted sex discrimination, often finding that it did not. Some cases ruled that supervisor sexual harassment resulted from individual proclivities over which organizations had little control. However, in 1980, using Title VII, the US Equal Employment Opportunity Commission (EEOC) published guidelines on sexual harassment. These guidelines clarified the illegality of harassment, describing two specific types as being unlawful sex discrimination: quid pro quo and hostile environment harassment.

In quid pro quo harassment, employment-related bribery or threat is used to obtain sexual compliance. The coercive nature of quid pro quo harassment requires that the harasser have some power over the target, thus most of such harassment is perpetrated by managers or supervisors. Hostile environment harassment occurs when sexual behaviors have "the purpose or effect of unreasonably interfering with an individual's work performance or creating an intimidating, hostile, or offensive" work environment. This type of harassment may be perpetrated by managers, supervisors, peers, or subordinates.

As is overt discrimination, sexual harassment is a persistent workplace problem for women worldwide. Numerous regions include prohibitions against such harassment (e.g., Canada, Israel, the United Kingdom, Australia), though with varying levels of stringency and application. Though specific prohibitions, terminology, and stringency vary worldwide, researchers have empirically identified three psychological dimensions of sexual harassment that persist across international boundaries: sexual coercion, gender harassment, and unwanted sexual attention. These dimensions have been confirmed in the US, Brazil, China, Canada, and other regions.

It is estimated that at least half of all US women and about 15% of men will be sexually harassed at some point during their careers....

Sexual harassment may contribute to the perpetuation of occupational sex segregation. Women may purposefully enter occupations typically dominated by women—occupations that have lower pay and fewer opportunities for advancement, in part to be safer from harassing co-workers....

The Glass Ceiling

The glass ceiling is the third form of discrimination that we discuss as affecting women in organizations and is an important factor in women's lack of access to power and status in organizations. The term "the glass ceiling" refers to invisible or artificial barriers that prevent women (and people of color) from advancing past a certain level. As discussed above, women comprise about 30% of all managers, but less than 5% of executive managers in the US. At the lowest levels, women comprise a larger percentage of managers, making more obvious the disparities between women in high and low-level managerial positions. The barriers that result in such disparities are often subtle, and include gender stereotypes, lack of opportunities for women to gain the job experiences necessary to advance, and lack of top management commitment to gender equity and equal employment initiatives. As with overt discrimination and sexual harassment, the glass ceiling exists in other regions of the world....

As an "invisible" barrier, the glass ceiling is difficult to eradicate through legislation. Informal networking and mentoring are frequently suggested as means of increasing the numbers of executive women, yet these suggestions have had limited time to demonstrate effectiveness for women. Further, networking with and mentoring offered by executive men can be less fruitful and more problematic for junior women, who may be assumed to be sexually involved with their mentors. These problems can be particularly difficult for women of color.

In sum, the relative lack of women managers and executives, the support roles many women workers provide to men workers, and occupational sex-segregation all facilitate sexual harassment. We propose that because overt discrimination, the glass ceiling, and sexual harassment are all forms of sex discrimination with (some) shared antecedents, measures to mitigate one will necessarily address the others. In the sections that follow, we discuss how having women in managerial and executive positions may be one particularly effective measure for reducing discrimination, for multiple reasons.

WOMEN EXECUTIVES AND HARASSMENT PREVENTION

In the previous sections we have discussed ways in which discrimination, the glass ceiling, and harassment affect women workers. Women who have attained executive positions have apparently achieved some measure of success against sex discrimination in matters of promotion and advancement. However, as evident by the existence of the glass ceiling, executive women are by no means discrimination free. Nonetheless, in the following sections, we propose that such executive women are uniquely positioned to address sexual harassment as illegal discrimination in their organizations in a variety of ways. From the perspective of the need for women executives in the battle against sexual harassment, we suggest that (1) women who work for male supervisors or managers report greater harassment and perceive their organizations as being more tolerant of harassment, (2) women rarely perpetrate harassment, (3) women view harassing behaviors differently from men and (4) women executives are more likely to have personal experience with sexual harassment than are men. Each is discussed below.

Supervisor Gender and Organizational Tolerance of Sexual Harassment

Research suggests that leader gender and behavior influence perceptions of organizational tolerance for sexual harassment and the actual existence of sexual harassment in an organization. For example, in Gutek's (1985) stratified random sample of workers in Los Angeles, women who had a male supervisor were more likely to report being harassed. Most of these women were harassed by male co-workers, who may have perceived that such behavior was tolerated (or condoned) by male supervisors. In Hulin et al.'s (1997) study, women who reported to

a male supervisor viewed the organization as being more tolerant of harassment than did women who reported to a female supervisor. Finally, in her study of women office workers who worked in male-dominated environments, Piotrkowski (1998) found that women whose supervisors were men experienced more frequent sexual harassment than did women whose supervisors were women. Further, the most frequent hostile environment harassment was reported by women whose supervisors were men whom they perceived as being biased against women (Piotrkowski, 1998). Gruber (1997, p. 95) reporting several studies, summarized the relationship between leader behavior and harassment, noting that "organizations whose leaders were perceived as discouraging harassment had a lower incidence of harassment." For those perceived as encouraging harassment and bias the opposite was true.

Supervisor Gender and Harassment Perpetration

Supervisor gender itself is also a factor in sexual harassment, in a fairly simplistic way. Women infrequently perpetrate sexual harassment; EEOC estimates suggest that female to male harassment comprises about 9% of harassment while male to female harassment comprises 90% of harassment, with the remainder being same sex harassment. Thus, it appears that merely employing women in managerial and executive positions would necessarily reduce sexual harassment to some extent—particularly sexual coercion.[3]

Gender Differences in Perceptions of Harassing Behaviors

In addition to differing in the experience and perpetration of sexual harassment, some gender differences exist in the determination of what behaviors constitute sexual harassment. These differences are less pronounced with sexual coercion; men and women view such behavior similarly and clearly, both perceiving it as harassment. Sexual coercion occurs less frequently than does hostile environment harassment. Whether the more frequent, but less clear cut behaviors, such as sexual joking, making obscene comments, and persistent requests for dates are deemed harassment depends largely on the pervasiveness and persistence of the behavior and the gender of the perceiver. Specifically, women are more likely to interpret ambiguous behaviors as harassing than are men; in situations where the behavior is less clear cut, women are more likely to label those behaviors as being harassing than are men. Thus, the types of behaviors that are more common are also the types of behaviors about which there are gender differences in perceptions of whether sexual harassment has occurred. These differences may help to explain the persistence of sexual harassment. Even though women are more likely than men to believe that certain behaviors do constitute harassment, they are unlikely to be in positions of power to influence behaviors, which contributes further to the persistence of sexual harassment. Further, women may not be treated fairly in organizations because the organizational culture may directly and indirectly communicate that they should not be. The absence of women in such positions may signal to potential harassers that women are not viewed as valuable members of the organization.

Women Executives and the Experience of Sexual Harassment

Despite being of higher level and status than most working women, as noted earlier, women executives remain far outnumbered by men executives and also experience sexual harassment. In addition to harassment from higher status executives and peers, women executives may also experience "contra-power" harassment, in which higher status women are harassed by lower status men. Galen et al. (1991) reported that 53% of the National Association of Female Executives in their survey had been sexually harassed. In a study of healthcare executives, twenty-nine percent of the women executives and five percent of the men executives reported having been harassed. Executive women in a 1992 survey by Working Women were also harassed at a higher rate than non-executive women. Working Women attributed this in part to the employment of such executive women in male-dominated companies. One respondent noted that "the higher up you climb, the worse the harassment gets," reflecting her belief that the harassment resulted from men's efforts to deter advancement of women. Finally, in a sample of professional and managerial Canadian women, Burke and McKeen (1992) found that sexual harassment was a significant problem and resulted in lower organizational commitment and less job satisfaction. Clearly, sexual harassment is not limited to women of low occupational status, which may be beneficial in cessation efforts.

Women executives, as persons who are more likely to have experienced harassment than are men executives, may have a greater ability to empathize with harassment targets than would men. In addition, regardless of whether they have personally experienced harassment, executive women will be likely to perceive harassing behaviors similarly to other women, who, as discussed earlier, view such behaviors differently from men. As policy-makers, regardless of a genuine intent to maintain a harassment free environment, executive men may be perceptually disadvantaged with regard to sexual harassment. Specifically, due to their position as men, and a lifetime of unfamiliarity with sexual harassment or fear of assault, executive men may be less able to perceive sexually harassing behaviors as do women....

INCREASING WOMEN EXECUTIVES: EQUITY AND POLICIES

We have discussed relationships between discrimination, harassment, and the glass ceiling, arguing that they are all factors that preclude women from occupying executive and managerial positions.

Thus, we are in a double-bind with respect to executive women, discrimination, and harassment. More women are needed in executive positions to help curb sexual harassment. At the same time, sexual harassment (along with other forms of discrimination against women) may be preventing or limiting the advancement of women to executive positions. In the following sections, we provide suggestions for coping with this conundrum, drawn from the literatures on sexual harassment, discrimination, and gender equity. We begin with organizational support of gender equity, which is an important factor in reducing discrimination and harassment. Given the small percentage of women in positions of power and decision-making in organizations, such a commitment to gender equity would necessarily require the commitment of men in such positions. The high costs of sexual harassment, in the forms of withdrawal behaviors and intentions, physical and psychological effects on harassed employees, lowered job satisfaction, litigation costs, and damage awards if found liable, should result in executives of both genders and other stakeholders being wholeheartedly in support of efforts to curb harassment.

Organizational Support of Gender Equity

Grundmann et al. (1997, p. 177) have argued that efforts to prevent sexual harassment would include equal numbers of women and men in various levels of authority, and clearly communicated job roles with expected duties and limits. Gutek and Morasch (1982) indeed found that women working in gender-integrated settings with approximately equal numbers of men and women reported the lowest levels of harassment. We thus propose that concerted organizational efforts be made to reduce sex segregation and to employ women and men in various levels of authority, across the organization. Women would be employed in non-stereotyped positions, in decision-making, and policy-making positions,

and earning pay comparable to men. Although overt efforts to employ women in male-dominated environments may initially increase levels of sexual harassment and backlash, over time, sexist barriers and hostile environments should be reduced. In their research on sexual harassment of women working in male-dominated fields, Mansfield et al. (1991) noted that the women who experienced the most harassment were working in more recently sex-integrated environments. We suggest that in organizations committed to gender equity, awareness of the potential for increased harassment would mean more concerted prevention efforts, including a strong harassment policy that reflects women's perspectives.

Sexual Harassment Policies

Strong sexual harassment policies have long been suggested as an important means of curbing sexual harassment. Stronger prohibitions and sanctions against harassment are associated with fewer reports of sexual harassment. Further, researchers have suggested that considering a feminist view of harassment in designing harassment policies is important. Despite large damage awards discussed in the media, most women who are harassed do not file lawsuits or even formally complain. Baugh (1997) and Riger (1991) have argued that women's failure to complain reflects gender bias in policies, stemming from perceptual differences in the way women and men view harassment and from women's belief that their complaints will not be taken seriously. Riger has also suggested that informal grievance procedures for sexual harassment complaints may be more successful than formal ones, given women's relative lack of power. In addition, rather than punishment or retribution, many harassed women simply want the behavior to stop. This suggests that in addition to formal grievance policies, organizations should include informal dispute resolutions that focus on harassment cessation for harassment targets who would be more comfortable with such measures.

WOMEN EXECUTIVES: AN UNTAPPED ADVANTAGE

Women Executives' Leadership Styles

A growing body of research indicates that women executives differ from men executives in many ways that enhance their management style and success, which may translate into how they address issues of sexual harassment. A woman is more likely to lead an organization from the center of a network of interrelated teams, rather than from the top of a traditional command hierarchy as do most male leaders. As such "centralist" leaders, women executives are more likely to gain information directly about harassing or discriminatory behaviors, and can thus be more responsive. As noted earlier, they may also be more likely to see such behaviors similarly to other women, rather than discounting or doubting them.

Another benefit of increased numbers of executive women may be higher satisfaction and retention of other managerial and professional women— those who would be future executives, shaping future policies. Burke and McKeen (1996) have reported that managerial and professional women working in organizations with predominantly men in higher level positions were less satisfied with their jobs and had greater intentions to quit than women in organizations with less skewed gender ratios in higher level positions. Burke and McKeen (1996) have also argued that the absence of women in executive positions may also result in the reluctance to create policies supportive of career goals of lower level managerial and professional women. We suggest that an under-representation of women may also result in reluctance or inability to create sexual harassment policies that meet the needs of women and men who are harassed. Regarding harassment of men, in McKinney's (1992) study of contrapower harassment, male participants thought that women who were harassed by persons of lower status would be more upset than men who were so harassed. Interestingly,

female participants thought that both men and women targets of contrapower harassment would be equally upset. That is, regardless of the target of harassment, women see harassing behaviors negatively. Thus, in situations where men are harassed by women, women executives would be expected to perceive this negatively rather than as flattering or innocuous as executive men might.

Feminist Perspective, Equity, and Effectiveness

Feminists and other researchers have long argued that viewing discrimination and its effects from a feminist rather than masculinist perspective would be beneficial in many ways. For example, Maier (1997, p. 943) has suggested that feminist alternatives be considered in organizations, rather than continuing to "take the prevailing masculinst managerial paradigm for granted." He also suggested that efforts toward gender equity would be beneficial for men as well as for women, given the prevailing (mis)perceptions and dysfunctionality inherent in masculinst assumptions. Maier (1997, p. 943) argued that these assumptions disadvantage women, parents (including men), and reduce overall organizational performance. He suggests that "feminist-based organizational transformation" would promote gender equity as well as more effective and ethical organizational behavior.

We suggest that women executives may increase organizational effectiveness in other areas as well. A climate of intolerance of sexual harassment is associated with a climate of tolerance for differences (e.g., in terms of race or ethnicity, culture, religion, or physical ability) and one that supports employee growth, participation, and empowerment through training, mentoring programs, and equitable pay for all employees. Such a climate is associated with a positive public image, and the concomitant attraction and retention of top talent (e.g., Fortune, 2000). In order to compete for human resources in today's tight labor market, men (as well as women) executives in other organizations will likely see the need to adopt similar policies that foster a healthy organizational climate. Policies and actions that promote gender equity may also be adopted in other organizations as the latest "management fashion" or trend. Thus, women executives have the potential to make sweeping, progressive changes, both within and beyond their organizations.

CONCLUSION

In this manuscript, we have discussed three forms of sex discrimination: overt discrimination, sexual harassment, and the glass ceiling. We have argued that women in executive leadership roles are uniquely positioned to reduce sex discrimination, and that because all three have some common antecedents, steps to reduce one form will likely affect the others. We focused on the reduction of sexual harassment in particular, and argued that not only should simply increasing the numbers of women in executive positions decrease sexual harassment, but also that women executives use their positions of influence to increase gender equity and reduce sexual harassment. A particularly important contribution of our work is our explication of how women executives are especially motivated and qualified to reduce sexual harassment and increase gender equity, and the specific steps that they may take to do so. Given the beneficial consequences of such actions, and the imitative nature of organizations, they will likely "spillover" and be adopted in other organizations as well.

NOTES

1   We acknowledge that the experience of sex discrimination and/or harassment is not limited to women, however, most discrimination and harassment involve women as targets. Thus, we focus our discussion on discrimination against and harassment of women.

2   We use the term overt discrimination to differentiate this type of discrimination from sexual harassment and the glass ceiling.

3   It could be argued that women do not perpetrate sexual harassment because they have not historically had the access to power and position that men have had; however, as women are 30% of all managers, but are estimated to be 9% of all harassers, it appears that managerial women are less likely to perpetrate sexual harassment than are men.

REFERENCES

Baugh, S.G.: 1997, 'On the Persistence of Sexual Harassment,' *Journal of Business Ethics* 16, 899–908.

Burke, R.J. and C.A. McKeen: 1992, 'Social-sexual Behaviors at Work: Experiences of Managerial and Professional Women,' *Women in Management Review* 7(3), 22–30.

Galen, M.J., J. Weber and A. Cuneo: 1991, 'Out of the Shadows, the Thomas Hearings Force Business to Confront an Ugly Reality,' *Business Week* (October 28), 30–31.

Gruber, J.E.: 1997, 'An Epidemiology of Sexual Harassment: Evidence from North America and Europe,' in W. O'Donohue (ed.), *Sexual Harassment: Theory, Research, and Treatment* (Allyn and Bacon, Boston), pp. 84–98.

Grundmann, E.O., W. O'Donohue and S.H. Peterson: 1997, 'The Prevention of Sexual Harassment,' in W. O'Donohue (ed.), *Sexual Harassment: Theory, Research, and Treatment* (Allyn and Bacon: Boston), pp. 175–184.

Gutek, B.A.: 1985, *Sex and the Workplace* (Jossey-Bass, San Francisco).

Gutek, B.A. and B. Morasch: 1982, 'Sex Ratios, Sex-role Spillover, and Sexual Harassment of Women at Work,' *Journal of Social Issues* 38, 55–74.

Hulin, C.L., L.F. Fitzgerald and F. Drasgow: 1997, 'Organizational Influences on Sexual Harassment,' in M.S. Stockdale (ed.), *Sexual Harassment in the Workplace*, Vol. 5 (Sage: Thousand Oaks, CA), pp. 127–150.

Maier, M.: 1997, 'Gender Equity, Organizational Transformation, and Challenger,' *Journal of Business Ethics* 16(9), 943–962.

Mansfield, P.K., P.B. Koch, J. Henderson, J.R. Vicary, M. Cohn and E.W. Young: 1991, 'The Job Climate for Women in Traditionally Male Blue-collar Occupations,' *Sex Roles* 25, 63–79.

McKinney, K.: 1992, 'Contrapower Sexual Harassment: The Effects of Student Sex and Type of Behavior or Faculty Perceptions,' *Sex Roles* 27, 1–17.

Piotrkowski, C.S.: 1998, 'Gender Harassment, Job Satisfaction, and Distress among Employed White and Minority Women,' *Journal of Occupational Health Psychology* 3, 33–43.

Riger, S.: 1991, 'Gender Dilemmas in Sexual Harassment Policies and Procedures,' *American Psychologist* 46(5), 497–505.

Wells, D.L. and B.J. Kracher: 1993, 'Justice, Sexual Harassment, and the Reasonable Victim Standard,' *Journal of Business Ethics* 12, 423–431.

—64—
THE SANITIZED WORKPLACE

Vicki Schultz

I. INTRODUCTION

DOES SEX HAVE A PLACE IN THE WORKPLACE? According to most management theorists and feminist lawyers, the answer is a resounding no. Progress, they say, means precisely driving sex out of the workplace—whether in the name of efficiency or equality.

It may seem paradoxical that such strange bedfellows would endorse the same sanitizing impulse; feminists are rarely viewed as close companions of corporate management. But upon further examination, it isn't ironic or strange at all. One of American society's most cherished beliefs is that the workplace is—or should be—asexual. The dominant ethic says, "Work is work, and sex is sex, and never the twain shall meet." Call it the ethic of workplace asexuality.

One may be tempted to attribute this ethic to Americans' prudishness, and, of course, conservative sexual sensibilities probably have played a role. But our commitment to workplace asexuality is, even more directly, a legacy of our historic commitment to a certain conception of organizational rationality. It wasn't Victorian churchwomen, but twentieth-century organization men who took the lead in creating the asexual imperative: men like Frederick Winslow Taylor, who saw managers as rational "heads" who would control the unruly "hands" and irrational "hearts" of those who assumed their places as workers in the modern organization. Although the necessity of bureaucratic organization has come under challenge in recent years, the drive toward asexuality is not

fading along with it. Today, as much as ever, sexuality is seen as something "bad"—or at least beyond the bounds of professionalism—that should be banished from organizational life. If sexuality cannot be banished entirely, then those who embody or display it must be brought under tight control and subjected to discipline.

Although the drive to sanitize the workplace raises a range of fascinating issues about the place of sexuality and other affective elements of human life in contemporary organizations, it is beyond the scope of this article to deal with most of them here. My goal is more modest: to show how sexual harassment law, as envisioned by some feminist reformers and implemented by many human resource (HR) managers, has become an important justification for a neo-Taylorist project of suppressing sexuality and intimacy in the workplace. To put it plainly, sex harassment policies now provide an added incentive and an increased legitimacy for management to control and discipline relatively harmless sexual behavior without even inquiring into whether that behavior undermines gender equality on the job.

This development was not (and I hope still is not) inevitable. Indeed, it is part of my aim to trace how it came about in order to reclaim some lost possibilities and chart a more promising path for the future. Although organizations are the main actors driving the sanitization process, the legal system has played an important role in providing incentive and cover for sanitization. In the United States, sex harassment has been viewed primarily as a form of sex discrimination under Title VII of the Civil Rights Act, the federal statute that prohibits sex discrimination in employment. Title VII says nothing about sexuality; it simply prohibits discrimination based on sex. Thus, under the statute, the concept of sex harassment might have been elaborated to cover the full range of hostile and discriminatory actions—both sexual and nonsexual—that tend to keep women (or men who fail to conform to prescribed gender roles) in unequal jobs or work roles. Such an approach would have paralleled developments in race discrimination law, where courts had already adopted a broad view of racial harassment that recognized its role in reproducing patterns of racial segregation and hierarchy that relegate minorities to lower-paid positions.

Instead, the federal agency and the lower courts charged with interpreting Title VII defined harassment primarily in terms of sexual advances and other sexual conduct—an approach I call the sexual model. In earlier work, I showed that this sexual model is too narrow, because the focus on sexual conduct has obscured more fundamental problems of gender-based harassment and discrimination that are not primarily "sexual" in content or design. In this Article, I show that the sexual model is also too broad, because the same focus on sexual conduct that has led courts to ignore these larger patterns of sexism and discrimination is also leading companies to prohibit a broad range of relatively harmless sexual conduct, even when that conduct does not threaten gender equality on the job. In the name of preventing sexual harassment, many companies are proscribing sexual conduct that would not amount to sexual harassment, let alone sex discrimination, under the law. Many firms are even banning or discouraging intimate relationships between their employees. Worst of all, companies are disciplining (and even firing) employees for these perceived sexual transgressions without bothering to examine whether they are linked to sex discrimination in purpose or effect....

The truth is that managers cannot succeed in banishing sexuality from the workplace: They can only subject particular expressions of it to surveillance and discipline. Although some groups suffer more than others when this occurs, everyone loses. It may well be true, as the libertarian critics of harassment law have charged, that punishing sexual language and conduct can infringe on employees' free expression, and, where that occurs, it is not a harm to be taken lightly. But, as Section V.A elaborates, I am equally concerned about the threats to human intimacy and the negative politics of sexuality that are ushered in by the drive toward sanitization. With the decline of civil society, the workplace is one of the few arenas left in our society where people from different walks of life can come to know one another well. Because people who work together come into close contact with each other for extended periods for the purpose of achieving common goals, work fosters extraordinarily intimate relationships of both the sexually charged and the more platonic varieties. When managers prohibit or discourage employees from dating each other, they deprive people of perhaps the single most promising avenue available for securing sexual partners. And, when managers punish employees for sexualized interactions with each other, they create a climate that may stifle workplace friendships and solidarity more generally. Evidence suggests that many employees fear that a simple expression of personal interest in a coworker may prompt an accusation of sexual harassment. We cannot expect diverse groups of people to form close bonds and alliances—whether sexual or nonsexual—if they must be concerned that reaching out to one another puts them at risk of losing their jobs or their reputations. Along with the loss of individual free expression comes an interference with intimacy and bonding.

Even more is at stake than whether or not people can form close friendships at work: The larger question is whether we as a society can value the workplace as a realm alive with personal intimacy, sexual energy, and "humanness" more broadly. The same impulse that would banish sexuality from the workplace also seeks to suppress other "irrational" life experiences such as birth and death, sickness and disability, aging and emotion of every kind.

But the old Taylorist dream of the workplace as a sterile zone in which workers suspend all their human attributes while they train their energies solely on production doesn't begin to reflect the rich, multiple roles that work serves in people's lives. For most people, working isn't just a way to earn a livelihood. It's a way to contribute something to the larger society, to struggle against their limits, to make friends and form communities, to leave their imprint on the world, and to know themselves and others in a deep way. As I have explained elsewhere, work isn't simply a sphere of production. It is also a source of citizenship, community, and self-understanding.

II. THE HISTORICAL DREAM OF A SANITIZED WORKPLACE

A. Divorcing Productivity and Passion

The idea that sex has no place in the workplace is not new. At least since the early 1900s, corporate managers have seen sexuality as something that properly lies "outside" the workplace—something that preexists and threatens it. This imperative was part of a larger wave of bureaucratization that rolled in with the twentieth century. The emergence of giant corporations with far-flung operations to be coordinated gave rise to a new class of professional managers. Lacking legitimacy rooted in firm ownership or ruling-class birthright, the new managers rested their authority on their technical expertise: As managers, they knew the "one best way" to organize work efficiently.

In contrast to the freewheeling intuitivism of some nineteenth-century entrepreneurs, the founding fathers of modern organizational theory imagined firms as spheres of "passionless" rationality. In the division of labor they invented, managers would use their brains to do the logical thinking-through and planning of organizational goals, and workers would use their bodies to implement them. In the words of Frederick Winslow Taylor, the steel company engineer-turned-consultant who invented the theory of scientific management, "[T]he workman who is best suited to actually doing the work is incapable of fully understanding [the science underlying it], without the guidance and help of those who are working with him or over him." Managers were to be the "heads" and workers the "hands" of the organization.

But as Max Weber recognized, it wasn't just people's hands that were to be controlled; it was also their hearts. Just as the proper use of the assembly line and time motion studies would help management harness workers' bodily capacities to the ends of production, so too could proper organizational structure suppress the personal elements of people's lives that threatened the smooth functioning of the firm. Work organizations were conceived as hierarchies of "jobs" or "slots" to be filled by generic "workers," who would suspend their human qualities while they were at work and focus their energies solely on production. According to Weber, such depersonalization was bureaucracy's special brilliance:

> Its specific nature ... develops the more perfectly the more bureaucracy is "dehumanized," the more completely it succeeds in eliminating from official business love, hatred, and all purely personal, irrational, and emotional elements which escape calculation. This is the specific nature of bureaucracy and it is appraised as its special virtue.[1]

... Decades later, this historical way of thinking about the place of sexuality in work organizations would provide challenging terrain for a women's movement that wanted to integrate women into equal roles at work. In a culture that viewed women as the walking embodiments of sexuality and regarded sexuality as a threat to organizational life, feminists faced a difficult choice: They could challenge the notion that the workplace is (or should be) asexual—and insist that sexuality is a common, not necessarily undesirable feature of organizational life that exists whether or not women are present. Or, they could embrace the ethic of asexuality—and join the struggle to stamp out sexual behavior, in the name of ensuring parity for women and productivity for the firm.

B. Equating Sexism and Sexuality

For the most part, the American women's movement has pursued the latter strategy. Instead of challenging the ethic of asexuality, a powerful strand of the movement mounted a legal campaign to curb men's sexual conduct. Feminist activists and lawyers invented a claim for sexual harassment, which holds companies responsible for unwanted sexual conduct as a form of sex discrimination in employment. Through this approach, feminists joined management's traditional drive to desexualize the workplace and demanded its contemporary completion. Management might believe the workplace was asexual, feminists claimed, but women's entrance had occasioned overt displays of heterosexual male predation. Men's sexual overtures subverted gender equality, feminists contended, for women could never be respected as employees so long as they were regarded as sexual objects. Not only did male sexuality threaten women's interests, it also interfered with everyone's productivity—men and women alike. Thus, feminists could claim, rationalizing the workplace required reining in male sexuality.

The centerpiece of this feminist strategy was equating unwanted sexual conduct with sex discrimination—a powerful maneuver that has crowded out other notions of workplace harassment and justified the drive to root sex out of the work world. Feminist lawyers focused on Title VII of the Civil Rights Act, which holds employers liable for sex discrimination and other forms of discrimination in employment. But Title VII does not mention sexuality or even sex harassment; its purpose was to end discriminatory job segregation. Thus, feminists might have pushed for a broad concept of sex harassment that encompassed the entire range of hostile and discriminatory actions—both sexual and nonsexual—through which supervisors and coworkers labeled women workers "different" and inferior, thereby helping to preserve historic patterns of sex segregation in employment that consigned women to lower-status, lower-paying, female-dominated jobs. Such an approach would have paralleled developments in race discrimination law, where courts had already taken such a broad view of racial harassment. In addition to this race discrimination precedent, there was a body of theoretical work, and at least one important precedent secured by a feminist lawyer in a sex discrimination case, that would have supported such a broad vision of sex harassment and its link to larger gender-based inequalities. That some lower courts would continue to adopt such a broad approach suggests that it would have been a viable strategy for feminists to pursue.

But as I have recounted elsewhere, most feminists did not pursue this path. Instead, feminist activists and lawyers pushed for a narrower understanding of sex harassment, defining the concept in terms of unwanted male-female sexual advances. They argued that such sexual advances were discriminatory and harmful to women—an argument that inspired sympathy among both liberal and socially conservative judges. Courts first accepted this line of argument in an early group of cases commonly known as quid pro quo harassment cases, in which male supervisors fired female subordinates for refusing their sexual advances. Although alternative lines of reasoning were available, the lower courts located the source of sex discrimination in the sexual desire presumed to motivate the supervisor's sexual advances. A heterosexual male boss's sexual come-on toward a female employee is discriminatory, said the courts, because the boss would not have been attracted to—and thus would not have made a sexual advance toward—a male employee. In the words of Judge Spottswood Robinson, writing for the D.C. Circuit in 1977, "[B]ut for her gender [the plaintiff] would not have been importuned.... [T]here is no suggestion that the allegedly amorous supervisor is other than heterosexual."[2]

The 1980 guidelines adopted by the Equal Employment Opportunity Commission (EEOC), the major federal agency responsible for enforcing and creating policies to implement Title VII, consolidated this approach. Building on the reasoning in the early quid pro quo cases, the guidelines defined sexual harassment as "[u]nwelcome sexual advances, requests for sexual favors, or other verbal or physical conduct of a sexual nature." Although these guidelines did not have the force of law, they were given broad deference by the lower courts—many of which read them to limit sex harassment to sexual conduct. By the time the Supreme Court decided its first sex harassment case in 1986, *Meritor Savings Bank v. Vinson*, the equation of sexual harassment with sexual advances was firmly established. Thus, the Justices could simply assume, without having to explain, why a bank manager's unwelcome sexual advances against a female employee would amount, if proven to be sufficiently hostile or abusive, to discrimination "because of sex" within the meaning of Title VII. In these sexually hostile work environment cases, as in the earlier quid pro quo harassment cases, it was the presumed presence of sexual desire that provided the inference of discriminatory intent necessary under the statute. As a result, the Court had no trouble reaching a unanimous decision holding that sexual harassment violated Title VII.

Over time, the sexualized understanding of harassment that arose out of the quid pro quo cases came to overwhelm the concept of hostile work environment harassment as well. As a result, courts have tended to single out sexual advances and other conduct of a sexual nature for disapproval, and have tended to exonerate even serious patterns of sexist misconduct that could not be easily characterized as sexually motivated. Thus, despite the fact that the Supreme Court has never expressly held that a Title VII claim for sex harassment requires conduct of a sexual nature for purposes of a harassment claim, systematic empirical research confirms that historically, in the lower federal courts, sexual harassment plaintiffs who complain about sexualized forms of behavior have been significantly more likely to win than plaintiffs who complain about other forms of sex-based misconduct.

C. Sanitizing the Workplace: A Summary of Current Developments

It would be one thing for companies to use sex harassment policies to create workplaces in which all men and women can work together as equal partners. To rid workplaces of sex-based harassment that conditions employment on sexual favors or creates a hostile work environment under Title VII would be something of which American companies—and, we, as a society—could be rightly proud. But it is another thing for organizations to prohibit or discourage workers from engaging in conduct simply because it is considered "sexual"—without regard to whether the conduct impinges on gender equality or rises to the level of sex discrimination under the law.

Yet, our nation's employers are being pressured to do just that. A huge (and growing) literature warns companies that they should go beyond the dictates of the law to curtail broad forms of sexual conduct—including conduct that does not satisfy the legal definition of sexual harassment and that does not necessarily undermine gender equality on the job—in order to avoid liability for sexual harassment. The bulk of this "how-to-avoid-liability" literature is put out by managers and HR professionals, but much of the legal literature also sounds this theme.

A 1992 article entitled Avoid Costly Lawsuits for Sexual Harassment, which appeared in the American Bar Association (ABA) publication, Law Practice Management, provides an illustration of the larger trends. It begins by cautioning managers that even benign, fully consensual sexual interactions can get the company into trouble:

> Sure, your office may be free from the traditional form of such harassment: an attorney or manager demanding sexual favors from an unwilling paralegal or subordinate in exchange for promotion or job retention. Yet courts

across the land are now deciding that a surprisingly wide range of other situations constitute sexual harassment, for which employers
are assessed big fines.

... [S]uccessful harassment lawsuits are
now resulting even when a subordinate was
the willing sexual partner of a supervisor.
Or when an office is deemed to be "hostile"
because of the presence of sexual joking, flirting or pin-ups. Or even when one employee
makes a practice of staring suggestively at
a co-worker.[3]

In response to legal incentives the Supreme Court
established as long ago as 1986 (and strengthened
in 1998), the article counsels companies to establish a policy to prohibit sexual harassment and to
set up a grievance procedure to punish those who
engage in it. The article recommends prohibiting
and punishing sexual conduct that, in and of itself,
would not necessarily amount to sexual harassment under Title VII. "Nip These Activities in the
Bud!" warns the bolded heading—and then, relying
on MacKinnon's expertise, goes on to command
companies not to let their employees "[t]ell sexual
jokes or make innuendoes," "[p]ost pin-up photographs on the walls," "[r]omance subordinates," or
"[r]equest sexual favors, touch or flirt with either
willing or unwilling subordinates."[4]

The article comes down hard on sexual joking,
which it refers to as "[i]nsensitive [s]ocializing."
"Recent court cases have shot down some workplace
traditions many people thought were good clean
fun or part of the normal socialization process,"
the article warns.[5] It then quotes Robert McCalla,
the chairman of the Labor and Employment Law
Section of the ABA, as saying: "Suggestive joking of
any kind simply must not be tolerated." Even if "the
joking occurs only with an employee who openly
welcomes the joking and joins in," the business is
still not protected against a sexual harassment suit,
the article cautions, because "[o]ther employees in
the office may file suit, claiming the joking creates a
hostile work environment."[6]

But it isn't simply sexual joking and interaction that must be curtailed. Companies must also
clamp down on consensual sexual relationships.
Even if an employee's affair is entirely welcome,
that doesn't mean the firm is protected from
sexual harassment lawsuits—quite the contrary.
"If the woman who engages in an affair receives
favors such as professional advancement, then
other women have causes of action, if they did not
submit and were not promoted," warns Lawrence
Katz, a partner in a Phoenix law firm (giving advice
contrary to the EEOC guidelines and some major
court decisions).[7] Furthermore, if the relationship
goes sour, the subordinate can retaliate by claiming
that the supervisor's advances were unwelcome, or
charging that a later failure to be promoted was
retaliation for her refusal to continue the relationship. Because of this threat of liability, the piece
cautions, companies must take steps to monitor
whether employees are intimately involved. With
this information in hand, management can separate the lovers, or, if they cannot be separated, "one
of the pair may be terminated."[8] ...

The effort to eliminate sex harassment by
punishing individual transgressors neglects larger
structural issues, such as the link between sex
segregation and sex harassment. Nowhere does the
article encourage companies to consider whether
the sexual conduct they are punishing is motivated
by sex bias or is a manifestation of larger forms of
sex discrimination in the company. Instead, echoing Susan Estrich's position, the article suggests
that sex harassment is different from sex discrimination—and that it is precisely the sexual nature of
sex harassment that presents the threat that must
be contained.

D. Punishing Sexual Transgressions

Just as many sexual harassment policies have been
crafted in an overzealous spirit, many are being
enforced in a similar spirit. When sexual harassment is defined in terms of conduct of a sexual
nature with no understanding of how harassment
is linked to larger forms of inequality such as

job segregation by sex, there is no incentive for companies to engage in structural reforms that might reduce the incidence of harassment, such as integrating their workforces. Instead, current law sets up incentives for employers to punish individual employees for engaging in any sexual conduct that might be seen as contributing to a hostile work environment—incentives that mesh well with many employers' preexisting inclinations to view sexual conduct as disruptive and out of place in the workplace....

In line with these incentives, there is evidence that, in the name of eliminating sexual harassment, many employees are being disciplined, and even discharged, for engaging in sexual conduct. According to a large national survey published in 1999 by the SHRM, fully 60% of all sexual harassment complaints resulted in some form of disciplinary action against the alleged harasser. That the majority of accused harassers are subjected to such discipline or training seems troubling, when we recall that in almost half of complaints, sexual remarks, teasing, and joking are the primary types of harassment alleged. Furthermore, the vast majority of all harassment complaints are filed against coworkers, not supervisors.

This systematic evidence of punishment finds confirmation in a wealth of anecdotal accounts. In the wake of the Clinton scandals, the press has reported countless stories of employees who have paid a high price for what look like harmless interactions. In one story, a male social worker was fired for imitating David Letterman and approaching a new female coworker with the comment, "I'm gonna flirt with ya." In another, a lesbian psychology professor's guest lecture on female masturbation prompted a sexual harassment lawsuit by a married, male Christian student, who claimed that he felt "raped and trapped" by the lecture. In another case, a male religion professor was reprimanded for "'engag[ing] in verbal conduct of a sexual nature' that had the effect of 'creating an intimidating, hostile or offensive' environment" when he recited a story from the Talmud, the writings that make up Jewish law. The story involved

a man who fell off a roof, accidentally landed on a woman, and had intercourse with her. The professor related that in the Talmud, the man is deemed innocent of sin because his act was unintentional. A female student in the class was offended by the story, and her sexual harassment complaint led the university to reprimand the professor and to record all his lectures to ensure that he did not say anything offensive in the future....

F. Disregarding Discrimination

Underneath this avalanche of no-dating policies and love contracts, zero-tolerance policies, self-policing, and discipline for conduct with sexual overtones, the most fundamental goal of employment discrimination law has been lost. Title VII should not be used to police sexuality; it was meant to guarantee women and men equal work roles. The drive to eliminate sexuality from the workplace has detracted from this important goal—and may even encourage organizations to act in ways that undermine genuine workplace equality.

At the level of the individual complaint, companies do not attempt to determine whether the alleged sexual harassment was linked to sex discrimination. They simply assume that any sexual conduct covered by their policies is discriminatory or harmful. Yet, in many of the cases in which men have been fired or disciplined for violating sexual harassment policies, the women who were the alleged targets of the harassment did not even object (or voiced only vague objections) to the conduct for which the offenders were punished. In the Monterey County arbitration, for instance, the female kitchen helper to whom the suspended financial officer brought cookies and blew kisses testified emphatically that his behavior was "not a problem"; it was others who were allegedly offended by his actions. In the case involving Arthur Andersen, it was the woman who supervised the flirtatious accountant—rather than the women he attempted to woo—who seemed most uncomfortable with his conduct. Similarly, in American Mail-Well Envelope, the leadman was suspended because he failed to discipline some men for viewing a sexually explicit magazine, despite the fact that no women were even exposed to it. In these and other cases, companies simply equated sexual content with sex discrimination—without bothering even to inquire into whether the offending conduct was intended or used to exclude women or otherwise interfere with their work opportunities on the basis of their sex.

At the organizational level, sexual harassment policies have taken on a life of their own, divorced from the larger goal of dismantling sex discrimination. As I have emphasized above and discuss more fully below, sex harassment is integrally linked to such sex segregation in employment. Sex segregation structures work environments in which harassment flourishes because numerical dominance encourages male job incumbents to associate their work with masculinity and to police their jobs by treating women and gender-nonconforming men as "different" and out of place. By the same token, sex harassment preserves segregation by driving away or denigrating the newcomers who would integrate the job. As a tool of segregation, sex harassment assumes many forms—not all of which can be easily or even best characterized as "sexual" in content or design.

V. TOWARD A NEW VISION

To find alternative visions, we don't have to look that far. Early in the twentieth century, a group of feminists and freethinkers who congregated in Greenwich Village championed women's right to participate equally in work, sexuality, and talk. They believed that women's ability to stand along-side men in the same paid work, to control their own sexuality, and to engage in free expression—including frank talk about sexuality—were the pillars upon which a good and egalitarian society rested. In the intervening decades, of course, it has become clear that these aspirations must be framed more broadly and that inequalities other than gender must be addressed. But the project of achieving a world in which all people have the capacity to participate meaningfully in work (both paid and unpaid), to pursue sexuality and intimacy on their own terms (both within and outside traditional family settings), and to practice free expression (both in politics and in more private realms) remains as powerful and as relevant as ever.

Unfortunately, the direction in which we are moving neglects the first goal (work equality) and threatens the second and third (sexual autonomy and free expression). We are not doing enough to promote gender equality in work roles, and what we are doing in the name of preventing sexual harassment threatens people's right to talk about—and even to participate in—many forms of sexual conduct that do not subordinate women. Although legal reform is an important part of what is needed, law alone is not enough. To change things for the better, we will have to alter our aspirations, as well as revise our legal and organizational approaches to workplace sexuality.

A. Aspiring to New Ideals

As we have seen, social movement politics has played a role in bringing about the sanitization process, and a new set of politics and ideals is needed to disrupt that process. It is time to reject the sanitizing impulse and strive, instead, for a world in which people are able to be more fully human while they are at work. This means countering the trend toward universal, across-the-board strictures on sexual interaction and creating ways for organizations to offer more sexually open, and more gender-egalitarian, environments. There are many good reasons for taking such a stance.

Today, work's passions pull at women and men alike. We work because we must, but also because most of us can't choose not to. Work isn't just a way to make a living; it's a way to create something of value, to struggle with our capacities and limits, to make friends and form intimate relationships, to contribute to our communities, to leave our imprint on the world, and to know ourselves and others in the way that humans can only be known through struggle and (sometimes) success. It isn't just that work is a stage where we as individuals can try to realize our dreams (and confront our demons); it's also one of the few arenas in which diverse groups of people can come together to find sustenance, solidarity, and shared meaning. Thanks to the partial success of forty years of social movements and legal reforms, our society has come to hold as an ideal the image—though not yet the reality—of the workplace as an arena of potential citizenship, a place where more and more groups have some claim to be included on equal terms. In the wake of this transformation, as sociologist Arlie Hochschild has chronicled, the workplace has become a central locus for many people's dreams and desires. Even for those who aren't fortunate enough to hold jobs that can foster self-realization, work remains vitally important to how they understand life. Like it or not, most people's lives are shaped profoundly—for better or worse—by their experiences in relation to the world of work.

In a world in which many relationships have become transitory and superficial, work can offer deep and meaningful connections. As sociologists are beginning to recognize, the workplace is a sphere characterized by extraordinarily intimate relations. For many people, work fosters exciting, erotically charged relationships. There is an electricity and a sense of connection that comes from working together closely, day in and day out, to achieve common goals. For other people, work offers close, not necessarily erotic, friendships that occur primarily at work but extend beyond workplace issues. Scores of people are involved in what researchers have called "non-sexual love relationships" with their coworkers, bosses, or subordinates. Whether they are sexual or nonsexual, the ties that emerge at work may be as intense as those that exist at home because, in both realms, the constant contact, coupled with the mutual recognition that can arise out of working on common projects, fosters close, self-disclosing relationships. As one important researcher put it, "With individuals increasingly oriented to their work as an extension of their core selves ... we are where we work. To use a worn metaphor, those who labor beside us become our kith and kin."

Of course, as this account suggests, intimacy is not synonymous with sexuality. Not all close ties create sexual energy, and not everyone in a sexually charged relationship consummates it physically. As a result, some readers may ask: Why should we care about whether employers prohibit sexual conduct? What would be wrong with preserving only workplace intimacy of the nonsexual variety?

One answer is that we may have to allow people to engage in sexual liaisons at work in order to find potential mates. In today's economy, many people work extremely long hours and have little time for social lives outside work. As a practical matter, these people may have to find potential partners through their employment. If prohibitions against workplace dating become universal, many people may find it difficult if not impossible to find marriage partners or to secure other long-term or short-term sexual relationships.

Yet, the problem isn't simply that rules against sexual conduct might pose a barrier to people forming traditional sexual relationships that would extend outside the workplace. The bigger problem is that such rules may pose barriers to people forming erotic and other close connections that would occur primarily inside the workplace. For, although intimacy and sexuality may be possible to separate as a theoretical matter, they are not so easy to disentangle at the level of experience or policy. For many people, the line between a platonic relationship and a sexual one is often porous, and friends may cross it once or even on occasion without becoming full-time partners or lovers. Furthermore, simply because intimacy doesn't require sexual relations does not mean it can thrive in the presence of the prohibitory sexual harassment measures many companies are adopting. Many employers' policies extend beyond prohibiting sexual relations to limit a broader set of personal interactions, such as sexual remarks and joking, and even looks and gestures, that can be interpreted as "sexual" (such as hugs). When people have to fear that they can be accused of sexual harassment on the basis of something minor they may say or do, no matter how harmless (or even affectionate) their intentions, working relationships can become mistrustful rather than intimate—just as some survey research suggests may be occurring. The sense of connection that work inspires can wither under the threat of sexual accusation.

Even if we could somehow separate out non-sexual intimacy from the more sexual variety, we should still be deeply concerned about across-the-board prohibitions on specifically sexual conduct. Workplace sexuality isn't solely a source of danger and disruption—it's also a source of vitality, creativity, and power. For many people, the sexual energy that work generates will be one of the most valued aspects of their work lives—one we should not sacrifice lightly. If sexuality were valued as it should be, we would celebrate, rather than seeking to snuff out, the erotic charge that often accompanies working. Sexuality is, to a large extent, what makes us alive. So, in the move to suppress workplace sexuality, what is at stake is the very idea of whether work can be a sphere of human energy, vitality, and connection. The very existence of work as a humanist enterprise is on the line, as is the value of sexuality to human experience.

Just as we are coming to realize the importance of workplace intimacy in people's lives, we are also beginning to recognize—however reluctantly and painfully—how desperately our society needs to embrace a new ethics of sexuality. As a new generation of queer theorists and feminists has eloquently shown, our society all too often induces sexual shame and creates moral panics about sexuality. Not only does the politics of shame harm some groups at the expense of others; it also induces social stigma and enforces sexual conformity in a way that impoverishes life for everyone. Viewed in this light, the contemporary campaign to drive sex out of the workplace becomes visible as a larger politics of sexuality. It is a politics that, in the name of protecting women from sexual discrimination and danger, privileges some people's notion of acceptable sexuality over others'; in the name of protecting firms from disorder and legal demise, gives management the power

to punish sexual transgressors upon pain of losing their jobs; and in the name of progress, enforces standardized, often stifling codes of appropriate sexual conduct that deprive employees of the capacity to create workplace cultures that reflect their own sexual norms.

This last realization raises an important point. Not only is the drive toward sexual sanitization part of a larger politics of sexuality; it is also part of a larger practice of managerial control. Firms are adopting sexual harassment policies in response to advice from lawyers and HR professionals, but without significant input from their own employees. In most cases, employees have little or no role in defining sex-based harassment, identifying its causes, or devising appropriate solutions. Managers sometimes even use accusations of sexual harassment as a pretext for firing workers whom they want to get rid of for other reasons. But even when no ulterior motives are present, sexual harassment law has given firms a newly progressive justification for punishing and even firing employees whose conduct can be said to interfere with productivity and order.

From a workers' rights perspective, there is cause for concern. These draconian practices put workers, as individuals, at risk of losing their jobs, their livelihoods, and a significant source of meaning and connection to others. But more is at stake, for such policies also put employees, as a group, at risk of losing the ability to forge their own workplace cultures and sexual norms—cultures and norms that may be mobilized, at least at times, as a source of solidarity, pleasure, and even resistance to managerial abuse of authority on the job.

NOTES

1   Max Weber, From *Max Weber,: Essays in Sociology* 215–16 (H.H. Gerth & C. Wright Mills ed. & trans., Routledge 1991) (1948).

2   *Barnes v. Costle*, 5671 F.2d 983, 989–90 & n.49 (D.C. Cir.1977) (holding, for the first time in an appellate case, that quid pro quo harassment is a form of sex discrimination actionable under Title VII).

3   Philip M. Perry, *Avoid Costly Lawsuits for Sexual Harassment*, LAW PRAC. MGMT., Apr. 1992, at 18, 18.

4   *Id.* at 24.

5   *Id.*

6   *Id.*

7   *Id.*

8   *Id.*

—65—

CASE STUDY

SEXUAL HARASSMENT IN THE WORKPLACE

Darci Doll

BACKGROUND

KEVIN HAD BEEN EMPLOYED AS A RESEARCH assistant at a biotechnology firm. Over the course of several years, Kevin received regular advancements in recognition of the positive contributions he had made for the company. Most recently, he was promoted as the Vice President of Research and Development. Shortly after this promotion, his associate Bridget began seeking him out more often than usual. She would initiate small talk or compliment him in passing. Believing that Bridget was innocently trying to initiate a friendly work relationship, Kevin thanked her for her compliments and would engage in conversation with her when work permitted. Over time, Bridget's compliments began to occur more frequently and became less innocent in nature. Bridget would make sexual innuendos toward Kevin and would openly express her sexual attraction to him. While the nature of these comments made Kevin uncomfortable, he believed that if he ignored them and let time take its course, Bridget would omit the sexual content from their conversations. After enduring these comments for several weeks, Kevin took Bridget aside and requested that she refrain from making sexual references toward him. He explained to her that in addition to making him uncomfortable, the comments were inappropriate for the work environment.

Initially, Kevin's intervention seemed to have had the desired results. Kevin's encounters with Bridget returned to their original nature and he began to feel comfortable at work again. However, a week later Bridget's sexual comments began to resurface. She repeatedly suggested they have an affair and that he leave his wife for her. Kevin would respond that he was happily married and that he was not interested in having an affair. In addition, he would remind Bridget that he was not comfortable engaging in dialogue containing sexual content. Despite his protests and requests that Bridget refrain from making suggestive comments, the intensity continued to increase. Her comments became more obscene and she started leaving notes for him at work. When it became apparent that Bridget was not going to respect his requests, Kevin began to consider taking action. While the content was of a sexual nature, Kevin was uncertain whether or not Bridget's behavior could be labeled as sexual harassment. First, Kevin was concerned that since Bridget did not hold a position of authority over him, his complaints would not be valid. Second, Kevin worried that gender standards would be detrimental to his position. Specifically, Kevin felt that the fact that the majority of sexual harassment cases are filed against men by women would weaken his case. In addition, the majority of his encounters with Bridget had gone unwitnessed. He feared that the situation would turn

523

into a case of his word against hers and that no one would give him the benefit of the doubt. With all the uncertainty, Kevin was hesitant to take action. While he was unbearably uncomfortable at work, Kevin did not want to risk his job over filing a sexual harassment claim, nor did he want to cause tension at work. On the other hand, his work was suffering because of Bridget's remarks. Fearing that he could lose his job if he did not remedy the problem, Kevin began to research sexual harassment. Upon weighing the consequences, Kevin decided to go forward with filing a sexual harassment complaint against Bridget.

ETHICAL ANALYSIS

Is Kevin's claim against Bridget justified? It is clear that the sexual nature of Bridget's comments were making Kevin uncomfortable at work. But is his discomfort sufficient grounds for filing a sexual harassment complaint? The following guidelines for sexual harassment are offered under Title VII of the 1964 Civil Rights Act:

> Unwelcome sexual advances, requests for sexual favors, and other verbal or physical conduct of a sexual nature constitute sexual harassment when (1) submission to such conduct is made either explicitly or implicitly a term or condition of an individual's employment, (2) submission to or rejection of such conduct by an individual is used as the basis for employment decisions affecting such individual, or (3) such conduct has the purpose or effect of unreasonably interfering with an individual's work performance or creating an intimidating, hostile, or offensive working environment.

From this, two types of sexual harassment have been established. The first part of the guidelines depict quid pro quo cases while the last part refers to a hostile work environment. Kevin's case clearly does not meet the criteria of being quid pro quo; his refusal or acceptance of Bridget's advances

does not have a direct effect on his position at work, nor do her suggestions constitute a term of his employment. Further, while Bridget's comments made Kevin uncomfortable, there is no evidence that his response to her advances would have a direct impact on his job in either a negative or positive way.

The second form of sexual harassment is less direct and seems more applicable to Kevin's situation. In Kevin's case, Bridget's suggestive comments resulted in an uncomfortable work setting. This discomfort caused Kevin's work to suffer which could have negative consequences on his employment status. Thus, it is arguable that Kevin's work performance suffered due to frequent harassment from Bridget. Bridget, however, argues that she was engaging in harmless flirting. In support of her position, she refers to the fact that in sexual harassment cases against men appeals are often made to the fact that men are by nature less sensitive about sexual dialogue. Bridget had assumed that Kevin would be able to handle her flirtation without being offended. In addition, Kevin's rejection of her attention was delayed; she was operating under the impression that they had an established friendship wherein this sort of banter would be appropriate. While this is a seemingly viable defense, its validity is called into question when compared with the fact that Kevin had repeatedly requested that Bridget omit sexual topics from their conversations. When the positions of the two parties are involved, the lines seem less clear. On the one hand, Kevin is clearly distressed about his relationship with Bridget and feels he is being harassed. On the other hand, Bridget is adamant that she was not intending to cause Kevin such discomfort. Instead, she maintains that she had been initiating harmless flirtation and her comments were not intended to be taken seriously. While fairness dictates that both positions be taken into consideration, it makes certainty difficult to attain. Ironically, it is this appeal to fairness that complicates the identification of sexual harassment.

DISCUSSION QUESTIONS

1. If you were on the committee that handled Kevin and Bridget's case, how would you rule? Upon your ruling, what methodology would you initiate to remedy the conflict? If you side with Kevin, what action would you take against Bridget? If, however, you feel Bridget has been unfairly accused, how would you handle the strife between the two coworkers?

2. If Kevin's accusations are correct and Bridget was behaving inappropriately, it is not certain that she intended to cause Kevin strife. To what extent should she be punished?

3. Sexual harassment is labeled as an infringement on a person's basic rights to freedom. What rights and freedoms are specifically compromised? Which ethical theories are most relevant to the issue of sexual harassment and why?

4. In your judgment, does sexual harassment qualify as a form of discrimination?

5. Do you feel that the current guidelines for sexual harassment are sufficient? If you were chosen to provide a more precise account of sexual harassment, what would it be?

6. Does one's right to free speech have priority over a person's right to be free from harassment? Explain your position.

FURTHER READINGS

Anderson, Elizabeth. 2006. "Recent Thinking about Sexual Harassment: A Review Essay." *Philosophy & Public Affairs* 34 (3).

Dromm, Keith. 2012. *Sexual Harassment: An Introduction to the Conceptual and Ethical Issues*. Peterborough, ON: Broadview Press.

Equal Employment Opportunity Commission, http://www.eeoc.gov.

MacKinnon, Catherine. 1979. *Sexual Harassment of Working Women: A Case of Sex Discrimination*. New Haven, CT: Yale University Press.

—66—
IS BUSINESS BLUFFING ETHICAL?

Albert Z. Carr

A RESPECTED BUSINESSMAN WITH WHOM I discussed the theme of this article remarked with some heat, "You mean to say you're going to encourage men to bluff? Why, bluffing is nothing more than a form of lying! You're advising them to lie!"

I agreed that the basis of private morality is a respect for truth and that the closer a businessman comes to the truth, the more he deserves respect. At the same time, I suggested that most bluffing in business might be regarded simply as game strategy—much like bluffing in poker, which does not reflect on the morality of the bluffer.

I quoted Henry Taylor, the British statesman who pointed out that "falsehood ceases to be falsehood when it is understood on all sides that the truth is not expected to be spoken"—an exact description of bluffing in poker, diplomacy, and business. I cited the analogy of the criminal court, where the criminal is not expected to tell the truth when he pleads "not guilty." Everyone from the judge down takes it for granted that the job of the defendant's attorney is to get his client off, not to reveal the truth; and this is considered ethical practice. I mentioned Representative Omar Burleson, the Democrat from Texas, who was quoted as saying, in regard to the ethics of Congress, "Ethics is a barrel of worms"[1]—a pungent summing up of the problem of deciding who is ethical in politics.

I reminded my friend that millions of businessmen feel constrained every day to say *yes* to their bosses when they secretly believe *no* and that this is generally accepted as permissible strategy when the alternative might be the loss of a job. The essential point, I said, is that the ethics of business are game ethics, different from the ethics of religion.

He remained unconvinced. Referring to the company of which he is president, he declared: "Maybe that's good enough for some businessmen, but I can tell you that we pride ourselves on our ethics. In 30 years not one customer has ever questioned my word or asked to check our figures. We're loyal to our customers and fair to our suppliers. I regard my handshake on a deal as a contract. I've never entered into price fixing schemes with my competitors. I've never allowed my salesmen to spread injurious rumors about other companies. Our union contract is the best in our industry. And, if I do say so myself, our ethical standards are of the highest!"

He really was saying, without realizing it, that he was living up to the ethical standards of the business game—which are a far cry from those of private life. Like a gentlemanly poker player, he did not play in cahoots with others at the table, try to smear their reputations, or hold back chips he owed them.

But this same fine man, at that very time, was allowing one of his products to be advertised in a way that made it sound a great deal better than it actually was. Another item in his product line was notorious among dealers for its "built-in obsolescence." He was holding back from the market a much-improved product because he did not want it to interfere with sales of the inferior item it would have replaced. He had joined with certain of his competitors in hiring a lobbyist to push a state legislature, by methods that he preferred not to know too much about, into amending a bill then being enacted.

In his view these things had nothing to do with ethics; they were merely normal business practice. He himself undoubtedly avoided outright falsehoods—never lied in so many words. But the entire organization that he ruled was deeply involved in numerous strategies of deception.

PRESSURE TO DECEIVE

Most executives from time to time are almost compelled, in the interests of their companies or themselves, to practice some form of deception when negotiating with customers, dealers, labor unions, government officials, or even other departments of their companies. By conscious misstatements, concealment of pertinent facts, or exaggeration—in short, by bluffing—they seek to persuade others to agree with them. I think it is fair to say that if the individual executive refuses to bluff from time to time—if he feels obligated to tell the truth, the whole truth, and nothing but the truth—he is ignoring opportunities permitted under the rules and is at a heavy disadvantage in his business dealings.

But here and there a businessman is unable to reconcile himself to the bluff in which he plays a part. His conscience, perhaps spurred by religious idealism, troubles him. He feels guilty; he may develop an ulcer or a nervous tic. Before any executive can make profitable use of the strategy of the bluff, he needs to make sure that in bluffing he will not lose self-respect or become emotionally disturbed. If he is to reconcile personal integrity and high standards of honesty with the practical requirements of business, he must feel that his bluffs are ethically justified. The justification rests on the fact that business, as practiced by individuals as well as by corporations, has the impersonal character of a game—a game that demands both special strategy and an understanding of its special ethics.

The game is played at all levels of corporate life, from the highest to the lowest. At the very instant that a man decides to enter business, he may be forced into a game situation, as is shown by the recent experience of a Cornell honor graduate who applied for a job with a large company:

> This applicant was given a psychological test which included the statement, "Of the following magazines, check any that you have read either regularly or from time to time, and double-check those which interest you most: *Reader's Digest, Time, Fortune, Saturday Evening Post, The New Republic, Life, Look, Ramparts, Newsweek, Business Week, US News & World Report, The Nation, Playboy, Esquire, Harper's, Sports Illustrated*."

> His tastes in reading were broad, and at one time or another he had read almost all of these magazines. He was a subscriber to *The New Republic*, an enthusiast for *Ramparts*, and an avid student of the pictures in *Playboy*. He was not sure whether his interest in *Playboy* would be held against him, but he had a shrewd suspicion that if he confessed to an interest in *Ramparts* and *The New Republic*, he would be thought a liberal, a radical, or at least an intellectual, and his chances of getting the job, which he needed, would greatly diminish. He therefore checked five of the more conservative magazines. Apparently it was a sound decision, for he got the job.

> He had made a game player's decision, consistent with business ethics.

A similar case is that of a magazine space salesman who, owing to a merger, suddenly found himself out of a job:

> This man was 58, and, in spite of a good record, his chance of getting a job elsewhere in a business where youth is favored in hiring practice was not good. He was a vigorous, healthy man, and only a considerable amount of gray in his hair suggested his age. Before beginning his job search he touched up his hair with a black dye to confine the gray to his temples. He knew that the truth about his age might well come out in time, but he calculated that he could deal with that situation when it arose. He and his wife decided that he could easily pass for 45, and he so stated his age on his resume.

This was a lie; yet within the accepted rules of the business game, no moral culpability attaches to it.

THE POKER ANALOGY

We can learn a good deal about the nature of business by comparing it with poker. While both have a large element of chance, in the long run the winner is the man who plays with steady skill. In both games ultimate victory requires intimate knowledge of the rules, insight into the psychology of the other players, a bold front, a considerable amount of self-discipline, and the ability to respond swiftly and effectively to opportunities provided by chance.

No one expects poker to be played on the ethical principles preached in churches. In poker it is right and proper to bluff a friend out of the rewards of being dealt a good hand. A player feels no more than a slight twinge of sympathy, if that, when—with nothing better than a single ace in his hand—he strips a heavy loser, who holds a pair, of the rest of his chips. It was up to the other fellow to protect himself. In the words of an excellent poker player, former President Harry

Truman, "If you can't stand the heat, stay out of the kitchen." If one shows mercy to a loser in poker, it is a personal gesture, divorced from the rules of the game.

Poker has its special ethics, and here I am not referring to rules against cheating. The man who keeps an ace up his sleeve or who marks the cards is more than unethical; he is a crook, and can be punished as such—kicked out of the game or,—in the Old West, shot.

In contrast to the cheat, the unethical poker player is one who, while abiding by the letter of the rules, finds ways to put the other players at an unfair disadvantage. Perhaps he unnerves them with loud talk. Or he tries to get them drunk. Or he plays in cahoots with someone else at the table. Ethical poker players frown on such tactics.

Poker's own brand of ethics is different from the ethical ideals of civilized human relationships. The game calls for distrust of the other fellow. It ignores the claim of friendship. Cunning deception and concealment of one's strength and intentions, not kindness and openheartedness, are vital in poker. No one thinks any the worse of poker on that account. And no one should think any the worse of the game of business because its standards of right and wrong differ from the prevailing traditions of morality in our society.

DISCARD THE GOLDEN RULE

This view of business is especially worrisome to people without much business experience. A minister of my acquaintance once protested that business cannot possibly function in our society unless it is based on the Judeo-Christian system of ethics. He told me:

> I know some businessmen have supplied call girls to customers, but there are always a few rotten apples in every barrel. That doesn't mean the rest of the fruit isn't sound. Surely the vast majority of businessmen are ethical. I myself am acquainted with many who adhere to strict codes of ethics based fundamentally

on religious teachings. They contribute to good causes. They participate in community activities. They cooperate with other companies to improve working conditions in their industries. Certainly they are not indifferent to ethics.

That most businessmen are not indifferent to ethics in their private lives, everyone will agree. My point is that in their office lives they cease to be private citizens; they become game players who must be guided by a somewhat different set of ethical standards.

The point was forcefully made to me by a Midwestern executive who has given a good deal of thought to the question:

So long as a businessman complies with the laws of the land and avoids telling malicious lies, he's ethical. If the law as written gives a man a wide-open chance to make a killing, he'd be a fool not to take advantage of it. If he doesn't, somebody else will. There's no obligation on him to stop and consider who is going to get hurt. If the law says he can do it, that's all the justification he needs. There's nothing unethical about that. It's just plain business sense.

This executive (call him Robbins) took the stand that even industrial espionage, which is frowned on by some businessmen, ought not to be considered unethical. He recalled a recent meeting of the National Industrial Conference Board where an authority on marketing made a speech in which he deplored the employment of spies by business organizations. More and more companies, he pointed out, find it cheaper to penetrate the secrets of competitors with concealed cameras and microphones or by bribing employees than to set up costly research and design departments of their own. A whole branch of the electronics industry has grown up with this trend, he continued, providing equipment to make industrial espionage easier.

Disturbing? The marketing expert found it so. But when it came to a remedy, he could only appeal to "respect for the golden rule." Robbins thought this a confession of defeat, believing that the golden rule, for all its value as an ideal for society, is simply not feasible as a guide for business. A good part of the time the businessman is trying to do unto others as he hopes others will not do unto him.[2] Robbins continued:

Espionage of one kind or another has become so common in business that it's like taking a drink during Prohibition—it's not considered sinful. And we don't even have Prohibition where espionage is concerned; the law is very tolerant in this area. There's no more shame for a business that uses secret agents than there is for a nation. Bear in mind that there already is at least one large corporation—you can buy its stock over the counter—that makes millions by providing counterespionage service to industrial firms. Espionage in business is not an ethical problem; it's an established technique of business competition.

"WE DON'T MAKE THE LAWS"

Wherever we turn in business, we can perceive the sharp distinction between its ethical standards and those of the churches. Newspapers abound with sensational stories growing out of this distinction:

· We read one day that Senator Philip A. Hart of Michigan has attacked food processors for deceptive packaging of numerous products.[3]
· The next day there is a Congressional to-do over Ralph Nader's book, *Unsafe At Any Speed*, which demonstrates that automobile companies for years have neglected the safety of car-owning families.[4]
· Then another Senator, Lee Metcalf of Montana, and journalist Vic Reinemer show in their book, *Overcharge*, the methods by

which utility companies elude regulating government bodies to extract unduly large payments from users of electricity.[5]

These are merely dramatic instances of a prevailing condition; there is hardly a major industry at which a similar attack could not be aimed. Critics of business regard such behavior as unethical, but the companies concerned know that they are merely playing the business game.

Among the most respected of our business institutions are the insurance companies. A group of insurance executives meeting recently in New England was startled when their guest speaker, social critic Daniel Patrick Moynihan, roundly berated them for "unethical" practices. They had been guilty, Moynihan alleged, of using outdated actuarial tables to obtain unfairly high premiums. They habitually delayed the hearings of lawsuits against them in order to tire out the plaintiffs and win cheap settlements. In their employment policies they used ingenious devices to discriminate against certain minority groups.[6]

It was difficult for the audience to deny the validity of these charges. But these men were business game players. Their reaction to Moynihan's attack was much the same as that of the automobile manufacturers to Nader, of the utilities to Senator Metcalf, and of the food processors to Senator Hart. If the laws governing their businesses change, or if public opinion becomes clamorous, they will make the necessary adjustments. But morally they have in their view done nothing wrong. As long as they comply with the letter of the law, they are within their rights to operate their businesses as they see fit.

The small business is in the same position as the great corporation in this respect. For example:

In 1967 a key manufacturer was accused of providing master keys for automobiles to mail-order customers, although it was obvious that some of the purchasers might be automobile thieves. His defense was plain and straightforward. If there was nothing in the law to prevent him from selling his keys to anyone who ordered them, it was not up to him to inquire as to his customers' motives. Why was it any worse, he insisted, for him to sell car keys by mail, than for mail-order houses to sell guns that might be used for murder? Until the law was changed, the key manufacturer could regard himself as being just as ethical as any other businessman by the rules of the business game.[7]

Violations of the ethical ideals of society are common in business, but they are not necessarily violations of business principles. Each year the Federal Trade Commission orders hundreds of companies, many of them of the first magnitude, to "cease and desist" from practices which, judged by ordinary standards, are of questionable morality but which are stoutly defended by the companies concerned.

In one case, a firm manufacturing a well-known mouthwash was accused of using a cheap form of alcohol possibly deleterious to health. The company's chief executive, after testifying in Washington, made this comment privately:

We broke no law. We're in a highly competitive industry. If we're going to stay in business, we have to look for profit wherever the law permits. We don't make the laws. We obey them. Then why do we have to put up with this 'holier than thou' talk about ethics? It's sheer hypocrisy. We're not in business to promote ethics. Look at the cigarette companies, for God's sake! If the ethics aren't embodied in the laws by the men who made them, you can't expect businessmen to fill the lack. Why, a sudden submission to Christian ethics by businessmen would bring about the greatest economic upheaval in history!

It may be noted that the government failed to prove its case against him.

CAST ILLUSIONS ASIDE

Talk about ethics by businessmen is often a thin decorative coating over the hard realities of the game:

Once I listened to a speech by a young executive who pointed to a new industry code as proof that his company and its competitors were deeply aware of their responsibilities to society. It was a code of ethics, he said. The industry was going to police itself, to dissuade constituent companies from wrongdoing. His eyes shone with conviction and enthusiasm.

The same day there was a meeting in a hotel room where the industry's top executives met with the "czar" who was to administer the new code, a man of high repute. No one who was present could doubt their common attitude. In their eyes the code was designed primarily to forestall a move by the federal government to impose stern restrictions on the industry. They felt that the code would hamper them a good deal less than new federal laws would. It was, in other words, conceived as a protection for the industry, not for the public.

The young executive accepted the surface explanation of the code; these leaders, all experienced game players, did not deceive themselves for a moment about its purpose.

The illusion that business can afford to be guided by ethics as conceived in private life is often fostered by speeches and articles containing such phrases as, "It pays to be ethical," or, "Sound ethics is good business." Actually this is not an ethical position at all; it is a self-serving calculation in disguise. The speaker is really saying that in the long run a company can make more money if it does not antagonize competitors, suppliers, employees, and customers by squeezing them too hard. He is saying that oversharp policies reduce ultimate gains. That is true, but it has nothing to do with ethics. The underlying attitude is much like that in the familiar story of the shopkeeper who finds an extra $20 bill in the cash register, debates with himself the ethical problem—should he tell his partner?—and finally decides to share the money because the gesture will give him an edge over the s.o.b. the next time they quarrel.

I think it is fair to sum up the prevailing attitude of businessmen on ethics as follows:

We live in what is probably the most competitive of the world's civilized societies. Our customs encourage a high degree of aggression in the individual's striving for success. Business is our main area of competition, and it has been ritualized into a game of strategy. The basic rules of the game have been set by the government, which attempts to detect and punish business frauds. But as long as a company does not transgress the rules of the game set by law, it has the legal right to shape its strategy without reference to anything but its profits. If it takes a long-term view of its profits, it will preserve amicable relations, so far as possible, with those with whom it deals. A wise businessman will not seek advantage to the point where he generates dangerous hostility among employees, competitors, customers, government, or the public at large. But decisions in this area are, in the final test, decisions of strategy, not of ethics.

THE INDIVIDUAL AND THE GAME

An individual within a company often finds it difficult to adjust to the requirements of the business game. He tries to preserve his private ethical standards in situations that call for game strategy. When he is obliged to carry out company policies that challenge his conception of himself as an ethical man, he suffers.

It disturbs him when he is ordered, for instance, to deny a raise to a man who deserves it, to fire an employee of long standing, to prepare advertising that he believes to be misleading, to conceal facts that he feels customers are entitled to know, to cheapen the quality of materials used in the manufacture of an established product, to sell as new a product that he knows to be rebuilt, to exaggerate the curative powers of a medicinal preparation, or to coerce dealers.

There are some fortunate executives who, by the nature of their work and circumstances, never have to face problems of this kind. But in one form or another the ethical dilemma is felt sooner or later by most businessmen. Possibly the dilemma is most painful not when the company forces the action on the executive but when he originates it himself—that is, when he has taken or is contemplating a step which is in his own interest but which runs counter to his early moral conditioning. To illustrate:

- The manager of an export department, eager to show rising sales, is pressed by a big customer to provide invoices which, while containing no overt falsehood that would violate a US law, are so worded that the customer may be able to evade certain taxes in his homeland.
- A company president finds that an aging executive, within a few years of retirement and his pension, is not as productive as formerly. Should he be kept on?
- The produce manager of a supermarket debates with himself whether to get rid of a lot of half-rotten tomatoes by including one, with its good side exposed, in every tomato six-pack.
- An accountant discovers that he has taken an improper deduction on his company's tax return and fears the consequences if he calls the matter to the president's attention, though he himself has done nothing illegal. Perhaps if he says nothing, no one will notice the error.
- A chief executive officer is asked by his directors to comment on a rumor that he owns stock in another company with which he has placed large orders. He could deny it, for the stock is in the name of his son-in-law and he has earlier formally instructed his son-in-law to sell the holding.

Temptations of this kind constantly arise in business. If an executive allows himself to be torn between a decision based on business considerations and one based on his private ethical code, he exposes himself to a grave psychological strain.

This is not to say that sound business strategy necessarily runs counter to ethical ideals. They may frequently coincide; and when they do, everyone is gratified. But the major tests of every move in business, as in all games of strategy, are legality and profit. A man who intends to be a winner in the business game must have a game player's attitude.

The business strategist's decisions must be as impersonal as those of a surgeon performing an operation—concentrating on objective and technique, and subordinating personal feelings. If the chief executive admits that his son-in-law owns the stock, it is because he stands to lose more if the fact comes out later than if he states it boldly and at once. If the supermarket manager orders the rotten tomatoes to be discarded, he does so to avoid an increase in consumer complaints and a loss of goodwill. The company president decides not to fire the elderly executive in the belief that the negative reaction of other employees would in the long run cost the company more than it would lose in keeping him and paying his pension.

All sensible businessmen prefer to be truthful, but they seldom feel inclined to tell the *whole* truth. In the business game truth-telling usually has to be kept within narrow limits if trouble is to be avoided. The point was neatly made a long time ago (in 1888) by one of John D. Rockefeller's associates, Paul Babcock, to Standard Oil Company executives who were about to testify before a government investigating committee: "Parry every question with answers which, while perfectly truthful, are evasive of *bottom* facts."[8] This was, is, and probably always will be regarded as wise and permissible business strategy.

FOR OFFICE USE ONLY

An executive's family life can easily be dislocated if he fails to make a sharp distinction between the ethical systems of the home and the office—or if his wife does not grasp that distinction. Many a businessman who has remarked to his wife, "I had to let Jones go today" or "I had to admit to the boss that Jim has been goofing off lately," has been met with an indignant protest. "How could you do a thing like that? You know Jones is over 50 and will have a lot of trouble getting another job." Or, "You did that to Jim? With his wife ill and all the worry she's been having with the kids?"

If the executive insists that he had no choice because the profits of the company and his own security were involved, he may see a certain cool and ominous reappraisal in his wife's eyes. Many wives are not prepared to accept the fact that business operates with a special code of ethics. An illuminating illustration of this comes from a Southern sales executive who related a conversation he had had with his wife at a time when a hotly contested political campaign was being waged in their state:

I made the mistake of telling her that I had had lunch with Colby, who gives me about half my business. Colby mentioned that his company had a stake in the election. Then he said, "By the way, I'm treasurer of the citizens' committee for Lang. I'm collecting contributions. Can I count on you for a hundred dollars?"

Well, there I was. I was opposed to Lang, but I knew Colby. If he withdrew his business I could be in a bad spot. So I just smiled and wrote out a check then and there. He thanked me, and we started to talk about his next order. Maybe he thought I shared his political views. If so, I wasn't going to lose any sleep over it.

I should have had sense enough not to tell Mary about it. She hit the ceiling. She said she was disappointed in me. She said I hadn't acted like a man, that I should have stood up to Colby.

I said, "Look, it was an either-or situation. I had to do it or risk losing the business."

She came back at me with, "I don't believe it. You could have been honest with him. You could have said that you didn't feel you ought to contribute to a campaign for a man you weren't going to vote for. I'm sure he would have understood."

I said, "Mary, you're a wonderful woman, but you're way off the track. Do you know what would have happened if I had said that? Colby would have smiled and said, 'Oh, I didn't realize. Forget it.' But in his eyes from that moment I would be an oddball, maybe a bit of a radical. He would have listened to me talk about his order and would have promised to give it consideration. After that I wouldn't hear from him for a week. Then I would telephone and learn from his secretary that he wasn't yet ready to place the order. And in about a month I would hear through the grapevine that he was giving his business to another company. A month after that I'd be out of a job."

She was silent for a while. Then she said, "Tom, something is wrong with business when a man is forced to choose between his family's security and his moral obligation to himself. It's easy for me to say you should have stood up to him—but if you had, you might have felt you were betraying me and the kids. I'm sorry that you did it, Tom, but I can't blame you. Something is wrong with business!"

This wife saw the problem in terms of moral obligation as conceived in private life; her husband saw it as a matter of game strategy. As a player in a weak position, he felt that he could not afford to indulge an ethical sentiment that might have cost him his seat at the table.

PLAYING TO WIN

Some men might challenge the Colbys of business—might accept serious setbacks to their business careers rather than risk a feeling of moral cowardice. They merit our respect—but as private individuals, not businessmen. When the skillful player of the business game is compelled to submit to unfair pressure, he does not castigate himself for moral weakness. Instead, he strives to put himself into a strong position where he can defend himself against such pressures in the future without loss.

If a man plans to take a seat in the business game, he owes it to himself to master the principles by which the game is played, including its special ethical outlook. He can then hardly fail to recognize that an occasional bluff may well be justified in terms of the game's ethics and warranted in terms of economic necessity. Once he clears his mind on this point, he is in a good position to match his strategy against that of the other players. He can then determine objectively whether a bluff in a given situation has a good chance of succeeding and can decide when and how to bluff, without a feeling of ethical transgression.

To be a winner, a man must play to win. This does not mean that he must be ruthless, cruel, harsh, or treacherous. On the contrary, the better his reputation for integrity, honesty, and decency, the better his chances of victory will be in the long run. But from time to time every businessman, like every poker player, is offered a choice between certain loss or bluffing within the legal rules of the game. If he is not resigned to losing, if he wants to rise in his company and industry, then in such a crisis he will bluff—and bluff hard.

Every now and then one meets a successful businessman who has conveniently forgotten the small or large deceptions that he practiced on his way to fortune. "God gave me my money," old John D. Rockefeller once piously told a Sunday school class. It would be a rare tycoon in our time who would risk the horse laugh with which such a remark would be greeted.

In the last third of the twentieth century even children are aware that if a man has become prosperous in business, he has sometimes departed from the strict truth in order to overcome obstacles or has practiced the more subtle deceptions of the half-truth or the misleading omission. Whatever the form of the bluff, it is an integral part of the game, and the executive who does not master its techniques is not likely to accumulate much money or power.

NOTES

1   *The New York Times*, March 9, 1967.
2   See Bruce D. Henderson, "Brinkmanship in Business," *Harvard Business Review* March-April 1967, 49.
3   *The New York Times*, November 21, 1966.
4   New York: Grossman Publishers, Inc., 1965.
5   New York: David McKay Company, Inc., 1967.
6   *The New York Times*, January 17, 1967.
7   Cited by Ralph Nader in "Business Crime," *The New Republic*, July 1, 1967, 7.
8   Babcock in a memorandum to Rockefeller (Rockefeller Archives).

—67—
SECOND THOUGHTS ABOUT BLUFFING

Thomas Carson

I. INTRODUCTION

In the United States it is common, perhaps even a matter of course, for people to misstate their bargaining positions during business negotiations. I have in mind the following kinds of cases, all of which involve deliberate false statements about one's bargaining position, intentions, or preferences in a negotiation: 1. I am selling a house and tell a prospective buyer that $90,000 is absolutely the lowest price that I will accept, when I know that I would be willing to accept as little as $80,000 for the house. 2. A union negotiator says that $13.00 an hour is the very lowest wage that his union is willing to consider when, in fact, he has been authorized by the union to accept a wage as low as $12.00 an hour. 3. I tell a prospective buyer that I am in no hurry to sell my house when, in fact, I am desperate to sell it within a few days.[1] Such statements would seem to constitute lies—they are deliberate false statements made with the intent to deceive others about the nature of one's own bargaining position. 1) and 2) clearly constitute lies according to standard dictionary definitions of lying. The *Oxford English Dictionary* defines the word "lie" as follows: "a false statement made with the intent to deceive." Also see *Webster's International Dictionary of the English Language,* (1929) "to utter a falsehood with the intent to deceive."

The cases described above should be contrasted with instances of bluffing which do not involve making false statements. An example of the latter case would be saying "I want more" in response to an offer which I am willing to accept rather than not reach an agreement at all. This paper will focus on cases of bluffing which involve deliberate false statements about one's bargaining position or one's "settlement preferences."

I will defend the following two theses:

1. Appearances to the contrary, this kind of bluffing typically does not constitute lying. (I will argue that standard dictionary definitions of lying are untenable and defend an alternative definition hinted at, but never clearly formulated, by W.D. Ross. On my definition, deliberate false statements about one's negotiating position usually do not constitute lies *in this society.*)
2. It is usually permissible to misstate one's bargaining position or settlement preferences when one has good reason to think that one's negotiating partner is doing the same and it is usually impermissible to misstate one's negotiating position if one does not have good reason to think that the other party is misstating her position (preferences).

There are significant puzzles and uncertainties involved in applying my definition of lying to cases of misstating one's bargaining position. Because of this, I intend to make my argument for b) independent of my argument for a). My arguments for b) are compatible with (but do not presuppose) the view that misstating one's position is lying and that lying is *prima facie* wrong. I will conclude the paper with a brief examination of other related deceptive stratagems in negotiations.

II. THE ECONOMIC SIGNIFICANCE OF BLUFFING

In a business negotiation there is typically a range of possible agreements that each party would be willing to accept rather than reach no agreement at all. For instance, I might be willing to sell my home for as little as $80,000. (I would prefer to sell the house for $80,000 *today*, rather than continue to try to sell the house.) My range of acceptable agreements extends upward without limit—I would be willing to accept any price in excess of $80,000 rather than fail to make the sale today. Suppose that a prospective buyer is willing to spend as much as $85,000 for the house. (She prefers to buy the house for $85,000 today rather than not buy it at all today.) The buyer's range of acceptable agreements presumably extends downward without limit—she would be willing to purchase the house for any price below $85,000. In this case the two bargaining positions overlap and an agreement is possible (today). Unless there is some overlap between the minimum bargaining positions of the two parties, no agreement is possible. For example, if the seller's lowest acceptable price is $80,000 and the buyer's highest acceptable price is $70,000 no sale will be possible unless at least one of the parties alters her position.

If there is an overlap between the bargaining positions of the negotiators, then the actual outcome will depend on the negotiations. Consider again our example of the negotiation over the sale of the house. The owner is willing to sell the house for as little as $80,000 and the prospective buyer is willing to pay as much as $85,000. Whether the house sells for $80,000, $85,000, somewhere between $80,000 and $85,000, or even whether it sells at all will be determined by the negotiations.

In this case, it would be very advantageous for either party to know the other person's minimum acceptable position and disadvantageous for either to reveal her position to the other. For example, if the buyer knows that the lowest price that the seller is willing to accept is $80,000, she can drive him towards the limit of his range of acceptable offers. She knows that he will accept an offer of $80,000 rather than have her break off the negotiations. In negotiations both buyer and seller will ordinarily have reason to keep their own bargaining positions and intentions secret.

It can sometimes be to one's advantage to mislead others about one's own minimum bargaining position. In the present case, it would be to the seller's advantage to cause the buyer to think that $85,000 is the lowest price that he (the seller) will accept. For in this case the buyer would offer $85,000 for the house—the best possible agreement from the seller's point of view. (It would also be easy to imagine cases in which it would be to the buyer's advantage to mislead the seller about her bargaining position.) There are various ways in which the seller might attempt to bluff the buyer in order to mislead her about his position. 1. He might set a very high "asking price," for example, $100,000. 2. He might initially refuse an offer and threaten to cut off the negotiations unless a higher offer is made while at the same time being prepared to accept the offer before the other person breaks off the negotiations. (I have in mind something like the following. The prospective buyer offers $80,000 and the seller replies: "I want more than that; I'm not happy with $80,000 why don't you think about it and give me a call tomorrow.") 3. He might misrepresent his own bargaining position.

The kind of deception involved in 1) and 2) does not (or need not) involve lying or making false statements. 3) involves a deliberate false statement intended to deceive the other party and thus constitutes lying according to the standard definition of lying.

Attempting to mislead the other person about one's bargaining position can backfire and prevent a negotiation from reaching a mutually acceptable settlement which both parties would have preferred to no agreement at all. For example, suppose that the seller tells the buyer that he won't accept anything less than $95,000 for the house. If the buyer believes him she will break off the negotiations, since, by hypothesis, she is not willing to pay $95,000 for the house. Unless he knows the other person's bargaining position, a person who misrepresents his own position risks losing the opportunity to reach an acceptable agreement. By misstating one's position one also risks angering the other party and thereby causing him to modify his position or even break off the negotiations. (Truthful statements about one's own position might be perceived as lies and thus also risk alienating one's counterpart.)

III. THE CONCEPT OF LYING

1. *The Standard Definition.* Standard dictionary definitions of lying are correct in holding that a lie must be a false statement. Showing that a statement is true is always sufficient to rebut the charge that one has told a lie. However, the two dictionary definitions cited earlier leave out an essential feature of lying. If a person's making a statement constitutes a lie, then it cannot be the case that she believes that it is true. Showing that one believed what one said is always sufficient to rebut a charge of lying.

According to most standard definitions of lying, telling a lie necessarily involves the intention to deceive others. See for example, the definitions from the *OED* and *Webster's* presented at the beginning of the paper. These definitions and other definitions which imply that the intent to deceive is a necessary condition of lying prove inadequate for dealing with certain kinds of cases in which one is compelled or enticed to make false statements. Suppose that I witness a crime and clearly see that a particular individual committed the crime. Later, the same person is accused of the crime and, as a witness in court, I am asked whether or not I saw the defendant

commit the crime. I make the false statement that I did not see the defendant commit the crime, for fear of being harmed or killed by him. It does not follow that I hope or intend that my false statements deceive anyone. (I may hope that he is convicted in spite of my testimony.) Deceiving the jury is not a means to securing my goal of preserving my life. Giving false testimony is a necessary means to achieving this goal, but deceiving others is not, it is merely an unintended "side effect." Clearly, in both the ordinary language sense of "intentional act" and in the standard philosophical sense of the term my deceiving the jury in such a case would not be intentional. But it seems clear that my false testimony would constitute a lie. This objection can be put more generally as follows. It is (or rather can be) a lie if I say x (where x is something that I know is false) in order to achieve objective (o), even if others coming to believe x is a foreseeable side effect of the action and neither a part of (o) nor a means to achieving (o).

2. *A New Definition of Lying.* I have defended an alternative analysis of the concept of lying in a paper written several years after the original paper on bluffing.[2] I still agree with much of this. I shall explain my definition here, repeating some of what I said in the paper on lying. I refer the reader to the paper on lying for a defense of my definition. My definition of lying is inspired by Ross's claim that the duty not to lie is a special case of the duty to keep promises. Ross holds that (at least in ordinary contexts) we make an implicit promise to be truthful when we use language to communicate with others. To lie is to break an implicit promise to be truthful.

Ross's view that making a statement (ordinarily) involves making an implicit promise that what one says is true suggests the following provisional definition of "lying" (Ross himself never attempts to define "lying"):

Y. A lie is a false statement which the "speaker" does not believe to be true made in a context in which the speaker warrants the truth of what he says.

This definition handles the earlier counter-example. Not only is the implicit warranty of truthfulness in force in the case of the witness's testimony in court, the witness explicitly warrants the truth of what he says by swearing an oath. Another virtue of the present analysis is that it makes sense of the common view that lying involves a violation of trust. To lie, in my view, is to invite trust and encourage others to believe what one says by warranting the truth of what one says and at the same time to betray that trust by making false statements which one does not believe to be true....

4. *The Concept of Warranting.* What does it mean to warrant the truth of what one says? I will not attempt to offer a definition with necessary and sufficient conditions. But I will try to sketch the outlines of an analysis. A warranty is a kind of promise. Following Austin and Searle, contemporary philosophers generally take promising to be a kind of performative act. To make a promise is to place oneself under an obligation to do something. This kind of analysis is claimed to be necessary in order to explain the difference between promising to do x and stating an intention to do x. But special problems arise if we attempt to extend this account of promising as an analysis of warranting the truth of a statement. If one promises to do x it is very clear *which action* one is placing oneself under an obligation to perform (one is placing oneself under an obligation to do x). But often when one warrants the truth of a statement it is unclear whether one is placing oneself under an obligation to perform any *particular action*. To warrant the truth of a statement x is not necessarily to place oneself under an obligation to make it true that x. For one is usually not in a position to affect the truth of the statements one makes. If I warrant the truth of my statement that the moon is 250,000 miles from the earth I am not placing myself under an obligation to make it the case that the moon is 250,000 miles from earth. Nor will it do to say that to warrant the truth of x is to place oneself under an obligation to perform acts of compensation in case x turns out not to be true and others are harmed as a result of believing our statements. There simply is no

general understanding about what (if anything) we owe others when they suffer harms or losses as a result of accepting false claims that we make. How can we characterize warranting the truth of a statement? To warrant a statement as true is to invite others to rely on it and assure them that it can be relied upon. When warranting a statement one is granting others permission to complain if the statement does not turn out to be true.

In our linguistic community and all others of which I am aware there is a presumption for thinking that the warranty of truth is in force in any situation. *Convention* dictates that one warrants the truth of one's statements, in the absence of special contexts, special signals, or cues to the contrary. In the context of a work of fiction, in games such as "Risk," or when saying something in jest, one is not guaranteeing the truth of what one says. So, for example, one is not implicitly guaranteeing that what one says is true if in the course of a game of "Risk" one makes the false statement that one will not attack one's opponent, or when one says something manifestly false to a friend in a joking tone of voice. In many cases it is unclear whether those who speak or communicate can be said to be warranting the truth of what they say. For example, suppose that I deliberately make a false statement to a person whom I know to be very gullible but give a very subtle indication that I might be joking (I might, for example, raise an eyebrow). In such a case it is unclear whether I am warranting the truth of what I say and, therefore, unclear whether or not this should be considered a lie. Such cases should be considered borderline cases for the concept of lying. It is a virtue of the present analysis that they count as such.

5. *Lying and Bluffing.* What are the implications of my analysis of lying for the issue of bluffing? Negotiations between experienced and "hardened" negotiators in our society (e.g., horse traders and realtors) are akin to a game of "Risk." It is understood that any statements one makes about one's role or intentions as a player during a game of "Risk" are not warranted to be true. In negotiations between hardened and cynical negotiators

statements about one's intentions or settlement preferences are not warranted to be true. But it would be too strong to hold that nothing that one says in negotiations is warranted to be true. Convention dictates that other kinds of statements concerning the transaction being contemplated, e.g., statements to the effect that one has another offer, are warranted as true. So, for example, in my view, it would be a lie if I (the seller) were to falsely claim that someone else has offered me $85,000 for my house.

I am strongly inclined to believe that statements about one's minimum negotiating position are not warranted to be true in negotiations between "hardened negotiators" who recognize each other as such. I cannot here propose general criteria for determining when one may be said to warrant the truth of what one says. Therefore, what follows is somewhat conjectural. A cynical negotiator typically does not expect (predict) that her counterpart will speak truthfully about his minimum negotiating position. This alone is not enough to remove the implicit warranty of truth. A pathological liar who denies his every misdeed warrants the truth of what he says, even if those he addresses do not *expect* (predict) that what he says is true. The crucial feature of a negotiation which distinguishes it from the foregoing case is that in ordinary negotiations each party *consents* to renouncing the ordinary warranty of truth. There are various ways in which people consent to removing the default warranty of truth. Business negotiations are ritualized activities to which certain unstated rules and expectations (both in the sense of predictions and demands) apply. It is not expected that one will speak truthfully about one's negotiating position. Those who understand this and who enter into negotiations with other parties who are known to share this understanding implicitly consent to the rules and expectations of the negotiating ritual. In so doing, they consent to remove the warranty of truth for statements about one's minimum negotiating position.

Here one might raise the following objection: "Of course I recognize that misstating one's position is *thought to be permissible*, but I strongly disapprove of that practice. I don't consent to being deceived when I enter into a negotiation simply because I know that others are likely to try to deceive me. In the old south it was an 'accepted' practice for blacks to be very deferential to whites in social interactions. But we cannot say that blacks who entered into social interactions with whites thereby gave their consent to abiding by the unwritten rules requiring deference."

Reply. There are relevant differences between the social code of the old south and our society's present rules and conventions for negotiations. Most people do not object to standard negotiating practices and those who enter into negotiations are justified in presuming acceptance of those practices by their counterparts. Further, those who do object to these practices can air their objections openly without fear of dire consequences. Most blacks objected very much to the social mores of the old south but were justifiably afraid of publicly airing their objections. Many whites deluded themselves into thinking that blacks did not object to their status, but few, if any, had adequate evidence for this view. My underlying principle here can be stated roughly as follows:

> Y implicitly consents to X's doing (act) *a* to him (Y) provided that: 1) X knows that: i) Y expects X to do *a* to him, ii) Y doesn't object to X's doing *a* to him, and iii) Y can, without fear of harm, object to X's doing *a* to him, and 2) Y knows that X knows that i)-iii).

Before moving on to other issues, I would again like to stress the following two points: 1. my application of my definition of lying to this case is tentative and conjectural, and 2. my arguments concerning the moral status of bluffing do not depend on the assumption that misstating one's bargaining position or intentions is (typically) not a case of lying (my arguments are compatible with the view that misstating one's position or intentions is lying)....

VII. VARIATIONS ON THE EXAMPLE

1. Is *Lying Worse than Mere Deception*? Consider the following case. Suppose that I want the other party to hold false beliefs about my minimum bargaining position. I want him to think that $90,000 is the lowest price that I'm willing to accept for my house when, in fact, I'm willing to sell it for as little as $80,000. However, I am very much averse to lying about this and I believe that misstating my own position would be a lie. I am willing to try to deceive or mislead him about my intentions, but I am not willing to lie about them. Here, as in many cases, it is possible to think of true but equally misleading things to say so as to avoid lying. Suppose that our lowest acceptable selling price is $80,000, but I want you to think that it is actually around $85,000. Instead of lying, I could say "my wife told me to tell you that $85,000 is absolutely the lowest price that we are willing to accept." The trick here would be to have my wife utter the words "tell the buyer that $85,000 is absolutely the lowest price that we will accept." In saying this she would not be stating our minimum position, but rather helping to create the ruse to fool the buyer. It is very doubtful that this is morally preferable to lying. Intuitively, it strikes me as worse. Many people (perhaps most) seem to believe that making true but deceptive statements is preferable to lying. This is demonstrated by the fact that many (most?) of us will, on occasion, go through verbal contortions or give very careful thought to exactly what we say in order to mislead others without lying. In this kind of case lying does not seem to be morally preferable to "mere deception."

Consider another example in which the difference between lying and mere deception does not seem to be morally significant. Suppose that two parents go out of town for the weekend leaving their two adolescent children home alone. The parents give their son strict orders that under no circumstances is he permitted to entertain his girlfriend in the house while they are away. The parents call during the weekend to "check up" on the children. They speak with their daughter. "What's going on there? What is your brother up to? He doesn't have Nora [his girlfriend] there does he?" The son is entertaining Nora in the house at the time that they call. The daughter does not want to get her brother in trouble, but, on the other hand, she doesn't want to lie. She does not answer the last question directly, but replies with the following true, but misleading, statement. "He's fine; he's watching the ball game with Bob." (Bob is a male friend who *is* there but is about to leave.)

2. *Claiming to have another offer.* In my view, the fact that misstating one's position is a very common practice can often help justify misstating one's own position. Because misstating one's bargaining position is such a widespread practice in our society, one is often justified in assuming that one's negotiating partner is misrepresenting her position. If the other person states a minimum bargaining position, then one is justified in thinking that she is misrepresenting that position, in the absence of reasons for thinking that she is not.

There are other ways of deceiving others about one's bargaining position which are not common practice. The following two cases are among the kinds that I have in mind here:

Case #1. I (the seller) say to a prospective buyer "I have another offer for $80,000, but I'll let you have it if you can beat the offer" when, in fact, I don't have another offer.

Case #2. I (the seller) want you to think that I have another offer. I have my brother come over and in your presence pretend to offer me $80,000 for the condo. (You don't know that he is my brother.) I say to my brother "the other person was here first. I'll have to let him/her see if he/she wants to meet the offer." I turn to the seller and say "It's yours for $80,000."

What I say in the first case is clearly a lie. It is a deliberate false statement which is warranted to be true and is intended to deceive others. My action in this case is *prima facie* very wrong. I am putting extreme pressure on the other person and may panic her into a rash decision. Falsely claiming to have another offer could, in principle, be justified by appeal to SD. If the buyer was falsely representing the possibility of another comparable deal, then a Rossian theory might conceivably justify me in doing the same. This is very unlikely in the ordinary course of things. This means that it is unlikely that one could defend lying in such a case by appeal to the need to defend one's own interests. My actions in case #2 seem intuitively even worse than those in #1. Case #2 does not involve lying but it does involve an elaborate scheme of deception and is potentially very harmful to the buyer. The same general things that I said about case #1 apply here. My actions in this case are *prima facie* very wrong. In principle, a Rossian theory could justify those actions, but that is very unlikely. I will not undertake a detailed examination of the implications of utilitarianism for these two cases. I would refer the reader to the arguments of section VI.2 which purport to show that AU implies that it would (usually) be wrong to misstate one's position to someone who has not first misstated her own position. A parallel, but much stronger, argument could be given for thinking that AU implies that the kind of lying or deception involved in these two cases would usually be wrong.

NOTES

1   This example is taken from "Shrewd Bargaining on the Moral Frontier: Towards a Theory of Morality in Practice," J. Gregory Dees and Peter C. Crampton, *Business Ethics Quarterly*, Vol. 1, No. 2, April 1991, 143.
2   "On the Definition of Lying: A Reply to Jones and Revisions," *Journal of Business Ethics*, 7, 509–14.

—68—
BUSINESS BLUFFING RECONSIDERED

Fritz Allhoff

1. INTRODUCTION

Imagine that I walk into a car dealership and tell the salesperson that I absolutely cannot pay more than $10,000 for the car that I want. And imagine further she tells me that she absolutely cannot sell the car for less than $12,000. Assuming that neither one of us is telling the truth, we are bluffing about our reservation prices, the price above or below which we will no longer be willing to make the transaction. This is certainly a common practice and, moreover, is most likely minimally prudent—whether our negotiating adversary is bluffing or not, it will always be in our interest to bluff. Discussions of bluffing in business commonly invoke reservation prices, but need not; one could misrepresent his position in any number of areas including the financial health of a company poised for merger, the authority that has been granted to him by the parties that he represents, or even one's enthusiasm about a project. The goal of bluffing is quite simple: to enhance the strength of one's position during negotiations.

Bluffing has long been a topic of considerable interest to business ethicists.[1] On the one hand, bluffing seems to bear a strong resemblance to lying, and therefore might be thought to be *prima facie* impermissible. On the other, many people have the intuition that bluffing is an appropriate and morally permissible negotiating tactic. Given this tension, what is the moral standing of bluffing in business? The dominant position has been that it is permissible and work has therefore been done to show why the apparent impermissibility is either mismotivated or illusory. Two highly influential papers have taken different approaches to securing the moral legitimacy of bluffing. The first, by Albert Carr, argued that bluffing in business is analogous to bluffing in poker and therefore should not be thought to be impermissible insofar as it is part of the way that the game is played. The second, by Thomas Carson, presented a more subtle argument wherein the author reconstrued the concept of lying to require an implied warrantability of truth and, since business negotiations instantiate a context wherein claims are not warranted to be true, bluffing is not lying.

I think that both papers are on the right track to the solution to the problem, but that both authors' positions are problematic. In this paper, I will consider the arguments of both Carr and Carson, and I will present my criticisms of their ideas. Drawing off of their accounts, I will then develop my own argument as to why bluffing in business is morally permissible, which will be that bluffing is a practice that should be endorsed by all rational negotiators.

2. ALBERT CARR

Carr's article is somewhat informal and therefore lacks clear and rigorous argumentation. His thesis, however, is that business is a game, just like poker, and that bluffing is permitted under the rules of the game. To strengthen the analogy between business and poker, he points out that both business and poker have large elements of chance, that the winner is the one who plays with steady skill, and that ultimate victory in both requires knowledge of the rules, insight into the psychology of the other players, a bold front, self-discipline, and the ability to respond quickly and effectively to opportunities presented by chance.[2]

Even if we grant Carr that there are no morally relevant disanalogies between poker and business, which seems dubious, he still has a problem by trying to legitimize bluffing on the grounds that it is permitted by the rules of the game.[3] As Carson has pointed out, Carr seems somewhat confused as to how we determine the rules of the game.[4] In some passages, Carr seems to think that convention determines the rules, whereas in others he seems to think that the law delineates boundaries and all acts within those boundaries are permissible. Regardless, neither of these standards can help to establish the moral legitimacy of bluffing.

The reason is that either one of these moves would violate a long standing principle in moral philosophy, dating back to David Hume, that one cannot reason from what is the case to what ought to be the case.[5] There have been numerous conventions, such as discrimination, that have nevertheless been immoral. And there have also been numerous practices, such as slavery, that have been legally sanctioned but that are also immoral. Facts about the way that the society operates or about the way that the law is, can not be used to derive values. The two supports that Carr gives for the moral permissibility of bluffing are precisely the sorts of considerations that are patently disallowed in moral philosophy.

Carr hints at, but does not discuss, a potentially more promising notion, that of consent. Certainly bluffing in poker, and most likely bluffing in business, is a practice to which all involved parties consent, which is more than can be said for other conventions. But since the fact-value divide makes convention wholly irrelevant, consent would have to do the entirety of the work, and not merely be used to identify a special kind of convention. This is clearly not what Carr has in mind, and I do not propose to read it into his argument. Furthermore, I still do not think that consent alone establishes permissibility. Just as I may consensually enter a poker game knowing full well that bluffing might happen, I may consensually travel to a dangerous neighborhood knowing full well that a crime against me might happen. Since my consent in the latter case does not provide moral license for the act against me, consent can similarly not be used to legitimize bluffing in the former.

3. THOMAS CARSON

Carson approaches the problem from a different direction, though he arrives at more or less the same conclusion. His strategy is to deny that bluffing is a form of lying and, in order to make this argument, he takes issue with the conventional idea that lying is a false statement made with the intent to deceive and proposes instead that "a lie is a false statement which the 'speaker' does not believe to be true made in a context in which the speaker warrants the truth or what he says."[6] Bluffing is certainly lying in the traditional definition; the bluffer's statement is false and it is intended to deceive. But Carson thinks that his definition of lying excludes bluffing. Why? He argues that the second requirement, the warrantability of truth, is largely absent in negotiations. There are some claims made during negotiations that convention dictates to be warranted as true, such as claims to have another offer on the table. If I were to claim that I had another offer while I did not, this would be a lie because it would satisfy both parts of Carson's requirements. Claims about reservation prices, however, do not carry implied warrantability of truth—as a matter of fact, nobody *ever* takes such claims to be literally true. Carson therefore thinks that bluffing is not lying and should therefore not hold the moral disapprobations that we confer on lying.

There are, I think, two problems with Carson's defense of bluffing. The most obvious one is that, even if bluffing is not lying, it does not follow that it is morally permissible. It might be wrong for some other reason. For example, we might want to distinguish between lying and other kinds of deception which are still morally objectionable. Imagine that I leave my children home for the weekend and tell my oldest son that his girlfriend is not allowed in the house. If I call home to ask my younger son what my older son is doing and am told "he is talking to his friend Robert," this might be strictly and literally true only because his girlfriend is in the kitchen getting something to drink and is currently unavailable for conversation. The answer, though true and not a lie, is deceptive insofar as it masks a fact that my younger son knows to be salient. Or I might ask my older son directly whether his girlfriend is in the house and he truthfully answers no because she is still in transit to the house. Again, this answer is not a lie, but is deceptive. If we find such behavior morally objectionable, which many of us would, then the absence of lying alone does not secure moral license. And if it is not morally objectionable, some argument has to be given as to why; it certainly is not intuitively obvious that all non-lying deceptions are morally permissible. Therefore, the most that Carson's argument can establish is that bluffing does not carry the same *prima facie* wrongness that lying does, not that it is morally permissible, which is his desired conclusion.

The second problem is that Carson's account still requires the same dependence convention that caused trouble for Carr. Carson admits that he will not pursue specific guidelines to determine whether a context involves implied warrantability of truth, but the examples that he gestures at are suggestive of conventionality playing a strong role.[7] For instance, he says that statements made in negotiations between experienced negotiators are understood to be not warranted as true. But this is only the case because it is a matter of convention; we could easily imagine another

society wherein negotiators do not bluff, but are honest about their reservation prices. We have already seen why convention alone cannot provide any reason to think that a practice is morally permissible.[8] To say it another way, we can meaningfully ask whether a practice is morally permissible *despite* its being conventional. A defense of bluffing must extend beyond mere conventionality and into the realm of moral philosophy, else it is doomed to violate the fact-value divide.

4. BLUFFING, ROLE-DIFFERENTIATED MORALITY, AND ENDORSEMENT

I will now develop what I think is the correct solution to the problem of bluffing in business. As I said earlier, I think that both Carr and Carson start off on the right track, but then go wrong for the reasons that I have presented.[9] In particular, both authors appeal to games in order to argue for the permissibility of bluffing in business; Carr uses a poker analogy and Carson argues that claims made during bluffing are similar to claims made during the game of Risk. But the problem that both authors have is that they infer moral legitimacy from the rules of their games, and this inference cannot be made. What we need is not an appeal to convention, but rather a moral argument that legitimizes bluffing within those games and that can be extended to bluffing in business.

One way that we could get this is to invoke what has become known as role-differentiated morality. Conventional wisdom within ethics has held that ethical rules are universal, and that everyone should be bound by the exact same moral laws. But work in professional ethics has recently come to challenge this idea.[10] These applications have come most auspiciously in legal ethics, where legal ethicists have often sought to defend ethically objectionable practices of lawyers (such as discrediting known truthful witnesses and/or enabling perjurious testimonies) on the grounds that the lawyer's role, that of zealous advocate, carries different moral rules than nonlawyer roles.[11] Though the applications have certainly been controversial, the underlying idea, role-differentiated morality, has garnered wide support.

Put simply, role-differentiated morality suggests the following three claims:

1. Certain roles make acts permissible that would otherwise be impermissible.
2. Certain roles make acts impermissible that would otherwise be permissible.
3. Certain roles make acts obligatory that would otherwise not be obligatory.

In this paper, I do not wish to provide an extended defense of the plausibility of role-differentiated morality; this has been done by other authors (including the two I cited above), and I do not feel that I have anything of value to add. What I will say in defense of the idea here is that it has tremendous intuitive resonance, as I think can be clearly shown through examples. In support of the first claim, we might say that soldiers fighting a just war are morally permitted to kill, whereas ordinary civilians are not. In support of the second claim, we could suggest that college professors should not have sexual relationships with their students (nor bosses with their subordinates), regardless of the act being consensual. In support of the third claim, we might claim that parents have special obligations to their children, such as providing for them and caring for them, that non-parents would not have towards the same child. I think the self-evidence of these examples gives strong support for the notion of role-differentiated morality.

Now, we can return to bluffing and ask whether some roles should allow for its moral permissibility.[12] I think that it is pretty clear that yes, some roles do allow for bluffing, while others definitely do not (though it remains, for now, an open question under which one bluffing in business falls). Some roles clearly do not morally permit bluffing. For example, consider a relationship between a husband and a wife. They have duties to each other to be honest and not to manipulate each other to secure advantages in negotiation. We might even want to say that negotiating, which is a

necessary precondition for bluffing, is not the sort of activity in which husbands and wives should partake. Negotiating assumes conflicting aims of the negotiators and pits them against each other as adversaries, whereas husbands and wives should, ideally, share the same goals and cooperate. When disagreements do occur (such as on how much to pay for a new house), they should not negotiate against each other to determine their collective reservation price but rather should debate the issue and build a consensus as a unified front. I think that husband or wife is a role in which bluffing is not morally permissible,[13] but there are others, such as any fiduciary role wherein one is morally bound to be fully open with another.

There are, on the other hand, roles under which bluffing is morally permitted. Both Carr and Carson suggested that bluffing is permitted in games, and I think that they are exactly right. But they got the reason wrong, convention alone cannot deliver moral permissibility. Whatever justifies bluffing in these cases needs to have moral, rather than merely descriptive, force. I think that the key to these cases is that the players involved in the game actually *endorse* the practice of bluffing; people play these games for fun, and bluffing makes the games much more fun. If bluffing did not exist in poker, and everyone's bet merely reflected the strength of their hands, there would be no game at all since the final results would all be made apparent. Thus, insofar as anyone even wants to play poker in a meaningful way, he is committed to endorsing the practice of bluffing. Bluffing in Risk is similarly explained; bluffing adds an exciting (though in this case non-essential) element to the game to which players are attracted. If this were not the case, we would certainly expect a proliferation in strategy games in which there were no bluffing via diplomacy, and this is certainly not what we see. Bluffing, in some games, is a welcome feature in which participants actually want to be involved.

Is endorsement a moral feature? Absolutely. Imagine that my son takes $20 out of my wallet. There could be two scenarios leading up to this act. In one, he asks me for the money and I endorse his taking it (to pay the delivery person for pizza, let's say) and, in the other, he does not ask and instead takes it without my permission. Obviously he acted permissibly in the first scenario and impermissibly in the second, and it was my approval, or endorsement, of his actions that is the *only* morally relevant difference. Therefore, endorsement carries with it the moral force to legitimize certain acts (or practices), and I think that it is precisely what is necessary to legitimize bluffing in games.[14]

I hope to have established both the plausibility of role-differentiated morality and that bluffing is permitted in some roles, but not in others. I can now return to my central aim and ask under which category bluffing in business falls. I think that bluffing in business is permissible for the same reason that it is permissible in games, namely that the participants endorse the practice. To explain why, let us return to the example with which I started. When I go to the car dealer with a reservation price of $12,000, what that means is that, all factors considered, that car has to me a utility marginally greater than the $12,000 does. *Ex hypothesi*, I am already willing to spend the $12,000; if that were the best that I could do, I would accept the offer. Any price that I can achieve below $12,000 would obviously be an improvement on the situation. Bluffing and negotiating are the mechanisms wherein I can achieve a final sale at a price beneath my reservation price and, insofar as any rational agent would welcome that end, he should also endorse its means.

Furthermore, other than bluffing, I cannot think of another reasonable procedure for the buyer to lower the sale price below my reservation price (or for the seller to raise the sale price above his reservation price). I might, for example, try to do so by force or threats, but these are obviously immoral. I might also make outright lies, such as to assert that the dealer across town has already guaranteed me a lower price. As Carson has already argued, this seems seriously immoral. So I think it is quite reasonable to suppose not only that the prospective buyer would endorse bluffing, but that there are no other reasonable alternatives.

One response to my position might be that bluffing does help the individual but that in negotiations there is not one, but two bluffers, and that the addition of the second cancels out all advantage to the first. Therefore, bluffing should not actually be endorsed, since it yields no expected improvement, and maybe even eschewed on the grounds that it takes time and energy. However, I do not see how the addition of another bluffer really changes anything. If the car dealer will go as low as $10,000 and I will pay as high as $12,000, then we would both agree to (and, *ex hypothesi*, be happy with) any transaction at any price between and including $10,000 and $12,000. Assuming that the reservation price of the buyer is higher than the reservation price of the seller, the issue is not whether the two parties will come to mutually agreeable terms, the question is just what those terms will be. Ideally, each party would like to be able to bluff while having his opponent's position be transparent, but since that is obviously not a possibility, both should welcome bluffing as an opportunity to improve their positions.

It is also interesting to note that, without bluffing, the idea of negotiations itself almost (though not quite) becomes incoherent. Suppose that bluffing were not practiced, but that parties merely met and announced their respective reservation prices. I tell the car dealer that I will give him $12,000 for the car and he tells me that he will take as little as $10,000 for the car. Now what? I do not even know how to settle on a transaction price other than to do something arbitrary such as splitting the reservation window in half and settling at $11,000. This seems like the wrong answer for a number of reasons. Such resolutions could be inefficient (i.e., not Pareto optimal), not utilitarian, unfair to those who negotiate well, etc.[15] Negotiating is, I think, an essential part of business. To reach a transaction price, it makes the most sense for the buyer to start low and the seller high, and to reach some agreement in the middle. By announcing reservation prices, we would be creating a system that I find less attractive and, furthermore, would give the participants every reason to transgress and to bluff.

Finally, I think that there really is a lot of merit in the analogies between business negotiating and games (despite the criticisms by Koehn and others). But I would go further than claiming that it is *like* a game, it seems to me that it is a game. Perhaps this is not true in the sense that negotiators are drawn to their work because they find it amusing, this is false in a wide number of cases and I certainly do not mean to trivialize many serious negotiations. But if two parties come to the negotiating table and the reservation price of the buyer is higher than the reservation price of the seller, then we already know that, *ceteris paribus*, the transaction will occur and, furthermore, it will occur at a price to which both parties are amenable. It seems to me that the occurrence of the transaction and the satisfaction of the parties is what is really important, where the price falls within the reservation window just determines what each party gains (in terms of money not spent or extra money earned) *in addition* to a mutually beneficial transaction. Whether the stakes are millions of dollars or not, the parties are still merely trying to secure money that they would otherwise be satisfied without.

NOTES

1   The first important paper was Albert Carr's "Is Business Bluffing Ethical?" *Harvard Business Review* (January/February 1968) 143–53. John Beach later reflects upon the treatment that the topic received in the years since Carr's publication (though Beach is somewhat critical of this response). See his "Bluffing: Its Demise as a Subject unto Itself," *Journal of Business Ethics* Vol. 4 (1985), 191–96. Then, Thomas Carson reconsiders Carr's classic treatment of the subject and proposes an alternative conception of business bluffing; see "Second Thoughts about Bluffing," *Business Ethics Quarterly* Vol. 3(4) (1993), 317–41. There are also numerous other examples within the literature, though I take these to be the most important.

2   Carr (1968), 72.

3   Daryl Koehn has, for example, argued that the analogy between business and poker is quite weak;

he takes nine features that exist in games and argues that few, if any, of these exist in business. For the sake of argument, I am willing to grant Carr's analogy; I think that, even with this analogy, he is unable to secure the conclusion that he desires. See Koehn's "Business and Game-Playing: The False Analogy," *Journal of Business Ethics* Vol. 16 (1997), 1447–52. Norman Bowie also argued against the legitimacy of adversarial models (such as poker) as proper characterizations of bargaining and negotiating. See his "Should Collective Bargaining and Labor Relations Be Less Adversarial?" *Journal of Business Ethics* Vol. 4 (1985), 283–91. Robert S. Adler and William J. Bigoness also challenge adversarial models in their work and find Carr's poker analogy to be flawed. See "Contemporary Ethical Issues in Labor-Management Issues in Labor-Management Relations," *Journal of Business Ethics* Vol. 11 (1992), 351–60.

4   Carson (1993), 324–25.

5   *A Treatise of Human Nature*, ed. P.H. Nidditch, 2nd ed. (Oxford: Oxford University Press, 1978), III.I.i.

6   Carson (1993), 320. I assume that speaker is placed in scare quotes in order to allow for the possibility of non-verbal lying, such as when someone gives false directions by pointing in the wrong direction without saying anything. This definition results partly from earlier work by Carson and a criticism that he consequently received from Gary Jones. To trace through this, start with Thomas Carson, Richard Wokutch, and James Cox's "An Ethical Analysis of Deception in Advertising," *Journal of Business Ethics* Vol. 4 (1985), 93–104. Jones's criticism can be found in "Lying and Intentions," *Journal of Business Ethics* Vol. 5 (1986), 347–49. And, finally, Carson's response is in "On the Definition of Lying: A Reply to Jones and Revisions," *Journal of Business Ethics* Vol. 7 (1988), 509–14.

7   Carson (1993), 321–22.

8   And, in an interesting recent article, Chris Provis argues that bluffing (or, more precisely, deception) is not as ubiquitous in business as everyone often assumes; he thinks that the appearance of bluffing can often be accounted for by genuine concessions. If Provis is correct, then Carson's reliance on conventionality is empirically flawed. Or, as I argue, the reliance on convention is conceptually flawed (in

order to secure moral permissibility). So, either way, the approach will not work. See Provis's "Ethics, Deception, and Labor Negotiation," *Journal of Business Ethics* Vol. 28(2) (2000), 145–58.

9   As I have indicated, other authors have also criticized the two approaches. What I have tried to do however, is be as charitable as possible: to grant all of their assumptions (the analogies, the adversarial nature of negotiating, Carson's definition of lying, etc.) and then aspired to show that they still cannot, even on their own terms, secure their desired conclusions.

10   An especially good and influential article is Richard Wasserstrom's "Lawyers as Professionals: Some Moral Issues," *Human Rights Quarterly* Vol. 5(1) (1975).

11   Monroe H. Freedman, "Professional Responsibility of the Criminal Defense Lawyer: The Three Hardest Questions," *Michigan Law Review* Vol. 27 (1966).

12   This step of my argument might be overly pedantic, and I might fare just as well if I skipped it and went directly to arguing for bluffing in business contexts specifically. However, I do think that it is an important part of the conceptual framework that I want to establish.

13   This is obviously not to say that husbands or wives cannot bluff in business situations, just that a husband cannot bluff *qua* husband nor a wife *qua* wife. The husband or wife who bluffs in business is not bluffing *qua* husband or *qua* wife, but rather *qua* businessperson.

14   John Rawls has argued that it is not morally permissible to sell oneself into slavery (i.e., *even if* I endorsed the sale, it is still immoral). See his *Theory of Justice* (Cambridge: Harvard University Press, 1971). This poses an interesting objection to my idea that endorsement alone suggests *prima facie* permissibility. There are two ways that I could respond. First, I could disagree with Rawls and argue that any decision made by free and rational agents should be honored (so long as it did not harm others), that to do otherwise would show lack of respect for the being's rational nature. I am personally inclined towards this view, though I know that many are not. The other way that I could go would be to argue

that Rawls' point merely indicates that people cannot voluntarily give up their rights and that consenting to being bluffed is not problematic since we do not have the moral right to be told the truth. I think that either of these responses could be profitably developed, though I will not do so here.

15   The "Split-the-Difference" theory of negotiating is discussed by Roger Bowlby and William Schriver in their "Bluffing and the 'Split-the-Difference' Theory of Wage Bargaining," *Industrial and Labor Relations Review* Vol. 31(2) (January 1978), 161–71. Their discussion, however, is quite empirical and numerical rather than normative.

REFERENCES

Adler, R.S. and W.J. Bigoness. 1992, "Contemporary Ethical Issues in Labor-Management Relations," *Journal of Business Ethics* 11.

Beach, J. 1985, "'Bluffing' Its Demise as a Subject unto Itself," *Journal of Business Ethics* 4.

Bowie, N.E. 1985, "Should Collective Bargaining and Labor Relations Be Less Adversarial?" *Journal of Business Ethics* 4.

Bowlby, R.L. and W.R. Schriver. 1978, "Bluffing and the 'Split-the-Difference' Theory of Wage Bargaining," *Industrial and Labor Relations Review* 31(2).

Carr, A. 1968, "Is Business Bluffing Ethical?" *Harvard Business Review* (January/February).

Carson, T.L. 1993, "Second Thoughts about Bluffing," *Journal of Business Ethics* 3(4).

Carson, T.L. 1988, "On the Definitions of Lying: A Reply to Jones and Revisions," *Journal of Business Ethics* 7.

Carson, T.L., R.E. Wokutch and J.E. Cox, Jr. 1985, "An Ethical Analysis of Deception in Advertising," *Journal of Business Ethics* 4.

Freedman, M. 1966, "Professional Responsibility of the Criminal Defense Lawyer: The Three Hardest Questions," *Michigan Law Review* 27.

Hume, D. 1978, *A Treatise of Human Nature* (2nd ed.). P.H. Nidditch (ed.). (Oxford: Oxford University Press).

Jones, G.E. 1986, "Lying and Intentions," *Journal of Business Ethics* 5.

Koehn, D. 1997, "Business and Game-Playing: The False Analogy," *Journal of Business Ethics* 16.

Post, F.R. 1990, "Collaborative Collective Bargaining: Toward an Ethically Defensible Approach to Labor Negotiations," *Journal of Business Ethics* 9.

Provis, C. 2000, "Ethics, Deception, and Labor Negotiation," *Journal of Business Ethics* 28.

Rawls, J. 1971, *A Theory of Justice* (Cambridge: Harvard University Press).

Wasserstrom, R. 1975, "Lawyers as Professionals: Some Moral Issues," *Human Rights Quarterly* 5(1).

—69—

THE ETHICS OF BLUFFING

Oracle's Takeover of PeopleSoft

Patrick Lin

BACKGROUND

ON JUNE 6, 2003, ORACLE AMBUSHED PEOPLESOFT with an unsolicited $5.1 billion cash offer to buy the rival technology company. This set the stage for the two Silicon Valley giants—both led by egos that were just as large—to play out a tale about power, drama, and deceit.

First, to introduce the players: Larry Ellison is Oracle's chairman, a swash-buckling personality known for his extravagance, such as financing the boat racing team that won in the America's Cup later in 2003. Equally aggressive, Craig Conway was PeopleSoft's CEO at the time and had once described Oracle, his former employer, as a "sociopathic company."

Just days before Oracle's hostile takeover bid, PeopleSoft had announced its agreement to buy another rival, J.D. Edwards, for $1.7 billion in stock—a deal which would make it the world's second-largest business software company behind SAP. PeopleSoft rejected Oracle's $16-per-share offer as too low a price to be taken seriously and therefore simply a marketing ploy or distraction.

For more than a year, Oracle and PeopleSoft fought in the courtroom and the boardroom. Oracle successfully fended off an antitrust trial that examined whether the proposed takeover would be anti-competitive and harm the industry as well as customers. This was followed by PeopleSoft's surprise vote of no-confidence in Conway by the board of directors, resulting in his firing in October 2004.

During the same period, Oracle had raised, re-raised, and even lowered its acquisition price, eventually tendering its "best and final" offer of $24 per share. PeopleSoft again rejected this offer, calling Oracle on its bluff. After more than twelve offers, Oracle's last bid of $26.50 per share was accepted by PeopleSoft in December 2004, and the merger was completed in 2005.

But Oracle was not the only one apparently bluffing in this bitter battle. Back in June 2003, PeopleSoft implemented a "poison pill" plan that, should the company be taken over, its customers would be entitled to a refund of up to five times the licensing fees they have paid to the company. This tactic would commit the company to costly future obligations, with the intention to dissuade Oracle from its takeover ambitions. PeopleSoft eventually let this policy expire less than a year later.

In another high-profile deal, a different kind of bluff was played out in the AOL-Time Warner merger, announced on January 10, 2000. The financial community was puzzled and shocked at how a scrappy New Economy start-up such as America Online could ever make a bid for Time Warner, a decades-old media empire, in a deal originally worth $165 billion. Many considered AOL's stock to be severely overvalued, but AOL had convinced Time Warner otherwise.

The AOL-Time Warner merger was cleared by regulators in early 2001, but the impending stock market crash, led by overvalued dot-com and technology companies, forced AOL-Time Warner to write off $99 billion in losses in 2002—causing some to observe that AOL had successfully "bluffed" that its 30 million dial-up Internet subscribers were worth Time Warner's much larger, established and iconic global business.

ANALYSIS

In the Oracle-PeopleSoft case, it is easy to see why bluffing would occur. The two parties were fierce adversaries, and there was personal animosity between the two company chiefs. As a result, the usual niceties in negotiation—such as trust and honesty—were replaced by a no-holds-barred fight. If all is fair in love and war, and business is war (at least in this case), then bluffing seems to be rather innocuous, compared to other tactics employed and that were possible.

Likewise, workforce negotiations also offer key opportunities for bluffing, since these relationships can be acrimonious. Some employee unions are quick to threaten a strike (or suggest that a strike is strongly possible) if their demands are not met. On the other side, the company may be bluffing when it refuses to negotiate further, insisting that its last offer was the best it could do or that it would be forced into bankruptcy or layoffs without more employee concessions. If one side has been bluffing, we would expect that a strike can be averted in last-minute negotiations—hiding the bluff by finding some token area of agreement or another face-saving reason.

But as the AOL-Time Warner deal shows, a negotiation need not involve adversaries. If "hype" or exaggeration counts as bluffing, then untold numbers of dot-com companies may have bluffed their way into key relationships and millions of dollars in private funding, ultimately unable to deliver on their sales and revenue forecasts. However, in order for this to count as a bluff, it seems that one must knowingly exaggerate, rather than really believing one's own hype.

It is not just soul-less corporations that bluff; we do it too. Any situation where one can state "This is my final offer" or "Do this, or else" is a potential opportunity to bluff. From negotiating salaries to buying a car, many of us might have bluffed our way into a better deal by suggesting that we might be unable to accept such a low offer (or to afford such a high price), when that amount really is acceptable.

But we should be careful not to completely confuse bluffing with lying, since not all cases of bluffing involve the making of false statements. Bluffing in poker does not, for example; it simply involves misdirection by taking an action that conceals the strength of one's cards, such as betting a lot of money when one has a weak hand. Depending on how AOL made its case to Time Warner, they might not have made a false statement—perhaps only overly optimistic forecasts. PeopleSoft implemented a poison-pill policy that could be renewed after a given date, but it didn't seem to make any (false) warranty that it would renew it. On the other hand, Oracle's "best and final" offer appears to be a false statement, since they subsequently raised that offer. Or maybe they just simply changed their mind. This highlights the difficulty of identifying even a failed bluff, much less discerning true intentions to determine whether a bluff is in progress.

DISCUSSION QUESTIONS

1. What exactly is bluffing—how should we define it? Where bluffing involves making false statements, where is the line between bluffing and lying, if one exists at all?
2. How else might one bluff in business without making a claim or threat that one has no intention of carrying out? Does creating doubt in the other party's mind, when a decision has already been made in one's own mind, count as a bluff?

3. Since the two are often compared, what are the relevant similarities as well as differences between poker and business? If bluffing (and even lying) might be permitted under the rules of a game, is business a game in which bluffing is permitted or even necessary?

4. We usually think of bluffing in the context of negotiations, but should intentional "hype" or exaggeration be thought of as bluffing too? Why doesn't story-telling count as bluffing?

5. If bluffing is so pervasive and conducted by otherwise ethical people such as ourselves, does that suggest that it is morally permissible?

6. Could we argue that bluffing (at least in the form that involves making false statements) is simply lying under mitigating circumstances—such as if the other party bluffs first, or if we believe the car dealer is making an unfairly high profit? Or are we simply rationalizing unethical behavior?

7. When we bluff by making a false statement, are our intentions different than if we were merely lying? If so, are these intentions morally relevant? If not, does that help make the case that there is no difference between the two?

FURTHER READINGS

Bowie, Norman E. 1993. "Does It Pay to Bluff in Business?" *Ethical Theory and Business* 3: 443–48.

Carson, Thomas L., Richard E. Wokutch, and Kent F. Murrmann. 1982. "Bluffing in Labor Negotiations: Legal and Ethical Issues." *Journal of Business Ethics* 1 (1): 13–22.

Koehn, Daryl. 1997. "Business and Game-Playing: The False Analogy." *Journal of Business Ethics* 16 (12–13): 1447–52.

—70—
ADVERTISING

The Whole or Only Some of the Truth?

Tibor R. Machan

WHEN COMMERCIAL ADVERTISING IS CRITICIZED, often some assumption surfaces that should be explored more fully. I have in mind in particular the hidden premises that advertising is first and foremost a means for conveying information. Another assumption which lingers in the background of criticisms of advertising is that ethics requires that those who sell goods and services should first of all help customers.

My aim here is to defend the approach to advertising that does not require of merchants that they tell all. So long as merchants are honest, do not mislead or deceive, they are acting in a morally satisfactory manner. It is not good for them—and there is nothing in morality that requires it of them—to take up the task of informing consumers of the conditions most favorable to them in the market place, to aid them in their efforts to find the best deal.

The following passage will help introduce us to the topic. It illustrates the kind of views that many philosophers who work in the field of business ethics seem to find convincing.

> Merchants and producers have many ways of concealing truth from the customers—not by lying to them, but simply by not telling them facts that are relevant to the question of whether they ought to purchase a particular product or whether they are receiving full value for their money.[1]

The author goes on to state that "it is certainly unethical for (salesmen and businessmen) to fail to tell their customers that they are not getting full value for their money."[2] He cites David Ogilvy, a successful advertiser, admitting that "he is 'continuously guilty' of *suppressio veri*, the suppression of the truth."[3] In other words, what advertisers do ethically or morally wrong is to fail to tell all, the whole truth, when they communicate to others about their wares, services, goods, products, or whatnot.

Yet there is something unrealistic, even farfetched, about this line of criticism. To begin with, even apart from advertising, people often enough advance a biased perspective on themselves, their skills, looks, and so on. When we go out on a first date, we tend to deck ourselves out in a way that certainly highlights what we consider our assets and diminishes our liabilities. When we send out our resumes in our job search efforts, we hardly tell all. When we just dress for the normal day, we tend to choose garb that enhances our looks and covers up what is not so attractive about our whole selves.

Burton Leiser, the critic we have been using to illustrate the prevailing view of advertising, is not wholly unaware of these points, since he continues with his quotation from Ogilvy, who says, "Surely it is asking too much to expect the advertiser to describe the shortcomings of his product. One must be forgiven for 'putting one's best foot forward.'" To this Leiser exclaims, "So the consumer is not to be told all the relevant information; he is not to be given all the facts that would be of assistance in making a reasonable decision about a given purchase...."[4] Nevertheless, Leiser does not tell us what is ethically wrong in such instance of *suppressio veri*. In fact, the claim that in all advertising one must present the whole truth, not just be truthful about one's subject matter, presupposes the very problematic ethical view that one ought to devote oneself *primarily* to bettering the lot of other people. What commerce rests on ethically, implicitly or explicitly, is the very different doctrine of *caveat emptor* (let him [the purchaser] beware), which assumes that prudence is a virtue and should be practiced by all, including one's customers. I will argue here that the merchant's ethical stance is more reasonable than that of the critics.

I. THE VICE OF *SUPPRESSIO VERI*

Leiser and many others critical of business and sales practices assume that in commercial transactions persons owe others the whole truth and nothing but the truth. This is why they believe that merchants act unethically in failing to tell their customers something that customers might ask about if they would only think of everything relevant to their purchasing activities. Leiser gives a good example:

> Probably the most common deception of this sort is price deception, the technique some high-pressure salesmen use to sell their goods by grossly inflating their prices to two, three, and even four times their real worth. Again, there may be no "untruth" in what they say; but they conceal the important fact that the same product, or one nearly identical to it, can be purchased for far less at a department or appliance store....

Before I discuss the ethical points in these remarks, a word, first, about the alleged simplicity of learning whether some item for sale by a merchant is in fact available for purchase "for far less" elsewhere.

The idea is, we may take it, that the customer will indeed obtain what he or she wants by purchasing this item from some other seller. This ignores the fact that it may be quite important for customers to purchase some items in certain places, in certain kinds of environments, even from certain types of persons (e.g., ones with good manners). Sheer accessibility can be crucial, as well as atmosphere, the merchant's demeanor, and so on. If it is legitimate for customers to seek satisfaction from the market, it is also legitimate to seek various combinations of satisfaction, not simply product or price satisfaction.

Let us, however, assume that a customer could have obtained all that she wanted by going elsewhere to purchase the item at a price "far less" than what it costs at a given merchant's store. Is there a responsibility on the merchant's part (if she knows this) to make the information available to the customer? Or even more demandingly, is it ethically required that the merchant become informed about these matters and convey the information to potential customers?

The answer depends on a broader ethical point. What are the standards by which human beings should conduct themselves, including in their relationship to others? If something on the order of the altruist's answer is correct, then, in general, *suppressio veri* is wrongful. Telling the whole truth would help other people in living a good human life. Altruism here means not the ideal of equal respect for everyone as a human being, advocated by Thomas Nagel.[5] Rather it is the earlier sense of having one's primary duty to advance the interest of others.[6] A merchant need not be disrespectful toward his customers by not informing them of something that perhaps they ought to have learnt in the first place. By volunteering information that quite conceivably a customer should, as a matter of his personal moral responsibility (as a prudent individual), have obtained, a merchant might be meddling in matters not properly his own, which could be demeaning.

But an altruism in terms of which one is responsible to seek and obtain the well-being of his fellow human beings would render *suppressio veri* morally wrong. Such an altruism is certainly widely advocated, if not by philosophers then at least by political reformers. For example, Karl Marx states, in one of his earliest writings, that "The main principle ... which must guide us in the selection of a vocation is the welfare of humanity ..." and that "man's nature makes it possible for him to reach his fulfillment only by working for the perfection and welfare of his society."[7] Here he states precisely the morality of altruism initially espoused by August Comte, who coined the term itself and developed the secular "religion" by which to promote the doctrine.[8]

Now only by the ethics of altruism does it follow unambiguously that a merchant who does not tell all "is certainly unethical." Neither the more common varieties of utilitarianism, nor Kant's theory, as it is often understood, implies this. If we are to live solely to do good for others, then when we have reason to believe that telling the whole truth will promote others' well-being (without thwarting the well-being of yet some other person), we morally ought to tell the whole truth to this person. So when a merchant has reason to believe that telling his customer about lower prices elsewhere (for goods which he sells at higher price) will benefit his customer, he ought morally to do so.

But for it to be established that this is what a merchant ought morally to do for any customer, and that not doing so "is certainly unethical," the sort of altruism Marx and Comte defended would have to be true. No other ethical viewpoint seems to give solid support to the above claim about what "is certainly unethical."

Still, might one perhaps be able to show the whole truth thesis correct by other means than depending on a strong altruistic moral framework? Not very plausibly.

Intuitionism, as generally understood, would not override the well entrenched belief that when one embarks on earning a living and deals with perfect strangers, one should not promote one's weaknesses, one should *not* volunteer information detrimental to one's prospects. I doubt anyone would seriously advise job seeking philosophers to list on their CVs rejected articles and denied promotions—that would be counterintuitive.

It is also doubtful that most versions of utilitarianism would support a very strong general principle of self-sacrifice from which it can be shown that it "is certainly unethical" not to tell the whole truth. There could be many good utilitarian reasons to support at least a substantial degree of *caveat emptor* in the marketplace. For example, if the classical and neo-classical defenses—and the Marxian explanation of the temporary necessity—of the unregulated market of profit seeking individuals have any merit, it is for utilitarian reasons that the competitive, self-interested conduct of market agents should be encouraged. This would preclude giving away information free of charge, as a matter of what is right from a utilitarian perspective of maximizing the good of society, which in this case would be wealth.

Even a Kantian deontological ethics, as generally understood, advises against talking over what is very plausibly another person's moral responsibility, namely, seeking out the knowledge to act prudently and wisely. The Kantian idea of moral autonomy may not require seeking one's personal happiness in life, as the Aristotelian concept of the good moral life does, but it does require leaving matters of morality to the discretion of the agent. Meddling with the agent's moral welfare would conceivably be impermissibly intrusive. By reference to the categorical imperative it is difficult to imagine why one should invite commercial failure in one's market transactions, a failure that is surely possible if one is occupied not with promoting one's success but with the success of one's potential customers.

It seems then, that the altruist ethics, which makes it everyone's duty to further the interests of other people, is indeed the most plausible candidate for making it "certainly unethical" to suppress the truth in commercial transactions. Yet, of course, troubles abound with altruism proper.

When properly universalized, as all *bona fide* moralities must be, the doctrine in effect obligates everyone to refuse any help extended. Such a robust form of altruism creates a veritable daisy-chain of self-sacrifice. None is left to be the beneficiary of human action. Perhaps, therefore, what should be considered is a less extreme form of altruism, one which obligates everyone to be helpful whenever he or she has good reason to think that others would suffer without help.

Specifically, the altruism that might be the underpinning of the criticism of advertising ethics illustrated above should be thought of more along Rawlsian lines. According to this view we owe help to others only if they are found in special need, following the lead of Rawls's basic principle that "All social values—liberty and opportunity, income and wealth, and the bases of self-respect—are to be distributed equally unless an unequal distribution of any, or all, of these values is to everyone's advantage."[9]

But this form of moderate egalitarianism no longer supports the prevailing idea of proper business ethics.[10] In complying with this principle the merchant should, in the main—except when informed of special disadvantages of potential customers—put a price on his product that will sell the most of his wares at the margin. That is exactly what economists, who assume that merchants are profit maximizers, would claim merchants will do. And this is the kind of conduct that the merchant has reason to believe will ensure the equal distribution of values, as far as she can determine what that would be. The reason is that from the perspective of each merchant qua merchant it is reasonable in the course of commerce to consider potential customers as agents with equal status to merchants who are interested in advancing their economic interests. From this, with no additional information about some possible special disadvantage of the customer, merchants must see themselves as having equal standing to customers and as having legitimate motives for furthering their own interests.[11]

Thus, the Rawlsian egalitarian moral viewpoint will not help to support the doctrine that merchants owe a service to customers. Only the robust form of altruism we find in Marx and some others is a good candidate for the morality that, for example, Leiser assumes must guide our merchant. Ethical views other than altruism might support the view that the merchant ought to be extra helpful to special persons—family, friends, associates, even neighbors—but not to everyone. Even a narrow form of subjective "ethical" egoism can lead merchants to regard it as their responsibility to be helpful toward *some* other people. For instance, a merchant might consider most of his customers close enough friends that the morality of friendship, which need not be altruistic and may be egoist, would guide him to be helpful even to the point of risking the loss of business. Or, alternatively, were it the case that having the reputation of being helpful leads to increased patronage from members of one's community, then in just such a community such a subjective egoist would properly engage in helping behavior, including now and then informing his customers of more advantageous purchases in other establishments.

II. THE MORALITY OF *CAVEAT EMPTOR*

In contrast to the assumption of altruism as a guide to business conduct, I wish to suggest a form of egoism as the appropriate morality in terms of which to understand commerce. I have in mind a form of egoism best called "classical" because, as I have argued elsewhere,[12] it identifies standards of (egoistic) conduct by reference to the teleological conception of the human self spelled out in the works of classical philosophers, especially Aristotle, but modified in line with an individualism that arises from the ontology of human nature.[13] The idea, briefly put, is that each individual should seek to promote his interests as a human being and as the individual he is.... Classical egoism regards the individual person as the ultimate, though not sole, proper beneficiary of that individual's own moral conduct. The standards of such conduct are grounded on the nature of the individual as a *human being*, as well as that particular person, thus in a moral universe which is coherent there need be no fundamental conflict between the egoistic conduct of one person and the egoistic conduct of another.

Accordingly, in the case of our merchant, he should abide by the basic moral principle of right reason, and the more particular implication of this namely the virtue of honesty, as he answers the questions his customer puts to him. He might, for example, even refuse to answer some question instead of either giving help or lying. It is a person's moral responsibility to promote his rational self-interest. And taking up the task of merchandising goods and services can qualify for various individuals with their particular talents and opportunities in life, as promoting one's rational self-interest. So a merchant could be acting with perfect moral propriety in not offering help to a customer with the task of information gathering (especially when it is clear that competing merchants are doing their very best to publicize such information as would be valuable to customers). The responsibility of merchants is to sell conscientiously their wares, not to engage in charitable work by carrying out tasks that other persons ought to carry out for themselves.

It might be objected that if someone asks an informed merchant, "Is the same product available for a lower price somewhere else?" no other alternative but letting the customer know the answer exists—it could be rather strained to refuse to answer. But there are many ways to deflect answering that do not mark someone as a deceiver. Smiling at the customer, the merchant might quietly put a question in response to the question: "Well, do you actually want me to help you to take your business elsewhere?" Should it be clear to the merchant that the customer isn't going to be satisfied with the wares available in his or her establishment, it would make perfectly good sense to offer help—and indeed countless merchants do frequently enough. Thus, when one looks for shoes, one frequently finds that one merchant will guide a customer to another where some particular style or size is likely to be available. Both good merchandising and ordinary courtesy would support such a practice, although it is doubtful that any feasible ethical system would make it obligatory!

In terms of the classical egoism that would seem to give support to these approaches to ethical issues in business, it does not follow that one would be acting properly by lying to avoid putting oneself at a competitive disadvantage. One's integrity, sanity, reputation, generosity and one's respect for others are more important to oneself than competitive advantage. Yet neither is prudence merely a convenience, and seeking a competitive advantage in the appropriate ways would indeed be prudent.[14]

Of course showing that this morality is sound would take us on a very long journey, although some work has already been done to that end.[15] As I have noted already, in numerous noncommercial situations human beings accept the form of conduct which characterizes ordinary but decent commercial transactions as perfectly proper. In introducing ourselves to people we have never met, for example, we do not advance information that would be damaging to the prospects of good relations. We do not say, "I am John Doe. When I am angry, I throw a fit, and when in a bad mood I am an insufferable boor." When we send an invitation to our forthcoming party, we do not say, "While this party may turn out to be pleasant, in the past we have had some very boring affairs that also set out to be fun." Innumerable noncommercial endeavors, including professional ones, are characterized by "putting our best foot forward," leaving to others the task of making sure whether they wish to relate to us. The fields of romance, ordinary conversation, political advocacy, and so forth all give ample evidence of the widespread practice of putting our best foot forward and letting others fend for themselves. We do not lie, mislead or deceive others by not mentioning to them, unsolicited, our bad habits, our foibles. As suggested before, we are not lying or misleading others when in sending along our resumes or CVs we do not list projects that have been rejected.

The exceptions to this are those cases in which we have special obligations arising out of special moral relationships such as friendship, parenthood, collegialty, and so on. In these—as well as in contractual relationships where the obligations arise out of explicitly stated intent instead of implied commitments and promises—one can have obligated oneself to be of assistance even in competition or contest. Friends playing tennis could well expect one another to lend a hand when skills are quite uneven. Parents should not allow their children to fend for themselves, with limited information, as the children embark upon various tasks. And in emergency cases it is also reasonable to expect strangers to set aside personal goals that ordinarily would be morally legitimate.

Commercial relationships usually take place between strangers. The only purpose in seeking out other persons is for the sake of a good deal. Even here, sometimes further bonds emerge, but those are essentially beside the point of commerce. So the moral aspects of personal intimacy would not be the proper ethics for commercial relationships, anymore than they would be for sport or artistic competitions.

Some, of course, envision the good human community as a kind of large and happy family, the "brotherhood of man," as Marx did (not only early in his life but, insofar as his normative model of the ultimately good human society was concerned, for all of his career). For them the fact that some human beings interact with others solely for "narrow," "selfish" economic purposes will be a lamentable feature of society—to be overcome when humanity reaches maturity, perhaps, or to be tolerated only if out of such selfishness some public good can be achieved.[16]

But this alleged ideal of social life cannot be made to apply to human beings as they in fact are found among us. That vision, even in Marx, is appropriate only for a "new man," not the actual living persons we are (in our time). For us this picture of universal intimacy must be rejected in favor of one in which the multifaceted and multidimensional possibility of pursuit of personal happiness—albeit in the tradition of Aristotle, not Bentham and contemporary microeconomists—is legally protected (not guaranteed, for that is impossible). For them commercial interaction or trade does not place the fantastic burden on the parties involved that would be required of them if they needed to "be forgiven for putting one's best foot forward."

I have tried to offer some grounds for conceiving of trade in such a way that the unreasonable burden of having to tell others the whole truth, blemishes and all, need not be regarded as morally required. None of the above endorse cheating, deception, false advertising, and the like. It does recommend that you look at the practice of commercial advertising—as well as other practices involving the presentation of oneself or one's skills and wares in a favorable light—as morally legitimate, justified, even virtuous (insofar as it would be prudent).

III. PRODUCT LIABILITY: SOME CAUTION

One line of objection that has been suggested to the above approach is the failing to tell all about the features of a commercial transaction on the part of those embarking on it is like not telling someone about a defect in a product. When a merchant sells an automobile tire, if he is aware that this tire is defective, the mere fact that his customer does not explicitly inquire about defects does not appear to be, on its face, sufficient justification for suppression of the truth of the fact. But is this not just what my analysis above would permit on egoistic grounds? And would that not be sufficient ground, as James Rachels argues[17] in another context against egoism, for rejecting the argument?

Without embarking on a full discussion of the topic of product liability, let me point out some possible ways of approaching the issues that are consistent with the moral perspective I have taken on truth telling. First, as in law, so in morality there is the "reasonable man" standard which can be appealed to considering personal responsibility.

After all, a merchant is selling an automobile tire and it is implicit in that act that he is selling something that will, to the best of available knowledge, function in that capacity when utilized in normal circumstances.

One problem with this response is that it comes close to begging the question. Just what the reasonable expectation is in such cases of commercial transaction is precisely at issue. If it is true that *caveat emptor* is justified, then why not go the full distance and make the buyer beware of all possible hitches associated with the transaction?

The answer to that question introduces the second approach to handling the product liability issue.... I am thinking here of the need for a distinction between what is essential about some item and what is incidental or merely closely associated with it. And when we are concerned about truth telling—and I have not tried to reject the requirement of honesty, only that of telling everything that one knows *and* that may be of help to the buyer—it is more than likely that in the very identification of what one is trading, one commits oneself to having to give any information that is pertinent to the nature of the item or service at hand. Concerning automobile tires, their function as reliable equipment for transport on ordinary roads is a good candidate for an essential feature. So not telling of a defect in tires pertaining to this feature would amount to telling a falsehood, that is, saying one is trading *x* when in fact one is trading *not-x* (inasmuch as the absence of an essential feature of *x* would render whatever is identified as *x* a fake, something that would in the context of commercial transactions open the party perpetrating the misidentification to charges of fraud).

This is not to claim that what is essential about items must remain static over time. The context has a good deal to do with the determination of essential attributes of items and services, and convention and practice are not entirely inapplicable to that determination. Here is where a certain version of the theory of rational expectations would be useful and may indeed already function in some instances of tort law. As J. Roger Lee puts it,

I have rights. They do not come out of agreements with others, being prior to and presupposed by such agreements. But standard relations with others, which I will call "rational expectations frameworks" fix the criteria of their application to situations in everyday life. And rational expectation frameworks are a guide to those criteria.

... For example, if I go into a bar and order a scotch on the rocks, then it is reasonable to expect that I'll get what I order and that neither it nor the place where I sit will be boobytrapped. There are countless examples of this.[18]

It is possible to show that from a robust or classical ethical egoist standpoint, *the truth about an item or service being traded should be told.* But this does not show that the whole truth should be told, including various matters associated with the buying and selling of the item or service in question—such as, its price elsewhere, its ultimate suitability to the needs of the buyer, its full value and so on. This perspective, in turn, does not imply that defective products or incompetent service are equally suitable objects of trade in honest transactions.[19]

NOTES

1   Burton Leiser, "Deceptive Practices in Advertising," in Tom L. Beauchamp and Norman Bowie (eds.), *Ethical Theory and Business* (Englewood Cliffs: Prentice-Hall, 1979), 479. Leiser's rendition of this view is perhaps the most extreme. Others have put the matter more guardedly, focusing more on the kind of suppression that conceals generally harmful aspects of products than on failure to inform the public of its comparative disadvantage vis-à-vis similar or even identical substitutes. Yet the general statements of the ethical point, in contrast to the examples cited, are very close to Leiser's own. See, e.g., Vincent Barry, *Moral Issues in Business* (Belmont: Wadsworth Publishing Company, 1983), Chapter 8. Barry chides advertisers "for concealing

fact … when its availability would probably make the desire, purchase, or use of a product less likely than in its absence" (278).

2   Leiser, *op. cit.*

3   Ibid., 484.

4   Ibid., 479.

5   Thomas Nagel, *The Possibility of Altruism* (Oxford: Clarendon Press, 1970).

6   This is the sense of the term as it occurs in the writings of August Comte who reportedly coined it. Thus the *Oxford English Dictionary* reports that the term was "introduced into English by the translators and expounders of Comte," e.g., Lewis' *Comte's Philosophy*, Sc. I. xxi. 224: "Dispositions influenced by the purely egotist impulses we call popularly 'bad,' and apply the term 'good' to those in which altruism predominates" (1853), *The Compact Edition*, 65.

7   Lloyd D. Easton and Kurt H. Guddat (eds.), *Writings of the Young Marx on Philosophy and Society* (Garden City: Anchor Books, 1967), 39. See, for a recent statement, W. Maclagan, "Self and Others: A Defense of Altruism," *The Philosophical Quarterly*, Vol. 4, No. 15 (1954), 109–27. As Maclagan states it, "I call my view 'altruism' assuming a duty to relieve the distress and promote the happiness of our fellows." He adds that such a virtue requires "that a man may and should discount altogether his own pleasure or happiness as such when he is deciding what course of action to pursue" (110).

8   Wilhelm Windelband, *A History of Philosophy*, Vol. II (New York: Harper Torchbooks, 1968), 650ff.

9   John Rawls, *A Theory of Justice* (Cambridge, MA: Harvard University Press 1971), 62.

10 Because of the intimate association of ethics and altruism (self-sacrifice), so defenders of the value of commerce or business have settled for a total disassociation of business and morality. See, e.g., Albert Carr, "Is Business Bluffing Ethical?" in Thomas Donaldson and Patricia H. Werhane (eds.), *Ethical Issues in Business* (Englewood Cliffs, NJ: Prentice-Hall, 1979), 46–52 (above pp. 526–34).

11 I believe that this point about the compatibility of Rawls' egalitarianism and the market economy has been argued in James Buchanan, "Hobbesian Interpretation of the Rawlsian Difference Principle," *Kyklos*, Vol. 29 (1976), 5–25.

12 Tibor R. Machan, "Recent Work in Ethical Egoism," *American Philosophy Quarterly*, Vol. 16 (1979), 1–15. See also T.R. Machan, "Ethics and the Regulation of Professional Ethics," *Philosophia*, Vol. 8 (1983), 337–48.

13 *Nicomachean Ethics*, 119a 12. This point is stressed in W.F.R. Hardie, "The First Good in Aristotle's Ethics," *Philosophy*, Vol. 40 (1965), 277–95.

14 For more elaborate development of these points, see Tibor R. Machan, *Human Rights and Human Liberties* (Chicago: Nelson-Hall, 1975), Chapter 3.

15 See, e.g., Eric Mack, "How to Derive Ethical Egoism," *The Personalist*, Vol. 59 (1971), 735–43.

16 The entire tradition of classical economics embodies this point, made forcefully by Mandeville's *The Fable of the Bees* and Adam Smith's *The Wealth of Nations*.

17 James Rachels, "Two Arguments Against Ethical Egoism," *Philosophia*, Vol. 4 (1974), 297–314.

18 J. Roger Lee, "Choice and Harms," in T.R. Machan and M. Bruce Johnston (eds.), *Rights and Regulations: Ethical, Political, and Economic Issues* (Cambridge, MA: Ballinger, 1983), 168–69.

19 For more on product liability, see Richard A. Epstein, *A Theory of Strict Liability* (San Francisco: Cato Institute, 1980). See, also, Tibor R. Machan, "The Petty Tyranny of Government Regulations," in M.B. Johnson and T.R. Machan (eds.), *Rights and Regulations, op. cit.*

—71—
ADVERTISING
AND BEHAVIOR CONTROL

Robert L. Arrington

CONSIDER THE FOLLOWING ADVERTISEMENTS:

1. "A woman in *Distinction Foundations* is so beautiful that all other women want to kill her."

2. Pongo Peach color for Revlon comes "from east of the sun ... west of the moon where each tomorrow dawns." It is "succulent on your lips" and "sizzling on your finger tips (and on your toes goodness knows)." Let it be your "adventure in paradise."

3. "Musk by English Leather—The Civilized Way to Roar."

4. "Increase the value of your holdings. Old Charter Bourbon Whiskey—The Final Step Up."

5. Last Call Smirnoff Style: "They'd never really miss us, and it's kind of late already, and it's quite a long way, and I could build a fire, and you're looking very beautiful, and we could have another martini, and it's awfully nice just being home ... you think?"

6. A Christmas Prayer. "Let us pray that the blessing of peace be ours—the peace to build and grow, to live in harmony and sympathy with others, and to plan for the future with confidence." New York Life Insurance Company.

These are instances of what is called puffery—the practice by a seller of making exaggerated, highly fanciful or suggestive claims about a product or service. Puffery, within ill-defined limits, is legal. It is considered a legitimate, necessary, and very successful tool of the advertising industry. Puffery is not just bragging; it is bragging carefully designed to achieve a very definite effect. Using the techniques of so-called motivational research, advertising firms first identify our often hidden needs (for security, conformity, oral stimulation) and our desires (for power, sexual dominance and dalliance, adventure) and then they design ads which respond to these needs and desires. By associating a product, for which we may have little or no direct need or desire, with symbols reflecting the fulfillment of these other, often subterranean interests, the advertisement can quickly generate large numbers of consumers eager to purchase the product advertised. What woman in the sexual race of life could resist a foundation which would turn other women envious to the point of homicide? Who can turn down an adventure in paradise, east of the sun when tomorrow dawns? Who doesn't want to be civilized and thoroughly libidinous at the same time? Be at the pinnacle of success—drink Old Charter. Or stay at home and dally a bit—with Smirnoff. And let us pray for a secure and predictable future, provided for by New York Life, God willing. It doesn't take very much motivational research to see the point of these sales pitches. Others are perhaps a little less obvious. The need to feel secure in one's home at night can be used to sell window air conditioners, which drown out small noises and provide a friendly, dependable companion. The fact that baking a cake is symbolic of giving birth to a baby used to prompt advertisements for cake mixes which glamorized the "creative" housewife. And other strategies, for example involving cigar symbolism, are a bit too crude to mention, but are nevertheless very effective.

Don't such uses of puffery amount to manipulation, exploitation, and downright control? In his very popular book *The Hidden Persuaders*, Vance Packard points out that a number of people in the advertising world have frankly admitted as much:

> As early as 1941 Dr. Dichter (an influential advertising consultant) was exhorting ad agencies to recognize themselves for what they actually were—"one of the most advanced laboratories in psychology." He said the successful ad agency "manipulates human motivations and desires and develops a need for goods with which the public has at one time been unfamiliar—perhaps even undesirous of purchasing." The following year *Advertising Agency* carried an ad man's statement that psychology not only holds promise for understanding people but "ultimately for controlling their behavior."[1]

Such statements lead Packard to remark: "With all this interest in manipulating the customer's subconscious, the old slogan 'let the buyer beware' began taking on a new and more profound meaning."[2] B.F. Skinner, the high priest of behaviorism, has expressed a similar assessment of advertising and related marketing techniques. Why, he asks, do we buy a certain kind of car?

> Perhaps our favorite TV program is sponsored by the manufacturer of that car. Perhaps we have seen pictures of many beautiful or prestigeful persons driving it—in pleasant or glamorous places. Perhaps the car has been designed with respect to our motivational patterns: the device on the hood is a phallic symbol; or the horsepower has been stepped up to please our competitive spirit in

enabling us to pass other cars swiftly (or, as the advertisements say, "safely"). The concept of freedom that has emerged as part of the cultural practice of our group makes little or no provision for recognizing or dealing with these kinds of control.[3]

In purchasing a car we may think we are free, Skinner is claiming, when in fact our act is completely controlled by factors in our environment and in our history of reinforcement. Advertising is one such factor.

A look at some other advertising techniques may reinforce the suspicion that Madison Avenue controls us like so many puppets. TV watchers surely have noticed that some of the more repugnant ads are shown over and over again, *ad nauseam*. My favorite, or most hated, is the one about A-1 Steak Sauce which goes something like this: Now, ladies and gentlemen, what is hamburger? It has succeeded in destroying my taste for hamburger, but it has surely drilled the name of A-1 Sauce into my head. And that is the point of it. Its very repetitiousness has generated what ad theorists call *information*. In this case it is indirect information, information derived not from the content of what is said but from the fact that it is said so often and so vividly that it sticks in one's mind—i.e., the information yield has increased. And not only do I always remember A-1 Sauce when I go to the grocers, I tend to assume that any product advertised so often has to be good—and so I usually buy a bottle of the stuff.

Still another technique. On a recent show of the television program "Hard Choices" it was demonstrated how subliminal suggestion can be used to control customers. In a New Orleans department store, messages to the effect that shoplifting is wrong, illegal, and subject to punishment were blended into the Muzak background music and masked so as not to be consciously audible. The store reported a dramatic drop in shoplifting. The program host conjectured whether a logical extension of this technique would be to broadcast subliminal advertising messages to the effect that the store's $15.99 sweater special is the "bargain of a lifetime." Actually, this application of subliminal suggestion to advertising has already taken place. Years ago in New Jersey a cinema was reported to have flashed subthreshold ice cream ads onto the screen during regular showings of the film—and, yes, the concession stand did a landslide business.[4]

Puffery, indirect information transfer, subliminal advertising—are these techniques of manipulation and control whose success shows that many of us have forfeited our autonomy and become a community, or herd, of packaged souls?[5] The business world and the advertising industry certainly reject his interpretation of their efforts. *Business Week*, for example, dismissed the charge that the science of behavior, as utilized by advertising, is engaged in human engineering and manipulation. It editorialized to the effect that "it is hard to find anything very sinister about a science whose principal conclusion is that you get along with people by giving them what they want."[6] The theme is familiar: businesses just give the consumer what he/she wants; if they didn't they wouldn't stay in business very long. Proof that the consumer wants the products advertised is given by the fact that he buys them, and indeed often returns to buy them again and again.

The techniques of advertising we are discussing have had their more intellectual defenders as well. For example, Theodore Levitt, Professor of Business Administration at the Harvard Business School, has defended the practice of puffery and the use of techniques depending on motivational research.[7] What would be the consequences, he asks us, of deleting all exaggerated claims and fanciful associations from advertisements? We would be left with literal descriptions of the empirical characteristics of products and their functions. Cosmetics would be presented as facial and bodily lotions—and powders which produce certain odor and color changes; they would no longer offer hope or adventure. In addition to the fact that these products would not then sell as well, they would not, according to Levitt, please us as much either. For it is hope and adventure we want when

we buy them. We want automobiles not just for transportation, but the feelings of power and status they give us. Quoting T.S. Eliot to the effect that "Human kind cannot bear very much reality," Levitt argues that advertising is an effort to "transcend nature in the raw," to "augment what nature has so crudely fashioned." He maintains that "everybody everywhere wants to modify, transform, embellish, enrich and reconstruct the world around him." Commerce takes the same liberty with reality as the artist and the priest—in all three instances the purpose is "to influence the audience by creating illusions, symbols, and implications that promise more than pure functionality." For example, "to amplify the temple in men's eyes, (men of cloth) have, very realistically, systematically sanctioned the embellishment of the houses of the gods with the same kind of luxurious design and expensive decoration that Detroit puts into a Cadillac." A poem, a temple, a Cadillac—they all elevate our spirits, offering imaginative promise and symbolic interpretations of our mundane activities. Seen in this light, Levitt claims, "Embellishment and distortion are among advertising's legitimate and socially desirable purposes." To reject these techniques of advertising would be "to deny man's honest needs and values."

Phillip Nelson, a Professor of Economics at SUNY-Binghamton, has developed an interesting defense of indirect information advertising.[8] He argues that even when the message (the direct information) is not credible, the fact that the brand is advertised, and advertised frequently, is valuable indirect information for the consumer. The reason for this is that the brands advertised most are more likely to be better buys—losers won't be advertised a lot, for it simply wouldn't pay to do so. Thus even if the advertising claims made for a widely advertised product are empty, the consumer reaps the benefit of the indirect information which shows the product to be a good buy. Nelson goes so far as to say that advertising, seen as information and especially as indirect information, does not require an intelligent human response. If the indirect information has been received and has had its impact, the consumer will purchase the better buy even if his explicit reason for doing so is silly, e.g., he naively believes an endorsement of the product by a celebrity. Even though his behavior is overtly irrational, by acting on the indirect information he is nevertheless doing what he ought to do, i.e., getting his money's worth. "'Irrationality' is rational," Nelson writes, "if it is cost-free."

I don't know of any attempt to defend the use of subliminal suggestion in advertising, but I can imagine one form such an attempt might take. Advertising information, even if perceived below the level of conscious awareness, must appeal to some desire on the part of the audience if it is to trigger a purchasing response. Just as the admonition not to shoplift speaks directly to the superego, the sexual virtues of TR-7's, Pongo Peach, and Betty Crocker cake mix present themselves directly to the id, bypassing the pesky reality principle of the ego. With a little help from our advertising friends, we may remove a few of the discontents of civilization and perhaps even enter into the paradise of polymorphous perversity.[9]

The defense of advertising which suggests that advertising simply is information which allows us to purchase what we want, has in turn been challenged. Does business, largely through its advertising efforts, really make available to the consumer what he/she desires and demands? John Kenneth Galbraith has denied that the matter is as straightforward as this.[10] In his opinion the desires to which business is supposed to respond, far from being original to the consumer, are often themselves created by business. The producers make both the product and the desire for it, and the "central function" of advertising is "to create desires." Galbraith coins the term "The Dependence Effect" to designate the way wants depend on the same process by which they are satisfied.

David Braybrooke has argued in similar and related ways.[11] Even though the consumer is in a sense, the final authority concerning what he wants, he may come to see, according to Braybrooke, that he was mistaken in wanting what he did. The statement "I want x," he tells us, is not incorrigible but is "ripe for revision." If the consumer had more objective information than he is provided by product puffing, if his values had not been mixed up by motivational research strategies (e.g., the confusion of sexual and automotive values), and if he had an expanded set of choices instead of the limited set offered by profit-hungry corporations, then he might want something quite different from what he presently wants. This shows, Braybrooke thinks, the extent to which the consumer's wants are a function of advertising and not necessarily representative of his real or true wants.

The central issue which emerges between the above critics and defenders of advertising is this: do the advertising techniques we have discussed involve a violation of human autonomy and a manipulation and control of consumer behavior, *or* do they simply provide an efficient and cost-effective means of giving the consumer information on the basis of which he or she makes a free choice. Is advertising information, or creation of desire?

To answer this question we need a better conceptual grasp of what is involved in the notion of autonomy. This is a complex, multifaceted concept, and we need to approach it through the more determinate notions of (a) autonomous desire, (b) rational desire and choice, (c) free choice, and (d) control or manipulation. In what follows I shall offer some tentative and very incomplete analyses of these concepts and apply the results to the case of advertising.

(a) Autonomous desire Imagine that I am watching TV and see an ad for Grecian Formula 16. The thought occurs to me that if I purchase some and apply it to my beard, I will soon look younger—in fact I might even be myself again. Suddenly want to be myself! I want to be young again! So I rush out and buy a bottle. This is our question: was the desire to be younger manufactured by the commercial, or was it "original to me" and truly mine? Was it autonomous or not?

F.A. von Hayek has argued plausibly that we should not equate nonautonomous desires, desires which are not original to me or truly mine, with those which are culturally induced.[12] If we did equate the two, he points out, then the desires for music, art, and knowledge could not properly be attributed to a person as original to him, for these are surely induced culturally. The only desires a person would really have as his own in this case would be the purely physical ones for food, shelter, sex, etc. But if we reject the equation of the nonautonomous and the culturally induced, as van Hayek would have us do, then the mere fact that my desire to be young again is caused by the TV commercial—surely an instrument of popular culture transmission—does not in and of itself show that this is not my own, autonomous desire. Moreover, even if I never before felt the need to look young, it doesn't follow that this new desire is any less mine. I haven't always liked 1969 Aloxe Corton Burgundy or the music of Satie, but when the desires for these things first hit me, they were truly mine.

This shows that there is something wrong in setting up the issue over advertising and behavior control as a question whether our desires are truly ours *or* are created in us by advertisements. Induced and autonomous desires do not separate into two mutually exclusive classes. To obtain a better understanding of autonomous and nonautonomous desires, let us consider some cases of a desire which a person does not *acknowledge* to be his own even though he *feels* it. The kleptomaniac has a desire to steal which in many instances he repudiates, seeking by treatment to rid himself of it. And if I were suddenly overtaken by a desire to attend an REO concert, I would immediately disown this desire, claiming possession or momentary madness. These are examples of desires which one might have but with which one would not identify. They are experienced as foreign to one's character or personality. Often a person will have what Harry Frankfurt calls a second-order desire, that is to say, a desire not to have another desire.[13] In such cases, the first-order desire is thought of as being nonautonomous, imposed on one. When on the contrary a person has a second-order desire to maintain and fulfill a first-order desire, then the first-order desire is truly his own, autonomous, original to him. So

there is in fact a distinction between desires which are the agent's own and those which are not, but this is not the same as the distinction between desires which are innate to the agent and those which are externally induced.

If we apply the autonomous/nonautonomous distinction derived from Frankfurt to the desires brought about by advertising, does this show that advertising is responsible for creating desires which are not truly the agent's own? Not necessarily, and indeed not often. There may be some desires I feel which I have picked up from advertising and which I disown—for instance, my desire for A-1 Steak Sauce. If I act on these desires it can be said that I have been led by advertising to act in a way foreign to my nature. In these cases my autonomy has been violated. But most of the desires induced by advertising I fully accept, and hence most of these desires are autonomous. The most vivid demonstration of this is that I often return to purchase the same product over and over again, without regret or remorse. And when I don't, it is more likely that the desire has just faded than that I have repudiated it. Hence, while advertising may violate my autonomy by leading me to act on desires which are not truly mine, this seems to be the exceptional case.

Note that this conclusion applies equally well to the case of subliminal advertising. This may generate subconscious desires which lead to purchases, and the act of purchasing these goods may be inconsistent with other conscious desires I have, in which case I might repudiate my behavior and by implication the subconscious cause of it. But my subconscious desires may not be inconsistent in this way with my conscious ones; my id may be cooperative and benign rather than hostile and malign.[14] Here again, then, advertising may or may not produce desires which are "not truly mine."

What are we to say in response to Braybrooke's argument that insofar as we might choose differently if advertisers gave us better information and more options, it follows that the desires we have are to be attributed more to advertising than to our own real inclinations? This claim seems empty.

It amounts to saying that if the world we lived in, and we ourselves, were different, then we would want different things. This is surely tame, but it is equally true of our desire for shelter as of our desire for Grecian Formula 16. If we lived in a tropical paradise we would not need or desire shelter. If we were immortal, we would not desire youth. What is true of all desires can hardly be used as a basis for criticizing some desires by claiming that they are nonautonomous.

(b) Rational desire and choice Braybrooke might be interpreted as claiming that the desires induced by advertising are often irrational ones in the sense that they are not expressed by an agent who is in full possession of the facts about the products advertised or about the alternative products which might be offered him. Following this line of thought, a possible criticism of advertising is that it leads us to act on irrational desires or to make irrational choices. It might be said that our autonomy has been violated by the fact that we are prevented from following our rational wills or that we have been denied the "positive freedom" to develop our true, rational selves. It might be claimed that the desires induced in us by advertising are false desires in that they do not reflect our essential, i.e., rational, essence.

The problem faced by this line of criticism is that of determining what is to count as rational desire or rational choice. If we require that the desire or choice be the product of an awareness of all the facts about the product, then surely every one of us is always moved by irrational desires and makes nothing but irrational choices. How could we know all the facts about a product? If it be required only that we possess all of the available knowledge about the product advertised, then we still have to face the problem that not all available knowledge is relevant to a rational choice. If I am purchasing a car, certain engineering features will be, and others won't be, relevant, *given what I want in a car.* My prior desires determine the relevance of information. Normally a rational desire or choice is thought to be one based upon relevant

information, and information is relevant if it shows how other, prior desires may be satisfied. It can plausibly be claimed that it is such prior desires that advertising agencies acknowledge, and that the agencies often provide the type of information that is relevant in light of these desires. To the extent that this is true, advertising does not inhibit our rational wills or our autonomy as rational creatures.

It may be urged that much of the puffery engaged in by advertising does not provide relevant information at all but rather makes claims which are not factually true. If someone buys Pongo Peach in anticipation of an adventure paradise, or Old Charter in expectation of increasing the value of his holdings, then he/she is expecting purely imaginary benefits. In no literal sense will the one product provide adventure and the other increased capital. A purchasing decision based on anticipation of imaginary benefits is not, it might be said, a rational decision, and a desire for imaginary benefits is not a rational desire.

In rejoinder it needs to be pointed out that we often wish to purchase subjective effects which in being subjective are nevertheless real enough. The feeling of adventure or of enhanced social prestige and value are examples of subjective effects promised by advertising. Surely many (most?) advertisements directly promise subjective effects which their patrons actually desire (and obtain when they purchase the product), and thus the ads provide relevant information for rational choice. Moreover, advertisements often provide accurate indirect information on the basis of which a person who wants a certain subjective effect rationally chooses a product. The mechanism involved here is as follows.

To the extent that a consumer takes an advertised product to offer a subjective effect and the product does not, it is unlikely that it will be purchased again. If this happens in a number of cases, the product will be taken off the market. So here the market regulates itself, providing the mechanism whereby misleading advertisements are withdrawn and misled customers are no longer misled. At the same time, a successful bit of puffery being one which leads to large and repeated sales, produces satisfied customers and more advertising of the product. The indirect information provided by such large-scale advertising efforts provides a measure of verification to the consumer who is looking for certain kinds of subjective effect. For example, if I want to feel well dressed and in fashion, and I consider buying an Izod Alligator shirt which is advertised in all of the magazines and newspapers, then the fact that other people buy it and that this leads to repeated advertisements shows me that the desired subjective effect is real enough and that I indeed will be well dressed and in fashion if I purchase the shirt. The indirect information may lead to a rational decision to purchase a product because the information testifies to the subjective effect that the product brings about.[15]

Some philosophers will be unhappy with the conclusion of this section largely because they have a concept of true, rational, or ideal desire which is not the same as the one used here. A Marxist, for instance, may urge that any desire felt by alienated man in a capitalistic society is foreign to his true nature. Or an existentialist may claim that the desires of inauthentic men are themselves inauthentic. Such concepts are based upon general theories of human nature which are unsubstantiated and perhaps incapable of substantiation. Moreover, each of these theories is committed to a concept of an ideal desire which is normatively debatable and which is distinct from the ordinary concept of a rational desire as one based upon relevant information. But it is in the terms of the ordinary concept that we express our concern that advertising may limit our autonomy in the sense of leading us to act on irrational desires, and if we operate with this concept we are driven again to the conclusion that advertising may lead, but probably most often does not lead, to an infringement of autonomy.

(c) Free choice It might be said that some desires are so strong or so covert that a person cannot resist them, and that when he acts on such desires he is not acting freely or voluntarily but is rather the victim of irresistible impulse or an unconscious drive. Perhaps those who condemn advertising feel that it produces this kind of desire in us and consequently reduces our autonomy.

This raises a very difficult issue. How do we distinguish between an impulse we *do* not resist and one we *could* not resist, between freely giving in to a desire and succumbing to one? I have argued elsewhere that the way to get at this issue is in terms of the notion of acting for a reason.[16] A person acts or chooses freely if he does so for a reason, that is, if he can adduce considerations which justify in his mind the act in question. Many of our actions are in fact free because this condition frequently holds. Often, however, a person will act from habit, or whim, or impulse, and on these occasions he does not have a reason in mind. Nevertheless he often acts voluntarily in these instances, i.e., he could have acted otherwise. And this is because if there *had been* a reason for acting otherwise of which he was aware, he would in fact have done so. Thus acting from habit or impulse is not necessarily to act in an involuntary manner. If, however, a person is aware of a good reason to do x and still follows his impulse to do y, then he can be said to be impelled by irresistible impulse and hence to act involuntarily. Many kleptomaniacs can be said to act involuntarily, for in spite of their knowledge that they likely will be caught and their awareness that the goods they steal have little utilitarian value to them, they nevertheless steal. Here their "out of character" desires have the upper hand, and we have a case of compulsive behavior.

Applying these notions of voluntary and compulsive behavior to the case of behavior prompted by advertising, can we say that consumers influenced by advertising act compulsively? The unexciting answer is: sometimes they do, sometimes not. I may have an overwhelming, TV induced urge to own a Mazda Rx-7 and all the while realize that I can't afford one without severely reducing my family's caloric intake to a dangerous level. If, aware of this good reason not to purchase the car, I nevertheless do so, this shows that I have been the victim of TV compulsion. But if I have the urge, as I assure you I do, and don't act on it, or if in some other possible world I could afford an Rx-7, then I have not been the subject of undue influence by Mazda advertising. Some Mazda Rx-7 purchasers act compulsively; others do not. The Mazda advertising effort in general cannot be condemned, then, for impairing its customers' autonomy in the sense of limiting free or voluntary choice. Of course the question remains what should be done about the fact that advertising may and does *occasionally* limit free choice. We shall return to this question later.

In the case of subliminal advertising we may find an individual whose subconscious desires are activated by advertising into doing something his calculating, reasoning ego does not approve. This would be a case of compulsion. But most of us have a benevolent subconsciousness which does not overwhelm our ego and its reasons for action. And therefore most of us can respond to subliminal advertising without thereby risking our autonomy. To be sure, if some advertising firm developed a subliminal technique which drove all of us to purchase Lear jets, thereby reducing our caloric intake to the zero point, then we would have a case of advertising which could properly be censured for infringing our right to autonomy. We should acknowledge that this is possible, but at the same time we should recognize that it is not an inherent result of subliminal advertising.

(d) Control or manipulation Briefly let us consider the matter of control and manipulation. Under what conditions do these activities occur? In a recent paper on "Forms and Limits of Control" I suggested the following criteria.[17]

A person C controls the behavior of another person P *if*

1. C intends P to act in a certain way A;
2. C's intention is causally effective in bringing about A; and
3. C intends to ensure that all of the necessary conditions of A are satisfied.

These criteria may be elaborated as follows. To control another person it is not enough that one's actions produce certain behavior on the part of that person; additionally one must intend that this happen. Hence control is the intentional production of behavior. Moreover, it is not enough just to have the intention; the intention must give rise to the conditions which bring about the intended effect. Finally, the controller must intend to establish by his actions any otherwise unsatisfied necessary conditions for the production of the intended effect. The controller is not just influencing the outcome, not just having input; he is as it were guaranteeing that the sufficient conditions for the intended effect are satisfied.

Let us apply these criteria of control to the case of advertising and see what happens. Conditions (1) and (3) are crucial. Does the Mazda manufacturing company or its advertising agency intend that I buy an Rx-7? Do they intend that a certain number of people buy the car? *Prima facie* it seems more appropriate to say that they hope a certain number of people will buy it, and hoping and intending are not the same. But the difficult term here is "intend." Some philosophers have argued that to intend A it is necessary only to desire that A happen and to believe that it will. If this is correct, and if marketing analysis gives the Mazda agency a reasonable belief that a certain segment of the population will buy its product, then, assuming on its part the desire that this happen, we have the conditions necessary for saying that the agency intends that a certain segment purchase the car. If I am a member of this segment of the population, would it then follow that the agency intends that I purchase an Rx-7? Or is control referentially opaque? Obviously we have some questions here which need further exploration.

Let us turn to the third condition of control, the requirement that the controller intend to activate or bring about any otherwise unsatisfied necessary conditions for the production of the intended effect. It is in terms of this condition that we are able to distinguish brainwashing from liberal education. The brainwasher arranges all of the necessary conditions for belief. On the other hand, teachers (at least those of liberal persuasion) seek only to influence their students—to provide them with information and enlightenment which they may absorb *if they wish*. We do not normally think of teachers as controlling their students, for the students' performances depend as well on their own interests and inclinations.

Now the advertiser—does he control, or merely influence, his audience? Does he intend to ensure that all of the necessary conditions for purchasing behavior are met, or does he offer information and symbols which are intended to have an effect only *if* the potential purchaser has certain desires? Undeniably advertising induces some desires, and it does this intentionally; but more often than not it intends to induce a desire for a particular object, given that the purchaser already has other desires. Given a desire for youth, or power, or adventure, or ravishing beauty, we are led to desire Grecian Formula 16, Mazda Rx-7's, Pongo Peach, and Distinctive Foundations. In this light, the advertiser is influencing us by appealing to independent desires we already have. He is not creating those basic desires. Hence it seems appropriate to deny that he intends to produce all of the necessary conditions for our purchases, and appropriate to deny that he controls us.[18]

Let me summarize my argument. The critics of advertising see it as having a pernicious effect on the autonomy of consumers, as controlling their lives and manufacturing their very souls. The defense claims that advertising only offers information and in effect allows industry to provide consumers with what they want. After developing some of the philosophical dimensions of this dispute, I have come down tentatively in favor of the advertisers. Advertising may, but certainly does not always or even frequently, control behavior, produce compulsive behavior, or create wants which are not rational or are not truly those of the consumer. Admittedly it may in individual cases do all of these things, but it is innocent of the charge of intrinsically or necessarily doing them or even, I think, of often doing so. This limited potentiality, to be sure, leads to the question whether advertising should be abolished or severely curtailed or regulated because of its potential to harm a few poor souls in the above ways. This is a very difficult question, and I do not pretend to have the answer. I only hope that the above discussion, in showing some of the kinds of harm that can be done by advertising and by indicating the likely limits of this harm, will put us in a better position to grapple with the question.

NOTES

1   Vance Packard, *The Hidden Persuaders* (New York: Pocket Books, 1958), 20–21.

2   Ibid., 21.

3   B.F. Skinner, "Some Issues Concerning the Control of Human Behavior: A Symposium," in Karlins and Andrews (eds.), *Man Controlled* (New York: The Free Press, 1972).

4   For provocative discussions of subliminal advertising, see W.B. Key, *Subliminal Seduction* (New York: The New American Library, 1973), and W.B. Key, *Media Sexploitation* (Englewood Cliffs, NJ: Prentice-Hall, Inc., 1976).

5   I would like to emphasize that in what follows I am discussing these techniques of advertising from the standpoint of the issue of control and not from that of deception. For a good and recent discussion of the many dimensions of possible deception in advertising, see Alex C. Michalos, "Advertising: Its Logic, Ethics, and Economics," in A. Blair and R.H. Johnson (eds.), *Informal Logic: The First International Symposium* (Pt. Reyes, CA: Edgepress, 1980).

6   Quoted by Packard, *op. cit.*, 220.

7   Theodore Levitt, "The Morality (?) of Advertising," *Harvard Business Review* 48 (1970), 84–92.

8   Phillip Nelson, "Advertising and Ethics," in Richard T. De George and Joseph A. Pichler (eds.), *Ethics, Free Enterprise, and Public Policy* (New York: Oxford University Press, 1978), 187–98.

9   For a discussion of polymorphous perversity see Norman O. Brown, *Life Against Death* (New York: Random House, 1969), chapter III.

10   John Kenneth Galbraith, *The Affluent Society*, reprinted in Tom L. Beauchamp and Norman

E. Bowie (eds.), *Ethical Theory and Business* (Englewood Cliffs: Prentice-Hall, 1979), 496–501.

11 David Braybrooke, "Skepticism of Wants, and Certain Subversive Effects of Corporations on American Values," in Sidney Hook (ed.), *Human Values and Economic Policy* (New York: New York University Press, 1967); reprinted in Beauchamp and Bowie (eds.), *op. cit.*, 502–08.

12 F.A. von Hayek, "The *Non Sequitur* of the 'Dependence Effect,'" *Southern Economic Journal* (1961); reprinted in Beauchamp and Bowie (eds.), *op. cit.*, 508–12.

13 Harry Frankfurt, "Freedom of the Will and the Concept of a Person," *Journal of Philosophy* LXVIII (1971), 5–20.

14 For a discussion of the difference between a malign and a benign subconscious mind, see P.H. Nowell-Smith, "Psychoanalysis and Moral Language," *The Rationalist Annual* (1954); reprinted in P. Edwards and A. Pap (eds.), *A Modern Introduction to Philosophy*, Revised Edition (New York: The Free Press, 1965), 86–93.

15 Michalos argues that in emphasizing a brand name—such as Bayer Aspirin—advertisers are illogically attempting to distinguish the indistinguishable by casting a trivial feature of a product as a significant one which separates it from other brands of the same product. The brand name is said to be trivial or unimportant "from the point of view of the effectiveness of the product or that for the sake of which the product is purchased" (*op. cit.*, 107). This claim ignores the role of indirect information in advertising. For example, consumers want an aspirin they can trust (trustworthiness being part of "that for the sake of which the product is purchased"), and the indirect information conveyed by the widespread advertising effort for Bayer Aspirin shows that this product is judged trustworthy by many other purchasers. Hence the emphasis on the name is not at all irrelevant but rather is a significant feature of the product from the consumer's standpoint, and attending to the name is not at all an illogical or irrational response on the part of the consumer.

16 Robert L. Arrington, "Practical Reason, Responsibility and the Psychopath," *Journal for the Theory of Social Behavior* 9 (1979), 71–89.

17 Robert L. Arrington, "Forms and Limits of Control," delivered at the annual meeting of the Southern Society for Philosophy and Psychology, Birmingham, Alabama, 1980.

18 Michalos distinguishes between appealing to people's tastes and molding those tastes (*op. cit.*, 104), and he seems to agree with my claim that it is morally permissible for advertisers to persuade us to consume some article *if* it suits our tastes (105). However, he also implies that advertisers mold tastes as well as appeal to them. It is unclear what evidence is given for this claim, and it is unclear what is meant by tastes. If the latter are thought of as basic desires and wants, then I would agree that advertisers are controlling their customers to the extent that they intentionally mold tastes. But if by molding tastes is meant generating a desire for the particular object they promote, advertisers in doing so may well be appealing to more basic desires, in which case they should not be thought of as controlling the consumer.

—72—

PERSUASIVE ADVERTISING, AUTONOMY, AND THE CREATION OF DESIRE

Roger Crisp

IN THIS PAPER, I SHALL ARGUE THAT ALL FORMS of a certain common type of advertising are morally wrong, on the ground that they override the autonomy of consumers. One effect of an advertisement might be the creation of a desire for the advertised product. How such desires are caused is highly relevant as to whether we would describe the case as one in which the autonomy of the subject has been overridden. If I read an advertisement for a sale of clothes, I may rush down to my local clothes store and purchase a jacket I like. Here, my desire for the jacket has arisen partly out of my reading the advertisement. Yet, in an ordinary sense, it is based on or answers to certain properties of the jacket—its colour, style, material. Although I could not explain to you why my tastes are as they are, we still describe such cases as examples of autonomous action, in that all the decisions are being made by me: What kind of jacket do I like? Can I afford one? And so on. In certain other cases, however, the causal history of a desire may be different. Desire can be caused, for instance, by subliminal suggestion. In New Jersey, a cinema flashed sub-threshold advertisements for ice cream onto the screen during movies, and reported a dramatic increase in sales during intermissions. In such cases, choice is being deliberately ruled out by the method of advertising in question.

These customers for ice cream were acting "automatonously," rather than autonomously. They did not buy the ice cream because they happened to like it and decided they would buy some, but rather because they had been subjected to subliminal suggestion. Subliminal suggestion is the most extreme form of what I shall call, adhering to a popular dichotomy, persuasive, as opposed to informative, advertising. Other techniques include puffery, which involves the linking of the product through suggestive language and images, with the unconscious desire of consumers for power, wealth, status, sex, and so on; and repetition, which is self-explanatory, the name of the product being "drummed into" the mind of the consumer.

The obvious objection to persuasive advertising is that it somehow violates the autonomy of consumers. I believe that this objection is correct, and that, if one adopts certain commonsensical standards for autonomy, non-persuasive forms of advertising are not open to such an objection. Very high standards for autonomy are set by Kant, who requires that an agent be entirely external to the causal nexus found in the ordinary empirical world, if his or her actions are to be autonomous. These standards are too high, in that it is doubtful whether they allow *any* autonomous action. Standards for autonomy more congenial to common sense will allow that my buying the jacket is autonomous, although continuing to deny that the people in New Jersey were acting autonomously. In the former case, we have what has come to be known in recent discussions of freedom of the will as *both* free will and free action. I both decide what to do, and am not obstructed in carrying through my decision into action. In the latter case, there is free action, but not free will. No one prevents the customers buying their ice cream, but they have not themselves made any genuine decision whether or not to do so. In a very real sense, decisions are made for consumers by persuasive advertisers, who occupy the motivational territory properly belonging to the agent. If what we mean by autonomy, in the ordinary sense, is to be present, the possibility of decision must exist alongside.

Arrington (1982) discusses, in a challenging paper, the techniques of persuasive advertising I have mentioned, and argues that such advertising does not override the autonomy of consumers. He examines four notions central to autonomous action, and claims that, on each count, persuasive advertising is exonerated on the charge we have made against it. I shall now follow in the footsteps of Arrington, but argue that he sets the standards for autonomy too low for them to be acceptable to common sense, and that the charge therefore still sticks.

(A) AUTONOMOUS DESIRE

Arrington argues that an autonomous desire is a first-order desire (a desire for some object, say, Pongo Peach cosmetics) accepted by the agent because it fulfils a second-order desire (a desire about a desire, say, a desire that my first-order desire for Pongo Peach be fulfilled), and that most of the first-order desires engendered in us by advertising are desires that we do accept. His example is an advertisement for Grecian Formula 16, which engenders in him a desire to be younger. He desires that both his desire to be younger and his desire for Grecian Formula 16 be fulfilled.

Unfortunately, this example is not obviously one of persuasive advertising. It may be the case that he just has this desire to look young again rather as I had certain sartorial tastes before I saw the ad about the clothes sale, and then decides to buy Grecian Formula 16 on the basis of these tastes. Imagine this form of advertisement: a person is depicted using Grecian Formula 16, and is then shown in a position of authority, surrounded by admiring members of the opposite sex. This would be a case of puffery. The advertisement implies that having hair coloured by the product will lead to positions of power, and to one's becoming more attractive to the opposite sex. It links, by suggestion, the product with my unconscious desires for power and sex. I may still claim that I am buying the product because I want to look young again. But the reasons for my purchase are my unconscious desires for power and sex, and the link made between the product and the fulfilment of those desires by the advertisement. These reasons are not reasons I could avow to myself as good reasons for buying the product, and, again, the possibility of decision is absent.

Arrington's claim is that an autonomous desire is a first-order desire which we accept. Even if we allow that it is possible for the agent to consider whether to accept or to repudiate first-order desires induced purely by persuasive advertising, it seems that all first-order desires induced purely by persuasive advertising will be non-autonomous in Arrington's sense. Many of us have a strong second-order desire not to be manipulated by others without our knowledge, and for no good reason. Often, we are manipulated by others without our knowledge but for a good reason, and one that we can accept. Take an accomplished actor: much of the skill of an actor is to be found in unconscious body language. This manipulation we see as essential to our being entertained, and thus acquiesce in it. What is important about this case is that there seems to be no diminution of autonomy. We can still judge the quality of the acting, in that the manipulation is part of its quality. In other cases, however, manipulation ought not to be present, and these are cases where the ability to decide is importantly diminished by the manipulation. Decision is central to the theory of the market-process: I should be able to decide whether to buy product A or product B, by judging them on their merits. Any manipulation here I shall repudiate as being for no good reason. This is not to say, incidentally, that once the fact that my desires are being manipulated by others has been made transparent to me, my desire will lapse. The people in New Jersey would have been unlikely to cease their craving for ice cream, if we had told them that their desire had been subliminally induced. But they would no longer have voice acceptance of this desire, and, one assumes, would have resented the manipulation of their desires by the management of the cinema.

It is no evidence for the claim that most of our desires are autonomous in this sense that we often return to purchase the same product over and over again. For this might well show that persuasive advertising has been supremely efficient in inducing non-autonomous desires in us, which we are unable even to attempt not to act on, being unaware of their origin. Nor is it an argument in Arrington's favour that certain members of our society will claim not to have the second-order desire we have postulated. For it may be that this is a desire which we can see is one that human beings *ought* to have, a desire which would be in their interests to have, and the lack of which is itself evidence of profound manipulation.

(B) RATIONAL DESIRE AND CHOICE

One might argue that the desires induced by advertising are often irrational, in the sense that they are not present in an agent in full possession of the facts about the product. This argument fails, says Arrington, because if we require all the facts about a thing before we can desire that thing, then all our desires will be irrational; and if we require only the relevant information, then prior desires determine the relevance of information. Advertising may be said to enable us to fulfil these prior desires, through the transfer of information, and the supplying of means to ends is surely a paradigm example of rationality.

But, what about persuasive, as opposed to informative, advertising? Take puffery. Is it not true that a person may buy Pongo Peach cosmetics, hoping for an adventure in paradise, and that the product will not fulfil these hopes? Are they really in possession of even the relevant facts? Yes, says Arrington. We wish to purchase subjective effects, and these are genuine enough. When I use Pongo Peach, I will experience a genuine feeling of adventure.

Once again, however, our analysis can help us to see the strength of the objection. For a desire to be rational, in any plausible sense, that desire must at least not be induced by the interference of other persons with my system of tastes, against my will and without my knowledge. Can we imagine a person, asked for a reason justifying their purchase of Pongo Peach, replying: "I have an unconscious desire to experience adventure and the product has been linked with this desire through advertising"? If a desire is to be rational, it is not necessary that all the facts about the object be known to the agent, but one of the facts about that desire must be that it has not been induced in the agent through techniques which the agent cannot accept. Thus, applying the schema of Arrington's earlier argument, such a desire will be repudiated by the agent as non-autonomous and irrational.

Arrington's claim concerning the subjective effects of the products we purchase fails to deflect the charge of overriding autonomy we have made against persuasive advertising. Of course, very often the subjective effects will be lacking. If I use Grecian Formula 16, I am unlikely to find myself being promoted at work, or surrounded by admiring members of the opposite sex. This is just straight deception. But even when the effects do manifest themselves, such advertisements have still overridden my autonomy. They have activated desires which lie beyond my awareness, and over behaviour flowing from which I therefore have no control. If these claims appear doubtful, consider whether this advertisement is likely to be successful: "Do you have a feeling of adventure? Then use this brand of cosmetics." Such an advertisement will fail, in that it appeals to a *conscious* desire, either which we do not have, or which we realise will not be fulfilled by purchasing a certain brand of cosmetics. If the advertisement were for a course in mountain-climbing, it might meet with more success. Our conscious self is not so easily duped by advertising, and this is why advertisers make such frequent use of the techniques of persuasive advertising.

(C) FREE CHOICE

One might object to persuasive advertising in that it creates desires so covert that an agent cannot resist them, and that acting on them is therefore neither free nor voluntary. Arrington claims that a person acts or chooses *freely* if they can adduce considerations which justify their act in their mind; and *voluntarily* if they had been aware of a reason for acting otherwise, they could have done so. Only occasionally, he says, does advertising prevent us making free and voluntary choices.

Regarding free action, it is sufficient to note that, according to Arrington, if I were to be converted into a human robot, activated by an Evil Genius who has implanted electrodes in my brain, my actions would be free as long as I could cook up some justification for my behaviour. I want to dance this jig because I enjoy dancing. (Compare: I want to buy this ice cream because I like ice cream.) If my argument is right, we are placed in an analogous position by persuasive advertising. If we no longer mean by freedom of action the mere non-obstruction of behaviour, are we still ready to accept that we are engaging in free action? As for whether the actions of consumers subjected to persuasive advertising are voluntary in Arrington's sense, I am less optimistic than he is. It is likely,

as we have suggested, that the purchasers of ice cream or Pongo Peach would have gone ahead with their purchase even if they had been made aware that their desires had been induced in them by persuasive advertising. But they would now claim that they themselves had not made the decision, that they were acting on a desire engendered in them which they did not accept, and that there was, therefore, a good reason for them not to make the purchase. The unconscious is not obedient to the commands of the conscious, although it may be forced to listen.

In fact, it is odd to suggest that persuasive advertising does give consumers a choice. A choice is usually taken to require the weighing-up of reasons. What persuasive advertising does is to remove the very conditions of choice.

(D) CONTROL OR MANIPULATION

Arrington offers the following criteria for control:

A person C controls the behaviour of another person P if

(1) C intends P to act in a certain way A

(2) C's intention is causally effective in bringing about A, and

(3) C intends to ensure that all of the necessary conditions of A are satisfied.

He argues that advertisements tend to induce a desire for X, given a more basic desire for Y. Given my desire for adventure, I desire Pongo Peach cosmetics. Thus, advertisers do not control consumers, since they do not intend to produce all of the necessary conditions for our purchases.

Arrington's analysis appears to lead to some highly counter-intuitive consequences. Consider again my position as human robot. Imagine that Evil Genius relies on the fact that I have certain basic unconscious desires in order to effect his plan. Thus, when he wants me to dance a jig, it is necessary that I have a more basic desire, say, ironically, for power. What the electrodes do is to jumble up my practical reasoning processes, so that I believe that I am dancing the jig because I like dancing, while, in reality, the desire to dance stems from a link between the dance and the fulfilment of my desire for power, forged by the electrodes. Are we still happy to say that I am not controlled? And does not persuasive advertising bring about a similar jumbling-up of the practical reasoning processes of consumers? When I buy Pongo Peach, I may be unable to offer a reason for my purchase, or I may claim that I want to look good. In reality, I buy it owing to the link made by persuasive advertising between my unconscious desire for adventure and the cosmetic in question.

A more convincing account of behaviour control would be to claim that it occurs when a person causes another person to act for reasons which the other person could not accept as good or justifiable reasons for the action. This is how brain-washing is to be distinguished from liberal education, rather than on Arrington's ground that the brain-washer arranges all the necessary conditions for belief. The student can both accept that she has the beliefs she has because of her education and continue to hold those beliefs as true, whereas the victim of brain-washing could not accept the explanation of the origin of her beliefs, while continuing to hold those beliefs. It is worth recalling the two cases we mentioned at the beginning of this paper. I can accept my tastes in dress, and do not think that the fact that their origin is unknown to me detracts from my autonomy, when I choose to buy the jacket. The desire for ice cream, however, will be repudiated, in that it is the result of manipulation by others, without good reason.

***

It seems, then, that persuasive advertising does override the autonomy of consumers, and that, if the overriding of autonomy, other things being equal, is immoral, then persuasive advertising is immoral.

An argument has recently surfaced which suggests that, in fact, other things are not equal, and that persuasive advertising, although it overrides autonomy, is morally acceptable. This argument was first developed by Nelson (1978), and claims that persuasive advertising is a form of informative advertising, albeit an indirect form. The argument runs at two levels: first, the consumer can judge from the mere fact that a product is heavily advertised, regardless of the form or content of the advertisements, that that product is likely to be a market-winner. The reason for this is that it would not pay to advertise market-losers. Second, even if the consumer is taken in by the content of the advertisement, and buys the product for that reason, he is not being irrational. For he would have bought the product anyway, since the very fact that it is advertised means that it is a good product. As Nelson says:

> It does not pay consumers to make very thoughtful decisions about advertising. They can respond to advertising for the most ridiculous, explicit reasons and still do what they would have done if they had made the most careful judgements about their behavior. "Irrationality" is rational if it is cost-free.

Our conclusions concerning the mode of operation of persuasive advertising, however, suggest that Nelson's argument cannot succeed. For the first level to work, it would have to be true that a purchaser of a product can evaluate that product on its own merits, and then decide whether to purchase it again. But as we have seen, consumers induced to purchase products by persuasive advertising are not buying those products on the basis of a decision founded upon any merit the products happen to have. Thus, if the product turns out to be less good than less heavily advertised alternatives, they will not be disappointed, and will continue to purchase, if subjected to the heavy advertising which induced them to buy in the first place. For this reason, heavy persuasive advertising is not a sign of quality, and the fact that a product is advertised does not suggest that it is good. In fact, if the advertising has little or no informative content, it might suggest just the opposite. If the product has genuine merits, it should be possible to mention them. Persuasive advertising as the executives on Madison Avenue know, can be used to sell anything regardless of its nature or quality.

For the second level of Nelson's argument to succeed, and for it to be in the consumer's interest to react even unthinkingly to persuasive advertising, it must be true that the first level is valid. As the first level fails, there is not even a *prima facie* reason for the belief that it is in the interest of the consumer to be subjected to persuasive advertising. In fact, there are two weighty reasons for doubting this belief. The first has already been hinted at: products promoted through persuasive advertising may well not be being sold on their merits, and may, therefore, be bad products, or products that the consumer would not desire on being confronted with unembellished facts about the product. The second is that this form of "rational irrationality" is anything but cost-free. We consider it a great cost to lose our autonomy. If I were to demonstrate to you conclusively that if I were to take over your life, and make your decisions for you, you would have a life containing far more of whatever you think makes life worth living, apart from autonomy, than if you were to retain control, you would not surrender your autonomy to me even for these great gains in other values. As we mentioned above in our discussion of autonomous desire, we have a strong second-order desire not to act on first-order desires induced in us unawares by others, for no good reason, and now we can see that that desire applies even to cases in which we would *appear* to be better off in acting on such first-order desires.

Thus, we may conclude that Nelson's argument in favour of persuasive advertising is not convincing. I should note, perhaps, that my conclusion concerning persuasive advertising echoes that of Santilli (1983). My argument differs from his, however, in centering upon the notions of autonomy and causes of desires acceptable to the agent, rather than upon the distinction between needs and desires. Santilli claims that the arousal of a desire is not a rational process, unless it is preceded by a knowledge of actual needs. This I believe, is too strong. I may well have no need of a new tennis-racket, but my desire for one, aroused by informative advertisements in the newspaper, seems rational enough. I should prefer to claim that a desire is autonomous and at least *prima facie* rational if it is not induced in the agent without his knowledge and for no good reason, and allows ordinary processes of decision-making to occur.

Finally, I should point out that, in arguing against all persuasive advertising, unlike Santilli, I am not to be interpreted as bestowing moral respectability upon all informative advertising. Advertisers of any variety ought to consider whether the ideological objections often made to their conduct have any weight. Are they, for instance, imposing a distorted system of values upon consumers, in which the goal of our lives is to consume, and in which success is measured by one's level of consumption? Or are they entrenching attitudes which prolong the position of certain groups subject to discrimination, such as women or homosexuals? Advertisers should also carefully consider whether their product will be of genuine value to any consumers, and, if so, attempt to restrict their campaigns to the groups in society which will benefit (see Durham, 1984). I would claim, for instance, that all advertising of tobacco-based products, even of the informative variety, is wrong, and that some advertisements for alcohol are wrong, in that they are directed at the wrong audience. Imagine, for instance, a liquor-store manager erecting an informative bill-board opposite an alcoholics' rehabilitation center. But these are secondary questions for prospective advertisers. The primary questions must be whether they are intending to employ the techniques of persuasive advertising, and, if so, how these techniques can be avoided.

REFERENCES

Arrington, R. 1982, "Advertising and Behaviour Control," *Journal of Business Ethics* I, 1.

Durham, T. 1984, "Information, Persuasion, and Control in Moral Appraisal of Advertising Strategy," *Journal of Business Ethics* III, 3.

Nelson, P. 1978, "Advertising and Ethics," in *Ethics, Free Enterprise, and Public Policy*, (eds.) R. De George and J. Pichler, New York: Oxford University Press.

Santilli, P. 1983, "The Informative and Persuasive Functions of Advertising. A Moral Appraisal," *Journal of Business Ethics* II, I.

—73—

MARKETING TO INNER-CITY BLACKS

PowerMaster and Moral Responsibility

George G. Brenkert

I. INTRODUCTION

THE NATURE AND EXTENT OF MARKETERS' MORAL obligations is a matter of considerable debate. This is particularly the case when those who are targeted by marketers live in disadvantaged circumstances and suffer various problems disproportionately with other members of the same society. An interesting opportunity to explore this difficult area of marketing ethics is presented by Heileman Brewing Company's failed effort to market PowerMaster, a malt liquor, to inner-city blacks. The story of PowerMaster is relatively simple and short. Its ethical dimensions are much more complicated.[1]

In the following, I wish to consider the moral aspects of this case within the context of a market society such as the US which permits the forms of advertising it presently does.[2] To do so, I first briefly evaluate three kinds of objections made to the marketing of PowerMaster. I contend that none of these objections taken by itself clearly justifies the criticism leveled at Heileman. Heileman might reasonably claim that it was fulfilling its economic, social and moral responsibilities in the same manner as were other brewers and marketers.

Accordingly, I argue that only if we look to the collective effects of all marketers of malt liquor to the inner-city can we identify morally defensible grounds for the complaints against marketing campaigns such as that of PowerMaster. The upshot of this argument is that marketers must recognize not only their individual moral responsibilities to those they target, but also a collective responsibility of all marketers for those market segments they jointly target. It is on this basis that Heileman's marketing of PowerMaster may be faulted. This result is noteworthy in that it introduces a new kind of moral consideration which has rarely been considered in discussions of corporate moral responsibilities.

II. HEILEMAN AND POWERMASTER

G. Heileman Brewing Co. is a Wisconsin brewer which produces a number of beers and malt liquors, including Colt Dry, Colt 45, and Mickey's. In the early 1990s, competition amongst such brewers was increasingly intense. In January 1991, Heileman was facing such economic difficulties that it filed for protection from creditors under Chapter 11 of the US Bankruptcy Code (Horovitz, 1991b: D1). To improve its financial situation, Heileman sought to market, beginning in June 1991, a new malt liquor called "PowerMaster." At that time there was considerable growth in the "up-strength malt liquor category." In fact, "this higher-alcohol segment of the business [had] been growing at an explosive 25% to 30% a year" (Freedman, 1991a: B1). To attempt to capitalize on this market segment, Heileman produced PowerMaster, a malt liquor that contained 5.9% alcohol, 31% more alcohol than Heileman's top-selling Colt 45 (4.5% alcohol). Reportedly, when introduced, only one other malt liquor (St. Ides) offered such a powerful malt as PowerMaster (Freedman, 1991a: B1).

Further, since malt liquor had become "the drink of choice among many in the inner city," Heileman focused a significant amount of its marketing efforts on inner-city blacks.[3] Heileman's ad campaign played to this group with posters and billboards using black male models. Advertisements assured consumers that PowerMaster was "Bold Not Harsh." Hugh Nelson, Heileman's marketing director, was reported to have claimed that "the company's research ... shows that consumers will opt for PowerMaster not on the basis of its alcohol content but because of its flavor. The higher alcohol content gives PowerMaster a 'bold not nasty' taste ..." (Freedman, 1991a: B4).

In response, a wide variety of individuals and groups protested against Heileman's actions. Critics claimed that both advertisements and the name "PowerMaster" suggested the alcoholic strength of the drink and the "buzz" that those who consumed it could get. Surgeon General Antonia Novello criticized the PowerMaster marketing scheme as "insensitive" (Milloy, 1991: B3). Reports in The Wall Street Journal spoke of community activists and alcohol critics branding Heileman's marketing campaign as "socially irresponsible" (Freedman, 1991b: B1). "Twenty-one consumer and health groups, including the Center for Science in the Public Interest, also publicly called for Heileman to halt the marketing of PowerMaster and for BATF to limit the alcohol content of malt liquor" (Colford and Teinowitz, 1991: 29). A reporter for the LA Times wrote that "at issue is growing resentment by blacks and other minorities who feel that they are being unfairly targeted—if not exploited—by marketers of beer, liquor and tobacco products" (Horovitz, 1991: D6). Another reporter for the same paper claimed that "[a]nti-alcohol activists contend that alcoholic beverage manufacturers are taking advantage of minority groups and exacerbating inner-city problems by targeting them with high-powered blends" (Lacey, 1992: A32). And Reverend Calvin Butts

of the Abyssinian Baptist Church in New York's Harlem said that "this [Heileman] is obviously a company that has no sense of moral or social responsibility" (Freedman, 1991a: B1).

Though the Bureau of Alcohol, Tobacco and Firearms (BATF) initially approved the use of "PowerMaster" as the name for the new malt liquor, in light of the above protests it "reacted by enforcing a beer law that prohibits labels 'considered to be statements of alcoholic content'" (Milloy, 1991: B3). It insisted that the word "Power" be removed from the "PowerMaster" name (Freedman, 1991b: B1). As a consequence of the actions of the BATF and the preceding complaints, Heileman decided not to market PowerMaster.

III. THE OBJECTIONS

The PowerMaster marketing campaign evoked three distinct kinds of moral objections:[4]

First, because its advertisements drew upon images and themes related to power and boldness, they were criticized as promoting satisfactions only artificially and distortedly associated with the real needs of those targeted. As such, the PowerMaster marketing campaign was charged with fostering a form of moral illusion.[5]

Second, Heileman was said to lack concern for the harm likely to be caused by its product. Blacks suffer disproportionately from cirrhosis of the liver and other liver diseases brought on by alcohol. In addition, alcohol-related social problems such as violence and crime are also prominent in the inner-city. Accordingly, Heileman was attacked for its lack of moral sensitivity.

Third, Heileman was accused of taking unfair advantage of those in the inner-city whom they had targeted. Inner-city blacks were said to be especially vulnerable, due to their life circumstances, to advertisements and promotions formulated in terms of power, self-assertion and sexual success. Hence, to target them in the manner they did with a product such as PowerMaster was a form of exploitation. In short, questions of justice were raised.

It is important not only for corporations such as Heileman but also for others concerned with such marketing practices to determine whether these objections show that the PowerMaster marketing program was morally unjustified. The economic losses in failed marketing efforts such as PowerMaster are considerable. In addition, if the above objections are justified, the moral losses are also significant.

The first objection maintained that by emphasizing power Heileman was, in effect, offering a cruel substitute for a real lack in the lives of inner-city blacks. PowerMaster's slogan, "Bold not Harsh," was said to project an image of potency. "The brewers' shrewd marketing," one critic maintained, "has turned malt liquor into an element of machismo" (Lacey, 1992: A1). George Hacker, Director of the National Coalition to Prevent Impaired Driving, commented that "the real irony of marketing PowerMaster to inner-city blacks is that this population is among the most lacking in power in this society" (Freedman, 1991a: B1).

This kind of criticism has been made against many forms of advertising. The linking of one's product with power, fame, and success not to mention sex is nothing new in advertising.[6] Most of those targeted by marketers lack (or at least want) those goods or values associated with the products being promoted. Further, other malt liquor marketing campaigns had referred to power. For example, another malt liquor, Olde English "800," claimed that "It's the Power." The Schlitz Red Bull was associated with the phrase "The Real Power" (Colford and Tenowitz, 1991: 1). Nevertheless, they were not singled out for attack or boycott as PowerMaster was.

Accordingly, however objectionable it may be for marketers to link a product with something which its potential customers (significantly) lack and which the product can only symbolically or indirectly satisfy, this feature of the PowerMaster marketing campaign does not uniquely explain or justify the complaints that were raised against the marketing of PowerMaster. In short, this objection appears far too general in scope to justify the

particular attention given PowerMaster. Heileman could not have reasonably concluded, on its basis, that it was being particularly morally irresponsible. It was simply doing what others had done and for which they had not been boycotted or against which such an outcry had not been raised. It is difficult to see how Heileman could have concluded that it was preparing a marketing program that would generate the social and moral protest it did, simply from an examination of its own plan or the similar individual marketing programs of other brewers.

The second objection was that the marketers of PowerMaster showed an especial lack of sensitivity in that a malt liquor with the potency of PowerMaster would likely cause additional harm to inner-city blacks. According to various reports, "alcoholism and other alcohol-related diseases extract a disproportionate toll on blacks. A 1978 study by the National Institute on Alcohol Abuse and Alcoholism found that black men between the ages of 25 and 44 are 10 times more likely than the general population to have cirrhosis of the liver" (*NY Times*, 1991). Fortune reported that "The Department of Health and Human Services last spring released figures showing a decline in life expectancy for blacks for the fourth straight year—down to 69.2 years, vs. 75.6 years for whites. Although much of the drop is attributable to homicide and AIDS, blacks also suffer higher instances of ... alcohol-related illnesses than whites" (*Fortune*, 1991: 100). Further, due to the combined use of alcohol and cigarettes, blacks suffer cancer of the esophagus at a disproportional rate than the rest of the population.[7] Similarly, assuming that black women would drink PowerMaster, it is relevant that the impact of alcohol use in the inner-city is also manifested in an increased infant mortality rate and by newborn children with fetal alcohol syndrome (*The Workbook*, 1991: 18). Finally, a malt liquor with a high percentage of alcohol was expected to have additional harmful effects on the levels of social ills, such as violence, crime, and spousal abuse. As such, PowerMaster would be further destructive of the social fabric of the inner-city.[8]

Under these circumstances, the second objection maintained, anyone who marketed a product which would further increase these harms was being morally obtuse to the problems inner-city blacks suffer. Accordingly, Heileman's PowerMaster marketing campaign was an instance of such moral insensitivity.

Nevertheless, this objection does not seem clearly applicable when pointed simply at PowerMaster. Surely inner-city blacks are adults and should be allowed, as such, to make their own choices, even if those choices harm themselves, so long as they are not deceived or coerced when making those choices and they do not harm others. Since neither deception nor coercion were involved in PowerMaster's marketing campaign, it is an unacceptable form of moral paternalism to deny them what they might otherwise wish to choose.

Further, those who raised the above complaints were not those who would have drunk PowerMaster, but leaders of various associations both within and outside the inner-city concerned with alcohol abuse and consumption.[9] This was not a consumer-led protest. Reports of the outcry over PowerMaster contain no objections from those whom Heileman had targeted. No evidence was presented that these individuals would have found PowerMaster unsatisfactory. Argument is needed, for example, that these individuals had (or should have had) overriding interests in healthy livers. Obviously there are many people (black as well as white) who claim that their interests are better fulfilled by drinking rather than abstinence.

Finally, argument is also needed to show that this increase in alcoholic content would have any significant effects on the targeted group. It might be that any noteworthy effects would be limited because the increased alcoholic content would prove undesirable to those targeted since they would become intoxicated too quickly. "Overly rapid intoxication undercuts sales volume and annoys consumers," *The Wall Street Journal* reported (Freedman, 1991a: B1). Supposedly this consequence led one malt brewer to lower the alcoholic content of its product (Freedman,

1991a: B1). Furthermore, malt liquor is hardly the strongest alcohol which blacks (or others) drink. Reportedly, "blacks buy more than half the cognac sold in the United States" (*The Workbook*, 1991: 18). Cheap forms of wine and hard liquor are readily available. Thus, it is far from obvious what significant effects PowerMaster alone would have in the inner-city.

One possible response to the preceding replies brings us to the third objection. This response is that, though inner-city blacks might not be deceived or coerced into drinking PowerMaster, they were particularly vulnerable to the marketing campaign which Heileman proposed. Because of this, Heileman's marketing campaign (wittingly or unwittingly) would take unfair advantage of inner-city blacks.

Little, if any attempt, has been made to defend or to explore this charge. I suggest that there are at least three ways in which inner-city blacks—or anyone else, for that matter—might be said to be specially vulnerable.

A person would be cognitively vulnerable if he or she lacked certain levels of ability to cognitively process information or to be aware that certain information was being withheld or manipulated in deceptive ways. Thus, if people were not able to process information about the effects of malt liquor on themselves or on their society in ways in which others could, they would be cognitively vulnerable.

A person would be motivationally vulnerable if he or she could not resist ordinary temptations and/or enticements due to his or her own individual characteristics. Thus, if people were unable, as normal individuals are, to resist various advertisements and marketing ploys, they would be motivationally vulnerable.

And people would be socially vulnerable when their social situation renders them significantly less able than others to resist various enticements. For example, due to the poverty within which they live, they might have developed various needs or attitudes which rendered them less able to resist various marketing programs.

Nevertheless, none of these forms of vulnerability was explored or defended as the basis of the unfair advantage which the PowerMaster marketers were said to seek.[10] And indeed it is difficult to see what account could be given which would explain how the use of the name "PowerMaster," and billboards with a black model, a bottle of PowerMaster and the slogan "Bold Not Harsh" would be enough to subvert the decision making or motivational capacities of inner-city blacks. To the extent that they are adults and not under the care or protection of other individuals or agencies due to the state of their cognitive or motivational abilities, there is a prima facie case that they are not so vulnerable. Accordingly, the vulnerability objection raises the legitimate concern that some form of unjustified moral paternalism lurks behind it.

In short, if we consider simply the individual marketing program of PowerMaster, it is difficult to see that the three preceding objections justified the outcry against Heileman. Heileman was seeking to satisfy its customers. As noted above, none of the reported complaints came from them. Heileman was also seeking to enhance its own bottom line. But in doing so it was not engaged in fraud, deception or coercion. The marketing of PowerMaster was not like other morally objectionable individual marketing programs which have used factually deceptive advertisements (e.g., some past shaving commercials), taken advantage of the target group's special vulnerabilities (e.g., certain television advertisements to children who are cognitively vulnerable), or led to unusual harm for the group targeted (e.g., Nestlé's infant formula promotions to Third World Mothers). Black inner-city residents are not obviously cognitively vulnerable and are not, in the use of malt liquor, uniformly faced with a single significant problem such as Third World Mothers are (viz., the care of their infants). As such, it is mistaken to think that PowerMaster's marketing campaign was morally offensive or objectionable in ways in which other such campaigns have been. From this perspective, then, it appears that Heileman could be said to be fulfilling its individual corporate responsibilities.

IV. ASSOCIATED GROUPS AND COLLECTIVE RESPONSIBILITY

So long as we remain simply at the level of the individual marketing campaign of PowerMaster, it is doubtful that we can grasp the basis upon which the complaints against PowerMaster might be justified. To do so, we must look to the social level and the collection of marketing programs of which PowerMaster was simply one part. By pushing on the bounds within which other marketers had remained,[11] PowerMaster was merely the spark which ignited a great deal of resentment which stemmed more generally from the group of malt liquor marketers coming into the inner-city from outside, aggressively marketing products which disproportionately harmed those in the inner-city (both those who consume the product and others), and creating marketing campaigns that took advantage of their vulnerabilities.[12]

As such, this case might better be understood as one involving the collective responsibility of the group of marketers who target inner-city blacks rather than simply the individual responsibility of this or that marketer. By "collective responsibility" I refer to the responsibility which attaches to a group (or collective), rather than to the individual members of the group, even though it is only through the joint action (or inaction) of group members that a particular collective action or consequence results. The objections of the critics could then more plausibly be recast in the form that the collection of the marketers' campaigns was consuming or wasting public health or welfare understood in a twofold sense: first, as the lack of illness, violence, and crime, and second, as the presence of a sense of individual self that is based on the genuine gratification of real needs. When the individual marketers of a group (e.g., of brewers) engage in their own individual marketing campaigns they may not necessarily cause significant harms—or if they do create harm, the customers may have willingly accepted certain levels of individual risk of harm. However, their efforts may collectively result in significant harms not consciously assumed by anyone.

Similarly, though the individual marketing efforts may not be significant enough to expose the vulnerabilities of individuals composing their market segment, their marketing efforts may collectively create a climate within which the vulnerabilities of those targeted may play a role in the collective effect of those marketing campaigns. Thus, it is not the presence of this or that billboard from PowerMaster which may be objectionable so much as the large total number of billboards in the inner-city which advertise alcohol and to which PowerMaster contributed. For example, it has been reported that "in Baltimore, 76 per cent of the billboards located in low-income neighborhoods advertise alcohol and cigarettes; in middle and upper-income neighborhoods it is 20 per cent" (*The Workbook*, 1991: 18). This "saturation advertising" may have an effect different from the effect of any single advertisement. Similarly, it is not PowerMaster's presence on the market as such, which raises moral questions. Rather, it is that alcohol marketers particularly target a group which not only buys "... more than half the cognac sold in the United States and ... consume[s] more than one-third of all malt liquor ..." (*The Workbook*, 1991: 18), but also disproportionately suffers health problems associated with alcohol. The connection between the amount of alcohol consumed and the alcohol related health problems is hardly coincidental. Further, if the level of alcohol consumption is significantly related to conditions of poverty and racism, and the consequent vulnerabilities people living in these conditions may suffer, then targeting such individuals may also be an instance of attempting to take unfair advantage of them.[13]

Now to make this case, it must be allowed that individual persons are not the only ones capable of being responsible for the effects of their actions. A variety of arguments have been given, for example, that corporations can be morally responsible for their actions. These arguments need not be recited here since even if they were successful, as I think some of them are, the marketers who target

inner-city blacks do not themselves constitute a corporation. Hence, a different kind of argument is needed.

Can there be subjects of responsibility other than individuals and corporations? Virginia Held has argued that under certain conditions random collections of individuals can be held morally responsible. She has argued that when it would be obvious to the reasonable person what a random collection of individuals ought to do and when the expected outcome of such an action is clearly favorable, then that random collection can be held morally responsible (Held, 1970: 476).

However, again the marketers of malt liquor to inner city blacks do not seem to fit this argument since they are not simply a random collection of individuals. According to Held, a random collection of individuals "... is a set of persons distinguishable by some characteristics from the set of all persons, but lacking a decision method for taking action that is distinguishable from such decision methods, if there are any, as are possessed by all persons" (Held, 1970: 471). The examples she gives, "passengers on a train" and "pedestrians on a sidewalk," fit this definition but are also compatible with a stronger definition of a group of individuals than the one she offers. For example, her definition would include collections of individuals with no temporal, spatial or teleological connection. Clearly marketers of malt liquor to inner-city blacks constitute a group or collection of individuals in a stronger sense than Held's random collection of individuals.

Consequently, I shall speak of a group such as the marketers who target inner-city blacks as an associated group. Such groups are not corporations. Nor are they simply random collections of individuals (in Held's sense). They are groups in a weaker sense than corporations, but a stronger sense than a random collection of individuals. I shall argue that such groups may also be the subject of moral responsibility. This view is based upon the following characteristics of such groups.

First, an associated group is constituted by agents, whether they be corporate or personal, who share certain characteristics related to a common set of activities in which they engage. Thus, the marketers who target inner-city blacks share the characteristic that they (and no one else) target this particular market segment with malt liquor. They engage in competition with each other to sell their malt liquor according to the rules of the (relatively) free market. Though they themselves do not occupy some single spatial location, the focus of their activities, the ends they seek, and their temporal relatedness (i.e., marketing to the inner-city in the same time period) are clearly sufficient to constitute them as a group.

Second, though such associated groups do not have a formal decision-making structure which unites them, Stanley Bates has reminded us that "there are other group decision methods, [that] ... are not formal ..." (Bates, 1971: 345).[14] For example, the brewers presently at issue might engage in various forms of implicit bargaining. These informal and implicit group decision methods may involve unstructured discussions of topics of mutual interest, individual group member monitoring of the expectations and intuitions of other group members, and recognition of mutual understandings that may serve to coordinate the expectations of group members (cf. Schelling, 1963). Further, brewers in the United States have created The Beer Institute, which is their Washington-based trade group, one of whose main purposes is to protect "the market environment allowing for brewers to sell beer profitably, free from what the group views as unfair burdens imposed by government bodies."[15] The Beer Institute provides its members with a forum within which they may meet annually, engage in workshops, discuss issues of mutual concern, agree on which issues will be lobbied before Congress on their behalf and may voluntarily adopt an advertising code to guide their activities.[16] Such informal decision-making methods amongst these brewers and suppliers are means whereby group decisions can be made.

Third, members of associated groups can be said to have other morally relevant characteristics which foster a group "solidarity" and thereby also

unify them as a group capable of moral responsibility (cf. Feinberg, 1974: 234). These characteristics take three different forms. a) Members of the group share a community of interests. For example, they all wish to sell their products to inner-city blacks.[17] They all seek to operate with minimal restrictions from the government on their marketing activities within the inner-city. They all are attempting to develop popular malt liquors. They all strive to keep the costs of their operations as low as possible. b) Further, they are joined by bonds of sentiment linked with their valuing of independent action and successfully selling their products. Though they may try to out-compete each other, they may also respect their competitors when they perform well in the marketplace. c) Finally, they can be said to share a common lot in that actions by one brewer that bring public condemnation upon that brewer may also extend public attention and condemnation to the other brewers as well as happened in the PowerMaster case. Similarly, regulations imposed on one typically also affect the others. Thus, heavy regulation tends to reduce all their profits, whereas light regulation tends to have the opposite effect.

The unity or solidarity constituted by the preceding characteristics among the various marketers would be openly manifested, for example, if the government were to try to deny them all access to the inner-city market segment. In such a circumstance, they would openly resist, take the government to court, and protest with united voice against the injustice done to them, both individually and as a group. In this sense, there is (at the least) a latent sense of solidarity among such marketers (cf. May, 1987: 37). When they act, then each acts in solidarity with the others and each does those things which accord with the kinds of actions fellow group members are inclined to take. All this may occur without the need for votes being taken or explicit directions given among the various brewers (cf. May, 1987: 40).

Fourth, associated groups like inner-city marketers can investigate the harms or benefits that their products and marketing programs jointly do to those who are targeted. They can also study the overall effects of their own individual efforts. They could do so both as individual businesses and as a group. In the latter case, The Beer Institute might undertake such studies. Similarly, these marketers might jointly commission some other organization to study these effects. In short, they are capable both as individual businesses and as a group, of receiving notice as to the effects of their individual and collective actions. In short, communication amongst the group members is possible.

Finally, associated groups can modify their activities. They are not simply inevitably or necessarily trapped into acting certain ways. For example, the inner-city malt liquor marketers might voluntarily reduce the number of billboards they use within the inner-city. They might not advertise in certain settings or in certain forms of media. They might not use certain appeals, e.g., touting the high alcoholic content of their products. As such, they could take actions to prevent the harms or injustices of which they are accused. At present brewers subscribe to an advertising code of ethics which The Beer Institute makes available and has recently updated. The Beer Institute might even lobby the government on behalf of this group for certain limitations on marketing programs so as to eliminate moral objections raised against such marketing programs.

The preceding indicates that this group can act: it has set up The Beer Institute; it may react with unanimity against new regulations; it may defend the actions of its members; it may investigate the effects its group members have on those market segments which they have targeted. It does not act as a group in marketing particular malt liquors. The law prevents such collective actions. However, marketing malt liquor to particular groups is an action which this group may approve or disapprove.[18] The group lobbies Congress on behalf of its members' interests. The group has organized itself such that through development and support of The Beer Institute

its interests are protected. There is no reason, then, that such a group may not also be morally responsible for the overall consequences of its members' marketing.

Does the preceding argument suggest that the group of marketers would run afoul of concerns about restraint of trade? The above argument need not imply that inner-city marketers are always a group capable of moral action and responsibility—only that under certain circumstances it could be. Hence, the above argument does not suggest that this group constitutes anything like a cartel. In addition, the above argument does not suggest that marketers agree on pricing formulas, on reserving certain distributional areas for this or that marketer, or similar actions which would constitute classic forms of restraint of trade. Further, the preceding argument leaves open what mechanisms might be legally used whereby these moral responsibilities are discharged. It might be that individual marketers voluntarily agree to such actions as they presently do with their advertising code. On the other hand, they might collectively appeal to the government to approve certain general conditions such that the playing field within which they compete would be altered to alleviate moral objections to their marketing campaigns, but would remain relatively level in comparison with their situations prior to the imposition of such conditions.

If the preceding is correct, then given the assumption that basic items of public welfare (e.g., health, safety, decision-making abilities, etc.) ought not to be harmed, two important conclusions follow regarding the marketing of malt liquor to inner-city blacks.

First, malt liquor marketers have a collective responsibility to monitor the effects of their activities and to ensure that they jointly do not unnecessarily cause harm to those they target or trade on their vulnerabilities. Assuming that malt liquor does harm inner-city blacks and that the marketing programs through which malt liquor is sold to this market segment play some significant causal role in creating this harm, then they have an obligation to alter their marketing to inner-city blacks in such a way that the vulnerabilities of inner-city blacks are not exploited and that unnecessary harm does not come to them.

Second, where the collective consequences of individual marketing efforts create the harms claimed for alcohol among inner-city blacks, and marketers as a group do not discharge the preceding collective responsibility, then there is a need for some agency outside those individual marketers to oversee or regulate their actions. Obviously, one form this may take is that of an industry or professional oversight committee; another form might be that of government intervention.

Two objections might be noted. It might be objected that the preceding line of argument faces the difficulty of determining the extent of harm which each marketer of malt liquor causes to the market segment targeted. Since this will be hard to determine, marketers of malt liquor may seek to escape the responsibility attributed to them. This difficulty, however, is no different in kind from other instances in which the actions of individual persons or businesses jointly produce a common problem. If the heavy trucks of several businesses regularly ply the city's streets contributing to the creation of potholes and broken asphalt, it will be difficult to determine the causal responsibility of each business. In all such instances there are difficult empirical and conceptual issues involved in establishing that harm has occurred, the levels at which it has occurred and the attendant moral responsibility. However, this is not to deny that such determinations can be made. I assume that similar determinations can be made in the present case.

Further, though it may be difficult to determine the harm which the marketing of a particular product may cause, it is less difficult—though by no means unproblematic—to determine the harm caused by the collection of marketing programs aimed at a particular market segment. Thus, though particular marketers may seek to escape individual responsibility for their actions, it will be much harder for them to escape their collective responsibilities. Still, we may anticipate that, in

some cases, the results will be that an individual marketer has met his or her individual *and* collective responsibilities.

It might also be objected that this group cannot be responsible since it lacks control of its members. However, various forms of moral control are available to this group. They may try to persuade each other to change their course of action. And indeed, this occurred in the PowerMaster case: "Patrick Stokes, president of Anheuser-Busch Cos.' Anheuser-Busch Inc. unit and chairman of The Beer Institute, asked … Heileman's president, to reconsider the strategy for PowerMaster, which 'appears to be intentionally marketed to emphasize high alcohol content'" (Freedman, 1991b: B1). They might seek to expel a member from The Beer Institute and the benefits which such membership carries.[19] Conceivably, they could turn to the public media to expose unethical practices on the part of that member. They might even, as with other groups within a nation state, seek outside help from the government. More positively, they could praise and hold up as models of marketing responsibility the marketing programs of certain group members. Thus, this group can be said to be able to exercise moral influence and control over its members which is not dissimilar to that which is exercised by other similar groups and more generally within society as a whole.

V. COLLECTIVE RESPONSIBILITY AND SHARED RESPONSIBILITY

The nature of the collective responsibility discussed in the preceding section deserves further elaboration. Why, for example, should we not consider the responsibility attributed above to all marketers who target inner-city blacks as a form of shared (rather than collective) responsibility? By shared responsibility I understand that the responsibility for a certain event (or series of events) is shared or divided among a number of agents (personal or corporate). Shared or divided responsibility does not require that we are able to identify any group which could be said to be itself responsible for that (or those) event(s). As such, under shared responsibility each of those identified is, at least partially, responsible for the event(s). Shared responsibility, then, is a distributional concept. Each agent involved is assumed to have played some causal role in the occurrence of the event(s) in question. This does not mean that each agent had to have done exactly what the others did. One person might have knowingly and secretly loaded a truck with toxic chemicals, another might have driven the truck to an unauthorized and dangerous dump site, and a third pulled the lever to dump the chemicals. Each one did something different, yet they all played contributory causal roles in the immoral (and illegal) dumping of toxic chemicals. They share responsibility for this event and their responsibility exhausts the responsibility which may be attributed under these circumstances. Such shared responsibility differs from individual responsibility in that when a number of moral agents participate together in the production of some event (or series of events) it may not be possible to determine what the contribution of each agent was and hence to establish the nature or extent of their individual responsibility (cf. May, 1992: 39). Thus, if several corporations each make one of their marketing experts available to solve a problem confronting a regional council on tourism, it may not be possible to determine the exact contribution of each expert or each corporation to the resolution of this problem. Still, to the extent that each corporation (and each marketing expert) contributed and was a necessary part of the solution, they all share responsibility for the solution.[20]

With collective responsibility, on the other hand, we must be able to identify some collective or group which itself has responsibility for the event (or series of events). Collective responsibility may or may not be distributional. Thus, some members of a group might be individually responsible as well as collectively responsible for what happens. In other instances, they may not be individually responsible, but only the group of which they are members be collectively responsible. For example, the members of some group might agree, by a divided vote, to undertake some project. Later, those who voted for the project may have died or left the group, while the negative voters (and others who have replaced the former members) remain. Still, that group remains responsible for (the completion of) the project, even though its individual members do not themselves have individual responsibilities for that project.[21]

Now with regard to the group of marketers who target inner-city blacks, we have seen that we can refer to this as a group, which, though it does not have a formal decision-making structure, may still act. Its members have common interests; they communicate with each other regarding those interests; they share a solidarity which unites them in approving various things their fellow members do and defending those members when criticized. Further, within this group we may distinguish four situations concerning the marketing program of individual brewers: (1) It itself harms inner-city blacks; (2) It contributes to the harm of inner-city blacks; (3) It is indeterminate in its harm, or contributory harm, to inner-city blacks; and (4) It does not itself harm, or contribute to the harm of, inner-city blacks. In the first case, the marketer is individually responsible for such harm as is caused. In the second case, the marketer has a shared responsibility with other marketers of this group. However, in the last two cases, though we may not speak of the individual or shared responsibility of the marketer, we may still speak of the collective responsibility of the group of marketers of which the last two are a part. We may also bring those in the first two cases under the same collective responsibility. The reason (in each of these cases) is that the group or collective of which they are members—whether they are individually responsible, share responsibility, or are responsible in neither of these cases—can collectively act, and could reduce such harms or evils by taking a stance against marketing practices which produce or foster them. For example, if Heileman dramatically revised its marketing campaign to inner-city blacks, but Pabst and Anheuser-Busch did not, then there might be little change in the results for inner-city blacks. Hence, it is only if the members of this group act in concert, as a group, that the objections raised against the marketing of malt liquors such as PowerMaster be responded to. This collective responsibility of the group of marketers will mean that individual marketers incur other individual responsibilities to act in certain ways as members of that group, e.g., to bring the harm created to the attention of other group members, to work within the group to develop ways to reduce or eliminate marketing practices which foster such harm, and to act in concert with other group members to reduce harm to targeted groups. Accordingly, it seems reasonable to attribute a collective responsibility to the group of these marketers, and not simply a shared responsibility.

It is also correct to say that the moral responsibility of the group of inner-city marketers does not replace or negate the individual responsibility of the members of this group. Still, the collective responsibility of this group does not simply reduce to the individual responsibility of its members in that, as argued above, an individual member of this group might fulfill his/her individual moral responsibilities and still the group might not fulfill its collective responsibilities. Accordingly, marketers of alcohol to inner-city blacks may have individual, shared and collective responsibilities to which they must attend.

VI. IMPLICATIONS AND CONCLUSION

The implications of this social approach to the PowerMaster case are significant:

First, marketers cannot simply look at their own individual marketing campaigns to judge their moral level. Instead, they must also look at their campaign within the context of all the marketing campaigns which target the market segment at which they are aiming. This accords with Garrett Hardin's suggestion that "the morality of an act is a function of the state of the system at the time it is performed" (Hardin, 1968: 1245; emphasis omitted). It is possible that marketers could fulfill their

individual responsibilities but not their collective responsibilities.

Second, when the products targeted at particular market segments cause consumers to suffer disproportionately in comparison with other comparable market segments, marketers must determine the role which their products and marketing programs play in this situation. If they play a contributory role, they should (both individually and as a group) consider measures to reduce the harm produced. One means of doing this is to voluntarily restrict or modify their appeals to that market segment. In the present case, industry organizations such as The Beer Institute might play a leading role in identifying problems and recommending counter measures. Otherwise when harm occurs disproportionately to a market segment, or members of that segment are especially vulnerable, outside oversight and regulation may be appropriate.

Third, marketers have a joint or collective responsibility to the entire market segment they target, not simply for the effects of their own products and marketing campaigns, but more generally for the effects of the combined marketing which is being done to that segment. The protests against PowerMaster are best understood against the background of this collective responsibility.

Thus, when we think of responsibility in the market we must look beyond simply the responsibility of individual agents (be they personal or corporate). We must look to the responsibility of groups of persons as well as groups of corporations. Such responsibility is not personal or individual, but collective. Examination of the case of PowerMaster helps us to see this.

Accordingly, the preceding analysis helps to explain both why PowerMaster was attacked as it was and also why it seemed simply to be doing what other marketers had previously done. Further, it helps us to understand the circumstances under which the above objections against marketing malt liquor to inner-city blacks might be justified. However, much more analysis of this form of collective harm and the vulnerability which is said to characterize inner-city blacks needs to be undertaken.

Finally, it should be emphasized that this paper advocates recognition of a new subject of moral responsibility in the market. Heretofore, moral responsibility has been attributed to individuals and corporations. Random collections of individuals have little applicability in business ethics. However the concept of associated groups and their collective responsibility has not been previously explored. It adds a new dimension to talk about responsibility within current discussions in business ethics.[22]

NOTES

1   Though the case of PowerMaster is admittedly several years old, its importance for this paper lies in gaining a better understanding of the moral responsibilities of marketers, rather than in the case itself.

2   As such, I do not attempt to raise far broader moral questions concerning the moral legitimacy of advertising itself. Instead, I wish to examine the marketing of PowerMaster as much as possible within the current, albeit vague, moral limits of advertising.

3   Marc Lacey, "Marketing of Malt Liquor Fuels Debate," *LA Times*, December 15, 1992, A31. Lacey also noted that "Blacks, who make up 12% of the US population, represent 10% of beer drinkers but 28% of malt liquor consumers, according to a study by Shanken Communications Inc. of New York City" (ibid.). It should be noted that Heileman was only one of a number of malt liquor manufacturers who directed marketing campaigns at this market segment.

4   This paper does not consider this legal aspect of the case. However, critics said that the reference to power in "PowerMaster" referred to the alcoholic strength of the drink. Such references were prohibited by a law passed in 1935. It was on this basis that BATF required that Heileman drop the word "power" from the name "PowerMaster."

5   The phrase "moral illusion" is not intended to suggest that those targeted by PowerMaster would have affirmed, had they been asked, that they gained the power they lacked by purchasing this malt liquor. On the other hand, critics did contend that an illegitimate form of value displacement or substitution was encouraged by advertisements such as those of PowerMaster.

6   It might be noted that the name "Powermaster" has been used for other products. Kleer-Flo uses it for water-based cleaning stations and Runnerless Molding Technology uses it for a filtering system designed to reroute electrical and nonelectrical disturbances. Needless to say, neither of these companies has been the object of protests against the use of the name "Powermaster."

7   The Reverend Jesse W. Brown claims that "African-Americans are twice as likely to die from cirrhosis of the liver than whites, and the rate of cancer of the esophagus is ten times higher for African-American males than for white males" (Brown, 1992: 17). These figures differ from others reported in this paper. I can only assume that they are due to differing "populations" being surveyed and different times during which the surveys were conducted.

8   An additional aspect of the objections against PowerMaster which only came out indirectly was the implication that the firms doing the marketing were based outside the inner-cities and were (presumably) predominately white. Thus, the impression given was that of outside whites marketing a product which might further harm poor blacks within the inner-city.

9   "'This is an activist reaction' to the product, said Heileman President Thomas Rattigan. 'I'm not sure anyone has a feel of the public reaction'" (Teinowitz and Colford, 1991, 35).

10 Among the questions we need to ask are: Is everyone in the inner-city vulnerable? Are they all vulnerable in the same way(s)? Are those who drink malt liquor specially vulnerable in a way relevant for the present case? Is their vulnerability the only relevant one for this case?

11 It did this by placing the word "power" within its name and not simply the various advertisements for its product. It also pushed the bounds by raising the alcohol content to the highest (or one of the highest) level(s) of malt liquors.

12   Suppose that malt liquors had harmed inner-city blacks *proportionately*—their rates of cirrhosis of the liver and other diseases were at the same levels of other people in society, whether whites, Hispanics or Asians and whether upper class, middle class or lower class. The upshot would be that one part of the present complex web of criticisms would have to be modified. It might still be, however, that the level of harm was unacceptably high in comparison with those who did not drink. This modification, however, would not, in itself, affect the other two criticisms having to do with the artificial gratifications being offered by the advertisements and with the vulnerability of those targeted. In the end, it appears, the vulnerability criticism is the criticism basic to this dispute.

13   Stanley I. Benn also distinguishes between the effects of individual advertisements and "the cumulative influence of an environment filled with a variety of advertisements all with the same underlying message...." Stanley I. Benn, "Freedom and Persuasion," *The Australasian Journal of Philosophy*, Vol. 45 (1967), 274. Benn maintains that the former might be resistible, whereas the latter might not be.

14   Bates refers to the work of Thomas Schelling, *The Strategy of Conflict* (New York: Oxford University Press, 1963), in making this point.

15   "The Beer Institute," *Encyclopedia of Associations*, Carolyn A. Fischer and Carol A. Schwartz (eds.), Vol. 1 (New York: Gale Research Inc., 1995), 27.

16   In 1995, The Beer Institute claimed to have 280 members (ibid.).

17   I leave vague here any more specific statement of this common interest: e.g., to make more profit, to fulfill the needs of their customers, to enlarge their market share, etc., etc. On the importance of a common interest or outlook to define a(n) (unorganized) group see May, 1987: 33.

18   When PowerMaster was under attack, the President of The Beer Institute defended Heileman's marketing of PowerMaster: "The strange inference drawn from these charges is that this product is somehow being marketed unfairly. That's not true. Everyone sells his product to the people who prefer them.... People can make up

their own minds about what product they prefer" (Farhi, 1991: A4).

19   In fact, this has never happened. One reason is that The Beer Institute might be sued by the expelled member for attempting to restrain trade.

20   The example is inspired by Michael J. Zimmerman, "Sharing Responsibility," *American Philosophical Quarterly*, Vol. 22, No. 2 (April, 1985).

21   This example is influenced by one from Joel Feinberg, "Collective Responsibility," in *Doing & Deserving* (Princeton: Princeton University Press, 1974), 249.

22   I am indebted to the following individuals for their helpful comments: James Bennett, Kathy Bohstedt, John Hardwig, John McCall, Betsy Postow, Leonard J. Weber, Andy Wicks and an anonymous reviewer for *Business Ethics Quarterly*. Barry Danilowitz helped in the identification and collection of relevant materials concerning the PowerMaster case.

BIBLIOGRAPHY

Bates, Stanley (1971), "The Responsibility of 'Random Collections,'" *Ethics*, 81, 343–49.

Benn, Stanley I. (1967), "Freedom and Persuasion," *The Australasian Journal of Philosophy*, 45, 259–75.

Brown, Jesse W. (1992), "Marketing Exploitation," *Business and Society Review*, Issue 83 (Fall), 17.

Colford, Steven W. and Teinowitz, Ira (1991), "Malt Liquor 'Power' Failure," *Advertising Age*, July 1, 1, 29.

Farhi, Paul (1991), "Surgeon General Hits New Malt Liquor's Name, Ads," *Washington Post*, June 26, A1, A4.

Feinberg, Joel (1974), "Collective Responsibility," in *Doing & Deserving*. Princeton: Princeton University Press, 222–51.

Fortune (1991), "Selling Sin to Blacks," October 21, 100.

Freedman, Alix (1991a), "Potent, New Heileman Malt Is Brewing Fierce Industry and Social Criticism," *Wall Street Journal*, June 17, B1, B4.

——(1991b), "Heileman, Under Pressure, Scuttles PowerMaster Malt," *Wall Street Journal*, July 5, B1, B3.

Hardin, Garrett (1968), "The Tragedy of the Commons," *Science*, 162, 1243–48.

Held, Virginia (1970), "Can a Random Collection of Individuals Be Morally Responsible?" *The Journal of Philosophy*, 67, 471–81.

Horovitz, Bruce (1991), "Brewer Faces Boycott Over Marketing of Potent Malt Liquor," *LA Times*, June 25, D1, D6.

Lacey, Marc (1992), "Marketing of Malt Liquor Fuels Debate," *LA Times*, December 15, A32, A34.

May, Larry (1987), *The Morality of Groups*. Notre Dame: University of Notre Dame Press.

——(1992), *Sharing Responsibility*. Chicago: The University of Chicago Press.

Milloy, Courland (1991), "Race, Beer Don't Mix," *The Washington Post*, July 9, B3.

New York Times, The (1991), "The Threat of Power Master," July 1, A12.

Schelling, Thomas (1963), *The Strategy of Conflict*. New York: Oxford University Press.

Teinowitz, Ira and Colford, Steven W. (1991), "Targeting Woes in PowerMaster Wake," *Advertising Age*, July 8, 1991, 35.

"The Beer Institute," *Encyclopedia of Associations* (1995), Carolyn A. Fischer and Carol A. Schwartz (eds.), Vol. 1, New York: Gale Research Inc.

Workbook, The (1991), "Marketing Booze to Blacks," Spring, 16, 18–19.

Zimmerman, Michael J. (1985), "Sharing Responsibility," *American Philosophical* Quarterly, 22, 115–22.

—74—

CHILDREN AS CONSUMERS

An Ethical Evaluation of Children's Television Advertising

Lynn Sharp Paine

TELEVISION SPONSORS AND BROADCASTERS began to identify children as a special target audience for commercial messages in the mid-1960s. Within only a few years, children's television advertising emerged as a controversial issue. Concerned parents began to speak out and to urge the networks to adopt codes of ethics governing children's advertising. By 1970, the issue had attracted the attention of the Federal Trade Commission (FTC) and the Federal Communications Commission (FCC). The FCC received some 80,000 letters in support of a proposed rule "looking toward the elimination of sponsorship and commercial content in children's programming."[1] Public attention to the controversy over children's television advertising peaked between 1978 and 1980, when the FTC, under its authority to regulate unfair and deceptive advertising, held public hearings on its proposal to ban televised advertising directed to or seen by large numbers of young children. More recently parents have complained to the FCC about so-called program-length commercials, children's programs designed around licensed characters.

As this brief chronology indicates, children's television advertising has had a history of arousing people's ethical sensibilities. In this paper I want to propose some explanations for why this is so and to argue that there are good ethical reasons that advertisers should refrain from directing commercials to young children. However, because so much of the public debate over children's advertising has focused on the FTC's actions rather than explicitly on the ethical aspects of children's advertising, a few preliminary remarks are called for.

First, it is important to bear in mind that the ethical propriety of directing television advertising to young children is distinct from its legality. Even if advertisers have a constitutional right to advertise lawful products to young children in a nondeceptive way, it is not necessarily the right thing to do. Our system of government guarantees us rights that it may be unethical to exercise on certain occasions. Terminology may make it easy to lose sight of the distinction between "having a right" and the "right thing to do," but the distinction is critical to constitutional governance. In this paper I will take no position on the scope of advertisers' First Amendment rights to freedom of speech. I am primarily interested in the moral status of advertising to young children.

A second preliminary point worth noting is that evaluating the ethical status of a practice, such as advertising to young children, is a different exercise from evaluating the propriety of governmental regulation of that practice. Even if a practice is unethical, there may be legal, social, economic, political, or administrative reasons that the government cannot or should not forbid or even regulate the practice. The public policy issues faced by the FTC or any other branch of government involved in regulating children's advertising are distinct from the ethical issues facing advertisers. The fact that it may be impossible or unwise for the government to restrict children's advertising does not shield advertisers from ethical responsibility for the practice.

Finally, I want to point out that public opinion regarding children's advertising is a measure neither of its ethical value nor of the propriety of the FTC's actions. Two critics of the FTC declared that it had attempted to impose its conception of what is good on an unwilling American public.[2] There is reason to doubt the writers' assumption about the opinions of the American public regarding children's advertising,[3] but the more critical point is the implication of their argument: that the FTC's actions would have been appropriate had there been a social consensus opposing child-oriented advertising. Majority opinion, however, is neither the final arbiter of justified public policy, nor the standard for assaying the ethical value of a practice like children's advertising. As pointed out earlier, constitutional limits may override majority opinion in the public policy arena. And although publicly expressed opinion may signal ethical concerns (as I suggested in mentioning the letters opposing commercial sponsorship of children's television received by the FCC), social consensus is not the test of ethical quality. We cannot simply say that children's advertising is ethically all right because many people do not object to it or because people's objections to it are relatively weak. An ethical evaluation requires that we probe our ethical principles and test their relation to children's advertising. Publicly expressed opposition may signal that such probing is necessary, but it does not establish an ethical judgement one way or the other.

... For purposes of this discussion, I will set aside the legal and public policy questions involved in government restrictions on children's advertising. Instead, as promised, I will explore the ethical issues raised by the practice of directing television advertising to young children. In the process of this investigation, I will necessarily turn my attention to the role of consumers in a free market economy, to the capacities of children as they relate to consumer activities, and to the relationships between adults and children within the family.

By *young children* I mean children who lack the conceptual abilities required for making consumer decisions, certainly children under eight. Many researchers have investigated the age at which children can comprehend the persuasive intent of advertising.[4] Depending on the questions employed to test comprehension of persuasive intent, the critical age has been set as low as kindergarten age or as high as nine or ten.[5] Even if this research were conclusive, however, it would not identify the age at which children become capable of making consumer decisions. Comprehending persuasive intent is intellectually less complex than consumer decision-making. Even if children appreciate the selling intent behind advertising, they may lack other conceptual abilities necessary for responsible consumer decisions. Child psychologists could perhaps identify the age at which these additional abilities develop. For purposes of this discussion, however, the precise age is not crucial. When I use the term child or children I am referring to "young children"—those who lack the requisite abilities.

Children's advertising is advertising targeted or directed to young children. Through children's advertising, advertisers attempt to persuade young children to want and, consequently, to request the advertised products. Although current voluntary guidelines for children's advertising prohibit advertisers from explicitly instructing children to request that their parents buy the advertised product, child-oriented advertising is designed to induce favorable attitudes that result in such requests. Frequently child-oriented ads utilize themes and techniques that appeal particularly to children: animation, clowns, magic, fantasy effects, superheroes, and special musical themes. They may involve simply the presentation of products, such as cereals, sweets, and toys that appeal to young children with announcements directed to them. The critical point in understanding child-directed advertising, however, is not simply the product, the particular themes and techniques employed, or the composition of the audience viewing the ad, but whether the advertiser intends to sell to or through children. Advertisers routinely segment their markets and target their advertising. The question at issue is whether children are appropriate targets.

Advertising directed to young children is a sub-category of advertising seen by them, since children who watch television obviously see a great deal of advertising that is not directed toward them—ads for adult consumer products, investment services, insurance, and so on. Occasionally children's products are advertised by means of commercials directed to adults. The toy manufacturer Fisher-Price, for example, at one time advertised its children's toys and games primarily by means of ads directed to mothers. Some ads are designed to appeal to the whole family. Insofar as these ads address young children they fall within the scope of my attention.

My interest in television advertising directed to young children, as distinct from magazine or radio advertising directed to them, is dictated by the nature of the medium. Television ads portray vivid and lively images that engage young children as the printed words and pictures of magazines, or even the spoken words of radio, could never do. Because of their immediacy television ads can attract the attention of young children who have not yet learned to read. Research has shown that young children develop affection for and even personal relationships with heavily promoted product characters appearing on television. At the same time, because of their immaturity, these children are unable to assess the status of these characters as fictional or real, let alone assess whatever minimal product information they may disclose. Technical limitations make magazine advertising and radio advertising inherently less likely to attract young children's attention. Consequently, they are less susceptible to ethical criticisms of the sort generated by television advertising.

CHILDREN AS CONSUMERS

The introduction of the practice of targeting children for televised commercial messages challenged existing mores. At the obvious level, the practice

was novel. But at a deeper level, it called into question traditional assumptions about children and their proper role in the marketplace. The argument advanced on behalf of advertising to children by the Association of National Advertisers (ANA), the American Association of Advertising Agencies (AAAA), and the American Advertising Federation (AAF) reflects the rejection of some of these traditional assumptions:

> Perhaps the single most important benefit of advertising to children is that it provides information to the child himself, information which advertisers try to gear to the child's interests and on an appropriate level of understanding. This allows the child to learn what products are available, to know their differences, and to begin to make decisions about them based on his own personal wants and preferences.... Product diversity responds to these product preferences and ensures that it is the consumer himself who dictates the ultimate success or failure of a given product offering.[6]

The most significant aspect of this argument supporting children's advertising is its vision of children as autonomous consumers. Children are represented as a class of consumers possessing the relevant decision-making capacities and differing from adult consumers primarily in their product preferences. Children are interested in toys and candy, while adults are interested in laundry detergent and investment services. That children may require messages tailored to their level of understanding is acknowledged, but children's conceptual abilities are not regarded as having any other special significance. Advocates of children's advertising argue that it gives children "the same access to the marketplace which adults have, but keyed to their specific areas of interest."[7] When children are viewed in this way—as miniature adults with a distinctive set of product preferences—the problematic nature of advertising to them is not apparent. Indeed, it appears almost unfair not to provide children with televised information about products available to satisfy their special interests. Why should they be treated differently from any other class of consumers?

There are, however, significant differences between adults and young children that make it inappropriate to regard children as autonomous consumers. These differences, which go far beyond different product preferences, affect children's capacities to function as responsible consumers and suggest several arguments for regarding advertising to them as unethical. For purposes of this discussion, the most critical differences reflect children's understanding of self, time, and money.

Child-development literature generally acknowledges that the emergence of a sense of one's self as an independent human being is a central experience of childhood and adolescence. This vague notion, "having a sense of one's self as an independent human being" encompasses a broad range of capacities—from recognition of one's physical self as distinct from one's mother to acceptance of responsibility for one's actions and choices. Nor do children acquire these capacities gradually in the course of maturation. While this mastery manifests itself as self-confidence and self-control in an ever-widening range of activities and relationships, it depends more fundamentally upon the emergence of an ability to see oneself as oneself. The reflexive nature of consciousness—the peculiar ability to monitor, study, assess, and reflect upon oneself and even upon one's reflections—underlies the ability to make rational choices. It permits people to reflect upon their desires, to evaluate them, and to have desires about what they shall desire. It permits them to see themselves as one among others and as engaging in relationships with others. Young children lack—or have only in nascent form—this ability to take a higher-order perspective on themselves and to see themselves as having desires or preferences they may wish to cultivate, suppress, or modify. They also lack the self-control that would make it possible to act on these higher-order desires if they had them.

Closely related to the sense of self, if not implicit in self-reflection, is the sense of time. Children's understanding of time—both as it relates to their own existence and to the events around them—is another area where their perspectives are special. Preschoolers are intrigued with "time" questions: "When is an hour up?" "Will you be alive when I grow up?" "When did the world begin and when will it end?" "Will I be alive for all the time after I die?" Young children's efforts to understand time are accompanied by a limited ability to project themselves into the future and to imagine themselves having different preferences in the future. It is generally true that children have extremely short time horizons. But children are also struggling with time in a more fundamental sense: they are testing conceptions of time as well as learning to gauge its passage by conventional markers. Young children's developing sense of time goes hand in hand with their developing sense of self. Their capacity for self-reflection, for evaluating their desires, and for making rational choices is intimately related to their understanding of their own continuity in time.

Young children are in many ways philosophers: they are exploring and questioning the very fundamentals of existence. Since they have not accepted many of the conventions and assumptions that guide ordinary commercial life, they frequently pose rather profound questions and make insightful observations. But although young children are very good at speculation, they are remarkably unskilled in the sorts of calculations required for making consumer judgements. In my experience, many young children are stymied by the fundamentals of arithmetic and do not understand ordinal relations among even relatively small amounts—let alone the more esoteric notions of selling in exchange for money. Research seems to support the observation that selling is a difficult concept for children. One study found that only 48 per cent of six-and-a-half- to seven-and-a-half-year-olds could develop an understanding of the exocentric (as distinct from egocentric) verb *to sell*.[8] A five-year-old may know from experience in making requests that a $5.00 trinket is too expensive, but when she concludes that $5.00 is also too much to pay for a piano, it is obvious that she knows neither the exchange value of $5.00, the worth of a piano, nor the meaning of *too expensive*.

What is the significance of the differences between adults and young children I have chosen to highlight—their differing conceptions of self, time, and money? In the argument for advertising quoted earlier, it was stated that advertising to children enables them "to learn what products are available, to know their differences, and to begin to make decisions about them based on [their] own personal wants and preferences." Ignore, for the moment, the fact that existing children's advertising, which concentrates so heavily on sugared foods and toys, does little either to let children know the range of products available or differences among them and assume that children's advertising could be more informative. Apart from this fact, the critical difficulty with the argument is that because of children's, shall we say, "naive" or "unconventional" conceptions of self, time, and money, they know very little about their own personal wants and preferences—how they are related or how quickly they will change or about how their economic resources might be mobilized to satisfy those wants. They experience wants and preferences but do not seem to engage in critical reflection, which would lead them to assess, modify, or perhaps even curtail their felt desires for the sake of other more important or enduring desires they may have or may expect to have in the future. Young children also lack the conceptual wherewithal to engage in research or deliberative processes that would assist them in knowing which of the available consumer goods would most thoroughly satisfy their preferences, given their economic resources. The fact that children want so many of the products they see advertised is another indication that they do not evaluate advertised products on the basis of their preferences and economic resources.

There is thus a serious question whether advertising really has or can have much at all to do with children's beginning "to make decisions about [products] based on [their] own personal wants and preferences" until they develop the conceptual maturity to understand their own wants and preferences and to assess the value of products available to satisfy them. If children's conceptions of self, time, and money are not suited to making consumer decisions, one must have reservations about ignoring this fact and treating them as if they were capable of making reasonable consumer judgements anyway....

CHILDREN'S ADVERTISING AND BASIC ETHICAL PRINCIPLES

My evaluation of children's advertising has proceeded from the principle of consumer sovereignty, a principle of rather narrow application. Unlike more general ethical principles, like the principle of veracity, the principle of consumer sovereignty applies in the specialized area of business. Addressing the issue of children's advertising from the perspective of special business norms rather than more general ethical principles avoids the problem of deciding whether the specialized or more general principles should have priority in the moral reasoning of business people. Nevertheless, children's advertising could also be evaluated from the standpoint of the more general ethical principles requiring veracity and fairness and prohibiting harmful conduct.

VERACITY

The principle of veracity, understood as devotion to truth, is much broader than a principle prohibiting deception. Deception, the primary basis of the FTC's complaint against children's advertising, is only one way of infringing the principle of veracity. Both critics and defenders of children's advertising agree that advertisers should not intentionally deceive children and that they should engage in research to determine whether children are misled by their ads. The central issue regarding veracity and children's advertising, however, does not relate to deception so much as to the strength of advertisers' devotion to truth. Advertisers generally do not make false statements intended to mislead children. Nevertheless, the particular nature of children's conceptual worlds makes it exceedingly likely that child-oriented advertising will generate false beliefs or highly improbable product expectations.

Research shows that young children have difficulty differentiating fantasy and reality[9] and frequently place indiscriminate trust in commercial characters who present products to them.[10] They also develop false beliefs about the selling characters in ads[11] and in some cases have unreasonably optimistic beliefs about the satisfactions advertised products will bring them.[12]

This research indicates that concern about the misleading nature of children's advertising is legitimate. Any parent knows—even one who has not examined the research—that young children are easily persuaded of the existence of fantasy characters. They develop (what seem to their parents) irrational fears and hopes from stories they hear and experiences they misinterpret. The stories and fantasies children see enacted in television commercials receive the same generous and idiosyncratic treatment as other information. Children's interpretations of advertising claims are as resistant to parental correction as their other fantasies are. One can only speculate on the nature and validity of the beliefs children adopt as a result of watching, for example, a cartoon depicting a pirate captain's magical discovery of breakfast cereal. Certainly, many ads are designed to create expectations that fun, friendship, and popularity will accompany possession of the advertised product. The likelihood that such expectations will be fulfilled is something young children cannot assess.

To the extent that children develop false beliefs and unreasonable expectations as a result of viewing commercials, moral reservations about children's advertising are justified. To the extent advertisers know that children develop false beliefs and unreasonable expectations, advertisers' devotion to truth and to responsible consumerism are suspect.

FAIRNESS AND RESPECT FOR CHILDREN

The fact that children's advertising benefits advertisers while at the same time nourishing false beliefs, unreasonable expectations, and irresponsible consumer desires among children calls into play principles of fairness and respect. Critics have said that child-oriented advertising takes advantage of children's limited capacities and their suggestibility for the benefit of the advertisers. As expressed by Michael Pertschuk, former chairman of the FTC, advertisers "seize on the child's trust and exploit it as weakness for their gain."[13] To employ as the unwitting means to the parent's pocketbook children who do not understand commercial exchange, who are unable to evaluate their own consumer preferences, and who consequently cannot make consumer decisions based on those preferences does indeed reflect a lack of respect for children. Such a practice fails to respect children's limitations as consumers, and instead capitalizes on them. In the language of Kant, advertisers are not treating children as "ends in themselves": they are treating children solely as instruments for their own gain.

In response to the charge of unfairness, supporters of children's advertising sometimes point out that the children are protected because their parents exercise control over the purse strings. This response demonstrates failure to appreciate the basis of the unfairness charge. It is not potential economic harm that concerns critics: it is the attitude toward children reflected in the use of children's advertising that is central. As explained earlier, the attitude is inappropriate or unfitting.

Another frequent response to the charge of unfairness is that children actually do understand advertising. A great deal of research has focused on whether children distinguish programs from commercials, whether they remember product identities, whether they distinguish program characters from commercial characters, and whether they recognize the persuasive intent of commercials. But even showing that children "understand" advertising in all these ways would not demonstrate that children have the consumer capacities that would make it fair to advertise to them. The critical questions are not whether children can distinguish commercial characters from program characters, or even whether they recognize persuasive intent, but whether they have the concepts of self, time, and money that would make it possible for them to make considered consumer decisions about the products they see advertised. Indeed, if children recognize that commercials are trying to sell things but lack the concepts to assess and deliberate about the products advertised, the charge that advertisers are "using" children or attempting to use them to sell their wares is strengthened. Intuitively, it seems that if children were sophisticated enough to realize that the goods advertised on television are for sale, they would be more likely than their younger counterparts to request the products.

HARM TO CHILDREN

Another principle to which appeal has been made by critics of television advertising is the principle against causing harm. The harmful effects of children's advertising are thought to include the parent-child conflict generated by parental refusals to buy requested products, the unhappiness and anger suffered by children whose parents deny their product requests, the unhappiness children suffer when advertising-induced expectations of product performance are disappointed, and unhappiness experienced by children exposed to commercials portraying life-styles more affluent than their own.

Replies to the charge that children's advertising is harmful to children has pinpointed weaknesses in the claim. One supporter of children's advertising says that the "harm" to children whose parents refuse their requests has not been adequately documented.[14] Another, claiming that

some experts believe conflicts over purchases are instructive in educating children to make choices denies that parent-child conflict is harmful.[15] As these replies suggest, demonstrating that children's advertising is harmful to children, as distinct from being misleading or unfair to them, involves much more than showing that it has the effects enumerated. Agreement about the application of the principle against causing harm depends on conceptual as well as factual agreement. A conception of harm must first be elaborated, and it must be shown to include these or other effects of advertising. It is not obvious, for example, that unhappiness resulting from exposure to more different life-styles is in the long run harmful.

Research indicates that children's advertising does contribute to the outcomes noted.[16] Certainly, child-oriented television advertising is not the sole cause of these effects, but it does appear to increase their frequency and even perhaps their intensity.[17] I believe that a conception of harm including some of these effects could be developed, but I will not attempt to do so here. I mention this argument rather to illustrate another general ethical principle on which an argument against children's advertising might be based....

CONCLUSION

How might advertisers implement their responsibilities to promote consumer satisfaction and consumer responsibility and satisfy the principles of veracity, fairness, and nonmaleficence? There are degrees of compliance with these principles: some marketing strategies will do more than others to enhance consumer satisfaction, for example. One way compliance can be improved is by eliminating child-oriented television advertising for children's products and substituting advertising geared to mature consumers. Rather than employing the techniques found in advertising messages targeted to children under eleven,[18] advertisers could include product information that would interest adult viewers and devise ways to let child viewers know that consumer decisions require responsible decision-making skills. If much of the information presented is incomprehensible to the five-year-olds in the audience, so much the better. When they reach the age at which they begin to understand consumer decision-making, they will perhaps have greater respect for the actual complexity of their responsibilities as consumers.

The problems of child-oriented advertising can best be dealt with if advertisers themselves recognize the inappropriateness of targeting children for commercial messages. I have tried to show why, within the context of a free market economy, the responsibilities of advertisers to promote consumer satisfaction and not to discourage responsible consumer decisions should lead advertisers away from child-oriented advertising. The problem of what types of ads are appropriate given these constraints provides a challenging design problem for the many creative people in the advertising industry. With appropriate inspiration and incentives, I do not doubt that they can meet the challenge.

Whether appropriate inspiration and incentives will be forthcoming is more doubtful. Children's advertising seems well entrenched and is backed by powerful economic forces, and it is clear that some advertisers do not recognize, or are unwilling to acknowledge, the ethical problems of child-focused advertising. The trend toward programming designed around selling characters is especially discouraging.

Even advertisers who recognize that eliminating child-oriented advertising will promote consumer satisfaction and consumer responsibility may be reluctant to reorient their advertising campaigns because of the costs and risks of doing so. Theoretically, only advertisers whose products would not withstand the scrutiny of adult consumers should lose sales from such a reorientation. It is clear that in the short run a general retreat from children's advertising would result in some lost revenues for makers, advertisers, and retail sellers of products that do not sell as well when advertised to adults. It is also possible that television networks, stations, and entrenched producers of children's shows would lose revenues and that children's programming might be jeopardized by the lack of advertisers' interest in commercial time during children's programs.

On the other hand, a shift away from children's advertising to adult advertising could result in even more pressure on existing adult commercial time slots, driving up their prices to a level adequate to subsidize children's programming without loss to the networks. And there are alternative means of financing children's television that could be explored. The extent to which lost revenues and diminished profits would result from recognizing the ethical ideals I have described is largely a question of the ability of all the beneficiaries of children's television advertising to respond creatively. The longer-term effect of relinquishing child-focused advertising would be to move manufacturers, advertisers, and retailers in the direction of products that would not depend for their success on the suggestibility and immaturity of children. In the long run, the result would be greater market efficiency.

NOTES

1   Richard Adler, "Children's Television Advertising: History of the Issue," in *Children and the Faces of Television*, ed. Edward L. Palmer and Aimee Dorr (New York: Academic Press, 1980), 243.

2   Susan Bartlett Foote and Robert H. Mnookin, "The 'Kid Vid' Crusade," *Public Interest* 61 (Fall 1980): 91.

3   One survey of adults found the following attitudes to children's commercials: strongly negative (23%); negative (50%); neutral (23%); positive (4%). These negative attitudes are most pronounced among parents of kindergarten-age children. The survey is cited in Thomas S. Robertson, "Television Advertising and Parent-Child Relations," in *The Effects of Television Advertising on Children*, ed. Richard P. Adler, Gerald S. Lesser, Laurene Krasay Meringoff, et al. (Lexington, MA: Lexington Books, 1980), 197; hereafter cited as Adler et al.

4   E.g., M. Carole Macklin, "Do Children Understand TV Ads?" *Journal of Advertising Research* 23

(February-March 1983): 63–70; Thomas Robertson and John Rossiter, "Children and Commercial Persuasion: An Attribution Theory Analysis," *Journal of Consumer Research* 1 (June 1974): 13–20. See also summaries of research in David Pillemer and Scott Ward, "Investigating the Effects of Television Advertising on Children: An Evaluation of the Empirical Studies," Draft read to American Psychological Assn., Div. 23, San Francisco, California, August 1977; John R. Rossiter, "The Effects of Volume and Repetition of Television Commercials," in Adler et al., 160–62; Ellen Wartella, "Individual Differences in Children's Responses to Television Advertising," in Palmer and Dorr, 312–14.

5   Wartella, 313.

6   Submission before the FTC, 1978, quoted in Emilie Griffin, "The Future is Inevitable: But Can It Be Shaped in the Interest of Children?" in Palmer and Dorr, 347.

7   Griffin, 344.

8   "FTC Final Staff Report and Recommendation," 27–28

9   See T.G. Bever, M.L. Smith, B. Bengen, and T.G. Johnson, "Young Viewers' Troubling Response to TV Ads," *Harvard Business Review*, November–December 1975, 109–20.

10   "FTC Final Staff Report and Recommendation" 21–22, n. 51, describes the work of Atkin supporting the conclusion that children trust selling characters. (See Charles K. Atkin, "Effects of Television Advertising on Children," in Palmer and Dorr.)

Atkin found in a group of three- to seven-year-olds that 70% of the three-year-olds and 60% of the seven-year-olds trusted the characters about as much as they trusted their mothers.

11   "FTC Final Staff Report and Recommendation," at 21–22, no. 51, describes the work of White, who found that many children in a group of four- to seven-year-olds she studied believe that the selling figures eat the advertised products and want the children to do likewise and that the selling figures want the children to eat things that are good for them.

12   Atkin, 300.

13   Quoted in Foote and Mnookin, 92.

14   Foote and Mnookin, 95.

15   *Comments of M & M/Mars*, Children's Television Advertising Trade Regulation Rulemaking Proceeding, Federal Trade Commission (November 1978), 64.

16   Atkin, 298–301. See also Scott Ward and Daniel B. Wackman, "Children's Purchase Influence Attempts and Parental Yielding," *Journal of Marketing Research*, August 1972, 318.

17   For example, one study found that heavy viewers of Saturday morning television got into more arguments with their parents over toy and cereal denials than did light viewers; Atkin 298–301.

18   The majority of advertising directed to children is targeted to children two-to-eleven or six-to-eleven years of age; "FTC Final Staff Report and Recommendation," 46.

—75—

JESUS IS A BRAND OF JEANS

Jean Kilbourne

A RECENT AD FOR THULE CAR-RACK SYSTEMS features a child in the backseat of a car, seatbelt on. Next to the child, assorted sporting gear is carefully strapped into a child's car seat. The headline says: 'We Know What Matters to You.' In case one misses the point, further copy adds: 'Your gear is a priority.'

Another ad features an attractive young couple in bed. The man is on top of the woman, presumably making love to her. However, her face is completely covered by a magazine, open to a double-page photo of a car. The man is gazing passionately at the car. The copy reads, 'The ultimate attraction.'

These ads are meant to be funny. Taken individually, I suppose they might seem amusing or, at worst, tasteless. As someone who has studied ads for a long time, however, I see them as part of a pattern: just two of many ads that state or imply that products are more important than people. Ads have long promised us a better relationship via a product: buy this and you will be loved. But more recently they have gone beyond that proposition to promise us a relationship with the product itself: buy this and it will love you. The product is not so much the means to an end, as the end itself.

After all, it is easier to love a product than a person. Relationships with human beings are messy, unpredictable, sometimes dangerous. 'When was the last time you felt this comfortable in a relationship?' asks an ad for shoes. Our shoes never ask us to wash the dishes or tell us we're getting fat. Even more important, products don't betray us. 'You can love it without getting your heart broken,' proclaims a car ad. One certainly can't say that about loving a human being, as love without vulnerability is impossible.

We are surrounded by hundreds, thousands of messages every day that link our deepest emotions to products, that objectify people and trivialize our most heartfelt moments and relationships. Every emotion is used to sell us something. Our wish to protect our children is leveraged to make us buy an expensive car. A long marriage simply provides the occasion for a diamond necklace. A painful reunion between a father and his estranged daughter is dramatized to sell us a phone system. Everything in the world—nature, animals, people—is just so much stuff to be consumed or to be used to sell us something.

The problem with advertising isn't that it creates artificial needs, but that it exploits our very real and human desires. Advertising promotes a bankrupt concept of relationships. Most of us yearn for committed relationships that will last. We are not stupid: we know that buying a certain brand of cereal won't bring us one inch closer to that goal. But we are surrounded by advertising that yokes our needs with products and promises us that things will deliver what in fact they never can. In the world of advertising, lovers are things and things are lovers.

It may be that there is no other way to depict relationships when the ultimate goal is to sell products. But this apparently bottomless consumerism not only depletes the world's resources, it also depletes our inner resources. It leads inevitably to narcissism and solipsism. It becomes difficult to imagine a way of relating that isn't objectifying and exploitative.

Most people feel that advertising is not something to take seriously. Other aspects of the media are serious—the violent films, the trashy talk shows, the bowdlerization of the news. But not advertising! Although much more attention has been paid to the cultural impact of advertising in recent years than ever before, just about everyone still feels personally exempt from its influence. What I hear more than anything else at my lectures is: 'I don't pay attention to ads ... I just tune them out ... they have no effect on me.' I hear this most from people wearing clothes emblazoned with logos. In truth, we are all influenced. There is no way to tune out this much information, especially when it is designed to break through the 'tuning out' process. As advertising critic Sut Jhally put it: 'To not be influenced by advertising would be to live outside of culture. No human being lives outside of culture.'

Much of advertising's power comes from this belief that it does not affect us. As Joseph Goebbels said: 'This is the secret of propaganda: those who are to be persuaded by it should be completely immersed in the ideas of the propaganda, without ever noticing that they are being immersed in it.' Because we think advertising is trivial, we are less on guard, less critical, than we might otherwise be. While we're laughing, sometimes sneering, the commercial does its work.

Taken individually, ads are silly, sometimes funny, certainly nothing to worry about. But cumulatively they create a climate of cynicism that is poisonous to relationships. Ad after ad portrays our real lives as dull and ordinary, commitment to human beings as something to be avoided. Because of the pervasiveness of this kind of message, we learn from childhood that it is far safer to make a commitment to a product than to a person, far easier to be loyal to a brand. Many end up feeling romantic about material objects yet deeply cynical about other human beings.

UNNATURAL PASSIONS

We know by now that advertising often turns people into objects. Women's bodies—and men's bodies too these days—are dismembered, packaged and used to sell everything from chainsaws to chewing gum, champagne to shampoo. Self-image is deeply affected. The self-esteem of girls plummets as they reach adolescence partly because they cannot possibly escape the message that their bodies are objects, and imperfect objects at that. Boys learn that masculinity requires a kind of ruthlessness, even brutality.

Advertising encourages us not only to objectify each other but to feel passion for products rather than our partners. This is especially dangerous when the products are potentially addictive, because addicts do feel they are in a relationship with their substances. I once heard an alcoholic joke that Jack Daniels was her most constant lover. When I was a smoker, I felt that my cigarettes were my friends. Advertising reinforces these beliefs, so we are twice seduced—by the ads and by the substances themselves.

The addict is the ideal consumer. Ten per cent of drinkers consume over sixty per cent of all the alcohol sold. Most of them are alcoholics or people in desperate trouble—but they are also the alcohol industry's very best customers. Advertisers spend enormous amounts of money on psychological research and understand addiction well. They use this knowledge to target children (because if you hook them early they are yours for life), to encourage all people to consume more, in spite of often dangerous consequences for all of us, and to create a climate of denial in which all kinds of addictions flourish. This they do with full intent, as we see so clearly in the 'secret documents' of the tobacco industry that have been made public in recent years.

The consumer culture encourages us not only to buy more but to seek our identity and fulfillment through what we buy, to express our individuality through our 'choices' of products. Advertising corrupts relationships and then offers us products, both as solace and as substitutes for the intimate human connection we all long for and need.

In the world of advertising, lovers grow cold, spouses grow old, children grow up and away—but possessions stay with us and never change. Seeking the outcomes of a healthy relationship through products cannot work. Sometimes it leads us into addiction. But at best the possessions can never deliver the promised goods. They can't make us happy or loved or less alone or safe. If we believe they can, we are doomed to disappointment. No matter how much we love them, they will never love us back.

Some argue that advertising simply reflects societal values rather than affecting them. Far from being a passive mirror of society, however, advertising is a pervasive medium of influence and persuasion. Its influence is cumulative, often subtle and primarily unconscious. A former editor-in-chief of Advertising Age, the leading advertising publication in North America, once claimed: 'Only eight per cent of an ad's message is received by the conscious mind. The rest is worked and re-worked deep within, in the recesses of the brain.'

Advertising performs much the same function in industrial society as myth did in ancient societies. It is both a creator and perpetuator of the dominant values of the culture, the social norms by which most people govern their behaviour. At the very least, advertising helps to create a climate in which certain values flourish and others are not reflected at all.

Advertising is not only our physical environment, it is increasingly our spiritual environment as well. By definition, however, it is only interested in materialistic values. When spiritual values show up in ads, it is only in order to sell us something. Eternity is a perfume by Calvin Klein. Infiniti is an automobile, and Hydra Zen a moisturizer. Jesus is a brand of jeans.

Sometimes the allusion is more subtle, as in the countless alcohol ads featuring the bottle surrounded by a halo of light. Indeed products such as jewelry shining in a store window are often displayed as if they were sacred objects. Advertising co-opts our sacred symbols in order to evoke an immediate emotional response. Media critic Neil Postman referred to this as 'cultural rape.'

It is commonplace to observe that consumerism has become the religion of our time (with advertising its holy text), but the criticism usually stops short of what is at the heart of the comparison. Both advertising and religion share a belief in transformation, but most religions believe that this requires sacrifice. In the world of advertising, enlightenment is achieved instantly by purchasing material goods. An ad for a watch says, 'It's not your handbag. It's not your neighbourhood. It's not your boyfriend. It's your watch that tells most about who you are.' Of course, this cheapens authentic spirituality and transcendence. This junk food for the soul leaves us hungry, empty, malnourished.

SUBSTITUTE STORIES

Human beings used to be influenced primarily by the stories of our particular tribe or community, not by stories that are mass-produced and market-driven. As George Gerbner, one of the world's most respected researchers on the influence of the media, said: 'For the first time in human history, most of the stories about people, life and values are told not by parents, schools, churches, or others in the community who have something to tell, but by a group of distant conglomerates that have something to sell.'

Although it is virtually impossible to measure the influence of advertising on a culture, we can learn something by looking at cultures only recently exposed to it. In 1980 the Gwich'in tribe of Alaska got television, and therefore massive advertising, for the first time. Satellite dishes, video games and VCRs were not far behind. Before this, the Gwich'in lived much the way their ancestors had for generations. Within 10 years, the young members of the tribe were so drawn by television they no longer had time to learn ancient hunting methods, their parents' language or their oral history. Legends told around campfires could not compete with Beverly Hills 90210. Beaded moccasins gave way to Nike sneakers, and 'tundra tea' to Folger's instant coffee.

As multinational chains replace local character, we end up in a world in which everyone is Gapped and Starbucked. Shopping malls kill vibrant downtown centres locally and create a universe of uniformity internationally. We end up in a world ruled by, in John Maynard Keynes's phrase, the values of the casino. On this deeper level, rampant commercialism undermines our physical and psychological health, our environment and our civic life, and creates a toxic society.

Advertising creates a world view that is based upon cynicism, dissatisfaction and craving. Advertisers aren't evil. They are just doing their job, which is to sell a product; but the consequences, usually unintended, are often destructive. In the history of the world there has never been a propaganda effort to match that of advertising in the past 50 years. More thought, more effort, more money goes into advertising than has gone into any other campaign to change social consciousness. The story that advertising tells is that the way to be happy, to find satisfaction—and the path to political freedom, as well—is through the consumption of material objects. And the major motivating force for social change throughout the world today is this belief that happiness comes from the market.

—76—

NESTLÉ AND ADVERTISING

An Ethical Analysis

Chris Ragg

BACKGROUND

SINCE THE 1970S, THE NESTLÉ CORPORATION HAS been the subject of an international boycott resulting from their methods of advertising. Nestlé, which owns Carnation, boasts that it is the world's largest food and beverage company. The set of products that have been the source of public outcry are newer versions of a product that Nestlé has been making since its inception in 1866: baby formula. Boycotters argue that the advertising campaigns promoting the formula in third world countries have been unethical, and have helped cause the death of millions of infants.

According to UNICEF and the World Health Organization, approximately 1.5 million infants die each year from bottle-feeding, many from what has been called "baby bottle disease." This disease is an effect of the combination of the diarrhea, dehydration, and malnutrition that result from unsafe bottle feeding. A typical case of baby-bottle disease might arise as follows: a poor set of parents purchase baby formula for their infant. Since the local water supply is contaminated and unsafe, however, the baby's ingestion of the diluted formula can soon lead to diarrhea, a common indicator of gastrointestinal distress and a cause of dehydration. Furthermore, due to the cost of the baby formula, the parents will often over-dilute it or spend less on additional food supplies, which can lead to malnutrition.

When growing up in an area with contaminated water, a bottle-fed child is 25 times more likely to die from diarrhea than a breastfed child. Even in areas with cleaner water, such as the United Kingdom, a bottle-fed child is ten times more likely to suffer the same fate. In most cases, in fact, doctors highly recommend that a mother breastfeed her child. Breastfed babies need no other food or drink for about the first six months of life, and have reduced risk of diabetes, pneumonia, ear infections, and some cancers. Further studies have shown that women who breastfeed may have a lower risk of breast and ovarian cancers. This does not imply, though, that bottle-feeding is never the best option. There are some cases where baby formula can be beneficial and, with the right information, mothers can decide whether or not theirs is such a case.

This requisite information, however, was not made available to many women in these poorer nations. In the 1960s and 1970s, Nestlé had extensive advertisement campaigns for its baby formula worldwide. Pamphlets were distributed highlighting the potential benefits of baby formula while ignoring the drawbacks. Free samples were also dispersed among the public. Nestlé's profit-driven actions began to outrage the public. Although they were not illegal, many of the boycotters claimed that Nestlé's actions were immoral and socially irresponsible. While corporations can justifiably try to turn the largest profit available, the boycotters claim that an ethical corporation must avoid deliberate harm in its pursuit of success.

ANALYSIS

Advertisements are all around us; it would be difficult to go even one day without coming into contact with at least one. In our capitalist society, a good marketing strategy can be the difference between a successful and failed business venture. In light of this, it is not all that surprising that in some countries Nestlé reportedly spends more money promoting their product than the government spends on health education. The information available to young mothers, then, can be biased. In the United States there are laws against false advertising, but these laws only protect consumers from lies and unsubstantiated claims. But these are not the only ways that companies can fool the public. Many companies choose to tell the truth, but not quite the whole truth. As was the case with Nestlé's pamphlets thirty-five years ago, an advertisement can explain all the potential benefits of the product while neglecting to mention its potential drawbacks.

In 1981 the policy-setting body of the World Health Organization adopted the International Code of Marketing of Breast-milk Substitutes. Those who agreed to the code swore that they would not provide free samples to hospitals or mothers, promote their product for use with children under six months of age, or promote their product to health workers. Nestlé has publicly agreed to abide by these standards. Nevertheless, it is claimed by IBFAN (the International Baby Foods Action Network) that Nestlé has repeatedly violated the code. In particular, there is evidence that Nestlé has aspired to win the approval of health care and hospital workers by giving them gifts, so that they will personally recommend Nestlé products to young mothers. This is often cheaper and more effective than trying to influence mothers one-by-one. Another strategy used by Nestlé has been to provide free samples to hospitals and maternity wards. A mother will then begin using the formula at the hospital, and by the time she leaves it will have interfered with her lactation process. Once home, the formula is no longer free and the mother is left without much choice but to purchase the product.

It does seem, however, that too many restrictions on advertising may lead us down a slippery slope. Nestlé's chocolate products, for instance, can help cause obesity, which leads to a host of health issues. It might be argued that, if all these restrictions apply to the advertisement of baby formula, then similar restrictions should apply to other unhealthy products. But then where will this proliferation of warnings and restrictions end? Surely manufacturers cannot be held accountable for all misuses of their product.

DISCUSSION QUESTIONS

1. Must a company be forthright with all of the potentially negative side effects of its products? If not all, which ones?
2. Although it is not clear that Nestlé has done anything illegal, have they done something unethical?
3. Are a corporation's only responsibilities to obey the law and attempt to make as much of a profit as possible? Do the basic tenets of capitalism require anything more?
4. Is there a difference in the cases of the baby formula and the chocolate? If so, what is it?

FURTHER READINGS

Britain, James E. 1984. "Product Honesty Is the Best Policy: A Comparison of Doctors' and Manufacturers' Duty to Disclose Drug Risks and the Importance of Consumer Expectations in Determining Product Defect." *Nw. UL Rev.* 79.

Hannon, Patrick. 1989. "The Ethics of Advertising." *The Furrow* 393–403.

Post, James E. 1985. "Assessing the Nestle Boycott: Corporate Accountability and Human Rights." *California Management Review* 27.

Sethi, S. Prakash. 2012. *Multinational Corporations and the Impact of Public Advocacy on Corporate Strategy: Nestle and the Infant Formula Controversy.* Vol. 6. Science & Business Media. New York: Springer.

WOMEN AND ADVERTISING

Sara De Vido

BACKGROUND

VIOLENCE AGAINST WOMEN IS STILL A WORRYING and widespread phenomenon. Intimate partner violence (IPV) or domestic violence, which includes different types of violence perpetrated by the current or former partner, represents the most severe form of violence against women in every society. According to the 2014 report prepared by the National Intimate Partner Sexual Violence Survey (NISVS), administered by the US Centers for Disease Control and Prevention, nearly 1 in 5 women (19.3%) and 1 in 59 men (1.7%) have been raped in their lifetime; one in 4 women (22.3%) have been the victim of severe physical violence by an intimate partner, while 1 in 7 men (14.0%) have experienced the same.[1] In Europe, a survey conducted by the European Union Agency for Fundamental Rights in 2014 showed that one in three women (33%) has experienced physical and/or sexual violence since she was 15 years old, and that 22% of all women who have a (current or previous) partner have experienced physical and/or sexual violence by the partner since the age of 15.[2] The report is based on 42,000 interviews with women living in the 28 EU Member States. At the international level, 35 per cent of women worldwide have experienced either physical and/or sexual intimate partner violence or non-partner sexual violence, according to a global review of available data prepared by the World Health Organization.[3]

Despite these disturbing statistics, business frequently produces and promotes products with images that objectify women, or portray domination of, or violence against, them. Media can influence consumers' behavior, and have the power to shape people's perception toward gender.[4] One major ethical concern is that advertisements and products depict and encourage, directly or indirectly, violence against women. A sample of recent ads from major companies illustrates this point.

In 2013 a web advertisement promoted Ford's Figo small car, the Indian version of the Fiesta. The ad, produced by the Indian advertising agency JWT, features three voluptuous women in a car boot with their mouths gagged and their hands tied. Sitting in the front seat, the former Italian Prime Minister, Silvio Berlusconi, who has been involved in numerous sex scandals, smiles making a V-sign. The caption reads: "Leave your worries behind with the Figo's extra-large boot." Ford replied that it had not authorized the publication which was "contrary to the standards of professionalism and decency within Ford and our agency partners."[5]

Another example is the online ad created by Dolce & Gabbana in 2007 and soon after banned from Italian publications. It shows a woman wearing black lingerie and stilettos, held down by a half-naked man. Three men are standing around them and looking at her. The image was criticized for simulating a "gang rape" for the purpose of promoting fashion. What is striking is the element of domination, of the strength of the man over the woman.

Other ads emphasize the domination of men over women that "evoke" rather than show episodes of violence.[6] Marc Jacobs' ad published in 2008 shows disembodied women's legs sticking out of a shopping bag. It is unclear whether or not the legs are attached to the body. A Blender's ad shows a naked female body hanging in pieces from the ceiling like meat stored in a butchery. A Calvin Klein ad depicts a woman elegantly dressed lying on the floor. An ominous male shape is approaching: is she waiting for him or is something bad about to happen? Belvedere, a Polish vodka brand, used a comedy video portraying a woman trying to wiggle out of a smiling man's grasp (supposedly her partner). The sentence accompanying the message can be read as a metaphor for a sexual act: "Unlike some people ... Belvedere always goes down smoothly." The ad was removed and Belvedere sent a donation to a women's charity.

Even examples that are meant to be "positive" can have a problematic message. Italy's football team Fiorentina joined the campaign to protect women from violence in November 2014. In a photo posted on Facebook the footballers (all men) stand with their arms crossed over their chest; they create a sort of "barrier" in order to protect some women, their arms along their body, standing in line. The caption reads: "In difesa ci siamo noi" ("we are your defense").[7] Messages posted on Facebook by several women were extremely positive, but some women's associations did not agree. The photo pictures women as vulnerable and defenseless persons, unable to save themselves from violence without the intervention of men.

The examples illustrated above are different in various ways, but they all represent women as weaker, and more vulnerable, than men. The question is then whether, and to what extent, media influence violence against women, and to provide an analysis from an international human rights law perspective.

ANALYSIS

One issue is that advertisement may influence attitudes that encourage violence toward women and reinforce sexist institutions. Radical feminists have argued that misogynistic images in advertising and entertainment create the cultural support for men's violence.[8] Depicting women as objects (for example as "parts" of a body), or in some forms of prostration, or as vulnerable subjects, can lead "men to be more accepting of violence towards women and less sympathetic towards women's viewpoints and feelings in the sexual and non-sexual arena."[9] The objectification of women's bodies in advertisements results in dehumanization, and it is the first step in justifying violence against them.[10]

In her work on pornography, Catherine MacKinnon emphasized the "social hierarchy of men over women," in particular the "so many distinctive features of women's status as second-class," including the servility and the display, and the requisite presentation of self as a beautiful thing.[11] She then posited that "male sexuality is apparently activated by violence against women and expresses itself in violence against women to a significant extent."[12] On her account, ads showing violence encourage violence by virtue of the representation of male domination over women. This position is reflected in the work of Jean Kilbourne who argued in 1999 that "male violence is subtly encouraged by ads that encourage men to be forceful and dominant and to value sexual intimacy more than emotional intimacy."[13]

In cases of computer games that simulate sexual acts, murders, and violence, sex can be viewed as "largely a spectator sport for its participants."[14] If it is entertainment, it gradually permeates the society, it becomes something that is part of our culture and is therefore accepted, and not questioned.

Decades of critiques by media studies scholars have not produced a significant reduction in negative representations of women in media and entertainment. If anything, today's girls grow up with a more amplified and widespread circulation of pornography, soft porn, graphic "entertainment" violence, and dead bodies.[15]

Feminist arguments are supported by meta-analyses that have investigated the relationship between media violence and aggression. For example, a group of psychologists of the American Psychological Society demonstrated that "exposure [to young people] to violent scenes may activate a complex set of associations that are related to aggressive ideas or emotions, thereby temporarily increasing the accessibility of aggressive thoughts, feelings, and scripts."[16] A recent report prepared by the Commission on Media Violence established by the International Society for Research on Aggression (ISRA) contends that if the violent content of a movie or an ad is seen as "fun," or "normal," then "aggression concepts will be classically conditioned with positive feelings [...] such as seeing aggression as a more acceptable response to provocation."[17] Watching a violent ad does not automatically lead men to assault women; it is not a simple "cause-effect" relationship. However, although findings vary according to the ages of the samples, the research paradigm, and the gender-role orientation of the participants, empirical work supports the thesis that exposure to media and ads is one risk factor for increased aggression in both the short and the long run.

Furthermore, even if social scientists still dispute the extent—if any—of the effects of some forms of advertising, many feminists contend that such ads constitute harm in themselves independently of their effects. Even if violent media cannot be shown to contribute to violence or discrimination, images that demean, degrade, or depict violence against women are still morally objectionable because their content is offensive.

If we grant that violence in the media can contribute to violent behavior or that violent media is in itself offensive, we face here the ethical conflict between freedom of expression and censorship. Should freedom of expression protect media's and advertising agencies' use of violent or degrading images? Or should measures be taken to eliminate or reduce images that encourage violence? If so, which images merit censorship? Only images that explicitly depict violence or images that can be interpreted as having violent meanings? What about images that objectify women or include

sexist images? Who answers these questions? How should laws and polices be enforced? Is law the instrument for prohibiting certain images which encourage violence or should companies voluntarily comply with standards?

It is useful to turn to international human rights law in order to understand whether or not it has a role in answering these questions. The UN Convention on the Elimination of All Forms of Discrimination against Women (CEDAW), adopted in 1979 by the UN General Assembly, is the first international legal instrument aimed to protect women, although it does not contain the definition of violence against women.[18] Even though the Convention does not include provisions on media, parties are required to take all necessary measures in order to "modify the social and cultural patterns of conduct of men and women" (Art. 5). Media can contribute to change social and cultural patterns. In 1995, the Beijing Platform for Action, a non-binding act, stressed the fact that "images in the media of violence against women, [...] as well as the use of women and girls as sex objects, including pornography, are factors contributing to the continued prevalence of such violence, adversely influencing the community at large, in particular children and young people."[19] Accordingly, one of the actions recommended is raising awareness of "the responsibility of the media in promoting non-stereotyped images of women and men, as well as in eliminating patterns of media presentation that generate violence, and encourage those responsible for media content to establish professional guidelines and codes of conduct."[20] The objectification or "commodification" of women has also been emphasized in the non-binding observations prepared by the CEDAW Committee regarding the implementation of the Convention in several states.[21] Furthermore, the Commission on the Status of Women encouraged media "to the extent consistent with freedom of expression, [...] to improve public awareness on violence against women and girls, to train those who work in the media and to develop and strengthen self-regulatory mechanisms to promote balanced and non-stereotypical portrayals of women."[22]

Guidelines for media are also mentioned in the Inter-American Convention on the Prevention, Punishment and Eradication of Violence against Women, adopted in 1994, in which States parties agree to undertake actions "to encourage the communications media to develop appropriate media guidelines in order to contribute to the eradication of violence against women in all its forms, and to enhance respect for the dignity of women" (Art. 8, letter g). The Council of Europe Istanbul Convention on Preventing and Combating Violence against Women and Domestic Violence, adopted in 2011 and entered into force on August 1, 2014, includes among States' obligations a provision on media: "Parties shall encourage the private sector, the information and communication technology sector and the media, with due respect for freedom of expression and their independence, to participate in the elaboration and implementation of policies and to set guidelines and self-regulatory standards to prevent violence against women and to enhance respect for their dignity" (Art. 17). In its recommendations of 2011, the Committee of Ministers of the Council of Europe posited that: "Media organizations should be encouraged to adopt self-regulatory measures, internal codes of conduct/ethics and internal supervision, and develop standards in media coverage that promote gender equality."[23]

The international community has clearly taken a position against gender-based violence; the same position is confirmed by numerous judgments rendered by regional courts of human rights. Instead of asking States to adopt new legislation, however, international legal instruments—both binding instruments such as conventions and non-binding instruments such as the Beijing Platform—have promoted a self-regulatory regime introduced and accepted by media. For example, in 2011 a group of both unions (including the International Federation of Journalists) and employers (including the European Broadcasting Union) adopted a "Framework of Actions on Gender Equality in the Audiovisual Sector in Europe" which affirms that

"European social partners support fair and balanced gender portrayal while defending the fundamental principle of freedom of creative expression for film and broadcast creative content."[24] Few concrete guidelines are provided, however. Furthermore, in the BBC "Advertising & Sponsorship Guidelines," effective as of June 22, 2015, there is no explicit prohibition of advertisements encouraging, directly or indirectly, violence against women.[25] A clearer example of a code of conduct addressing gender issues is the "Canadian Code of Advertising Standards," which includes an entire section on "Gender Portrayal" and stresses that "caution should be taken to ensure that the overall impression of an ad does not violate the spirit of gender equality even though the individual elements of the ad may not violate any particular guideline."[26]

DISCUSSION QUESTIONS

1. If you were asked to write a code of conduct for media regarding gender issues, which guidelines will you elaborate? Will these guidelines only prohibit clear images of violence or also discriminatory images that emphasize domination of men over women?

2. One possible instrument to avoid sexist advertisements is to establish a gender committee in the newsroom. How would this committee balance freedom of expression, on the one hand, and prohibition of violence against women, on the other hand?

3. Luce Irigaray posited in her famous work *This Sex which Is Not One* that "the feminine occurs only within models and laws devised by male subjects. Which implies that there are not really two sexes, but only one. A single practice of the sexual." Watching contemporary ads, is it correct to say that there is only a single practice of the sexual?

4. Compare Chapter IV of the Beijing Platform for Action with the Council of Europe Istanbul Convention. What are the main differences between the two instruments? Which one creates States' obligations?

NOTES

1   Breiding, Matthew J, et al. "Prevalence and Characteristics of Sexual Violence, Stalking, and Intimate Partner Violence Victimization—National Intimate Partner and Sexual Violence Survey, United States, 2011." Surveillance Summaries. Centers for Disease Control and Prevention. September 5, 2014 / 63(SS08); 1–18. http://www.cdc.gov/mmwr/preview/mmwrhtml/ss6308a1.htm?s_cid=ss6308a1_e.

2   FRA. 2014. *Violence against Women: An EU-wide Survey.* 2014. Luxembourg: Publication Office of the EU.

3   World Health Organization. 2013. Global and Regional Estimates of Violence against Women. http://apps.who.int/iris/bitstream/10665/85239/1/9789241564625_eng.pdf, p. 2.

4   Crisp, Roger, and Arrington, Robert L., in this volume.

5   Nelson, Dean. 2013. "Ford Criticised for Indian Advert with Women Stuffed in the Boot." *Telegraph,* March 24. http://www.telegraph.co.uk/news/worldnews/asia/india/9950940/Ford-criticised-for-Indian-advert-with-women-stuffed-in-the-boot.html.

6   See Huffington post. *Women and Advertising*: http://www.huffingtonpost.com/news/women-and-advertising/. Also see Dominic, Green. 2013. "15 Recent Ads That Glorify Sexual Violence Against Women." *Business Insider,* May 18. http://www.businessinsider.com/sex-violence-against-women-ads-2013-5#ixzz3lAaV3hi7.

7   ACF Fiorentina, "In difesa ci siamo noi." https://www.facebook.com/ACFFiorentina/photos/a.469901579707710.114326.334348116596391/860686980629166/?type=1.

8   Bridges, Ana J., and Jensen, Robert. 2011. "Pornography." In: Renzetti et al. (eds). *Sourcebook on Violence against Women.* Thousand Oaks: Sage. 137.

9   Gunter, Barrie. 2002. *Media Sex: What Are the Issues?* Abingdon: Routledge. Experiments were conducted as early as the 1980s.

10 Seamans, Skyla. 2010. "We're Not Buying What You're Selling: Violence against Women in Advertisements." Violence against Women in the Media, Susan B. Anthony Women's Center at MCLA Newsletter. https://www.mcla.edu/Assets/uploads/MCLA/import/www.mcla.edu/Student_Life/uploads/textWidget/1020.00045/documents/Oct.2010.Violence_in_Media.pdf. See also the documentary by Kilbourne, Jean. *Killing Us Softly.* 1979. http://www.jeankilbourne.com/videos/.

11 MacKinnon, Catherine. 1989. "Sexuality, Pornography, and Method: 'Pleasure under Patriarchy." *Ethics* 99 (2): 316–317.

12 Ibid., p. 334.

13 Kilborne, Jean. 1999. *Can't Buy My Love: How Advertising Changes the Way We Think and Feel.* New York: Touchstone. 272.

14 MacKinnon, note 15, 327.

15 Dillman, Joanne Clarke. 2014. *Women and Death in Film, TV, and News.* New York: Palgrave. 82.

16 Anderson, Craig A., et al. 2003. "The Influence of Media on Youth." *Psychological Science in the Public Interest* 4 (3): 81–110, 95.

17 Barbara Krahé, Barbara, Chair, ISRA Commission on Media Violence. 2012. "Report of the Media Violence Commission International Society for Research on Aggression (ISRA)." *Aggressive Behaviour* 38 (5): 335–341, 338.

18 Definition that was introduced in the "UN Declaration on the Elimination of Violence against Women," adopted by the UN General Assembly on December 20, 1993. A/RES/48/104.

19 "Beijing Platform for Action. 1995." Chapter IV: "Strategic Objectives and Actions." Par. 118. http://www.un-documents.net/bpa-4-d.htm.

20 Ibid., para. 125, letter j.

21 For example, "Report on Italy. 2011." CEDAW/C/ITA/CO/6. Para. 22; report on Norway. 2012. CEDAW/C/NOR/CO/8. Para. 21.

22 UN Commission on the Status of Women. 2013. "Report on the Fifty-seventh Session" (4–15 March 2013). E/2013/27, E/CN.6/2013/11. Part B (vv).

23 Recommendation CM/Rec(2013)1 of the Committee of Ministers to member states on gender equality

and media, adopted by the Committee of Ministers on July 10, 2013 at the 1176th meeting of the Ministers' Deputies.

24 https://www3.ebu.ch/files/live/sites/ebu/files/Events/WEM/AVSDC_GEF0A_Executive%20Summary.pdf.

25 http://www.bbcworldwide.com/advertising.aspx.

26 The *Canadian Code of Advertising Standards* sets the criteria for acceptable advertising in Canada. Created by the advertising industry in 1963 to promote the professional practice of advertising, the *Code* is the cornerstone of advertising self-regulation in Canada. http://www.adstandards.com/en/standards/theCode.aspx.

FURTHER READINGS

Charlesworth, Hilary, and Chinkin, Christine. 2000. *The Boundaries of International Law.* Manchester: Manchester University Press.

Council of Europe Convention on Preventing and Combating Violence against Women and Domestic Violence. Istanbul. 2011. http://conventions.coe.int/Treaty/EN/Treaties/Html/210.htm.

De Vido, Sara. 2014. "States' Due Diligence Obligations to Protect Women from Violence: A European Perspective in Light of the 2011 CoE Istanbul Convention." In: *European Yearbook on Human Rights 2014.* Antwerp, Vienna, Graz: Intersentia Nwv.

Edwards, Alice. 2011. *Violence Against Women under International Human Rights Law.* Cambridge: Cambridge University Press. Chap. 1, 2, 3, 4.

Goffman, Erving. 1979. *Gender Advertisements.* New York: Harper & Row.

Irigaray, Luce. 1985. *This Sex Which Is Not One.* New York: Cornell University Press.

MacKinnon, Catherine A. 1998. "The Roar on the Other Side of Silence." In: MacKinnon, Catherine A., Dworkin, Andrea, *In Harm's Way. The Pornography Civil Rights Hearings.* Cambridge, MA: Harvard University Press.

Siebel Newson, Jennifer. 2011. Documentary "Miss Representation." Updated 2014. http://therepresentationproject.org/films/miss-representation/.

Women's Media Center. *The Status of Women in US Media 2015.* http://wmc.3cdn.net/7d-039991d7252a5831_0hum68k6z.pdf.

CASE STUDY

CHILDREN AND TARGETING

Is It Ethical?

Brennan Jacoby

BACKGROUND

ON JUNE 3, 2001, JENNIFER SMITH BEGAN WORK at a large advertising firm. The following fall she was assigned to help with an ad campaign for Puff Fluffs, a new sugar cereal. As she researched her new subject, Jennifer found that previous studies done by the makers of Puff Fluffs showed children ages 6 to 10 enjoying the taste of Puff Fluffs. Since Jennifer's job was to do whatever she could to sell Puff Fluffs, her task became trying to get American youth ages 6 to 10 to buy the cereal, or have it purchased for them.

Jennifer soon started work on devising a full line of television and magazine ads, promoting Puff Fluffs. Being highly skilled in her job Jennifer knew what American youth would be drawn to. Following this knowledge, her advertisements consisted of bright colors, quick transitions, and she even invented a singing mascot to represent the sugar cereal.

In the spring of 2002 when Jennifer's ad campaign was complete, it was broadcast and distributed all over America. Every Saturday morning her television commercials were shown between the most popular cartoons, and her magazine ads could be seen in some of the newest comic books. As a result of Jennifer's advertising, Puff Fluffs saw a year of record sales.

Puff Fluff cereal sales were not the only records made in 2002. The number of obese adolescents in America soared to an all time high. Soon the media began pointing fingers at Jennifer's advertising firm saying that they should be held at least partly responsible for the health issues facing American children. After all, they were the ones targeting children with the unhealthy junk food product: Puff Fluffs.

Perplexed, Jennifer thought to herself, "I was just doing what I was supposed to. I was just doing my job ... wasn't I? Those kids can decide what to eat, or at least their parents should be able to help them! And besides, this is a free country. I was just exercising my First Amendment rights when I advertised Puff Fluffs."

In the following days legislation was passed barring advertisers from targeting youth with products that may have negative effects on their health. Jennifer has since lost her job, and the world of advertising has had to rethink their practices.

While the story of Jennifer and Puff Fluffs is fictitious, the outcome is quite close to reality. The health of America's youth has been dropping, and some have argued that advertisers are to be held partly responsible since they target youth with unhealthy food products. In fact the number of overweight children in America aged 6 to 11 more than doubled in the past 20 years, going from 7% in 1980 to 18.8% in 2004.[1] In addition, in December of 2005, The National Academy of Science issued a report stating that the advertising of junk food poses a threat to the health of young children.[2]

Made up of respected nutritionists, educators, psychologists and lawyers, the authors of the NAS report urged Congress to consider restrictions on the marketing of junk food to children. It was thought that the food industry could play a large role in turning around the eating habits of youth. One of the authors of the National Academy of Science study wrote regarding the food industry, "If voluntary efforts by industry fail to successfully shift the emphasis of television advertising during children's programming away from high-calorie, low-nutrient products to healthier fare, Congress should enact legislation to mandate this change on both broadcast and cable television."[3] As of yet, legislation barring the targeting of youth by advertisers has not been made.

ANALYSIS

If it is agreed that the targeting of youth by advertisers of unhealthy products has negative consequences, one must next consider what action should be taken. It seems that there are three possible responses.

First, it may be argued that each individual is an autonomous being with the ability to make decisions for him or herself. If children are unable to navigate such grounds as to what food to eat, parents or closely related individuals may be there to give direction. In other words, health begins at home, advertisers should not be held responsible.

Second, as was suggested by the National Academy of Science, advertisers could be expected to create and monitor their own set of ethical guidelines. Advertisers as a whole might decide that marketing less healthy foods is acceptable but specifically targeting youth with such products is not.

Third, as has been the case in other arenas of advertising, government legislated limitations could be placed on ads targeting youth. Bans have already been enacted that bar the targeting of youth with cigarette advertisements. Such legislation was formed on the basis that cigarettes are poor for one's health. If foods offering virtually no nutrition are viewed in the same light as cigarettes, it would not be too much to respond in the same way.

In her book, *Diet for a Small Planet*, Francis Moore Lappe articulated that, "There is virtually unanimous opinion that high sugar, low nutrition foods—those which monopolize TV advertising threaten our health. So why not ban advertising of candy, sugared cereals, soft drinks, and other sweets?"[4]

How might advertisers respond to Lappe? From the advertisers' perspective, it may seem that they are only doing their job. Companies award advertising firms with large amounts of funding in return for selling their product. Indeed, it is assumed that advertisers will use all the tools they have at their disposal. Regardless of how much sugar is in a product, advertisers are trying to get the product into the world of the consumer the best that they can.

Do advertisers have a right to advertise how they want and target who they will? When advertisers target youth are they doing nothing more than exercising their First Amendment Rights? Again, Lappe asks "... should we include in the definition of 'free speech' the capacity to dominate national advertising? Isn't there something amiss in this definition of rights?"[5]

Certainly, there may be far reaching repercussions of a decision to ban the advertising of junk food to children. Optimistically, such a ban might raise societal awareness to the effect advertising has on individuals of all ages and spark a new breed of consumers who think for themselves.

Pessimistically, advertising that negatively targets youth might be hard to distinguish from a form of targeting that does not harm the consumer. While it may be a rather simple task to count the calories on the panel of a cereal box to see if it is healthy or not, it may not be as easy to discern which toys, or books will help or hurt the constituencies they are aimed at.

DISCUSSION QUESTIONS

1. How far reaching should First Amendment rights be in cases such as advertising to youth?
2. What might be the strengths and weaknesses of government legislating boundaries on advertising to children?
3. What sort of ramifications might occur from a ban on advertising less healthy products to children?
4. Should advertisers be held responsible if children become unhealthy after consuming a product they advertised?

NOTES

1   "Healthy Youth!" 2006. *Center for Disease Control and Prevention.* http://www.cdc.gov/healthyyouth/obesity.

2   "Food Marketing Aimed at Kids Influences Poor Nutritional Choices, IOM Study Finds; Broad Effort Needed to Promote Healthier Products and Diets." 2005. *The National Academies.* http://www4.nas.edu/news.nsf/6a3520dc2dbfc2ad85256ca8005c1381/e16a92687989758385257oocf00535d29?OpenDocument.

3   The National Academies.

4   Lappe, Francis Moore. 1975. *Diet for a Small Planet.* New York: Ballantine Books, 140–57.

5   Lappe (1975), 155.

FURTHER READINGS

Kelly, Bridget, Jason C.G. Halford, Emma J. Boyland, Kathy Chapman, Inmaculada Bautista-Castano, Christina Berg, and Margherita Caroli. 2010. "Television Food Advertising to Children: A Global Perspective." *American Journal of Public Health* 100 (9): 1730–36.

Livingstone, S., and E.J. Helsper. 2006. "Does Advertising Literacy Mediate the Effects of Advertising on Children? A Critical Examination of Two Linked Research Literatures in Relation to Obesity and Food Choice." *Journal of Communication* 56 (3): 560–84.

Macklin, M. Carole, and Les Carlson. 1999. *Advertising to Children: Concepts and Controversies.* Thousand Oaks, ON: Sage Publications.

Moore, Elizabeth S. 2004. "Children and the Changing World of Advertising." *Journal of Business Ethics* 52 (2): 161–67.

DISTRIBUTIVE JUSTICE

INTRODUCTION

Fritz Allhoff

DISTRIBUTIVE JUSTICE, MOST FUNDAMENTALLY, is about how to distribute the social product, by which I mean all of the things that society produces. The social product consists in material goods, social goods (e.g., health care), financial goods (e.g., money), and services (e.g., the police force). Every social product is finite, so the amount that any individual member could have might be far lower than that which she or he would prefer. Because of the finitude of the social product, society has to make decisions about how to allocate it, and the morality of such allocations might be judged. In this unit on distributive justice, we will try to get clear on some of the options that are available, as well as some of the moral arguments for each approach.

Since the above discussion might sound abstract, let us consider a more concrete example: salaries and wages. Take all of the salaries and wages that everyone in society earns, and then add them up. Now, we can try to figure out what to do with that money. One obvious idea is that we should return the salaries and wages to the people who earn them: if you make $40,000 a year, then we would give you back $40,000. Or, more to the point, there might not be any *distribution* at all since you would just keep what you made.

But there is a problem with such an approach: no public goods (e.g., roads) would ever be funded since all the money was returned to whoever earned it. This then suggests a refinement on the above practice, taxes. Through taxation, some centralized authority will retain some of the earnings

of the citizenry, and those revenues will be spent on projects to serve that citizenry. This now leads to two important questions: what is the appropriate level of taxation? And how should that burden be distributed?

There is widespread disagreement about answers to the first question. One approach would be to favor a minimal level of taxation in which few goods and services would be provided by the government; this is often called a libertarian approach, and is advocated in this volume by Robert Nozick (with John Locke as an important predecessor). The libertarian might think that the government should retain money for some things (e.g., roads), but not for others (e.g., the National Endowment of the Arts), because some people would be forced to pay for things they don't want. This is not to say that libertarians would not support, for example, the arts; it's just that they would oppose compulsory funding for it through taxes.

While this might sound like a good argument for libertarianism, things get a little more tricky when we consider some of the programs that would probably not be part of the minimal state, such as an extensive welfare system. Here, the problem might be that tax revenues to support welfare would be taken from workers to benefit the unemployed, perhaps against the will of the former. But, consider the alternative: that there is no welfare system and that the most vulnerable members of society are not provided for. This, we might think, is morally problematic insofar as society has an obligation to provide for all of its members and, therefore, the government should be allowed to redistribute some of the social produce from workers to provide for those in need.

John Rawls defends substantial redistribution, arguing that the well-off should only be able to benefit insofar as the lot of the least well-off is also improved. More technically, Rawls held that social and economic inequalities are to be of the greatest benefit to the least advantaged members of society (what he calls the "difference principle"). Many people have interpreted the difference principle as allowing people to respond to economic incentives that create inequalities if this will generate more wealth overall and permit redistribution (e.g., through progressive tax rates) so that the least well-off people do better than they would under conditions of strict inequality. Rawls' position can

be made even more radical. The Marxian philosopher Kai Nielsen argues that Rawls still allows for significant inequality if it in fact benefits the worst off. Instead, he proposes a Marxian egalitarianism that prescribes a far more extensive redistribution based on the democratic control of means of production.

These are some of the questions that arise in discussions of distributive justice and which will be addressed by the selections in this section. The first section surveys some of the major historical figures who set the debate about distributive justice. The second section incorporates contemporary work that builds on these classics. We have also included a discussion about intellectual property which has become more and more important in our era.

—79—
EXCERPTS FROM *LEVIATHAN*

Thomas Hobbes

CHAPTER XIII: OF THE NATURAL CONDITION OF MANKIND AS CONCERNING THEIR FELICITY AND MISERY

NATURE HATH MADE MEN SO EQUAL IN THE faculties of body and mind as that, though there be found one man sometimes manifestly stronger in body or of quicker mind than another, yet when all is reckoned together the difference between man and man is not so considerable as that one man can thereupon claim to himself any benefit to which another may not pretend as well as he. For as to the strength of body, the weakest has strength enough to kill the strongest, either by secret machination or by confederacy with others that are in the same danger with himself.

And as to the faculties of the mind, setting aside the arts grounded upon words, and especially that skill of proceeding upon general and infallible rules, called science, which very few have and but in few things, as being not a native faculty born with us, nor attained, as prudence, while we look after somewhat else, I find yet a greater equality amongst men than that of strength. For prudence is but experience, which equal time equally bestows on all men in those things they equally apply themselves unto. That which may perhaps make such equality incredible is but a vain conceit of one's own wisdom, which almost all men think they have in a greater degree than the vulgar; that is, than all men but themselves, and a few others, whom by fame, or for concurring with themselves, they approve. For such is the nature of men that howsoever they may acknowledge many others to be more witty, or more eloquent or more learned, yet they will hardly believe there be many so wise as themselves; for they see their own wit at hand, and other men's at a distance. But this proveth rather that men are in that point equal, than unequal. For there is not ordinarily a greater sign of the equal distribution of anything than that every man is contented with his share.

From this equality of ability ariseth equality of hope in the attaining of our ends. And therefore if any two men desire the same thing, which nevertheless they cannot both enjoy, they become enemies; and in the way to their end (which is principally their own conservation, and sometimes their delectation only) endeavour to destroy or subdue one another. And from hence it comes to pass that where an invader hath no more to fear than another man's single power, if one plant, sow, build, or possess a convenient seat, others may probably be expected to come prepared with forces united to dispossess and deprive him, not only of the fruit of his labour, but also of his life or liberty. And the invader again is in the like danger of another.

And from this diffidence of one another, there is no way for any man to secure himself so reasonable as anticipation; that is, by force, or wiles, to master the persons of all men he can so long till he see no other power great enough to endanger him: and this is no more than his own conservation requireth, and is generally allowed. Also, because there be some that, taking pleasure in contemplating their own power in the acts of conquest, which they pursue farther than their security requires, if others, that otherwise would be glad to be at ease within modest bounds, should not by invasion increase their power, they would not be able, long time, by standing only on their defence, to subsist. And by consequence, such augmentation of dominion over men being necessary to a man's conservation, it ought to be allowed him.

Again, men have no pleasure (but on the contrary a great deal of grief) in keeping company where there is no power able to overawe them all. For every man looketh that his companion should value him at the same rate he sets upon himself, and upon all signs of contempt or undervaluing naturally endeavours, as far as he dares (which amongst them that have no common power to keep them in quiet is far enough to make them destroy each other), to extort a greater value from his contemners, by damage; and from others, by the example.

So that in the nature of man, we find three principal causes of quarrel. First, competition; secondly, diffidence; thirdly, glory.

The first maketh men invade for gain; the second, for safety; and the third, for reputation. The first use violence, to make themselves masters of other men's persons, wives, children, and cattle; the second, to defend them; the third, for trifles, as a word, a smile, a different opinion, and any other sign of undervalue, either direct in their persons or by reflection in their kindred, their friends, their nation, their profession, or their name.

Hereby it is manifest that during the time men live without a common power to keep them all in awe, they are in that condition which is called war; and such a war as is of every man against every man. For war consisteth not in battle only, or the act of fighting, but in a tract of time, wherein the will to contend by battle is sufficiently known: and therefore the notion of time is to be considered in the nature of war, as it is in the nature of weather. For as the nature of foul weather lieth not in a shower or two of rain, but in an inclination thereto of many days together: so the nature of war consisteth not in actual fighting, but in the known disposition thereto during all the time there is no assurance to the contrary. All other time is peace.

Whatsoever therefore is consequent to a time of war, where every man is enemy to every man, the same consequent to the time wherein men live without other security than what their own strength and their own invention shall furnish them withal. In such condition there is no place for industry, because the fruit thereof is uncertain: and consequently no culture of the earth; no navigation, nor use of the commodities that may be imported by sea; no commodious building; no instruments of moving and removing such things as require much force; no knowledge of the face of the earth; no account of time; no arts; no letters; no society; and which is worst of all, continual fear, and danger of violent death; and the life of man, solitary, poor, nasty, brutish, and short.

It may seem strange to some man that has not well weighed these things that Nature should thus dissociate and render men apt to invade and destroy one another: and he may therefore, not trusting to this inference, made from the passions, desire perhaps to have the same confirmed by experience. Let him therefore consider with himself: when taking a journey, he arms himself and seeks to go well accompanied; when going to sleep, he locks his doors; when even in his house he locks his chests; and this when he knows there be laws and public officers, armed, to revenge all injuries shall be done him; what opinion he has of his fellow subjects, when he rides armed; of his fellow citizens, when he locks his doors; and of his children, and servants, when he locks his chests. Does he not there as much accuse mankind by his actions as I do by my words? But neither of us accuse man's nature in it. The desires, and other passions of man, are in themselves no sin. No more are the actions that proceed from those passions till they know a law that forbids them; which till laws be made they cannot know, nor can any law be made till they have agreed upon the person that shall make it.

It may peradventure be thought there was never such a time nor condition of war as this; and I believe it was never generally so, over all the world: but there are many places where they live so now. For the savage people in many places of America, except the government of small families, the concord whereof dependeth on natural lust, have no government at all, and live at this day in that brutish manner, as I said before. Howsoever, it may be perceived what manner of life there would be, where there were no common power to fear, by the manner of life which men that have formerly lived under a peaceful government use to degenerate into a civil war.

But though there had never been any time wherein particular men were in a condition of war one against another, yet in all times kings and persons of sovereign authority, because of their independency, are in continual jealousies, and in the state and posture of gladiators, having their weapons pointing, and their eyes fixed on one another; that is, their forts, garrisons, and guns upon the frontiers of their kingdoms, and continual spies upon their neighbours, which is a posture of war. But because they uphold thereby the industry of their subjects, there does not follow from it that misery which accompanies the liberty of particular men.

To this war of every man against every man, this also is consequent; that nothing can be unjust. The notions of right and wrong, justice and injustice, have there no place. Where there is no common power, there is no law; where no law, no injustice. Force and fraud are in war the two cardinal virtues. Justice and injustice are none of the faculties neither of the body nor mind. If they were, they might be in a man that were alone in the world, as well as his senses and passions. They are qualities that relate to men in society, not in solitude. It is consequent also to the same condition that there be no propriety, no dominion, no mine and thine distinct; but only that to be every man's that he can get, and for so long as he can keep it.

And thus much for the ill condition which man by mere nature is actually placed in; though with a possibility to come out of it, consisting partly in the passions, partly in his reason.

The passions that incline men to peace are: fear of death; desire of such things as are necessary to commodious living; and a hope by their industry to obtain them. And reason suggesteth convenient articles of peace upon which men may be drawn to agreement. These articles are they which otherwise are called the laws of nature, whereof I shall speak more particularly in the two following chapters.

CHAPTER XIV: OF THE FIRST AND SECOND NATURAL LAWS, AND OF CONTRACTS

THE right of nature, which writers commonly call jus naturale, is the liberty each man hath to use his own power as he will himself for the preservation of his own nature; that is to say, of his own life; and consequently, of doing anything which, in his own judgement and reason, he shall conceive to be the aptest means thereunto.

By liberty is understood, according to the proper signification of the word, the absence of external impediments; which impediments may oft take away part of a man's power to do what he would, but cannot hinder him from using the power left him according as his judgement and reason shall dictate to him.

A law of nature, lex naturalis, is a precept, or general rule, found out by reason, by which a man is forbidden to do that which is destructive of his life, or taketh away the means of preserving the same, and to omit that by which he thinketh it may be best preserved. For though they that speak of this subject use to confound jus and lex, right and law, yet they ought to be distinguished, because right consisteth in liberty to do, or to forbear; whereas law determineth and bindeth to one of them: so that law and right differ as much as obligation and liberty, which in one and the same matter are inconsistent.

And because the condition of man (as hath been declared in the precedent chapter) is a condition of war of every one against every one, in which case every one is governed by his own reason, and there is nothing he can make use of that may not be a help unto him in preserving his life against his enemies; it followeth that in such a condition every man has a right to every thing, even to one another's body. And therefore, as long as this natural right of every man to every thing endureth, there can be no security to any man, how strong or wise soever he be, of living out the time which nature ordinarily alloweth men to live. And consequently it is a precept, or general rule of reason: that every man ought to endeavour peace, as far as he has hope of obtaining it; and when he cannot obtain it, that he may seek and use all helps and advantages of war. The first branch of which rule containeth the first and fundamental law of nature, which is: to seek peace and follow it. The second, the sum of the right of nature, which is: by all means we can to defend ourselves.

From this fundamental law of nature, by which men are commanded to endeavour peace, is derived this second law: that a man be willing, when others are so too, as far forth as for peace and defence of himself he shall think it necessary, to lay down this right to all things; and be contented with so much liberty against other men as he would allow other men against himself. For as long as every man holdeth this right, of doing anything he liketh; so long are all men in the condition of war. But if other men will not lay down their right, as well as he, then there is no reason for anyone to divest himself of his: for that were to expose himself to prey, which no man is bound to, rather than to dispose himself to peace. This is that law of the gospel: Whatsoever you require that others should do to you, that do ye to them. And that law of all men, quod tibi fieri non vis, alteri ne feceris.

To lay down a man's right to anything is to divest himself of the liberty of hindering another of the benefit of his own right to the same. For he that renounceth or passeth away his right giveth not to any other man a right which he had not before, because there is nothing to which every man had not right by nature, but only standeth out of his way that he may enjoy his own original right without hindrance from him, not without hindrance from another. So that the effect which redoundeth to one man by another man's defect of right is but so much diminution of impediments to the use of his own right original.

Right is laid aside, either by simply renouncing it, or by transferring it to another. By simply renouncing, when he cares not to whom the benefit thereof redoundeth. By transferring, when he intendeth the benefit thereof to some certain person or persons. And when a man hath in either manner abandoned or granted away his right, then is he said to be obliged, or bound, not to hinder those to whom such right is granted, or abandoned, from the benefit of it: and that he ought, and it is duty, not to make void that voluntary act of his own: and that such hindrance is injustice, and injury, as being sine jure; the right being before renounced or transferred. So that injury or injustice, in the controversies of the world, is somewhat like to that which in the disputations of scholars is called absurdity. For as it is there called an absurdity to contradict what one maintained in the beginning; so in the world it is called injustice, and injury voluntarily to undo that which from the beginning he had voluntarily done. The way by which a man either simply renounceth or transferreth his right is a declaration, or signification, by some voluntary and sufficient sign, or signs, that he doth so renounce or transfer, or hath so renounced or transferred the same, to him that accepteth it. And these signs are either words only, or actions only; or, as it happeneth most often, both words and actions. And the same are the bonds, by which men are bound and obliged: bonds that have their strength, not from their own nature (for nothing is more easily broken than a man's word), but from fear of some evil consequence upon the rupture.

Whensoever a man transferreth his right, or renounceth it, it is either in consideration of some right reciprocally transferred to himself, or for some other good he hopeth for thereby. For it is a voluntary act: and of the voluntary acts of every man, the object is some good to himself. And therefore there be some rights which no man can be understood by any words, or other signs, to have abandoned or transferred. As first a man cannot lay down the right of resisting them that assault him by force to take away his life, because he cannot be understood to aim thereby at any good to himself. The same may be said of wounds, and chains, and imprisonment, both because there is no benefit consequent to such patience, as there is to the patience of suffering another to be wounded or imprisoned, as also because a man cannot tell when he seeth men proceed against him by violence whether they intend his death or not. And lastly the motive and end for which this renouncing and transferring of right is introduced is nothing else but the security of a man's person, in his life, and in the means of so preserving life as not to be weary of it. And therefore if a man by words, or other signs, seem to despoil himself of the end for which those signs were intended, he is not to be understood as if he meant it, or that it was his will, but that he was ignorant of how such words and actions were to be interpreted.

The mutual transferring of right is that which men call contract.

There is difference between transferring of right to the thing, the thing, and transferring or tradition, that is, delivery of the thing itself. For the thing may be delivered together with the translation of the right, as in buying and selling with ready money, or exchange of goods or lands, and it may be delivered some time after.

Again, one of the contractors may deliver the thing contracted for on his part, and leave the other to perform his part at some determinate time after, and in the meantime be trusted; and then the contract on his part is called pact, or covenant: or both parts may contract now to perform hereafter, in which cases he that is to perform in time to come, being trusted, his performance is called keeping of promise, or faith, and the failing of performance, if it be voluntary, violation of faith.

When the transferring of right is not mutual, but one of the parties transferreth in hope to gain thereby friendship or service from another, or from his friends; or in hope to gain the reputation of charity, or magnanimity; or to deliver his mind from the pain of compassion; or in hope of reward in heaven; this is not contract, but gift, free gift, grace: which words signify one and the same thing.

Signs of contract are either express or by inference. Express are words spoken with understanding of what they signify: and such words are either of the time present or past; as, I give, I grant, I have given, I have granted, I will that this be yours: or of the future; as, I will give, I will grant, which words of the future are called promise.

Signs by inference are sometimes the consequence of words; sometimes the consequence of silence; sometimes the consequence of actions; sometimes the consequence of forbearing an action: and generally a sign by inference, of any contract, is whatsoever sufficiently argues the will of the contractor.

Words alone, if they be of the time to come, and contain a bare promise, are an insufficient sign of a free gift and therefore not obligatory. For if they be of the time to come, as, tomorrow I will give, they are a sign I have not given yet, and consequently that my right is not transferred, but remaineth till I transfer it by some other act. But if the words be of the time present, or past, as, I have given, or do give to be delivered tomorrow, then is my tomorrow's right given away today; and that by the virtue of the words, though there were no other argument of my will. And there is a great difference in the signification of these words, volo hoc tuum esse cras, and cras dabo; that is, between I will that this be thine tomorrow, and, I will give it thee tomorrow: for the word I will, in the former manner of speech, signifies an act of the will present; but in the latter, it signifies a promise of an act of the will to come: and therefore the former words, being of the present, transfer a future right; the latter, that be of the future, transfer nothing. But if there be other signs of the will to transfer a right besides words; then, though the gift be free, yet may the right be understood to pass by words of the future: as if a man propound a prize to him that comes first to the end of a race, the gift is free; and though the words be of the future, yet the right passeth: for if he would not have his words so be understood, he should not have let them run.

In contracts the right passeth, not only where the words are of the time present or past, but also where they are of the future, because all contract is mutual translation, or change of right; and therefore he that promiseth only, because he hath already received the benefit for which he promiseth, is to be understood as if he intended the right should pass: for unless he had been content to have his words so understood, the other would not have performed his part first. And for that cause, in buying, and selling, and other acts of contract, a promise is equivalent to a covenant, and therefore obligatory.

He that performeth first in the case of a contract is said to merit that which he is to receive by the performance of the other, and he hath it as due. Also when a prize is propounded to many, which is to be given to him only that winneth, or money is thrown amongst many to be enjoyed by them that catch it; though this be a free gift, yet so to win, or so to catch, is to merit, and to have it as due. For the right is transferred in the propounding of the prize, and in throwing down the money, though it be not determined to whom, but by the event of the contention. But there is between these two sorts of merit this difference, that in contract I merit by virtue of my own power and the contractor's need, but in this case of free gift I am enabled to merit only by the benignity of the giver: in contract I merit at the contractor's hand that he should depart with his right; in this case of gift, I merit not that the giver should part with his right, but that when he has parted with it, it should be mine rather than another's. And this I think to be the meaning of that distinction of the Schools between meritum congrui and meritum condigni. For God Almighty, having promised paradise to those men, hoodwinked with carnal desires, that can walk through this world according to the

precepts and limits prescribed by him, they say he that shall so walk shall merit paradise ex congruo. But because no man can demand a right to it by his own righteousness, or any other power in himself, but by the free grace of God only, they say no man can merit paradise ex condigno. This, I say, I think is the meaning of that distinction; but because disputers do not agree upon the signification of their own terms of art longer than it serves their turn, I will not affirm anything of their meaning: only this I say; when a gift is given indefinitely, as a prize to be contended for, he that winneth meriteth, and may claim the prize as due.

If a covenant be made wherein neither of the parties perform presently, but trust one another, in the condition of mere nature (which is a condition of war of every man against every man) upon any reasonable suspicion, it is void: but if there be a common power set over them both, with right and force sufficient to compel performance, it is not void. For he that performeth first has no assurance the other will perform after, because the bonds of words are too weak to bridle men's ambition, avarice, anger, and other passions, without the fear of some coercive power; which in the condition of mere nature, where all men are equal, and judges of the justness of their own fears, cannot possibly be supposed. And therefore he which performeth first does but betray himself to his enemy, contrary to the right he can never abandon of defending his life and means of living.

But in a civil estate, where there is a power set up to constrain those that would otherwise violate their faith, that fear is no more reasonable; and for that cause, he which by the covenant is to perform first is obliged so to do.

The cause of fear, which maketh such a covenant invalid, must be always something arising after the covenant made, as some new fact or other sign of the will not to perform, else it cannot make the covenant void. For that which could not hinder a man from promising ought not to be admitted as a hindrance of performing.

He that transferreth any right transferreth the means of enjoying it, as far as lieth in his power. As he that selleth land is understood to transfer the herbage and whatsoever grows upon it; nor can he that sells a mill turn away the stream that drives it. And they that give to a man the right of government in sovereignty are understood to give him the right of levying money to maintain soldiers, and of appointing magistrates for the administration of justice.

To make covenants with brute beasts is impossible, because not understanding our speech, they understand not, nor accept of any translation of right, nor can translate any right to another: and without mutual acceptation, there is no covenant.

To make covenant with God is impossible but by mediation of such as God speaketh to, either by revelation supernatural or by His lieutenants that govern under Him and in His name: for otherwise we know not whether our covenants be accepted or not. And therefore they that vow anything contrary to any law of nature, vow in vain, as being a thing unjust to pay such vow. And if it be a thing commanded by the law of nature, it is not the vow, but the law that binds them.

The matter or subject of a covenant is always something that falleth under deliberation, for to covenant is an act of the will; that is to say, an act, and the last act, of deliberation; and is therefore always understood to be something to come, and which judged possible for him that covenanteth to perform.

And therefore, to promise that which is known to be impossible is no covenant. But if that prove impossible afterwards, which before was thought possible, the covenant is valid and bindeth, though not to the thing itself, yet to the value; or, if that also be impossible, to the unfeigned endeavour of performing as much as is possible, for to more no man can be obliged.

Men are freed of their covenants two ways; by performing, or by being forgiven. For performance is the natural end of obligation, and forgiveness the restitution of liberty, as being a retransferring of that right in which the obligation consisted.

Covenants entered into by fear, in the condition of mere nature, are obligatory. For example, if I covenant to pay a ransom, or service for my life, to an enemy, I am bound by it. For it is a contract, wherein one receiveth the benefit of life; the other is to receive money, or service for it, and consequently, where no other law (as in the condition of mere nature) forbiddeth the performance, the covenant is valid. Therefore prisoners of war, if trusted with the payment of their ransom, are obliged to pay it: and if a weaker prince make a disadvantageous peace with a stronger, for fear, he is bound to keep it; unless (as hath been said before) there ariseth some new and just cause of fear to renew the war. And even in Commonwealths, if I be forced to redeem myself from a thief by promising him money, I am bound to pay it, till the civil law discharge me. For whatsoever I may lawfully do without obligation, the same I may lawfully covenant to do through fear: and what I lawfully covenant, I cannot lawfully break.

A former covenant makes void a later. For a man that hath passed away his right to one man today hath it not to pass tomorrow to another: and therefore the later promise passeth no right, but is null.

A covenant not to defend myself from force, by force, is always void. For (as I have shown before) no man can transfer or lay down his right to save himself from death, wounds, and imprisonment, the avoiding whereof is the only end of laying down any right; and therefore the promise of not resisting force, in no covenant transferreth any right, nor is obliging. For though a man may covenant thus, unless I do so, or so, kill me; he cannot covenant thus, unless I do so, or so, I will not resist you when you come to kill me. For man by nature chooseth the lesser evil, which is danger of death in resisting, rather than the greater, which is certain and present death in not resisting. And this is granted to be true by all men, in that they lead criminals to execution, and prison, with armed men, notwithstanding that such criminals have consented to the law by which they are condemned.

A covenant to accuse oneself, without assurance of pardon, is likewise invalid. For in the condition of nature where every man is judge, there is no place for accusation: and in the civil state the accusation is followed with punishment, which, being force, a man is not obliged not to resist. The same is also true of the accusation of those by whose condemnation a man falls into misery; as of a father, wife, or benefactor. For the testimony of such an accuser, if it be not willingly given, is presumed to be corrupted by nature, and therefore not to be received: and where a man's testimony is not to be credited, he is not bound to give it. Also accusations upon torture are not to be reputed as testimonies. For torture is to be used but as means of conjecture, and light, in the further examination and search of truth: and what is in that case confessed tendeth to the ease of him that is tortured, not to the informing of the torturers, and therefore ought not to have the credit of a sufficient testimony: for whether he deliver himself by true or false accusation, he does it by the right of preserving his own life.

The force of words being (as I have formerly noted) too weak to hold men to the performance of their covenants, there are in man's nature but two imaginable helps to strengthen it. And those are either a fear of the consequence of breaking their word, or a glory or pride in appearing not to need to break it. This latter is a generosity too rarely found to be presumed on, especially in the pursuers of wealth, command, or sensual pleasure, which are the greatest part of mankind. The passion to be reckoned upon is fear; whereof there be two very general objects: one, the power of spirits invisible; the other, the power of those men they shall therein offend. Of these two, though the former be the greater power, yet the fear of the latter is commonly the greater fear. The fear of the former is in every man his own religion, which hath place in the nature of man before civil society. The latter hath not so; at least not place

enough to keep men to their promises, because in the condition of mere nature, the inequality of power is not discerned, but by the event of battle. So that before the time of civil society, or in the interruption thereof by war, there is nothing can strengthen a covenant of peace agreed on against the temptations of avarice, ambition, lust, or other strong desire, but the fear of that invisible power which they every one worship as God, and fear as a revenger of their perfidy. All therefore that can be done between two men not subject to civil power is to put one another to swear by the God he feareth: which swearing, or oath, is a form of speech, added to a promise, by which he that promiseth signifieth that unless he perform he renounceth the mercy of his God, or calleth to him for vengeance on himself. Such was the heathen form, Let Jupiter kill me else, as I kill this beast. So is our form, I shall do thus, and thus, so help me God. And this, with the rites and ceremonies which every one useth in his own religion, that the fear of breaking faith might be the greater.

By this it appears that an oath taken according to any other form, or rite, than his that sweareth is in vain and no oath, and that there is no swearing by anything which the swearer thinks not God. For though men have sometimes used to swear by their kings, for fear, or flattery; yet they would have it thereby understood they attributed to them divine honour. And that swearing unnecessarily by God is but profaning of his name: and swearing by other things, as men do in common discourse, is not swearing, but an impious custom, gotten by too much vehemence of talking.

It appears also that the oath adds nothing to the obligation. For a covenant, if lawful, binds in the sight of God, without the oath, as much as with it; if unlawful, bindeth not at all, though it be confirmed with an oath.

—80—

EXCERPTS FROM *THE SECOND TREATISE OF HUMAN GOVERNMENT*

John Locke

CHAPTER V: OF PROPERTY

SEC. 25. WHETHER WE CONSIDER NATURAL reason, which tells us, that men, being once born, have a right to their preservation, and consequently to meat and drink, and such other things as nature affords for their subsistence: or revelation, which gives us an account of those grants God made of the world to Adam, and to Noah, and his sons, it is very clear, that God, as king David says, Psal. cxv. 16. has given the earth to the children of men; given it to mankind in common. But this being supposed, it seems to some a very great difficulty, how any one should ever come to have a property in any thing: I will not content myself to answer, that if it be difficult to make out property, upon a supposition that God gave the world to Adam, and his posterity in common, it is impossible that any man, but one universal monarch, should have any property upon a supposition, that God gave the world to Adam, and his heirs in succession, exclusive of all the rest of his posterity. But I shall endeavour to shew, how men might come to have a property in several parts of that which God gave to mankind in common, and that without any express compact of all the commoners.

Sec. 26. God, who hath given the world to men in common, hath also given them reason to make use of it to the best advantage of life, and convenience. The earth, and all that is therein, is given to men for the support and comfort of their being. And tho' all the fruits it naturally produces, and beasts it feeds, belong to mankind in common, as they are produced by the spontaneous hand of nature; and no body has originally a private dominion, exclusive of the rest of mankind, in any of them, as they are thus in their natural state: yet being given for the use of men, there must of necessity be a means to appropriate them some way or other, before they can be of any use, or at all beneficial to any particular man. The fruit, or venison, which nourishes the wild Indian, who knows no enclosure, and is still a tenant in common, must be his, and so his, i.e., a part of him, that another can no longer have any right to it, before it can do him any good for the support of his life.

Sec. 27. Though the earth, and all inferior creatures, be common to all men, yet every man has a property in his own person: this no body has any right to but himself. The labour of his body, and the work of his hands, we may say, are properly his. Whatsoever then he removes out of the state that nature hath provided, and left it in, he hath mixed his labour with, and joined to it something that is his own, and thereby makes it his property. It being by him removed from the common state nature hath placed it in, it hath by this labour something annexed to it, that excludes the common right of other men: for this labour being the unquestionable property of the labourer, no man but he can have a right to what that is once joined to, at least where there is enough, and as good, left in common for others.

Sec. 28. He that is nourished by the acorns he picked up under an oak, or the apples he gathered from the trees in the wood, has certainly appropriated them to himself. No body can deny but the nourishment is his. I ask then, when did they begin to be his? when he digested? or when he eat? or when he boiled? or when he brought them home? or when he picked them up? and it is plain, if the first gathering made them not his, nothing else could. That labour put a distinction between them and common: that added something to them more than nature, the common mother of all, had done; and so they became his private right. And will any one say, he had no right to those acorns or apples, he thus appropriated, because he had not the consent of all mankind to make them his? Was it a robbery thus to assume to himself what belonged to all in common? If such a consent as that was necessary, man had starved, notwithstanding the plenty God had given him. We see in commons, which remain so by compact, that it is the taking any part of what is common, and removing it out of the state nature leaves it in, which begins the property; without which the common is of no use. And the taking of this or that part, does not depend on the express consent of all the commoners. Thus the grass my horse has bit; the turfs my servant has cut; and the ore I have digged in any place, where I have a right to them in common with others, become my property, without the assignation or consent of any body. The labour that was mine, removing them out of that common state they were in, hath fixed my property in them.

Sec. 29. By making an explicit consent of every commoner, necessary to any one's appropriating to himself any part of what is given in common, children or servants could not cut the meat, which their father or master had provided for them in common, without assigning to every one his peculiar part. Though the water running in the fountain be every one's, yet who can doubt, but that in the pitcher is his only who drew it out? His labour hath taken it out of the hands of nature, where it was common, and belonged equally to all her children, and hath thereby appropriated it to himself.

Sec. 30. Thus this law of reason makes the deer that Indian's who hath killed it; it is allowed to be his goods, who hath bestowed his labour upon it, though before it was the common right of every one. And amongst those who are counted the civilized part of mankind, who have made and multiplied positive laws to determine property, this original law of nature, for the beginning of property, in what was before common, still takes place; and by virtue thereof, what fish any one catches in the ocean, that great and still remaining common of mankind; or what ambergrise any one takes up here, is by the labour that removes it out of that common state nature left it in, made his property, who takes that pains about it. And even amongst us, the hare that any one is hunting, is thought his who pursues her during the chase: for being a beast that is still looked upon as common, and no man's private possession; whoever has employed so much labour about any of that kind, as to find and pursue her, has thereby removed her from the state of nature, wherein she was common, and hath begun a property.

Sec. 31. It will perhaps be objected to this, that if gathering the acorns, or other fruits of the earth, &c. makes a right to them, then any one may ingross as much as he will. To which I answer, Not so. The same law of nature, that does by this means give us property, does also bound that property too. God has given us all things richly, 1 Tim. VI. 12. is the voice of reason confirmed by inspiration. But how far has he given it us? To enjoy. As much as any one can make use of to any advantage of life before it spoils, so much he may by his Tabour fix a property in: whatever is beyond this, is more than his share, and belongs to others. Nothing was made by God for man to spoil or destroy. And thus, considering the plenty of natural provisions there was a long time in the world, and the few spenders; and to how small a part of that provision the industry of one man could extend itself, and ingross it to the prejudice of others; especially keeping within the bounds, set by reason, of what might serve for his use; there could be then little room for quarrels or contentions about property so established.

Sec. 32. But the chief matter of property being now not the fruits of the earth, and the beasts that subsist on it, but the earth itself; as that which takes in and carries with it all the rest; I think it is plain, that property in that too is acquired as the former. As much land as a man tills, plants, improves, cultivates, and can use the product of, so much is his property. He by his labour does, as it were, inclose it from the common. Nor will it invalidate his right, to say every body else has an equal title to it; and therefore he cannot appropriate, he cannot inclose, without the consent of all his fellow-commoners, all mankind. God, when he gave the world in common to all mankind, commanded man also to labour, and the penury of his condition required it of him. God and his reason commanded him to subdue the earth, i.e., improve it for the benefit of life, and therein lay out something upon it that was his own, his labour. He that in obedience to this command of God, subdued, tilled and sowed any part of it, thereby annexed to it something that was his property, which another had no title to, nor could without injury take from him.

Sec. 33. Nor was this appropriation of any parcel of land, by improving it, any prejudice to any other man, since there was still enough, and as good left; and more than the yet unprovided could use. So that, in effect, there was never the less left for others because of his enclosure for himself: for he that leaves as much as another can make use of, does as good as take nothing at all. No body could think himself injured by the drinking of another man, though he took a good draught, who had a whole river of the same water left him to quench his thirst: and the case of land and water, where there is enough of both, is perfectly the same.

Sec. 34. God gave the world to men in common; but since he gave it them for their benefit, and the greatest conveniencies of life they were capable to draw from it, it cannot be supposed he meant it should always remain common and uncultivated. He gave it to the use of the industrious and rational, (and labour was to be his title to it) not to the fancy or covetousness of the quarrelsome and contentious. He that had as good left for his improvement, as was already taken up, needed not complain, ought not to meddle with what was already improved by another's labour: if he did, it is plain he desired the benefit of another's pains, which he had no right to, and not the ground which God had given him in common with others to labour on, and whereof there was as good left, as that already possessed, and more than he knew what to do with, or his industry could reach to.

Sec. 35. It is true, in land that is common in England, or any other country, where there is plenty of people under government, who have money and commerce, no one can inclose or appropriate any part, without the consent of all his fellowcommoners; because this is left common by compact, i.e., by the law of the land, which is not to be violated. And though it be common, in respect of some men, it is not so to all mankind; but is the joint property of this country, or this parish. Besides, the remainder, after such enclosure, would not be as good to the rest of the commoners, as the whole was when they could all make use of the whole; whereas in the beginning and first peopling of the great common of the world, it was quite otherwise. The law man was under, was rather for appropriating. God commanded, and his wants forced him to labour. That was his property which could not be taken from him where-ever he had fixed it. And hence subduing or cultivating the earth, and having dominion, we see are joined together. The one gave title to the other. So that God, by commanding to subdue, gave authority so far to appropriate: and the condition of human life, which requires labour and materials to work on, necessarily introduces private possessions.

Sec. 36. The measure of property nature has well set by the extent of men's labour and the conveniencies of life: no man's labour could subdue, or appropriate all; nor could his enjoyment consume more than a small part; so that it was impossible for any man, this way, to intrench upon the right of another, or acquire to himself a property, to the prejudice of his neighbour, who would still have room for as good, and as large a possession (after the other had taken out his) as before it was appropriated. This measure did confine every man's possession to a very moderate proportion, and such as he might appropriate to himself, without injury to any body, in the first ages of the world, when men were more in danger to be lost, by wandering from their company, in the then vast wilderness of the earth, than to be straitened for want of room to plant in. And the same measure may be allowed still without prejudice to any body, as full as the world seems: for supposing a man, or family, in the state they were at first peopling of the world by the children of Adam, or Noah; let him plant in some inland, vacant places of America, we shall find that the possessions he could make himself, upon the measures we have given, would not be very large, nor, even to this day, prejudice the rest of mankind, or give them reason to complain, or think themselves injured by this man's incroachment, though the race of men have now spread themselves to all the corners of the world, and do infinitely exceed the small number was at the beginning. Nay, the extent of ground is of so little value, without labour, that I have heard it affirmed, that in Spain itself a man may be permitted to plough, sow and reap, without being disturbed, upon land he has no other title to, but only his making use of it. But, on the contrary, the inhabitants think themselves beholden to him, who, by his industry on neglected, and consequently waste land, has increased the stock of corn, which they wanted. But be this as it will, which I lay no stress on; this I dare boldly affirm, that the same rule of propriety, (viz.) that every man should have as much as he could make use of, would hold still in the world, without straitening any body; since there is land enough in the world to suffice double the inhabitants, had not the invention of money, and the tacit agreement of men to put a value on it, introduced (by consent) larger possessions, and a right to them; which, how it has done, I shall by and by shew more at large.

Sec. 37. This is certain, that in the beginning, before the desire of having more than man needed had altered the intrinsic value of things, which depends only on their usefulness to the life of man; or had agreed, that a little piece of yellow metal, which would keep without wasting or decay, should be worth a great piece of flesh, or a whole heap of corn; though men had a right to appropriate, by their labour, each one of himself, as much of the things of nature, as he could use: yet this could not be much, nor to the prejudice of others, where the same plenty was still left to those who would use the same industry. To which let me add, that he who appropriates land to himself by his labour, does not lessen, but increase the common stock of mankind: for the provisions serving to the support of human life, produced by one acre of inclosed and cultivated land, are (to speak much within compass) ten times more than those which are yielded by an acre of land of an equal richness lying waste in common. And therefore he that incloses land, and has a greater plenty of the conveniencies of life from ten acres, than he could have from an hundred left to nature, may truly be said to give ninety acres to mankind: for his labour now supplies him with provisions out of ten acres, which were but the product of an hundred lying in common. I have here rated the improved land very low, in making its product but as ten to one, when it is much nearer an hundred to one: for I ask, whether in the wild woods and uncultivated waste of America, left to nature, without any improvement, tillage or husbandry, a thousand acres yield the needy and wretched inhabitants as many conveniencies of life, as ten acres of equally fertile land do in Devonshire, where they are well cultivated?

Before the appropriation of land, he who gathered as much of the wild fruit, killed, caught, or tamed, as many of the beasts, as he could; he that so imployed his pains about any of the spontaneous products of nature, as any way to alter them from the state which nature put them in, by placing any of his labour on them, did thereby acquire a propriety in them: but if they perished, in his possession, without their due use; if the fruits rotted, or the venison putrified, before he could spend it, he offended against the common law of nature, and was liable to be punished; he invaded his neighbour's share, for he had no right, farther than his use called for any of them, and they might serve to afford him conveniencies of life.

Sec. 38. The same measures governed the possession of land too: whatsoever he tilled and reaped, laid up and made use of, before it spoiled, that was his peculiar right; whatsoever he enclosed, and could feed, and make use of, the cattle and product was also his. But if either the grass of his enclosure rotted on the ground, or the fruit of his planting perished without gathering, and laying up, this part of the earth, notwithstanding his enclosure, was still to be looked on as waste, and might be the possession of any other. Thus, at the beginning, Cain might take as much ground as he could till, and make it his own land, and yet leave enough to Abel's sheep to feed on; a few acres would serve for both their possessions. But as families increased, and industry inlarged their stocks, their possessions inlarged with the need of them; but yet it was commonly without any fixed property in the ground they made use of, till they incorporated, settled themselves together, and built cities; and then, by consent, they came in time, to set out the bounds of their distinct territories, and agree on limits between them and their neighbours; and by laws within themselves, settled the properties of those of the same society: for we see, that in that part of the world which was first inhabited, and therefore like to be best peopled, even as low down as Abraham's

time, they wandered with their flocks, and their herds, which was their substance, freely up and down; and this Abraham did, in a country where he was a stranger. Whence it is plain, that at least a great part of the land lay in common; that the inhabitants valued it not, nor claimed property in any more than they made use of. But when there was not room enough in the same place, for their herds to feed together, they by consent, as Abraham and Lot did, Gen. XIII. 5. separated and inlarged their pasture, where it best liked them. And for the same reason Esau went from his father, and his brother, and planted in mount Seir, Gen. XXXVI. 6.

Sec. 39. And thus, without supposing any private dominion, and property in Adam, over all the world, exclusive of all other men, which can no way be proved, nor any one's property be made out from it; but supposing the world given, as it was, to the children of men in common, we see how labour could make men distinct titles to several parcels of it, for their private uses; wherein there could be no doubt of right, no room for quarrel.

Sec. 40. Nor is it so strange, as perhaps before consideration it may appear, that the property of labour should be able to over-balance the community of land: for it is labour indeed that puts the difference of value on every thing; and let any one consider what the difference is between an acre of land planted with tobacco or sugar, sown with wheat or barley, and an acre of the same land lying in common, without any husbandry upon it, and he will find, that the improvement of labour makes the far greater part of the value. I think it will be but a very modest computation to say, that of the products of the earth useful to the life of man nine tenths are the effects of labour: nay, if we will rightly estimate things as they come to our use, and cast up the several expences about them, what in them is purely owing to nature, and what to labour, we shall find, that in most of them ninety-nine hundredths are wholly to be put on the account of labour.

Sec. 41. There cannot be a clearer demonstration of any thing, than several nations of the Americans are of this, who are rich in land, and poor in all the comforts of life; whom nature having furnished as liberally as any other people, with the materials of plenty, i.e., a fruitful soil, apt to produce in abundance, what might serve for food, raiment, and delight; yet for want of improving it by labour, have not one hundredth part of the conveniencies we enjoy: and a king of a large and fruitful territory there, feeds, lodges, and is clad worse than a day-labourer in England.

Sec. 42. To make this a little clearer, let us but trace some of the ordinary provisions of life, through their several progresses, before they come to our use, and see how much they receive of their value from human industry. Bread, wine and cloth, are things of daily use, and great plenty; yet notwithstanding, acorns, water and leaves, or skins, must be our bread, drink and cloathing, did not labour furnish us with these more useful commodities: for whatever bread is more worth than acorns, wine than water, and cloth or silk, than leaves, skins or moss, that is wholly owing to labour and industry; the one of these being the food and raiment which unassisted nature furnishes us with; the other, provisions which our industry and pains prepare for us, which how much they exceed the other in value, when any one hath computed, he will then see how much labour makes the far greatest part of the value of things we enjoy in this world: and the ground which produces the materials, is scarce to be reckoned in, as any, or at most, but a very small part of it; so little, that even amongst us, land that is left wholly to nature, that hath no improvement of pasturage, tillage, or planting, is called, as indeed it is, waste; and we shall find the benefit of it amount to little more than nothing.

This shews how much numbers of men are to be preferred to largeness of dominions; and that the increase of lands, and the right employing of them, is the great art of government: and that prince, who shall be so wise and godlike, as by established laws of liberty to secure protection and encouragement to the honest industry of mankind, against the oppression of power and narrowness of party, will quickly be too hard for his neighbours: but this by the by. To return to the argument in hand,

Sec. 43. An acre of land, that bears here twenty bushels of wheat, and another in America, which, with the same husbandry, would do the like, are, without doubt, of the same natural intrinsic value: but yet the benefit mankind receives from the one in a year, is worth 5l. and from the other possibly not worth a penny, if all the profit an Indian received from it were to be valued, and sold here; at least, I may truly say, not one thousandth. It is labour then which puts the greatest part of value upon land, without which it would scarcely be worth any thing: it is to that we owe the greatest part of all its useful products; for all that the straw, bran, bread, of that acre of wheat, is more worth than the product of an acre of as good land, which lies waste, is all the effect of labour: for it is not barely the plough-man's pains, the reaper's and thresher's toil, and the baker's sweat, is to be counted into the bread we eat; the labour of those who broke the oxen, who digged and wrought the iron and stones, who felled and framed the timber employed about the plough, mill, oven, or any other utensils, which are a vast number, requisite to this corn, from its being feed to be sown to its being made bread, must all be charged on the account of labour, and received as an effect of that: nature and the earth furnished only the almost worthless materials, as in themselves. It would be a strange catalogue of things, that industry provided and made use of, about every loaf of bread, before it came to our use, if we could trace them; iron, wood, leather, bark, timber, stone, bricks, coals, lime, cloth, dying drugs, pitch, tar, masts, ropes, and all the materials made use of in the ship, that brought any of the commodities made use of by any of the workmen, to any part of the work; all which it would be almost impossible, at least too long, to reckon up.

Sec. 44. From all which it is evident, that though the things of nature are given in common, yet man, by being master of himself, and proprietor of his own person, and the actions or labour of it, had still in himself the great foundation of property; and that, which made up the great part of what he applied to the support or comfort of his being, when invention and arts had improved the conveniencies of life, was perfectly his own, and did not belong in common to others.

Sec. 45. Thus labour, in the beginning, gave a right of property, wherever any one was pleased to employ it upon what was common, which remained a long while the far greater part, and is yet more than mankind makes use of. Men, at first, for the most part, contented themselves with what unassisted nature offered to their necessities: and though afterwards, in some parts of the world, (where the increase of people and stock, with the use of money, had made land scarce, and so of some value) the several communities settled the bounds of their distinct territories, and by laws within themselves regulated the properties of the private men of their society, and so, by compact and agreement, settled the property which labour and industry began; and the leagues that have been made between several states and kingdoms, either expresly or tacitly disowning all claim and right to the land in the others possession, have, by common consent, given up their pretences to their natural common right, which originally they had to those countries, and so have, by positive agreement, settled a property amongst themselves, in distinct parts and parcels of the earth; yet there are still great tracts of ground to be found, which (the inhabitants thereof not having joined with the rest of mankind, in the consent of the use of their common money) lie waste, and are more than the people who dwell on it do, or can make use of, and so still lie in common; tho' this can scarce happen amongst that part of mankind that have consented to the use of money.

Sec. 46. The greatest part of things really useful to the life of man, and such as the necessity of subsisting made the first commoners of the world look after, as it doth the Americans now, are generally things of short duration; such as, if they are not consumed by use, will decay and perish of themselves: gold, silver and diamonds, are things that fancy or agreement hath put the value on, more than real use, and the necessary support of life. Now of those good things which nature hath provided in common, every one had a right (as hath been said) to as much as he could use, and property in all that he could effect with his labour; all that his industry could extend to, to alter from the state nature had put it in, was his. He that gathered a hundred bushels of acorns or apples, had thereby a property in them, they were his goods as soon as gathered. He was only to look, that he used them before they spoiled, else he took more than his share, and robbed others. And indeed it was a foolish thing, as well as dishonest, to hoard up more than he could make use of. If he gave away a part to any body else, so that it perished not uselessly in his possession, these he also made use of. And if he also bartered away plums, that would have rotted in a week, for nuts that would last good for his eating a whole year, he did no injury; he wasted not the common stock; destroyed no part of the portion of goods that belonged to others, so long as nothing perished uselessly in his hands. Again, if he would give his nuts for a piece of metal, pleased with its colour; or exchange his sheep for shells, or wool for a sparkling pebble or a diamond, and keep those by him all his life he invaded not the right of others, he might heap up as much of these durable things as he pleased; the exceeding of the bounds of his just property not lying in the largeness of his possession, but the perishing of any thing uselessly in it.

Sec. 47. And thus came in the use of money, some lasting thing that men might keep without spoiling, and that by mutual consent men would take in exchange for the truly useful, but perishable supports of life.

Sec. 48. And as different degrees of industry were apt to give men possessions in different proportions, so this invention of money gave them the opportunity to continue and enlarge them: for supposing an island, separate from all possible commerce with the rest of the world, wherein there were but an hundred families, but there were sheep, horses and cows, with other useful animals, wholsome fruits, and land enough for corn for a hundred thousand times as many, but nothing in the island, either because of its commonness, or perishableness, fit to supply the place of money; what reason could any one have there to enlarge his possessions beyond the use of his family, and a plentiful supply to its consumption, either in what their own industry produced, or they could barter for like perishable, useful commodities, with others? Where there is not some thing, both lasting and scarce, and so valuable to be hoarded up, there men will not be apt to enlarge their possessions of land, were it never so rich, never so free for them to take: for I ask, what would a man value ten thousand, or an hundred thousand acres of excellent land, ready cultivated, and well stocked too with cattle, in the middle of the inland parts of America, where he had no hopes of commerce with other parts of the world, to draw money to him by the sale of the product? It would not be worth the enclosing, and we should see him give up again to the wild common of nature, whatever was more than would supply the conveniencies of life to be had there for him and his family.

Sec. 49. Thus in the beginning all the world was America, and more so than that is now; for no such thing as money was any where known. Find out something that hath the use and value of money amongst his neighbours, you shall see the same man will begin presently to enlarge his possessions.

Sec. 50. But since gold and silver, being little useful to the life of man in proportion to food, raiment, and carriage, has its value only from the consent of men, whereof labour yet makes, in great part, the measure, it is plain, that men have agreed to a disproportionate and unequal possession of the earth, they having, by a tacit and voluntary consent, found out, a way how a man may fairly possess more land than he himself can use the product of, by receiving in exchange for the overplus gold and silver, which may be hoarded up without injury to any one; these metals not spoiling or decaying in the hands of the possessor. This partage of things in an inequality of private possessions, men have made practicable out of the bounds of society, and without compact, only by putting a value on gold and silver, and tacitly agreeing in the use of money: for in governments, the laws regulate the right of property, and the possession of land is determined by positive constitutions.

Sec. 51. And thus, I think, it is very easy to conceive, without any difficulty, how labour could at first begin a title of property in the common things of nature, and how the spending it upon our uses bounded it. So that there could then be no reason of quarrelling about title, nor any doubt about the largeness of possession it gave. Right and conveniency went together; for as a man had a right to all he could employ his labour upon, so he had no temptation to labour for more than he could make use of. This left no room for controversy about the title, nor for encroachment on the right of others; what portion a man carved to himself, was easily seen; and it was useless, as well as dishonest, to carve himself too much, or take more than he needed.

—81—

EXCERPTS FROM *AN INQUIRY INTO THE NATURE AND CAUSES OF THE WEALTH OF NATIONS*

Adam Smith

BOOK I, CHAPTER I: OF THE DIVISION OF LABOUR

THE GREATEST IMPROVEMENT IN THE PRODUCTIVE powers of labour, and the greater part of the skill, dexterity, and judgment with which it is any where directed, or applied, seem to have been the effects of the division of labour.

The effects of the division of labour, in the general business of society, will be more easily understood, by considering in what manner it operates in some particular manufactures. It is commonly supposed to be carried furthest in some very trifling ones; not perhaps that it really is carried further in them than in others of more importance: but in those trifling manufactures which are destined to supply the small wants of but a small number of people, the whole number of workmen must necessarily be small; and those employed in every different branch of the work can often be collected into the same workhouse, and placed at once under the view of the spectator. In those great manufactures, on the contrary, which are destined to supply the great wants of the great body of the people, every different branch of the work employs so great a number of workmen, that it is impossible to collect them all into the same workhouse. We can seldom see more, at one time,

than those employed in one single branch. Though in such manufactures, therefore, the work may really be divided into a much greater number of parts, than in those of a more trifling nature, the division is not near so obvious, and has accordingly been much less observed.

To take an example, therefore, from a very trifling manufacture; but one in which the division of labour has been very often taken notice of, the trade of the pin-maker; a workman not educated to this business (which the division of labour has rendered a distinct trade), nor acquainted with the use of the machinery employed in it (to the invention of which the same division of labour has probably given occasion), could scarce, perhaps, with his utmost industry, make one pin in a day, and certainly could not make twenty. But in the way in which this business is now carried on, not only the whole work is a peculiar trade, but it is divided into a number of branches, of which the greater part are likewise peculiar trades. One man draws out the wire, another straights it, a third cuts it, a fourth points it, a fifth grinds it at the top for receiving the head; to make the head requires two or three distinct operations; to put it on, is a peculiar business, to whiten the pins is another; it is even a trade by itself to put them into the paper; and the important business of making a pin is, in this manner, divided into about eighteen distinct operations, which, in some manufactories, are all performed by distinct hands, though in others the same man will sometimes perform two or three of them. I have seen a small manufactory of this kind where ten men only were employed, and where some of them consequently performed two or three distinct operations. But though they were very poor, and therefore but indifferently accommodated with the necessary machinery, they could, when they exerted themselves, make among them about twelve pounds of pins in a day. There are in a pound upwards of four thousand pins of a middling size. Those ten persons, therefore, could make among them upwards of forty-eight thousand pins in a day. Each person, therefore, making a tenth part of forty-eight thousand pins, might be considered as making four thousand eight hundred pins in a day. But if they had all wrought separately and independently, and without any of them having been educated to this peculiar business, they certainly could not each of them have made twenty, perhaps not one pin in a day; that is, certainly, not the two hundred and fortieth, perhaps not the four thousand eight hundredth part of what they are at present capable of performing, in consequence of a proper division and combination of their different operations.

In every other art and manufacture, the effects of the division of labour are similar to what they are in this very trifling one; though, in many of them, the labour can neither be so much sub-divided, nor reduced to so great a simplicity of operation. The division of labour, however, so far as it can be introduced, occasions, in every art, a proportionable increase of the productive powers of labour. The separation of different trades and employments from one another, seems to have taken place, in consequence of this advantage. This separation too is generally carried furthest in those countries which enjoy the highest degree of industry and improvement; what is the work of one man in a rude state of society, being generally that of several in an improved one. In every improved society, the farmer is generally nothing

but a farmer; the manufacturer, nothing but a manufacturer. The labour too which is necessary to produce any one complete manufacture, is almost always divided among a great number of hands. How many different trades are employed in each branch of the linen and woollen manufactures, from the growers of the flax and the wool, to the bleachers and smoothers of the linen, or to the dyers and dressers of the cloth! The nature of agriculture, indeed, does not admit of so many subdivisions of labour, nor of so complete a separation of one business from another, as manufactures. It is impossible to separate so entirely, the business of the grazier from that of the corn-farmer, as the trade of the carpenter is commonly separated from that of the smith. The spinner is almost always a distinct person from the weaver; but the plough-man, the harrower, the sower of the seed, and the reaper of the corn, are often the same. The occasions for those different sorts of labour returning with the different seasons of the year, it is impossible that one man should be constantly employed in any one of them. This impossibility of making so complete and entire a separation of all the different branches of labour employed in agriculture, is perhaps the reason why the improvement of the productive powers of labour in this art, does not always keep pace with their improvement in manufactures. The most opulent nations, indeed, generally excel all their neighbours in agriculture as well as in manufactures; but they are commonly more distinguished by their superiority in the latter than in the former. Their lands are in general better cultivated, and having more labour and expence bestowed upon them, produce more in proportion to the extent and natural fertility of the ground. But this superiority of produce is seldom much more than in proportion to the superiority of labour and expence. In agriculture, the labour of the rich country is not always much more productive than that of the poor; or, at least, it is never so much more productive, as it commonly is in manufactures. The corn of the rich country, therefore, will not always, in the same degree of goodness, come cheaper to market than that of the poor. The corn of Poland, in the same degree of goodness, is as cheap as that of France, notwithstanding the superior opulence and improvement of the latter country. The corn of France is, in the corn provinces, fully as good, and in most years nearly about the same price with the corn of England, though, in opulence and improvement, France is perhaps inferior to England. The corn-lands of England, however, are better cultivated than those of France, and the corn-lands of France are said to be much better cultivated than those of Poland. But though the poor country, notwithstanding the inferiority of its cultivation, can, in some measure, rival the rich in the cheapness and goodness of its corn, it can pretend to no such competition in its manufactures; at least if those manufactures suit the soil, climate, and situation of the rich country. The silks of France are better and cheaper than those of England, because the silk manufacture, at least under the present high duties upon the importation of raw silk, does not so well suit the climate of England as that of France. But the hardware and the coarse woollens of England are beyond all comparison superior to those of France, and much cheaper too in the same degree of goodness. In Poland there are said to be scarce any manufactures of any kind, a few of those coarser household manufactures excepted, without which no country can well subsist.

This great increase of the quantity of work which, in consequence of the division of labour, the same number of people are capable of performing, is owing to three different circumstances; first to the increase of dexterity in every particular workman; secondly, to the saving of the time which is commonly lost in passing from one species of work to another; and lastly, to the invention of a great number of machines which facilitate and abridge labour, and enable one man to do the work of many.

First, the improvement of the dexterity of the workman necessarily increases the quantity of the work he can perform; and the division of labour, by reducing every man's business to some one simple operation, and by making this operation the sole employment of his life, necessarily increases very much the dexterity of the workman. A common smith, who, though accustomed to handle the hammer, has never been used to make nails, if upon some particular occasion he is obliged to attempt it, will scarce, I am assured, be able to make above two or three hundred nails in a day, and those too very bad ones. A smith who has been accustomed to make nails, but whose sole or principal business has not been that of a nailer, can seldom with his utmost diligence make more than eight hundred or a thousand nails in a day. I have seen several boys under twenty years of age who had never exercised any other trade but that of making nails, and who, when they exerted themselves, could make, each of them, upwards of two thousand three hundred nails in a day. The making of a nail, however, is by no means one of the simplest operations. The same person blows the bellows, stirs or mends the fire as there is occasion, heats the iron, and forges every part of the nail: In forging the head too he is obliged to change his tools. The different operations into which the making of a pin, or of a metal button, is subdivided, are all of them much more simple, and the dexterity of the person, of whose life it has been the sole business to perform them, is usually much greater. The rapidity with which some of the operations of those manufactures are performed, exceeds what the human hand could, by those who had never seen them, be supposed capable of acquiring.

Secondly, the advantage which is gained by saving the time commonly lost in passing from one sort of work to another, is much greater than we should at first view be apt to imagine it. It is impossible to pass very quickly from one kind of work to another; that is carried on in a different place, and with quite different tools. A country weaver, who cultivates a small farm, must lose a good deal of time in passing from his loom to the field, and from the field to his loom. When the two trades can be carried on in the same workhouse, the loss of time is no doubt much less. It is even in this case, however, very considerable. A man commonly saunters a little in turning his hand from one sort of employment to another. When he first begins the new work he is seldom very keen and hearty; his mind, as they say, does not go to it, and for some time he rather trifles than applies to good purpose. The habit of sauntering and of indolent careless application, which is naturally, or rather necessarily acquired by every country workman who is obliged to change his work and his tools every half hour, and to apply his hand in twenty different ways almost every day of his life; renders him almost always slothful and lazy, and incapable of any vigorous application even on the most pressing occasions. Independent, therefore, of his deficiency in point of dexterity, this cause alone must always reduce considerably the quantity of work which he is capable of performing.

Thirdly, and lastly, every body must be sensible how much labour is facilitated and abridged by the application of proper machinery. It is unnecessary to give any example. I shall only observe, therefore, that the invention of all those machines by which labour is so much facilitated and abridged, seems to have been originally owing to the division of labour. Men are much more likely to discover easier and readier methods of attaining any object, when the whole attention of their minds is directed towards that single object, than when it is dissipated among a great variety of things. But in consequence of the division of labour, the whole of every man's attention comes naturally to be directed towards some one very simple object. It is naturally to be expected, therefore, that some one or other of those who are employed in each partic- ular branch of labour should soon find out easier and readier methods of performing their own particular work, wherever the nature of it admits of such improvement. A great part of the machines made use of in those manufactures in which labour is most subdivided, were originally the inventions of common workmen, who, being each of them employed in some very simple operation, naturally turned their thoughts towards finding out easier and readier methods of performing it. Whoever has been much accustomed to visit such manu- factures, must frequently have been shewn very pretty machines, which were the inventions of such workmen, in order to facilitate and quicken their own particular part of the work. In the first fire- engines, a boy was constantly employed to open and shut alternately the communication between the boiler and the cylinder, according as the piston either ascended or descended. One of those boys, who loved to play with his companions, observed that, by tying a string from the handle of the valve which opened this communication, to another part of the machine, the valve would open and shut without his assistance, and leave him at liberty to divert himself with his play-fellows. One of the greatest improvements that has been made upon this machine, since it was first invented, was in this manner the discovery of a boy who wanted to save his own labour.

All the improvements in machinery, however, have by no means been the inventions of those who had occasion to use the machines. Many improvements have been made by the ingenuity of the makers of the machines, when to make them became the business of a peculiar trade; and some by that of those who are called philos- ophers or men of speculation, whose trade it is not to do any thing, but to observe every thing; and who, upon that account, are often capable of combining together the powers of the most distant and dissimilar objects. In the progress of society, philosophy or speculation becomes, like every other employment, the principal or sole trade and occupation of a particular class of citizens. Like every other employment too, it is subdivided into a great number of different branches, each of which affords occupation to a peculiar tribe or class of philosophers; and this subdivision of employment in philosophy, as well as in every other business, improves dexterity, and saves time. Each individual becomes more expert in his own peculiar branch, more work is done upon the whole, and the quan- tity of science is considerably increased by it.

It is the great multiplication of the productions of all the different arts, in consequence of the divi- sion of labour, which occasions, in a well-governed society, that universal opulence which extends itself to the lowest ranks of the people. Every workman has a great quantity of his own work to dispose of beyond what he himself has occasion for; and every other workman being exactly in the same situation, he is enabled to exchange a great quantity of his own goods for a great quantity, or, what comes to the same thing, for the price of a great quantity of theirs. He supplies them abundantly with what they have occasion for, and they accommodate him as amply with what he has occasion for, and a general plenty diffuses itself through all the different ranks of the society.

Observe the accommodation of the most common artificer or day-labourer in a civilized and thriving country, and you will perceive that the number of people of whose industry a part, though but a small part, has been employed in procuring him this accommodation, exceeds all computation. The woollen coat, for example, which covers the day-labourer, as coarse and rough as it may appear, is the produce of the joint labour of a great multitude of workmen. The shepherd, the sorter of the wool, the wool-comber or carder, the dyer, the scribbler, the spinner, the weaver, the fuller, the dresser, with many others, must all join their different arts in order to complete even this homely production. How many merchants and carriers, besides, must have been employed in transporting the materials from some of those workmen to others who often live in a very distant part of the country! how much commerce and navigation in particular, how many ship-builders, sailors, sail-makers, rope-makers, must have been employed in order to bring together the different drugs made use of by the dyer, which often come from the remotest corners of the world! What a variety of labour too is necessary in order to produce the tools of the meanest of those workmen! To say nothing of such complicated machines as the ship of the sailor, the mill of the fuller, or even the loom of the weaver, let us consider only what a variety of labour is requisite in order to form that very simple machine, the shears with which the shepherd clips the wool. The miner, the builder of the furnace for smelting the ore, the feller of the timber, the burner of the charcoal to be made use of in the smelting-house, the brick-maker, the brick-layer, the workmen who attend the furnace, the mill-wright, the forger, the smith, must all of them join their different arts in order to produce them. Were we to examine, in the same manner, all the different parts of his dress and household furniture, the coarse linen shirt which he wears next his skin, the shoes which cover his feet, the bed which he lies on, and all the different parts which compose it, the kitchen-grate at which he prepares his victuals, the coals which he makes use of for that purpose, dug from the bowels of the earth, and brought to him perhaps by a long sea and a long land carriage, all the other utensils of his kitchen, all the furniture of his table, the knives and forks, the earthen or pewter plates upon which he serves up and divides his victuals, the different hands employed in preparing his bread and his beer, the glass window which lets in the heat and the light, and keeps out the wind and the rain, with all the knowledge and art requisite for preparing that beautiful and happy invention, without which these northern parts of the world could scarce have afforded a very comfortable habitation, together with the tools of all the different workmen employed in producing those different conveniencies; if we examine, I say, all these things, and consider what a variety of labour is employed about each of them, we shall be sensible that without the assistance and co-operation of many thousands, the very meanest person in a civilized country could not be provided, even according to what we very falsely imagine, the easy and simple manner in which he is commonly accommodated. Compared, indeed, with the more extravagant luxury of the great, his accommodation must no doubt appear extremely simple and easy; and yet it may be true, perhaps, that the accommodation of an European prince does not always so much exceed that of an industrious and frugal peasant, as the accommodation of the latter exceeds that of many an African king, the absolute master of the lives and liberties of ten thousand naked savages.

BOOK I, CHAPTER II: OF THE PRINCIPLE WHICH GIVES OCCASION TO THE DIVISION OF LABOUR

This division of labour, from which so many advantages are derived, is not originally the effect of any human wisdom, which foresees and intends that general opulence to which it gives occasion. It is the necessary, though very slow and gradual, consequence of a certain propensity in human nature which has in view no such extensive utility; the propensity to truck, barter, and exchange one thing for another.

Whether this propensity be one of those original principles in human nature, of which no further account can be given; or whether, as seems more probable, it be the necessary consequence of the faculties of reason and speech, it belongs not to our present subject to enquire. It is common to all men, and to be found in no other race of animals, which seem to know neither this nor any other species of contracts. Two greyhounds, in running down the same hare, have sometimes the appearance of acting in some sort of concert. Each turns her [the hare being hunted] towards his companion, or endeavours to intercept her when his companion turns her towards himself. This, however, is not the effect of any contract, but of the accidental concurrence of their passions in the same object at that particular time. Nobody ever saw a dog make a fair and deliberate exchange of one bone for another with another dog. Nobody ever saw one animal by its gestures and natural cries signify to another, this is mine, that yours; I am willing to give this for that. When an animal wants to obtain something either of a man or of another animal, it has no other means of persuasion but to gain the favour of those whose service it requires. A puppy fawns upon its dam, and a spaniel endeavours by a thousand attractions to engage the attention of its master who is at dinner, when it wants to be fed by him. Man sometimes uses the same arts with his brethren, and when he has no other means of engaging them to act according to his inclinations, endeavours by every servile and fawning attention to obtain their good will. He has not time, however, to do this upon every occasion. In civilized society he stands at all times in need of the cooperation and assistance of great multitudes, while his whole life is scarce sufficient to gain the friendship of a few persons. In almost every other race of animals each individual, when it is grown up to maturity, is entirely independent, and in its natural state has occasion for the assistance of no other living creature. But man has almost constant occasion for the help of his brethren, and it is in vain for him to expect it from their benevolence only. He will be more likely to prevail if he can interest their self-love in his favour, and show them that it is for their own advantage to do for him what he requires of them. Whoever offers to another a bargain of any kind, proposes to do this. Give me that which I want, and you shall have this which you want, is the meaning of every such offer; and it is in this manner that we obtain from one another the far greater part of those good offices which we stand in need of. It is not from the benevolence of the butcher, the brewer, or the baker, that we expect our dinner, but from their regard to their own interest. We address ourselves, not to their humanity but to their self-love, and never talk to them of our own necessities but of their advantages. Nobody but a beggar chuses to depend chiefly upon the benevolence of his fellow-citizens. Even a beggar does not depend upon it entirely. The charity of well-disposed people, indeed, supplies him with the whole fund of his subsistence. But though this principle ultimately provides him with all the necessaries of life which he has occasion for, it neither does nor can provide him with them as he has occasion for them. The greater part of his occasional wants are supplied in the same manner as those of other people, by treaty, by barter, and by purchase. With the money which one man gives him he purchases food. The old cloaths which another bestows upon him he exchanges for other old cloaths which suit him better, or for lodging, or for food, or for money, with which he can buy either food, cloaths, or lodging, as he has occasion.

As it is by treaty, by barter, and by purchase, that we obtain from one another the greater part of those mutual good offices which we stand in need of, so it is this same trucking disposition which originally gives occasion to the division of labour. In a tribe of hunters or shepherds a particular person makes bows and arrows, for example, with more readiness and dexterity than any other. He frequently exchanges them for cattle or for venison with his companions; and he finds at last that he can in this manner get more cattle and venison, than if he himself went to the field to catch them. From a regard to his own interest, therefore, the making of bows and arrows grows to be his chief business, and he becomes a sort of armourer. Another excels in making the frames and covers of their little huts or moveable houses. He is accustomed to be of use in this way to his neighbours, who reward him in the same manner with cattle and with venison, till at last he finds it his interest to dedicate himself entirely to this employment, and to become a sort of house-carpenter. In the same manner a third becomes a smith or a brazier; a fourth a tanner or dresser of hides or skins, the principal part of the clothing of savages. And thus the certainty of being able to exchange all that surplus part of the produce of his own labour, which is over and above his own consumption, for such parts of the produce of other men's labour as he may have occasion for, encourages every man to apply himself to a particular occupation, and to cultivate and bring to perfection whatever talent or genius he may possess for that particular species of business.

The difference of natural talents in different men is, in reality, much less than we are aware of; and the very different genius which appears to distinguish men of different professions, when grown up to maturity, is not upon many occasions so much the cause, as the effect of the division of labour. The difference between the most dissimilar characters, between a philosopher and a common street porter, for example, seems to arise not so much from nature, as from habit, custom, and education. When they came into the world, and for the first six or eight years of their existence, they were perhaps, very much alike, and neither their parents nor playfellows could perceive any remarkable difference. About that age, or soon after, they come to be employed in very different occupations. The difference of talents comes then to be taken notice of, and widens by degrees, till at last the vanity of the philosopher is willing to acknowledge scarce any resemblance. But without the disposition to truck, barter, and exchange, every man must have procured to himself every necessary and conveniency of life which he wanted. All must have had the same duties to perform, and the same work to do, and there could have been no such difference of employment as could alone give occasion to any great difference of talents.

As it is this disposition which forms that difference of talents, so remarkable among men of different professions, so it is this same disposition which renders that difference useful. Many tribes of animals acknowledged to be all of the same species, derive from nature a much more remarkable distinction of genius, than what, antecedent to custom and education, appears to take place among men. By nature a philosopher is not in genius and disposition half so different from a street porter, as a mastiff is from a greyhound, or a greyhound from a spaniel, or this last from a shepherd's dog. Those different tribes of animals, however, though all of the same species, are of scarce any use to one another. The strength of the mastiff is not in the least supported either by the swiftness of the greyhound, or by the sagacity of the spaniel, or by the docility of the shepherd's dog. The effects of those different geniuses and talents, for want of the power or disposition to barter and exchange, cannot be brought into a common stock, and do not in the least contribute to the better accommodation and conveniency of the species. Each animal is still obliged to support and defend itself, separately and independently, and derives no sort of advantage from that variety of talents with which nature has distinguished its fellows. Among men, on the contrary, the most dissimilar geniuses are of use to one another; the different produces of their respective talents, by the general disposition to truck, barter, and exchange, being brought, as it were, into a common stock, where every man may purchase whatever part of the produce of other men's talents he has occasion for.

BOOK IV, CHAPTER II: OF RESTRAINTS UPON THE IMPORTATION FROM FOREIGN COUNTRIES OF SUCH GOODS AS CAN BE PRODUCED AT HOME

... Every individual is continually exerting himself to find out the most advantageous employment for whatever capital he can command. It is his own advantage, indeed, and not that of the society, which he has in view. But the study of his own advantage naturally, or rather necessarily, leads him to prefer that employment which is most advantageous to the society ...

As every individual, therefore, endeavours as much as he can both to employ his capital in the support of domestic industry, and so to direct that industry that its produce may be of the greatest value; every individual necessarily labours to render the annual revenue of the society as great as he can. He generally, indeed, neither intends to promote the public interest, nor knows how much he is promoting it. By preferring the support of domestic to that of foreign industry, he intends only his own security; and by directing that industry in such a manner as its produce may be of the greatest value, he intends only his own gain, and he is in this, as in many other cases, led by an invisible hand to promote an end which was no part of his intention. Nor is it always the worse for the society that it was no part of it. By pursuing his own interest he frequently promotes that of the society more effectually than when he really intends to promote it. I have never known much good done by those who affected to trade for the public good. It is an affectation, indeed, not very common among merchants, and very few words need be employed in dissuading them from it.

—82—
ESTRANGED LABOR

Karl Marx

WE HAVE STARTED OUT FROM THE PREMISES OF political economy. We have accepted its language and its laws. We presupposed private property; the separation of labor, capital, and land, and likewise of wages, profit, and capital; the division of labor; competition; the conception of exchange value, etc. From political economy itself, using its own words, we have shown that the worker sinks to the level of a commodity, and moreover the most wretched commodity of all; that the misery of the worker is in inverse proportion to the power and volume of his production; that the necessary consequence of competition is the accumulation of capital in a few hands and hence the restoration of monopoly in a more terrible form; and that, finally, the distinction between capitalist and landlord, between agricultural worker and industrial worker, disappears and the whole of society must split into the two classes of *property owners* and propertyless *workers*.

Political economy proceeds from the fact of private property. It does not explain it. It grasps the *material* process of private property, the process through which it actually passes, in general and abstract formulae which it then takes as *laws*. It does not *Comprehend* these laws—*i.e.*, it does not show how they arise from the nature of private property. Political economy fails to explain the reason for the division between labor and capital. For example, when it defines the relation of wages to profit, it takes the interests of the capitalists as the basis of its analysis—*i.e.*, it assumes what it is supposed to explain. Similarly, competition is frequently brought into the argument and explained in terms of external circumstances.

Political economy teaches us nothing about the extent to which these external and apparently accidental circumstances are only the expression of a necessary development. We have seen how exchange itself appears to political economy as an accidental fact. The only wheels which political economy sets in motion are *greed*, and the *war of the avaricious—Competition*.

Precisely because political economy fails to grasp the interconnections within the movement, it was possible to oppose, for example, the doctrine of competition to the doctrine of monopoly, the doctrine of craft freedom to the doctrine of the guild, and the doctrine of the division of landed property to the doctrine of the great estate; for competition, craft freedom, and division of landed property were developed and conceived only as accidental, deliberate, violent consequences of monopoly, of the guilds, and of feudal property, and not as their necessary, inevitable, and natural consequences.

We now have to grasp the essential connection between private property, greed, the separation of labor, capital and landed property, exchange and competition, value and the devaluation [*Entwertung*] of man, monopoly, and competition, etc.—the connection between this entire system of estrangement [*Entfremdung*] and the *money* system.

We must avoid repeating the mistake of the political economist, who bases his explanations on some imaginary primordial condition. Such a primordial condition explains nothing. It simply pushes the question into the grey and nebulous distance. It assumes as facts and events what it is supposed to deduce—namely, the necessary relationships between two things, between, for example, the division of labor and exchange. Similarly, theology explains the origin of evil by the fall of Man—*i.e.*, it assumes as a fact in the form of history what it should explain.

We shall start out from a *present-day* economic fact.

The worker becomes poorer the more wealth he produces, the more his production increases in power and extent. The worker becomes an ever cheaper commodity the more commodities he produces. The *devaluation* of the human world grows in direct proportion to the *increase in value* of the world of things. Labor not only produces commodities; it also produces itself and the workers as a *commodity* and it does so in the same proportion in which it produces commodities in general.

This fact simply means that the object that labor produces, it product, stands opposed to it as *something alien*, as a power independent of the producer. The product of labor is labor embodied and made material in an object, it is the *objectification* of labor. The realization of labor is its objectification. In the sphere of political economy, this realization of labor appears as a *loss of reality* for the worker, objectification as loss of and bondage to the object, and appropriation as estrangement, as *alienation* [*Entausserung*].

So much does the realization of labor appear as loss of reality that the worker loses his reality to the point of dying of starvation. So much does objectification appear as loss of the object that the worker is robbed of the objects he needs most not only for life but also for work. Work itself becomes an object which he can only obtain through an enormous effort and with spasmodic interruptions. So much does the appropriation of the object appear as estrangement that the more objects the worker produces the fewer can he possess and the more he falls under the domination of his product, of capital.

All these consequences are contained in this characteristic, that the worker is related to the product of labor as to an *alien* object. For it is clear that, according to this premise, the more the worker exerts himself in his work, the more powerful the alien, objective world becomes which he brings into being over against himself, the poorer he and his inner world become, and the less they belong to him. It is the same in religion. The more man puts into God, the less he retains within himself. The worker places his life in the object; but now it no longer belongs to him, but to the object. The greater his activity, therefore, the fewer objects the worker possesses. What the product of his labor is, he is not. Therefore, the greater this product, the less is he himself. The externalization [*Entausserung*] of the worker in his product means not only that his labor becomes an object, an external existence, but that it exists *outside* him, independently of him and alien to him, and begins to confront him as an autonomous power; that the life which he has bestowed on the object confronts him as hostile and alien.

Let us not take a closer look at objectification, at the production of the worker, and the estrangement, the loss of the object, of his product, that this entails.

The workers can create nothing without nature, without the sensuous external world. It is the material in which his labor realizes itself, in which it is active and from which, and by means of which, it produces.

But just as nature provides labor with the means of life, in the sense of labor cannot live without objects on which to exercise itself, so also it provides the means of life in the narrower sense, namely the means of physical subsistence of the worker.

The more the worker appropriates the external world, sensuous nature, through his labor, the more he deprives himself of the means of life in two respects: firstly, the sensuous external world becomes less and less an object belonging to his labor, a means of life of his labor; and, secondly, it becomes less and less a means of life in the immediate sense, a means for the physical subsistence of the worker.

In these two respects, then, the worker becomes a slave of his object; firstly, in that he receives an object of labor, *i.e.*, he receives work, and, secondly, in that he receives means of subsistence. Firstly, then, so that he can exist as a worker, and secondly as a physical subject. The culmination of this slavery is that it is only as a worker that he can maintain himself as a physical subject and only as a physical subject that he is a worker.

(The estrangement of the worker in his object is expressed according to the laws of political economy in the following way:

the more the worker produces, the less he has to consume;
the more value he creates, the more worthless he becomes;
the more his product is shaped, the more misshapen the worker;
the more civilized his object, the more barbarous the worker;
the more powerful the work, the more powerless the worker;
the more intelligent the work, the duller the worker and the more he becomes a slave of nature.)

Political economy conceals the estrangement in the nature of labor by ignoring the direct relationship between the worker (labor) and production. It is true that labor produces marvels for the rich, but it produces privation for the worker. It produces palaces, but hovels for the worker. It produces beauty, but deformity for the worker. It replaces labor by machines, but it casts some of the workers back into barbarous forms of labor and turns others into machines. It produces intelligence, but it produces idiocy and cretinism for the worker.

The direct relationship of labor to its products is the relationship of the worker to the objects of his production. The relationship of the rich man to the objects of production and to production itself is only a *consequence* of this first relationship, and confirms it. Later, we shall consider this second aspect. Therefore, when we ask what is the essential relationship of labor, we are asking about the relationship of the worker to production.

Up to now, we have considered the estrangement, the alienation of the worker, only from one aspect—*i.e.*, his relationship to the products of his labor. But estrangement manifests itself not only in the result, but also in the act of production, within the activity of production itself. How could the product of the worker's activity confront him as something alien if it were not for the fact that in the act of production he was estranging himself from himself? After all, the product is simply the resume of the activity, of the production. So if the product of labor is alienation, production itself must be active alienation, the alienation of activity, the activity of alienation. The estrangement of the object of labor merely summarizes the estrangement, the alienation in the activity of labor itself.

What constitutes the alienation of labor?

Firstly, the fact that labor is external to the worker—*i.e.*, does not belong to his essential being; that he, therefore, does not confirm himself in his work, but denies himself, feels miserable and not happy, does not develop free mental and physical energy, but mortifies his flesh and ruins his mind. Hence, the worker feels himself only when he is not working; when he is working, he does not feel himself. He is at home when he is not working, and not at home when he is working. His labor is, therefore, not voluntary but forced, it is *forced labor*. It is, therefore, not the satisfaction of a need but a mere *means* to satisfy needs outside itself. Its alien character is clearly demonstrated by the fact that as soon as no physical or other compulsion exists, it is shunned like the plague. External labor, labor in which man alienates himself, is a labor of self-sacrifice, of mortification. Finally, the external character of labor for the worker is demonstrated by the fact that it belongs not to him but to another, and that in it he belongs not to himself but to another. Just as in religion the spontaneous activity of the human imagination, the human brain, and the human heart, detaches itself from the individual and reappears as the alien activity of a god or of a devil, so the activity of the worker is not his own spontaneous activity. It belongs to another, it is a loss of his self.

The result is that man (the worker) feels that he is acting freely only in his animal functions—eating, drinking, and procreating, or at most in his dwelling and adornment—while in his human functions, he is nothing more than animal.

It is true that eating, drinking, and procreating, etc., are also genuine human functions. However, when abstracted from other aspects of human activity, and turned into final and exclusive ends, they are animal.

We have considered the act of estrangement of practical human activity, of labor, from two aspects: (1) the relationship of the worker to the product of labor as an alien object that has power over him. The relationship is, at the same time, the relationship to the sensuous external world, to natural objects, as an alien world confronting him, in hostile opposition. (2) The relationship of labor to the *act of production* within labor. This relationship is the relationship of the worker to his own activity as something which is alien and does not belong to him, activity as passivity [*Leiden*], power as impotence, procreation as emasculation, the worker's own physical and mental energy, his personal life—for what is life but activity?—as an activity directed against himself, which is independent of him and does not belong to him. Self-estrangement, as compared with the estrangement of the object [*Sache*] mentioned above.

We now have to derive a third feature of estranged labor from the two we have already examined.

Man is a species-being, not only because he practically and theoretically makes the species—both his own and those of other things—his object, but also—and this is simply another way of saying the same thing—because he looks upon himself as the present, living species, because he looks upon himself as a universal and therefore free being.

Species-life, both for man and for animals, consists physically in the fact that man, like animals, lives from inorganic nature; and because man

is more universal than animals, so too is the area of inorganic nature from which he lives more universal. Just as plants, animals, stones, air, light, etc., theoretically form a part of human consciousness, partly as objects of science and partly as objects of art—his spiritual inorganic nature, his spiritual means of life, which he must first prepare before he can enjoy and digest them—so, too, in practice they form a part of human life and human activity. In a physical sense, man lives only from these natural products, whether in the form of nourishment, heating, clothing, shelter, etc. The universality of man manifests itself in practice in that universality which makes the whole of nature his inorganic body, (1) as a direct means of life and (2) as the matter, the object, and the tool of his life activity. Nature is man's inorganic body—that is to say, nature insofar as it is not the human body. Man lives from nature—*i.e.*, nature is his body—and he must maintain a continuing dialogue with it if he is not to die. To say that man's physical and mental life is linked to nature simply means that nature is linked to itself, for man is a part of nature.

Estranged labor not only (1) estranges nature from man and (2) estranges man from himself, from his own function, from his vital activity; because of this, it also estranges man from his species. It turns his species-life into a means for his individual life. Firstly, it estranges species-life and individual life, and, secondly, it turns the latter, in its abstract form, into the purpose of the former, also in its abstract and estranged form.

For in the first place labor, life activity, productive life itself, appears to man only as a means for the satisfaction of a need, the need to preserve physical existence. But productive life is species-life. It is life-producing life. The whole character of a species, its species-character, resides in the nature of its life activity, and free conscious activity constitutes the species-character of man. Life appears only as a means of life.

The animal is immediately one with its life activity. It is not distinct from that activity; it is that activity. Man makes his life activity itself an object of his will and consciousness. He has conscious life activity. It is not a determination with which he directly merges. Conscious life activity directly distinguishes man from animal life activity. Only because of that is he a species-being. Or, rather, he is a conscious being—*i.e.*, his own life is an object for him, only because he is a species-being. Only because of that is his activity free activity. Estranged labor reverses the relationship so that man, just because he is a conscious being, makes his life activity, his being [*Wesen*], a mere means for his existence.

The practical creation of an *objective world*, the fashioning of inorganic nature, is proof that man is a conscious species-being—*i.e.*, a being which treats the species as its own essential being or itself as a species-being. It is true that animals also produce. They build nests and dwelling, like the bee, the beaver, the ant, etc. But they produce only their own immediate needs or those of their young; they produce only when immediate physical need compels them to do so, while man produces even when he is free from physical need and truly produces only in freedom from such need; they produce only themselves, while man reproduces the whole of nature; their products belong immediately to their physical bodies, while man freely confronts his own product. Animals produce only according to the standards and needs of the species to which they belong, while man is capable of producing according to the standards of every species and of applying to each object its inherent standard; hence, man also produces in accordance with the laws of beauty.

It is, therefore, in his fashioning of the objective that man really proves himself to be a species-being. Such production is his active species-life. Through it, nature appears as *his* work and his reality. The object of labor is, therefore, the objectification of the species-life of man: for man produces himself not only intellectually, in his consciousness, but actively and actually, and he can therefore contemplate himself in a world he himself has created. In tearing away the object of his production from man, estranged labor therefore tears away from him his species-life, his true

species-objectivity, and transforms his advantage over animals into the disadvantage that his inorganic body, nature, is taken from him.

In the same way as estranged labor reduces spontaneous and free activity to a means, it makes man's species-life a means of his physical existence.

Consciousness, which man has from his species, is transformed through estrangement so that species-life becomes a means for him.

(3) Estranged labor, therefore, turns man's species-being—both nature and his intellectual species-power—into a being alien to him and a means of his individual existence. It estranges man from his own body, from nature as it exists outside him, from his spiritual essence [*Wesen*], his human existence.

(4) An immediate consequence of man's estrangement from the product of his labor, his life activity, his species-being, is the estrangement of man from man. When man confronts himself, he also confronts other men. What is true of man's relationship to his labor, to the product of his labor, and to himself, is also true of his relationship to other men, and to the labor and the object of the labor of other men.

In general, the proposition that man is estranged from his species-being means that each man is estranged from the others and that all are estranged from man's essence.

Man's estrangement, like all relationships of man to himself, is realized and expressed only in man's relationship to other men.

In the relationship of estranged labor, each man therefore regards the other in accordance with the standard and the situation in which he as a worker finds himself.

We started out from an economic fact, the estrangement of the worker and of his production. We gave this fact conceptual form: estranged, alienated labor. We have analyzed this concept, and in so doing merely analyzed an economic fact.

Let us now go on to see how the concept of estranged, alienated labor must express and present itself in reality.

If the product of labor is alien to me, and confronts me as an alien power, to whom does it then belong?

To a being *other* than me.

Who is this being?

The gods? It is true that in early times most production—*e.g.*, temple building, etc., in Egypt, India, and Mexico—was in the service of the gods, just as the product belonged to the gods. But the gods alone were never the masters of labor. The same is true of nature. And what a paradox it would be if the more man subjugates nature through his labor and the more divine miracles are made superfluous by the miracles of industry, the more he is forced to forgo the joy or production and the enjoyment of the product out of deference to these powers.

The alien being to whom labor and the product of labor belong, in whose service labor is performed, and for whose enjoyment the product of labor is created, can be none other than man himself.

If the product of labor does not belong to the worker, and if it confronts him as an alien power, this is only possible because it belongs to a man other than the worker. If his activity is a torment for him, it must provide pleasure and enjoyment for someone else. Not the gods, not nature, but only man himself can be this alien power over men.

Consider the above proposition that the relationship of man to himself becomes objective and real for him only through his relationship to other men. If, therefore, he regards the product of his labor, his objectified labor, as an alien, hostile, and powerful object which is independent of him, then his relationship to that object is such that another man—alien, hostile, powerful, and independent of him—is its master. If he relates to his own activity as unfree activity, then he relates to it as activity in the service, under the rule, coercion, and yoke of another man.

Every self-estrangement of man from himself and nature is manifested in the relationship he sets up between other men and himself and nature. Thus, religious self-estrangement is necessarily manifested in the relationship between layman and priest, or, since we are dealing here with the spiritual world, between layman and mediator, etc. In the practical, real world, self-estrangement can manifest itself only in the practical, real relationship to other men. The medium through which estrangement progresses is itself a practical one. So through estranged labor man not only produces his relationship to the object and to the act of production as to alien and hostile powers; he also produces the relationship in which other men stand to his production and product, and the relationship in which he stands to these other men. Just as he creates his own production as a loss of reality, a punishment, and his own product as a loss, a product which does not belong to him, so he creates the domination of the non-producer over production and its product. Just as he estranges from himself his own activity, so he confers upon the stranger and activity which does not belong to him.

Up to now, we have considered the relationship only from the side of the worker. Later on, we shall consider it from the side of the non-worker.

Thus, through estranged, alienated labor, the worker creates the relationship of another man, who is alien to labor and stands outside it, to that labor. The relation of the worker to labor creates the relation of the capitalist—or whatever other word one chooses for the master of labor—to that labor. Private property is therefore the product, result, and necessary consequence of alienated labor, of the external relation of the worker to nature and to himself.

Private property thus derives from an analysis of the concept of alienated labor—*i.e.*, alienated man, estranged labor, estranged life, estranged man.

It is true that we took the concept of alienated labor (alienated life) from political economy as a result of the movement of private property. But it is clear from an analysis of this concept that, although private property appears as the basis and cause of alienated labor, it is in fact its consequence, just as the gods were originally not the cause but the effect of the confusion in men's minds. Later, however, this relationship becomes reciprocal.

It is only when the development of private property reaches its ultimate point of culmination that this, its secret, re-emerges; namely, that is (a) the product of alienated labor, and (b) the means through which labor is alienated, the realization of this alienation.

This development throws light upon a number of hitherto unresolved controversies.

(1) Political economy starts out from labor as the real soul of production and yet gives nothing to labor and everything to private property. Proudhon has dealt with this contradiction by deciding for labor and against private property [see his 1840 pamphlet, *Qu'est-ce que la propriété?*]. But we have seen that this apparent contradiction is the contradiction of estranged labor with itself and that political economy has merely formulated laws of estranged labor.

It, therefore, follows for us that wages and private property are identical: for there the product, the object of labor, pays for the labor itself, wages are only a necessary consequence of the estrangement of labor; similarly, where wages are concerned, labor appears not as an end in itself but as the servant of wages. We intend to deal with this point in more detail later on: for the present we shall merely draw a few conclusions.

An enforced rise in wages (disregarding all other difficulties, including the fact that such an anomalous situation could only be prolonged by force) would therefore be nothing more than better pay for slaves and would not mean an increase in human significance or dignity for either the worker or the labor.

Even the equality of wages, which Proudhon demands, would merely transform the relation of the present-day worker to his work into the relation of all men to work. Society would then be conceived as an abstract capitalist.

Wages are an immediate consequence of estranged labor, and estranged labor is the immediate cause of private property. If the one falls, then the other must fall too.

(2) It further follows from the relation of estranged labor to private property that the emancipation of society from private property, etc., from servitude, is expressed in the political form of the emancipation of the workers. This is not because it is only a question of their emancipation, but because in their emancipation is contained universal human emancipation. The reason for this universality is that the whole of human servitude is involved in the relation of the worker to production, and all relations of servitude are nothing but modifications and consequences of this relation.

Just as we have arrived at the concept of private property through an analysis of the concept of estranged, alienated labor, so with the help of these two factors it is possible to evolve all economic categories, and in each of these categories—*e.g.,* trade, competition, capital, money—we shall identify only a particular and developed expression of these basic constituents.

But, before we go on to consider this configuration, let us try to solve two further problems.

(1) We have to determine the general nature of private property, as it has arisen out of estranged labor, in its relation to truly human and social property.

(2) We have taken the estrangement of labor, its alienation, as a fact and we have analyzed that fact. How, we now ask, does man come to alienate his labor, to estrange it? How is this estrangement founded in the nature of human development? We have already gone a long way towards solving this problem by transforming the question of the origin of private property into the question of the relationship of alienated labor to the course of human development. For, in speaking of private property, one imagines that one is dealing with something external to man. In speaking of labor, one is dealing immediately with man himself. This new way of formulating the problem already contains its solution.

As to (1): The general nature of private property and its relationship to truly human property.

Alienated labor has resolved itself for us into two component parts, which mutually condition one another, or which are merely different expressions of one and the same relationship. Appropriation appears as estrangement, as alienation; and alienation appears as appropriation, estrangement as true admission to citizenship.

We have considered the one aspect, alienated labor in relation to the worker himself—*i.e.,* the relation of alienated labor to itself. And as product, as necessary consequence of this relationship, we have found the property relation of the non-worker to the worker and to labor. Private property as the material, summarized expression of alienated labor embraces both relations—the relation of the worker to labor and to the product of his labor and the non-workers, and the relation of the non-worker to the worker and to the product of his labor.

We have already seen that, in relation to the worker who appropriates nature through his labor, appropriation appears as estrangement, self-activity as activity for another and of another, vitality as a sacrifice of life, production of an object as loss of that object to an alien power, to an *alien* man. Let us now consider the relation between this man, who is *alien* to labor and to the worker, and the worker, labor, and the object of labor.

The first thing to point out is that everything which appears for the worker as an activity of alienation, of estrangement, appears for the non-worker as a situation of alienation, of estrangement.

Secondly, the real, practical attitude of the worker in production and to the product (as a state of mind) appears for the non-worker who confronts him as a theoretical attitude.

Thirdly, the non-worker does everything against the worker which the worker does against himself, but he does not do against himself what he does against the worker.

Let us take a closer look at these three relationships.

—83—
THE IDEA AND IDEAL
OF CAPITALISM

Gerald Gaus

1. CAPITALISM, BUSINESS AND ETHICS

CONSIDER A STYLIZED CONTRAST BETWEEN medical and business ethics. Both fields of applied ethics focus on a profession whose activities are basic to human welfare. Both enquire into obligations of professionals, and the relations between goals intrinsic to the profession and ethical duties to others and to the society. I am struck, however, by a fundamental difference: whereas medical ethics takes place against a background of almost universal consensus that the practice of medicine is admirable and morally praiseworthy, the business profession is embedded within the framework of firms in a capitalist market economy, and for the last century and a half there has been sustained debate about the moral and economic justifiability of such an economy. To be sure, even under socialism there might be an "ethics of socialist managers," and there would be some overlap between such an ethic and contemporary business ethics. Nevertheless, many of the characteristic problems of business ethics—e.g., what are the obligations of a corporation to its shareholders?—arise only in the context of a private property-based market economy.

This raises a deep problem for business ethics: can one develop an account of ethical practices for an activity (i.e., business) while ignoring that the context in which this activity occurs (i.e., capitalism) is morally controversial? It is as if the work in medical ethics proceeded in the midst of widespread disagreement whether medicine was a good thing. Another way of thinking about the problem is: if one teaches business ethics, does this commit you to accepting that business can be ethical? And doesn't this commit you to accepting that capitalism is justifiable? I suspect that this is a serious problem for many teachers of business ethics. Many were trained in academic philosophy, and within academic philosophy there are many who think—or at least suspect—that capitalism is basically unjust, or perhaps that only a greatly modified capitalism would be acceptable. The great economist, John Maynard Keynes articulated a view that is probably shared by many teachers of business ethics:

> For my part I think that capitalism, wisely managed, can probably be made more efficient for attaining economic ends than any alternative system yet in sight, but that in itself is in many ways extremely objectionable. Our problem is to work out a social organisation which shall be as efficient as possible without offending our notions of a satisfactory way of life.[1]

Indeed, many teachers and students of business ethics may not even incline as far as Keynes in thinking that capitalism can be made acceptable: in the end, Keynes was more a liberal reformer than a radical critic of capitalism. If the practice of business ethics is embedded in a capitalist economic system, students and teachers of business ethics should have an appreciation of what a relatively pure form of capitalism would look like. We can then begin to think about what would be required for its justification. Knowing that, we will then be in a position to reflect on whether we think there can be truly ethical business practices. If, after seeing what a pure form of capitalism would be, and what would be required for its justification, a student or teacher of business ethics concludes that such justification is not to be had, then her task is basically Keynes's: to determine what, if any, alteration of this system retains the important benefits of capitalist business while conforming to her notion of "a satisfactory way of life." Perhaps, reflecting on contemporary versions of capitalism she will decide that the current versions depart from the pure form, and because of that they are consistent with her notion of a satisfactory way of life; then again, it is possible that contemporary capitalism is objectionable just because it departs too much from the pure form. My task in this chapter is to sketch what I see as the elements of a pure form of capitalism, and to indicate some of the ways that proponents of capitalism have sought to justify these elements. The rather vague idea of "capitalism" is better grasped if we analyze it into distinct elements. And each element might be justified in different ways. As the reader will see, I believe that once we reflect on the elements of capitalism we will see that Keynes and many others have woefully underestimated its power as an ideal way to organize economic—and indeed many social—relations. However, my main aim is not to defend capitalism as an ideal, but to analyze capitalism into its constitutive elements. This will not only allow us to better understand the context in which business occurs, but it will help the reader to better identify just what aspect of capitalism, if any, offends her notion "of a satisfactory way of life." This chapter, then, is not so much an essay in business ethics as it is an essay on the foundations of

the very practice of business and business ethics—the idea of a capitalist economic order.

2. PRIVATE PROPERTY

Maximally Extensive Feasible Property Rights: Capitalist Ownership

Classical debates about the justifiability of capitalism, and especially the contrast between capitalism and communism, focused on the right to private property. John Stuart Mill (a defender of a modified version of capitalism) and Karl Marx (the most famous critic of all) supposed that capitalism is essentially defined by a system that relies on private property rights, and so they thought that the rejection of capitalism just is the rejection of private property. "Communism is the positive abolition of private property," wrote Marx.[2] The complete abolition of private property has rarely been advocated. In Plato's ideal republic, it is true, the ruling class were to live under complete communism—including communism of wives—but that is an extreme view indeed. Even Soviet Communism recognized personal private property in the form of consumer goods such as clothes, household items, and books. Perhaps, then, capitalism requires private property in non-personal goods—we might think that capitalism is characterized by the private ownership of capital goods (i.e., goods required for the production of other goods). Although there is something to this, throughout almost all of human history capital goods such as tools and farm equipment have been privately owned, yet we wouldn't want to say that capitalism has been the dominant mode of production throughout all human history. Just what is the relation between capitalism and private property?

The ideal of capitalism—that is, a pure version of capitalism—is characterized by maximally extensive feasible property rights along two different dimensions. The first dimension concerns the extent of an individual's ownership right or, as philosophers often put it, the extent of the bundle of rights that make up a person's property. Most scholars today conceive of property in terms of a set of rights that might vary. For Alf to have full private property rights over P, Alf must have:[3]

- The right to use P as he wishes so long as this is not harmful to others or their property;
- The right to exclude others from using P;
- The right to manage: Alf may give permission to any others he wishes to use P, and determine how it may be used by them;
- The right to compensation: If someone damages or uses P without Alf's consent, Alf has a right to compensation for the loss of P's value from that person.
- The rights to destroy, waste or modify: Alf may destroy P, waste it or change it.
- The right to income: Alf has a right to the financial benefits of forgoing his own use of P and letting someone else use it.
- Immunity from expropriation: P (or any part of P) may not be made the property of another or the government without Alf's consent, with the exception of a few items such as taxation.
- Liability to execution: P may be taken away from Alf by authorized persons for repayment of a debt.
- Absence of term: Alf's rights over P are of indefinite duration.
- Rights to rent and sale (transfer rights): Alf may temporarily or permanently transfer all or some of his rights over P to anyone he chooses.

To say that someone who holds these rights over P has maximally extensive feasible property rights over P is to say that his control over P is as complete as possible (the maximal claim) given the like control of others over their property (the feasibility claim). If we drop the feasibility requirement we can give Alf an even more extensive control over P: he might have the right to use his property in ways that harm others, or has no liability to execution. But this increase in his control would limit others' control over their property. If Alf has the right to use his property in ways harmful to others, their use of their property will be impaired. If Alf is free from liability to execution, he can avoid paying compensation when he damages the property of others.

So we can think of the above as approaching the maximally extensive control of Alf over P consistent with the like control of others over their property.

Maximally extensive feasible property rights is part of an ideal, pure conception of capitalism. Real world economic systems, even those that we would all agree are appropriately deemed "capitalist," may limit Alf's control over P by limiting, or even removing, some of these rights. Zoning laws limit the uses to which Alf may put his property; historical district regulations limit his rights to destroy, waste or modify his residence; business licensing laws limit his ability to transfer his property; laws setting a maximum interest rate limit his right to an income. Sometimes, however, real-world systems actually expand these rights. A long-established public policy has been to limit the extent to which consumers can claim rights to compensation against harm from certain public utilities; thus the utilities have less liability than other property owners. All these are rightly seen as ways of qualifying full capitalist ownership of some people. It is clear, though, that as these qualifications accumulate, we are apt to wonder whether the remaining property rights are sufficiently extensive to provide the basis for capitalism. And certainly some of these rights are more fundamental to capitalism than others. The rights to use, to exclude, to income, to modify, to manage, to transfer, to compensation and immunity from expropriation are basic to a capitalist order. An economic system that is based on some qualifications on them may still be recognizably capitalist: one that drastically curtails any of them over a wide range of property begins to lose its capitalist character. A system that does not generally recognize the rights to income or to transfer, for example, may be said to have a sort of private property, but not capitalist property.

The right against expropriation raises deep questions about the justifiability of taxation. Nonconsensual takings of property limit or abridge this right; if such takings are extensive, the resulting system will be far from the capitalist ideal. As John Locke insisted, if government may legitimately take away people's property without their consent, "this would be in effect to leave them no Property at all."[4] Given this, the most extreme capitalist position is "anarcho-capitalism," which maintains that, because all taxation is non-consensual, government is inherently illegitimate. Locke took a more moderate view. Though he held that government may not raise taxes without the people's consent, insofar as a legitimate legislature rests on the consent of the governed, taxation approved by a representative legislature does not constitute an expropriation, and so is not a violation of property rights. Thus the famous rallying cry of the American Revolution—"No taxation without representation!"—expresses a strong commitment to capitalist property rights. Only if government is organized in a certain way can its taxes, which take a citizen's property, be legitimate.

Maximally Extensive Feasible Property Rights: What Can Be Owned

One dimension along which the ideal of capitalism endorses maximally extensive feasible property rights is, then, the extent of the bundle of rights one has over P. The other dimension concerns the range of objects over which one can have property rights. The capitalist ideal is to extend as far as possible the range of things that are privately owned. Of course under the capitalist ideal, consumer and productive goods are privately owned. So too are natural resources. Recently advocates of capitalism have argued that many of our environmental problems stem from the absence of private property rights over such resources. Many environmental problems concern what are called "common pool resources," which are characterized by (1) relatively open ("public") access and (2) private consumption. Clean air and fresh water are common pool resources: they are accessible to everyone but consumed privately. The "tragedy of the commons" arises in situations in which individuals (or groups) make individually rational decisions about how much of the relevant resource (e.g., water, air) to consume that, collectively, leads to the over-harvesting of that resource and depleting its

sustainable capacity. Pollution is a prime example of a common pool problem: over-use of the air's ability to dissipate waste gasses leads to the depletion of that ability. When goods remain in the common pool, if some restrain their current consumption (e.g., fish less) while others do not, those who restrain themselves will not only end up with less today, but very likely will have no more in the future: those who do not restrain themselves may well overharvest the resource, depleting future stocks. If so, no one has an incentive to restrain themselves today and all will over-harvest. Most of our worst resource depletion problems—the ability of the atmosphere to absorb carbon dioxide, fresh air, fresh water, fisheries, coral reefs, wild animals—stem from lack of private property rights. When a resource is privately owned, the owner will be confident that she will benefit from her restraint on present use: she will reap less today but she will gain the benefit—future sustainable yields. As David Schmidtz has convincingly argued, only if resources are taken out of the common pool will depletions be minimized. As he tellingly puts it, "leaving goods in the common practically ensures their destruction."[5] When dealing with resources that cannot be renewed such as petroleum, capitalist ownership induces efficient pricing (see section 3, below), which in turn encourages both search for additional supplies and alternative technologies.

Advocates of the capitalist ideal thus have sought to extend as far as feasible the range of objects subject to private property rights. This includes maximal rights over one's body and labor, so that one is free to sell any services to others that do not harm third parties (again, one's use of one's property does not uncontroversially extend to harmful uses). Although Marx sometimes saw private property as characteristic of capitalism, at other times he stressed that capitalism's truly distinctive feature was the "commodification of labor": that labor itself is a commodity to be bought and sold like any other good. This "commodification" of labor and services is embraced by capitalism: defenders of capitalism not only endorse the sale of labor in the usual contexts, but may also support—even strongly support—more controversial applications such as the right to sell sexual services in the form of prostitution, sell pornography, create clubs with strippers, and so on. The terms "sex industry" and "workers in the sex industry" expresses this "commodification" of sexual services. Indeed, many friends of capitalism push the "commodification" even further, arguing for property rights in body parts, and thus for the right to sell parts of one's body such as a kidney—or, more radically, any body part. The upshot of this conception of capitalism is a "permissive society": in "competitive capitalism ... the businessman will make money by catering to for whatever it is people wish to do—by providing pop records, or nude shows, or candyfloss."[6] At the extreme, this leads some advocates of capitalism to allow that an individual may transfer the property over himself to another, becoming a slave or a source of many body parts for research and transplantation.

Justifying Capitalist Property Rights: The Space of Capitalist Property

I have been describing a regime of maximally extensive feasible property rights; as Figure 1 shows, there are numerous regimes of property that lie between such a regime (point A) and communism (point D):

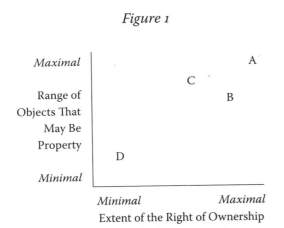

Figure 1

One might speculate that, say current American capitalism is closer to point C than to A, the capitalist ideal: the range of things that can be owned is quite extensive (though certainly not maximal—think of the absence of property over heroin, certain sexual services, and kidneys), but ownership rights are qualified in numerous ways (licensing regulations, environmental regulations, health and safety rules, and so on). On the other hand, John Stuart Mill seemed to support a system closer to B: something like full property rights over what can be owned but significant limitations on what should be owned. For Mill, the justification of private property—that people deserve the fruits of their labor—does not apply to land: "No man made the land. It is the original inheritance of the whole species."[7]

To justify a non-pure regime of capitalist property rights, then, is to justify a system of property rights somewhere in the neighbourhood of point A. To justify the capitalist ideal is to justify the sort of maximally extensive feasible property rights at A. Although we cannot even begin to fully survey the arguments that have been advanced to justify such extensive property rights, it will help to get some idea of why advocates of capitalism have thought property rights approaching point A can be justified. I consider briefly two important lines of justification advanced by political philosophers (I turn to economists in section 3).

Self-ownership. Perhaps the most influential justification holds that (1) to be a free person is to have maximally extensive feasible property rights over oneself and (2) there is some mechanism that allows these extensive self-ownership rights to yield extensive rights over objects in the world. For Locke, one's property is not just one's "estates" but one's "life," "liberty," and "person."[8] In this sense we are self-owners, and our ownership over parts of the world is an extension of our self-ownership. For Locke, when a person mixes his labor (which is his property) with unowned parts of the world, he can extend his property in his person to include those parts of the world. This type of view was by no means unique to Locke. As Stephen Buckle shows in his study of the natural law theories of property, Hugo Grotius, Samuel Pufendorf, and Locke all insisted on an intimate connection between a person's rights and what "belongs" to her. This idea of what belongs to a person or her "suum" concerns a set of "essential possessions": life, limbs, and liberty. Thus understood, says Buckle, the suum is "what naturally belongs to a person because none of these things can be taken away without injustice."[9] Now, crucially, natural law theorists held that one's suum could be—indeed, if we are to survive, must be—extended into the world. As Buckle says, concerning Locke, "[t]he property in one's own person thus has a dynamic quality, in that it needs to grow to survive—it requires the acquisition of certain things. The suum must be extended—'mixed' with things—in order to be maintained."[10] Thus by extending one's suum into the external world—in Locke's theory, by mixing one's labor with parts of the world—external private property in goods is generated. External ownership involves property rights over things that are as extensive as property rights over oneself: they are an extension of the attributes of personhood itself.

If the self-ownership argument is to justify the sort of extensive capitalist property rights we have been analyzing, (1) it must be shown that the extension process applies a suitably wide range of objects and (2) that these new property rights are characterized by the full bundle of capitalist rights. Both of these tasks look daunting. As Buckle notes, at the heart of self-ownership theories such as Locke's was the idea that our right of self-ownership is inalienable: we have property in our own person, but no right to destroy or waste it.[11] But if one's property rights over one's self constitutes less than full capitalist property, it is hard to see how one's extension of this right of self-ownership creates full capitalist property rights: the extended property rights would be more complete than the property right on which they are based. Moreover, if the point of the extension of one's suum is to provide for our maintenance, then it seems that this process could not justify property rights that would ultimately be harmful to us, such

as property rights over heroin or alcohol. To be sure, some advocates of the self-ownership view have insisted that a pure self-ownership doctrine would accord us full capitalist property rights over our body and labor. An implication of this position would be that others would have a right of execution over your body for purpose of compensation and non-payment of debts—a radical view.

Agency Justifications. A more adequate justification of maximally extensive property seeks to derive them from the very idea of agency. Loren Lomasky, for example, argues that persons, understood as pursuers of projects, have a natural and important interest in possessing things:

> Persons ... have a natural interest in having things. The relation of having is conceptually more basic and not to be confused with a property right. It amounts to the actual ability to employ some object in the furtherance of one's designs and does not presuppose the existence of any structure of rights. Having I and enjoying property rights in I are conceptually and empirically distinguishable.... However, these are not two unrelated concepts. It is because of a person's interests in having objects that there is an interest in being accorded property rights.[12]

Thus, as Lomasky understands them, property rights protect one's possession of things. "Property rights demarcate a moral space within which what one has is marked as immune from predation."[13] Such morally secure possession is required for successful project pursuit.

The crucial task for the agency justification is to move from a general argument that some property is necessary for agency to a defense of maximally extensive property rights. The agency argument has an easier time than self-ownership accounts in showing that our rights of ownership should approximate full property rights (our first dimension of capitalist property rights): agency requires that one be able to control parts of the world as part of one's projects, and full capitalist property maximizes control. But can it also be shown that the agency justification leads to the desirability of maximal property rights over the other dimension—the things over which one can have property? This looks more dubious. The key, it would seem, is to show that (1) agency is a great, perhaps the supreme value and (2) to limit what parts of the world a person may own, or what services she may sell, always to some extent limits her agency and so (3) it takes a extremely strong case, in terms of competing values, to justifiably set a limit on what can be owned, or what services can be sold. Thus, for example, an advocate of the agency justification may object to John Rawls's suggestion that one's interest in agency is adequately advanced by a system that grants private property over personal items but prohibits it over productive goods.[14] Such a socialist system prohibits "capitalist acts between consenting adults"[15]—and that looks like a significant limitation on the types of projects that one is free to pursue.

3. CAPITALISM AND MARKETS

Markets and Efficient Property: Full Capitalist Property Rights

To fully understand why capitalism endorses maximally extensive property rights we need to turn from philosophic justifications to the analysis of the market and efficiency. In his classical paper on "The Problem of Social Cost" R.M. Coase showed that, regardless of the initial distribution of property rights, if there are no transaction costs, free exchange in the market yields an efficient outcome.[16] Consider an example. As we all know, there is a great demand for solar panels in the West; environmentalists, those concerned about global warming, and those interested in national energy independence all are urging increased use of solar power. Now the production of solar panels requires polysilcon, but manufacturing polysilcon produces toxic waste. In western countries this waste is recycled; in China, however, recycling technologies are not well developed, and recycling

is not required by law.[17] Waste is either stored or, after minimal reprocessing, released into the environment. It is estimated that to recycle the waste would increase the cost of Chinese polysilcon by somewhere between 50 to 400%. It is disputed how great the resulting pollution is, but it is safe to say that enough waste leaks on to adjoining land to severely curtail agriculture on surrounding farms. Suppose, as does Coase, that we ignore transaction and bargaining costs; and simply focus on the Polysilcon Factory and say, the group of Affected Farmers. The Polysilcon Factory clearly produces what economists call a negative externality on the Affected Farmers: its productive activity negatively impacts their livelihood. Now if the Polysilcon Factory does not take this negative impact into account it has an incentive to produce polysilcon up to the point where its marginal costs equal its marginal benefits: that is, up to the point where its costs for producing another ton of polysilcon equals the profits of doing so. (That this is so is a standard axiom of economics.) If the Polysilcon Factory is at a level of production such that the benefits of producing another ton of polysilcon exceed the total costs of producing that unit, it clearly has an incentive to produce that additional ton; if it is at the point where the total costs of producing another ton of polysilcon exceed the benefits of producing that unit, it clearly has an incentive not to produce that ton. But the problem for society is that at the point at which the Polysilcon Factory's marginal costs equal its marginal benefits, the total social costs will have exceeded the total social benefits. This is because the Polysilcon Factory does not take into account the costs imposed on the Affected Framers; if it considers these costs in its calculations, it would have ceased production at a lower level of output (at an extreme, zero).

To see this better, let us assume some figures. Suppose that a Polysilcon Factory would incur a one-time cost of $500,000 to build an improved storage facility that would not leak on to neighboring properties: suppose such a facility would last 20 years, so the yearly cost is roughly $25,000.

Now assume that the pollution causes a collective loss of $40,000 a year to the Affected Farmers. Even if there is no law against the pollution, an efficient result can still be achieved: the Farmers can pay the Factory $25,000 a year to build the improved facility. They will be $15,000 a year better off, and the factory will be no worse off (if they pay $26,000, both will be better off than in the current situation). It is important that this "theorem" applies regardless of how the property rights are divided between the two parties. An efficient outcome can be reached whether the Factory has a right to pollute or the Farmers have a right that it not pollute. Suppose that there is indeed a law against pollution, but to totally stop pollution would require a much larger expenditure, say $10,000,000; suppose the Factory could not afford to pay this and would close down. Assume that the Farmers still suffer a total loss of $25,000 a year and that the Farmers have the right to bring suit against the Factory. Now it is efficient for the Factory to pay the Farmers something more than $25,000 a year not to bring suit. This would be better for both the Farmers and the Factory than shutting down the Factory.

According to Coase, then, in the absence of transaction and bargaining costs, parties to activities with negative externalities will agree to some efficient allocation of resources regardless of the initial distribution of property rights. Coase's theorem challenges one of the main principled justifications for government activity. In the absence of a perfect scheme of property rights that fully internalizes costs and benefits (i.e., an economic actor reaps the full benefits, but also pays the full costs, of his activity), it has been widely argued that government action is necessary to regulate the "market failure" that results from externalities (when an actor imposes costs on another that are not considered in his calculations). But Coase argues that, at least ideally, market transactions can solve the problem of externalities and get us to efficient outcomes (though the actual costs involved in negotiation, etc. may preclude this, and then government action may be required as a

second-best strategy). But—and this is the important point—if markets are to approach efficient outcomes in which people are compensated for externalities, people must have extensive rights to make agreements. Restrictions on to what they can agree to—what trades they can make, what aspects of their rights they can transfer to others, how they can use their property, and so on—will undermine efficiency and the possibility of mutual benefit. Suppose that the Factory is doing $1,000,000 damage to the Farmers, but that strict enforcement of the pollution code would raise the price of Factory's polysilcon by 200%, which would drive it out of business. It would obviously be mutually beneficial for the Factory and the Framers to agree to, say, a payment to the Farmers of $1,500,000 a year: both would be better off than if the factory closed. If such agreements are precluded—if the parties cannot trade their rights in these ways—then the efficient outcome may not be possible. Thus we see how full capitalist ownership rights are conducive to efficiency—and "efficiency" is simply a term for mutual benefit. Unless each is free to trade her rights as she sees fit, opportunities for mutually beneficial exchanges will be blocked.

Markets, Mutual Benefit, and Mutual Respect

The account I have been stressing conceives of markets as arenas of mutual benefit. The idea that exchange is generally mutually beneficial is at the heart of what we might call that capitalist view of social life (and most of modern economics). In contrast, in the eyes of many opponents of capitalist markets, market exchanges are what game theorists call "zero-sum" transactions: for every gain by one party, there is a corresponding loss by another. The market is seen as a realm of dog-eat-dog competition: some win by devouring others, but the devoured lose. For every one who eats there is someone who is eaten. In the words of a former French prime minister, "What is the market? It is the law of the jungle, the law of nature."[18] Capitalism rejects this conflict-ridden view of social life and the market. If I possess two bottles of beer, and you possess two slices of pizza, an exchange of a slice of pizza for a bottle of beer will make us both better off. As Adam Smith saw it, our propensity to "truck, barter and exchange one thing for another"[19] is at the root of mutual benefit, and the growth of wealth.

> Give me that which I want and you shall have this which you want, is the meaning of every such offer; and it is in this manner that we obtain from one another the far greater part of those good offices which we stand in need of. It is not from the benevolence of the butcher, the brewer, or the baker, that we expect our dinner, but from their regard to their own interest.... Nobody but a beggar chooses to depend chiefly on the benevolence of his fellow-citizens.[20]

In commenting on this passage Stephen Darwall stresses that, though certainly it is about mutual advantage, it presumes far more than mere self-interested agency. Smith stresses that exchange relations presuppose agents who conceive of each other of having distinct points of view, which demand respect. "Smith evidently thinks of exchange as an interaction in which both parties are committed to various normative presuppositions, for example, that the exchange is made by free mutual consent, that neither party will simply take what the other has.... Both parties must presume that the other is dealing fairly."[21] Market transactions are built on a foundation of trust and a type of mutual respect: without that, we are apt to invade for gain (a true zero-sum interaction) rather than trade for mutual gain.

As Smith famously shows, markets both rely on, and provide the main impetus to, the division of labor. If someone is a butcher, another a brewer, and another a baker, an immensely greater amount of food and drink is available than if each is her own butcher, brewer, and baker. According to David Hume, this is the very essence of society: "By the partition of employments, our ability encreases."[22] Indeed, for Hume market relations are even more basic than property or justice: the rules of property and justice evolve out of market relations based on the division of labor. As cooperation proceeds, conventions arise about the terms of our cooperative interactions—hence the genesis of our principles of justice.

Are Market Exchanges Always Beneficial?

A fundamental claim of capitalism, then, is that markets respect full private property rights and allow for mutual benefit among independent agents. We have been assuming that each of the parties to the exchange has full information about what they are exchanging. Economists generally assume that both parties to an exchange are equally informed; only recently has there been a sustained interest in how asymmetric information can affect market transactions. To the extent that one party does not know what he is buying, we can no longer suppose that market exchanges are truly mutually beneficial. Of course classical exponents of the market economy insisted that mutual gain through markets presupposed the absence of fraud and force (recall the idea that markets are based on trust and a sort of mutual respect), but the problems of asymmetric information run deeper.

A related problem is asymmetric bargaining power. One of the main justifications for labor laws regulating hours and factory conditions in the early part of twentieth century was that employers and workers had asymmetric bargaining power, so that workers were forced to accept disadvantageous bargains. This line of analysis is more complex and controversial than it first appears. Hardly any bargains are made from equality of bargaining power, yet the fact that some need the bargain more than others does not show that the exchange is not mutually beneficial. On the other hand, in extreme cases unequal bargaining power can undermine the moral legitimacy of market outcomes. As Robert Nozick, a staunch defender of capitalism argued, "a person may not appropriate the only water hole in a desert and charge what he will.

Nor may he charge what he will if he possesses one, and unfortunately it happens that all the water holes in the desert dry up but his."[23] Under these conditions an offer of a glass of water for all your property would be a coercive offer: an offer that exploits one's bargaining power and simply cannot be refused.[24] Instead of mutual advantage we have a sort of exploitation of those in great need.

Thus far we have been considering the conditions under which an individual market transaction is genuinely mutually beneficial. But it might be objected that a series of market transactions, each of which is unobjectionable, may have an outcome in which some (i.e., the workers) have no real choices, and so their freedom and self-ownership is undermined...

A defender of markets must, I think, show that the overall effect of markets, far from radically decreasing options, is to increase them, providing a greater range of choice. To be sure, just what we mean by a greater range of choice is open to various interpretations: it might mean simply how many options a person has, how many options a person values, the breadth of options (not simply a lot of options to do basically similar things), and so on. These are difficult issues in the philosophy of freedom. However, on almost any interpretation, modern capitalist-like market economies have astronomically increased people's range of options. Consider Eric Beinhocker's comparison of two tribes: the Yanomamö, a tribe living along the Orinoco River between Brazil and Venezuela, and the New Yorkers, a tribe living on the Hudson River along the border of New York and New Jersey. The Yanomamö have an average income of $90 a year, the New Yorker $36,000:

> But it is not just the absolute level of income that makes the New Yorkers so wealthy: it is also the incredible variety of things their wealth can buy. Imagine you had the income of a New Yorker, but you could only spend it on things in the Yanomamö economy. If you spent your $36,000 fixing up your mud hut, buying the best clay pots in the village, and eating the finest Yanomamö cuisine, you would be extraordinarily wealthy by Yanomamö standards, but you would still feel far poorer than a typical New Yorker with his or her Nike sneakers, televisions and vacations in Florida. The number of economic choices the average New Yorker has is staggering. The Wal-Mart near the JFK Airport has over 100,000 different items in stock, there are over 200 television channels offered on cable TV, Barnes and Noble lists over 8 million titles, the local supermarket has 275 varieties of breakfast cereal, the typical department store offers 150 types of lipstick, and there are over 50,000 restaurants in New York City alone.[25]

Beinhocker points out that the 400-fold difference in income does not even begin to estimate the difference in options; the New Yorker, he estimates, has an order of 1010 more choices—an astronomical number. And with these consumer choices come occupational, educational, and religious ones as well. When we compare capitalist modern market economies with simple non-market economies (and Soviet-type planned economies), what is striking is not simply the difference in the absolute level of wealth, but in the range of options—the jobs one can perform, the goods one can consume, the lives one can have.

Markets and Efficiency: The Extent of Property

As we have already seen in the case of common pool resources, extending the range of things that can be privately owned is of fundamental importance if our aim is to ensure efficient sustainable use. Efficiency is also nearly always enhanced when services are privately rather than publicly provided. There is evidence of the greater efficiency of private over public ownership in, among other things, airlines, banks, municipal bus services, cleaning services, debt collection, fire protection, hospitals, housing insurance claims processing, military aircraft repair, ocean tanker maintenance, preschool education, garbage collection, removal of abandoned vehicles, slaughterhouses and weather forecasting.

Hayek provides one of the most compelling arguments for extending as far as possible the range of things subject to private ownership. As Hayek understands a modern society, each individual has her own projects and plans (think again of the agency justification in section 2); whether she is successful depends on whether she can mesh her plans with those of others. If plans come into constant conflict, people will find their aims and projects frustrated. Two things are needed for this meshing. First, there must be settled rules of conduct that allow each to anticipate the actions of others: repeated interventions by government to change regulations and the rules of the market undermine our ability to anticipate others. Second, however, we require knowledge: we need to know what others are doing. If we are to efficiently pursue our own goals we must have an idea of whether the resources necessary for our plans are being demanded by others, whether others will be interested in the outputs of our plans and projects, and so on. But how can we know that? Modern society is literally composed on hundreds of millions of people; the knowledge required for meshing the plans of these great societies is of an incredible magnitude.

The economic problem of society is thus not merely a problem of how to allocate "given" resources—if "given" is taken to mean given to a single mind which deliberately solves the problem set by these "data." It is rather a problem of how to secure the best use of resources known to any of the members of society, for ends whose relative importance only these individuals know. Or, to put it briefly, it is a problem of the utilization of knowledge which is not given to anyone in its totality.

The problem is this: each of us has both personal and local knowledge not generally available to others, and yet the success of our plans often depends on knowing the personal and local knowledge of others. Personal knowledge consists of one's knowledge of one's own plans and goals. Local knowledge is "the knowledge of the particular circumstances of time and place. It is with respect to this that practically every individual has some advantage over all others because he possesses unique information of which beneficial use might be made, but of which use can be made only if the decisions depending on it are left to him or are made with his active cooperation."[26] I wish to employ my local knowledge to exploit those possibilities of which I know. But for me to successfully do this requires that I know about events in far off places that might affect my plans: what do others want, what alternative uses do they have for resources, what local new possibilities do they see that I don't? How can I possibly know all this? Now—and here is Hayek's great contribution—this knowledge of remoter events is conveyed by the price system. The relative prices for goods do not tell us why goods are wanted, or why they are in short supply: it is a summary measure conveying just the crucial information—that others want the good, or that they are having a hard time getting hold of enough. "The marvel [of the market] is that in a case like that of a scarcity of one raw material, without an order being issued, without more than perhaps a handful of people knowing the cause, tens of thousands of people whose identity could not be ascertained by months of investigation, are made to use the material or its products more sparingly; i.e., they move in the right direction."[27] The market, then, sums up the local and personal knowledge of actors across the world, and converts it into the crucial information that each of us must have so that we can use our own local and personal knowledge to efficiently satisfy our aims. If, though, the market is to convey as much information as possible about the plans, resources, and opportunities, as many resources as possible must be subject to the price mechanism. To take something out of the market limits the spread of information about it, impairing the effectiveness of plans throughout the market....

4. THE HIERARCHICAL, PROFIT-MAXIMIZING FIRM

The Master-Servant Relation

It might seem that once we have described a market based on maximally extensive property rights we have completed our task of characterizing the capitalist ideal. Not so. In his Principles of Political Economy—the most influential economic text of the nineteenth century—John Stuart Mill sketches an alternative to capitalism that embraces both private property and markets. Mill endorsed the private ownership of firms, but not firms in which some were hired and were required to obey the instructions of the owners—the "master."

> Hitherto there has been no alternative for those who lived by their labour, but that of labouring either each for himself alone, or for a master. But the civilizing and improving influences of association, and the efficiency and economy of production on a large scale, may be obtained without dividing the producers into two parties with hostile interests and feelings, the many who do the work being mere servants under the command of the one who supplies the funds, and having no interest of their own in the enterprise except to earn their wages with as little labour as possible.... [T]here can be little doubt that the status of hired labourers will gradually tend to confine itself to the description of workpeople whose low moral qualities render them unfit for anything more independent: and that the relation of masters and workpeople will be gradually superseded by partnership, in one of two forms: in some cases, association of the labourers with the capitalist; in others, and perhaps finally in all, association of labourers among themselves.[28]

As workers become better educated and more public-spirited, Mill argued, the master/servant relation characteristic of the capitalist firm will be replaced by a regime of worker cooperatives: worker-owned firms that compete in the market. The idea was that workers would be collective owners of the firms and democratically decide important strategic matters, though-day-to-day operations would still be directed by a manger instructing workers what to do—but a manger that could be dismissed by the workers. Thus the worker cooperatives were privately held firms in a competitive market economy without the master-servant relation (in which the owners are masters and the workers simply hired servants). Unfortunately for this view, the worker cooperative movement barely outlived Mill; worker cooperatives appear to have succumbed to the greater efficiency of capitalist firms based on the master-servant relation.

Hierarchy and Efficiency

Why did Mill's hope for the future—firms owned by the workers and, ultimately, managed by them—succumb to traditional capitalist firms in which, either, the owner managed the firm and hired workers as his "servants," or (see below) the owners hired managers, who in turn instructed the workers about what to do, when to do it, and so on? As we have seen, Coase had a fundamental impact on our thinking about markets, property and efficiency. Another of his papers fundamentally changed our thinking about "The Nature of the Firm."[29] Coase agrees with Mill: the "master and servant" relation is fundamental to the capitalist firm (it is widely thought that this relation is at least partly constitutive of capitalism).[30] This, of course, is a hierarchical, authority, relation: those who own (or at the behest of the owners, who manage) make the decisions about what is to be produced, how, by whom etc. The job of the workers is to do as they are instructed by their "boss." Coase and his followers show that organization via such an authority relation reduces transaction costs. Transactions organized through the market and its price mechanism entail, for instance, negotiating costs and information costs: we must find out who is selling a product, whether we wish to pay his price, and so on. Typically these costs are not so great as to make market exchange inefficient; however in some cases the negotiations would be quite costly. Suppose that one is building a new computer. One might buy all the components in the market, but perhaps one's aim is to design a new computer. This would involve a new motherboard unit, a video display that works well with it, effective power sources, and so on. Now these new units must work well together, and this may require constant cooperation by the individual design teams (focusing on the motherboard, display, etc.) as they are building the unit. If so, it may greatly reduce transaction costs to have a central coordinator who directs each specialist team and their activities, giving them design parameters so that the designs work well together. And so one may organize a hierarchical firm. The firm, then, is a way to decrease some transaction costs. In this sense the hierarchical firm is an engine of efficiency.

The "Socialist" Character of the Capitalist Firm

The division of labor in the market is based on individual producers and consumers, each contracting with each other; one's reward is directly based on one's production of what others want. The division of labor in the firm is very different. It is based on a central coordinator—the boss—who decides the relevant targets, and then designs systems that divide up tasks in order to achieve the goals. Of course the boss may seek input and feedback from her subordinates, but this is up to her. Those with authority make plans and instruct the "servants" how to go about implementing them. The values within the firm are in many ways the opposite of the values between participants in the market: whereas the latter stress independence, contract, and reward based satisfaction of demand, the former stresses the values of leadership, teamwork

(directed by leaders), tasks based on instruction from above, and reward based on the boss' evaluation of the subordinates' usefulness to the firm.

It is interesting that the values within the firm were attractive to many communists. N.I. Bukharin and Evgenii Preobrazhensky sought to organize all of society as one large factory. They wrote in their ABC of Communism:

> We must know in advance how much labour to assign to the various branches of industry; what products are required and how much of each it is necessary to produce; how and where machines must be provided. These and similar details must be thought out beforehand, with approximate accuracy at least; and the work must be guided in accordance with calculations.... Without a general plan, without a general directive system, and without careful calculation and book-keeping, there can be no organization. But in the communist social organization, there is such a plan.[31]

Just as a factory manager seeks to organize and plan production, so too, it was thought, must communist planners organize and plan production for the entire economy. Thus early communists had great regard for capitalist techniques of production within enterprises; it was the "anarchy" of the market that provoked their deepest ire.[32]

Because most people in capitalist societies spend their lives within large corporations, in non-profit organizations such as universities, or in government service, we arrive at the surprising conclusion that most people in capitalist societies spend their lives in organizations whose values are in many ways more "socialist" than "capitalist." This is an important theme in Hayek's work. In large organizations subordinates expect to be rewarded according to their merit: they were given tasks to perform and if, on some set of criteria, they performed well, they merit a higher pay. As Hayek points out, this is very different than reward in the market: "Reward for merit is reward for obeying the wishes of others in what we do, not compensation for the benefits we have conferred upon them by doing what we thought best."[33] In the market one's reward does depend on how much others benefit from your action; and a good deal of luck may be involved in this. An entrepreneur may gain because she was in the right place and the right time, and so able to perceive a way to satisfy others' wants. In the market two entrepreneurs may have tried equally hard, done everything in their power, and one entirely fail and the other be a great success. It is not the case that such luck is simply about the way a "deliberate gamble" works out: the luck may be that the entrepreneur's local situation was such that she had possibilities of gain that were simply unknowable by others.

Because most of us spend most of our time in organizations not informed by market values, when we come to politics—where market outcomes are often the subject of debate—we tend to apply our "socialist" (i.e., non-market) values to market outcomes. For example, in contemporary political philosophy one of the most influential doctrines of distributive justice is that property should track the distinction between "choice and chance": although one should be held responsible for one's choices, one should not be held responsible for what results from mere brute chance. Distributive justice, it is said, should compensate people for bad brute luck. This claim resonates with all of us who have spent our life within large organizations: if things go wrong for us and it was through no fault of our own, then we insist that this does not detract from our merit, or the rewards we are due from our bosses. "It was simply bad luck" is a relevant reply in one's end-of-the-year review. But, as Hayek points out, this makes no sense in the market, which in many ways runs by brute luck. Entrepreneurs are confronted by options many of which are not of their own devising; efficiency is promoted by them taking advantage of this "brute luck" (a sort of local knowledge) to satisfy additional wants and aims. To "compensate" entrepreneurs for their bad luck (not having the same local knowledge as others)

would undermine the very core of the market as a device for generating information. For the market to function, differential local knowledge must crucially enter into an entrepreneur's profits. In Hayek's eyes the upshot of this is a certain moral instability of capitalism: most people in capitalist economic systems have moral views about justice and distribution that they apply to the market, and are destructive of the very economic prosperity on which all depend.

NOTES

1. John Maynard Keynes, "The End of Laissez-Faire," in his *Essays in Persuasion* (London: Macmillan, 1972), 294.

2. Karl Marx, *Economic and Philosophic Manuscripts of 1844*, in *Marx/Engels Collected Works* (London: Lawrence & Wishart, 1975–2002), vol. 4, p. 293. Compare John Stuart Mill, *Principles of Political Economy with Some of Their Applications to Social Philosophy*, in *The Collected Works of John Stuart Mill*, edited by J.M. Robson (Toronto: University of Toronto Press, 1977), vol. 2, Book II, chap. 1.

3. This list draws on A.M. Honoré, "Ownership" in *Oxford Essays in Jurisprudence*, edited by A.G. Guest (Oxford: Clarendon Press, 1961), pp. 107–47; and Frank Snare, "The Concept of Property," *American Philosophical Quarterly*, vol. 9 (April 1972), pp. 200–206. For an excellent and accessible discussion, see Lawrence C. Becker, *Property Rights: Philosophical Foundations* (London: Routledge & Kegan Paul, 1977), chapter 2.

4. John Locke, *Second Treatise of Government*, edited by Peter Laslett (Cambridge: Cambridge University Press, 1960), section 139. Emphasis in original.

5. David Schmidtz, *The Limits of Government: An Essay on the Public Goods Argument* (Boulder, CO: Westview Press, 1991), p. 21.

6. Samuel Brittan, *A Restatement of Economic Liberalism* (Atlantic Highlands, NJ: Humanities Press, 1988), p. 1.

7. Mill, *Principles of Political Economy*, book 2, chapter 2, section 6. Emphasis added.

8   Locke, *Second Treatise*, sections 27, 123.

9   Stephen Buckle, *Natural Law and the Theory of Property* (Oxford: Clarendon Press, 1991), p. 29.

10   Buckle, *Natural Law and the Theory of Property*, p. 171. Buckle argues for the applicability of the concept of suum to Locke's theory on pp. 168–74. See also A. John Simmons, *The Lockean Theory of Rights* (Princeton: Princeton University Press, 1992), pp. 226–27.

11   Buckle, *Natural Law and the Theory of Property*, pp. 191ff.

12   Loren E. Lomasky, *Persons, Rights and the Moral Community* (New York: Oxford University Press, 1987), pp. 120–21. Emphasis in original.

13   Lomasky, *Persons, Rights and the Moral Community*, p. 121.

14   John Rawls, *Justice as Fairness: A Restatement*, edited by Erin Kelly (Cambridge, MA: Harvard University Press, 2001), pp. 136ff. I have in mind here Rawls's support of "liberal (democratic) socialism."

15   Nozick, *Anarchy, State and Utopia*, p. 163.

16   See Ronald Coase, "The Problem of Social Cost," *Journal of Law and Economics*, vol. 3 (1960): 1–44. My explication follows Dennis Mueller, *Public Choice III* (Cambridge: Cambridge University Press, 2003), pp. 27–30.

17   See Ariana Eunjung Cha, "Solar Energy Firms Leave Waste Behind in China," *The Washington Post*, March 9, 2008, page A1.

18   Edouard Balladur quoted in Martin Wolf, *Why Globalization Works* (New Haven: Yale University Press, 2004), p. 4.

19   Adam Smith, *An Inquiry Into the Nature and Causes of the Wealth of Nations*, edited by W.B. Todd (Indianapolis: Liberty Fund, 1981), book I, chapter 2, paragraph 1.

20   Smith, *Wealth of Nations*, book I, chapter 2, paragraph 2.

21   Stephen Darwall, *The Second-person Standpoint: Morality, Respect, and Accountability* (Cambridge: Harvard University Press, 2006), p. 47.

22   David Hume, *A Treatise of Human Nature*, second edition, edited by L.A. Selby-Bigge and P.H. Nidditch (Oxford: Oxford University Press, 1978), book 3, part 2, section 2, paragraph 3.

23   Nozick, *Anarchy, State and Utopia*, p. 180.

24   Joel Feinberg, *The Moral Limits of the Criminal Law*, vol. 3, Harm to Self (New York: Oxford University Press, 1986), p. 250.

25   Eric D. Beinhocker, *The Origin of Wealth* (Cambridge, MA: Harvard Business School Press, 2006), 9.

26   Hayek "The Use of Knowledge in Society," p. 522.

27   Hayek "The Use of Knowledge in Society," p. 527.

28   Mill, *Principles*, book 4, chapter 7, section 4.

29   Coase, *The Firm, The Market and the Law*, chapter 2.

30   See, for example, Talcott Parsons's "Introduction" to Max Weber, *The Theory of Social and Economic Organization*, translated by A.M. Henderson and Talcott Parsons (New York: Free Press, 1947), p. 51; Niehaus, *A History of Economic Theory*, p. 144; Karl Marx, *Capital*, chapter 14, section 5.

31   Nikolai Bukharin and Evgenii Preobrazhensky, *The ABC of Communism*, quoted in Michael Ellman, *Socialist Planning* (Cambridge: Cambridge University Press, 1979), p. 9. Emphasis added.

32   See Bukharin and Preobrazhensky's views on the "anarchy of production" in Ellman, *Socialist Planning*, p. 8. See also Marx, Capital, chap. 14, section 4.

33   F.A. Hayek, *The Constitution of Liberty* (London: Routledge and Kegan Paul, 1960), p. 100.

—84—
EXCERPTS FROM
A THEORY OF JUSTICE

John Rawls

3. THE MAIN IDEA OF THE THEORY OF JUSTICE

MY AIM IS TO PRESENT A CONCEPTION OF JUSTICE which generalizes and carries to a higher level of abstraction the familiar theory of the social contract as found, say, in Locke, Rousseau, and Kant. In order to do this we are not to think of the original contract as one to enter a particular society or to set up a particular form of government. Rather, the guiding idea is that the principles of justice for the basic structure of society are the object of the original agreement. They are the principles that free and rational persons concerned to further their own interests would accept in an initial position of equality as defining the fundamental terms of their association. These principles are to regulate all further agreements; they specify the kinds of social cooperation that can be entered into and the forms of government that can be established. This way of regarding the principles of justice I shall call justice as fairness.

Thus we are to imagine that those who engage in social cooperation choose together, in one joint act, the principles which are to assign basic rights and duties and to determine the division of social benefits. Men are to decide in advance how they are to regulate their claims against one another and what is to be the foundation charter of their society. Just as each person must decide by rational reflection what constitutes his good, that is, the system of ends which it is rational for him to pursue, so a group of persons must decide once and for all what is to count among them as just and unjust. The choice which rational men would make in this hypothetical situation of equal liberty, assuming for the present that this choice problem has a solution, determines the principles of justice.

In justice as fairness the original position of equality corresponds to the state of nature in the traditional theory of the social contract. This original position is not, of course, thought of as an actual historical state of affairs, much less as a primitive condition of culture. It is understood as a purely hypothetical situation characterized so as to lead to a certain conception of justice. Among the essential features of this situation is that no one knows his place in society, his class position or social status, nor does anyone know his fortune in the distribution of natural assets and abilities, his intelligence, strength, and the like. I shall even assume that the parties do not know their conceptions of the good or their special psychological propensities. The principles of justice are chosen behind a veil of ignorance. This ensures that no one is advantaged or disadvantaged in the choice of principles by the outcome of natural chance or the contingency of social circumstances. Since all are similarly situated and no one is able to design principles to favor his particular condition, the principles of justice are the result of a fair agreement or bargain. For given the circumstances of the original position, the symmetry of everyone's relations to each other, this initial situation is fair between individuals as moral persons, that is, as rational beings with their own ends and capable, I shall assume, of a sense of justice. The original position is, one might say, the appropriate initial status quo, and thus the fundamental agreements reached in it are fair. This explains the propriety of the name "justice as fairness": it conveys the idea that the principles of justice are agreed to in an initial situation that is fair. The name does not mean that the concepts of justice and fairness are the same, any more than the phrase "poetry as metaphor" means that the concepts of poetry and metaphor are the same.

Justice as fairness begins, as I have said, with one of the most general of all choices which persons might make together, namely, with the choice of the first principles of a conception of justice which is to regulate all subsequent criticism and reform of institutions. Then, having chosen a conception of justice, we can suppose that they are to choose a constitution and a legislature to enact laws, and so on, all in accordance with the principles of justice initially agreed upon. Our social situation is just if it is such that by this sequence of hypothetical agreements we would have contracted into the general system of rules which defines it. Moreover, assuming that the original position does determine a set of principles (that is, that a particular conception of justice would be chosen) it will then be true that whenever social institutions satisfy these principles those engaged in them can say to one another that they are cooperating on terms to which they would agree if they were free and equal persons whose relations with respect to one another were fair. They could all view their arrangements as meeting the stipulations which they would acknowledge in an initial situation that embodies widely accepted and reasonable constraints on the choice of principles. The general recognition of this fact would provide the basis for a public acceptance of the corresponding principles of justice. No society can, of course, be a scheme of cooperation which men

enter voluntarily in a literal sense; each person finds himself placed at birth in some particular position in some particular society, and the nature of this position materially affects his life prospects. Yet a society satisfying the principles of justice as fairness comes as close as a society can to being a voluntary scheme, for it meets the principles which free and equal persons would assent to under circumstances that are fair. In this sense its members are autonomous and the obligations they recognize self-imposed.

One feature of justice as fairness is to think of the parties in the initial situation as rational and mutually disinterested. This does not mean that the parties are egoists, that is, individuals with only certain kinds of interests, say in wealth, prestige, and domination. But they are conceived as not taking an interest in one another's interests. They are to presume that even their spiritual aims may be opposed, in the way that the aims of those of different religions may be opposed. Moreover, the concept of rationality must be interpreted as far as possible in the narrow sense, standard in economic theory, of taking the most effective means to given ends. I shall modify this concept to some extent, as explained later (§25), but one must try to avoid introducing into it any controversial ethical elements. The initial situation must be characterized by stipulations that are widely accepted.

In working out the conception of justice as fairness one main task clearly is to determine which principles of justice would be chosen in the original position. To do this we must describe this situation in some detail and formulate with care the problem of choice which it presents. These matters I shall take up in the immediately succeeding chapters. It may be observed, however, that once the principles of justice are thought of as arising from an original agreement in a situation of equality, it is an open question whether the principle of utility would be acknowledged. Offhand it hardly seems likely that persons who view themselves as equals, entitled to press their claims upon one another, would agree to a principle which may require lesser life prospects for some simply for the sake of a greater sum of advantages enjoyed by others. Since each desires to protect his interests, his capacity to advance his conception of the good, no one has a reason to acquiesce in an enduring loss for himself in order to bring about a greater net balance of satisfaction. In the absence of strong and lasting benevolent impulses, a rational man would not accept a basic structure merely because it maximized the algebraic sum of advantages irrespective of its permanent effects on his own basic rights and interests. Thus it seems that the principle of utility is incompatible with the conception of social cooperation among equals for mutual advantage. It appears to be inconsistent with the idea of reciprocity implicit in the notion of a well-ordered society. Or, at any rate, so I shall argue.

I shall maintain instead that the persons in the initial situation would choose two rather different principles: the first requires equality in the assignment of basic rights and duties, while the second holds that social and economic inequalities, for example inequalities of wealth and authority, are just only if they result in compensating benefits for everyone, and in particular for the least advantaged members of society. These principles rule out justifying institutions on the grounds that the hardships of some are offset by a greater good in the aggregate. It may be expedient but it is not just that some should have less in order that others may prosper. But there is no injustice in the greater benefits earned by a few provided that the situation of persons not so fortunate is thereby improved. The intuitive idea is that since everyone's well-being depends upon a scheme of cooperation without which no one could have a satisfactory life, the division of advantages should be such as to draw forth the willing cooperation of everyone taking part in it, including those less well situated. The two principles mentioned seem to be a fair basis on which those better endowed, or more fortunate in their social position, neither of which we can be said to deserve, could expect the willing cooperation of others when some workable scheme is a necessary condition of the welfare of all. Once we decide to look for a conception

of justice that prevents the use of the accidents of natural endowment and the contingencies of social circumstance as counters in a quest for political and economic advantage, we are led to these principles. They express the result of leaving aside those aspects of the social world that seem arbitrary from a moral point of view.

The problem of the choice of principles, however, is extremely difficult. I do not expect the answer I shall suggest to be convincing to everyone. It is, therefore, worth noting from the outset that justice as fairness, like other contract views, consists of two parts: (1) an interpretation of the initial situation and of the problem of choice posed there, and (2) a set of principles which, it is argued, would be agreed to. One may accept the first part of the theory (or some variant thereof), but not the other, and conversely. The concept of the initial contractual situation may seem reasonable although the particular principles proposed are rejected. To be sure, I want to maintain that the most appropriate conception of this situation does lead to principles of justice contrary to utilitarianism and perfectionism, and therefore that the contract doctrine provides an alternative to these views. Still, one may dispute this contention even though one grants that the contractarian method is a useful way of studying ethical theories and of setting forth their underlying assumptions.

Justice as fairness is an example of what I have called a contract theory. Now there may be an objection to the term "contract" and related expressions, but I think it will serve reasonably well. Many words have misleading connotations which at first are likely to confuse. The terms "utility" and "utilitarianism" are surely no exception. They too have unfortunate suggestions which hostile critics have been willing to exploit; yet they are clear enough for those prepared to study utilitarian doctrine. The same should be true of the term "contract" applied to moral theories. As I have mentioned, to understand it one has to keep in mind that it implies a certain level of abstraction. In particular, the content of the relevant agreement is not to enter a given society or to adopt a given form of government, but to accept certain moral principles. Moreover, the undertakings referred to are purely hypothetical: a contract view holds that certain principles would be accepted in a well-defined initial situation.

The merit of the contract terminology is that it conveys the idea that principles of justice may be conceived as principles that would be chosen by rational persons, and that in this way conceptions of justice may be explained and justified. The theory of justice is a part, perhaps the most significant part, of the theory of rational choice. Furthermore, principles of justice deal with conflicting claims upon the advantages won by social cooperation; they apply to the relations among several persons or groups. The word "contract" suggests this plurality as well as the condition that the appropriate division of advantages must be in accordance with principles acceptable to all parties. The condition of publicity for principles of justice is also connoted by the contract phraseology. Thus, if these principles are the outcome of an agreement, citizens have a knowledge of the principles that others follow. It is characteristic of contract theories to stress the public nature of political principles. Finally there is the long tradition of the contract doctrine. Expressing the tie with this line of thought helps to define ideas and accords with natural piety. There are then several advantages in the use of the term "contract." With due precautions taken, it should not be misleading.

A final remark. Justice as fairness is not a complete contract theory. For it is clear that the contractarian idea can be extended to the choice of more or less an entire ethical system, that is, to a system including principles for all the virtues and not only for justice. Now for the most part I shall consider only principles of justice and others closely related to them; I make no attempt to discuss the virtues in a systematic way. Obviously if justice as fairness succeeds reasonably well, a next step would be to study the more general view suggested by the name "rightness as fairness." But even this wider theory fails to embrace all moral relationships, since it would seem to include only our relations with other persons and to leave out of account how we are to conduct ourselves toward animals and the rest of nature. I do not contend that the contract notion offers a way to approach these questions which are certainly of the first importance; and I shall have to put them aside. We must recognize the limited scope of justice as fairness and of the general type of view that it exemplifies. How far its conclusions must be revised once these other matters are understood cannot be decided in advance.

4. THE ORIGINAL POSITION AND JUSTIFICATION

I have said that the original position is the appropriate initial status quo which insures that the fundamental agreements reached in it are fair. This fact yields the name "justice as fairness." It is clear, then, that I want to say that one conception of justice is more reasonable than another, or justifiable with respect to it, if rational persons in the initial situation would choose its principles over those of the other for the role of justice. Conceptions of justice are to be ranked by their acceptability to persons so circumstanced. Understood in this way the question of justification is settled by working out a problem of deliberation: we have to ascertain which principles it would be rational to adopt given the contractual situation. This connects the theory of justice with the theory of rational choice.

If this view of the problem of justification is to succeed, we must, of course, describe in some detail the nature of this choice problem. A problem of rational decision has a definite answer only if we know the beliefs and interests of the parties, their relations with respect to one another, the alternatives between which they are to choose, the procedure whereby they make up their minds, and so on. As the circumstances are presented in different ways, correspondingly different principles are accepted. The concept of the original position, as I shall refer to it, is that of the most philosophically favored interpretation of this initial choice situation for the purposes of a theory of justice.

But how are we to decide what is the most favored interpretation? I assume, for one thing, that there is a broad measure of agreement that principles of justice should be chosen under certain conditions. To justify a particular description of the initial situation one shows that it incorporates these commonly shared presumptions. One argues from widely accepted but weak premises to more specific conclusions. Each of the presumptions should by itself be natural and plausible; some of them may seem innocuous or even trivial. The aim of the contract approach is to establish that taken together they impose significant bounds on acceptable principles of justice. The ideal outcome would be that these conditions determine a unique set of principles; but I shall be satisfied if they suffice to rank the main traditional conceptions of social justice.

One should not be misled, then, by the somewhat unusual conditions which characterize the original position. The idea here is simply to make vivid to ourselves the restrictions that it seems reasonable to impose on arguments for principles of justice, and therefore on these principles themselves. Thus it seems reasonable and generally acceptable that no one should be advantaged or disadvantaged by natural fortune or social circumstances in the choice of principles. It also seems widely agreed that it should be impossible to tailor principles to the circumstances of one's own case. We should insure further that particular inclinations and aspirations, and persons' conceptions of their good do not affect the principles adopted. The aim is to rule out those principles that it would be rational to propose for acceptance, however little the chance of success, only if one knew certain things that are irrelevant from the standpoint of justice. For example, if a man knew that he was wealthy, he might find it rational to advance the principle that various taxes for welfare measures be counted unjust; if he knew that he was poor, he would most likely propose the contrary principle. To represent the desired restrictions one imagines a situation in which everyone is deprived of this sort of information. One excludes the knowledge

of those contingencies which sets men at odds and allows them to be guided by their prejudices. In this manner the veil of ignorance is arrived at in a natural way. This concept should cause no difficulty if we keep in mind the constraints on arguments that it is meant to express. At any time we can enter the original position, so to speak, simply by following a certain procedure, namely, by arguing for principles of justice in accordance with these restrictions.

It seems reasonable to suppose that the parties in the original position are equal. That is, all have the same rights in the procedure for choosing principles; each can make proposals, submit reasons for their acceptance, and so on. Obviously the purpose of these conditions is to represent equality between human beings as moral persons, as creatures having a conception of their good and capable of a sense of justice. The basis of equality is taken to be similarity in these two respects. Systems of ends are not ranked in value; and each man is presumed to have the requisite ability to understand and to act upon whatever principles are adopted. Together with the veil of ignorance, these conditions define the principles of justice as those which rational persons concerned to advance their interests would consent to as equals when none are known to be advantaged or disadvantaged by social and natural contingencies.

There is, however, another side to justifying a particular description of the original position. This is to see if the principles which would be chosen match our considered convictions of justice or extend them in an acceptable way. We can note whether applying these principles would lead us to make the same judgments about the basic structure of society which we now make intuitively and in which we have the greatest confidence; or whether, in cases where our present judgments are in doubt and given with hesitation, these principles offer a resolution which we can affirm on reflection. There are questions which we feel sure must be answered in a certain way. For example, we are confident that religious intolerance and racial discrimination are unjust. We think that we have examined these things with care and have reached what we believe is an impartial judgment not likely to be distorted by an excessive attention to our own interests. These convictions are provisional fixed points which we presume any conception of justice must fit. But we have much less assurance as to what is the correct distribution of wealth and authority. Here we may be looking for a way to remove our doubts. We can check an interpretation of the initial situation, then, by the capacity of its principles to accommodate our firmest convictions and to provide guidance where guidance is needed.

In searching for the most favored description of this situation we work from both ends. We begin by describing it so that it represents generally shared and preferably weak conditions. We then see if these conditions are strong enough to yield a significant set of principles. If not, we look for further premises equally reasonable. But if so, and these principles match our considered convictions of justice, then so far well and good. But presumably there will be discrepancies. In this case we have a choice. We can either modify the account of the initial situation or we can revise our existing judgments, for even the judgments we take provisionally as fixed points are liable to revision. By going back and forth, sometimes altering the conditions of the contractual circumstances, at others withdrawing our judgments and conforming them to principle, I assume that eventually we shall find a description of the initial situation that both expresses reasonable conditions and yields principles which match our considered judgments duly pruned and adjusted. This state of affairs I refer to as reflective equilibrium. It is an equilibrium because at last our principles and judgments coincide; and it is reflective since we know to what principles our judgments conform and the premises of their derivation. At the moment everything is in order. But this equilibrium is not necessarily stable. It is liable to be upset by further examination of the conditions which should be imposed on the contractual situation and by particular cases which may lead us to revise our judgments. Yet

for the time being we have done what we can to render coherent and to justify our convictions of social justice. We have reached a conception of the original position.

I shall not, of course, actually work through this process. Still, we may think of the interpretation of the original position that I shall present as the result of such a hypothetical course of reflection. It represents the attempt to accommodate within one scheme both reasonable philosophical conditions on principles as well as our considered judgments of justice. In arriving at the favored interpretation of the initial situation there is no point at which an appeal is made to self-evidence in the traditional sense either of general conceptions or particular convictions. I do not claim for the principles of justice proposed that they are necessary truths or derivable from such truths. A conception of justice cannot be deduced from self-evident premises or conditions on principles; instead, its justification is a matter of the mutual support of many considerations, of everything fitting together into one coherent view.

A final comment. We shall want to say that certain principles of justice are justified because they would be agreed to in an initial situation of equality. I have emphasized that this original position is purely hypothetical. It is natural to ask why, if this agreement is never actually entered into, we should take any interest in these principles, moral or otherwise. The answer is that the conditions embodied in the description of the original position are ones that we do in fact accept. Or if we do not, then perhaps we can be persuaded to do so by philosophical reflection. Each aspect of the contractual situation can be given supporting grounds. Thus what we shall do is to collect together into one conception a number of conditions on principles that we are ready upon due consideration to recognize as reasonable. These constraints express what we are prepared to regard as limits on fair terms of social cooperation. One way to look at the idea of the original position, therefore, is to see it as an expository device which sums up the meaning of these conditions and helps us to extract their consequences. On the other hand, this conception is also an intuitive notion that suggests its own elaboration, so that led on by it we are drawn to define more clearly the standpoint from which we can best interpret moral relationships. We need a conception that enables us to envision our objective from afar: the intuitive notion of the original position is to do this for us....

11. TWO PRINCIPLES OF JUSTICE

I shall now state in a provisional form the two principles of justice that I believe would be agreed to in the original position. The first formulation of these principles is tentative. As we go on I shall consider several formulations and approximate step by step the final statement to be given much later. I believe that doing this allows the exposition to proceed in a natural way.

The first statement of the two principles reads as follows.

First: each person is to have an equal right to the most extensive scheme of equal basic liberties compatible with a similar scheme of liberties for others.

Second: social and economic inequalities are to be arranged so that they are both (a) reasonably expected to be to everyone's advantage, and (b) attached to positions and offices open to all.

There are two ambiguous phrases in the second principle, namely "everyone's advantage" and "open to all." Determining their sense more exactly will lead to a second formulation of the principle in §13. The final version of the two principles is given in §46; §39 considers the rendering of the first principle.

These principles primarily apply, as I have said, to the basic structure of society and govern the assignment of rights and duties and regulate the distribution of social and economic advantages. Their formulation presupposes that, for the

purposes of a theory of justice, the social structure may be viewed as having two more or less distinct parts, the first principle applying to the one, the second principle to the other. Thus we distinguish between the aspects of the social system that define and secure the equal basic liberties and the aspects that specify and establish social and economic inequalities. Now it is essential to observe that the basic liberties are given by a list of such liberties. Important among these are political liberty (the right to vote and to hold public office) and freedom of speech and assembly; liberty of conscience and freedom of thought; freedom of the person, which includes freedom from psychological oppression and physical assault and dismemberment (integrity of the person); the right to hold personal property and freedom from arbitrary arrest and seizure as defined by the concept of the rule of law. These liberties are to be equal by the first principle.

The second principle applies, in the first approximation, to the distribution of income and wealth and to the design of organizations that make use of differences in authority and responsibility. While the distribution of wealth and income need not be equal, it must be to everyone's advantage, and at the same time, positions of authority and responsibility must be accessible to all. One applies the second principle by holding positions open, and then, subject to this constraint, arranges social and economic inequalities so that everyone benefits.

These principles are to be arranged in a serial order with the first principle prior to the second. This ordering means that infringements of the basic equal liberties protected by the first principle cannot be justified, or compensated for, by greater social and economic advantages. These liberties have a central range of application within which they can be limited and compromised only when they conflict with other basic liberties. Since they may be limited when they clash with one another, none of these liberties is absolute; but however they are adjusted to form one system, this system is to be the same for all. It is difficult, and perhaps impossible, to give a complete specification of these liberties independently from the particular circumstances—social, economic and technological—of a given society. The hypothesis is that the general form of such a list could be devised with sufficient exactness to sustain this conception of justice. Of course, liberties not on the list, for example, the right to own certain kinds of property (e.g., means of production) and freedom of contract as understood by the doctrine of laissez-faire are not basic; and so they are not protected by the priority of the first principle. Finally, in regard to the second principle, the distribution of wealth and income, and positions of authority and responsibility, are to be consistent with both the basic liberties and equality of opportunity.

The two principles are rather specific in their content, and their acceptance rests on certain assumptions that I must eventually try to explain and justify. For the present, it should be observed that these principles are a special case of a more general conception of justice that can be expressed as follows.

All social values—liberty and opportunity, income and wealth, and the social bases of self-respect—are to be distributed equally unless an unequal distribution of any, or all, of these values is to everyone's advantage.

Injustice, then, is simply inequalities that are not to the benefit of all. Of course, this conception is extremely vague and requires interpretation.

As a first step, suppose that the basic structure of society distributes certain primary goods, that is, things that every rational man is presumed to want. These goods normally have a use whatever a person's rational plan of life. For simplicity, assume that the chief primary goods at the disposition of society are rights, liberties, and opportunities, and income and wealth. (Later on in Part Three the primary good of self-respect has a central place.) These are the social primary goods. Other primary goods such as health and vigor, intelligence and imagination, are natural goods; although their possession is influenced by the basic structure, they are not so directly under its control. Imagine, then, a hypothetical initial arrangement in which all the social primary goods are equally distributed: everyone has similar rights and duties, and income and wealth are evenly shared. This state of affairs provides a benchmark for judging improvements. If certain inequalities of wealth and differences in authority would make everyone better off than in this hypothetical starting situation, then they accord with the general conception.

Now it is possible, at least theoretically, that by giving up some of their fundamental liberties men are sufficiently compensated by the resulting social and economic gains. The general conception of justice imposes no restrictions on what sort of inequalities are permissible; it only requires that everyone's position be improved. We need not suppose anything so drastic as consenting to a condition of slavery. Imagine instead that people seem willing to forego certain political rights when the economic returns are significant. It is this kind of exchange which the two principles rule out; being arranged in serial order they do not permit exchanges between basic liberties and economic and social gains except under extenuating circumstances (§§26, 39).

For the most part, I shall leave aside the general conception of justice and examine instead the two principles in serial order. The advantage of this procedure is that from the first the matter of priorities is recognized and an effort made to find principles to deal with it. One is led to attend throughout to the conditions under which the absolute weight of liberty with respect to social and economic advantages, as defined by the lexical order of the two principles, would be reasonable. Offhand, this ranking appears extreme and too special a case to be of much interest; but there is more justification for it than would appear at first sight. Or at any rate, so I shall maintain (§82). Furthermore, the distinction between fundamental rights and liberties and economic and social benefits marks a difference among primary social goods that suggests an important division in the social system. Of course, the distinctions drawn and the ordering proposed are at best only approximations. There are surely circumstances in which they fail. But it is essential to depict clearly the main lines of a reasonable conception of justice; and under many conditions anyway, the two principles in serial order may serve well enough.

The fact that the two principles apply to institutions has certain consequences. First of all, the rights and basic liberties referred to by these principles are those which are defined by the public rules of the basic structure. Whether men are free is determined by the rights and duties established by the major institutions of society. Liberty is a certain pattern of social forms. The first principle simply requires that certain sorts of rules, those defining basic liberties, apply to everyone equally and that they allow the most extensive liberty compatible with a like liberty for all. The only reason for circumscribing basic liberties and making them less extensive is that otherwise they would interfere with one another.

Further, when principles mention persons, or require that everyone gain from an inequality, the reference is to representative persons holding the various social positions, or offices established by the basic structure. Thus in applying the second principle I assume that it is possible to assign an expectation of well-being to representative individuals holding these positions. This expectation indicates their life prospects as viewed from their social station. In general, the expectations of representative persons depend upon the distribution of rights and duties throughout the basic structure. Expectations are connected: by raising the prospects of the representative man in one position we presumably increase or decrease the prospects of representative men in other positions. Since it applies to institutional forms, the second principle (or rather the first part of it) refers to the expectations of representative individuals. As I shall discuss below (§14), neither principle applies to distributions of particular goods to particular individuals who may be identified by their proper names. The situation where someone is considering how to allocate certain commodities to needy persons who are known to him is not within the scope of the principles. They are meant to regulate basic institutional arrangements. We must not assume that there is much similarity from the standpoint of justice between an administrative allotment of goods to specific persons and the appropriate design of society. Our common sense intuitions for the former may be a poor guide to the latter.

Now the second principle insists that each person benefit from permissible inequalities in the basic structure. This means that it must be reasonable for each relevant representative man defined by this structure, when he views it as a going concern, to prefer his prospects with the inequality to his prospects without it. One is not allowed to justify differences in income or in positions of authority and responsibility on the ground that the disadvantages of those in one position are outweighed by the greater advantages of those in another. Much less can infringements of liberty be counterbalanced in this way. It is obvious, however, that there are indefinitely many ways in which all may be advantaged when the initial arrangement of equality is taken as a benchmark. How then are we to choose among these possibilities? The principles must be specified so that they yield a determinate conclusion. I now turn to this problem....

20. THE NATURE OF THE ARGUMENT FOR CONCEPTIONS OF JUSTICE

The intuitive idea of justice as fairness is to think of the first principles of justice as themselves the object of an original agreement in a suitably defined initial situation. These principles are those which rational persons concerned to advance their interests would accept in this position of equality to settle the basic terms of their association. It must be shown, then, that the two principles of justice are the solution for the problem of choice presented by the original position. In order to do this, one must establish that, given the circumstances of the parties, and their knowledge, beliefs, and interests, an agreement on these principles is the best way for each person to secure his ends in view of the alternatives available.

Now obviously no one can obtain everything he wants; the mere existence of other persons prevents this. The absolutely best for any man is that everyone else should join with him in furthering his conception of the good whatever it turns out to be. Or failing this, that all others are required to act justly but that he is authorized to exempt himself as he pleases. Since other persons will never agree to such terms of association these forms of egoism would be rejected. The two principles of justice, however, seem to be a reasonable proposal. In fact, I should like to show that these principles are everyone's best reply, so to speak, to the corresponding demands of the others. In this sense, the choice of this conception of justice is the unique solution to the problem set by the original position.

By arguing in this way one follows a procedure familiar in social theory. That is, a simplified situation is described in which rational individuals with certain ends and related to each other in certain ways are to choose among various courses of action in view of their knowledge of the circumstances. What these individuals will do is then derived by strictly deductive reasoning from these assumptions about their beliefs and interests, their situation and the options open to them. Their conduct is, in the phrase of Pareto, the resultant of tastes and obstacles. In the theory of price, for example, the equilibrium of competitive markets is thought of as arising when many individuals each advancing his own interests give way to each other what they can best part with in return for what they most desire. Equilibrium is the result of agreements freely struck between willing traders. For each person it is the best situation that he can reach by free exchange consistent with the right and freedom of others to further their interests in the same way. It is for this reason that this state of affairs is an equilibrium, one that will persist in the absence of further changes in the circumstances. No one has any incentive to alter it. If a departure

from this situation sets in motion tendencies which restore it, the equilibrium is stable.

Of course, the fact that a situation is one of equilibrium, even a stable one, does not entail that it is right or just. It only means that given men's estimate of their position, they act effectively to preserve it. Clearly a balance of hatred and hostility may be a stable equilibrium; each may think that any feasible change will be worse. The best that each can do for himself may be a condition of lesser injustice rather than of greater good. The moral assessment of equilibrium situations depends upon the background circumstances which determine them. It is at this point that the conception of the original position embodies features peculiar to moral theory. For while the theory of price, say, tries to account for the movements of the market by assumptions about the actual tendencies at work, the philosophically favored interpretation of the initial situation incorporates conditions which it is thought reasonable to impose on the choice of principles. By contrast with social theory, the aim is to characterize this situation so that the principles that would be chosen, whatever they turn out to be, are acceptable from a moral point of view. The original position is defined in such a way that it is a status quo in which any agreements reached are fair. It is a state of affairs in which the parties are equally represented as moral persons and the outcome is not conditioned by arbitrary contingencies or the relative balance of social forces. Thus justice as fairness is able to use the idea of pure procedural justice from the beginning.

It is clear, then, that the original position is a purely hypothetical situation. Nothing resembling it need ever take place, although we can by deliberately following the constraints it expresses simulate the reflections of the parties. The conception of the original position is not intended to explain human conduct except insofar as it tries to account for our moral judgments and helps to explain our having a sense of justice. Justice as fairness is a theory of our moral sentiments as manifested by our considered judgments in reflective equilibrium. These sentiments presumably affect our thought and action to some degree. So while the conception of the original position is part of the theory of conduct, it does not follow at all that there are actual situations that resemble it. What is necessary is that the principles that would be accepted play the requisite part in our moral reasoning and conduct.

One should note also that the acceptance of these principles is not conjectured as a psychological law or probability. Ideally anyway, I should like to show that their acknowledgment is the only choice consistent with the full description of the original position. The argument aims eventually to be strictly deductive. To be sure, the persons in the original position have a certain psychology, since various assumptions are made about their beliefs and interests. These assumptions appear along with other premises in the description of this initial situation. But clearly arguments from such premises can be fully deductive, as theories in politics and economics attest. We should strive for a kind of moral geometry with all the rigor which this name connotes. Unhappily the reasoning I shall give will fall far short of this, since it is highly intuitive throughout. Yet it is essential to have in mind the ideal one would like to achieve.

A final remark. There are, as I have said, many possible interpretations of the initial situation. This conception varies depending upon how the contracting parties are conceived, upon what their beliefs and interests are said to be, upon which alternatives are available to them, and so on. In this sense, there are many different contract theories. Justice as fairness is but one of these. But the question of justification is settled, as far as it can be, by showing that there is one interpretation of the initial situation which best expresses the conditions that are widely thought reasonable to impose on the choice of principles yet which, at the same time, leads to a conception that characterizes our considered judgments in reflective equilibrium. This most favored, or standard, interpretation I shall refer to as the original position. We may conjecture that for each traditional conception of justice there exists an interpretation of the initial

situation in which its principles are the preferred solution. Thus, for example, there are interpretations that lead to the classical as well as the average principle of utility. These variations of the initial situation will be mentioned as we go along. The procedure of contract theories provides, then, a general analytic method for the comparative study of conceptions of justice. One tries to set out the different conditions embodied in the contractual situation in which their principles would be chosen. In this way one formulates the various underlying assumptions on which these conceptions seem to depend. But if one interpretation is philosophically most favored, and if its principles characterize our considered judgments, we have a procedure for justification as well. We cannot know at first whether such an interpretation exists, but at least we know what to look for....

24. THE VEIL OF IGNORANCE

The idea of the original position is to set up a fair procedure so that any principles agreed to will be just. The aim is to use the notion of pure procedural justice as a basis of theory. Somehow we must nullify the effects of specific contingencies which put men at odds and tempt them to exploit social and natural circumstances to their own advantage. Now in order to do this I assume that the parties are situated behind a veil of ignorance. They do not know how the various alternatives will affect their own particular case and they are obliged to evaluate principles solely on the basis of general considerations.

It is assumed, then, that the parties do not know certain kinds of particular facts. First of all, no one knows his place in society, his class position or social status; nor does he know his fortune in the distribution of natural assets and abilities, his intelligence and strength, and the like. Nor, again, does anyone know his conception of the good, the particulars of his rational plan of life, or even the special features of his psychology such as his aversion to risk or liability to optimism or pessimism. More than this, I assume that the parties do not know the particular circumstances of their own society. That is, they do not know its economic or political situation, or the level of civilization and culture it has been able to achieve. The persons in the original position have no information as to which generation they belong. These broader restrictions on knowledge are appropriate in part because questions of social justice arise between generations as well as within them, for example, the question of the appropriate rate of capital saving and of the conservation of natural resources and the environment of nature. There is also, theoretically anyway, the question of a reasonable genetic policy. In these cases too, in order to carry through the idea of the original position, the parties must not know the contingencies that set them in opposition. They must choose principles the consequences of which they are prepared to live with whatever generation they turn out to belong to.

As far as possible, then, the only particular facts which the parties know is that their society is subject to the circumstances of justice and whatever this implies. It is taken for granted, however, that they know the general facts about human society. They understand political affairs and the principles of economic theory; they know the basis of social organization and the laws of human psychology. Indeed, the parties are presumed to know whatever general facts affect the choice of the principles of justice. There are no limitations on general information, that is, on general laws and theories, since conceptions of justice must be adjusted to the characteristics of the systems of social cooperation which they are to regulate, and there is no reason to rule out these facts. It is, for example, a consideration against a conception of justice that, in view of the laws of moral psychology, men would not acquire a desire to act upon it even when the institutions of their society satisfied it. For in this case there would be difficulty in securing the stability of social cooperation. An important feature of a conception of justice is that it should generate its own support. Its principles should be such that when they are embodied in the basic structure of society men tend to acquire the corresponding sense of justice and develop a desire to act in accordance with its principles. In this case a conception of justice is stable. This kind of general information is admissible in the original position.

The notion of the veil of ignorance raises several difficulties. Some may object that the exclusion of nearly all particular information makes it difficult to grasp what is meant by the original position. Thus it may be helpful to observe that one or more persons can at any time enter this position, or perhaps better, simulate the deliberations of this hypothetical situation, simply by reasoning in accordance with the appropriate restrictions. In arguing for a conception of justice we must be sure that it is among the permitted alternatives and satisfies the stipulated formal constraints. No considerations can be advanced in its favor unless they would be rational ones for us to urge were we to lack the kind of knowledge that is excluded. The evaluation of principles must proceed in terms of the general consequences of their public recognition and universal application, it being assumed that they will be complied with by everyone. To say that a certain conception of justice would be chosen in the original position is equivalent to saying that rational deliberation satisfying certain conditions and restrictions would reach a certain conclusion. If necessary, the argument to this result could be set out more formally. I shall, however, speak throughout in terms of the notion of the original position. It is more economical and suggestive, and brings out certain essential features that otherwise one might easily overlook.

These remarks show that the original position is not to be thought of as a general assembly which includes at one moment everyone who will live at some time; or, much less, as an assembly of everyone who could live at some time. It is not a gathering of all actual or possible persons. If we conceived of the original position in either of these ways, the conception would cease to be a natural guide to intuition and would lack a clear sense. In any case, the original position must be interpreted so that one can at any time adopt its perspective. It must make no difference when one takes up this viewpoint, or who does so: the restrictions must be such that the same principles are always chosen. The veil of ignorance is a key condition in meeting this requirement. It insures not only that the information available is relevant, but that it is at all times the same.

It may be protested that the condition of the veil of ignorance is irrational. Surely, some may object, principles should be chosen in the light of all the knowledge available. There are various replies to this contention. Here I shall sketch those which emphasize the simplifications that need to be made if one is to have any theory at all. (Those based on the Kantian interpretation of the original position are given later, §40.) To begin with, it is clear that since the differences among the parties are unknown to them, and everyone is equally rational and similarly situated, each is convinced by the same arguments. Therefore, we can view the agreement in the original position from the standpoint of one person selected at random. If anyone after due reflection prefers a conception of justice to another, then they all do, and a unanimous agreement can be reached. We can, to make the circumstances more vivid, imagine that the parties are required to communicate with each other through a referee as intermediary, and that he is to announce which alternatives have been suggested and the reasons offered in their support. He forbids the attempt to form coalitions, and he informs the parties when they have come to an understanding. But such a referee is actually superfluous, assuming that the deliberations of the parties must be similar.

Thus there follows the very important consequence that the parties have no basis for bargaining in the usual sense. No one knows his situation in society nor his natural assets, and therefore no one is in a position to tailor principles to his advantage. We might imagine that one of the contractees threatens to hold out unless the others agree to principles favorable to him. But how does he know which principles are especially in his interests?

The same holds for the formation of coalitions: if a group were to decide to band together to the disadvantage of the others, they would not know how to favor themselves in the choice of principles. Even if they could get everyone to agree to their proposal, they would have no assurance that it was to their advantage, since they cannot identify themselves either by name or description. The one case where this conclusion fails is that of saving. Since the persons in the original position know that they are contemporaries (taking the present time of entry interpretation), they can favor their generation by refusing to make any sacrifices at all for their successors; they simply acknowledge the principle that no one has a duty to save for posterity. Previous generations have saved or they have not; there is nothing the parties can now do to affect that. So in this instance the veil of ignorance fails to secure the desired result. Therefore, to handle the question of justice between generations, I modify the motivation assumption and add a further constraint (§22). With these adjustments, no generation is able to formulate principles especially designed to advance its own cause and some significant limits on savings principles can be derived (§44). Whatever a person's temporal position, each is forced to choose for all.

The restrictions on particular information in the original position are, then, of fundamental importance. Without them we would not be able to work out any definite theory of justice at all. We would have to be content with a vague formula stating that justice is what would be agreed to without being able to say much, if anything, about the substance of the agreement itself. The formal constraints of the concept of right, those applying to principles directly, are not sufficient for our purpose. The veil of ignorance makes possible a unanimous choice of a particular conception of justice. Without these limitations on knowledge the bargaining problem of the original position would be hopelessly complicated. Even if theoretically a solution were to exist, we would not, at present anyway, be able to determine it.

The notion of the veil of ignorance is implicit, I think, in Kant's ethics (§40). Nevertheless the problem of defining the knowledge of the parties and of characterizing the alternatives open to them has often been passed over, even by contract theories. Sometimes the situation definitive of moral deliberation is presented in such an indeterminate way that one cannot ascertain how it will turn out. Thus Perry's doctrine is essentially contractarian: he holds that social and personal integration must proceed by entirely different principles, the latter by rational prudence, the former by the concurrence of persons of good will. He would appear to reject utilitarianism on much the same grounds suggested earlier: namely, that it improperly extends the principle of choice for one person to choices facing society. The right course of action is characterized as that which best advances social aims as these would be formulated by reflective agreement, given that the parties have full knowledge of the circumstances and are moved by a benevolent concern for one another's interests. No effort is made, however, to specify in any precise way the possible outcomes of this sort of agreement. Indeed, without a far more elaborate account, no conclusions can be drawn. I do not wish here to criticize others; rather, I want to explain the necessity for what may seem at times like so many irrelevant details.

Now the reasons for the veil of ignorance go beyond mere simplicity. We want to define the original position so that we get the desired solution. If a knowledge of particulars is allowed, then the outcome is biased by arbitrary contingencies. As already observed, to each according to his threat advantage is not a principle of justice. If the original position is to yield agreements that are just, the parties must be fairly situated and treated equally as moral persons. The arbitrariness of the world must be corrected for by adjusting the circumstances of the initial contractual situation. Moreover, if in choosing principles we required unanimity even when there is full information, only a few rather obvious cases could be decided. A conception of justice based on unanimity in these circumstances would indeed be weak and trivial. But once knowledge is excluded, the requirement of unanimity is not out of place and the fact that it can be satisfied is of great importance. It enables us to say of the preferred conception of justice that it represents a genuine reconciliation of interests.

A final comment. For the most part I shall suppose that the parties possess all general information. No general facts are closed to them. I do this mainly to avoid complications. Nevertheless a conception of justice is to be the public basis of the terms of social cooperation. Since common understanding necessitates certain bounds on the complexity of principles, there may likewise be limits on the use of theoretical knowledge in the original position. Now clearly it would be very difficult to classify and to grade the complexity of the various sorts of general facts. I shall make no attempt to do this. We do however recognize an intricate theoretical construction when we meet one. Thus it seems reasonable to say that other things equal one conception of justice is to be preferred to another when it is founded upon markedly simpler general facts, and its choice does not depend upon elaborate calculations in the light of a vast array of theoretically defined possibilities. It is desirable that the grounds for a public conception of justice should be evident to everyone when circumstances permit. This consideration favors, I believe, the two principles of justice over the criterion of utility.

—85—
EXCERPTS FROM
ANARCHY, STATE AND UTOPIA

Robert Nozick

DISTRIBUTIVE JUSTICE

THE MINIMAL STATE IS THE MOST EXTENSIVE state that can be justified. Any state more extensive violates people's rights. Yet many persons have put forth reasons purporting to justify a more extensive state. It is impossible within the compass of this book to examine all the reasons that have been put forth. Therefore, I shall focus upon those generally acknowledged to be most weighty and influential, to see precisely wherein they fail. In this chapter we consider the claim that a more extensive state is justified, because necessary (or the best instrument) to achieve distributive justice; in the next chapter we shall take up diverse other claims.

The term "distributive justice" is not a neutral one. Hearing the term "distribution," most people presume that some thing or mechanism uses some principle or criterion to give out a supply of things. Into this process of distributing shares some error may have crept. So it is an open question, at least, whether *redistribution* should take place; whether we should do again what has already been done once, though poorly. However, we are not in the position of children who have been given portions of pie by someone who now makes last minute adjustments to rectify careless cutting. There is no *central* distribution, no person or group entitled to control all the resources, jointly deciding how they are to be doled out. What each person gets, he gets from others who give to him in exchange

for something, or as a gift. In a free society, diverse persons control different resources, and new holdings arise out of the voluntary exchanges and actions of persons. There is no more a distributing or distribution of shares than there is a distributing of mates in a society in which persons choose whom they shall marry. The total result is the product of many individual decisions which the different individuals involved are entitled to make. Some uses of the term "distribution," it is true, do not imply a previous distributing appropriately judged by some criterion (for example, "probability distribution"); nevertheless, despite the title of this chapter, it would be best to use a terminology that clearly is neutral. We shall speak of people's holdings; a principle of justice in holdings describes (part of) what justice tells us (requires) about holdings. I shall state first what I take to be the correct view about justice in holdings, and then turn to the discussion of alternate views.

SECTION I: THE ENTITLEMENT THEORY

The subject of justice in holdings consists of three major topics. The first is the *original acquisition of holdings*, the appropriation of unheld things. This includes the issues of how unheld things may come to be held, the process, or processes, by which unheld things may come to be held, the things that may come to be held by these processes, the extent of what comes to be held by a particular process, and so on. We shall refer to the complicated truth about this topic, which we shall not formulate here, as the principle of justice in acquisition. The second topic concerns the *transfer of holdings* from one person to another. By what processes may a person transfer holdings to another? How may a person acquire a holding from another who holds it? Under this topic come general descriptions of voluntary exchange, and gift and (on the other hand) fraud, as well as reference to particular conventional details fixed upon in a given society. The complicated truth about this subject (with placeholders for conventional details) we shall call the principle of justice in transfer. (And we shall suppose it also includes principles governing how a person may divest himself of a holding, passing it into an unheld state.)

If the world were wholly just, the following inductive definition would exhaustively cover the subject of justice in holdings.

1. A person who acquires a holding in accordance with the principle of justice in acquisition is entitled to that holding.
2. A person who acquires a holding in accordance with the principle of justice in transfer, from someone else entitled to the holding, is entitled to the holding.
3. No one is entitled to a holding except by (repeated) applications of 1 and 2.

The complete principle of distributive justice would say simply that a distribution is just if everyone is entitled to the holdings they possess under the distribution.

A distribution is just if it arises from another just distribution by legitimate means. The legitimate means of moving from one distribution to another are specified by the principle of justice in transfer. The legitimate first "moves" are specified by the principle of justice in acquisition. Whatever arises from a just situation by just steps is itself just. The means of change specified by the principle of justice in transfer preserve justice. As correct rules

of inference are truth-preserving, and any conclusion deduced via repeated application of such rules from only true premises is itself true, so the means of transition from one situation to another specified by the principle of justice in transfer are justice-preserving, and any situation actually arising from repeated transitions in accordance with the principle from a just situation is itself just. The parallel between justice-preserving transformations and truth-preserving transformations illuminates where it fails as well as where it holds. That a conclusion could have been deduced by truth-preserving means from premises that are true suffices to show its truth. That from a just situation a situation *could* have arisen via justice-preserving means does *not* suffice to show its justice. The fact that a thief's victims voluntarily *could* have presented him with gifts does not entitle the thief to his ill-gotten gains. Justice in holdings is historical; it depends upon what actually has happened. We shall return to this point later.

Not all actual situations are generated in accordance with the two principles of justice in holdings: the principle of justice in acquisition and the principle of justice in transfer. Some people steal from others, or defraud them, or enslave them, seizing their product and preventing them from living as they choose, or forcibly exclude others from competing in exchanges. None of these are permissible modes of transition from one situation to another. And some persons acquire holdings by means not sanctioned by the principle of justice in acquisition. The existence of past injustice (previous violations of the first two principles of justice in holdings) raises the third major topic under justice in holdings: the rectification of injustice in holdings. If past injustice has shaped present holdings in various ways, some identifiable and some not, what now, if anything, ought to be done to rectify these injustices? What obligations do the performers of injustice have toward those whose position is worse than it would have been had the injustice not been done? Or, than it would have been had compensation been paid promptly? How, if at all, do things change if the beneficiaries and those made worse off are not the direct parties in the act of injustice, but, for example, their descendants? Is an injustice done to someone whose holding was itself based upon an unrectified injustice? How far back must one go in wiping clean the historical slate of injustices? What may victims of injustice permissibly do in order to rectify the injustices being done to them, including the many injustices done by persons acting through their government? I do not know of a thorough or theoretically sophisticated treatment of such issues. Idealizing greatly, let us suppose theoretical investigation will produce a principle of rectification. This principle uses historical information about previous situations and injustices done in them (as defined by the first two principles of justice and rights against interference), and information about the actual course of events that flowed from these injustices, until the present, and it yields a description (or descriptions) of holdings in the society. The principle of rectification presumably will make use of its best estimate of subjunctive information about what would have occurred (or a probability distribution over what might have occurred, using the expected value) if the injustice had not taken place. If the actual description of holdings turns out not to be one of the descriptions yielded by the principle, then one of the descriptions yielded must be realized.

The general outlines of the theory of justice in holdings are that the holdings of a person are just if he is entitled to them by the principles of justice in acquisition and transfer, or by the principle of rectification of injustice (as specified by the first two principles). If each person's holdings are just, then the total set (distribution) of holdings is just. To turn these general outlines into a specific theory we would have to specify the details of each of the three principles of justice in holdings: the principle of acquisition of holdings, the principle of transfer of holdings, and the principle of rectification of violations of the first two principles. I shall not attempt that task here. (Locke's principle of justice in acquisition is discussed below.)

HISTORICAL PRINCIPLES AND END-RESULT PRINCIPLES

The general outlines of the entitlement theory illuminate the nature and defects of other conceptions of distributive justice. The entitlement theory of justice in distribution is *historical*, whether a distribution is just depends upon how it came about. In contrast, *current time-slice principles* of justice hold that the justice of a distribution is determined by how things are distributed (who has what) as judged by some *structural* principle(s) of just distribution. A utilitarian who judges between any two distributions by seeing which has the greater sum of utility and, if the sums tie, applies some fixed equality criterion to choose the more equal distribution, would hold a current time-slice principle of justice. As would someone who had a fixed schedule of trade-offs between the sum of happiness and equality. According to a current time-slice principle, all that needs to be looked at, in judging the justice of a distribution, is who ends up with what; in comparing any two distributions one need look only at the matrix presenting the distributions. No further information need be fed into a principle of justice. It is a consequence of such principles of justice that any two structurally identical distributions are equally just. (Two distributions are structurally identical if they present the same profile, but perhaps have different persons occupying the particular slots. My having ten and your having five, and my having five and your having ten are structurally identical distributions.) Welfare economics is the theory of current time-slice principles of justice. The subject is conceived as operating on matrices representing only current information about distribution. This, as well as some of the usual conditions (for example, the choice of distribution is invariant under relabeling of columns), guarantees that welfare economics will be a current time-slice theory, with all of its inadequacies.

Most persons do not accept current time-slice principles as constituting the whole story about distributive shares. They think it relevant in assessing the justice of a situation to consider not only the distribution it embodies, but also how that distribution came about. If some persons are in prison for murder or war crimes, we do not say that to assess the justice of the distribution in the society we must look only at what this person has, and that person has, and that person has, ... at the current time. We think it relevant to ask whether someone did something so that he *deserved* to be punished, deserved to have a lower share. Most will agree to the relevance of further information with regard to punishments and penalties. Consider also desired things. One traditional socialist view is that workers are entitled to the product and full fruits of their labor; they have earned it; a distribution is unjust if it does not give the workers what they are entitled to. Such entitlements are based upon some past history. No socialist holding this view would find it comforting to be told that because the actual distribution *A* happens to coincide structurally with the one he desires *D*, *A* therefore is no less just than *D*; it differs only in that the "parasitic" owners of capital receive under *A* what the workers are entitled to under *D*, and the workers receive under *A* what the owners are entitled to under *D*, namely very little. This socialist rightly, in my view, holds onto the notions of earning, producing, entitlement, desert, and so forth, and he rejects current time-slice principles that look only to the structure of the resulting set of holdings. (The set of holdings resulting from what? Isn't it implausible that how holdings are produced and come to exist has no effect at all on who should hold what?) His mistake lies in his view of what entitlements arise out of what sorts of productive processes.

We construe the position we discuss too narrowly by speaking of *current* time-slice principles. Nothing is changed if structural principles operate upon a time sequence of current time-slice profiles and, for example, give someone more now to counterbalance the less he has had earlier. A utilitarian or an egalitarian or any mixture of the two over time will inherit the difficulties of his more myopic comrades. He is not helped by the fact that *some* of the information others consider relevant in assessing a distribution is reflected, unrecoverably, in past matrices. Henceforth, we shall refer to such unhistorical principles of distributive justice, including the current time-slice principles, as *end-result principles* or *end-state principles.*

In contrast to end-result principles of justice, *historical principles* of justice hold that past circumstances or actions of people can create differential entitlements or differential deserts to things. An injustice can be worked by moving from one distribution to another structurally identical one, for the second, in profile the same, may violate people's entitlements or deserts; it may not fit the actual history.

PATTERNING

The entitlement principles of justice in holdings that we have sketched are historical principles of justice. To better understand their precise character, we shall distinguish them from another subclass of the historical principles. Consider, as an example, the principle of distribution according to moral merit. This principle requires that total distributive shares vary directly with moral merit; no person should have a greater share than anyone whose moral merit is greater. (If moral merit could be not merely ordered but measured on an interval or ratio scale, stronger principles could be formulated.) Or consider the principle that results by substituting "usefulness to society" for "moral merit" in the previous principle. Or instead of "distribute according to moral merit," or "distribute according to usefulness to society," we might consider "distribute according to the weighted sum of moral merit, usefulness to society, and need," with the weights of the different dimensions equal. Let us call a principle of distribution *patterned* if it specifies that a distribution is to vary along with some natural dimension, weighted sum of natural dimensions, or lexicographic ordering of natural dimensions. And let us say a distribution is patterned if it accords with some patterned principle. (I speak of natural dimensions, admittedly without a general criterion for them, because for any set of holdings some artificial dimensions can be gimmicked up to vary along with the distribution of the set.) The principle of distribution in accordance with moral merit is a patterned historical principle, which specifies a patterned distribution. "Distribute according to I.Q." is a patterned principle that looks to information not contained in distributional matrices. It is not historical, however, in that it does not look to any past actions creating differential entitlements to evaluate a distribution; it requires only distributional matrices whose columns are labeled by I.Q. scores. The distribution in a society, however, may be composed of such simple patterned distributions, without itself being simply patterned. Different sectors may operate different patterns, or some combination of patterns may operate in different proportions across a society. A distribution composed in this manner, from a small number of patterned distributions, we also shall term "patterned." And we extend the use of "pattern" to include the overall designs put forth by combinations of end-state principles.

Almost every suggested principle of distributive justice is patterned: to each according to his moral merit, or needs, or marginal product, or how hard he tries, or the weighted sum of the foregoing, and so on. The principle of entitlement we have sketched is *not* patterned. There is no one natural dimension or weighted sum or combination of a small number of natural dimensions that yields the distributions generated in accordance with the principle of entitlement. The set of holdings that results when some persons receive their marginal products, others win at gambling, others receive a share of their mate's income, others receive gifts from foundations, others receive interest on loans, others receive gifts from admirers, others receive returns on investment, others make for themselves much of what they have, others find things, and so on, will not be patterned. Heavy strands of patterns will run through it; significant portions of the variance in holdings will be accounted for by pattern-variables. If most people most of the time choose to transfer some of their entitlements to others only in exchange for something from them, then a large part of what many people hold will vary with what they held that others wanted. More details are provided by the theory of marginal productivity. But gifts to relatives, charitable donations, bequests to children, and the like, are not best conceived, in the first instance, in this manner. Ignoring the strands of pattern, let us suppose for the moment that a distribution actually arrived at by the operation of the principle of entitlement is random with respect to any pattern. Though the resulting set of holdings will be unpatterned, it will not be incomprehensible, for it can be seen as arising from the operation of a small number of principles. These principles specify how an initial distribution may arise (the principle of acquisition of holdings) and how distributions may be transformed into others (the principle of transfer of holdings). The process whereby the set of holdings is generated will be intelligible, though the set of holdings itself that results from this process will be unpatterned.

To think that the task of a theory of distributive justice is to fill in the blank in "to each according to his _____" is to be predisposed to search for a pattern, and the separate treatment of "from each according to his _____" treats production and distribution as two separate and independent issues. On an entitlement view these are *not* two separate questions. Whoever makes something, having bought or contracted for all other held resources used in the process (transferring some of his holdings for these cooperating factors), is entitled to it. The situation is *not* one of something's getting made, and there being an open question of who is to get it. Things come into the world already attached to people having entitlements over them. From the point of view of the historical entitlement conception of justice in holdings, those who start afresh to complete "to each according to his _____" treat objects as if they appeared from nowhere, out of nothing. A complete theory of justice might cover this limit case as well; perhaps here is a use for the usual conceptions of distributive justice.

So entrenched are maxims of the usual form that perhaps we should present the entitlement conception as a competitor. Ignoring acquisition and rectification, we might say:

From each according to what he chooses to do, to each according to what he makes for himself (perhaps with the contracted aid of others) and what others choose to do for him and choose to give him of what they've been given previously (under this maxim) and haven't yet expended or transferred.

This, the discerning reader will have noticed, has its defects as a slogan. So as a summary and great simplification (and not as a maxim with any independent meaning) we have:

From each as they choose, to each as they are chosen.

HOW LIBERTY UPSETS PATTERNS

It is not clear how those holding alternative conceptions of distributive justice can reject the entitlement conception of justice in holdings. For suppose a distribution favored by one of these non-entitlement conceptions is realized. Let us suppose it is your favorite one and let us call this distribution D_1; perhaps everyone has an equal share, perhaps shares vary in accordance with some dimension you treasure. Now suppose that Wilt Chamberlain is greatly in demand by basketball teams, being a great gate attraction. (Also suppose contracts run only for a year, with players being free agents.) He signs the following sort of contract with a team: In each home game, twenty-five cents from the price of each ticket of admission goes to him. (We ignore the question of whether he is "gouging" the owners, letting them look out for themselves.) The season starts, and people cheerfully attend his team's games; they buy their tickets, each time dropping a separate twenty-five cents of their admission price into a special box with Chamberlain's name on it. They are excited about seeing him play; it is worth the

total admission price to them. Let us suppose that in one season one million persons attend his home games, and Wilt Chamberlain winds up with $250,000, a much larger sum than the average income and larger even than anyone else has. Is he entitled to this income? Is this new distribution D_2, unjust? If so, why? There is *no* question about whether each of the people was entitled to the control over the resources they held in D_1; because that was the distribution (your favorite) that (for the purposes of argument) we assumed was acceptable. Each of these persons *chose* to give twenty-five cents of their money to Chamberlain. They could have spent it on going to the movies, or on candy bars, or on copies of *Dissent* magazine, or of *Monthly Review*. But they all, at least one million of them, converged on giving it to Wilt Chamberlain in exchange for watching him play basketball. If D_1 was a just distribution, and people voluntarily moved from it to D_2, transferring parts of their shares they were given under D_1 (what was it for if not to do something with?), isn't D_2 also just? If the people were entitled to dispose of the resources to which they were entitled (under D_1), didn't this include their being entitled to give it to, or exchange it with, Wilt Chamberlain? Can anyone else complain on grounds of justice? Each other person already has his legitimate share under D_1. Under D_1, there is nothing that anyone has that anyone else has a claim of justice against. After someone transfers something to Wilt Chamberlain, third parties *still* have their legitimate shares; *their* shares are not changed. By what process could such a transfer among two persons give rise to a legitimate claim of distributive justice on a portion of what was transferred, by a third party who had no claim of justice on any holding of the others *before* the transfer? To cut off objections irrelevant here, we might imagine the exchanges occurring in a socialist society, after hours. After playing whatever basketball he does in his daily work, or doing whatever other daily work he does, Wilt Chamberlain decides to put in *overtime* to earn additional money. (First his work quota is set; he works time over that.) Or imagine it is a skilled juggler people like to see, who puts on shows after hours.

Why might someone work overtime in a society in which it is assumed their needs are satisfied? Perhaps because they care about things other than needs. I like to write in books that I read, and to have easy access to books for browsing at odd hours. It would be very pleasant and convenient to have the resources of Widener Library in my back yard. No society, I assume, will provide such resources close to each person who would like them as part of his regular allotment (under D_1). Thus, persons either must do without some extra things that they want, or be allowed to do something extra to get some of these things. On what basis could the inequalities that would eventuate be forbidden? Notice also that small factories would spring up in a socialist society, unless forbidden. I melt down some of my personal possessions (under D_1) and build a machine out of the material. I offer you, and others, a philosophy lecture once a week in exchange for your cranking the handle on my machine, whose products I exchange for yet other things, and so on. (The raw materials used by the machine are given to me by others who possess them under D_1, in exchange for hearing lectures.) Each person might participate to gain things over and above their allotment under D_1. Some persons even might want to leave their job in socialist industry and work full time in this private sector. I shall say something more about these issues in the next chapter. Here I wish merely to note how private property even in means of production would occur in a socialist society that did not forbid people to use as they wished some of the resources they are given under the socialist distribution D_1. The socialist society would have to forbid capitalist acts between consenting adults.

The general point illustrated by the Wilt Chamberlain example and the example of the entrepreneur in a socialist society is that no end-state principle or distributional patterned principle of justice can be continuously realized without continuous interference with people's lives. Any favored pattern would be transformed into one unfavored by the principle, by people choosing to act in various ways; for example, by people exchanging goods and services with other people, or giving things to other people, things the transferrers are entitled to under the favored distributional pattern. To maintain a pattern one must either continually interfere to stop people from transferring resources as they wish to, or continually (or periodically) interfere to take from some persons resources that others for some reason chose to transfer to them. (But if some time limit is to be set on how long people may keep resources others voluntarily transfer to them, why let them keep these resources for *any* period of time? Why not have immediate confiscation?) It might be objected that all persons voluntarily will choose to refrain from actions which would upset the pattern. This presupposes unrealistically (1) that all will most want to maintain the pattern (are those who don't, to be "reeducated" or forced to undergo "self-criticism"?), (2) that each can gather enough information about his own actions and the ongoing activities of others to discover which of his actions will upset the pattern, and (3) that diverse and far-flung persons can coordinate their actions to dovetail into the pattern. Compare the manner in which the market is neutral among persons' desires, as it reflects and transmits widely scattered information via prices, and coordinates persons' activities.

It puts things perhaps a bit too strongly to say that every patterned (or end-state) principle is liable to be thwarted by the voluntary actions of the individual parties transferring some of their shares they receive under the principle. For perhaps some *very* weak patterns are not so thwarted. Any distributional pattern with any egalitarian component is overturnable by the voluntary actions of individual persons over time; as is every patterned condition with sufficient content so as actually to have been proposed as presenting the central core of distributive justice. Still, given the possibility that some weak conditions or patterns may not be unstable in this way, it would be better to formulate an explicit description of the kind of interesting and contentful patterns under discussion, and to prove a theorem about their instability. Since the weaker the patterning, the more likely it is that the entitlement system itself satisfies it, a plausible conjecture is that any patterning either is unstable or is satisfied by the entitlement system....

—86—

A MORAL CASE FOR SOCIALISM

Kai Nielsen

I

IN NORTH AMERICA SOCIALISM GETS A BAD PRESS. It is under criticism for its alleged economic inefficiency and for its moral and human inadequacy. I want here to address the latter issue. Looking at capitalism and socialism, I want to consider, against the grain of our culture, what kind of moral case can be made for socialism.

The first thing to do, given the extensive, and, I would add, inexcusably extensive, confusions about this, is to say what socialism and capitalism are. That done I will then, appealing to a cluster of values which are basic in our culture, concerning which there is a considerable and indeed a reflective consensus, examine how capitalism and socialism fare with respect to these values. Given that people generally, at least in Western societies, would want it to be the case that these values have a stable exemplification in our social lives, it is appropriate to ask the question: which of these social systems is more likely stably to exemplify them? I shall argue, facing the gamut of a careful comparison in the light of these values, that, everything considered, socialism comes out better than capitalism. And this, if right, would give us good reason for believing that socialism is preferable—indeed morally preferable—to capitalism if it also turns out to be a feasible socio-economic system.

What, then, are socialism and capitalism? Put most succinctly, capitalism requires the existence of private *productive* property (private ownership of the means of production) while socialism works toward its abolition. What is essential for socialism is public ownership and control of the means of production and public ownership means just what it says: *ownership by the public*. Under capitalism there is a domain of private property rights in the means of production which are not subject to political determination. That is, even where the political domain is a democratic one, they are not subject to determination by the public; only an individual or a set of individuals who own that property can make the final determination of what is to be done with that property. These individuals make the determination and not citizens at large, as under socialism. In fully developed socialism, by contrast, there is, with respect to productive property, no domain which is not subject to political determination by the public, namely by the citizenry at large. Thus, where this public ownership and control is genuine, and not a mask for control by an elite of state bureaucrats, it will mean genuine popular and democratic control over productive property. What socialism is *not* is *state* ownership in the absence of, at the very least, popular sovereignty, i.e., genuine popular control over the state apparatus including any economic functions it might have.

The property that is owned in common under socialism is the means of existence—the productive property in the society. Socialism does not proscribe the ownership of private personal property, such as houses, cars, television sets and the like. It only proscribes the private ownership of the means of production.

The above characterizations catch the minimal core of socialism and capitalism, what used to be called the essence of those concepts. But beyond these core features, it is well, in helping us to make our comparison, to see some other important features which characteristically go with capitalism and socialism. Minimally, capitalism is private ownership of the means of production but it is also, at least characteristically, a social system in which a class of capitalists owns and controls the means of production and hires workers who, owning little or no means of production, sell their labor-power to some capitalist or other for a wage. This means that a capitalist society will be a class society in which there will be two principal classes: capitalists and workers. Socialism by contrast is a social system in which every able-bodied person is, was or will be a worker. These workers commonly own and control the means of production (this is the characteristic form of public ownership). Thus in socialism we have, in a perfectly literal sense, a classless society for there is no division between human beings along class lines.

There are both pure and impure forms of capitalism and socialism. The pure form of capitalism is competitive capitalism, the capitalism that Milton Friedman would tell us is the real capitalism while, he would add, the impure form is monopoly or corporate capitalism. Similarly the pure form of socialism is democratic socialism, with firm workers' control of the means of production and an industrial as well as a political democracy, while the impure form is state bureaucratic socialism.

Now it is a noteworthy fact that, to understate it, actually existing capitalisms and actually existing socialisms tend to be the impure forms. Many partisans of capitalism lament the fact that the actually existing capitalisms overwhelmingly tend to be forms of corporate capitalism where the state massively intervenes in the running of the economy. It is unclear whether anything like a fully competitive capitalism actually exists—perhaps Hong Kong approximates it—and it is also unclear whether many of the actual players in the major capitalist societies (the existing capitalists and their managers) want or even expect that it is possible

to have laissez-faire capitalism again (if indeed we ever had it). Some capitalist societies are further down the corporate road than other societies, but they are all forms of corporate, perhaps in some instances even monopoly, capitalism. Competitive capitalism seems to be more of a libertarian dream than a sociological reality or even something desired by many informed and tough-minded members of the capitalist class. Socialism has had a similar fate. Its historical exemplifications tend to be of the impure forms, namely the bureaucratic state socialisms. Yugoslavia is perhaps to socialism what Hong Kong is to capitalism. It is a candidate for what might count as an exemplification, or at least a near approximation, of the pure form.

This paucity of exemplifications of pure forms of either capitalism or socialism raises the question of whether the pure forms are at best unstable social systems and at worse merely utopian ideals. I shall not try directly to settle that issue here. What I shall do instead is to compare *models* with *models*. In asking about the moral case for socialism, I shall compare forms that a not inconsiderable number of the theoretical protagonists of each take to be pure forms but which are still, they believe, historically feasible. But I will also be concerned to ask whether these models—these pure forms—can reasonably be expected to come to have a home. If they are not historically feasible models, then, even if we can make a good theoretical moral case for them, we will have hardly provided a good moral case for socialism or capitalism. To avoid bad utopianism we must be talking about forms which could be on the historical agenda. (I plainly here do not take "bad utopianism" to be pleonastic.)

II

Setting aside for the time being the feasibility question, let us compare the pure forms of capitalism and socialism—that is to say, competitive capitalism and democratic socialism—as to how they stand with respect to sustaining and furthering the values of freedom and autonomy, equality, justice, rights and democracy. My argument shall be that socialism comes out better with respect to those values.

Let us first look at freedom and autonomy. An autonomous person is a person who sets ends for herself and, in optimal circumstances, is able to pursue those ends. But freedom does not only mean being autonomous; it also means the absence of unjustified political and social interference in the pursuit of one's ends. Some might even say that it is just the absence of interference with one's ends. Still it is self-direction—autonomy—not non-interference which is *intrinsically* desirable. Non-interference is only valuable where it is an aid to our being able to do what we want and where we are sufficiently autonomous to have some control over our wants.

How do capitalism and socialism fare in providing the social conditions which will help or impede the flourishing of autonomy? Which model society would make for the greater flourishing of autonomy? My argument is (a) that democratic socialism makes it possible for more people to be more fully autonomous than would be autonomous under capitalism; and (b) that democratic socialism also interferes less in people's exercise of their autonomy than any form of capitalism. All societies limit liberty by interfering with people doing what they want to do in some ways, but the restrictions are more extensive, deeper and more undermining of autonomy in capitalism than in democratic socialism. Where there is private ownership of productive property, which, remember, is private ownership of the means of life, it cannot help but be the case that a few (the owning and controlling capitalist class) will have, along with the managers beholden to them, except in periods of revolutionary turmoil, a firm control, indeed a domination, over the vast majority of people in the society. The capitalist class with the help of their managers determines whether workers (taken now as individuals) can work, how they work, on what they work, the conditions under which they work and what is done with what they produce (where they are producers) and what use is made of their

skills and the like. As we move to welfare state capitalism—a compromise still favoring capital which emerged out of long and bitter class struggles—the state places some restrictions on some of these powers of capital. Hours, working conditions and the like are controlled in certain ways. Yet whether workers work and continue to work, how they work and on what, what is done with what they produce, and the rationale for their work are not determined by the workers themselves but by the owners of capital and their managers; this means a very considerable limitation on the autonomy and freedom of workers. Since workers are the great majority, such socio-economic relations place a very considerable limitation on human freedom and indeed on the very most important freedom that people have, namely their being able to live in a self-directed manner, when compared with the industrial democracy of democratic socialism. Under capitalist arrangements it simply cannot fail to be the case that a very large number of people will lose control over a very central set of facets of their lives, namely central aspects of their work and indeed in many instances, over their very chance to be able to work.

Socialism would indeed prohibit capitalist acts between consenting adults; the capitalist class would lose its freedom to buy and sell and to control the labor market. There should be no blinking at the fact that socialist social relations would impose some limitations on freedom, for there is, and indeed can be, no society without norms and some sanctions. In any society you like there will be some things you are at liberty to do and some things that you may not do. However, democratic socialism must bring with it an industrial democracy where workers by various democratic procedures would determine how they are to work, on what they are to work, the hours of their work, under what conditions they are to work (insofar as this is alterable by human effort at all), what they will produce and how much, and what is to be done with what they produce. Since, instead of there being "private ownership of the means of production," there is in a genuinely socialist society "public ownership of the means of production," the means of life are owned by everyone and thus each person has a *right* to work: she has, that is, a right to the means of life. It is no longer the private preserve of an individual owner of capital but it is owned in common by us all. This means that each of us has an equal right to the means of life. Members of the capitalist class would have a few of their liberties restricted, but these are linked with owning and controlling capital and are not the important civil and political liberties that we all rightly cherish. Moreover, the limitation of the capitalist liberties to buy and sell and the like would make for a more extensive liberty for many, many more people.

One cannot respond to the above by saying that workers are free to leave the working class and become capitalists or at least petty bourgeoisie. They may indeed all in theory, taken *individually*, be free to leave the working class, but if many in fact try to leave the exits will very quickly become blocked. Individuals are only free on the condition that the great mass of people, taken collectively, are not. We could not have capitalism without a working class and the working class is not free within the capitalist system to cease being wage laborers. We cannot all be capitalists. A people's capitalism is nonsense. Though a petty commodity production system (the family farm writ large) is a logical possibility, it is hardly a stable empirical possibility, and, what is most important for the present discussion, such a system would not be a capitalist system. Under capitalism, most of us, if we are to find any work at all, will just have to sell (or *perhaps* "rent" is the better word) our labor-power as a commodity. Whether you sell or rent your labor power or, where it is provided, you go on welfare, you will not have much control over areas very crucial to your life. If these are the only feasible alternatives facing the working class, working class autonomy is very limited indeed. But these are the only alternatives under capitalism.

Capitalist acts between consenting adults, if they become sufficiently widespread, lead to severe imbalances in power. These imbalances in power tend to undermine autonomy by creating differentials in wealth and control between workers and capitalists. Such imbalances are the name of the game for capitalism. Even if we (perversely I believe) call a system of petty commodity production capitalism, we still must say that such a socio-economic system is inherently unstable. Certain individuals would win out in this exchanging of commodities and in fairly quick order it would lead to a class system and the imbalances of power—the domination of the many by the few—that I take to be definitive of capitalism. By abolishing capitalist acts between consenting adults, then (but leaving personal property and civil and political liberties untouched), socialism protects more extensive freedoms for more people and in far more important areas of their lives.

III

So democratic socialism does better regarding the value that epitomizes capitalist pride (*hubris*, would, I think, be a better term), namely autonomy. It also does better, I shall now argue, than capitalism with respect to another of our basic values, namely democracy. Since this is almost a corollary of what I have said about autonomy I can afford to be briefer. In capitalist societies, democracy must simply be *political* democracy. There can in the nature of the case be no genuine or thorough workplace democracy. When we enter the sphere of production, capitalists and not workers own, and therefore at least ultimately control, the means of production. While capitalism, as in some workplaces in West Germany and Sweden, sometimes can be pressured into allowing an ameliorative measure of worker control, once ownership rights are given up, we no longer have private productive property but public productive property (and in that way social ownership): capitalism is given up and we have socialism. However, where worker control is restricted to a few firms, we do not yet have socialism. What makes a system socialist or capitalist depends on what happens across the whole society, not just in isolated firms. Moreover, managers can become very important within capitalist firms, but as long as ownership, including the ability to close the place down and liquidate the business, rests in the hands of capitalists we can have no genuine workplace democracy. Socialism, in its pure form, carries with it, in a way capitalism in any form cannot, workplace democracy. (That some of the existing socialisms are anything but pure does not belie this.)

Similarly, whatever may be said of existing socialisms or at least of some existing socialisms, it is not the case that there is anything in the very idea of socialism that militates against political as well as industrial democracy. Socialists are indeed justly suspicious of some of the tricks played by parliamentary democracy in bourgeois countries, aware of its not infrequent hypocrisy and the limitations of its stress on purely legal and formal political rights and liberties. Socialists are also, without at all wishing to throw the baby out with the bath water, rightly suspicious of any simple reliance on majority role, unsupplemented by other democratic procedures and safeguards. But there is nothing in socialist theory that would set it against political democracy and the protection of political and civil rights; indeed there is much in socialism that favors them, namely its stress on both autonomy and equality.

The fact that political democracy came into being and achieved stability within capitalist societies may prove something about conditions necessary for its coming into being, but it says nothing about capitalism being necessary for sustaining it. In Chile, South Africa and Nazi Germany, indeed capitalism has flourished without the protection of civil and political rights or anything like a respect for the democratic tradition. There is nothing structural in socialism that would prevent it from continuing those democratic traditions or cherishing those political and civil rights. That something came about under certain conditions does not establish that these conditions are necessary for its continued existence. That men initially took an interest in chess does not establish that women cannot quite naturally take an interest in it as well. When capitalist societies with long-flourishing democratic traditions move to socialism there is no reason at all to believe that they will not continue to be democratic. (Where societies previously had no democratic tradition or only a very weak one, matters are more problematic.)

IV

I now want to turn to a third basic value, equality. In societies across the political spectrum, *moral* equality (the belief that everyone's life matters equally) is an accepted value. Or, to be somewhat cynical about the matter, at least lip service is paid to it. But even this lip service is the compliment that vice pays to virtue. That is to say, such a belief is a deeply held considered conviction in modernized societies, though it has not been at all times and is not today a value held in all societies. This is most evident concerning moral equality.

While this value is genuinely held by the vast majority of people in capitalist societies, it can hardly be an effective or functional working norm where there is such a diminishment of autonomy as we have seen obtains unavoidably in such societies. Self-respect is deeply threatened where so many people lack effective control over their own lives, where there are structures of domination, where there is alienated labor, where great power differentials and differences in wealth make for very different (and often very bleak) life chances. For not inconsiderable numbers, in fact, it is difficult to maintain self-respect under such conditions unless they are actively struggling against the system. And, given present conditions, fighting the system, particularly in societies such as the United States, may well be felt to be a hopeless task. Under such conditions any real equality of opportunity is out of the question. And the circumstances are such, in spite of what is often said about these states, that equality of condition is an even more remote possibility. But without at least some of these things moral equality cannot even be approximated. Indeed, even to speak of it sounds like an obscene joke given the social realities of our lives.

Although under welfare-state capitalism some of the worst inequalities of capitalism are ameliorated, workers still lack effective control over their work, with repercussions in political and public life as well. Differentials of wealth cannot but give rise to differentials in power and control in politics, in the media, in education, in the direction of social life and in what options get seriously debated. The life chances of workers and those not even lucky enough to be workers (whose ranks are growing and will continue to grow under capitalism) are impoverished compared to the life chances of members of the capitalist class and its docile professional support stratum.

None of these equality-undermining features would obtain under democratic socialism. Such societies would for starters, be classless, eliminating the power and control differentials that go with the class system of capitalism. In addition to political democracy, industrial democracy and all the egalitarian and participatory control that goes with that would in turn, reinforce moral equality. Indeed it would make it possible where before it was impossible. There would be a commitment under democratic socialism to attaining or at least approximating, as far as it is feasible, equality of condition; and this, where approximated would help make for real equality of opportunity, making equal life chances something less utopian than it must be under capitalism.

In fine, the very things, as we have seen, that make for greater autonomy under socialism than under capitalism, would in being more equally distributed, make for greater equality of condition, greater equality of opportunity and greater moral equality in a democratic socialist society than in a capitalist one. These values are values commonly shared by both capitalistically inclined people and those who are socialistically inclined. What the former do not see is that in modern industrial societies, democratic socialism can better deliver these goods than even progressive capitalism.

There is, without doubt, legitimate worry about bureaucratic control under socialism. But that is a worry under any historically feasible capitalism as well, and it is anything but clear that state bureaucracies are worse than great corporate bureaucracies. Indeed, if socialist bureaucrats were, as the socialist system requires, really committed to production for needs and to achieving equality of condition, they might, bad as they are, be the lesser of two evils. But in any event democratic socialism is not bureaucratic state socialism, and there is no structural reason to believe that it must—if it arises in a society with skilled workers committed to democracy—give rise to bureaucratic state socialism. There will, inescapably, be some bureaucracy, but in a democratic socialist society it must and indeed will be controlled. This is not merely a matter of optimism about the will of socialists, for there are more mechanisms for democratic control of bureaucracy within a democratic socialism that is both a political and an industrial democracy, than there can be under even the most benign capitalist democracies—democracies which for structural reasons can never be industrial democracies. If, all that notwithstanding, bureaucratic creepage is inescapable in modern societies, then that is just as much a problem for capitalism as for socialism.

The underlying rationale for production under capitalism is profit and capital accumulation. Capitalism is indeed a marvelous engine for building up the productive forces (though clearly at the expense of considerations of equality and autonomy). We might look on it, going back to earlier historical times, as something like a forced march to develop the productive forces. But now that the productive forces in advanced capitalist societies are wondrously developed, we are in a position to direct them to far more humane and more equitable uses under a socio-economic system whose rationale for production is to meet human needs (the needs of everyone as far as this is possible). This egalitarian thrust, together with the socialists' commitment to attaining, as far as that is possible, equality of condition, makes it clear that socialism will produce more equality than capitalism.

V

In talking about autonomy, democracy and equality; we have, in effect, already been talking about justice. A society or set of institutions that does better in these respects than another society will be a more just society than the other society.

Fairness is a less fancy name for justice. If we compare two societies and the first is more democratic than the second; there is more autonomy in the first society than in the second; there are more nearly equal life chances in the first society than in the second and thus greater equality of opportunity; if, without sacrifice of autonomy, there is more equality of condition in the first society than in the second; and if there is more moral equality in the first society than in the second, then we cannot but conclude that the first society is a society with more fairness than the second and, thus, that it is the more just society. But this is exactly how

socialism comes out vis-à-vis even the best form of capitalism.

A society which undermines autonomy, heels in democracy (where democracy is not violating rights), makes equality impossible to achieve and violates rights cannot be a just society. If, as I contend, that is what capitalism does, and cannot help doing, then a capitalist society cannot be a just society. Democratic socialism, by contrast, does not need to do any of those things, and we can predict that it would not, for there are no structural imperatives in democratic socialism to do so and there are deep sentiments in that tradition urging us not to do so. I do not for a moment deny that there are similar sentiments for autonomy and democracy in capitalist societies, but the logic of capitalism, the underlying structures of capitalist societies—even the best of capitalist societies—frustrate the realization of the states of affairs at which those sympathies aim. A radical democrat with a commitment to human rights, to human autonomy and moral equality and fair equality of opportunity ought to be a democratic socialist and a firm opponent of capitalism—even a capitalism with a human face.

—87—

ILLUSIONS ABOUT PRIVATE PROPERTY AND FREEDOM

G.A. Cohen

1. IN CAPITALIST SOCIETIES EVERYONE OWNS something, be it only his own labour power, and each is free to sell what he owns and to buy whatever the sale of it enables him to buy.[1] Many claims made on capitalism's behalf may reasonably be doubted, but here is a freedom which it certainly bestows.

It is clear that under capitalism everyone has this freedom, unless being free to sell something is incompatible with being forced to sell it: but I do not think it is. For one is in general free to do anything which one is forced to do.

There are several reasons for affirming this possibly surprising thesis. The most direct argument in favour of it is as follows: you cannot be forced to do what you are not able to do, and you are not able to do what you are not free to do. Hence you are free to do what you are forced to do.

I am not, in the foregoing argument, equating being free to do something with being able to do it.[2] Being free to do *A* is a necessary but not a sufficient condition of being able to do *A*. I may be unable to do something not because I am unfree to, but because I lack the relevant capacity. Thus I am no doubt free to swim across the English Channel, but I am nevertheless unable to. If I were a much better swimmer, but forbidden by well-enforced law to swim it, then, again, I would be unable to swim it. The argument of the last paragraph goes through on what is often called the "negative" or "social" conception of freedom, according to which I am free to do whatever nobody would prevent me from doing. I have no quarrel with that conception in this paper.

A second argument for the claim that I am free to do what I am forced to do is that one way of frustrating someone who would force me to do something is by rendering myself not free to do it: it follows, by contraposition, that if I am forced to do it, I am free to do it. To illustrate: I commit a crime, thereby causing myself to be gaoled, so that I cannot be forced by you to do something I abhor. If you still hope to force me to do it you will have to make me free to do it (by springing me from jail).

Look at it this way: before you are forced to do *A*, you are, at least in standard cases, free to do *A* and free not to do *A*. The force removes the second freedom, but why suppose that it removes the first? It puts no obstacle in the path of your doing *A*, and you therefore remain free to do it.

We may conclude, not only that being free to do *A* is compatible with being forced to do *A*, but that being forced to do *A entails* being free to do *A*. Resistance to this odd-sounding but demonstrable result reflects failure to distinguish the idea of *being free to do something* from other ideas, such as the idea of *doing something freely*. I am free to do what I am forced to do even if, as is usually true,[3] I do not do it freely, and even though, as is always true, I am not free with respect to whether or not I do it.

I labour this truth—that one is free to do what one is forced to do—because it, and failure to

695

perceive it, help to explain the character and the persistence of a certain ideological disagreement. Marxists say that working class people are forced to sell their labour power. Bourgeois thinkers celebrate the freedom of contract manifest not only in the capitalist's purchase of labour power but also in the worker's sale of it. If Marxists are right[4] working class people are importantly unfree: they are not free *not* to sell their labour power. But it remains true that (unlike chattel slaves) they are free to sell their labour power. The unfreedom asserted by Marxists is compatible with the freedom asserted by bourgeois thinkers. Indeed: if the Marxists are right the bourgeois thinkers are right, unless they also think, as characteristically they do, that the truth they emphasise refutes the Marxist claim. The bourgeois thinkers go wrong not when they say that the worker is free to sell his labour power, but when they infer that the Marxist cannot therefore be right in his claim that the worker is forced to. And Marxists[5] share the bourgeois thinkers' error when they think it necessary to deny what the bourgeois thinkers say. If the worker is not free to sell his labour power, of what freedom is a foreigner whose work permit is removed deprived?

2. Freedom to buy and sell is one freedom, of which in capitalism there is a great deal. It belongs to capitalism's essential nature. But many think that capitalism is, quite as essentially, a more comprehensively free society. Very many people, including philosophers, who try to speak carefully, use the phrase "free society" as an alternative name for societies which are capitalist.[6] And many contemporary English-speaking philosophers and economists call the doctrine which recommends a purely capitalist society "libertarianism," not, as might be thought more apt, "libertarianism with respect to buying and selling."

It is not only the libertarians themselves who think that is the right name for their party. Many who reject their aims concede the name to them: they agree that unmodified capitalism is comprehensively a realm of freedom. This applies to *some* of those who call themselves "liberals."

These liberals assert, plausibly, that liberty is a good thing, but they say that it is not the only good thing. So far, libertarians will agree. But liberals also believe that libertarians wrongly sacrifice other good things in too total defence of the one good of liberty. They agree with libertarians that pure capitalism is liberty pure and simple, or anyway *economic* liberty pure and simple, but they think the various good things lost when liberty pure and simple is the rule justify restraints on liberty. They want a capitalism modified by welfare legislation and state intervention in the market. They advocate, they say, not unrestrained liberty, but liberty restrained by the demands of social and economic security. They think that what they call a free economy is too damaging to those, who, by nature or circumstance, are ill placed to achieve a minimally proper standard of life within it, so they favour, within limits, taxing the better off for the sake of the worse off, although they believe that such taxation reduces liberty. They also think that what they call a free economy is subject to fluctuations in productive activity and misallocations of resources which are potentially damaging to everyone, so they favour measures of interference in the market, although, again, they believe that such interventions diminish liberty. They do not question the libertarian's description of capitalism as the (economically) free society. But they believe that economic freedom may rightly and reasonably be abridged. They believe in a compromise between liberty and other values, and that what is known as the welfare state mixed economy achieves the right compromise.

I shall argue that libertarians, and liberals of the kind described, misuse the concept of freedom. This is not a comment on the attractiveness of the institutions they severally favour, but on the rhetoric they use to describe them. If, however, as I contend, they misdescribe those institutions, then that is surely because the correct description of them would make them less attractive, so my critique of the defensive rhetoric is indirectly a critique of the institutions the rhetoric defends.

My central contention is that liberals and libertarians see the freedom which is intrinsic to capitalism, but do not give proper notice to the unfreedom which necessarily accompanies it.

To expose this failure of perception, I shall criticise a description of the libertarian position provided by Antony Flew in his *Dictionary of Philosophy*. It is there said to be "whole-hearted political and economic liberalism, opposed to any social or legal constraints on individual freedom."[7] Liberals of the kind I described above would avow themselves unwhole-hearted in the terms of this definition. For they would say that they support certain (at any rate) legal constraints on individual freedom.

Now a society in which there are *no* "social and legal constraints on individual freedom" is perhaps imaginable, at any rate by people who have highly anarchic imaginations. But, be that as it may, the Flew definition misdescribes libertarians, since it does not apply to defenders of capitalism, which is what libertarians profess to be, and are.

For consider. If the state prevents me from doing something I want to do, it evidently places a constraint on my freedom. Suppose, then, that I want to perform an action which involves a legally prohibited use of your property. I want, let us say, to pitch a tent in your large back garden, because I have no home or land of my own, but I have got hold of a tent, legitimately or otherwise. If I now try to do what I want to do, the chances are that the state will intervene on your behalf. If it does, I shall suffer a constraint on my freedom. The same goes for all unpermitted uses of a piece of private property by those who do not own it, and there are always those who do not own it, since "private ownership by one person ... presupposes non-ownership on the part of other persons."[8] But the free enterprise economy advocated by libertarians rests upon private property: you can sell and buy only what you respectively own and come to own. It follows that the Flew definition is untrue to its *definiendum*, and that "libertarianism" is a questionable name for the position it now standardly denotes.

How could Flew publish the definition I have criticised? I do not think he was being dishonest. I would not accuse him of appreciating the truth of this particular matter and deliberately falsifying it. Why then is it that Flew, and libertarians like him, see the unfreedom in prospective state interference with your use of your property, but do not see the unfreedom in the standing intervention against my use of it entailed by the fact that it *is* your private property? What explains their monocular vision?

One explanation is a tendency to take as part of the structure of human existence in general, and therefore as no "social or legal constraint" on freedom, any structure around which, *merely as things are*, much of our activity is organised. In capitalist society the institution of private property is such a structure. It is treated as so *given* that the obstacles it puts on freedom are not perceived, while any impingement on private property itself is immediately noticed. Yet private property pretty well *is* a distribution of freedom *and* unfreedom. It is necessarily associated with the liberty of private owners to do as they wish with what they own, but it no less necessarily withdraws liberty from those who do not own it. To think of capitalism as a realm of freedom is to overlook half of its nature. (I am aware that the tendency to this failure of perception is stronger, other things being equal, the more private property a person has. I do not think really poor people need to have their eyes opened to the simple conceptual truth I emphasise. I also do not claim that anyone of sound mind will for long deny that private property places restrictions on freedom, once the point has been made. What is striking is that the point so often needs to be made, against what should be *obvious* absurdities, such as Flew's definition of "libertarianism.")

I have supposed that to prevent someone from doing something he wants to do is to make him, in that respect, unfree: I am unfree whenever someone interferes, *justifiably or otherwise*, with my actions. But there is a definition of freedom which is implicit in much libertarian writing,[9] and which entails that interference is *not* a sufficient condition of unfreedom. On that definition, which I shall call the *moralised* definition, I am unfree only when someone does or would *unjustifiably* interfere with me. If one now combines this moralised definition of freedom with a moral endorsement of private property, one reaches the result that the protection of legitimate private property cannot restrict anyone's freedom. It will follow from the moral endorsement of private property that you and the police are justified in preventing me from pitching my tent on your land, and, because of the moralised definition of freedom, it will then further follow that you and the police do not thereby restrict my freedom. So here we have another explanation of how intelligent philosophers are able to say what they do about capitalism, private property and freedom. But the characterisation of freedom which figures in the explanation is unacceptable. For it entails that a properly convicted murderer is not rendered unfree when he is justifiably imprisoned.

Even justified interference reduces freedom. But suppose for a moment that, as libertarians say or imply, it does not. On that supposition one cannot readily argue that interference with private property is wrong *because* it reduces freedom. For one can no longer take for granted, what is evident on a morally neutral account of freedom, that interference with private property *does* reduce freedom. Under a moralised account of freedom one must abstain from that assertion until one has shown that private property is morally defensible. Yet libertarians tend *both* to use a moralised definition *and* to take it for granted that interference with private property diminishes the owner's freedom. Yet they can take that for granted only on an account of freedom in which it is equally obvious that the protection of private property diminishes the freedom of nonowners, to avoid which consequence they retreat to a moralised definition of the concept.

Still, libertarians who embrace the moralised definition of freedom need not occupy this inconsistent position. They can escape it by justifying private property on grounds other than considerations of freedom. They can contrive, for example, to represent interference with rightfully held private property as unjust, and *therefore*, by virtue of the moralised definition, invasive of freedom. This is a consistent position. But it still incorporates an unacceptable definition of freedom, and the position is improved[10] if that is eliminated. We then have a defence of private property on grounds of justice. Freedom falls out of the picture.[11]

3. I now want to consider a possible response to what I said about pitching a tent on your land. It might be granted that the prohibition on my doing so restricts my freedom, but not, so it might be said, my *economic* freedom. If the connection between capitalism and freedom is overstated by libertarians and others, the possibility that capitalism is *economic* freedom still requires consideration.

The resurrected identification will survive only if the unavailability to me of your garden is no restriction on my economic freedom. I can think of only one reason for saying so. It is that I am not here restricted with respect to whether I may sell something I own, or buy something in exchange for what I own. If that is economic freedom, then my lack of access to your garden does not limit my economic freedom.

A different definition of economic freedom would include in it freedom to use goods and services. It is hard to say whether such a definition is superior to the less inclusive one just considered, since "neither the tradition of political philosophy nor common understanding provides us with a ... set of categories of economic liberty" comparable to the acknowledged set of categories of political liberty,[12] perhaps because the boundary of the economic domain is unclear.[13] A reasoned attempt to construct a clear concept of economic freedom might be a valuable exercise, but it is not one which I can report having completed. I am accordingly unable to recommend any particular characterisation of economic freedom.

I can nevertheless reply to the present claim, as follows: either economic freedom includes the freedom to use goods and services, or it does not. If it does, then capitalism withholds economic freedom wherever it grants it, as the tent case shows. If, on the other hand, economic freedom relates only to buying and selling, then the case for identifying economic freedom and free enterprise looks better. But we have to define "economic freedom" narrowly to obtain this result. On a wide but eligible definition of economic freedom, capitalism offers a particular limited form of it. On a narrow definition, the limitations recede, but we are now talking about a much narrower freedom.

To those who do not think this freedom is narrow, I offer three comments, which may move them a little:

(i) The freedom in question is, fully described, freedom to sell what I own and to buy whatever the sale of what I own enables me to buy. Importantly, that freedom is not identical with freedom to buy and sell just anything at all, which is much broader, and which is not granted by capitalism. For first, one is evidently not free to sell what belongs to somebody else. This is, to be sure, true by definition: there logically *could* not be that freedom, in any society. But this does not diminish the importance of noticing that capitalism does not offer it.[14] And secondly, one is free to buy, not anything at all, but only that which the sale of what one owns enables one to buy. A poor man is not free to buy a grand piano, even if one necessary condition of that freedom—he is not legally forbidden to do so—is satisfied.

(ii) It is an important fact about freedom in general, and hence about the freedom under discussion, that it comes in degrees. That I am free to do something does not say *how* free I am to do that thing, which might be more or less. To cite just one dimension in which freedom's degree varies, my freedom to do *A* is, other things equal, smaller, the greater is the cost to me of doing *A*. It might be true of both a poor man and a rich man that each is free to buy an £8 ticket to the opera, yet the rich man's freedom to do so is greater, since, unlike the poor man, he will not have to give up a few decent meals, for example, in order to buy the ticket. Since it is consistent with the capitalist character of a society that it should contain poor people, the buying and selling freedom which capitalism grants universally can be enjoyed in very limited degrees.

Now some will disagree with my claim that freedom varies in degree in the manner just described. They will deny that some people have a higher degree of a certain freedom than others (who also have that freedom), and will say, instead, that for some people it is relatively easy to exercise a freedom which others, who also have it, find it difficult to exercise. But even if they are right, the substance of my case is unweakened. For it is scarcely intelligible that one should be interested in how much freedom people have in a certain form of society without being interested in how readily they are able to exercise it.

(iii) Finally, we should consider the *point* of the freedom to buy and sell, as far as the individual who has it is concerned. For most citizens, most of the time, that point is to obtain goods and services of various sorts. When, therefore, goods and services are available independently of the market, the individual might not feel that his lack of freedom to *buy* them is a particularly significant lack. A lack of freedom to buy medical services is no serious restriction on liberty in a society which makes them publicly available on a decent scale. In a socialist society certain things will be unbuyable, and, consequently, unsellable. But, as long as they are obtainable by other means, one should not exaggerate the gravity of the resulting restrictions on freedom.

Still, restrictions on freedom do result. I may not *want* to buy a medical or an educational service, but I am nevertheless unfree to, if the transaction is forbidden. Note that I would not be unfree to if a certain popular account of freedom were correct, according to which I am unfree only when what I *want* to do is something I shall or would be prevented from doing. But that account is false.[15] There are important connections between freedom and desire, but the straightforward one maintained in the popular account is not among them. Reference to a man's desires is irrelevant to the question "What is he free to do?" but it is, I believe, relevant to the question "How much freedom (comprehensively) does he have?" and consequently to the politically crucial question of comparing the amounts of freedom enjoyed in different societies. As far as I know, the vast philosophical literature on freedom contains no sustained attempt to formulate criteria for answering questions about quantity of freedom. I attempted a discussion of such criteria in an earlier draft of this paper, but the response to it from many friends was so skeptical that I decided to abandon it. I hope to return to it one day, and I hope that others will address it too.

4. I have wanted to show that private property, and therefore capitalist society, limit liberty, but I have not shown that they do so more than communal property and socialist society. Each *form* of society is by its nature congenial and hostile to various sorts of liberty, for variously placed people. And *concrete* societies exemplifying either form will offer and withhold additional liberties whose presence or absence may not be inferred from the nature of the form itself. Which form is better for freedom, all things considered, is a question which may have no answer in the abstract: it may be that which form is better for freedom depends entirely on the historical circumstances.

I am here separating two questions about capitalism, socialism, and freedom. The first, or *abstract* question, is which form of society is, just as such, better for freedom, not, and this is the second, and *concrete* question, which form is better for freedom in the conditions of a particular place and time.[16] The first question is interesting, but difficult and somewhat obscure. I shall try to clarify it presently. I shall then indicate that two distinct ranges of consideration bear on the second question, about freedom in a particular case, considerations which must be distinguished not only for theoretical but also for political reasons.

Though confident that the abstract interpretation of the question, which form, if any, offers more liberty, is meaningful, I am not at all sure what its meaning is. I do not think we get an answer to it favouring one form if and only if that form would in all circumstances provide more freedom than the other. For I can understand the claim that socialism is by nature a freer society than capitalism even though it would be a less free society under certain conditions.

Consider a possible analogy. It will be agreed that sports cars are faster than jeeps, even though jeeps are faster on certain kinds of terrain. Does the abstract comparison, in which sports cars outclass jeeps, mean, therefore, that sports cars are faster on *most* terrains? I think not. It seems sufficient for sports cars to be faster in the abstract that there is some unbizarre terrain on which their maximum speed exceeds the maximum speed of jeeps on any terrain. Applying the analogy, if socialism is said to be freer than capitalism in the abstract, this would mean that there are realistic concrete conditions under which a socialist society would be freer than *any* concrete capitalist society would be. This, perhaps, is what some socialists mean when they say that socialism is a freer society, for some who say that would acknowledge that in some conditions socialism, or what would pass for it,[17] would be less free than at any rate some varieties of capitalism.

There are no doubt other interesting abstract questions, which do not yield to the analysis just given. Perhaps, for example, the following intractably rough prescription could be made more useable: consider, with respect to each form of society, the sum of liberty which remains when the liberties it withholds by its very nature are subtracted from the liberties it guarantees by its very nature. The society which is freer in the abstract is the one where that sum is larger.

So much for the abstract issue. I said that two kinds of consideration bear on the answer to concrete questions, about which form of society would provide more freedom in a particular here and now. We may look upon each form of society as a set of rules which generates, in particular cases, particular enjoyments and deprivations of freedom. Now the effect of the rules in a particular case will depend, in the first place, on the resources and traditions which prevail in the society in question. But secondly, and distinctly, it will also depend on the ideological and political views of the people concerned. (This distinction is not always easy to make, but it is never impossible to make it.) To illustrate the distinction, it could be that in a given case collectivisation of agriculture would provide more freedom on the whole for rural producers, were it not for the fact that they do not *believe* it would, and would therefore resist collectivisation so strongly that it could be introduced only at the cost of enormous repression. It could be that though socialism might distribute more liberty in Britain now, capitalist ideology is now here so powerful, and the belief that socialism would reduce liberty is, accordingly, so strong, that conditions *otherwise* propitious for realising a socialism with a great deal of liberty are not favourable in the final reckoning, since the final reckoning must take account of the present views of people about how free a socialist society would be.

I think it is theoretically and politically important to attempt a reckoning independent of that final reckoning.

It is theoretically important because there exists a clear question about whether a socialist revolution would expand freedom whose answer is not determined by people's beliefs about what its answer is. *Its* answer might be "yes," even though most people think its answer is "no," and even though, as a result, "no" is the correct answer to the further, "final reckoning" question, for whose separateness I am arguing. Unless one separates the questions, one cannot coherently evaluate the ideological answers to the penultimate question which help to cause the ultimate question to have the answer it does.

It is also politically necessary to separate the questions, because it suits our rulers not to distinguish the two levels of assessment. The Right can often truly say that, all things considered, socialism would diminish liberty, where, however, the chief reason why this is so is that the Right, with its powerful ideological arsenal, have convinced enough people that it is so. Hence one needs to argue for an answer which does not take people's conviction into account, partly, of course, in order to combat and transform those convictions. If, on the other hand, you want to defend the status quo, then I recommend that you confuse the questions I have distinguished.

The distinction between concrete questions enables me to make a further point about the abstract question, which *form* of society provides more freedom. We saw above that a plausible strategy for answering it involves asking concrete questions about particular cases. We may now add that the concrete questions relevant to the abstract one are those which prescind from people's beliefs about their answers.

I should add, finally, that people's beliefs about socialism and freedom affect not only how free an achieved socialist society would be, but also how much restriction on freedom would attend the process of achieving it. (Note that there is a somewhat analogous distinction between how much freedom we have in virtue of the currently maintained capitalist arrangements, and how much we have, or lose, because of the increasingly repressive measures used to maintain them.) Refutation of bourgeois ideology is an imperative task for socialists, not as an alternative to the struggle for socialism, but as part of the struggle for a socialism which will justify the struggle which led to it.

5. I said above that capitalism and socialism offer different sets of freedoms, but I emphatically do not say that they provide freedom in two different senses of that term. To the claim that capitalism gives people freedom some socialists respond that what they get is *merely bourgeois* freedom. Good things can be meant by that response: that there are important particular liberties which capitalism does not confer; and/or that I do not have freedom, but only a necessary condition of it, when a course of action (for example, skiing) is, though not *itself*

against the law, unavailable to me anyway, because other laws (for example, those of private property, which prevent a poor man from using a rich man's unused skis) forbid me the means to perform it. But when socialists suggest that there is no "real" freedom under capitalism, at any rate for the workers, or that socialism promises freedom of a higher and as yet unrealised kind, then I think their line is theoretically incorrect and politically disastrous. For there is freedom under capitalism, in a plain, good sense, and if socialism will not give us more of it, we shall rightly be disappointed. If the socialist says he is offering a new variety of freedom, the advocate of capitalism will carry the day with his reply that he prefers freedom of the known variety to an unexplained and unexemplified rival. But if, as I would recommend, the socialist argues that capitalism is, all things considered, inimical to freedom *in the very sense* of "freedom" in which, as he should concede, a person's freedom is diminished when his private property is tampered with, then he presents a challenge which the advocate of capitalism, by virtue of his own commitment, cannot ignore.

For it is a contention of socialist thought that capitalism does not live up to its own professions. A fundamental socialist challenge to the libertarian is that pure capitalism does not protect liberty in general, but rather those liberties which are built into private property, an institution which also limits liberty. And a fundamental socialist challenge to the liberal is that the modifications of modified capitalism modify not liberty, but private property, often in the interest of liberty itself. Consequently, transformations far more revolutionary than a liberal would contemplate might be justified on the very same grounds as those which support liberal reform.

A homespun example shows how communal property offers a differently shaped liberty, in no different sense of that term, and, in certain circumstances, more liberty than the private property alternative. Neighbours *A* and *B* own sets of household tools. Each has some tools which the other lacks. If *A* needs tools of a kind which only *B* has, then, private property being what it is, he is not free to take *B*'s one for a while, even if *B* does not need it during that while. Now imagine that the following rule is imposed, bringing the tools into partly common ownership: each may take and use a tool belonging to the other without permission provided that the other is not using it and that he returns it when he no longer needs it, or when the other needs it, whichever comes first. *Things being what they are* (a substantive qualification: we are talking, as often we should, about the real world, not about remote possibilities) the communising rule would, I contend, increase tool-using freedom, on any reasonable view. To be sure, some freedoms are removed by the new rule. Neither neighbour is as assured of the same easy access as before to the tools that were wholly his. Sometimes he has to go next door to retrieve one of them. Nor can either now charge the other for use of a tool he himself does not then require. But these restrictions probably count for less than the increase in the range of tools available. No one is as sovereign as before over any tool, so the privateness of the property is reduced. But freedom is probably expanded.

It is true that each would have more freedom still if he were the sovereign owner of *all* the tools. But that is not the relevant comparison. I do not deny that full ownership of a thing gives greater freedom than shared ownership of that thing. But no one did own all the tools before the modest measure of communism was introduced. The kind of comparison we need to make is between, for example, sharing ownership with ninety-nine others in a hundred things and fully owning just one of them. I submit that which arrangement nets more freedom is a matter of cases. There is little sense in one hundred people sharing control over one hundred toothbrushes. There is an overwhelming case, from the point of view of freedom, in favour of our actual practice of public ownership of street pavements. Denationalising the pavements in favour of private ownership of each piece by the residents adjacent to it would be bad for freedom of movement.

But someone will say: ownership of private property is the only example of *full* freedom. Our practice with pavements may be a good one, but no one has full freedom with respect to any part of the pavement, since he cannot, for instance, break it up and put the result to a new use, and he cannot prevent others from using it (except, perhaps, by the costly means of indefinitely standing on it himself, and he cannot even do that when laws against obstruction are enforced). The same holds for all communal possessions. No one is fully free with respect to anything in which he enjoys a merely shared ownership. Hence even if private property entails unfreedom, and even if there is freedom without private property, *there is no case of full freedom which is not a case of private property*. The underlined thesis is unaffected by the arguments against libertarianism in sections 2 and 3 of this paper.

There are two things wrong with this fresh attempt to associate freedom and private property. First, even if it is true that every case of full freedom is a case of private property, a certain number of full freedoms need not add up to more freedom overall than a larger number of partial freedoms: so it is not clear that the underlined thesis supports any interesting conclusion.

The thesis is, moreover, questionable in itself. It is a piece of bourgeois ideology masquerading as a conceptual insight The argument for the thesis treats freedom fetishistically, as control over *material things*. But freedom, in the central sense of the term with which we have been occupied, is freedom to *act*, and if there is a concept of full freedom in that central sense, then it is inappropriate, if we want to identify it, to focus, from the start, on control over *things*. I can be fully free to walk to your home when and because the pavement is communally owned, even though I am not free to destroy or to sell a single square inch of that pavement. To be sure, action requires the use of matter, or at least space,[18] but it does not follow that to be fully free to perform an action with certain pieces of matter in a certain portion of space I need full control over the matter and the space, since some forms of control will be unnecessary to the action in question. The rights I need over things to perform a given action depend on the nature of that action.

The thesis under examination is, then, either false, or reducible to the truism that one has full freedom *with respect to a thing* only if one privately owns that thing. But why should we be especially interested in full freedom with respect to a *thing*, unless, of course, we are already ideologically committed to the overriding importance of private property?

6. Recall the example of the tools, described above. An opponent might say: the rules of private property allow neighbours to *contract* in favour of the stated arrangement. If both would gain from the change, and they are rational, they will agree to it. No communist property rule, laid down independently of contract, is needed.

This is a good reply with respect to the case at hand. For that case my only counter is the weakish one that life under capitalism tends to generate an irrationally strong attachment to purely private use of purely private property, which can lead to neglect of mutually gainful and freedom-expanding options.

That point aside, it must be granted that contracts often establish desirably communal structures, sometimes with transaction costs which communist rules would not impose, but also without the administrative costs which often attach to public regulation.

But the stated method of achieving communism cannot be generalised. We could not by contract bring into shared ownership those non-household tools and resources which Marxists call means of production. They will never be won for socialism by contract,[19] since they belong to a small minority, to whom the rest can offer no quid pro quo. Most of the rest must lease their labour power to members of that minority, in exchange for some of the proceeds of their labour on facilities in whose ownership they do not share.

So we reach, at length, a central charge with respect to freedom which Marxists lay against capitalism, and which is, in my view, well founded: that in capitalist society the great majority of people are forced, because of the character of the society, to sell their labour power to others. In properly refined form, this important claim about capitalism and liberty is, I am sure, correct. I have attempted to refine it elsewhere.[20]

NOTES

1 The present paper rewrites and extends arguments first presented on 9–17 of "Capitalism, Freedom and the Proletariat," which appeared in Alan Ryan (ed.), *The Idea of Freedom: Essays in Honour of Isaiah Berlin*, Oxford, 1979. The position of the proletariat with respect to freedom, discussed on 17–25 of that paper, is not treated here. I return to that issue in a forthcoming article on "The Structure of Proletarian Unfreedom."

2 I point this out because the argument was thus misinterpreted by Galen Strawson in a review of *The Idea of Freedom* which appeared in *Lycidas*, the journal of Wolfson College, Oxford. See *Lycidas*, 7, 1978–79, 35–36.

3 It is not true that whenever I am forced to do something I act unfreely, not, at any rate, if we accept Gerald Dworkin's well-defended claim that "*A* does *X* freely if ... *A* does *X* for reasons which he doesn't mind acting from" ("Acting Freely," *Nous*, 1970, 381). On this view some forced action is freely performed: if, for example, I am forced to do something which I had wanted to do and had fully intended to do, then, unless I resent the supervenient coercion, I do it freely.

4 I consider whether they are right in the latter half of "Capitalism, Freedom and the Proletariat," and in "The Structure of Proletarian Unfreedom."

5 Such as Ziyad Husami, if he is a Marxist, who says of the wage worker: "Deprived of the ownership of means of production and means of livelihood, he is forced (not free) to sell his labour power to the capitalist" ("Marx on Distributive Justice," *Philosophy and Public Affairs*, Fall, 1978, 51–52). I contend that the phrase in parentheses introduces a falsehood into Husami's sentence, a falsehood which Karl Marx avoided when he said of the worker that "the time for which he is free to sell his labour power is

the time for which he is forced to sell it" (*Capital*, I, Moscow, 1961, 302).

6 See, for example, Jan Narveson, "A Puzzle about Economic Justice in Rawls' Theory," *Social Theory and Practice*, 1976, 3; James Rachels, "What People Deserve," in J. Arthur and W. Shaw (eds.), *Justice and Economic Distribution*, Englewood Cliffs, 1978, 151.

7 *A Dictionary of Philosophy*, London, 1979, 188.

8 Karl Marx, *Capital*, III, Moscow, 1970, 812.

9 And sometimes also explicit: see Robert Nozick, *Anarchy, State and Utopia*, New York, 1974, 262.

10 It is improved intellectually in that a certain objection to it no longer applies, but ideologically speaking it is weakened, since there is more ideological power in a recommendation of private property on grounds of justice *and* freedom—however confused the relationship between them may be—than in a recommendation of private property on grounds of justice alone.

11 The justice argument for private property is not examined in what follows. I deal with it at length in "Respecting Private Property."

12 Thomas Scanlon, "Liberty, Contract and Contribution," in G. Dworkin et al. (eds.), *Markets and Morals*, Washington, 1977, 54; and see also 57.

13 This suggestion is due to Chris Proviso.

14 Cheyney Ryan's discussion of "capacity rights" is relevant here. See his "The Normative Concept of Coercion," *Mind*, forthcoming.

15 See Isaiah Berlin, *Four Essays on Liberty*, Oxford, 1969, xxxviii ff., 139–40. The point was originally made by Richard Wollheim, in a review of Berlin's *Two Concepts of Liberty*. See too Hillel Steiner, "Individual Liberty," *Proceedings of the Aristotelian Society*, 1974–75, 34.

16 One may also distinguish not, as above, between the capitalist form of society and a particular capitalist society, but between the capitalist form in general and specific forms of capitalism, such as competitive capitalism, monopoly capitalism, and so on (I provide a systematic means of generating specific forms in *Karl Marx's Theory of History*, Oxford, 1978, Chapter III, sections [6] and [8]). This further distinction is at the abstract level, rather than

between abstract and concrete. I prescind from it here to keep my discussion relatively uncomplicated. The distinction would have to be acknowledged, and employed, in any treatment which pretended to be definitive.

17   Which way they would put it depends on how they would define socialism. If it is defined as public ownership of the means of production, and this is taken in a narrowly juridical sense, then it is compatible with severe restrictions on freedom. But if, to go to other extreme, it is defined as a condition in which the free development of each promotes, and is promoted by, the free development of all, then only the attempt to institute socialism, not socialism, could have negative consequences for freedom.

18   This fact is emphasised by Hillel Steiner in section III of his "Individual Liberty," but he goes too far when he says: "My theorem is ... that *freedom is the personal possession of physical objects*" (48). I claim that the "theorem" is just bourgeois ideology. For further criticism of Steiner, see Onora O'Neill, "The Most Extensive Liberty," *Proceedings of the Aristotelian Society*, 1979–80, 48.

19   Unless the last act of this scenario qualifies as a contract: in the course of a general strike a united working class demands that private property in major means of production be socialised, as a condition of resumption of work, and a demoralised capitalist class meets the demand. (How, by the way, could "libertarians" object to such a revolution? For hints see Robert Nozick, "Coercion," in P. Laslett et al. [eds.], *Philosophy, Politics and Society*, Fourth Series, Oxford, 1972.)

20   See note 1 above.

—88—

DISTRIBUTIVE JUSTICE

The Case of Café Feminino

Kyle Johannsen

BACKGROUND

FAIR TRADE SOMETIMES GETS A BAD RAP. Though the label is meant to help conscientious consumers avoid supporting exploitive trade relationships with producers in the Global South, the idea of Fair Trade is commonly abused by companies seeking to take advantage of its marketing potential. By selling only a couple of Fair Trade certified products or by creating similar sounding labels, companies can market themselves as ethically minded without taking on the corresponding commitments that Fair Trade is supposed to embody. This phenomenon is frequently referred to as "fair washing." However, as an examination of coffee production in the Andean foothills of northern Peru reveals, Fair Trade can sometimes yield significant economic and social benefits.

A number of Fair Trade coffee producers in that region operate under the brand name "Café Feminino." As the name suggests, producers are committed to improving local Peruvian women's socio-economic status. Money generated through the sale of their products is used to fund a number of development initiatives, including the creation of community spaces for women, workshops designed to develop women's leadership abilities, and a respiratory health initiative that targets the improvement of air quality in home kitchens.[1] Café Feminino imposes a unique requirement: members must be women who hold title to their coffee growing land. This has created a powerful incentive for female land ownership and a corresponding increase in women's economic independence.

In response to the crisis of falling prices and oversupply for coffee in the 1990s, Peruvian coffee cooperatives organized themselves under the umbrella cooperative CECANOR to gain fair-trade certification. Convinced that they produced a better product than the male members of CECANOR, female members created their own separate label in order to differentiate their product.[2] Though based in Peru, Café Feminino has extended its activities to benefit coffee producers in over 10 other countries through an extensive grants program. Examples include a respiratory health initiative in Colombia similar to the one in Peru, and an income diversification initiative in the Dominican Republic designed to increase women's economic independence.[3]

In addition to female ownership, other special features distinguish Café Feminino from other Fair Trade coffee labels. A second unique feature is that an extra two cents per pound on top of the standard fair-trade premium goes directly to female producers who decide how to use it in their community. This means that, in total, Café Feminino secures 17 cents more per pound of coffee than is typically the case for coffee producers in the Global South. A third unique feature is Café Feminino's commitment to supporting women in the Global North. One of the ways it exercises this concern is by securing an extra two cents per pound to fund women's shelters in the communities where its coffee is sold. Another way is by encouraging its Northern business partners to be more inclusive of women. In particular, Café Feminino requires that a woman sign the contract between them on behalf of the partner.[4]

ANALYSIS

Promoters of fair trade assume that existing trade relations between businesses in the Global North and producers in the Global South are morally problematic, and that the right way to tackle the problem is via a consumer driven approach. Given these assumptions, Café Feminino appears to be an exemplar of a socially responsible brand. The benefits secured by Café Feminino for its members and other women in the rural communities of northern Peru far exceed the benefits normally secured through North-South trade, and even those normally secured through Fair Trade as well. What's more, by focusing on a historically disadvantaged group (women in the Andean foothills of Peru), Café Feminino ensures that the benefits it secures impact those who really need them.

The assumption that there is something morally problematic with standard trade relations between businesses in the Global North and producers in the Global South is debatable, however. To fully evaluate this assumption requires reflecting on broader questions and theories of distributive justice, the branch of justice that examines the fair distribution of benefits and burdens. How one responds to cases like Café Feminino depends in part on whether one subscribes to a view of distributive justice that sees transactions in the free market as a just basis for distributing goods, or to a view that accords government a significant role in regulating the market and redistributing goods to remediate inequalities, or to a view that sees current economic institutions as instantiating structural injustice based on unequal power relationships between the South and North.

According to most libertarians, economic transactions are only problematic in cases of theft or fraud. So long as the parties to a transaction did not acquire their holdings either directly or indirectly through theft or fraud, and so long as they do not commit theft or fraud against each other, then the outcome of their transaction is fair. It arguably follows that benefitting the less well-off by purchasing Fair Trade products is not a requirement of justice, but a matter of charity: possibly praiseworthy but not morally required.

A second, very different sort of conclusion one might draw is that Fair Trade, even when conducted in accordance with the exceptionally high standards exemplified by Café Feminino, doesn't go nearly far enough. Instead, what's needed is a considerable degree of state level redistribution from those in the Global North to those in the South. There are a number of routes via which this conclusion might be reached. From a libertarian perspective focused on the historical injustices of, say, colonialism, it could be argued that current holdings are tainted by previous unjust transactions: the Global North has its current wealth in part because of past acts of theft and fraud against populations in the Global South. If so, then a considerable amount of redistribution may be needed for the sake of rectifying past injustice.

Redistribution could also be grounded in a liberal egalitarian perspective such as the one argued for by John Rawls. On his view, economic inequalities between citizens of the same society are only just when (a) they are consistent with equality of opportunity, and (b) they maximally benefit those who are worst off. If those with less did not have the same opportunities to attain wealth as those with more, and if the greater share of those who have more does not work to the benefit of those who have less, e.g., by incentivizing the use of productive talents that raise everyone's absolute position, then the inequality between them is unjust. Though Rawls himself did not extend his view to the global context, philosophers such as Charles Beitz and Thomas Pogge have argued from a Rawlsian perspective that it is clear that these inequalities should also be deemed unjust. The citizens of countries in the Global South do not have the same opportunities to acquire wealth as citizens in the North, and even if there's some sense in which existing inequalities benefit the global poor, it's highly doubtful that the benefit is maximal.

From another perspective, opting for state level redistribution is almost as unsatisfying as settling for Fair Trade. It might be argued that the root problem is not an unequal distribution of wealth, but rather the global capitalist framework within which that inequality is situated. From a socialist viewpoint focused on the means of production, inequality is certainly a bad thing, but addressing it without also addressing the system of property underlying it is like treating the symptoms without providing a cure. A socialist might note that, first, global private ownership of the means of production has led to an unequal distribution of it between the Global North and South. While the North has various means of adding value to raw goods, e.g., advanced manufacturing facilities, the South largely does not. As a result, those in the Global South have no choice but to participate in exploitive trade relationships, as there are few productive options for them to choose from aside from producing and exporting largely unprocessed goods, for example, coffee.

A second point that someone with a socialist perspective might emphasize is that private ownership of the means of production amongst Southern producers puts them in competition with each other, thereby creating a race to the bottom. If a producer tries to raise her prices, she'll be undercut by the other producers she's in competition with. Private ownership is thus arguably responsible for sustaining the exploitive trade relations that Fair Trade is a response to.

Our discussion thus far presents a choice between two starkly opposed points of view. On the one hand, a libertarian proponent of the view that voluntary transactions are fair transactions would likely maintain that purchasing Fair Trade products, Café Feminino coffee included, does nothing to increase the amount of justice in the world. On this view, so long as Northern businesses don't defraud Southern producers, then all is fine as far as justice is concerned. In contrast, liberal egalitarians and socialists would likely maintain that Fair Trade falls dramatically short of what justice requires. If justice requires either large transfers of wealth from the better off to the worse off or common ownership of the means of production, then Fair Trade is arguably a distraction that diverts attention away from what we really ought to be concerned with.

Suppose we were to reject the view that voluntary transactions are always fair. However, suppose we also take for granted the background conditions we currently find ourselves in, i.e., conditions characterized by private ownership of the means of production and insufficient political will to implement a substantial international system of redistributive transfers. Though we might prefer either common ownership or a system of redistributive transfers, our moral analysis would be fairly superficial were we merely to lament the fact that this preference hasn't been satisfied. There remains an important, unanswered question about what Northern businesses and consumers owe to Southern producers in our present political and economic circumstances. And if we can agree that we have an obligation to benefit those in the South who are badly off, then we need to ask ourselves whether securing Fair Trade arrangements and buying Fair Trade products, especially in accordance with the more ambitious standards set by Café Feminio, would help us to fulfill that obligation.

There are at least two sides to this issue. One is whether Fair Trade would tangibly benefit socio-economically disadvantaged groups in the South. In this respect, Fair Trade seems superior to typical North-South trade relations, and the more ambitious form of Fair Trade exemplified by Café Feminino seems superior to standard Fair Trade. To fully assess the merits of Café Feminino–style Fair Trade, however, we would need to know what other feasible means of benefitting Southern producers are available to Northern businesses and consumers, and whether these means are more or less effective than Fair Trade. For example, does Fair Trade sometimes have negative effects that offset its positive effects? Paying a higher price to Fair Trade producers may disadvantage Southern producers who don't sell Fair Trade products. It may also remove some of the incentive for Southern producers to shift toward more lucrative forms of production. Would it be better for consumers to donate a portion of their earnings to reliable charities, rather than paying Fair Trade prices? Questions like these need to be answered before we can make a comprehensive assessment.[5]

The second side of this issue concerns the relationship between Fair Trade and the relevant background conditions themselves, e.g., ownership of the means of production. How would Fair Trade affect these conditions? Would it affect them in a positive way? These are complicated questions, but there are some things that can tentatively be said in reply. According to J.J. McMurtry, one of the problems with Fair Trade as it's normally practiced is that it leaves intact the structural conditions that create the need for Fair Trade in the first place.[6] For example, a Fair Trade label that increases wages and improves work conditions for female factory workers in the clothing industry benefits them, but it does so in a potentially temporary manner if it does not address the circumstances that make them vulnerable to exploitation. If their employers suddenly decided to pay less, these women would not have the economic independence necessary to refuse work. In this respect, however, Café Feminino is an important exception. Since the use of their label by any Peruvian producer is conditional upon female land ownership, Café Feminino has placed an important means of production into the hands of a disadvantaged group, thereby increasing their economic independence. Elevating the socio-economic position of women in this comparatively permanent way gives them a platform upon which to implement improvements on their own. It may also help to ensure that future measures taken to benefit the producers of northern Peru, e.g., monetary transfers, have a greater chance of benefitting women, and not just those who have traditionally held a position of power in the area.

Though transferring ownership of one means of production to a disadvantaged group is admittedly a far cry from common ownership, it is nonetheless responsive to the socialist worry that lack of access to the means of production is the real issue. What's more, it's responsive to the liberal egalitarian view that the better off have an obligation to benefit the worst off. Across at least some of the perspectives discussed above, then, the sort of Fair Trade exemplified by Café Feminino arguably counts as a significant improvement in justice. Still, it's worth asking whether alternative approaches would bring us closer to that ideal.

DISCUSSION QUESTIONS

1. Are voluntary transactions always fair? If not, what conditions must they satisfy in order to be fair?
2. Assuming there's an obligation to benefit producers in the Global South, whose obligation is it? Is it a consumer obligation? A corporate obligation? A state obligation? A mixture of all three?
3. Is Fair Trade the best feasible way for consumers to benefit producers in the Global South? What other options are available to them?
4. Are current standards associated with the Fair Trade label high enough? What are the advantages and disadvantages of adopting higher standards?
5. What lessons can we learn from the case of Café Feminino? Should Café Feminino be used as a model by other Fair Trade producers, or are the circumstances of different producers too dissimilar for any single approach to be generally applied?

NOTES

1   Café Feminino Foundation. Available at http://www.
    coffeecan.org/our-work/peru.
2   Organic Products Trading Company. Available
    at http://www.optco.com/cafe_femenino.htm.
3   Café Feminino Foundation. Available at http://www.
    coffeecan.org/.
4   For a comprehensive description of Café Feminino,
    see McMurtry, J.J. "Ethical Value-Added: Fair Trade
    and the Case of Café Feminino." *Journal of Business
    Ethics*, 86, S1, 2009, pp. 27–49 at pp. 38–42.
5   Moore, Geoff. 2004. "The Fair Trade Movement:
    Parameters, Issues and Future Research." *Journal of
    Business Ethics*, 53, 1/2, pp. 27–49 at p. 76.
6   McMurtry, "Ethical Value-Added," pp. 31–32.

FURTHER READINGS

Beitz, Charles R. 1979. *Political Theory and International
    Relations*. Princeton: Princeton University Press.
McMurtry, J.J. 2009. "Ethical Value-Added: Fair Trade
    and the Case of Café Feminino." *Journal of Business
    Ethics* 86 (S1): 27–49.
Moore, Geoff. 2004. "The Fair Trade Movement:
    Parameters, Issues and Future Research." *Journal of
    Business Ethics* 53 (1/2): 73–86.
Pogge, Thomas. 1989. *Realizing Rawls*. Ithaca: Cornell
    University Press.
Pogge, Thomas. 2008. *World Poverty and Human Rights*,
    2nd ed. Malden: Polity Press.
Rawls, John. 1999. *The Law of Peoples*. Cambridge, MA:
    Harvard University Press.
St. Pierre, Eric. 2012. *Fair Trade: A Human Journey*.
    Barbara Sandilands, trans. Fredericton: Goose
    Lane Editions.

—89—
JUSTIFYING
INTELLECTUAL PROPERTY

Edwin C. Hettinger

PROPERTY INSTITUTIONS FUNDAMENTALLY SHAPE a society. These legal relationships between individuals, different sorts of objects, and the state are not easy to justify. This is especially true of intellectual property. It is difficult enough to determine the appropriate kinds of ownership of corporeal objects (consider water or mineral rights); it is even more difficult to determine what types of ownership we should allow for noncorporeal, intellectual objects, such as writings, inventions, and secret business information. The complexity of copyright, patent, and trade secret law reflects this problem.

According to one writer "patents are the heart and core of property rights, and once they are destroyed, the destruction of all other property rights will follow automatically, as a brief postscript."[1] Though extreme, this remark rightly stresses the importance of patents to private competitive enterprise. Intellectual property is an increasingly significant and widespread form of ownership. Many have noted the arrival of the "post-industrial society"[2] in which the manufacture and manipulation of physical goods is giving way to the production and use of information. The result is an ever-increasing strain on our laws and customs protecting intellectual property.[3] Now, more than ever, there is a need to carefully scrutinize these institutions.

As a result of both vastly improved information handling technologies and the larger role information is playing in our society, owners of intellectual property are more frequently faced with what they call "piracy" or information theft (that is, unauthorized access to their intellectual property). Most readers of this article have undoubtedly done something considered piracy by owners of intellectual property. Making a cassette tape of a friend's record, videotaping television broadcasts for a movie library, copying computer programs or using them on more than one machine, photocopying more than one chapter of a book, or two or more articles by the same author—all are examples of alleged infringing activities. Copyright, patent, and trade secret violation suits abound in industry, and in academia, the use of another person's ideas often goes unacknowledged. These phenomena indicate widespread public disagreement over the nature and legitimacy of our intellectual property institutions. This article examines the justifiability of those institutions.

COPYRIGHTS, PATENTS,
AND TRADE SECRETS

It is commonly said that one cannot patent or copyright ideas. One copyrights "original works of authorship," including writings, music, drawings, dances, computer programs, and movies; one may not copyright ideas, concepts, principles, facts, or knowledge. Expressions of ideas are copyright-able; ideas themselves are not.[4] While useful, this notion of separating the content of an idea from its style of presentation is not unproblematic.[5] Difficulty in distinguishing the two is most apparent in the more artistic forms of authorship (such as fiction or poetry), where style and content interpenetrate. In these mediums, more so than in others, *how* something is said is very much part of *what* is said (and vice versa).

A related distinction holds for patents. Laws of nature, mathematical formulas, and methods of doing business, for example, cannot be patented. What one patents are inventions—that is, processes, machines, manufacturers, or compositions of matter. These must be novel (not previously patented); they must constitute nonobvious improvements over past inventions; and they must be useful (inventions that do not work cannot be patented). Specifying what sorts of "technological recipes for production"[6] constitute patentable subject matter involves distinguishing specific applications and utilizations from the underlying unpatentable general principles.[7] One cannot patent the scientific principle that water boils at 212 degrees, but one can patent a machine (for example, a steam engine) which uses this principle in a specific way and for a specific purpose.[8]

Trade secrets include a variety of confidential and valuable business information, such as sales, marketing, pricing, and advertising data, lists of customers and suppliers, and such things as plant layout and manufacturing techniques. Trade secrets must not be generally known in the industry, their nondisclosure must give some advantage over competitors, and attempts to prevent leakage of the information must be made (such as pledges of secrecy in employment contracts or other company security policies). The formula for Coca-Cola and bids on government contracts are examples of trade secrets.

Trade secret subject matter includes that of copyrights and patents: anything which can be copyrighted or patented can be held as a trade secret, though the converse is not true. Typically a business must choose between patenting an invention and holding it as a trade secret. Some advantages of trade secrets are

1. they do not require disclosure (in fact they require secrecy), whereas a condition for granting patents (and copyrights) is public disclosure of the invention (or writing);
2. they are protected for as long as they are kept secret, while most patents lapse after seventeen years; and
3. they involve less cost than acquiring and defending a patent.

Advantages of patents include protection against reverse engineering (competitors figuring out the invention by examining the product which embodies it) and against independent invention. Patents give their owners the *exclusive* right to make, use, and sell the invention no matter how anyone else comes up with it, while trade secrets prevent only improper acquisition (breaches of security).

Copyrights give their owners the right to reproduce, to prepare derivative works from, to distribute copies of, and to publicly perform or display the "original work of authorship." Their duration is the author's life plus fifty years. These rights are not universally applicable, however. The most notable exception is the "fair use" clause of the copyright statute, which gives researchers, educators, and libraries special privileges to use copyrighted material.[9]

INTELLECTUAL OBJECTS AS NONEXCLUSIVE

Let us call the subject matter of copyrights, patents, and trade secrets "intellectual objects."[10] These objects are nonexclusive: they can be at many places at once and are not consumed by their use. The marginal cost of providing an intellectual object to an additional user is zero, and though there are communications costs, modern technologies can easily make an intellectual object unlimitedly available at a very low cost.

The possession or use of an intellectual object by one person does not preclude others from possessing or using it as well.[11] If someone borrows your lawn mower, you cannot use it, nor can anyone else. But if someone borrows your recipe for guacamole, that in no way precludes you, or anyone else, from using it. This feature is shared by all sorts of intellectual objects, including novels, computer programs, songs, machine designs, dances, recipes for Coca-Cola, lists of customers and suppliers, management techniques, and formulas for genetically engineered bacteria which digest crude oil. Of course, sharing intellectual objects does prevent the original possessor from selling the intellectual object to others, and so this sort of use is prevented. But sharing in no way hinders *personal* use.

This characteristic of intellectual objects grounds a strong *prima facie* case against the wisdom of private and exclusive intellectual property rights. Why should one person have the exclusive right to possess and use something which all people could possess and use concurrently? The burden of justification is very much on those who would restrict the maximal use of intellectual objects. A person's right to exclude others from possessing and using a physical object can be justified when such exclusion is necessary for this person's own possession and unhindered use. No such justification is available for exclusive possession and use of intellectual property.

One reason for the widespread piracy of intellectual property is that many people think it is unjustified to exclude others from intellectual objects.[12] Also, the unauthorized taking of an intellectual object does not feel like theft. Stealing a physical object involves depriving someone of the object taken, whereas taking an intellectual object deprives the owner of neither possession nor personal use of that object—though the owner is deprived of potential profit. This non-exclusive feature of intellectual objects should be kept firmly in mind when assessing the justifiability of intellectual property.

OWNING IDEAS AND RESTRICTIONS ON THE FREE FLOW OF INFORMATION

The fundamental value our society places on freedom of thought and expression creates another difficulty for the justification of intellectual property. Private property enhances one person's freedom at the expense of everyone else's. Private intellectual property restricts methods of acquiring ideas (as do trade secrets), it restricts the use of ideas (as do patents), and it restricts the expression of ideas (as do copyrights)—restrictions undesirable for a number of reasons. John Stuart Mill argued that free thought and speech are important for the acquisition of true beliefs and for individual growth and development.[13] Restrictions on the free flow and use of ideas not only stifle individual growth, but impede the advancement of technological innovation and human knowledge generally.[14] Insofar as copyrights, patents, and trade secrets have these negative effects, they are hard to justify. Since a condition for granting patents and copyrights is public disclosure of the writing or invention, these forms of intellectual ownership do not involve the exclusive right to possess the knowledge or ideas they protect. Our society gives its inventors and writers a legal right to exclude others from certain uses of their intellectual works in return for public disclosure of these works. Disclosure is necessary if people are to learn from and build on the ideas of others. When they bring about disclosure of ideas which would have otherwise remained secret, patents and copyrights enhance rather than restrict the free flow of ideas (though they still restrict the idea's widespread use and dissemination). Trade secrets do not have this virtue. Regrettably, the common law tradition which offers protection for trade secrets encourages secrecy. This makes trade secrets undesirable in a way in which copyrights or patents are not.[15]

LABOR, NATURAL INTELLECTUAL PROPERTY RIGHTS, AND MARKET VALUE

Perhaps the most powerful intuition supporting property rights is that people are entitled to the fruits of their labor. What a person produces with her own intelligence, effort, and perseverance ought to belong to her and to no one else. "Why is it mine? Well, it's mine because I made it, that's why. It wouldn't have existed but for me."

John Locke's version of this labor justification for property derives property rights in the product of labor from prior property rights in one's body.[16] A person owns her body and hence she owns what it does, namely, its labor. A person's labor and its product are inseparable, and so ownership of one can be secured only by owning the other. Hence, if a person is to own her body and thus its labor, she must also own what she joins her labor with—namely, the product of her labor.

This formulation is not without problems. For example, Robert Nozick wonders why a person should gain what she mixes her labor with instead of losing her labor. (He imagines pouring a can of tomato juice into the ocean and asks whether he thereby ought to gain the ocean or lose his tomato juice.)[17] More importantly, assuming that labor's fruits are valuable, and that laboring gives the laborer a property right in this value, this would entitle the laborer only to the value she added, and not to the *total* value of the resulting product. Though exceedingly difficult to measure, these two components of value (that attributable to the object labored on and that attributable to the labor) need to be distinguished.

Locke thinks that until labored on, objects have little human value, at one point suggesting that labor creates 99 per cent of their value.[18] This is not plausible when labor is mixed with land and other natural resources. One does not create 99 per cent of the value of an apple by picking it off a tree, though some human effort is necessary for an object to have value for us.

What portion of the value of writings, inventions, and business information is attributable to the intellectual laborer? Clearly authorship, discovery, or development is necessary if intellectual products are to have value for us; we could not use or appreciate them without this labor. But it does not follow from this that all of their value is attributable to that labor. Consider, for example, the wheel, the entire human value of which is not appropriately attributable to its original inventor.[19]

The value added by the laborer and any value the object has on its own are by no means the only components of the value of an intellectual object. Invention, writing, and thought in general do not operate in a vacuum; intellectual activity is not creation *ex nihilo*. Given this vital dependence of a person's thoughts on the ideas of those who came before her, intellectual products are fundamentally social products. Thus even if one assumes that the value of these products is entirely the result of human labor, this value is not entirely attributable to *any particular laborer* (or small group of laborers).

Separating out the individual contribution of the inventor, writer, or manager from this historical/social component is no easy task. Simply identifying the value a laborer's labor adds to the world with the market value or the resulting product ignores the vast contributions of others. A person who relies on human intellectual history and makes a small modification to produce something of great value should no more receive what the market will bear than should the last person needed to lift a car receive full credit for lifting it. If laboring gives the laborer the right to receive the market value of the resulting product, this market value should be shared by all those whose ideas contributed to the origin of the product. The fact that most of these contributors are no longer present to receive their fair share is not a reason to give the entire market value to the last contributor.[20]

Thus an appeal to the market value of a laborer's product cannot help us here. Markets work only after property rights have been established and enforced, and our question is what sorts of property rights an inventor, writer, or manager should have, given that the result of her labor is a joint product of human intellectual history.

Even if one could separate out the laborer's own contribution and determine its market value, it is still not clear that the laborer's right to the fruits of her labor naturally entitles her to receive this. Market value is a socially created phenomenon, depending on the activity (or nonactivity) of other producers, the monetary demand of purchasers, and the kinds of property rights, contracts, and markets the state has established and enforced. The market value of the same fruits of labor will differ greatly with variations in these social factors.

Consider the market value of a new drug formula. This depends on the length and the extent of the patent monopoly the state grants and enforces, on the level of affluence of those who need the drug, and on the availability and price of substitutes. The laborer did not produce these. The intuitive appeal behind the labor argument—"I made it, hence it's mine"—loses its force when it is used to try to justify owning something others are responsible for (namely, the market value). The claim that a laborer, in virtue of her labor, has a "natural right" to this socially created phenomenon is problematic at best.

Thus, there are two different reasons why the market value of the product of labor is not what a laborer's labor naturally entitles her to. First, market value is not something that is produced by those who produce a product, and the labor argument entitles laborers only to the products of their labor. Second, even if we ignore this point and equate the fruits of labor with the market value of those fruits, intellectual products result from the labor of many people besides the latest contributor, and they have claims on the market value as well.

So even if the labor theory shows that the laborer has a natural right to the fruits of labor, this does not establish a natural right to receive the full market value of the resulting product. The notion that a laborer is naturally entitled as a matter of right to receive the market value of her product is a myth. To what extent individual laborers should be allowed to receive the market value of their products is a question of social policy; it is not solved by simply insisting on a moral right to the fruits of one's labor.[21]

Having a moral right to the fruits of one's labor might also mean having a right to possess and personally use what one develops. This version of the labor theory has some force. On this interpretation, creating something through labor gives the laborer a *prima facie* right to possess and personally use it for her own benefit. The value of protecting individual freedom guarantees this right as long as the creative labor, and the possession and use of its product, does not harm others.

But the freedom to exchange a product in a market and receive its full market value is again something quite different. To show that people have a right to this, one must argue about how best to balance the conflicts in freedoms which arise when people interact. One must determine what sorts of property rights and markets are morally legitimate. One must also decide when society should enforce the results of market interaction and when it should alter those results (for example, with tax policy). There is a gap—requiring extensive argumentative filler—between the claim that one has a natural right to possess and personally use the fruits of one's labor and the claim that one ought to receive for one's product whatever the market will bear.

Such a gap exists as well between the natural right to possess and personally use one's intellectual creations and the rights protected by copyrights, patents, and trade secrets. The natural right of an author to personally use her writings is distinct from the right, protected by copyright, to make her work public, sell it in a market, and then prevent others from making copies. An inventor's natural right to use the invention for her own benefits is not the same as the right, protected by patent, to sell this invention in a market and exclude others (including independent inventors) from using it. An entrepreneur's natural right to use valuable business information or techniques that she develops is not the same as the right, protected by trade secret, to prevent her employees from using these techniques in another job.

In short, a laborer has a *prima facie* natural right to possess and personally use the fruits of her labor. But a right to profit by selling a product in the market is something quite different. This liberty is largely a socially created phenomenon. The "right" to receive what the market will bear is a socially created privilege, and not a natural right at all. The natural right to possess and personally use what one has produced is relevant to the justifiability of such a privilege, but by itself it is hardly sufficient to justify that privilege.

DESERVING PROPERTY RIGHTS BECAUSE OF LABOR

The above argument that people are naturally entitled to the fruits of their labor is distinct from the argument that a person has a claim to labor's fruits based on desert. If a person has a natural right to something—say her athletic ability—and someone takes it from her, the return of it is something she is *owed* and can rightfully demand. Whether or not she deserves this athletic ability is a separate issue. Similarly, insofar as people have natural property rights in the fruits of their labor, these rights are something they are owed, and not something they necessarily deserve.[22]

The desert argument suggests that the laborer deserves to benefit from her labor, at least if it is an attempt to do something worthwhile. This proposal is convincing, but does not show that what the laborer deserves is property rights in the object labored on. The mistake is to conflate the created object which makes a person deserving of a reward with what that reward should be. Property rights in the created object are not the only possible reward. Alternatives include fees, awards, acknowledgment, gratitude, praise, security, power status, and public financial support.

Many considerations affect whether property rights in the created object are what the laborer deserves. This may depend, for example, on what is created by labor. If property rights in the very things created were always an appropriate reward for labor, then as Lawrence Becker notes, parents would deserve property rights in their children.[23] Many intellectual objects (scientific laws, religious and ethical insights, and so on) are also the sort of thing that should not be owned by anyone.

Furthermore, as Becker also correctly points out, we need to consider the purpose for which the laborer labored. Property rights in the object produced are not a fitting reward if the laborer does not want them. Many intellectual laborers produce beautiful things and discover truths as ends in themselves.[24] The appropriate reward in such cases is recognition, gratitude, and perhaps public financial support, not full-fledged property rights, for these laborers do not want to exclude others from their creations.

Property rights in the thing produced are also not a fitting reward if the value of these rights is disproportional to the effort expended by the laborer. "Effort" includes

1. how hard someone tries to achieve a result,
2. the amount of risk voluntarily incurred in seeking this result, and
3. the degree to which moral consideration played a role in choosing the result intended.

The harder one tries, the more one is willing to sacrifice, and the worthier the goal, the greater are one's deserts.

Becker's claim that the amount deserved is proportional to the value one's labor produces is mistaken.[25] The value of labor's results is often significantly affected by factors outside a person's control, and no one deserves to be rewarded for being lucky. Voluntary past action is the only valid basis for determining desert.[26] Here only a person's effort (in the sense defined) is relevant. Her knowledge, skills, and achievements insofar as they are based on natural talent and luck, rather than effort expended, are not. A person who is born with extraordinary natural talents, or who is extremely lucky, *deserves* nothing on the basis of these characteristics. If such a person puts forward no greater effort than another, she deserves no greater reward. Thus, two laborers who expend equal amounts of effort deserve the same reward, even when the value of the resulting products is vastly different.[27] Giving more to workers whose products have greater social value might be justified if it is needed as an incentive. But this has nothing to do with giving the laborer what she deserves.

John Rawls considers even the ability to expend effort to be determined by factors outside a person's control and hence a morally impermissible criterion for distribution.[28] How hard one tries, how willing one is to sacrifice and incur risk, and how much one cares about morality are to *some extent* affected by natural endowments and social circumstances. But if the ability to expend effort is taken to be entirely determined by factors outside a person's control, the result is a determinism which makes meaningful moral evaluation impossible. If people are responsible for anything, they are responsible for how hard they try, what sacrifices they make, and how moral they are. Because the effort a person expends is much more under her control than her innate intelligence, skills, and talents, effort is a far superior basis for determining desert. To the extent that a person's expenditure of effort is under her control, effort is the proper criterion for desert.[29]

Giving an inventor exclusive rights to make and sell her invention (for seventeen years) may provide either a greater or a lesser reward than she deserves. Some inventions of extraordinary market value result from flashes of genius, while others with little market value (and yet great social value) require significant effort.

The proportionality requirement may also be frequently violated by granting copyright. Consider a five-hundred-dollar computer program. Granted, its initial development costs (read "efforts") were high. But once it has been developed, the cost of each additional program is the cost of the disk it is on—approximately a dollar. After the program has been on the market several years and the price remains at three or four hundred dollars, one begins to suspect that the company is receiving far more than it deserves. Perhaps this is another reason so much illegal copying of software goes on: the proportionality requirement is not being met, and people sense the unfairness of the price. Frequently, trade secrets (which are held indefinitely) also provide their owners with benefits disproportional to the effort expended in developing them.

THE LOCKEAN PROVISOS

We have examined two versions of the labor argument for intellectual property, one based on desert, the other based on a natural entitlement to the fruits of one's labor. Locke himself put limits on the conditions under which labor can justify a property right in the thing produced. One is that after the appropriation there must be "enough and as good left in common for others."[30] This proviso is often reformulated as a "no loss to others" precondition for property acquisition.[31] As long as one does not worsen another's position by appropriating an object, no objection can be raised to owning that with which one mixes one's labor.

Under current law, patents clearly run afoul of this proviso by giving the original inventor an exclusive right to make, use, and sell the invention. Subsequent inventors who independently come up with an already patented invention cannot even personally use their invention, much less patent or sell it. They clearly suffer a great and unfair loss because of the original patent grant. Independent inventors should not be prohibited from using or selling their inventions. Proving independent discovery of a publicly available patented invention would be difficult, however. Nozick's suggestion that the length of patents be restricted to the time it would take for independent invention may be the most reasonable administrative solution.[32] In the modern world of highly competitive research and development, this time is often much shorter than the seventeen years for which most patents are currently granted.

Copyrights and trade secrets are not subject to the same objection (though they may constitute a loss to others in different ways). If someone independently comes up with a copyrighted expression or a competitor's business technique, she is not prohibited from using it. Copyrights and trade secrets prevent only mimicking of other people's expressions and ideas.

Locke's second condition on the legitimate acquisition of property rights prohibits spoilage. Not only must one leave enough and as good for others, but one must not take more than one can use.[33] So in addition to leaving enough apples in the orchard for others, one must not take home a truckload and let them spoil. Though Locke does not specifically mention prohibiting waste, it is the concern to avoid waste which underlies his proviso prohibiting spoilage. Taking more than one can use is wrong because it is wasteful. Thus Locke's concern here is with appropriations of property which are wasteful.

Since writings, inventions, and business techniques are nonexclusive, this requirement prohibiting waste can never be completely met by intellectual property. When owners of intellectual property charge fees for the use of their expressions or inventions, or conceal their business techniques from others, certain beneficial uses of these intellectual products are prevented. This is clearly wasteful, since everyone could use and benefit from intellectual objects concurrently. How wasteful private ownership of intellectual property is depends on how beneficial those products would be to those who are excluded from their use as a result.

SOVEREIGNTY, SECURITY, AND PRIVACY

Private property can be justified as a means to sovereignty. Dominion over certain objects is important for individual autonomy. Ronald Dworkin's liberal is right in saying that "some sovereignty over a range of personal possessions is essential to dignity."[34] Not having to share one's personal possessions or borrow them from others is essential to the kind of autonomy our society values. Using or consuming certain objects is also necessary for survival. Allowing ownership of these things places control of the means of survival in the hands of individuals, and this promotes independence and security (at least for those who own enough of them). Private ownership of life's necessities lessens dependence between individuals, and takes power from the group and gives it to the individual. Private property also promotes privacy. It constitutes a sphere of privacy within which the individual is sovereign and less accountable for her actions. Owning one's own home is an example of all of these: it provides privacy, security, and a limited range of autonomy.

But copyrights and patents are neither necessary nor important for achieving these goals. The right to exclude others from using one's invention or copying one's work of authorship is not essential to one's sovereignty. Preventing a person from personally using her own invention or writing, on the other hand, would seriously threaten her sovereignty. An author's or inventor's sense of worth and dignity requires public acknowledgment by those who use the writing or discovery, but here again, giving the author or inventor the exclusive right to copy or use her intellectual product is not necessary to protect this.

Though patents and copyrights are not directly necessary for survival (as are food and shelter), one could argue that they are indirectly necessary for an individual's security and survival when selling her inventions or writings is a person's sole means of income. In our society, however, most patents and copyrights are owned by institutions (businesses, universities, or governments). Except in unusual cases where individuals have extraordinary bargaining power, prospective employees are required to give the rights to their inventions and works of authorship to their employers as a condition of employment. Independent authors or inventors who earn their living by selling their writings or inventions to others are increasingly rare.[35] Thus arguing that intellectual property promotes individual security makes sense only in a minority of cases. Additionally, there are other ways to ensure the independent intellectual laborer's security and survival besides copyrights and patents (such as public funding of intellectual workers and public domain property status for the results).

Controlling who uses one's invention or writing is not important to one's privacy. As long as there is no requirement to divulge privately created intellectual products (and as long as laws exist to protect people from others taking information they choose not to divulge—as with trade secret laws), the creator's privacy will not be infringed. Trying to justify copyrights and patents on grounds of privacy is highly implausible given that these property rights give the author or inventor control over certain uses of writings and inventions only after they have been publicly disclosed.

Trade secrets are not defensible on grounds of privacy either. A corporation is not an individual and hence does not have the personal features privacy is intended to protect.[36] Concern for sovereignty counts against trade secrets, for they often directly limit individual autonomy by preventing employees from changing jobs. Through employment contracts, by means of gentlemen's agreements among firms to respect trade secrets by refusing to hire competitors' employees, or simply because of the threat of lawsuits, trade secrets often prevent employees from using their skills and knowledge with other companies in the industry.

Some trade secrets, however, are important to a company's security and survival. If competitors could legally obtain the secret formula for Coke, for example, the Coca-Cola Company would be severely threatened. Similar points hold for copyrights and patents. Without some copyright protection, companies in the publishing, record, and movie industries would be severely threatened by competitors who copy and sell their works at lower prices (which need not reflect development costs). Without patent protection, companies with high research and development costs could be underpriced and driven out of business by competitors who simply mimicked the already developed products. This unfair competition could significantly weaken incentives to invest in innovative techniques and to develop new products.

The next section considers this argument that intellectual property is a necessary incentive for innovation and a requirement for healthy and fair competition. Notice, however, that the concern here is with the security and survival of private companies, not of individuals. Thus one needs to determine whether, and to what extent, the security and survival of privately held companies is a goal worth promoting. That issue turns on the difficult question of what type of economy is most desirable. Given a commitment to capitalism, however, this argument does have some force.

THE UTILITARIAN JUSTIFICATION

The strongest and most widely appealed to justification for intellectual property is a utilitarian argument based on providing incentives. The constitutional justification for patents and copyrights—"to promote the progress of science and the useful arts"[37]—is itself utilitarian. Given the shortcomings of the other arguments for intellectual property, the justifiability of copyrights, patents, and trade secrets depends, in the final analysis, on this utilitarian defense.

According to this argument, promoting the creation of valuable intellectual works requires that intellectual laborers be granted property rights in those works. Without the copyright, patent, and trade secret property protections, adequate incentives for the creation of a socially optimal output of intellectual products would not exist. If competitors could simply copy books, movies, and records, and take one another's inventions and business techniques, there would be no incentive to spend the vast amounts of time, energy, and money necessary to develop these products and techniques. It would be in each firm's self-interest to let others develop products, and then mimic the result. No one would engage in original development, and consequently no new writings, inventions, or business techniques would be developed. To avoid this disastrous result, the argument claims, we must continue to grant intellectual property rights.

Notice that this argument focuses on the users of intellectual products, rather than on the producers. Granting property rights to producers is here seen as necessary to ensure that enough intellectual products (and the countless other goods based on these products) are available to users. The grant of property rights to the producers is a mere means to this end.

This approach is paradoxical. It establishes a right to restrict the current availability and use of intellectual products for the purpose of increasing the production and thus future availability and use of new intellectual products. As economist Joan Robinson says of patents: "A patent is a device to prevent the diffusion of new methods before the original investor has recovered profit adequate to induce the requisite investment. The justification of the patent system is that by slowing down the diffusion of technical progress it ensures that there will be more progress to diffuse.... Since it is rooted in a contradiction, there can be no such thing as an ideally beneficial patent system, and it is bound to produce negative results in particular instances, impeding progress unnecessarily even if its general effect is favorable on balance."[38] Although this strategy may work, it is to a certain extent self-defeating. If the justification for intellectual property is utilitarian in this sense, then the search for alternative incentives for the production of intellectual products takes on a good deal of importance. It would be better to employ equally powerful ways to stimulate the production and thus use of intellectual products which did not also restrict their use and availability.

Government support of intellectual work and public ownership of the result may be one such alternative. Governments already fund a great deal of basic research and development, and the results of this research often become public property. Unlike private property rights in the results of intellectual labor, government funding of this labor and public ownership of the result stimulate new inventions and writings without restricting their dissemination and use. Increased government funding of intellectual labor should thus be seriously considered.

This proposal need not involve government control over which research projects are to be pursued. Government funding of intellectual labor can be divorced from government control over what is funded. University research is an example. Most of this is supported by public funds, but government control over its content is minor and indirect. Agencies at different governmental levels could distribute funding for intellectual labor with only the most general guidance over content, leaving businesses, universities, and private individuals to decide which projects to pursue.

If the goal of private intellectual property institutions is to maximize the dissemination and use of information, to the extent that they do not achieve this result, these institutions should be modified. The question is not whether copyrights, patents, and trade secrets provide incentives for the production of original works of authorship, inventions, and innovative business techniques. Of course they do. Rather, we should ask the following questions: Do copyrights, patents, and trade secrets increase the availability and use of intellectual products more than they restrict this availability and use? If they do, we must then ask whether they increase the availability and use of intellectual products more than any alternative mechanism would. For example, could better overall results be achieved by shortening the length of copyright and patent grants, or by putting a time limit on trade secrets (and on the restrictions on future employment employers are allowed to demand of employees)? Would eliminating most types of trade secrets entirely and letting patents carry a heavier load produce improved results?

Additionally, we must determine whether and to what extent public funding and ownership of intellectual products might be a more efficient means to these results.[39]

We should not expect an across-the-board answer to these questions. For example, the production of movies is more dependent on copyright than is academic writing. Also, patent protection for individual inventors and small beginning firms makes more sense than patent protection for large corporations (which own the majority of patents). It has been argued that patents are not important incentives for the research and innovative activity of large corporations in competitive markets.[40] The short-term advantage a company gets from developing a new product and being the first to put it on the market may be incentive enough.

That patents are conducive to a strong competitive economy is also open to question. Our patent system, originally designed to reward the individual inventor and thereby stimulate invention, may today be used as a device to monopolize industries. It has been suggested that in some cases "the patent position of the big firms makes it almost impossible for new firms to enter the industry"[41] and that patents are frequently bought up in order to suppress competition.[42]

Trade secrets as well can stifle competition, rather than encourage it. If a company can rely on a secret advantage over a competitor, it has no need to develop new technologies to stay ahead. Greater disclosure of certain trade secrets—such as costs and profits of particular product lines—would actually increase competition, rather than decrease it, since with this knowledge firms would then concentrate on one another's most profitable products.[43] Furthermore, as one critic notes, trade secret laws often prevent a former employee "from doing work in just that field for which his training and experience have best prepared him. Indeed, the mobility of engineers and scientists is often severely limited by the reluctance of new firms to hire them for fear of exposing themselves to a lawsuit."[44] Since the movement of skilled workers between companies is a vital mechanism in the growth and spread of technology, in this important respect trade secrets actually slow the dissemination and use of innovative techniques.

These remarks suggest that the justifiability of our intellectual property institutions is not settled by the facile assertion that our system of patents, copyrights, and trade secrets provides necessary incentives for innovation and ensures maximally healthy competitive enterprise. This argument is not as easy to construct as one might at first think; substantial empirical evidence is needed. The above considerations suggest that the evidence might not support this position.

CONCLUSION

Justifying intellectual property is a formidable task. The inadequacies of the traditional justifications for property become more severe when applied to intellectual property. Both the nonexclusive nature of intellectual objects and the presumption against allowing restrictions on the free flow of ideas create special burdens in justifying such property.

We have seen significant shortcomings in the justifications for intellectual property. Natural rights to the fruits of one's labor are not by themselves sufficient to justify copyrights, patents, and trade secrets, though they are relevant to the social decision to create and sustain intellectual property institutions. Although intellectual laborers often deserve rewards for their labor, copyrights, patents, and trade secrets may give the laborer much more or much less than is deserved. Where property rights are not what is desired, they may be wholly inappropriate. The Lockean labor arguments for intellectual property also run afoul of one of Locke's provisos—the prohibition against spoilage or waste. Considerations of sovereignty, security, and privacy are inconclusive justifications for intellectual property as well.

This analysis suggests that the issue turns on considerations of social utility. We must determine whether our current copyright, patent, and trade secret statutes provide the best possible mechanisms for ensuring the availability and widespread dissemination of intellectual works and their resulting products. Public financial support for intellectual laborers and public ownership of intellectual products is an alternative which demands serious consideration. More modest alternatives needing consideration include modifications in the length of intellectual property grants or in the strength and scope of the restrictive rights granted. What the most efficient mechanism for achieving these goals is remains an unresolved empirical question.

This discussion also suggests that copyrights are easier to justify than patents or trade secrets. Patents restrict the actual usage of an idea (in making a physical object), while copyrights restrict only copying an expression of an idea. One can freely use the ideas in a copyrighted book in one's own writing, provided one acknowledges their origin. One cannot freely use the ideas a patented invention represents when developing one's own product. Furthermore, since inventions and business techniques are instruments of production in a way in which expressions of ideas are not, socialist objections to private ownership of the means of production apply to patents and trade secrets far more readily than they do to copyrights. Trade secrets are suspect also because they do not involve the socially beneficial public disclosure which is part of the patent and copyright process. They are additionally problematic to the extent that they involve unacceptable restrictions on employee mobility and technology transfer.

Focusing on the problems of justifying intellectual property is important not because these institutions lack any sort of justification, but because they are not so obviously or easily justified as many people think. We must begin to think more openly and imaginatively about the alternative choices available to us for stimulating and rewarding intellectual labor.

NOTES

1   Ayn Rand, *Capitalism: The Unknown Ideal* (New York: New American Library, 1966), 128.

2   See, for example, John Naisbitt's *Megatrends* (New York: Warner Books, 1982), chap. 1.

3   See R. Salaman and E. Hettinger, *Policy Implications of Information Technology*. NTIA Report 84–144, US Department of Commerce, 1984, 28–29.

4   For an elaboration of this distinction see Michael Brittin, "Constitutional Fair Use," in *Copyright Law Symposium*, No. 28 (New York: Columbia University Press, 1982), 142ff.

5   For an illuminating discussion of the relationships between style and subject, see Nelson Goodman's *Ways of Worldmaking* (Indianapolis: Hackett, 1978), chap. II, esp. sec. 2.

6   This is Fritz Machlup's phrase. See his *Production and Distribution of Knowledge in the United States* (Princeton: Princeton University Press, 1962), 163.

7   For one discussion of this distinction, see Deborah Johnson, *Computer Ethics* (Englewood Cliffs, NJ: Prentice-Hall, 1985), 100–01.

8   What can be patented is highly controversial. Consider the recent furor over patenting genetically manipulated animals or patenting computer programs.

9   What constitutes fair use is notoriously bewildering. I doubt that many teachers who sign copyright waivers at local copy shops know whether the packets they make available for their students constitute fair use of copyrighted material.

10   "Intellectual objects," "information," and "ideas" are terms I use to characterize the "objects" of this kind of ownership. Institutions which protect such "objects" include copyright, patent, trade secret, and trademark laws, as well as socially enforced customs (such as sanctions against plagiarism) demanding acknowledgment of the use of another's ideas. What is owned here are objects only in a very abstract sense.

11   There are intellectual objects of which this is not true, namely, information whose usefulness depends precisely on its being known only to a limited group of people. Stock tips and insider trading information are examples.

12   Ease of access is another reason for the widespread piracy of intellectual property. Modern

information technologies (such as audio and video recorders, satellite dishes, photocopiers, and computers) make unauthorized taking of intellectual objects far easier than ever before. But it is cynical to submit that this is the major (or the only) reason piracy of information is widespread. It suggests that if people could steal physical objects as easily as they can take intellectual ones, they would do so to the same extent. That seems incorrect.

13 For a useful interpretation of Mill's argument, see Robert Ladenson, "Free Expression in the Corporate Workplace," in *Ethical Theory and Business*, 2nd ed., eds. T. Beauchamp and N. Bowie (Englewood Cliffs, NJ: Prentice-Hall, 1983), 162–69.

14 This is one reason the recent dramatic increase in relationships between universities and businesses is so disturbing: it hampers the disclosure of research results.

15 John Snapper makes this point in "Ownership of Computer Programs," available from the Center for the Study of Ethics in the Professions at the Illinois Institute of Technology. See also Sissela Bok, "Trade and Corporate Secrecy," in *Ethical Theory and Business*, 176.

16 John Locke, *Second Treatise of Government*, chap. 5. There are several strands to the Lockean argument. See Lawrence Becker, *Property Rights* (London: Routledge and Kegan Paul, 1977), chap. 4, for a detailed analysis of these various versions.

17 Robert Nozick, *Anarchy, State, and Utopia* (New York: Basic Books, 1974), 175.

18 Locke, *Second Treatise*, chap. 5, sec. 40.

19 Whether ideas are discovered or created affects the plausibility of the labor argument for intellectual property. "I discovered it, hence it's mine" is much less persuasive than "I made it, hence it's mine." This issue also affects the cogency of the notion that intellectual objects have a value of their own not attributable to intellectual labor. The notion of mixing one's labor with something and thereby adding value to it makes much more sense if the object preexists.

20 I thank the Editors of *Philosophy & Affairs* for this way of making the point.

21 A libertarian might respond that although a natural right to the fruits of labor will not by itself justify a right to receive the market value of the resulting product, that right plus the rights of free association and trade would justify it. But marketplace interaction presupposes a set of social relations, and parties to these relations must jointly agree on their nature. Additionally, market interaction is possible only when property rights have been specified and enforced, and there is no "natural way" to do this (that is, no way independent of complex social judgments concerning the rewards the laborer deserves and the social utilities that will result from granting property rights). The sorts of freedoms one may have in a marketplace are thus socially agreed-upon privileges rather than natural rights.

22 For a discussion of this point, see Joel Feinberg, *Social Philosophy* (Englewood Cliffs, NJ: Prentice-Hall, 1973), 116.

23 Becker, *Property Rights*, 46.

24 This is becoming less and less true as the results of intellectual labor are increasingly treated as commodities. University research in biological and computer technologies is an example of this trend.

25 Becker, *Property Rights*, 52. In practice it would be easier to reward laborers as Becker suggests, since the value of the results of labor is easier to determine than the degree of effort expended.

26 This point is made nicely by James Rachels in "What People Deserve," in *Justice and Economic Distribution*, eds. J. Arthur and W. Shaw (Englewood Cliffs, NJ: Prentice-Hall, 1978), 150–63.

27 Completely ineffectual efforts deserve a reward provided that there were good reasons beforehand for thinking the efforts would pay off. Those whose well-intentioned efforts are silly or stupid should be rewarded the first time only and then counseled to seek advice about the value of their efforts.

28 See John Rawls, *A Theory of Justice* (Cambridge: Harvard University Press, 1971), 104: "The assertion that a man deserves the superior character that enables him to make the effort to cultivate his abilities is equally problematic; for his character depends in large part upon fortunate family and social circumstances for which he can claim no

credit." See also 312: "the effort a person is willing to make is influenced by his natural abilities and skills, and the alternatives open to him. The better endowed are more likely, other things equal, to strive conscientiously."

29   See Rachels, "What People Deserve," 157–58, for a similar resistance to Rawls's determinism.

30   Locke, *Second Treatise*, chap. 5, sec. 27.

31   See Nozick, *Anarchy*, 175–82, and Becker, *Property Rights*, 42–43.

32   Nozick, *Anarchy*, 182.

33   Locke, *Second Treatise*, chap. 5, sec. 31.

34   Ronald Dworkin, "Liberalism," in *Public and Private Morality*, ed. Stuart Hampshire (Cambridge: Cambridge University Press, 1978), 139.

35   "In the United States about 60 per cent of all patents are assigned to corporations" (Machlup, *Production*, 168). This was the case twenty-five years ago, and I assume the percentage is even higher today.

36   Very little (if any) of the sensitive information about individuals that corporations have is information held as a trade secret. For a critical discussion of the attempt to defend corporate secrecy on the basis of privacy see Russell B. Stevenson, Jr., *Corporations and Information* (Baltimore: Johns Hopkins University Press, 1980), chap. 5.

37   US Constitution, sec. 8, para. 8.

38   Quoted in Dorothy Nelkin, *Science as Intellectual Property* (New York: Macmillan, 1984), 15.

39   Even supposing our current copyright, patent, and trade secret laws did maximize the availability and use of intellectual products, a thorough utilitarian evaluation would have to weigh all the consequences of these legal rights. For example, the decrease in employee freedom resulting from trade secrets would have to be considered, as would the inequalities in income, wealth, opportunity, and power which result from these socially established and enforced property rights.

40   Machlup, *Production*, 168–69.

41   Ibid., 170.

42   See David Noble, *America by Design* (New York: Knopf, 1982), chap. 6.

43   This is Stevenson's point in *Corporations*, 11.

44   Ibid., 23. More generally, see ibid., chap. 2, for a careful and skeptical treatment of the claim that trade secrets function as incentives.

—90—

TRADE SECRETS AND THE JUSTIFICATION OF INTELLECTUAL PROPERTY

A Comment on Hettinger

Lynn Sharp Paine

IN A RECENT ARTICLE EDWIN HETTINGER considers various rationales for recognizing intellectual property.[1] According to Hettinger, traditional justifications for property are especially problematic when applied to intellectual property because of its nonexclusive nature.[2] Since possessing and using intellectual objects does not preclude their use and possession by others, there is, he says, a "strong prima facie case against the wisdom of private and exclusive intellectual property rights." There is, moreover, a presumption against allowing restrictions on the free flow of ideas.

After rejecting several rationales for intellectual property, Hettinger finds its justification in an instrumental, or "utilitarian," argument based on incentives. Respecting rights in ideas makes sense, he says, if we recognize that the purpose of our intellectual property institutions is to promote the dissemination and use of information. To the extent that existing institutions do not achieve this result, they should be modified. Skeptical about the effectiveness of current legal arrangements, Hettinger concludes that we must think more imaginatively about structuring our intellectual property institutions—in particular, patent, copyright, and trade secret laws—so that they increase

the availability and use of intellectual products. He ventures several possibilities for consideration: eliminating certain forms of trade secret protections, shortening the copyright and patent protection periods, and public funding and ownership of intellectual objects.

Hettinger's approach to justifying our intellectual property institutions rests on several problematic assumptions. It assumes that all of our intellectual property institutions rise or fall together—that the rationale for trade secret protection must be the same as that for patent and copyright protection. This assumption, I will try to show, is unwarranted. While it may be true that these institutions all promote social utility or wellbeing, the web of rights and duties understood under the general heading of "intellectual property rights" reflects a variety of more specific rationales and objectives.

Second, Hettinger assumes that the rights commonly referred to as "intellectual property rights" are best understood on the model of rights in tangible and real property. He accepts the idea, implicit in the terminology, that intellectual property is like tangible property, only less corporeal. This assumption leads him to focus his search for the justification of intellectual property on the traditional arguments for private property. I will try to show the merits of an alternative approach to thinking about rights in ideas—one that does not depend on the analogy with tangible property and that recognizes the role of ideas in defining personality and social relationships.

The combined effect of these assumptions is that trade secret law comes in for particular serious criticism. It restricts methods of acquiring ideas; it encourages secrecy; it places unacceptable restrictions on employee mobility and technology transfer; it can stifle competition; it is more vulnerable to socialist objections. In light of these deficiencies, Hettinger recommends that we consider the possibility of "eliminating most types of trade secrets entirely and letting patents carry a heavier load." He believes that trade secrets are undesirable in ways that copyrights and patents are not.

Without disagreeing with Hettinger's recommendation that we reevaluate and think more imaginatively about our intellectual property institutions, I believe we should have a clearer understanding of the various rationales for these institutions than is reflected in Hettinger's article. If we unbundle the notion of intellectual property into its constituent rights, we find that different justifications are appropriate for different clusters of rights. In particular, we find that the rights recognized by trade secret law are better understood as rooted in respect for individual liberty, confidential relationships, common morality, and fair competition than in the promotion of innovation and the dissemination of ideas. While trade secret law may serve some of the same ends as patent and copyright law, it has other foundations which are quite distinctive.

In this article, I am primarily concerned with the foundations of trade secret principles. However, my general approach differs from Hettinger's in two fundamental ways. First, it focuses on persons and their relationships rather than property concepts. Second, it reverses the burden of justification, placing it on those who would argue for treating ideas as public goods rather than those who seek to justify private rights in ideas. Within

this alternative framework, the central questions are how ideas may be legitimately acquired from others, how disclosure obligations arise, and how ideas become part of the common pool of knowledge. Before turning to Hettinger's criticisms of trade secret principles, it will be useful to think more broadly about the rights of individuals over their undisclosed ideas. This inquiry will illustrate my approach to thinking about rights in ideas and point toward some of the issues at stake in the trade secret area.

THE RIGHT TO CONTROL DISCLOSURE

If a person has any right with respect to her ideas, surely it is the right to control their initial disclosure. A person may decide to keep her ideas to herself, to disclose them to a select few, or to publish them widely. Whether those ideas are best described as views and opinions, plans and intentions, facts and knowledge, or fantasies and inventions is immaterial. While it might in some cases be socially useful for a person to be generous with her ideas, and to share them with others without restraint, there is no general obligation to do so. The world at large has no right to the individual's ideas.

Certainly, specific undertakings, relationships, and even the acquisition of specific information can give rise to disclosure obligations. Typically, these obligations relate to specific types of information pertinent to the relationship or the subject matter of the undertaking. A seller of goods must disclose to potential buyers latent defects and health and safety risks associated with the use of the goods. A person who undertakes to act as an agent for another is obliged to disclose to the principal information she acquires that relates to the subject matter of the agency. Disclosure obligations like these, however, are limited in scope and arise against a general background right to remain silent.

The right to control the initial disclosure of one's ideas is grounded in respect for the individual. Just as a person's sense of herself is intimately connected with the stream of ideas that constitutes consciousness, her public persona is determined in part by the ideas she expresses and the way she expresses them. To require public disclosure of one's ideas and thoughts—whether about "personal" or other matters—would distort one's personality and, no doubt, alter the nature of one's thoughts. It would seriously interfere with the liberty to live according to one's chosen life plans. This sort of thought control would be an invasion of privacy and personality of the most intrusive sort. If anything is private, one's undisclosed thoughts surely are.

Respect for autonomy, respect for personality, and respect for privacy lie behind the right to control disclosure of one's ideas, but the right is also part of what we mean by freedom of thought and expression. Frequently equated with a right to speak, freedom of expression also implies a *prima facie* right not to express one's ideas or to share them only with those we love or trust or with whom we wish to share. These observations explain the peculiarity of setting up the free flow of ideas and unrestricted access as an ideal. Rights in ideas are desirable insofar as they strengthen our sense of individuality and undergird our social relationships. This suggests a framework quite different from Hettinger's, one that begins with a strong presumption against requiring disclosure and is in favor of protecting people against unconsented-to acquisitions of their ideas. This is the moral backdrop against which trade secrecy law is best understood.

CONSEQUENCES OF DISCLOSURE

Within this framework, a critical question is how people lose rights in their ideas. Are these rights forfeited when people express their ideas or communicate them to others? Surely this depends on the circumstances of disclosure. Writing down ideas in a daily journal to oneself or recording them on a cassette should not entail such a forfeiture. Considerations of individual autonomy,

privacy, and personality require that such expressions not be deemed available for use by others who may gain access to them.

Likewise, communicating an idea in confidence to another should not render it part of the common pool of knowledge. Respect for the individual's desire to limit the dissemination of the idea is at stake, but so is respect for the relationship of trust and confidence among the persons involved. If *A* confides in *B* under circumstances in which *B* gives *A* reason to believe she will respect the confidence, *A* should be able to trust that *B* will not reveal or misuse the confidence and that third parties who may intentionally or accidentally discover the confidence will respect it.

The alternative possibility is that by revealing her ideas to *B*, *A* is deemed to forfeit any right to control their use or communication. This principle is objectionable for a couple of reasons. First, it would most certainly increase reluctance to share ideas since our disclosure decisions are strongly influenced by the audience we anticipate. If we could not select our audience, that is, if the choice were only between keeping ideas to ourselves and sharing them with the world at large, many ideas would remain unexpressed, to the detriment of individual health as well as the general good.

Second, the principle would pose an impediment to the formation and sustenance of various types of cooperative relationships—relationships of love and friendship, as well as relationships forged for specific purposes such as education, medical care, or business. It might be thought that only ideas of an intimate or personal nature are important in this regard. But it is not only "personal" relationships, but cooperative relationships of all types, that are at stake. Shared knowledge and information of varying types are central to work relationships and communities—academic departments and disciplines, firms, teams—as well as other organizations. The possession of common ideas and information, to the exclusion of those outside the relationship or group, contributes to the group's self-definition and to the individual's sense of belonging. By permitting and protecting the sharing of confidences, trade secret principles, among other institutions, permit "special communities of knowledge" which nurture the social bonds and cooperative efforts through which we express our individuality and pursue common purposes.

Of course, by disclosing her idea to *B*, *A* runs the risk that *B* or anyone else who learns about the idea may use it or share it further. But if *B* has agreed to respect the confidence, either explicitly or by participating in a relationship in which confidence is normally expected, she has a *prima facie* obligation not to disclose the information to which she is privy. Institutions that give *A* a remedy against third parties who appropriate ideas shared in confidence reduce the risk that *A*'s ideas will become public resources if she shares them with *B*. Such institutions thereby support confidential relationships and the cooperative undertakings that depend on them.

Yet another situation in which disclosure should not be regarded as a license for general use is the case of disclosures made as a result of deceit or insincere promises. Suppose *A* is an entrepreneur who has created an unusual software program with substantial sales potential. Another party, *B*, pretending to be a potential customer, questions *A* at great length about the code and other details of her program. *A*'s disclosures are not intended to be, and should not be deemed, a contribution to the general pool of knowledge, nor should *B* be permitted to use *A*'s ideas. Respect for *A*'s right to disclose her ideas requires that involuntary disclosures—such as those based on deceit, coercion, and theft of documents containing expressions of those ideas—not be regarded as forfeitures to the common pool of knowledge and information. In recognition of *A*'s right to control disclosure of her ideas and to discourage appropriation of her ideas against her wishes, we might expect our institutions to provide *A* with a remedy against these sorts of appropriation. Trade secret law provides such a remedy.

Competitive fairness is also at stake if *B* is in competition with *A*. Besides having violated standards of common morality in using deceit to gain access to *A*'s ideas, *B* is in a position to exploit those ideas in the marketplace without having contributed to the cost of their development. *B* can sell her version of the software more cheaply since she enjoys a substantial cost advantage compared to *A*, who may have invested a great deal of time and money in developing the software. Fairness in a competitive economy requires some limitations on the rights of firms to use ideas developed by others. In a system based on effort, it is both unfair and ultimately self-defeating to permit firms to have a free ride on the efforts of their competitors.

PROBLEMATIC ISSUES

Respect for personal control over the disclosure of ideas, respect for confidential relationships, common morality, and fair competition all point toward recognizing certain rights in ideas. Difficult questions will arise within this system of rights. If *A* is not an individual but an organization or group, should *A* have the same rights and remedies against *B* or third parties who use or communicate information shared with *B* in confidence? For example, suppose *A* is a corporation that hires an employee, *B*, to develop a marketing plan. If other employees of *A* reveal in confidence to *B* information they have created or assembled, should *A* be able to restrain *B* from using this information to benefit herself (at *A*'s expense)? Does it matter if *A* is a two-person corporation or a corporation with 100,000 employees? What if *A* is a social club or a private school?

Hettinger seems to assume that corporate *A*'s should not have such rights—on the grounds that they might restrict *B*'s employment possibilities. It is certainly true that giving *A* a right against *B* if she reveals information communicated to her in confidence could rule out certain jobs for *B*. However, the alternative rule—that corporate *A*'s should have no rights in ideas they reveal in confidence to others—has problems as well.

One problem involves trust. If our institutions do not give corporate *A*'s certain rights in ideas they reveal in confidence to employees, *A*'s will seek other means of ensuring that competitively valuable ideas are protected. They may contract individually with employees for those rights, and if our legal institutions do not uphold those contracts, employers will seek to hire individuals in whom they have personal trust. Hiring would probably become more dependent on family and personal relationships and there would be fewer opportunities for the less well connected. Institutional rules giving corporate *A*'s rights against employees who reveal or use information given to them in confidence are a substitute for personal bonds of trust. While such rules are not cost-free and may have some morally undesirable consequences, they help sustain cooperative efforts and contribute to more open hiring practices.

Contrary to Hettinger's suggestion, giving corporate *A*'s rights in the ideas they reveal in confidence to others does not always benefit the strong at the expense of the weak, or the large corporation at the expense of the individual, although this is surely sometimes the case. Imagine three entrepreneurs who wish to expand their highly successful cookie business. A venture capitalist interested in financing the expansion naturally wishes to know the details of the operation—including the prized cookie recipe—before putting up capital. After examining the recipe, however, he decides that it would be more profitable for him to sell the recipe to CookieCo, a multinational food company, and to invest his capital elsewhere. Without money and rights to prevent others from using the recipe, the corporate entrepreneurs are very likely out of business. CookieCo, which can manufacture and sell the cookies much more cheaply, will undoubtedly find that most of the entrepreneurs' customers are quite happy to buy the same cookies for less at their local supermarket.

NON-PROPERTY FOUNDATIONS OF TRADE SECRET LAW

To a large extent, the rights and remedies mentioned in the preceding discussion are those recognized by trade secret law. As this discussion showed, the concept of property is not necessary to justify these rights. Trade secret law protects against certain methods of appropriating the confidential and commercially valuable ideas of others. It affords a remedy to those whose commercially valuable secrets are acquired by misrepresentation, theft, bribery, breach or inducement of a breach of confidence, espionage or other improper means.[3] Although the roots of trade secret principles have been variously located, respect for voluntary disclosure decisions and respect for confidential relationships provide the best account of the pattern of permitted and prohibited appropriations and use of ideas.[4] As Justice Oliver Wendell Holmes noted in a 1917 trade secret case, "The property may be denied but the confidence cannot be."[5] Trade secret law can also be seen as enforcing ordinary standards of morality in commercial relationships, thus ensuring some consistency with general social morality.

It may well be true, as Hettinger and others have claimed, that the availability of trade secret protection provides an incentive for intellectual labor and the development of ideas. The knowledge that they have legal rights against those who "misappropriate" their ideas may encourage people to invest large amounts of time and money in exploring and developing ideas. However, the claim that trade secret protection promotes invention is quite different from the claim that it is grounded in or justified by this tendency. Even if common law trade secret rights did not promote intellectual labor or increase the dissemination and use of information, there would still be reasons to recognize those rights. Respect for people's voluntary disclosure decisions, respect for confidential relationships, standards of common morality, and fair competition would still point in that direction.

Moreover, promoting the development of ideas cannot be the whole story behind trade secret principles, since protection is often accorded to information such as customer data or cost and pricing information kept in the ordinary course of doing business. While businesses may need incentives to engage in costly research and development, they would certainly keep track of their customers and costs in any event. The rationale for giving protection to such information must be other than promoting the invention, dissemination, and use of ideas. By the same token, trade secret principles do not prohibit the use of ideas acquired by studying products available in the marketplace. If the central policy behind trade secret protection were the promotion of invention, one might expect that trade secret law, like patent law, which was explicitly fashioned to encourage invention, would protect innovators from imitators.

The fact that Congress has enacted patent laws giving inventors a limited monopoly in exchange for disclosure of their ideas without at the same time eliminating state trade secret law may be a further indication that trade secret and patent protection rest on different grounds. By offering a limited monopoly in exchange for disclosure, the patent laws implicitly recognize the more fundamental right not to disclose one's ideas at all or to disclose them in confidence to others.

REASSESSING HETTINGER'S CRITICISM OF TRADE SECRET LAW

If we see trade secret law as grounded in respect for voluntary disclosure, confidential relationships, common morality, and fair competition, the force of Hettinger's criticisms diminishes somewhat. The problems he cites appear not merely in their negative light as detracting from an ideal "free flow of ideas," but in their positive role as promoting other important values.

Restrictions on Acquiring Ideas

Hettinger is critical, for example, of the fact that trade secret law restricts methods of acquiring ideas. But the prohibited means of acquisition—misrepresentation, theft, bribery, breach of confidence, and espionage—all reflect general social morality. Lifting these restrictions would undoubtedly contribute to the erosion of important values outside the commercial context.

How much trade secrecy laws inhibit the development and spread of ideas is also open to debate. Hettinger and others have claimed that trade secrecy is a serious impediment to innovation and dissemination because the period of permitted secrecy is unlimited. Yet, given the fact that trade secret law offers no protection for ideas acquired by examining or reverse-engineering products in the marketplace, it would appear rather difficult to maintain technical secrets embodied in those products while still exploiting their market potential. A standard example used to illustrate the problem of perpetual secrecy, the Coke formula, seems insufficient to establish that this is a serious problem. Despite the complexity of modern technology, successful reverse-engineering is common. Moreover, similar technical advances are frequently made by researchers working independently. Trade secret law poses no impediment: in either case independent discoverers are free to exploit their ideas even if they are similar to those of others.

As for nontechnical information such as marketing plans and business strategies, the period of secrecy is necessarily rather short since implementation entails disclosure. Competitor intelligence specialists claim that most of the information needed to understand what competitors are doing is publicly available.[6] All of these considerations suggest that trade secret principles are not such a serious impediment to the dissemination of information.

Competitive Effects

Hettinger complains that trade secret principles stifle competition. Assessing this claim is very difficult. On one hand, it may seem that prices would be lower if firms were permitted to obtain cost or other market advantages by using prohibited means to acquire protected ideas from others. Competitor access to the Coke formula would most likely put downward pressure on the price of "the real thing." Yet, it is also reasonable to assume that the law keeps prices down by reducing the costs of self-protection. By giving some assurance that commercially valuable secrets will be protected, the law shields firms from having to bear the full costs of protection. It is very hard to predict what would happen to prices if trade secret protection were eliminated. Self-protection would be more costly and would tend to drive prices up, while increased competition would work in the opposite direction. There would surely be important differences in morale and productivity. Moreover, as noted, any price reductions for consumers would come at a cost to the basic moral standards of society if intelligence-gathering by bribery, misrepresentation, and espionage were permitted.

Restrictions on Employee Mobility

Among Hettinger's criticisms of trade secret law, the most serious relate to restrictions on employee mobility. In practice, employers often attempt to protect information by overrestricting the post-employment opportunities of employees. Three important factors contribute to this tendency: vagueness about which information is confidential; disagreement about the proper allocation of rights to ideas generated by employees using their employers' resources; and conceptual difficulties in distinguishing general knowledge and employers specific knowledge acquired on the job. Courts, however, are already doing what Hettinger recommends, namely, limiting the restrictions that employers can place on future employment in the name of protecting ideas. Although the balance between employer and employee interests is a delicate one not always equitably struck, the solution of eliminating trade secret protection altogether is overbroad and undesirable, considering the other objectives at stake.

Hypothetical Alternatives

Hettinger's discussion of our intellectual property institutions reflects an assumption that greater openness and sharing would occur if we eliminated trade secret protection. He argues that trade secret principles encourage secrecy. He speaks of the "free flow of ideas" as the ideal that would obtain in the absence of our intellectual property institutions. This supposition strikes me as highly unlikely. People keep secrets and establish confidential relationships for a variety of reasons that are quite independent of any legal protection these secrets might have. The psychology and sociology of secrets have been explored by others. Although much economic theory is premised on complete information, secrecy and private information are at the heart of day-to-day competition in the marketplace.

In the absence of something like trade secret principles, I would expect not a free flow of ideas but greater efforts to protect information through contracts, management systems designed to limit information access, security equipment, and electronic counterintelligence devices. I would also expect stepped-up efforts to acquire intelligence from others through espionage, bribery, misrepresentation, and other unsavory means. By providing some assurance that information can be shared in confidence and by protecting against unethical methods of extracting information and undermining confidentiality, trade secret principles promote cooperation and security, two important conditions for intellectual endeavor. In this way, trade secret principles may ultimately promote intellectual effort by limiting information flow.

The Burden of Justification

We may begin thinking about information rights, as Hettinger does, by treating all ideas as part of a common pool and then deciding whether and how to allocate to individuals rights to items in the pool. Within this framework, ideas are conceived on the model of tangible property. Just as, in the absence of social institutions, we enter the world with no particular relationship to its tangible *assets* or natural resources, we have no particular claim on the world's ideas. In this scheme, as Hettinger asserts, the "burden of justification is very much on those who would restrict the maximal use of intellectual objects."

Alternatively, we may begin, as I do, by thinking of ideas in relation to their originators, who may or may not share their ideas with specific others or contribute them to the common pool. This approach treats ideas as central to personality and the social world individuals construct for themselves. Ideas are not, in the first instance, freely available natural resources. They originate with people, and it is the connections among people, their ideas, and their relationships with others that provides a baseline for discussing rights in ideas. Within this conception, the burden of justification is on those who would argue for disclosure obligations and general access to ideas.

The structure of specific rights that emerges from these different frameworks depends not only on where the burden of justification is located, but also on how easily it can be discharged. It is unclear how compelling a case is required to overcome the burden Hettinger sets up and, consequently, difficult to gauge the depth of my disagreement with him. Since Hettinger does not consider the rationales for trade secret principles discussed here, it is not clear whether he would dismiss them altogether, find them insufficiently weighty to override the presumption he sets up, or agree that they satisfy the burden of justification.

One might suspect, however, from the absence of discussion of the personal and social dimension of rights in ideas that Hettinger does not think them terribly important, and that his decision to put the burden of justification on those who argue for rights in ideas reflects a fairly strong commitment to openness. On the assumption that our alternative starting points reflect seriously held substantive views (they are not just procedural devices to get the argument started) and that both frameworks require strong reasons to overcome the initial presumption, the resulting rights and obligations are likely to be quite different in areas where neither confidentiality nor openness is critical to immediate human needs.

Indeed, trade secrecy law is an area where these different starting points would be likely to surface.

The key question to ask about these competing frameworks is which is backed by stronger reasons. My opposition to Hettinger's allocation of the burden of justification rests on my rejection of his conception of ideas as natural resources and on different views of how the world would look in the absence of our intellectual property institutions. In contrast, my starting point acknowledges the importance of ideas to our sense of ourselves and the communities (inducting work communities) of which we are a part. It is also more compatible with the way we commonly talk about ideas. Our talk about disclosure obligations presupposes a general background right not to reveal ideas. If it were otherwise, we would speak of concealment rights. To use the logically interesting feature of non exclusiveness as a starting point for moral reasoning about rights in ideas seems wholly arbitrary.

CONCLUSION

Knives, forks, and spoons are all designed to help us eat. In a sense, however, the essential function of these tools is to help us cut, since without utensils, we could still consume most foods with our hands. One might be tempted to say that since cutting is the essential function of eating utensils, forks and spoons should be designed to facilitate cutting. One might even say that insofar as forks and spoons do not facilitate cutting, they should be redesigned. Such a modification, however, would rob us of valuable specialized eating instruments.

Hettinger's train of thought strikes me as very similar. He purports to examine the justification of our various intellectual property institutions. However, he settles on a justification that really only fits patent and, arguably, copyright institutions. He then suggests that other intellectual property rights be assessed against the justification he proposes and redesigned insofar as they are found wanting. In particular, he suggests that trade secret principles be modified to look more like patent principles. Hettinger fails to appreciate the various rationales behind the rights and duties understood under the heading "intellectual property," especially those recognized by trade secret law.

I agree with Hettinger that our intellectual property institutions need a fresh look from a utilitarian perspective. The seventeen-year monopoly granted through patents is anachronistic given the pace of technological development today. We need to think about the appropriate balance between employer and employee rights in ideas developed jointly. Solutions to the problem of the unauthorized copying of software may be found in alternative pricing structures rather than in fundamental modifications of our institutions. Public interest considerations could be advanced for opening access to privately held information in a variety of areas. As we consider these specific questions, however, I would urge that we keep firmly in mind the variety of objectives that intellectual property institutions have traditionally served. If, following Hettinger's advice, we single-mindedly reshape these institutions to maximize the short-term dissemination and use of ideas, we run the risk of subverting the other ends these institutions serve.

NOTES

1   Edwin C. Hettinger, "Justifying Intellectual Property," *Philosophy & Public Affairs* 18, No. 1 (Winter 1989): 31–52.

2   Thomas Jefferson agrees. See Jefferson's letter to Isaac McPherson, 13 August 1813, in *The Founder's Constitution*, ed. Philip B. Kurland and Ralph Lerner (Chicago: University of Chicago Press, 1987), 3: 42.

3   *Uniform Trade Secrets Act with 1985 Amendments*, sec. 1, in *Uniform Laws Annotated*, Vol. 14 (1980 with 1988 Pocket Part). The *Uniform Trade Secrets Act* seeks to codify and standardize the common law principles of trade secret law as they have developed in different jurisdictions.

4   See Ramon A. Klitzke, "Trade Secrets: Importing Quasi-Property Rights," *Business Lawyer* 41 (1986): 557–70.

5   *E.I. DuPont de Nemours Powder Co. v. Masland*, 244 US 100 (1917).

6   See, e.g., the statement of a *manager* of a competitor surveillance group quoted in Jerry L. Wall, "What the Competition Is Doing: Your Need to Know," *Harvard Business Review* 52 (November–December 1974): 34. See generally Leonard M. Fuld, *Competitor Intelligence: How to Get It—How to Use It* (New York: John Wiley and Sons, 1985).

—91—

INTELLECTUAL PROPERTY AND PHARMACEUTICAL DRUGS

An Ethical Analysis

Richard T. De George

THE NOTION OF INTELLECTUAL PROPERTY (IP) IS contentious. Nonetheless there is justification for granting exclusive rights to some original useful products or processes if the result benefits the common good. This is recognized in Article 1, Section 8 of the US Constitution, which establishes the power of Congress "to promote the progress of science and useful arts, by securing for limited times to authors and inventors the exclusive right to their respective writings and discoveries." The length of time is somewhat arbitrary, has varied over the past century, and is vastly different for copyright than for patents, the latter offering much stronger protection for a shorter period of time.

THE MORAL JUSTIFICATION OF INTELLECTUAL PROPERTY

Because intellectual property is significantly different from other kinds of property,[1] the ethical defenses of intellectual property differ from the defenses—such as the Lockean—of other kinds of property, and traditions in different parts of the world treat intellectual property differently. Nonetheless, there is a two-part argument in defense of the ethical legitimacy of limited intellectual property rights that is intuitively attractive, widely held, and, I believe, sound. The first part

is a fairness, or justice, argument that says that, within the economic system of free enterprise, those who spend time and/or money in developing a product or the expression of an idea deserve a chance to receive recompense if the result they achieve is useful and beneficial to others who are willing to pay for it. It would be unfair or unjust for others to take that result, market it as their own, and profit from it without having expended comparable time or money in development, before the original developer has a chance to recoup his investment and possibly make a profit. Intellectual property protection gives innovators this chance.

The second part of the argument is based on consequences. It states that unless developers are allowed a period during which to recoup their investment and make a profit, the incentive to produce new products beneficial to society will be greatly reduced. Society benefits from new products, both initially and after they are no longer protected and fall into the public domain. Hence, the greatest benefit to the common good or to society is achieved by offering inventors and developers of new products a period during which they can make their profits without the competition of free riders. Both arguments together lead to the conclusion that protection of intellectual property for a limited period of time is just and produces more good for society than an absence of such protection.

I shall call the two arguments together the Standard Argument (SA). For the sake of argument, let us accept SA as a valid moral justification for intellectual property. It is general in form, and applies to pharmaceutical products as well as to inventions, machines, and other types of intellectual property. There have been many studies by economists to support the second part of the Standard Argument. The pharmaceutical industry and some economist have persuasively argued that more new drugs are developed when pharmaceutical companies make sufficient profits to invest in research and development, and the pharmaceutical industry argues that the large profits for which the industry is known are necessary to underwrite both the high cost of developing a new drug and the large number of initial attempts that never turn into successful, marketable drugs.

The industry then builds on the Standard Argument to develop what I shall call the Status Quo Approach (SQA), which is a legal-economic approach, to reply to critics of their policies who adopt not an economic but a moral approach to pharmaceuticals. The Status Quo Approach takes existing intellectual property law, especially patent law, as setting the appropriate parameters within which to view and answer all challenges to the practices of pharmaceutical companies. Taking this approach leads to concentration on using the law to help these companies protect and increase their profits so that they can develop new drugs. Thus they defend their techniques to extend the time before which generic drugs can be introduced, to extend patent protection on an international level through the World Trade Organization (WTO), to produce me-too drugs or drugs that are only marginally different from existing drugs rather than concentrating on breakthrough drugs, and so on. Morally based attacks that make a link between patents and the availability of drugs for the poor are rejected as misconceived. Nonetheless, there is an attempt to diffuse the latter attacks by giving away some drugs in some circumstances. These giveaway programs are presented as the industry's or a particular company's living up to its social responsibility. Social responsibility is the surrogate for moral responsibility, is part of the Status Quo Approach, and is seen by the industry as answering morally based criticism.

The SQA is an approach that pharmaceutical companies are comfortable with, as well as one that is widely accepted. It has the benefits of tradition, of requiring no change in current practices or law, and of having produced beneficial results in the past. Hence, one can argue, it is more likely than untried alternative schemes of intellectual property protection to produce beneficial results in the future. The approach thus entrenches and sanctifies the status quo.

Both the Standard Argument and the Status Quo Approach, however, are coming under increased strain and attack, and in this paper I shall attempt to examine the direction of those strains and the validity of these attacks. Only if we fully appreciate the Standard Argument and the Status Quo Approach, and their shortcomings, can we make sense of the continuing charges made by critics and the responses made by the pharmaceutical industry. My aim is to bring some order to a very confused and confusing public discussion on the actions of pharmaceutical companies, the obligations attributed to them, and the claimed right of the public with respect to needed drugs. Although clarifying the discussion is my main purpose, I shall also make some suggestions for improving the situation.

THE LIMITS OF THE STANDARD ARGUMENT

Patents, I have argued, can be justified from an ethical point of view. But that justification is limited. Despite the constitutionally stated basis for patents, neither common good (nor utilitarian) considerations form part of what is required for a patent. Nor have ethical considerations been a dominant consideration in changes that have been made in patent law. Hence the details of how patent protection has developed do not follow from the ethical justification. It is not that the way in which patent law has developed is unethical, but that it is only one of many sets of ethically justifiable ways of protecting pharmaceuticals.

Discussions of intellectual property are very complex and involve knowledge of convoluted laws, legal decisions, and economic and business analyses. Typically, at any negotiation involving intellectual property prior to the drafting of legislation, the parties are government officials, lawyers, and corporate representatives. Thus the best defense of those policies is given not in ethical but in legal and economic terms. This is why the SQA uses these. Critics, however, fail to be convinced by such considerations. It is not clear to them who, if anyone, represents the general public in the general process. It is difficult for any government to represent both the consumer and the industry, and the public's trust in government as representing the public's interest is lessened when the industry present in the negotiations is the pharmaceutical industry, which is known for being one of the most successful lobbying groups and for being among the top spenders of lobbying money.

The complaint about the Standard Argument is not that it is wrong, but that it is taken to prove too much and to respond to all objections. The mantra that is repeated by industry representatives in every context and in reply to every criticism with respect to intellectual property protection, pricing, and access is that unless the pharmaceutical companies are profitable enough to have the funds to do so and can expect future profits from their products, they will not engage in R&D and will not develop new drugs, which, of course, benefit society as a whole. When critics point to the fact that the industry has the highest rate of profit of any industry year after year, this is the primary answer. When critics complain about the high cost of drugs and the fact that the price of drugs increases much faster than the inflation rate, this is their answer. When the critics claim that the developed nations are forcing the less-developed ones to adopt standards of intellectual protection

that go against their traditions and may not be in their best interests, this is their answer. When critics say that the reason for intellectual property protection is not private profit but the common good, this is the answer. And all this makes some sense because there is ample evidence that, without profits, there are few new drugs developed. Yet the answer covers over a good deal, as I shall try to show....

THE RIGHT-TO-HEALTH CARE ARGUMENT

Just as the Standard Argument is often assumed by the pharmaceutical industry, the defense of the right to health care is often assumed by its critics. The critics do not deny the overall validity of the SA and the SQA, but at its limits the critics challenge the application of the argument and the defenses of their practices given by representatives of the pharmaceutical industry. The central claim is that although the Standard Argument justifies the right to intellectual property, the right is only a prima facie and not an absolute right. In many cases the right holds sway and trumps other considerations. But in the case of pharmaceuticals it comes up against other prima facie rights, namely the right to life, the right to adequate health care, and the right to access essential lifesaving drugs; it comes up against the obligation to aid those in need; and it comes up against competing claims made in the name of the common good. The right to life, the right to adequate healthcare, the right to access to essential lifesaving drugs, and the obligation to aid those in need, critics note, must be given at least as much consideration as intellectual property rights. Not only do IP rights not necessarily trump those other rights, but they are in fact often trumped by them. The pharma industry tends to argue that intellectual property rights are always sacrosanct, when they are not. Although critics sometimes give too little weight to the actual strength of IP rights, the rights to health and to health care raise serious issues in certain circumstances about the pharma industry's claims. Hence the discussion does not end with simply asserting the Standard Argument and the SQA.

What then are the arguments in support of the right to health and health care and the right to access, and how can they be weighed against the right to intellectual property?

There is considerable confusion in the literature, and although the basic ethical claims are usually fairly clear, how they are justified is not.

We can start by distinguishing two different rights that are often confused. They are related but are not identical. One is the right to health; the other is the right to health care. The UN Declaration of Human Rights, Article 25, states

> (1) Everyone has the right to a standard of living adequate for the health and well-being of himself and of his family, including food, clothing, housing, and medical care and necessary social services, and the right to security in the event of unemployment, sickness, disability, widowhood, old age, or other lack of livelihood in circumstances beyond his control.

Although there are a number of different rights included in this sentence, for our purposes two are central. One is the right to health; the other is the right to medical or health care. It is generally agreed that the rights stated in the Declaration are primarily rights that members of a state enjoy vis-a-vis their governments. Thus, the primary obligation that is correlative to the right to health falls on the state. The right to health has perhaps received so little attention in developed nations because in its most plausible sense these nations face no problem with respect to it. Most plausibly the right to health is analogous to the right to life. The state cannot give anyone health. Its obligation, rather, is to ensure that the conditions necessary for maintaining good health are provided and to prevent any party from damaging the health of another. Understood in this way, the state has the obligation to provide those conditions that promote the health of its citizens, such as ensuring clean water and air, providing sewers and sanitation, and taking other basic measures necessary to promote and protect the health of its members. But although states may have that general obligation, their obligation does not exhaust the obligation of others. The rights impose obligations on business, individuals, and others as well. It is a violation of the human right to health, for instance, for manufacturers to dump toxic waste that will infiltrate a community's water supply and cause people to fall ill. The obligation not to cause harm to people's health and thus not to act in this way is a negative obligation. Positively, companies are bound to provide safe and healthy working conditions for their employees. Providing these conditions is an obligation imposed on them by their employees' right to health, whether or not it is also required by law. And positively, the government has the obligation to pass and enforce such laws.

If one reads the right to health care in the same way, then it is an obligation of states or governments to see that medical care is available to their people, whether or not the governments actually provide it. Although states are generally held responsible for protecting the health of their citizens by providing the common goods of clean drinking water and sewers and other general sanitation facilities, they are not usually held responsible for providing health care in the same way. The reason is that the principle of subsidiarity comes into play. The principle of subsidiarity states that one does not call on a higher level to do a job that can be done at a lower level. With respect to health care, it is usually applied intuitively, even by those who do not use that term. Thus, when children get sick, for instance, it is typical for their parents to care for them, and family members usually are the primary caregivers, rather than the state. When a family is unable to adequately care for someone who needs medical care, they might first go to the circle of friends, or to the larger community. When the community cannot handle the need, they go to the city or the state or federal level. Although in a developed society the structures are in place to handle the needs of people at the appropriate level, they are considerably different in a country that has a socialized medicine program than in a country that does not. If a government is unable to handle the need or needs it faces, it might appeal to the international community. Also assumed by this process is that individuals have not only the right to health and health care, but they also have the obligation to do what they can to preserve their health and to care for themselves to the extent they are able to do so. Thus the rights to health and to health care impose correlative obligations on many parties. So far the obligations of pharmaceutical companies are no different from the obligations of other companies. But this is only part of the story.

Another argument comes into play here that develops the obligation to help others in serious need to the extent that one can do so. There are two versions of this. One is a weak version which says that one has the obligation to help others in serious need to the extent that one can do so with little or moderate cost to oneself. A stronger version says that one must do so even at great expense to oneself, although one does not have to make oneself worse off than the person or persons one is helping. The obligation to aid others in serious need can be justified by either a rule-utilitarian approach, which argues that more good is achieved overall if this rule is followed than if it is not; or by a deontological approach, which bases it on the respect due others as persons and beings worthy of respect. The obligation is one that is widely acknowledged. Intuitively, if one sees a child drowning and one can save the child's life by extending a hand, one has the obligation to do so. Not to do so would be characterized by most people as inhuman or barbaric. The obligation holds even if one will be late to an appointment, or if one will get one's shoes wet in the process of saving the child. The obligation becomes less clear as the cost to oneself increases, and most would agree that one is not obliged to save the child at the risk of one's drowning oneself.

The application of this principle with respect to an individual vis-a-vis a drowning child is straightforward. It becomes more and more problematic as the case becomes more complex. What if the child is drowning in the water of a crowded beach, with a thousand people on it? Is it the obligation of each of the thousand to save the child? Is the obligation greater for those closer? Is it exculpatory for someone who is dressed to say that the obligation falls on those in bathing suits? Would all be equally blameworthy if no one did anything and the child drowned? Now increase the number of children drowning, say from an overturned boat, to twenty. Each person on the beach can save at most one of the children. Is it the obligation of every person on the beach to save all the children, or to save only one, and, if the latter, which one? When we then move to millions of people in danger of death from the lack of medical care in the world and ask what is the obligation of developed countries, of those living in developed countries, of NGOs, and of pharmaceutical companies with respect to the needy, the arguments tend to get more and more tenuous. This is not to say that there is no obligation to help based on the right of the people to health or medical care. But the complexity of the situation suggests the need for action by many parties on many levels.

If one accepts the obligation of aid, then it is not difficult to argue that those in the best position to help have the greatest obligation to do so. Now join that with the fact that those in the health professions have special obligations with respect to health and health care. They have these special obligations because of the field they have freely chosen, because they are related to health care in a way others are not, because they have the expertise that others lack, and because they make their living or profit from health-related activities. A doctor, for instance, has a greater obligation to help an accident victim if other aid is not available, than does someone without medical training. A hospital has a greater obligation to help an accident victim brought through its doors than does a bank or a department store, and people naturally would bring such victims to a hospital rather than to some other kind of enterprise....

With this background we can develop the right to access to needed medicines. But the argument works differently with respect to life-saving medicines, to those which are necessary for health but which treat non-life-threatening illnesses, and to those that are neither and are simply life-enhancing.

The strongest case can be made for the right to access to those drugs that are essential for the preservation of life. If one has the right to life, then one has the right to that which is necessary to sustain one's life—be it food and shelter, or medicines and medical care. Medicines, obviously, are included in medical care. The right of access to available lifesaving medicine has both a negative and a positive aspect. Negatively, all have the obligation not to prevent anyone from having access to what they need to sustain their lives. The positive obligation to ensure that access is available, as in the earlier case, falls on a variety of parties (applying the principle of subsidiarity) and is practically limited by the goods and resources available in a given situation....

I shall call the set of arguments I have sketched out above the Moral Argument.

People typically invoke something like the above general arguments with respect to the drug industry and drug companies. The various claims are that the industry as a whole and the individual companies that make it up have special obligations; that these are related to what they produce, namely pharmaceutical drugs; that they are in a special position to help and that therefore they have the special obligation to do so; and that those in dire need, because of their right to health care, impose obligations on those able to help, including the pharmaceutical industry.

We can apply this claimed right to access both on the international and on the national level in the United States and see how we can weigh it against the right to intellectual property.

We should note that approaching ethical issues relating to the pharmaceutical industry from the perspective of the Moral Right to Access dramatically changes the issues that rise to the surface as opposed to those that arise when taking the Standard Argument and the Status Quo Approach. To see how, we can start with the pharmaceutical companies' use of the term "social responsibility."

THE MORAL RESPONSIBILITY OF PHARMACEUTICAL COMPANIES

With this background, we can now ask: What are the obligations, from an ethical point of view, of the pharmaceutical industry as a whole and of individual pharmaceutical companies? The above discussion forms the background that is generally understood by critics, even though they do not often articulate their arguments very clearly. Can we come up with general obligations that stem from the rights of those in need of medical care? Clearly, pharmaceutical companies are not the only healthcare providers and the entire obligation to fulfill the rights in question does not fall on them. And clearly if they have special obligations, that does not mean that governments, individuals, families, NGOs, and so on do not also have obligations. Since governments have the primary responsibility to provide for the health care of their citizens, they bear the primary obligation. They may either meet this obligation directly or indirectly by ensuring the needs of the public are met in some other way.

Given present structures, the pharmaceutical industry, as part of the health-care system, arguably has two basic ethical obligations. I shall call the first the Production Obligation and the second the Access Obligation. The obligations of the industry with respect to health care are broader and more general than the obligations of any particular pharmaceutical company. The industry's obligations can only be met to the extent that individual companies take the appropriate action. Yet the two levels—industry and company—should be kept distinct, even though many critics conflate the two.

THE PRODUCTION OBLIGATION

The Production Obligation consists in the obligation to develop and produce beneficial drugs. This is the area of the industry's expertise and it is that which the companies in the industry can do that others cannot. Moreover, in this regard one can argue that the pharmaceutical industry as well as individual companies have the obligation to pursue needed new lifesaving drugs more than to pursue alternatives to drugs that already exist and are effective, namely, so-called me-too drugs. Benefit to the patient, and hence to the public and the common good, should play a greater role in the case of health care than in other industries, just as safety is paramount in the engineering industries, whether it be in airplane or building and bridge safety. This first obligation is not an unjust imposition by society, but simply reflects part of the role of pharmaceutical companies in society. The obligation is one that is arguably shared by governments also. The United States Government funds billions of dollars worth of medical research, and it is appropriate that it does so because of its obligation to fulfill the rights of its citizens to health and to health care. In a free enterprise system governments do not engage directly in production, although they can encourage and promote production through their system of intellectual property protection and their tax system, among others. To the extent that the pharmaceutical industry fails to produce needed drugs, it is up to governments to ensure that they are produced.

Many pharma companies and the industry in general, as well as government-sponsored programs, are engaged in the search for cures or remedies for cancer, various kinds of heart disease, new and improved antibiotics to fight infections, and so on. The industry as a whole, therefore, not only is actively engaged in fulfilling this obligation, but individual pharmaceutical companies have an economic interest in pursuing breakthrough and essential new drugs. The market for such drugs, if they treat diseases suffered by large numbers of people in the developed countries, is potentially lucrative.

Nonetheless the market incentive fails with respect to orphan drugs. Diseases which are life threatening but in which the market is either small or the potential recipients poor, require a different approach.

In the United States the Orphan Drug Act has proven to be a successful marriage of government and pharmaceutical companies. The government provides tax incentives and guarantees 7 years of exclusivity (after FDA approval) to encourage drug makers to develop drugs that affect fewer than 200,000 people and are generally unprofitable. The result has been, on the whole, positive, despite abuses....

The market similarly fails with respect to the development of drugs for diseases restricted to those living in tropical countries. Although the governments in such countries have the responsibility for providing for the health of their people, they have insufficient funds to promote research and in addition they lack the facilities and the expertise needed. With minimal budgets for health care, they have difficulty providing the bare essentials of clean water and sanitation and developing an adequate delivery system for health care, regardless of the cost of drugs. Under these conditions the obligation of aid comes to the surface. In this case the appropriate aid is the development of drugs for the diseases in question. The obligation does not clearly fall on any particular pharmaceutical company, and how it is to be apportioned among countries and the pharmaceutical industry worldwide is a topic that urgently needs addressing. The first step in any solution, however, is to recognize the obligation. Perhaps something comparable to an international orphan drug act can be agreed upon; perhaps governments can subsidize special research in these areas; perhaps companies can agree to fund joint research for drugs that would not be covered by patents and would be produced and distributed at cost. The actual action taken should be the result of negotiations among all the interested and affected parties. The pharmaceutical industry clearly has an important role to play in any such negotiations. But approaching the problem from the point of view of the Moral Argument brings to the fore obligations in this regard that the Standard Argument and the Status Quo Approach do not.

Although I have indicated the financial incentive that drug companies have to pursue important new drugs, critics of the pharmaceutical industry have concentrated on whether the drug industry is actually doing either all it can and should do, or all it claims to be doing with respect to the development of new drugs. The issue arises in part because of the industry's use of the Standard Argument and the Status Quo Approach. The many tactics used by pharmaceutical companies to produce profits are justified, the SA and SQA claim, because these profits are necessary to fund the research that has led to and will lead to the development of new essential drugs. The industry thus implicitly acknowledges that the production of such drugs is its goal, even if it does not acknowledge that it is also its obligation.

It is in this context that some critics claim that the amount that the industry spends on R&D is less than the amount that it spends on marketing (including advertising, free samples to doctors, etc.), that the amount may even be less than the amount it spends on lobbying government officials; that most of the profits it makes are not in fact plowed back into research but distributed as dividends to shareholders; and that most of the research that leads to new drugs comes from government-funded research, the results of which are appropriated for private gain. All of this may be appropriate. But it is not self-evidently so, and this is what most concerns the critics. The industry in its blanket claims fails to be convincing.

According to a 2002 study of the National Institute for Health Care Management Research and Educational Foundation for the period 1989–2000, only 35 percent of new drug applications contained new active ingredients (of which only 15 percent were considered to provide "significant improvement over existing drugs"), while 54 percent were incremental modifications of existing drugs (and under Hatch-Waxman get up to 3 years of market exclusivity) and 11 percent were identical to existing drugs.[2] Although these facts by themselves prove nothing with respect to the obligation to provide new drugs, they are used by critics to offset the image that the pharmaceutical industry suggests by its use of the SA to justify its approach to the development of new drugs.

To be convincing the industry must first acknowledge its obligations; but even more important it must be willing to show why the above activities are necessary to produce new drugs. Simply pointing to new drugs as proof is an instance of a logical fallacy. Simply because new drugs have been produced and the industry has been profitable using its advertising, lobbying, and other techniques, does not show that these techniques are necessary to produce new drugs.

If one takes the obligation to produce new lifesaving drugs seriously, then one might consider changes in the status quo with respect to IP. Essential, lifesaving drugs can and arguably should be distinguished from other drugs for a variety of purposes. Me-too drugs and incremental changes, as well as cosmetic changes, do not clearly deserve the same protection or the same encouragement and inducement on the part of government....

THE ACCESS OBLIGATION

The second obligation, the Access Obligation, is the obligation to make the drugs the industry or a company develops available to those who need them. Simply developing them would not serve any purpose otherwise. Fulfilling this obligation may be compatible with the existing structures relating to existing practices concerning intellectual property, pricing, government regulation, charity, and so on. Yet critics claim that both the industry and the market fail to some extent with regard to this obligation, and they claim that if and when current practices impede the fulfillment of this obligation, then the right to access and the concomitant obligation to provide access take precedence over IP and other rights.

The argument as we have developed it so far imposes a stronger obligation on governments to ensure access than it does on the pharmaceutical industry. As we have developed the argument to aid, it comes into play most clearly in times of dire need. This would apply most clearly with respect to essential lifesaving drugs. The obligation to help those in need in less dire circumstances is proportionately weaker. But the obligation of governments is not to ensure access only for lifesaving drugs, but for all drugs needed for health. Governments are obliged to ensure their people have access, whether by actually buying and supplying the drugs or by other means—such as making sure the price of drugs makes them accessible. The right to access puts a strain on any strong claim to intellectual property rights in drugs, if what stands in the way of people receiving lifesaving drugs is maximizing corporate profit.

(a) Let us look at the poor countries first. The question of access to many medicines is a pressing need. Although governments have the responsibility to enable or provide access, it is beyond the ability of many of them to do so. Hence the obligation falls on others able to do so. Included in that number are pharmaceutical companies, especially those that manufacture the needed drugs. The issue was brought to global attention by the AIDS epidemic. The drugs in question are very expensive and only a few are on the current WHO list of essential drugs because of that. The most widely used such drug in poor countries is a combination of three generic drugs produced by the Indian pharmaceutical company Cipla. Nonetheless, it is clear from the Moral Argument that when millions of people are dying and can benefit substantially from available medicines, they have a right to access with respect to them. A consensus is emerging that many parties are ethically responsible for access—the patient, the local government, other governments that can help, NGOs, international organizations, and the drug companies. The problem is clearly not only the result of practices of pharmaceutical companies. Even if the drugs were given away free, access by many of the needy would still be a problem. And a number of pharmaceutical companies have instituted plans to give away antiretroviral drugs, to sell them at cost, or to license them for production by generic manufacturers in less developed countries under

certain conditions. Arguably they are at least to some extent meeting their obligation to be part of the solution. (We have already seen the arguments of critics to the industry's approach that it is being socially responsible by its programs.)

Both nations and companies seem to acknowledge in principle the obligation to respond in case of dire need. Thus, for instance, a provision of the TRIPS agreement states that mandatory licensing of necessary medicines is justifiable in times of extreme national emergencies (such as epidemics) as decided by the country in question. Yet despite the Agreement the right to access is not being met and the pharmaceutical industry bears part of the blame. The TRIPS Agreement, despite its recognition of the obligation to aid, has in practice had little effect and has been faulted for a number of reasons. In 2001 PhRMA and a group of pharmaceutical companies charged South Africa with violating the WTO's rules on patents by producing the drugs needed by their people and 40 companies filed suit. After much adverse publicity, the charges and the suit were withdrawn. But neither the industry nor the companies involved ever acknowledged the right of the South African government to provide access to the needed lifesaving drugs in accord with the spirit of TRIPS, if not with its letter.

The TRIPS Agreement requires that poor countries adopt the type of IP protection found in the developed countries. They must do so whether or not it impedes the government of the country in question from meeting its obligation to provide access to needed drugs for its people. In this way it fails to consider the common good of the people of the country in question. For instance, while strong defenses of intellectual property with respect to pharmaceuticals may produce the best results overall for developed countries, they do not seem to do so for poor and developing countries, such as India. If, as drug companies claim, new drugs cost $800,000,000 to develop, then developing countries are probably not able to develop any. They are better served by developing generic drugs or by requiring compulsory licensing of drugs or by some other strategy. Compulsory licensing and parallel importing policies—with measures adopted to prevent the development of a gray market—would arguably benefit poor countries more than present arrangements. The Moral Argument puts these as well as other suggestions on the table for consideration, while the Standard Argument and the Status Quo Approach—used in negotiating TRIPS—in effect prevent their being raised....

(b) As opposed to poor countries that cannot afford drugs, the United States can afford to pay for drugs. In fact the United Stated both pays more for drugs and contributes more to the profit of the pharmaceutical companies than any other nation. So the aspect of the right to access that has received the greatest attention is the barrier of high prices to access, even though access and price are not the same thing. Even if drugs were free, access requires that the drugs be transported, distributed, and administered to patients. At issue is accessibility, especially of the newer drugs for which no competitive generic drug is available. Although the lack of accessibility for the poor and elderly on restricted incomes gets most publicity, more and more people are complaining that the high cost of drugs is limiting accessibility by putting the cost of insurance out of their reach. As insurance prices rise, employers are less and less willing to pay the escalating costs and are forcing employees to bear a larger and larger portion of the cost. The complaints against the pharmaceutical industry focus especially on two issues that are seen as limiting access. One is the high and ever increasing price of new drugs covered by patents. Not only the poor and elderly, but even middle-class families find that the "co-pay" portion of medicines is increasing at a rate so much faster than inflation that they are having a harder time keeping up. The second is what is seen as illegitimate attempts by drug companies to "extend" their patents and to prevent generic drugs from entering the market, thereby keeping prices high and restricting access for those who can afford only the lower cost of the generics.

The Status Quo Approach simply applies market economics, assuming the force of law in protecting intellectual property rights with respect to patents, and adding that the overall result is not only fair but produces the most good for society. A rights approach to health care yields a different focus. If the right to access to needed drugs is more important than the right to property, then the status quo is up for evaluation and becomes a candidate for change, rather than for passive acceptance. The issue then is not what does market economics prescribe, but how should the status quo be changed to do justice to the right to access to needed drugs. This means once again that intellectual property rights with respect to pharmaceutical drugs should be carefully scrutinized and perhaps changed....

i. *Access and the Cost of Drugs.* My earlier argument distinguished between those drugs that are necessary for life and those that are important for illnesses that are not life-threatening. In the United States critics of pharmaceutical industry pricing are critical of both, and for the most part insurance plans do not distinguish clearly between the two kinds of drugs. The assumption—and as we have seen a dubious assumption—of most Americans is that they are entitled or have a right to the best drugs available for their condition. The relation between the cost of health insurance and the price of medicines and between the cost of health care and the price of medicines is complicated. But the cost of medicines has increased much faster than the cost of health care generally, and the justification for the increase is not obvious, except if one invokes market economics and produces the not-surprising result that the market has been willing to pay the higher prices.

The right to access argument in the US is joined to a fairness argument. That argument says that fairness involves all parties paying their fair share for medicines, including paying sufficient amounts so that drug companies have a continuing incentive to produce more beneficial drugs. The complaint is not that American consumers are subsidizing drugs for the poor countries, or even that they are subsidizing the pharmaceutical companies' compassionate programs. That would be acceptable, and the better off—such as Americans in general—may well have the obligation to bear this cost. But under the Status Quo Approach, in effect, Americans are subsidizing not only poor countries but also seem to bear a disproportionate load. Japan, Canada, and the countries of Europe all negotiate much lower prices than are available in the United States. Americans are increasingly finding it not only ironic but unfair that US drugs cost more in the United States than in other developed countries. This leads to such anomalies as the US government presently prohibiting the importation of US-made drugs from Canada for personal use, while various state governments attempt to find ways of making it legal for senior US citizens to buy US-made drugs from Canada, where the government helps keep the price lower than it is in the United States....

The standard reply to all questions about the high cost of drugs is to appeal to the SA and the SQA and claim that unless there are the profits brought about by high prices, there will be many fewer future drugs. The Status Quo Approach tends to present a questionable dichotomy: either protect drugs and drug pricing to the maximum or face a future with fewer new innovative drugs. The claim is made no matter what the percent of profit, no matter what the prices, no matter how much the industry spends on lobbying and advertising to consumers. The claims are blanket, the justification is blanket, and the public is asked to take the claims on faith. The consuming public must take it on faith that money spent on the recently developed technique of advertising prescription drugs to the general public, for instance, is necessary to produce the profits that will lead to new drugs. They must take it on faith that money spent on researching minor changes in existing drugs is necessary to produce the profits that will lead to new drugs. They must take it on faith that the various tactics that seek loopholes in legislation—whether with respect to the Orphan Drug Act to garner windfall profits or Hatch-Waxman or other legislation to keep competition at bay as long as

possible—are necessary to produce the profits that will lead to new drugs.

That faith has been shaken. Because there is very little transparency in drug pricing economics, the claims have worn thin. That the industry needs the highest rate of profit of any industry is not obvious, even for the production of new products.[3] The lack of adequate transparency exacerbates the communication gap and hinders fruitful dialogue. Abuses and attempts at gaming the system further erode trust....

ii. *Access and Patents.* If there is a difference between different kinds of drugs, and if people have a greater right to access to the more essential drugs than to the less essential ones, then at least it becomes an open question what the best means of protecting the different kinds is. If one takes seriously the Moral Argument, then the assumption of the SQA that all drugs deserve the same length or strength of protection and that they should be treated the same as all other patents in all other areas, is on the table for discussion. Although the laws governing patents are uniform for all products and processes, the range of processes and products is extensive, the differences among them considerable, and so the argument for a one-size-fits-all approach is questionable. Moreover, the pressure on pharmaceutical patents is different from the pressure on patents in general. No one has a right to a better mousetrap, and the market may legitimately determine who gets one; but the right to access to essential medicines places an obligation on all those who can satisfy that right to come up with an equitable means of doing so....

Since access and price are related, attempts to extend the protected life of a drug by introducing slight modifications to get new patents or to delay the entry of generic competitors—which would lower the price and increase accessibility—are not justified by the Standard Argument and are more appropriately seen as taking advantage of the system....

The task with respect to pharmaceutical products is to balance claims to intellectual property rights against the rights to access to needed medicines, the common good, and the obligation to aid. The economic argument that unless companies can make a profit from their research in discovering, developing, and producing drugs, they will not produce them, is only a partial defense of the existing patent system and one that focuses only on property rights. It is only a partial defense because patent protection is not the only conceivable way of either protecting intellectual property or of guaranteeing profits. It does not show that other alternatives—public financing of research and development, cooperation instead of competition on some drug development, government regulation of prices or guarantees of profits at a certain level for certain drugs, and so on, are not viable alternatives. In particular, the SA and SQA do not show that intellectual property rights, no matter how strong and justifiable, trump the right to basic health care and the right of access to needed medicines or that the right to profits trumps these, the common good, or the obligation to aid....

NOTES

1   Unlike other property, intellectual property is infinitely shareable. It can be stolen, borrowed, copied, and one still has it. Intellectual property refers to some products of the mind. But arguably the most important products—ideas—cannot be claimed as one's property. Only the expressions of ideas or their embodiment in some product or process can with any plausibility be said to constitute property in any sense. Even in these cases, no expression or invention is developed completely independently. In the realm of knowledge one always builds on what has gone and has been developed before and is part of the public domain.

2   NIHCM, "Changing Patterns of Pharmaceutical Innovation," p. 3 at http://www.nihem. org/ innovations.pdf.

3   According to the Fortune 500 Report, in 2001, the pharmaceutical industry was the most profitable industry again for several years running. In 2001 the profit of the top 10 drug makers increased 33 percent, and drug prices increased 10 percent, even though the rate of inflation was only 1.6 percent. *The Public Citizen* (April 18, 2002, "Pharmaceutical Industry Ranks as Most Profitable Industry—Again" at http://www.citizen.org/congress/refoirn/drug_ industry/profits) notes that "The drug industry maintains that it needs extraordinary profits to fuel risky R&D into new medicines. But companies plow far more into profits than into R&D. Fortune 500 drug companies channeled 18.5 percent of revenue into profits last year. Yet they spent just 12.5 percent of revenue on R&D." It also reports that for 2002 the industry had return on assets of 14.1 percent (compared with a median of 2.3 percent for Fortune 500 companies); that it spent 30.8 percent of its revenue on marketing and administration, but only 14.1 percent on R&D; and that its direct-to-consumer advertising increased from $800 million in 1996 to $2.7 billion in 2001. (Public Citizen, Congress Watch, June 2003, "2002 Drug Industry Profits: Hefty Pharmaceutical Company Margins Dwarf Other Industries," at http://www.citizen. org/ congress/reform/drug_industry/r_d/articles. cfm?ID=9923.)

INTELLECTUAL PROPERTY ACROSS NATIONAL BORDERS

John Weckert and Mike Bowern

DESCRIPTION

BECAUSE OF THE INTERNET, NATIONAL BORDERS are becoming transparent. This is creating some interesting, and urgent, ethical problems, given the often conflicting moral and legal customs and structures in different countries. This case covers two associated news items about intellectual property issues across national borders. This first news item, paraphrased from Cochrane,[1] is about proposed legislation which allows hacking to protect IP.

A bill before the US House of Representatives would "give American copyright holders freedom to hack PCs used to illicitly share files over peer-to-peer (P2P) networks, without fear of prosecution or litigation." "A copyright owner shall not be liable in any criminal or civil action for disabling, interfering with, blocking, diverting or otherwise impairing the unauthorized distribution, display, performance or reproduction of his or her copyrighted work on a publicly accessible peer-to-peer file-trading network," the bill says.

The global nature of file sharing means people in other countries otherwise outside the reach of US authorities will in effect be directly subject to US law. There is no provision in the bill to protect or isolate PCs in other countries.

The bill protects copyright holders from most claims by PC owners, provided the US Attorney-General is given seven days' notice of their interdiction. Copyright holders must say what methods they will use—such as a worm or denial of service—but that information would not be made public. They will not be permitted to disrupt the operation of the targeted PCs or networks generally, "except as may be reasonably necessary" to protect their copyrighted works. That loophole could foreseeably allow disabling of a PC's normal operations—its operating system, hardware such as the processor chip, attacking Internet routers or deleting the user's file-sharing software. The Attorney-General may veto copyright holders' hacking rights if they engage in a "pattern or practice of impairing ... computer files or data without a reasonable basis to believe that infringement of copyright has occurred."

Those whose PCs are disabled will be unable to claim damages if the total is less than USD 50 for each "impairment" to an interdicted copyright work. For amounts greater than USD 250 they must appeal to the US Attorney-General, who will have 120 days to determine if the complaint has merit, before they can file suit in a US court.

The second news item is paraphrased from Hamdan,[2] and describes how a minister in the Malaysian government may encourage the use of pirated software in schools.

The Domestic Trade and Consumer Affairs Ministry of Malaysia may consider allowing schools and social organisations to use pirated computer software for educational purposes. Minister Tan Sri Muhyiddin Yassin said the exemption for such institutions and organizations was to encourage usage among Malaysians and speed up computer literacy among students.

However, he stressed that other sectors, especially the commercial sector like companies and factories, would be booked if they were found to be using pirated software. "We are concerned over the rampant sale and use of pirated computer software in the country and will continue to conduct raids to curb it. But for educational purposes and to encourage computer usage, we may consider allowing schools and social organisations to use pirated software," he said.

Muhyiddin said the ministry would launch another joint raid with the Business Software Alliance to check the illegal use of pirated computer software soon. He said it was not easy to curb such piracy and the computer software industry had noted that the problem was worse in the United States.

ANALYSIS

Given that the two stories in this case involve legal systems in various countries, it might be argued that the important issues are legal and not moral. That they are legal is not in question, but it does not follow that they are not also moral. In an ideal situation the legal system codifies, to some extent, the moral mores of the society—the moral precedes the legal. The moral should also precede the legal in interactions between countries. The situation here is of course a little different, because there is often disagreement about what is moral in these cases, and when attempts are made to develop a legal framework, these differences will almost certainly come to the fore. It is important to examine the moral questions so that there is a firmer foundation on which to build the legal structure between nations. A variety of ethical issues are raised by the case, but here we will limit the analysis, and just consider in turn, intellectual property and cultural imperialism.

The case illustrates quite starkly a dramatic difference in attitudes to intellectual property in different countries. On the one hand there is a country considering using pirated software in its schools, and on the other, a country contemplating enforcing its copyright laws globally.

To justify this enforcement, unauthorized copying must really be quite wicked. But is it? Ownership of intellectual property is defended most strongly by those most wedded to capitalism, for the obvious reason that intellectual property is seen as a commodity with monetary value. Not all cultures, however, see things this way, and therefore, in some cultures, there is a much greater tendency for intellectual property to be in the public domain, so copying is not seen as a particular evil.

Consider the Malaysian example. Suppose that pirated software is used in schools. What is the problem? No other users are deprived of its use, and no one is losing any sales because of it. The schools have no money to buy the software (or the government does not have the money to give them), so either they use it without paying, or they do not use it at all. So by copying, they gain and nobody loses. It is not difficult to understand this point of view. It is however, very different from the view of the supporters of the proposed bill in the US, as outlined in the first report.

The second issue is cultural imperialism, which can be described as one society imposing its cultural values on another society. The case illustrates a situation that could be interpreted in this way. The original report about the new US law, which was in the Australian press, says: "File sharing's global nature means Australians otherwise outside the reach of US authorities will in effect be directly subject to US law. There are no provisions to protect or isolate PCs in other countries."

The proposed US copyright law would, it seems, make people worldwide subject to US law, regardless of intellectual property laws in their own countries. This does seem to be a clear case where one society is imposing its cultural values on another, but probably without realizing that this is what it is doing. It believes that it is upholding a value that is universal, or ought to be. There is no suggestion that the proposed US bill is directed at Malaysia. The two news reports coincidentally came out more or less at the same time.

What should be done about these, and similar global issues? Raising the problems is easy; knowing how to solve them justly is not. In the case described, all countries could be forced to abide by intellectual property laws as they operate in most Western countries. But it is not clear that this would be just. There is nothing sacred about the notion of intellectual property, and not all societies see it as important. If such laws are enforced this would need to be done in the light of individual societies' customs and their ability to pay.

This brief analysis indicates that solutions acceptable globally will be difficult, if not impossible, to find. But given that the Internet is global, more or less, these problems must be faced. There is no way of avoiding them.

DISCUSSION QUESTIONS

1. In the case of the US copyright law, the available technology could allow the US view to be imposed on Malaysia, and schools could have their computers disabled, and so on, by the copyright owners. In the case of the Malaysian schools, should this be allowed to happen?
2. Should there be a law that allows any American copyright holder to hack into any computer, regardless of where in the world that computer is?
3. Should the Malaysian government allow the use of pirated software in the country's schools?

NOTES

1 Cochrane, Nathan, 2002, "Hollywood Seeks the Right to Hack," *The Age*, 30 July, http://www.theage.com.au/articles/2002/07/26/ 1027497416300.html.
2 Hamdan Raja Abdullah, 2002, "Schools May Get to Use Pirated Software," 28 July, http://pgoh.free.fr/pirated.html.

—93—

CASE STUDY

COPY THAT, RED LEADER

Is File-Sharing Piracy?

David Meeler and Srivatsa Seshadri

BACKGROUND

IN 1999, AN 18-YEAR-OLD COLLEGE DROP-OUT SET a course of events in motion that shook the recording industry. Shawn Fanning had just penned the computer code for Napster®. According to *Time*, Fanning was nicknamed "Napster" because of his hairstyle. Shawn's idea was fairly simple: find a way to coordinate users so they could share computer files with one another. Computer users have always been in search of ways to easily move files from one computer to another. Most of this is innocuous enough. You write a paper in your apartment, copy it to your flash-drive, and go to campus to print it. Sometimes, of course, we share files with friends or acquaintances. When we create these files, there is no problem. But when the file you share is the creative property of someone else, you may have infringed the author's copyright.

What made Napster® so effective is that it provided a platform upon which users could search and share the files of countless others. Napster's® initial plan was elegant. First, it created a catalog of each user's "shared" files, then allowed all users to search this "master-list" of files. In effect, Napster® operated like an introduction service. If you wanted a certain hit-song you "told" Napster® by entering a search string; Napster® would then find a user who had the file you wanted to download, and "introduce" the two of you: one user who has the file, and another user who wants the file.

The underlying problem is that music recordings—which the vast majority of Napster® users were interested in sharing with one another—are copyrighted material. Copyright is a difficult concept for some to grasp. It merely creates and regulates one form of intellectual property. It allows people to own their creativity in the same way we can own physical property. Copyright generally covers such things as music, films, sound recordings and broadcasts, and literary and artistic works; it is sometimes thought to include software and multimedia. Any transaction requires that parties exchange goods of value. If I hand over my hard-earned cash to buy a music-recording, then it seems that I *own* the recording. If not, what have I bought? While it is true that I own the physical recording itself, it does not follow that I own the *content* recorded on the medium. It's the difference between owning this copy of the book you are reading and owning the picture on the cover. As it turns out, most musical artists don't own the copyrights to their songs. Rather, the labels who produce the recordings often own them. So Napster® facilitated the practice of illegally depriving recording labels of their rightful fees. Napster® lost its court battles and its servers were shut down. It is now owned by media behemoth Bertelsmann—who owns BMG and Sony—and offers a paid subscription service for sharing legally copyrighted files.

Due to the simplicity of its set-up, Napster® was easily shut down. All of its files were on a

749

single server. Later file-sharing networks, such as Fasttrack, operate on a decentralized network, so they are incredibly difficult to shut down. But in June 2005 the US Supreme Court ruled against distributed file-sharing networks, in the case of *Metro-Goldwyn-Mayer Studios Inc. v. Grokster, Ltd.*

ANALYSIS

In 1984, Sony Corp. was exonerated when Universal Studios sued them for contributing to copyright infringements with their Betamax® technology. The Supreme Court's ruling then was based on the fact that most people used VCRs to record television broadcasts so they could watch them at a later time. This innocent practice is known as time-shifting. As the Supreme Court saw things, comparatively few VCR owners were pirating movies. This decision rested on the fact that VCRs had "substantial non-infringing uses." However, it is widely known that the vast majority of file-sharing involves copyright infringement, and is therefore plainly illegal.

DISCUSSION QUESTIONS

1. Does it seem natural to you to justify intellectual property with traditional arguments for private property? Why or why not?

2. Patents issued for new inventions usually last for 20 years. When they expire, others may use the patent to make their own versions of the invention. Copyright, however, usually lasts for the author's lifetime plus 50 to 100 years. Would a shorter time-limit on copyright be justifiable? Or should copyright protections continue to exist in perpetuity? Why or why not?

3. Suppose the copied music files are used by a teacher in a music class. Does the educational use change your moral assessment of the copyright violation?

4. How does your ethical assessment of copyright violation change if we consider copying a movie? A book? Computer code?

FURTHER READINGS

Lessig, L. 2004. *Free Culture*. New York: The Penguin Press.

Smith, Seagrumn. 2003. "From Napster to Kazaa: The Battle over Peer-to-Peer Filesharing Goes International." *Duke Law & Technology Review* 2(1): 1–9.

PERMISSIONS ACKNOWLEDGMENTS

Allhoff, Fritz. "Business Bluffing: Reconsidered," from *Journal of Business Ethics* 45 (4) 2003: 283–89. Reprinted with the permission of Springer-Verlag Dordrecht, via Copyright Clearance Center, Inc.

Arnold, Denis G., and Keith Bustos. "Business, Ethics, and Global Climate Change," from *Business and Professional Ethics Journal* 24 (1/2), Spring/Summer 2005: 103–30. DOI: 10.5840/bpej2005241/26. Reprinted with the permission of the Philosophy Documentation Center.

Arrington, Robert L. "Advertising and Behavior Control," from *Journal of Business Ethics* 1 (1) 1982: 3–12. Reprinted with the permission of Springer-Verlag, via Copyright Clearance Center, Inc.

Bell, Myrtle P., Mary E. McLaughlin, and Jennifer M. Sequeira. Excerpt from "Discrimination, Harassment, and the Glass Ceiling: Women Executives as Change Agents," in *Journal of Business Ethics* 37 (1) 2002: 65–76. Reprinted with the permission of Springer-Verlag Dordrecht, via Copyright Clearance Center, Inc.

Bowern, Mike. "Email and Privacy: A Novel Approach," reprinted with the permission of Mike Bowern.

Brenkert, George G. "Marketing to Inner-City Blacks: Power Master and Moral Responsibility," from *Business Ethics Quarterly* 8 (1) January 1998: 1–18. Copyright © Society for Business Ethics 1998. Reprinted with the permission of Cambridge University Press. "Private Corporations and Public Welfare," from *Public Affairs Quarterly* 6 (2) 1992: 155–68. Reprinted with the permission of Public Affairs Quarterly, University of Pittsburgh. "Whistle-Blowing, Moral Integrity, and Organizational Ethics," Part VII, # 19 from *The Oxford Handbook of Business Ethics*, edited by George G. Brenkert. Oxford: Oxford University Press, 2009. Reprinted with the permission of Oxford University Press.

Carr, Albert Z. "Is Business Bluffing Ethical?" from *Harvard Business Review*, January/February 1968. Copyright © 1968 by Harvard Business Publishing. Reprinted with permission. All rights reserved.

Carson, Thomas. "Second Thoughts about Bluffing," from *Business Ethics Quarterly* 3 (4) October 1993: 317–41. Copyright © Society for Business Ethics 1993. Reprinted with the permission of Cambridge University Press.

Chan, Gary Kok Yew. Excerpt from "The Relevance and Value of Confucianism in Contemporary Business Ethics," in *Journal of Business Ethics* 77 (3) 2007: 347–60. Reprinted with the permission of Springer-Verlag Dordrecht, via Copyright Clearance Center, Inc.

Charters, Darren. "Electronic Monitoring and Privacy Issues in Business-Marketing: The Ethics of the DoubleClick Experience," from *Journal of Business Ethics* 35 (4) 2002: 243–54. Reprinted with the permission of Springer-Verlag Dordrecht, via Copyright Clearance Center, Inc.

Cohen, G.A. "Illusions About Private Property and Freedom," from Volume IV of *Issues in Marxist Philosophy*, edited by J. Mepham and D. Ruben. Atlantic Highlands, NJ: Humanities Press, 1979. Sussex: Harvester Press, 1981.

Cragg, A.W. Excerpt from "Business, Globalization, and the Logic and Ethics of Corruption," in *International Journal* 53 (4) 1998: 643–60. Copyright © 1998 by Sage Publications, Ltd. Reprinted with the permission of Sage Publications.

Cranford, Michael. "Drug Testing and the Right to Privacy," from *Journal of Business Ethics* 17 (16) 1998: 1805–15. Reprinted with the permission of Springer-Verlag Dordrecht, via Copyright Clearance Center, Inc.

Crisp, Roger. "Persuasive Advertising, Autonomy, and the Creation of Desire," from *Journal of Business Ethics* 6 (5) 1987: 413–18. Reprinted with the permission of Springer-Verlag Dordrecht, via Copyright Clearance Center, Inc.

De George, Richard T. "Intellectual Property and Pharmaceutical Drugs: An Ethical Analysis," from *Business Ethics Quarterly* 15 (4), October, 2005: 549–75. Copyright © 2005 Society for Business Ethics. Reprinted with the permission of Cambridge University Press. Excerpt from "Chapter 14: Whistleblowing," in *Business Ethics*, 7th edition, copyright © 2010. Reprinted by permission of Pearson Education, Inc., New York, New York.

Dees, J. Gregory. "The Meaning of Social Entrepreneurship," 2001. As seen at https://centers.fuqua.duke.edu/case/knowledge_items/the-meaning-of-social-entrepreneurship/. Reprinted with the permission of the Center for the Advancement of Social Entrepreneurship, Duke University Fuqua School of Business.

DesJardins, Joseph, and Ronald Duska. "Drug Testing in Employment," from *Business and Professional Ethics Journal* 6 (3) Fall 1987: 3–21. DOI: 10.5840/bpej19876324. Reprinted with the permission of the Philosophy Documentation Center.

Doll, Darci. "Sexual Harassment in the Workplace," reprinted with the permission of Darci Doll.

Donaldson, Thomas. "Values in Tension: Ethics Away from Home," from *Harvard Business Review*, September/October 1996. Copyright © 1996 by Harvard Business Publishing. Reprinted with permission. All rights reserved.

Elegido, Juan M. Excerpt from "Does It Make Sense to Be a Loyal Employee?" in *Journal of Business Ethics* 116 (3) 2013: 495–511. Reprinted with the permission of Springer-Verlag Dordrecht, via Copyright Clearance Center, Inc.

Epstein, Richard A. "In Defense of the Contract at Will," from *The University of Chicago Law Review* 51 (4) 1984: 947–82. Reprinted with the permission of The University of Chicago Press, via Copyright Clearance Center, Inc.

Freeman, R. Edward. "Managing for Stakeholders," copyright © 2011 by R. Edward Freeman. Reprinted with the permission of R. Edward Freeman.

French, Samantha. "Genetic Testing in the Workplace: The Employer's Coin Toss," from *Duke Law & Technology Review* 1 (1) 2002: 1–13.

Friedman, Milton. "The Social Responsibility of Business Is to Increase Its Profits," from *The New York Times Magazine*, September 13, 1970. Copyright © 1970, The New York Times. All rights reserved. Used by permission and protected by the Copyright Laws of the United States. The printing, copying, redistribution, or retransmission of this Content without express written permission is prohibited.

Garriga, Elisabet, and Domènec Melé. Excerpt from "Corporate Social Responsibility Theories: Mapping the Territory," in *Journal of Business Ethics* 53 (1) 2004: 51–71. Republished with the permission of Springer-Verlag Dordrecht, via Copyright Clearance Center, Inc.

Gaus, Gerald. Excerpt from "The Idea and Ideal of Capitalism," Part II, # 3 of *The Oxford Handbook of Business Ethics*, edited by George G. Brenkert. Oxford: Oxford University Press, 2009. Reprinted with the permission of Oxford University Press.

Ghoshal, S. Excerpt from "Bad Management Theories Are Destroying Good Management Practices," in *Academy of Management Learning & Education* 4 (1): 75–91. Reprinted with permission.

Glatz, Richard. "Aristotelian Virtue Ethics and the Recommendations of Morality." Copyright © 2006 by Richard Glatz. Reprinted with the permission of Richard Glatz.

Griffith, Stephen. "Sexual Harassment and the Rights of the Accused," from *Public Affairs Quarterly* 13 (1) 1999: 43–71. Reprinted with the permission of Public Affairs Quarterly, University of Pittsburgh.

Hawken, Paul. "Natural Capitalism," from *Mother Jones*, March/April 1997. As seen at http://www.motherjones.com/politics/1997/03/natural-capitalism. Reprinted with the permission of Mother Jones and The Foundation for National Progress.

Heath, Joseph. "Business Ethics Without Stakeholders," from *Business Ethics Quarterly* 16 (4), October 2006: 533–57. Copyright © 2006 Society for Business Ethics. Reprinted with the permission of Cambridge University Press.

Hettinger, Edwin C. "What Is Wrong with Reverse Discrimination?" from *Business and Professional Ethics Journal* 6 (3), Fall 1987: 39–55. DOI: 10.5840/bpej19876323. Reprinted with the permission of the Philosophy Documentation Center. "Justifying Intellectual Property," from *Philosophy and Public Affairs* 18 (1) 1989: 31–52. Reprinted with the permission of Blackwell Publishing Inc. via Copyright Clearance Center, Inc.

Jacoby, Brennan. "Children and Targeting: Is It Ethical?" Reprinted with the permission of Brennan Jacoby.

Kilborne, Jean. "Jesus is a Brand of Jeans," from *New Internationalist*, September 2006. As seen at http://newint.org/features/2006/09/01/culture/. Reprinted with the permission of New Internationalist Canada.

Lin, Patrick. "The Ethics of Bluffing: Oracle's takeover of PeopleSoft," reprinted with the permission of Patrick Lin.

Machan, Tibor R. "Human Rights, Workers' Rights, and the 'Right' to Occupational Safety," from *Moral Rights in the Workplace*, edited by Gertrude Ezorsky.

Copyright © 1972 the State University of New York Press. Reprinted with the permission of the State University of New York Press. "Advertising: The Whole Truth or Only Some of the Truth?" from *Public Affairs Quarterly* 1 (4) 1987: 59–71. Reprinted with the permission of Public Affairs Quarterly, University of Pittsburgh.

Maitland, Ian. "The Great Non-Debate Over International Sweatshops," from *The British Academy of Management Annual Conference Proceedings*: 240–64, 1997. Reprinted with the permission of Ian Maitland.

Manning, Rita C. "Caring as an Ethical Perspective," from *Business in Ethical Focus*, 1st edition, edited by F. Allhoff and A.J. Vaidya. Broadview Press, 2008. Reprinted with the permission of Rita C. Manning.

Mayer, Don, and Anita Cava. "Ethics and the Gender Equality Dilemma for US Multinationals," from *Journal of Business Ethics* 12 (9) 1993: 701–08. Reprinted with the permission of Springer-Verlag Dordrecht, via Copyright Clearance Center, Inc.

McCall, John J. "Employee Voice in Corporate Governance: A Defense of Strong Participation Rights," from *Business Ethics Quarterly* 11 (1), January 2001: 195–213. Copyright © Society for Business Ethics 2001. Reprinted with the permission of Cambridge University Press.

Meeler, David. "Utilitarianism," from *Business in Ethical Focus*, 1st edition, edited by F. Allhoff and A.J. Vaidya. Broadview Press, 2008. Reprinted with the permission of David Meeler.

Meeler, David, and Srivatsa Seshadri. "Actions Speak Louder Than Words: Rebuilding Malden Mills"; "Charity Begins at Home: Nepotism"; "Copy That, Red Leader: Is File-Sharing Piracy?"; and "Lifestyles and Your Livelihood: Getting Fired in America," reprinted with the permission of David Meeler and Srivatsa Seshadri.

Nielsen, Kai. "A Moral Case for Socialism," from *Critical Review: A Journal of Politics and Society* 3 (3–4), Summer/Fall 1989: 542–52. Reprinted with the permission of Critical Review.

Nozick, Robert. Excerpts from "Distributive Justice," in *Anarchy, State, and Utopia*. New York: Basic Books, 1977. Copyright © 1977 by Robert Nozick.

Paine, Lynn Sharp. "Children as Consumers: An Ethical Evaluation of Children's Television Advertising," from *Business and Professional Ethics Journal* 3 (3/4), Spring/Summer 1984: 119–45. DOI: 10.5840/bpej198433/429. Reprinted with the permission of the Philosophy Documentation Center. "Trade Secrets and the Justification of Intellectual Property: A Comment on Hettinger," from *Philosophy and Public Affairs* 20 (3) 1991: 247–63. Reprinted with the permission of Blackwell Publishing Inc. via Copyright Clearance Center, Inc.

Poff, Deborah C. "Reconciling the Irreconcilable: The Global Economy and the Environment," from *Journal of Business Ethics*, 13 (6) 1994: 439–45. Reprinted with the permission of Springer-Verlag Dordrecht, via Copyright Clearance Center, Inc.

Pojman, Louis P. "The Moral Status of Affirmative Action," from *Public Affairs Quarterly* 6 (2) 1992: 181–206. Reprinted with the permission of Public Affairs Quarterly, University of Pittsburgh.

Ragg, Chris. "Nestlé and Advertising: An Ethical Analysis," reprinted with the permission of Chris Ragg.

Rawls, John. Excepts from *A Theory of Justice: Revised Edition*. Cambridge, MA: The Belknap Press of Harvard University Press, copyright © 1971, 1999 by the President and Fellows of Harvard College. Reprinted with permission.

Rhode, Deborah L., and Amanda K. Packel. "Ethics and Non-Profits," from *Stanford Social Innovation Review* 7 (3), Summer 2009. Reprinted with the permission of Stanford Social Innovation Review.

Rice, Gillian. Excerpt from "Islamic Ethics and the Implications for Business," in *Journal of Business Ethics* 18 (4) 1999: 345–58. Reprinted with the permission of Springer-Verlag Dordrecht, via Copyright Clearance Center, Inc.

Salazar, Heather. "Kantian Business Ethics," from *Business in Ethical Focus*, 1st edition, edited by F. Allhoff and A.J. Vaidya. Broadview Press, 2008. Reprinted with the permission of Heather Salazar.

Schultz, Vicki. "The Sanitized Workplace," from *The Yale Law Journal* 2061 (2003); as seen at http://www.yalelawjournal.org/article/the-sanitized-workplace. Reprinted with the permission of The Yale Law Journal.

Sen, Amartya. "Does Business Ethics Make Economic Sense?" from *Business Ethics Quarterly* 3 (1), January 1993: 45–54. Copyright © 1993 Society for Business Ethics. Reprinted with the permission of Cambridge University Press.

Shrader-Frechette, Kristin. "A Defense of Risk-Cost-Benefit Analysis," from *Environmental Ethics: Readings in Theory and Applications*, 3rd edition, edited by Louis P. Pojman. Wadsworth, 2001.

Spurgin, Earl W. Excerpt from "Occupational Safety and Paternalism: Machan Revisited," in *Journal of Business Ethics* 63 (2) 2006: 155–73. Reprinted with the permission of Springer-Verlag Dordrecht, via Copyright Clearance Center, Inc.

Steidlmeier, P. Excerpt from "Gift Giving, Bribery and Corruption: Ethical Management of Business Relationships in China," in *Journal of Business Ethics* 20 (2) 1999: 121–32. Reprinted with the permission of Springer-Verlag Dordrecht, via Copyright Clearance Center, Inc.

Stout, Lynn A. "The Shareholder Value Myth," from *The European Financial Review*, April-May, 2013. As seen at http://papers.ssrn.com/sol3/papers.cfm?abstract_id=2277141. Reprinted with the permission of The European Financial Review.

Superson, Anita M. "The Employer-Employee Relationship and the Right to Know," from *Business and Professional Ethics Journal* 3 (1), Fall 1983: 45–58. DOI: 10.5840/bpej19833144. Reprinted with the permission of the Philosophy Documentation Center. "A Feminist Definition of Sexual Harassment," from *Journal of Social Philosophy* 24 (1) 1993: 46–65. Reprinted with the permission of Blackwell Publishing, Inc., via Copyright Clearance Center, Inc.

Treviño, Linda Klebe, and Michael E. Brown. Excerpt from "Managing to Be Ethical: Debunking Five Business Ethics Myths," in *Academy of Management Executive* 18 (2): 69–80. Reprinted with the permission of the Academy of Management via Copyright Clearance Center, Inc.

Vaidya, Anand Jayprakash. "Ill-Founded Criticisms of Business Ethics." Copyright © 2006 by Anand Jayprakash Vaidya. Reprinted with the permission of the author.

Velasquez, Manuel. "International Business, Morality, and the Common Good," from *Business Ethics Quarterly* 2 (1), January 1992: 45–54. Copyright © 1992 Society for Business Ethics. Reprinted with the permission of Cambridge University Press.

Weckert, John, and Mike Bowern. "Intellectual Property Across National Borders," reprinted with the permission of John Weckert and Mike Bowern.

Weissinger, S.E. Excerpt from "Gender Matters. So Do Race and Class: Experiences of Gendered Racism on the Wal-Mart Shop Floor," in *Humanity & Society* 33 (4) 2009: 341–62. Copyright © 2009 by Sage Publications. Reprinted with the permission of Sage Publications, Inc.

Werhane, Patricia H., and Tara J. Radin. "Employment at Will and Due Process," from *Ethical Issues in Business*, edited by T. Donaldson and P. Werhane. Upper Saddle River, NJ: Prentice-Hall, 1999. Reprinted with the permission of Patricia Werhane and Tara Radin.

Zsolnai, Laszlo. Excerpt from "Western Economics versus Buddhist Economics," in *Society and Economy* 29 (2), 2007: 145–53. Reprinted with the permission of Akadémiai Kiadó Zrt., Budapest, Hungary.

From the Publisher

A name never says it all, but the word "Broadview"
expresses a good deal of the philosophy behind our company.
We are open to a broad range of academic approaches and
political viewpoints. We pay attention to the broad impact
book publishing and book printing has in the wider world;
we began using recycled stock more than a decade ago,
and for some years now we have used 100% recycled paper
for most titles. Our publishing program is internationally
oriented and broad-ranging. Our individual titles often
appeal to a broad readership too; many are of interest as
much to general readers as to academics and students.

Founded in 1985, Broadview remains a fully independent
company owned by its shareholders—not an imprint or
subsidiary of a larger multinational.

For the most accurate information on our books (including
information on pricing, editions, and formats) please visit
our website at www.broadviewpress.com. Our print books
and ebooks are also available for sale on our site.
On the Broadview website we also offer several goods that
are not books—among them the Broadview coffee mug, the
Broadview beer stein (inscribed with a line from Geoffrey
Chaucer's *Canterbury Tales*), the Broadview fridge magnets
(your choice of philosophical or literary), and a range
of T-shirts (made from combinations of hemp, bamboo,
and/or high-quality pima cotton, with no child labor,
sweatshop labor, or environmental degradation
involved in their manufacture).

All these goods are available through the "merchandise"
section of the Broadview website. When you buy Broadview
goods you can support other goods too.

broadview press

www.broadviewpress.com